The Balkans

The Balkans: A Post-Communist History is a country-by-country treatment of the contemporary history of each of the Balkan states: Albania, Bulgaria, Romania, Croatia, Serbia, Bosnia and Herzegovina, Macedonia, Montenegro and Kosova.

This survey focuses on political and economic continuities and changes since the 1980s. It includes brief overviews of the history of each state prior to the 1980s to provide the background to enable readers to make sense of the more recent devel - opments. The book has a distinctive conceptual framework for explaining divergent patterns of historical change. This shifts the emphasis away from traditional cultural explanations, especially cultural and national stereotyping, and instead concentrates on the pervasive influence of strongly entrenched vertical power structures and powe relations.

The Balkans is an excellent companion volume to the successful *A History of Eastern Europe*, by the same authors. This is an invaluable book for all students of Eastern European history.

Robert Bideleux is a Reader in the School of Humanities and **Ian Jeffries** is a Reader in the School of Business, Economics and Law at the University of Wales, Swansea. Their publications include *A History of Eastern Europe: Crisis and Change* (Routledge, 1998).

The Balkans

A post-Communist history

Robert Bideleux and Ian Jeffries

Routledge
Taylor & Francis Group

LONDON AND NEW YORK

First published 2007
by Routledge
2 Park Square, Milton Park, Abingdon, Oxon OX14 4RN

Simultaneously published in the USA and Canada
by Routledge
711 Third Avenue, New York, NY 10017

Routledge is an imprint of the Taylor and Francis Group, an informa business

© 2007 Robert Bideleux and Ian Jeffries

Typeset in Times New Roman by
Keystroke, 28 High Street, Tettenhall, Wolverhampton

British Library Cataloguing in Publication Data
A catalogue record for this book is available from the British Library

Library of Congress Cataloging in Publication Data
Library of Congress Cataloging-in-Publication Data
Bideleux, Robert.
   The Balkans : a post-communist history / Robert Bideleux and Ian Jeffries. – 1st ed.
      p. cm.
   ISBN 0–415–22962-6 (hardback) — ISBN 0–415–22963–4 (pbk.) 1. Balkan
Peninsula–History–1989– 2. Post-communism–Balkan Peninsula. I. Jeffries, Ian.
II. Title.
   DR48.6.B53 2006
   949.6–dc22   2006011073

ISBN10: 0-415-22962-6 (hbk)
ISBN10: 0-415-22963-4 (pbk)
ISBN10: 0-203-96911-1 (ebk)

ISBN13: 978-0-415-22962-3 (hbk)
ISBN13: 978-0-415-22963-0 (pbk)
ISBN13: 978-0-203-96911-3 (ebk)

For Catherine Lee, with love from Robert and with heartfelt thanks from both of us for helping to make the completion of this huge project possible

Contents

List of tables		viii
Preface		x
List of abbreviations		xv
Map		xx

1 Conceptual frameworks: 'The Balkans' and the nature of post-Communist democratization and economic transformations — 1

2 Albania: between a rock and a hard place — 22

3 Bulgaria: the Devil has all the best tunes — 73

4 Romania: the road to the EU is paved with good intentions — 125

5 Croatia: paying a price — 183

6 Serbia: from Serbdom to pariahdom — 233

7 Bosnia and Herzegovina: the travails of coexistence — 329

8 Macedonia: towards a bi-national state? — 405

9 Montenegro: to be or not to be? — 471

10 Kosova: the forging of a nation and a state — 512

11 The post-Communist Balkans, the West and the EU: major challenges and contradictions between rhetoric and reality — 581

Bibliography — 595
Index — 609

Tables

1.1	Key economic statistics, 2004	6
1.2	The post-Communist Balkans: population and indicators of economic growth, economic recovery and privatization	20
2.1	Albania: selected economic indicators, 1990–2005	44
2.2	Albanian people's assembly election, 22 and 29 March 1992	45
3.1	Ethnic and religious aff liation of population of Bulgaria	74
3.2	Bulgaria: selected economic indicators, 1990–2005	95
3.3	Bulgarian grand national assembly election, 10 and 17 June 1990	96
3.4	Bulgarian national assembly election, 13 October 1991	99
3.5	Bulgarian parliamentary election, 18 December 1994	103
3.6	Bulgarian parliamentary election, 17 June 2001	112
3.7	Bulgarian parliamentary election, 25 June 2005	120
4.1	Romanian assembly of deputies election, 20 May 1990	146
4.2	Romania: selected economic indicators, 1990–2005	148
4.3	Romanian assembly of deputies election, 27 September 1992	151
4.4	Romanian presidential election, 3 and 17 November 1996	155
4.5	Romanian house of deputies election, 3 November 1996	156
4.6	Romanian presidential election, 26 November and 10 December 2000, f rst round results	165
4.7	Romanian chamber of deputies election, 26 November 2000	166
4.8	Romanian municipal election, 2 and 20 June 2004	172
4.9	Romanian chamber of deputies election, 29 November 2004	174
4.10	Romanian presidential election, 28 November and 12 December 2004, first round result	175
5.1	Ethnic affiliations of population of Croatia, 1991 and 200	183
5.2	Croatian house of representatives election, 2 August 1992	204
5.3	Croatian house of representatives election, 29 October 1995	207
5.4	Republic of Croatia: selected economic indicators, 1990–2005	209
5.5	Croatian parliamentary election, 3 January 2000	216
5.6	Croatian house of representatives election, 23 November 2003	225
6.1	Ethnic aff liations of population of Serbia, 2002	233
6.2	Serbian presidential election, 9 December 1990	244
6.3	Serbian parliamentary election, 8 and 23 December 1990	245
6.4	Federal parliament election, 31 May 1992	247
6.5	Skupstina (Serbian parliamentary) election, 20 December 1992	248
6.6	Serbian parliamentary election, 19 and 26 December 1993	250
6.7	Serbia and Montenegro: selected economic indicators, 1990–2005	251

6.8	Federal parliamentary election, 3 November 1996	255
6.9	Serbian parliamentary election, 21 September 1997	259
6.10	Federal parliamentary election, 24 September 2000	270
6.11	(a) and (b) Federal presidential election, 24 September 2000	271
6.12	Serbian parliamentary election, 23 December 2000	279
6.13	Serbian presidential election, 29 September, 2002, first roun	297
6.14	Serbian parliamentary election, 28 December 2003	309
7.1	Bosnia-Herzegovina parliamentary election, 18 and 25 November 1990	342
7.2	All-Bosnian parliamentary election, 14 September 1996	363
7.3	FBiH parliamentary election, 14 September 1996	363
7.4	Republika Srpska national assembly election, 14 September 1996	363
7.5	Republika Srpska national assembly election, 22–23 November 1997	369
7.6	All-Bosnian house of representatives election, 12–13 September 1998	373
7.7	FBiH house of peoples election, 12–13 September 1998	373
7.8	Republika Srpska national assembly election, 12–13 September 1998	374
7.9	All-Bosnian house of representatives election, November 2000	376
7.10	FBiH house of representatives election, November 2000	377
7.11	Republika Srpska national assembly election, November 2000	377
7.12	All-Bosnian house of representatives election, 5 October 2002	385
7.13	Bosnia and Herzegovina: selected economic indicators, 1993–2005	398
8.1	Ethnic aff liations of population of Macedonia, 1981–2002	406
8.2	Macedonian parliamentary election, 11 and 25 November and 9 December 1990	411
8.3	Macedonian parliamentary election, 16 and 30 October 1994	417
8.4	Macedonian parliamentary election, 18 October and 1 November 1998	420
8.5	Macedonian parliamentary election, 15 September 2002	450
8.6	Republic of Macedonia: selected economic indicators, 1990–2005	459
9.1	Ethnic affiliations of population of Montenegro, 1953–200	472
9.2	Montenegrin parliamentary election, 9 and 16 December 1990	477
9.3	Montenegrin parliamentary election, 20 December 1992	478
9.4	Montenegrin parliamentary election, 3 November 1996	481
9.5	Montenegrin parliamentary election, 31 May 1998	484
9.6	Montenegrin parliamentary election, 22 April 2001	493
10.1	Kosovan parliamentary election, 17 November 2001	565
10.2	Kosovan parliamentary election, 23 October 2004	573

Preface

This book has been over seventeen years in the making. Since 1989 we have both been deeply engrossed in the momentous and sometimes gruesome dramas which were being acted out by the formerly Communist-ruled peoples on the Balkan Peninsula – in an awesome Greek tragedy which unfolded in slow motion. These peoples have not only had to battle with the arduous challenges of post-Communist democratization and establishing more 'horizontally structured' liberal market economies and civil societies based upon the rule of law, but have also been engaged (for the most part involuntarily) in grim struggles to survive or to avoid getting sucked into the terrible vortex of Yugoslav disintegration. While the global media have mainly focused on the gore, the systematic killings, the ethnic cleansing and the profoundly cynical manipulation and exploitation of highly emotive issues and problems by the region's ruthless, lethal, clientelistic and corrupt power-holders (usually for ill-gotten personal gains), we have been more impressed by the stoic courage, powers of endurance and determination to pull through and build new lives displayed by the 53 million inhabitants of the countries under consideration.

This book has been written as a companion to our *History of Eastern Europe* (1998), which deals with the Balkans and East Central Europe more thematically – a panoramic view rather than the country-by-country treatment offered here in *The Balkans*. The country-by-country approach results in a very different 'take' on the region. By changing the angle of vision, the substantive focus and the types of sources used, many issues appear in a very different light or guise than they did in our thematic volume. An extensively revised and updated second edition of *A History of Eastern Europe* is being published almost simultaneously with this volume. We have attempted to maintain a reasonable division of labour between the two books, in order to minimize the duplication or overlap and maximize their complementarity, for the benefit of thos who wish to acquire or read both books – as we hope most readers will. Therefore, fuller treatments of certain themes concerning Balkan identity and the Balkans as a whole will be found in *A History of Eastern Europe*, especially in the new edition. The latter also takes account of recent 'revisionist' writing and research on the Ottoman Empire and its legacies in the Balkan Peninsula. In addition, partly in response to requests from the many readers of the f rst edition, it provides expanded coverage of the cataclysmic impact of the two world wars and of the systematic genocide and ethnic cleansing perpetrated during the early 1940s. The peoples of the Balkan Peninsula (in common with various peoples in other parts of Europe) are still engaged in painfully slow and difficult processes of coming to terms with what occurred during the Firs and especially the Second World War, partly because they are still overcoming the effects of several decades of suppression, censorship, selective amnesia and 'denial' fostered by the Communist regimes. These themes are also apparent in *The Balkans*. It is necessary to bear in mind that the peoples of this peninsula are currently grappling not only with the legacies of four decades of Communist rule and so-called 'transitions' to democracy, liberal governance and market economies, but also with even older unresolved legacies. It inevitably takes decades to heal the scars and repair the damage to the social fabric from political, social and economic conflicts and convulsions as enormous as those which ravaged the Balkan Peninsula during the 1910s, the 1940s and the 1990s. It takes even longer to fully understand and come to terms with what occurred, as the whole of Europe is still discovering, in relation to the Third Reich and the Holocaust. There are neither 'quick fixes' to, nor easy black-and-whit explanations of, such phenomena.

At the same time, *The Balkans* is profoundly concerned to avoid and guard against the widespread cultural, religious, national and ethnic caricatures and stereotyping of the supposed 'behaviour', 'conduct', 'mentalities', 'attitudes', 'syndromes' and 'mindsets' of the peoples of the Balkan Peninsula. These cultural caricatures and stereotypes are mainly (sometimes scurrilously) deployed by Western writers, politicians, journalists and academics, often as means of affirming and validating unwarranted, complacent and arrogant assumptions about the supposed cultural or moral superiority, 'exceptionalism' and 'civility' of the West and the presumed right of the Western powers to exercise a conscious moral, political, economic and ide- ological tutelage over the Balkan peoples, who are widely portrayed as not willing or not able to conduct or govern themselves in sufficiently 'civilized' ways. Looking a the Balkan Peninsula through such distorting lenses (almost through the wrong end of a telescope) is a profoundly lazy, arrogant, ignorant and dangerous substitute for more thorough and open-minded empirical investigation of the terrible afflictions that repeatedly ravaged Balkan peoples during the twentieth century. It has the unfortunate (and often undoubtedly deliberate) effect of tarring whole peoples with the same brush and thus holding them largely (and to varying degrees collectively) responsible for the crimes perpetrated in their names. It presents the Balkan peoples themselves as the root causes of affictions of which they have more often been victims than instigators. It thereby deflects attention (perhaps in some cases deliberately) from the large roles of the major Western powers plus Russia and Austria in deciding how Balkan polities and Balkan political and human geography were (re)structured in 1878, 1913, 1918–19, 1945, 1991–2, 1994–5, 1999 and 2001 and how they may be restructured yet again in 2006–7, in attempts to settle the future of Montenegro, Kosova and Bosnia (which in turn could have significant repercussions for Serbia and possibly Macedonia and Albania, bringing attendant risks of wider Balkan conf icts). We are not suggesting that the major Western powers and Russia and Austria have necessarily had evil intentions towards the Balkans, but merely that these powers have been the major brokers or even architects of the new political architecture and human geography of the peninsula ever since the end of Ottoman and Habsburg rule – including the most recent architectural alterations and boundary revisions. These powers have thus had the major roles in and responsibility for creating (or at least structuring) the situations which have produced the terrible inter-ethnic and other conflicts which afflicted the peninsula during the twentieth century. They should therefore bear much of the blame for 'what has gone wrong'. In particular, it is quite untenable for these powers and their Western apologists to see and portray the terrible problems which the Balkan peoples have suffered as being largely *of their own making* or largely a consequence of supposedly innate popular ' *mentalities*', '*mindsets*' or '*attitudes*' which are peculiarly 'Balkan'. To do so is to mistake victims for perpetrators.

As Anthony Giddens has forcefully argued, nation-states should be seen as 'power containers' (Giddens 1985). The ways in which not just individual nation-states but a whole constellation or system of nation-states has been fostered and structured by the major Western powers plus Russia and Austria has strongly influenced the way in which the polities, power relations, power structures, economies and societies which have emerged within these Balkan states have been structured. Nevertheless, the influence of the Western powers plus Russia and Austria has not been the onl factor at play. The other major factor is that highly clientelistic, corrupt and 'vertically structured' power relations and power structures were the norm during nearly 1,000 years of Byzantine ascendancy and influence in the Balkans and again during the subsequent 500 years of Ottoman ascendancy and influence in the Balkans. This 'verticality of power', which became so deeply entrenched and self-perpetuating for 1,500 years, was largely reproduced in new guises by the (post-Ottoman) nationalist and Communist regimes during the nineteenth and twentieth centuries, with the active connivance of the major powers who brokered or even designed the new Balkan states systems established in 1877–8, 1913, 1918–19, 1945 and 1991–5.

Crucially, the Balkan peoples themselves can only be held very marginally responsible for the many ways in which these arrangements and power structures subsequently either produced or failed to prevent catastrophic results, primarily because the great mass of the population were allowed little or no say in what kinds of arrangements, power structures and policies were adopted in each state and had very little hand in the ways in which they were subsequently administered and altered. In any case, even if the twentieth-century Balkan peoples really had been characterized by particularly querulous, intemperate, uncivil, violent or murderous 'mentalities', 'attitudes' or 'mindsets' (which we very much doubt), this would only have had a very marginal influence on political and societal outcomes. To even greater degrees tha in Western and East Central Europe, the mass of the population were scarcely allowed to play any independent or determining roles in political, economic or social life. They were 'the passive object' rather than 'an active subject of history' (Kormos 1944: 112). They inhabited 'power containers' which had repeatedly been designed and foisted upon them, either 'from above' (by their social 'superiors') or 'from outside' (by Europe's major powers) or by varying combinations of the two. In saying this, we are not trying to whitewash or completely exonerate the Balkan peoples. The Balkan populations have undoubtedly included just as many xenophobes, thugs, hatemongers, religious bigots, murderers, psychopaths and rapists as other European peoples. However, contrary to the prevailing images and impressions fostered and purveyed by many Western journalists, politicians, academics and other writers and pundits (especially since 1990), we have yet to find any evidence that the Balkan nations contained significantly higher proportions of such sick persons than most other European peoples did during the twentieth century – a century in which many more Europeans were killed than ever before.

It is also untenable simply to blame the much-publicized religious and ethnic heterogeneity of the twentieth-century Balkan states for the recurrent instability and strife which they suffered. The populations of these states were indeed religiously and ethnically heterogeneous, but (i) most nations are mongrels, comprising amal-gamations of culturally, ethnically and religiously diverse elements, and heterogeneity is therefore the norm rather than an unusual condition; (ii) it is questionable whether the populations of the Balkan states really have been much more ethnically and religiously heterogeneous than those of many other European states, especially France, the UK, Spain and Italy (see Stavrianos 1958: 12–13, 32; Bideleux and Jeffries 1998: 40–1); and (iii) ethnic and religious heterogeneity in itself need not lead to instability and strife. It is significant that in the early modern era, when ethnic and national identities were still inchoate, fluid and much less important than religious identities there was far less inter-denominational religious strife in the Balkans than in either Central or Western Europe (Banac 1984: 410; Gagnon 2004: 31). Even twentieth-century Albania, which was 70 per cent Muslim, 20 per cent Eastern Orthodox Christian and 10 per cent Catholic and which experienced recurrent internal strife, was notable for the almost complete absence of specifically religious strife. It is also strikin that Macedonian Slavs (who were predominantly Orthodox Christians) and ethnic Albanians (who were predominantly Muslim) managed to keep religion almost completely out of the major armed conflict which took place between them in the Republic of Macedonia between February and August 2001 (*IHT*, 22 August 2001, p. 4; *The Guardian*, 22 August 2001, p. 10). In these instances, religious diversity was *not* automatically conducive to religious strife. By the same token, ethnic hetere geneity has not been an automatic recipe for inter-ethnic strife. It has only become a source of strife when the prevailing power structures and modes of governance, which in the case of the Balkan Peninsula have mostly been imposed from above or outside, have been incapable of accommodating such ethnic diversity. This manifestly became the case in several of the post-Ottoman Balkan states, for reasons we have examined elsewhere (Bideleux and Jeffries 1998: 2–7, 25–6, 37–108, 407–18, 458–96). This book endeavours to explain why it became so again in several of the post-Communist Balkan states.

The text of this book has largely been shaped and synthesized by Robert Bideleux, who also wrote the whole of Chapters 1 and 11, all the pre-1990s material in the country studies (Chapters 2–10), the whole of Kosova up to 1997 and the introductory and concluding sections of each of the country studies. Ian Jeffries furnished vast amounts of text and information on individual countries during the 1990–2005 period – indeed, much more than it has been possible to include in this already long book. Ian's text, which was mainly factual and included innumerable and extensive quotations, was restructured, thematized, drastically condensed and almost completely rewritten by Robert in the course of combining and reconciling it with substantial amounts of information and text of his own on the 1990–2006 period. However, Robert takes sole responsibility for Chapters 1 and 11, for the book's overall structure, themes and conceptual frameworks, and for all the views, judgements, arguments and interpretations put forward.

We aim not only to provide a great deal of information on this fascinating and deeply troubled part of the world, but also to provide challenging interpretations and explanations of what has happened there, why, and what might be possible in the near future. Several of the country studies could easily be books in their own right, and might indeed become such in due course.

We would like to express our warmest thanks to Eve Setch and Vicky Peters at Routledge for guiding this book through the various production stages. Eve, in particular, has shown great patience with Robert's many delays in completing the fina text of this long book. We would also like to thank the authors of the readers' reports for their helpful suggestions and Liz O'Donnell for her very thorough and astute editing.

This book is dedicated to Robert's wife, Catherine Lee. Without her invaluable support and inputs on many fronts during the writing of this book, including proof-reading, suggesting new ideas and source materials and making countless comments on the themes and the text, the book would have been both poorer and even longer in the making.

Robert Bideleux and Ian Jeffries

April 2006

Abbreviations

AAK	Alliance for the Future of Kosova
AIC	agrarian-industrial complex
AKSh	Armata Kombetare Shquiptare (Albanian National Army, in the ROM)
APC	agricultural producer cooperative
ARFY	Alliance of Reform Forces of Yugoslavia (Savez reformskih snaga Jugoslavije)
AVNOJ	Anti-Fascist Council for the National Liberation of Yugoslavia
BANU	Bulgarian Agrarian National/Popular Union
BCE	Business Central Europe
BCP	Bulgarian Communist Party
BK	Balli Kombetar (National Front, in 1940s Albania and Kosova)
BND	Federal Intelligence Service (Germany)
BOSS	Bosnian Party
BSDP	Bulgarian Social Democratic Party
BSP	Bulgarian Socialist Party ('successor' to the old Communist Party)
CDR	Democratic Convention of Romania
CDU	Christian Democratic Union (CDU)
CIS	Commonwealth of Independent States
CNSLR	National Confederation of the Free Trade Unions of Romania
CPA	Communist Party of Albania
CPR	Communist Party of Romania
CPSU	Communist Party of the Soviet Union
CPY	Communist Party of Yugoslavia
CSCE	Committee for Security and Cooperation in Europe
DA	Truth and Justice Alliance (Romania)
DEPOS	Democratic Movement of Serbia
DM	Deutschmark
DNZ (BiH)	Democratic People's Union (Bosnia)
DOS	Democratic Opposition of Serbia
DP	Democratic Party (of Albania)
DPA	Democratic Party of Albanians (in the ROM)
DPS	Democratic Party of Socialists (Montenegro)
DS	Democratic Party (Serbia)
DSA	Democratic Socialist Alliance
DSS	Democratic Party of Serbia

DUI	Democratic Union for Integration (in the ROM)
DZVM	Democratic Union of Vojvodina Hungarians (in Serbia)
EBRD	European Bank for Reconstruction and Development
EC	European Community
EEN	*Eastern Europe Newsletter*
EFTA	European Free Trade Association
EP	Ecological Movement (Bosnia)
EU	European Union
EUFOR	European Union Force (successor to SFOR in Bosnia)
EUPM	European Union Police Mission (successor to UNIPTF in Bosnia)
FBiH	Federation of Bosnia and Herzegovina (the predominantly Bosniak and Croat 'entity' in Bosnia)
FDI	foreign direct investment
FDSN	Democratic National Salvation Front (Romania)
FRY	Federal Republic of Yugoslavia (Serbia and Montenegro only, 1992–2003)
FSN	National Salvation Front (Romania)
FT	*Financial Times*
FYROM	Former Yugoslav Republic of Macedonia (officially, the ROM
G7	Group of seven major advanced capitalist states
G8	Group of 8 (seven major advanced capitalist states plus Russia)
G17 Plus	Serbian think tank turned technocratic political party
GDP	gross domestic product
GMP	gross material product (measure of national income favoured by Communist regimes)
GSS	New Democracy and the Civic Alliance of Serbia
GSZ	ground safety zone (the buffer zone along Serbia's borders with Kosova and the ROM, 1999–)
GZP	Group for Changes (think tank turned political party in Montenegro)
HDS	Croatian Democratic Party
HDZ	Croatian Democratic Union
HNS	Croatian People's Party
HPSS	*Hrvatska Pucka Seljacka Stranka* (Croatian People's Peasant Party)
HSLS	Croatian Social Liberal Party
HSP	Croatian Party of Rights
HSS	Croatian Peasant Party
ICB	International Commission on the Balkans
ICC	International Criminal Court
ICG	International Crisis Group (inf uential Brussels-based NGO)
ICTY	International Criminal Tribunal for former Yugoslavia
IDPs	internally displaced persons
IDS	Istrian Democratic Assembly (political party in Croatia)
IFOR	Implementation Force for Bosnia
IHT	*International Herald Tribune*
IMF	International Monetary Fund
IMRO	Internal Macedonian Revolutionary Organization

JAT	Yugoslav (later Serb) national airline
JMO	Yugoslav Muslim Organization (in inter-war Bosnia)
JNA	Yugoslav People's Army
JSO	Special Operations Unit, Serbia's notorious 'Red Berets'
JUL	Yugoslav United Left (Serbia)
KAP	*Kombinat Aluminijuma Podgorica* (Podgorica aluminium combine, Montenegro)
KAT	*Kombinat Aluminijuma Titograd* (Titograd aluminium combine, Montenegro)
KFOR	Kosova Peace Implementation Force (established by NATO in 1999)
KLA	Kosova Liberation Army (Ushtria Climatare e Kosoves)
KNS	Coalition for National Accord
LCC	League of Communists of Croatia
LCK	League of Communists of Kosovo
LCS	League of Communists of Serbia
LCY	League of Communists of Yugoslavia
LDK	Democratic League of Kosova
LDP	Liberal Democratic Party (in the ROM)
LNC	National Liberation Front (Albania)
LPK	*Levizja Popullore e Kosoves* Popular Movement for Kosovo (the militant Kosovar movement behind the KLA)
LS	Liberal Party
MBO	Muslim Bosniak Organization
MRF	Movement for Rights and Freedoms (Turkish party in Bulgaria)
NATO	North Atlantic Treaty Organization
NCB	National Commercial Bank (Albania)
ND	New Democracy (Serbia)
NDH	Independent State of Croatia (1941–5)
NDS	National Movement for Simeon II (Bulgaria)
NGO	non-governmental organization
NHI	New Croatian Initiative (a Croatian party in Bosnia)
OHR	Office of the High Representative (of the UN in Bosnia
OSCE	Organization for Security and Cooperation in Europe
PCNU	Provisional Council of National Unity
PD	Democratic Party (Romania)
PDA	Party of Democratic Action (Muslim party in Serbia and Bosnia)
PDK	Democratic Party of Kosova
PDP	Party for Democratic Prosperity (ethnic Albanian party in ROM)
PDPr	Party of Democratic Progress (a reformist party in Bosnia, especially RS)
PDS	Party of Democratic Socialists (Serbia)
PDSR	Party of Romanian Social Democracy
PfP	Partnership for Peace (NATO affiliates
PLA	Party of Labour of Albania (Albania's Communist Party, 1946–91)
PNL	National Liberal Party (Romania)

PNR	Romanian National Party
PNT	National Peasant Party (Romania)
PRM	Greater Romania Party
PSD	Party of Social Democracy
PSM	Socialist Labour Party (Romania)
PUNR	Party of Romanian National Unity
PUR	Romanian Humanist Party
reg.	reign
ROM	Republic of Macedonia
RS	Republika Srpska (the predominantly Bosnian Serb 'entity' in Bosnia)
RSK	Republika Srpska Krajina
RTS	Radio Television Serbia
SAA	stabilization and association agreement (a tailored treaty of association with the EU)
SANU	Serbian Academy of Arts and Sciences
SBiH	Party for Bosnia and Herzegovina
SDA	Party of Democratic Action (Bosnia, Montenegro, Serbia)
SDP	Social Democratic Party (in various countries)
SDS	Serbian Democratic Party (Bosnia and Croatia)
SDUM	Social Democratic Union of Macedonia
SFOR	Stabilization Force for Bosnia
SFRY	Socialist Federal Republic of Yugoslavia (the former Communist-ruled Yugoslavia)
SKH	League of Communists of Croatia
SNP	Socialist People's Party (pro-Serb, partly pro-Milosevic, party in Montenegro)
SNS	Serbian People's Union
SNSD	Party of Independent Social Democrats (in Bosnia)
SPA	Socialist Party of Albania
SPO	Serbian Movement of Renewal
SPRS	Socialist Party of Republika Srpska
SPS	Socialist Party of Serbia
SPU	Pensioners Party (Bosnia)
SRS	Serbian Radical Party
SRSJ	Alliance of Reform Forces of Yugoslavia
SRT	Serbian Radio and Television network (in Pale, Bosnia)
TO	Territorial Defence units (in Yugoslavia and its successor states)
TOL	Transitions Online (www.tol.cz) (a very useful information service on Europe's post-Communist states)
UCK	Ushtria Climatare Kombetare (National Liberation Army)
UCPMB	Liberation Army of Presevo, Medvedya and Bujanovac
UDB	Uprava Drzavne Bezbednosti (the SFRY's state security service)
UDF	Union of Democratic Forces (Bulgaria)
UDMR	Democratic Union of Hungarians of Romania
UJDI	Association for Yugoslav Democratic Initiative
UN	United Nations

UNEP	United Nations Environment Programme
UNHCR	UN High Commission for Refugees
UNIPTF	UN International Police Task Force (in post-Dayton Bosnia)
UNMIK	UN Mission in Kosova
UNPREDEP	UN Preventative Deployment Force
UNPROFOR	UN Protection Force (in Bosnia and Croatia)
USD	Union of Social Democrats (Romania)
VAT	value added tax
VJ	Yugoslav Army (army of the Serbian rump FRY)
VMRO	Internal Macedonian Revolutionary Organization
VMRO-DPMNE	Internal Macedonian Revolutionary Organization–Democratic Party for Macedonian National Unity
WEU	Western European Union
WTO	World Trade Organization
ZOP	centralized payments/clearing system used in the SFRY and, for a time, in its successor states.

The post-Communist Balkans and adjacent states

1 Conceptual frameworks

'The Balkans' and the nature of
post-Communist democratization
and economic transformations

This book describes, analyses and assesses the history, accomplishments, problems and challenges of the post-Communist states in the Balkan Peninsula. In order to 'set the scene' and establish an overarching framework for our country studies, this Introduction briefly assesses (i) what does and does not constitute 'the Balkans'; (ii) the place of the Balkan Peninsula in Europe; (iii) the nature, context and trajectories of democratization and liberalization in the post-Communist Balkan states; and (iv) the nature of the economic transformations in the post-Communist Balkans. The Introduction concludes with brief explanations of our selective coverage of the history of the Balkans prior to the 1990s and of the reasons for our omission of Greece and Slovenia from this book.

What does and does not constitute 'the Balkans'

This book endeavours to use the expression 'the Balkan Peninsula' in a culturally neutral territorial or geographical sense to refer to a particularly rugged and mountainous promontory jutting out south-eastwards from Europe, which is itself merely a peninsular appendage to the vast Eurasian landmass. Nevertheless, we are fully aware that the words 'Balkan' and 'the Balkans' are heavily laden with multiple cultural meanings, connotations and stereotypical images, that some of these meanings and images are quite rightly considered to be demeaning, condescending, derogatory or at best ambiguous, and that the terms 'Balkan' and 'the Balkans' are therefore by no means fully accepted by this peninsula's inhabitants. These people understandably feel even less happy with the more obviously pejorative uses of the term 'Balkanization'. This has come into widespread use to signify the onset of endemic propensities towards highly debilitating (and often self-perpetuating) political, cultural and socio-economic fragmentation, deeply destructive and often fratricidal inter-communal conflict, political destabilization, intemperate or intolerant attitudes an mentalities, pervasive clientelism and corruption, a preponderance of relatively oppressive *vertical* power relations and power structures, weak development of the rule of law, stunted development of impersonal *horizontally structured* 'civil', legal and 'associational' ties and relationships, the exercise of unstable and strongly personalized power and influence, a prevalence of polities with strong coercive but wea 'infrastructural' capabilities and widespread feelings of victimization, vindictiveness and fatalism. There are some limited respects in which the term 'Balkanization' is illuminating and helpful, but we fully recognize that it can also be used in unwarrantedly pejorative or dangerously misleading senses, from which we wish to dissociate this book at the outset.

Even though our attraction to and high regard for the peoples of the Balkan Peninsula has encouraged both of us to devote more than thirty years of our working lives to studying them, we sadly accept that the concept of 'Balkanization' does convey some significant aspects of the predicaments in which the peoples and polities on thi peninsula have had the misfortune to find themselves since the nineteenth century (Bideleux and Jeffries 1998: 2–7, 25–8, 37–41 and 97–108). At the same time, we emphasize that this is not the whole story and that the notion of 'Balkanization' is fraught with dangers of crude and highly misleading *cultural stereotyping* and *national caricatures*. This book is highly critical of the often crude, arrogant and profoundly ignorant generalizations about so-called Balkan 'mentalities', 'attitudes' and 'mind-sets' which emanate mainly (though not exclusively) from Western observers. It has been all too easy for outside observers to consider 'Balkanization' to be a congenital condition of the peoples of the Balkan Peninsula and, by attributing it to innate or genetically determined 'Balkan' characteristics and mentalities, to succumb to facile and fatalistic assumptions that the inhabitants of this peninsula are somehow incapable of thinking and behaving in more peaceful and 'civilized' ways. Assumptions of this sort have underlain most Western and Central European perceptions of politics and conf ict in the Balkans since the late nineteenth century. Such perceptions were strongly aroused for the frst time by the so-called 'Bulgarian atrocities' of April 1876, when irregular forces known as *bashibazouks* in the service of the Ottoman Empire were accused of having killed around 5,000 Bulgarian Christians (mainly women and children), many of whom were burned alive in a church in which they had taken refuge (Crampton 1997: 81–2). These perceptions were reinforced by the grisly murder of the King and Queen of Serbia during a military *coup d'état* in 1903, and were strengthened still further by the gruesome atrocities that armed combatants in the Balkan Peninsula inflicted on many thousands of civilians during the Balkan Wars o 1912–13, during the First and Second World Wars, during the aftermaths of those wars, during the Yugoslav conflicts of 1991–5, and in Kosova in 1999. There is n denying that such actions were extremely barbaric and shocking. Nevertheless, the often prurient Western accounts of such terrible occurrences too easily portray them as peculiarly 'Balkan', 'alien', 'other', 'un-European' and even exotic and 'Oriental', apparently forgetting that similar or far greater atrocities have been committed more than once in twentieth-century Germany, Austria, Poland, Hungary, Czechoslovakia, Spain, Ireland, France, the Netherlands, Belgium and Italy, to name only the most obvious cases, and that (appalling though they were) all such occurrences in the Balkan Peninsula were dwarfed by the scale of the barbarism and atrocities committed by hundreds of thousands of ethnic Germans and their mostly Austrian, French, Italian, Dutch, Belgian, Baltic, Hungarian, Croat, Romanian, Ukrainian and Belorussian collaborators against millions of (mostly but not exclusively Jewish and Gypsy) civilians during the Second World War. This is *not* said in order to excuse or play down in any way the many barbarities committed by inhabitants of the Balkan Peninsula, but simply to keep things in perspective and to emphasize that the latter have no monopoly on barbarism, ethnic cleansing and genocide, which need to be seen as products of broader 'European' rather than narrowly 'Balkan' 'civilization'. Western and Central Europeans have no grounds whatsoever to feel either morally superior to, or more 'civilized' than, the inhabitants of the Balkans. Rather than being fundamentally 'alien' or 'essentially different', the post-Communist Balkans have been a microcosm of Europe as a whole and a very revealing mirror in which Western and Central Europeans have been uncomfortably reminded of the dangerous currents of xenophobia, bigotry, inter-communal violence and racist violence which still lurk not far below the surface in their own societies and cultures. As Mohandas Gandhi famously replied to the Western journalist who asked him 'What do you think about Western civilization?', 'That would be a good idea!'. The perverted, sadistic and degrading acts of barbarity committed by some Western soldiers against Iraqi detainees in 2003–4 are merely the most recent proofs of his point.

In using the expressions 'the Balkans' and 'Balkan', therefore, this book is in no way suggesting that the peoples, states and societies of the Balkan Peninsula are morally or culturally 'inferior' to the peoples, states and societies of Western and Central Europe, nor that the inhabitants of the Balkan Peninsula are more culturally conditioned or genetically programmed to kill one another than are their Western or Central European 'cousins'. Quite the contrary, although Balkan strife is still fresh in the memory, in a slightly longer historical time-frame, the scale of the ethnic cleansing, genocide and wanton killing carried out in the Balkan Peninsula has been utterly dwarfed by the scale of similar types of atrocity perpetrated in many other parts of Europe since the late Middle Ages. Indeed, for all its arrogance and ill-founded conceits, no other part of the world has been more prone to racism, bigotry and violent inter-communal conf ict than Europe.

The main practical reason why this book refers to this peninsula as 'the Balkans' is that this is the name that most immediately and precisely conveys to most people the region under discussion. If a less loaded but generally recognized collective designation for these countries were available, that would be used instead. The principal problem with the more neutral-sounding designation 'South-eastern Europe' (which some writers prefer precisely because they think it has fewer negative connotations; e.g., Lampe 2006) is that it refers to a much larger area which commonly includes Turkey, Cyprus and Moldova and ought also to include Georgia, Armenia and Ukraine. Another problem (albeit largely ignored in the West) is that the term 'South-eastern Europe' (*Südosteuropa*) 'became an important concept in the geopolitical views of the Nazis', which resulted in 'the complete discrediting of this term in its German usage' (Todorova 1997: 28).

In any case, it ought to become possible to use 'the Balkans' not as a pejorative term, but as one which encapsulates much that is positive, beautiful, inspiring, admirable, vibrant and exciting, even though many of the region's strengths, virtues and cultural achievements have not yet gained as much international recognition as they deserve. In so far as this book uses the term 'the Balkans' in something more than the purely geographical sense, it is in predominantly positive and admiring ways. Other valuable discussions of 'Balkanism' and 'Balkanness' include: Maria Todorova (1997), Dusan Bjelic and Obrad Savic (eds) (2002), Vesna Goldsworthy (1998), Milica Bakic-Hayden (1995) and John Allcock (2000a).

The relative standing of the Balkan Peninsula in Europe

The Western European Industrial Revolution, coupled with Balkan and East European specialization in the exportation of unsophisticated and less remunerative primary products, widened Europe's east–west disparity in per-capita GDP (at market prices) from about 2:1 to about 3:1 during the nineteenth century (Berend 1986: 339). By 2004, these economic disparities had widened enormously, to a ratio of around 14:1 or 15:1 (at market prices) for Albania and Bosnia, 1:13 for Macedonia, 12:1 for Serbia and Montenegro, 11:1 for Bulgaria, 10:1 for Romania and 1:5 for Croatia (World Bank

2005: 292–3). Therefore, unless Western Europe were to suffer some currently unforeseen catastrophe, these massive east–west economic disparities are bound to persist for another 50 to 100 years from now. This would be the case even if the Balkan economies were to grow by historically exceptional rates of 5 or 6 per cent per annum for several decades to come.

Substantial reductions of the huge east–west economic disparities which currently exist will take even longer if the Balkans continue to be dogged by the recurrent warfare and political and economic crises which they repeatedly experienced during the twentieth century. Of course, we fervently hope that such crises and warfare will not recur. Unfortunately the odds are strongly stacked against a prospectus of continuous peace and economic growth. As the International Commission on the Balkans rightly warned in its powerful report on *The Balkans in Europe's Future* (April 2005), the post-Communist Balkan states are currently grappling with mass poverty, very extensive unemployment and under-employment, severely damaged social fabrics, glaring inequalities, seriously restricted mobility and (most alarmingly of all) major criminal gangs and networks which engage in widespread racketeering and have a powerful hold on large parts of these economies and societies and even on parts of their security forces, judiciaries and political systems. These countries are in part being 'held captive' by organized crime and various forms of racketeering, and they desperately need sustained external help in order to break free from their mostly quite ruthless and dangerous captors. Furthermore, the foreseeable future is still fraught with dangers of renewed economic breakdown, societal breakdown, political instability and violent inter-ethnic or inter-state conf ict.

The economic benefits from the major externally funded reconstruction programme which were launched in the aftermath of the confcts in Croatia and in Bosnia between 1991 and 1995 and following the Kosova war in March–June 1999 had run their course by 2003 or 2004. Much of the damage to physical infrastructure had been repaired, and the temporary (artificial) economic stimuli by reconstruction work and by ne inflows of economic aid were beginning to dry up. Unemployment rates, which fell temporarily during the reconstruction booms, then started rising again – to offial rates exceeding 30 per cent in Bosnia, Serbia and Macedonia and exceeding 50 per cent in Kosova. In addition, it was becoming much harder for unemployed and impoverished inhabitants of the Balkan states and the Kosova protectorate to escape to other parts of Europe as refugees, asylum-seekers or economic migrants. The very fact that the f ghting in the Balkans had at least temporarily stopped made it harder for inhabitants of the post-Communist Balkan states to claim refugee or asylum status in European Union (EU) states, and increasing xenophobia and rising restrictions on migration into EU states were having a similar effect. In addition, many hundreds of thousands of refugees and economic migrants from the Yugoslav successor states, Kosova and Albania either returned voluntarily or were sent 'back home' after the ghting stopped. Partly for these reasons, the hitherto relatively large inflows of remittances from Yugoslavs, Kosovars, Albanians and other displaced persons and economic migrants working in Western Europe and North America began to diminish and were expected to fall even further. The International Commission on the Balkans therefore rightly warned that the economic recovery which had begun in the later 1990s and resumed after the Kosova crisis might not be sustained and could even go into reverse and that mass poverty, mass unemployment, glaring inequalities, organized criminal racketeering and restricted mobility, along with the resultant loss of hope for future improvement in these harrowing conditions and uncertainties about the future status of Kosova, Montenegro and the Bosnian confederation, could easily reignite the kinds of inter-ethnic and inter-state conflict and intra-state insurgency that struck the Balkan in 1991–5, 1998–9 and 2001. These sobering perspectives were backed up by the International Crisis Group and other professional 'watchers' of the Balkans. Therefore, even though the major insurgency in Macedonia in 2001 was followed by several years of relative tranquillity in the Balkans, there were no grounds for complacent optimism regarding the future of the Balkans. We return to these themes in Chapter 11.

Explaining divergent patterns of post-Communist democratization and liberalization

Since the end of Communist rule, the most crucial political and economic challenges in East Central Europe, the Balkans and in the CIS (the Commonwealth of Independent States, alias 'Eastern Europe') have been to break away from the primacy of 'vertical' power relations, 'vertical' power structures, 'ethnic collectivism' and often gang-sterish 'power clans' based upon large-scale and clientelistic use of patronage and corruption, in order to establish more 'horizontally structured' civil societies and civil economies based upon the rule of law. Changes of this order have been needed in order to lay the indispensable foundations for more liberal, accountable and law-governed forms of democracy and market economy. Such changes can be characterized most graphically (and in a nutshell) as shifts from vertically to horizontally structured polities, economies and societies.

The widely differing degrees and trajectories of post-Communist democratization and liberalization, as well as the major impediments to such changes (especially in the Balkans and in the CIS), have widely been explained and portrayed *in cultural or so-called 'civilizational' terms* – that is to say, in terms of *attitudes, mentalities, mindsets, value systems* and *religious-cum-political cultures.* For example, in a widely acclaimed study of the illiberal yet elective regime maintained by Slobodan Milosevic in Serbia from 1987 to 2000, Lenard Cohen has argued that Milosevic's

> political ascendancy and consolidation of power depended primarily on factors having more to do with the cultural underpinnings, rather than the structural features, of the Serbian polity ... Although it is analytically difficult, even dangerous, to extrapolate from ... the historically conditioned Serbian mindset directly to contemporary and current political dynamics, the importance of cultural factors in understanding Serbian politics should not be ignored .. Indeed, while enthusiasm for 'instinctive democracy', 'self-determination', and 'democratic participation' are often noted as major components of the Serbian 'national character', historically Serbian political culture placed even more emphasis on the value of strong leaders ... who can pursue the community's national mission ... Deeply engrained facets of Serbian political culture clearly provided especially fertile soil for Milosevic's populist leadership style and appeal.
>
> (Cohen 2002: 128)

It is easy to find similar emphases on nationalism and illiberal 'political cultures' a the chief determinants of political, societal and economic outcomes in many other recent studies of Serbian, Croatian, Bosnian, Macedonian, Albanian, Romanian and Bulgarian politics and history, as also for Russia, Belarus, Moldova the Caucasus and Central Asia.

1.1 Key economic statistics, 2004

	GDP per capita (PPP) ($)	Distribution of workforce by occupation (%)			Unemployment (%)	Foreign debt ($ bn)	Public debt (% GDP)
		Agriculture	Industry	Services			
Albania	4,900	58.0	19.0	23.0	14.8 (30)[2]	1.4	–
Bulgaria	8,200	11.0	32.7	56.3	12.7	16.1	42.0
Romania	7,700	31.6	30.7	37.7	6.3	24.6	23.6
Croatia	11,200	2.7	32.8	64.5	13.8	26.4	41.7
Serbia[1]	2,400	–	–	–	30.0	13.0	80.0
Bosnia	6,500	–	–	–	44.0[3]	3.0	–
Macedonia	7,100	–	–	–	38.0	1.9	20.0

1. Including Montenegro and Vojvodina
2. Unofficial estimates exceeded 30 per cent.
3. Unofficial estimates allowing for grey economy reduced the actual rate to 25–30 per cent.

For purposes of comparison:

	GDP per capita (PPP) ($)	Distribution of workforce by occupation (%)			Unemployment (%)	Foreign debt ($ bn)	Public debt (% GDP)
		Agriculture	Industry	Services			
Slovenia	19,600	6.0	40.0	55.0	6.4	14.7	31.5
Russia	9,800	12.3	22.7	65.0	8.3	169.6	28.2
Portugal	17,900	10.0	30.0	60.0 (1999)	6.5	274.7	61.5
Greece	21,300	12.0	20.0	68.0	10.0	67.2	112.0
Spain	23,300	5.3	30.1	64.6	10.4	771.1	53.2
Italy	27,700	5.0	32.0	63.0 (2001)	8.6	913.9	105.6
France	28,700	4.1	24.4	71.5	10.1	–	67.7
UK	29,600	1.5	19.1	79.5	4.8	4710.0	39.6

Note: GDP per capita at purchasing power parity.

Source: CIA (2005).

However, our thirty or more years of research on political and economic change
in the post-Communist Balkans, East Central Europe and Russia have revealed
fundamental flaws and inadequacies in this influential but misleading emphasis
the allegedly pivotal importance of 'political culture', 'mindsets' and popular 'attitudes' and 'mentalities' as major explanatory factors or independent variables. In our
view (which has elements in common with the work of some other Balkan specialists,
such as V. P. Gagnon and Eric Gordy), such explanations implicitly or explicitly rely
on caricature and cultural stereotyping as substitutes for more concrete and circum-
spect observation and analysis. Protracted study of each of the post-Communist Balkan
states has convinced us that attitudes, mentalities and mindsets are for the most
part highly malleable and manipulable *dependent variables*, rather than determining
independent variables, and that they change over time in response to changes in power
relations, power structures and resultant behavioural incentives and opportunities.
We have found that (i) the impediments to – and the differing degrees and trajectories
of – democratization and liberalization can be much more concretely and cogently
explained in terms of prevailing power relations and power structures, including the
influence of 'ethnic collectivism' understood more as a power structure than as a
mentality; and (ii) the incidence of vertically structured power relations and power
structures does not neatly correspond to cultural or supposedly 'civilizational'
demarcation lines, but rather cuts across them.

In the East Central European states that joined the EU in May 2004, the struggles
to fulfil the 'Copenhagen criteria' and 'Madrid criteria' for EU membership helpe
to foster growing cross-party consensuses on macro-economic policies, privatization,
restructuring of institutions and industries, judicial and legal reform and promotion
and protection of human and minority rights, which in turn helped to promote the
rule of law, equal citizenship (equal civil rights and equality before the law), political
stability, democracy and the development of more 'level playing fields' and more
fully marketized and liberalized economies. This in turn helped slowly to *restructure
and reorientate* these candidate countries away from the prevalence of 'vertical' power
relations and power structures, from the primacy of 'primordial' ethno-cultural ties,
and from clientelistic and 'ethnic collectivist' conceptions of the polity, towards
stronger horizontally structured impersonal ties and civil societies and civil econo -
mies based upon the rule of law. This was inherently complex and far from easy
to accomplish, but it has nevertheless been accomplished to remarkable degrees. It
was implicitly on this basis that it was decided at Copenhagen in December 2002 to
let them enter the EU in May 2004.

Starting in the immediate aftermath of the Kosova war of March–June 1999,
and reinforced by the formal pledge given at the Thessaloniki European Council
in 2003, the 'dangled carrot' of eventual EU membership has been giving the formerly Communist-ruled Balkan countries powerful incentives and political leverage
to carry out similar but very difficult changes. This is probably the main reason
why such changes have latterly made much more headway in the Balkans than
in the CIS (Commonwealth of Independent States, the former Soviet republics
other than the Baltic states), which have thus far been given few grounds for
hoping that they can realistically aspire to eventual membership of the EU. The EU
is therefore having much less impact on the post-Soviet CIS than on the Balkan states.
This is strongly reinforced by the fact that the Balkan states are much closer to the
EU and a great deal smaller than countries such as Russia and Ukraine. Any given
amount of EU economic aid and political leverage can have far greater effects on

the mostly very small Balkan states than it can on the vastness of Russia or even on Ukraine.

The main impediments which have damaged and constrained the democratization and liberalization of the post-Communist Balkans states, seriously delaying their admission into the EU, have been the closely inter-linked legacies of deeply entrenched 'vertical' power structures, 'vertical' power relations, ethnic collectivism and pervasive clientelism, corruption and gangsterism.

These are features which the post-Communist Balkans have shared with all but three of the former Soviet republics (the three exceptions being Estonia, Latvia and Lithuania). In current academic writing in and on post-Communist Russia, this deeply entrenched legacy from both tsarist and Soviet times is aptly referred to as the problem of 'the verticality of authority', which has been skilfully deployed to perpetuate the dominance of Russia's tenacious and highly clientelistic 'power clans' (Shevtsova 2005: 7, 10). As Mikhail Gorbachev's former close colleague and political adviser Alexander Yakovlev once put it, 'Russia's great misfortune is always to have been ruled by men rather than by laws' (although he should have added that during the eighteenth century it was also ruled by some exceedingly powerful women).

Sadly, while the post-Communist East Central European states have largely accomplished the critical shift from a preponderance of 'vertical' power relations and power structures to horizontally structured civil societies and civil economies based upon the rule of law, and while the post-Communist Balkan states are also moving in this direction under the impact of quite extraordinary levels of Western (mainly EU) leverage-cum-tutelage, Russia under Putin is moving in the opposite direction. Putin is steadily reinforcing the 'verticality of authority' in Russia. Buoyed up by surging oil and gas revenues, which increasingly accrue directly to the Russian state and to Putin as executive president of that state, Putin is gradually turning Russia into a 'rentier state'. This is not only superf cially reviving parts of the Russian economy on the basis of increased state spending and tax remissions, but is also rendering the Russian state (and President Putin himself) increasingly independent from taxpayers' scrutiny and control. This reverses the 'normal' healthier relationship between the state and civil society. In Russia, instead of the state being substantially accountable to and dependent upon civil society, the state finds itself i an ever-stronger position to exercise patronage, control and tutelage over civil society. Whatever the inscrutable Mr Putin's personal inclinations and ambitions might be, this fundamentally keeps Russian democratization and liberalization 'in reverse gear'.

In response to the important question of why the Balkans and the CIS regions have been characterized by such a deeply entrenched predominance of 'vertical' power structures and 'vertical' power relations, reinforced by the pervasive dominance of ethnic collectivism, the short (but not glib) answer is that this has been the 'normal' condition of more than f ve-sixths of humanity. What *really* needs to be explained is the nature of the relatively few polities and societies (comprising less than one-sixth of the world's population) which have managed against the odds to escape the usual 'verticality of power', but readers will be relieved to hear that this lies far beyond the remit of the present book! However, a region-specific explanation for the prevalenc of long-standing and deeply entrenched power relations and power structures in the Balkan states has been offered elsewhere (Bideleux 2005a: 667–81).

Against cultural or 'civilizational' explanations

Most of the Balkan states and the most populous former Soviet republics are pre-dominantly Eastern Orthodox by religion and can therefore be seen as belonging to (and indeed constituting) 'Eastern Orthodox Christendom'. There are therefore strong temptations to attribute the great difficulties which they have experienced i establishing robustly liberal and law-governed forms of civil society, democracy and market capitalism to their shared Byzantine (autocratic) and Eastern Orthodox Christian heritage, along the lines that Toynbee, Huntington and their followers have done. It is very easy (albeit simplistic) to win cheap applause from Western politi-cians and the media by pedalling crudely stereotypical or caricatured contrasts between an allegedly liberal, tolerant, individualistic, law-governed, societally autonomous and easily democratized and marketized 'Latin West', on the one hand, and the sup-posedly illiberal, autocratic, personalistic and collectivist *political cultures*, *attitudes* and *mentalities* which allegedly prevail among the Eastern Orthodox peoples, on the other. It has been even easier (and even more simplistic) for Toynbee, Huntington and their followers to contrast the 'Latin West' with the (often stereotyped or caricatured) illiberal and personalistic 'Oriental despotisms' which have allegedly been characteristic of 'Islamic' peoples and cultures (Toynbee 1935–54; Huntington 1993, 1998).

Nevertheless, these so-called 'civilizational' perspectives are seriously unsound and misleading. Strongly Roman Catholic countries or regions such as Croatia, southern Italy and (until relatively recently) Portugal and Spain have experienced almost as much difficulty in establishing robustly liberal and law-governed forms of civil society, democracy and market capitalism as have the Eastern Orthodox and Muslim peoples of the Balkans and the former Soviet Union. In crudely conceived 'civilizational' terms, both Croatia and southern Italy have belonged to 'the Latin West' rather than to 'the Orthodox East', yet this has not helped them to become markedly more liberal or democratic or law-governed than Eastern Orthodox post-Communist states such as Bulgaria or Romania. Conversely, Greece has already managed to establish, and Turkey appears to be establishing, increasingly robust, liberal and law-governed forms of democracy, civil society and market capitalism, even though Greece is predominantly Eastern Orthodox and Turkey is largely Muslim.

A focus on 'vertical' versus 'horizontally structured' power structures and power relations as the major explanatory factors or 'independent variables' which can account for why some parts of Europe have experienced much greater difficulty in establishin robustly liberal and law-governed forms of civil society, democracy and market capitalism is thus not only more cogent but also offers a much better 'fit' than do so-called 'cultural' explanations that are couched in terms of religion and the so-called 'civilizational' characteristics, which are often crudely attributed to different religions. Furthermore, *none* of the enduringly dynamic and successful 'civilizations' in world history has ever been culturally *monolithic* or *homogeneous*; and much of the vigour and dynamism of these civilizations has in fact stemmed from their being *culturally heterogeneous* (usually multi-denominational or multi-cultural or both). This makes it all the more misleading to label or characterize 'civilizations' in terms of a single 'marker', such as a predominant religion or language grouping.

Instead of treating supposedly culturally determined attitudes, mindsets and 'mentalities' as 'independent variables' or as relatively fixed or immutable determi nants of political and economic behaviour and performance, it is both sounder and more fruitful to treat them as relatively malleable 'dependent variables', especially as responses to long-standing or deeply entrenched power relations, power structures and structures of opportunities and incentives which are capable of being changed by sufficiently persistent and determined policies, actions and reforming elites. The literature based upon cultural and 'civilizational' stereotyping has been far too fatalistic (i.e., pessimistic) about the scope for changing societal power relations and power structures, and hence for changing the attitudes, 'mentalities' and behaviour which they evoke. This is not only true in relation to the southern, east central, south-eastern and eastern regions of Europe, but even more so in relation to the so-called 'Confucian civilizations' of East Asia, which were until recently regarded as irredeemably rigid, conservative, 'Oriental', despotic, stultifying and lethargic, yet have spectacularly confounded the cultural caricatures and stereotypes imposed upon them by major currents of Western thought from Montesquieu and François Guizot through Max Weber to Karl Wittfogel.

Instead of finding profound and tenacious differences in attitudes, mentalities, values and aspirations between the predominantly Catholic, the predominantly Eastern Orthodox and the predominantly Muslim areas of Europe, many surveys on attitudes, values, opinions, concerns, preoccupations and aspirations in the eastern half of Europe during the 1990s found that these did not differ very greatly from those prevalent in the western half of Europe (see, for example, Miller et al. 1998; Sakwa 2002: 343–4). Studies of Serbia and Croatia during the Yugoslav conficts of 1991–5 found that most people were preoccupied with mundane bread-and-butter issues rather than with fratricidal hatred (Gordy 1999; Gagnon 2004). Public-opinion research conducted in the multi-ethnic Republic of Macedonia in 2005, which came close to being torn apart by conflict between ethnic Albanian insurgents and predominantl Slavic state security forces (in 2001), similarly revealed that the major *popular* preoccupations were (i) unemployment, (ii) poverty and (iii) corruption, rather than inter-communal hatreds (Stavrova and Alagjozovski 2005f).

The curse of ethnic collectivism

Contrary to the dominant media caricatures of Europe's post-Communist states, the curse of ethnic collectivism is not an affliction peculiar to the Balkans, or to the Balkan plus East Central Europe and the former Soviet republics, even though the great upheavals of 1989–2001 have sometimes caused 'ethnic collectivism' to appear much more salient or even rampant in the eastern than in the western half of Europe. The pernicious consequences of 'ethnic collectivism' pervade the whole of Europe (and several other sub-continents and continents as well, for that matter). We are therefore only confronted by continually fluctuating differences in saliency rather tha 'chalk-and-cheese' differences in kind.

Dwelling on the pernicious effects of 'ethnic collectivism' is not a matter of apportioning blame or postulating that some ethnic groups are or have been inherently worse-behaved than others. On the contrary, today's victims have all too often been yesterday's villains, and vice versa; and this largely invalidates the frequent claims that certain ethnic groups have been innately worse than others. The root of the problem is not the (often appalling) conduct of certain ethnic groups towards other ethnic groups, but the pernicious effects of 'ethnic collectivism' per se. As remarked by Rudolf Rocker, the French Revolution of 1789 freed

the people from the yoke of royal power, but in doing so it merely plunged them
into deeper bondage to the national state. And this chain proved more effective
than the straightjacket [sic] of the absolute monarchy, because it was anchored,
not in the power of the ruler, but in the abstract idea of the 'common will', which
sought to fit all efforts of the people to a definite nor

(Rocker 1937: 43)

In present-day Europe, the post-Communist Balkan states are the ones which most
need 'to free human beings from the bondage of ethnic collectivism – that source of
all strife and enslaver of human individuality', as Vaclav Havel aptly put it (Havel
1996: 40). They also need to be freed from the straitjacket of the nation-state. In
large measure, this is because in the Balkans (as also in East Central Europe), 'ethnic
collectivism', ethnic discrimination and the preferential status of dominant ethnic
groups are not just unfortunate and regrettable lapses or aberrations. On the contrary,
since the Berlin Congress of 1878 ratif ed the creation of several newly independent
states on an 'ethnic' basis in the Balkans in 1878, and even more markedly since
President Woodrow Wilson formally proclaimed in January 1918 that the doctrine of
'national self-determination' would be the guiding principle of the post-1918 peace
settlements, the result has been to make ethnic collectivism, ethnic discrimination
and the preferential status of numerically dominant ethnic groups *the very basis* of
the state, of democratic representation, of public employment and of many (perhaps
most) social, political and economic rights and entitlements in the so-called 'successor
states' of the Balkans and East Central Europe (Bideleux and Jeffries 1998: 407–17).
It is this 'ethnocratic' basis of the post-Habsburg and post-Ottoman 'new order' in
the Balkans and East Central Europe, rather than the frequently over-stated contrasts
between 'Eastern' and 'Western' forms of nationalism, which has done most to
differentiate Western Europe from the Balkans and East Central Europe (Bideleux
2001c: 25–32). As a consequence, most states in the Balkans and East Central Europe
have tended to attach greater importance to the perceived *collective rights, interests
and values and aspirations* of the dominant ethnic (and sometimes religious) groups
than to the *rights, interests and values of individuals* (Ramet 1997). From their
inception, the *new* nation-states established in the Balkans and East Central Europe
clung tenaciously to archaic self-images and Quixotic conceptions of national valour,
while nationalists became increasingly messianic and collectivist, claiming rights
for the nation rather than for individual citizens and demanding obedient service to
the nation, which was seen as having a 'historic' or 'God-given' mission or destiny
to fulfil (Sugar 1971: 11). To question or reject this 'mission' became tantamount t
'treason', and individuals who held out against this national messianism and ethnic
(or religious) collectivism were often regarded as 'traitors' to their nation.

The concept of 'ethnocracy' was coined in relation to inter-war Romania by the
Romanian nationalist intellectual Nichifor Crainic (1938: 283–4), but similarly
dangerous notions became deeply entrenched and influential in most of the Balka
and East Central European states at that time:

Romania has been, and must be, the ethnic state of the Romanians. The state is
the dynamic organization of the nation through the will and power of native
Romanians . . . A nationalist state is an ethnocratic state .. . The ethnocratic state
is the will for power and increase of the Romanian people. Its principal factors
are: soil, blood, soul, faith. The soil of the Romanian people has today inhabitants

of other races and faiths, as well. They came here through invasion (like the Hungarians), colonization (like the Germans), through crafty infiltration (like the Jews). Every one of them, fonder of its own people than of ours, presents no guarantees of security for the official organism of the state. The Jews are permanent danger for every national state. The experience of other states teaches us that any unassimilated member of a minority, active in the organism of the state, is an element of dissolution and ruin. It follows from these judgements that it is a vital necessity for Romania to be an exclusively ethnocratic state. Only native Romanians, who have created it through their sacrifice, guarante the durability of the state.

> (Crainic 1938: 283–4; extracts translated
> by James P. Niessen in Sugar 1995: 274–5)

This messianic ethnic collectivism became illiberal, exclusive and xenophobic, and it rendered the Balkan and East Central European nation-states very prone to various forms of nationalist and fascist authoritarianism. The region's dominant ethnic groups rejoiced in their new-found 'national freedom', even when this took the form of repressive dictatorship, and their ascendant power-holders hegemonically promoted the languages and cultures of their own ethnic group, whilst doing as little as possible (or worse) for the languages and cultures of long-standing ethnic minorities. Indeed, having won (or having recently regained) independent statehood after what the triumphant nationalists saw as several centuries of 'national' oppression by alien over-lords, the potentates of the newly ascendant ethnic groups felt quite justifd in keeping the lion's share of any political, cultural or economic spoils for themselves. Even more perniciously, individuals and the rights and interests of individuals (including those of the individual members of dominant ethnic groups) came to be seen as subordinate to the rights and interests of ethnic (or religious) collectivities, for which individuals and individual rights could sometimes be sacrificed. Most of the Balkan and East Central European states became 'ethnocracies', in the sense that they (especially their more-or-less nationalist rulers and intelligentsias) regarded the state and the other major institutions of each country as exclusively belonging to a dominant ethnic group, to considerably greater degrees than was the case in the more inclusive and 'civic' states which gradually came to prevail in most of Western Europe. (By this criterion, Germany and Austria were far more 'Central' than 'Western' European.)

During the early 1990s, as a result of the disintegration of the former Soviet, Yugoslav and Czechoslovak federations, political authority in Central and Eastern Europe was further reconfigured along putatively national lines – there was a 'massiv "nationalization" of political space' (Brubaker 1996: 3). For nationalists, this was a cause for euphoria and celebration, but even for them the prosaic and often grim realities gradually struck home. Unchecked 'ethnic collectivism' is stif ing, stultify-ing, intimidating and sometimes lethal – most obviously for minorities, but also to lesser degrees for the dominant ethnic group(s) as well. The region's 'free spirits' felt boxed in or imprisoned by the confining ethnic identities which were forced upon the more (a)stringently than ever before. The 'Croatian' writer Slavenka Drakulic famously described the consequences in personal terms:

> Being Croat has become my destiny . . . I am defined by my nationality, and
> by it alone . . . Along with millions of other Croats, I was pinned to the wall of
> nationhood – not only by outside pressure from Serbia and the Federal Army,

but by national homogenization within Croatia itself . . . reducing us to one dimension – the Nation . . . Whereas before I was defined by my education, m job, my ideas, my character – and yes, my nationality too – now I feel stripped of all that.

(Drakulic 1993: 50–2)

In that context, many Yugoslav males who had previously thought of themselves simply as Yugoslavs, free to work and reside in any part of former Yugoslavia, in 1992 suddenly found themselves pinned down to the much smaller, narrower and more restrictive *ethnic* identities specified in each Yugoslav male's military-service docu ments (Serb, Croat, Slovene, Bosniak, Montenegrin, etc.). They quickly discovered that they were not only no longer free to move around the Yugoslav lands, but that they were now expected to back (and if necessary fight for) their own ethnic grou against other Yugoslav ethnic groups whom they had hitherto regarded as fellow citizens, friends, compatriots or even lovers. It was surreal and, for many people, it had catastrophic practical consequences which in some cases threatened careers, livelihoods or even physical survival. Citizens of Romania and Bulgaria similarly found themselves in milder versions of this predicament, as ethnic Romanians and ethnic Bulgarians found themselves ranged against ethnic Hungarian and ethnic Turkish minorities, respectively, during the 1990s.

Taken to extremes, as it was in parts of former Yugoslavia during the 1990s, 'ethnic collectivism' spawned what the Romanian-Hungarian Gaspar Tamás aptly charac-terized as 'ethnarchy' or 'ethno-anarchy', emphasizing its volatile, destabilizing and anarchic properties:

Ethnarchy means here that the source of all power is . . the racially or ethnically pure dominant majority within any arbitrarily given territory . . Countries, states, nations can be reshaped at will, regardless of their ancient traditions or present interests, regardless of ancient ties . . . Only natural identity counts.

The chief concern of those he called 'ethno-anarchists' was to establish

a turf of their own where total identity, total equality, total and magical non-politics reigns supreme. It is a truly radical tendency that . . . has changed the terms of political debate for a long time to come . . The old rules of diplomacy and warfare do not apply, because the aim is not pre-eminence, advantage, or control of alien territory, but delimitation, distance, exit from the world of politics... as we knew it . . . The new ethnarchic power is very frail and volatile, precisely because there are no real arguments there to argue for obedience to authority. After all, anybody within the group is *us* and can and does lay claim to power.

(Tamás 1996: 172–4)

Furthermore, 'The absolute unquestioned power of ethnarchy is apolitical and anti-political.' In contrast to nineteenth-century liberal nationalism, which built states, brought about unifications and fostered high culture, late twentieth-century ethno-anarchism 'destroys states, smashes them into smithereens, and fails to replace them with *anything*. The sheer fact of collective physical existence suff ces . . . This is the end of politics as we know it' (Tamás 1996: 180–3).

This conceptualization vividly conveys the magnitude of the threat posed by the gangsterish, predatory and ostensibly 'ethnic nationalist' paramilitary movements which (once entrenched in power in particular localities) not only targeted former old neighbours transmogrified into 'enemies', but increasingly preyed upon 'their ow people' as well by engaging in mafia-style protection rackets, drug-dealing, arms-smuggling, sex-slavery and people trafficking. As Bill Berkeley has written apropo contemporary Africa, ethnic conflict is 'a form of organized crime . . akin to that of the Sicilian Mafia . . Inflamed ethnic passions are not the cause of political conflic but its consequence' (Berkeley 2001: 15). Like their counterparts in Africa, inter-ethnic conflict, genocide and ethnic cleansing in twentieth-century Europe have been driven and orchestrated by (usually quite educated) criminal entrepreneurs who personally profit from their enterprise in various ways and in the process exploit, manipulate and prey upon many of 'their own kind' as well as on their prime targeted victims. Similar phenomena are to be found in the Americas and Asia: they are global phenomena, rather than culturally specif c, and they manifest themselves in particular circumstances (especially power structures) rather than in particular cultures.

The entrenchment of 'ethnic collectivism' in the Balkans (and East Central Europe) does not mean that whole populations in this region have been more rabidly nationalistic or xenophobic than elsewhere in Europe. The deep-seated ethnic, religious or cultural *collectivism*, which has rightly been seen as the bane of Balkan societies (Sugar and Lederer 1971: Chapter 1; Haddock and Caraiani, 1999), should not be perceived as something intrinsic to Balkan 'psyches', 'mentalities', 'mindsets' or 'political culture', but rather as a not-uncommon dysfunctional phenomenon whose saliency in the Balkans has been magnif ed by the prevalence of highly clientelistic 'vertical' power relations and power structures on that peninsula, including powerful maf a-like criminal networks and protection rackets. 'Ethnic collectivism' has never been primarily a matter of 'popular attitudes' or 'popular mentalities'. It refers much more to the ways in which political and economic power is structured, to elite and intelligentsia attitudes and mindsets or mentalities, to off cial or quasi-off cial con-ceptions of the nature of the polity and to assumptions that the rights and interests of all individuals (not just members of minorities) should be subordinate to the officiall perceived (or even prescribed) rights and interests of the dominant ethnic collectivity. In the Balkans (and East Central Europe), the population at large has never had much say on these matters – or, indeed, on much else. On the contrary, the strong preva - lence of 'vertical' power relations and power structures has ensured that state power holders and relatively narrow elite circles have largely been able to monopolize political decision-making and policy-making. Thus, even if it could be shown that Balkan (and East Central European) popular attitudes and mentalities had indeed been more f ercely nationalistic, intolerant or xenophobic than those of Western Europeans (a claim which is much more open to dispute than is commonly supposed), this need not have impinged very strongly or directly on politics, because (for better or worse) the bulk of the population has played very limited and largely passive roles in political life. This is not to deny that xenophobic ultra-nationalist attitudes and mentalities have also been at work lower down the socio-political scale. Quite manifestly, there were numerous xenophobes and hatemongers among each of the Balkan peoples during the 1990s. However, we have found no evidence that such people have been any more numerous, as percentages of the population, than supporters of the Front National in France, the Freedom Party in Austria, the People's Party in Denmark, the

List Pym Fortyn in the Netherlands, or the Vlams Bloc in Belgium, to name only the most obvious examples of xenophobic movements in Western Europe.

Scholars such as V. P. Gagnon (2004) have demonstrated quite cogently that the levels of popular 'ethnic hatred', xenophobia and 'ethnic mobilization' in countries such as Serbia and Croatia during the 1990s have been greatly exaggerated by the Western media and by balefully sensationalist writers such as Robert Kaplan (1993) and Andre Gerolymatos (2004). For example, it has been convincingly demonstrated that, even though Milosevic *initially* attained power in 1987–90 by mobilizing Serbian nationalism in relation to the allegedly beleaguered plight of the Serb minority in Kosova, he thereafter retained power by ruthlessly exploiting his dominance of *state power structures*, the divisions between his opponents, and a first-past-the-post electoral system, while actively *demobilizing* (rather than mobilizing) an increasingly disaffected, weary and demoralized Serb population (Gordy 1999). The violent conflicts in the Yugoslav lands during the 1990s were manipulated and exploited b power elites

> not in order to mobilize people, but rather as a way to *demobilize* those who were pushing for changes in the structures of economic and political power . . . The goal of this strategy was to silence, marginalize, and demobilize challengers and their supporters . . . This in turn enabled conservatives to maintain control of existing structures of power, as well as to reposition themselves by converting state-owned property into privately held wealth . . . The wars and violence seen in the 1990s were thus not the expression of grass-roots sentiment . . They were also far from being the democratic expression of the political and cultural preferences of the wider population.
>
> (Gagnon 2004: xv)

President Tudjman did much the same in 1990s Croatia (Gagnon 2004: xv, xviii, Chapter 5). Far from being ignited by nationalist fervour, in all the Yugoslav successor states there was very little public support for war and even less enthusiasm for fight ing. In Serbia as a whole, between 50 and 80 per cent of the men called up to f ght refused to serve and 'even among those who did serve there were massive desertions from the battlefield'. Many reservists either rebelled when called up or were shippe off 'to the Bosnian front against their wills' (Gagnon 2004: 2). 'The conflicts in Bosnia were not the result of ethnic hatreds, but rather of purposeful attempts by the Serbian regime to foment conflict as a way of imposing a conservative leadership that would allow recentralization of the federation' (Gagnon 2004: 77). The aim was to thwart and suppress the forms of anti-regime popular mobilization which swept many ex-Communists out of office in other hitherto Communist-ruled states i Europe by reconstructing political space in such a way that 'the only legitimate and authentic political and ideological position was the one held by the ruling party' (Gagnon 2004: 87–8).

> The key here is to focus on the ability of those who control power resources . . . to shape and construct images of interest; the way in which those with power can structure situations such that some interests can or cannot be expressed; the ability of power-elites to set the political agenda and limit options.
>
> (Gagnon 2004: 26)

As mentioned above, public-opinion research in the Republic of Macedonia following the major violent confrontations between members of the ethnic Albanian minority and the Slav-controlled security forces in 2001 showed that the major popular preoccupations were focused not on ethnic hatreds but on bread-and-butter issues: (i) unemployment, (ii) poverty and (iii) corruption (Stavrova and Alagjozovski 2005f). Much the same was true during and after the major violent attacks on the Turkish and Hungarian minorities in Bulgaria and in Romania, respectively, during the early 1990s.

Seen in this light, the pernicious effects of ethnic collectivism in the Balkans (as also in East Central Europe) have largely been determined by the calculations, attitudes and conduct of relatively small ruling elites and of often criminal 'ethnic entrepreneurs', rather than by those of the population at large. Thus the problem of 'ethnic collectivism' in the Balkans and East Central Europe is *not* primarily one of *popular* mentalities and attitudes, but another important manifestation of the prevalence of strongly 'vertical' power relations and power structures. It is also closely tied in with the highly clientelistic and clannish organization of political parties, politics and the state.

Unfortunately, in nations and nation-states that are conceived in exclusive 'ethnic' rather than in more inclusive 'civic' terms, formal 'liberal democracy' has a particularly marked tendency to degenerate into 'ethnocracy', by instituting oppressive new 'collectivist tyrannies of ethnic majorities over ethnic minorities' – especially when the going gets tough and competition for scarce resources and state employment intensifies. In these circumstances, the closed and exclusive notion of the *ethnos* (ethnic group) gets thoroughly confused with and eventually envelops the more open and inclusive notion of the *demos* ('the people'), which comprises all the people who live under a particular jurisdiction (the inclusive concept of 'the nation' proclaimed by the Declaration of the Rights of Man and Citizen during the French Revolution). Furthermore, it has often been a remarkably short step even from democratic 'ethnic collectivism' and 'ethnocracy' to 'ethnic cleansing' or genocide, as Michael Mann has cogently argued in *The Dark Side of Democracy* (2005). The scope for such evils is still far from exhausted and may be resurgent in an increasingly multi-racial, multi-ethnic and multi-denominational Western Europe.

In relation to 'ethnic collectivism', democracy is much more *part of the problem* than part of the solution. This is primarily because *democracy inevitably addresses, empowers and safeguards the rights, interests and aspirations of the dominant ethnic (or religious) collectivities* much more than it empowers and safeguards the rights, interests and aspirations of ethnic and other minorities, but it is also because democracy has a tendency to arouse demons that are best left safely asleep.

The nature of the economic transformations in the post-Communist Balkans

It is usually assumed that the so-called economic 'transitions' that have occurred in each of Europe's formerly Communist-ruled countries since 1989 have involved moves from various forms of 'socialism' to 'capitalism' or market economies. However, it is profoundly misleading to suggest that the economic systems established by the former Communist regimes were in any meaningful sense 'socialist' rather than 'capitalist'. Socialism as a fully fledged radical alternative to capitalism has not yet been tried out anywhere, and it is therefore premature (if not dishonest) to proclaim either the 'failure' or the 'demise' of any meaningful form of 'socialism'.

The economic systems established by the former Communist regimes replaced heavy reliance on market systems and relatively unfettered market forces to allocate resources and to motivate managers and employees with varying forms and degrees of economic planning and state or social ownership of the means of production. However, they continued to employ wage labour to generate and appropriate 'surplus value', albeit mainly in the hands of state or party bureaucracies rather than private capitalists, and they did so primarily in order to produce commodities for sale on state-regulated markets. These economic systems were just as hierarchical and exploitative as the wide range of Western economic systems which go under the name of 'capitalism' or 'the market economy' and treated 'their own' workers and peasants far more brutally and oppressively than did Western market economies (Bideleux 1985: 81, 115–27, 133–4, 144–63, 205–11). The exploitative, hierarchical, corrupt and self-serving nature of the European Communist regimes was conf rmed by the leading Yugoslav Communist-turned-dissident Milovan Djilas, in his famous Marxist critique *The New Class* (Djilas 1957), which followed in the distinguished footsteps of Leon Trotsky's devastating Marxist critique of Stalin's Soviet Union (Trotsky 1937). The economic systems which most Western writers on the former Communist regimes choose to call 'socialism', for reasons that range from concep - tual wooliness to cynical attempts to discredit socialism (which has never yet been put to the test), were hugely oppressive and inefficient bureaucratic travesties of 'socialism' fiercely exploitative, hierarchical and based on piece-rates

Therefore, although the term 'socialism' is often applied to the economic systems established by Europe's former Communist regimes as a convenient shorthand, even by specialists who know full well that these systems were anything but socialist, it is deeply misleading to do so. It thoroughly misunderstands and misrepresents the nature and dynamics of the systems that operated under so-called 'socialism' or rule by self-styled 'Communist parties', as well as the nature of the recent so-called 'transitions' away from those mainly state capitalist systems.

The situation in Communist-ruled Yugoslavia was even more ambiguous. An abortive attempt to establish a centrally planned economy and carry out Soviet-style forced industrialization in the late 1940s, in def ance of Stalin's wishes, brought the Yugoslav Federation to the verge of collapse and had to be abandoned in the early 1950s. It was gradually superseded by a system which came to be called 'workers self-management' because it involved considerable degrees of 'social ownership' and supposedly 'self-managed' enterprises, within which elected workers' councils exer cised some inf uence on managerial power, autonomy and decision-making, especially from *c.*1966 to *c.*1978 (see Lydall 1987, 1989; Estrin 1983, 1991; and a briefer assess-ment in Bideleux 1987: 176–88). From 1976 to 1988, the autonomy of the ostensibly 'self-managed' enterprises became increasingly circumscribed and ossified by prolif erating 'basic organizations of associated labour', 'social compacts' and bureaucratic controls on credit, investment, imports and prices. Most of these controls emanated from the constituent republics rather than from the central (federal) government, but that did not prevent them contributing to the processes by which Yugoslavia's market system became increasingly mired in bureaucracy, cronyism, corruption, inflationary rampant credit creation, over-manning, rigidities, stagflation and mountin unemployment (Lampe 1996: 310–33). Communist-ruled Yugoslavia nevertheless remained a market economy, albeit an increasingly dysfunctional one.

In partial acknowledgement of the problems of calling the economic systems established by the Communist regimes 'socialist', many Western writers on these economic systems resorted to calling them either 'centrally planned economies' or even *sui generis* siege economies or 'war economies in time of peace'. This at least had the virtue of implicitly acknowledging that these systems owed more to the systems and practices developed by certain European states (especially Germany) during the two world wars than they did to the ideas of any of the major socialist thinkers. This was partly because Marx and Engels, who were powerful critics of capitalism, had little to say on the nature of either a 'socialist' or a 'planned' economy. However, calling these systems 'centrally planned economies' is almost as problematic as calling them 'socialist'. Most of the countries examined in this book never became 'centrally planned economies' in reality for any major length of time, so it would be a complete misnomer to think of them as having had to engage in a so-called 'transition' from 'central planning' to 'capitalism' or 'the market'. These Yugoslav successor states were already very hierarchical and exploitative economies based on wage labour and production for (albeit poorly functioning) market systems when Communist rule ended.

Even in Bulgaria, Romania and especially Albania, the 'centrally planned economy' remained largely an aspiration, instead of becoming an actual attainment. These countries, which were not yet highly industrialized and well educated when their Communist parties came to power, generally lacked the human expertise, therfancial wherewithal and the institutional capabilities to centrally plan their economies, even though at that stage their economies were still simple enough to be amenable to central planning (in principle). They were also mired in clientelism, political in-fighting an corruption, which often frustrated the intentions of the central planners. Therefore, while some economic activities were formally brought under the control of central planners, the (often terrifying) pressure to fulfil over-ambitious and arduous plan targets often obliged enterprise directors to improvise, to resort to expedients, to mobilize resources and to engage in (sometimes illegal) horse-trading with one another, and all of this (virtually by definition) could not have been part of 'the plan' or eve envisaged and asked for by the central planners. These planners lacked the supernatural powers of clairvoyance which would have been necessary to draw up internally consistent and viable plans for whole economies f ve years ahead. In addition, political interventions and in-fighting frequently resulted in arbitrary and incompatibl alterations to so-called 'five-year plans'. Furthermore, enterprise directors had majo incentives to protect their backs and their autocratic autonomy and to boost their bonuses by falsifying records, by hoarding hidden reserves of resources and production capacity, and by fostering corrupt 'cosy family relationships' with Communist party and state officials and with customers and suppliers (including black-marketeers). I these factors and unremitting pressure to fulfil the most high-profile plan targets entailed large-scale reliance on and proliferation of unplanned activities (i.e., activities which had not been envisaged or embodied in the plan, some of which were illegal or relied on the black economy), it is somewhat meaningless to think of these as 'centrally planned economies' in practice.

Higher levels of economic, institutional and educational achievement failed to facilitate the attainment of centrally planned economies. The presumed advantages of increased planning expertise, resources and institutional efficacy at higher level of economic and technological development were more than cancelled out by the intrinsic complications caused by the exponentially increasing diversity and complexity of more advanced and industrialized economies. Marxist assumptions that 'centrally planned economies' would become more feasible as economies became more advanced were sheer naivety – the opposite was the case. Not even the advent of mathematical programming and computers enabled Communist central planners to produce five-year plans that were accurately informed and internally consistent a the outset and accurately implemented and fulfilled in practice. Economic information knowledge is too fragmented, incomplete and endlessly changing to lend itself to being incorporated into accurate and internally consistent comprehensive economic plans several years in advance. Therefore, our occasional use of the terms 'centrally planned economy' or 'central planning' refers mainly to the aspirations rather than the attainments of these highly regimented economies, which are more aptly called 'command economies', although reality fell far short even of that aspiration! The capacity of Communist regimes to command and to regiment was continually outmatched by human ingenuity in devising and engaging in ever-more sophisticated forms of passive resistance and evasion. However, this maintains our faith in the ultimate indomitability of human beings, especially the millions of workers and peasants who steadfastly refused to become the obedient and mindless morons that the Communist regimes endeavoured to make them.

In this book we have for these reasons refrained from applying the word 'socialist' to the economic systems of the formerly Communist-ruled countries. Other than in the Yugoslav successor states, the changes have mainly been from varying forms and degrees of centrally directed 'state capitalism' to varying forms and degrees of market system. In the Yugoslav successor states, which make up two-thirds of the post-Communist Balkan countries considered in this book, the so-called 'transitions' after 1989 were *not* from so-called 'centrally planned economies' or even 'state capitalism' to market economies, but rather from one form of market economy to another. As anyone acquainted with Yugoslavia in the 1960s to 1980s should know, the Yugoslav peoples became very familiar with market mechanisms and, even during the mounting economic crises of the 1980s, often displayed considerable entrepreneurial flair and dynamism. The Yugoslav 'transitions' have thus mainly been from various forms of overregulated and dysfunctional market economy and predominantly 'social ownership' of the means of production (other than land, which mostly remained privately owned), to other forms of market system. By 2005 these were mainly based on private enterprise and private ownership of the means of production in each of the successor states. It is noteworthy that economic recovery from the post-Communist economic collapse has been stronger, and the share of the private sector in GDP is now greater, in the formerly state capitalist and nominally 'central planned economies' (Albania, Bulgaria and Romania) than in the already decentralized and at least semi-marketized former Yugoslav republics (see Table 1.2). This must be attributed in large measure to the retarding effects of the Yugoslav conficts of 1991–2001 on the pace of economic change in the Yugoslav successor states, but it is also a warning against glibly assuming that the already-decentralized and semi-marketized economies of the Yugoslav successor states were bound to win this particular 'race'.

These caveats do not imply that the widely misunderstood and misconceived economic changes in the post-Communist Balkans did not involve massive economic (and hence social) upheavals, but they do imply that it is highly misleading to characterize them as shifts from 'socialism' or 'centrally planned economies' to 'capitalism'. The changes entailed introducing more horizontal power relations, the rule of law, competition and harsher financial discipline

1.2 The post-Communist Balkans: population and indicators of economic growth, economic recovery and privatization

	Population (m)		Average GDP growth (%)			Real GDP in 2004 as % of 1989 level	Private sector share of GDP (%), 2005
	1991	*2004*	*1992–6*	*1997–8*	*1999–2004*		
Albania	3.3	3.2	5.4	0.5	6.4	131	75
Bulgaria	9.0	7.8	−3.2	0.8	4.4	89	75
Romania	23.2	21.7	1.6	−5.8	4.0	100	70
Croatia	4.8	4.4	−1.0	4.5	3.6	94	60
Serbia[1]	7.7	7.5	−9.0	6.0	4.8	55	55
Montenegro	0.6	0.6	–	–	–	–	–
Kosova	2.0	2.0	–	–	–	–	–
Bosnia and Herzegovina	4.4	3.8	–	–	6.0	60	55
Macedonia	2.0	2.0	−4.9	2.4	1.4	80	65

Note:
[1] Includes Vojvodina. The economic data include Montenegro, for which separate data were not found.

Sources: Lampe (2006: 291); EBRD *Transition Reports*, various years; Europa (1992).

A note on our selective coverage of the history of the Balkans prior to the 1990s

This book is primarily concerned with the changes that have occurred in the post-Communist Balkan states. However, these changes cannot be understood or explained satisfactorily in isolation from their earlier history, which has in many ways helped to shape their responses to the end of Communist rule, especially their attempts to democratize, liberalize and reconstitute their polities and societies and to liberalize, marketize, privatize and restructure their economies. Furthermore, many of the most salient issues, debates, processes and conflicts that have taken place in the post-Communist states either relate to or are products of earlier eras. We have therefore considered it important to provide rather more than mere thumbnail sketches of the previous history of these states and their precursors. Nevertheless, we have also had to respect the space constraints of a single volume, as well as the patience of readers who are primarily interested in the post-Communist period. We have therefore been fairly selective in our treatment of the earlier history of these states, their precursors and their peoples.

Our coverage has concentrated on setting the scene for the post-Communist era and on giving more detailed consideration to themes, issues, traditions, problems and perspectives which we consider to have had important bearings on political and economic patterns, changes, options or concerns during the 1990s and early 2000s.

A brief explanation of our omission of Greece and Slovenia

Greece is obviously an important component of the Balkan Peninsula and in some respects it is a pity that it has been excluded from this book. The main reason for this omission is that the book's main focus is on democratization and liberalization in the formerly Communist-ruled Balkan states. The fact that Greece did not undergo several decades of Communist rule and the subsequent problems of readjustment to the goals of liberal democratic government and a fully fledged market economy has given i very different challenges to deal with. However, Robert Bideleux has addressed these elsewhere (Bideleux 1996: 127–53, 1998: 205–27, and 2004: 299–341).

More controversially, we have also omitted Slovenia from this volume, on the grounds that Slovenia is more 'East Central European' than 'Balkan'. In terms of lifestyle, living standards, attitudes, cultural ties, landscape and (most importantly) power relations, power structures and the rule of law, Slovenia has long had even more in common with other parts of Central Europe (especially Austria) than with the more central and southerly parts of the Balkan Peninsula, even though much of Slovenia's nineteenth- and twentieth-century history was intimately intertwined with that of the other Yugoslav peoples. This was the implicit reason why Slovenia was included in the May 2004 'eastward enlargement' of the EU, along with the other post-Communist states in East Central Europe and the Baltic region. This is also the basis on which major international organizations such as the European Bank for Reconstruction and Development (EBRD) off cially classify Slovenia as part of East Central Europe, rather than as part of the Balkans or South-eastern Europe.

Regrettably, pressure of space has made it necessary to omit an overview of Yugoslavia as a whole and its disintegration during the 1990s. What is offered here, instead, is an unusually comprehensive treatment of the rich diversity of the Yugoslav successor states and their individual precursors, along with separate treatments of Albania, Bulgaria and Romania.

2 Albania

Between a rock and a hard place

Introductory 'country profile'

Albania is a small country with a population estimated at 3.2 million in 2004 and a land area of 28,748 square kilometres (12 per cent of the size of the UK, 5 per cent of the size of France). The mainly rugged and inhospitable terrain has been aptly described as the rock garden of South-eastern Europe. About 70 per cent of its land area consists of hills and mountains, which support sheep, goats, forest and scrub. Trees cover nearly half of Albania's territory. Its coastal plains and river basins, which are mainly located in the south and west, are warm and potentially fertile. About 57 per cent of Albania's workforce was engaged in agriculture in 2004, but arable land made up only 21 per cent of its territory, and Albania has had to import most of its food requirements in recent years. The country is relatively well endowed with minerals and energy resources, especially chrome (of which it had the world's third-largest output in 1985), nickel, copper, iron ore, manganese, oil, gas and coal. It also has considerable hydroelectric power potential, which now accounts for over 90 per cent of the country's electricity generation and permits some electricity to be exported, and a lot of untapped tourism potential.

Albania's population was 3.2 million in 1989. During the 1980s it had grown by 1.9 per cent per annum (the fastest rate of population growth in Europe and one of the highest rates in the world). However, its population has ceased growing since the early 1990s, mainly because the fearful post-Communist economic and social collapse, greatly increased poverty and political and economic turmoil led to sharply reduced birth rates and several waves of emigration. Just over 25 per cent of the population was estimated to be under the age of ffteen in 2005 (an unusually high proportion for a European country).

According to the most recent census (1989), the ethnic affiliations of the populatio were 98 per cent ethnic Albanian, 1.7 per cent ethnic Greek and 0.3 per cent ethnic Macedonian, Vlach, Gypsy, Serb or Montenegrin (Hall 1994: 25). However, the intense nationalism of the Communist regime may have led the census authorities to understate the ethnic Greek share (Greek nationalists have variously claimed it to be 6 to 10 per cent). Besides the 3.2 million or so Albanians living in 'Albania proper', between 2.5 and 3 million ethnic Albanians live in neighbouring Kosova, Montenegro, Macedonia and north-western Greece. These communities are not considered to be part of the large Albanian diaspora, comprising ethnic Albanian émigrés and descendants of previous ethnic Albanian émigrés. Rather, they are seen as members of ethnic Albanian communities who have lived for hundreds of years in territories which were deliberately not included in the small Albanian state established by negotiation between

Europe's major powers in 1913 and again in 1921. However, the sizeable Albanian diaspora numbers at least 1 million in Turkey, 350,000 in the USA, 250,000 in Italy and 150,000 each in Germany and Switzerland.

Who are the Albanians? And should Albania include Kosova and western Macedonia?

Most writing on Albania begins by claiming that in ancient times the present-day territory of Albania, Kosova, western Macedonia, Montenegro, north-western Greece (Epirus) and southern Serbia was inhabited by one or more Indo-European peoples called 'the Illyrians', that these people(s) spoke a language or languages called 'Illyrian', that this 'Illyrian' language or group of languages belonged to the Indo-European 'family' of languages, and that the ancient 'Illyrian' people(s) were the lineal forebears of the modern Albanians. In particular the 'authorized' nationalist versions of Albanian history, which have been part of the curriculum in Albanian schools since the 1930s and have been embodied in official Albanian publication and television programmes since the 1960s, have taught modern-day Albanians to think of themselves as the lineal descendants of the supposedly Indo-European 'Illyrian tribes' who settled in the western Balkans during the second or perhaps even the third millennium BC. They thus claim to be the oldest 'indigenous people' of the western Balkans, with a long and illustrious 'lineage' dating back to ancient times – indeed, almost as old as that of the Greeks (Pollo and Puto 1981: 2–4; Wilkes 1992: 11–12). From a combination of archaeological evidence and the sparse comments of ancient Greek and Roman writers (most of which appear to be no more than hearsay), it has been *conjectured* that the presumed 'Illyrians' were 'honest', 'hospitable' and 'polytheistic', spoke an 'Illyrian' Indo-European language and mainly lived in fortifie places of refuge protected by thick walls built with huge rough-hewn stones, either on the tops of hills or mountains or in river valleys or beside roads. They are said to have used pottery and later iron weapons and armour, but had 'no real sculpture' until later centuries, when they came under the infuence of the ancient Greeks (Pollo and Puto 1981: 3–7).

These perspectives, which feed into the identity and self-image of modern-day Albanians, also underpin Kosovar and Macedonian Albanian claims to a state of their own in Kosova, preferably including the mainly Albanian-inhabited areas in western Macedonia. They have also encouraged *some* Albanian nationalists to dream of eventually uniting almost all the ethnic Albanian inhabitants of the western Balkans in a 'Greater Albania', on the logic that being 'the oldest inhabitants' of the western Balkans gives Albanians some sort of 'prior claim' to a large slice of this region. However, these Albanian claims and aspirations are *mainly* based on the principle of *national self-determination* and on the consideration that at least since the late nineteenth century ethnic Albanians have constituted the *vast majority* of the population in Kosova and much of western Macedonia, rather than on historical arguments.

The Albanian-born and Albanian-educated writer and broadcaster Paulin Kola has strongly argued that there has never been much interest in or support for the creation of a 'Greater Albania' within the present-day Republic of Albania (Kola 2003). If so, the main practical political implications of Albanian claims and beliefs that modern-day ethnic Albanians are the 'oldest inhabitants' of the western Balkans (and thus implicitly hold 'prior claims' to the territories which they now inhabit) chief concern

Kosovar and Macedonian Albanian agitation and demands for international recognition of Kosova as an independent Kosovar state, the conversion of the current Republic of Macedonia into a bi-national Albanian-and-Slav federal state and the future 'unification of an Albanian-ruled Kosova with the predominantly Albanian-inhabited western areas of the current Republic of Macedonia, more than the creation of a 'Greater Albania'. However, public-opinion surveys conducted in late 2004 somewhat contradicted Kola's claims, indicating 'a relatively high acceptance of the idea of a "Greater Albania" among the Albanian populations of both Kosova and Albania', although 'a great majority of Albanians in Macedonia reject the idea of dividing the country' and '77.5 % of ethnic Albanians (and 85 % of ethnic Macedonians) support the territorial integrity of the Macedonian state' (International Commission on the Balkans 2005: 17–18, 43–45).

Nevertheless, all the historical claims and assumptions are sheer conjecture, based on very little reliable information and a great deal of wishful thinking. In fact, as the Albanian authors of a major English-language history of Albania acknowledged, 'little is known about the language of the Illyrians. We still have not found inscriptions or documents written in this language' (Pollo and Puto 1981: 6). Moreover, even if one or more ancient 'Illyrian' languages *did* exist, this in itself would not prove the existence of an ancient 'Illyrian' people or peoples. It would have been perfectly possible for a diversity of peoples to have spoken a common 'Illyrian' language or group of languages and, since references to ancient 'Illyrians' span many centuries, the people(s) who spoke an 'Illyrian' language in this region could well have changed dramatically over time. Much the same occurred in Europe's other 'language zones', whose diverse inhabitants have recurrently migrated, assimilated, interbred and mutated.

In his major book on the ancient 'Illyrians', the archaeologist John Wilkes argues that

> They spoke a language of which almost no trace has survived . . .We cannot be sure that any of them actually called themselves Illyrians: in the case of most of them, it is near certain that they did not . . Illyrians have tended to be recognized from a negative standpoint, in that they were manifestly not Celts, Dacians or Thracians, or Greeks or Macedonians.
>
> (Wilkes 1992: 3)

If they were ever a distinct 'people' at all, 'Illyrians were not an homogeneous ethnic entity' (Wilkes 1992: 38). No ancient Greek writer 'is known to have made a serious study of Illyrians in their homeland and what has been transmitted [from the ancient Greeks] is mainly nonsense' (Wilkes 1992: 167). Much the same seems to have been true of the Romans. Under Roman rule (167 BC to AD 378), 'the Illyrians disappeared into the Roman Empire. When we next hear of them, they are Roman Illyrians, army commanders and emperors repelling invaders' (Wilkes 1992: 218, 265).

In order to 'pacify' the 'Illyrian' lands, much of the indigenous population was massacred, expelled or sold into slavery by the Romans and replaced by military-cum-agricultural colonies recruited from other parts of the Roman Empire. These transformed Illyricum into a major source of food and mineral exports and military personnel for the empire, including in due course many outstanding Roman commanders and military dictators. In order to exploit their new Balkan domains more effectively, the Romans built up a very impressive infrastructure – primarily networks of roads, towns, aqueducts, and irrigation and drainage works. Starting from the Adriatic port of Dyrrachion (which acquired the Latin name of Durrachium) and the slightly inland port of Apollonia (which was linked to the Adriatic by the navigable river Aoos or Viosa), the Romans gradually built the famous two-pronged Via Ignatia eastwards across the Balkans to Thessaloniki via Elbasan (where the two prongs joined together), the Shkumbi river and lake Ohrid. This paved road was eventually extended as far south-east as Constantinople, the new capital of the Roman Empire inaugurated in AD 325, and it became the main artery of east–west trade and communication across the Balkan Peninsula.

Starting in the second century AD, the inhabitants of Illyricum were gradually converted to Christianity, which became the official imperial religion inAD 313. The country was overrun and devastated by Goths and Huns during the fourth century. When the Roman Empire was divided into two in AD 395, Illyricum came under the political jurisdiction of the East Roman (Byzantine) Empire centred on Constantinople (Istanbul). It came formally under the ecclesiastical jurisdiction of the Eastern Orthodox Patriarch in Constantinople from AD 734.

From AD 548 onward, the lands now known as Albania began to be overrun from the north by ever-increasing numbers of Slavs who gradually settled in the western Balkans. They displaced, killed or (most commonly) subjugated and absorbed most of the pre-existing non-Slavic communities, be they Illyrian, Latin, Greek or Macedonian. 'The new settlers did not strive to eradicate the existing Illyrian and Roman cultures, and several of their major settlements grew up on the sites of Roman cities.' This gave rise to new cultural fusions and syntheses, which in turn gave the future Yugoslavs as much claim as the Albanians to be the inheritors of the Roman-Illyrian heritage (Wilkes 1992: 268–71). Nevertheless, Illyricum's ports, commerce, waterworks, irrigated agriculture, craft industries and urban civilization declined through growing disruption and neglect between AD 548 and 900. Parts of the indigenous population appear to have shifted from Albania's increasingly marshy and malarial lowlands to its relatively remote and impenetrable mountains, where 'tribal' or clan-based communities practised relatively meagre pastoralism on poor soils.

The modern Albanians, rather than being lineal descendants of the ancient Illyrians, were products of a new medieval synthesis with multiple roots (Wilkes 1992: 280). The modern name 'Albania' *probably* derives from that of a so-called 'tribe' known as the 'Albanoi' or 'Arbanitai' in Byzantine Greek, and as the 'Albanenses' or 'Arbanenses' in medieval Latin. This 'tribe', which lived in the vicinity of the present-day city of Durres, was first mentioned in written sources during the eleventh and twelfth centuries AD (Malcolm 1998: 28–29). Although the second-century Roman geographer Ptolemy also mentioned a tribe called the 'Albanoi' and located their main town ('Albanopolis') somewhere to the east of Durres (Malcolm 1998: 29), it cannot safely be assumed that these 'Albanoi' were the ancestors of their medieval namesakes – not least because almost nothing is known about them and *there is absolutely no mention of them in historical sources of any kind during the intervening nine centuries.* It is possible that these 'Albanoi' *took* their name from (rather than *gave* it to) the mountainous areas they inhabited and that the 'Alb-' element in the name 'Albania' derives from an ancient Indo-European root word for 'a type of mountainous terrain, from which the word "Alps" is also derived . . The continuity of this name is a striking fact; but it does not amount to proof that Albanians have lived continuously in Albania.

Place-names can endure while populations literally come and go' (Malcolm 1998: 29). Indeed, countries are akin to busy railway stations with very transient populations, rather than the fixed essences imagined by nationalists

In any case, modern Albanians call themselves *shqipëtarë*, their language *shqip*, and their country *Shqipëria*. These names bear no resemblance whatsoever to the above-mentioned 'tribal' names and seem to have come into use only after the conquest of the Albanians by the Ottoman Turks during the fifteenth century AD (Hall 1994: 26). These new names are often claimed to derive either from the Albanian word for an eagle (*shqipe*), perhaps to signify that they are a mountain people, or alternatively from the Albanian verb 'to speak' (*më shquiptue*), perhaps to signify those who speak languages or dialects that are supposedly descended from an ancient Illyrian language. However, even these notions are *mere conjecture*, no matter how confidently or dogmatically they are asserted. Archaeologists have found some evidence of continuities of material culture in this area, 'but material remains do not tell us what language people spoke (unless they include inscriptions, which these do not), and the main cultural affinities here seem to have been with the Latin-speakin Romano-Byzantine towns' rather than with the ancient 'Albanoi' or the 'Illyrians' (Malcolm 1998: 30).

It is thus unlikely that there were major connections between ancient 'Illyrian' and modern Albanian, let alone between the peoples who spoke these languages. The modern-day Albanian language (like modern-day Armenian and Farsi) represents a distinct sub-category within the Indo-European family of languages, and over the centuries neighbouring countries naturally supplied many Latin, Turkish, Greek and Slavic 'loan words'. Modern Albanian has two main dialects, that used by the Gheg clans in the very mountainous north and that used by the Tosks in the less mountainous, more populated and more economically developed south and coastal plains. During the eleventh and twelfth centuries a feudal chiefdom system emerged, as did a sense of Albanian identity, despite repeated invasions of the Albanian domains by the Normans. After a brief subjugation by Serbia from 1344 to 1355, foreign domination was shaken off and powerful clans re-emerged.

In common with other Balkan Christian peoples, however, the Albanians were subsequently subjugated by the Ottoman Turks, who inflicted a succession of devastating assaults on them between 1385 and 1501. Albanian resistance, especially that led by Gjergj Kastrioti Skenderbeg from 1442 until his death in 1468, has been immortalized in Albanian folklore and epic verse, in which Albania has traditions comparable to those of neighbouring Serbia and Montenegro. This resistance led to Turkish reprisals, to significant Albanian emigration (mainly to Italy, where Albanian communities have survived to the present) and to concerted campaigns to convert the Albanians into loyal Muslim subjects of the Ottoman sultan and caliph, starting in the seventeenth century. By then, the Tosk lowlanders of southern and coastal Albania (Shqiperi) had mostly become Greek Orthodox Christians, while the Gheg highland clans of northern and central Albania remained predominantly Roman Catholic. During this period the Roman Catholic Church did much to develop and protect the Albanian language – it even produced the first Albanian books an dictionaries. By 1800, however, most Ghegs and Tosks had at least nominally converted to Islam, although some adopted Muslim names and customs while covertly maintaining Christian traditions in private. The inducements to adopt Islam included land grants and lower tax burdens – there is little evidence of extensive 'forced conversions'. Many joined the (heterodox) Bektashi Muslim sect, which did not require

strict observance of Muslim prayer and fasting and permitted women to mix socially
with men and to be seen unveiled in public. It also took a relatively relaxed and tolerant
view of Christianity, which may have contributed to the remarkably low incidence of
sectarian strife (whether Christian–Muslim or Catholic–Orthodox) in modern multi-
confessional Albania, in sharp contrast to the inter-confessional conflicts which
afflicted some of the neighbouring Yugoslav Lands during the twentieth century. This
is an important warning against making ill-founded generalizations about alleged
propensities towards sectarian conflict in the Balkans. Such strife has been largel
confined to just some of the regions with religiously heterogeneous populations
and has by no means been an endemic problem. Since the end of Ottoman rule in
1912, Albania's inhabitants are said to have been roughly 70 per cent Muslim, 20 per
cent Greek Orthodox and 10 per cent Roman Catholic by (increasingly nominal)
religious aff liation, but these figures are merely 'guesstimates'

Under the Ottoman regime, Albania was administratively fragmented into several
separate *sanjaks* and *vilayets*. Landownership was increasingly concentrated in the
hands of a Muslim landlord class. Ottoman control was reinforced by fiscal, educationa
and occupational discrimination in favour of Muslims, primarily at the expense of
Roman Catholic rather than Eastern Orthodox Christians. Catholic sponsorship
of the Albanian language and Albanian church schools, not to mention Catholic links
with hostile European powers, aroused intense irritation and mistrust in Ottoman
circles, whereas the captive and subservient Greek Orthodox Church was much more
readily tolerated. Moreover, since the Ottoman Empire was structured on the basis
of religious communities ('millets') rather than ethnic or national groupings, the
only educational institutions open to Islamicized Albanians were Muslim ones, which
taught in Turkish and Arabic. The Ottoman regime endeavoured to suppress the
Albanian language, Albanian schools, publications in Albanian and the development of any kind of Albanian national identity, unity, consciousness or political
leadership. However, persistent suppression, increasingly burdensome taxation,
compulsory five-year military service for adult males (from the 1840s), and the growin
impoverishment of most Albanian peasants and pastoralists engendered debilitating
cycles of violence and counter-violence.

The Albanian 'national awakening'

Albanian expatriate communities in Italy, Romania, metropolitan Turkey and the USA
perceived that the mid-nineteenth-century expansion of Muslim-Turkic and Greek
Orthodox schooling in the Ottoman Empire threatened to extinguish Albania's distinct
linguistic identity. Therefore, starting in the 1860s and 1870s, they sponsored (often
clandestine) Albanian language schools and publications. Albanian nationalists
looked to the national language and secular linguistic nationalism as unifying forces
that could weld together the disparate Albanian *vilayets* and religious communities
and transcend clan/tribal and religious divisions. The Habsburg Empire also started
financing Albanian-language Catholic church schools in northern Albania, Kosova
and western Macedonia. This spurred Italy to sponsor Italo-Albanian Catholic schools
and act as a 'patron' of the incipient Albanian*Risorgimento* (resurgence). Starting in
the mid-1850s, moreover, German, Austrian and Italo-Albanian philologists and
historians advanced plausible philological arguments that Albanians were neither
'mountain Turks' nor Greeks nor Slavs, but rather a distinct ethnic group with an Indo-
European language which could be traced back to the ancient 'Illyrians'. This enhanced

Albanian standing and self-esteem, even though the claims to lineal descent from the ancient 'Illyrians' were ill founded.

However, the emergence of independent Greek, Serbian, Italian, Montenegrin and Bulgarian nation-states posed dire threats to Albania's future, as all of them had predatory designs on Albanian homelands. Through Russia's victories in the Russo-Turkish War of 1877–8, Serbia, Montenegro, Greece and (briefly) Bulgaria acquire territories inhabited by Albanians. Albanian notables and political leaders reacted by convening a meeting at Prizren (in Kosova) in 1878, where they launched a nationalist Albanian league to seek great power intervention and to mobilize popular resistance to these encroachments on Albanian homelands. The Ottomans initially supported this 'League of Prizren', hoping that Albanian resistance to Greek and South Slav expansionism might help to stem the contraction of Ottoman control in the Balkans. However, when it became clear that it was seeking Albanian autonomy and unity, the league was crushed by Turkish troops in 1881. Thousands of Albanians were killed and over 4,000 were imprisoned or exiled.

Leaders of the Albanian 'national awakening' convened a linguistic congress in Monastir in 1908. This adopted a unified, standardized and simple-to-use Latin alphabet, which replaced the diverse scripts in use and differentiated Albanian from the Greek, Cyrillic and Muslim-Turkic scripts used by most of the Balkan peoples. This was also an important preparatory step towards launching a national education system, even though only about 10 per cent of ethnic Albanians could read or write at that time.

In addition, Albanian national leaders supported the Young Turk Revolution of 1908, in the mistaken belief that the Young Turks would in return grant the Albanian *vilayets* far-reaching administrative, fscal and educational autonomy under Ottoman protection. In 1909, 1910 and 1911, the nationalistic Young Turks repeatedly reneged on their promises, provoking Albanian uprisings which were brutally suppressed. However, the major crises and territorial losses that engulfed the Ottoman Empire in 1911–12 forced the Young Turks to concede most of the demands of a large Albanian insurrection in the summer of 1912. This in turn aroused fears in Montenegro, Serbia, Greece and Bulgaria that the Albanian national movement was becoming a force strong enough to thwart their own territorial aspirations, and these four states therefore decided to take joint military action to realize those aspirations at Ottoman and Albanian expense before it was too late to do so. On 17 October 1912 the Balkan alliance of Serbia, Bulgaria, Greece and Montenegro declared war on the Ottoman Empire, and by May 1913 they had brought Ottoman power in the Balkans to an end. This spurred the Albanians to seek independent national statehood, in an attempt to prevent further Greek, Serbian and Montenegrin encroachments on their homelands.

A self-appointed national assembly proclaimed Albanian independence and established a provisional government in the town of Vlore on 28 November 1912. An international commission was set up to determine the boundaries of this independent Albanian nation-state. On 29 July 1913 a great-power 'Conference of Ambassadors' in London confirmed and guaranteed Albanian independence, albeit under the nomina 'protection' of an international control commission, but it also decided to award the mainly Albanian-inhabited territories of Kosova and western Macedonia to Serbia and the partly Albanian-inhabited territory of southern Epirus (including Janina) to Greece. The international control commission ignored the existing Albanian provisional government and invited Prince Wilhelm of Wied, a thirty-five-year-old German arm off cer, to found a constitutional monarchy in Albania, following the well-worn pattern that established monarchies in nineteenth-century Greece, Romania and Bulgaria. But he encountered such resentment that he only remained in Albania from 21 February to 3 September 1914, during which time the country lapsed into anarchy.

During the First World War, various parts of Albania were occupied by Greece, Italy, Serbia, Montenegro, Austria and France. The south was invaded by Greece, while Italy occupied the coastal lowlands and the main seaports. Central and northern Albania were occupied twice by Serbia and Montenegro and, in between, by Austria. The Bolshevik publication of the secret April 1915 Treaty of London in November 1917 revealed that Albania was slated for partition between Greece, Italy, Montenegro and Serbia at the war's end, but this intensified Albanian efforts to secure the re-establishment of an independent Albanian state in late 1918, aided by support from President Woodrow Wilson (Pano 1992: 21). The mutual incompatibility of Serb and Italian territorial ambitions also helped to prevent the planned partition of Albania among its neighbours.

On 25 December 1918 an Albanian national congress, convened in Durres, appointed the Albanian notable Turkhan Pasha as provisional president of Albania. However, his administration was little more than an Italian-controlled 'puppet regime' (Vickers 1999: 94). An Albanian national congress convened in Lushnja in late January 1920 refused to recognize his authority and established a provisional government under the presidency of Suleiman Bey Delvino (Vickers 1999: 94). The Lushnja congress also voted unanimously to fight foreign domination, assert Albanian nationa sovereignty and reject any form of foreign tutelage or protectorate. Tirana, which then had only 17,000 inhabitants but was seen to have a fairly central location close to Durres and to be acceptable to both northern Ghegs and southern Tosks, became the capital city. Between June and September 1920, poorly armed but tenacious Albanian irregular forces pushed out the Italian forces ensconced in parts of coastal Albania. Greek and Yugoslav occupation forces withdrew in 1921 under international pressure but having secured 'territorial adjustments' in favour of their own states (including the highly controversial allocation of the whole of Kosova to Yugoslavia).

Independent statehood, 1921–39

On 17 December 1920, Albania was admitted to full membership of the League of Nations. In November 1921, a great-power 'ambassadors conference' reaffirmed Albania's independence and its 1913 boundaries, but (rather ominously) acknowledged Italy's 'special interest' in 'protecting' Albania. Albania's f rst parliamentary elections in April 1921 were followed by a power struggle between conservative landowning interests in the Progressive Party led by Shefqet Verlaci and the radical-liberal Democratic Party led by Fan Noli (1882–1965). Noli was a historian, a linguist and a Harvard-educated bishop in the US Albanian Orthodox Church.

The minister of the interior in the provisional government of Albania established in Lushnje in early 1920 was Ahmed Zogu (1895–1961), the twenty-five-year-old son of the head of the Muslim Mati clan in the river Mat basin. Zogu had his own retinue of armed men, through whom he played leading roles both in the restoration of 'law and order' and in the expulsion of foreign occupation forces in 1920. He was the emerging 'strongman', allied to the conservative landowning interests led by Shefqet Verlaci, whose daughter he married. In December 1922 Zogu became prime minister and corruptly 'stage-managed' parliamentary elections in December 1923. Nevertheless, the conservative landowning interests were overthrown and forced into exile in May 1924, amid serious crop failures, peasant unrest and allegations that a leading opposition politician (Avni Rustem) had been murdered by Zogu's armed followers.

Fan Noli's Democratic Party governed Albania from June to December 1924. However, Noli neglected to legitimize his government by calling fresh elections. He introduced censorship, attempted to confiscate the property of his exiled opponents failed to act on his promises of agrarian reform and failed to obtain aid from the League of Nations. His radical rhetoric and diplomatic recognition of the Soviet Union in July 1924 alarmed conservatives, potential Western investors and aid donors, and neighbouring Balkan states. In December 1924, aided by weapons, money and soldiers provided by the Yugoslav government, Zogu overthrew and exiled Noli and his associates. In January 1925, Zogu had himself elected president by a rump parliament, pushed through a constitution conferring sweeping presidential powers on himself, suppressed civil liberties, banned political parties and imposed even stricter censorship. In May 1925 he ditched his erstwhile Yugoslav allies and, in return for promises of substantial economic assistance, signed a wide-ranging economic agreement with Fascist Italy. This granted Italian companies and colonists extensive preferential trading, agricultural and mineral exploitation rights in Albania. Fascist Italy subsequently established, f nanced and controlled the National Bank of Albania, the oil industry, the main mining companies and the Society for the Economic Development of Albania, which carried out considerable public-works programmes – building roads, bridges, harbours, dams, hydroelectric-power facilities and irrigation/drainage canals. These economic agreements were reinforced by a Treaty of Friendship and Mutual Defence in November 1926 and by a full-scale military alliance in November 1927, which committed Italy to train and equip Albania's armed forces, while allowing the Italian navy to use the port of Vlore.

In 1928, Zogu had himself crowned 'Zog I, King of the Albanians', a title which made implicit irredentist claims on Kosova and northern Greece (Epirus). However, his corrupt authoritarian rule and his ever-expanding 'civil list' aroused derision and opposition. He promulgated secular civil (1929), penal (1930) and commercial (1931) legal codes, which largely superseded Albania's Islamic laws, but Islamic courts continued to function until 1944. He also abolished the veiling of women and curbed brigandage and blood feuds. Highland clansmen were gradually disarmed or integrated into the regular security forces, while clan heads were bought off with military or civil-service sinecures. Zog's agrarian-reform law of 1930 was a joke – in all, 6,375 hectares were redistributed to 8,763 persons (Sjöberg 1991: 30). During the 1930s, about 3 per cent of the rural population owned 40 per cent of arable land, while 14 per cent owned no land at all (Prescott 1986: 5). 'Peasants were obliged to contribute labour and produce to a private landlord, to the state or to a religious institution' (Cungu and Swinnen 1999: 607).

Relations with Fascist Italy were in crisis from 1931 to 1936, because Zog dismissed his Italian military 'advisers', nationalized church schools, concluded trade pacts with Greece and Yugoslavia, and rejected Mussolini's demands for an Italo-Albanian customs union, increased Italian colonization and teaching of Italian in Albanian schools. Mussolini retaliated by halting Italian economic aid and sailing the Italian navy (uninvited) into Durres harbour in 1934. However, Mussolini backed down and resumed Italian aid to Albania in 1936, during his Abyssinian (Ethiopian) war. Zog's resistance to Italian pressure gained him some popularity, allowing him to relax his authoritarian rule somewhat in 1935–7. However, on 25 March 1939 Mussolini gave

Zog an ultimatum demanding acceptance of an Italian military protectorate over
Albania. Zog dithered and Italy invaded Albania on 7 April 1939. At first, the onl
major resistance to the Italian occupation was in Durres, partly because Zog had suppressed possession of firearms and Albanians were thus ill equipped to resist. Withi
three years, however, the Albanians began to attract attention as one of the European
nations most resistant to foreign military occupation. Zog's 'royal family' went into
exile.

In 1939 Albania was still the poorest and least-developed country in Europe.
About 85 per cent of its 1 million inhabitants lived in rural areas, and 80 per cent
depended on agriculture and herding. Around 90 per cent of national income was
derived from agriculture. Average life expectancy was thirty-eight years. Around
80 per cent of adults were illiterate and only 37 per cent of school-age children
attended schools. The country had only eighteen secondary schools, no university,
155 doctors, forty-four dentists, eleven hospitals and 15,000 non-agricultural workers.
Albania's per capita national income was only about half that of Yugoslavia and
Greece. In 1938, industry accounted for just 4.4 per cent of national income (Schnytzer
1982: 1, 14, 65).

Foreign occupation and civil war, 1939–44

Other European governments barely reacted to Mussolini's invasion of Albania.
London and Paris sought to propitiate Mussolini. Zog was prevented from setting up
an Albanian royalist 'government in exile', even though he spent the war years in
London.

The Italians established an Albanian quisling regime under Shefqet Verlaci
(Albania's biggest landowner) and an appointed 'national assembly', which promptly
voted for full political and economic union with Italy and handed the Albanian crown
to Italy's King Vittorio Emanuele III. Albania's army and police were merged into
their Italian counterparts. All Albanians serving the Italian occupiers were required
to join a fascist party of Albania, which became the sole legally authorized political
party, and over 200,000 Italians moved to Albania in 1939–40 in order to make
preparations for further Italian colonization and conquests in the Balkans. On 28
October 1940, Italy's forces in Albania invaded Greece, but they proved ill equipped
to fight in such rugged terrain, which was ideal for guerrilla warfare. Albanians
also staged sabotage attacks in support of the Greeks, whose military ruler General
Metaxas vowed not merely to defend Greece but also to 'liberate' Albania. However,
having repelled the Italians with Albanian assistance, Greek forces then proceeded
to occupy southern Albania as conquerors rather than as 'liberators' and set up entirely
Greek administrations in several southern Albanian towns.

In April 1941, Fascist Italy was rescued from ignominious defeat when Nazi
Germany invaded Greece as well as Yugoslavia. This enabled Italy to propitiate its
Albanian fascist collaborators by incorporating Kosova and parts of northern Greece
and western Macedonia into a fascist-controlled 'Greater Albania'. These territories
were subjected to systematic expulsion or killing of their Slavic and Greek inhabitants,
i.e., 'ethnic cleansing'.

In the wake of Germany's invasion of the Soviet Union in June 1941, two Yugoslav
Communists were despatched to Albania and persuaded several scattered and feuding
Albanian Marxist cells to form the first-ever Communist Party of Albania (CPA) i
November 1941. The CPA launched a Communist-led 'national liberation front'

(LNC) under Yugoslav Communist tutelage in September 1942. The CPA and the LNC were both headed by Enver Hoxha (1908–85), commonly described as a 'cosmopolitan intellectual' from a southern Muslim Tosk family, who had been 'converted to Communism' while he was a university student in Montpellier, Paris and Brussels from 1931 to 1936.

The CPA and the LNC initially recruited support among southern Albanian workers, students and educated townspeople. Acts of sabotage and assassination committed by Communist-led 'partisans' provoked indiscriminate Italian reprisals, driving ever-increasing numbers of Albanians to join the partisans. Since Albania had only about 15,000 workers in 1938 and few educated townspeople, the survival and expansion of the CPA and LNC increasingly depended on successful mobilization of support among peasants, farm labourers and highland pastoralists. This brought it into direct competition and eventual conflict with the republican-nationalist Balli Kombetar (BK, National Front) guerrilla movement, which was launched by Midhat Frasheri in October 1942 and drew its main support from rural areas. In 1943–4 these rival resistance movements may have inflicted more casualties on each other than on th foreign occupiers, who nevertheless retaliated with ferocious punitive expeditions to repress rural insurgency by burning or vandalizing whole villages and executing or interning anyone suspected of supporting either the LNC or the BK. The magnitude of the reprisals and the willingness of many conservative nationalists and property-owners to collaborate with the foreign occupiers gradually radicalized much of the population, whose allegiance mainly gravitated towards the Communist-led partisans. In 1943 the CPA was renamed the Party of Labour of Albania (PLA). When Fascist Italy capitulated to the Allies in August 1943, many Italian soldiers in Albania abandoned their weapons to the partisans, whereupon Nazi Germany invaded Albania in order to pre-empt potential Allied landings there. The Western Allies then switched their support from the somewhat ineffectual BK to the more single-minded and effective Albanian partisans. Growing Albanian conservative and nationalist collaboration with or reluctance to fight against the Germans made it easier for the partisan to discredit and defeat their conservative-nationalist rivals, to mobilize support for a Communist-led Anti-Fascist Council for National Liberation and to gain control of southern and central Albania during 1944. In November 1944, the partisans captured Tirana from the retreating Germans and installed a PLA government under Enver Hoxha, before crushing the remnants of the nationalist, conservative and royalist movements in northern Albania in 1945. According to Marmullaku (1975: 59), the f ghting in Albania during the Second World War had cost over 28,000 Albanian and 26,000 German or Italian lives, along with the destruction of 52,000 homes and 'almost every bridge, port and mine'.

Albania under Enver Hoxha, November 1944 to April 1945

Flushed with military victory, the Communist-led LNC was swiftly transformed into a 'democratic front' representing the 'anti-fascist' forces which had 'liberated' Albania from foreign occupation. Enver Hoxha became prime minister, foreign minister and commander-in-chief. The new Communist-controlled state took control of the still tiny industrial, banking and transport sectors in December 1944. The land reform enacted in August 1945 prohibited the buying and selling of land, assigned each agricultural household 12 acres of land and started confiscating all landholdings i excess of that amount, eliminating the old landlord class. Nevertheless, from 1945 to

1948 the PLA was under the tutelage of the Communist Party of Yugoslavia (Vickers 1999: 163), and Albanians paid a heavy price for this. The politically mobilized Albanian population and their new Communist rulers experienced several years of arrogant and offensive Yugoslav Communist dictation and economic exploitation, and there was no question of (re)incorporating Albania's 'lost homelands' (Kosova, western Macedonia and southern Montenegro) into a 'Greater Albania', as the Yugoslavs were militarily much stronger ('might was right').

Meanwhile, Albania's relations with Britain and the USA rapidly deteriorated. Despite the crucial role of the largely US-funded United Nations Relief and Rehabilitation Administration in saving Albania from complete economic collapse and mass starvation between September 1945 and spring 1947 and initial attempts to maintain the wartime 'anti-fascist alliance', mutual enmity soon gained the upper hand. The PLA and other patriotic Albanians resented Anglo-US support for Greek nationalist and royalist territorial claims to southern Albania (which Greek nationalists called 'Northern Epirus'), while Britain and the USA were increasingly alarmed by Albanian Communist support for the Greek Communist forces in the incipient Greek civil war. There has been a long and acrimonious debate between the various Britons who were involved in (and have therefore tended to defend) British military, technical and economic support to Albania's Communist-led LNC during the Second World War, and anti-Communist Britons who argued that by supporting the LNC, Britain effectively 'delivered' Albania into Communist hands. Actually, both sides are 'right': British aid to the Communist-led LNC *did* help to ensure the defeat of the Axis Powers as quickly as possible, thereby saving many Allied lives, but it *also* left Albania under Communist control when the war ended. However, British and American policy-makers missed several potential opportunities to lure Communist Albania into the Western camp by resuming economic, technical and even military assistance, as was done so successfully in the case of Yugoslavia after its expulsion from the Soviet bloc in 1948. War-ravaged and impoverished Albania was even more desperately in need of Western assistance than was Yugoslavia, and the poverty and the very small size of Albania's population meant that the offer of even quite small amounts of Western assistance would have been very enticing and could have reduced the rigours of Communist rule in Albania just as surely as it did in 1950s Yugoslavia.

On 2 December 1945, elections were held to a constituent assembly to draw up a new constitution. Almost all candidates were chosen by the Communist-controlled Democratic Front, which allegedly won 93 per cent of the votes cast. This victory consolidated a massive shift of power from the 'clannish' northern Ghegs, who had dominated inter-war Albania under Zog, to southern Albania's more educated and urbanized Tosks, who then made up about three-quarters of PLA members. This shift disempowered northern Albania's Roman Catholic community, which main - tained pockets of armed anti-Communist resistance in Albania's barely accessible northern mountains until 1949. Most of the pre-1945 political and economic elites, including most of the Muslim and Christian clergy, were expropriated, imprisoned, executed or driven into exile by the Communist regime between 1945 and 1950. The constituent assembly formally abolished the monarchy and proclaimed a 'people's republic' in January 1946.

During 1947 and the first half of 1948, the state-security chief and party organ izational secretary, Koçi Xoxe, served as the chief collaborator of Albania's Yugoslav overlords. Xoxe championed the economic union of Albania with Yugoslavia, perceived as a prelude to full political incorporation of Albania into the Yugoslav Federation and a Yugoslav-dominated Balkan federation. In 1948, however, Hoxha seized the opportunity of Tito's quarrel with Stalin to denounce the Yugoslav Communist leaders as 'anti-Communist renegades'. Irksome Yugoslav tutelage encouraged him to turn to Stalin for support, protection and inspiration. However, Hoxha's severance of Communist Albania's hitherto-extensive links with Communist Yugoslavia in 1948 led to even more irksome dependence on Soviet economic and technical aid during the 1950s. In 1950, tipped off by the British double agent Kim Philby, Hoxha crushed a major Anglo-US attempt to overthrow his regime.

Albania broke with the Soviet Union in 1961, following Soviet criticisms of Mao's China and the ensuing 'Sino-Soviet split'. Other 'sins' and 'heresies' committed by the Soviet Union included Khrushchev's famous denunciation of Stalin's cult of personality in 1956, Soviet acceptance of the need for 'peaceful coexistence' with the 'imperialist' USA and Soviet moves towards reconciliation with Yugoslavia between 1955 and 1961. In retaliation, the Soviet Union terminated all Soviet-bloc aid to and trade with Albania. Hoxha then turned to China for aid and technicians to replace those withdrawn by the Soviet bloc.

In 1967, Hoxha banned all religious institutions and practices and proclaimed the world's f rst completely atheistic state. He also redoubled his efforts to stamp out all Western influences, whether Christian or consumerist, and continued to keep pay differentials within very narrow limits. These policies enabled Communist Albania to avoid the so-called 'capitalist scourges' of inflation, unemployment, foreign debt and private cars, but it paid dearly for doing so. Albanian society became increas ingly closed off and regimented, and its living standards remained abysmally low. Until his death in April 1985, Hoxha maintained one of the most paranoid, xenophobic, repressive, puritanical and isolationist dictatorships in the Communist world.

Following the death of Mao Zedong in 1976, Hoxha also fell out with the new (more pragmatic) Chinese leadership in 1978, thereby completing Albania's international isolation. He accused Mao's successors of sucking up to the USA, adopting 'social revisionism' and taking the 'capitalist road' in economic policy. Chinese aid to Albania therefore came to an abrupt halt and the Chinese engineers and technicians working in Albania were repatriated. By this time, however, previous Soviet and Chinese aid had helped Albania to develop a comprehensive modern education system (the most valuable legacy of Communist rule), collectivized and extensively irrigated agriculture, major hydroelectric power supplies and some large-scale and centrally planned extractive and processing industries. Economic relations with China were not restored until 1983, and no Albanian foreign minister visited China again until January 1991. Nevertheless, the sharp contraction of foreign assistance and external trade after 1978 led to severe stagnation and infrastructural decay, with the result that by 1989, 39 per cent of Albanian children were reportedly suffering from malnutrition (World Health Organisation Report, quoted in *FT*, 14 December 1991, p. xx).

Albania under Ramiz Alia, 1985–91

The monolithic façade of the Hoxha regime began to show cracks in the early 1980s. In December 1981 it was announced that Hoxha's long-time closest associate and prime minister, Mehmet Shehu, had committed suicide. However, rumours imme- diately spread that Shehu had actually been shot by Hoxha himself or one of his bodyguards during a heated argument, conceivably over conficting economic priorities

(Hoxha favoured complete isolationism, whereas his more pragmatic ex-general favoured opening up the economy to foreign trade, capital and technology in order to overcome its growing shortages, dysfunctionality and technological obsolescence). As a result of Shehu's death, the hardline Communist Adil Carcani was promoted to the now-vacant post of prime minister in January 1982. In November 1982 another seemingly dogmatic Communist, Ramiz Alia, was promoted to the post of chairman of the *presidium* of the people's assembly (de-facto head of state), quite possibly because Alia's daughter was married to Hoxha's son. The Hoxha regime, like the Ceauşescu regime in Romania and the Zhivkov regime in Bulgaria, became a highly incestuous and degenerative 'socialism in one family'. As early as the mid-1950s, over half of the fifty-three members of the PLA central committee were connected to on another by family ties (Vickers 1999: 181).

Following Hoxha's death in 1985, power passed to President Ramiz Alia, while Hoxha's widow Nexhmije continued to wield considerable hardline influence behin the scenes. Adil Carcani remained prime minister. After becoming First Secretary of the PLA in April 1985, Alia initially ruled out radical forms of political liberaliza-tion and economic reform, although something of a thaw in domestic and foreign relations had already begun, breaking out of Communist Albania's long-standing self-imposed isolation and autarky. For example, a freight ferry link with mainland Italy was established in 1983. Relations with Greece improved following bilateral negotiations conducted in 1984. Diplomatic relations were established with Spain in September 1986 and with Canada and West Germany in September 1987. Two accords were signed with Turkey, one on economic, scientifc and technological cooperation and the other on road transport.

Albania took part in the Balkan conference of foreign ministers hosted by Yugoslavia from 24 to 26 February 1988, signalling its readiness to improve its rela-tions with its neighbours. This conference aimed at increasing regional stability and cooperation in the spheres of economic and cultural relations, tourism, the environ-ment, and transport and communications. Albania hosted a second Balkan conference of foreign ministers on 24–25 October 1990.

The 'revolutions of 1989' affected even the 'hermit state' of Albania. In November 1989 the regime signalled a slight relaxation of political and cultural controls by announcing an amnesty for certain categories of political prisoners and allowing the publication of a novel by Neshat Tozai, in which he implicitly criticized human-rights violations by the Interior Ministry and its notorious security police, the Sigurimi. At a literary conference that same month, Albania's most celebrated writer Ismail Kadare publicly called for literary freedom. This slight 'thaw' seems to have opened the door to stronger expressions of public discontent. In December 1989 anti-government demonstrations took place in Shkoder and other towns. Anti-government demonstrations were violently suppressed in Shkoder between 11 and 14 January 1990.

At the plenary meeting of the PLA central committee held on 22 January 1990, President Alia made a speech in which he blamed the collapse of Communist rule in East Central and South-eastern Europe, not on the failure of socialism as such, but on 'revisionism'. He rejected a multiparty system and freely contested elections, but put forward Gorbachev-style reforms, including the holding of open meetings by grass-roots party organizations, the promotion of the most able and devoted people, limited terms of office for key PLA officials, the principle that there should be more than o candidate for each seat in the forthcoming elections to the people's assembly, decentralization of authority within the PLA, economic decentralization, price reforms, payment of bonuses to workers in key industries and increased priority for the production and importation of food and other consumer goods.

On 22 February 1990, Albania's Communist regime admitted for the first time that it was holding political prisoners, and releases of political prisoners ensued. In May 1990 the criminal code was liberalized. Attempting to leave the country illegally had hitherto been a treasonable offence carrying punishments of ten to fiftee years of imprisonment, but the penalty was reduced to a maximum of five years o imprisonment.

At a plenary meeting of the PLA central committee held on 17 April 1990, President Alia announced a further relaxation of economic controls, and in May 1990 it was announced that religious services and other acts of worship were no longer to be criminal offences; in the same month, the people's assembly liberalized the penal code, decriminalized religious evangelism and relaxed the constitutional prohibition on foreign loans and investment. The Ministry of Justice, which had been abolished in 1965, was re-established in the summer of 1990 in order to signal Albania's new-found concern for law, justice and human rights.

In June 1990, Albania applied for membership of the Commission on Security and Cooperation in Europe (CSCE), the forerunner of the OSCE, declaring its willingness to comply with all the human-rights provisions of the 1975 Helsinki Final Act. This request was not immediately granted, but Albania was given observer status at the CSCE meeting held in Copenhagen on 5 June 1990 and it became a full member of that organization on 19 June 1991. It was announced on 12 June 1990 that henceforth any adult citizen of Albania would be eligible to apply for a passport. However, considerable practical obstacles to travel and emigration would remain: in particular, the dire poverty of most Albanians, the acute scarcity of hard currency and the f erce travel and immigration restrictions that Western states apply to would-be travellers and migrants from poor countries. Albania restored diplomatic relations with the Soviet Union on 30 July 1990, and President Alia addressed the UN General Assembly in New York on 29 September 1990.

Police repression of a fresh eruption of popular unrest in Tirana and other major cities in July 1990 resulted in several thousand Albanians seeking asylum in foreign embassies, demanding to be allowed to leave the country. These internationally televised 'embassy invasions' by Albanians frantic to be allowed to go abroad were defused by permitting about 6,000 would-be emigrants to leave the country.

In November 1990 Alia finally conceded that the forthcoming election should be multi-candidate. Individuals would be allowed to run either as independents or as candidates for recognized social organizations such as trade unions. There was to be democracy and free debate within the PLA, and churches and mosques were to be (re)opened. In Shkoder on 23 November 1990, thousands of people attended the f rst public celebration of Mass in a Catholic church since 1967. The fst officially sanctioned Muslim religious service since 1967 was held in Tirana on 18 January 1991.

However, such modest changes merely whetted the appetite for more far-reaching liberalization and democratization. Large student-led 'pro-democracy' protests erupted in Tirana in December 1990 and spread to Shkoder, Kavaje and Elbasan. Copies of Enver Hoxha's books were publicly burned and there were attacks on public buildings. The violence was contained by the police and the army. Over 150 people were arrested and tried, receiving prison sentences of f ve to twenty years.

On 11 December 1990 the PLA central committee announced that 'it is to the benefi of the further democratization of the country's life and of pluralism to create political organizations in accordance with the laws in force'. The Democratic Party of Albania (DP) was founded the next day by students and intelligentsia led by the charismatic cardiologist Sali Berisha, who was from the Gheg north, and the economist Gramoz Pashko, who came from the Tosk south. This was the first independent political party to have been established in Albania since 1944, and its name harked back to the Democratic Party founded and led by Fan Noli in 1923–4. Its newspaper *Rilindja Demokratike* ('Democratic Revival') was first published on 5 January 1991, following the formal authorization of opposition newspapers on 28 December 1990. The DP's membership reached 60,000 by the March 1991 election campaign, when the PLA claimed to have 130,000 members – considerably less than the 147,000 members it had claimed in 1986 (Vickers 1999: 217).

Other political parties emerged in the wake of the meteoric rise of the DP, most notably the Albanian Ecology Party, the Christian Democratic Party, the Republican Party of Albania, the Social Democratic Party, and Omonia (the Democratic Union of the Greek Minority). There also emerged a Forum for the Defence of Human Rights. However, the decree legalizing the formation of independent parties, which was issued on 17 December 1990 and ratifed by parliament two days later, stipulated that parties could not be 'fascist, racist or anti-national', could not be founded from abroad and could not aim 'to overthrow the constitution of the Socialist Republic of Albania'.

In December 1990 there also began another mass exodus from Albania, this time mainly involving members of Albania's Greek and Jewish minorities. Some people perished while trying to get out of Albania. By mid-April 1991, all 300 or so members of Albania's small Jewish community had left for Israel, and around 5,000 Greek Albanians had crossed the mountainous border between Albania and Greece into northern Greece. Although most of these ethnic Greeks possessed or could lay claim to Greek passports, the Greek state was not at all keen to grant them visas for entry into Greece, which was experiencing economic and social problems of its own.

The PLA held a special conference on 26 December 1990 in order to draw up a new party programme in anticipation of the parliamentary election to be held on 10 February 1991. It promised 'non-stop' democratic reform, the separation of party and state, 'freedom of conscience and faith', and legal recognition and protection of human rights. The economic proposals included: 'replacing the system of centralized direction and administration with the mechanisms of a market economy', 'a balance between the state sector and free initiative', 'coordination' as well as competition between the state sector and the cooperative and private sectors, the breaking up of state enterprises into smaller units in order to increase competition, designing the f scal system as well as economic reform in such a way as to 'ensure an equal distri bution of income', a reorientation of investment priorities away from heavy industry towards tourism, services and consumer goods, the seeking of foreign loans, gradually making the national currency (the lek) convertible and the retention of agricultural producer cooperatives (APCs), albeit as 'independent' farms and with provision to be made for other forms of ownership, including private ownership. A draft constitution with guarantees for multiparty democracy and economic liberalization was published on 31 December.

In January 1991 the country was gripped by a wave of strikes, particularly in the mining and public-transport sectors. These were only resolved by conceding wage increases, by legalizing the right to strike on 23 January and by making the reform-minded economists Fatos Nano and Skleqim Cani deputy prime ministers in charge of economic reform on 31 January. On 16 January, the government announced that, in response to demands from the new political parties and their supporters among Albanian professional people, the student population and striking workers, the multiparty parliamentary elections scheduled for 10 February 1991 would be post-poned until 31 March 1991 in order to give the newly formed parties more time to get organized and funded for the election contest. In return, the opposition parties agreed that, until 1 May 1991, they would refrain from calling and supporting workers' strikes. Independent trade unions were formally legalized on 18 February.

Nevertheless, fresh protests at the Enver Hoxha University of Tirana in early February 1991 culminated in a major hunger strike by over 700 students and lecturers, demanding the removal of Enver Hoxha's name from that of the university and an end to the obligatory study of Marxism-Leninism. On 20 February several thousand protestors marched to Tirana's central square, where they pulled down the giant statue of Enver Hoxha. Within hours, statues of Hoxha were being pulled down in other towns as well. In response, President Alia denounced the demonstrators as 'vandals' and declared 'presidential rule'. Undeterred, the following day demonstrators zestfully burned Communist literature and portraits of Hoxha on street bonfires in central Tirana. The unrest was contained by a combination of half-hearted repression and further concessions. The latter included the formation of a new government headed by the 'reform Communist' Fatos Nano on 22 February, pay rises for striking workers and the renaming of the Enver Hoxha University of Tirana. At the same time, bitter divisions began to open up within the PLA and the armed forces. Over 100 off cers went on hunger strike in protest against the use of force against demonstrators, and at least three people were killed when demonstrators stormed the Tirana military academy. In response, hardline Communists and 'Enverists' staged counter-demonstrations and rallies demanding the re-erection of the demolished statues of Hoxha and reaffirmation of loyalty to his ideology (Vickers 1999: 219–20)

In late February and early March 1991, about 20,000 Albanians commandeered ships in the ports of Durres and Vlore and sailed to the Italian port of Brindisi, demanding aid, jobs and asylum, and the Albanian authorities initially did little to discourage this new exodus. The Italian public were shocked by the television images of thousands of destitute and malnourished Albanians seeking refuge in Italy, and premier Giulio Andreotti suggested that Italians should 'adopt' refugees and take them into their homes, while a hospital in Brindisi treated many Albanian migrants for dysentery, hepatitis and scabies. However, the initial wave of sympathy soon wore off, not least because Italian media attention was diverted and public attitudes were hardened by the 1991 Gulf War. When the Italian government announced a new policy of forcible repatriation and demanded that action be taken in Albania to stem the f ow of refugees, President Alia placed the ports of Durres and Vlore under military and police control on 7 March, established a committee for employment and emigration, and imposed an ineffectual ban on mass gatherings in Tirana, Durres, Vlore and Shengjin. By that stage, however, most Albanians were redirecting their hopes and energies to the hard-fought political campaigns that led up to the three-stage parliamentary election held on 31 March, 7 April and 14 April 1991. In March 1991 diplomatic relations were resumed with the USA (they had been severed in June 1939, following the Italian invasion of Albania) and it was announced that Albania's remaining political prisoners were to be freed.

President Alia's economic reforms, 1989–90

There was now belated recognition of the need for reform, but sweeping economic reforms and restructuring like those in the Soviet Union under Gorbachev were still being rejected. In September 1989 President Alia accepted the need for unemployment in the case of 'idlers' and the 'irresponsible'. The following month it was accepted that indirect rather than direct steering would characterize the new economic system. In January 1990 Alia proposed the election of enterprise managers by workers, a decentralization of economic decision-making, greater retention of profits by enter prises, wages linked to performance and the freeing of prices for some non-essential goods. In April 1990 he advocated greater self-financing for enterprises (provision o long-term credits by the state banks, in place of grants and subsidies from the state budget) and increased roles for private enterprise. In mid-1990, private craftspeople and traders were allowed, although only family labour was to be employed (a restriction subsequently removed), and foreign direct investment (FDI) was permitted. Free markets were allowed for the sale of agricultural products from private plots. Other changes included the enlargement of private plots and the termination of restrictions on private holdings of livestock herds.

The three-round parliamentary election of 31 March, 7 April and 14 April 1991

Albania's first-ever freely contested parliamentary election witnessed a 96 per cen turn-out in the f rst round on 31 March. It is undeniable that the opposition parties were seriously disadvantaged by their very recent formation and, as a consequence, by their relative lack of political experience, funding and organizational infrastructure. Nevertheless, most of the 260 independent Western observers present confirmed th overall fairness of the frst round, claiming that fraud and manipulation were minimal, despite the PLA's control of election scrutineers in some rural areas and its control of the media (Vickers 1999: 223).

The ruling PLA won 56 per cent of the votes cast in the first round, mainly thanks to its continuing hold on the Tosk-dominated south and on the hearts and minds of the agricultural population, many of whom (rather unrealistically) feared that a DP victory would result in descendants of Albania's former big private landowners regaining possession of most of the country's agricultural land. Nevertheless, the fledgling DP won a significant 'moral victory' by gaining 39 per cent of the vote cast in the first round (and a majority of votes in the much freer urban constituencies including almost all of the nineteen seats in the capital). The election was essentially a two-horse race between the PLA and the DP.

The DP manifesto pledged a Western-style political democracy. It made no bones about the fact that it favoured the rapid introduction of a market economy based on private ownership. It promised a free distribution of land to farmers and, in relation to the privatization of industry, a discounted or even free distribution of shares to workers. For the state sector, it envisaged a standard five-day, forty-hour week. Th DP complained that the PLA was employing scare tactics, alleging that the DP would bring back large landowners and sell the country out to foreigners.

Prior to the further rounds of voting which were held on 7 and 14 April in seventeen constituencies where no candidate had managed to win more than 50 per cent of the vote in the first ballot and two others where no vote had taken place, the DP instigate large demonstrations in Shkoder on 2 April 1991 to protest against the widespread electoral fraud and intimidation which it claimed that the PLA had perpetrated during the first ballot. Police opened fire on this DP-inspired demonstration, killing four peop and injuring many others. About 3,000 demonstrators were also forcibly dispersed by the police in Tirana on the same day, but without loss of life. DP members expressed fears that conservative hardliners within the PLA, who had apparently won more seats than the more liberal and reform-minded members of the PLA in the first round, wer in the process of succumbing to the temptation to make use of their sizeable electoral victory on 31 March to bring the whole process of reform and liberalization to an abrupt halt as soon as the rest of the election was completed.

Following this 'massacre' of peaceful protestors by hardline Communists ruthlessly determined not to relinquish power (as the DP and its major daily newspaper imme- diately portrayed it), a conciliatory President Alia appealed to the DP to join with the PLA in forming a 'coalition government of national salvation' after the election was completed. However, the DP rejected Alia's appeal, calling instead for those responsible for the shootings to be identified and brought to trial – something whic Alia initially felt unwilling or perhaps unable to do. The rest of the election thus took place in a highly charged, poisonous atmosphere, with mutual recrimination on both sides. The f nal distribution of seats in the 250-member people's assembly was as follows: PLA, 169; DP, seventy-five; Omonia, five; and the National Veteran Organization, one (Pano 1997: 311). The PLA had the two-thirds majority needed to alter the constitution.

The new people's assembly and the new 'constitutional law' of 29 April 1991

The new people's assembly f rst met on 10 April, but the DP refused to take part in it until effective steps were taken to track down those responsible for the shootings in Shkoder on 2 April 1991. This stand-off was resolved a week later by an inter- party agreement on the appointment of an offcial commission which would investigate the shootings and apportion blame. 'It reported within a week that the police were to blame for provoking violence from initially peaceful demonstrators' (Vickers 1999: 224).

The draft of a new constitution was presented to the newly elected but still PLA- controlled people's assembly in late April. However, the non-Communist parties vigorously objected to making such a change so soon after Albania's first post- Communist multiparty elections and while hardline Communists still dominated the assembly. On 29 April, as a pragmatic compromise, the people's assembly passed an interim 'constitutional law' to modify the 1976 Constitution without pretending that this law would be accepted as defnitive. Thus Albania became simply 'The Republic of Albania' (in place of 'The People's Socialist Republic of Albania') and the 'leading role' of the PLA was abolished, as was the role of Marxism-Leninism as the officia state ideology. The state was redefined as 'democratic and juridical, based on socia equality, on the defence of freedom and the rights of man and on political pluralism'. Private property was endorsed and reference was made to the fundamental rights and duties of citizens and their rights to strike, demonstrate and emigrate. The people's assembly was to be responsible for electing (by a two-thirds majority) the president of the republic, who, once elected, would be required to relinquish any party affiliation and positions which he or she might still hold.

Even though President Alia humiliatingly failed to get elected in the Tirana constituency in which he had stood as a parliamentary candidate, he was nevertheless elected president of the republic by a large majority in the PLA-dominated people's assembly on 31 April 1991 (the opposition parties abstained from the vote). Alia duly relinquished his positions as the first secretary (leader) of the PLA and as a membe of the PLA politburo and central committee.

The socialist government headed by Fatos Nano, early May to 4 June 1991

Although the new government was composed entirely of PLA personnel, the govern-ment programme presented to the people's assembly by premier Fatos Nano in May 1991 'envisaged fundamental reforms, including extensive privatization and a rapid shift to a market economy' (Vickers 1999: 225). However, the Nano govern-ment was almost immediately overwhelmed by seemingly insurmountable demands and problems. The 'no-strike agreement' which had been reached with Albania's non-Communist parties on January 1991 expired on 1 May. On 16 May the newly established Independent Trade Union Federation called for a general strike, demanding a 50 per cent pay rise for workers, a reduction in the working week from forty-eight to thirty-six hours, a ban on women working night shifts, and the resignation of the PLA government. By late May it was claiming that 70 per cent of the urban workforce was participating in the strike (Vickers 1999: 225) and that 90 per cent of enterprises had ceased operation. This protest movement, in which the student population also played a prominent part, was further fuelled by an increasingly widespread belief (propounded primarily by the DP) that the elections in rural constituencies on 31 March 1991 had in effect been rigged by the ruling PLA. Finding himself increasingly unable to govern the country in the face of such an effective general strike and student-led demonstrations, Nano resigned as prime minister on 4 June 1991.

The six-party 'Government of National Stability' headed by Ylli Bufi, June to December 1991

The minister of food Ylli Buf (a technocrat and an engineer by profession) was asked to try to put together a 'government of national stability'. Large (18–20 per cent) pay rises were immediately granted to all state employees and there was a swift 'return to work', as part of a hastily negotiated no-strike deal which was to last until fresh elections were held in mid-1992. Buf succeeded in assembling an interim six-party coalition government on 12 June. It was agreed that the individual ministers would act independently of their party affliations during the government's period of offce. It appears that the non-Communist parties only agreed to participate in a coalition government because they hoped that this might prevent a descent into complete anarchy, which they feared would lead to the declaration of a state of emergency or even a military takeover. The PLA, which had changed its name to the Socialist Party of Albania (SPA), was allotted twelve of the twenty-four ministerial port-folios, including the important ministries of internal and foreign affairs. The DP was given seven ministries, including the important defence and economic portfolios. The economist and former university professor Gramoz Pashko became the deputy prime minister with overall responsibility for the economy, and Genc Ruli became finance minister. The remaining five portfolios were shared out between the Republica Party, the Social Democratic Party and the Agrarian Party. Ylli Bufstressed the need for political reconciliation and rehabilitation, the restoration of order and stability, further democratization, austerity measures, price reform, a return to work, foreign aid and the privatization of small enterprises and some land. In July he talked of privatizing agriculture and liberalizing prices by the autumn of 1991. The government's plans also included foreign-trade liberalization, limited convertibility of the lek and the creation of a social safety net.

At the tenth and final party congress of the PLA, which took place from 10 to 1 June 1991, the party was renamed the SPA and Fatos Nano became in effect the new party leader. In addition, a new party programme was adopted, aligning the socialists with the principles advocated by European social democratic parties. It supported the creation of a market economy, while stressing that reforms were to be introduced gradually and that economic planning was still to play an important role. Privatization received support, but the party favoured the retention of agricultural cooperatives and state control of vital industries.

James Baker, the US secretary of state, visited Tirana on 22 June 1991. The UK established diplomatic relations with Albania in June 1991, as did the EU in July. As the year wore on, however, the economic situation turned increasingly desperate, with looting, rioting and growing lawlessness. The exodus of Albanians to other countries revived in August 1991 and, overall, more than 40,000 Albanians fled to Italy in th course of 1991 (*IHT*, 16 April 1997, p. 5).

Sali Berisha pulled the seven DP ministers out of the coalition government on 4 December 1991, protesting that there was a need to bring forward the next election, that the socialists were destabilizing society in the hope of discrediting democracy and that more should be done to bring former Communist officials to book. However the DP itself started to split, with Gramoz Pashko at loggerheads with Berisha over (i) the wisdom of leaving the coalition and (ii) Berisha's increasingly authoritarian and 'clannish' conduct. Berisha was from the north of Albania, which was still to a large extent controlled by Gheg 'clans', whereas Pashko was from the more-developed and less 'clannish' south, dominated by the Tosks. Pashko was later expelled from the DP on 29 June 1992, after the election, and he and other ex-DP personnel launched a rival 'Democratic Alliance' in November 1992.

The interim 'Government of National Stability' headed by Vilson Ahmeti, December 1991 to March 1992

On 11 December 1991, the food minister Vilson Ahmeti took Ylli Bufi's place as prime minister. Ahmeti was a non-partisan technocrat, an engineer by profession. A new election was arranged. Since under the constitution no party was allowed to represent an ethnic minority, Omonia was not eligible to participate in its own right. A 'Union for Human Rights in Albania' was therefore formed to contest the election.

By March 1992 Albania's economy had largely collapsed. Both industrial and agricultural output fell to about 20 to 30 per cent of their (already very low) 1990 levels during 1992, and over 30 per cent of the workforce became unemployed. Inflation, i a country which under Hoxha had proudly claimed to have banished inflation, spiralle to over 200 per cent in 1992, partly because tax revenues were now only covering about 20 per cent of public expenditure. Nearly 10 per cent of Albania's population emigrated in 1991–2. And much of Albania's peasantry embarked on a largely unregulated (free-for-all) land grab, involving thousands of bitter disputes, physical casualties and social injustices. In this crisis, the PLA lost control of its hitherto-loyal rural constituencies and most of the incumbents lost their seats in the next parliamentary elections.

The economic policies of the two 'Governments of National Stability', June 1991 to March 1992

The central planks of the economic programme adopted by the Ylli Buf government in June 1991 were (i) rapid macro-economic stabilization by means of a balanced budget, price liberalization and currency convertibility and (ii) privatization. Small enterprises such as shops, restaurants, bars and cafés were to be rapidly auctioned off, with preference being given to their current operator-occupants, while the privatization of most large-scale industry was to proceed by means of free distribution of shares via investment funds. The privatization of *small enterprises* proceeded very quickly from mid-1991 onward, and by January 1992 almost three-quarters of retail trade and small-scale services were in private hands (Pashko 1996: 69) and many such enterprises were taken over by their employees (EBRD 1994: 16). However, the privatization of *large state enterprises* got off to a slow start, although many of these were broken up and some were even partly closed down. In June 1992 a much delayed banking law, which separated the functions of the central bank and the commercial banks, granted the National Bank of Albania formal independence on the model of the German Bundesbank. Finding themselves suddenly starved of state credits, most state-owned industrial enterprises ceased operation and industrial output more than halved (see Table 2.1). A bankruptcy law was also adopted in 1992, but in practice no bankruptcies were allowed to take place during the early 1990s. A rapid accumulation of inter-enterprise arrears in 1991–2 was halted in early 1993 by adopting a settlement system relying on payment before delivery (EBRD 1994: 16).

The privatization of agriculture and 'real estate', 1990–2

Agriculture experienced 'a virtual collapse' in 1990–1 (Cungu and Swinnen 1999: 608). This forced the Buf government to initiate a major restructuring of the agricultural sector. Under the Land Law of 22 July 1991, all land formally in the possession of APCs, amounting to about 80 per cent of all arable land, was to be redistributed by local committees to members of those APCs free of charge at the rate of 0.1 hectares per family member. This land was to become inheritable and permitted to be sold after five years, although the sale and purchase of agricultural land was initially prohibited. Legal division of land was not supposed to have started until June 1992, but by that date 77 per cent of cultivated land was already de-facto in private hands. Most of Albania's APCs were abandoned spontaneously and their assets (including the land) were simply taken over by their members. Uncertainty over land titles contributed to a 24 per cent reduction in agricultural output in 1991 (Table 2.1). By the end of 1992, 90 per cent of agricultural land had been grabbed by or distributed to peasant households, 80 per cent of whom had become landholders (UN Economic Commission for Europe 1993: 203). Collectivized farmland was restituted to former (pre-Communist) owners in some mountainous regions (Cungu and Swinnen 1999: 639).

2.1 Albania: selected economic indicators, 1990–2005

	1990	1991	1992	1993	1994	1995	1996	1997	1998	1999	2000	2001	2002	2003	2004	2005
								% growth/rate								
GDP	−10.0	−27.7	−7.2	9.6	8.3	13.3	9.1	−7.0	8.0	10.1	7.3	7.2	3.4	6.0	5.9	5.5
Industrial output	−7.6	−42.0	−51.2	−10.0	−2.0	6.0	13.6	−5.6	4.1	34.2	0.5	7.1	−7.9	2.7	3.1	4.0
Agricultural output	6.9	−17.4	18.5	10.4	8.3	13.2	3.0	1.0	5.0	0.4	4.5	2.2	2.1	3.0	3.8	3.0
Annual inf ation rate	0.0	35.5	226.0	85.0	22.6	7.8	12.7	33.2	20.6	0.4	0.1	3.1	5.2	2.4	2.9	2.3
Budget surplus (+) / def cit (−) as % of GDP	−3.7	−44.0	−23.1	−15.5	−12.6	−10.1	−12.1	−12.6	−10.4	−12.2	−9.2	−8.5	−7.2	−4.4	−5.0	3.3
Unemployment rate	9.5	9.2	27.9	28.9	19.6	16.9	12.4	14.9	17.8	18.4	16.8	14.5	15.8	15.0	14.5	14.7
Foreign debt as % of GDP	–	56.0	124.0	78.0	56.0	31.0	30.0	37.0	32.0	32.3	31.8	29.3	26.3	24.7	22.0	20.0
Share of industry in GDP	–	–	–	–	–	–	–	–	–	8.4	8.1	7.8	7.7	7.5	7.3	–
Share of agriculture in GDP	–	–	–	–	–	–	–	–	–	34.1	32.0	31.9	28.4	27.6	26.8	–
Share of private sector in GDP	5.0	5.0	10.0	40.0	50.0	60.0	75.0	75.0	75.0	75.0	75.0	75.0	75.0	75.0	75.0	75.0
Private-sector share employment	–	–	–	–	–	–	–	–	–	80.0	80.0	80.0	80.0	80.0	80.0	–
FDI inf ow (net, $ m)	–	–	20.0	45.0	65.0	89.0	97.0	42.0	45.0	51.0	143.0	204.0	135.0	178.0	343.0	288.0
Foreign debt ($ bn)	–	0.6	0.8	0.9	1.0	0.8	0.8	0.8	1.0	1.1	1.2	1.2	1.2	1.4	1.7	1.7
Population (m)	–	3.3	3.2	3.2	3.2	3.2	3.3	3.3	3.4	3.1	3.1	3.1	3.2	3.2	3.2	3.2

Sources: Various issues of the annual EBRD *Transition Report*, supplemented by UN Economic Commission for Europe, *Economic Survey of Europe*; UN *World Economic and Social Survey*; and IMF *World Economic Outlook*. Figures for 2004 and 2005 are provisional estimates.

In the case of state-farm land, at first only 50,000 hectares were distributed amon state-farm employees, with most of the remainder put into joint ventures with foreign capital. However, when these joint ventures failed (as most did), state-farm employees initially received cultivation rights and were eventually awarded full property rights to what had been state-farm land (Cungu and Swinnen 1999: 610–11, 640). From October 1991, the land and other property of religious institutions, which had been confiscated in 1967, were returned to the former owners

Elections to the 140-seat people's assembly, 22 and 29 March 1992

There were 100 constituency seats allocated on a first-past-the-post basis and 40 seat allocated by proportional representation. The turn-out in the first round was 95 per cent (Carlson and Betts 2002: 53). The DP, together with its allies (the SDP and the Albanian Republican Party), secured the two-thirds of seats necessary to change the constitution. Ramiz Alia resigned as president on 3 April 1992. The results are listed in Table 2.2.

2.2 Albanian people's assembly election, 22 and 29 March 1992

Party	Share of vote (%)	Seats
Democratic Party of Albania (DP)	62.1	92
Socialist Party of Albania	25.7	38
Social Democratic Party	4.4	7
Union for Human Rights	2.9	2
Albanian Republican Party	3.1	1

Source: Pano (1997: 320).

Albania under Sali Berisha, April 1992 to July 1997

The charismatic forty-seven-year-old ex-Communist cardiologist and DP-leader Sali Berisha was elected president of Albania by the new DP-controlled parliament on 9 April. Presidential prerogatives were increased: for example, he gained the power to give direct orders to members of the government. The engineer Alexander Meksi, who became prime minister on 14 April, outlined an economic programme of marketization and privatization on 18 April.

At the beginning of July 1992 around 6,000 people tried to commandeer ships in two ports, and in January 1993 several thousand again tried to flee to Italy. In Ma 1992 it was announced that all buildings belonging to the SPA, which had inherited the property of the old PLA (Albania's former Communist party), were to be con-f scated by the state. Ex-President Alia was placed under house arrest on 12 September 1992 for alleged abuse of power, including corruption, while in January 1993 Nexhmije Hoxha (the widow of Enver Hoxha) was jailed for nine years for misappropriation of state funds (her sentence was increased to eleven years the following May).

The Berisha regime soon began to show worrying signs of authoritarianism. On 12 July 1993, for instance, the leader of a small opposition party was sentenced to six months in prison for denouncing President Berisha in the party newspaper. On 27 July 1993 parliament voted to deprive former prime minister Fatos Nano of his parliamentary immunity from arrest. Criminal proceedings were then started against him for alleged 'abuse of duty and the falsifcation of offcial documents in connection with Italian aid'. An agency which he was said to have insisted on using allegedly overcharged and delivered some foodstuffs which were unfit for human consumption He was arrested on 30 July (followed by other members of the Socialist Party), and on 3 April 1994 he was sentenced to twelve years in prison. After Nano's arrest, public political rallies were banned, other than those of the DP, and indoor meetings organized by opposition parties were routinely disrupted or banned (*The Economist*, 9 April 1994, p. 39).

On 19 August 1993, seven senior Communists were placed under arrest, including Ramiz Alia (who was already under house arrest for abuse of power) and Foto Cami (who was also already under house arrest). The trial of Alia and nine other people, including former prime minister Adil Carcani, began on 21 May 1994. Alia was charged with misappropriation of state funds and abuse of power, including the policy of shooting Albanians trying to fee the country. On 2 July 1994 he was given a jail sentence of nine years, but he was released on 7 July 1995.

In November 1993 'Leka I', the son of ex-King Zog (who died in 1961), visited Albania for the first time since his family fled in April 1939. The authorities order him to leave after just one day.

On 6 November 1994 Berisha called a referendum on a new constitution which, if approved, would have granted increased powers to himself as president, including the right to nominate the prime minister, appoint or dismiss ministers at the suggestion of the prime minister, preside over the cabinet on special occasions and set the agenda, and to dismiss or arrest the chairman and members of the supreme court and constitutional court with the approval of parliament. The proposed new constitution also separated judicial, executive and legislative powers and granted freedom of religion. Berisha had been unable to achieve a two-thirds majority for it in parliament. However, only just over 40 per cent voted 'yes', on a turn-out of 84 per cent. In December 1994, after the failure of the referendum, nine out of nineteen cabinet ministers were replaced. Berisha's administration lost much of its support when the Republican Party (one representative) and the Social Democratic Party (SDP) (seven representatives) pulled out of the ruling coalition on the grounds that the government was incapable ofghting corruption and ineff ciency.

Around 1,000 young Albanians stormed the US embassy in Tirana on 26 March 1995, amid rumours that visas and work permits were about to be issued. Police opened fire and two demonstrators were reportedly injured

On 5 June 1995 the government announced a ban on the street sales of newspapers and magazines in Tirana. Newspapers were henceforth only to be distributed through state-controlled kiosks and bookshops.

A 'Law on Communist Genocide', passed on 22 September 1995, prohibited anyone who had been, prior to 31 March 1991, a member of the old PLA politburo or central committee or the Communist-controlled parliament from participating in national or local elections and holding jobs in the judiciary or state media until 2002. Those affected by this law included Fatos Nano, the leader of the Socialist Party, and Skender Gjinushi, the leader of the SDP, who had been the Communist regime's last education minister. The law was later reviewed by the constitutional court.

Parliament passed a 'Law on Dossiers' on 30 November 1995. Anyone deemed by a vetting committee to have worked in the past as a Sigurimi (Communist security organization) collaborator was to be banned from political and state office until th year 2002 (*EEN*, 1995, vol. 9, no. 25, p. 9). The law permitted the opening of Sigurimi f les on public fgures. A state committee would check the files of all persons who ra for parliament, anyone who was appointed to leading local and central government posts and anybody who was employed by the courts. The files on all other citizen were to be closed for thirty years (*Albanian Life*, 1996, no. 60, p. 35).

On 31 January 1996 the constitutional court ruled in favour of the so-called Law on Communist Genocide and also supported a law calling for the creation of a nine-member committee with exclusive access to former secret-police files. This committe was to be empowered to issue certificates to politicians stating they had not collaborate with the former Communist regime, thus allowing them to stand in elections.

On 24 May 1996, an Albanian court convicted three former senior Communist officials of crimes against humanity and of political persecution (e.g., ordering internal exile for dissidents). The death penalty was ordered for Aranit Cela (former supreme-court chairman), Rrapi Mino (former prosecutor geneal) and Zylyftar Ramizi (former deputy interior minister and head of the Sigurimi secret police). Haxhi Lleshi (president 1953–82) and Manush Myftiu (former deputy prime minister) were sentenced to life in prison. On 24 July 1996, however, the death sentences were revoked. Instead, Cela and Mino were sentenced to twenty-five years in prison, while Ramizi was give a life sentence.

The two-stage parliamentary election of 26 May and 2 June 1996

The 140 seats were divided into 115 constituency (first-past-the post) seats and 2 determined by proportional representation. The 4 per cent threshold for party representation remained.

Opposition parties pulled out of the election on 26 May (polling day). Six of them issued a joint statement which referred to 'a climate of terror, psychological pressure and physical violence' (*IHT*, 27 May 1996, p. 6). The SPA and the Democratic Alliance alleged that the DP had practised intimidation and electoral manipulation. The parties would neither take their seats in parliament nor contest the run-off on 2 June. Nevertheless, the turn-out in the first round was allegedly 89 per cent (Carlson an Betts 2002: 53).

An OSCE (Organization for Security and Cooperation in Europe) preliminary report on the election, published on 29 May 1996, stated:

> During the counting process observers noted several instances where the voter register was altered to bring it in line with the number of votes cast. In some polling stations the number of ballots cast exceeded the number of signatures on the voter register. Also, there were widespread reports of the alteration of ballots to make them invalid . . . in many instances the implementation of the law failed to meet its own criteria . . . The presence of armed individuals and unidentified persons inside polling stations did have an intimidating effect on voters and polling commission officials . . . In direct violation of the law, observers noted that decisions of the polling station were not made by majority vote, but by the arbitrary decisions of the government-appointed chairman and secretary.
>
> (*IHT*, 30 May 1996, p. 11; *FT*, 30 May 1996, p. 2)

The next day the acting president of OSCE called on political parties to 'examine, for the sake of democratic stability, all measures, including the possibility of partial repetition of elections' (*IHT*, 31 May 1996, p. 6). On 31 May the Italian foreign ministry, on behalf of the EU, advocated 'the repetition, in compliance with the current electoral rules in Albania, of elections in constituencies in which grave irregularities were ascertained' (*IHT*, 1 June 1996, p. 2). The official OSCE report came to the conclusion that the conduct of the election violated thirty-two of the seventy-nine articles in Albania's election law. The poll also failed to meet five of the nine electio commitments made by OSCE member countries (*FT*, 13 June 1996, p. 2). On 9 June Berisha announced that there would be reruns in seventeen constituencies on 16 June. On 16 June the DP won all seventeen of the rerun constituency elections.

The final distribution of the 140 seats was as follows, with the percentage of th votes cast shown in brackets: Democratic Party, 122 seats (55.5 per cent); Socialist Party, ten seats (20.4 per cent); the Republican Party led by Sabri Godo, three seats (5.7 per cent); the Human Rights Party, successor to the banned Omonia ethnic Greek party, three seats (4 per cent); Balli Kombetar (National Front), the right-wing monarchist party led by Hysen Selfo, two seats (5 per cent) *FT*, Survey, 19 February 1997, p. 15). Other parties obtained a total of 9.4 per cent of the votes but no seats. On 16 June the International Helsinki Federation for Human Rights called for fresh elections, as did the OSCE parliamentary assembly in July. The conduct of the elections had made a mockery of the Council of Europe's decision in July 1995 to admit Albania. Albania was also the only post-Communist Balkan state in which the government still controlled the airwaves and private radio and television were still not permitted (*IHT*, 29 October 1996, p. 2).

The local elections held on 20 and 27 October 1996

The run up to the October 1996 local elections was tense. On 16 September 1996 four Albanians were jailed for the offence of trying to re-establish a Communist party and conspiring to overthrow the government, while five former leading figures in the PLA were put on trial for 'genocide' *EEN*, 1996, vol. 10, no. 19, p. 5). In September 1996 there was all-party agreement on amendments to the local election law: the deputy chairmen of the central election commission and all district commissioners were to be appointed by the opposition parties, and they would sign the f nal vote-count tally at every polling booth and keep a copy of the document; and the Law on Communist Genocide, which previously barred anyone deemed to have participated in the Communist regime from standing, was amended.

The OSCE announced on 17 October that it would not monitor the local elections because the Albanian government wanted to halve the OSCE team of thirty observers. The only international organization to monitor the elections would be the Council of Europe, but in the event there were 350 international monitors.

Turn-out in the first round was 75 per cent. The DP won 52.5 per cent of the vot and claimed fairly to have won thirty-seven of the sixty-four mayorships, as against the Socialist Party's four, and 193 of 309 the local councils. After the run-off, the DP had won twenty-one of the twenty-two city halls and seventy-three of the ninety-six districts. Only one large city, Shkoder, elected a mayor who was not from the ruling party (*IHT*, 20 October 1996, p. 5; *FT*, Survey, 19 February 1997, p. 15). A Council of Europe delegation, which coordinated the monitoring by 350 international observers, said it was on the whole satisfied with the way the local elections had been conducte but referred to a few cases of irregularities which were serious enough to warrant examination by the central electoral commission (*IHT*, 23 October 1996, p. 5).

The deterioration of Greek–Albanian relations, 1993–4

Greek–Albanian relations deteriorated seriously during the early 1990s. It is difficul
to know how many ethnic Greeks there were in Albania before the exodus of refugees
during the early to mid-1990s. The Albanian government claimed that there were only
60,000, based on the biased 1989 census, whereas the Greek government claimed
that there were upwards of 300,000. Most Western estimates were around the 200,000
mark (*Independent*, 25 August 1993, p. 35).

On 25 June 1993 Albania expelled a Greek Orthodox priest, accusing him of stirring
up secessionist feeling among the minority Greeks in southern Albania. He had
allegedly distributed literature claiming that the area was Greek territory. The next
day, in retaliation, Greece began to expel up to 30,000 (mostly illegal) Albanian
immigrants. *EEN* put the total number eventually deported at over 120,000 (*EEN*, 15
March 1995, vol. 9, no. 6, p. 4).

Two Albanian border guards were killed in a raid on a training camp near the border
with Greece on 10 April 1994, possibly by members of the Greek nationalist North
Epirus Liberation Front, which demanded the annexation of the area by Greece.
Reciprocal expulsions of diplomats followed. On 30 May 1994 Greece lodged a formal
complaint about arrests of members of the Greek minority in Albania. A Greek soldier
was wounded in another border incident on 7 July 1994.

On 15 August 1994 there began a trial of fve ethnic Greeks (members of Omonia)
who were charged with (i) treason and military espionage on behalf of the Greek secret
service; (ii) attempting to change Albania's frontiers; and (iii) illegal possession
of weapons. Although the charge of treason was dropped because it derived from
the penal code adopted in the Communist era, they were still accused of attempting
to 'annex southern Albania'. On 7 September they were convicted of 'collaborating
with Greek secret services to arm the Greek minority in Albania' and of informing
Greek intelligence of Albanian troop movements, and were given prison sentences of
six to eight years each. One was pardoned in December 1994 and the other four had
their sentences suspended by the supreme court on 8 February 1995.

Greek retaliation took a number of forms: (i) the expulsion of more Albanians;
(ii) the blocking of EU fnancial aid worth 35 million ecu to Albania (until November
1994); and (iii) the closing of one of the main crossing points to Albanians and a
slowing of commercial traffic

Greek–Albanian reconciliation, 1995–7

During 1995 and 1996, however, the Greek government adopted a more conciliatory
stance towards its Balkan neighbours (not just Albania but also Macedonia), both
in order to shore up its diminished standing in the eyes of other EU member states
and in order to exploit more effectively its expanding potential to reap economic
benefits from the new opportunities that were opening up for it in the post-Communist
Balkans. On 13–14 March 1995, the Greek foreign minister Carolos Papoulos visited
Albania. The visit was a success, and both sides promised to work towards a treaty
of peace and friendship. Key issues agreed on were the establishment of private Greek
language schools, economic cooperation (such as protection of foreign investment
and the creation of a joint Greek–Albanian bank) and the settlement by negotiation
of the legal status of Albanian migrant workers in Greece (*EEN*, 1995, vol. 9, no. 6,
p. 4). On 21 March 1996 the presidents of Albania and Greece signed a 'friendship

and cooperation' treaty. Albania agreed that schools in southern Albania should provide Greek-language teaching and that visa requirements for Greek businessmen should be lifted. Greece promised legislation to allow at least 150,000 Albanians to be issued with temporary work permits in Greece (*FT*, 21 March 1996, p. 4). On 5 August 1997 Greece agreed to issue temporary work permits to Albanians working illegally in Greece, in return for cooperation in combating cross-border crime (*FT*, 6 August 1997, p. 2).

Foreign policy under Berisha, 1992–7

During the war in Bosnia-Herzegovina, Berisha received generally strong support from Western countries, especially the USA, for keeping Albania out of the line of f re. Even though Albania profited by largely ignoring international sanctions agains the Bosnian Serbs and Federal Republic of Yugoslavia, Berisha won international acclaim for refraining from stirring up nationalist passions about the plight of ethnic Albanians in Kosova and Macedonia. In October 1993 the USA and Albania signed an accord on military cooperation. It affirmed a 'readiness to broaden and expand defence and military relations between the two countries' with training programmes for Albanian off cers and high level meetings on 'the international security environ- ment'. After the Bosnian war, however, Western states (and the USA in particular) became critical of Berisha's increasingly authoritarian behaviour.

On 22 February 1996 an agreement was announced concerning the return of 1.5 tonnes of gold ingots and coins (worth around 20 million US dollars) which had been seized by the Germans during the Second World War and subsequently by the Allies (held in trust by the Bank of England). In return, the UK received 2 million US dollars from Albania as compensation for the two destroyers lost in 1946 when they hit mines in the Corfu channel.

Economic policies under President Berisha, 1992–7

The Berisha regime's IMF (International Monetary Fund)-inspired economic-reform programme was supposed to have been introduced on 1 July 1992, but its imple- mentation was delayed by the imminence and the results of the local elections held on 26 July 1992, in which the DP share of the vote plummeted. The main planks of the reform programme introduced in the course of 1992–5 included:

1. *Austerity measures to reduce the huge budget deficit.* These measures included the phasing out of the generous unemployment compensation scheme. The law on social assistance did not become fully operational until July 1992. Unemployment pay was to be limited to one year, at a rate of 70 per cent of the previous year's average wage for the frst six months and 60 per cent for the next six months. A wage-inflation tax was put into operation. A nominal wage ceilin was introduced in September 1992, which was permitted to be exceeded only by certain relatively successful enterprises. An agreement was reached between the government and the largest trade union to index government wages to the prices of twenty-four basic consumer goods (EBRD 1996b: 136). The total strength of the armed forces was reduced from 90,000 to 35,000 personnel and the 600,000-strong reserve force was disbanded (*FT*, Survey, 19 February 1997, p. 16).

2. *Flotation of the lek.* The lek became convertible on current account, although strict controls were retained on the capital account.
3. *Foreign-trade liberalization.* Albania signed a ten-year trade and cooperation agreement with the EU in May 1992 and a free-trade agreement with EFTA in December 1992.
4. *Rapid price liberalization.* In August 1992 almost all prices were freed and the few controlled prices of basic food products were raised by 300 to 400 per cent (United Nations Economic Commission for Europe 1993: 221). Price liberalization was comprehensive, although twenty-five items remained subject to administrative price-setting (EBRD 1994: 17). The prices of bread, gas and kerosene were liberalized in July 1996. However, some price controls and subsidies (amounting to less than 1 per cent of GDP) were retained on public transport, rail fares, postal tariffs, electricity and rural water supply (EBRD 1996b: 136). Price controls on food were temporarily reimposed during the state of emergency in 1997.
5. *Rapid expansion of the private sector*, although it remained 'extremely hard for any businessman in Albania to succeed independently of the mafia or of government corruption' (*EEN*, 12 October 1996, vol. 10, no. 20, p. 4).
6. *A new bankruptcy law was passed in October 1995.* It defined bankruptcy procedures for all enterprises (the previous one covering only state enterprises), although no bankruptcies were allowed actually to take place in 1995–6 (EBRD 1996b: 136).

Privatization of industry and services, 1992–7

A voucher-based mass-privatization programme was approved in early 1995, with voucher distribution to start in June 1995. In the programme, a total of 400 medium and large enterprises were to be privatized through auctions. By July 1996, a total of ninety-seven enterprises had been sold under this programme (EBRD 1996b: 11). Emphasis was placed on finding strategic investors for the remaining large enterprises, but up to 1997 only one large-scale privatization had been completed (EBRD 1997b: 148). The enterprise-restructuring agency set up in 1993 to deal with thirty-two problem firms was 'relatively successful in restructuring these firms, reduci employment from 50,000 at their peak to 7,000 at the end of 1995'. However, only ten of these were privatized and only one smaller enterprise was liquidated (EBRD 1998b: 148). Strategic industries such as telecommunications were to be handled separately (*FT*, Survey, 2 October 1995, p. iv). A stock exchange was opened on 2 May 1996, initially dealing only in treasury bills and privatization vouchers.

Foreign aid, workers' remittances and external debt, 1992–7

Between 1991 and 1996, Albania rapidly became heavily dependent on Western economic aid and on remittances from émigré workers. Italy, the country most directly affected by the successive outpourings of Albanian refugees, provided generous food aid and other assistance, partly in attempts to stem these outflows. Food aid amounted to more than 600 million US dollars in 1991–2, a sum equivalent to 63 per cent of Albania's GDP (Pashko 1996: 70).

Remittances from Albanians working abroad rose from virtually zero in 1991 to 334 million US dollars in 1993 (*FT*, 29 June 1994, p. 3) and 500 million US dollars in 1994 (*BCE*, May 1994, p. 80). In 1996 some 400,000 Albanians worked abroad, mostly illegally, sending home more than 450 million US dollars a year (*The Economist*, 18 May 1996, p. 51). Emigrant workers accounted for an estimated 18 per cent of Albania's workforce in 1995 (EBRD 2000a: 37). Albania also profite considerably from being the biggest sanctions-buster for fuel delivered to the Federal Republic of Yugoslavia during the Bosnian conflict (*IHT*, 3 April 1995, p. 1). In 1995 foreign aid, remittances from Albanians working abroad and earnings from sanctions-busting altogether accounted for three-quarters of Albania's national income (*IHT*, 1 April 1995, p. 11).

Gross foreign debt stood at around 900 million US dollars in late 1994. Albania barely serviced its outstanding foreign debt.

Agriculture and 'real estate' under the Berisha regime, 1992–7

A major impediment to agricultural restructuring was the slow pace of reforms to settle compensation claims from pre-Communist and pre-collectivization property-owners. The lack of clear title deeds complicated the acquisition of land or buildings or the offering of such assets as collateral for bank loans. This legal vacuum also delayed the consolidation of land holdings that would make agriculture more efficient (*FT*, Survey, 18 May 2004, p. 32). Pre-Communist landowners were only allowed to reclaim a maximum of 15 hectares from their pre-Communist land holdings. Alternatively they could seek compensation for up to 30 hectares. Compensation was to be in the form of bonds (*EEN*, 21 September 1994, vol. 8, no. 19, p. 6).

In May 1993 the Berisha regime approved a restitution law under which expro-priated urban property was to be returned to the original owners or their heirs in 1995; in the meantime, existing domestic or commercial tenants were to pay rent to the former owners. However, the law only provided for compensation of up to 10 per cent for owners of rural property, and even then only in the form of bank guarantees. The sale and purchase of land was forbidden in order to prevent 'tenants' from selling the pre-1946 landowners' land. Families wanting to repossess land expropriated by the Communist regime during the 1940s had to pay vast bribes to acquire titles to that land (*EEN*, 16 February 1997, vol. 11, no. 3, p. 3). According to the laws passed in 1993, many former owners or their heirs could claim either compensation for, or restitution of, non-agricultural land. In the case of property that had already been privatized, there was the possibility of co-ownership between the new and former owners (EBRD 1994: 16).

A new agrarian law passed in summer 1995 allowed the buying and selling of farmland for the frst time and converted the titles to usage of land into property titles (EBRD 1996b: 136). In order to encourage land consolidation, the law required any farmer wishing to sell land to offer it f rst of all to relatives of the current owner, to owners of neighbouring properties, to other villagers or to former owners of the land, before it could be offered for sale to anyone else. A few informal sales did take place (EBRD 1997b: 148).

By the end of 1993, 92 per cent of agricultural land had been privatized, and by the end of 1996 this proportion had risen to 98 per cent, but as yet no land market had developed and land still could not be traded effectively. The main obstacles were the absence of clear mechanisms for establishing the legality of land transactions and the requirement that all land holdings in a village be registered before any could be sold; in fact only 3 per cent of privatized land had been so registered by mid-1997

(*FT*, Survey, 2 October 1995, p. iii). By 1995, 95 per cent of agricultural production was being contributed by private farmers, whereas in 1990, 50 per cent had come from 'agricultural producer cooperatives' (collective farms) (Deutsche Bank, 15 February 1995, no. 125, p. 4).

Cungu and Swinnen argued that Albania's agricultural restructuring was the most radical among Europe's post-Communist states. Virtually all land was transferred to small individual farmers, whereas in other Central and Eastern European countries large-scale cooperatives, joint stock companies and limited liability companies continued to occupy an important share of the land (Cungu and Swinnen 1999: 605). All agricultural producer cooperatives and most of the state farms were completely broken up into individual farms. By 1998 more than 95 per cent of land was being used by 'approximately 490,000 individual private farms in at least 1.9 million separate parcels, with an average of about 3.3 separately located parcels for each farm'. The average size was '1.0 hectares, ranging between 1.3 hectares in valley and foothill regions to 0.8 hectares in the mountains' (Cungu and Swinnen 1999: 611).

Foreign direct investment, 1992–7

FDI was actively sought after, but even before the crisis of 1996–7 the response was poor (see Table 2.1). Attempts were made to improve the economic environment. In July 1995, for example, a law was passed which allowed foreign individuals or companies to buy land if they combined the purchase with a three-times-as-large investment in the use of that land (EBRD 1995b: 33). In 1997, Premier Oil (UK) and Preussag (Germany) agreed to invest 250 million US dollars in a joint venture with the state oil company Albpetrol to develop Albania's largest onshore oil field, making this the largest single FDI in Albania.

The pyramid-scheme crisis of 1996–7 and the insurgency of 1997

Pyramid schemes are inherently fraudulent investment schemes which pay out artificially high returns to early investors using money paid in by subsequent investors. Pure pyramid schemes are backed by nothing but the ability to attract fresh funds until their inevitable demise. Early players in the game who withdraw their funds and gains in time benefit at the expense of later participants. When later investors try t get their money out, the pyramid scheme collapses – and this is often accompanied by acts of outright theft by the operators, if they are not caught first.

During the mid-1990s, some Albanian companies were or became pure pyramid schemes, with no real assets. Pyramid schemes were by no means peculiar to Albania. What distinguished Albania was the scale on which pyramid schemes emerged, the seriousness of the consequences and the extent of government involvement. 'At their peak the nominal value of the pyramid schemes' liabilities amounted to almost half of the country's GDP. Many Albanians – about two-thirds of the population – invested in them . . . Albanians sold their houses to invest in the schemes; farmers sold their livestock.' Indeed, due to the combined effects of the bureaucratic slowness of the payments system inherited from the Communist regime, the fact that Albanians were receiving about 300 million US dollars a year as remittances (c.12 per cent of GDP), and the widespread distrust of banks, Albanians 'tended to hold an unusually high proportion of their financial assets in cash'. At the same time, 'with the bank

family ties and financed by remittances grew'. In addition, some of the largest of th
companies (VEFA Holdings, Gjallica and Kamberi) were widely believed to be
engaged in criminal activities, including violating UN sanctions by illegally smuggling
goods into the Yugoslav successor states. This enabled them to offer initial high returns.
However, at the end of 1995 UN sanctions against Serbia and Montenegro were
suspended, greatly reducing one of the schemes' main sources of revenue (smuggling).
In addition, the regulatory framework for Albania's financial institutions was ver
inadequate. It was unclear who had responsibility for supervising the informal market.
Although in February 1996 a new banking law formally empowered the Bank of
Albania to close illegal deposit-taking institutions, it did not obtain the government's
support to exercise this power, because during the 1996 election several pyramid
companies made campaign contributions to the DP and it was alleged that 'many
government off cials benefited personally from the companies'. Moreover, the finan
ministry not only did not warn the public about the schemes until October 1996,
but even then 'drew a false and misleading distinction between companies with real
investments and "pure pyramid schemes"'. In November 1996 Sude (which had no
real investments) defaulted on its payments, and in early January both Sude and
Gjallica declared bankruptcy (Jarvis 2000: 3, 6, 15, 46–8).

During January 1997 about half of all Albanian families lost some money and
over a third lost most of their savings as a result of the collapse of these pyramid
schemes (*The Economist*, 25 January 1997, p. 43, and 1 February 1997, p. 4). On 23
January the government belatedly prohibited the creation of any more pyramid savings schemes and froze the assets of the two schemes which were bankrupt, but it
still dared not close down those which had remained in business. Violent protests
erupted on 25 January, especially in Vlore, where Gjallica was based, and in Tirana,
where VEFA Holdings was based. Parliament authorized the use of troops to guard
roads and government buildings. On 29 January President Berisha announced that
only the poorest investors would receive cash payments from the two pyramid schemes
whose bank accounts had been frozen (*IHT*, 30 January 1997, p. 7).

Opposition parties and organizations on 30 January formed an alliance called the
Forum for Democracy, whose main aims were to persuade the government to set
up a caretaker government of technical experts and then hold fresh elections, but
arrests continued. Another scheme went bankrupt on 4 February. On 5 February the
prime minister promised to start refunding investors' frozen deposits using the assets
of the frozen pyramid schemes. Two inmates were killed in prison riots, while a
high-ranking member of the Socialist Party was critically wounded (*FT*, 5 February
1997, p. 2). In February parliament passed a law banning pyramid schemes, but without
def ning them, while the government tried to differentiate between companies with
real investments and pure pyramid schemes. This was misleading because even
pyramid scheme companies with real investments were being funded by unsound
and unsustainable methods.

Larger anti-government protests occurred in Vlore on 5 February. A man died there
after being beaten up during clashes between riot police and demonstrators on
9 February, and the following day the police lost control of the city. This resulted in
further deaths. 'As the riots intensified and spread, the remaining schemes ceased pay
ments' (Jarvis 2000: 15). The growing anarchy and bloodshed caused the lek to lose
a third of its value against the US dollar and prices to rise by 40 to 50 per cent (*IHT*,
1 March 1997, p. 2).

Berisha accused the Socialist Party of fomenting the insurgency, and senior opposition politicians, including Rexhep Meidani (secretary-general of the SPA), Gjinushi Skender (chairman of the SDP) and Arben Imami (of the Democratic Alliance), were arrested. Nevertheless, President Berisha dismissed the Meksi government on 1 March and offered to consult the Forum for Democracy about the formation of a new government. The following day parliament declared a state of emergency. Among the measures taken were a dusk-to-dawn curfew, media censorship, suspension of the international television satellite link (until 3 March), a ban on meetings of more than four people in any one place, permission for security personnel to shoot without warning anyone who defied the emergency regulations and the exclusion of foreigner from the south.

Weapons were looted from police and army barracks in Vlore and Sarande, where some 200 prisoners were released by demonstrators, on 2 March. The next day the DP-dominated parliament defiantly re-elected Berisha as president. The following day he dismissed the army chief of staff. On 5 March, however, Berisha and his government completely lost control of Vlore, Tepelene, Sarande and Delvina. The same was true of Gjirokaster, Permet, Berat and Kucove by 10 March.

As the insurgency escalated, over half a million weapons of various sorts fell into civilian hands through the looting of army depots (*FT*, Survey, 23 February 2000, p. 16). This made it increasingly impossible for the state security forces to restore order, and some soldiers and police either deserted or went over to the insurgents. Many of the looted weapons would eventually end up in the hands of Kosovar Albanian insurgents in Kosova in 1998 and early 1999 (see Chapter 10), not only because of Albanian political sympathy with the plight of the Albanian Kosovars, but also because the Kosovars and their émigré support networks in Germany and Switzerland paid good prices for weapons and many Albanians were desperate for cash.

An EU delegation arrived in Albania on 7 March. Faced with the growing impossibility of restoring order by force, Berisha was persuaded to appear on television on 9 March, accompanied by opposition leaders, and to accept the need for an interim 'government of national reconciliation' representing all political parties and fresh parliamentary elections within two months. The next day Italian diplomats met with insurgent leaders in Vlore, who agreed to try to restore order and to encourage civilians to lay down their weapons in return for a swift implementation of the agreement in Tirana, but it was not known how representative these leaders were and demonstrators elsewhere continued to demand Berisha's resignation, while the leaders of the insurgency in Vlore denied that any agreement had been reached.

More than 1,500 lives were lost between March and June 1997, as direct results of the insurgency precipitated by the collapse of the pyramid schemes (*IHT*, 27 June 1997, p. 6), while about 13,000 people f ed to Italy and over 10,000 (mostly ethnic Greeks) fled to Greece *IHT*, 3 April 1997, p. 5). Albania's GDP contracted by 7 per cent during 1997 (Table 2.1). With regard to the causes, it is 'impossible to separate out the supply side effects of the civil disorder from the demand-side effects from the loss of savings in the pyramid schemes' (Jarvis 2000: 23). The pyramid-scheme crisis, the subsequent insurgency and the massive looting of weapons inflicted huge damag on the social fabric, from which it took several years to recover. There was a lasting escalation of organized criminal networks, smuggling, drug-dealing, arms-dealing, people-trafficking and white-slave-trading (exportation of prostitutes from the Commonwealth of Independent States (CIS) to Western Europe, as virtual captives of their pimps), which Albania has not yet been able to bring under control.

Winding up Albania's pyramid schemes proved difficult. The major pyramid schemes clung to their assets, proclaimed their solvency and continued trading. The interim government set up in March 1997 encountered resistance both from the operators and from parliamentarians, many of whom were reported to have invested in the schemes. Consequently it was not until July 1997 that a newly elected parliament passed a law mandating the appointment of foreign administrators from the international accounting firm Pricewaterhouse Coopers to liquidate the schemes. Th administrators did not gain full control of the companies until March 1998, and the sale of their residual assets did not begin until mid-1998. By then the assets were apparently sufficient to cover less than 10 per cent of the companies' nominal liabilitie (Jarvis 2000: 25, 29, 46–8).

The interim cross-party government headed by Bashkim Fino, 11 March to 28 July 1997

On 11 March 1997 Bashkim Fino of the Socialist Party was named as interim prime minister. Fino was formerly the mayor of Gjirokaster. The presidential adviser declared that Berisha would resign only if the opposition won the forthcoming parliamentary elections, but by this stage Berisha's position was weakening daily. About 70 per cent of the military had either deserted or transferred its support to the rebels(*The Guardian*, 12 March 1997, p. 11).

On 12 March rebel leaders in fourteen southern towns formed the National Committee for Public Salvation, based in Gjirokaster. Its main aims were the resig-nation of Berisha and participation in the Tirana talks. Anti-government rebels pillaged an arms depot near Elbasan. 'In some parts of the south the rebellion ... deteriorated into lawlessness, with armed gangs roaming through towns' (*IHT*, 13 March 1997, p. 6). In Tirana itself groups of men entered the military academy and removed small arms, but there were strong suspicions that the arming of civilians on 13 March was organized by Berisha (*IHT*, 14 March 1997, p. 7).

The new government was sworn in on 13 March. Berisha and the opposition parties issued a joint appeal to the Western European Union (WEU) (the European members of NATO, the North Atlantic Treaty Organization) to intervene militarily, admitting that the country was beyond their control. Lawlessness spread rapidly throughout the country, including Tirana (despite the presence of army tanks). Berisha sent his wife and children to Italy, and the exodus of foreign nationals was speeded up. Hundreds of prisoners broke out of jail, including Ramiz Alia. (Fellow prisoners broke down the door to Fatos Nano's prison cell on 13 March, but he refused to leave until the prison director offered to drive him home!) In late March 1997 the government approved an amnesty for some 700 of the estimated 1,300 prisoners who had escaped, while those who returned to jail by 5 April 1997 had their sentences reduced by one-third (*The Times*, 29 March 1997, p. 15). Thousands of people fed abroad, especially through the port of Durres, where greater calm prevailed.

US, Italian and German rescue helicopters came under fire on 14 March and operations were suspended. German troops exchanged fire with armed attackers. The head of the OSCE mission, former Austrian chancellor Franz Vranitzsky, called for international military intervention. The government tripled the wages of security personnel, which helped to restore calm in Tirana. On 16 March the OSCE recom-mended international military intervention. Javier Ruperez, president of the OSCE assembly, proposed that a 'modest NATO force could provide security and disarm the population while the EU provides economic assistance, primarily in food and medicine, and the OSCE can prepare for internationally supervised elections' (*IHT*, 22 March 1997, p. 6). EU foreign ministers agreed to send a small team of advisers to help restore civilian structures and law and order, and to join the OSCE, Greece and Turkey in sending a delegation to act as mediators. Italy, France, the Netherlands, Denmark and Greece advocated military intervention, but the UK, Germany and Sweden strongly opposed this.

Berisha issued a presidential pardon to Fatos Nano on 16 March, and Nano moderated his hitherto-vengeful attitude towards Berisha the next day, merely stating that free and fair elections were the ideal way of removing the president and that Berisha should either step aside or stop interfering with the work of the coalition government. There was a peace rally in an increasingly calm Tirana, where shops reopened and public transport resumed. Tirana airport reopened on 20 March. Government representatives began talks with rebel leaders in different parts of the country.

Italy declared a state of emergency from 19 March to 30 June 1997 in order to cope with large inflows of Albanian refugees. Provision was made to expel those 'deemed to be a danger to public security', but also to send food and medicine to Albania. The head of the EU mission warned Albania that it had to put its house in order before the EU could help it. On 21 March the National Committee for Public Salvation withdrew its threats to march on Tirana and form an alternative government. Instead it declared its support for the coalition government (provided it proved to be independent of Berisha) and demanded that Berisha resign and be replaced by a presidential council until the elections. Italian and Albanian politicians reached agreement on an Italian naval blockade of Albania on 24 March, in an attempt to stem the flood of refugees, but vessels filled with refugees (usually organized criminal gangs for payment) continued to set sail for Italy. EU foreign ministers approved a food and medical aid package (*The Times*, 25 March 1997, p. 12). On 28 March the UN Security Council approved, for three months, an Italian-led inter - national force to protect aid deliveries to Albania. An Albanian vessel carrying refugees sank after colliding with an Italian warship, and eighty-three people were drowned. The Albanian parliament approved the UN force on 30 March.

Fino announced on 1 April that the pro-Berisha state-security force, Shik, had been disbanded. On 4 April about twenty DP parliamentarians signed a statement that they would no longer 'accept the diktat' of President Berisha (*The Guardian*, 5 April 1997, p. 15). On 9 April SPA deputies attended parliament for the first tim since the May–June 1996 election.

The Italian government, with some difficulty, obtained parliamentary approval on 9 April 1997 to send a 2,500-strong force to Albania. The initial aims were to secure the ports of Durres and Vlore and the airport at Tirana. Advance contingents of Italian and French troops arrived in Albania on 11 and 12 April, respectively. The main international force started arriving on 15 April. It eventually comprised *c.*2,500 troops from Italy, *c.*1,000 from France, *c.*800 from Greece, *c.*700 from Turkey, *c.*450 from Spain, *c.*400 from Romania, *c.*120 from Austria and *c.*60 from Denmark.

The ten main political parties signed an agreement on 9 May to hold a parliamentary election on 29 June 1997. The Law on Communist Genocide was to be repealed and the 'national salvation committees' were to be dissolved at least forty-six days before the election. However, on 13 May the DP used its majority in parliament to vote for an electoral law similar to the previous one. The number of seats was to increase from 140 to 155, with 115 seats to be decided on a first-past-the-post basi and 40 by proportional representation.

Berisha dissolved parliament on 21 May 1997 and scheduled the election for 29 June, as agreed. The Socialist Party declared the next day that it would contest the election provided there was full international monitoring. Instead, Berisha announced that the caretaker government could appoint the members of the central electoral commission, which in turn would appoint local electoral officials. The president als signed a decree allowing a referendum on the monarchy to be held at the same time as the parliamentary election. The DP, the SPA and the SDP signed an agreement on the fair conduct of elections on 23 June.

The parliamentary elections of 29 June and 6 July 1997 and the referendum on restoring the monarchy

There was a 66 per cent turn-out in the first round of the parliamentary elections. There were some 500 OSCE observers on 29 June and around 150 on 6 July, but not all polling stations were covered. The international peacekeeping force undertook escort duties. OSCE concluded that the first round of the election (held on 29 Jun 1997) had been conducted acceptably, despite minor f aws in many areas and major problems in a few areas. Voters had generally managed to vote without fear or intimidation, but there had been reports of serious problems with the vote-counting process in some areas.

During his campaign, Fatos Nano made 'an utterly implausible promise that all savings lost in the pyramid schemes would be refunded. The sum is at least half of Albania's GDP and no reliable record of individual losses exists'*The Times*, 3 July 1997, p. 25). However, he subsequently claimed that he had never told the voters they would get all their money back and had merely talked of 'dishing out what is left' (*The Economist*, 5 July 1997, p. 42). Through the first two rounds of votin the SPA obtained over 50 per cent of the votes cast and 100 of the 155 seats, while its allies won another eighteen seats. The DP obtained only 25 per cent of the votes and twenty-four seats (Carlson and Betts 2001: 58). Only 7.1 per cent of parliamentary seats were won by women, down from 15 per cent in 1996 and over 30 per cent in 1990 (Jouan 2003: 56). In the referendum on whether or not to restore the monarchy, an overwhelming 66.8 per cent of voters voted in favour of remaining a republic. Ex-King Zog's gigantic son Leka Zog led protests against the verdict, armed with a pistol and a sub-machine gun. However, he returned hurriedly to his home in South Africa when police sought to question him in connection with a shooting death.

Decisively rejected by the electorate, Berisha resigned as president on 23 July, but he decided to stay on as leader of the DP. In the short space of four years (1993–7) Berisha had created what Human Rights Watch called 'a one-party state based on fear and corruption'. He had turned the judicial system into a political instrument, and he had expanded the National Intelligence Service to a force of 3,000 agents, supported by a further 3,000 informers which operated as an arm of his party (*IHT*, 5 August 1997, p. 7). The former director of the Shik, the state-security service, fle abroad just before the SPA victory was confirmed, as did the commander of the presidential guard and the national police director (*IHT*, 5 August 1997, p. 7). The opening session of parliament was boycotted by the DP. On 21 July the constitutional court declared that the election should be rerun in part of northern Albania and that a number of other official results should be revised *EEN*, 1997, vol. 11, no. 14, p. 2). Parliament elected Rexhep Meidani, a leading figure in the SPA, as president of Albania on 24 July and lifted the state of emergency and the curfew.

The centre-left coalition government headed by Fatos Nano, 29 July 1997 to 28 September 1998

The new governing coalition comprised the SPA, the Democratic Alliance (led by interior minister Neritan Ceka), the SDP (led by Skender Gjinushi), the Agrarian Party (led by agriculture minister Lufter Xhuveli) and the Union for the Protection of Human Rights (led by Vasil Melo). Other important members of the government included Bashkim Fino (deputy prime minister), Paskal Milo (foreign minister), Sabit Brokaj (defence minister), Arben Malaj (finance minister) and Ylli Bu (privatization and economics minister).

The last troops of the international force departed on 11 August, although about 600 Italian troops moved in subsequently to guard ports and border-crossings. The next day the Nano government sent Albanian troops to Vlore, Gjirokaster, Sarande and Tepelene to restore order. The DP ended its boycott of parliament on 13 August.

The new government claimed on 14 August that the police had restored order in Vlore, and on 17 August the government issued orders that all the heavy weapons distributed by the police after the collapse of the state were to be surrendered by 31 August and all light weapons by 30 September. On 22 August the government appointed administrators to each of the surviving pyramid schemes, but on 17 September VEFA Holdings won a case in the appeals court to prevent state administrators from assuming managerial control. Four major investment funds were still in operation, albeit offering lower interest rates than before and without receiving new deposits. On 7 October the IMF signed a six-month agreement for 'post-conflct' assistance.

On 18 September an SPA deputy shot a DP deputy in parliament, and the DP executive subsequently decided to boycott parliamentary proceedings again.

A Tirana court acquitted Ramiz Alia *in absentia* (along with three other senior officials) of charges of 'genocide and crimes against humanity' on 20 October 1997. The state prosecution dropped the charges against him. Alia had been accused of deporting hundreds of his opponents between 1982 and 1986 and of ordering the killing of Albanians who sought to fee Albania between 1986 and 1991. He was believed to have fled to France in March 1997 *IHT*, 21 October 1997, p. 5; *The Times*, 21 October 1997, p. 15).

The DP announced on 29 January 1998 that it would end its boycott of parliament, but it did not actually do so until 5 March 1998 (in order to attend a debate on the brewing crisis in Kosova). Demonstrations in Shkoder demanding the release of two senior Berisha supporters from detention on 22 February developed into a riot, but the next day interior-ministry troops wrested control of Shkoder from the armed gangs of Berisha supporters.

Parliament approved an amendment legalizing the Communist Party on 9 April 1998. Berisha supporters saw this as proof that the SPA were crypto-Communists, but the move was in fact a healthy sign that Albania was becoming a more pluralistic state.

The DP began another boycott of parliament in July 1998, following the publication of an official report which pinned the main blame for the pyramid-scheme crisis and the February–March 1997 insurgency on ex-President Berisha and the Meksi government. On 22 August the former defence minister Safet Zhulali and five other senior members of the previous DP government were arrested. They were charged with 'crimes against humanity' before and during the February–March 1997 insurgency (*EEN*, 1998, vol. 12, no. 10, pp. 2, 8).

About 2,000 DP supporters set fire to cars outside the interior ministry and to th prime minister's office in Tirana on 13 September, accusing the SPA government o being behind the assassination of Azem Hajdari (a leading DP deputy) the day before. The prime minister and other cabinet ministers fled. A protestor was killed and fou of the prime minister's guards were wounded, two of whom later died. The government offered a 100,000-dollar reward for information leading to the arrest of the culprits. Azem Hajdari's funeral took place in Tirana the next day (along with those of two of his bodyguards). Armed pro-Berisha supporters temporarily took control of the parliament building, the offices of the prime minister and the state television and radio station, and government forces killed three rioters. Fatos Nano claimed that this was an attempted coup. On 15 September about 3,000 pro-Berisha supporters staged an unauthorized but peaceful demonstration in Tirana. The government aimed to prosecute Berisha for leading what it considered to be an attempted coup. The OSCE tried to persuade the DP to end its boycott of parliament and renew talks on amending Albania's constitution. 'This was a serious attempt to overthrow the government', according to Timothy Isles, deputy head of the OSCE mission in Tirana, but to 'put in perspective there was a band of no more than 500 militants bent on creating chaos and anarchy. The rest of the country was quiet and they got no widespread support' (*FT*, 16 September 1998, p. 2). On 16 September about 3,000 pro-Berisha supporters staged another peaceful demonstration in Tirana. According to the interior ministry, however, the three days of unrest (13–16 September) had left eight dead and eighty injured (*IHT*, 17 September 1998, p. 4).

Parliament lifted Berisha's immunity from prosecution on 18 September, clearing the way for prosecutors to charge him with attempting a coup. Of the 113 members participating in the vote, 108 voted in favour. The DP was still boycotting parlia - ment. Berisha faced the death penalty or life imprisonment if convicted of attempting to overthrow the government. Before the vote Berisha led a peaceful march of about 3,000 people in Tirana's Skanderbeg Square (*IHT*, 19 September 1998, p. 2).

Fatos Nano resigned as prime minister on 28 September 1998, claiming that political in-f ghting had made it impossible to construct a new cabinet of his ve-party coalition government. He accepted responsibility 'for everything this government has not done' and acknowledged that 'the chances of coming out of the crisis are small' *FT*, 30 September 1998, p. 3). The fall of his government had become a racing certainty after his brief loss of nerve and disappearance following the mid-September coup attempt by the opposition DP. Nano had been taken wholly by surprise when a DP-incited mob stormed his office. Having fled the building and reportedly driven to Macedonia or Greece, he went to ground for a couple of days, leaving President Meidani and Pandeli Majko to hold the ring. It had been left to Meidani to address the nation on television and, in his role as commander-in-chief of the armed forces, to call in the special forces which put Berisha's motley army to f ight (*EEN*, 1998, vol. 12, no. 11, pp. 1–2).

The centre-left coalition government headed by Pandeli Majko, October 1998 to October 1999

The thirty-year-old secretary-general of the SPA was chosen to succeed Fatos Nano as prime minister of the five-party governing coalition. He had been active in the 1990–1 street protests that helped topple the country's Stalinist regime and, being so young, he was the f rst prime minister to have had no connections with Albania's deceased Communist regime (Berisha, like Nano, had been a long-serving member of the PLA). Although he lacked ministerial experience, Majko had made a name for himself as a mediator in feuds between the government and the opposition leader, Sali Berisha. The SPA still held a comfortable majority in the 155-seat parliament (*IHT*, 30 September 1998, p. 5). A priority was to sack the deputy premier Bashkim Fino, the former mayor of Girokaster who became premier after the March 1997 collapse and whose corruption and abuse of patronage were considered second to none. The former interior minister Neritan Ceka had enough information on Fino to do far more than sack him, and Majko's new cabinet duly excluded him*EEN*, 1998, vol. 12, no. 11, p. 2).

A new constitution drawn up by the left-of-centre coalition reduced the powers of the president and increased the element of proportional representation for future parliamentary elections. It was overwhelmingly approved in a referendum held on 22 November 1998, but the turn-out was only around 50 per cent, partly because Berisha and the DP appealed to the electorate to boycott the referendum. Nevertheless, the OSCE upheld the result, and President Meidani approved the new constitution on 28 November (*EEN*, 1998, vol. 12, no. 13, p. 6).

On 13 January 1999 parliament approved legislation aimed at stemming an unsafe and illegal exodus of people to Italy. It banned boats of less than 70 horsepower from sailing further than 2 miles off the coast unless they had advised the border police first *The Times*, 14 January 1999, p. 13).

During the Kosova crisis of 1998–9 (described in Chapter 10), tens of thousands and eventually over 400,000 Kosovar Albanians took refuge in Albania where, despite the country's poverty and the damaging impact of the Kosova crisis on the Albanian economy, they were given much sympathy and hospitality. The influx during the first half of 1999 imposed an enormous strain on Albania's social services and state budget. However, the termination of the conflict in June was quickly followed by the return of the vast majority of these refugees to Kosova by the end of July 1999 (EBRD 1999b: 183). In addition, the Albanian government refrained from criticizing NATO's rather clumsy and inept handling of the crisis and supported the NATO intervention in just about every way that it could. The NATO powers, the EU and the Western media were suitably impressed by all of this and, in return, gave Albania increased economic aid and made encouraging noises 'about the rewards Albania might expect for its cooperation'. In April 1999 EU officials stated that Albania would be allowe to sign a stabilization and association agreement (SAA) with the EU 'very soon', and on 25 May the EU commissioner for external affairs told Prime Minister Majko that 'the EU would discuss the timetable for Albania's accession to the EU', while in September 1999 the US government pledged its support for Albania's efforts to join the WTO. The Kosova crisis brought not only NATO troops and increased Western aid into Albania, but also a measure of order. Nevertheless, once NATO's Kosova operation was completed and a measure of order was restored, France vetoed Albania's entry into the WTO in October 1999 and the EU backtracked on its promise of an SAA, contending that Albania needed to undergo considerable reform and restructuring before it would be fit to enter such a state of grace (Crampto 2002: 307).

The DP ended its twelve-month boycott of parliament on 21 July 1999. On 28 September the DP deputy chairman Genc Pollo resigned his party position in protest at Berisha's dictatorial style, but Berisha was nevertheless comfortably re-elected chairman of the party.

Fatos Nano decided to embark on a political comeback in the autumn of 1999 and challenged Prime Minister Pandeli Majko to a contest for the SPA leadership. Nano narrowly defeated Majko on 11 October and two weeks later Majko resigned from the premiership. However, the SPA decided to nominate not Nano but the even younger deputy prime minister, Ilir Meta, as Majko's successor. This choice was confirme by parliament on November 5.

The centre-left coalition government headed by Ilir Meta, November 1999 to June 2001

From the start, the Meta government gave priority to carrying out the types of economic and judicial reform that were needed to make Albania more eligible for membership of the EU and NATO in due course, and EU and US government circles came to prefer Meta to Albania's much more clientelistic and corrupt political dinosaurs, such as Fatos Nano, Sali Berisha and Bashkim Fino. Nevertheless, the dinosaurs gave him a rough ride.

On 6 November 1999 a faction within the DP, led by Genc Pollo, set up the 'Democratic Alternative' to oppose the Berisha wing of the party. On 7 December the DP suspended the party membership of Genc Pollo, accusing him of having failed to disclose the origin of the private funds which he had used to buy real estate in Tirana. The opposition DP thus split, with the moderates under Genc Pollo forming a 'Democratic Alternative' faction which attended parliament, while the bulk of the DP under Berisha maintained its parliamentary boycott (*EEN*, 1999, vol. 12, no. 21, pp. 4, 7).

Local elections, 1 and 15 October 2000

The elections were monitored by OSCE which reported that the conduct of the election marked 'significant progress toward meeting the standards for democratic elections' The Council of Europe and OSCE reported that voting had taken place in 'a tense but remarkably peaceful atmosphere, with only a few isolated incidents of violence' (*IHT*, 3 October 2000, p. 5). On 2 October the SPA claimed that it had won 52 per cent of the vote. A second round of voting took place on 15 October, involving those seats where candidates failed to get more than 50 per cent of the vote. However, the opposition DP declined to participate in the second round, so the ruling SPA obtained 75 per cent of the seats contested at that point. They also wrested control of the municipality of Tirana from the DP (*The Economist*, 28 October 2000, p. 48).

Overall, 43 per cent of the vote went to the SPA and 34 per cent to the DP. Irregularities were noted by observers brought in by OSCE, but not on the scale claimed by the DP. The DP's massive loss of local-authority seats threatened Berisha's dominance of his party. In February 2000 he had expelled the reformist deputies from the parliamentary DP, but the reformists had nevertheless not opposed officia DP candidates in these local elections and thereby not only gained stature among the DP membership for not splitting the vote, but also could blame the defeat squarely on Berisha. The October 2000 mayoral elections were in large measure conducted on programmes of municipal improvement. The victory of the parties of the governing coalition in 280 of the 378 towns and communes brought some likelihood of implementation. Edi Rama, who was elected as an 'independent' mayor of Tirana (albeit with SPA support), quickly initiated a major programme of investment in the capital whose population had rocketed from 243,000 in 1990 to some 600,000 in 2000 (Kaser 2001: 10–13, 51).

The parliamentary elections of June and July 2001

The 140-seat parliament comprised 100 first-past-the-post single-member constituenc seats and 40 allocated by proportional representation from party lists. The threshold for representation in parliament was 2.5 per cent of the votes cast in the first roun for individual parties and 4 per cent for coalitions. This was one of the country's most peaceful elections since the end of Communist rule. Although gunmen broke into a polling station in the north and burned ballot papers and two men were injured in a shooting outside a polling station in Tirana, these were minor incidents by past standards (*The Guardian*, 25 June 2001, p. 10). However, due to widespread electoral irregularities, in some constituencies the voting extended to five rounds, giving ris to the most protracted election contest in Albania's recent history. During the campaign Sali Berisha expressed strong support for ethnic Albanian insurgents in Macedonia (*The Times*, 25 June 2001, p. 10) and alleged widespread electoral fraud and intimidation of polling-station officials by the police in the first round, but an OS preliminary report noted only 'isolated incidents of violence' (*The Guardian*, 26 June 2001, p. 10).

The turn-out in the first round (24 June) was 54 per cent and in the second (8 July was 48 per cent, well down from the 1990s levels, reflecting widespread disillusion ment with both of the major parties, the DP and the SPA. Ultimately, the SPA obtained 73 of the 140 seats. The DP-led Union for Victory coalition comprising the DP, the monarchist Legality Movement Party, the National Front Party and the Republican Party obtained only forty-six seats, the breakaway New Democratic Party formed and led by the former DP deputy leader Genc Pollo obtained six seats, four small centrist parties (the SDP, the Human Rights Union, the Agrarian Party and the Democratic Alliance) obtained thirteen seats between them, and independents won two seats (Carlson and Betts 2002: 52–3).

The second socialist government headed by Ilir Meta, August 2001 to January 2002

Prime Minister Ilir Meta announced on 9 July that the SPA had won at least 71 seats in the 140-member house and about 42 per cent of the vote, as against 42 seats and 36 per cent for the DP. The socialists decided to continue to govern in coalition with three small centrist parties. 'Our priorities are still the same – to become a candidate for EU membership, to go on improving infrastructure and to fight corruption an trafficking.' OSCE reported that the polls had been 'generally peaceful and there was no serious violence, although there were some irregularities', but the DP claimed widespread fraud in both rounds (*FT*, 10 July 2001, p. 6). Berisha continued to allege that fraud had been widespread, but instead of urging his supporters to demonstrate in the streets of Tirana he threatened to take his case to the European Court of Human Rights. With the support of the pro-EU Democratic Alliance and SDP, the socialist-led coalition had the eighty-four parliamentary votes needed to elect a new president in 2002 (*The Economist*, 14 July 2001, p. 45).

On 27 June 2001 the governments of Albania, Bosnia, Bulgaria, Croatia, Romania, Macedonia and Yugoslavia signed an agreement aimed at liberalizing trade in at least 90 per cent of goods traded between them, under the EU's Stability Pact for

South-eastern Europe aimed at enhancing stability in the region through economic growth (*FT*, 28 June 2001, p. 8).

On 9 December 2001, two reports drawn up by independent French and Italian consultants and carried out on behalf of Europe Aid, which was set up by the EU for external affairs commissioner Chris Patten in 2001 to speed up disbursement of aid and develop a long-term strategy, stated that EU aid programmes to Macedonia and Albania lacked clear strategies, were bogged down in bureaucratic delays and in-fighting and competed with other international financial institutions. EU aid of 1. billion euros since 1991 to these countries so far had had little impact, failing to build up civil society institutions or to tackle corruption. As one of the poorest countries in Europe, with an annual per capita GDP of 1,100 US dollars, Albania had received 1 billion euros of aid between 1991 and 2000, yet there had been little attempt to work jointly with other donors such as the World Bank on sector-wide programmes (*FT*, 10 December 2001, p. 6).

On 21 December 2001 Prime Minister Ilir Meta accused Fatos Nano, the leader of the Socialist Party, of trying to bring down the socialist-led government and force early elections after Nano had blocked the appointment of new ministers. The power struggle peaked when deputies loyal to Nano prevented a vote to confirm new ministers backed by Meta by boycotting a parliamentary session (*IHT*, 22 December 2001, p. 2).

Prime Minister Ilir Meta resigned on 29 January 2002 after a six-month feud with Fatos Nano. This power struggle had crippled Meta's government, blocking the thirty-two-year-old reformist's efforts to deal with economic problems. It began when Nano challenged Meta's right to govern, despite having won the June 2001 parliamentary elections. Nano persistently accused Meta's government of corruption and incompetence, demanding that the cabinet be restructured and that his own appointees be installed. Four ministers resigned in the second half of 2001 in attempts to appease Meta's foes, but Nano blocked efforts to replace them, and their posts remained vacant (*IHT*, 30 January 2002, p. 6). Nano intensified the crisis when Meta refused t support him for the presidency. When Nano announced on 29 January that he would only back a new Meta cabinet if Meta supported his own presidential bid, Meta resigned. Meta's government had won Western praise for its handling of the economy and its campaigns against corruption, smuggling and other crimes, but this was to no avail against Nano's barracking and factionalism (*Independent*, 30 January 2002, p. 15).

The SPA-led government headed by Pandeli Majko, February 2002 to July 2005

Pandeli Majko returned to the premiership in February 2002, but the Majko gov - ernment was from the outset wracked by factional conf ict within the SPA between the discontented supporters of the previous prime minister, Ilir Meta, and supporters of Fatos Nano. This reached a climax on 19 March 2002, when the faction led by Meta supported a DP motion to force the resignation of the prosecutor-general Arben Rakipi, a Nano supporter who had initiated corruption investigations against several of Meta's supporters (including former ministers) and who was himself accused by Sali Berisha of actually having allowed corruption to go unchecked. On 25 April the constitutional court ruled that Rakipi's dismissal by parliament had been unconstitutional, but parliament later overturned the court ruling (Jouan 2003: 57).

Leka Zog, the son of Albania's ex-King Zog, was allowed to return to Albania with his family on 28 June 2002. He had previously been in Albania in June 1997, campaigning for a 'yes' vote in the referendum on whether to restore the monarchy. He was granted an amnesty for the weapons charge brought against him at that time and parliament approved his return (*Independent*, 29 June 2002, p. 13).

A major political crisis was averted on 23 June 2002. President Rexhep Meidani's term of office was due to expire on 24 June. The SPA and its allies no longer had enough reliable supporters in parliament to obtain the three-fifths majority needed t secure the election of their presidential candidate. However, failure to obtain cross-party agreement on a generally acceptable compromise candidate would have forced Albania into holding a parliamentary election. Furthermore, the EU had made the election of a consensus candidate to the presidency a precondition for opening negotiations with Albania for an SAA in February 2003. Against the odds, the mutually hostile SPA and DP managed to find a mutually acceptable candidate: Alfred Moisiu the former defence minister (1990–1) who now headed the Albanian North Atlantic Association, an organization campaigning to secure Albania's admission to NATO. On 25 July President Moisiu asked Fatos Nano to form a new SPA-led government.

The SPA-led government headed by Fatos Nano, July 2002 to August 2005

In August 2002 it was reported that at least 200,000 of the weapons looted during the uprising in Albania in February–March 1997 remained at large, despite threats of prison sentences if they were not handed in by 4 August (*The Times*, 5 August 2002, p. 12).

In December 2002 there was mounting international concern over Albania's major role in drug-smuggling, mainly heroin from Afghanistan, which was arriving via Turkey, Bulgaria and Macedonia. There had been a crackdown on the drugs trade in response to increasing EU pressure on the Albanian government to halt it as a precondition for starting negotiations with Brussels on an SAA in February 2003. The port of Vlora was a high-profle centre for illegal traffcking in drugs, contraband cigarettes, illegal migrants and involuntary prostitutes (*FT*, Survey, 18 December 2002, pp. 28–9).

Political feuding between the factions headed by Fatos Nano, Ilir Meta and Sali Berisha during 2003 and 2004 severely impeded Albania's progress in negotiations towards signing an SAA with the EU, by delaying the passage of much-needed judicial/legal and economic reforms and measures to curb crime and corruption. The negotiations were inaugurated in February 2003, but in March 2004 the EU Commission accused Albania's leaders of lacking the political will to carry out the reforms which were a precondition for concluding an SAA. The commission also accused the opposition leader Sali Berisha of being partly to blame for paralysing the work of parliament in protest at the results of the 2003 local elections. The SAA talks dragged on for over two years without substantive progress being made in the critical areas of justice and home affairs, especially on measures to crack down on organized crime and to reform the poorly trained, corrupt and deeply politicized judiciary. Control of the media by Albania's business 'oligarchs' was also criticized (*FT*, Surveys, 18 May 2004, pp. 32–3, and 12 April 2005, pp. 31–2).

Albania signed an agreement with the USA on 2 May 2003, exempting each other's citizens from prosecution by the new International Criminal Court. Albania was the thirty-second country to do this. US officials had warned that military aid would b cut off unless such an agreement was signed by July 2003. The US Secretary of State Colin Powell then joined the foreign ministers of Albania, Croatia and Macedonia in signing a 'US–Adriatic Partnership Charter', designed to accelerate the entry of these three countries into NATO (*IHT*, 3 May 2003, p. 4).

In July 2003 ex-premier Ilir Meta resigned from the post of foreign minister, accusing Prime Minister Nano of cronyism and interference with foreign policy. Meta subsequently managed to block the appointment of a successor by persuading a group of SPA deputies to vote against or abstain from approving the candidacy of Marko Bello, a close ally of Nano. The minister of European integration resigned along with Meta.

Efforts to sell off big state-owned companies, build better roads, collect more taxes and overcome a chronic power shortage (some of the main reasons for the failure to attract FDI) slowed under Nano. The speedboats which had been used to transport thousands of illegal immigrants from the port of Vlora to Italy were suppressed, but international drugs and cigarette smugglers still used Albania as a transit route and warehouse (*The Economist*, 30 August 2003, pp. 28–9). Transparency International's 2003 'Corruption Perception Index' ranked Albania ninety-second out of 133 countries (EBRD 2004b: 90).

Growing perceptions that the existing parties did not – and could not – reflect voters needs contributed to the launching of an opposition civic movement called Mjaft! (Enough!) in March 2003 by half a dozen Albanian graduates who had recently returned from Western European and American universities. Western embassies had provided the movement with 200,000 dollars in funding (*FT*, Survey, 18 May 2004, pp. 32–3).

There were celebrations on 8 December 2004, when Edi Rama, the socialist mayor of Tirana, beat 400 rival candidates to be voted World Mayor 2004. First elected in 2000, he had 'changed a whole city', promoting 'a new Tirana, colourful and happy, with a new and improved infrastructure and cultural life' (*Independent*, 9 December 2004, p. 27).

A new electoral law was passed on 10 January 2005 to promote freer and fairer parliamentary elections in mid-2005, in the hope of preventing the two major parties from accusing each other of electoral fraud (*IHT*, 1 January 2005, p. 4). The votes of internal migrants were bound to strongly influence the election result, but many home in the sprawling squatter suburbs around Tirana and other cities lacked street addresses and f xed-wire telephones (*FT*, Survey, 12 April 2005, p. 31).

Economic affairs under the SPA-led governments, 1997–2005

Despite the chronic in-f ghting and rampant crime and corruption, Albania's economy grew remarkably strongly under the SPA-led governments (Table 2.1). Although the economy ran large and growing trade deficits (equal to more than 20 per cent of GDP by 2002–5, EBRD 1995b: 95, 97), over half of these deficits were covered b large remittances from the 500,000 or more Albanians working abroad. These remittances amounted to about 500 million dollars in 2002 (*The Economist*, 2 February 2002, p. 37) and to 700 million dollars or 13–14 per cent of GDP in 2004 (EBRD 2005b: 95). In addition, during the later 1990s international aid donors provided Albania with grants and soft loans worth roughly 300 million dollars per annum (*FT*, Survey, 23 February 2000, p. 13). Even though Albania's foreign debt rose from

1.1 billion dollars in 1999 to 1.7 billion dollars in 2004, strong economic growth dramatically reduced its ratio to GDP from 32 per cent in 1999 to 22 per cent in 2004 (Table 2.1; EBRD 2005b: 97).

In 1998 Albania's total tax revenues were the lowest in Europe, at around 13 per cent of GDP. In an effort to boost them, the government introduced a new tax law in January 1999. This raised the top rate of income tax to 30 per cent and also set the rate of taxation of company profits at that same (comparatively moderate) level. Strict limits on exemptions from profit tax were introduced and tax holidays were abolished (EBRD 1999b: 182). Tax revenue still remained the lowest in Europe in 2004, at only 20 per cent of GDP, and taxes were 'not applied equally to all enter-prises', thereby fuelling the growth of the informal sector (*FT*, Survey, 18 May 2004, p. 32). However, the tax regime reflected a conscious attempt by Albania's SPA led government to lure foreign companies to Albania and to encourage successful Albanian entrepreneurs and investors to remain in Albania by keeping corporate and personal taxation levels low. The corporate tax rate was reduced from 25 per cent to 23 per cent in 2005, with the aim of reducing it further to 20 per cent in 2006 (*FT*, Survey, 12 April 2005, p. 31). Nevertheless, these rates were higher than those in several other post-Communist states.

There continued to be a managed foating exchange rate. Excise taxes on imported and domestically produced goods were harmonized from 1 January 1999, and the maximum tariff on imports was reduced from 30 per cent to 20 per cent from 1 April 1999, with most goods rated at 10 per cent or less. In December 1999 Albania further reduced the maximum tariff rate on goods from 20 per cent to 18 per cent, with the unweighted average tariff rate declining to 13 per cent (EBRD 2000b: 126). The gov-ernment simultaneously took steps to improve the collection of customs revenues. Training courses for tax inspectors were established with the assistance of the International Monetary Fund (IMF) and World Bank, and an EU Customs Assistance Mission also helped in a number of areas (EBRD 1999b: 182).

From October 1999 the EU granted unilateral trade preferences to Albania, includ-ing exemptions from duties and abolition of quantitative restrictions for industrial goods, special concessions for selected agricultural and f shery products and provi-sion of specific ceilings for textiles. About 90 per cent of all exports from Albania to the EU were now duty-free. About 90 per cent of Albania's imports were from the EU, which absorbed about 94 per cent of Albania's exports (these mainly went to Italy, Greece and Germany) (Kaser 2001: 53; EBRD 2000b: 126). On 18 September 2000 EU foreign ministers approved an EU package granting duty-free access to 95 per cent of imports from Albania, Bosnia, Croatia, Macedonia and Montenegro. This package included the abolition of tariffs on exports of most industrial and farm products to the EU, the main exceptions being fish products and wine (*FT*, 19 September 2000, p. 10).

Privatization and foreign direct investment under the socialists, 1997–2005

The privatization programme focused on selling off the remaining small and medium state enterprises as well as public monopolies in strategic sectors such as tele-communications, copper and chrome. However, the 1998–9 Kosova crisis further delayed the privatization of large state enterprises (EBRD 1999b: 182–3). The energy sector was dominated by the state-owned Albanian power generation and distribution company, KESH, which was on the verge of bankruptcy because of non-payment and theft of electricity, but the Italian company ENEL was awarded a contract to manage KESH in May 2000 in a bid to reduce losses and theft (EBRD 2000b: 126–7). Electricity prices were doubled in December 2001.

In October 1999 parliament passed a law which specified competitive tenderin as the standard method of privatization for shares in enterprises operating in non-strategic sectors. During 2000 a state-owned brewery, winery, dairy factory, pharmaceutical factory and cement factory were put up for sale; an 85 per cent stake in the state-owned mobile phone company was sold to a foreign consortium; the government set about privatizing or liquidating all copper and chrome mines; and parts of the oil industry were made ready for sale (EBRD 2001a: 44).

Low levels of foreign investor interest and high levels of political uncertainty led to further delays in the large-scale privatization programme in 2001 and 2002, notably in the oil industry (EBRD 2002b: 110–11). 'Poor governance, especially corruption and inadequacies in the legal framework, remained the main obstacles to both private sector development and foreign investment' (EBRD 2003b: 108–9).

A report published in 2003 by the International Crisis Group estimated that nearly half of Albania's GDP was accounted for by illegal (mostly criminal) activity. Since 2001 the government had been cracking down on traffcking and smuggling, but it had failed to tackle the links between crime and state officials, the police and politician (*IHT*, 24 October 2003, p. 3).

Until 1999 Albania's banking sector was dominated by the state-owned National Commercial Bank (NCB) and the Savings Bank, which together accounted for over 70 per cent of banking assets. However, control of the NCB was sold to Kent Bank of Turkey by competitive tender in 1999, and the Savings Bank was sold to the Austrian Raiffeisen Group in December 2003, thus bringing the entire banking sector under private management (EBRD 2004b: 90). Nevertheless, this system still played only modest roles in an economy which had a large informal sector and in which most business transactions were conducted in cash (*FT*, Survey, 18 May 2004, p. 32).

Inflows of FDI dwindled to about 45 million dollars per annum following the pyramid-scheme crisis of 1996–7 (Table 2.1). By 2000, however, Albania's new-found (if precarious) stability was beginning to lure back Greek and Italian investors who had pulled out after the pyramid schemes collapsed in 1997. In 1999–2000 Turkish and North American firms invested in copper-mining concessions, a British compan reopened a cobalt and nickel mine, and a Greek–Norwegian consortium bought Albanian Mobile Communications, Albania's state mobile operator (*The Economist*, 29 April 2000, p. 49; Kaser 2001: 30, 48, 51).

Agriculture under the socialists, 1997–2005

The pyramid-scheme crisis and the resultant descent into anarchy during 1997 had relatively little effect on Albanian agriculture, whose output continued to grow impressively in the later 1990s (Cungu and Swinnen 1999: 610). A new land law was passed in May 1998. Whereas previously land could not be sold until all plots in a district had been registered, the new law permitted the sale of land on an individual basis (EBRD 1998b: 148). The programme of land registration, which had been initiated under IMF pressure in 1998 to facilitate the emergence of a functioning land market, took much longer than originally expected and was especially slow in the remote areas (Kaser 2001: 46–7). By March 1999, however, land registration had been completed for about 40 per cent of the total land area, enabling a visible market in agricultural land to emerge (EBRD 1999b: 182). By 2001 the allocation of title deeds to agricultural land was almost complete (EBRD 2001b: 106).

The privatization process left land ownership highly fragmented. An agricultural survey conducted in 1999 showed that there were 466,766 holdings with an average area of 4.1 hectares each, of which 1.8 hectares was agricultural land, 2.2 hectares forest and 0.1 hectares either built on or in other use. The land-registration process generated conflicting claims over assets previously held on quasi-feudal terms, especially in the Gheg north and central uplands. Fewer registration problems arose in the south and on the coastal plain, where private ownership had been more clearly established before the Second World War and a great deal of former marsh and waste land had been reclaimed under the state auspices between the 1930s and the 1970s. Peasant self-sufficiency, which had in effect been forced on Albania's collective farmers by the former Communist regime's prohibitions on private trade in farm produce, remained very high. A survey conducted in 1999 indicated that '48.5 per cent of farm households never bought arable or animal produce from outside' and that '42 per cent of farmers still tilled their land with the aid of animal and manpower alone' (Kaser 2001: 46–7). However, about 800 'water users' associations' were established to rehabilitate and manage irrigation systems, and other associations were established to assist the new private smallholders with the buying and selling of seeds, fertilizers and pesticides. There were also about 100 livestock associations with more than 200 sheep each (*FT*, Survey, 23 February 2000, p. 14).

The parliamentary election of 3 July and 21 August 2005 and the formation of a new centre-right government under Sali Berisha, September 2005

The first ballot was marred by allegations of major electoral irregularities. After som wrangling, a rerun was ordered for three seats (*IHT*, 23 August 2005, p. 5). Victory in all three of these seats capped a decisive victory for the DP led by sixty-year-old Sali Berisha. His coalition obtained 80 of the 140 seats, as against 59 for the centre-left coalition headed by the SPA under Fatos Nano. The election commission certifie the final result on 2 September. The newly formed Socialist Movement for Integration a splinter group of the socialists headed by the former socialist prime minister Ilir Meta, obtained f ve seats. Among the coalition partners of the DP, the Republican Party obtained eleven seats, while parties allied with the socialists obtained twelve. Parliament did not meet until 2 September 2005 – two months after the first ballot o 3 July! During the election campaign, Berisha had promised to tackle widespread poverty, to stimulate business and, by lowering corporate taxes, to combat corruption and organized crime, and to save taxpayers' money by reducing the number of ministries from eighteen to fourteen. He also accused Fatos Nano of being deeply implicated in corruption and a wide range of illicit business(*Independent*, 2 September 2005, p. 22).

By early 2006 the Berisha government's promised campaigns against corruption, nepotism and tax evasion appeared to be delivering tangible results. The government made a point of excluding politicians with major business interests from holding ministerial office and curbing the links between business and deputies in the rulin coalition which had flourished under the preceding SPA-led coalitions, although link between the new governing coalition and business interests were of course likely to grow over time. Holders of high office were now required to declare their assets an to make this information publicly accessible on-line. Berisha personally headed a government task force to f ght corruption, 'promoted a new concept of governing, namely viewing it as a public function and not as a way to make money', and secured the passage of 'four laws in .. . five months targeting nepotism in public administration (Puto 2006a). Customs revenue rose by 20–30 per cent between September and December 2005, mainly as a result of more stringent inspection. Nevertheless, payment of bribes remained endemic and almost mandatory, especially in education, health care and the judicial service; and, despite the accusations of rampant corruption which Berisha had levelled against the preceding SPA-led governments, there were hardly any prosecutions of those accused (Puto 2006a). Only time would tell how far the anti-corruption drive was real, how far it was mere window-dressing, and how far Berisha himself had turned over a new leaf.

After three years of foot-dragging, the EU Commission president José Manuel Barroso and the EU enlargement commissioner Olli Rehn visited Tirana on 18 February 2006 to finalize and sign off the text of an SAA between Albania and th EU, in readiness for ratif cation by the EU in the spring. It was stated that four main conditions had to be judged to have been met in order to obtain this SAA: a function ing rule of law with enshrined human and minority rights, a functioning market economy, substantial harmonization of Albanian legislation with EU rules and an administrative capacity to implement EU standards. At the same time, Albania was told that it would have to strengthen its judiciary and democratic institutions, promote increased cooperation with other western Balkan countries and step up its campaigns against organized crime and corruption if it wanted to proceed to officia candidacy for EU membership in due course. The main quid pro quo offered by the EU was a relaxation of its visa regime, especially for students and researchers wishing to study in EU member states, although the grim reality was a seemingly inexorable increase in restrictions on travel by Albanians to EU countries, seemingly to keep Albanians at arms' length or in a sort of quarantine (Puto 2006b).

Concluding reflections

Post-Communist Albania's economic roller-coaster ride

At the end of the 1980s Albania was still the poorest country in Europe. It became the only European country ever to be categorized by the UN as a 'least-developed nation'. The World Bank estimate of its per-capita income in mid-1991 was just 600 dollars. By way of comparison, in 1989 the corresponding figure for Portugal, the poorest country in Western Europe, was 4,250 dollars, while that for Turkey was 1,370 dollars (Åslund and Sjöberg 1991: 6, 8). The proportion of the population who were living below the poverty line was estimated to be 11.8 per cent in 2002 (EBRD 2004b: 92) and about 25 per cent in 2005 (FT, Survey, 12 April 2005, p. 31). Unemployment was rife during the 1990s (see Table 2.1), although estimates of its magnitude have varied considerably. Some sources have maintained that the real level of unemployment (i.e., including those without remunerated work who were excluded from the statistics) was at least 30 per cent at the end of 1993 (Deutsche Bank, *Focus: Eastern Europe*, no. 125, p. 3). Roughly 44 per cent of the non-agricultural labour force may have been unemployed by mid-1993, contributing to the exodus of 200,000 to 300,000 Albanians seeking work in other countries (Sjöberg

1996: 91–2). By early 2005, however, the official unemployment rate had fallen t about 14 per cent (*FT*, Survey, 12 April 2005, p. 31).

Some of the worst socio-economic problems have stemmed from sudden and rapid urbanization. During the first half of the 1990s there was a dramatic and uncontrolle exodus from highland villages to the towns. The great majority of migrants to the poor and unhygienic shanty towns were from the northern and central highlands. The DP, whose leader Sali Berisha was from the north-eastern district of Tropoja, did nothing to prevent the migration – first, because these people came from districts tha were identified with the DP establishment and, secondly, because it was considere opportune that DP-voting northerners should settle in the opposition's urban strongholds. Government statistics suggested that the urban population had increased from 35 per cent to 44 per cent of the total and that the proportion could reach over 50 per cent by the end of 1996 (*EEN*, 18 January 1996, vol. 10, no. 2, p. 7). Tirana grew from 350,000 in 1991 to more than 600,000 residents in 2001, as people from Albania's impoverished mountainous north migrated south in search of jobs. Shanty towns, without water or electricity, sprang up on Tirana's northern edge. The 6,000 inhabitants of Porto Romano, a fast-growing township on the Adriatic Sea about 5 kilometres from Durres, built their homes next to an abandoned chemicals plant which produced pesticides and chemicals. The United Nations Environment Programme (UNEP) classified Porto Romano as 'one of the worst environmental hotspots in th Balkans' (*FT*, Survey, 18 December 2002, pp. 28–9).

After dramatic drops in output between 1990 and 1992, the economy (especially agriculture) appeared to make a strong recovery between 1992 and 1995. Positive GDP growth was achieved as early as 1993 (Table 2.1). Post-Communist Albania managed to avoid the hyperinf ation experienced by some of the other post-Communist states during the 1990s. Inflation peaked in 1992 at 226 per cent, which was very painful but not catastrophic. However, output fell back by 7 per cent in 1997 as a result of the collapse of the pyramid schemes and the resultant explosion of violent and anarchic unrest, beginning in earnest in January of that year.

Nevertheless, consumer prices had more or less stabilized by 1999 and GDP had bounced back again by 2000, when it surpassed the 1989 level for therßt time (EBRD 2001a: 15). By 2004 Albania's real GDP was 31 per cent above its (admittedly depressed) 1989 level, the second highest increase for any of Europe's post-Communist states. Lithuania (42 per cent) and Slovenia (21 per cent) were in first and third place, respectively (EBRD 2005b: 48). Booms in construction and services were buoyed up by renewed inf ows of FDI, by the receipt of about 700 million dollars per annum in remittances from Albanians working in other countries, and by an informal sector which was roughly half the size of the country's registered GDP of 6 billion dollars (*FT*, Survey, 18 May 2004, p. 32). About one-quarter of Albania's citizens were working in other countries by 2004. An estimated 800,000 worked in Western Europe, primarily in Greece and Italy. Besides unskilled workers, the Albanian diaspora included more than 10,000 professional people (especially doctors, dentists, teachers and academics). In 2004 migrants' remittances exceeded 750 million euros, or 13–14 per cent of GDP *FT*, Survey, 12 April 2005, p. 31; EBRD 2005b: 95). Despite (or perhaps because of) the extensive corruption and insider-dealing at play in its privatization programmes, the relative importance of Albania's private sector increased rapidly, from 5 per cent of GDP in mid-1991 to 40 per cent in mid-1993, to 75 per cent since 1996 (EBRD 2002b: 20, 112; 2004b: 6, 92).

Albanian democratization in comparative perspective

In countries such as Serbia, Montenegro, Bulgaria and Romania, the power structures and power networks inherited from the Communist era have remained in large measure intact and have continued to operate. Many large state-owned enterprises which make no profit and fail to innovate have nevertheless remained in existence as employer and as producers, while the administrative structures inherited from the Communist regimes have also survived.

In Albania, by contrast, all the structures bequeathed by the Communist regime were destroyed or swept away during the 1990s, especially during the explosion of violent conflict in 1997. What replaced the old structures that disintegrated in Albania however, was not liberal democracy and a new more horizontally structured legal order, but lawlessness, disorder and (especially in the mountainous north, where the Kosova Liberation Army (KLA) was trained) a kind of gangsterland anarchy. Unlike most of the other post-Communist Balkan polities, therefore, Albania's current ongoing struggle to establish a truly*liberal* democracy and a civil society based upon the rule of law is hampered less by a continuing stranglehold of deeply entrenched vertical power structures and power relations than by a serious deficiency of powe structures and social moorings of any kind.

That said, a rude yet very vigorous democracy of sorts has gradually established itself in post-Communist Albania. Albanian political parties 'play rough' in their parliamentary and local elections and there have been frequent allegations of electoral malpractice, yet all this noise and fury has tended to obscure some important *positive* developments. Even if they are very roughly conducted, democratic elections have become 'the only game in town', in that since 1999 Albanian politicians and voters have not looked to violent confict, the army, paramilitary forces orcoups d'état to determine political outcomes. Furthermore, the levels of popular engagement in democratic deliberation and debate have been relatively high, especially during the 1990s, and slightly higher than in some outwardly more 'consolidated' democracies such as Poland and the Czech Republic. In the circumstances, this is a notable achievement.

3 Bulgaria

The Devil has all the best tunes

Introductory 'country profile'

Bulgaria is a small state with a land area of 110,550 square kilometres (about one-fifth of the size of France or over two-fifths of the size of the UK). Its population ha shrunk quite significantly during the post-Communist period, from 9 million in 199 to 7.8 million in 2004. This is partly attributable to a dramatic fall in birth rates, as in most of the post-Communist states. In addition, however, an estimated 700,000 Bulgarians emigrated in the fifteen years from November 1989 to November 200 (*FT*, Survey, 16 November 2004, p. 33).

Bulgaria is located on the Black Sea, and the river Danube flows along much o its northern border with Romania. During most of its history, however, the country has been somewhat cut off from Europe's major trade routes, partly because its access to the Mediterranean has long been at the mercy of whoever controlled Istanbul (formerly Constantinople) and the Turkish straits, but also because until quite recently the Danube has not been readily navigable upstream (towards Central Europe). It is nevertheless an important transit and trans-shipment point for many of the drugs illegally exported from Asia via Turkey and Bulgaria to other parts of Europe.

Although Bulgaria contains some fertile low-lying farmland, over half of its terrain is mountainous or hilly, and arable land makes up only 39 per cent of its total land area. It is a major producer and exporter of both cool temperate and Mediterranean agricultural products. Forests and woodland cover about 38 per cent of its land area. Viticulture has been a significant activity for at least 2,500 years. It had some significa deposits of non-ferrous metals (bauxite, copper, lead, zinc) which contributed to the growth of its metallurgical and engineering industries during the era of Communist rule (1946–89), but it became heavily dependent on oil and gas imported from the Soviet Union, as well as on electricity generated by dangerous Chernobyl-type nuclear power plants. Bulgaria is now poorly endowed with minerals.

Who are the Bulgarians?

Ethnic Bulgarians, southern Slavs, made up 83.9 per cent of Bulgaria's population in 2001 (see Table 3.1). Their language, which is written in the Cyrillic script also used by Russia, Ukraine, Belarus, Serbia, Montenegro and Macedonia, has close aff nities with these other east and south Slavic languages. Most Bulgarians are Eastern Orthodox Christians by declared religious affiliation, but most are not regular church goers. As a result of more than a century of vigorous secularization and occasional public disillusionment with the sometimes corrupt and disreputable conduct of the

74 *Bulgaria*

3.1 Ethnic and religious affiliation of population of Bulgaria (per cent

	1981	2001
Ethnic affiliation		
Bulgarians (excluding Pomaks)	82.3	83.9
Turks	8.5	9.4
Roma (Gypsies)	2.6	4.7
Pomaks (Islamicized Slavs)	3.0	n.a.
Macedonians	2.5	n.a.
Others	1.1	2.0
Religious affiliations		
Orthodox	–	82.6
Other Christian	–	1.2
Muslim	–	12.2
Other/unaffiliate	–	4.0

Sources: Europa (1992: 97) and CIA (2005).

church, religious affiliation and observance have become either somewhat nomina or more private and personal than public. Bulgaria also has a few Roman Catholics (during Pope John Paul II's visit to Bulgaria in May 2002, they numbered *c*.60,000, well under 1 per cent of the population (*HT*, 25 May 2002, p. 5)) as well as a substan tial and underprivileged Muslim minority (12 per cent, three-quarters of whom are Turks).

Bulgaria's substantial Roma (Gypsy) minority, whose size is widely believed to be understated by census returns, has incurred varying levels of discrimination, harassment and persecution for decades. Bulgaria's small but significant Jewish community incurred some Nazi-inspired persecution during the Second World War, but far less than the Jewish minorities in most other Balkan and East Central European countries at that time. Unusually for these regions, almost all the 48,000 Jews living in Bulgaria proper in 1939 survived the Second World War (other than those who died from natural causes).

The seventh-century Bulgar conquerors and settlers who gave this country its medieval and modern name were Turkic, not Slavic. The crises which aff icted the Byzantine Empire from the seventh to ninth centuries created a power vacuum which was f lled by two short-lived Bulgarian 'empires', the first of which was founde by Khan (Prince) Boris (AD 852–89). Gradual conversion to Eastern Orthodox Christianity and the adoption of a written 'Church Slavonic' language gradually forged the Bulgar and Slavic inhabitants of medieval Bulgaria into one of Europe's earliest linguistically unified nations (Fine 1983: 127–9; Crampton 1997: 22). Two Byzantin monks, named Cyril and Methodius, were invited to neighbouring Moravia in AD 862 to counteract growing Germanic and Roman Catholic influence in the Czech lands Cyril had devised the first-ever Slavonic alphabet/script ('Glagolitic') in around AD 855, for the purpose of translating Byzantine religious writings from the Greek into Slavonic languages. However, their proselytizing mission aroused strong German/ Roman Catholic opposition and in 885, after Cyril and Methodius died, their Orthodox Christian disciples were hounded out of Moravia and were given sanctuary in Bulgaria. Here they resumed the work of translating Byzantine religious literature – this time into 'Old Bulgarian', alias 'Church Slavonic'. Khan Boris had decided to adopt Byzantine Orthodox Christianity as his country's official religion and to foste a Bulgarian Slavonic written language. For this purpose, the Glagolitic and Greek alphabets were adapted to create the so-called 'Cyrillic' script (named after St Cyril). With modifications, this became the template on which the written national language of several Eastern Orthodox Slavs were forged (Hristov 1985: 33–40). That in turn fostered enduring linguistic and spiritual bonds (as well as rivalries) between the Bulgarian, Montenegrin, Russian, Belorussian and Ukrainian peoples, all of whom still use archaic 'Church Slavonic' for ecclesiastical purposes.

Tsar Simeon (reg. 893–927), the Byzantine-educated son of Khan Boris, vigorously promoted the new Slavic literary culture and an 'autocephalous' (self-governing) Bulgarian Orthodox Church. In 926 he established a Bulgarian Orthodox patriarchate at Preslav, his showy new capital city. He also conquered most of Macedonia, Serbia, Albania, Wallachia (Vlachia) and Thrace, pronounced himself 'Tsar of the Bulgars and Autocrat of the Romans' (i.e., Byzantine Orthodox Christians) and made several unsuccessful attempts to capture Constantinople. Simeon's son Peter (AD 927–69) made peace with Byzantium and gained recognition both of the Bulgarian Orthodox patriarchate and of himself as Tsar of the Bulgarians. However, his dominions were repeatedly ravaged by Magyar and Pecheneg marauders; Preslav was captured by Kiev Rus in 968–9; and most of Bulgaria was brought back under Byzantine control in 970–1. The last bastions of Bulgarian resistance were savagely subjugated by the Byzantine emperor 'Basil the Bulgar Slayer' between 1014 and 1019. This led to the abolition of the Bulgarian Orthodox patriarchate and the Hellenization of the Orthodox clergy, while Bulgaria's big landowners (*boyars*) mostly collaborated and enriched themselves at their peasants' expense.

An uprising begun by a group of Bulgarian *boyars* in Trnovo in 1185 elicited reluctant Byzantine recognition in 1187 of a new Bulgarian kingdom centred on Trnovo and ruled by the Asen family. Taking advantage of conflicts precipitated by the Third Crusade (1187–92) and the sacking of Constantinople by west European crusaders in 1204, Bulgaria's new rulers rapidly expanded their domains. In 1205 they defeated and captured the new 'Latin' emperor, who had attempted to subjugate Bulgaria in 1204. By 1231 Tsar Ivan Asen II (1218–41) had gained control of Macedonia, Albania, Serbia, southern Wallachia and northern Greece. He proclaimed himself 'Tsar and Autocrat of the Bulgarians and Romans' and restored an autocephalous Bulgarian Orthodox Church and patriarchate in 1235. Starting in 1237 and 1242, however, this second Bulgarian empire was devastated by a succession of Mongol/Tatar invasions and rapidly disintegrated. The quarrelsome self-serving *boyars* were unwilling either to accept a strong central administration and standing army or to unite against external foes.

In 1330 Bulgaria was subjugated by an emerging Serbian empire established by the Serb rulers Stefan Urosh III (1321–31) and Stefan Dusan (1331–55), but after the latter's death in 1355 this far-from-unifed state disintegrated almost as rapidly as it had been assembled. The major defeats suffered by Balkan Christian forces at the hands of the Ottoman Turks in 1371 and during the 1380s and 1390s allowed the Ottoman Empire to fill the power vacuum created in the Balkans by the decline of bot Byzantium and the flimsy South Slav empires

Under the impact of 481 years of Ottoman Turkish overlordship (1396–1877) and widespread conversion of Bulgarian Slavs to Islam, Bulgaria developed a rich and varied Turkic and Muslim culture alongside its predominant Slavic and Eastern Orthodox Christian culture. The eminent Turkish historian Kemal Karpat has controversially claimed that the 'Greater Bulgaria' established by Russia's military victories over Ottoman Turkey in 1877–8 had 1.5 million Muslim inhabitants, mainly comprising Turks and so-called Pomaks (Bulgarian Slavic converts to Islam), but also Circassian, Tatar and Roma (Gypsy) converts to Islam, as against 1.25 million non-Muslim inhabitants (mainly Eastern Orthodox Christians), and that 'During the war of 1877–78 approximately half of the Muslim population was forced to emigrate, and some 300,000 were killed by Bulgarian bands and Russian troops' (Karpat 1990: 12). He has also claimed that as late as 1888 Muslims made up about 35 per cent of the population of the truncated autonomous Bulgarian state whose creation was ratifie by the Berlin Congress of 1878, along with the province of East Rumelia which was annexed by Bulgaria in 1885 (Karpat 1990: 13).

Between the 1820s and the 1860s, as Serbia, Greece and Romania gradually gained full independence from the Ottoman Empire, Bulgaria was able to take over their former roles in supplying grain, honey, wax, wine, cattle, leather goods, footwear, metalwork, woollen textiles and clothing to the Ottoman market (especially nearby Constantinople), thereby strengthening the economic basis of the emerging Bulgarian nation. Bulgarian merchants and peasants began to buy farmland from their local Muslim overlords and to send their offspring to local church schools and to the proliferating 'modern' Bulgarian or Graeco-Bulgarian schools sponsored by pros - pering Eastern Orthodox merchants. Some went on to higher schools and universities in Central Europe, France and Russia. This growth of schooling helped to disseminate Bulgarian nationalist and pan-Slavic ideas and also stimulated interest in liberal and socialist doctrines. The resultant campaign for an autocephalous Bulgarian national church, involving Bulgarian bishops and use of the Bulgarian language, triumphed in 1870–2. However, Ottoman appeasement of growing Bulgarian nationalism encour aged Bulgarian nationalists to raise their sights still higher. Violent repression of a Bulgarian uprising in the Balkan mountain region in 1876 unleashed an international outcry against Ottoman 'Bulgarian atrocities' (although thousands were killed o*both* sides) and contributed to the outbreak of the 1877–8 Russo-Turkish War. Russia defeated the Ottoman Turks and the ensuing Russo-Turkish Treaty of St Stefano (1878) bestowed 'independence' on Serbia, Romania, Montenegro and a 'Greater Bulgaria' (including most of Macedonia, Thrace and Eastern Rumelia), albeit under Russian tutelage. However, this Russian-backed 'Greater Bulgaria' straddling the Balkan Peninsula proved unacceptable to Europe's other powers, who at the 1878 Berlin Congress separated off Eastern Rumelia as an autonomous Ottoman dominion and returned Macedonia and Thrace to full Ottoman control, whilst conf rming Serbian, Romanian and Montenegrin independence and granting Bulgaria the status of an *autonomous principality* under nominal Ottoman suzerainty. Thenceforth, the ultimate goal of many Bulgarian nationalists was to recreate this 'Greater Bulgaria', including Eastern Rumelia and most of Thrace and Macedonia, but this was an outcome which Bulgaria's neighbours were equally determined to avoid.

The relatively liberal 'Turnovo Constitution' of 1879 remained in force (with interruptions) until 1934. It established an independent judiciary, freedom of expression, assembly and association, security of property and person, and elective local self-government. The national assembly, elected by universal manhood suffrage, enjoyed full control of the state budget and taxation, joint control of ministers and full rights to initiate, veto and amend legislation. The monarch was to conduct foreign policy and appoint ministers (who were also accountable to the national assembly) and provincial prefects. However, this constitution invested the constitutional monarch not only with the functions of head of state and commander in chief, but also with powers to approve and promulgate laws and to control the executive . . . without bearing responsibility for its decisions. These powers created a permanent tension between the advocates of popular sovereignty and those who saw the ruler as the ultimate arbiter and authority.

(Pundeff 1992: 66)

In one fell swoop Bulgaria had achieved national autonomy, a liberal constitution, the virtual elimination of the largely Turkish and Muslim landlord class and a radical redistribution of almost all large landed properties to peasant proprietors. By 1910, 93 per cent of agrarian households were landholders and under 10 per cent depended primarily on wage work, and by 1914 the 1879 constitution's commitment to universal, free, compulsory schooling had found expression in a nationwide network of primary schools and the third highest school enrolment ratio in the Balkans and East Central Europe (only the Czech lands and Austria had signif cantly higher ratios) (Bideleux 1985: 227–9). Thus Bulgaria had acquired one of the most equal distributions of property, income and opportunity in Europe, even *before* it came under radical 'peasantist' rule in 1919–23 or under Communist rule from 1946 to 1989.

From 1879 to 1886 Bulgaria was ruled by Prince Aleksandur of Battenberg, who brought about the union of Bulgaria with Eastern Rumelia in 1885–6. However, this union defied the expressed wishes of Russia's Tsar Alexander III, who force this young prince to abdicate. His wily successor, Prince Ferdinand of Saxe-Coburg-Gotha (1887–1918), instigated railway construction, protective tariffs and tax incentives in order to encourage industrial development. In 1908, while the Ottoman Empire was preoccupied by the Young Turk revolution and Austria-Hungary's full annexation of Bosnia-Herzegovina, Ferdinand declared Bulgaria's full political independence and assumed the title of tsar. However, the atrocious living and working conditions of Bulgaria's nascent industrial proletariat fuelled the growth of a (Marxist) Social Democratic Party, which was established in 1891 and obtained thirty-seven seats in the national assembly in the parliamentary election of 1913. Bulgaria's craft industries declined, having lost their erstwhile privileged position in the Ottoman market and suffered a mass exodus of Turkish craftsmen. Also grain exports, which had accounted for two-thirds of Bulgaria's total exports from 1886 to 1911, faced increasingly intense international competition, which contributed to growing agricultural hardships and unrest. Over 100 peasants died in 1899–1900, when the army suppressed peasant protests and revolts against the rapidly rising burden of both direct and indirect taxation of peasant incomes. This in turn stimulated the growth of a radical peasantist Agrarian Union, founded by Aleksandur Stamboliski in 1899.

The Balkan War of 1912–13, through which the Balkan states expelled the Ottoman Empire from most of its remaining Balkan territory (other than Constantinople/Istanbul and its environs), enabled an alliance of Bulgarian royalists, nationalists and military forces to re-establish much of the 'Greater Bulgaria' which had been briefly establishe under Russian auspices in 1877–8. In the Balkan War of 1913, however, Bulgaria's similarly victorious Balkan neighbours ganged up against it and forced it to relinquish most of its territorial gains, to the chagrin of the ruling coalition, the armed forces and Tsar Ferdinand, who became bent on reversing these losses. By allying itself with the central powers during the First World War, the Bulgarian state and its armed forces succeeded in re-establishing a 'Greater Bulgaria' in 1915–17, only to be deprived of these territorial gains once more in September 1918 – by which time

Bulgaria had nothing to show for almost six years of strenuous, costly and devastating warfare. In order to sustain this warfare, nearly 40 per cent of Bulgaria's young adult males had been conscripted into armed forces between 1912 and 1918, and of these over 150,000 had perished and over 400,000 had been wounded (Bell 1977: 122). Seething peasant anger against the fruitless sacrifices, exactions, corruptness and ineptitudes of the ruling nationalist-royalist coalition finally erupted in the Radomi rebellion of September 1918 and was only partly assuaged by Tsar Ferdinand's consequent abdication in favour of his son Boris (1918–43), who had been brought up as an Eastern Orthodox Christian in order to propitiate Russia and Bulgarian nationalists. Opposition to Bulgaria's involvement in these wars came mainly from the Agrarian Union led by Aleksandur Stamboliski, who had been imprisoned from 1915 to 1918 (primarily for his anti-war stance and activities).

From October 1918 to June 1923 Bulgaria was ruled by Stamboliski's Bulgarian National Agrarian Union (BANU, which was also known as the Peasant Union). Perceiving towns to be decadent and parasitic, Stamboliski's 'peasantist' regime rapidly degenerated into a brutal and increasingly dictatorial expression of pent-up peasant bitterness and resentments. His fascistic paramilitary 'Orange Guard' became the scourge of the 'parasitic' bourgeoisie and of his political opponents and rivals. 'He almost appeared to be less interested in benef ting the peasants than in harassing the other classes' (Rothschild 1974: 338). The increasingly violent Stamboliski regime nevertheless left some positive legacies. Foremost among these were: a land distribution even more egalitarian than that of 1878–80; an enduring expansion of rural schooling, credit facilities and cooperatives; a lasting system of compulsory national labour service (in lieu of military service); and the displacement of what Stamboliski and his followers saw as parasitic and exploitative private grain dealers by a fairer state grain procurement corporation. Stamboliski's land reforms enacted in June 1920 and April 1921 broke up the few remaining large landed estates (Thompson 1993: 843). As of 1926, however, these measures had redistributed 'only 1 per cent of all land held in the country' (Crampton 1997: 154), because nearly all the large landholdings had already been redistributed by the radical land reforms of the late 1870s. According to the Bulgarian land census of 1926, 97.6 per cent of Bulgarian farms held less than 20 hectares of farmland, while 85 per cent held less than 10 hectares; farms exceeding 30 hectares in size accounted for only 5.3 per cent of all farmland, while those exceeding 20 hectares accounted for only 12.6 per cent (Rothschild 1974: 330).

Stamboliski's violent excesses were perpetrated *in the name* of the peasantry, who then comprised about 80 per cent of the population. However, unjust allegations that this violence was *approved or supported* by the Bulgarian peasantry in general are refuted by the fact that Stamboliski's Peasant Union obtained only 32 per cent of the vote in the elections of 1919, 38 per cent in those of 1920 and 53 per cent in those of 1923, even though the Peasant Union's Orange Guard widely resorted to harassment and intimidation during the parliamentary election campaigns of 1920 and 1923. These voting figures indicate that many (perhaps most) peasants did *not* support him, even though his supporters' violent excesses briefly brought the peasantry as a whole into disrepute and were exploited by 'anti-peasant' parties to try to tar all peasants with the same brush. Far from telling us anything definite about the supposed characte and proclivities of the peasantry and peasantist parties and regimes, the Stamboliski regime illustrates the grave dangers of trying to mobilize and rally support for a regime on the basis of preaching and exploiting any kind of class hatred (whether it be peasant, proletarian or propertied). This was made all too clear by the subsequent much greater wave of retaliatory violence and terror *against* the peasantry, supporters of the Peasant Union and many of their allies and sympathizers, from 1923 to 1926.

In June 1923 Stamboliski and thousands of his activists were butchered in a very bloody military coup. Stamboliski himself was tortured and hacked to pieces by his captors (Pundeff 1992: 85). This coup was actively assisted and supported by a vengeful bourgeoisie and by the terrorist International Macedonian Revolutionary Organization (IMRO), which had been established in 1894 with the principal aim of promoting the incorporation of an ill-defined 'Macedonia' into a 'Greater Bulgaria' At first the leaders of the substantial Bulgarian Communist Party (BCP) and the considerable Bulgarian Social Democratic Party (BSDP) gloated on the sidelines, relishing the nemesis of their peasantist rivals. In September 1923, however, the BCP belatedly staged an abortive ten-day insurrection against the repressive new regime formed by the 'bourgeois' National Alliance (Naroden Sgovar), which had been established in 1922 and was headed by the economics professor Aleksandur Tsankov (Crampton 1997: 157). The failure of the Communist-led insurrection merely intensifed the Tsankov regime's murderous 'White Terror' against both peasant and proletarian parties from 1923 to 1926. Around 16,000 Agrarians and Communists were killed by the regime and its supporters between June 1923 and late 1925 (Bell 1977: 245).

The Tsankov regime was succeeded by less ferocious governments headed by Andrei Lyapchev (1926–31) and Nikolai Mushanov (1931–4). However, these govern-ments were undermined by their inability to restrain IMRO terrorism, which culminated in the assassination of Yugoslavia's King Aleksandar during his royal visit to France in October 1934, as well as by the severe economic distress inflicted on Bulgaria's peasant farmers by the devastating decline in global grain and tobacco prices between 1927 and 1933 (tobacco having overtaken grain as Bulgaria's prin - cipal export during the 1920s). In all, 'feuding between various Macedonian factions' resulted in over 800 political murders between 1924 and 1934 (Crampton 1997: 164). These assassinations were mostly directed against peasants, workers and members of peasant and proletarian parties.

In May 1934 another military coup established a government of 'national regen-eration', headed by colonels Damian Velchev and Kimon Georgiev and by a group of civilian technocrats known as Zveno (Link). This regime managed not only to suppress the IMRO, but also to patch up Bulgaria's severely damaged relations with most of its Balkan neighbours (in particular Yugoslavia, whose King Aleksandar IMRO had assassinated), and in June 1934 with the Soviet Union, which had been antagonized by Bulgarian state terrorism against the Communist Party.

In January 1935, however, the colonels' regime was swept aside by Tsar Boris, who scrapped the 1879 constitution, banned political parties and went on to establish a quasi-fascist royal dictatorship. Boris had been angered by the usurpation of poli - tical power by the military and was determined to restore the ascendancy of civilian politicians (albeit neither liberals nor democrats). The arrest of Colonel Velchev in November 1935 on charges of conspiring against the tsar, for which Velchev was given a (subsequently suspended) death sentence in February 1936, facilitated the dissolution of the Military League and the consolidation of Tsar Boris's personal rule (Crampton 1997: 165). Boris allowed local government elections to be held in January 1937, but the franchise was restricted to possessors of a secondary education in urban areas and possessors of a full primary education in rural areas, all voters had to sign statements that they were not Communists, and voting was spread over three Sundays to facilitate supervision by the police and other officials (Crampton 1997: 166). Roya and government satisfaction with the tame outcome of these local elections led to the holding of similarly controlled first-past-the-post parliamentary elections in Marc 1938 and in December 1939/January 1940. Once elected, however, the new parliaments proved less pliable than Boris and his government had anticipated, and fi e Communist and five Agrarian deputies were expelled from the March 1938 parliamen (Crampton 1997: 167–8).

In foreign policy, Tsar Boris's chief concerns were much the same as those of the colonels' regime in 1934: to improve relations with all of Bulgaria's neighbours and to keep out of potentially risky entanglements in Europe's emerging power blocs. In 1936, as a goodwill gesture towards Yugoslavia, his prime minister banned all demonstrations demanding revision of the punitive Treaty of Neuilly (1919), paving the way for the signing of a Friendship Treaty with Yugoslavia in 1937. The 'Salonika Accords' concluded between Bulgaria and Greece in July 1938 allowed Greece to remilitarize Thrace while liberating Bulgaria from the arms restrictions imposed by the Treaty of Neuilly. When the Second World War broke out in September 1939, Bulgaria immediately declared its neutrality. Boris turned down the Soviet offer of a mutual-assistance pact and support for Bulgarian reacquisition of South Dobrudja in October 1939, as well as an offer of accession to the Balkan entente in February 1940. 'Boris believed Bulgaria's best interests were served by peace or, failing that, neutrality', not least because 'My army is pro-German, my wife is Italian, my people are pro-Russian. I alone am pro-Bulgarian'! (Crampton 1997: 169).

From 1933 to 1943, nevertheless, Bulgaria allowed itself to become drawn into steadily increasing commercial dependence on Germany. Following the German–Bulgarian trade agreement of February 1933 (which *pre-dated* the coming to power of the Nazis), Bulgarian exports were granted preferential access to the German market. In return, however, Bulgaria's farmers came under pressure to specialize in intensive cultivation of the industrial, oil-bearing, fodder, fruit, tobacco and horticultural crops which Germany needed. By 1937 such 'specialist crops' occupied 16 per cent of Bulgaria's cropland, were generating nearly half its agricultural income and were reinforcing the transition from relatively unremunerative and extensive grain cultivation and sheep-rearing to more lucrative and intensive forms of agriculture and horticulture. This transition was facilitated by Bulgaria's relatively ample rural education provisions and by the growth of peasant cooperatives in the 1920s and 1930s, which laid the foundations of Bulgaria's latter-day success as an exporter of specialist intensive products such as wine, bottled fruits and the rose petals used for the manufacture of certain perfumes. Furthermore, under the terms of this bilateral trading system, Bulgaria was obliged to accept payment for its exports to Germany in over-valued and non-convertible German 'blocked marks'. These marks could only be used to purchase German goods chosen from lists drawn up by the German government – increasingly, as time went by, goods which were obsolete or unattractive or no longer needed by Nazi Germany, including second-hand machinery and sub-standard weapons. As a result of its (fully understandable) desperation to obtain secure markets for its agricultural exports, Germany's share of total Bulgarian exports increased from 30 per cent in 1929 to 36 per cent in 1933, 43 per cent in 1937 and 71 per cent in 1939. Conversely, Germany's share in Bulgaria's imports rose from 22 per cent in 1929 to 38 per cent in 1933, 55 per cent in 1937 and 70 per cent in 1939 (Berend and Ranki 1974: 281–2). The 1939 figures were inflated by the Nazi annexation of Austria and the Sudetenland in 1938 and of the rest of the Czech lands in March 1939, as Austria and Czechoslovakia were also significant trade partner for Bulgaria, but the resultant increase in Bulgarian economic dependence on an expanding Third Reich was nonetheless real and Bulgaria found it increasingly difficul to extricate itself from it.

The Nazi–Soviet Pact of August 1939 was greeted enthusiastically in Bulgaria, which remained strongly Russophile despite its increasingly close economic alignment with Nazi Germany. As a result of this notorious pact, the position of the BCP was much enhanced, several Bulgarian leftists who had volunteered to fight for th republic in the Spanish Civil War had their citizenship restored, and the country was opened up to Soviet films, newspapers and books (Gross 2000: 17), while nine Communists and allies of the BCP were elected to Bulgaria's national assembly in the elections of December 1939 (Todorov 2001: 4).

In the course of 1941, Tsar Boris and his government headed by Bogdan Filov signed up to the German–Italian–Japanese tripartite pact and recreated 'Greater Bulgaria' by militarily occupying South Dobruja and much of Macedonia and Thrace (ostensibly on behalf of the Axis powers). They also declared war on the Western Allies, 'effectively closing the ways of escape behind them' (Chary 1972: 18). In supporting this, Prime Minister Filov seems to have been motivated more by pragmatic calculation than by his undoubted ideological leanings towards the Axis states. He wrote in his diary on 7 January 1941:

> War is unavoidable. If, however, we realize this, it is best that we follow it under the conditions that are the least complicated for us. If we allow the Germans simply to pass through our country, they will treat us as an occupied land, like Rumania, and this will be much worse than if we ally with them. We cannot gain anything from an English victory, for a failure of German arms inevitably means that we shall be 'Bolshevized'.
>
> (quoted by Chary 1972: 21)

However, partly in deference to Bulgarian Russophilia, Boris still prudently refused to get drawn into Hitler's war against the Soviet Union. Hitler proved willing to accept this, as a small price to pay for ensuring Bulgarian compliance with Germany's ever-expanding economic demands. Under pressure from Nazi Germany, Boris's government also passed anti-Semitic laws which discriminated against Jews in state employment, education and economic life, required Jews to wear the Star of David as identification and forced them to congregate in ghettoes and/or join militar 'labour battalions'. During March 1943, under pressure from the Nazi Schutzstaffel (SS), Bulgarian officials, military forces and police rounded up and deported nearl all the 11,355 Jewish residents of newly occupied Macedonia and Thrace to the Nazi death camps in Poland. Only twelve of these Thracian and Macedonian Jews survived the war (Todorov 2001: 8–9).

In early March 1943 Boris's government started taking steps to prepare a similar fate for the Jewish citizens of Bulgaria proper, who (according to a census conducted in 1934) numbered about 48,400 people or 0.8 per cent of the population (Todorov 2001: 4). However, these moves against Bulgarian Jews quickly unleashed growing waves of protest from Bulgarian parliamentarians, church leaders, the liberal pro-fessions and the intelligentsia who, to their great credit, put up a remarkably strong and successful defence of their Jewish compatriots. On the basis of the conduct of the

Bulgarian state and Bulgarian ultra-nationalists from the Balkan War of 1912 to the late 1930s, the country had become renowned more for the *weakness* than for the strength of its liberal traditions. Nevertheless, many of Bulgaria's leading parliamentarians, intelligentsia, newspapers and churchmen discovered hitherto-latent or dormant liberal convictions and summoned up the courage to denounce and resist anti-Semitism both volubly and effectively. However, Frederick Chary added a note of scepticism concerning the courage of Bulgaria's philo-Semites, stating that the fate of Bulgarian Jews hinged far more on the changing military fortunes of Nazi Germany 'than on the political fortunes of the anti-Semites in Sofia' (Chary 1972: 3) The stance taken by many seemingly courageous educated Bulgarians can be *partly* explained by: (i) growing perceptions that the tide of the war was turning against Nazi Germany; and (ii) the circumstance that Bulgarian Christians and nationalists had long regarded Turks and other Muslim minorities (rather than Bulgaria's not very numerous Jews) as the most problematic 'resident aliens' or 'enemies within', with the result that Bulgarians were (by contemporary Western as well as Central European standards) relatively free from anti-Semitic prejudices and traditions. Whatever the motives, however, these protests prompted Boris III and his government to start dragging their feet over the rounding up of Jews within Bulgaria proper and, when chastised by their Nazi overlords for this apparent display of defiant non-compliance, either to procrastinate or even to justify their inaction by claiming that more vigorous implementation of the Final Solution would severely impede and disrupt Bulgaria's capacity to comply with Germany's voracious economic demands, which were by then crucially important to the German war effort. The German legation in Sofia was fairly relaxed about this and took no reprisals. 'Under the circumstances', it recorded on 5 April 1943, 'the actual outcome, 11,343 Jews deported [from Thrace and Macedonia] must be considered satisfactory' (Todorov 2001: 11).

Tsar Boris III died at the age of forty-nine on 28 August 1943, just thirteen days after his return on 15 August from a stressful meeting with Hitler. The timing of his death almost immediately aroused suspicions that Boris had been poisoned by the Nazis, who were becoming increasingly irritated by his persistent refusal both to declare war on the Soviet Union and to cooperate fully in their 'Final Solution of the Jewish problem'. Many Bulgarians have no doubt wanted to believe that Boris was poisoned, because that would put both their former tsar and their country in a better light, by suggesting that they were really 'victims' of (rather than 'collaborators with) Nazism. Nevertheless, there is 'no frm proof' that Boris's death was caused by 'foul play' (Crampton 1997: 177) and, like Prime Minister Filov, Boris III seems to have been motivated mainly by considerations of *Realpolitik*. After all, in early March 1943 Boris had been ready to comply fully with the German demand for the deportation of 20,000 Jews, half to come from Bulgaria proper and half from the occupied territories. 'Boris appears to have played a less heroic role than his admirers ascribe to him . . . What motivated him was national interest as he understood it, not humanitarian principles' (Todorov 2001: 23).

Although it may well have been largely beyond their power to save the Jews of Bulgarian-occupied Macedonia and Thrace from the gas chambers, Bulgarians did successfully resist German pressure for mass deportation of Jews from Bulgaria proper to the Nazi death camps. Bulgaria was the only European Axis-aligned state in which there were more Jews alive at the end of the war than at its start (Chary 1972: xiii). However, Tzvetan Todorov concluded his incisive study of this remarkable episode with a profound warning:

a community is powerless without leaders, without those individuals within its midst who exercise responsibility – in this case, the metropolitans, the deputies, the politicians who were ready to accept the risks that their actions entailed. All this was necessary for good to triumph, in a certain place and at a certain time; any break in the chain and their efforts might well have failed.

(Todorov 2001: 40)

Thus this 'triumph of good over evil' also depended in large measure on a fortuitous constellation of political, economic, social and moral forces, which even the slightest false move or mistiming could easily have jeopardized.

Since Boris III's son Simeon was only six years old when he succeeded his father as tsar in August 1943, a regency council was established to rule on Simeon's behalf. However, the regents continued Bulgaria's increasingly conscious policy of procrastination and foot-dragging.

The emergence of an anti-fascist 'Fatherland Front'

Between 1927 and 1932 the two main 'popular' movements, the fragmented but semi-legal Agrarian Union and the illegal but more unif ed BCP (operating through a legal 'front organization' known as the Bulgarian Workers Party), gradually recovered from the repression that had been inflicted upon them by the quasi-fascist Tsanko regime from June 1923 to 1926. They also capitalized on the social distress caused by the world depression of 1929–33; the Bulgarian Workers Party even won the municipal elections of 1931–2. However, this precipitated further bouts of repression, culminating in the near annihilation of Bulgaria's Communist movement in 1942.

In the summer of 1942, the battered remnants of still mutually mistrustful left-leaning Agrarians under Nikola Petkov, a few Communists and some members of Zveno (including Kimon Georgiev) finally decided to sink their differences and work together in an anti-fascist 'Fatherland Front', whose programme called for strict Bulgarian neutrality between the two armed camps in the war, the cessation of Bulgarian military operations against Yugoslavia's Communist-led partisan move - ment, the termination of food exports to Germany, the restoration of civil liberties and the prohibition of all fascist organizations. However, the Fatherland Front had neither leverage nor military muscle until the summer of 1944, when (i) a Bulgarian anti-fascist partisan movement began to get off the ground; and (ii) the Soviet Red Army's liberation of Ukraine in late 1943 and early 1944 and its occupation of Romania on 20 August 1944 raised the spectre of an impending Soviet invasion of Bulgaria (Crampton 1997: 178–81).

Meanwhile, the Western Allies had started carrying out heavy bombing raids from Italy on Bulgaria's main cities in November 1943 and on a much larger scale (using incendiary bombs) in January and March 1944, in order to cause chaos and put pressure on Bulgaria to switch sides in the way that Italy had done between July and September 1943. Bulgaria's rulers did indeed put out peace-feelers to the Western Allies in October 1943 and again in February and March 1944, but the peace terms offered by the Western Allies (unconditional surrender, withdrawal of Bulgarian forces from the Greek and Yugoslav territories they had occupied and an Allied occupation) were considered (i) too harsh to be acceptable to the bulk of Bulgaria's population; and (ii) impossible to implement so long as significant German military forces were still presen in Bulgaria.

Finally on 17 August 1944, in anticipation of the Soviet invasion of Romania which began on 20 August, the Bulgarian royalist government declared its neutrality in the war, amnestied all political prisoners, repudiated the policies of its predecessors and revoked all anti-Semitic legislation, but this proved insufficient to propitiate the Sovie Union. After an anti-Axis and anti-Antonescu coup enabled Romania to switch sides in the war on 23–24 August (see Chapter 3), allowing Soviet forces to advance swiftly and unimpeded to Bulgaria's northern border, the Bulgarian royalist government ordered the withdrawal of German forces from Bulgarian soil on 25 August and began to disarm those that remained there, but this too proved insufficient to avert a Sovie declaration of war on Bulgaria on 5 September. As a final throw, Bulgaria's royalis government declared war on Germany on 7 September, too late to avert a Soviet invasion of Bulgaria on 8 September and the seizure of power by Bulgaria's Fatherland Front, its burgeoning partisan movement and sections of the official Bulgarian armed forces on 9 September. The new Fatherland Front government was headed by the Zveno leader Kimon Georgiev, who had similarly organized the successful coup in Bulgaria in 1934. It comprised five Zvenari, four Agrarians, three Social Democrats and four Communists. The politically strategic ministries of the interior and justice were allocated to the Communists, who rapidly made use of them to establish their own 'police state' as a semi-autonomous 'state within a state' and to imprison or summarily execute thousands of actual or alleged fascists and 'collaborators', thereby eliminating many of their strongest opponents and preparing the ground for a gradual Communist takeover by stealth.

A nation taken captive by the Communist Party and the Soviet Union, late 1944–December 1989

Even though the Soviet Union invaded northern Bulgaria on 8 September 1944, its overriding objective was neither a complete conquest nor a 'liberation' of Bulgaria as such, but rather the swift passage of its forces across Bulgaria to drive the Germans out of northern Yugoslavia and blaze a new trail into Central Europe. This was what left the Bulgarian 'Fatherland Front' and the Bulgarian military free to depose Bulgaria's royalist regime on 8–9 September 1944, even though that regime had belatedly declared war on Germany. Furthermore, as part of their infamous 'percentages agreement' concluded in Moscow in October 1944, the British Prime Minister Winston Churchill and the Soviet war leader Iosif Stalin implicitly agreed (i) that Bulgaria would become part of the Soviet 'sphere of infience' (for the time being in Churchill's thinking, but in perpetuity in Stalin's); and (ii) that Britain would deliberately delay taking up its seat on the newly established Allied Control Commission for Bulgaria, precisely in order to give the Soviet Union a freer hand there. For the Western Allies, understandably, the paramount need was to defeat Nazi Germany in the shortest time and with as few Western casualties as possible. To that end, they were prepared to concede a virtual free hand to Stalin in his own neck of the woods. The fate of countries such as Bulgaria and Romania was of little concern at that time to the vast majority of British and North American politicians and voters (most of whom barely knew who or where these countries were), while both Churchill and the US President Roosevelt were keen to be re-elected at the end of the war. This was an important (albeit ignoble) aspect of the emerging East–West division of Europe, under which countries such as Bulgaria, Romania, Hungary and Poland were consigned to the Soviet 'sphere'. As a consequence, they had little or no realistic hope of durably (re-)establishing democratic forms of governance at that time, even if that was not yet apparent to the desperately unfortunate inhabitants of these countries.

The Communist minority within the Fatherland Front regime rapidly took the lead in mobilizing military and logistical support for further Soviet advances into East Central Europe in late 1944 and early 1945. In total, this placed 340,000 Bulgarian troops at the disposal of the Soviet armed forces, out of whom 200,000 served at the front and 32,000 of these perished (McIntyre 1988: 88). However, these casualties were only small fractions of those incurred by states such as Hungary and Romania. As Istvan Deak has profoundly observed, 'the extent of the material and human losses suffered by European states, and their postwar treatment, depended on luck, geography and great power politics. At no time was their postwar fate a function of wartime merits and demerits' (Deak 2000: 55).

Indeed, Bulgaria came out of the Second World War in a much better condition and position than either Romania or Hungary. Overall, it incurred relatively few casualties and relatively little war damage (Berend and Ranki 1974: 340). Partly as punishment for having been an 'enemy state' allied to Nazi Germany from 1941 to 1944, the peace treaty imposed on Bulgaria by the Western Allies and the Soviet Union in February 1947 required it to relinquish Macedonia and Thrace to Yugoslavia and Greece, respectively, but allowed it to keep South Dobrudja. Bulgaria was also supposed to pay 'reparations' to Yugoslavia, Greece and the Soviet Union, but in practice not much was paid. Bulgaria was shielded considerably: (i) by its traditional Russophilia, which had strongly contributed to Bulgaria's refusal to participate in the Axis invasion of the USSR in 1941–3; (ii) by the relatively high standing of the Bulgarian Communist leader Georgi Dimitrov in the Soviet Union, after his virtuoso performances in the German 'Reichstag fire' trial in 1934 (in which he managed t make a fool of the Nazi bigwig Hermann Goering) and in the wartime Comintern; and (iii) by its sheer subservience to Stalin.

The Fatherland Front nevertheless decided to make Bulgaria the first European state to institute criminal trials of 'fascists', 'war criminals' and their 'collaborators'. Relative to its population size, Bulgaria reportedly tried and either imprisoned or executed more 'fascists', 'war criminals' and 'collaborators' than any other country in Europe (Oren 1973: 88). Officially, by March 1945, 10,897 people had been subjected to trials of this nature, 2,138 of these had been executed, and 1,940 had received sentences of at least twenty years in prison (McIntyre 1988: 67). According to Patrick Moore, these trials were used as part of a 'particularly ruthless and bloody consolidation of power' by the BCP and its collaborators (Moore 1984: 194). According to Nissan Oren,

> The desire to prove to the world Bulgaria's determination to cleanse herself of pro-German and cryptofascist elements was undoubtedly the . . . primary motive in holding the trials . . . Even though the large majority of the victims deserved punishment, the arbitrary settling of accounts produced an atmosphere of terror and insecurity . . . A sizeable segment of Bulgaria's tiny intelligentsia was exterminated. That most were people with rightist leanings and profascist sympathies did not alter the fact that many also were people of talent . . . a loss which a small peasant people could ill afford.
>
> (Oren: 88–9)

However, some scholars who have been more inclined to excuse or even justify the conduct of the BCP have sought to parry such criticisms. According to Robert McIntyre:

> These are certainly large numbers by the standards of other European countries, but I know of no evidence that these trials were used to destroy anti-fascist but non-Communist political forces. The large number of individuals tried is to some extent explained by the precipitous German collapse in Romania and the speed of the arrival of the Red Army in Bulgaria, leaving no time for the government and police officials to escape or conceal themselves. The BCP took revenge fo both Gestapo-directed repression during the war and the massacres of earlier decades by indigenous fascists and their allies.
>
> (McIntyre 1988: 67)

Either way, the scale and severity of the retribution meted out was out of all proportion to the nature and conduct of the wartime Bulgarian royalist regime, which had not been particularly brutal towards its own subjects and had even spared the lives of a higher proportion of its Jewish subjects than did any other Balkan or East Central European regime. The new 'people's courts' were established by the Communists ostensibly to punish 'collaborators and war criminals'. However,

> as Bulgaria had not been occupied by a foreign power and had not been engaged on the eastern front, there were few Bulgarians who fell into either category. Yet per capita more Bulgarians were accused of these crimes than any other East European nation. For the Communists the problem was that the local intelligentsia and political establishment had not been decimated by the Gestapo or its local equivalent, and therefore the potential pool of opposition [to the Communist Party] was greater than in other states; the Bulgarian intelligentsia and political classes were now paying the price for their relatively easy war.
>
> (Crampton 1997: 185–6)

This offers a much more convincing interpretation of what occurred. It was the very *mildness* of the Bulgarian royalist regime and its reluctance to allow its non-Jewish subjects to be pointlessly slaughtered on the Russian front, as well as the Bulgarians' successful (albeit partly self-interested) resistance to the deportation of their Jewish compatriots to the Nazi death camps, which allowed the Bulgarian intelligentsia and political classes to survive the war largely intact. This in turn posed a major challenge to the Bulgarian Communists and helps to explain the ferocity with which they used the 'people's courts' and the pretext of prosecuting of 'collaborators and war criminals' to terrify and dispose of thousands of potential opponents. In early 1945 the by-then Communist-controlled police services arrested the former regents, former royal advisers, all members of Bulgaria's wartime parliament and anyone who had served in government at any time since 1941, and then put most of these unfortunate people on trial in the Communist-controlled people's courts, which in turn judged most of them to be guilty of 'crimes' of various sorts. About 100 of them were summarily shot on the very day that the verdicts were pronounced (Crampton 1997: 186), thereby maximizing the already massive scope for miscarriages of justice.

This rough justice and blood-letting, followed by extensive nationalization of public utilities and industrial enterprises, strengthened the Fatherland Front's pervasive control over Bulgarian society and helped it to obtain 88 per cent of the votes cast in the single-list parliamentary election held in November 1945. In a referendum on the future of the monarchy held in September 1946, 85 per cent of the electorate supposedly voted in favour of a republic, although many – including the deposed King Simeon II – have often claimed that the ballot was rigged by the Communists who controlled the ministry of the interior at the time. This in turn paved the way for the proclamation of a Communist-controlled 'people's democracy' and a 'people's republic', in which the Communist Party claimed to be *vox populi*.

In the highly skewed October 1946 election for a 'grand national assembly' which would ratify the constitution drawn up by the Communists in 1947, the Communists gained 53 per cent of the votes cast, their coalition partners won 17 per cent, and the opposition 30 per cent. In June 1947 Communist control was consolidated by (i) the arrest and subsequent execution of the leader of the democratic opposition, the Agrarian Party leader Nikola Petkov on charges of espionage; (ii) the expulsion of twenty-three other Agrarians from the grand national assembly; and (iii) the inauguration of a reign of terror. The cowed remnants of the Agrarian Union were nevertheless preserved as emasculated junior partners in an all-encompassing Communist-controlled Fatherland Front.

During the period 1947–53, while experiencing the full rigours of Stalinism, Bulgaria was ruled by doctrinaire 'Moscow Communists'. They were headed first of all by premier Georgi Dimitrov (reg. 1947–9) and his ally Vasil Kolarov and then, after their deaths in 1949 and 1950 respectively, by Dimitrov's brother-in-law Vulko Chervenkov, who succeeded Dimitrov both as premier (1949–56) and as party leader (1949–54). All three had spent the 1930s and the early 1940s in the Soviet Union, close to Stalin and his acolytes, and were inclined to lord it over the less-travelled and less-sophisticated 'home Communists' – as those who spent the 1930s and the Second World War in Bulgaria came to be called. In 1949 the leading home Communist Traicho Kostov was tried and executed on trumped-up charges of 'nationalist deviation' and 'Titoism'. His real 'crimes' consisted of having a mind of his own and resenting the unwarranted condescension and tutelage of the increasingly paranoid Moscow Communists, who feared that the so-called home Communists aspired (with good reason!) to oust them. The 'show trial' and execution of Kostov was the opening shot in an over-kill offensive against the home Communists. Out of a recorded Communist Party membership of 495,658 in 1948 (McIntyre 1988: 55), over 100,000 were expelled from the party, demoted, imprisoned, sent to forced-labour camps or even executed, in a quest to establish total and unquestioning ideological conformity and blind obedience to Moscow and to the doctrinaire Moscow Communists during the purges of 1949–52. Even greater numbers of people 'from the civil service, the armed forces and all sections of society were purged at the same time' (Crampton 1997: 193). In fact, even the Communist terror against alleged collaborators and war criminals in 1944–6 was small beer by comparison with this bloody and traumatic assault on Bulgaria's body politic.

Simultaneously, starting with a two-year plan in 1947–8 and a first five-year plan in 1949–53, Bulgaria embarked on a classic Stalinist programme of large-scale and lopsided industrialization and the establishment of a centrally planned command economy which placed overriding emphasis on the development of large-scale capital- and energy-intensive heavy and extractive industries, to the relative neglect of services and light industry. The nationalization of all large-scale enterprises was completed in 1947–8.

Furthermore, in return for unquestioning and often obsequious loyalty to the Soviet Union and later also for steadily growing exports of the fresh and processed Mediterranean agricultural and horticultural products (which were always in extremely short supply in the Soviet Union), Bulgarian industrialization and economic growth were amply assisted by Soviet 'technology transfers' and steadily increasing deliveries of Soviet oil, gas, coal, metal ores, machinery and equipment, often through barter arrangements or on exceptionally favourable terms. (In the 1970s–1980s, however, this was how Bulgaria also acquired its highly dangerous Soviet nuclear power plants.) This greatly reduced the otherwise potentially crippling foreign-exchange costs of this very lopsided and capital- and energy-intensive pattern of industrialization. As a consequence, Bulgaria became the European Communist state most dependent upon the Soviet Union, which accounted for well over 50 per cent of Bulgaria's imports and exports (by value) from the 1950s to the 1980s. By 1977, 78 per cent of Bulgaria's external trade was with other members of Comecon (Osmova and Faminsky 1980: 120).

After Stalin's death in 1953, workers' unrest in Plovdiv in May 1953 and Soviet demands for a New Course (coded language for partial de-Stalinization) helped to restore Bulgarian home Communists to power and favour. Thus Todor Zhivkov, who served as Bulgaria's indigenous Communist Party leader from 1954 to 1989, gradually ousted or demoted the doctrinaire Moscow Communists and promoted new generations of more pragmatic home Communists, with the full approval of the new Soviet Communist Party leader Nikita Khrushchev (reg. 1953–64). Indeed, Zhivkov was initially regarded as a Bulgarian Khrushchev, although he totally lacked Khrushchev's redeeming qualities (elements of humanity, honesty, integrity, sound judgement and idealism). In spite of presiding over an unsuccessful Chinese-style 'Great Leap Forward' from 1958 to 1960, which ran the risk of alienating his Soviet patron Khrushchev, Zhivkov became prime minister from 1962 to 1971, while continuing to serve as party leader until 1989. By the time of Khrushchev's downfall in 1964, Zhivkov had consolidated his power sufficiently to weather the change of ruler in th Moscow Kremlin. In 1971 Zhivkov relinquished the premiership and opted for the more honorif c post of president of the state council (de-facto head of state) of the newly proclaimed 'Socialist Republic of Bulgaria', while again remaining party leader. Until the accession of the liberal reform Communist Mikhail Gorbachev to the leadership of the Communist Party of the Soviet Union in 1985, Zhivkov was grovellingly obsequious towards each of the successive rulers of the Soviet Union, and Russians and Bulgarians began jokingly to refer to Bulgaria as the 'sixteenth republic' of the Soviet Union. What they did not know for sure was that on two occasions, once to Khrushchev and once to his successor Leonid Brezhnev, Zhivkov proposed in all seriousness that Bulgaria should formally join the Soviet Union (Pundeff 1992: 105).

During Zhivkov's long rule, there was a continuous stream of modest reforms to the Bulgarian economic system. However, for all its intermittent talk of economic decentralization and incentives and of opening the economy up to Western products, technology and investment, the Zhivkov regime clung tenaciously to central control of the allocation of output and input assignments, investment and prices – the key elements of a command economy. During the 1980s, Bulgaria's hitherto-dynamic economy had begun to stagnate, and in 1987 even the Zhivkov regime felt obliged to start emulating (however hypocritically) elements of Gorbachev's *perestroika* programme, with effect from 1 January 1988. 'Strategic' matters were to remain the prerogative of the centre and enterprises would still receive mandatory 'state orders' (i.e., there would still be a 'command economy'), but state enterprises were to be allowed greater leeway in deciding how to fulfil them and prices were expected t move towards world levels. From January 1988 Bulgarians were permitted to establish private firms, provided they did not employ more than ten permanent employees (although employment of additional casual labour was permitted). This 'ten perma-nent employees' restriction on private employment remained in force until 23 March 1992, more than two years after the end of the Communist regime. In January 1989 there was also a decree calling for the transformation of enterprises into 'firms' o various kinds, including joint stock and limited liability companies, and provision was made for the distribution of shares to each firm's employees

Bulgarian agriculture, 1946–89

A distinctive feature of the Zhivkov regime was its solicitude (at least in comparison with most Communist regimes) towards the agricultural sector, which regularly absorbed over 20 per cent of Bulgaria's gross investment. This came about partly to ensure adequate food supplies and agricultural exports to the Soviet Union and partly to strengthen the role of the purged and emasculated Agrarian Union as the Communist Party's junior partner in the 'Fatherland Front'. At the start of de-facto Communist rule, the 1946 land reform affected only 3.6 per cent of arable land, as the pattern of landholding was already unusually equal in Bulgaria. The country also already boasted 3,000 peasant credit and marketing cooperatives with roughly 1 million members. Nevertheless, a conventionally Stalinist collectivization of agriculture was carried out between 1948 and 1957. Although offially acknowledged 'excesses' and 'distortions of Party policy' (Brown 1970: 174–204) did occur in 1948–50, the massive resistance and the destruction of livestock which had accompanied rural collectivization in Stalin's Soviet Union were avoided. In addition, there was less de-kulakization, not least because Bulgaria had comparatively few *kulaks* (rich peasants).

When Comecon began to promote greater specialization (socialist division of labour) between the economies of its member states during the 1960s, Bulgaria (unlike Romania and Albania) readily accepted its assigned role/specialization as a major supplier of relatively remunerative and intensive Mediterranean agricultural and horticultural products, in return for considerable economic and technological assis - tance from the more developed Comecon members, who helped Bulgaria to develop computer, robotics, forklift truck, petrochemical and nuclear power industries from the later 1960s to 1989.

In 1957–8, however, Bulgaria began to depart from the standard Stalinist models by promoting the so-called 'industrialization of agriculture'. Most of Bulgaria's 3,450 collective farms were merged to form just 644 new farms averaging 7,700 hectares each (the world's largest farms at that time). Furthermore, from 1970 onwards the entire agricultural sector was reorganized into gigantic 'agrarian-industrial complexes' (AICs), which in 1982 averaged 16,000 hectares in size. The objectives were to promote economies of scale, rural industries, vertical integration between industry and agriculture, more 'scientific' management, rural construction enterprises, the industrialization of agricultural life, more urban forms of housing and service pro - vision in the countryside, more effective delivery of rural services and the reduction of differences between town and country. However, critics claimed that these AICs were unwieldy, bureaucratic and stultifying, and that they contributed to a noticeable falling off in Bulgaria's previously impressive agricultural advance and a decline in the quality of some of its agricultural products (most noticeably, for foreign consumers, with regard to its wines). To some extent, Communist-ruled Bulgaria was being used as a small test bed for new forms of agricultural organization which, ten to fifteen year later, were to be adopted on a vaster scale in Brezhnev's Soviet Union.

The festering socio-economic and environmental crisis of the 1980s

During the 1980s, as Bulgaria's hitherto-dynamic economy stagnated, the mounting inefficiency, energy intensity and obsolescence of Bulgaria's bloated heavy-industrial sector caused fuel imports to soar, at the very time when mounting difficulties in the Soviet oil and coal industries were increasing Bulgaria's dependence on much higher-priced fuel imports from countries accustomed to payment in hard currency rather than through barter deals. From 1984 onwards Bulgaria was afflicted by mount ing shortages of manufactured consumer goods, foodstuffs and electricity (exacerbated by scarcity of hard currency), accelerating inflation and massive misuse and mis - appropriation of public funds by Zhivkov's 'kleptocracy'. In addition, there was growing public awareness of the costly cumulative environmental damage caused by the over-expansion of the country's 'dirty' metallurgical, chemical and power-generating industries, growing use of poor quality but cheap and locally available lignite as power-station fuel, overuse of chemical fertilizers and pesticides in agri - culture and irresponsible and dangerous neglect of environmental safeguards. This has left signif cant areas of post-Communist Bulgaria looking like industrial waste - lands, seriously disfiguring the natural beauty of some of its landscapes. The cost o 'cleaning up' these landscapes has been and continues to be high.

Bulgaria did not borrow wildly from the West during the 1970s, unlike Romania, Yugoslavia, Poland and Hungary. Indeed, its hard currency debt fell from 3.7 billion dollars in 1979 to 0.9 billion dollars in 1984. After 1984, however, Bulgaria started to borrow heavily from abroad and its foreign debt surged to 5.3 billion dollars in 1987 and over 10 billion dollars in 1989, by which time over half of its hard-currency earnings were being absorbed by debt service. Because the size of the debt was hidden from the public, the revelation of its magnitude in 1990 came as a shock both to Bulgarians and to Western creditors. This burdensome debt has remained a major millstone round post-Communist Bulgaria's neck. The problems were further compounded by Bulgaria's relative lack of success in attracting FDI, despite the passage of legislation in March 1980 to permit majority ownership of Bulgarian fms by foreigners and further legislation in January 1989 allowing the establishment of wholly foreign-owned companies.

The Zhivkov regime's virulent Bulgarian nationalism and xenophobia during the 1980s

The more sordid and disreputable the Zhivkov regime became, and the deeper it became mired in social and economic failings during the 1970s and 1980s, the more it endeavoured to bolster its sagging legitimacy by promoting crude Bulgarian national chauvinism and xenophobia. This infected relations with Bulgaria's Turkish, Roma and Pomak minorities. There also emerged an unholy alliance between the increasingly corrupt, effete and nationalistic Bulgarian Orthodox Church hierarchy and the equally corrupt, effete and nationalistic Communist regime.

During the 1980s Zhivkov tried to deflect mounting public discontent with his regime and with the deepening socio-economic and environmental crises by stirring up Bulgarian nationalism and xenophobia towards ethnic and religious minorities, especially Turks and other Muslims. This did not come out of the blue. The Communist regime had begun applying pressure to Vlachs and to Islamicized Roma (Gypsies) to 'Bulgarianize' their names and identities during the 1950s. Furthermore, many Turkish schools catering for the Turkish minority were closed in 1958, while the regime's campaigns against organized religion helped to reduce the number of active Muslim clergy in Bulgaria from 2,715 in 1956 to 570 in 1982 and 400 in 1987 (Pundeff 1992: 106). The regime next turned its attention to the Pomaks, usually regarded as the descendants of Slavic Bulgarians who had converted to Islam under Ottoman rule and who still comprised around 3 per cent of the population in 1981. During the 1970s they were required to change their Turkish, Arabic or Muslim names to Slavic Christian ones, the term 'Pomak' was banned, 'Pomaks' ceased to be included as a category on subsequent census forms, and the 'Socialist Constitution' adopted in 1971 dropped all references to ethnic minorities in Bulgaria. By 1974 '500 of the 1,300 inmates of the notorious Belene labour camp were Pomaks who had resisted pressure to change their names' (Crampton 1997: 201). Under the terms of an agreement with the Turkish government, the Zhivkov regime also secured the 'voluntary' emigration of around 130,000 ethnic Turks to Turkey between 1968 and 1978 (Pundeff 1992: 106).

In 1984–5 the Zhivkov regime launched a so-called 'regenerative process' (this can also be translated as the 'purificatory process'), directed against Bulgaria's 850,00 ethnic Turks, who still comprised about 10 per cent of the population (Crampton 1997: 210). The regime propagated the view that Bulgaria's last 'genuine' ethnic Turks had emigrated during the 1970s, that the residual Muslim population was 'really' only made up of ethnic Bulgarians and other non-Turks whose ancestors had been converted to Islam under Ottoman Turkish rule, and that it was now time to forcibly reassimilate them into an ethno-culturally monolithic Bulgarian nation. Paradoxically, Zhivkov's ostensibly *atheist* but actually *xenophobic-nationalist* 'Communist regime' perceived the Bulgarian nation to be defined in large measure by its Orthodox *Christian* heritage, and even *required* Bulgaria's supposedly Communist historians to write in this vein! In 1985 Bulgaria's Turks (and other Muslims) were ordered to choose new names drawn from an officially approved list of acceptable Slavic/Christian names. Those who dragged their feet or refused to choose new names from this list were liable to have names imposed on them by the authorities. Persistent refusal often resulted in demotion, denial of employment, rejection of applications for public housing, public sanctions against the daughters and sons of 'refusers', or even incarceration in labour and concentration camps such as Belene and Lovech. In addition, the regime restricted or closed schools which had been teaching in Turkish, and it halted all public broadcasting and publications in the Turkish language, while circumcision (required by Islamic doctrine) and the use of the Turkish language in public were prohibited. This was a wholesale assault on outward expressions of Turkic and Islamic identity. Laudably, far from being eagerly supported by the rest of the population, these measures provoked the emergence of the first significant Bulgari dissident movements (Todorov 2001: 33). Not surprisingly, the campaign evoked some violent resistance from Turkish communities, and in some areas the regime even deployed troops, tanks and elite red-beret commando units against the protesters.

This unleashed a growing chorus of international condemnation from Turkey and other predominantly Muslim countries, as well as from Western human-rights organizations and the UN. As a by-product, powerful international spotlights were turned on the vast range and scale of human-rights violations in Bulgaria, and the reviled Zhikov regime was exposed in all its crude barbarity, although this did not stop the capitalist West from simultaneously lending ever-larger sums of money to this increasingly insolvent regime!

Zhivkov whipped up the Bulgarian nationalist anti-Turkish campaign into an even greater frenzy in May 1989, in an attempt to divert public attention from the escalating socio-economic and environmental crises and the manifest moral and financial bankruptcy of his regime. Growing numbers of Turks were driven from their homes, with only the possessions they could carry in person, and many sought refuge in Turkey. The Turkish government responded by declaring that all those Bulgarian Turks who wished to emigrate to Turkey would be made welcome. Zhivkov called their bluff and by the time Turkey was f nally obliged to close its doors in August 1989, over 300,000 Bulgarian Turkish refugees had crossed the border from Bulgaria into Turkey. Among other things, this gave the lie to the Zhivkov regime's claims that there were no 'genuine' Turks left in Bulgaria! Furthermore, Bulgaria's economy was thrown even deeper into crisis by this massive haemorrhage of valuable Turkish labour and skills. It appears that about half of the Turks who fled returned to Bulgaria by the lat autumn of 1989, but many found that their homes had been vandalized or even destroyed by Bulgarian nationalist hoodlums during their absence (*EEN*, 5 October 1992, p. 7).

The fall of the Communist regime, 1989–90

The severe environmental damage incurred by Bulgaria spawned ecological pressure groups, the most famous of which was 'Ecoglasnost'. An internationally televised police crackdown on the organization's demonstrators on 26 October 1989 unleashed another international outcry against the Zhivkov regime and accelerated moves within Zhivkov's entourage to carry out a 'palace revolution' and force his resignation both as party leader and as president of the state council.

On 10 November 1989, Petur Mladenov, who had served as foreign minister from 1971 until mid-1989, took Zhivkov's place both as leader of the Communist Party and as president of the state council.

On 14 November various dissident groups and embryonic political parties, plus an independent trade-union movement called Podkrepa (Support), jointly launched a Union of Democratic Forces (UDF) which quickly established itself as the main political challenger to the ruling Communist Party. The leading figure in the UD during its f rst years was Bulgaria's best-known dissident, Zheliu Zhelev. In 1981 he had published a book called *Fascism*, which had dared to highlight the generic resemblances between Communist and fascist totalitarianisms. He went on to found Ecoglasnost and to denounce the regime's persecution of the Turkish minority. An internationally and domestically respected figure, Zhelev was an important force for stability, integrity, liberalism and self-critical reflection in post-Communist Bulgaria. He championed the emergence of a strong political centre ground and helped to marginalize Bulgaria's nationalist and neo-Communist xenophobes.

A plenary meeting of the Communist Party's central committee from 11 to 13 December publicly acknowledged the glaring deficiencies of the Zhivkov regime and promised to turn over a new leaf, but without as yet committing itself to the holding of free multiparty elections. The plenum also divulged that the foreign debt had rocketed to 12 billion dollars, rather than the figure of 3 billion dollars falsely pu about by the Zhivkov regime. President Mladenov graphically declared the Bulgarian economy to be 'on the verge of cardiac arrest'.

Zhivkov was expelled from the Communist Party on 13 December, and on 18 January 1990 a warrant was issued for his arrest on charges of 'incitement to ethnic hostility and hatred, unwarranted receiving of excessive amounts of public property and gross malfeasance'. The 'incitement to ethnic hostility' charge referred mainly to his 'regenerative campaign'. His trial started on 25 February 1991, and in 1992 he was convicted of embezzlement and sentenced to seven years in prison. Saved from jail by poor health, he spent several years under house arrest. In February 1996 Bulgaria's highest court acquitted him of the embezzlement charges, although he remained indicted on charges of human-rights abuses. He died on 5 August 1998.

On 29 December 1989 the rights of Bulgaria's Turks were restored, including being able to reclaim their former jobs and properties. However, the Communist 'old guard' in the provinces responded by transporting large numbers of xenophobic Bulgarian nationalist and Communist 'rent-a-crowd' workers and peasants to Sof a on 7 January 1990 to take part in mass demonstrations against these concessions. Counter-demonstrations in favour of the Turks took place a week later. Fears that the polarized country was on the brink of civil unrest led to the inauguration of round-table negotiations between the ruling Communists and the UDF leadership, headed by Zhelev, in order to prepare the ground for multiparty elections. It is quite con - ceivable that without the continuing strong show of Bulgarian public support for the Turkish minority, the Communist Party would have sought to retain its political monopoly. The Turkish minority and all those who championed their rights performed a great service to the causes of both liberalism and democracy (these should not be conflated, as they are not the same thing)

During 1992, yet more ethnic Turks emigrated to Turkey, but this time mainly because of Bulgaria's accelerating economic collapse and laws designed to return property to its pre-Communist owners, which deprived some Bulgarian Turks of their livelihoods (*The Times*, 29 December 1994, p. 11). However, the scale of the net exodus should not be exaggerated. According to the 2001 census returns, 9.4 per cent of Bulgaria's population was still Turkish by ethnicity and 9.6 per cent spoke Turkish as its mother tongue, while 12.2 per cent of the population (including Pomaks, Tatars and Circassians as well as Turks) were still declared to be Muslim by religious affiliation

On 15 January 1990 the national assembly removed the clause in the constitution which described the Communist Party as 'the guiding force in society and the state'. However, even though numerous new parties had been established by then, the national assembly did not formally authorize their formation until 3 April 1990. Furthermore, although an extraordinary congress of the Communist Party held in late January 1990 decided to embrace a course of political and economic liberalization, including the authorization of multiparty elections and a *gradual* transformation of the economy into a privatized, market-based system, it did so without much conviction or enthusiasm. Mladenov, aiming to become president of the republic, relinquished the Communist Party leadership to the 'reform Communist', Aleksandur Lilov.

In April 1990 the national assembly duly elected Mladenov to the new post of president of the republic. It also decided that multiparty elections to a grand national assembly (constituent assembly), which would sit for eighteen months and draw up a new constitution, would take place in June 1990. In late April, the Communist Party voted to 'reinvent itself' as a more social democratic Bulgarian Socialist Party (BSP). A new (and unsuccessful) Bulgarian Communist Party was launched by a few hardliners in June 1990.

The 'reform Communist' government headed by Andrei Lukanov, February to November 1990

Andrei Lukanov, who had been minister for foreign economic relations since August 1987 and was a protégé of President Mladenov, was installed as prime minister on 4 February 1990. Faced with a gargantuan economic crisis, inability to service Bulgaria's ballooning foreign debt, and the need to introduce painful austerity mea-sures, Lukanov attempted to involve the UDF in a coalition 'government of national unity' with suff cient support to carry through far-reaching reforms. However, even though the original orientation of the UDF had been left of centre, many of its members had suffered in various ways under the Zhivkov regime (harassment, imprisonment, forced labour) and were, understandably, fiercely anti-Communist. Furthermore, the UDF had no wish to incur popular opprobrium for the impending collapse in living standards, which the collapse of the centrally planned economy, the disintegration of Comecon (whose markets had accounted for over half Bulgaria's exports), the incipient default on debt-service payments and the long-overdue austerity measures had rendered unavoidable. They especially did not want to incur unpopularity on these accounts in the run up to the parliamentary elections scheduled for June 1990.

First steps towards a privatized market economy, 1990

The UDF took the view that, since the BCP had got the country into this mess, the ex-Communists in the BSP could reap the main flack for having to deal with th consequences. The Lukanov government duly suspended repayments on the foreign debt in March 1990 and interest payments on it in June. This made it virtually impossible for Bulgaria to obtain any new loans. The government continued to honour its internal financial commitments, but it was only able to do so by printing a lot mor money. This stoked up inflation, rapidly eroded the real value of wages, personal savings and pensions and aroused widespread discontent and industrial unrest.

In February and March 1990 the Lukanov government abolished compulsory sale or delivery of farm produce to the state, removed restrictions on the size of private landholdings and on the number of people who could be employed privately and abolished the state monopoly of foreign trade. The collapse of Comecon in 1990 hit Bulgaria particularly hard. Exports to the former Comecon countries fell by about 66 per cent in 1991 and by a further 15 to 25 per cent in 1992 (Borenzstein et al. 1993: 6) (see Table 3.2). But in 1992 the EU still only accounted for only 31 per cent of Bulgaria's foreign trade (*FT*, Survey, 5 May 1993, p. 31).

The two-stage elections to a 400-seat 'grand national assembly' (constituent assembly), 10 and 17 June 1990

The UDF expected to have an easy victory, riding on a wave of popular revulsion against forty-f ve years of Communist misrule. However, the UDF was a divided and

3.2 Bulgaria: selected economic indicators, 1990–2005

	1990	1991	1992	1993	1994	1995	1996	% rise/rate 1997	1998	1999	2000	2001	2002	2003	2004	2005
GDP	-9.1	-11.7	-7.3	-1.5	1.8	2.9	-9.4	-5.6	4.0	2.3	5.4	4.0	4.8	4.5	5.6	5.8
Industrial output	-16.5	-27.3	-6.4	-6.2	5.9	-5.4	-11.8	-11.3	4.3	-4.3	12.0	0.7	2.6	12.0	15.0	7.3
Agricultural output	-6.0	-0.3	-14.8	-30.2	7.1	16.0	10.9	13.7	-0.6	2.7	-9.1	-0.1	4.2	-1.4	5.6	-8.6
Annual inflation rate	26.3	333.5	82.0	73.0	96.3	62.0	123.0	1082	22.2	0.7	9.9	7.4	5.9	2.3	6.1	5.0
Budget surplus (+) / deficit (−) as % of GDP	-12.8	-14.7	-2.9	-8.7	-3.9	-5.7	-10.4	-2.1	0.9	-0.9	-0.5	1.4	-0.2	0.6	1.3	2.4
Unemployment	1.8	10.5	15.3	16.4	12.8	11.1	12.5	13.7	12.2	17.0	16.4	19.5	16.8	13.7	12.0	9.9
Foreign debt as % of GDP	–	157.0	146.0	128.0	118.0	78.0	97.0	95.0	93.0	84.2	88.6	78.4	72.7	67.7	69.3	68.2
Private sector as % of GDP	10.0	20.0	25.0	35.0	40.0	50.0	55.0	60.0	65.0	70.0	70.0	70.0	70.0	75.0	75.0	75.0
Private sector as % of employment	–	–	–	–	–	–	–	–	–	46.0	55.0	59.0	61.0	62.0	66.0	–
FDI inflow (net, $ million)	4.0	56.0	42.0	40.0	105.0	98.0	138.0	507.0	537.0	802.0	998.0	803.0	876.0	2070.0	1232.0	1991.0
Foreign debt ($ billion)	–	11.8	12.5	13.9	11.4	10.3	9.5	9.7	10.1	10.9	11.2	10.6	11.3	13.4	16.7	17.9
Population (m)	–	8.6	8.5	8.5	8.4	8.4	8.3	8.3	8.2	8.2	8.1	7.9	7.8	7.8	7.8	7.8

Sources: Various issues of the annual EBRD *Transition Report*, supplemented by UN Economic Commission for Europe, *Economic Survey of Europe*; UN *World Economic and Social Survey*; and IMF *World Economic Outlook*. Figures for 2004 and 2005 are provisional estimates.

unwieldy coalition, and it underestimated the sheer weight of power, influence, patronage and infrastructure which the BSP inherited from the Zhivkov regime, especially in the countryside. The BSP won the election on a platform of a Gorbachev-style 'humane and democratic socialism' and a very cautious approach to economic transformation. It claimed that the costs of conversion to a more market-orientated economy would be minimized by a gradual process of change, combined with state provision of generous social safety nets, although it accepted the need to expand the private sector. The UDF favoured a more rapid transition to a market economy and more vigorous promotion of private enterprise. BANU advocated 'a socially orientated market economy' and the return of land to former owners (or their heirs), but with the stipulation that they had to farm it themselves (partly to prevent a re-emergence of landlordism). The UDF won a plurality of votes in the major cities, especially among professional, young and educated people, but its overall support was a crushing disappointment (see Table 3.3).

3.3 Bulgarian grand national assembly election, 10 and 17 June 1990

Party	Share of vote (%)	Seats
Bulgarian Socialist Party (BSP)	47.2	211
Union of Democratic Forces (UDF)	36.2	144
Bulgarian Agrarian National Union (BANU)	8.0	16
Movement for Rights and Freedoms (MRF)	6.0	23
Others	2.6	6

Note: Turn-out was 90.6 per cent. Source: Bell (1997: 369).

For the BSP, however, this quickly proved to be a pyrrhic victory. In July 1990 Mladenov was forced to step down as president, after a videotape which was repeatedly broadcast on television appeared to show him calling for tanks to be used to suppress anti-Communist demonstrations by force in December 1990 (though the sound quality on the tape was so poor that it is impossible to be certain what he really said). After much wrangling, the grand national assembly finally chose the UD leader Zheliu Zhelev to be the new president, and he then stood down as leader of the UDF. During the autumn of 1990, furthermore, the independent trade union Podkrepa (Support) organized a wave of strikes to protest against soaring inflation and unemployment and plummeting living standards. Bulgaria became almost ungovernable, prompting the Lukanov government to throw in the towel on 29 November 1990.

The caretaker coalition government headed by Dimitar Popov, December 1990 to October 1991

On 7 December, Dimitar Popov, a non-party judge, was appointed as caretaker prime minister until a new parliamentary election could be held. His coalition government, which included members of the BSP, the UDF and the BANU, was approved on 20 December 1990.

Further steps towards a privatized market economy

In January 1991 agreement was reached on a 200-day 'social pact' between the government, trade unions and employers. This included a ban on strikes until July 1991, but with automatic partial (70 per cent) wage compensation for price rises. Wage levels were to be determined by a trilateral commission representing unions, employers and government. Potentially inflationary pay increases were to be curbed by a 'wage inflation tax'. Unemployment compensation was to be provided by the state for up to a year, after which social assistance was available. The level of unionization continued to be high in the state sector of the workforce, but the newly emerging private sector was largely ununionized (EBRD 1997b: 160).

The de-collectivization of Bulgarian agriculture, 1991–9

A land law adopted in late January 1991 made provision for the restitution of land which had been forcibly collectivized by the Communist regime to its former owners or their heirs. Financial compensation was to be provided by the state where physical restitution was impossible. Provision was also made for auctioning off about 400,000 hectares of state land to agriculturalists who had never previously owned any land. However, Bulgarian agricultural productivity and yields were adversely affected by the fragmentation and minute average size of the re-established private smallhold-ings, as well as by (often inevitable) long delays in granting full and undisputed titles to restituted property. By late 1993 around 30 per cent of the land was being worked by farmers who owned their own land (*Employment Observatory*, December 1993, no. 5, p. 4). There were more than 1.7 million conf icting restitution claims, but more than 90 per cent of the land which passed into private hands was in tiny plots of less than 1 hectare each. Furthermore, because much of the land was transferred on a temporary basis pending f nal decisions on claims, the land could not be used as collateral or sold (*The Economist*, 7 August 1993, p. 63). By early 1994 around 50 per cent of farmland was in private hands, and about 25 per cent of land had been returned to former owners (*Transitions*, 1994, vol. 5, no. 4, pp. 9–10). Roughly 60 per cent of the new landowners lived in cities or towns and many were unable or unwill-ing to 'return' to farming. Some worked their new plots of land only at weekends and with simple implements. The average size of restituted landholdings was only 1.6 hectares (*FT*, Survey, 13 October 1994, p. 14). Livestock formerly belonging to collective farms was redistributed somewhat indiscriminately, often to people who could not feed and did not know how to look after their newly acquired animals, causing the number of cattle to fall from 648,000 in 1989 to 358,000 at the end of 1996. Private producers accounted for over 70 per cent of farm output, but on holdings averaging less than 1 hectare each (*FT*, 15 July 1997, p. 33). Although 80 per cent of the farmland available for restitution had been returned to its pre-collectivization owners by the end of 1998, still only 24 per cent of restituted land had been registered and titled and only about 5 per cent of private farms exceeded 2 hectares in size. In addition, more than half of Bulgaria's agro-industrial enterprises (in terms of assets) and virtually all its grain warehouses had been privatized *FT*, Survey, 8 March 1999, p. iii; EBRD 1999b: 202). Most of the new landholdings remained tiny, 'good for nothing but subsistence', and, since most farmers still had no official title to their land, they could not sell it, nor could they use it as collateral to borrow money to invest in their farms. Therefore, spending on fertilizer and seed, not to mention equipment, largely dried up (*BCE*, July–August 1999, p. 48). 'By the end of 1999 land restitution was 96 per cent complete' (EBRD 2000b: 146).

All in all, the *de-collectivization* of Bulgarian agriculture initiated by the Popov government at the start of the 1990s was probably at least as disruptive and damaging to agricultural performance as the Communist*collectivization* of Bulgarian agriculture had been during the 1950s, and the net reduction (by slaughter and non-replacement) of livestock herds resulting from de-collectivization may even have exceeded the loss of livestock during the 1950s collectivization campaigns! Furthermore, the ineffi ciencies and demerits of 'de-collectivized' agriculture appear to have been even more debilitating than the inefficiencies and dysfunctional attributes for which mos Western critics of the former Communist regimes used to berate the Communist systems of collectivized agriculture. The main conclusions to be drawn from both of these experiences are that any fundamental change of system (in whichever direction) is profoundly disruptive and damaging to agricultural performance, and that the results of this disruption and damage far outweigh any intrinsic demerits of collectivized agriculture as compared with non-collectivized agriculture, at least in the short to medium term (cf. Bideleux 1985, Chapter 12). Indeed, Communist-ruled Bulgaria developed one of the more successful systems of collectivized agriculture, whereas since 1991 it has been painfully rediscovering the major deficiencies and drawbacks of 'uncollectivized' agriculture, which are not at all easy to avoid or over- come. (The grass is always greener on the other side of the fence.) The large-scale, highly mechanized, capital-intensive and energy-intensive systems of Western capitalist 'agribusiness', which Western hyperbole used to contrast so favourably with the many alleged deficiencies of the various Communist systems of collective farming were merely pie-in-the-sky fantasies pedalled by armchair critics of Communism, rather than truly feasible or realistic options in the 'really existing conditions' of the Balkans and East Central Europe, where for the time being the only realistic alternative to Communist systems of collectivized agriculture seems to be small-scale subsistence farming carried out on relatively fragmented, dysfunctional, overmanned, under - capitalized, unproductive and unremunerative dwarf-holdings – quite a depressing prospect. The most promising means of mitigating the manifest and manifold defi ciencies of 'de-collectivized' agriculture would be to emulate the highly successful Danish model of farmers' marketing, purchasing, dairying and food-processing cooperatives (the classic expositions are Jensen 1937 and Skrubbeltrang 1953). That would be a way forward which the region's relatively well-educated but acutely capital- deficient post-Communist smallholders should be well able to manage in order to pull themselves up by their own bootstraps, instead of simply selling out to highly exploitative Western 'agribusiness' companies or passively waiting for a f nancial milchcow called 'Brussels' to bail them out.

Price liberalization, February 1991

The prices of goods accounting for around 90 per cent of retail turnover were substantially freed from state control on 1 February 1991. The main exceptions were public utility prices, including energy, telecommunications, water and trans- port. Even the prices that remained subject to controls were dramatically increased, as subsidies were reduced, e.g., milk prices rose by 500 per cent and fares on public transport rose by 1,100 per cent (*Transitions*, April 1994, vol. 5, no. 4, p. 9). Import quotas were largely removed in February 1991, foreign trade was liberalized, and on

1 February 1991 the lev was floated at a unified rate. The Popov programme gain IMF approval and credits in February 1991. In addition, because servicing the 12 billion-dollar foreign debt inherited from the Zhivkov regime was an impossible burden on post-Communist Bulgaria, creditor governments had to agree to a re-scheduling in April 1991.

Overall, however, the Popov government wasted too much time and energy on petty wrangling over trivial issues and on long and inconclusive deliberations on the major ones. Bulgaria thus missed a valuable 'window of opportunity' for more radical economic reform.

The new constitution adopted in July 1991

The new constitution adopted in July 1991 established a directly elected president of the republic, a unicameral 240-seat national assembly elected by proportional representation but with a 4 per cent threshold, and a constitutional court to adjudicate on disputes between the executive and the national assembly. In order to forestall the possibility that Bulgaria's former King Simeon might be tempted to enter the next presidential election, it stipulated that all presidential candidates would have to have lived in Bulgaria for at least fve years beforehand. The grand national assembly then dissolved itself, to clear the way for parliamentary elections.

Meanwhile Petur Beron, Zheliu Zhelev's successor as leader of the UDF, had been forced to resign following disclosures that he had been a police informer under the Zhivkov regime. The new leader of the UDF was Filip Dimitrov, a Green Party politician. He was unable to 'bring back into the fold' the radical liberal and centrist groupings which had seceded from the UDF and, as a consequence, the UDF shifted further to the right of centre in the political spectrum. By narrowing its previously very broad base (almost everyone who opposed Communist dictatorship), this realign ment effectively deprived the UDF of its earlier potential for winning a working majority in the October 1991 elections (see Table 3.4).

3.4 Bulgarian national assembly election, 13 October 1991

Party	Share of vote (%)	Seats
Union of Democratic Forces (UDF)	34.4	110
Bulgarian Socialist Party (BSP)	33.1	106
Movement for Rights and Freedoms (MRF)	7.6	24

Parties that failed to pass the 4 per cent threshold for representation in parliament:

Bulgarian Agrarian National Union (United)	3.9
Bulgarian Agrarian National Union (Nikola Petkov)	3.5
UDF (centrists)	3.2
UDF (radical liberals)	2.8
Kingdom of Bulgaria Party	1.8
Business Bloc	1.3
Others	7.3

Note: Turn-out 79 per cent.

Source: Bell (1997: 377).

The centrist government headed by Filip Dimitrov, November 1990 to October 1992

The UDF-led national movement headed by Filip Dimitrov formed a minority government with a pledge of parliamentary support from the Movement for Rights and Freedoms (MRF), which was not given seats because of Bulgarian nationalist sensitivities about the Turkish minority which it represented. Dimitrov worked hard to accelerate economic liberalization, restructuring and privatization, which had been much delayed by political wrangling, but his government was handicapped by its lack of a secure majority and by policy disagreements. The UDF was in favour of restoring land to previous owners or their heirs (which disadvantaged the Turkish minority, which had owned relatively little land per capita in pre-Communist Bulgaria), whereas the MRF and the BSP wanted land to be allocated to members of the agricultural producer cooperatives in proportion to their respective labour contributions. A slump in demand for Bulgarian tobacco, produced mainly by the country's Turkish minority, further strained relations with the increasingly discontent MRF.

In April 1992 the IMF reacted favourably to the economic liberalization and macroeconomic stabilization policies initiated by the Popov government in 1991, and a stand-by loan was approved. In October 1992 Bulgaria was able to resume interest payments on its foreign debt, and on 16 December the Paris Club of Western creditor nations agreed to reschedule their share of Bulgaria's foreign debt. Legislation intended to encourage and attract foreign investment was passed in February 1992, but Bulgaria's still confused, restrictive and dysfunctional economic legislation resulted in poor responses.

The privatization of small urban businesses was accelerated by a restitution law introduced in 1992. By June 1992, 65 per cent of shops had been returned to former owners or their heirs (*Employment Observatory*, 1992, no. 3, p. 2), and by July 1993 the proportion was 83 per cent for shops and restaurants (Wyzan 1996: 58). In addition, a law to accelerate privatization of industry was approved by parliament on 8 May 1992. However, this law was barely implemented. Only one out of sixteen large enterprises and seventeen out of 870 medium enterprises had been privatized by mid-1994 (EBRD 1994: 20). Less than 6 per cent of state enterprise assets were privatized up to mid-1996 (EBRD 1996b: 142).

The Dimitrov government adopted a more vindictive stance towards the past misdeeds of former senior members of the Zhivkov regime than did the earlier leaders of the UDF (especially Zheliu Zhelev, whose priorities were institutional reform and burying of hatchets, rather than vengeance or retribution against individuals). Ex-premier Andrei Lukanov was arrested in July 1992 on charges of having misappropriated state funds during the Communist era, but mainly by granting aid to countries such as Cuba and Vietnam when he served as minister for foreign economic relations under Zhivkov. In November 1992, Zhivkov's former premier Georgi Atanosov was sentenced to ten years in jail for alleged misuse of state funds.

Dimitrov's government lost a vote of no confidence (120 to 111) on 29 Octobe 1992, after allegations that it had tried to supply arms to Macedonia in breach of the UN embargo.

The technocratic government headed by Lyuben Berov, December 1992 to September 1994

On 23 December 1992, Lyuben Berov, a professor of economic history and presidential economic adviser who enjoyed the support of the MRF, was asked to try to form a government committed to more rapid economic restructuring and privatization. Berov published an 'action plan' in February 1993, but his government was all plan and very little action.

Bulgaria signed a 'Europe Agreement' (an 'enhanced' association agreement) with the EU on 8 March 1993, with effect from 1 February 1995. This obliged Bulgaria to open up its market to imports from the EU. In return, the EU agreed to eliminate 90 per cent of all quotas and tariffs on industrial imports from Bulgaria, while retaining restrictions on imports of agricultural products and so-called 'sensitive goods' (coal, steel, chemicals, textiles, footwear and processed foods) from Bulgaria. Economically, this asymmetrical agreement was a poor bargain for Bulgaria, but it marked the first step on Bulgaria's long road towards the coveted goal of eventua EU membership, and it committed the EU to periodic political consultation with Bulgaria. All the political parties represented in parliament approved EU membership as a goal.

A new privatization programme was announced in August 1993, but it was not approved by parliament until June 1994. Mass privatization based on the free distribution of vouchers was ruled out, but citizens were to be allowed to buy some vouchers, other vouchers were to be used for restitution purposes, and foreign investors were to be allowed to participate. The privatization of 3,485 enterprises was initiated in September 1994. Management and employees were allowed to bid for up to 20 per cent of shares at a 50 per cent discount. Brady bonds and 'Zunk bonds' (domestic bad-loan bonds) became usable as payment (EBRD 1996a: 142).

Price controls were reintroduced in the form of ceiling prices for fuels (1993), as well as controls on tobacco and certain other products (March 1994). In mid-1994, government 'monitoring' of basic food prices and restrictions on profit margins strongly expanded, reducing the share of genuinely free prices to about 54 per cent of all prices (EBRD 1995b: 37).

During 1993 there were some delays in paying interest on the 9 billion-dollar debt owed to the London Club of Western creditor banks, but a rescheduling agreement was reached with them on 25 November. In June 1994 Bulgaria signed an agreement with the London Club, which provided for a 47.1 per cent reduction in its debt to them. In April 1994 the Paris Club of Western creditor governments also agreed to reschedule repayments on Bulgaria's 3 billion dollars to them. IMF-inspired austerity measures were implemented to try to reduce the budget deficit. Value added tax (VAT was introduced on 1 April 1994.

In March 1994 the government took steps to refinance some of the bad loans arranged in the Communist era by state banks to state enterprises, issuing bonds to convert enterprise debt into government debt (*FT*, 29 March 1994, p. 3). Banks were recapitalized using Zunk bonds to cover non-performing bank assets. The bonds had a twenty-five-year maturity period and a five-year grace period, and paid only a fractio of market rates of interest for the first seven years. These low interest rates create severe liquidity problems for the banks, which the Berov government addressed by repeated cash infusions (EBRD 1995: 54). A bankruptcy law was passed by parliament in July 1994, but no bankruptcy procedures were initiated against any major enterprise before July 1996 (EBRD 1996b: 143). In April 1994 an increasingly frustrated President Zhelev accused the Berov government of failing to push forward economic reforms and called for its resignation (*IHT*, 14 May 1994, p. 11). After surviving six no-confidence votes tabled by the UDF, the Berov government finally resigned in September 1994, when an exasperated MRF finally withdrew its support and backe calls for an early parliamentary election.

On 17 October 1994 Reneta Indzhova was chosen to serve as interim prime minister until the 18 December 1994 general election. A former director of the priva-tization programme, she had helped the UDF draw up its economic programme and was Bulgaria's first female premier

Delays in 'open' privatization allowed 'hidden', 'spontaneous' or '*nomenklatura* privatization' to thrive under the Berov government. The former Communist*nomen-klatura* exploited business and political connections to become fabulously rich by running private trading companies that supplied fuels and raw materials to, and marketed the products of, Bulgaria's state-owned industries. They fostered a bizarre economic sub-system in which production was state-run but profits were private. The private trading companies controlled most of what was sold to state-owned industries and marketed their production too. Such enterprises could be highly lucrative through kickbacks and manipulation of antiquated accounting methods (*HT*, 14 May 1994, p. 11). Although formal privatization was slow, private companies supplied state enterprises with artificially high-priced inputs and marketed their heavily subsidized output for resale at market prices. In this way, state enterprises accumu-lated ever-growing inter-enterprise losses and debts, while a new class of traders made huge fortunes. This process of 'nationalizing losses' and 'privatizing profits' was t be found throughout the former Soviet bloc, but it was most blatant and most rife in Bulgaria and Romania (*FT*, Survey, 13 October 1994, p. 14). It became increasingly obvious that Bulgaria's state enterprises were being 'comprehensively asset-stripped by managers and private businessmen with close ties to the former Communists' (*The Guardian*, 17 December 1994, p. 9). The economic power of the *nomenklatura* was particularly strong in Bulgaria and this was resulting in 'what the Bulgarians call the "maf aization" of the economy' (*The Economist*, 7 January 1995, p. 33). The Russian 'mafia' also became extensively involved in Bulgaria's large 'grey' econom (*The Economist*, 19 October 1996, p. 55). Officially, the private sector contribute only 22 per cent of GDP in 1994, but the World Bank estimated illegal and quasi-legal activities outside the government tax net lifted the actual scale of private economic activity to around 50 per cent of GDP and that at least 90 per cent of profs in the economy accrued to the informal private sector. After 1991, as a general rule, private firms took over distribution, marketing and foreign-trade functions in the economy, and huge private income and wealth was concentrated in very few hands by siphoning off prof ts from state-owned enterprises (*Transitions*, 1995, vol. 6, no. 3, pp. 4, 6).

The parliamentary election of 18 December 1994

After the failure of three successive centre-right governments to deliver on their promises of rapid economic liberalization, restructuring and privatization, the BSP, led by Zhan Videnov since December 1991, obtained an absolute majority of seats in the national assembly, aided by an electoral pact with the Bulgarian Agrarian Party 'Aleksandur Stamboliski' and the political club Ecoglasnost. Filip Dimitrov resigned

3.5 Bulgarian parliamentary election, 18 December 1994

Party	Share of vote (%)	Seats
BSP-led 'Coalition of the Democratic Left'	43.2	125
Union of Democratic Forces (UDF)	24.2	69
Popular Union	6.5	18
Movements for Rights and Freedoms (MRF)	5.4	15
Bulgarian Business Bloc	4.7	13
Others beneath 4 per cent threshold	16.0	0

Note: Turn-out 74 per cent.

Source: Bell (1997: 390).

as leader of the UDF as a result of its very poor electoral performance. He was succeeded by its former finance minister, Ivan Kostov. The election results are show in Table 3.5.

The socialist government led by Zhan Videnov, December 1994 to December 1996

The new government included Roumen Getchev (vice premier in charge of the economy and privatization, favouring growth over a lower rate of inflation), Dimitar Kostov (finance), Kyril Tsochev (trade), Georgi Pirinski (foreign affairs) and Dimitar Pavlov (defence). The Bulgarian Business Bloc also joined government.

At this time, Bulgaria's post-Communist economic recession seemed to be 'bottoming out' and hopes ran high that, with its secure parliamentary majority, the new government would finally be able to tackle mounting crime and corruption and delive the economic restructuring that the country so desperately needed. Videnov affirme that his priorities were to curb crime, reverse the economic decline and promote Bulgarian integration into the EU. However, he was less keen on NATO and sought instead to placate the Russophile neo-Communists in his party by promising closer trade, energy and defence ties with Russia (to balance the Europe Agreement with the EU). In May 1995 the Videnov government concluded several trade and energy agreements with Russia and announced an action programme which expressed support for a 'social market economy'. A programme for the mass voucher-based privatization of medium enterprises was submitted to parliament on 22 March 1995. Roughly 150 enterprises were to be selected for privatization between November 1995 and October 1996. However, Videnov was doctrinally opposed to privatizing public utilities, military-industrial complexes and the major state banks, and the implementation of his privatization programme was repeatedly postponed. In the municipal elections held in 1995, the BSP won 195 of the 255 mayoralties, while the opposition UDF under its new leader Ivan Kostov was beaten into third place, winning fewer seats than the MRF. During 1995 Bulgaria's GDP rose 3 per cent, the inflation rate fell to its lowest level since 1991, interest rates were repeatedly reduced, the value of its currency (the lev) appreciated, and for six months there was a trade surplus.

Nevertheless, all was not well. The Videnov government tried at least partially to reverse the privatization of agriculture by introducing amendments to the 1991 land legislation which would allow new APCs to be formed. President Zhelev had these amendments referred to the constitutional court, which struck them down on the grounds that they infringed private-property rights. However, the ensuing uncertainties caused farms to hold back from cultivating as much land as in previous years. At the same time, large swathes of the semi-marketized industrial sector had fallen under the control of financial conglomerates, known colloquially as 'the mafia', which h close links (dating back to Soviet times) with the Russian 'mafia'. These conglomerate used their inside knowledge and connections in high places to siphon off ever-larger subsidies from the state budget, obtain low-interest loans from the state banks and buy up grain and obtain grain export permits, thereby creating acute bread shortages on Bulgaria's home market. In addition, these conglomerates had become heavily involved in sanctions-busting trade with former Yugoslavia, in illicit trade in drugs, arms, people-trafficking, mass production of pirated CDs and in a lot of shady deals in the Russian and Caucasian energy and pipeline industries. Ex-premier Andrei Lukanov was prominent in these energy and pipeline dealings and became very wealthy.

In early 1996, however, everything started falling apart. Banks got into difficultie as a result of ever-proliferating non-performing loans being siphoned off by the 'maf'. The budget def cit and borrowing by increasingly insolvent state industries ballooned out of control, and the inflation rate accelerated dramatically. Interest rates were repeatedly raised in unsuccessful attempts to restrain borrowing, to dampen the strong inflationary pressures and to shore up the value of the lev

The major economic crisis of May 1996 to mid-1997, and the governmental crises of December 1996 to February 1997

In early May 1996 the lev plunged to fresh lows, and there was a run on the banks on 9 May, when many banks were unable to meet the scramble for cash. Shopkeepers refused to accept payment in leva for goods other than food (*IHT*, 10 May 1996, p. 15). The exchange rate fell from 70 leva to the US dollar in January 1996 to 487.4 at the end of 1996, and to 2,936.7 on 12 February 1997 (Wyzan 1998: 6, 24), before stabilizing at around 1,500 lev to the US dollar in February 1997 (*FT*, 5 May 1997, p. 2). The crisis reached its apogee in February 1997, when the monthly inflation rat was 242.7 per cent, the payment of rapidly depreciating wages, salaries and state pensions fell increasingly into arrears, turf wars between rival gangs and 'mafia' group escalated into a major violent crime wave, and unemployment increased dramatically. By late 1996 soup kitchens had become necessary in many towns to feed growing numbers of malnourished and unemployed inhabitants.

According to the EBRD, 'Bulgaria's severe economic crisis was fundamentally the result of years of delays in necessary enterprise restructuring, with mounting losses f nanced by the largely state-owned banking system (amounting to an estimated 15 per cent of GDP in 1995)' (EBRD 1997b: 159). 'In 1996 Bulgaria slid into eco - nomic crisis, rooted in continued massive bank lending to loss-making state enterprises and a general lack of structural reforms' (EBRD 1997a: 7). Bulgaria's crisis was 'caused by increasingly accommodating refinance policies toward distressed com mercial banks, along with an attempt by the authorities to decrease interest rates significantly. Downward pressure on the exchange rate depleted foreign exchange reserves in the course of 1996, which, in turn, led to panic and runs on many com-mercial banks' (OECD, *Economic Outlook*, December 1996, p. 124). The crisis had 'its origins in the ineff cient and unviable state-owned sector of the economy, but due to soft budget constraints and repeated bail-outs it spread to the public finances, th banking system and the financial markets' (UN ECE 1997: 81). The crisis was cause by 'a mixture of ill-judged lending, over-expansion . . corruption . . . lax supervision, inadequate regulation and industrial chaos . . . . In 1993 the country's banks were recapitalized with $2.7 billion of so-called "zunk" bonds. That money... disappeared down Bulgaria's black hole' (*The Economist*, 20 April 1996, p. 90).

The IMF was closely involved in Bulgaria's battle to overcome this economic crisis. On 29 May 1996 Prime Minister Videnov announced a draconian IMF-backed austerity programme comprising: an increase in the rate of VAT from 18 per cent to 22 per cent, the introduction of a 5 per cent import levy from 1 July 1996 to 30 June 1997, a continuation of Bulgaria's restrictive incomes policy, increased petrol prices, the liquidation of 64 enterprises employing 24,000 people and responsible for 25 per cent of state enterprise losses in 1995, accelerated privatization (42 per cent of all state enterprises were to be sold for cash or privatization vouchers), and the consolidation of the banking sector, including the closure of up to fe insolvent banks. In addition, 71 enterprises employing 230,000 people (10 per cent of the workforce) and responsible for 50 per cent of state enterprise losses in 1995 were to be cut off from fresh f nance from the state budget or the state banking system from July 1996. These enterprises were given one year in which to devise restructuring plans, with the successful ones to be privatized and the unsuccessful ones to be liquidated. This 'financial isolation' programme was largely successful in reimposing financial discipline and in forcing the downsizing of enterprises and the preparation of restructuring and privatization plans., while the even more drastic 'liquidation' programme' was largely completed by July 1997 (*FT*, 14 May 1996, p. 2; *FT*, 17 May 1996, p. 2; EBRD 1996b: 143; EBRD 1997a: 27; and EBRD 1997b: 159).

Under a stabilization and mass privatization programme agreed with the IMF in May–June 1996, all state enterprises except the utilities and a small number of 'strategic' enterprises were to be transferred into private hands by mid-1998. In October 1996 shares in 968 enterprises (with a book value equivalent to 11 per cent of GDP) were offered to the public and eighty-one specialized investment funds, which had attracted two-thirds of the vouchers that had been issued to the population (EBRD 1997a: 27). This first round of mass privatization came to an end in July 1997, and privatization vouchers became tradable on the stock exchange on 3 March 1998. Bulgaria became a member of the WTO in December 1996.

On 15 July 1996 President Zhelev warned of possible mass unrest in the autumn because of mounting political and economic chaos, and he appealed for the introduction of strong presidential rule (*IHT*, 16 July 1996, p. 5), but his request was refused. On 24 September the central bank raised its base interest rate to 300 per cent (from the 108 per cent set in May 1996) and put nine banks under special supervision (*FT*, 25 September 1996, p. 2), while Bulgaria's nouveaux riches increasingly squirreled much of their capital out of the country (*IHT*, 29 October 1996, p. 8).

Ex-premier Andrei Lukanov, who had become one of Bulgaria's major *nomenklatura capitalists*, with close links to the increasingly intertwined Bulgarian and Russian mafias, was murdered outside his home on 2 October 1996. The murder wa widely seen as resulting from 'conflict between powerful economic interests' (FT, 3 October 1996, p. 2).

In the two-stage presidential election held on 27 October and 3 November 1996, the UDF decided to back Petar Stoyanov in preference to the incumbent Zheliu Zhelev as its presidential candidate. Stoyanov won in the second round with 59.73

per cent of the vote, against 40.27 per cent for the BSP candidate Ivan Marazo, on a turn-out of 61 per cent.

Prime minister Zhan Videnov survived a vote of no confidence at a plenum of th Socialist Party (by eighty-nine votes to sixty-nine, with two abstentions) on 12 November 1996, but the next day Georgi Pirinski resigned as foreign minister, claiming that the government no longer enjoyed public confidence. On 15 November there was a run on the state savings bank, amid rumours that the government was using its deposits to repay government debt.

Zhan Videnov resigned as prime minister and as leader of the BSP on 21 December 1996. Three days later Georgi Parvanov accepted the leadership of the BSP but not the premiership. On 2 January 1997 the headless BSP government announced that from mid-February 1997 it would deal with rampant inflation and the collapse of th lev by introducing a currency board system, which would tie the money supply to the level of hard currency reserves (*FT*, 4 January 1997, p. 2). The next day demonstrators in Sof a called for early parliamentary elections, as the next ones were not due until December 1998.

Unsuccessful attempts to form a new BSP-led government, January–February 1997

The BSP nominated the interior minister Nikolai Dobrev as prime minister on 6 January 1997, but the next day 1 million people in Sofia took part in protest demon strations, which continued daily. On 10 January the national assembly voted against holding an extraordinary debate on an opposition motion calling for an early general election, and opposition deputies stomped out. Protestors attacked the parliament building, and next day many were injured as riot police cleared crowds from around the parliament and escorted BSP deputies out of the building. On 12 January the BSP leader Georgi Parvanov agreed to talks with the opposition about holding an early general election, but tried to insist that he should be allowed to form a new government which would be allowed to last at least a year to deal with the mounting economic crisis. The next day the BSP issued a statement declaring its readiness 'to accept in principle the idea of holding early parliamentary elections in the context of implementing a national anti-crisis programme for the economic and financial stabilization of Bulgaria' On 15 January BSP deputies returned to parliament and agreed to hold elections at the end of 1997. However, protest strikes broke out in coal mines, steelworks, hospitals, schools and government off ces, while several trade-union federations threatened to call a general strike if the BSP remained in office *EEN*, 1997, vol. 11, no. 2, p. 3).

President Petar Stoyanov declared on 19 January 1997 that he was convinced that the country needed 'early parliamentary elections and a new agreement between social forces and between the government and the governed . . . People are demonstrating in the streets because their poverty has reached desperate levels.' He later added: 'Although the first UDF government under Filip Dmitrov started serious reform, mos of the last seven years we only had the pretence of reform. We deluded ourselves that we could survive without great sacrifices. But things kept getting tougher and we go deeper and deeper into debt.' January 1997 'marked the turning point when we shed our illusions' (*FT*, Survey, 21 October 1997, p. 32). Although Bulgaria had become accustomed to free elections and free media, the power of the 'mafia' over large swathes of the economy and the escalation of crime and corruption in economic life under the BSP had reached alarming proportions. Unfortunately, Bulgaria had missed its initial 'window of opportunity' to embark on rapid economic liberalization and privatization between 1990 and 1994, and this failure to implement sufficiently bol economic reforms had brought Bulgaria to its knees economically.

President Stoyanov announced on 27 January that he would give a mandate to the BSP to form a new government, but he appealed to the BSP to return the mandate immediately in order to allow a caretaker government to take office until fresh elec tions could be held. On 28 January Nikolai Dobrev accepted the mandate to form a new government, whereupon a one-hour general strike broke out across the country (*EEN*, 1997, vol. 11, no. 2, p. 4). Next day Dobrev warned of 'an explosive situation ... The chaos and power vacuum may cause a threat to civil peace. The deadlock is so complicated and the confidence in the government so low that the only alternativ is new elections.' He proposed that a caretaker government should take over for three to f ve months. A one-hour general strike took place on 29 January. The next day Dobrev announced that he was willing to give up the mandate and allow President Stoyanov to assemble a coalition government, but the strikes spread further. On 31 January parliament passed a bill which permitted a doubling of state salaries(*IHT*, 1 February 1997, p. 4).

The UDF rejected the BSP's offer of more talks on a coalition on 2 February, insisting that the BSP must f rst hand back its mandate. Under the constitution, that would have paved the way for elections within two months of a new government being formed (*IHT*, 4 February 1997, p. 5). On 4 February a joint statement was issued by the BSP and opposition parties asking President Stoyanov to call a parliamentary election in April. The BSP then tried unsuccessfully to form an interim government. 'We were never so close to civil war,' President Stoyanov declared (*FT*, 5 February 1997, p. 2).

The UDF ended its boycott of parliament on 5 February, but the next day most of the BSP deputies began a boycott of their own, in protest against the agreement to hold an early election (*IHT*, 7 February 1997, p. 5). On 7 February Ivan Kostov, the leader of the UDF, declined the president's invitation to form a government, and three days later the Popular Union did likewise. Now that three invitations to form a government had been refused, Stoyanov was constitutionally empowered to appoint a caretaker government and to call an election.

On 12 February the president asked Stefan Sofianski, the UDF mayor of Sofia, to head a caretaker government to run the country until the parliamentary election called for 19 April. Two days later the government banned the export of food and fuels, and on 17 February it announced that it would seek full membership of NATO. An IMF-backed stabilization programme was announced by Sofianski on 17 March Its austerity measures were accompanied by liberalization of all prices, other than for bread, milk, chicken and cheese, which continued to benefit from temporary subsidies On 21 April all remaining price controls were abolished, other than for bread, milk, cheese and salami (*FT*, 25 April 1997, p. 2). The IMF and the Sof anski government agreed a budget deficit of 6.2 per cent of GDP for 1997, and this was approved b parliament at the end of June 1997.

The parliamentary election held on 19 April 1997

The turn-out was 60 per cent. The UDF-led coalition, comprising Ivan Kostov's UDF and the People's Union (comprising Stefan Safov's Democratic Party and Anastasia Moser's Agrarian Party), won 52.26 per cent of the vote and 137 seats, of which 123 seats went to the UDF and fourteen to the People's Union. The BSP led by Georgi Purvanov won 22.07 per cent of the vote and fifty-eight seats (relying mainly on suppor in the countryside and among the elderly). The Alliance for National Salvation (a coalition of the MRF, monarchists, republicans and environmentalists) won 7.6 per cent of the vote and nineteen seats. Euro-Left won 5.5 per cent of the vote and fourteen seats. The Bulgarian Business Bloc (led by George Ganchev) won 4.93 per cent of the vote and twelve seats.

The centre-right UDF government headed by Ivan Kostov, May 1997 to June 2001

Parliament approved the appointment of Ivan Kostov as prime minister on 21 May 1997. His cabinet was also approved. He and President Stoyanov set a fm course for macro-economic stabilization, economic reform and restructuring and membership of the EU and NATO.

After several failed stabilization attempts, a currency board was introduced on 1 July 1997, with the lev fxed at 1,000 to the Deutschmark. Controversial and difficul to implement amid Bulgaria's serious structural problems, the currency board was 'a crucial factor in the success of the . . . stabilization programme'. It combined 'a traditional rule-based exchange arrangement with legal and structural measures that addressed pressing banking sector and fiscal issues . . . Under the currency board Bulgaria reduced annual inflation to 13 per cent by mid-1998 and to 1 per cent by th end of 1998 while rebuilding foreign exchange reserves from less than $800 million to more than $3 billion.' The Bulgarian National Bank basic interest rate, which had exceeded 200 per cent in late 1996 and early 1997, fell to 5.2 per cent by the end of 1998, and 'Bulgaria's stabilization was not disrupted by Russia's crisis of mid-1998, despite close economic ties between Bulgaria and Russia' (Gulde 1999: 36–9).

Bulgaria was not included among the countries which the EU Commission recommended on 16 July 1997 to be allowed to begin EU membership negotiations in early 1998. However, along with Slovakia, Latvia, Lithuania and Romania, Bulgaria was to be given special EU aid to help meet the conditions necessary for membership negotiations to begin. These recommendations were ratified by a meeting of EU head of government (European Council) in Luxembourg on 13 December 1997.

The Kostov government announced a new privatization programme on 7 October 1997. This envisaged the privatization of 80 per cent of state enterprises by the end of 1998. Under Kostov, privatization became faster, more transparent and more concerned with corporate governance, with the acquisition by Western investors of majority stakes in Bulgaria's biggest steelworks, the state-owned telecoms operator and two state banks (*FT*, 13 October 1999, p. 34).

In October 1997 an agreement was reached between Gazprom (the Russian gas monopoly) and Bulgargas (the state gas company), which guaranteed Russian gas supplies to Bulgaria for the next ten to fifteen years. It also cleared the way for th construction of a new transit gas pipeline between Russia and western Turkey by the year 2000. The deal left a question hanging over the future of Topenergy, the energy company set up in 1994 as a joint venture between Gazprom and Bulgargas. The Kostov government insisted that any deals should be done directly between Gazprom and Bulgargas, cutting out Topenergy, and it forced Bulgarian investors in Topenergy to sell their shares to Bulgargas. On 20 March 1998, however, thegovernment signed an agreement with Gazprom for delivery of Russian gas in return for Gazprom's acquisition of 100 per cent of Topenergy (*EEN*, 1998, vol. 12, no. 5, p. 5).

On 22 October the interior minister 'named and shamed' twenty-three leading public figures who had served in the intelligence services during the Communist era Among them were fourteen members of parliament (including four from the BSP and the MRF leader Ahmed Dogan), four magistrates and a banker. Only a few were accused of informing on compatriots. Kostov declared that officials who worked fo the Communist state security services would be dismissed.

The IMF decided on 15 May 1998 to release the final tranche of a stand-by loan thereby signaling that Bulgaria was out of 'financial quarantine' and would be allowe to start borrowing again.

The high court on 4 June 1998 allowed Bulgaria's exiled ex-King Simeon II to resume possession of the Saxe-Coburg family property, which had been conf scated in 1947. From 25 May to 17 June 1996, Simeon II had visited Bulgaria for the firs time since being forced into exile in 1946 and large numbers of people had turned out to see him. He paid a second visit on 16 April 1997. He had become king at the age of six after the death of his father Boris III in 1943, but the Communists had forced him to leave Bulgaria in 1946, when it became a republic after a referendum. He had never formally abdicated. During his exile in Spain, he had spent thirteen years as chairman of the Spanish subsidiary of Thomson CSF, the French defence and electronics group (*IHT*, 13 July 2001, p. 5).

A law barring former senior Communist officials from holding public office f f ve years came into force on 4 November 1998. However, the constitutional court later annulled a controversial clause that would have banned former Communist off cials from working in the public administration, even in junior posts (*FT*, Survey, 8 March 1999, p. ii).

The second round of mass privatization started in January 1999, with foreign investors being eligible to participate this time. Strategic foreign investors had started to play larger roles in the Bulgarian economy, fostering patterns of corporate governance that increased the roles of outside institutions. At the same time, management–employee buy-outs proliferated in 1998 (EBRD 1999b: 202–3). In 1999 major progress was made in privatization, with several of the largest enterprises being sold (including Balkan Airlines and the large Kremikovtski steel works). During 1999 reforms of the tax system and the customs service helped to reduce the previously dominant role played by the half-dozen shadowy 'conglomerates' in Bulgaria's economy. The withdrawal of the conglomerates from sectors such as banking and energy created a more level playing field for investors, including foreigners*FT*, Survey, 8 March 1999, p. ii). A 'new leva', exactly equal in value to the Deutschmark, was introduced on 5 July 1999. One new lev was made equal to 1,000 old leva. The old and the new currencies circulated in parallel until the end of 1999 (*BCE*, July–August 1999, p. 11).

On 13 October 1999 the EU Commission recommended that EU leaders meeting in Helsinki in December 1999 should allow Bulgaria to begin accession negotiations in early 2000, along with Latvia, Lithuania, Malta, Romania and Slovakia. A fully flexible, multi-speed accession process was envisaged, whereby each candidate country would be allowed

> to proceed on merit, including the possibility for those which join the negotiations from 2000 to catch up with the others . . . Whether the first accessions can tak

place as from 1 January 2003 will then depend entirely on the speed with which
the applicant countries can make progress on meeting the criteria.

The EU Commission considered that Bulgaria's economy was making 'substantial
progress', but starting 'from a very low level', and that its time horizon for coping
with competitive pressures would therefore have to extend 'beyond the medium term'.
In addition, the Commission stipulated that, before starting negotiations, Bulgaria
should make further progress with economic restructuring and reform and commit
itself to 'acceptable' closure dates for the four Soviet-built and environmentally
hazardous nuclear reactors at the Kozloduy nuclear power station, which were then
providing 40 per cent of Bulgaria's electricity. More specifically, the EU insisted tha
the two oldest reactors at Kozloduy nuclear plant be shut down before 2003 and that
'the equally obsolete reactors 3 and 4 be closed by 2006' (*FT*, 14 October 1999,
pp. 1, 10; *IHT*, 14 October 1999, p. 5; *IHT*, 3 October 2002, p. 8).

Kostov announced a major reshuffle on 20 December 1999. Ten ministers, includin
three deputy prime ministers, were dismissed from the sixteen-member cabinet.
Petar Jotev, the new economics minister and deputy prime minister, was put in charge
of an economics 'super-ministry' with overarching responsibility for the ministries
of industry, commerce and tourism. Kostov himself took direct responsibility for
reform of state administration, which was seen to be crucial to Bulgaria's chances of
gaining admission to the EU.

The BSP congress in early May 2000 for the first time publicly supported eventua
Bulgarian membership of NATO, subject to approval by a referendum. In late May
Ecoglasnost ended its alliance with the BSP in protest against this decision.

In May 2000 the UDF government was 'seriously rocked by public allegations
of high-level corruption and nepotism, particularly around Kostov's own family'. The
governing elite around Kostov was denounced as 'self-serving, corrupt and arrogant'
(*EEN*, 2000, vol. 12, no. 23, pp. 3, 5). President Stoyanov joined in the criticisms:
'My most intimate fear is corruption. If our reforms are accompanied by corruption,
democracy itself will be threatened' (*The Economist*, 17 June 2000, p. 56). However,
on 18 May a BSP-proposed vote of no confidence in the government failed by a wid
margin.

The second of the EU Commission's regular annual reports on Bulgaria'*Progress
Towards Accession* stated on 8 November 2000 that Bulgaria had made progress
but was still ranked second to last (just ahead of Romania) among the official candidate
for EU membership.

> Bulgaria has clearly made further progress towards becoming a functioning market
> economy. It is not yet able to cope with competitive pressure and market forces
> within the Union in the medium term. Bulgaria is establishing a satisfactory track
> record of macro-economic stabilization and performance. Good progress has
> been made in privatization, especially as regards banks . . . However, structural
> reforms still need to be taken further and enterprise restructuring needs to be
> advanced . . . Major efforts are needed to develop a strong, independent, effective
> and professional judicial system. The fight against corruption needs to be
> strengthened.

With regard to the Roma, 'further concrete actions and adequate financial resource
are still required' (EU Commission,*Progress Towards Accession*, 8 November 2000,
p. 87).

In December 2000 the EU member states decided to take Bulgaria off the list of countries whose citizens needed visas to enter the EU for visits lasting up to three months, but they maintained such visa requirements for Romanians. Bulgarians still could not take jobs in the EU. 'In return, Bulgaria agreed to restrict the entry of people from farther east, such as Moldovans and Ukrainians' (*The Economist*, 9 December 2000, p. 54).

In January 2001 the BSP launched an electoral 'Coalition for Bulgaria', bringing together fourteen other groups and civil-society movements to fight the forthcomin June 2001 parliamentary election on a joint platform (*BCE*, February 2001, p. 13).

On 8 February 2001 Bulgaria's constitutional court ruled that ex-King Simeon II could not stand in the November 2001 presidential elections as he had not been resident in Bulgaria for the requisite six months per year over the previous five years. However, the following month ten deputies launched the 'For Dialogue and Partnership' parliamentary group as a potential vehicle for Simeon II. The ruling UDF suffered several defections to Simeon II's camp. Two such defectors, Khristo Biserov and Dimitur Ivanov, floated the idea of Simeon II standing as the leader of new party, with a view to becoming prime minister after the June 2001 parliamentary elections. In March 2001 the UDF signed an electoral alliance with the MRF (*EEN*, 2001, vol. 13, no. 4, pp. 5–6).

Ex-King Simeon II, who was also henceforth officially known by his Bulgarianize name (Simeon Saxecoburggotski), formally launched a National Movement for Simeon II (NDS) on 6 April 2001. He was the first ex-king to enter politics in th former Communist states. He made his live television announcement from the symbolic setting of his former royal palace in Vrania (Sofia), which had been returne to his family in June 1998. He lamented that 'By European standards most of our people live in misery, while some politicians bathe in inexplicable luxury', and he expressed the hope that his 'movement' would win enough votes in the June 2001 election to enable it to amend the constitution to restore the monarchy (*FT*, 7 April 2001, p. 6; *The Times*, 7 April 2001, p. 19). However, on 23 April the Sofia city cour rejected the National Movement for Simeon II's application to take part in elections in June, citing nine 'substantial violations' of the law governing the formation and registration of political parties. Saxecoburggotski's legal team decided to appeal, but the deadline for registration of parties as contestants in the election was 2 May and the supreme court upheld the Sofia city court's ruling. On 29 April his team hi upon a way to circumvent these barriers. His movement would nominally form a coalition with two tiny parties which gave him their unconditional support and their legally registered names: the Party of Bulgarian Women and the Oborishte Party for National Revival. The two parties merged and chose as their joint name... the National Movement for Simeon II. On 30 April the election commission ruled that the movement could indeed use the merged parties as a 'flag of convenience'*IHT*, 7 May 2001, p. 5).

In June 2001 the governments of Bulgaria, Croatia, Romania, Macedonia, Albania, Bosnia-Herzegovina and Yugoslavia signed an agreement aimed at liberalizing trade in at least 90 per cent of goods between them, under the auspices of the EU's Stability Pact for South-eastern Europe, which aimed to enhance stability in the region through economic growth (*FT*, 28 June 2001, p. 8).

The parliamentary election of 17 June 2001

The contest was for the 240 seats in the unicameral parliament. The electoral system was based on proportional representation, but with a 4 per cent threshold. The turn-out was 67 per cent. The head of the OSCE election observers' mission stated that the election had gone 'extremely well' (*IHT*, 19 June 2001, p. 5). Only four group-ings cleared the 4 per cent threshold and gained representation in parliament (see Table 3.6).

Over the preceding four years (1997–2001) the centre-right Kostov government had pulled Bulgaria out of an economic crisis and put it on track for eventual NATO and EU membership. However, like so many economic reformers before him, Kostov had been punished 'for being too slow in delivering the fruits of reform'. Even though the economy had grown by more than 5 per cent in 2000, ordinary Bulgarians felt let down by the other realities ('rising unemployment, low pay and pensions and miser-able living standards') and by the 'widespread corruption' (*FT*, 16 June 2001, p. 15). The defeated UDF suffered for having 'failed to translate the reforms into a better standard of living for the country's 8 million people' (*FT*, 18 June 2001, p. 1). 'The Kostov government . . . privatized a lot – but mostly to politically favoured managers and dubious investors, foreign and local' (*The Economist*, 16 June 2001, p. 51). On 26 June Kostov resigned as leader of the UDF and Ekaterina Mikhailova took his place.

Saxecoburggotski ended up just one seat short of an overall majority in parliament. However, some of his opponents had resorted to electoral trickery in order to deny him an outright majority. No less than three movements bearing the name Simeon II were registered as contestants by the central electoral commission! 'Two of these movements were false ones created to divert votes from NDS. If these false move - ments had not been there, NDS would have won 134 seats out of the 240 in parliament.' Nearly 5 per cent of the NDS vote was lost to these false movements (*EEN*, 2001, vol. 13, no. 5, p. 2).

The sixty-four-year-old Saxecoburggotski fought his campaign on a promise to raise the average monthly pay packet to 400 levs within 800 days. Ivan Kostov accused him of 'wild populism' (*The Times*, 16 June 2001, p. 20), but Saxecoburggotski explained that 'The 800 days is simply a normal economic parameter': the first year would be for 'damage control or assessment', to see what has to be done; the second year would be to 'start building and put in place the trend'; and in the third year the 'shareholders' would reap their 'dividends' (*Independent*, 16 June 2001, p. 18; *The Times*, 18 June 2001, p. 15). He promised 'to create jobs and spur invest-ment in a country where living standards are plummeting' (*IHT*, 16 June 2001, p. 2). He certainly benefited from widespread disillusionment with the BSP, the UDF an

3.6 Bulgarian parliamentary election, 17 June 2001

Party	Share of vote (%)	Seats
National Movement for Simeon II (NDS)	43.4	120
Union of Democratic Forces (UDF)	18.3	51
BSP-led 'Coalition for Bulgaria'	17.4	48
Movement for Rights and Freedoms (MRF)	6.7	21

the old elite. Part of his appeal was 'simply that the other parties are so unloved and distrusted. Some nine out of ten voters think that the UDF is corrupt. The Socialists have also lost any credit that they might once have enjoyed' (*Independent*, 16 June 2001, p. 18). While not ruling out a restoration of the monarchy, Simeon 'said the country must concentrate its energies on building the economy' (*IHT*, 18 June 2001, p. 4). According to opinion polls, there was 'only about 15 per cent support for restoring the monarchy' (*Independent*, 19 June 2001, p. 11). Indeed, the election result 'was not a public endorsement for reinstating the monarchy – there is little support for that. It was a massive protest against existing political parties from a nation tired of living in poverty' (*Independent*, 13 July 2001, p. 13). As Ivan Kostov stated in hindsight: 'We have taken a lot of unpopular decisions and also made mistakes. We wanted the voter to pay a higher price than he was prepared to pay' (*Independent*, 19 June 2001, p. 11).

During the previous three years, Saxecoburggotski had built up a team of Western-educated economists in their early thirties who had worked for British and American banks. A City of London pub had been home to the Bulgarian City Club, a group of expatriate economists and bankers who had largely drafted Saxecoburggotski's economic strategy. Members of the group were also approached for important positions in heading the privatization agency (*FT*, 26 July 2001, p. 6). This team devised a radical neo-liberal reform programme, including tax cuts, public-spending cuts and a target of zero public borrowing. They intended 'to follow a similar road to the UDF but faster, more efficiently and with less corruption'. They promised to accelerate the privatization programme (*FT*, 18 June 2001, p. 1), to introduce incen tives for small and medium enterprises and fight corruption and organized crime (*The Times*, 16 June 2001, p. 20) and to provide 'early increases in public pay and pensions and, most controversially, interest-free loans of 5,000 levs available to all' (*FT*, 16 June 2001, p. 15). However, on the day after the election, they had already started hedging and backtracking on their promises! (*Independent*, 19 June 2001, p. 11).

At the core of Saxecoburggotski's economic team were Nikolai Vasilev, a thirty-two-year-old f nancial analyst from Lazard Capital Markets in the City of London, and Milen Velchev, a thirty-five-year-old vice president of the emerging-markets unit of Merrill Lynch in London. Both Vasilev and Velchev had studied at universities in the USA before arriving in London as analysts of emerging markets (*FT*, 25 July 2001, p. 6). They were intent on reducing licensing requirements to cut down on bureaucratic red tape and the scope for bribe-taking, exempting reinvested profits and capital gains from tax, and cutting taxes, while reducing the budget deficit to zero, providing interest-free loans to aspiring entrepreneurs and maintaining the currency board. They drove voter expectations 'sky-high, encouraged by Simeon's populist campaign promises' (*BCE*, July–August 2001, pp. 39–40).

In view of the fact that the Saxecoburggotski government was punished in the June 2005 parliamentary election for failing to deliver on its promise of a tangible leap in living standards within four years and for failing to act with sufficient vigou against the corruption for which it had so strongly criticized the Kostov government, it is significant that from the start some economists claimed that Saxecoburggotski' financial programme was 'unrealistic' and that his figures simply did not add up, i promising 'zero-rate corporate tax to attract foreign investment and lower personal income tax – but also a balanced budget' *Independent*, 18 June 2001, p. 11). President Stoyanov was also critical of Saxecoburggotski from the outset, 'accusing him of dealing in fairy tales at a time when the country needs firm stewardship' (*Daily Telegraph*, 18 June 2001, p. 11).

The centre-right government headed by Simeon Saxecoburggotski, August 2001 to June 2005

In spite of his team's vaunted 'preparations for government' and their electoral promises to move fast and deliver tangible benefits for ordinary Bulgarians within 80 days, the Saxecoburggotski team actually got off to a very slow start and wasted much valuable time. In order to maintain the considerable momentum of the UDF-initiated reform programme of 1997–2001, it might well have been much more advantageous for Bulgaria to have re-elected the far more experienced Kostov government, but democratic elections rarely result in the wisest of choices. The reality was that Saxecoburggotski had entered the parliamentary contest somewhat opportunistically, at almost the last possible moment, and was therefore actually very ill prepared for government. Until shortly before the election, he had been aspiring to become president and possibly king of Bulgaria, rather than head of government, while his economic team was dominated by young City of London bankers with no prior experience of governing a country, a task whose complexity rarely lends itself to simplistic bankers' nostrums! Saxecoburggotski had not even prepared the ground by aligning himself in advance with a would-be coalition partner. By the time he had resolved the choice of partner (needed to secure a working majority), parliament was preparing for its summer recess. The government's programme was not fully worked out and presented to parliament until autumn 2001.

The MRF leader Ahmed Dogan offered to enter a coalition with the NDS on 5 July. On 12 July Saxecoburggotski was nominated as prime minister and was required to put together a government by 22 July. On 15 July Saxecoburggotski stated that he hoped the outgoing UDF would participate in his government (*FT*, 16 July 2001, p. 6). Saxecoburggotski named his proposed cabinet on 22 July. His declared intention was to include as many 'experts' as possible, ignoring political affiliations. It included two ethnic Turks from the MRF, whose seats gave the coalition 141 seats in the 240-seat chamber. The deputy prime ministers included Nikolai Vasilev, who was also to be economics minister. Milen Velchev was named finance minister. Other deputy prime ministers included forty-year-old Kostadin Paskalev, a former BSP mayor of the university city of Blagoevgrad, who also held the regional development and urbanization portfolio, and forty-four-year-old Lydia Shuleva, who headed the ministry of labour and social affairs (*IHT*, 23 July 2001, p. 4). While the economy would be in new hands, the appointment of Solomon Passy as foreign minister underscored Saxecoburggotski's 'desire for continuity in Bulgaria's drive to join NATO and the EU'. Passy was the founding director of the Atlantic Club, an NGO which had spearheaded Bulgaria's drive for NATO membership (*FT*, 25 July 2001, p. 6). However, the inclusion of two experts from the BSP prompted the UDF to refuse to take part in the coalition (*FT*, 23 July 2001, p. 9).

Milen Velchev reiterated that their economic philosophy was much the same as the UDF's, but that their policy for implementing it would be more radical, and he reeled off a list of measures he hoped to enact: 'abolishing taxes on profits reinveste in the company; lowering income tax gradually from a top rate of 38 per cent to 29 per cent; removing capital gains taxes; letting foreigners buy land; and rapidly privatizing . . . telecoms, the tobacco monopoly, gas distribution, energy utilities and two big banks' (*The Economist*, 21 July 2001, p. 39).

On 24 July parliament approved Saxecoburggotski by 141 votes to 50, with 46 abstentions, and the ex-king took an oath of allegiance to the republican constitution in front of Patriarch Maxim of the Bulgarian Orthodox Church (*IHT*, 25 July 2001, p. 1). The UDF voted against the new government and criticized Saxecoburggotski for nominating two members of the BSP as ministers, but its leaders gave assurances that 'they would cooperate with the new government' in continuing 'the reformist programme of the past four years'. Saxecoburggotski affirmed his coalition's deter mination to fight corruption by introducing strict procedures and 'one-stop-shops' for processing new investments (*FT*, 25 July 2001, p. 6).

Saxecoburggotski unveiled more of his economic programme on 20 August 2001, promising to cut taxes, to raise the minimum wage, to double child-welfare payments, to reduce the state payroll by 10 per cent and to raise electricity prices. Finance-ministry off cials claimed that 'increased spending would be funded by more efficient revenue collection and by fighting corruption' *Daily Telegraph*, 21 August 2001, p. 12). However, this package dashed hopes of any early increases in pensions and public-sector wages, and it promised to cut income tax in ways that seemed 'to help the rich more than the poor. The government honoured a pledge of zero tax on reinvested profits, but then had to back down under pressure from the IMF which also insisted on a smaller 2002 budget deficit than the government wanted.' I addition, the privatization law was 'amended to eliminate some unwise privileges for management-employee buy-outs' (*The Economist*, 24 November 2001, p. 48).

Thousands of demonstrators from across the country marched through Sofia on November 2001, the hundredth day of Saxecoburggotski's term as prime minister, to protest against his perceived failure to act on his election-campaign pledges. The protest was organized by the two main trade unions. 'Transportation workers, doctors . . . and teachers gathered to protest against "poverty, destitution and unemployment" . . . Protesters demanded a minimum 20 per cent pay rise for the next year and payments of delayed salaries.' However, the tough talks with the IMF over a funding deal had 'forced the government to agree to measures that curbed plans to increase spending and eased the tax burden on business', while Saxecoburggotski's anti-corruption drive had so far 'failed to achieve a single conviction' and no reform legislation had as yet reached parliament (*IHT*, 2 November 2001, p. 6).

In the f rst round of the presidential election on 11 November 2001, the incumbent Petar Stoyanov (35 per cent) and the Bulgarian Socialist Party leader Georgi Parvanov (36 per cent) went through to the second round (*IHT*, 19 November 2001, p. 5). In the second round on 18 November Georgi Parvanov won 53.3 per cent of the vote compared with Petar Stoyanov's 46.7 per cent, on a turn-out of 54.5 per cent. Saxecoburggotski was 'ditheringly late and lukewarm in backing . . . Stoyanov' (*The Economist*, 24 November 2001, p. 48). The victorious Parvanov promised to work to speed up the negotiations on membership of the EU and NATO, 'naturally on the basis of meeting their criteria', but declared that it was 'also extremely important to revive Bulgaria's relations with Russia, Ukraine and other strategic partners' (*IHT*, 20 November 2001, p. 2). He also pledged to work 'for a stronger role of the state' in alleviating economic burdens. He was backed by the MRF, several Gypsy organizations and pensioners' organizations, as well as by the BSP (*IHT*, 20 November 2001, p. 2).

The EU published the third of its regular annual progress reports on the twelve applicants negotiating for EU membership on 13 November 2001. As many as ten countries were deemed likely to be ready to join the EU in 2004, but Bulgaria and Romania were not among them. On the face of it, this should have dealt a further blow to Saxecoburggotski's reform and restructuring programme, but in practice it helped to shake the government out of its complacency and galvanize it into activity.

A Bulgarian court jailed two members of the former Communist security police on 11 April 2002 for having destroyed 140,000 files in 1990, some of which relate to the murder of the exiled Bulgarian dissident Georgi Markov in London on 11 September 1978. (Markov's killer has never been caught.) The shredded files almos certainly also contained information on the alleged plot to kill Pope John Paul II. In June 1992 a former chief of Communist Bulgaria's intelligence service had been sentenced to sixteen months in jail for destroying ten volumes of material, while a second suspect had 'committed suicide rather than face trial for destroying the files and another former member of the Bulgarian intelligence service died in an unexplained car crash' (*The Times*, 12 April 2002, p. 16). By this time Mehmet Ali Agca, the Turk who tried to kill the Pope in St Peter's Square in Rome on 13 May 1981, had repeatedly stated that the Soviet KGB and the Bulgarian Communist government of Todor Zhivkov were behind the attack (*IHT*, 2 November 2001, p. 6). However, during his papal visit to Bulgaria on 23–25 May 2002, Pope John Paul II declared that he had never believed that Mehmet Ali Agca was working for the Bulgarian secret service (*IHT*, 25 May 2002, p. 5).

In September 2002 a *Financial Times* survey on Bulgaria reported that the Saxecoburggotski government had 'seen its support fade for failing to deliver on an election promise to raise living standards and a perceived failure in tackling corruption . . . While the new government seems to be corruption-free at the top and has taken action against alleged bribe-takers, bribery among bureaucrats remains widespread' (*FT*, Survey, 2 October 2002, p. 14). However, the Saxecoburggotski government was tenacious in delivering its neo-liberal agenda. It 'kept tight control of public finances'. Taxes were cut and simplified, and utility charges were rais towards commercial levels. The maximum rate of income tax was 29 per cent, and there was no capital gains tax for stock-market investments (*FT*, Survey, 2 October 2002, p. 14).

The Bulgarian parliament defied the government and the EU on 2 October 2002 by voting not to close two Soviet-designed reactors before joining the EU, despite EU demands that the reactors be decommissioned by 2006. 'The Bulgarian parliament insisted that the closing date for the third and fourth reactors "must take into account the country's socio-economic capacities and must not take place before Bulgaria's full and complete entry into the EU"' (*IHT*, 3 October 2002, p. 8). A week later the EU Commission recommended that the potential accession of Bulgaria and Romania to the EU should be delayed until 2007, although in November 2002 (partly as a sort of 'consolation prize') Bulgaria was accepted for entry into NATO in March 2004. In its October 2002 report on Bulgaria's *Progress Towards Accession,* the Commission reaffirmed tha

> Bulgaria is a functioning market economy. It should be able to cope with competitive pressure and market forces within the Union in the medium term, provided that it continues implementing its reform programme to remove remaining difficulties . . Further efforts are needed to improve the flexibility o markets. In particular, the efficiency of the administrative and judicial syste has to be reinforced, to allow economic agents to make decisions in a climate of

stability and flexibility . . . Administrative capacity has developed, although significant further efforts remain to be made. More attention needs to be paid to how laws will be implemented and enforced. In this regard, progress on public administration and judicial reform needs to be sustained . . Bulgaria needs to make sustained efforts to develop sufficient administrative and judicial capacity to implement and enforce the *acquis communautaire* [the accumulated body of EU legislation] . . . Corruption . . . remains a cause for serious concern . . . Concerning the Roma community, little has been done to remedy problems of social discrimination or to take action to improve very poor living conditions.

(EU Commission, *Progress Towards Accession,*
9 October 2002, pp. 127–30).

In July 2003 the IMF described Bulgaria's economic performance under the Saxecoburggotski government as 'excellent', with fairly steady economic growth of 5 per cent per annum, while expressing concern that the government's falling popularity was sapping its will to persevere with its neo-liberal reform programme (*The Economist*, 1 November 2003, p. 42).

On 7 August f nance minister Milen Velchev announced that he wished to resign due to insufficient support for tough fiscal discipline and to pressure to postpone crackdown on customs fraud. It was initially unclear whether Saxecoburggotski would accept his resignation. Krassimir Katev, the deputy finance minister responsible for ref nancing the country's foreign debt, had already said that he planned to leave the government and there was also speculation that Nikolai Vasilev, who had recently been demoted to transport minister, would also quit. However, Velchev withdrew his resignation on 20 August, after Saxecoburggotski rallied support for maintaining tight wage policies in 2004 and legislation to close a network of duty-free shops which were regarded as channels for smuggling of cigarettes, alcohol and coffee.

In the two-round municipal elections held in October 2003, the BSP obtained about 33 per cent of the votes cast, followed by the UDF with about 21 per cent, while the MRF gained a respectable 11 per cent. Saxecoburggotski's movement also obtained 11 per cent – only one-third of the level of support it had garnered in the June 2001 parliamentary election. The turn-out was 47 per cent in the first round and 50 per cen in the second (Krastev 2004: 160), the lowest level since the fall of Communism but not as poor as in some East Central European states.

In its November 2003 annual report on Bulgaria's *Progress Towards Accession*, the EU Commission warned that

Sustained efforts will be necessary to further implement the public administration reform and to fulf l Bulgaria's aim to have a qualif ed and eff cient civil service in the medium term . . . Bulgaria needs to continue to make sustained efforts to develop sufficient administrative and judicial capacity to implement and enforc the *acquis*. . . Corruption remains a problem . . . In particular the efficiency o the administrative and judicial system has to be improved . . . Determined and sustained efforts are needed to fight discriminatory attitudes and behaviour an to address the widespread social disadvantage affecting the Roma community... The Bulgarian economy has achieved a high degree of macro-economic stability due to a good policy mix brought about by the currency board, a tight fiscal stanc and wage moderation . . . The flexibility of product and labour markets needs t be further enhanced . . . The privatization programme needs to be completed . . . Over the past year Bulgaria has continued to make good progress in most areas of the *acquis* and is on track to complete the required legislative transposition before the planned date of accession if the current pace of progress is maintained. Regarding the internal market, Bulgaria has made further progress. In free movement of goods progress continued . . . As regards free movement of persons, progress was limited and considerable further work is needed concerning mutual recognition of qualifications . . and the establishment of the necessary administrative bodies for the future co-ordination of social security systems. . . In the area of free movement of capital Bulgaria has made good progress in adopting new legislation on capital movements and payments, and anti-money laundering.

(EU Commission, *Progress Towards Accession*,
5 November 2003, pp. 121–4).

The commission reaffirmed that Bulgaria could be ready to join the EU by 2007

Bulgaria acceded to NATO on 29 March 2004, along with Romania, Estonia, Latvia, Lithuania, Slovakia and Slovenia.

In August 2004 an EU report on crime in Europe concluded that Bulgaria 'constitutes the weakest link in the fight against organized crime in the Balkans'. It gangs had turned mainly to smuggling, drug-trafficking and prostitution rackets an had become embroiled in conflicts during which dozens of powerful criminals ha been assassinated since the beginning of 2003. The minister of the interior claimed that 128 of the 260 gangs believed to be operating in Bulgaria had been 'neutralized' during 2003, but Bulgaria's minister for European integration expressed fears that failure to end gang wars and reform an inefficient justice system, rampant crim and the inability of the courts and law-enforcement off cials to address the problem could delay entry into the EU until 2008 (*IHT*, 25 August 2004, p. 3). Nevertheless, in October 2004 the EU Commission declared that Romania and Bulgaria were still on track for potential entry into the EU in 2007 and that it was aiming to conclude its membership negotiations with these two states by the end of 2004. In its *Strategy Paper of the European Commission on Progress in the Enlargement Process* published on 6 October 2004, the commission affirmed tha

Bulgaria and Romania are an integral part of this enlargement process which was launched in 1997 . . . The EU's objective is to welcome both countries in January 2007, if they are ready . . They need to continue their efforts to develop sufficient administrative and judicial capacity to implement and enforce the *acquis*.

However, since 'the period between the end of the negotiations and Bulgaria's and Romania's expected date of accession is likely to be long, and given the large number of commitments that still need to be fulfilled', the commission considered that as a precaution their accession treaties had to contain '*safeguard clauses*' which would allow the commission to recommend a one-year postponement of their accession 'if there is clear evidence that there is a serious risk that Bulgaria or Romania will be manifestly unprepared to meet the requirements of membership' (pp. 2–4).

In its October 2004 *Regular Report on Bulgaria's Progress Towards Accession*, the commission also warned that

Certain key parts of the reform of the judiciary remain to be adopted. The complexity and efficiency of the penal structures, in particular in the pre-trial stage, is a matter of concern. Strong efforts will be necessary to foster Bulgaria's capacity to prosecute organized crime and corruption, which involves further reforms in the structures of the judiciary and of the police. Bulgaria has implemented several measures in the fight against corruption, but it remains a problem Renewed efforts are needed, including tackling high level corruption . . .
Trafficking in human beings is a serious problem . . . Efforts have been made in the past years to develop a framework to tackle the problems faced by minorities, but the situation on the ground has not evolved much. Sustained efforts including allocation of appropriated financial resources will be necessary to effectively implement the intentions and to combat in particular anti-Roma prejudice . . . Efforts to improve the framework in the f ght against money laundering should be maintained.

(pp. 140–4).

The government responded by immediately announcing that, prior to entering the EU, Bulgaria would introduce a new penal code which would (among other things) end the immunity of judicial offcials from criminal prosecution (*FT*, 7 October 2004, p. 10). Bulgaria and Romania were both allowed to sign treaties of accession to the EU on 25 April 2005, albeit with the aforementioned 'safeguard clauses'.

In November 2004 parliament approved a cut in corporation tax from 19.5 per cent to 15 per cent, which for a time gave Bulgaria the lowest tax rate for business in South-east Europe. Personal income tax rates were also cut, the highest bracket from 29 per cent to 24 per cent (*FT*, Survey, 16 November 2004, p. 33).

Around 15,000 workers demonstrated in Sofia on 10 November 2004, calling fo the Saxecoburggotski government to resign for having failed to improve living stand ards (*IHT*, 11 November 2004, p. 4). However, the government, which by then stood very little chance of winning the fast-approaching parliamentary elections of June 2005, decided to stick to its guns and 'go down ghting' by maintaining a very stringent f scal policy in the run-up to the planned accession to the EU in 2007.

Bulgaria's growing cooperation with the USA, 2001–5

The government headed by Ivan Kostov from 1997 to 2001 pursued a strongly pro-USA and pro-NATO foreign policy, and on 22 November 1999 Bill Clinton became the first US president ever to visit Bulgaria. In a similar vein, following the 11 September 2001 terrorist attacks on the USA the Saxecoburggotski government seized every opportunity to support and assist the USA. In 2001, Bulgarian airspace was made available to US bombers carrying out attacks on the Taliban regime in Afghanistan and Bulgarian airbases were made available to fly food parcels to Afghanistan, while in 2002 Bulgaria also sent soldiers to Kabul(*FT*, Survey, 2 October 2002, p. 14). US tanker aircraft, which refuelled US warplanes operating over Afghanistan, started operating from a Bulgarian military airport on the Black Sea, which became, de-facto, a US airbase. This was the first time since 1918 that Bulgari had ever provided a base from which foreign forces could operate from Bulgarian soil – something it had managed to avoid even during the Second World War and during the Warsaw Pact era. Both Bulgaria and Romania opened up their airspace to the USA unconditionally, offered the USA the use of all their land and seaport facilities, sent troops to Afghanistan and tripled the size of their forces in the international peacekeeping missions in the Balkans in order to free up US forces for use in Afghanistan. The Bulgarian government also provided a specialized mountain unit for service in Iraq in 2003 (*IHT*, 26 March 2002, pp. 1, 4).

By October 2004, 480 Bulgarian troops had been deployed in Iraq. Two Bulgarian truck drivers were beheaded in Iraq in July 2004 and seven Bulgarian soldiers were killed there in December 2003 and autumn 2004. By then, opinion polls were indicating that almost two-thirds of voters opposed Bulgarian military involvement in the US-led occupation of Iraq, but the calls for the recall of Bulgarian troops were 'relatively muted' (*IHT*, 28 October 2004, p. 3).

In May 2005, after Bulgaria had suffered its tenth military fatality in Iraq, an opinion poll reported that 70 per cent of Bulgarians wanted their country's troops with-drawn and parliament voted by 110 to 53 (with 45 abstentions) to pull 462 Bulgarian troops out of Iraq by 31 December 2005. The defence minister announced that negotiations on other forms of participation in the Iraqi operation were underway and that Bulgaria would help to rebuild Iraq and train its armed forces (*IHT*, 6 May 2005, p. 4).

The parliamentary election of 25 June 2005

Despite the unpopularity of Saxecoburggotski's participation in the US-led occupation of Iraq, this did not seem to have a major impact on his movement's performance in the election, in which it actually obtained far more votes than almost anyone anticipated – thereby improving its chances of entering a new coalition government (see Table 3.7). In fact, bread-and-butter issues and perceived failure to reduce corruption appeared to weigh much more heavily with Bulgarian voters. Furthermore, while viewing Bulgaria's participation in the Iraq operation with considerable distaste, many Bulgarians seem to have understood or even accepted the pragmatic advantages of subservience to the world's only superpower and the leader of NATO. This reduced their sense of international isolation, given that they had not yet been definitely accepted into the EU.

The BSP failed to gain the overall majority that it had been anticipating. Although the MRF soon declared its willingness to join a coalition with the BSP, even this was insufficient to assure a working majority. Saxecoburggotski also indicated his willingness to take part in a coalition government, but tried to insist on remaining prime minister. A seven-week stand-off ensued between Saxecoburggotski and Sergei Stanishev, the BSP leader, as each held out for the post of prime minister.

3.7 Bulgarian parliamentary election, 25 June 2005

Party	Share of vote (%)
Bulgarian Socialist Party (BSP), led by Sergei Stanishev	31.0
National Movement for Simeon II, led by Simeon Saxecoburggotski (NDS)	19.9
Movement for Rights and Freedoms (MRF)	12.8
Union of Democratic Forces (UDF)	7.7
Ataka (Attack) coalition, led by the ultra-nationalist Volen Siderov	8.1
Democrats for a Strong Bulgaria, led by the former UDF premier Ivan Kostov	6.4
The Bulgarian People's Union	5.2

Note: Turn-out 56 per cent.

The national assembly approved the nomination of Stanishev as prime minister by 120 votes to 119 on 27 July 2005, but it subsequently voted down his proposed cabinet. Saxecoburggotski was then given a chance to form a government, but he too was unsuccessful. Finally, on 15 August 2005 Bulgaria's three largest parties agreed to form a coalition government headed by Sergei Stanishev, after the seven-week deadlock threatened to delay Bulgaria's entry to the EU from 2007 to 2008 under the 'safeguard clause' in the treaty of accession. The new government appeared to be backed by 169 of the 240 deputies (*IHT*, 16 August 2005, p. 3). The following day parliament confirmed Stanishev as the new prime minister, by 168 votes to 67. Thi alliance of Bulgaria's three biggest parties was 'a last resort after two failed attempts at forming a government threatened to push the country into new elections' (*IHT*, 17 August 2005, p. 4).

The privatization of the banking sector was almost complete in 2005, 'with over 80 per cent of banking assets in the hands of foreign-owned institutions'. In late 2005 the central bank announced that Bulgaria would adopt the euro in 2010, three years after the target EU entry date of 2007. The currency board arrangement remained f rmly in place (EBRD 2005b: 114–15).

The EU Commission's annual progress reports on 25 October 2005 warned that both Bulgaria and Romania risked having their accession to the EU delayed until 2008 if fraud, bribery, piracy of intellectual property and organized crime were not brought under control by the time that EU governments decided in April 2006 whether to allow them to become members in 2007. The commission's reports high-lighted the slow pace of judicial reform in both countries, worryingly large backlogs of cases in their court systems, and rampant organized crime and human-trafficking The reports highlighted continuing deficiencies in administrative capacity, press freedom, access of Roma (Gypsies) to jobs and housing, privatization, bankruptcy procedures, use of regional-development funds and labour-market f exibility. They asked both countries to speed up the implementation of laws in areas ranging from environmental protection and treatment of psychiatric patients to justice and home affairs. The Romanian and Bulgarian governments immediately vowed to redouble their campaigns against crime and corruption. The EU Commission warned that Bulgaria's failure to get organized crime under control was undermining its chances of joining the EU on schedule in January 2007. Over sixty mobsters had been assassinated in car bombings and shoot-outs in Sofia and other cities in Bulgaria ove the previous three years, without any arrests. The pace of such killings was accelerating, with eight murders in the previous three months. Two reasons for the scale of the problem were that Bulgaria was a conduit between Turkey and Europe for traffickin in people and drugs and that it had a corrupt, ineff cient judiciary. Parliament f nally pushed through a new criminal code, drawn up after consultations with Brussels. The very next day, however, Emil Kyulev, chairman of DZI-Rosexim, the country's biggest f nancial group, was shot dead in the centre of Sof a. The gunman escaped. Kyulev had 'apparently shaken off a shady past to become a high-flying banker', i which capacity he served as a financial adviser to President Georgi Parvanov *The Economist*, 29 October 2005, p. 42).

Concluding reflections

The biggest surprise in the June 2005 parliamentary election was the 8.1 per cent share of the vote won by the Ataka coalition headed by the charismatic, racist, xenophobic,

Turkophobic and anti-EU television broadcaster and maverick journalist Volen Siderov, who had only founded Ataka two months before the election. His strong showing was based on support from the growing pool of unemployed and impoverished Bulgarians and other marginal groups who felt let down by the recurrent crises and austerities in post-Communist Bulgaria and by perceptions that the country was gripped by endemic and largely unchecked or uncontrolled corruption at all levels of government and in business, whichever of the big parties was in government. The sudden emergence of this rather nasty movement was widely interpreted as a timely warning to Bulgaria's governing elites that they would have to redouble their efforts to bring off cial and business corruption under control and deliver tangible socio-economic rewards to Bulgaria's long-suffering population for the seemingly endless succession of crises and hardships that it had endured since the 1980s.

However, the eventual decision of the three reform-minded political parties to form a viable coalition government in late August 2005, in a bid to avoid jeopardizing Bulgaria's chance to enter the EU in January 2007 and to safeguard the very substantial economic, political and legal advances that had been achieved since the massive socio-economic convulsion and crisis of mid-1996 to mid-1997, attested to the paramount importance of the prospect of EU membership in focusing minds on what had to be done in order to strengthen the rule of law, democracy and the emerging market economy. It also demonstrated the growing willingness of Bulgaria's political elites to sink their (no longer very great) differences, in order to maintain the basically sound and advantageous course on which Bulgaria had embarked under the UDF government led by Ivan Kostov from May 1997 to June 2001 and which continued under the Saxecoburggotski government from July 2001 to June 2005.

During the early 1990s Bulgaria largely missed the initial 'window of opportunity' to get radical political and economic liberalization, privatization and painful economic restructuring over and done with fairly quickly, while the population was still relatively sanguine, confident and ready to take risks and make sacrifices. By 1994–5, wh Bulgaria's political elites (even within the BSP) began to recognize the need for more radical and far-reaching changes, much of the population was suffering great hard - ship and was deeply disillusioned, anxious, risk-averse and less able (let alone willing) to make short-term sacrifices for greater long-term reward. By then, too, much of th economy had fallen into the hands of organized crime – mainly mafia networks wh had created their own 'vertical' and highly clientelistic power relations and power networks, and who had their own reasons for being averse to radical change.

It is tempting for Western observers, in particular, to attribute this missed oppor - tunity to Bulgarian mentalities, attitudes or mindsets, which are often claimed to have been less Westernized, more obdurate, less sophisticated, more Russophile or in some way or other *deficient* by comparison with their counterparts in other Balkan post-Communist states and more especially in the East Central European states. Perhaps this has been the case – or perhaps not. It would be very hard to demonstrate scientifically either way. Our own subjective experiences have not borne ou such claims, but perhaps that is merely what we want to believe – wishful thinking. In our view, however, all such judgements are based on subjective perceptions, preconceptions and ideologically tinted lenses. Investigators usually 'discover' what they *want* to find. However, other types of explanation are available which do no depend on these forms of cultural caricature and stereotyping. It is relatively easy and (in our view) more convincing to explain Bulgaria's missed opportunity in *structural* terms.

Bulgaria under Communist rule retained strongly 'vertical', clientelistic and 'ethnic collectivist' power relations and power structures, which were preserved fairly intact through most of the 1990s. Particularly when in power, the BSP largely represented a perpetuation of those structures, which rarely came close to collapsing as completely and dramatically as they did in Albania, at the opposite pole. Even when centre-right coalitions held office, prior to 1997 these coalitions were too weak and divided to take strong stands against Bulgaria's very strongly entrenched 'vertical' power relations and power structures. The party system in Bulgaria from 1990 to 1997 was strongly polarized between the BSP and the centre-right, with each camp tending to 'demonize' the other, making cross-party cooperation and consensus on reform and restructuring especially difficult to achieve

It was not until the election of the Kostov government in April 1997 that this situation began to change fundamentally. Since then, spurred on by increasingly tough-minded governing elites and especially by the desire not to be left out of the EU, Bulgaria has been changing at impressive rates. However, this has obliged Bulgarians to start sprinting furiously to try to catch up with a train that had already left the station a year or two earlier. It was a phenomenally tall order. The organized criminal networks which had gained control of a major slice of the economy still appeared to be powerful and firmly entrenched. The EU decision on whether Bulgaria had reformed its institutions, laws, procedures and practices sufficiently to gain a positiv recommendation from the EU enlargement commissioner Olli Rehn to be allowed to proceed towards entry into the EU on 1 January 2007 was postponed from May to September 2006.

EU membership would reap recognition and reward for the huge efforts that Bulgarians have made and the hardships that they have endured on the economic front, and the reduced political polarization of Bulgaria's major political parties ought to make close cooperation and programmatic consensus between centre-right and centre-left increasingly feasible. However, there is a broad agreement that, following the rejection of the proposed EU constitution in the referendums held in France and the Netherlands in May/June 2005, the inconclusive parliamentary-election result in August 2005 and the subsequent two months of protracted wrangling over forming a new government, Bulgaria's vital judicial and institutional reform programmes seriously lost momentum – so much so, that Bulgaria suddenly became considerably less certain than Romania to be admitted to the EU on 1 January 2007.

On 16 May 2006 the EU Commission stipulated that, in order to be admitted into the EU in January 2007, Bulgaria would have to show clear results and achievements in the following areas by early October 2006: (i) investigating and prosecuting organized criminal networks, including trafficking in women, children and drugs; (ii) reforms to increase judicial efficiency, probity and independence; (iii) more effective and systematic implementation of laws and mechanisms for f ghting fraud and corruption and for preventing money laundering and the embezzlement of EU funds; (iv) strengthening border security; (v) improving conditions in psychiatric institutions; and (vi) carrying out reforms in the agricultural sector, including effective animal registration and facilities for the collection and treatment of animal by-products. There was little doubt that Bulgaria was exhibiting major problems or deficiencies i each of these areas, as well as a lack of coherent, resolute and well-focused strategies for dealing with them. The commission lamented that there had been no tangible results in investigating and prosecuting organized crime networks in Bulgaria. It noted that since 2001 over 100 maf a-style contract killings in Bulgaria had gone unpunished and that this represented a serious challenge to the rule of law. The commission warned that if problems persisted in these areas, it would propose withholding EU aid from Bulgaria even after it joined the EU (Bulgaria was expecting to receive 661 million euros in EU financial transfers during its first year of EU membership) *IHT*, 17 May 2006, p. 7). It also warned that the EU could impose so-called 'safeguard clauses' or monitoring mechanisms to ensure that conditions were met before Bulgaria was allowed full access to the benefits of EU membership. The 'safeguard clauses' coul restrict Bulgarian participation in EU decision-making. In addition, the commission could put in place a special monitoring mechanism during the first three years of Bulgarian EU membership if implementation of reforms in the justice system was deemed to be insufficiently robust before its accession, or if the fight against corrupti had not yet yielded sufficient tangible results. The monitoring system would entai annual reports by the commission to EU governments and the European parliament. A major potential penalty would be that judgements or warrants issued by Bulgarian courts would no longer be automatically recognized in other EU states. Such close monitoring of a new member state would be unprecedented in the EU (*FT*, 17 May 2006, p. 6). In theory, the EU could also postpone Bulgarian and/or Romanian entry into the EU until January 2008, but such a postponement was unlikely in Bulgaria's case because it would require*unanimous* agreement by all twenty-fve member states. However, nine of the EU's twenty-five member states (including Germany, Franc and the Netherlands) had not yet ratified the Bulgarian and Romanian accession treaties, and the potential refusal of one or more to do so could still prevent or delay Bulgarian and/or Romanian accession to the EU.

If the belated yet strong and purposeful momentum of reform built up by the Kostov and Saxecoburggotski governments from 1997 to 2005 really has dissipated, Bulgaria could easily find itself completely sidelined for a considerable time to come considering the ominous growth of xenophobia and 'enlargement fatigue' among the Western European members of the EU in 2004–6. Such an outcome could seriously diminish or throw away many of the potential rewards that Bulgaria should be reaping from the very considerable changes it has already made. In early September 2006 the EU commission made it known that it would be recommending that Bulgaria (as well as Romania) be allowed to enter the EU in January 2007, even though it was disappointed with the meagre headway Bulgaria had made in bringing corruption in high circles and organized crime under control. However, Bulgaria would be closely monitored and subject to post-accession legal and fnancial sanctions if it was judged to have failed to make further headway.

4 Romania

The road to the EU is pa ved
with good intentions

Introductory 'country profile'

By European standards, Romania is a medium-sized country with an area of 237,500 square kilometres (slightly smaller than the UK and less than half the size of France) and 21.7 million inhabitants in 2004. Its population has been declining since 1992, due to a combination of sharply reduced birth rates and considerable net emigration (which itself partly accounts for the lower birth rates, because young adults are the age group most likely to emigrate). Birth rates have been depressed mainly by grim living conditions, economic insecurity and fear for the future, as in most former Communist states. Over 5 million ethnic Romanians live outside Romania, including almost 3 million in Moldova, almost 500,000 in Ukraine, between 10,000 and 20,000 in Hungary, 40,000 in Serbia's Vojvodina, and over 1 million in Western Europe (especially Germany) and the USA (Boia 2001: 224).

Romania has a relatively mountainous terrain: 31 per cent of the land surface is classified as mountain, 36 per cent as hills and tablelands and only 33 per cent as lowland plains (primarily the Lower Danubian Plain, through which the river Danube f ows into the Black Sea). About 29 per cent of the country's total land area is classif as forest and woodland, 41 per cent as arable land, and 21 per cent as pasture, while 3 per cent is given over to permanent crops and 6 per cent to buildings and wasteland. In 1998 the population was 55 per cent urban and 45 per cent rural. Bucharest, the capital city, had just over 2 million inhabitants in 1998. The other cities with populations exceeding 200,000 inhabitants were: Iasi (349,000), Constanta (344,000), Cluj-Napoca (333,000), Galati (332,000), Timisoara (327,000), Brasov (316,000), Craiova (314,000), Ploiesti (253,000), Braila (234,000), Oradea (224,000) and Bacau (209,000) (all above data from Romania Factbook 2000 and Romania Factbook 2005). In 2004, 31.6 per cent of the workforce was employed in agriculture, 30.7 per cent in industry (including construction), and 37.7 per cent in services (CIA 2005). In 2003, agriculture accounted for only 11.7 per cent of GDP, industry for 28.4 per cent, and services for 59.9 per cent (EBRD 2005b: 169). In 2004 its per-capita GDP was 8,190 dollars at purchasing power parity (World Bank 2005: 293).

According to the 2002 population census, ethnic Romanians comprised 89.5 per cent of the population, ethnic Hungarians (Magyars) 6.6 per cent, Gypsies (Roma) 2.5 per cent, ethnic Germans 0.3 per cent, ethnic Ukrainians 0.3 per cent, ethnic Russians 0.2 per cent and ethnic Turks 0.2 per cent. The Holocaust and the subsequent emigration of most of the Jews who managed to survive it had reduced the formerly significant Jewish minority (by ethnic rather than religious affiliation) to just 0.04 pe cent of the population by the 1992 census. Only about 9,000 remained in 2001 (Boia 2001: 208).

According to the 1992 census, 70 per cent of the population were Eastern Orthodox by declared religious affiliation, 6 per cent Roman Catholic and 6 per cent Protestant while 18 per cent were declared to be unaffiliated or to have other affiliations (Roman Factbook 2005). According to the 2002 census, however, 87 per cent of the population were declared to be Eastern Orthodox ('including all sub-denominations'), 6.8 per cent Protestant, 5.6 per cent Roman Catholic, 0.4 per cent were classified as belongin to other religious affiliations (mostly Muslim), and only 0.2 per cent were unaffiliat (CIA 2005). All these figures should be taken with a pinch of salt. As elsewhere i Europe, active religious observance and belief have been steadily declining since the mid-twentieth century, and for many (perhaps most) Romanians nominal religious affiliations are no more than that. Most of the Catholics and Protestants in Romania are members of the Magyar and German minorities.

On Romania's eastern fank, the largely Romanian-inhabited territory described by tsarist Russia as 'Bessarabia' but regarded by Romanians as Eastern Moldavia was annexed to the Russian Empire from 1812 to 1918. It became part of the unified kingdom of Romania from 1918 to 1940, but was (re-)annexed by the Soviet Union in 1940–1. It returned to Romanian control in late summer 1941, following the Nazi-led invasion of the Soviet Union, but it was reoccupied by the Soviet Union in mid-1944 and reconstituted as the Soviet Socialist Republic of Moldavia from 1945 to 1991. Since its secession from the USSR in 1991, it has become universally known as Moldova. There have been no serious attempts to reunite it with the rest of Romania, partly because most Romanians regard Moldova as even less developed, less liberal, less democratic, less law-abiding, and even more gangster-ridden and corrupt than 'Romania proper'. For their part, Moldova's Romanians have had their hands tied by the fact that about 15 per cent of their country is controlled by secessionist-minded Russo-Ukrainian and Gaugaz minorities. The de-facto autonomy of this self-styled 'Republic of Transdnestria' is buttressed by the presence of substantial Russian armed forces, who are ostensibly there to guard the stockpiles of former Soviet weaponry left there by the former USSR. Partly in sober recognition of these recalcitrant 'facts on the ground', an overwhelming 95 per cent of Moldova's electorate voted in favour of Moldova remaining a formally independent state in a referendum held in March 1994 (Roper 2000: 125). This largely neutralized pan-Romanian nationalist aspirations to 'reunite' Moldova with Romania, although Romania's President Basescu (elected in December 2004) reasserted Romania's interest in Moldova.

Who are the Romanians?

At least since the mid-nineteenth century, if not earlier, Romanians have tended to see their nation as a beleaguered outpost of Latin Romance/Latin civilization amid a sea of Slavs. The name 'Romania' proclaims the country's 'Roman' heritage, harking back to a time when Romania was a distant Danubian frontier colony of the Roman Empire (formally, from AD 106 to 271). Romanian is a Romance language, with numerous resemblances to and loan words from Italian/Latin and, to lesser degrees, French. Up to the mid-nineteenth century, Romanian was written in Cyrillic script, reflecting the country's close contacts and links with its Greek and Slavic neighbours and the prevalence of Eastern (Greek) Orthodox Christianity, but since the later nineteenth century it has been written in Roman (Western) script.

The 'ethnogenesis' of the Romanians is a matter of ongoing controversy, especially between Romanian and Hungarian nationalists. Romanian nationalist histories and textbooks (especially those published under the Communist regime) have long claimed that the modern Romanian nation is lineally descended from the Roman colonists who came from all over the Roman Empire and mixed and interbred with the indigenous 'Geto-Dacian' (alias 'Thracian') inhabitants of the Roman colony of Dacia, which was established by conquest in AD 101–6 as a Danubian outpost of the Roman Empire. This claim underpins Romanian beliefs that (i) they have an ancient Western/Latin 'pedigree'; (ii) they settled in 'Dacia' (including/especially Transylvania) *long before* the settlement of Magyar (Hungarian) tribes in Transylvania in the late ninth and early tenth centuries AD; and (iii) this gives Romanians an 'ancient' and 'prior' territorial claim to Transylvania. However, Hungarian nationalist histories and textbooks claim with equal conviction that (i) there is very little hard information on the ethno-cultural characteristics of the inhabitants of Dacia (including Transylvania) between the Roman Empire's formal evacuation and liquidation of its exposed and vulnerable Dacian colony in AD 271 and the appearance of more clearly identifiabl ethnic precursors of the modern Romanians during the eleventh and twelfth centuries AD; (ii) there is no hard evidence of any direct/lineal connections between the inhabitants of ancient Dacia and those of modern Romania (including Transylvania); (iii) Transylvania's Magyar (Hungarian) inhabitants are thus the oldest *continuous* inhabitants of Transylvania and have a 'prior' territorial claim to it. There is no way of resolving these disputes here, and they may never be resolved to the satisfaction of both sides.

It is sometimes alleged that the medieval Romanian principalities of Wallachia and Moldavia, which emerged during the thirteenth and fourteenth centuries, developed various forms of serfdom in order to exploit peasant labour for the benefit of majo landholders known as *boyars* during the f fteenth and sixteenth centuries. However, Peter Sugar has argued that the economically dependent Romanian peasantry who worked on landed estates in these Danubian principalities at that time 'cannot really be called serfs because they retained some right to property and could even change their place of domicile' (Sugar 1977: 117). Admittedly, as Romanian *boyars* (estate-owners) became more powerful and increased their demands for dues in cash, kind and labour during the seventeenth century, 'the peasantry was pushed down almost to the level of serfdom' (Sugar 1977: 126). Nevertheless, even then persistently high peasant mobility (including ease of flight to adjacent territories) rendered the serf law enacted in 1600 largely unenforceable (McGowan 1997: 683). Between 1741 and 1746, for example, Wallachia lost half its peasant families through emigration (Sugar 1977: 137). Consequently, the full juridical (re-)enserfment of the Romanian peasantry on the 'second serfdom' model did not take place until the second half of the eighteenth century (Sugar 1977: 137–8), when Wallachia and Moldavia became more integrated into the international economy and the opportunities for agricultural exports produced by forced labour expanded signif cantly.

These principalities were to varying degrees isolated from the mainstream of European development and culture and fell under mainly indirect Ottoman overlordship (suzerainty) from the fifteenth to the nineteenth century. From 1711 to 1821 Ottoman suzerainty was exercised mainly through Greek clergy, servitors and merchant princes, under a mercenary and sometimes rapacious system known to historians as the 'Phanariot regime', named after the Greek merchants and clergy who came from the Phanar (lighthouse) district of Constantinople/Istanbul. The Phanariot rulers corruptly and parasitically siphoned off taxes, fines and bribes for their own enrich ment, while paying tribute to the Ottomans for the privilege of doing so. Partly as a consequence, they largely neglected to develop the principalities' physical and social infrastructure. It is sometimes claimed that these relatively parasitic and stultifying systems (both serfdom and the Phanariot system) retarded the economic development of the Danubian principalities from the sixteenth to the eighteenth century, despite their considerable agricultural potential and mineral resources. However, such claims need to be regarded as tentative until there has been further historical research on early Romanian serfdom and the effects of the Phanariot regime.

Starting in the late eighteenth century, Romanian *boyars* and their commercial intermediaries began to take advantage of growing opportunities for profitable large scale production of grain on the fertile Danubian plains for export – both to West European markets (chiefly in Italy) and to Istanbul (alias Constantinople). This large scale agriculture was based increasingly upon (re-)enserfed peasant labour until 1864, when Romania became the last major European state to abolish serfdom. Nevertheless, the participation of the Phanariot ruling classes in the eighteenth-century European Enlightenment disseminated liberal ideas and helped to sow the seeds of a modern Romanian national consciousness, which germinated during the nineteenth century.

In 1821 Ottoman suppression of a Greek revolt prompted the Ottoman Empire to terminate the Phanariot regime. From 1822 to 1864 the increasingly autonomous Danubian principalities were mainly ruled by prospering and increasingly powerful Romanian *boyars* through their councils *(divans)*. From 1829 to 1853 the Danubian principalities became Russian protectorates, experiencing Russian military occupation and rule in 1829–34 and in 1849–51. However, when Russia became embroiled in the disastrous Crimean War of 1853–6, the Danubian principalities were subjected to Austrian military occupation from 1854 to 1857.

The 'core territories' of modern Romania, the so-called Danubian principalities of Wallachia and Moldavia, were brought together under a single ruler, Alexandru Ioan Cuza, in 1859. They became a de-facto Romanian state under the patronage of the French Emperor Napoleon III during the 1860s and gained recognition as an independent state by the Berlin Congress of 1878 following Russia's victory over the Ottoman Empire in the Russo-Turkish War of 1876–7, but the predominantly Romanian-inhabited region known as Transylvania remained part of the Habsburg-ruled Kingdom of Hungary until 1918. Cuza accomplished full administrative and political unification of his principalities in 1861–2, secularized the landed estates o the Orthodox Church in 1863 (about a quarter of Romania's total land area) and won a plebiscite to broaden the franchise and augment his powers in 1864. He then launched a national schooling system, established the universities of Iasi and Bucharest, promulgated a civil code modelled on France's Code Napoléon and formally dissolved serfdom in 1864–5.

In 1866, however, Cuza was deposed and exiled by powerful Romanian *boyars*, who felt threatened by his modernizing reforms. Consequently, not only did the 5,000 largest landowners retain control of 49 per cent of Romania's arable land up to 1919, but retrograde agrarian legislation enacted in 1866 and 1872 also fostered new forms of peasant servitude (mainly peonage) to large landowners, who continued to profit from the accelerating grain export boom. By 1900–5 Romania was the world's fifth-largest grain exporter (grain provided three-quarters of its export earnings) and widespread absentee landlordism had resulted in over 70 per cent of *boyar* landholdings being leased out to intermediaries known as *arendasi*, about 27 per cent of whom were Jewish (some of whom gradually become part of the landlord class). These in turn sub-let land (mainly to very insecure share-croppers) and mercilessly exploited the peasantry. This hated *arenda* system, together with a growth of (mainly Jewish) money-lending and an influx of over 100,000 Jewish refugees from Russia, stimulate widespread Christian, anti-capitalist and xenophobic anti-Semitism. In 1907 peasant anger at this tragic perversion of the seemingly 'enlightened' 1864 agrarian reforms erupted into a massive peasant revolt, repressed by General Averescu at a cost of over 10,000 lives.

From 1866 to 1914 Romania was consolidated by Prince Carol of Hohenzollern-Sigmaringen, scion of the Catholic branch of Prussia's royal family. Carol basked in the reflected glory when Hohenzollern Prussia defeated Austria (1866) and Franc (1870) and established a German Empire (1871). German and Austrian influence an investment eclipsed that of France and drew Romania into a military alliance with Austria and Germany (the central powers) from 1883 to 1914. Romania became a fully independent state in 1878, after the defeat of the Ottoman Empire in the Russo-Turkish War of 1877–8, and (with Prussian backing) a kingdom in 1881.

The 1866 constitution, which effectively remained in force (with amendments) until 1938, allowed the monarch to appoint and dismiss ministers and governments, to dissolve the indirectly elected parliament and to veto parliamentary legislation. Carol alternated the landed conservatives and the more urban, professional and bour geois property-owning liberals in office, playing one off against the other and allowin neither to become a truly independent force. Royal patronage and control of the state apparatus, the army and the police ensured that almost any government appointed by the monarch could pre-arrange electoral outcomes and be sure of a parliamentary majority. For the most part this continued to be the case even in the 1920s and 1930s, after the introduction of universal manhood suffrage in 1918.

Between 1860 and 1910 Romania's population grew from 3.9 million to 7 million, the urban population from 313,000 (8 per cent of the total) to 1.2 million (17 per cent), and Bucharest (the capital) from 122,000 to 293,000. The railway network had expanded to 3,437 kilometres by 1910. Romanian industrialization was assisted by the adoption of protective import tariffs and discriminatory subsidies and taxation in 1885–7 and by the meteoric growth of an oil industry (92 per cent foreign-owned). Romania's annual oil output rose from 5,000 tonnes in 1860–9 to 24,600 tonnes in 1880–9, 102,900 in 1890–9, 711,000 tonnes in 1900–9, and 1.7 million tonnes in 1910–14. It ranked third in the world up to 1885, fourth from 1886 to 1909, and fift from 1910 to 1914. Buoyant export earnings assisted the establishment of a stable currency in 1880, the adoption of the gold standard in 1890, and the attraction of considerable foreign investment in physical infrastructure and extractive industries from the 1880s to 1914. During the Balkan Wars of 1912–13, in which Serbia, Montenegro, Greece and Bulgaria expelled the Ottoman Turks from nearly all their remaining Balkan territories, Romania annexed South Dobrudja (mainly inhabited by Bulgarians).

From 1914 to 1927 Romania was ruled by Carol's Prussian nephew Ferdinand of Hohenzollern, who was related to Germany's Kaiser Wilhelm II (reg. 1890–1918). During the First World War, despite King Ferdinand's German ties and Romania's 1887 treaty allying it with the central powers, the country was initially neutral. In August 1916, however, calculating that the war was turning against the central powers, Romania entered the war on the side of the Entente, hoping to seize Transylvania from Austria-Hungary, but Romania's armed forces were no match for the central powers. In December 1917, having lost over 300,000 lives and any hope of relief from Russia (by then Bolshevik-ruled), a severely mauled and outgunned Romania capitulated to the central powers, who occupied and plundered Romania's valuable oilfields and extracted forced deliveries of grain and other strategic commodities

In order to be rewarded with additional territory by the victorious Western powers, Romania briefly re-entered the First World War on the winning side in Novembe 1918. When challenged for control of Transylvania by Bela Kun's aggressively expansionist 'National Bolshevik' regime in Hungary (March–July 1919), Romanian troops occupied southern Hungary and Budapest from August to November 1919. The acquisition of Transylvania, Bessarabia and Bukovina and the reacquisition of South Dobrudja roughly doubled Romania's territory and population, but also brought in ethnic minorities who comprised nearly one-third of the expanded state's population. According to the 1930 census, the country contained 1.4 million Hungarians (8 per cent of the population), 1 million Russians and Ukrainians (5.5 per cent), 757,000 Jews (4.2 per cent), 745,000 Germans (4.1 per cent), 366,000 Bulgarians (2.0 per cent), and 263,000 Roma (1.5 per cent). The problems of fully integrating the disparate 'old' and 'new' territories, which had been under separate jurisdictions for centuries past, were greatly exacerbated by the rise of ultra-nationalist and fascist movements in inter-war Romania, most notably the fascist Iron Guard and its murderous Legion of the Archangel Michael, founded by Corneliu Codreanu in 1927 (see Bideleux and Jeffries 1998: 485–7, 492–3).

Romania experienced several major upheavals between 1907 and 1919: the massive peasant revolt of 1907; the military mobilizations of 1913, 1916–17, 1918 and 1919; the Austrian–German military occupation of 1917–18; and Romania's occupation of Transylvania and much of Hungary in 1918–20. These and the repercussions of the Russian revolutions of February and October 1917 and Bela Kun's short-lived soviet republic in Hungary in 1919 fuelled peasant and proletarian class consciousness, unrest and demands for radical change and eroded deference to social 'superiors'. Peasants and workers increasingly attributed their sufferings 'to the failures of their betters as leaders and administrators' (Mitrany 1930: 98).

King Ferdinand and the ruling classes endeavoured to appease the underprivileged classes and head off a potential revolution by promising electoral and agrarian reform. Universal *manhood* suffrage was enacted in 1918, while between 1920 and 1923 the third most radical land reform in inter-war Europe (after Bulgaria and Bolshevik Russia) redistributed over 66 per cent of the estate owners' arable land to peasants who had hitherto possessed little or no land. The reforms also expropriated the land of non-Romanians in newly acquired Transylvania, Bukovina and Bessarabia, who had for centuries cruelly oppressed Romanian peasants and labourers in the eyes of Romania's militant peasant, proletarian and nationalist parties. By 1930, 75 per cent of Romania's landholdings were under 5 hectares each (Roberts 1951: 370) and over 90 per cent of peasant farmers farmed their own landholdings (Bideleux 1985: 229).

From 1920 to 1928, Romania was dominated by the National Liberal Party (PNL) under Ionel Bratianu. This was the party of Romania's rising urban bourgeoisie, brash nouveaux riches who were voraciously committed to self-enrichment, industrialization, economic nationalism (a combination of protectionism and 'nostrification', involvin the transfer of company assets from foreign to native private ownership), embezzle-ment, nepotism and corruption. They introduced a new constitution in 1923, but perpetuated deeply corrupt, clientelistic and repressive modes of governing. Peasant and proletarian radicalism and discontent was not assuaged, and Romania remained under martial law from 1920 to 1928 and again from 1933 to 1945, while elections continued to be rigged by governments enjoying royal favour.

The 1923 constitution and the 1924 mining law restricted foreign ownership, especially in the oil industry, and precipitated a damaging British, French and American financial boycott of Romania. The national-liberal government backed dow in 1927. Romanian oil output nevertheless regained its 1912–14 average annual level (1.8 million tonnes) in 1924 and then climbed to 4.8 million tonnes in 1929 (seventh in the world) and 8.7 million tonnes in 1936 (fourth in the world), before slipping to 6.2 million tonnes in 1939.

In 1927, King Ferdinand, the PNL's royal patron, died. Ionel Bratianu also died. Since Crown Prince Carol had been exiled in 1926 (partly because of an allegedly 'scandalous' love life), exceptional circumstances allowed the reformist and relatively 'clean' national peasant party (PNT) led by Iuliu Maniu (a Romanian nationalist from Transylvania) to come to power in 1928 on a wave of revulsion against PNL malpractices, xenophobia, protectionism and neglect of both social reform and the needs of the 'new territories' (Transylvania, Bessarabia and Bukovina). As in most industrializing countries, protectionism had enriched inefficient and corrupt local industrialists and monopolists at the expense of peasant farmers and urban consumers.

The National Peasant Party government headed by Iuliu Maniu, December 1928 to October 1930

The new PNT government lifted martial law and decisively won the unusually free election of December 1928, riding on the crest of a huge wave of popular excitement and enthusiasm. It was fervently hoped that this was the start of a new era of 'genuine' democracy, 'clean' government and long-overdue reforms that would soon mark out Romania as one of Europe's most progressive and innovative democratic states. Like the UK Labour Party, but unlike most radical and socialist parties in Europe, the PNT took the view that the 'toiling classes' had more to gain from free trade than from protectionism. The PNT was also refreshingly free of xenophobic mis-trust towards foreign investors. It was strongly committed to public probity and accountability, the rule of law, universal schooling and health care, administrative decentralization, agricultural extension services, peasant marketing and credit cooperatives, freer trade and the attraction of foreign capital and technology, mainly to benefit peasants and urban consumers. The PNL had championed étatism, pro - tectionism, monopolistic prof ts, corruption and other 'closed-in' forms of prosperity for the few. The social democratic, Communist and nationalist parties and the fascist Iron Guard were propounding forms of étatism and autarky which in practice would not have been very different from the national liberal policies. The PNT, especially its f nance minister Virgil Madgearu (who was subsequently murdered by the fascist Iron Guard), was the only major party championing open-door policies and an 'open society' as the keys to greater liberty, economic health and prosperity for the bulk of the population. It combined this with policies to counteract 'urban bias' to assist and empower the peasantry (over two-thirds of the population) through rural extension services, mass education, peasant cooperatives, decentralized governance and vigorous grass-roots democracy. It was strongly influenced by Russian *narodnichestvo* (populism) and Alexander Chayanov (see Bideleux 1987: 2–11, 29–47, 53–7), while also aspiring to emulate the influential and hugely successful late nineteenth- and earl twentieth-century Danish agrarian-development model.

This bold, attractive and potentially trail-blazing socio-economic experiment was tragically ill timed. The 1930s depression slashed export earnings, peasant incomes and state revenues, caused widespread bankruptcies, unemployment and labour unrest, exacerbated inter-ethnic tensions, increased support for fascist movements, scuppered plans for trade liberalization and increased public spending on social reforms and welfare provisions, and bitterly disappointed and divided the PNT and its initially enthusiastic supporters. Largely due to global conditions beyond its control, Romania lost its best chance in decades to break out of the vicious circles of poverty, ignorance, clientelism, corruption and authoritarianism in which it had been trapped by its rapacious ruling classes. Instead, the 1930s depression launched Romania on a course towards nationalist, fascist and ultimately Communist étatism, clientelism, corruption and authoritarianism. However, the failure of the brief peasantist experiment cannot be blamed entirely on circumstances beyond anyone's control. The prime minister Iuliu Maniu was a somewhat vain, hidebound and strait-laced man of limited ability and imagination, who had risen to power as the leader of the conservative Transylvanian Romanian *nationalist* wing of the PNT, rather than its larger and more radical *peasantist* wing. A bolder and more inspiring leader could have risen to the occasion by persuading his constituents to pull together, accept material sacrif ces and press on with radical reform, even in the face of daunting economic adversity, on the grounds that all the available alternatives were greatly inferior to the peasantist programme. Even in the midst of a global economic depression, much could still have been achieved though radical mobilization and empowerment of the peasantry through education, cooperatives and rural extension services, in order to raise agri - cultural incomes and efficiency and promote rapid diversification from the low-val and worst-hit grain crops into rural industries and more intensive and lucrative production of fruit, vegetables, industrial crops and livestock products. However, Maniu had long been unenthusiastic towards the party's radical peasantist commit - ments and simply used the depression as a pretext to shelve reform until easier times, to the anger and frustration of radical peasantists.

King Carol's destabilizing and damaging 'divide-and-rule' tactics: October 1930 to August 1940

Crown Prince Carol took advantage of the incipient crisis to reclaim his throne in June 1930, to accept prime minister Maniu's pusillanimous resignation in October 1930, and to play the deeply divided parties and politicians off against each other until Romania's democracy was destroyed. Carol then established a royal-fascist dictatorship in 1938–40. Meanwhile, economic and geopolitical circumstances pushed Romania into rapidly growing commercial dependence on Nazi Germany, which by 1939 was taking 43 per cent of its exports and supplying 56 per cent of its imports (Berend and Ranki 1974: 282).

For reasons of *Realpolitik* and under the terms of the notorious Nazi–Soviet Pact (1939), the Soviet Union occupied and annexed Bessarabia (present-day Moldova) and Bukovina on 28–30 June 1940. Two months later Hitler forced King Carol to cede northern Transylvania to Hungary (on 30 August) and South Dobrudja to Bulgaria (on 7 September). In all, Romania was deprived of one-third of its previous population and territory. These losses completely discredited King Carol in the eyes of his subjects – left, right and centre. He handed the throne to his nineteen-year-old son Mihai on 6 September and f ed abroad in disgrace the following day (Hitchins 1994: 445–55).

Ion Antonescu's military-fascist dictatorship, 6 September 1940 to 23 August 1944

On 6 September 1940 King Mihai appointed General Ion Antonescu as leader (*conducator*) of the Romanian state, with full powers to govern as he saw fit (Hitchin 1994: 455, 476). Antonescu received full support from Iuliu Maniu and the PNL leader Constantin Bratianu because they believed that (i) he was 'the one person capable of establishing a working relationship with Germany that would not require the total subordination of the country to Hitler's war aims'; and (ii) 'the prevailing international situation required a temporary accommodation with Germany in order to preserve the Romanian state'. However, although Antonescu*nominally* preserved a Romanian state, he did so at the price of *completely subordinating* that state and its economy to the requirements of Nazi Germany, not only as the main supplier of liquid fuel and imported food for the German war effort, but as the 'southern anchor of the German eastern front' (Hitchins 1994: 456–8), at massive human cost. He committed twenty-seven army divisions to Germany's war against the Soviet Union, in which 300,000 Romanians perished and 200,000 were wounded (Rothschild 1974: 318). Over 150,000 Romanians were killed, lost or wounded in the Battle of Stalingrad alone (Deletant 1990: 127). Hitler, who was fighting an increasingly difficult war on several front greatly preferred the effcient, disciplined and dependable Romanian military-fascists under Antonescu to the more fanatical, wayward and disruptive fascist Iron Guard, which had repeatedly proved itself to be much more of a liability than an asset to the German war effort. It was thus with Hitler's blessing that Antonescu brutally crushed Romania's unruly Iron Guard when it rose up against him in January 1941.

Furthermore, in contrast to the royalist and pro-Axis regime in neighbouring Bulgaria, General Antonescu and his government cooperated in large measure with Hitler's 'Final Solution' of the Jewish question. There were probably about 800,000 Jews living in Romania in early 1940. After Romania lost one-third of its territory and population to the USSR, Hungary and Bulgaria in June–September 1940, only about 315,000 Jews remained under Romanian rule (Hitchins 1994: 483). About 330,000 Jews were living in Bessarabia and northern Bukovina when these territories were annexed by the USSR in late June 1940 (Mann 2005: 305). Some of these Jews quite understandably 'collaborated' with or even become members of the Soviet regime, the Red Army or the Communist Party of the Soviet Union (CPSU), because (as Jews) they naturally felt much safer from annihilation under Soviet rule than under either Nazi German or Romanian military-fascist rule. This probably meant that *some* Jews participated in the atrocities committed by the Soviet military and civil authorities against Romanians, Hungarians and Germans in Bessarabia and northern Bukovina (especially against known or suspected Romanian, Hungarian and German nationalists and fascists). However, although anti-Semitic Romanian nationalists and fascists ranted continually against 'Judaeo-Bolshevism', they greatly exaggerated the proportion of Jews who became Communists and the proportion of Communists who were Jews, in much the same way that Polish nationalists greatly exaggerated the numbers of Jews who participated in Soviet atrocities against Poles in eastern Poland between September 1939 and June 1941 and subsequently used this as a bogus pretext for anti-Semites to take savage reprisals against Jews (Gross 2000: 92–115). Consequently, when the USSR lost Bessarabia and northern Bukovina to the German–Romanian–Hungarian invasion launched in June 1941, over one-third of the Jewish inhabitants of these territories ('perhaps as many as 130,000', according to Hitchins

(1994: 485)) prudently fled eastwards with the retreating Red Army and the CPS and thus survived the war – other than those who subsequently perished either fightin for the Soviet Union, or in Soviet captivity or as prisoners captured by the Axis forces. Nevertheless, about half the 330,000 Jews of Bessarabia and northern Bukovina were killed by the Romanian–German invasion force between June and September 1941 (Mann 2005: 305). Most of the surviving Jews in these two provinces, along with 'as many as 100,000 Jews' from Romania's core territories (the Regat) and southern Transylvania, were then deported to camps in Romanian-run 'Transnistria', where from autumn 1941 to autumn 1944 about 200,000 Jews 'suffered waves of killings, deliberate starvation and cruel treatment . . . Only 50,000 Jews survived to the end of 1943' (Hitchins 1994: 485; Mann 2005: 305). Ultimately, over 80 per cent of the Jews in Romanian-controlled Transnistria were killed (Gallagher 2005: 39). During 1941 Antonescu had called repeatedly for 'the purifĉation of our Nation from all those elements foreign to its heart' (Mann 2005: 303, 305). The biggest single anti-Semitic massacre in the entire Holocaust was carried out by Romanian forces in Odessa in October 1941, where 60,000 Jews were killed in three days, using machine guns and grenades (Ioanid 2000: 178–9).

However, as soon as the tide of the war began to turn against Germany in September 1942, Antonescu rejected German demands for the deportation of Romanian Jews to the Nazi death camps; and from December 1942 he sought ways to dispatch them to Palestine instead of the Nazi gas chambers. The surviving Jews thenceforth became bargaining chips in Antonescu's fumbling and ultimately unsuccessful pursuit of a 'separate peace' with the Allies (Mann 2005: 306; Hitchins 1994: 486).

Professor Istvan Deak has estimated that at least 200,000 Jews perished on Romanian-controlled territory between 1940 and 1945. In addition, around 150,000 formerly 'Romanian' (but actually mainly Hungarian-speaking) Jews were deported to the Nazi death camps from northern Transylvania after it was annexed by Hungary in September 1940, but Romania and the Antonescu regime self-evidently cannot be made responsible for those deaths (*NYRB*, vol. 39, no. 10, 28 May 1992). Professor Lucian Boia reckons that around 300,000 Romanian Jews survived the Holocaust (Boia 2001: 210). This is consistent with a claim that by the 1950s around 300,000 Romanian Jews were living in Israel, while 23,000 remained in Romania (*NYRB*, vol. 39, no. 10, 28 May 1992). Overall, therefore, the Jewish survival rate was probably higher in Romanian-controlled territory than in most of the Nazi-occupied areas of Europe (Mann 2005: 303).

Nevertheless, the Antonescu regime and the Iron Guard undeniably had a great deal of Jewish blood on their hands. It is therefore disturbing that many Romanians continued to revere Antonescu as a saviour f gure and as a national hero of whom they felt proud during the 1990s, even going so far as to name streets after him, erect public statues to him, make nostalgic flms about him and deny that many Romanians were willing accomplices in the Holocaust (*HT*, 2 August 2002, p. 3). The continuing reverence and nostalgia towards Antonescu in 1990s Romania revealed that many Romanians were still 'in denial' towards the magnitude of their country's active complicity in the Holocaust and in Hitler's 'new order'. To some extent, these attitudes were a reflection of the extent to which the Communist regime and the subsequen Iliescu regime suppressed the evidence that around 200,000 Jews perished at the hands of the Antonescu regime and the Iron Guard.

The reversal of alliances, August 1944 to May 1945

In early 1943, as the tide turned decisively against the Axis Powers, Romanian anti-fascists formed an underground patriotic front, in which the hitherto-minuscule Romanian Communist Party (RCP) played an increasingly important role. On 23 August 1944, as the steadily advancing Soviet Red Army began to invade Romania, young King Mihai, in collusion with a small group of conspirators linked mainly to the liberal and social democratic parties and the PNT, deposed General Antonescu and appointed an anti-fascist coalition government under General Sanatescu. Books and other publications produced under the Communist regime generally portrayed the overthrow of Antonescu as the result of a 'national anti-fascist armed insurrection' carried out under the auspices of 'the patriotic national forces of Romania, whose principal nucleus was the Romanian Communist Party' (Romania 1974: 9). What actually occurred was quite literally a 'palace revolution' (the conspirators lured Antonescu into the royal safe to admire young King Mihai's stamp collection and then locked the door on him). The RCP, which had less than 1,000 members at that time, was far too small to have spearheaded a 'national anti-fascist armed insurrection' at that time. The only Communist participant in the arrest of General Antonescu was Emil Bodnaras, a Ukrainian former army officer who had been flown into Roman from Moscow earlier that summer. The only RCP member to obtain a ministerial post in the new government was the moderate and relatively 'bourgeois' lawyer Lucretiu Patrascanu, who became minister of justice. Thus this 'palace revolution' was not part of a covert plan to bring the Communists to power, even though (primarily to propitiate the Soviet Union) Bodnaras and Patrascanu were allowed to play cameo roles in it. Rather, it was a desperate last-ditch attempt by Romanian patriots to prevent their country from falling into the hands of the Red Army and a Soviet-sponsored Communist regime. In July 1945, significantly, Stalin awarded King Mihai a ruby studded Soviet Order of Victory in recognition of his pivotal role in the deposition of Antonescu, which rapidly halted Romanian resistance to the Soviet invasion and thus saved many Soviet and Romanian lives as well as valuable time in ending the war in Europe.

General Sanatescu's coalition government (23 August to 2 November 1944) concluded an armistice with the Soviet Union in Moscow on 12 September 1944 and quickly re-entered the war on the side of the Allies, thereby dramatically opening up East Central Europe, Bulgaria and north-eastern Yugoslavia to the Red Army. The Soviet Union 'liberated' these lands from fascist control with the active assistance of 540,000 Romanian troops, at the heavy cost of 110,000 Romanian lives and 60,000 wounded (Rothschild 1974: 318; Romania 1974: 9). The continuation of Germany's war effort was very severely impaired by Germany's sudden loss of access to Romanian oil and oil products. Henceforth, the combat performance of German planes and tanks was fatally damaged by mounting fuel shortages and increased dependence on inferior synthetic fuels.

In late 1944 and early 1945, in view of the paramount role of the Soviet Union in 'liberating' Romania, Bulgaria and East Central Europe from fascist control, the Western Allies gave Stalin a fairly free hand in Romania. Seeing which way the wind was blowing, and perhaps in some cases genuinely impressed by the policies and military prowess of Soviet Communism, Romanians focked to join the RCP – whose membership rocketed from less than 1,000 in 1944 to over 800,000 by the end of 1947 (King 1980: 64). The Soviet military were the real power in the land, appointing

Communists, 'fellow travellers' and cynical careerist collaborators to local positions of power and authority. In February 1945 the RCP orchestrated mass demonstrations in Bucharest demanding larger roles for the Communists in central government. When Romanian police dispersed these demonstrations, the Soviet deputy foreign minister Andrei Vyshinsky was dispatched to Bucharest to order King Mihai to appoint a pro-Soviet government, while the royal palace was surrounded by Soviet tanks. Mihai had no option but to comply.

The leftist coalition government headed by Petru Groza, March 1945 to December 1947

The new prime minister was Petru Groza, leader of the Ploughman's Front and a socialist 'fellow traveller' with the RCP. A prominent Moscow Communist Teohari Georgescu took over the crucial ministry of the interior, which controlled the police and intelligence services. The most prominent of the so-called home Communists, Gheorghe Gheorghiu-Dej, became minister of communications, while Patrascanu remained minister of justice and thereby established steadily increasing Communist control over the judiciary.

The Groza government enacted a land reform on 22 March 1945. The land (and any machinery thereon) belonging to German citizens, war criminals, collaborators and absentee landowners, as well as all private landholdings in excess of 50 hectares. were also expropriated, in order to eliminate the last vestiges of landlordism and German landownership. By January 1947 1,443,911 hectares of land (about 10 per cent of the cultivated area) had been expropriated from 143,219 former proprietors. Thus the average amount of land expropriated was only about 10 hectares per pro - prietor. In total, 1,057,674 hectares of land were distributed to 796,000 peasants with little or no land. This means that, on average, the latter received only 1.3 hectares each, not nearly enough to establish fully viable farms. Thus the magnitude of the 1945–6 land reform was much less than that of 1919–21, which – within the equivalent territory – had expropriated 4,312,911 hectares, and 2,824,962 hectares had been distributed to 1,036,367 peasants, who had received an average of 2.7 hectares each. This was mainly because the 1919–21 land reform had already largely eliminated landlordism (Roberts 1951: 296; Berend and Ranki, 1974: 345; Tsantis and Pepper 1979: 228).

In the spring of 1945, the Groza government began to harass and arrest opponents and curb press freedom; General Antonescu and his closest colleagues were put on trial, and Antonescu was executed on 1 June 1946. However, as lip-service to the undertakings given by Stalin to the Western Allies at Yalta and Potsdam in February and July 1945, respectively, to uphold freedom and democracy in Eastern Europe (largely in the hope of receiving sorely needed American reconstruction aid), the RCP and the Soviet occupation forces still avoided excessive displays of power, routinely labelled those who opposed them as 'fascists', and equated democracy with 'struggle against fascism' (Fischer-Galati 1975: 316–17).

In mid-1945 Romania was forced formally to cede Bessarabia and Bukovina to the Soviet Union, while South Dobrudja was awarded to Bulgaria. However, partly by way of compensation, Stalin backed Romania's claims to northern Transylvania.

In August 1945 King Mihai tried unsuccessfully to force the Communist-dominated government to resign on the grounds that it was overstepping the bounds of democratic governance, but thenceforth it simply bypassed him.

In November 1945 there were huge pro-democracy demonstrations. The following month, prodded by the US and the UK (who were still represented on Romania's Allied Control Commission) as well as by Stalin, who was still hoping to receive US reconstruction aid, Groza brought additional non-Communist ministers into the government. Nevertheless, despite Stalin's pledge at Yalta in February 1945 to allow 'free elections' in the countries assigned to the Soviet 'sphere of influence', no parliamentary election were held in Romania until November 1946, when the Communist-dominated 'National Democratic Front' (NDF) supposedly won 80 per cent of the vote. Although this result was obtained partly by ballot-rigging and intimidation, that was not the whole story:

> because of the continuing policies of moderation and identification of the Romanian people's interests with the policies of the Groza government and the Soviet Union, the Communists were able to persuade most people to vote for the candidates of the National Democratic Front . . . The Communists and their electoral allies were quite successful in . . . pre-empting the political platforms of the National Peasant and National Liberal Parties and promising the voters more than these parties could.
>
> (Fischer-Galati 1975: 318–19)

Having legitimized their power through 'democratic' (i.e., anti-fascist) elections and by the formal signature of a peace treaty between Romania and the Allies in February 1947, the Romanian Communists and their Soviet backers considered it was safe to engage in more blatant displays of power and repression (Fischer-Galati 1975: 318–19). By the end of 1947, the civil service, the judiciary, the police and the armed forces had been purged, the leaders of parties opposed to the Communists had mostly been imprisoned or driven into exile, the PNL and the PNT had been outlawed, and the PNT leaders (including Iuliu Maniu and Ion Mihalache) had been put on trial. Some of the leading opponents of the nascent Communist regime were tried before a 'judge' who had previously been a senior off cial in charge of Antonescu's prisons and concentration camps.

The Petru Groza dictatorship, December 1947 to March 1952

In November 1947 the purged Social Democratic Party was forcibly merged with the Communist Party, to form the Romanian Workers Party (which did not revert to the name Romanian Communist Party until 1965). On 30 December 1947 King Mihai was forced to abdicate and a Romanian people's republic under a 'dictatorship of the proletariat' was proclaimed. Between 1946 and 1952 some 60,000 Romanians were summarily executed, while about 180,000 were dispatched to punitive forced labour camps (Ionescu 1964). In 1948 the notorious Securitate (security police) was established, and almost all large enterprises were nationalized. In 1949 a 'centrally planned economy' was launched in order rapidly to expand heavy industry and transport infrastructure, to the relative neglect of the consumer, housing and service sectors. Many large enterprises became Soviet–Romanian joint ventures known as *sovroms*. These developed and exploited Romania's considerable natural resources largely for the benefit of the Soviet Union, but with the assistance of substantial inputs of Soviet equipment and technology – especially in the oil industry (Montias 1967: 290–306).

The Gheorghiu-Dej dictatorship, May 1952 to March 1965

In May 1952 so-called home Communists, who had spent the 1930s and the war years in Romania, supplanted Groza and the so-called Moscow Communists, who had spent the 1930s and the war years in the Soviet Union. Led by Gheorghe Gheorghiu-Dej, the home Communists dissolved the hated *sovroms* in 1953–4.

Romania's 'loyal' participation in Soviet suppression of the Hungarian revolution of October–November 1956 was rewarded by the full withdrawal of Soviet troops from Romania in 1958 (though Soviet air and naval bases still remained and Soviet forces could arrive from Ukraine and the Moldavian Republic within hours). The last Warsaw Pact troop exercise on Romanian soil took place in 1962.

In the early 1960s Gheorghiu-Dej felt sufficiently confident of his hold on pow to defiantly reject Soviet proposals that Romania should specialize in agriculture an food exports in a proposed 'socialist division of labour' among the Comecon states. Instead, he continued to give overriding priority to the development of heavy industry and mining. Consequently, Romania's light industries, service industries and agri- culture suffered from chronic lack of investment, with very damaging effects on living standards. Romania also largely missed out on not-insignificant technological and economic assistance which the Soviet Union lavished on its slavishly subservient neighbour, Bulgaria.

Agriculture was forcibly collectivized in stages between 1949 and 1962, in effect 're-enserfing' the peasantry by subjecting them to regimented forced labour and under-priced compulsory deliveries to state agencies. In 1961, Gheorghiu-Dej publicly admitted that the security services had coerced the peasantry into accepting collec - tivization and that 80,000 peasants had been arrested and put on trial for opposing it, but he blamed these 'excesses' on the ousted and disgraced Moscow Communists.

The 'reign' of Nicolae Ceauşescu, March 1965 to December 1989: from initial 'Pepsi-Cola Communism' to 'obsessive compulsive despotic disorder'

When Gheorghiu-Dej died unexpectedly in March 1965, he was replaced by a little known home Communist, Nicolae Ceauşescu, who had become close to Gheorghiu-Dej while they were imprisoned together during the Second World War. Ceau şescu continued to promote the stridently 'national' Communism initiated by Gheorghiu-Dej in 1961–2.

Nevertheless, he initially retreated from the rigours of Stalinism. Romania enjoyed a brief relaxation in the censorship of books, films and plays, an upsurge in the screening of Western f lms and television series, and an enduring rehabilitation of both native and Western literary classics. Romania's first Pepsi-Cola plant was opene in 1968, and sales of televisions, refrigerators and washing machines and construction of (ugly) apartment blocks soared. From the outset, Ceaus ,escu also dissociated Romania as much as possible from Soviet foreign policy and played up Romanian cultural affinities with the 'Latin' West (especially Italy and France) as against th Slav countries. Unlike other members of the Soviet bloc, Ceauşescu refused to break off relations either with China (in the Sino-Soviet dispute of the 1960s) or with Israel (over the Arab–Israeli War of 1967).

Ceauşescu's stock soared on 21 August 1968, when he delivered a speech to 100,000 people assembled in the Piata Republici, not only defending the right of each

Communist-ruled state to chart its own 'national' road to socialism, but also loudly condemning the August 1968 Warsaw Pact invasion of Czechoslovakia (in which Romania refused to participate) as a dangerous violation of Czechoslovakia's sovereignty:

> The penetration of the troops of five socialist countries into Czechoslovakia is great mistake and a grave danger to peace in Europe, to the fate of socialism ... There is no justification whatsoever and no reason can be given for admitting fo even a single moment the idea of a military intervention in the affairs of a fraternal socialist state . . . The problem of choosing the roads to socialism is a problem of the respective party, the respective state, the respective people. Nobody can pose as adviser, as a guide to the way in which socialism has to be built in another country. We maintain that in order to place the relations between the socialist countries, between the Communist parties, on a truly Marxist-Leninist basis, an end must be put for good and all to interference in the affairs of other states, in other parties . . . We have decided to start from today forming armed patriotic detachments of workers, peasants and intellectuals, defenders of the independence of our socialist homeland . . . Be sure, comrades, be sure, citizens of Romania, that we shall never betray our homeland.
>
> (quoted in Catchlove 1972: 108–9)

This seemingly courageous stance considerably raised Ceauşescu's standing both domestically and internationally, even though Romanians knew that their relatively poor country was even more vulnerable to Soviet invasion than either Czechoslovakia or Hungary. As a result, Ceauşescu was courted not merely by China, but also by the West, which for a time mistook his assertive nationalism for liberalism and regarded him as a valuable thorn in the Soviet Union's side. President Richard Nixon visited Romania in August 1969; President Gerald Ford did so in August 1975; Ceaus,escu was received at Buckingham Palace to be decorated by Queen Elizabeth II; and President de Gaulle of France admitted him to the Lêgion d'Honneur. Romania was also admitted to the World Bank and the IMF in 1972; the USA awarded it Most Favoured Nation status in 1975; and the country gained preferential access to Western credits.

Western states were slow to recognize the ever-increasing corruptness, ruthlessness and rapacity of the Ceauşescu regime, as well as the prodigious scale on which it wasted Western credits and other resources on 'white elephants' such as the monstrous Palace of the Republic in central Bucharest and hugely over-expanded and highly capital-intensive oil-ref ning and petrochemical industries. Consequently, the West went on lending the regime too much money for too long, and Western loans were used as *substitutes for* (rather than as aids to) meaningful economic restructuring and reform, with the result that instead of improving, Romania's economic perfor - mance deteriorated rapidly. Between 1976 and 1981 this former major net exporter of foodstuffs became increasingly dependent on imports of food, and in 1977 it also became a net importer of oil. The foreign debt rose from 3.6 billion dollars in 1977 to 10.2 billion dollars in 1981 (Gallagher 2005: 63). In response, during the 1980s Romanians were subjected to a draconian and hugely debilitating austerity programme in order to repay the foreign debt, which Ceau şescu claimed had been repaid in full on 31 March 1989. To this end, industrial, agricultural and especially public service and infrastructural investment was squeezed to the bone, with particularly dire consequences for tens of thousands of abandoned children in state orphanages and the inmates of mental hospitals, as the international media discovered in 1990. This manic obsession with repaying the debt partly stemmed from a desire to minimize the scope for Western monitoring of and 'interference' in Romania's increasingly oppressive internal policies.

At the same time, the regime became increasingly xenophobic and nationalistic. It fostered an ultra-nationalist rewriting of the country's official histories and gave fre rein to ultra-nationalist writers and propagandists, such as Ceaus,escu's unsavoury 'court poet' Corneliu Vadim Tudor, who in turn contributed to the idolization of Ceauşescu as the great *Conducator* ('Leader', the title previously used by the fascist General Antonescu). The chief victims of the intensification of 'ethnic collectivism were Romania's 1.6 million ethnic Hungarians, located mainly in Transylvania. They incurred mounting personal harassment by the regime and the suppression of Hungarian-language schools, university teaching and broadcasting. This was seen by the Hungarian minority as threatening to terminate the cultural reproduction and preservation of their Hungarian identity and communities.

Ceauşescu tightened still further his already vice-like political grip during the 1980s, partly in response to the emergence of the anti-Communist Solidarity movement in Poland in 1980–1. However, while Ceauşescu undoubtedly constituted a particularly severe case of 'obsessive compulsive despotic disorder', he did not revert to full-blown Stalinism. He instigated no mass executions, no large-scale Stalinist purges of the party and state apparatus, and no mass deportations to forced labour camps, even though his prisons and detention camps were awash with political prisoners by the 1980s.

In October 1985 the military took control of thermal and hydroelectric power plants and two years later a state of emergency was declared in the energy sector, in order to 'militarize' it. Thereafter, the party took increasing control of the economy in an attempt to head off demands for radical (liberalizing and/or decentralizing) reforms like those taking place in the USSR under Gorbachev's *perestroika* (1985–91).

Under Ceauşescu, there was very little legitimate private economic activity outside agriculture, although semi-private black-marketeering naturally flourished. Joint ventures with foreign companies were few in number, despite the enactment of a law in 1971 allowing them (with foreign ownership limited to a maximum of 49 per cent).

Despite the repressiveness of his regime, Romanians did not meekly acquiesce in Ceauşescu's policies. A strike by coal miners in the Jiu valley in July 1977, in protest against reduced pay and disability pensions, a raised retirement age and bad working conditions and demanding a six-hour day, resulted in the area being sealed off by the army and subjected to reprisals: several hundred workers were relocated to other areas and some were sent to the forced labour camps (Deletant 1998: 184–7). Strikes by miners against wage cuts in the Maramures region of northern Transylvania were broken up by the Securitate in September 1983. Pay cuts precipitated strikes in Cluj in November 1986 and in Iasi in February 1987. In November 1987 there were major protests against heating restrictions and pay cuts in Brasov (Deletant 1998: 189–91). In fact, strikes and unrest occurred throughout the 1980s, owing to the deteriorating economic climate.

A much-publicized feature of the Ceauşescu era was a so-called 'systematization' programme. In a speech on 3 March 1988 Ceauşescu declared that 'we must reduce the number of villages from about 13,000 at present to 5,000 to 6,000 at most' (Deletant

1998: 208). The official aims were to increase the amount of cultivable land, improv
rural infrastructure (including the construction of apartment blocks), and homogenize
society by eliminating the differences between town and country. The more sinister
underlying motives were to enhance police surveillance and control, especially against
the Hungarians of Transylvania. 'Systematization' allegedly had its origins in visits
made by Ceauşescu to Mao's China and to Kim Il-Sung's North Korea in 1971, during
which he was impressed by Mao's 'people's communes'. There was a conference
on the idea in 1972, but it was only made law in 1978 and a concrete timetable was
announced in March 1988. The plans evoked international protests, which were
orchestrated by the Operation Villages Romains organization. The process had barely
got off the ground before the regime fell in 1989, but about twenty-nine villages were
destroyed and thirty-seven were 'crippled', losing between a quarter and half of their
older buildings (*The Guardian*, 2 March 1994, p. 12).

An indication of the scale of official statistical falsification under Cea ‚escu can
be seen in the f gure for the 1989 grain harvest. In the autumn of 1989 Ceaus ‚escu
announced a record harvest of over 60 million tonnes, whereas the actual figure turne
out to be only 18.4 million tonnes (*FT*, 17 May 1990, p. 42).

Romania's deeply entrenched vertical power relations and power structures,
clientelism, corruption and 'ethnic collectivism' undoubtedly accelerated the degen-
eration of its Communist regime into a particularly vicious, venal, inbred, clientelistic,
personalistic, repressive and xenophobic form of 'ethnic collectivism', exacerbated
by a crassly incompetent form of 'socialism in one family'. Over a dozen members
of the Ceauşescu family held high official positions and abused them to line their
own pockets or for corrupt and clientelistic puposes and cracked down heavily on
anyone who dared to criticize them for doing so.

The power relations, power structures and practices of the Ceaus ‚escu regime
reflected the enduring strength of the deeply entrenched, clientelistic and corrupt
vertical power structures and power relations which Romania inherited from the
Byzantine and Ottoman eras, and which had been perpetuated in the highly centralized,
clientelistic, corrupt and 'ethnic collectivist' nation-state power structures maintained
between the 1860s and the 1940s. Successive Romanian regimes have relied primarily
on the coercive and centralized but brittle 'despotic power' of the state, instead
of developing more dispersed, autonomous, liberal and resilient 'infrastructural
capabilities' in Romanian society as a whole (to borrow a valuable distinction drawn
by Michael Mann 1988). These features have been buttressed by the corresponding weakness or stunted development of *the kinds of horizontal ties, voluntary
associations, limited government and rule of law*, which in genuinely *liberal* democracies provide the essential legal and institutional infrastructure of more liberal forms
of governance and society and are the basis of vigorous and healthy civil societies
and 'civil economies' (Parekh 1993; Rose 1992). They constrain and set limits on the
power of the state and governing elites by sharing that power and thereby dispersing
or de-concentrating it. It is in these respects, rather than with respect to easily
caricatured or stereotyped national attitudes, characteristics and 'mentalities', that
Romania has been crucially deficient. This does not mean that 'ordinary Romanians
were paragons of liberal and democratic virtue, but rather that (i) they are not
'essentially' different from other Europeans, warts and all; and (ii) popular 'attitudes'
and 'mentalities' have been much less decisively important than elite attitudes and
deeply entrenched power relations and power structures in determining political
outcomes, to which popular attitudes and 'mentalities' have mainly tended to adjust

or accommodate themselves. In other words, popular attitudes and 'mentalities' have been 'dependent variables' rather than independent determinants of public policy and the nature of the polity.

Romania's 'stolen revolution', December 1989

At the party congress held on 20–24 November 1989, Ceaus¸escu was unanimously re-elected leader of the 4 million-member RCP (nearly one-fifth of the population) Within a month, however, his power was crumbling.

The spark that lit the fuse of the Romanian revolution came from the historic cosmo-politan Transylvanian city of Timisoara, where Lazlo Tokes, a dissident Hungarian Reformed Church pastor, had been campaigning for Hungarian educational rights since 1986 and against the systemization programme since March 1988. His causes had been taken up by the media and politicians in Hungary, and he had succeeded in mobilizing joint Hungarian, Romanian, Protestant, Catholic and Eastern Orthodox opposition to systematization. Starting on 15 December 1989, the regime's attempts to remove him from his church there to a less infiential posting in the back of beyond evoked tenacious spontaneous mass protests by the ethnic Hungarian community, as well as an impressive display of cross-cultural and inter-denominational solidarity from ethnic Romanians and even Serbs in support of the Hungarians. International television reports at the time stated that thousands of protesters were being killed by the Securitate and the army, which opened fire on large crowds on 17 December although subsequent investigations established that a total of 122 had been killed – still appalling, but far fewer than initially believed (Deletant 1998: 223–30).

A large crowd was assembled in front of the Communist Party headquarters in Bucharest on 21 December to hear Ceaus¸escu give a set-piece speech which was broadcast 'live' to the nation. However, the speech was heckled, the nervous crowd panicked and the broadcast was interrupted for several minutes, but millions of Romanians realized that the despot had lost control of his 'rent-a-crowd' audience. This signalled to Romanians and to the world at large that Ceau şescu had lost his authority and that many Romanians were no longer cowed by his regime. Street barricades were erected, demonstrators were fired upon by Securitate and army units and several other cities were by then in revolt: Timisoara, Cluj, Arad, Sibiu and Cugir. On 22 December hostile crowds booed Ceaus¸escu when he appeared on a balcony of the central committee building, and the Ceauşescus had to escape from the roof by helicopter as the building was stormed. The same day, a self-styled National Salvation Front (FSN) took over the running of the country. Ion Iliescu, a little-known fifty nine-year-old Communist Party apparatchik who had fallen out with Ceau şescu in 1971, appeared on television and somewhat mysteriously 'emerged' in the role of interim president. A couple of days later Dr Petre Roman, a telegenic forty-three-year-old university lecturer, similarly 'emerged' as interim prime minister. Ceauşescu and his wife were taken prisoner on 23 December and were executed on 25 December (Christmas Day in the West, but not in predominantly Eastern Orthodox Romania), following a very destructive pitched battle for control of central Bucharest and a swift makeshift trial by a kangaroo court of dubious legality. It is widely believed that the Ceauşescus were executed so hastily in order to prevent them from 'talking' and implicating key members of the FSN in their crimes. This led some people to see the emerging Iliescu regime as morally compromised from the outset (Deletant 1998: 240). Communist Party rule was formally ended on 27 December, and the 'Socialist

Republic of Romania' dropped the word 'socialist' from its title on 29 December. Freedom to travel abroad was announced on 3 January 1990.

Among the 'revolutions of 1989', Romania's was the only one that involved major violence. An official investigation concluded that 1,033 people had perished (includin 270 soldiers) and 2,383 were wounded (including 673 soldiers) during the revolution (Deletant 1998: 233). Students and sections of the largely conscript army (most of whom 'defected' to the rebels) played leading roles in the unrest, while thousands of Securitate snipers (so-called 'terrorists') fought back in vain. However, not one of these murderous 'terrorists' was ever brought to trial for the heavy casualties they inflicted. Moreover, the RCP headquarters (the central committee building) an the state television headquarters escaped largely unscathed, whereas many nearby buildings were badly damaged or destroyed. Critics of the FSN soon concluded that 'a bogus mini-war' had been stage-managed in order 'to legitimize the new power' and present it as 'the saviour of the revolution' (Gallagher 2005: 72). There is ongoing debate as to how spontaneous the revolution was. The most widespread view is that what began as a popular revolution in Timisoara was quickly 'stolen' or 'hijacked' in Bucharest by the self-styled FSN, which had apparently been formed by Communist apparatchiks some six months earlier, evidently with the connivance of large sections of the Securitate and the military.

A different 'take' is provided by Aurelian Craiutu:

> The fact that in Romania the transition had been initiated not through negotiations as in Poland or Hungary, but through the sudden collapse of the regime, had a strong impact . . . As a result there were no institutional arrangements in place capable of providing channels for collective action and bargaining in an uncertain and highly volatile environment. The lack of pacts and negotiations before 1989 could account for the rhetoric of intransigence and the winner-take-all mentality of the main political actors after 1989, which delayed the consolidation of the new democratic regime.
>
> (Craiutu 2000: 172)

The emasculation of civil society in Romania during the Communist era, combined with the legacies of mounting social and economic hardship and an increasingly obsolete, run-down and dysfunctional economic system, was to make the testing challenges of democratization and marketization especially tortuous and difficult fo Romania. This made it much easier for the well-prepared FSN to 'steal a march' on the numerous rival movements and political parties which mushroomed in late December 1989 and in January 1990.

The multi-ethnic composition and the inter-ethnic cooperation of the groups that brought about the downfall of the Ceaușescus in December 1989 initially aroused high hopes that the new Romania would rise above the vicious and debilitating 'ethnic collectivism' and xenophobia of the Ceaus,escu regime. This prompted neighbouring Hungary (Romania's traditional enemy), which was understandably concerned over the plight of the 1.7 million ethnic Hungarians in Romania, to be therßt country in the world to recognize the new FSN government (22 December) and to send its foreign minister to visit Romania (29 December). In return, on 4 January the FSN government issued decrees that in areas inhabited by ethnic minorities public decisions were to be promulgated in the respective minority language(s), and that public broadcasting in Hungarian and German was to resume (Gallagher 2005: 75–6). The next day, the FSN even issued a statement that:

> The revolution in Romania, an historic act of the entire people, of the Romanian nation and of the national minorities, attests to the unity and solidarity of all the homeland's sons who have wished freedom and democracy . . . The National Salvation Front solemnly declares that it shall achieve and guarantee the individual and collective rights and liberties of all the national minorities.
>
> (Gallagher 2005: 75–6)

If the FSN had adhered to these principles, Romania would have become a much more peaceful and prosperous country and an earlier entrant into the EU.

As early as 25 December 1989, the ethnic Hungarian communities in Transylvania launched a Democratic Union of Hungarians in Romania (UDMR), which has remained their primary vehicle of political expression and representation ever since. Geza Domokos, its founder leader, prudently sought to reassure Romanians that the UDMR aimed 'to achieve the rights of the Hungarians with due respect for the territorial integrity and sovereignty of a free and democratic Romania' (Gallagher 2005: 77). There was no assertion by the ethnic Hungarians of a right to secede or to rejoin Hungary. This policy of ethnic Hungarian loyalty to the Romanian revolution and inter-ethnic and inter-denominational cooperation with predominantly Eastern Orthodox Romanians culminated in the thirteen-point 'Timisoara Declaration', drawn up by liberal Hungarian and Romanian intelligentsia and adopted at a rally in Timisoara on 11 March 1990.

> Signed by almost four million citizens, the Timisoara Declaration pointed out that the true goal of the Revolution had not been the replacement of Nicolae Ceauşescu with second-rank members of the nomenklatura, but a clear-cut break with the communist past. It also stressed the need for the consolidation of genuine pluralism.
>
> (Craiutu 2000: 174)

However, in their excessive haste to restore teaching through the Hungarian language in some of the best secondary schools in Transylvania in late January 1990, the Hungarian community and Romania's liberal-minded education minister com - mitted serious blunders, inasmuch as these over-hasty moves resulted in substantial numbers of ethnic Romanian schoolchildren being displaced to greatly inferior institutions – some of which were not even proper schools. This understandably angered and antagonized many parents of suddenly disadvantaged ethnic Romanian teenagers, especially in Cluj and Tirgu Mures. Xenophobic Romanian ultra-nationalist organizations such as Vatra Romaneasca (Romanian Hearth) and the Partitul Romania Mare (PRM, Greater Romania Party) immediately seized on this issue and accused the ethnic Hungarian minority of plotting to call in undercover agents provocateurs from Hungary and to break up Romania's unity. At this point, instead of urging retreat and restraint, the FSN government allowed and even encouraged inter-ethnic conflict to culminate in serious bloodshed in Tirgu Mures. On 19 Marc 1990, peaceful (albeit somewhat imprudent and provocative) Hungarian celebrations of the anniversary of the start of the Hungarian nationalist revolution of 1848 gave Romanian thugs organized by Vatra Romaneasca a pretext to besiege the off ces of the UDMR, with many serious injuries and some loss of life, with the implicit cooperation of the Romanian authorities. President Iliescu and Prime Minister Roman jumped on the nationalist bandwagon by repeatedly accusing Romania's 1.7 million ethnic Hungarians of seeking to undermine the country's unity and bring about Hungarian repossession of northern Transylvania (Gallagher 2005: 76–89). The internationally televised pictures of the violence carried out against unarmed Hungarian civilians by Romanian ultra-nationalist thugs and police inherited from the Ceausescu regime quickly tarnished the international reputation of Romania in general and the FSN regime in particular.

On 23 January Iliescu and the FSN announced that, supposedly in response to pressure from below, the FSN would compete as a political party in the elections scheduled for April 1990. This provoked furious street protests and complaints from Romania's 'historic parties', the National Liberal Party (PNL) and the National Peasant Party (PNT), because it reneged on earlier assurances that the FSN would only serve as an interim government (Gallagher 2005: 79). During the street confrontations between FSN supporters and supporters of the 'historic parties' between 25 and 29 January, the FSN leaders appealed on television to miners and factory workers (with whom the FSN inherited old Communist Party links) to come to central Bucharest to defend the FSN government against its rivals. As a result, on 28 January unarmed protestors against the FSN were beaten up by miners and other workers. The following day the offices of the PNL and the PNT were attacked (Gallagher 2005: 80).

On 2 February a token provisional council of national unity (PCNU) was established with the aim of providing a forum or channel of participation for representatives of other parties and groups besides the FSN, which made up half the members, but this PCNU was given little say in government appointments and decisions, which were reserved almost entirely to the self-appointed FSN. However, on 14 March the PCNU did postpone the elections until 20 May. It then decided that these would elect an assembly of deputies (lower house) by proportional representation, a senate (upper house) and a relatively strong president. The new parliament was to enact a new constitution within eighteen months and hold fresh elections within thirty months (Roper 2000: 66).

Elections to the assembly of deputies (lower house), 20 May 1990

The FSN obtained two-thirds of the votes for the lower house (Table 4.1), as well as 92 seats (out of 119) in the senate. On the same day, Ion Iliescu obtained over 85 per cent of the votes in the presidential election. Although the election campaigns and the ballots themselves were fawed, international observers accepted that opinion polls and the exceptionally large margin of victory indicated clear majority support for the FSN and Iliescu. The Iliescu/FSN platform attracted widespread popular support mainly by claiming to embody the 'revolution' and by promising *a cautious ('gradualist') approach to economic restructuring and reform.* Large-scale unemployment was to be avoided by what was promised would be a relatively slow and judicious transition to a mixed economy, in which the state sector would remain dominant but private enterprise would also be encouraged, albeit extensively regulated by the state. Generous social security was to be offered to those adversely affected, such as the unemployed. Foreign investment would not be vigorously promoted, but was instead

4.1 Romanian assembly of deputies election, 20 May 1990

Party	Share of vote (%)	Seats
FSN, led by Ion Iliescu and Petre Roman	66.3	263
Hungarian Democratic Union of Romania (UDMR)	7.2	29
National Liberal Party (PNL)	6.4	29
National Peasant Party (PNT) under Corneliu Coposu	2.7	12
Romanian Ecological Movement	2.6	12
Alliance for a United Romania	2.1	9
Democratic Agrarian Party of Romania	1.8	9
Romanian Ecological Party	1.7	8
Romanian Socialist Democratic Party	1.1	5

Note: Turn-out was 86 per cent.

Source: Roper (2000: 68).

regarded warily. 'We shall not sell off the country' became one of Iliescu's catch-phrases. Agricultural producer cooperatives were not to be speedily disbanded, although their members and former owners of farmland were to be allowed to obtain smallholdings of their own (up to a maximum of 10 hectares apiece).

Despite this gradualism, the diff cult conditions took their toll. Anti-government demonstrations continued, inspired by widespread worries that so many of Ceaușscu's apparatchiks were still quite obviously in power. In April 1990 young protesters established a 'tent city' in University Square in central Bucharest. When President Iliescu denounced them as *golani* (hooligans) in a television broadcast, they proudly adopted that name. However, there was a major international outcry when large numbers of coal miners from the Jiu valley were bused into Bucharest in June 1990 and used by the authorities to beat up, arrest and disperse the *golani* with gratuitous brutality and bloodshed. This so-called *mineriada*, combined with the over-hasty execution of the Ceaușescus on 25 December 1989 and the pogrom against Hungarians in Tirgu Mures on 19 March 1990 shocked international television audiences, Western governments and international NGOs (non-governmental organizations), dragging Romania into even deeper international disrepute. Western responses to the FSN regime were increasingly tinged with distaste for what was widely perceived to be an authoritarian, corrupt and brutal neo-Communist regime.

Perhaps because he was stung by suspicions and accusations that the June 1990 *mineriada* must have been assisted, f nanced or even coordinated by at least some members of the FSN regime (possibly including Roman and Iliescu), from June 1990 onwards Prime Minister Petre Roman began to dissociate himself from the more conservative, corporatist and 'gradualist' President Iliescu. Roman now called for rapid marketization of the economy, to the great annoyance of the neo-Communist elements within the FSN:

> Our foremost mission is to make a historic transition of an unprecedented scope, namely from a super-centralized to a market economy. The state must abandon to the greatest possible extent its role as proprietor and manager . . . The present state of the economy can only be overcome by radical reform, carried out in quick steps. Plastic surgery and artif cial adjustments cannot but deepen our crisis.

In a speech to parliament in October 1990 he announced a 'leap to a market economy', to be accomplished by June 1992. At the FSN's first national convention held in Marc 1991, Roman was re-elected party leader and gained approval for the reshaping of the FSN into a social democratic party committed to a market-based economy.

Romania's initial steps towards a market economy, 1990–1

The central planning system broke down very quickly, and the state planning commission was abolished in January 1990. In the absence of either a functioning command economy (whose commands had suddenly ceased to be obeyed as the veil of fear lifted) or functioning capitalist market, financial and legal institutions an infrastructure, the situation initially became chaotic and rudderless. Relative to countries such as Hungary, Poland and even former Yugoslavia, Romania had comparatively few citizens with much understanding or experience of the institutional and legal requirements and workings of a market economy. In February 1990 state and private enterprises were declared free to engage in foreign trade on their own. A series of devaluations of the Romanian currency (the leu) paved the way for internal convertibility of the leu, which was inaugurated in November 1991.

It has been argued that, 'As Romania entered the 1990s, the country was in many ways in a better position to pursue economic restructuring than other East European countries', primarily because Ceauşescu had repaid the external debt during the 1980s and the country had a 2.8 billion-dollar current account surplus in 1989 (Roper 2000: 87–8). However, these paper advantages were more than offset by the moribund run-down state of the economy and the exhaustion, malnutrition and acute poverty of much of the population. As Roper himself points out, the 2.8 billion-dollar surplus of 1989 had already given way to a 1.6 billion-dollar current account deficit in 1990 (Rope 2000: 89) and Romania rapidly accumulated a new external debt (10.2 billion dollars by 2000 and 22.8 billion dollars by 2004 – see Table 4.2).

A privatization bill was passed in late July 1990. It envisaged: (i) the conversion of 80 per cent of state enterprises into joint stock 'commercial enterprises', in preparation for eventual privatization; (ii) continued state control of about 20 per cent of enterprises ('strategic' state-owned semi-autonomous enterprises, including mines, public utilities, armaments and energy); (iii) the distribution of 30 per cent of the value of the capital of these joint stock companies to adult citizens in the form of vouchers exchangeable for shares; (iv) the allocation of around 30 per cent of the shares of most enterprises to their employees in exchange for cash or vouchers; and (v) setting aside a block of shares for purchase by foreigners. Voucher distribution was scheduled to start in the first quarter of 1991, while the sale of shares would begin in the last quarter. However, implementation of the July 1990 privatization programme was very slow. Only ffteen enterprises had been privatized by the end of 1992 (UN ECE 1993: 223).

Most Romanian state enterprises made substantial losses during the 1990s, but enterprise debts and losses were, in effect, continuously rolled over or written off by means of new credit infusions from the state banks, and no bankruptcy law was enacted until 21 March 1995. As a result, there was little pressure on enterprises either to restructure or to become efficient, profitable or even frugal (Ronnas 1996: 25

There were some price increases in July 1990, e.g., for petrol, luxury goods and newspapers. About half of all prices were freed from price controls in November 1990 (EBRD 1994: 33), and by mid-1991 this proportion had risen to about 80 per cent. As

4.2 Romania: selected economic indicators, 1990–2005

	1990	1991	1992	1993	1994	1995	1996	1997	1998	1999	2000	2001	2002	2003	2004	2005
								% rises/rates								
GDP	-5.6	-12.9	-8.8	1.5	3.9	7.1	3.9	-6.1	-5.4	-1.2	1.8	5.3	4.9	5.2	8.3	4.0
Industrial output	-23.7	-22.8	-21.9	1.3	3.3	9.5	9.8	-5.6	-17.3	-8.8	8.2	8.2	6.0	3.1	5.3	2.1
Agricultural output	-2.9	0.8	-13.3	12.9	0.2	4.5	1.3	3.4	-7.6	5.5	-14.1	22.7	-3.5	3.0	–	-13.9
Annual inflation rate	5.1	170.2	210.4	256.1	136.7	32.3	38.8	154.8	59.1	45.8	45.7	34.5	22.5	15.4	11.9	9.5
Unemployment rate	0.0	3.1	8.2	10.4	10.1	8.2	6.6	8.9	10.3	6.8	7.1	6.6	8.4	7.0	6.2	5.9
Budget surplus (+) / deficit (−) (as % of GDP)	1.2	0.6	-4.6	-0.4	-2.2	-2.5	-3.9	-4.6	-5.0	-2.1	-3.8	-3.5	-2.0	-2.0	-1.4	-0.8
Foreign debt share of GDP	–	7.4	16.6	16.1	18.3	18.3	23.6	26.9	23.7	25.9	28.8	31.0	35.0	36.0	36.2	34.8
Private-sector share of GDP	15.0	25.0	25.0	35.0	40.0	45.0	55.0	60.0	60.0	60.0	60.0	65.0	65.0	65.0	70.0	70.0
Private-sector share in employment	–	–	–	–	–	–	–	–	–	72	75	75	–	–	–	–
FDI inflow (net, $ m)	18.0	37.0	73.0	87.0	341.0	417.0	415.0	1267.0	2079.0	1025.0	1051.0	1154.0	1080.0	2156.0	5020.0	5230.0
Foreign debt ($ bn)	–	2.1	3.2	4.2	5.5	6.5	8.3	9.5	9.9	9.2	10.7	12.5	16.0	20.6	26.5	32.5
Population (m)	23.2	22.8	22.7	22.6	22.6	22.6	22.6	22.6	22.5	22.5	22.4	22.4	21.8	21.7	21.7	21.7

Sources: Various issues of the annual EBRD *Transition Report*, supplemented by UN Economic Commission for Europe, *Economic Survey of Europe*; UN *World Economic and Social Survey*; and IMF *World Economic Outlook*. Figures for 2004 and 2005 are provisional estimates.

a result, the annual inflation rate surged from 5.1 per cent in 1990 to 170 per cent i 1991 and 210 per cent in 1992 (see Table 4.2), but these rates were quite modest compared with those in countries such as Poland and the Yugoslav successor states.

With regard to external financial support, it would appear that for a time Wester governments consciously 'penalized' Romania for having elected a neo-Communist government in May 1990. However, from 1990 to 1996 little was done actively to attract Western direct investment. Indeed, until 1997 there was a constitutional prohibition on foreign ownership of land (or any other form of real estate), with the partial exception of cases where Romanian enterprises had majority foreign ownership and Romanian partners contributed land as their share (EBRD 1996b: 169).

Controls on the movement of labour were abolished in 1990 and free collective bargaining was introduced the following year. However, the rise of independent trade unions, which pushed up wage rates and reduced average working hours, also exacerbated inflation and the general laxity of financial discipline. In response, a wag inf ation tax and austerity measures were introduced.

In agriculture, one of the first acts was to scrap the notorious systematization programme (on 26 December 1989). In addition, food exports were prohibited from 1990 to 1994 as a quick expedient to improve the domestic food supplies, which had been depressed by agricultural inefficiency, lack of incentives and investment and the use of food exports to help repay Romania's foreign debt during the 1980s. A land restitution law was passed in February 1991, stipulating that some 80 per cent of arable land would be eligible for return to former owners or their heirs (*EEN*, 20 August 1991, p. 4). Others eligible for land included people who had worked in agricultural producer cooperatives for at least the three previous years. Land received from the state was limited to a maximum of 10 hectares of farmland and 1 hectare of forestland per household, although acquisition of up to 100 hectares of land (all kinds) was allowed through purchase or inheritance. Romania took 1947 as the cut-off year for restitution, partly with the aim of denying restitution claims by descendants of big landowners (including the royal family) from the inter-war years, but also with the effect (whether intended or not) of denying restitution claims by any surviving relatives of the hundreds of thousands of Romanian Jews wiped out by the Holocaust (Swinnen 1999: 642–3). Former foreign landowners were denied land restitution (Swinnen 1999: 646). About two-thirds of Romania's state-owned farmland had been reclaimed for agricultural use by the Communist regime through land improvements and drainage investments, especially in the Danube valley. This land was initially retained in state ownership (Swinnen 1999: 652). During 1991 agricultural producer cooperatives were dissolved, while state farms were transformed into state commercial companies (Frydman et al. 1993: 231). Over 80 per cent of all farmland had been privatized by late 1992 (UN ECE 1993: 223).

The *mineriada* of September 1991 and the demise of Petre Roman

In September 1991 there was another violent *mineriada* by a large group of Jiu valley coal miners (supported by other citizens) who demanded improved pay and working conditions, a price freeze and the resignations of Iliescu and Roman. Their violent rampage through Bucharest, allegedly orchestrated by the wayward miners' leader and ultra-nationalist thug Miron Cozma, left several people dead and many injured.

Petre Roman handed in his prime ministerial mandate in order to form a new cabinet more capable of dealing with this crisis. However, wily Iliescu tricked Roman by announcing publicly that he had accepted the resignation of the Roman government and then refusing to allow Roman to form a new government (Roper 2000: 70), thereby making Roman a scapegoat for the crisis and clipping the wings of his chief rival. Roman's political career never recovered from this setback.

The government headed by Theodor Stolojan, October 1991 to October 1992

Theodor Stolojan, a non-party economist and a staunch advocate of rapid marketization of the Romanian economy, became prime minister on 1 October 1991. His coalition government involved technocrats and members of the PNL, who were broadly in tune with his own (neo-)liberal economic orientation. Stolojan vowed not to stand in the next parliamentary election, which was scheduled for September 1992 (he subsequently took up a job with the World Bank). The political disturbances of autumn 1991 led to a temporary freeze on the prices of basic goods and services, but the remaining subsidies on basic consumer goods were removed in May 1992 and most of the remaining consumer subsidies ended on 1 May 1993 (EBRD 1994: 33).

In November 1991 the new government secured the passage of the new constitution, which had been drawn up under the Petre Roman government before it fell and which more or less maintained the status quo while further increasing the powers and patronage wielded by President Iliescu. This was approved by 78.5 per cent of the voters in a referendum held on 8 December 1991 (Gallagher 2005: 101).

However, local elections held in February 1992 registered a major swing of public support from the FSN to the Democratic Convention of Romania (CDR), which was a broad coalition of centrist and centre-right parties. The FSN vote slumped from the 66 per cent share it had obtained in 1990 to just 33 per cent and would have been even lower but for the resilience of support among the elderly and in the countryside, where the influence of local potentates over voters 'often counted in its favour'. In the wake of these results, the FSN acrimoniously split into two separate parties. Ex-premier Roman's support among local FSN branches was sufficient to enable hi faction to retain the FSN name and emblem. However, most of the FSN's elite and members of parliament joined a new Democratic National Salvation Front (FDSN), launched in April 1992 in order to mobilize support for the re-election of Iliescu in the forthcoming presidential election. Roman posed as 'the genuine partisan of democracy' while casting Iliescu in the role of the 'nostalgic Communist', but they were merely rivals for political power (Gallagher 2005: 102).

The presidential election of 27 September and 11 October 1992

In the first round, Ion Iliescu won 47.34 per cent of the votes, as against the 31.24 per cent share obtained by Professor Emil Constantinescu, the rector of Bucharest University and candidate of the more liberal and reform-minded Democratic Convention of Romania (CDR). The CDR comprised seventeen groupings, including the PNT-Christian Democrats, the Civic Alliance, and the UDMR. Gheorghe Funar, the leader of the ultra-nationalist Party of Romanian National Unity (PUNR), obtained 10.9 per cent of the vote, creating the need for a run-off contest between Iliescu and Constantinescu. In the second round, Iliescu won 61.4 per cent of the votes, as against

38.6 per cent for Constantinescu. Iliescu's main support was (i) in the rural areas, where he fed fears that, if the CDR were to win, they would restore the old landlord class and take away the land of the existing farm population; (ii) among workers fearful of mounting unemployment, especially in areas where mining and/or heavy industry were dominant; and (iii) among the elderly, who feared that the economic neo-liberals in the Constantinescu camp would further reduce the various forms of public support on which they felt heavily dependent. Constantinescu's support came mainly from the big cities, the better-educated intelligentsia/white-collar classes and younger voters.

The assembly of deputies election, 27 September 1992

The results of the fiercely fought election were as follows

4.3 Romanian assembly of deputies election, 27 September 1992

Party	Share of votes (%)	Seats
Democratic National Salvation Front (FDSN)	27.7	117
The Democratic Convention of Romania (CDR)	20.0	82
National Salvation Front (FSN, led by Petre Roman)	10.2	43
Party of Romanian National Unity (PUNR, led by Gheorghe Funar)	7.7	30
Democratic Union of Hungarians in Romania (UDMR)	7.5	27
Greater Romania Party (PRM, ultra-nationalist, led by Corneliu Vadim Tudor)	3.9	16
Socialist Workers Party (PSM, neo-Communist)	3.0	13
Others	20.0	0

Notes: Turn-out was 74 per cent. There was proportional representation, with a 3 per cent threshold.

Source: Roper (2000: 74).

The government headed by Nicolae Vacaroiu, November 1992 to November 1996

Nicolae Vacaroiu, a senior civil servant (head of taxation) in the ministry of finance was made prime minister of a somewhat precarious FDSN-led minority government on 4 November 1992. (Theodor Stolojan left Romanian politics as promised and took a job with the World Bank.) Vacaroiu had begun his career in the railways and in the state planning commission under Ceauşescu and had little enthusiasm for economic liberalization, restructuring or privatization. His cabinet was largely made up of other senior civil servants and members of the FDSN. Misu Negritoiu, a reform-minded independent technocrat, initially served as the deputy prime minister in charge of economic reform, but he resigned in August 1993 (along with some other reformist ministers) when several members of the government were accused of corruption.

The Romanian government signed a 'Europe Agreement' (an 'enhanced' association agreement) with the EU on 1 February 1993, with effect from 1 February 1995. This obliged Romania to open up its market to imports from the EU. In return, the EU agreed to eliminate 90 per cent of all quotas and tariffs on industrial imports from Romania, but the EU retained restrictions on imports of agricultural products and so-called 'sensitive goods' (coal, steel, chemicals, textiles, footwear and processed foods) from Romania. Economically, this asymmetrical agreement was quite a poor bargain for Romania, as its main exports were 'sensitive goods'. Nevertheless, this marked the first step on Romania's long road towards eventual membership of th EU and it committed the EU to intermittent political consultation with Romania. All of the political parties represented in parliament approved EU membership as a goal on 21 June 1995, and the next day Romania formally submitted its application for full membership of the EU.

An internal accord improving the rights of the ethnic minorities was signed on 20 July 1993, e.g., more elementary-school lessons in history and geography were to be taught in minority languages, bilingual street signs were to be erected in areas where minorities represented at least 30 per cent of the population, and more university places were to be provided for training Hungarian teachers. Partly on the strength of this, the Council of Europe voted to admit Romania as the thirty-second member on 4 October 1993 (Hungary abstained in the vote).

In January 1994 Romania became one of the first signatories of NATO's 'Partnership for Peace' (PfP) programme, and in 1995 it hosted two major PfP joint exercises and participated in six PfP activities in other countries. This was a relatively undemanding and low-cost substitute for more substantive integration into the EU and NATO, while in the longer run it prepared the ground for acceptance of Romania into NATO in 2002.

Even though it had to propitiate the Hungarian minority in order to make Romania a more acceptable partner for the EU and NATO states, Vacaroiu's minority government depended for its survival on parliamentary support from Gheorghe Funar's xenophobic/ultra-nationalist PUNR, the neo-Communist Socialist Labour Party (PSM) and, less often, the more violently ultra-nationalist PRM. However, neither Vacaroiu nor President Iliescu wanted the FDSN-led government to be seen to be formally associated with such unsavoury parties – especially in the West, where formal links to ultra-nationalist and neo-Communist parties would have been seen as grounds for ostracizing Romania from Western organizations such as the Council of Europe and the EU. Vacaroiu's government was subjected to several parliamentary votes of 'no confidence' between June 1993 and December 1994, but it skilfully contrived to survive. The FDSN, which had been renamed the Social Democracy Party of Romania (PDSR) in July 1993, entered a more formal pact with the PUNR in January 1994, although this was kept secret until two 'moderate' members of the PUNR joined the Vacaroiu government, as ministers of agriculture and communications, in 19 August 1994. In January 1995 the PDSR signed a broader pact including the PRM and the Socialist Labour Party (PSM) as well, committing them to support the government in return for consultation and more consensual four-party decision-making. In January 1996 the PRM received some minor (non-cabinet) ministerial posts. By mid-1996, however, this arrangement was undermined by the PRM's recurrent personal attacks on President Iliescu, accusing him of having been a KGB agent, of involvement in a Zionist conspiracy against Romania, of running down Romania's armed forces at NATO's behest and of selling out to the Hungarians.

In August 1996 Romania and Hungary finally reached agreement on a 'basic treaty of mutual reconciliation and friendship, mainly in order to meet EU and NATO requirements that Romania and Hungary had to resolve their differences and accord respect and substantial minority rights to each other's ethnic groups before either country could even be considered for membership of the EU or NATO. Perhaps with forced smiles and clenched teeth, the prime ministers of Romania and Hungary signed the 'basic treaty' in Timisoara on 15 September 1996. Hungary finally recognize the permanence of Romania's current borders (i.e., permanent Romanian possession of Transylvania) in return for Romanian pledges to respect and protect the rights of the ethnic Hungarians in Romania. Although these ethnic Hungarians were granted human rights, the treaty did not recognize their 'collective rights' or grant territorial autonomy along ethnic lines. The treaty required both countries to protect the civil liberties and cultural identity of national minorities. Ethnic minorities were to have guaranteed rights to be educated in their own languages at all levels of the education system and to use 'historic languages' in local administrative and judicial proceedings in regions where such minorities were concentrated. The same went for road signs, print and broadcast media and virtually every other aspect of communal life. Each country committed itself to supporting NATO and EU membership for the other (*IHT*, 19 September 1996, p. 8).

The PUNR ministers of justice, agriculture and communications were dismissed from the Vacaroiu government on 2 September 1996 after they refused to distance themselves from statements by the party's president, Gheorghe Funar, calling the proposed signing of the basic treaty with Hungary 'an act of treason' and demanding the impeachment of President Iliescu for supporting it (*FT*, 3 September 1996, p. 2), although the PUNR transport minister retained his position after announcing his resignation from the party. The Vacaroiu government and the PDSR severed their unhealthy ties with the PSM as well, partly in an attempt to clean up their soiled image before the November 1996 parliamentary and presidential elections.

Meanwhile, at the end of May 1993 Petre Roman's FSN merged with the Democratic Party (PD) as the PD-FSN. In March 1996, in preparation for the November 1996 parliamentary and presidential elections, Petre Roman forged a Union of Social Democrats (USD), comprising his own PD-FSN and the small Social Democratic Party led by Sergiu Cunescu. He also entered a tactical alliance with the Civic Democratic Party (led by Nicolae Manulescu).

The local elections held on 2, 16 and 30 June 1996

The turn-out was 56.5 per cent in the first round and 54.7 per cent in the second round while some additional run-off elections had to be held on 30 June. The ruling PDSR performed poorly. It lost in most of the larger towns and cities – even in Bucharest, where its mayoral candidate Ilie Nastase (who had been the world's most famous and charismatic tennis star during the 1970s) was decisively defeated by Victor Ciorbea, the plain-speaking 'Mr Clean' candidate of the PNT–Christian Democrats (the main party in the Democratic Convention of Romania). The PDSR retained more support in the countryside, but lost a lot of ground even there.

The Romanian economy under the Vacaroiu government, November 1992 to November 1996

By mid-1996 Romania had become the least privatized and least liberalized economy in the whole of the Balkans and East Central Europe. Vacaraoiu was a staunchly 'corporatist' believer in and defender of Romania's state monopolies, especially the semi-autonomous '*regies autonomies*' (modeled on their French counterparts), which were notorious for their low productivity and poor public service. Furthermore, potential Western investors and donors of economic assistance inexorably came to the conclusion that, under Vacaroiu, 'reforms were agreed to unwillingly and then only to secure funds from international donors which were put to uses other than those intended' (Gallagher 2005: 114–15). This made Western lenders and investors increasingly reluctant to assist Romania with loans and investment.

Vacaroiu presented his stance as prudent caution, gradualism and self-reliance, stressing the need to take a long-term view, to show sensitivity towards the social costs of economic liberalization, surgery and restructuring, and to avoid incurring large new foreign debts or selling out the Romanian economy to foreigners. He had been dismissed from Petre Roman's government for opposing the lifting of state subsidies and price controls, but he encouraged voters to see this as reflecting his concern fo the plight of workers, pensioners and the poor.

Nevertheless, the political stasis achieved by Iliescu and Vacaroiu helped to initiate a modest recovery in 1993–5 (Table 4.2). An austerity package agreed with the IMF in December 1993 and approved by parliament in January 1994 committed the govern ment to float the leu, to reduce the budget deficit to 3.5 per cent of GDP, to curb t trade def cit, and to speed up privatization and restructuring. Partly in consequence, the leu was stable against the dollar during 1994 (*IHT*, 17 March 1995, p. 8). A foating exchange-rate regime was introduced on 8 April 1994, with the exchange rate determined on daily auctions. The leu became almost fully convertible for the purpose of foreign-trade transactions, but there remained controls on capital account trans-actions (EBRD 1994: 33, 109). The 1995 budget, approved on 1 March 1995, set a target budget def cit of 2.7 per cent of GDP and a target infation rate of 29 per cent, in line with IMF advice (*IHT*, 17 March 1995, p. 8). The inflation rate was substan tially reduced in 1994 and 1995, due mainly to the relatively tight monetary policies pursued by Mugur Isarescu, who served as governor of the central bank from 1990 to 1999 (when he became prime minister).

Vacaroiu was the first of Romania's post-Communist prime ministers to serve a full four-year term in office, although voters massively rejected his government a the end of its tenure in November 1996. In effect, government cushioned and cocooned the Romanian economy against painful adjustments, but it could only do so by postponing the painful privatization and restructuring that Romanians would have to undergo sooner or later, if they really wanted to reap in full the potential benefits o fully integrating their country and its economy into the workings of the European and global capitalist economic systems. In 1993, for example, only 250 (mainly small) enterprises were sold off, as against a target of 800–1,000 (*FT*, Survey, 3 May 1994, p. 30). As a result of postponing painful adjustments during the critical 'window of opportunity' of the early to mid-1990s, during which most of the Balkan and East Central European post-Communist governments gritted their teeth and pressed forward with very painful yet quite rapid restructuring, the Romanian economy remained relatively unchanged. This ensured that Romania would not and could not be included among the five 'front-runners' for EU membership designated by the EU in October/December 1997. Romania paid a heavy price in terms of low FDI and financia transfers, reduced competitiveness and restricted access to Western markets and technology.

Nevertheless, a trade agreement was negotiated with the European Free Trade Association (EFTA) in December 1992, with effect from 1 May 1993, while a 'Europe Agreement' (an enhanced treaty of association) was signed with the EU on 1 February 1993, with effect from 1 February 1995. The USA granted Romania Most Favoured

Nation status in October 1993. By 1994 the EU accounted for 47.1 per cent of exports and 50.3 per cent of imports.

In 1996, in an attempt to halt a depreciation of the leu, the authorities imposed restrictions on enterprises' access to foreign currency. In mid-July 1996 an energy crisis led to the introduction of stringent foreign exchange controls (*FT*, 13 August 1996, p. 2). 'Credit policies loosened considerably in 1996 as subsidization of the agriculture and energy sectors through directed credits and the financing of part o the budget def cit by the national bank accelerated', but this increased year-end inflatio to 57 per cent (EBRD 1997a: 9, 32). Resurgent inflation and controls reduced suppor for the PDSR.

There was considerable labour unrest under Vacaroiu. There were strikes by steel workers in May and rail workers in June 1993. In August 1993 there were serious strikes by coal miners in the Jiu valley and by train drivers, but a tough approach by the government resulted in moderate pay awards. On 18 November 1993 large numbers of workers demonstrated against the government and its economic policies. There was a one-day strike by an estimated 2 million workers on 28 February 1994. There were also worker demonstrations in Bucharest between 14 and 16 June 1994. Trade unions wanted improved pay and social-security payments, but also (significantly) faster economic reform. In December 1994 there were strikes by steel workers, coal miners and oil workers. In March 1995 workers protested in Bucharest at a government decision to limit public-sector wage increases, while energy workers went on strike 3–5 June 1995. The largest trade-union groupings were CNSLR–Fratia, claiming 3.7 million members, and Alfa Cartel, claiming 1.2 million members. Both favoured marketizing reform. Total trade-union membership may have been as high as 5.5 million, out of a total workforce of 10.5 million (*FT*, Survey, 3 May 1994, p. 30).

The presidential election of 3 and 17 November 1996

The percentage distribution of votes in the first round is shown in Table 4.4

There was a 75.9 per cent turn-out for the run-off contest between Constantinescu and Iliescu on 17 November 1996, which Constantinescu won with 54.4 per cent of the vote to Iliescu's 45.6 per cent. Petre Roman and Gyorgy Frunda openly declared their support for Constantinescu in the second round. As before, Iliescu played on the fears of farmers, workers, pensioners and nationalists. Many rural voters, espe-cially the elderly who constituted the largest component of the rural population, feared that the opposition might take back land which they had received under the

4.4 Romanian presidential election, 3 and 17 November 1996, f rst round results

Candidate and party	Share of vote (%)
Ion Iliescu, Social Democracy Party of Romania (PDSR)	32.3
Emil Constantinescu, Democratic Convention of Romania (CDR)	28.2
Petre Roman, Union of Social Democrats (USD)	20.5
Gyorgy Frunda, Democratic Union of Hungarians in Romania (UDMR)	6.0
Corneliu Vadim Tudor, Greater Romania Party (PRM)	4.7
Gheorghe Funar, Party of Romanian National Unity (PUNR)	3.2
Tudor Mohora, Socialist Labour Party	1.3
Adrian Paunescu, Socialist Workers Party	0.7

1991 restitution law. Iliescu claimed that the opposition would close large enterprises and threaten the country's unity by including ethnic Hungarians in the government (*FT*, 19 November 1996, p. 21). However, Iliescu's scaremongering no longer carried conviction, and Constantinescu's more liberal stance carried the day. Exit polls on 3 November indicated that Iliescu had won more than half the votes of peasant farmers and 42 per cent of the over sixty-fives, while his challengers obtained overwhelmin support among city dwellers, the young and private entrepreneurs (*FT*, 9 November 1996, p. 2).

Elections to the house of deputies, 3 November 1996

There was proportional representation, with a 3 per cent threshold and fifteen seat reserved for representatives of minorities. The results are shown in Table 4.5.

During the campaign, the CDR advocated faster economic and political reform, a drive against corruption, removal of barriers to private enterprise, reforms of the welfare system, and tax reductions (*FT*, 19 November 1996, p. 21). The CDR and the USD signed a coalition agreement on 7 November 1996. Their priorities were to 'free the exchange rate, tighten monetary policy and overhaul the fiscal system, including a sharp reduction in direct taxes' (*FT*, 8 November 1996, p. 2).

4.5 Romanian house of deputies election, 3 November 1996

Party	Share of vote (%)	Seats
Democratic Convention of Romania (CDR)[1]	30.2	122
Union of Social Democracy (USD)[2] led by Petre Roman	12.9	53
Democratic Union of Hungarians in Romania (UDMR)	6.6	25
Party of Social Democracy of Romania (PDSR)	21.5	91
Greater Romania Party (PRM), led by Corneliu Vadim Tudor	4.5	19
Party of Romanian National Unity (PUNR), led by Gheorghe Funar	4.4	18

Notes: In addition, fifteen seats were allocated to ethnic minorities
1. Dominated by the National Peasant Party–Christian Democrats and the National Liberal Party.
2. Dominated by the Democratic Party (led by Roman), but also including the Romanian Social Democratic Party (led by Sergiu Cunescu) and the Romanian Ecological Convention (led by Dan Hazaparu).

Source: Roper (2000: 80).

The presidency of Emil Constantinescu, November 1996 to November 2000

Professor Emil Constantinescu, the former rector of the University of Bucharest, was an eminent liberal who promised a 'clean break' with Romania's Communist and recent neo-Communist past. He achieved only a very limited success in this regard. The multiparty centrist or centre-right coalition governments that Constantinescu appointed during his term of office were bedevilled by in-fighting and gradually tainted by much the same corruption and clientelism that they had criticized in their neo-Communist and ultra-nationalist predecessors. One of the major consequences was that economic restructuring and privatization proceeded far more slowly than promised. Therefore, when Romania's thoroughly disillusioned voters handed the direction of their country back to the pragmatic and clientelistic neo-Communists led by Ion Iliescu and Adrian Nastase in November 2000, the economy was almost as unrestructured as it had been in 1996.

The government headed by Victor Ciorbea, November 1996 to March 1998

President Constantinescu chose Victor Ciorbea, who had led a high-profile anti-corruption drive as mayor of Bucharest, to become prime minister on 19 November 1996. Unfortunately, Ciorbea soon proved to be a very poor communicator and an ineffective chair of the cabinet, whose interminable meetings frequently went no-where. On 27 November 1996 Petre Roman was rewarded for his crucial support for Constantinescu and the Democratic Convention by being elected speaker of the senate (upper house) by eighty-seven votes to f fty-two.

The new coalition government approved by parliament on 10 December 1996 comprised: foreign minister Adrian Severin, defence minister Victor Babiuc, interior minister Gavril Dejeu, finance minister Mircea Ciumara, industry and commerce minister Calin Popescu Tariceanu, transport minister Traian Basescu, reform and privatization minister Ulm Spineanu. The UDMR was given the portfolios for national minorities and tourism.

On 10 January 1997 the new government secured the arrest of Miron Cozma, the coal miners' leader from the Jiu valley, who had led the *mineriadas* that killed or wounded several people in Bucharest in June 1990 and September 1991. CDR supporters were angry that for six years Cozma had gone unpunished for his crucial role in those actions. However, the charges against him were vaguely and timidly focused on constitutional infringements rather than violations of particular laws and were dropped altogether in June 1998.

On 21 February 1997 the Ciorbea government restored Romanian citizenship to ex-King Mihai. President Iliescu had forced him to leave almost immediately when he visited Romania in 1991 and refused him entry in October 1994. Mihai paid a low-key private visit to Romania from 28 February to 5 March 1997, and on 2 January 1998 Ciorbea announced that the ex-king would be allowed permanent residence in Romania. Next day, however, President Constantinescu reassured republicans that he would not try to restore the monarchy (*EEN*, 1998, vol. 11, no. 25, p. 8).

Economic austerity and reform, 1997–8

On 17 February 1997 Prime Minister Ciorbea announced what he described as a 'programme of national economic salvation', combining austerity measures with ambitious promises to speed up economic restructuring, privatization and reform. He declared:

> We have prepared a comprehensive programme of economic reforms, with the goal of stabilizing the economy and launching the structural reforms necessary for growth . . . We inherited a budget deficit (including implicit subsidies) of 13 per cent of gross domestic product from the previous government. Our programmes for 1997 will be to eliminate hidden subsidies and cut the total defici to roughly one-third last year's level, to 4.5 per cent of GDP. To achieve this

we will cut agricultural subsidies, end most price controls, eliminate tax breaks
and substantially reduce the public sector . . . At the same time we will put in
place programmes of social support to see people through these difficult times

(*FT*, 18 February 1997, p. 20)

In February 1997 subsidies were withdrawn from fuel, electricity, public transport
and telecommunications. By April 1997, all price controls were removed, other than
on electricity, heat, public services, transport and mail (Deutsche Morgan Grenfell,
Focus: Eastern Europe, 11 June 1997, p. 31). On 1 May 1997 even the prices of gas
and heating were increased fivefold, bringing them closer to international levels
(*FT*, 10 May 1997, p. 2). On 17 April parliament formally approved the austerity
programme, which aimed to reduce the budget deficit (excluding implicit/hidden
subsidies) from 5.7 per cent of GDP in 1996 to 4.5 per cent in 1997 and was accompanied by a major devaluation of the leu. Its value fell from 4,000 lei to the US dollar
in late 1996 to a low of *c*.9,000, before stabilizing at just over 7,000 lei to the US
dollar in mid-1997 (*FT*, Survey, 25 June 1997, p. iii).

The government also claimed that it would put 75 per cent of the economy into
private hands within two years (*BCE*, April 1997, p. 15). To this end, control of the
state-ownership fund was transferred from parliament to the cabinet and an anti-
corruption committee was established, partly in an attempt to head off accusations that
privatization would be used simply to enrich the government's friends and relations
(*The Economist*, 3 May 1997, p. 36).

On 23 April 1997 the IMF agreed a standby loan of 430 million US dollars,
conditional on meeting or at least working towards such goals as inflation of 2 per
cent a month in the second half of 1997 (*FT*, 24 April 1997, p. 3), while the World
Bank agreed to loans totalling 530 million dollars. More funds were to be allotted to
the social sector (including health, education and social benef ts), to cushion some
of the pain of economic liberalization, restructuring and privatization. Employees
laid off as a result of restructuring were to be eligible for compensation of up to
twelve months' wages (*EEN*, 5 September 1997, pp. 38–41). In August 1997 Ciorbea
announced the immediate closure of seventeen large state enterprises, including
engineering enterprises, food-processing enterprises and three of Romania's eleven
oil refineries, but the whole list was later whittled down from seventeen to twelve
(*BCE*, March 1998, p. 28).

Overall, however, Coirbea's programme was more smoke than f re. In 1998 the
share of GDP generated by the private sector was no higher than when his government
took office (EBRD 1999b: 24, 256), and during his term of office the economy
contracted severely without realizing tangible compensatory benefts (see Table 4.2).

Foreign affairs, 1997–8

In foreign policy, Ciorbea sought to mend fences and win support for integration
of Romania into the EU and NATO. On 22 February 1997, at the end of a two-day
visit to Romania, President Chirac of France announced his support for the proposed
early admission of Romania to NATO. On 2 June 1997 the presidents of Romania
and Ukraine signed a friendship treaty, including mutual recognition of existing land
frontiers. Romania finally recognized Ukrainian sovereignty over the parts of Bukovin
and Bessarabia annexed by the USSR in 1945. Sea frontiers were to be settled by
negotiations to be completed by 1999. One issue concerned the delimitation of

economic zones in the Black Sea, with its possible reserves of oil and gas. However, both sides 'pledged to resolve the issue within two years, or failing this, to accept the judgement of the International Court at the Hague' (*FT*, Survey, 25 June 1997, p. iv).

On 8 July 1997, however, NATO invited the Czech Republic, Hungary and Poland, but *not* Romania, to begin accession talks. A majority of NATO countries, led by France, had supported the admission of Romania and Slovenia, but the USA insisted that only three post-Communist states should be invited to join in the first instance However, during a visit to Bucharest on 11 July 1997, President Clinton described Romania as one of the 'strongest candidates' for the second wave of invitations, provided it kept to the path of reform.

On 16 July 1997, even more woundingly to Romanian hopes and self-esteem, the EU Commission recommended that Romania should *not be included* among the former Communist countries to be invited to open membership negotiations with the EU in early 1998. The invitations to Estonia, the Czech Republic, Hungary and Slovenia were formally approved at an EU summit in Luxembourg on 13 December 1997, where it was decided that Slovakia, Latvia, Lithuania, Bulgaria and Romania were to be given special EU aid to help them meet the conditions necessary for membership negotiations to begin.

Home affairs, 1997–8

On 18 October 1997 the Ciorbea government decided to open the files of the Securitate Under a law passed by the previous government, the files were closed for thirty years. The new law allowed citizens immediate access to their own files and to thos of public f gures, from the president down to local councillors (*FT*, 20 October 1997, p. 2). The government also decided to reduce the official privileges of so-called 'revolutionaries' or 'f ghters with special merit' – the people who had (supposedly) taken part in the overthrow of Ceauşescu in 1989. More than 30,000 people had been granted tax exemptions, a free hectare of land, free housing, preferential access to office space and free public-transport passes. The new government believed that many had received such privileges simply because they had supported Iliescu (or had bribed officials to get them) and that only those who had been wounded or imprisone in the uprising and close relatives of those killed should receive tax exemptions (*FT*, 20 October 1997, p. 2). After protests, however, the government agreed not to amend the law on privileges until all those on the offial lists were checked to see if recipients had genuinely taken part in the revolution (*FT*, 31 October 1997, p. 3).

On 2 December 1997 there was a cabinet reshuffle prompted largely by failings i the privatization programme, caused by wrangling within the governing coalition. The sense of urgency which Premier Ciorbea had tried to inject into privatization when he took off ce had already evaporated (*EEN*, 1997, vol. 11, no. 23, pp. 4, 8). Trade unions were protesting against the government's social policies and the way restructuring was being carried out, but the protests had for the most part been poorly attended, while golden handshakes had blunted resistance to closures. Nevertheless, industrial restructuring was usually only occurring under external pressure and was producing botched, last-minute decisions on closures. In the first nine months of 1997 1,120 (mainly small) firms had been privatized, but there was little progress on broade industrial restructuring – even of privatized firms. Sales of big companies were stil rare. Few doubted the government's will to reform, but questions were 'starting to be asked about its competence' (*BCE* December, 1997 pp. 39–40).

A political crisis began in December 1997 when Roman's USD demanded the replacement of Prime Minister Ciorbea, after the removal of two USD ministers. (The foreign minister Adrian Severin was forced to resign after failing to substantiate allegations that senior politicians were foreign agents, while the transport minister Traian Basescu, a future president of Romania, was sacked for publicly criticizing Ciorbea.) On 14 January 1998 the UDR gave Prime Minister Ciorbea an ultimatum 'to step down to pave the way for a government more intent on proceeding with market reforms (*IHT*, 15 January 1998, p. 5), but the next day Ciorbea's PNT rejected his offer to resign. In fact, the clash was only partly about 'different approaches to economic reform'. Personal rivalries, feuding between parties and 'the deeply entrenched clientilism of Romanian politics, with politicians acting on behalf of opposing business and industrial interests', were delaying key reforms, from the restructuring of the oil industry to the redistribution of agricultural land. The PNT was insisting on further restitution of agricultural land to its former owners, while the Civic Alliance was pressing for the opening of Securitate f les and the barring from politics of people found to have been Securitate officers or informers, all of which th USD (dominated by former Communist apparatchiks) opposed. The USD leaders, although proponents of the free market, were mostly drawn from younger members of the former Communist elite, regarded themselves as progressive technocrats, and looked down on the PNT as 'backward-looking, romantic, inexperienced and incompetent'. The PNT, for its part, viewed the USD 'as corrupt former Communist apparatchiks who jumped ship from the Ceaus,escu dictatorship at the last possible moment' (*FT*, 27 January 1998, p. 3). The suspicion was that Roman wanted to block reform 'because it would damage his cronies in business and finance'*BCE*, February 1998, p. 7).

The USD withdrew its remaining ministers from the cabinet on 29 January, but on 6 February the DCR and the USD signed a new cooperation agreement, with the USD no longer insisting on the replacement of Prime Minister Ciorbea. Finally, on 29 March the PNL called on Ciorbea to resign the premiership. He did so the next day, having lost the support even of his own PNT.

The Radu Vasile government, April 1998 to December 1999

A new cabinet headed by Radu Vasile, the deputy chairman of the NPP–Christian Democrats, was approved by parliament on 15 April 1998. The respected non-party economist Daniel Daianu (nominated by the PNL) became minister of finance. However, Daianu formally resigned on 23 September 1998, after the PNL withdrew its backing. The PNL advocated lower taxes, a policy that Daianu rejected owing to the growing budget deficit *FT*, 24 September 1998, p. 3). Daianu was fired ostensibl because he had failed to cut taxes. However, he had put some noses out of joint by refusing to authorize a 1.5 billion-dollar order for ninety-six US helicopters, while his calls for tax rises and spending cuts had further reduced both his and the government's popularity (*BCE*, November 1998, pp. 45–6). The privatization minister Sorin Dimitru resigned on 19 October 1998, less than a month later, amid widespread criticism of continuing delays in carrying out privatization. While both ministers were widely criticized for failing to implement reforms, both blamed other ministers and bureaucratic foot-dragging for their lack of progress. Their departures removed two of Romania's major advocates of reform. Dimitru complained that he had received no support for privatization either from the government or from parliament. His agency had privatized 825 companies by the end of August 1998, as against a target for the year of 1,600 (*FT*, 20 October 1998, p. 3).

The **mineriada** *of January and February 1999*

On 18 December 1998 the government announced that it planned to close twenty-nine coal mines. A miners' strike began in the Jiu valley on 4 January 1999, after the government refused to increase pay by 35 per cent and halt the planned pit closures. On 15 January a district court ruled the strike to be illegal. Police helicopters sprayed tear gas and dropped smoke bombs on an estimated 10,000 striking miners on 18 January, as they marched on Bucharest. Premier Vasile appealed to the miners to return home, promising to talk to them personally. Organized rallies and demonstrations by miners had been banned in Bucharest since the *mineriada* of September 1991 (*FT*, 19 January 1999, p. 2).

On 19 January the Romanian government threatened to deploy troops to halt the 20,000 workers marching towards Bucharest, after riot police failed to stall their advance. Jiu valley miners had been joined by others from the Oltenia coalf elds as well as workers from other regions and industries. It was estimated 70,000 people could lose their jobs if the planned closures and restructuring of forty-nine loss-making state-owned companies were carried out. Another 70,000 workers in the steel industry were set to lose their jobs as part of a five-year plan to restructure the steel sector (*FT*, 20 January 1999, p. 3).

Miners clashed violently with police and smashed through barricades on 21 January. The interior minister, unable to halt this 'march on Bucharest', resigned. President Constantinescu threatened to call a state of emergency if the miners did not turn back to the Jiu valley. The next day, after hours of talks between Prime Minister Radu Vasile and the militant miners' leader Miron Cozma in an Orthodox monastery outside the town of Rimnicu Vilcea in central Romania, the government announced that it had reached a deal with the miners. 'Neither the miners nor the government won,' Premier Vasile declared. 'Only the country won, because there will be peace.' He did not give details of the deal, saying they would be ironed out in Bucharest in the coming weeks, but he conceded that the proposal 'went in the direction of the miners' claims'. However, it would not become final until a plan to reduce production costs in the mine was completed. One miner claimed that they had secured a 30 per cent wage increase, but the government insisted that it could not afford such demands, because miners already earned double the average salary and the coal industry was making losses (*IHT*, 23 January 1999, p. 2). The agreement involved pledges to keep many un-prof table mines open for at least f ve years and provide wage increases, but it made the proposed pay rises contingent upon a five-year plan to turn round the performanc of the Jiu valley mining industry. Mine managers and the miners' unions were given thirty days to work out a plan to cut losses by 20 per cent a year for f years, according to government spokespersons (*IHT*, 25 January 1999, p. 5).

However, many miners and ultra-nationalists saw the deal which Cozma negotiated with Vasile as a sell-out that had scuppered a golden opportunity to bring down a hated hard-nosed neo-liberal government, and Cozma suddenly found himself very isolated and excoriated by both sides. He was expelled from Tudor's Greater Romania Party. The government then seized this opportunity to prosecute him for his leading role in what had obviously been another attempt to overthrow an elected government by force. On 15 February Romania's supreme court sentenced Miron Cozma to eighteen years in jail, having found him guilty of undermining state authority, illegal possession of firearms and violent offences committed in June 1991, when he led the violent miners' rampage through Bucharest that left several people dead, invaded parliament, set government buildings on fire and brought down the Petre Roman government (*IHT*, 16 February 1999, p. 6). Cozma went into hiding, unable to appeal against the jail sentence because of the nature of the charges against him. Tudor, meanwhile, was suspended from parliament (and thus lost his parliamentary immunity) for making allegations about President Constantinescu's private life *FT*, 16 February 1999, p. 2).

An estimated 4,000 Romanian coal miners launched another 'march on Bucharest' on 16 February, defiantly led by Cozma, and most of the coal mines in the wester Jiu valley shut down as a consequence *IHT*, 17 February 1999, p. 5). However, Cozma was arrested the next day, following clashes between paramilitary police units and miners that left one miner dead and dozens injured. More than 500 arrests were reported (*IHT*, 18 February 1999, p. 7).

In the end, the initially unnerved Vasile government mustered enough resolve to face down the threat to its existence and restore its governmental authority, but this *mineriada* blew a gaping hole in its economic programme and made it exceedingly diff cult for it to regain its chosen course. Any further challenges of this sort could be expected to finish it off

Back to politics as usual, April to December 1999

From 7 to 9 May 1999, Pope John Paul II made the first papal visit to a predominantl Orthodox country since 1054, when the Eastern Orthodox Church split from the Catholic Church. However, despite his request to visit the concentrations of Catholics in Transylvania and Moldova, the visit was restricted to Bucharest and was not without tensions. Romania's Orthodox Church was at loggerheads with the 300,000-strong Uniate ('Eastern rite') Catholic Church, which was seeking the return of over 2,000 churches seized by the Communist regime in 1948 and given to the Orthodox Church, while their congregations were forced to revert to Orthodoxy. 'Eastern rite' Uniate Catholics, who broke away from the Orthodox faith in the seventeenth century, still worshipped according to Orthodox-style rites, but recognized the Pope as their spiritual leader.

The Vasile government announced an accelerated privatization programme on 16 May 1999. The f rst sixty-four large and medium state companies to be privatized represented about 14 per cent of GDP. The list was headed by the national airline Tarom, the giant Sidex steelworks of Galati and two aluminium companies. Next in line were the electricity, oil and gas, transportation, tobacco, postal services and water corporations, including the country's biggest companies: the power company Conel, the oil company Petrom and the natural-gas company Romgaz. Petrom was Romania's largest company, accounting for *c*. 10 per cent of GDP (*FT*, 17 May 1999, p. 3; *IHT*, Survey, 26 October 1999, pp. 18–20). The June 1999 privatization law provided for the use of investment banks as sales agents and eliminated minimum sales prices linked to book value (thereby allowing sale at market value). It contained provisions for debt workouts and gave minority shareholders the right to more information and control, which were intended to reduce the power of the 'insiders' who had previously gained effective control of most privatized enterprises (EBRD 1999b: 254–5).

During the March–June 1999 Kosova war, Romania shrewdly offered NATO important help and valuable use of Romanian facilities. Romania had also given the EU states help to subdue the major insurgency in Albania in 1997. In addition, the EU Commission and the governments of the EU member states were rapidly becoming more aware of the fragility of Balkan stabilization efforts, the damaging effects of continuing Balkan instability on their own societies and economies, of the demoralizing and destabilizing effects of their decision in 1997 to open membership negotiations with just five of the thirteen applicants for EU membership and of th need to be seen to be taking much bolder and more decisive action to bring more of the former Communist states into the EU fold and to give the governing elites of the candidate countries greater encouragement and incentives to persevere with economically, socially and politically painful reforms and restructuring. Britain and France, which were bearing the brunt of European military interventions, Italy, which had intervened in Albania, and Germany, which had much to gain economically and in other ways from greater stability in East Central Europe and the Balkans – each had strong motivations to bring about a fundamental change of tune. This was the context in which the EU Commission recommended on 13 October that the December 1999 European Council meeting in Helsinki should allow Romania (along with Bulgaria, Latvia, Lithuania, Malta and Slovakia) to begin accession negotiations in March 2000. The 'principle of differentiation' was to apply to each candidate, recognizing their differing states of readiness for EU entry. 'Each country will be able to proceed on merit, including the possibility for those which join the negotiations from 2000 to catch up with the others' (*FT*, 14 October 1999, p. 1; *IHT*, 14 October 1995, p. 9). Nevertheless, the commission's recommendations warned that Romania's situation gave considerable cause for concern and that Romania would have to make up a lot of economic ground before it could be deemed ready for accession. Most immediately, Romania was required to take steps to deal with its weak economic and budgetary position and to improve the lot of 100,000 children in child-care institutions, before being allowed even to begin negotiations. Many observers believed at the time that Romania was still far from ready to take on the arduous obligations and challenges of EU membership, but these misgivings were quite rightly overridden by an even stronger belief that Romania's querulous and restructuring-averse elites had to be offered a major new inducement to act decisively to break out of the country's debilitating vicious circles and inertia.

There were violent workers' demonstrations in Brasov on 8 November 1999 and in Iasi on 23 November, a national rail strike started on 6 December, and students also mounted protests against the Vasile government that month *EEN*, 2000, vol. 12, no. 21, pp. 6, 8). According to an opinion poll published in early December 1999, 61 per cent of Romanians believed that their living standards had been higher under Communist rule. About 66 per cent were worried that the country was moving in the wrong direction and about 80 per cent said they were unhappy with their lives. However, around 85 per cent were still in favour of a market economy, but 88 per cent believed that the market system had benefited only the few *Transitions*, 1999, vol. 10, no. 3, p. 33).

President Constantinescu decided to dismiss Premier Vasile on 14 December, following the resignation of seven cabinet ministers. Vasile was deemed no longer able to carry out his duties and to have failed in his quest to revive the economy (*IHT*, 15 December 1999, p. 4). Vasile was also dismissed from the deputy leadership of his own party and banned from standing for re-election to senior posts over the next two years. Vasile objected that a prime minister could only be sacked by parliament and that the president's action was unconstitutional and Ion Iliescu, as leader of the opposition, agreed and threatened to withdraw his party from both chambers of parliament until Constantinescu revoked the dismissal (*FT*, 15 December 1999, p. 10). However, Vasile soon realized that the game was up. He formed a 'Popular Group' faction within the PNT–Christian Democrats, claiming over thirty MPs, but for this he was expelled from the party on 27 December. In January 2000 he launched a rival party, which was joined by a dozen defectors from the PNT–Christian Democrats, but in August his new party (re)joined the CDR-led coalition.

The Mugur Isarescu government, December 1999 to December 2000

On 16 December 1999 President Constantinescu nominated Mugur Isarescu, governor of the Romanian central bank since 1990, as the new prime minister. He was widely respected and credited with having successfully upheld sufficient degrees o monetary discipline and central-bank independence to bring about considerable macroeconomic stabilization. He had endeavoured to resuscitate the privatization programme by seeking to broker a cross-party consensus on economic policy. He was also considered the ideal person to solicit increased Western economic assistance and inspire confidence that Romania could use it effectively *IHT*, 28 December 1999, p. 8). Nevertheless, the Isarescu government inherited a very difficult situation. In 2000 Romania had 'the highest proportion of people in Europe below the off cial poverty line, outside the former Soviet Union'. About 40 per cent of its 22 million inhabitants could barely afford to feed themselves, according to the World Bank *FT*, 9 February 2001, p. 8).

In April 2000, in order to increase Romania's chances of admission to the EU, Iliescu's PDSR backed a cross-party, medium-term economic programme. This envisaged keeping budget deficits below 3 per cent of GDP and further deregulatio and privatization. Nevertheless, Iliescu criticized the fraudulent 'insider' privatizations allegedly orchestrated by Radu Sirbu (former head of the state property fund) and signalled that, if he and his party were returned to power (as expected) in the November 2000 elections, he intended to reverse some recent privatizations and increase public assistance for the poor (*FT*, 24 November 2000, p. 12).

The PDSR made major gains in the local elections held on 4 June 2000 and even obtained control of Bucharest for the f rst time. The turn-out was only 47 per cent (*The Economist*, 10 June 2000, p. 57). Later, especially after the November 2000 elections, many hundreds of local councillors and mayors 'defected' to the PDSR, giving it almost complete control of local as well as central government in Romania by 2001 (Pralong and Apostol 2003: 475–8).

President Constantinescu announced on 17 July 2000 that he would not run for a second term of office in November 2000. He said his decision had been 'prompted b setbacks in his attempts to fight what he called a Mafia-type system of "official corruption, with links to high-ranking state institutions" ' (*IHT*, 18 July 2000, p. 7). However, Constantinescu had failed to use his presidential power and prestige to give much stronger and clearer leadership and guidance to the country and to the querulous ministers whom he chose to govern it.

In November 2000 the EU Commission made particularly scathing and distressing criticisms of Romania in its annual report on the country' *Progress Towards Accession*:

Little progress has been made in reducing levels of corruption . . . There has been little progress in developing administrative capacity . . . Romania cannot be regarded as a functioning market economy and is not able to cope with competitive pressure and market forces within the Union in the medium term. It has not substantially improved its future economic prospects . . . The fragile macroeconomic environment, the uncertain legal and institutional framework and the uneven commitment to reforms continue to hinder economic development. Many institutions required to ensure the functioning of a market economy either do not exist or are too weak to be effective. Insufficient reforms and a growin black market economy have undermined progress made on macroeconomic stabilization. The absence of a sound and well functioning financial system hampers economic activity. A very large part of the enterprise sector has yet to start restructuring or is still in the process of doing so. Investment has continued to fall, delaying the required modernization of the supply side of the economy . . . In the case of agriculture a major structural reform of the sector is needed. In the case of the treatment of Roma, the continued high levels of discrimination are a serious concern . . . Further progress still needs to be made with regard to demilitarization of the police and other bodies subordinated to the ministry of interior.

(EU Commission, *Progress Towards Accession*,
8 November 2000, pp. 87–9)

As a consequence, Romania was ranked last among the twelve countries negotiating for admission to the EU. The force of these criticisms contributed to the CDR's total meltdown in the November 2000 elections.

The presidential election of 26 November and 10 December 2000

There was a marked swing away from the centre-right parties, which split their vote in the f rst round of the presidential election and meant that they were therefore unable to continue to the second round. The chief beneficiaries were Ion Iliescu an the ultra-nationalist Corneliu Vadim Tudor, who managed to exceed even the combined share of the vote for the main liberal candidates, Theodor Stolojan and Mugur Isarescu. The percentage distribution of votes is shown in Table 4.6.

Iliescu comfortably won the presidential run-off held on 10 December 2000, with 66.9 per cent of the vote to Tudor's 33.1 per cent, on a turn-out of 57.5 per cent. Both domestic and international attention focused not on Iliescu but on his thuggish

4.6 Romanian presidential election, 26 November and 10 December 2000, f rst round results

Candidate and party	Share of votes (%)
Ion Iliescu, Party of Social Democracy	37.0
Corneliu Vadim Tudor, leader of the ultranationalist Greater Romania Party	28.5
Theodor Stolojan, National Liberal Party	12.0
Mugur Isarescu, independent banker/technocrat	9.0
Gyorgy Frunda, Hungarian Democratic Union of Romania	6.0
Petre Roman, Democratic Party	3.0

quasi-fascist challenger, who secured an alarmingly high share of the votes cast – even higher than Jean-Marie Le Pen's 19 per cent share in the rather similar presidential run-off in France in May 2002 (Cole 2005: 43). However, this comparison points to striking similarities as well as differences between Balkan and Western European politics. In this election, like Le Pen in France in 2002, Tudor skilfully 'moderated his tone and portrayed himself as a nationalist determined to fight corruption, red tape and mismanagement' (*FT*, 29 November 2000, p. 10). Nevertheless, in 1998 Tudor had declared that Romania needed to be governed 'from the barrel of a gun', and in his election campaign he stated: 'Romania is caught between anarchy and the Mafia. I will liquidate the Mafia so fast that they won't even have time to glance a their watches to let them know that Romania is ruled by an iron fist' *Independent*, 29 November 2000, p. 15). His election broadcasts concentrated on his 'liquidate the Maf a' message and promises to create 500,000 jobs by producing goods needed in the developing world (*IHT*, 29 November 2000, p. 6). He also promised a tough law-and-order policy and state compensation 'for savers hurt by a string of bank failures', while blaming privatization for most of the public corruption which he lambasted (*The Economist*, 2 December 2000, p. 60).

Elections to the chamber of deputies, 26 November 2000

For this election, the number of seats was increased to 345, 18 of which were earmarked for representatives of ethnic minorities. Proportional representation was retained, but the threshold was raised from 3 per cent to 5 per cent for free-standing political parties, 8 per cent for two-party coalitions, 9 per cent for three-party coalitions and 10 per cent for those involving four or more parties. In accepting these changes, the CDR virtually cut its own throat. Even its chief component, the PNT–Christian Democrats, failed to pass the raised threshold and was therefore not represented at all in the new parliament. The results are shown in Table 4.7.

Like the PNT–Christian Democrats, the ultra-nationalist PUNR also failed to pass the threshold and therefore obtained no seats. The upshot was that Iliescu's PDSR, which was led in parliament by the prime-minister-designate Adrian Nastase (a former senior member of Ceaus ̦escu's regime), faced a very fragmented and ineffectual opposition and was able to take full control of the entire state apparatus, including almost all local councils and mayoralties. Nevertheless, the OSCE election monitors felt able to report that 'The 2000 polls further demonstrated that democratic elections are firmly entrenched in Romania. Important features of the legal and

4.7 Romanian chamber of deputies election, 26 November 2000

Party	Share of votes (%)	Seats
Party of Social Democracy of Romania (PDSR)	44.9	155
Greater Romania Party (PRM, led by Tudor)	24.3	84
Democratic Party (PD)	8.9	31
National Liberal Party (PNL)	8.7	30
Democratic Union of Hungarians in Romania (UDMR)	7.8	27
Ethnic-minority parties	5.2	18

Note: Turn-out 65.3 per cent.

Sources: Pralong and Apostol (2002: 314; 2003: 477–9).

administrative framework produce an election process that is accountable, transparent, free, fair and equal' (Pralong and Apostol 2003: 475–9). This provided another classic illustration of the feasibility of even well-conducted democratic procedures producing outcomes that are clientelistic, illiberal and conducive to 'state capture' by a single self-serving and corrupt political party. Within two weeks of the election, hordes of civil servants were dismissed en masse and replaced by PDSR political appointees.

The government of Adrian Nastase and the third presidency of Ion Iliescu, November 2000 to November 2004

In forging a working majority in parliament, the PDSR chose not to seek the support of either the Democratic Party or Tudor's Greater Romania Party (PRM). Instead it formed a minority government shored up by cooperation pacts with the UDMR and the PNL, which pledged their support for a year. The Nastase government's pact with the UDMR dovetailed neatly with the EU's insistence on respect and protection for minority rights as a prerequisite for future accession to EU, and the government therefore agreed to promote Hungarian-language education (including a Hungarian-language university) and the use of Hungarian in public administration wherever the Hungarian minority comprised 20 per cent or more of the local population (*EEN*, 2001, vol. 13, no. 2, p. 3). In addition, from early on, the Nastase government encouraged (and benefited from) numerous defections from other parties to its own rank (Pralong and Apostol 2003: 476–8). The opposition became very ineffectual after the ousting of Petre Roman as leader of the PD, which precipitated 'mass defections' from the PD to Nastase's PDSR (*EEN*, 2001, vol. 13, no. 5, p. 4).

Nevertheless, during 2001 Romania had a much better year than many of its citizens had dared to hope when the Iliescu–Nastase team was first elected. The new ruler provided some much-needed political stability. Within a month of taking off ce the new government introduced tax breaks for small and medium enterprises and a new property-restitution bill. Its economic policies, still based on the above-mentioned cross-party medium-term development programme, were virtually unchanged from those of the previous government. However, the tax breaks for small companies were new, and the budget deficit for 2001 was set to exceed 4 per cent of GDP, breachin the IMF-inspired limit of 3 per cent (*BCE*, February 2001, p. 37).

In February 2001 Premier Nastase negotiated a comprehensive 'social pact' or 'stability pact' with the main trade unions and employers' associations by offering to create jobs quickly by building more roads, dams and housing. The pact set out principles which the unions, employers and government agreed to abide by. The aim was to secure a stable framework, so that negotiations rather than strikes would be used to solve industrial disputes. The unions agreed that wage rises should be linked to output and to corporate profitability. The government also promised to reduce business taxes and bureaucratic red tape, to cut inf ation to less than 25 per cent and to hold the budget deficit at 3–4 per cent of GDP, in the hope of striking a new dea with the IMF by mid-May, thereby unfreezing credits suspended in autumn 2000 (*IHT*, 12 February 2001, p. 4; *BCE*, April 2001, p. 50).

The PDSR merged with the tiny Romanian Social Democratic Party and adopted the name Social Democratic Party (PSD), under the chairmanship of premier Adrian Nastase, on 16 June 2001. This merger was motivated by the PDSR's 'desire to be admitted into the Socialist International, in which the smaller party was already a member', in order to acquire international respectability. Due to its neo-Communist legacy and chequered record, 'the PDSR had been refused membership repeatedly since 1990. The trick paid off' (Pralong and Apostol 2002: 314). In the same month, a showy public statue of Romania's wartime fascist dictator Marshal Ion Antonescu was unveiled in Bucharest (*IHT*, 2 June 2001, p. 4). But two months later, in response to warnings that Romania's chances of being admitted to NATO could be damaged by the erection of statues and the naming of streets in honour of Antonescu, the government banned any further public displays of his image (*IHT*, 2 August 2002, p. 3).

Internationally, steps were being taken to reduce Romania's marginalization. On 15 March 2001 the EU conditionally removed visa requirements for Romanians visiting the EU for up to three months (and did the same unconditionally for Bulgarians), pending further progress on tackling illegal immigration/people trafficking (*IHT*, 16 March 2001, p. 4). On 27 June 2001 the governments of Romania, Albania, Bosnia, Bulgaria, Croatia, Macedonia and Yugoslavia signed an agreement aimed at liberalizing trade in at least 90 per cent of goods traded between them, under the auspices of the EU's stability pact for South-eastern Europe, in order to enhance regional stability through economic growth. Moldova was expected to join the arrangement shortly, thereby reducing the drawbacks of its continued amputation from Romania (*FT*, 28 June 2001, p. 8).

In October 2001, at a conference on the stability pact for South-eastern Europe hosted in Bucharest, financial support totalling 2.4 billion euros (mostly loans) wa announced for twenty-seven infrastructural projects to deepen integration among the Balkan states. The funding was targeted on transport, energy and environmental projects. Romania was to receive about 535 million euros (*FT*, 25 October 2001, p. 14).

The EU Commission, which in November 2000 had branded Romania as the worst performer among the candidate states, delivered a more upbeat assessment of its progress and prospects in its November 2001 report.

In June 2002 Romania abandoned its plans to build a Count Dracula theme park at Sighisoara – one of the outstanding intact medieval citadels of Europe, the birthplace of the eponymous Vlad the Impaler, and a UNESCO-funded world heritage site. The theme park would have involved the destruction of a forest of ancient oak trees, some believed to be 800 years old. The Romanian authorities decided to develop ecologically friendly tourism there and seek an alternative site for Dracula Land (*Independent*, 29 June 2002, p. 13). In January 2003 the consultancy frm PricewaterhouseCoopers recommended that it would be more commercially viable to locate the project nearer to Bucharest (*IHT*, 27 January 2003, p. 2), and in October 2003 it was announced that the Count Dracula amusement park would be built in Snagov, 35 kilometres north of the capital, starting in 2004 (*IHT*, 29 October 2003, p. 2).

Wooing the USA, 2001–3

Following the 11 September 2001 terrorist attacks on the USA, Romania (like Bulgaria) opened up its airspace unconditionally to US aircraft and offered the use of all land and port facilities. Bulgarian and Romanian troops were already serving as peace-keepers in Kabul. Both tripled their presence in international peacekeeping missions in the Balkans in order to free up allied troops for Afghanistan, while a Romanian military facility in the Black Sea city of Constanza was under preparation to become a staging ground for the rotation of US troops in and out of the Balkans and other theatres (*IHT*, 26 March 2002, pp. 1, 4). By 2002 Romania's armed forces had been cut to less than half their 1989 peak of 230,000 personnel (*FT*, 24 June 2002, p. 6).

On 1 August 2002 Romania became the first country to sign an 'Article 98' agreement with the USA, promising not to extradite to the International Criminal Court in The Hague any 'American soldiers or peacekeeping personnel allegedly involved in crimes against humanity while serving abroad' (*FT*, 2 August 2002, p. 6). A week later an EU Commission spokesman declared: 'We deplore that a candidate country to the EU has not waited for the EU to establish its final position, which will be take in early September' (*FT*, 12 August 2002, p. 6).

In August 2002, with a view to the decision in November 2002 on whether to admit Romania to NATO, the Romanian government ended a moratorium on foreign adoptions of Romanian children. The EU had asked for this ban, claiming such adoptions were little more than 'baby selling' (*FT*, 24 August 2002, p. 6). Yet, partly in response to this obsequious grovelling, the USA duly backed Romania's admission to NATO when the time came and President George W. Bush visited Romania on 23 November 2002.

In February 2003 Romania supported the US-led occupation of Iraq, and Romanian forces have consistently taken part in that occupation, even surviving the change of government in January 2005.

In June 2003 Romania's ministry of public information provoked international controversy by issuing a statement that 'within the borders of Romania between 1940 and 1945 there was no Holocaust' (*Daily Telegraph*, 15 June 2003). Jean Ancel, a leading Israeli specialist on the Holocaust in Romania, protested that in his estimation 420,000 of the 760,000 Jews whom he estimated were living in Romanian-controlled territories in 1939 had been killed by 1945. He also claimed to have documentary evidence that the Antonescu regime was directly involved in the systematic extermination of Jews. Indeed, 'Romania was the only ally of Germany that had its own plan of destruction and used its own army to exterminate Jews' (Associated Press, 15 June 2003). However, even though Ancel's claims were in one sense accurate, his way of presenting them was misleading, because of his estimated total of 420,000 Romanian Jews killed, up to half were killed by Germans and Hungarians, rather than by Romanians. Distorting facts in order to present Romania in the blackest possible light may be counterproductive as a means of getting Romanians to face up to unpalatable truths. The continuing reluctance of many Romanians fully to acknowledge and come to terms with this terrible chapter in their country's past remains a major problem, but one that is by no means peculiar to Romania. For example, similar problems have been present in the politics of France, which has only quite recently began fully to face up to (i) the magnitude of French support for the Vichy regime and (ii) French complicity in the Holocaust, which for a long time was too easily blamed almost entirely on Nazi Germany. Even countries such as Switzerland, Portugal and Sweden, which were formally neutral during the Second World War and not parties to the Holocaust, have only quite recently begun to confront the ways in which they profit from the Holocaust or contributed to Hitler's new order. In formerly Communist-ruled countries such as Romania, Hungary and even Poland, however, public ignorance or denial of such occurrences has been compounded by the refusal of their former Communist regimes to allow these subjects either to be properly acknowledged and taught in the education system or to be fully reported and debated in the media. All 'blame' was very conveniently deflected onto Nazi Germany and a few conveientl scapegoated 'collaborators'. Continuing Romanian admiration and nostalgia for

Antonescu is also a sad testimony to the depths of hardship, suffering and despair to which most Romanians were later reduced by the Communist and Iliescu regimes. Denial and selective amnesia vis-à-vis the recent past is nevertheless a major barrier to mutual and self-understanding in the present.

The vicissitudes of integration into the EU, 2002–3

In its October 2002 annual report on Romania's *Progress Towards Accession*, the EU Commission complimented Romania on 'positive developments' in the treatment of minorities and continuing 'progress towards being a functioning market economy'. However, the report also emphasized the need to 'give priority to establishing a track record on macroeconomic stabilization grounded on further disinflation, by maintaining an appropriate policy mix and underpinning it with the enforcement of enterprises' financial discipline', to accelerate privatization, to liquidate loss-makin enterprises, to strengthen the capacity of Romanian public administration to implement the *acquis communautaire*, to strengthen border infrastructure and management, to increase the eff ciency of the judiciary, and to crack down on money laundering and corruption. 'Administrative capacity building will require a comprehensive, structural reform of both the public administration and the judicial system' (EU Commission, *Progress Towards Accession,* 9 October 2002, pp. 127–30). On the basis of this mixed report, the European Council in Copenhagen in December 2002 decided to exclude Romania from the first wave of the 'eastward enlargement' of the EU in May, and t put back its target date for entry (as well as that of Bulgaria) to January 2007.

In its November 2003 annual report on Romania's *Progress Towards Accession,* the EU Commission emphasized the continuing impediments to EU membership. Romania was told it could not yet be considered a functioning market economy, that its courts were not fully independent, and that it was mired in corruption and mismanagement:

> The judicial system needs to improve the management of cases and the consistency of judgements as well as to increase the independence of the judiciary. .   . . Corruption in Romania continues to be widespread and affects all aspects of society. A number of high-profile measures were launched . . . but the implementation of anti-corruption policy as a whole has been limited . . . While some progress can be reported in meeting the priorities relating to respect for human rights and protection of minorities, a considerable amount of work still remains to be done . . . In addition, a vigorous and sustained implementation of its structural reform programme is required in order for Romania to be able to cope with competitive pressure and market forces within the Union in the near term . . . Particular attention must be paid to developing the ability to administer the public procurement, the foodstuffs and food safety *acquis*. Progress of the free movement of persons has been limited and additional efforts should now be focused on preparations for implementing the *acquis* on mutual recognition of professional qualifications. Work to identify barriers to the free movement of services has continued – although only a few restrictions have been removed. While alignment with the *acquis* on free movement of capital is steadily improving, greater efforts are needed to improve payments systems and the figh against money laundering.
>
> (*Progress Towards Accession*, 5 November 2003, pp. 121–6)

If this somewhat damning assessment had been made in November 2002, on the eve of the European Council in Copenhagen, rather than a year later, it might well have scuppered Romania's chances of EU membership before 2010.

Meanwhile, back at the ranch . . .

On 18–19 October 2003 there was a referendum in which 89.7 per cent of those who voted approved a new constitution, which had been designed to promote marketizing and democratic reforms and was seen as crucial to Romania's EU membership prospects. The turn-out of 55.7 per cent exceeded the 50 per cent needed to make the referendum result valid. Fearing that a low vote turn-out could invalidate the vote, the PSD had campaigned hard from door to door, urging reluctant voters to cast their vote. Even priests and doctors went door to door in some regions. However, NGOs, the media and opposition politicians criticized what they saw as heavy-handed tactics and excessive use of mobile ballot boxes. There were widespread allegations of voters being offered television sets, seats at football matches and even firewood as incentive to vote (*IHT*, 20 October 2003, p. 3; *Independent*, 22 October 2003, p. 12). While not opposed to the constitutional changes, the PNL leader Theodor Stolojan and the PD leader Traian Basescu accused the government of 'taking illegal and improper steps to ensure the 50 per cent turn-out necessary for a valid referendum' (*FT*, 22 October 2003, p. 16). Three government ministers resigned amid allegations of corruption(*The Times*, 21 October 2003, p. 18).

In February 2004 the prominent ultra-nationalist, anti-Semite, xenophobe and leader of the opposition, Corneliu Vadim Tudor, announced that he would lead a pilgrimage to the Auschwitz death camp to express his remorse and to ask for forgiveness for having denied for so long that a holocaust had taken place in Romania during the Second World War and for his 'terrible words' against Jewish leaders. Tudor was still leader of the extreme-right PRM and was preparing to run again in the November 2004 presidential election. The popularity of Tudor's party's had risen, especially in rural areas, where people were increasingly tired of persistent poverty and corruption (*IHT*, 14 February 2004, p. 6).

On 15 June 2004 the chamber of deputies approved a new law stipulating that Romanian children could be adopted by foreigners only after every attempt had been made to make it possible for them to remain with their natural family or be placed with a Romanian family (*The Times*, 15 May 2004, p. 19). The new law bowed to EU insistence that the lucrative trade in children had to be stamped out and defl pressure from the USA for regulated foreign adoption. The law was to take effect from January 2005. It allowed Romanian orphans to be adopted abroad only by their grandparents and only after a search for Romanian adoptive parents had failed (*The Guardian*, 16 June 2004, p. 17). Some 40,000 children remained in the Romanian state orphanage system, which had been accused of selling orphan babies to the highest bidders (*FT*, 15 May 2004, p. 7).

The municipal elections held on 2 and 20 June 2004

The distribution of votes in these elctions is shown in Table 4.8. The PSD suffered major losses, paying a price for persistent corruption and malpractice, but remained the largest single party. The PSD foreign minister Mircea Geoana was trounced in the mayoral contest for Bucharest, obtaining only 30 per cent of the vote, whereas the

4.8 Romanian municipal election, 2 and 20 June 2004

Party	Share of votes (%)
Social Democratic Party (PSD)	35
National Liberals (PNL)	17
Democratic Party (PD)	13
Greater Romania Party (led by Corneliu Vadim Tudor)	8
Democratic Union of Hungarians of Romania (UDMR)	7
Humanist Party of Romania (PUR)	5

Democratic Party incumbent Traian Basescu won 60 per cent (*FT*, 8 June 2004, p. 9; *IHT*, 9 June 2004, p. 5).

Privatization made significant headway during 2004. Austria's ÖMV corporatio acquired a 33 per cent stake in the national oil and gas company SNP Petrom in July 2004 and majority control in December 2004. This was Romania's largest privatization to date. Progress was also made with the privatization of half the electricity-distribution companies and the two natural-gas distributors. The remaining four state-owned electricity distribution companies were scheduled for privatization in 2006 (EBRD 2005b: 166).

Press freedom resurfaced as a widely discussed issue in Romania in September 2004 after journalists at *Evenimenttul Zilei* and *Romania Libera*, two of the biggest dailies, accused their foreign owners (Switzerland's *Ringier* and Germany's *Westdeutsche Allgemeine Zeitung*) of trying to suppress negative coverage of the PSD government and alleged that the government was using state-controlled advertising budgets and selective enforcement of tax laws to influence the media in the run-up t the parliamentary and presidential elections scheduled for November 2004. In its October 2003 progress report on Romania, the EU Commission had warned that, by allowing foreign-owned media companies to delay paying their taxes, the government had rendered them 'dependent on the good will of the Romanian authorities' (*FT*, 28 September 2004, p. 8).

The *Strategy Paper of the European Commission on Progress in the Enlargement Process* published on 6 October 2004 claimed that Romania was back on track for admission to the EU in January 2007. The paper was nevertheless critical. Corruption remained 'a serious and widespread problem which affects almost all aspects of society' and was hard to root out because of 'integrity problems' among law enforee ment officials. Although press freedom had improved in some respects after the abolition of the catch-all crime of 'insult' in May 2004, there was a rising trend of 'serious physical attacks against journalists'. The report also found that 'a majority of judges had come under political pressure', while organized crime remained rampant: 'Romania remains the country of origin, transit and destination for victims of traff cking in human beings.' The strategy paper reaffirmed that 'Bulgaria and Romani are an integral part of this enlargement process which was launched in 1997' and stated that the commission was aiming to complete the membership negotiations with Bulgaria and Romania before the end of 2004, which would make it feasible for them to join in 2007.

They need to continue their efforts to develop sufficient administrative and judicia capacity to implement and enforce the *acquis* . . . Additional efforts are needed in particular in the competition chapter as regards state aid and in the justice and home affairs chapter as regards judicial cooperation, fight against corruptio and organized crime, border management.

However, because 'the period between the end of the negotiations and Bulgaria's and Romania's expected date of accession is likely to be long, and given the large number of commitments that still need to be fulfilled', the commission considered that thei accession treaties should as a precaution contain 'safeguard clauses' that would

> allow the Commission to recommend to the Council . . to postpone the envisaged date of accession of Bulgaria or Romania by one year to January 2008 if there is clear evidence that there is a serious risk that Bulgaria or Romania will be manifestly unprepared to meet the requirements of membership by 1 January 2007 in a number of important areas.
>
> (EU Commission, *Strategy Paper of the European Commission on Progress in the Enlargement Process*, October 2004, pp. 2–4)

The commission's *Regular Report on Romania's Progress Towards Accession*, published on 6 October 2004, was more upbeat:

> Macroeconomic stability has been achieved, profound economic reforms have been carried out, while the Romanian authorities' commitment to the economic requirements of EU accession has been sustained. Hence, it is concluded that Romania complies with the criterion of being a functioning market economy. Vigorous implementation of its structural reform programme should enable Romania to cope with competitive pressure and market forces within the EU .. . Organizational and legislative changes introduced in Romania's judicial system should help make it more independent and efficient. Their implementation on the ground is a matter of priority . . . Substantial progress in the functioning of the judiciary and the public administration, including an even and predict- able application of law, is required to create an enabling business environment with a level playing field . . . The economic situation of many mass media organizations remains precarious and further efforts are necessary to guarantee media independence. Although the restitution of agricultural land is almost completed, a more speedy and transparent approach is needed to further the restitution of buildings and religious property. Efforts to address the problems of ill-treatment in custody, trafficking in human beings and prison overcrowdin should be sustained . . . De facto discrimination against the Roma minority remains widespread . . . Romania is generally meeting the commitments that it has made during the negotiations, although delays have been noted in specif areas. Bearing in mind the progress achieved . . . the level of alignment and administrative capacity that Romania has achieved at this point in time, and its track record in implementing the commitments that it had made in the negotiations . . . the Commission expects Romania to assume the obligations of membership in accordance with the envisaged timescale.
>
> (EU Commission, *Strategy Paper of the European Commission on Progress in the Enlargement Process*, October 2004, pp. 146–50)

Elections to the chamber of deputies, 29 November 2004

The incumbent PSD, led by Adrian Nastase, was allied to the small Romanian
Humanist Party (PUR), while the PNL and the PD formed a coalition called the Truth
and Justice Alliance (DA). The other major contenders were Tudor's ultra-nationalist
PRM and the UDMR. The official results are shown in Table 4.9

Neither of the major alliances obtained a parliamentary majority. Both the
DA and the PSD ruled out any coalition or cooperation with the ultra-nationalist
PRM (whose 13 per cent share of the vote was no higher than that obtained by
major ultra-nationalist parties in France, Italy, the Netherlands, Belgium, Austria and
Denmark).

The PSD prime minister Adrian Nastase behaved as if his party had won the election
and would form the next government in coalition with the PUR and possibly the
UDMR as well. Nastase and the PSD had benefited from almost non-stop coverag
by state television and by some of the private networks owned by wealthy Romanian
businessmen. Romanian NGOs accused the government of allowing politically
connected business groups to escape taxation, rigging state contracts and manipulating
the media. Many Romanians felt the campaign had been 'unfair, because of biased
media coverage in favour of the PSD, especially from state-run television and radio'
(*FT*, 29 November 2004, p. 6). The PSD foreign minister Mircea Geoana was expected
to succeed Nastase as prime minister, on the widely held assumption that Nastase
would win the second round of the presidential election on 12 December (*IHT*,
27 November 2004, p. 3). The PSD was embarrassed by an eve-of-election leaking
of transcripts of party-leadership meetings which (if genuine) showed that it had
'routinely manipulated the justice system and the media' (*The Economist*, 4 December
2004, pp. 40–1).

OSCE observers judged that, overall, the conduct of the elections 'seemed pro -
fessional and efficiently organized', although they urged the authorities to investigat
reports of multiple voting: for example, some voters had shown identity documents
rather than registration cards at polling stations, opening the way to multiple voting,
but the OSCE considered that resultant distortions had probably been too small to
affect the result, even if they slightly boosted the SDP vote, and that 'administrative
and judicial' remedies should suff ce (*The Economist*, 4 December 2004, pp. 40–1).

By contrast, Romania's main civil-rights group, Pro Democratia, claimed that it
had been inundated with fraud allegations. It alleged that as much as 5 per cent of the
vote might have been affected and that the PSD had resorted to widespread ballot-
rigging, transporting voters from one polling station to another and thus enabling them

4.9 Romanian chamber of deputies election, 29 November 2004

Party	*Share of vote (%)*	*Seats*
PSD+PUR Alliance	36.6	132
PSD	–	(113)
PUR	–	(19)
Truth and Justice Alliance (DA)	31.3	113
Greater Romania Party (PRM)	12.9	48
Democratic Union of Hungarians (UDMR)	6.2	21

Source: Mungiu-Pippidi (2005).

to vote more than once, while hundreds of ballot papers had disappeared (*IHT*, 30 November 2004, p. 3). On 30 November the DP leader Basescu called for a rerun of the elections (*The Guardian*, 1 December 2004, p. 14). The opposition parties accepted the results in the end, however, because they managed to turn them to their own advantage.

The two-round presidential election held on 28 November and 12 December 2004

The distribution of votes in the first round is shown in Table 4.10

The main presidential rival to Nastase was the mayor of Bucharest and former ship's captain, Traian Basescu. Although he had been a member of the RCP, Basescu had held no party posts under Ceauşescu. He had served as transport minister (1996–7), but he mainly made his mark on Romanian voters as the hard-working and plain-speaking mayor of Bucharest (2000–4) by improving public services and ridding the capital of its large packs of stray dogs. He entered the presidential election only two months before polling day, after Theodor Stolojan (then leader of the PNL and the presidential candidate of the Truth and Justice Alliance) decided to pull out of the race for health reasons – and probably also because Basescu was emerging as a stronger DA presidential candidate. By default Calin Popescu-Tariceanu, the deputy leader of the PNL, became the DA's most likely prime-ministerial candidate.

During the campaign, Basescu pledged to continue Romania's quest to join the EU in 2007 and to keep Romania's 700 troops in Iraq at least until elections were held. He talked a great deal about forming a 'Washington–London–Bucharest axis', implicitly downgrading Romania's 'traditional' links with France. (President Chirac's arrogant 'lecture' to the Balkan and East Central European states in February 2003 concerning their support for the US-led occupation of Iraq had alienated many people in the region.) Basescu also proposed a single 16 per cent flat-rate tax both on compan profits and on personal incomes, with the stated aim of drawing Romania's substantial black economy back into the open (*FT*, 14 December 2004, p. 10). He went 'to the heart of the issues preoccupying the majority of Romanians: poverty and corruption at the highest level'. He claimed that the manner in which privatization had been carried out had served the interests of the ruling elite, because it had lacked transparency and the enterprise managers had close links with the PSD. He promised 'zero tolerance' towards sleaze/corruption and vowed to annul any state contracts that had been awarded illegally (*IHT*, 27 November 2004, p. 3, and 14 December 2004, p. 1).

The capital, the educated young, the urban middle classes and western Romania mainly supported Basescu and the DA, whereas Nastase and the PSD were mainly supported by the rural poor, the elderly, Romania's poorer southern and eastern regions,

4.10 Romanian presidential election, 28 November and 12 December 2004, first round results

Candidate	Share of vote (%)
Adrian Nastase, incumbent PSD prime minister	40.9
Traian Basescu, leader of the PD and of the DA alliance	33.9
Corneliu Vadim Tudor, leader of the Greater Romania Party	12.6
Bela Marko, leader of Democratic Union of Hungarians of Romania	5.1

Source: Mingiu-Pippidi (2005).

and the still sizeable class of former Communist apparatchiks *FT*, 29 November 2004, p. 6). In the presidential run-off held on 12 December 2004, contrary to expectations, Basescu obtained 51.23 per cent of the votes to Adrian Nastase's 48.77 per cent. Election monitors reported irregularities, but fewer than before. More than 3,000 observers monitored the vote (*IHT*, 13 December 2004, p. 3). Nastase bowed out gracefully the next day. Mircea Geoana, the former PSD foreign minister, took over as PSD leader in 2005. A burst of intense political lobbying ensued, as the DA sought support from the UDMR and the PUR, both of which had been considered likely to join a PSD-led government (*FT*, 14 December 2004, p. 10).

On 16 December 2004, just before leaving office, Iliescu issued a presidential pardon to the former miners' leader Miron Cozma, who had been jailed for his roles in the violent *mineriadas* of September 1991 and January 1999. However, after loud protests from politicians and the media, the pardon was revoked the next day.

On 22 December 2004 President Basescu nominated as prime minister the PNL leader Calin Popescu-Tariceanu, who forged a coalition between the DA and the smaller UDMR and PUR (both of which had been expected to join a PSD-led government), with further support among the eighteen ethnic-minority deputies.

The government headed by Calin Popescu-Tariceanu, December 2004–

Calin Popescu-Tariceanu named his cabinet on 26 December 2004. The PNL obtained six portfolios, besides the premiership. The PD had a deputy premiership and six portfolios. The PUR had another deputy premiership and the economy ministry. The non-party historian Mihai-Razvan Ungureanu became foreign minister, while the non-party human-rights activist Monica Macovei became justice minister. But on 28 December 2004 Cristina Parvulescu, nominated to the post of European inte - gration minister, was judged to be too young and inexperienced, so she was replaced by the economics professor Emila Dinga. The new government was mainly made up of unknown young technocrats with little or no previous experience of government (*IHT*, 29 December 2004, p. 3).

The new government was sworn in on 29 December 2004. Using the government's power to make law by emergency ordinance, Calin Popescu-Tariceanu immediately introduced the promised 16 per cent flat rate of taxation both on personal income and on company prof ts with effect from 1 January 2005, in an attempt to stimulate increased investment and to draw out into the open much of the country's sizeable 'black economy', estimated at 40–50 per cent of the real economy. The existing tax rate on corporate prof ts was 25 per cent, while personal income taxes ranged from 20 per cent to 40 per cent (*FT*, 30 December 2004, p. 5; *FT*, 14 January 2005, p. 7).

In February 2005 the government lifted the immunity from prosecution of former cabinet ministers, and in March it started opening up millions of fes compiled by the former Securitate, which was said to have used 'half a million officers and million of informers to spy on their fellow Romanians' (*IHT*, 11 March 2005, p. 5).

In early 2005 President Basescu made visits to London, Moscow, Berlin and Washington, endeavouring to give substance to his proposed 'Washington–London–Bucharest axis'. In Moscow on 14–15 February he reasserted Romanian interest in Black Sea region cooperation, in the future of Moldova and in a resolution of the Transnistria/Transdnestria problem (its Russian-backed de-facto autonomy). The USA and Romania signed an agreement on 7 December 2005, allowing the USA to use and develop three military bases in Romania (*FT*, 8 December 2005, p. 8). However, by early 2006 Basescu had retreated from his 'Washington–London–Bucharest axis' vision, in order not to alienate the founder members of the EU and to concentrate single-mindedly on pursuing Romanian admission into the EU on 1 January 2007.

The most pressing task of the new government was to complete the preparations for Romania's accession to the EU. On 25 April 2005 Romania, like Bulgaria, signed its treaty of accession to the EU, although this would not take effect until January 2007 at the earliest. However, during the summer of 2005 three reforms, which (if adopted) would have helped to combat corruption and strengthen the independence of the judiciary, were rejected by still PSD-controlled constitutional court, on the grounds that they were incompatible with the constitution. This ruling meant that President Basescu could not sign into law the seventeen bills passed on 22 June to overhaul the judiciary, compensate citizens for property taken under Communism, align anti-trust laws with the EU and f ght corruption.

On 14 June 2005 a Romanian court ordered the release of the former miners' leader Miron Cozma, imprisoned for his roles in the violent *mineriadas* of September 1991 and January 1999, after seven years of his eighteen-year sentence. Upon his release, Cozma accused Ion Iliescu and Petre Roman of having planned the September 1991 *mineriada* and of having consistently manipulated the Jiu valley miners for their own ends (Ameriei 2005a).

Prime Minister Popescu-Tariceanu took most people by surprise on 7 July 2005 by announcing that he would resign and request a fresh parliamentary election. In such circumstances, the president was supposed to nominate a new prime minister and, if that person also failed to form a government capable of governing, the president was supposed to call an election (*FT*, 8 July 2005, p. 10).

However, on 19 July 2005 Tariceanu announced that he had changed his mind and would ask parliament for a vote of confidence in a bid to remain prime minister and continue to lead the reform and restructuring of Romania in preparation for EU membership. He declared that his government's top priority was to help those in need, after floods swept through central and eastern Romania, killing twenty-one people (*IHT*, 20 July 2005, p. 4). However, it appears most likely that he resumed office – and was accepted on that basis – because both he and President Basescu were warned by the EU that the turmoil and uncertainty of putting together a new government and risking new elections at that critical juncture could well result in Romania being deemed not ready for accession to the EU by January 2007. Tariceanu, the Romanian parliament and the constitutional court appear to have decided that they all had no choice but to bite the bullet and persevere with the requisite reforms.

On 25 October 2005 the EU Commission's annual progress reports warned that Bulgaria and Romania risked having their accession to the EU delayed until 2008 if fraud, bribery, piracy of intellectual property and organized crime were not brought under control by the time that EU governments decided in April 2006 whether to allow them to become members in 2007. The commission's reports highlighted the slow pace of judicial reform in both countries, worryingly large backlogs of cases in their court systems and rampant organized crime and human trafficking. The report highlighted continuing deficiencies in administrative capacity, press freedom, acces of Roma (Gypsies) to jobs and housing, privatization, bankruptcy procedures, use of regional development funds and labour market flexibility. They asked both countrie to speed up the implementation of laws in areas ranging from environmental protection and treatment of psychiatric patients to justice and home affairs. Transparency International had ranked Romania as the most corrupt of the EU member and accession states. The Romanian and Bulgarian governments immediately vowed to redouble their campaigns against crime and corruption (Ameriei 2005c;*IHT*, 26 October 2005, p. 3).

On 25 October President Basescu refused to sign and referred back to parliament an anti-racism bill which failed to mention Roma (Gypsies) among the victims of the Holocaust. The previous week, rights activists and EU parliamentarians had signed an open letter objecting to the wording of the legislation, which banned Holocaust denial and aimed to make racism illegal (*IHT*, 26 October 2005, p. 4).

In January 2006, perhaps partly to provide a virtuoso demonstration of Romanian determination to fight corruption on the eve of potential EU entry, the state prosecu tion service began corruption investigations into deputy prime minister George Copos, ex-prime minister Adrian Nastase and the former economy minister Dan Ioan Popescu (Ameriei 2006). By April 2006 many foreign observers were commenting that Romania's chances of being able to enter the EU on schedule in January 2007 had improved signif cantly, whereas several high-profile street killings and loss o reforming momentum had diminished Bulgaria's chances. It was even being contemplated that Romania might join in January 2007 without Bulgaria.

Nevertheless, on 16 May 2006 the EU decision on whether to admit Romania in January 2007 was postponed until early October 2006. The EU Commission emphasized that Romania still had to increase its efforts to combat corruption, carry out judicial reform, stop human trafficking and improve conditions in psychiatric institutions. A special monitoring system could be put in place during the first thre years of Romanian EU membership, if the implementation of reforms in the justice system was deemed to be insufficiently advanced before accession, or if the fight against corruption in the judiciary had not yielded suff cient tangible results. Such close monitoring of a new member state would be unprecedented in the EU. The mechanism would be in place for three years, and would involve annual reports by the commission to EU governments and the European parliament. A major potential penalty would be that judgements or warrants issued by Romanian courts would no longer be automatically recognized in the rest of Europe. In addition, the so-called 'safeguard clauses' could restrict Romanian participation in EU decisions on such areas as justice, home affairs and food safety, or could even postpone its accession to the EU until January 2008 (although this was considered unlikely because it would require majority agreement among the twenty-five member states). Furthermore, failure to speed up reform in these areas could result in limits being introduced on Romanian access to EU aid. Romania was expecting to receive 1.7 billion euros (2.2 billion US dollars) in EU financial transfers during its first year of EU membershi and the 10.69 billion euros of EU fnancing that Romania was due to receive between 2007 and 2009 was equivalent to the total amount of FDI that the country had received during the previous ten years (*IHT*, 17 May 2006, p. 7).

There also remained four other areas of serious concern (so-called 'red flags') whic Romania was required to tackle before entry into the EU, but these were essentially technical in nature: (i) to make its computer systems for VAT collection interoperable with those in other EU states, in order to permit effective collection of VAT; (ii) to establish fully operational payment agencies for disbursing EU farm aid to farmers; (iii) to achieve an effective system of animal registration, necessary both for the payment of EU farm subsidies and for the maintenance of acceptable veterinary standards; and (iv) to put in place adequate facilities for the collection and treatment of animal by-products, mainly to guard against bovine spongiform encephalopathy (BSE, or 'mad cow disease'). Lurking in the background was a further potential hurdle on the road to EU accession: nine of the twenty-five EU member states, includin Germany, France and the Netherlands, had not yet ratified the Romanian and Bulgaria accession treaties (*IHT*, 16 May 2006, pp. 1, 5; *IHT*, 17 May 2006, p. 7; www.bbc. co.uk, 16 May 2006).

The non-party human-rights lawyer Monica Macovei, who had been appointed Romania's justice minister in January 2005, was accorded much of the credit for Romania's vaunted successes in combating corruption and crime during 2005 and early 2006. Her most potent weapon against corruption had been the new requirement that politicians, senior civil servants, judges and customs officers had to publicly declare their assets, 'right down to details of banks accounts and art collections'. Nevertheless, it was of crucial importance that her efforts had been 'sustained by public support and solid backing from President Traian Basescu' (*FT*, 15 May 2006, p. 8).

Concluding reflections: democratization and liberalization in Romania

It is all too easy to pass harsh judgements on Romania. However, from 1990 to 1999, the West did 'little but watch as post-Communist Romania stagnated, mired in appalling poverty and systemic corruption'. This inaction was made possible by the fact that, unlike some of its Balkan neighbours, Romania remained politically stable and free from the civil warfare, insurgency and genocide that tend to trigger international concern and intervention (*IHT*, 28 December 1999, p. 8). However, if it is borne in mind that Romania lacked the head-starts provided by the development of an autonomous civil society in Communist-ruled Poland or of a semi-marketized economy and considerable freedom of travel in Communist-ruled Hungary and Slovenia, or of a relatively sound and stable economy in the case of Communist-ruled Czechoslovakia, it could be argued that, in terms of 'the sheer amount of social, political and economic change', Romania travelled much further than these other countries did during the 1990s (*IHT*, 28 December 1999, p. 8). Even though Daniel Nelson made these observations (in the*IHT*) as long ago as 1999, they remain pertinent today.

According to an opinion survey published in early November 1999, 61 per cent of Romanians believed that they were better off under Communism. About 66 per cent were worried that the country was moving in the wrong direction, with 75 per cent dissatisf ed with living standards; 80 per cent said they were unhappy with their lives. Around 85 per cent were still in favour of a market economy, but 88 per cent believed that the market only benefited high-ranking officials (*Transitions*, 1999, vol. 10, no. 3, p. 33). In 2004 Transparency International reported that, on average, Romanians were having to spend about 10 per cent of their monthly wages on routine bribes*The Guardian*, 29 November 2004, p. 14). Romania's GDP in 2004 was estimated merely to have reached 99 per cent of the already depressed level which it was at in 1989 (EBRD 2005a: 13). Clearly, there has been no shortage of indicators of poor perfor-mance since 1989.

Nevertheless, post-Communist Romania underwent far-reaching changes. Despite all the gradualism and foot-dragging with respect to economic liberalization and privatization during the 1990s, the private-sector share of the formal economy had risen from just 5 per cent in 1989 (Deutsche Bank,*Focus: Eastern Europe*, 1994, no. 100, p. 30) to 15 per cent in 1990, 55 per cent in 1996 and 60 per cent in 1997–9 (see Table 4.2). Furthermore, if the semi-legal 'informal sector' and the illegal 'black economy' are taken into account, private enterprise became even more dominant. In February 1997, Prime Minister Ciorbea spoke of the (informal) 'grey economy' representing 40 per cent of GDP, while the chief of the main state security agency reckoned that the 'black economy' represented 35–38 per cent of GDP(*EEN*, 11 April 1997, vol. 11, no. 7, p. 4). In early 2000 the 'black economy' accounted for an estimated 40 per cent of GDP (*BCE*, March 2000, p. 42). The importance of the private sector varied considerably between sectors. In early 1995 its share of value added was only 12 per cent for industry, but it was 46 per cent for services, 50 per cent for construction and 69 per cent for domestic trade. In 1996 the private-sector share was estimated at 24 per cent for agriculture and 75 per cent for trade and services (EBRD 1994: 10; 1995b: 11; 1996b: 53, 167; and 1997b: 14, 192).

Politically, the nature and direction of the dominant trends have been more difficult to characterize. In some respects, Romania appeared to achieve more impressive democratization than most of the other formerly Communist-ruled states in the Balkans and East Central Europe. In particular, the OSCE has frequently complimented Romania on the relatively fair and rigorous conduct of its elections, even though there were apparently some glitches in the elections held on 26 November 2004. Election turn-outs were considerably higher in Romania during the late 1990s and early 2000s than they were in several East Central European states. If the best measures of the state of health and vigour of a democracy are the levels of political participation and engagement of its *demos*, then Romania comes out relatively well.

Nevertheless, Romanian politics and power structures have continued to be dominated by 'power clans', clientelism, patronage, 'insider privatization', corruption, personalism, dependence and *vertical* power relations (as they were under medieval princely, Ottoman, nationalist and Communist rule), rather than by the rule of law and the *horizontal* ties, contractual relations and rich associational life which are the essential underpinnings of the more liberal forms of governance that came to prevail in the modern West. Post-Communist Romania achieved a relatively high degree of electoral democracy, but just how liberal, responsive, transparent and accountable it has become is another matter. It has certainly become more liberal, responsive, transparent and accountable than the widespread forms of 'illiberal democracy' and 'delegative democracy' identified by writers such as Fareed Zacharia (1998) and Guillermo O'Donnell (1996), but it still leaves much to be desired. The unchallenged political ascendancy of the political forces associated with Ion Iliescu and the FSN from 1990 to 1996 had a baleful impact on the Romanian polity. The FSN had been

> created from the top down with the expectation that it could – and should – control or closely supervise the emergent political competition. It also sought to continue a pattern of politics whose main goal was to elicit popular acquiescence in elite-determined politics, which put a low emphasis on political accountability and responsiveness . . . Opposition parties were tolerated, but they were not viewed as equal partners in the competition for power.
>
> (Craiutu 2000: 175)

The configuration of the first freely elected parliament in May 1990 did not encoura 'the emergence of a politics based on bargaining, compromise and self-restraint', but on the contrary encouraged intolerance and an adversarial politics 'which politicized nearly every issue on the legislative agenda to the point of excluding enlightened pragmatism and cooperation across party lines' (Craiutu 2000: 176). The result was a worst-of-both-worlds combination of (i) highly clientelistic and elite-dominated conglomerate parties centred on prominent individuals with (ii) high levels of intemperate ideological polarization focusing on non-negotiable *ideological* positions, stances and issues, rather than on more negotiable *distributional* ones. 'Romanian political parties appeared more as vehicles for polarizing polemics than interest aggregation and compromise' (Craiutu 2000: 177). Unfortunately, these entrenched patterns and power relations were perpetuated rather than overcome by the Democratic Convention of Romania coalition that replaced Iliescu and his colleagues after the elections of November 1996.

Fortunately, the intensifying quest among the greater part of Romania's political elite from the late 1990s onward for acceptance of Romania into the EU by 2007 or 2008 appears to have strongly increased their motivation and willingness to accept and promote greater degrees of liberalization, privatization, restructuring, account - ability, rule of law, and cross-party cooperation and consensus and, thus, to make possible a momentous shift from a polity, society and economy based upon *vertical* power structures, power relations, dependence, patronage, clientelism and corruption to one based much more on the rule of law, *horizontal* ties, contractual relations, associational vitality and a civil society, civil economy and liberal polity. The galvanizing and mind-concentrating effects of the 'dangled carrot' of EU membership on the Romanian political classes since the late 1990s has been quite remarkable. Such consequences, occurring not just in Romania but almost throughout the Balkan Peninsula, have helped to justify the existence of the EU far more than is realized in the West – even among Europhiles.

Considering how far from ready for EU membership Romania was in November 1999, when the country was invited to commence formal accession negotiations the following year, the catalytic decision formally to include it in the 'enlargement pro-cess' must have been taken for (geo)political and strategic reasons. In the wake of the major crises in Albania in 1997 and in Kosova during 1998 and the first half of 1999, the commission and EU heads of government became convinced that Balkan destabilization was contagious, that the rest of Europe was unable to insulate itself from the consequences and that drastic action had to be taken to reinforce the faltering efforts and incentives of Balkan elites to persevere with politically, socially and economically painful restructuring and liberalization. Furthermore, EU and NATO heads of government seem to have appreciated (i) the considerable value of the strategic and logistical support given by Romania and Bulgaria to EU and NATO efforts to deal with the crises in Albania 1997 and in Kosova in 1998–9, and (ii) the importance of being seen to reward these countries for having offered and provided this valuable support. More generally, the EU Commission and EU heads of government quickly recognized that the 1997 decision to initiate formal accession negotiations in 1998 with just five of the twelve applicant states was having (and was bound to have) potentially demoralizing, demotivating, stigmatizing, marginalizing and destabilizing effects on the candidates who had been excluded from those negotiations, because they somewhat invidiously separated the favoured 'sheep' from the considerably disadvantaged 'goats' and erected new 'walls in the mind' as well as new policed and fortified territorial frontiers and barriers between them. For all these reasons, in autumn 1999 it was decided to make the 'eastward enlargement' of the EU a much broader and more inclusive project, within which each candidate country would be recurrently assessed on its own (shifting) merits and the perceived laggards would be allowed chances to draw level with the perceived front-runners. In adopting this momentous change of tack, the commission and the EU heads of government took considerable (indeed courageous!) gambles and risks. However, the political classes of Romania and especially Bulgaria (which were by common consent perceived to be by far the weakest and least prepared candidates for EU membership) have richly rewarded the faith that was placed in them by belatedly making quite heroic, hectic and largely successful efforts to diminish the distance between themselves and the perceived 'front-runners'. To be sure, Romania and Bulgaria have not been alone in this regard. The political elites of the republics of Macedonia, Montenegro, post-1997 Albania, post-Dayton Bosnia, post-Tudjman Croatia and even post-Milosevic Serbia have also made strenuous, courageous and often successful headway in the same direction. In the Romanian case, the most striking achievements have arisen out of the considerable but long-overdue efforts made by Romania's political elites from 1996 onward to break with old vertical power structures and power relations and to promote the rule of law, horizontal ties, contractual relations, economic liberalization and level playing fields. Even the instinctively corporatist, nationalist and clientelistic Democratic National Salvation Front/Social Democratic Party, which remained under the baleful tutelage of Ion Iliescu from 1990 to 2004, belatedly attempted to kick some of its old habits during Iliescu's final term of office (December 2000–December 2004). Maj cross-party efforts had substantially reduced the proverbial 'gaps' between Romania and the post-Communist avant-garde by May 2006. As a result, in early September 2006, the EU commission made it known that it would be recommending that Romania (and, less deservedly, Bulgaria) be allowed to join the EU on schedule in January 2007. This was a remarkable achievement for the Popescu-Tariceanu government and President Basescu. The drive to attain accession has provided powerful reinforcements of the quest to entrench more strongly the rule of law, level playing fields, legal curb on clientelism and corruption and the decisive restructuring of power structures from vertical to horizontal axes, needed to transform Romania (for the fst time in its history) into a robust civil society with a fourishing civil economy and polity. Even the issues of the plight of the Transylvanian Hungarians and who 'owns' Transylvania would be defused considerably by Romanian entry into the EU. This would make a 'Europe without frontiers' and free movement of persons much more of a reality for people on either side of the border between Romania and Hungary and would make Magyars and Romanians equal citizens of the EU, with the same rights and obligations and subject to the same 'cosmopolitan' supranational legal order, policy frameworks and jurisdiction. This could help to lay the 'demons' of Romanian and Magyar nationalism and ethnic collectivism to rest – finally

5 Croatia

Paying a price

Introductory 'country profile'

Croatia is a small country, with an area of 56,538 square kilometres (about one-tenth of the size of France and one-fifth of the size of former Yugoslavia). It had a population of 4.5 million in 2005. Only 26 per cent of Croatia's territory was arable land in 2001, but overall the country has been fairly well provided with grape-vines, olive groves, fruit trees and (since the late eighteenth century) maize. Croatia's capital city is Zagreb (855,568 inhabitants in 1981). Its other major cities include Split, Rijeka, Osijek, Cakovec, Zadar, Slavonski Brod, Varazdin, Sisak, Sibenik, Karlovac, Dubrovnik (formerly known by its Italian name, Ragusa), Vukovar and Pula. Croatia's economy is quite highly developed. In 2004 64.5 per cent of the workforce was engaged in services (including transport and the large tourism sector), 32.8 per cent was employed in industry (including construction) and only 2.7 per cent was engaged in agriculture. In 1989, with 21 per cent of the Yugoslav Federation's population, Croatia contributed 26 per cent of Yugoslavia's GDP. Its per-capita income was about 30 per cent above the Yugoslav average. In 2004 Croatia's per-capita GDP at purchasing power parity was 11,670 dollars, a little over one-third that of France, Germany and the UK (World Bank 2005: 296).

According to the 2001 census, by ethnic affiation 89.6 per cent of Croatia's inhabitants were Croats, 4.5 per cent were Serbs and 5.9 per cent had other ethnic affiliations However, 96.1 per cent stated that Croat was their f rst language and only 1 per cent recorded Serbian as their first language, while the remaining 2.9 per cent said the primarily spoke other languages. By declared religious affiliation, 87.8 per cent wer Roman Catholic, 4.4 per cent were Eastern Orthodox, 0.4 per cent had other Christian affiliations, 1.3 per cent were Muslim, 5.2 per cent atheist and the remaining 0.9 per cent were unspecified

The 1991 and 2001 census returns show that the campaigns of 'ethnic cleansing' carried out in 1991–5 had major effects on the composition of Croatia's population by ethnic affiliation (see Table 5.1)

5.1 Ethnic affiliations of population of Croatia, 1991 and 2001 (per cent

	Croats	Serbs	Yugoslavs	Others
1991	78.1	12.2	2.2	7.5
2001	89.6	4.5	–	5.9

Source: Lampe (1996: 330); CIA (2005).

Who are the Croatians?

Modern Croatians are brought up and educated to think of themselves as descendants of the Slavs who from the sixth to the ninth centuries AD settled in the lands which have come to be known as Croatia. Like every other people, however, the Croatians are mongrels. Ancient Greeks, so-called 'Illyrians', Celts, Romans, Italians, Austro-Germans and Hungarians have contributed significantly to Croatia's ethno-cultura heritage.

By the second millennium BC, the main inhabitants of what is now Croatia are generally claimed to have been so-called Illyrians, speaking what may have been an Indo-European language, but no one really knows who they were or even the language they spoke – there is a dearth of reliable information (see Chapter 2). Between the eighth and the fourth centuries BC, ancient Greek seamen, wanderers and traders founded significant settlements on the Adriatic islands and coasts. During the fourt century BC, parts of the western Balkans were also settled by Celts.

Crushing defeats inflicted by Rome on mutinous protégés in southern 'Illyria' i 168 BC and on the kingdom of Macedon in 146 BC resulted in gradual extension of Roman control over the whole of Illyria, which eventually became the Roman prefecture of Illyricum. Following the suppression of major revolts inAD 9, Illyricum was sub-divided into a coastal province known as Dalmatia and an inland province of Pannonia, comprising what are now Croatia's Slavonia region, Serbia's Vojvodina and Hungary's southern plain. Parts of the intermittently rebellious indigenous Illyrian population were gradually killed, expelled or sold into slavery by the Romans and replaced by substantial numbers of military and agricultural colonists recruited from all over the Roman Empire. The Romans also built up a very impressive infra-structure, including roads, drainage, irrigation aqueducts, running water, baths, and some f ne public buildings and amphitheatres. Illyricum became one of the Roman Empire's major sources of food, metals, salt, wine, olives and military recruits, some of whom became outstanding military commanders or even Roman emperors. The major Roman towns were often redevelopments of existing Greek or Illyrian towns. The inhabitants of Illyricum were gradually converted to Christianity, which became the official imperial religion in AD 313. However, Illyricum was overrun and exten-sively looted and vandalized by Goths and Huns during the fourth century AD, and from the sixth to the ninth century it experienced sometimes destructive invasions by (Turkic) Avars, Slavs, (Iranian) Croats and (Iranian) Serbs, comprising variable mixtures of mobile warriors and relatively primitive agriculturalists. Some Graeco-Roman maritime trading-cum-piratical communities survived along the Dalmatian and Istrian coasts or decamped to the relative safety of the Adriatic islands, while others mixed and interbred with (and were thus gradually assimilated by) the new predominantly Slavic settlers.

From the seventh to the twelfth century the history of the predominantly Slavic settlers in Dalmatia and Pannonia was primarily one of struggles between their various clans, each under a *zupan* (initially, a clan 'chief', later a more territorially based 'duke'). These Slavs were gradually converted to Christianity by Catholic clergy and townspeople from Dalmatia's increasingly Italianate port cities and by Catholic missionaries from Italy, Austria, Germany and later Hungary, all of which promoted extensive (but not exclusive) cultural and commercial communion with western (Catholic) Christendom. But there was also trade and cultural contact with Byzantium and other Slavs. Autonomous 'South Slavic' zupanates began to appear in what is now

Croatia during the ninth and tenth centuries. Some of these engaged in piracy against Venetian merchant shipping, whose most profitable trade was in slaves captured alon the Dalmatian coast. This initiated a 600-year struggle between Venice and the Dalmatian and Istrian ports for ascendancy in the Adriatic sea and its South Slav hinter-land. An independent Croatian kingdom survived from 924 to 1091, when it submitted to Hungarian suzerainty (formalized by a 'Union of Crowns' in 1102). From 1091 to the 1520s and again from 1718 to 1918, parts of Croatia retained a semi-autonomous status under predominantly 'South Slavic' landed nobilities, who were allowed to retain their own diet (Sabor) and viceroy (Ban) under the suzerainty (overlordship)*either* of the kingdom of Hungary (1091–1526, 1718–67, 1790–1809, 1814–48 and 1868–1918) *or* of the Austrian emperor (1527–30, 1767–90 and 1849–67).

The Dalmatian port cities that participated vigorously in Adriatic, Italian and eastern Mediterranean trade up to the sixteenth century maintained close cultural contacts with Italy and Constantinople, producing a major 'flowering' of Renaissance humanis scholarship, poetry (in several languages), fine art, music and architecture during the fifteenth and sixteenth centuries. The republic of Ragusa, centred on the magnif cent port city of Dubrovnik, and the writer Marko Marulic of Split were especially prominent. Ragusan humanists also pioneered conceptions of pan-Slav and South Slav unity. Thereafter, unfortunately, most of coastal Dalmatia came under economically restrictive Venetian control (*c.*1429–1797) and then under equally debilitating Austrian Habsburg rule (1797–1805, 1814–1918). The resultant stagnation and decline of the Dalmatian port cities was exacerbated by the stultifying impact of the Catholic counter-reformation, which began in the 1570s and was perpetuated by reactionary Catholic-absolutist Habsburg rule from the 1690s onward, as well as by long-term agricultural stagnation and the atrophy of Dalmatia's once-flourishing maritime activities (shipping, shipbuilding, piracy and fishing), although Dubrovnik retaine its independence until 1797. The rest of Croatia succumbed to economically damag-ing Ottoman Turkish encroachments from 1493 and Ottoman conquest from 1526, until it was 'liberated' (i.e., subjugated) by the Catholic-absolutist Habsburg Empire during the 1690s. This paved the way for renewed subordination of inland Croatia to a Habsburg-controlled kingdom of Hungary for most of the period from 1718 to 1918. Croatia was a relatively stagnant cultural and economic 'backwater' during the seventeenth and eighteenth centuries.

From 1591 to 1848, the Croatian landed nobility and the noble-dominated Croatian diet preferred semi-subordination to the Hungarian diet, which included representatives from the Croatian diet and helped to preserve decentralized but oligarchic forms of local self-administration (a 'county system') in Croatia, to their brief experience of more centralized absolutist rule by Habsburg Vienna from 1767 to 1778. However, Hungarian domination increased considerably after the Sabor voluntarily surrendered the important prerogatives of voting taxes ('contributions') and joint control of the 'common affairs' of Croatia and Hungary to the Hungarian diet in 1790. The Sabor even resolved in 1827 that Magyar (Hungarian) should be taught (mainly in place of Latin) in Croatian schools, and in 1830 that a knowledge of Magyar (again, mainly in place of Latin) should be required of Croatian officials. Until then, ther was more collusion than hostility between the Magyar and the Croatian nobili-ties. Croatian landed nobles cooperated with the Magyar nobility in joint defence of their local autonomy and class privileges against perceived threats both 'from above' (the Habsburg monarchy and imperial bureaucracy) and 'from below' (from the downtrodden and increasingly restive peasantry).

Out of the blue, between 1805 and 1809 the main Croatian- and Slovene-inhabited lands were conquered by Napoleonic forces. From 1809 to 1814 they were united under French jurisdiction as *les provinces illyriennes,* a name harking back to Roman Illyricum and the ancient Illyrians. French rule introduced civil equality before the law, abolished craft-guild monopolies and servile obligations and initiated schooling in the Illyrian language (as Croatian became known at that time). *Kraljski Dalmatin,* the first newspaper in the Illyrian (Croatian) language, was published in French-rule Dalmatia from 1806 to 1810. In these ways, and by serving as an inspiring example to later generations, the short-lived French conquest reawakened the Croatian and broader South Slavic ethno-cultural consciousness which had diminished during the seventeenth and eighteenth centuries (Djilas 1991: 20–1). 'Illyrianism' was launched as a broad-church South Slav movement in 1835–6 by the indefatigable Croatian publicist Ludevit Gaj (1814–72) through the inf uential *Novine Horvatzke* (Croatian News) and its literary supplement *Danica Ilirska* (Illyrian Morning Star). Like-minded South Slav intelligentsia were publishing patriotic verse and instigated the standard-ization and codification of a shared Serbo-Croat language which was written in tw different scripts (in Latin script by Croats and in Cyrillic by Serbs and Montenegrins). The north-west Balkan Illyrianism was the precursor of an even broader 'Yugoslav' consciousness, which culminated in the establishment of the f rst unif ed Yugoslav state in 1918 (Wachtel 1998: 4–9, 24–9, 32–3, 63–6).

During the 1830s and 1840s Croatia's nobility began to resent increasingly overbearing and heavy-handed Magyar attempts to foist far-reaching 'Magyarization' on Croatia, as this threatened Croatia's separate and autonomous institutions, traditions and cultural identity. Magyar nationalism drove the Croatian nobility into the arms of the Habsburgs. Indeed, despite their long-standing alliance with the Magyar nobility, the Croatian nobility had developed traditions of service in the Habsburg armed forces and of loyalty to the Habsburg emperor. This was also true of the mainly Serb 'frontiersmen' who were encouraged to settle in Croatia's *Vojna Krajina* (military borderland) from the late sixteenth century onward, as part of the Habsburg counter-offensive against the Ottoman Empire.

In 1847 the Croatian Sabor finally declared the Croatian Slavic language to be the official language of Croatia-Slavonia (in place of both Latin and Magyar), thereb directly challenging the 'Magyar supremacist' aspirations of the Hungarian diet. In 1848, the Croatian ban (viceroy) Josip Jelacic, backed by the Croatian Sabor, even provided around 40,000 Croatian troops for use by the Habsburg monarchy in the suppression of the Hungarian nationalist revolution of 1848–9. This led Hungary's nationalistic ruling classes to feel 'betrayed' by their formerly subservient Croatian allies. However, the subsequent failure of the Habsburg monarchy to reward the 'Habsburg loyalism' of the Croatian Sabor and nobility in 1848–9, either by fully restoring Croatian autonomy in the 1850s or by protecting Croatia against the resumption of aggressive 'Magyarization' from 1875 onwards (*a fortiori* from 1883), drove many would-be conservative loyalist Croats towards a cultural and political rapprochement with their Orthodox South Slav 'cousins', the Serbs, from whom they had hitherto been separated by a seemingly unbridgeable religious chasm. A more viable basis for a Croat–Serb cultural and political rapprochement was prepared (albeit unintentionally) by the high-minded liberal-cosmopolitan 'Yugoslavism' promoted by Bishop Josip Strossmayer (1815–1905), who founded the first Yugosla Academy of Sciences and Arts (1867) and Croatia's first university (1874), both i Zagreb. Strossmayer himself was somewhat tetchy towards the Serbs, but his assiduous championship of a conception of Yugoslav cultural unity which could transcend religious differences and ethnic parochialism clearly offered a basis on which Serbs and Croats could come together and collaborate against their common oppressors, especially in the decade or two following his death in 1905.

In parallel, however, anti-Serb integral nationalist conceptions of the Croatian 'ethnic nation' were propagated from 1852 onwards by Ante Starcevic (1823–96), Eugen Kvaternik (d. 1872) and Josip Frank (1844–1911). Starcevic considered the Catholic minority in Bosnia-Herzegovina to be 'ethnic Croats' and part of a 'greater' Croatian nation. He also considered Slovenes merely to be 'mountain Croats', and 'Bosnian Muslims' (Bosniaks) merely to be Islamicized Croats. He even 'argued that the Serbs of Bosnia and the Military Border were really Orthodox Croats who, like the Bosnian Muslims, would voluntarily acknowledge their tie to the historical Catholic nation once it was shown to them' (Lampe 1996: 61). This dangerous pan-Croatian nationalism initiated by Starcevic eventually culminated in the annexation of Bosnia-Herzegovina by the 'Independent State of Croatia' established by Ante Pavelic's Croatian fascist Ustasa in April 1941, with the help of its Nazi and Italian Fascist patrons. 'Following the teachings of Starcevic, the Ustasa leaders believed the Muslims were ethnically pure Croats who needed to be brought back into the fold' (Tanner 1997: 148). A similar mentality was to result in President Tudjman's blatant attempts to partition Bosnia-Herzegovina between Croatia and Serbia in 1992–4, rather than accept and respect Bosnia-Herzegovina's right to an existence, identity and statehood of its own. This tendency for pan-Croatian nationalists to regard most of Bosnia-Herzegovina as being 'rightfully' part of Croatia resulted in great loss of life and human suffering under the Ustasa in 1941–5 and under Tudjman in 1992–5.

The later nineteenth century witnessed the beginnings of significant economic development in northern and eastern Croatia, spurred by the construction of north–south railways from the 1860s onwards. These integrated the main towns more closely with each other and with their Hungarian counterparts. Zagreb's population rocketed from *c.*20,000 in 1868 to *c.*80,000 in 1910. However, Dalmatia's age-old shipbuilding industry declined as a result of the worldwide switch from wooden sailing ships to iron-hulled steamships, while in the 1890s Dalmatian viticulture was ravaged by phylloxera, which further increased emigration and rural depopulation. The resulting socio-economic hardships in Dalmatia, concurrent with the accelerating economic development of the Zagreb region and Slavonia, radicalized Croats and rendered them more receptive to new political options and strategies.

The Hungarian Count Khuen-Hedervary, who served as the ban (governor) of Croatia from 1883 to 1903, revived the aggressive Magyarization policies of 1830–48 and heavy-handedly repressed Croatian national self-expression. He also wooed Croatia's substantial Serbian minority, which comprised nearly 25 per cent of Croatia's population at that time (63 per cent were Croats, 5 per cent were Germans and 4 per cent were Magyars). He promoted Serbian nationalism, the publication of Serbian newspapers, the establishment of Serbian Orthodox Church schools and the use of the Serbian Cyrillic script, in an attempt to divide and rule the South Slavs. A Croatian nationalist backlash against the Khuen-Hedervary regime led to anti-Serb riots in Zagreb (Agram) in 1902 and contributed to the establishment of the strongly anti-Serb Croatian People's Peasant Party (Hrvatska Pucka Seljacka Stranka, HPSS) under Stjepan and Ante Radic in 1904. Dedicated to radical agrarian reform and Croatian unity, coupled with resistance to potential further encroachments on Croatia by Serb colonists and Hungarian landowners and offcials, this party later became the leading political force in inter-war Croatia and built up a very extensive Croatian peasant co-operative movement.

During the decade from 1905 to 1914, however, in the face of increasing Austrian as well as Hungarian intransigence and expansionism vis-à-vis the Yugoslav lands, there was in fact closer cooperation between the Croats and the Serbs living within Croatia than at any time before or since. From 1905 onwards, their political leaders endeavoured to unite in a common struggle for greater South Slav unity, dignity and autonomy. Croat and Serb politicians in economically depressed Dalmatia took the lead, seeking the union of Dalmatia with Slavonia and the rest of Croatia, albeit within the protective/paternalist framework of the Austro-Hungarian Empire. Croats and Serbs in the Zagreb region and in Slavonia emulated Dalmatia's growing Serb–Croat collaboration, and Serb–Croat coalitions won major victories in the elections to the Dalmatian and Croatian sabors in 1906 and 1908. In 1908 many Croats and Serbs united in denouncing Austria-Hungary's full annexation of Bosnia and Herzegovina and the arrest and trial of fifty-two Croatian Serbs in Zagreb on bogus charges of treason, and they jointly rejoiced in the momentous victories of Serbia, Montenegro, Bulgaria and Greece over the Ottoman Empire in the Balkan Wars of 1912–13.

On 28 June 1914, however, Serb–Croat relations were suddenly soured by the assassination in Sarajevo of Archduke Franz Ferdinand and his wife by Gavrilo Princip, a Bosnian member of the predominantly Serb and fiercely nationalistic Black Han (Crna Ruka) society. This double murder unleashed a wave of Croatian revulsion against so-called 'Serbdom' – particularly in Zagreb, where there were pogroms against Serbian homes, newspapers and businesses, and Serbs were attacked or insulted in the streets (Guldescu 1970: 69). Many Croats feared that the ensuing diplomatic and military stand-off between Serbia and the Habsburg Empire would drag them into a major war in which, if Austria-Hungary were to disintegrate or lose, Croatia (including Slavonia and Dalmatia) risked being 'carved up' between Italy and a Greater Serbia (Tanner 1997: 114).

Croatian political leaders responded to the Sarajevo assassinations with fierce displays of loyalty to the Habsburg monarchy. Moreover, 'Of the sixty-odd divisions that Austria-Hungary put into the field at the beginning of the war, no less than four teen were Croatian'; and, in the course of the war, '1,200,000 Croatians out of a total population of 5,800,000 rendered military service . . . No other nationality in the Monarchy had such a high proportion of front-line f ghters . . . Serbians complained bitterly that it was their "Croatian brothers" who fought them most relentlessly' (Guldescu 1970: 70, 73–4). This is consistent with the view that politically conscious Croatians on the whole strongly preferred membership of the predominantly Catholic Habsburg Empire to any form of incorporation into a predominantly Orthodox or Serb–Montenegrin polity.

Croatia's role in the creation of the 'Triune Kingdom of Serbs, Croats and Slovenes'

Historians have long debated how much (or how little!) initial Croatian support there was for the formation of the first Yugoslavia, which survived from 1919 to April 1941 Many Croats have maintained that: (i) they were duped or bullied into joining the first Yugoslavia against their wishes (Tanner 1997: 120); and (ii) this explained and justif ed the open hostility shown towards it by Croats of various persuasions from the 1920s to the mid-1940s, during the late 1960s and early 1970s, and again in the late 1980s and the early 1990s. Furthermore, some Western historians have argued that the first Yugoslavia was an artificial state which wa*stupidly foisted* upon *reluctant* South Slavs by the victorious Allies in 1918–19, and that this Western folly was an underlying cause of the fratricidal conflict that accompanied the dismemberment of this allegedly 'artif cial' Yugoslav state in 1941 and the disintegration of its allegedly 'artificial' Communist successor in 1991–2 (for example, Almond 1994)

Both of these perspectives greatly underestimate the initial Croatian support for the creation of Yugoslavia. In August 1918 General Stefan Sarkotic, the Habsburg military governor of Bosnia-Herzegovina, reckoned that around 60 per cent of the inhabitants of Croatia-Slavonia and almost all those of Dalmatia had embraced the Yugoslav idea (Ekmecic 1980: 25–26; Lampe 1996: 106, 369–70). Other accounts report initial *rejoicing* in Croatia at the creation of a Yugoslav union. Although there were Croatian peasant revolts in late 1918, these were directed against the big (mainly Magyar or German) landlords, not against the Serbs. The largely Croatian 'national council' in Zagreb actually called in Serbian troops to restore order (Lampe 1996: 116). Leroy King, an American sent by the state department to investigate the mood in Croatia, reported on 20 March 1919 that the 'vast majority of Croatians are strongly supporting a united Jugoslavia', although 'the city of Zagreb . . . has a predominant autonomist sentiment because the people would like to see Zagreb as the most important city in Jugoslavia and do not like the idea of being second to Belgrade' (quoted by Tanner 1997: 120). Croatia-Slavonia and Dalmatia acceded*voluntarily* to the 'Triune Kingdom of Serbs, Croats and Slovenes' in December 1918, albeit partly out of fear of Hungarian and Italian annexationist designs on Croatia-Slavonia-Dalmatia-Slovenia and partly in the (ill-founded) belief that they would be allowed a great deal of *regional autonomy*.

Croatia in the inter-war Yugoslavia

The f rst Yugoslavia did not become the federal 'triple monarchy' which its off cial title seemed to portend and which many Croats had genuinely anticipated. Quite the opposite: Croatia finally lost the considerable (albeit oligarchic) autonomy whic it had retained during several centuries of Hungarian, Ottoman and Austrian over-lordship, and Croats therefore had ample reason to feel aggrieved.

The Croatian Peasant Party (HSS) led by Ante and Stjepan Radic quickly estab - lished itself as the major champion of Croatian autonomist aspirations, for which its leaders were subjected to official harassment and occasional imprisonment. Croatia resentment of Serb dominance of inter-war Yugoslavia intensified after the fatal shooting of Stjepan Radic, his nephew Pavle and another Croatian deputy by a way-ward Montenegrin member of the ruling Serbian radical party during a heated parliamentary debate on 20 June 1928. The HSS reacted by boycotting parliament and forswearing allegiance to the 1921 constitution. This exacerbated the breakdown of parliamentary government, which gave King Aleksandar an excuse to establish a royal dictatorship in 1929.

During the 1930s the autonomist HSS, now led by Vladko Macek, continued to provide the main opposition to the royalist regime in Belgrade. In 1931 Macek and twenty-four other Croats were tried on bogus charges of complicity in terrorism. However, this trial and Macek's subsequent acquittal rebounded against the regime, as did revelations that some Croats had been tortured to extract confessions. Macek also spent much of 1933 and 1934 in prison on trumped-up charges. After 1934, the HSS concentrated on promoting its cooperative movement and other practical activities to assist depression-stricken Croatian farmers.

In 1929 Ante Pavelic, a Croatian ultra-nationalist deputy, responded to King Aleksandar's declaration of a Serbian royal dictatorship by going into exile and establishing the Croatian Catholic-fascist Ustasa (Insurrection) movement, dedicated to the establishment of an independent Croatia. This movement attracted support from Fascist Italy and revisionist Hungary, both of which had designs on Yugoslav territory, and it sponsored or perpetrated anti-Serb acts of terrorism, sometimes in collusion with the Internal Macedonian Revolutionary Organization (IMRO). The joint Ustasa–IMRO terrorist campaign culminated in the assassination of King Aleksandar during his state visit to France on 9 October 1934. This aroused a wave of condemnation across 'respectable' Europe, and Pavelic was placed under house arrest, while several hundred other Ustasa members resident in Italy were placed in detentions of varying severity (Rothschild 1974: 245–6; Lampe 1996: 172–3).

The murdered King Aleksandar was succeeded by a regent, Prince Pavle. His attempts to appease the Croatian-Catholic opposition to the Serbian-royalist regime backfred, souring Serb–Croat relations still further. In 1937, mass demonstrations orchestrated by the Serbian Orthodox Church forced the government to abandon a concordat which it had negotiated with the Vatican. In 1939 Macek played a *triple* game, supporting Serb-opposition demands for political liberalization while simultaneously seeking Fascist Italy's support for Croatian secession and negotiating with the Yugoslav government for regional autonomy for Croatia. However, the autonomy which Macek obtained for Croatia in August 1939 incensed most Serbs without fully satisfying many Croats. By striking a bilateral deal with the royalists, Macek and the HSS had dashed any hope of a more far-reaching liberalization of Yugoslavia as a whole for the benefit of all ethnic groups (including Serbs).

Terrible vengeance, 1941–5

During the Second World War, Croatian Catholic ultra-nationalists took fearful revenge on the Serbs and Montenegrins, over 300,000 of whom were killed on the territory of the 'Independent State of Croatia' (NDH). This was established by Ante Pavelic and his fascist Ustasa with the active support of many Catholics, Bosniaks (Bosnian Muslims) and the Axis powers, during the Axis dismemberment and occupation of Yugoslavia in April 1941. The NDH comprised not only 'Croatia proper', but also much of Slovenia, Slavonia, Bosnia and Herzegovina, within which the Ustasa and its Catholic collaborators carried out many forced conversions to Catholicism (on pain of death) and widespread 'ethnic cleansing'.

In the late 1940s, the Yugoslav Communist regime informed the UN that the number of war deaths in Yugoslavia had been 1.7 million, including about 600,000 Serbs, Montenegrins and Jews who had allegedly perished at the Ustasa concentration camp at Jasenovac. This greatly inflated estimate of the death toll was uncritically accepte in most foreign writing on Yugoslavia (including our own). This exaggerated figur was used to reinforce the claim of the Communist-ruled Yugoslav federal system to be the most efficacious 'cure' for Serb supremacism as well as the genocidal Croatia and Bosniak backlash that it provoked.

More recently, estimates of the numbers of Yugoslavs killed by fellow Yugoslavs during the 1940s have been revised downwards, not only by Franjo Tudjman and other

Croatian ultra-nationalists eager to play down the enormity of Croatian and Bosniak crimes against humanity, but also by Serbian and Croatian historians and demographers who appear to be primarily interested in veracity. On the basis of census data from before and after the Second World War, the Serbian émigré academic Bogoljub Kocevic estimated that the number of Yugoslav deaths attributable to the Ustasa regime and the Second World War was around 1 million. Implicitly, the rest of the 'demographic deficit' for that period reflected the wartime reduction in birth rates rather th increased mortality (Lampe 1996: 380). This was broadly supported by subsequent calculations (by Vladimir Zerjavic and other Croatian academics, but based on work by Serb as well as Croat historians) that about 947,000 Yugoslavs perished between 1941 and 1945, including about 487,000 Serbs, 50,000 Montenegrins, 207,000 Croats, 86,000 Muslims (Bosniaks), 60,000 Jews and 30,000 Slovenes. On these estimates, 78 per cent of Yugoslavia's Jews, 8.1 per cent of its Bosniaks, 7.3 per cent of its Serbs and 5.0 per cent of its Croats perished (Covic 1991: 35). The Croatian historian Ivo Goldstein reckons that out of 2.1 million ethnic Serbs resident on NDH territory, about 330,000 perished: 217,000 as victims of fascist terror (124,000 in their towns or villages and 93,000 in prisons or camps), 82,000 as partisan combatants, and 23,000 as actual or suspected 'collaborators' killed by partisans; and that, out of 3.4 million ethnic Croats resident on NDH territory, about 135,000 perished: 46,000 as partisan combatants, 19,000 in prisons or camps (indicating that many Croats opposed or were victims of the Ustasa) and about 70,000 as actual or suspected 'collaborators' killed by partisans (Goldstein 1999: 158).

However, these revisions do not mean that the plight of the Serbs and Montenegrins was not far worse than that of the Croats and the Bosniaks. Most of the Serbs, Montenegrins and Jews who perished did so *either as victims of, or in the struggle against*, fascist and ultra-nationalist aggression, ethnic cleansing and genocide. Conversely, most of the Croats and Bosniaks who perished did so either as *perpetrators* or as *accomplices* of fascist aggression, ethnic cleansing and genocide. It is difficul to see much (if any) 'moral equivalence' between the casualties incurred on the two sides of this murderous divide. *Croatian* estimates of the numbers of people who perished in NDH concentration camps range from 60,000 (Tudjman) to 120,000 (Banac) and 215,000 (Covic) (Lampe 1996: 207, 380; Tanner 1997: 152). Even Tudjman's controversially low estimate is evidence that the Ustasa committed crimes against humanity on a monstrous scale, even though he was seeking to clear the Croats' bad name.

Another ongoing controversy concerns the relations of the Catholic clergy and especially the archbishop of Zagreb, Alojzije Stepinac, with the Ustasa regime. Stepinac was kept either in prison or under house arrest from 1947 until his death in 1960, because of his alleged collaboration with the Ustasa. Paradoxically, having vilif ed Stepinac in his lifetime, the Communist regime performed a volte-face after his death, perhaps in order to curry favour with the West. In 1991 Croatia's fst post-Communist government hailed him 'as a hero and a martyr, the victim of Communist attempts to suppress the church and stifle the national aspirations of the Croatian people', while Croatia's Jewish community (c.30,000 of whose members had perished under the NDH) expressed gratitude to him for helping to save Jewish lives, but beyond that refused to pass judgement either way (*IHT*, 3 October 1998, p. 2). Stepinac was beatified in 1998 by Pope John Paul II for having helped to save the lives of many Jews and Serbs. But for many Orthodox Serbs this beatification was offensiv and provocative because Cardinal Stepinac *did* initially give signif cant public support and respectability to the Ustasa regime and *never* denounced Ustasa crimes anywhere near as strongly or as volubly as he subsequently denounced the (much smaller) crimes of the Communist regime. However, he did not merit outright vilification because h *did* engage in private interventions which helped to save the lives of a few hundreds (not thousands) of Serbs, Montenegrins and Jews, albeit mainly by allowing and encouraging them to save themselves by converting to Catholicism, and he did try (largely in vain) to restrain the Ustasa's programmes of genocide and religious and ethnic 'cleansing'. As a fervent anti-Communist, Stepinac had publicly praised the Ustasa regime as 'God's hand at work', but when the scale of its crimes became clear, he did start criticizing Ustasa excesses *privately* in 1942 (once in a letter to Pavelic) and *semi-publicly* in sermons and letters to priests in 1943. Yet, as a prominent and protected public figure, he could probably have done much more than he did to halt the slaughter. After all, Orthodox Church leaders in fascist Bulgaria, as well as Lutheran Church leaders in Nazi-occupied Denmark, strongly and successfully resisted anti-Semitic genocide. However, these are very murky waters, and there is a need to be wary of simplistic 'black-and-white' judgements as well as the opposite dangers of moral relativism.

With regard to other Croatian Catholic clergy, all too many were active members of the Ustasa, publicly carrying out and sanctifying its forced conversions of Serbs and Montenegrins to Catholicism on pain of expropriation or death and directly perpetrating crimes against humanity. However, many other Catholic clergy kept their heads down, finding it expedient to avoid publicly taking sides, while a few courage ously opposed and spoke out against the Ustasa or risked their lives to save people who might otherwise have fallen prey to the Ustasa.

Many of the Croatian and Bosnian Serbs and Montenegrins who managed to escape the barbarities of the Ustasa and their Catholic collaborators, together with those Croats, Slovenes and Bosniaks who were repulsed by the crimes against humanity committed by their fanatical compatriots and co-religionists, eventually gravitated towards the Communist-led partisan resistance movement which operated under the overall command of the Croat Josip Broz, alias Tito. The partisans deservedly won renown for their extraordinary endurance and courage and for drawing adherents from almost all the major ethnic groups within Yugoslavia – the major exception being the Kosova Albanians, who fought their own ethnic war against the Serbs and the Montenegrins and who, with some justification, viewed the partisan movement as a new vehicle for Slav domination of Kosova. However, this should not blind us to the fact that many partisans took their own murderous and sometimes indiscriminate revenge against Croatian and Slovene Catholics and Bosniaks, both when they 'liberated' Croatia, Slovenia and Bosnia-Herzegovina in 1944–5 and as the new masters of Communist-ruled Yugoslavia. Partly to save their skins, many thousands of Domobrans (soldiers in the NDH regular army) and other Croats f ocked to join the partisans in 1944–5. In May 1945, over 100,000 Croats who had reason to fear reprisals from the Communist regime or the partisans sought refuge in British-controlled areas of Austria, where they were interned in camps. However, most of them were later handed over to the Yugoslav authorities by the British, and it appears that most of these were either executed or perished on so-called 'death marches' to prisons in various parts of Yugoslavia (Goldstein 1999: 155). British actions in this matter were later f ercely condemned in books by Nicholas Bethell (1974) and Nikolai Tolstoy (1978). Formally, Britain felt 'morally' obligated by agreements it had made with its wartime Communist allies to hand back such prisoners, but it used duplicity to get the prisoners to cooperate. Instead of continuing to hand over even more such prisoners for likely execution, the British could and should have reneged on those agreements once it was realized that many of the prisoners were being summarily killed after their return to Yugoslav soil.

Croatia under Communist rule, 1945–90

After the Second World War, Croatia became one of the six constituent republics of the Communist-ruled Yugoslav Federation. The Communist regime deliberately drew the boundaries of these republics in such a way as to make the Serbian Republic as small as possible (which was to become a major bone of contention for many Serbs). Partly in consequence, the Republic of Croatia included a substantial (15 per cent) Serb minority. These Serbs were denied autonomous status, even though they were concentrated in particular localities, but they were recognized as one of the constituent 'nations' of the republic, enjoying the same formal rights as Croats.

In the wake of the Ustasa genocide, any expression of Croatian nationalism was liable to reawaken harrowing memories and anxieties and was widely regarded as almost synonymous with fascism. Up to the mid-1980s, it was often repressed with severity. Even the statue of the Croatian national hero Ban Josip Jelacic (of 1848–9 fame) was symbolically removed from Zagreb's central square in 1945. The fact that all expressions of Croatian nationalism were tarred with the same brush became a major source of frustration and resentment for many Croatian nationalists – not just the few who remained unrepentant admirers of the Ustasa regime. Perhaps because he was himself a Croat and was thus wary of being seen to favour 'his own people', President Tito came down hard on any expression of Croatian nationalism.

The removal of the Serb 'police chief' Aleksandar Rankovic from his position as the widely feared/hated head of Yugoslav state security in January 1966 opened the way for greatly increased autonomy for 'worker self-managed' enterprises and decentralization of power to the federation's constituent republics. This in turn unleashed a Croatian 'national revival' from 1967 to 1972, which came to be known as the 'Croatian spring', by analogy with the 1963–8 'Prague spring' in Czechoslovakia. A major catalyst was the 'Declaration on the Name and Position of Croatian Standard Language', signed by 180 leading Croatian academics and cultural institutions in early 1967. This demanded recognition of Croatian as a language equal to and separate from Serbian, Slovene and Macedonian, contrary to the official Communist-cum-Yugoslavist line that there was a single Serbo-Croatian language (albeit written in two different scripts: Cyrillic and Latin). The 'Croatian spring' combined national assertion with political, economic and cultural liberalization. It was spearheaded by the Croatian cultural organization Matica Hrvatska (literally, 'the Croatian bee'). In 1971 this started publishing a weekly journal, *Hrvatski Tjednik*, which became the major mouthpiece for Croatian nationalists and non-Communist intellectuals (Goldstein 1999: 177–82).

In November 1971 President Tito decided to suppress the 'Croatian spring', which was seriously challenging Communist political control. Croatian nationalist effusions were also ringing alarm bells among Croatia's Serbs, some of whom detected echoes of the Ustasa NDH (1941–5) and were rearming (Goldstein 1999: 179). There were large-scale purges of the ruling Croatian League of Communists and Croatian cultural organizations from late 1971 though much of 1972. Over 400 league members were forced to resign or were expelled, and 'several thousand people were detained, harassed in various ways or forced into the sidelines of public life'. Many thousands of Croats emigrated (although over a million Yugoslavs of all sorts did so anyway between 1960 and 1980, mainly for economic reasons). A few Croatian nationalists even tried to incite rebellion or engaged in acts of terrorism, but they were hunted down. 'Croatia descended into a political apathy from which it did not emerge for almost two decades' (Goldstein 1999: 183–4).

'The silent republic', 1972–88

Again denied full scope for specifically national or cultural self-expression, Croatia energies and intelligence were redirected into an ever-widening range of money-making activities during the 1970s and early 1980s, despite the onset of global economic recessions in 1974 and 1979. Reinforced by soaring emigrants' remittances from the West and by Dalmatia's booming tourist industry, Croatia enjoyed the fastest per-capita growth of 'social product' of any of the Yugoslav republics (5 per cent per annum from 1952 to 1985). By 1990 Croatia's per-capita GDP was 7,179 US dollars, compared with 4,870 US dollars for Serbia and a Yugoslav average of 5,434 US dollars (*FT*, 9 September 1991, p. 15). However, instead of promoting inter-ethnic harmony and reconciliation, Croatia's growing prosperity stoked up Croat resentment of Belgrade's tutelage.

During the 1980s Croatia experienced a resurgence of Roman Catholicism and secessionist nationalism. The stimuli included the Communist regime's vilificatio and subsequent rehabilitation of Cardinal Stepinac (which gave Croatia's Catholic nationalists a new national hero/martyr), large-scale Catholic celebrations of 'Thirteen Centuries of Christianity among the Croats' in 1976, big celebrations in Nin in 1979 to commemorate the 1,100th anniversary of the founding of its bishopric and 'authen ticated sightings' of the Virgin Mary by some young Catholic girls in 1981 in the village of Mejdugore, located in a Croat-inhabited area of neighbouring Herzegovina. These 'miracles' subsequently attracted millions of Catholic pilgrims from all over the world to Mejdugore, generating an annual income of 80 million US dollars in revenues from 'religious tourism' (Goldstein 1999: 195–6), and were seen by some as signs of divine favour towards the Croats.

Alarmed by what it saw as a resurgence of 'reactionary' religious fervour, nationalism and testing of the limits of what was permitted, in 1984 the Croatian League of Communists published a so-called 'White Book' attacking 200 leading cultural f gures and the tendencies they represented. However, this merely highlighted how 'out of touch' Croatia's (partly Serb) Communist leadership had become. This became even more obvious when they tried to suppress the making and public screening of the f lm *Zivot sa stricem* (Life with Uncle), which analysed Communist repression in post-1944 Croatia and was shown to packed cinemas in 1988, and the 1988 fil based on the stage play *Sokol ga nije volio* (The Falcon Does not Love Him), which treated the fate of Croatian Domobrans and Ustasa supporters during the 'death marches' of 1945 (Goldstein 1999: 196–7). There was also a major burst of strike activity by industrial workers in Croatia, following a strike by 1,000 coal miners in the Croatian town of Labin in 1987. This broke previous taboos on television reporting of strikes. The League of Communists was evidently losing its grip on Croatian society and the veil of fear was lifting.

The emergence of opposition parties, 1989–90

New non-Marxist political parties mushroomed in Croatia, as elsewhere in Communist-ruled Europe, during 1989. An Association for Yugoslav Democratic Initiative (UJDI) was founded in Zagreb in February 1989 by the widely respected left-liberal academics Branko Horvat and Predrag Matvejevic. The UJDI sought the democratic trans-formation of Yugoslavia as a whole (branches were established in other republics as well), but it did not become a fully fledged party and soon lost members to othe movements (Goldstein 1999: 204). The Croatian Social Liberal Party (HSLS) was founded in May 1989 under Drazen Budisa. It attached more importance to liberalism and universal civil rights than to Croatian nationalism. In October 1989, however, it caught the public's imagination by launching a public petition demanding the return of the statue of Ban Josip Jelacic to its 'rightful place' in Zagreb's central square. 'On a rainy morning', it collected 70,000 signatures, and this 'seems to have been the key moment in conquering the fears of people in Zagreb and other towns about joining opposition parties' (Goldstein 1999: 206).

However, having helped to vanquish these fears, the HSLS rapidly lost ground to its major rival, the Croatian Democratic Union (HDZ), which was launched in Zagreb in June 1989 under Dr Franjo Tudjman (1922–99). He had served with the Communist-led partisans during the Second World War and subsequently lived in Belgrade. He had attained the rank of general in the Yugoslav People's Army (JNA) in 1960, at the age of thirty-eight. Soon afterwards he resigned from the JNA to carry out 'revisionist' research on the notorious Croatian Ustasa and its NDH (1941–5). As an ardent pan-Croatian nationalist, he went to great lengths to try to whitewash the Ustasa and the NDH, claiming that fewer than 60,000 Serbs and others died in Croatia's extermina-tion camps. He actively supported the 'Croatian spring' of 1967–72 and signed the controversial Croatian-language petition in 1967. He had been periodically imprisoned for his nationalist activities. He had travelled extensively abroad, establishing close links with nationalists among the 3-million-strong Croatian diaspora in Germany and the USA, which generously fnanced the HDZ (Cohen 1997: 75). 'Tudjman reassured Croats that they should not feel uncomfortable about Croatia's World War II pro-fascist affiliations, or exhibiting nationalist sentiments.' He preached 'national reconciliation', but by this he meant reconciliation between those Croats who had supported the Ustasa and those who had supported the Communist movement, rather than between Croats and Serbs (Cohen 1997: 76–7).

Another significant party established at that time was the Croatian Democratic Part (HDS), led by former Communists who had been ousted by Tito in late 1971 for having tolerated the 'Croatian spring'. This soon joined the Croatian Social Liberal Party (HSLS) and some smaller centre-left parties to form the Coalition for National Accord (KNS).

At the Eleventh Congress of the League of Communists of Croatia (SKH) on 12–13 December 1989, the liberal-minded 'reform Communist' Ivica Racan became the 'new-broom' leader of the league, which adopted the suffix 'Party of Democratic Change'. These changes were much influenced by the cataclysmic events of late 198 in East Central Europe. That same month, the Croatian Sabor declared Croatian 'sovereignty' and abolished the Communist monopoly of political power by legalizing the formation and registration of non-Communist parties, while two-stage multiparty elections were scheduled for April–May 1990. The sudden disintegration of the ruling League of Communists of Yugoslavia (LCY) was precipitated by the dramatic withdrawal of Milan Kucan's Slovene delegation from an emergency LCY congress held in January 1990, followed by the secession of Ivica Racan's Croatian delegation. This ushered in the holding of multiparty elections in all the Yugoslav republics during 1990.

In February 1990, a Serbian Democratic Party (SDS) was launched under Jovan Raskovic to represent Croatia's 14 per cent Serbian minority (including those who described themselves as 'Yugoslav'), although half of Croatia's Serbs voted for the cosmopolitan League of Communists in the April–May 1990 elections while only one-third voted for the SDS (Meier 1999: 146; Gagnon 2004: 35). In contrast to Tudjman's uncompromisingly Jacobin unitarist stance (*la nation unie et indivisible*), the SDS demanded equal rights and status for Serbs and Croats and recognition of Serbs as one of the constituent nations of the Republic of Croatia (as in the republic's Communist-era constitution). Tudjman offered Raskovic 'cultural autonomy' for the Serb minority and a token seat in government, but he was adamant that Croatia had to become the state of the Croats in an exclusive proprietorial sense, rather than a civic, bi-national or multinational state. Tudjman's intransigence undercut the moderate and conciliatory stance taken by Raskovic, who was soon to be eclipsed by the more secessionist Serbian nationalist Milan Babic as leader of the Croatian Serbs. Babic emerged as the leader of Serb unrest and armed road blockades in the Knin area (in the 'Krajina', or 'Borderland') in August and September 1990 (Cohen 1997: 80–3; Meier 1999: 153–7).

Nevertheless, the Yugoslav Federation was not yet dead, even though the LCY had disintegrated. Ante Markovic, a Croatian economic reformer who served as prime minister of Croatia from 1982 to 1988 and as the last prime minister of the Yugoslav Federation from January 1989 to 20 December 1991, made a heroic attempt to 'save' the Yugoslav economy and federation from complete collapse. During 1989 Yugoslavia had experienced hyperinfation (1,256 per cent per annum). To deal with this crisis, Premier Markovic initiated a remarkably successful IMF-inspired macro-economic stabilization and austerity programme in December 1989. During 1990 the hyperinfation was stopped in its tracks by draconian restrictive fscal and monetary policies, a six-month pay freeze and the simultaneous introduction of a new currency on 1 January 1990. The international exchange rate of this 'new dinar' was pegged one for one to the value of the Deutschmark, and wages and salaries were fixed accord ingly. This fixed exchange rate was intended to hold until 30 June 1990, but in th event it did so until 1 January 1991. Foreign trade was simultaneously liberalized and the main banks were transformed into either private or limited liability joint stock companies. At the same time, even though 80 per cent of retail and 76 per cent of producer goods' prices were decontrolled, the annual infation rate plummeted to 121 per cent in 1990 (Jeffries 1993: 471–3). By May 1990 inflows of foreign exchang were exceeding outfows (a good indication of reviving domestic and international confdence), and summer 1990 witnessed record levels of foreign tourist arrivals in Yugoslavia (Lampe 1996: 348). Although the January–June 1990 pay freeze was painful, there was palpable relief and gratitude that wages and salaries were once again worth something and the public mood was broadly optimistic (as one of the authors, RB, saw for himself in August 1990). As a result, at least until mid-1990, the liberal 'Yugoslavist' Ante Markovic was the most popular politician not only in Yugoslavia as a whole, but even in Serbia (Lampe 1996: 349; Miller 1997: 158) and in Croatia, along with his liberalizing and non-nationalist policies (Gagnon 2004: 35, 39). Furthermore, in a brave endeavour to unite educated liberal-minded Yugoslavs behind his reform programme, thwart the pernicious champions of intolerant 'ethnic collectivism' (principally Tudjman and Milosevic), and 'relaunch' the Yugoslav Federation on a new liberal-cosmopolitan non-Communist footing, on 29 July 1990 Markovic founded an Alliance of Reform Forces of Yugoslavia (ARFY). Tragically, in most of the multiparty elections held in Yugoslavia during 1990, including those in Croatia, fewer voters voted for the ARFY and similarly cosmopolitan (non-nationalist) parties than for parties wedded to 'ethnic collectivism'. This undermined Markovic's liberal-cosmopolitan brand of 'Yugoslavism' and gave 'ethnic collectivism' its head. Some misguided people positively *welcomed* the demise of the Markovic programme as the final death knell of the Yugoslavia they disliked, but with it died the best chance of avoiding the terrible bloodshed and enormous socio-economic destruction from which Slovenia is the only one of the former Yugoslav republics that can be said to have recovered sixteen years later, partly because it alone managed to escape with relatively little human and economic destruction, but also because it was the least 'Balkan' of the Yugoslav republics in terms of its internal power relations and power structures.

Two-stage multiparty elections to Croatia's Sabor, 24 April and 7–8 May 1990

Franjo Tudjman's HDZ obtained f fty-four of the eighty seats in the (main) socio-political chamber of the Croatian Sabor. The League of Communists of Croatia-Party of Democratic Change (LCC-SDP) obtained only twenty seats, while the SDS obtained only five seats (Cohen 1997: 80, 108)

The Sabor elected Franjo Tudjman to the office of president of the republic by 281 votes to 50 on 30 May 1990. 'Tudjman and the HDZ leadership viewed their electoral victory not only as a change in the governing party, but as a mandate to prepare Croatia's departure from the already enfeebled Yugoslav Federation', and 'the new regime rapidly initiated a purge of Serbs in the police, judiciary, media, and educational system' (Cohen 1997: 80). Serb political representation was now confed to some members of the depleted League of Communists and the five deputies of th SDS, whose leader Jovan Raskovic turned down Tudjman's offer of a (token) position in government (Cohen 1997: 80).

The problem of Croatia's Serb minority, 1990–5

The distinguished Balkan analyst Viktor Meier, who knew Tudjman personally, has stated that 'Tudjman was aware that the Serbs, who constituted about 14 per cent of the population, would present the greatest problem in Croatia' (Meier 1999: 146). Croatia's Serbs were greatly over-represented in the police, the military, the judiciary, the state bureaucracy, education and the media and were understandably regarded by Croat nationalists as a potential Serbian 'fifth column' or internal 'threat to the republic. The scale of the Communists' defeat in the parliamentary election of April–May 1990 was partly attributable to the unpopularity of their long-standing reliance on Croatia's Serbian minority to maintain control over Croatian political and cultural life.

Serb unrest and armed road blockades emerged in the Knin area of the mainly Serb-inhabited Krajina (Borderland) in August and September 1990, deploying weapons supplied by General Ratko Mladic, the Serbian commander of nearby JNA forces (Cohen 1997: 80–3; Meier 1999: 153–7). In consequence, the large numbers of tourists in Croatia at that time (including RB, one of the authors of this book) were being redirected around or away from the Krajina, which roughly corresponds to the old Habsburg military borderland, a chain of thirteen communes stretching from northern Dalmatia through eastern Lika, the Kordun and the Banija to Western Slavonia. The Krajina had been settled by (mainly Serbian) 'frontiersmen' from the late sixteenth to the nineteenth century, to help protect the Habsburgs' southern flan against the Ottoman Empire. These 'frontiersmen' and their descendants gained reputations for being rough-hewn, wayward and fiercely independent. They had bee the main focus of ethnic cleansing and genocide by and resistance to the NDH in 1941–4 (Lampe 1996: 208), and they had maintained their*Cetnik* (Serbian nationalist) and partisan (Yugoslav Communist) traditions of resistance to recurrent Croat attempts to subjugate them. Their perfectly legitimate aspirations were for territorial autonomy within Croatia or, if that was denied them, secession from Croatia and union with a 'Greater Serbia'.

In April 1990, when Tudjman's f ercely nationalistic HDZ looked likely to win the republic's first free elections and proclaim Croatian independence, the Serb-dominated JNA secretly ordered all weapons held by Croatia's local territorial defence units to be handed over to local JNA barracks in an attempt to prevent their potential use to secure Croatia's secession. The territorial defence units in neighbouring Slovenia resisted a similar command, and only 40,000 weapons were handed over there, but in Croatia (where Serbs dominated the security forces) over 200,000 weapons were handed in. The Croats were thus effectively disarmed by the JNA, while Croatia's Serbian enclaves were allowed to retain or even increase their weaponry. When the Krajina communes began to declare their autonomy from Croatia in August 1990, they were better armed than the Croatian authorities and were thus in a strong position to help the JNA take control of a quarter of the republic.

However, Tudjman's government handled the Serb minority insensitively and provocatively: by launching concerted media campaigns against it, by indiscriminately purging Serbs from key occupations, by belittling the terrible atrocities that many Croats had committed against large numbers of Serbs and Montenegrins between 1941 and 1945, by ordering imposition of Catholic instruction in all of Croatia's state schools (even in predominantly Serb-inhabited areas), and by blowing up some of the houses of Serbs in communes that wished to secede from Croatia. In December 1990, the Croatian Sabor adopted a new constitution which was designed (according to its chief author) to create an exclusively Croatian 'ethnic state' rather than a civil one. It implicitly downgraded the Serbs (previously recognized as a 'constituent nation', conferring equal status with Croats) to just one of several ethnic minorities (Cohen 1997: 82–3). In addition, by adopting symbols resembling those of the Ustasa regime, the Tudjman regime appeared to be saying that Croat nationalism had nothing to be ashamed of and could ignore the sensibilities of its former victims. The fact that Tudjman's strongest backers were Germany and Austria, the countries which had given the Ustasa the power to carry out a programme of genocide from 1941 to 1944, further inflamed Serb and Montenegrin fears that history might be abou to be repeated. This gave Croatia's Serbs some grounds for taking pre-emptive action. While it would be wrong to try to exonerate or to whitewash the often barbaric conduct of many of Croatia's Serbs and the JNA between July and December 1991, it is equally beyond doubt that many (perhaps most) of Croatia's Serbs saw themselves as a beleaguered minority acting in legitimate self-defence against a Croatian nationalist regime which looked likely to discriminate against them or even oppress them.

These Serbian anxieties regarding the nature of the Tudjman regime cannot simply be dismissed as fantasies and anxieties scurrilously stirred up by Serbian demagogues and the Serbian media (even though the latter certainly fostered and played upon such fears). General Martin Spegelj, who was Croatia's defence minister from 1 September 1990 to 15 June 1991, chief superintendent of the Croatian army from 25 September 1991 to 1 January 1993, and 'the creator of the strategic basis for the successful defence of Croatia' (Magas and Zanic 2001: xii, xxii), has confirme the presence of Ustasa elements in the Tudjman regime of which he was an uncomfortable member:

> The Ustasha ideology was imported from abroad with the return of extremist émigrés – not those who really had been NDH officials, but those who though they could use this ideology for their own benef now that a new order was being established in Croatia. And they did indeed benefit and acquire power; becaus of them, because of their presence in politics . . . That fact, together with the blowing up of Serbian houses in the spring of 1991, caused greater damage to Croatia's defence than the entire JNA aggression, and the aftermath can be felt even today in neo-fascist manifestations of various kinds.
>
> (Spegelj 2001: 31)

The generally very bad press given to Serb resistance to incorporation into a Jacobin unitarist Croatia largely ignored another crucial consideration: as equal human beings, *Croatia's Serb minority had just as much right to 'national self-determination' as did the Croat majority*. The desire of most of Croatia's ethnic Serbs to be included in a 'Greater Serbia' rather than in a secessionist Croatia was *in principle* no more treasonable or reprehensible than the desire of most ethnic Croats to secede from the Yugoslav Federation. Indeed, the desire of most of the ethnic Serbs was merely to maintain their status quo, to remain citizens of the same state as their 'Serb cousins' in Serbia, whereas Croats were seeking to overturn the status quo. Serbs were invoking exactly the same rights as the Croats, namely to decide their own status and to belong to a state with which they felt that they could identify and within which they could expect their status and identity (and not just their civil rights) to be fully respected and safeguarded. Western expectations that the Serb-inhabited enclaves within Croatia should agree to remain part of secessionist Croatia, merely on condition that the new Croatian state accorded them equal civil rights, woefully missed the point. Even if Croatia's new rulers had granted the Croatian Serbs extensive civil rights and full civil equality with Croats (notions which the Tudjman regime fiercely opposed), th Serb minority would still have remained wholly dependent on Croatian grace and favour. They would still only have had a very minor 'say' in Croatia's affairs, and they would still have found it very difficult to identify with or 'belong to' this essentiall Croatian state, whose new rulers (not only Tudjman but also his successors) adamantly rejected any notion of Croatia as a bi-national or multinational state. Furthermore, Western-backed arguments that conflicts on these matters had to be resolved withi the framework of existing political boundaries ignored the very well-known fact that those boundaries were deliberately drawn by the Tito regime in 1945 in such a way as to disadvantage the Serbs and diminish Serbia as much as possible. There was therefore was no reason why Serbs should have respected such inherently unacceptable boundaries as unalterable 'givens'. Given that Croatian Serbs lived in mainly rural borderland regions (as the name 'Krajina' implied), it would have been quite feasible as well as reasonable to have redrawn republican boundaries in such a way as to attach most of the ethnic Serb enclaves to a 'Greater Serbia', along the lines proposed by the (admittedly obnoxious) Milosevic regime. There were few Croats or Bosniaks in Serbia, precisely because all the mixed Serb–Croat and Serb–Bosniak areas had deliberately been included in Croatia and Bosnia, respectively, in order to diminish Serbia as much as possible. The reasonable compromise in 1991–2 would have been for the 'international community' (the favoured euphemism for the Western powers) to have mediated a negotiated division of these ethnically mixed areas between a 'Greater Serbia', on the one hand, and a slightly diminished Croatia and Bosnia-Herzegovina, on the other, with a bit of give and take all round. This would not have satisf ed the intransigent Serbian, Croatian and Bosniak ultra-nationalists, all of whom regarded their respective claims as non-negotiable, but it could have averted wars in which over 130,000 people were killed, over 300,000 were wounded, and over 2 million were 'ethnically cleansed' or rendered homeless. (For views diametrically opposite to these, see Meier 1999: 155–6.)

Unfortunately, reasonable give-and-take compromises were not on the Yugoslav menu in 1991. The problems resided in the intransigent leaders who had elbowed their way up the existing power structures and in the nature of those power relations and power structures, rather than in the various Yugoslav peoples, whose major preoccupations were with the problems of day-to-day survival, peaceful coexistence and mundane security, rather than with ethnic hatreds and nationalist bigotry (Gagnon 2004: xv–xix, 34–9, 51, 88, 178). Martin Spegelj has written that:

> The aims of the [Yugoslav People's] army and the Serbian, on the one hand, and the leaderships of the western [Yugoslav] republics, on the other, were absolute in the sense that both sides were determined to achieve them at any price. Some think it was possible to act politically to reconcile these opposing positions and thus avoid military conf ict. I was not then, nor am I now, an adherent of this view, although I deeply respect all attempts at a peaceful resolution.
>
> (Spegelj 2001: 23)

Overall, this appears to have been a very accurate assessment. However, President Milosevic exhibited rather more pragmatic f exibility in these matters than did presidents Tudjman and Izetbegovic, who took up and adhered to intransigent positions, perhaps calculating (correctly) that at the end of the day the Western powers would give greater backing to them than to the more widely detested Milosevic.

Tragically, the 'international community' greatly inflamed this already highly combustible situation by choosing to apply *double standards* – by supporting maximal rights for some ethnic groups and minimal rights for others, rather than identical rights of self-determination for each of the major ethnic groups in the Yugoslav Federation. Partly under pressure from Germany and Austria, the Western powers implicitly favoured the interests of some ethnic groups (Croats, Slovenes, Bosniaks and, after 1998, ethnic Albanians) over others (Serbs and, before 1998, ethnic Albanians). Not surprisingly, Western double standards and favouritism with regard to rights of self-determination poured petrol on the highly combustible inter-ethnic tensions in 1990s Yugoslavia. If it is to be used at all, the potentially explosive and destabilizing doctrine of national self-determination has to be applied with enormous care and circumspection and as equitably as possible, rather than on the basis of which ethnic groups the Western powers currently 'like' or in such a way as to enormously favour some ethnic groups at the expense of others (we have argued this more fully elsewhere: Bideleux and Jeffries 1998; Bideleux 2001a and 2001b). Otherwise, it is a recipe for inter-ethnic strife, for which in this instance (as in so many others) the Western powers bear a large (largely unacknowledged) share of responsibility. They are mostly too 'superior' to recognize their own blunders and culpability.

The drift into war, March to July 1991

Serious clashes between Croatian Serbs and the Tudjman regime took place from early March 1991 onwards. As punishment for Croatian Serb armed defiance of th will of Croatia's duly elected president and government, the Tudjman regime started 'blowing up . . . Serbian houses in the spring of 1991' (Spegelj 2001: 31). On 12 March the federal 'collective presidency' declared itself paralysed, and Serb leaders tried to prevent Stipe Mesic (later president of Croatia) from taking his turn in the rotating presidency of the federal 'collective presidency' on 15 May 1991.

A referendum on whether to declare Croatia independent was held on 19 May 1991. It produced a 93 per cent 'yes' vote, on an 86 per cent turn-out. However, most Croatian Serbs refused to vote, because they were being denied the same rights of self-determination as the Croats. Croatian independence was declared on 25 June, synchronized with parallel moves in Slovenia. However, on 7 July the European Community persuaded both republics to accept a three-month moratorium, in order to allow more time for EC-mediated negotiations. The independence declarations were activated on 8 October 1991, when the moratorium expired.

Croatia's 'homeland war', July 1991 to January 1992, and the disintegration of Yugoslavia

The JNA fought briefly in Slovenia in July 1991, in a bid to prevent Slovenia's secession from Yugoslavia. However, when Slovenian secession was accepted as a fait accompli on 18 July, the JNA redirected its forces to supporting the beleagured Serbian minority in Croatia. The Serb-controlled JNA's prime concern was to protect and hold onto the Serb-inhabited areas of Croatia. This was a major reason why it decided to cut its losses by pulling out of Slovenia, which contained very few Serbs and was not contiguous with Serbia. It is worth noting that Slovenia, which received no support from the Tudjman regime in June–July 1991, simply took its easily won independence and did little to help Croatia attain the same goal. There was remarkably little solidarity between the two breakaway republics. Worse still, General Martin Spegelj has recorded that, before it intervened in Slovenia, the JNA leadership obtained a valuable assurance from President Tudjman that 'We shan't meddle in your dispute with Slovenia.' Spegelj adds: 'I was horrified by this, and it was then that I began t consider resigning, because it was too stupid to remain passive when it was obvious what would follow after the intervention in Slovenia' (Spegelj 2001: 26). Sadly, this was to be an 'each people for itself' struggle. General Spegelj wryly commented:

> It was by the goodwill of the Slovene leadership that the JNA was able to with-
> draw some of its heavy weapons from Slovenia to Bosnia-Herzegovina, Serbia
> and parts of Croatia ... I once debated on TV Ljubljana with Slovenia's President

Milan Kucan and a few other politicians and I told them: 'You had a good breakfast (meaning you successfully faced up to armed intervention); you had a still better lunch (you defeated it); but you had no dinner (you did not hold on to your armour and put it at our disposal, so that we too could defend ourselves).' Kucan's reply was brilliant: 'You know, General, after a good breakfast and a good lunch, it is best to omit dinner, because then one sleeps more easily'.

(Spegelj 2001: 27)

Warren Zimmerman, the last US ambassador to the Yugoslav Federation (1985–92), emphasized that 'The fighting in Croatia began with the illusion of evenhanded ness. The Yugoslav army would step in to separate the Serbian and Croatian combatants. During the summer of 1991, however, it soon became apparent that the JNA, while claiming neutrality, was in fact turning territory over to Serbs' (Zimmerman 1995: 13). By August 1991, however, it was obvious that the JNA was neither strong enough nor cohesive enough to halt Croatia's secession from Yugoslavia. The main reason was that, contrary to recent Western caricatures and stereotypes of the Serbs, the programme to create a 'Greater Serbia' and the wars needed to attain it never aroused strong popular support among Serbs, many of whom actively opposed them (Thomas 1999: 107, 111–13; Magas and Zanic 2001: xxiv, xxix; Spegelj 2001: 24; Tus 2001: 57; Gagnon 2004: xv, 51; see also pp. 15, 253–4, 262–3, 324–5).

By mid-September 1991 the JNA and Croatian Serb forces controlled about a quarter of Croatia. The JNA should have concentrated on the limited objective of consolidating that control. Instead, it pursued too many (ultimately mutually incon - sistent) goals at once. It started shelling the cities of Vukovar on 24 August and Dubrovnik in October 1991. It captured territory around Dubrovnik in October and early November and Vukovar itself on 19 November, but in so doing exhausted and overreached itself (Tus 2001: 48, 54, 57).

The EC mediator David Owen cogently argued that NATO missed a brief but crucial window of opportunity to intervene militarily and nip this rapidly escalating conf ict in the bud during July or August 1991 (Owen 1996: 375–6). US ambassador Zimmerman came to the same view, albeit too late to make a difference:

The use of force [by NATO] was simply too big a step to consider in late 1991. I did not recommend it myself – a major mistake. The JNA's artillery on the hills surrounding Dubrovnik and its small craft on the water would have been easy targets. Not only would damage to the city have been averted, but the Serbs would have been taught a lesson about Western resolve that might have deterred at least some of the aggression against Bosnia. As it was, the Serbs learned another lesson – that there was no Western resolve, and that they could push about as far as their power could take them.

(Zimmerman 1995: 14)

Instead of backing a timely military intervention by NATO, which at relatively low cost could have averted major loss of life and massive destruction, the European Community imposed a leaky and ineffectual arms embargo on the belligerent Yugoslav republics in July 1991 and the UN Security Council followed suit on 25 September 1991. Numerous ceasefires were attempted, but it took until April 1992 for UN peacekeeping forces to occupy the Serb-inhabited areas of Croatia and establish a fragile cessation of hostilities.

During the siege of Vukovar and its aftermath, soldiers in the JNA and Serb irregulars committed numerous war crimes and crimes against humanity. However, the concentration of Milosevic and the JNA on capturing Vukovar 'at all costs' during October and the first half of November 1991 was so draining that, instead of becomin the springboard for JNA offensives against Zagreb and Varazdin (as planned), it left the JNA unable to advance any further and gave Croatia a breathing space in which 'to strengthen defence in depth' and prepare counter-offensives which recaptured parts of western Slavonia in December 1991 and southern Dalmatia in 1992 (Tus 2001: 57–63). On 10 October Alija Izetbegovic, the Muslim president of Bosnia, made a televised appeal to all Bosnian soldiers and conscripts to refuse to serve in the JNA against Croatia: 'I call upon you to find the courage to refuse to take part in evil deeds. Remember, this is not our war. Let those who want it, wage it. We do not want this war' (quoted by Tus 2001: 58). This further exacerbated the JNA recruitment crisis (and provided further refutation of Western caricatures of Balkan peoples as congenitally warmongering). By the end of December 1991 'the JNA was on the verge of collapse, since all its non-Serb members had left. They were unable to carry out any further mobilization in Serbia, so they opted for UN peacekeeping forces', thereby shrewdly placing the main Serb-inhabited parts of Croatia under UN protection for three years (Tus 2001: 64–5).

Meanwhile, the disintegration of the Yugoslav Federation had been completed, with damaging economic consequences (due to the high interdependence between the republics). The Croatian representative Stipe Mesic formally resigned from the federal collective presidency on 5 December 1991, declaring that 'Yugoslavia no longer exists'. Finally, the (Croatian) federal prime minister Ante Markovic resigned on 20 December.

Under strong pressure from Germany and Austria, the European Community formally recognized Croatia and Slovenia as independent states on 15 January 1992, despite strong and well-founded fears in the West that the ultra-nationalist and increasingly authoritarian Tudjman regime would not respect and uphold human and minority rights – especially those of Serbs. This abandonment of the initial Western stance of neutrality and even-handedness reinforced the temporary abatement of the Serb–Croat war and the consolidation of Croatian independence, which in turn encouraged the West's politicians and media to view the policy shift as having been vindicated by 'events on the ground'. However, the policy shift also encouraged Croats to regard Tudjman's increasingly authoritarian nationalism as having been justif ed, and it further encouraged Tudjman to prepare for the 'ethnic cleansing' of eastern Croatia in 1995, when Croatia's armed forces (re-equipped by the West) drove nearly 200,000 Croatian Serbs out of Croatia. It also further alienated and isolated Serbian nationalists from the West and made them even less amenable to appeals to desist from barbaric conduct in Bosnia-Herzegovina and Kosova. Thus the human costs of the West's abandonment of its initial attempts to remain neutral and even-handed greatly exceeded the short-term benefits from temporary curtailment of th Serb–Croat conflict

There was another – more sinister – reason for the abatement of the Serb–Croat 'homeland war' in January 1992. On 26 December 1991 and again on 2 January 1992, just when the military tide of the Serb–Croat war was turning dramatically in Croatia's favour, President Tudjman ordered Croatia's armed forces to stop fighting the Serbs so as to be able instead to cooperate with his enemy-turned-ally Milosevic in 'carving up' Bosnia-Herzegovina between Croatia and Serbia. Tudjman's decision delayed by three years Croatia's recovery of the territory it had lost. Croatia's able military commanders were utterly disgusted, infuriated and frustrated with him on this account, as was his future successor Stipe (Stjepan) Mesic (Mesic 2001: 11–12; Spegelj 2001: 35–6, 39; Tus 2001: 63–6). General Tus, as commander-in-chief of the Croatian armed forces, told President Tudjman that 'To go to war in Bosnia-Herzegovina with a new opponent while the Serb aggressor held more than a quarter of our state territory would be madness.' Tudjman replied that 'these were political, not military, issues, and that the world did not want a Muslim state in the heart of Europe!' In the military perceptions of General Tus, Tudjman's pan-Croatian *folie de grandeur* resulted in the Serbs retaining control of a quarter of Croatia until 1995, while the proportion of Bosnia-Herzegovina under Croat control actually *fell* from over 20 per cent in 1992 to under 10 per cent in 1995 (Tus 2001: 65–6). Thus, even in terms of crude *Realpolitik*, Tudjman's ultra-nationalist megalomania brought Croats and Bosniaks nothing but harm.

The presidential election of 2 August 1992

Nevertheless, by fully exploiting the siege atmosphere, generous funding from nationalists in the Croatian diaspora and his political control of the state-owned media, Tudjman obtained 57 per cent of the vote and a first-round victory over the libera centre-left candidate Drazen Budisa, who obtained only 22 per cent. The ultra-nationalist Dobroslav Paraga obtained 5.4 per cent. There was a 79.4 per cent turn-out (Cohen 1997: 93).

Elections to the house of representatives (lower house), 2 August 1992

Croatia's Sabor was henceforth to comprise a house of representatives (lower house) and a house of governors (upper house). This election was only for the 138-seat house of representatives. Half of its seats were to be fled by proportional representation and half by frst-past-the-post contests in single-member constituencies. Parties had to win at least 5 per cent of the votes cast, in order to gain any of the seats filled by proportiona representation. The ex-Communists' share of the vote slumped to 5.4 per cent (down from 28 per cent in April 1990). The final distribution of seats in the house of representatives is shown in Table 5.2.

5.2 Croatian house of representatives election, 2 August 1992

Party	Seats
Croatian Democratic Union (HDZ)	85
Croatian Social Liberal Party (HSLS)	14
Ex-Communists (SDP)	11
Croatian People's Party (HNS)	6
Croatian Party of Rights (HSP)	5
Small regional parties	6
Croatian Peasant Party (HSS)	3
Serbian Democratic Party	3
Others	5

Source: Cohen (1997: 93, 108).

**The second HDZ government, August 1992 to October 1995,
and the Croatian 'war of independence', 1993–5**

On 22 January 1993, Croatian offensives were launched against several Serb-controlled areas of Croatia, violating the UN ceasefire lines. The Tudjman regime justified th on the basis that the Serbs had taken back the heavy weapons which they had been required to hand over to the UN and had broken their promise to relinquish control of the proposed demilitarized buffer zones around the edges of the 'Serb autonomous regions'. In addition, other conditions laid down as part of the UN-brokered truce had not been fulfilled, notably the return of Croatian refugees and the rebuilding of the Maslenica bridge linking the northern and southern coastal regions of Croatia, which had been destroyed in November 1991. The Croat offensive recaptured the Maslenica area. On 6 April the Croatian forces agreed to withdraw behind the 1992 ceasefire line, while the Serb forces agreed to return their heavy weapons to UN custody. So-called 'pink zones' were to be placed under the control of a UN protection force (UNPROFOR), instead of being under the authority of the Serbian police.

On 18 July 1993, fears of renewed conflict between Croats and Serbs were allaye by an agreement to replace the Maslenica bridge with a pontoon bridge, to place Zemunik airport (near Zadar) under UN protection, and to withdraw Croat forces from recaptured territory by 31 July, provided the Serbs placed their heavy weapons in UN depots. However, much of this remained on paper, and periodic shelling continued.

A Croat offensive on 9 September 1993 captured three Serbian villages on the *Krajina* front line. The Serbs retaliated with intensive shelling and surface-to-surface missile attacks, one of which hit a Zagreb suburb. A ceasefire was agreed on 15 September 1993, but the Croatian withdrawal was accompanied by massive destruction and many civilian deaths, which were later classified as atrocities by the UN human rights investigator Tadeuz Mazowiecki.

Milan Martic, backed by Serbia's President Milosevic, became 'president' of the Krajina in an election held on 23 January 1994. A new ceasefire was agreed on 3 March 1994. UN forces were to be deployed in buffer zones along the edges of the Krajina. Croatia signed an economic agreement with the Croatian Serbs on 2 December 1994, restoring road and rail links, water and gas supplies, and the use of the oil pipeline. However, the Croatian Serbs refused to implement the second stage of this accord unless the UN agreed to keep its troops in the buffer zones (*The Economist*, 4 March 1995, p. 14). Croatia rejected further extensions of the UN peacekeeping mandate on 12 January 1995 and called for the 15,000 UN troops in Serb-controlled areas of Croatia to leave by the end of June 1995, on the grounds that: (i) the existing arrangements could result in an unacceptable permanent partition of Croatia; and (ii) 'Krajina' Serbs had not allowed Croat refugees to return home.

Representatives of the USA, Russia, the EU and the UN put forward fresh peace proposals on 30 January 1995. In return for full guarantees of human and minority rights and recognition of Croatia's sovereignty and international borders, the Croatian Serbs would be granted substantial autonomy in two of their four UN-protected enclaves (Knin and Glina), where the Croatian Serbs would have their own president, parliament, flag, education system, police force and currency (albeit one issued b the central bank of Croatia). However, Croatia's Serbs refused even to consider these proposals unless guarantees were given that UN forces would remain. In an attempt to break the deadlock, the US state department stepped up discussions with President

Tudjman, who announced on 12 March 1995 that he was willing to allow UN troops to remain in the Serb enclaves for another six months provided: (i) the UN troop deployment was reduced from around 12,000 to 5,000; (ii) the UN troops were also to control Krajina's borders with Bosnia and the Federal Republic of Yugoslavia (FRY) and the overland passage of aid to Bosnia; (iii) recent agreements with the Croatian Serbs were implemented and the reintegration of Croatia was encouraged.

'Operation Flash', 1–2 May 1995

On 1 May 1995 Croat forces launched a three-pronged attack on the most isolated and vulnerable Serb-held area, namely 'Sector West Krajina' in western Slavonia. They catured Okucani, the main Serb-held town in Western Slavonia. In response, the Croatian Serbs shelled or rocket-attacked Zagreb, Karlovac, Sisak and other Croatian towns, killing at least seven civilians and wounding nearly 200. They also made prisoners of a number of UN civilian and military personnel. However, the UN brokered a 'cessation of hostilities'.

The Bosnian town of Bihac was besieged on 19 July 1995 by Bosnian Serbs, Croatian Serbs and forces loyal to Fikret Abdic, former director of Agrokomerc (see pp. 341–2). In response, on 22 July President Tudjman and Bosnia's President Izetbegovic concluded a major pact on military cooperation, with Croatia agreeing to support the Bosnian government militarily. On 27 July Bosnian Croats, backed by units of the Croatian army, duly launched a major offensive to relieve Bihac. They also captured the Serb-held Bosnian towns of Grahovo and Glamoc the next day.

'Operation Storm', 4–7 August 1995

While talks proceeded between the Croatian government and the Croatian Serbs, Bosnian Serbs continued to shell the outskirts of Dubrovnik and Croatia's armed forces launched a full-scale military assault on Serb-held areas of the Krajina. They made spectacular gains, capturing Knin, Petrinje and Ubdina airbase on 6 August. NATO assisted the Croat counter-offensive, for example by knocking out Croatian Serb anti-aircraft positions. However, despite (false) assurances of good treatment given by the Croatian government, there took place a mass exodus of Croatian Serbs; some estimates put the figure as high as 200,000. This exodus was encouraged by ruthles Croatian attacks on feeing Croatian Serb civilians, as well as by Croatian looting and destruction of Croatian Serb homes and off ces. Claims were later made that mass graves of Croatian Serbs had been found. Officially, 118 members of the Croatia armed forces lost their lives in the operation. A report by EU monitors published on 2 October 1995 stated that the Croatian army had carried out a systematic campaign of indiscriminate killing, arson and looting against the Croatian Serbs and had deliberately targeted a UN observation post, killing three UN troops, while others had allegedly been used as human shields.

The UN brokered a ceasefire on 8 August. The UN collected heavy weapons from the Croatian Serb forces in return for the safe passage of about 40,000 Croatian Serb refugees from the northern part of the war zone. On 9 August the UN reported that the last major pocket of Croatian Serb resistance had ended with the fall of Dvor. However, there were further reports of a number of atrocities committed by Croatian and Bosnian government forces. On 12 August Croatia's armed forces attacked Croatian Serb positions in the hills overlooking Dubrovnik, whose outskirts had come under renewed attack. On 25 August Serbia and Croatia signed a ceasefire with regar to Eastern Slavonia, but further skirmishing was reported. On 29 August the UN Security Council agreed to reduce the number of UN peacekeepers in Croatia from around 12,000 to no more than 2,500.

In March 1999 investigators at the International Criminal Tribunal for former Yugoslavia (ICTY) concluded that, during the August 1995 Croatian offensive, the Croatian army had carried out summary executions, indiscriminate shelling of civilian populations and 'ethnic cleansing'. They recommended that generals Ante Gotovina, Mirko Norac and Ivan Cermak, who were national heroes in Croatia for having 'won' the 'war of independence', should be indicted.

> Croatian armed forces and special police committed numerous violations of international humanitarian law . . . During and in the 100 days following the military offensive, at least 150 Serb civilians were summarily executed, and many hundreds disappeared . . . In a widespread and systematic manner, Croatian troops committed murder and other inhumane acts upon and against Croatian Serbs.
>
> (*IHT*, 22 March 1999, p. 5)

Elections to the house of representatives, 29 October 1995

Among the 127 seats in the house of representatives, eighty were to be filled by proportional representation (party lists), twenty-eight on a first-past-the-post constituency basis, twelve by parts of the Croatian 'diaspora', and seven by ethnic minorities (instead of thirteen previously). The seven ethnic minority seats included three to be elected by Croatian Serbs (instead of seven previously), one by ethnic Italians (mainly in Istria), one by ethnic Hungarians (mainly in northern Croatia), one by ethnic Germans, and one by Western and Eastern Slavs (Czechs, Slovaks, Russian and Ukrainians). There was still a 5 per cent threshold for parties, but an 11 per cent threshold was set for alliances. The turn-out was 65 per cent.

Reaping political rewards from recent military victories, Tudjman's HDZ won seventy-five seats, including ten of the twelve 'diaspora' seats, but its victory fell short of the two-thirds majority needed to change the constitution to increase further the powers of the president. The party performed badly in Zagreb and other major cities, where the opposition parties (while complaining of lack of proper access to the media) successfully played on socio-economic problems such as unemployment and criticized the increasingly blatant corruption of the Tudjman regime. See Table 5.3 for the results of the election.

5.3 Croatian house of representatives election, 29 October 1995

Party	Share of vote (%)	Seats
HDZ, led in parliament by Prime Minister Zlatko Mateson	45.23	75
Croatian Peasants Party (HSS), led by Zlatko Tomcic	18.25	10
Croatian Social Liberal Party (HSLS), led by Drazen Budisa	11.55	12
Social Democratic Party of Croatia (SDP), led by Ivica Racan	9.08	10
Croatian Party of Rights (HSP) (ultra-nationalist)	5.10	4
Representatives of Serb minority	–	3

The human and economic costs of the wars of 1991–5

In June 2001, Croatia's Institute of Social Studies estimated that Croatia had lost 20,091 citizens (including ethnic Serbs) during the 1991–5 war. This was the first attempt to count victims on both sides in the war. The Tudjman regime's death counts had ignored about 4,000 Serb war casualties (*Daily Telegraph*, 19 June 2001, p. 12). In addition, over 300,000 Croats and over 200,000 Serbs became refugees. By December 1991 Croatia's official unemployment rate was 19 per cent of the workforce. 'Collatera damage' to industry and infrastructure was equal to over a year's output. The pre - viously very lucrative annual inflows of Western tourists dried up, and the value o the currency plummeted as a result of hyperinflation. By 1993 Croatia's industria production was only half the 1987 level (see Table 5.4). About 10 per cent of fixe industrial capital was destroyed by the war (*BCE*, June 1996, p. 18). About 10 per cent of the housing stock (more than 170,000 homes and apartments) was destroyed or damaged (*FT*, Survey, 14 December 1998, p. 28).

'Normalization' of relations with the Serbs, November 1995 to August 1996

On 12 November 1995 Croatia and the Croatian Serbs signed an agreement relating to Eastern Slavonia, which had been drafted by presidents Tudjman and Milosevic during their talks in the USA. Eastern Slavonia would return to Croatian control after a transitional term of no more than two years (albeit with the possibility of an additional year if either side requested it). During the transitional period there would be a UN administration, and the Security Council would determine the implementation force of peacekeepers and police. Demilitarization would be carried out within thirty days of their deployment. Eastern Slavonia would have a multi-ethnic character, with refugees to be allowed to return to their old homes. The UN mandate expired on 15 January 1996, but the UN Security Council authorized a new force of up to 5,000 personnel (up from 1,600) for Eastern Slavonia, able to call on the support of NATO airpower.

In January 1996 the UN Security Council acknowledged that there had been an exodus of roughly 180,000 Serbs from Croatia and that their 'rights to return in safety and dignity' were being 'severely curtailed'. It condemned Croatia for its system-atic atrocities against Serbs, called for the repeal of laws making the return of Croatian Serb property to its owners conditional, and demanded the extradition of six Croats to the ICTY to be tried for war crimes and crimes against humanity (*FT*, 10 January 1996, p. 2). The Zagreb–Belgrade motorway (the 'Highway of Unity and Brotherhood') was reopened in May 1996, although only for international traffic The Adriatic oil pipeline between the Croatian port of Rijeka and the Serbian town of Pancevo was also reopened (*FT*, 8 May 1996, p. 2). Presidents Tudjman and Milosevic met on 7 August 1996 and agreed to restore diplomatic relations. A mutual recognition accord was signed on 23 August. Ambassadors were to be exchanged and refugees were to be allowed to return to their homes.

The Tudjman regime's increasing authoritarianism, 1996–7

On 24 April 1996 the parliamentary assembly of the Council of Europe voted to admit Croatia, but with the stipulation that Croatia would have to ratify the European

5.4 Republic of Croatia: selected economic indicators, 1990–2005

	1990	1991	1992	1993	1994	1995	1996	1997	1998	1999	2000	2001	2002	2003	2004	2005
								% rise/rate								
GDP	-7.1	-21.1	-11.7	-8.0	5.9	6.8	6.0	6.5	2.5	-0.9	2.9	4.4	5.2	4.3	3.8	4.0
Industrial output	-11.3	-28.5	14.6	-6.0	-2.7	0.3	3.1	6.8	3.7	-1.4	1.7	6.0	5.4	5.0	4.8	5.0
Agricultural output	-3.2	-7.2	-13.5	4.9	-0.3	0.7	1.3	4.0	10.2	-3.5	2.8	8.7	4.5	1.7	3.2	–
Annual inflation rate	609.5	123.0	665.5	1517.5	97.6	2.0	3.5	3.6	5.7	4.2	6.2	4.9	2.2	1.8	2.1	5.3
Unemployment rate	–	14.1	17.8	16.6	17.3	17.6	15.9	17.6	18.6	13.6	16.1	15.8	14.8	14.3	13.8	–
Budget surplus (+)/def cit (−) (as % of GDP)	–	-5.0	-3.9	-0.8	1.2	-1.4	-1.0	-1.9	-1.0	-8.2	-6.5	-6.7	-5.0	-6.3	-4.9	-4.5
Foreign debt as % of GDP	–	16.4	26.7	22.8	20.7	20.2	26.7	37.1	44.3	55.0	61.0	60.0	69.0	86.0	88.0	86.0
Private sector as % of GDP	15.0	20.0	25.0	30.0	40.0	40.0	50.0	55.0	55.0	60.0	60.0	60.0	60.0	60.0	60.0	60.0
Private-sector share in employment	–	–	–	–	–	–	–	–	–	58.0	56.0	58.0	58.0	60.0	–	–
FDI (net, $ m)	–	13.0	102.0	110.0	109.0	486.0	347.0	835.0	1445.0	1420.0	1085.0	1407.0	591.0	1700.0	898.0	2000.0
Foreign debt ($ bn)	–	3.0	2.7	2.5	3.0	3.8	5.3	7.5	9.6	10.1	11.3	11.9	15.6	24.8	30.2	32.0
Population (m)	–	4.8	4.5	4.6	4.6	4.7	4.5	4.6	4.5	4.6	4.4	4.4	4.4	4.4	4.4	4.4

Sources: Various issues of the annual EBRD *Transition Report*, supplemented by UN Economic Commission for Europe, *Economic Survey of Europe*; UN *World Economic and Social Survey*; and IMF *World Economic Outlook*. Figures for 2004 and 2005 are provisional estimates.

Convention on Human Rights within a year of joining. It would also have to recognize the right of citizens to petition the European Court of Human Rights and abolish the death penalty in peacetime within three years of joining (*IHT*, 25 April 1996, p. 5).

Zagreb's city council, which appointed the mayor and was dominated by the opposition, was dissolved on 30 April 1996 by President Tudjman, who subsequently appointed one of his own nominees as mayor of the capital city. The move was part of a drive to recentralize power, removing the large state-owned firms in the capita from municipal jurisdiction, and was accompanied by a series of new press laws which made it difficult to criticize the president and government officials. Tudjm claimed that he was obliged to dissolve the Zagreb city council after the constitutional court, dominated by HDZ appointees, had ruled that the city budget drawn up by the anti-HDZ majority was illegal. The struggle centred on power, patronage and the privatization of state-owned businesses and properties, many of which had ended up in the hands of Tudjman's cronies and henchmen. Tudjman was not ready to allow his opponents to take over the city administration, which could monitor these transfers (*IHT*, 3 May 1996, p. 12).

In response, on 14 May 1996 the Council of Europe's Committee of Ministers decided to postpone the admission of Croatia to the Council of Europe. On 5 June the Council of Europe set fve additional conditions for Croatia's admission: the handing over of war-crimes suspects; full cooperation in the holding of free elections in Bosnia; allowing the return of Serb refugees; dropping prosecutions against the independent media; and allowing the opposition-controlled Zagreb city council freely to elect a mayor. The Tudjman regime reluctantly complied, and Croatia finally became the fortieth member of the Council of Europe on 6 November 1996.

On 26 September 1996 two journalists were prosecuted (unsuccessfully) on the charge of defaming President Tudjman, under a new clause in the criminal code allowing a maximum sentence of three years for insulting high offials. A series of stringent press laws were passed, including one to limit the residency visas of the handful of foreign correspondents based in Croatia to three months and one promulgated in October 1996 which contained provisions to allow the government to set the qualifa-tions needed to become a chief editor and to force newspapers to run corrections or clarifications (*IHT*, 9 October 1996, p. 7). On 20 November, moreover, the government refused to renew the licence of Radio 101, Croatia's last independent radio station, claiming that the station was insufficiently 'objective' (it was finally granted a n license in 1997).

Elections to the upper house, 13 April 1997

UN observers declared the elections to be generally free and fair. Voting in Eastern Slavonia was extended by a day to allow all ethnic Serbs who wished to vote the chance to do so. The HDZ gained 40 per cent of the vote but obtained forty-one of the sixty-eight seats in the upper house (four more than in 1993). The Croatian Peasant Party obtained ten seats, the SDP five, the Croatian Social Liberal Party five and the Istri Democratic Forum two. The president nominated five seats, two of which were reserved for Serbs.

Local elections held on 13 April 1997

There was a 71 per cent turn-out. The HDZ won nineteen of Croatia's twenty-one counties and narrowly gained control of the Zagreb city assembly, winning twenty-four seats (just two short of an absolute majority) to the SDP's fourteen, the Croatian Social Liberal Party's nine and the Croatian Peasant Party's three, two of whom later defected to the CDU (*FT*, 20 May 1997, p. 3). However, the HDZ lost in almost every other city or big town.

Eastern Slavonia, September 1995 to 1999

Of the 120,000 ethnic Serbs who had lived in Eastern Slavonia up to 1995, nearly half had left (*IHT*, 20 March 1998, p. 4). Croatia granted not only citizenship but in many cases abandoned Serb houses to its Bosnian Croat refugees. Poverty was rife in Eastern Slavonia and the unemployment rate was nearly 80 per cent. Foreign reconstruction aid was a tiny fraction of aid to Bosnia.

The UN transitional administration concluded agreements with Croatia to encourage Serbs native to Eastern Slavonia to remain there. About 40 per cent of jobs in the public sector were reserved for Serbs, and the Serb community was permitted half an hour per day of television airtime.

During the autumn of 1997, the Eastern Slavonian Serbs boycotted state schools to protest against Croatia's off cial history curriculum, which taught that the Serbs had been the aggressors in the wars of 1991–5, and the UN administration brokered a deal to suspend the teaching of recent history for five years. The OSCE sent 25 monitors into Croatia, of whom 100 were for Eastern Slavonia alone, in order to encourage it to treat its minorities well. At Croatia's own request, 180 UN police monitors were retained in Eastern Slavonia to allay foreign suspicions that the local police would mistreat the Serb community there (*The Economist*, 10 January 1998, pp. 37–8). In July 1997 the UN transitional administration in Eastern Slavonia was extended until 15 January 1998, when it finally ended. By then the Croatian authori ties had fulfiled promises to establish police, judiciary and school systems that ref ected pre-1991 population splits and voter sentiment. The regional police force was almost half Serb, as were local judicial appointments, and schoolbooks had become available in Cyrillic as well as Latin script (*IHT*, 12 January 1998, p. 5). In February 1998, however, an OSCE spokesman stated that Serbs in Eastern Slavonia were 'very much concerned about their future' due to growing 'economic discrimination', such as discriminatory lay-offs and problems with pensions and social benefits *FT*, 20 February 1998, p. 2). In July 1998 the Croatian Sabor approved a comprehensive programme for the return and accommodation of persons forced to flee their home in Croatia during the wars of 1991–5 *FT*, Survey, 7 July 1998, pp. i and iii). However, Serb refugees who returned to their old homes in Croatia continued to be denied citizenship and rights to work, vote or own property and therefore had to survive on 'handouts and the charity of local relatives' (*FT*, 30 December 1999, p. 4).

The presidential election of 15 June 1997

Tudjman won a second five-year term as president. In 1996 he had been treated in Washington clinic for what American sources said was stomach cancer, but he denied it. He won 61.42 per cent of the votes cast, but on a 57 per cent turn-out. Zdravko

Tomac (leader of the Social Democratic Party) received 21.1 per cent of the vote, while Vlado Gotovac (leader of the Social Liberal Party) received 17.7 per cent (*IHT*, 17 June 1997, p. 6). An OSCE report on the election concluded that the electoral process had conferred enormous advantages on the incumbent and limited the ability of the opposition candidates to campaign effectively, as did state control of the media (especially television) and the disparity in campaign resources. Ethnic Serbs who had fled the country were disenfranchised, whereas ethnic Croats resident in Bosni were allowed to vote.

The mounting costs of pariah status, 1997–9

Croatia's growing isolation during the second half of Tudjman's 'reign' resulted in its exclusion from NATO's Partnership for Peace, loss of access to economic and technical aid from the EU PHARE programme and, most damagingly of all, exclusion from the f rst wave of 'eastward enlargement' of the EU. These exclusions, furthermore, strongly discouraged Western firms from investing in Croatia, not only becaus of Croatia's growing pariah status, but because without the prospect of EU membership, the returns on any FDI in Croatia looked uncertain and insecure. On 25 July 1997 the IMF withheld a 40-million-dollar loan, due to 'the unsatisfactory state of democracy in Croatia' (*FT*, 31 July 1997, p. 2).

The 'international community' was also concerned about Croatia's poor record of cooperation with the ICTY. On 6 October 1997, however, ten Bosnian Croats left Croatia to surrender to the ICTY. As a result, on 10 October the IMF decided to release almost 80 million dollars in loans. Ironically, Croatia then decided not to make use of them.

During 1998, Hrvoje Sarinic, former prime minister and a leader of the liberal wing of the HDZ, resigned after 'allegations that the military intelligence service had been used to undermine moderates within the HDZ', while the defence minister Andrija Hebrang resigned due to damaging internal divisions and the ascendancy of hardline nationalists led by Ivic Pasalic, Tudjman's 'presidential adviser' (*FT*, Survey, 14 December 1998, p. 25).

In late January 1999 an OSCE report on Croatia highlighted restrictive HDZ/ government control of the media (including 90 per cent of television), 'distrust and hostility' towards the ICTY, weak rule of law, lack of respect for human rights and mistreatment of minorities, especially ethnic Serbs (*IHT*, 4 March 1999, p. 9).

The demise of Tudjman and his regime, November 1999 to January 2000

Tudjman, who had been secretly treated for cancer in Washington in 1996, underwent an emergency intestinal operation in Zagreb on 1 November 1999 and subsequently suffered fatal complications. On 24 November, 85 of the 127 members of the Sabor voted for a constitutional amendment providing for some presidential powers to be transferred to the speaker of parliament (Vlatko Pavletic) should Tudjman become 'temporarily unfit to perform his duties' *IHT*, 25 November 1999, p. 6). There was no post of vice president and Tudjman had never allowed an heir-apparent to be named. He had run the country through an extensive team of 'presidential advisers' headed by Ivic Pasalic, who controlled internal security and media matters, but Pasalic was unpopular and not a viable successor. Parliamentary elections were scheduled to take place on 22 December 1999, but the HDZ played for time while its leaders squabbled over which of them would run for the presidency. The political paralysis was exacerbated by the growing unpopularity of the ruling HDZ, economic recession, high unemployment and rampant corruption (*IHT*, 26 November 1999, p. 7). The parliamentary term was due to expire on 27 November 1999 and an election was supposed to be held by 27 December, but no date had been set due to the president's illness. The HDZ favoured holding the parliamentary election on 28 December, when many Croatian expatriates (its strongest supporters) would be home for Christmas (*FT*, 25 November 1999, p. 10).

On 26 November the constitutional court decided that Tudjman was 'temporarily incapacitated', whereupon the speaker, Vlatko Pavletic, became acting president. On 1 December 1999 six main opposition parties formally agreed to form a coalition government if they did well enough in the forthcoming parliamentary election, which was finally scheduled for 3 January. Tudjman died on 10 December 1999, an his funeral took place on 13 December. The only foreign head of state present was the president of Turkey. The prime ministers of Hungary, Macedonia, Slovenia and Montenegro attended, along with the Croat member of the three-person presidency of Bosnia. On 21 December the Croatian parliament set 24 January 2000 as the date for a presidential election, hard on the heels of the parliamentary election.

The Croatian economy under Tudjman, 1990–9

After the economic collapse accompanying the end of Communist rule and the break-up of the Yugoslav Federation, Croatia's GDP started growing again in 1994. However, growth decelerated sharply in 1998 and became negative during the 1999 Kosova war. In addition, the Croatian economy was much damaged by 'insider privatizations' and corrupt 'tycoon capitalism'. Reckless borrowing contributed to a banking crisis in 1998.

Monetary, currency and anti-inflation policies

A new currency, the Croatian dinar, was launched in December 1991. In mid-October 1993 parliament controversially voted to rename it the *kuna* ('marten'), the name of the currency issued by the fascist Ustasa regime from 1941 to 1944. The taming of inflation, which peaked at an annual rate of 1,517 per cent in 1993, was a high priority. This was successfully accomplished between October 1993 and mid-1995 (see Table 5.4). The stabilization plan involved a major devaluation of the dinar accompanied by tight monetary, fiscal and incomes policies, whose effects were reinforced by high unemployment (over 17 per cent of the workforce in 1994–5). A managed floating exchange-rate regime was introduced in late 1993, and the *kuna* exchange rate was gradually pegged to the Deutschmark. Current-account conver - tibility was high, but some capital controls remained. All direct price controls were removed, although some indirect controls remained, particularly in the energy sector. Wage controls remained in place for the state sector, supported until November 1994 by a 'social contract' with the trade unions. Financial discipline on state agencies and public enterprises was hardened from late 1993 onward and a bankruptcy law took effect from January 1997 (EBRD 1994: 21; 1996b: 145).

Privatization of 'real estate' and agriculture

As in the other Yugoslav republics, most farms and some small-scale service enterprises were already privately owned in Croatia under Communist rule, so there was little pressure to make major changes here. Privatization of 'socially owned' land was slowed down by the need to reregister in the name of the state land which had officially been owned by cooperatives under Communist rule. The governmen aimed to encourage consolidation in agriculture, as most private farms were small(*FT*, Survey, 24 June 2002, p. 11). In October 1996 a law was passed providing compensation for property confiscated or nationalized by the Communist regime and regulating the denationalization of such property. It gave preference to restitution of property where this was most feasible (primarily in relation to agricultural land, forests, and some housing, shops and restaurants) and provided for compensation in other cases, such as offices, factories and larger residences, shops and restaurants. The privatization of housing which had formerly been socially owned was almost complete by 1997 (EBRD 1997a: 28).

Privatization of industry and services

The system of 'worker self-management' for which Yugoslavia had been famous was rapidly dismantled in 1990–1, when more autocratic management boards took power away from elected workers' councils in industrial enterprises. In April 1991 a law on 'the transformation of enterprises with social capital' was enacted, requiring the conversion of almost all socially owned enterprises into joint stock companies and allowing workers to buy shares of up to 20,000 Dentschmarks by book value at a 20 per cent discount (plus 1 per cent for every year they had worked). The remaining shares in each enterprise were to be divided between the pension funds and the Croatian privatization fund (EBRD 1994: 20; *FT*, 31 March 1994, p. 32). Most of the early privatizations were management or worker buy-outs. The deadline for the privatization of all socially owned enterprises was originally the end of June 1992; all shares not sold by then (around 50 per cent of the value of all socially owned enterprises) were to have been transferred to state funds without compensation (UN ECE 1993: 224).

During 1992, however, the economy was put on a war footing and most Croatian enterprises were taken into state ownership. Ironically, the end of Communist rule was thus initially followed by a significant *increase* in state ownership. Some 200 publicly owned enterprises which had not lodged proposals for privatization passed completely into the hands of the privatization fund. The privatization of small enterprises was largely completed by 1994, but no large social-sector enterprises were privatized until 1995 (Bartlett 1996: 162).

A new privatization ministry was established in January 1995 with the task of accelerating privatization (EBRD 1995a: 54). By the end of 1995 about 1,200 out of a total of 2,750 enterprises had been sold to their employees or management. In a further 900 enterprises the state retained only a minority stake (EBRD 1995b: 38). INA (the state oil company), public utilities and health-care organizations were earmarked for privatization in the future, but large industrial combines were to be restructured and divided into smaller units before being privatized. By early 1997 the state still accounted for about 40 per cent of the net asset value and the workforce of the 2,550 commercialized enterprises, but over 1,000 had been fully privatized and the state retained only a minority stake in another 1,350. Most of the fully privatized enterprises were small (EBRD 1997b: 161–2).

Croatia's privatization policy was subject to two lines of criticism. Journalists complained that Tudjman's privatization policy merely succeeded in 'concentrating vast economic power in the hands of a small oligarchy' (*The Times*, 7 August 1996, p. 14), or that privatized state assets 'disappeared into the pockets of the chosen few, including members of Tudjman's family' (*EEN*, 31 December 1996, vol. 10, no. 25, p. 6). The EBRD complained that much of the privatization completed by the end of 1995 had failed to significantly accelerate industrial restructuring and that the pace of both privatization and restructuring had remained relatively slow (EBRD 1997b: 162). In most privatized enterprises, restructuring was inhibited by the 'poor corporate governance that typically results from the absence of a strong majority shareholder and from large residual state holdings'. As a result of a privatization process dominated by management and employee buy-outs, small shareholders (mainly employees) owned the vast majority of shares in privatized companies, while the state privatization fund and the state pension fund (which remained the largest shareholders in many largely privatized companies) took no active role in enterprise restructuring (EBRD 1998b: 160). Few frms 'received fresh capital or outside shareholders with an interest in pressurizing management to focus on profit'. Most ended up with such arcane shareholder structures that it was hard for them to restructure at all (*BCE*, February 1998, pp. 44, 46). The 'grey economy' amounted to about 25 per cent of GDP by 1996 (EBRD 1996b: 144, 161).

A new privatization law was approved in February 1996. It provided a framework for the privatization of large public enterprises, including the oil and gas conglomerate, electricity generation and distribution, television and radio, and telecommunications. It was decided to use vouchers (exchangeable for shares or able to be placed in investment funds) rather than cash to compensate some 300,000 victims of the wars of 1991–5 (refugees, war invalids and other displaced persons) and about 4,400 people who had been political prisoners under the former Communist regime. They could bid for shares either directly or via investment funds. The new law extended purchase by instalment from f ve years to twenty, and it was envisaged that foreign bidding would be permitted for some of these enterprises (*FT*, 10 April 1996, p. 2; EBRD 1996b: 144–5). However, this voucher-based mass-privatization programme was not implemented until mid-1998, when about 225,000 voucher holders acquired shares in 471 f rms, either directly or through one of seven competing privatization funds, and about 80 per cent of the assets were sold in three bidding rounds (EBRD 1998b: 160). In 1998, about 50 per cent of enterprise employees worked in fully private enterprises, 20 per cent in f rms with minority stakes owned by the state and 30 per cent in fully state-owned enterprises, mainly public utilities (EBRD 1998b: 160). In 2000 the state still held direct stakes in 1,610 enterprises, 851 of which were loss-making, as well as additional indirect stakes through pension funds and banks (EBRD 2000a: 48; 2000b: 150).

Despite slow privatization of industry, the private sector grew rapidly from 15 per cent of GDP in 1990 to 40 per cent in 1994 and 60 per cent by 1999 (see Table 5.4). Croatia attracted very little FDI from 1990 to 1994, but inflows of FDI were muc higher from 1995 onward. Foreigners were permitted to own or lease land, subject to reciprocity and usage restrictions (EBRD 1996b: 146).

Foreign trade

Even before the end of Communist rule, Croatia already traded mainly with the West. The Tudjman regime adopted a liberal foreign-trade regime. There were no quantitative restrictions on imports, and most imports and exports were tariff-free. An import tax of 10 per cent was introduced as part of the government's macro-economic stabilization programme in autumn 1993 (EBRD 1994: 21, 109). A later trade law applied import quotas to less than 1 per cent of tariff items, mainly petroleum derivatives, fertilizers and cement, but export quotas still applied to thirty-five items, mainly timber crude oil and natural gas (EBRD 1996b: 145).

Croatia after the Tudjman regime, 2000 onward

The parliamentary election of 3 January 2000

The turn-out was over 78 per cent. The overall conduct of the election was praised by the OSCE, although concern was expressed at the treatment of minorities, media bias and the large numbers of votes from Bosnia and Herzegovina (*FT*, 5 January 2000, p. 8). Under an electoral law passed in October 1999, 140 seats were to be filled by proportional representation (in ten electoral districts, each with fourteen seats), six were allocated to the Croatian diaspora (most of whom voted for the HDZ), and five were reserved for ethnic minorities. The HDZ was swept from offic partly because the economy was in deep recession, unemployment was over 20 per cent, the pension fund was virtually bankrupt, and there was a large budget def cit (*IHT*, 7 January 1997, p. 5).

The final distribution of the 151 seats in the house of representatives is shown in Table 5.5.

The biggest gainer was the SDP. Its leader Ivica Racan had won respect for his astute and liberal-minded conduct as the last leader of the old Croatian League of Communists from December 1989 onward. Instead of trying to crack down on opposition to Communist rule, he had paved the way for Croatia's f rst multiparty

5.5 Croatian parliamentary election, 3 January 2000

Party	Seats
Croatian Democratic Union (HDZ)	46
Six-Party Anti-HDZ Alliance:	
Social Democratic Party (SDP) (ex-Communists), led by Ivica Racan	44
Croatian Social Liberal Party (HSLS), led by Drazen Budisa	24
Croatian Peasant Party (HSS)	16
Istrian Democratic Congress (IDS, mainly Italian)	4
Liberal Party (LS)	2
Croatian People's Party (HNS)	2
Others:	
Croatian Party of Rights (HSP, ultra-nationalist)	4
Croatian Christian Democratic Union (HKDU)	1
Serbian People's Union (SNS)	1
Regional parties	3
Independents	4

Source: Forto (2003: 200).

elections in April-May 1990. In January 2000 Racan pledged that (if elected) he would cut public spending by 17 per cent, promote economic restructuring as a matter of urgency, reduce unemployment (which exceeded 20 per cent), reduce onerous taxes, establish more open and honest methods of privatization of state industries and banks, reduce the salaries of politicians and senior officials by up to 50 per cent, cooperate more fully with the ICTY, end Croatia's previous meddling in the internal affairs of Bosnia and Herzegovina, increase the power of parliament, reduce the power of the presidency, establish a fairer justice system, strengthen minority and human rights, speed up the rehabilitation of refugees, and end the previous role of state television as a propaganda tool for the government/president (*IHT*, 3 January 2000, p. 7; *IHT*, 5 January 2000, p. 4). The second big gainer was the Croatian Social Liberal Party (HSLS), whose leader Drazen Budisa was the presidential candidate of the 'the Opposition of Six' alliance.

The two-stage presidential election, 24 January and 7 February 2000

Nine candidates took part in the first round. The three front-runners obtained the following percentage shares of the votes: Stipe Mesic, 41.6 per cent; Drazen Budisa, 28 per cent; Mate Granic, 21 per cent. All three promised an open and democratic Croatia with closer ties to the EU and the USA and a curtailment of presidential power (*IHT*, 26 January 2000, p. 7).

Stipe Mesic, a member of the Croatian People's Party, was backed by four centre parties. He had brief y been president of Yugoslavia on the eve of its disintegration. He then joined the HDZ and became the speaker of the Croatian parliament, before resigning in 1994 in protest at Tudjman's 'meddling' in Bosnia. Mesic was also the only Croat to have given evidence for the prosecution at the ICTY, and he campaigned openly for all ICTY indictees to be extradited to The Hague. Mesic's platform rejected the crude nationalism of the HDZ, and he was married to a Serb. The HDZ saw him as a major threat to their/Croatia's interests in Bosnia-Herzegovina (where the party remained strong), because he had emphasized the need to treat Bosnia as a fully independent sovereign state, to stop allowing Bosnian Croats to vote in Croatian elections, and to stop the spending of 150 million dollars per annum supporting the Bosnian Croats and their armed forces. Mesic declared: 'I sent a blunt message to the Croats in Bosnia-Herzegovina that they have to turn toward Sarajevo; they must lose all illusions that they will one day be part of Croatia.' He had started to pull away from Tudjman after the infamous March 1991 meeting in Karadgeorgevon, at which Tudjman and Milosevic plotted to partition Bosnia between Croatia and Serbia (*IHT*, 8 February 2000, p. 7; 9 February 2000, p. 2).

Drazen Budisa was the joint candidate of his own HSLS and Racan's SDP. Like Mesic, he also supported a strengthening of democratic governance, including a reduction in the powers of the president, and favoured Croatian membership of the EU and NATO. Both Budisa and Mesic had been jailed for nationalist activities during the early 1970s, but Budisa was the more nationalistic of the two and the more conservative on issues such as drug use and abortion. Both vowed to cooperate with Ivica Racan to achieve political and economic liberalization *(The Guardian*, 25 January 2000, p. 15). Mate Granic, Croatia's former foreign minister, was from the liberal pro-EU wing of the HDZ. He ignored Western advice to run as an independent. In the run-off, Stipe Mesic obtained 56.2 per cent of the vote, against Budisa's 43.8 per cent.

On taking office, President Mesic appealed to the 300,000 ethnic Serb refugees t return to Croatia, where he would endeavour to ensure that they would be welcomed back to their old homes (*The Economist*, 12 February 2000, p. 4). On 23 March 2000 he also visited Bosnia to assure the Bosnian authorities that Croatia would stop interfering in their internal affairs.

When Mesic and his staff moved into the presidential palace, they found 'an archive of some 830 tapes and 17,000 transcripts of conversations between Tudjman and just about every single person who had visited him since 1991 . . Tudjman was obsessed with history. That is why he taped everything.' Ironically, even though it was widely assumed that much of the most sensitive material had been removed during the three weeks between Tudjman's death and the election of the new government, the surviving records still revealed that 'the HDZ elite pillaged every public institution in sight and virtually bankrupted the country'. At least fifteen financial institutions were 'in a state of collapse'. In just under a decade, Tudjman and his cronies had run up 'a $15.1 billion domestic and foreign debt'. Tudjman had assisted Miroslav Kutle, a former barman with no money of his own, to buy 157 companies. Tudjman's cronies 'either had no idea how to make money or simply stripped what they had acquired of assets'. In addition, Tudjman had repeatedly considered calling 'an international conference in which Bosnia would now be formally divided between Serbia and Croatia'. The Bosniaks were to be given a small rump territory to be called 'Muslimania', while Kosova was to be 'divided between Serbia and Albania' (*NYRB*, 2000, vol. 47, no. 13, pp. 20–2).

The Racan government later confrmed that Tudjman and his cronies had plundered billions of dollars from the treasury and had 'enriched friends, family members and political allies by manipulating the privatization of state-owned companies and handing out lucrative contracts and suspect loans'. The regime 'allowed the politically well-connected to acquire big banks and plunder them.' State funds were also secretly funnelled to Tudjman's favoured causes, such as the ethnic Croatian paramilitaries fighting in Bosnia and Herzegovina. 'The state accumulated large debts off the books, and there was no treasury ministry to monitor or control how money was spent from the government's 3,000 bank accounts' (*IHT*, 14 June 2000, p. 13). Tudjman's tapes and transcripts were said to provide ample proof that 'he and his close circle were directly involved in perpetrating war crimes'. According to President Mesic, who handed copies of the transcripts to the ICTY, the tapes implicated Tudjman's senior military commanders in 'extensive atrocities and then the subsequent cover-up of these crimes'. The major revelation was that Tudjman had covered up his involvement in ethnic cleansing in the Bosnian village of Ahmici. The tapes and a Croatian intelligence report backed up claims by General Tomas Blaskic that the killers in Ahmici were 'clandestine Croatian forces under Tudjman's command'. Another set of tapes showed 'how Tudjman and his cronies skimmed off $100 million' from the privatization of Croatia's telecommunications corporation. Tapes also recorded that, even after the Dayton Accords of 1995, Tudjman and Milosevic continued plotting to carve Bosnia up between them (*Independent*, 1 November 2000, p. 16).

The first centre-left coalition government headed by Ivica Racan, February 2000 to July 2002

Racan's SDP-led coalition government initially enjoyed the support of nearly two-thirds of the 151 deputies in the house of representatives. Among its f rst steps was the imprisonment of the former tourism minister Ivan Herak on charges of embezzlement, and of the tycoon Miroslav Kutle, who was part of Tudjman's corrupt inner circle, on 3 February. Both Kutle and Ivic Pasalic were alleged to have been involved in a banking scandal. The new interior minister Sime Lucin assured Croatian journalists that their phones would no longer be tapped. Although Racan warned that cutting aid to the Bosnian Croats too suddenly could precipitate an expensive wave of immigration to Croatia, which he wished to avoid, he vowed that all Croatian payments to Bosnia would henceforth be channelled through Bosnian state institutions.

On 6 February 2000 Prime Minister Racan tried to fulfil its promises of social equality and justice by announcing that officials' salaries were to be cut by up to 40 per cent and that allegations of corruption against former ministers and official would be pursued, even if the targets (such as Tudjman's former aide Ivic Pasalic) still held parliamentary seats and offcial positions. Racan announced that his government would try gradually to bring Croatia's overvalued currency to a more realistic exchange rate and then tie its value to the euro/(*HT*, 7 February 2000, p. 5). The Racan government presented its first budget on 8 March 2000. It aimed to cut the budge deficit to 1 per cent of GDP in 2000, partly by reducing defence spending from its 1999 level (7 per cent of GDP). Croatia joined NATO's Partnership for Peace programme in May 2000.

In March 2000 a refugee swap was signed to allow 2,000 Croatian Serbs to return to Croatia and 2,000 Croats to return to Serb-administered Republika Srpska by June 2000 (*IHT*, 6 April 2000, p. 4). The Racan government had a plan for some 16,500 Croatian Serb refugees to return to Croatia, assisted by Western cash to rebuild their homes and improve services, but it proceeded very slowly and half-heartedly (*The Economist*, 15 July 2000, p. 46). However, a report issued by the Council of Europe in July 2001 highlighted and criticized continuing institutionalized Croatian discrimination against Croatian Serbs who returned to their former homes *FT*, 9 July 2001, p. 6).

Mate Granic and other disaffected HDZ deputies launched a new 'Democratic Centre Party' in March 2000, claiming that the HDZ had been hijacked by the corrupt and authoritarian ultra-nationalists led by Tudjman's former henchman Ivic Pasalic.

On 12 September 2000 sixteen suspected Croatian war criminals were arrested, including several high-ranking army officers. Since only one (General Ivan Andabak was wanted by the ICTY, the government took steps to hold war-crimes trials in Croatia. The arrests mainly related to atrocities committed by Croatian nationalists in Bosnia-Herzegovina. In response, on 28 September twelve serving and retired Croatian generals published an open letter accusing President Mesic and the Racan government of 'waging a campaign to smear the independence struggle'. The next day President Mesic sacked the seven signatories who were still serving off cers for 'complaining that the government was insulting the memory of the country's war for independence by prosecuting alleged war criminals for atrocities committed against Serbs' (*The Guardian*, 30 September 2000, p. 19).

A major Balkan–EU summit was held in Zagreb on 24 November 2000. Albania, Bosnia, Macedonia and the FRY were represented and Macedonia signed the first so-called stabilization and association agreement (SAA) with the EU, a new kind of agreement intended for western Balkan countries. Croatia started negotiating a similar SAA with the EU to further liberalize trade with and gain increased funding from the EU. It was signed in May 2001.

Thousands of public-sector workers went on strike in December 2000 in protest against plans to freeze public-sector wages for a year and then raise them only in line with economic growth. Over 60 per cent of Croatian workers belonged to trade unions, so they were still a force to be reckoned with (Forto 2003: 206). The previous government had promised public-sector workers an 8.5 per cent pay rise. Bound by a legal contract, Racan eventually agreed to honour the promise. Indeed, he had to suspend the public-sector wage freeze 'just to get unions to come to the table' (*BCE*, February 2001, pp. 13, 39–40).

On 7 February 2001 a Zagreb court ordered the arrest of General Mirko Norac and his deputy Milan Canic, both of whom were indicted for alleged crimes committed in autumn 1991. Croatian police launched a search for Norac after he failed to give himself up. On 11 February over 100,000 Croatians took part in HDZ-organized protests in Split and elsewhere against these and other attempts to bring alleged war criminals to trial (*IHT*, 12 February 2001, p. 4). Norac finally gave himself up on 21 February, after Prime Minister Racan gave assurances that his case would be heard in a Croatian court because the ICTY did not want him (*The Guardian*, 23 February 2001, p. 18). On 24 March 2003 Norac was sentenced to twelve years in jail, having been found guilty of organizing the killing of at least f fty ethnic Serb civilians in 1991. He was the highest ranking Croatian offcer to have been sentenced by a Croatian court for crimes committed during the 1991–5 wars. Four courts had been empowered to try such cases.

The house of representatives passed a constitutional amendment in March 2001 abolishing the senate (the Sabor's upper house) when its term expired. The senate, which had delaying powers, was still dominated by the HDZ and refused to debate the motion. Its delaying powers were transferred to local assemblies: provided one-third of them agreed to do so, they could force the house of representatives to reconsider a bill (*BCE*, May 2001, p. 44).

Local (county) elections, 20 May 2001

The turn-out was only 46.9 per cent, far below the 75.3 and 63 per cent for the 2000 parliamentary and presidential elections, respectively. The HDZ performed sur-prisingly well, winning the largest share of votes in sixteen of Croatia's twenty counties (as in the local elections of 1997). However, the HDZ was hampered by lack of potential coalition partners and gained overall control of only four counties, whereas the ruling coalition gained overall control of f fteen (Forto 2003: 203; *IHT*, 22 May 2001, p. 5).

Nevertheless, the results made it obvious that the Racan government had already disappointed many Croatians. It had appeared timid on several fronts and had 'failed' to reduce unemployment (although this was a totally unrealistic popular expecta-tion, given the dire state in which ten years of Tudjman's corrupt, bigoted and belligerent pan-Croatian nationalism and authoritarianism had left the Croatian economy). One-quarter of voters had voted for the HDZ, while another quarter had expressed their disillusionment by not voting at all, raising doubts as to whether the fractious coalition government would survive until the next parliamentary elections, which were due in 2004 (*FT*, Survey, 19 June 2001, pp. 39, 41).

Racan acknowledged on 4 June 2001 that there might have to be early elections, after the Istrian Democratic Congress left the ruling coalition. This party had striven to make Italian an official language (at least on the partly Italian-inhabited Istrian peninsula), but the government had challenged the legality of a local Istrian law proclaiming Istria to be bilingual. The government claimed that it violated Croatia's extant Tudjman constitution, which envisaged Croatia as a one-nation state, and that it would set a 'dangerous precedent' (*IHT*, 5 June 2001, p. 6).

The governments of Croatia, Albania, Bosnia-Herzegovina, Bulgaria, Romania, Macedonia and the FRY signed an agreement on 27 June 2001 aimed at liberalizing trade in at least 90 per cent of visible trade between them, under the aegis of the EU's Stability Pact for South-eastern Europe. This was designed to enhance stability in the region through economic growth. Croatia, Bosnia and the FRY also agreed on measures to help resettle their remaining 1.2 million refugees and 'internally displaced persons' (IDPs) in their former homes (*FT*, 28 June 2001, p. 8).

On 6 July 2001 the chief prosecutor of the ICTY, Carla del Ponte, announced during a visit to Zagreb that two Croatian generals (war heroes) had been indicted for alleged war crimes. Neither she nor Prime Minister Racan would disclose their names. The next day, the government decided (by nineteen votes to four) to consent to the extradition of these two indictees to The Hague, as did President Mesic. This precipitated the resignation of four ministers. However, the Dayton Accords, which Franjo Tudjman had signed on Croatia's behalf, included a pledge of full cooperation with the ICTY. Racan had written to the ICTY, requesting permission for these indictees to be tried in Croatia, but his request was rejected (*IHT*, 9 July 2001, p. 9). The four cabinet ministers who resigned were members of the HSLS. This party's withdrawal from the governing coalition deprived the government of its parliamentary majority. However, the HSLS deputy prime minister subsequently changed his mind and remained in government, rejecting his party's stance. At the same time, war veterans threatened mass protests (*The Economist*, 14 July 2001, p. 46). Up to this point, Croatia had cooperated with the ICTY by extraditing a dozen Bosnian Croat indictees to The Hague. It had also taken action of its own against Croatian generals suspected of war crimes. However, it had not as yet extradited any of its indicted 'war heroes' to The Hague (*The Times*, 9 July 2001, p. 10; *The Guardian*, 9 July 2001, p. 9).

Racan announced on 9 July 2001 that one of the indicted generals, General Rahim Ademi (an ethnic Albanian from Kosova), was willing to surrender voluntarily. The second (still unnamed) indictee, who was widely reported to be retired General Ante Gotovina, was quoted as saying that he did not recognize the ICTY and refused to surrender himself to it. The HDZ then demanded a debate on the future of cooperation with the ICTY. The HDZ had enacted a constitutional clause pledging cooperation with the ICTY in 1996, but it now wanted this clause to be changed to prevent the extradition of indictees who were perceived to be wanted primarily because of their seniority – as the men who had either ordered or turned a blind eye to war crimes and crimes against humanity, but who had not necessarily carried them out in person. On 11 July the HSLS leader Drazen Budisa resigned from the government to publicize his opposition to its plans. However, two opinion polls showed that about half of Croatia's population was in favour of full cooperation with the ICTY, and on 15 July the government won a vote of confidence by ninety-three votes to thirty-six (*Independent*, 17 July 2001, p. 11). General Rahim Ademi turned himself over to the ICTY on 25 July.

The presidents of Croatia and Italy agreed on 9 October 2001 that a long-standing dispute over Croatia's non-payment of war reparations to Italy should no longer be allowed to prevent closer ties between these two states. Italy's president praised Croatia's stability and expressed his support for its efforts to join the EU and NATO.

The second centre-left coalition government headed by Ivica Racan, July 2002 to November 2003

Prime Minister Racan suddenly resigned on 5 July 2002, declaring that he wanted to form a new governing coalition which would exclude the HSLS members who opposed cooperation with the ICTY, so that he could get on with enacting much-needed reforms before the next elections (due in January 2004). He explained that this resignation had been made necessary by the deep rifts and infighting within his previous governin coalition, especially regarding cooperation with the ICTY and the status of Croatia's minorities, which had increasingly incapacitated the government over the previous year (*FT*, 6 July 2002, p. 8). President Mesic gave Racan a mandate to form a new government omitting Drazen Budisa and the HSLS, whereupon the HSLS then split and nine of the twenty-four HSLS deputies joined the new coalition as members of a newly constituted party (Libra). The new government was able to count on 75 of the 151 deputies in the house of representatives.

The presidents of Croatia, the FRY and Bosnia-Herzegovina attended a summit in Sarajevo on 15 July 2002, the first such meeting since 1991. They pledge to strengthen peace, trust and trade, to respect each other's borders, to cooperate against crime and to help refugees and IDPs return to their old homes (*IHT*, 16 July 2002, p. 5).

Ivo Sanader, the leader of the moderate 'modernizing' wing of the HDZ, defeated the corrupt ultra-nationalist Ivic Pasalic in a contest for the HDZ leadership in September 2002. Pasalic then left the HDZ and launched an ultra-nationalist 'Croatian Bloc', taking with him many ultra-nationalist HDZ supporters and four former HDZ deputies in the house of representatives. This cleared the way for Sanader to start energetically rebuilding the HDZ as a moderate pro-EU and pro-NATO conservative party modelled on Germany's Christian Democratic Union (CDU). That in turn provided additional cross-party parliamentary backing for the Racan government's efforts to reform Croatia in ways that would make it eligible to join both NATO and the EU in due course.

On 24 September 2002 the Croatian government refused to extradite the eighty-three-year-old war hero General Janko Bobetko to The Hague to be tried for alleged war crimes. Prime Minister Racan defended his stance on two grounds: General Bobetko was an old man with serious heart problems and diabetes, and this extradition would infringe the constitution. Indeed, the Racan government had been greatly weakened politically by the relentless pressure from the ICTY and its Western backers for more and more extraditions, which in turn had led to the government being increasingly denounced as 'traitors' by Croatian nationalists for having complied with ICTY demands and to the governmental crisis in July 2002 which sharply reduced its parliamentary majority. Racan was therefore rightly afraid that, if he complied with this latest ICTY demand, a Croatian nationalist backlash could bring down his reforming government (*FT*, 25 September 2002, p. 14; *IHT*, 4 December 2002, p. 6). General Bobetko had been Croatia's army chief of staff and thus one of the architects of Croatia's eventual victory in the wars of 1991–5. In the short term, the Racan government was let off the hook by General Bobetko's timely death on 29 April 2003. The ICTY had suspended the indictment after the government's claim that the general was too ill to face trial was corroborated by Dutch doctors(*The Guardian*, 30 April 2003, p. 15). In the longer term, unfortunately, Racan's understandable refusal to cooperate with the ICTY in the case of Bobetko led the Western powers to take a much tougher line with Croatia regarding full compliance with the ICTY. This eventually undermined and tore apart Croatia's liberal reforming coalition government, which was obliged to call early elections which in turn brought the still more nationalistic HDZ back to power. This trajectory was very similar to what was happening concurrently in Serbia. There, uncompromising Western insistence that Serbia had to comply fully with ICTY demands not only discredited and steadily undermined the post-Milosevic liberal reforming coalition but also directly contributed to the assassination of Serbia's only charismatic reforming leader, Prime Minister Zoran Djindjic. In both countries, the cause of liberal reform was set back several years by blinkered Western intransigence about extraditions to the ICTY, but the Western powers have repeatedly contrived to offload the blame for these grave setbacks ont alleged Croatian and Serbian obduracy instead of acknowledging their own share of responsibility.

Croatia and Serbia-Montenegro signed an agreement on 10 December 2002 about the disputed Prevlavka peninsula, which enabled the UN peacekeeping mission there to leave. The peninsula was to be demilitarized and subject to joint sea-police patrols (*The Times*, 11 December 2002, p. 18).

A law was passed on 13 December 2002 to increase the political representation of minorities and to grant them the right to have their children educated in their own languages (*Independent*, 14 December 2002, p. 11). Serbs were henceforth to have three designated seats in the house of representatives, while five seats were earmarke for other minorities, including one each for Italians and Hungarians. However, as the Freedom House rapporteur Edin Forto has rightly pointed out, 'the three seats that Serbs now hold are still insufficient to provide them with the necessary influence to restore the rights they enjoyed prior to the 1991 hostilities' (Forto 2004: 184). In order to ensure parity with the preconditions regarding recognition and representation of minorities which have been laid down for Turkish and Macedonian entry into the EU, Croatia probably ought not to be allowed to enter the EU until it has made more radical alterations to its 'Tudjman constitution'. The massive 'ethnic cleansing' perpetrated against Croatia's Serbs between 1991 and 1995, which reduced the Serb share of the population from 14 per cent in the 1991 census to 4.5 per cent in the 2001 census, was regarded by the Tudjman regime as an enduring fait accompli. This resulted in the passing of a law in 1999 which reduced Serb representation in the house of representatives to just one designated representative (0.67 per cent of the seats). The December 2002 legislation provided very incomplete redress. If Serb refugees are genuinely to be encouraged to return to their former homes or home areas in Croatia, Croatia will need to pass legislation restoring the Croatian Serbs' former status as one of the constituent nations of Croatia and granting Serbs political representation proportionate to the 14 per cent share of the population that they comprised in the 1991 census, just before the start of the 'ethnic cleansing'. In the long term, full acceptance that Croatia is a plurinational state could be a lot more constructive than the obsessive EU, US and ICTY insistence on the extradition of Croatian 'war heroes' to The Hague to be tried for alleged war crimes and crimes against humanity. This obsession with retribution is backward-looking, whereas proper recognition and accommodation of minorities is forward-looking.

Croatia's quest for EU membership from 2003 onward

The year 2003 began with EU officials discouraging the Racan government from applying for EU membership, but on 21 February 2003 the Racan government 'made the bold decision to submit its application anyway' (Forto 2004: 175). From that time onward, the quest for EU membership has been the overriding driving force in Croatian political and economic life. Almost everything done by government has become geared to achieving that goal, which has been commanding cross-party support. That in turn has been the main reason why the EU has taken the Croatian application seriously (despite the commission's prior misgivings) and why Croatia eventually succeeded in gaining official candidate status in October 2005

At the Jasenovac concentration camp on 11 May 2003, President Stipe Mesic expressed his 'deepest regret for the innocent victims of those who tarnished Croatia's name'. This was the first time a Croatian head of state had expressed remorse in thi way. Without wishing to cast doubt on his sincerity, it would appear that the quest for EU membership contributed to his desire to demonstrate that Croatia was turning over a new leaf.

After further criticism from the ICTY chief prosecutor Carla del Ponte in June 2003, the Racan government posted a reward of 50,000 euros for information leading to the arrest of General Ante Gotovina, who had been indicted for failing to halt the killings of Serbian civilians in 1995 (*IHT*, 6 June 2003, p. 4). This too was done partly to propitiate the gods of the EU. On 9 October 2003 the USA offered a 5 million dollar reward for information leading to the arrest of General Gotovina.

President Mesic held talks with Svetozar Marovic, the federal president of Serbia and Montenegro, on 10 September 2003. The two presidents apologized for 'all the evils' committed by their citizens during the wars of 1991–5. The thorniest issues concerned the return of refugees, including the 300,000 ethnic Serbs displaced from Croatia to Serbia. Croatia had registered 100,000 returns (nearly one-third of those displaced), but many had remained only a short time before returning to Serbia. Many had found their old homes were destroyed or had new occupants (*FT*, 10 September 2003, p. 12; *The Times*, 11 September 2003, p. 16). Mending fences with neighbours was seen as not only desirable in itself, but also as yet another way of pleasing the EU.

Elections to the house of representatives, 23 November 2003

Eight seats were reserved for members of ethnic minorities and up to fourteen for representatives of the Croatian diaspora. There was a system of proportional representation, with a 5 per cent threshold for representation in parliament. The turn-out was 59.6 per cent, well below the 75.3 per cent turn-out in the January 2000 elections. The final distribution of the 152 seats in the house of representatives is shown in Table 5.6.

Although the Racan government had implemented economic reforms designed to extend and strengthen a market system, the chief results had been negative: the closure of unprofitable factories, stubbornly high unemployment and an average monthly wage that remained just 625 dollars. The Racan coalition had also been continually disrupted and distracted by internal quarrels over its failure to prosecute people implicated in corruption scandals under Tudjman and over the tribulations of extraditing Croatian war heroes to The Hague for trial by the ICTY (*IHT*, 24 November 2003, p. 3).

5.6 Elections to the Croatian house of representatives, 23 November 2003

Party	Seats
Croatian Democratic Union (HDZ), led by Ivo Sanader	66
Croatian Pensioners Party (HSU), allied to the HDZ	3
Social Democratic Party (SDP), led by Ivica Racan	34
Croatian Peasant Party (HSS)	10
Croatian People's Party (HNS)	10
Croatian Social Liberal Party (HSLS)	2
Istrian Democratic Assembly (IDS)	4
Liberal Party (LS)	2
LIBRA – Party of Liberal Democrats	3
Democratic Centre	1
Party of Democratic Action (SDA)	1
Croatian Party of Rights (HSP, ultra-nationalist)	8
Independent Democratic Serbian Party (SSDS)	1
Small regional parties	1
Independents	3

Source: Peranic (2005: 8).

By purging authoritarian and ultra-nationalist elements from the HDZ leadership, Sanader had moved the HDZ back towards its pre-1991 ideological roots as a moderate centrist democratic party. He claimed it was no longer a nationalist party. It had not been founded as the corrupt, clientelistic, authoritarian and charismatic ultra-nationalist party it became under Franjo Tudjman. He wanted it to be seen as just another Christian democratic party, and had replaced nationalist rhetoric with emphasis on the crucial importance of deeper integration into the EU and NATO. He also hinted to the Serbian SDS that he might give it a post in government. This impressed the EU, but it played less well with many of the older HDZ members, whom the Croatian political analyst Davor Gjenero characterized as old-style nationalists, even if Sanader had 'moved on' (*The Economist*, 29 November 2003, p. 49; *IHT*, 25 November 2003, p. 3; *FT*, Survey, 13 July 2004, p. 34).

The centre-right government headed by Ivo Sanader, from December 2003 onward

On 23 December 2003 the prime minister Ivo Sanader pledged to spur economic growth and strengthen human rights in Croatia, after his government was approved by eighty-eight votes to twenty-nine. He gave the key foreign-affairs portfolio to Miomir Zuzul, Croatia's former ambassador to the USA. Zuzul declared that he would seek reconciliation with former enemies and invite NATO to establish bases in Croatia, as a prelude to NATO membership (*FT*, 24 December 2003, p. 5). However, Zuzul had to resign on 4 January 2005, following allegations that he was involved in a bribery scandal. He rejected the allegations (*IHT*, 5 January 2005, p. 3). On 12 January 2004 Prime Minister Sanader set 2007 as Croatia's target date for joining the EU and declared that it would meet all the entry requirements, including judicial reforms, respecting the Serb minority and full cooperation with the ICTY (*FT*, 13 January 2004, p. 9).

Sanader struck a deal with the Serbian Democratic Party, appointing Serbs as junior ministers and promising financial aid for Serb refugees seeking to repossess and repair war-damaged homes. Symbolically, he publicly celebrated the Eastern Orthodox

Christmas with the Serb community (*FT*, 30 January 2004, p. 9). He appealed to Serb refugees, more than 200,000 of whom still lived outside the country, to return to Croatia. He also visited families who had recently returned to their rebuilt houses – something no previous Croat prime minister had done (*FT*, Survey, 13 July 2004, p. 34).

In early 2004 Croatia dispatched fifty military-police officers to assist the NAT led occupation forces in Afghanistan and also donated rifles and ammunition to the new Afghan army. American officials explored whether Croatia might send troops to Iraq, a prospect that the Croatian military was willing to embrace but which was unpopular with the public (*IHT*, 9 February 2004, p. 5). On 19 November 2004, moreover, Croatia's defence minister announced that the government had signed a pact in July granting extensive rights for US forces to use the country's airspace, territorial waters and training facilities. The deal had been struck without the know-ledge of President Mesic, who was Croatia's supreme commander but was also Croatia's most prominent opponent of the US-led occupation of Iraq (*IHT*, 20 November 2004, p. 4).

On 8 March Croatia agreed to extradite Mladen Markac and Ivan Cermak, two retired army generals indicted by the ICTY for their roles in the Croat recapture of Knin in 1995, which had been accompanied by savage reprisals against its Serb inhabitants (*FT*, 9 March 2004, p. 8).

The *Jasenovac Flower*, a giant rose with petals extending skywards, was unveiled in a field at the site of the Jasenovac concentration camp on 16 March 2004, in homag to the tens of thousands of Jews, Gypsies, Serbs and others killed there by Croatian fascists from 1941 to 1945.

The EU Commission published its third annual report on Croatia's stabilization and association process on 30 March 2004. It stated:

> Croatia is a functioning democracy, with stable institutions guaranteeing the rule of law . . . The 2000 and 2003 elections were free and fair . . . Croatia can be regarded as a functioning market economy. It should be able to cope with competitive pressure and market forces within the EU in the medium term, provided that it continues implementing its reform programme . . . Croatia's economy is already well integrated with that of the EU. However, the working of market mechanisms still needs some improvement . . . Full integration in the single market and the adoption of the *acquis* would, at this stage, cause difficultie for a number of sectors in withstanding the competition within the single market.

The report stressed that Croatia's shipbuilding and agricultural sectors needed to be modernized, that its judicial sector needed to be strengthened, and that Croatia needed to 'make additional efforts in the fields of minority rights, refugees returns, judicia reform, regional co-operation and the f ght against corruption' (pp. 1–4).

On 20 April 2004 the EU Commission recommended that Croatia could start accession negotiations with the EU in the autumn of 2004, provided the governments of the member states formally accepted the commission's recommendations at the EU European Council meeting in June 2004 (*FT*, 21 April 2004, p. 16). However, the European Council decided on 17 June that accession negotiations with Croatia would not start until early 2005 (*FT*, 18 June 2004, p. 6).

The government ordered the removal of two plaques erected to commemorate officials from the Ustasa/NDH era on 27 August 2004. This was hailed as the first ac of 'de-Nazif cation' to have been undertaken by independent Croatia.

On 23 November 2005 Carla del Ponte, the chief prosecutor at the ICTY, questioned the seriousness of Croatia's efforts to arrest General Ante Gotovina. She had previously praised Croatia for handing over eight other indictees and implementing new measures to help track down the former army commander (*HT*, 24 November 2004, p. 3). Prime Minister Sanader protested that his government was fully committed to tracking down and extraditing the general.

The two-round presidential election held on 2 and 16 January 2005

In the first round, the turn-out was just over 50 per cent. There were thirteen candidates The electorate of about 4.4 million people included 400,000 Croats living abroad. For the first time it was felt unnecessary for international observers to monitor the election. In the first round, seventy-year-old Stipe Mesic won 48.9 per cent of th votes, narrowly failing to reach the minimum 50 per cent needed to validate the result. The runner-up was Jadranka Kosor of the HDZ, with just over 20 per cent. Boris Miksic came third with 17.8 per cent. All three backed Croatia's efforts to join NATO and the EU (*FT*, 3 January 2005, p. 5). The third-placed candidate, Boris Miksic, was a populist Croatian American millionaire who had recently returned to Croatia to run for the presidency and was a sharp critic of the country's ruling parties, accusing them of 'selling out the country to foreigners' and plunging it into 'even greater misery' than it had endured under Communism (*FT*, 3 January 2005, p. 5).

Both Mesic and Kosor opposed the deployment of Croatian troops in Iraq; and both supported cooperation with the ICTY (*IHT*, 15 January 2005, p. 3). However, Mesic had made enemies among Croatian nationalists, who considered him a traitor for insisting that any Croat who had committed war crimes should be punished (*HT*, 3 January 2005, p. 3). He was the candidate of a coalition of eight centre-left, non-nationalist, reform-orientated parties, and he warned that, if Kosor were to win, the HDZ would have too much power (*HT*, 15 January 2005, p. 3). By contrast, Jadranka Kosor was 'proud' of Tudjman (*HT*, 3 January 2005, p. 3) and appealed to the Croatian diaspora, who made up 400,000 of Croatia's electorate of 4.4 million (*HT*, 15 January 2005, p. 3). She was a close ally of prime minister Ivo Sanader, serving as his deputy prime minister responsible for war veterans and families. She campaigned hard to win the support of nationalist voters who backed other candidates in the first round Mild-mannered and moderate, she personified the transformation of the HDZ into a European-style conservative party (*IHT*, 4 January 2005, p. 3; 15 January 2005, p. 3). However, she only made it to the second round with the votes of the diaspora, mainly in Bosnia, amongst whom widespread vote rigging was subsequently dis - covered (*The Guardian*, 17 January 2005, p. 12). Mesic won the second round on 16 January 2005, obtaining 66.6 per cent of the vote to Kosor's 33.4 per cent.

In January 2005 it was revealed that, in cooperation with a Novi Sad-based Serbian law firm called MiS-NS, which represented refugees from Krajina, Croatia's state-ru real-estate agency (APN) had sold over 10,000 houses of Croatian Serb refugees without their knowledge and using forged papers (*Independent*, 3 January 2005, p. 17). In February 2005 it was disclosed that of the 300,000 Croatian Serb refugees who had left Croatia in 1991–5, only 115,000 had officially returned. However, th real number of returnees was thought to be as low as 30,000, as the official figu included those who had only returned to claim a Croatian passport. Only 200,000 Serbs were now living in Croatia (*Independent*, 4 February 2005, p. 23), as against 700,000

at the time of the 1991 census. These figures implied that Croatia's Serb populatio
had actually declined by about 500,000 since early 1991.

General Gotovina announced in a letter on 12 January 2005 that he was ready
to surrender 'immediately' if he was granted a trial in Croatia rather than at the ICTY,
but his offer was rejected by the ICTY (*IHT*, 13 January 2005, p. 4). On 31 January
the EU Commission gave Croatia six weeks in which to deliver Ante Gotovina to the
ICTY, failing which the membership negotiations scheduled to start on 17 March
would be postponed (*FT*, 1 February 2005, p. 8). On 14 March the Croatian government froze Ante Gotovina's assets but not his army pension, which was being used
to support his two families.

On 16 March 2005, EU foreign ministers formally delayed the start of accession
negotiations with Croatia, due to its failure to cooperate fully in tracking down and
handing over Ante Gotovina to the ICTY, after Carla del Ponte stated in writing that
Croatia was not doing enough to find him. They declared that accession negotiations could only begin once it was established that Croatia was 'co-operating fully
with the ICTY'. Austria, Hungary, Slovenia, Slovakia, Malta, Ireland and Cyprus
favoured starting talks straightaway (even without Gotovina), but the UK (which
then held the EU presidency) and Germany opposed this. Meanwhile, a Eurobarometer
opinion survey found that only 38 per cent of Croats believed that EU membership would benefit Croatia *IHT*, 17 March 2005, p. 36; *The Times*, 17 March 2005,
p. 36). President Mesic suggested that Gotovina might be in Paraguay, beyond
Croatia's reach. Most EU leaders believed that they had to take a tough line, if
only to avoid undermining the credibility of their insistence that Serbia had to cooperate
fully with the ICTY as a precondition for the opening of negotiations on an SAA.
However, Croatian veterans' organizations and other nationalists attacked the
Sanader government for being too subservient towards the ICTY and threatened to
form a veterans' party with the potential to undermine Sanader's position as leader
of the HDZ.

On 12 September 2005 a Croatian court charged eight former military police with
torturing and killing Serb prisoners at the Lora military prison near Split in 1992. The
eight had already been 'tried and acquitted by a county court in Split in 2002, amid
allegations by human rights groups of bias, mishandling of evidence and harassment
of witnesses'. However, Croatia's supreme court had overturned their acquittal in
September 2004 and ordered a retrial. The prosecution announced that it would now
call in witnesses from Serbia, who had refused to appear at the previous trial because
of fears for their safety. Only half the defendants appeared in court on 12 September.
The other four had gone into hiding after their acquittal was overturned (*IHT*, 12
September 2005).

Montenegro's assembly on 28 September approved President Filip Vujanovic's
decision in June to pay damages to Croatia for the part played by Montenegrins in
the 1991 war. Montenegro's pro-Serbian opposition were infuriated, because paying such damages would be an implicit admission of Montenegrin culpability for
some of the war crimes committed around Dubrovnik in 1991 (*IHT*, 29 September
2005, p. 8).

Carla del Ponte declared on 3 October 2005: 'I can say that, for a few weeks now,
Croatia has been co-operating fully with us and is doing everything it can to locate
and arrest Ante Gotovina' (*IHT*, 4 October 2005, p. 4). This finally gave the gree
light for the EU formally to initiate membership negotiations with Croatia on 4 October
2005 (*FT*, 5 October 2005, p. 6).

The ICTY issued an arrest warrant for one of five Croatian journalists charged with repeatedly ignoring judicial secrecy orders. All five were charged in 2005 with 'knowingly and wilfully' publishing the name of a protected witness and publishing excerpts from private testimony by that witness. The ensuing news stories and head-lines were evidently designed to intimidate witnesses. Four of the indicted journalists went to the ICTY on 3 October to plead 'not guilty'. ICTY officials had also repeatedl complained that defence lawyers and the police in Croatia and Serbia had damagingly leaked information (*IHT*, 4 October 2005, p. 3).

The EU Commission's fourth annual progress report on Croatia, published in November 2005, warned that 'the ability of Croatia to adequately prosecute transferred war crimes cases remains to be seen'. The commission also pointed out that the 'vast majority of these cases had been against Serbs, with little appetite to try Croats, and many cases have been tried *in absentia* as well as based on unsubstantiated evidence'. The commission reported that ethnic bias remained a problem in Croatian prosecution of war crimes.

> In 2004 around 55 per cent of local court verdicts in war crimes cases were reversed by the supreme court. In the frst seven months of 2005 the fgure stands at more than 60 per cent. While a good sign that justice is eventually done, such a reversal rate reflects poorly on what is happening at the local level

President Mesic replied that the Croatian judiciary was sufficiently impartial to continue to try war crimes in Croatia (*IHT*, 22 November 2005, p. 3).

President Mesic attacked the government on 29 November 2005 for having initialled an agreement with Austria regarding claims for compensation and restitution of property lost by Austrian Germans kicked out of Croatia in 1945. He warned that if this agreement were to be ratified by the Croatian Sabor, it could open a floodgat Italy and Germany would also seek to reopen property compensation and restitution issues, which could be f nancially ruinous for Croatia. However, the agreement had yet to be ratified by a two-thirds parliamentary majority. The government 'pledge that only property still in state hands could be returned' *The Guardian*, 30 November 2005, p. 18).

Ante Gotovina was f nally arrested on 7 December at a luxury hotel in Tenerife. On 10 December he was f own to The Hague in a Spanish military aircraft. Major protests ensued in Croatia, where many nationalists still saw him as a war hero. On 11 December about 70,000 people demonstrated in Split, demanding that Gotovina be provisionally set free pending a trial in Croatia. The protests, organized by veterans of Croatia's war of independence, were peaceful. The charges against Gotovina included the killing of at least 150 civilians, the burning and pillaging of more than a dozen towns and villages, and the expulsion of 150,000 Serb inhabitants (*IHT*, 12 December 2005, pp. 1, 10; *Independent*, 12 December 2005, p. 20).

Croatian economic affairs after Tudjman, 2000–5

Positive GDP growth was restored in 2000, with the subsidence of the Kosova crisis and the emergence of a less corrupt and more liberal post-Tudjman regime. By 2004, Croatia's GDP had recovered to about 94 per cent of its 1989 level (EBRD 2005a: 13).

The privatization of the banking sector was largely complete by 2001 (EBRD 2002a: 50). Following a round of bank acquisitions and mergers in 2002, eight

EU-based foreign banking groups were in control of just over 90 per cent of banking assets in Croatia by 2003 (EBRD 2003b: 132–3; *FT*, Survey, 13 July 2004, p. 35). However, privatization came to a near standstill in 2003, after the Croatian Peasant Party (HSS), the second biggest party in the ruling coalition, forced the Racan government to annul the sale of the Suncani Hvar tourist resort to a Slovenian company in February. The row between the Social Democratic Party and HSS (which was doctrinally lukewarm towards privatization) prompted the Croatian privatization fund's entire board to resign.

In May 2003 the government approved large bail-out package for Croatia's loss-making state-owned shipyards, less than a year after a previous large bail-out, which it had promised would be the last. The five state-owned shipyards depended on annua government bail-outs, each of which exceeded the 17,000 shipyard workers' yearly gross wage bill (*FT*, Survey, 17 June 2003, p. 32). Some state-owned companies were privatized in 2004, but several tenders were unsuccessful. The Croatian privatiza-tion fund aimed to complete all small-scale privatizations by June 2005 (EBRD 2004b: 114). The privatization process regained some momentum in 2005, with the sale of several agricultural and food-processing companies and the Suncani Hvar tourist resort, but the objective of completing all small-scale privatizations by June 2005 was not achieved (EBRD 2005b: 118).

Foreign trade was further liberalized as part of the (re)integration of Croatia with the Balkan and EU economies. In September 2000 EU foreign ministers approved an EU package granting duty-free access to 95 per cent of imports from Croatia, along with Albania, Bosnia, Macedonia and Montenegro, although limits remained on exports of fish products and wine *FT*, 19 September 2000, p. 10). Under the terms of the SAA signed with the EU in October 2001, Croatia committed itself to the gradual abolition of import tariffs on industrial goods from the EU (EBRD 2002a: 50).

Concluding reflections: democratization and marketization in Croatia

Croatia was, next to Slovenia, one of the most prosperous, economically developed, marketized and Westernized of all the formerly Communist-ruled states. Due to its rich tourism assets and potential, its relatively strong civil society and its extensive contacts with Germany, Austria and Italy, it enjoyed major potential advantages over nearly all of the other formerly Communist-ruled states. Other things being equal, therefore, it could have had a running start in its moves towards liberal democracy and a more fully privatized, marketized and liberalized economy following the end of Communist rule, and it should have been a front-runner (perhaps even *the* front-runner) for inclusion in the May 2004 'eastward enlargement' of the EU. But this was not to be.

Tragically, by repeatedly voting into presidential off ce the corrupt, authoritarian and obsessively nationalistic Dr Franjo Tudjman, a substantial section of Croatia's electorate squandered a golden opportunity, threw away Croatia's major potential advantages and allowed the country to become mired in hugely debilitating inter-ethnic conflicts, designs on Bosnian territory, authoritarianism, corruption and a large 'black economy'. The Tudjman regimes perpetuated strongly vertical and clientelistic power relations and power structures and a form of 'ethnic collectivism'. These were far from conducive to liberal and horizontally structured forms of democracy, civil society, civil economy and the rule of law. Implicitly, these were the main reasons why Croatia was excluded from the first 'eastward enlargement' of the EU in May 2004. If thos who voted for Tudjman could have foreseen the full consequences of the choice which they repeatedly made, they might have voted differently, but we cannot be completely sure of that. The illiberal and clientelistic power relations, power structures and ethnic collectivism that held large parts of Croatia's economy and society in their grip were still very powerful and deeply entrenched during the 1990s. There had long been powerful and dangerous illiberal currents in Croatian culture, politics and intellectual life, dating back to the fascist-terrorist Ustasa movement-turned-regime and its nineteenth-century nationalist progenitors. Croatians as a whole, however, have paid a heavy price politically, economically and culturally for the continuing power and influence of these illiberal, clientelistic and 'ethnic collectivist' power relations and power structures under Tudjman during the 1990s, and it will take many years for the country to recoup what it has lost.

Since 2000 Croatia's rulers have worked hard to get the country back onto the track it could have taken much sooner. Large swathes of the political classes, the business community and the electorate have perceived all too clearly the economic and political price that Croatia paid for the Tudjman regime, especially when Croatia was excluded from the accelerating process of 'eastward enlargement' of the EU between 1997 and 2002. The lesson was driven home with particular force when neighbouring Slovenia was included in the first wave of EU enlargement, whereas Croatia had not even bee recognized as an official candidate or been given a date on which to begin membershi negotiations.

However, in the wake of the momentous political, economic and social restructuring and reforms carried out by successive Croatian governments between 2000 and 2005, on 3 October 2005 Croatia was rewarded by the opening of negotiations for admission to the EU, which could take place as early as 2009. It was particularly significant tha it had not been felt necessary for international observers to monitor the presidential elections held on 2 and 16 January 2005. Nevertheless, there still remain a few lingering doubts over the depth and wholeheartedness of the country's commitment to this course. In order to be truly eligible for admission to the EU, Croatia's rulers and voters will need to convince other Europeans that they have finally turned their backs on the pernicious 'ethnic collectivism' and on the corruptingly clientelistic 'vertical' power relations and power structures which repeatedly impaired the country's prospects during the twentieth century.

For its part, the EU has rendered the challenges facing the various Croatian liberals and reformers who have been in government since 2000 a great deal harder by so adamantly insisting that the Croatian state must cooperate fully with the ICTY in tracking down Croatians indicted for war crimes, genocide and other crimes against humanity. Other things being equal, of course, it is highly desirable to bring to trial those accused of having committed terrible crimes. Real life, however, is rarely so cut and dried. Several of the prominent Croats who have been indicted for war crimes or crimes against humanity by the ICTY are national heroes in the eyes of many (possibly most) Croats, because several of these indicted persons played pivotal roles in reconquering the territory which Croatia lost to Serbia in 1991. If and when these indictees are handed over to the ICTY and found guilty, it does not encourage their Croatian admirers either to feel penitent or to accept that justice has been done. On the contrary, the whole process arouses strong feelings that grave injustices are being done by a court whose impartiality and legitimacy many patriotic Croats question, while the fact that the trials are conducted in The Hague greatly diminishes the Croats' sense of being active participants in the judicial process. To that extent, the whole process may in fact turn those found guilty by the ICTY into national-martyr figure and, as a consequence, deflect many or most Croats from acknowledging and trul facing up to the crimes of which their compatriots have been accused, thereby rendering the process somewhat counterproductive.

Furthermore, this process makes those Croatian liberals or reformers who have cooperated with the ICTY appear to be 'unpatriotic' or even 'traitors' to their country in the eyes of many patriotic Croats. This makes it even more difficult for such politicians to push through the much-needed liberal reforms which the EU has stipulated as a condition of membership, and it also reduces the chances that these liberals and reformers will manage to remain in power. Although it is conceivable that (in spite of this) they might nevertheless manage to complete the implementation of the liberalizing reform programme needed to gain entry to the EU, it would be utterly myopic and counterproductive for the EU to force Croatian liberals and reformers to use up all their public goodwill and political capital on tracking down and handing over those indicted by the ICTY. Taking the longer view, there are even more important matters at stake than bringing these controversial national heroes to trial. On the other hand, if the EU really cannot be deflected from this hazardous and potentially counterproductive course, the sooner the processes of catching the criminals and 'bringing them to justice' are completed and got out of the way, the sooner the country will be able to concentrate on the more urgent and important challenges of liberalizing its polity, economy and society, provided the Western powers and the ICTY have not succeeded in totally undermining and discrediting Croatia's remaining liberal reformers by then.

6 Serbia

From Serbdom to pariahdom

Introductory 'country profile'

The Republic of Serbia, including Vojvodina but excluding Kosova and Montenegro, is a small country with a land area of 88,361 square kilometres, just over one-third of the size of the UK and of the former Communist-ruled Yugoslav Federation and just over one-sixth of the size of France. In 2002, according to the population census of that year, Serbia (excluding Kosova and Montenegro) had a population of 7.5 million. Apart from the capital city Belgrade, which had 1.6 million inhabitants in 2002, Serbia's major cities are Novi Sad (299,294), Nis (250,518), Kragujevac (175,802), Leskovac (156,252) and Subotica (148,401). In 2000, about 55 per cent of land area was cultivated (mainly in the fertile plains of Vojvodina), about 15 per cent was either grassland or under permanent tree crops (e.g., orchards, olive groves), and the remaining 30 per cent was forest and woodland. About 17.3 per cent of the working population was engaged in agriculture in 2002 (Web site of the Serbian Government: Facts about Serbia, 2005).

According to the census conducted in 2002, the ethnic affliations of the Republic of Serbia's population (excluding Kosova and Montenegro) were as shown in Table 6.1.

6.1 Ethnic affiliations of population of Serbia, 200

Serbs	82.9
Hungarians (Magyars)	3.9
Bosniaks (Muslims)	1.9
Roma	1.4
Croats	0.9
Albanians	0.8
Slovaks	0.8
Vlachs	0.5
Romanians	0.5
Bulgarians	0.3
Others	6.1

Source: Web site of Serbian Government: Facts about Serbia (2005).

Who are the Serbs?

Modern-day Serbs regard themselves as descendants of the illiterate, pagan and predominantly agricultural Slavs who first settled on the territories of latter-day Serbi in substantial numbers during the late sixth and especially the seventh centuriy AD, particularly in the area which came to be known as Raska during the tenth century and as the Sandzak of Novi Pazar during the nineteenth and early twentieth century (the area is still known as 'Sandzak' for short). The Byzantine Emperor Heraclius (reg. 610–41) appears to have recognized Slavic possession of this territory in return for the Slavs' submission to Byzantine overlordship, which in turn prepared the ground for their subsequent gradual conversion to Byzantine Orthodox Christianity. For the next five centuries, the history of the Slavs in these areas was to be primarily one o 'struggles between their various clans, each under a chieftain or *zupan*. Sometimes a more powerful *zupan* would absorb his weaker neighbours and take the title of grand zupan" (*veliki zupan*), but such unions were followed by disruption and regrouping, and the whole period was turbulent and confused' (Darby 1968: 87–9). Early in the tenth century most of this territory became part of the short-lived Eastern Orthodox and South Slavic empire established by Bulgaria's Tsar Simeon (reg. 893–927), but it reverted to the control of local *zupans* allied to Byzantium in the mid-tenth century. The first independent and recognizably 'Serbian' polities emerged in 1037–8 in Zahumlje and Travunia, which later came to be known as Herzegovina and Zeta (later still, Montenegro, respectively). A local potentate called Stefan Nemanja established himself as the 'grand zupan' of Raska in 1169. This was the embryo of the future Serbian state. He also founded the Nemanja dynasty, which created a Serbian empire in the Balkans under the Raskan Serbian rulers Stefan Uros III (reg. 1321–31) and Stefan Dusan 'the Great' (reg. 1331–55). The latter's empire embraced Serbia, Montenegro, Macedonia, Bulgaria, Albania and northern Greece and had its capital in Skopje (capital of the present-day Republic of Macedonia).

The hurriedly assembled Serbian empire rapidly fell apart after Stefan Dushan's death in 1355. This and the seemingly irretrievable decline of Byzantium left a Balkan power vacuum which the advancing Ottomans Turks gradually fled during the 1370s and 1380s. South Slav and especially Serbian nationalist historiography maintains that, on 15 June 1389 by the Eastern Orthodox calendar (i.e., 28 June by the Western calendar), the Ottomans decisively defeated a major alliance of Serb and other Balkan Orthodox Christian forces on Kosova plain, shattering the last remnants of the long-defunct Serbian empire. However, even though 'Serbian myth and poetry have presented this battle as a cataclysmic defeat in which the flower of Balkan chivalr perished', in fact the losses were 'heavy on both sides' (Malcom 1994: 20). Never-theless, whereas the Serbs had lost a large part of their forces in holding the Turks to a temporary draw, the Ottomans could still draw upon large reserves of fresh troops and were thus able to complete their conquest of the Orthodox and Serb-speaking lands (other than Bosnian-ruled Hum and parts of Zeta/Montenegro) by 1392. In that sense, Orthodox Christian and Serbian nationalist historiography were right to com-memorate this most famous Balkan battle as a decisive landmark defeat for Balkan Orthodox Christendom (Fine 1987: 411–18). The weak, shrinking and fissipar-ous Orthodox Christian states were unable to command much loyalty or support, and the Ottomans either encouraged or compelled many of the weak and vulnerable Orthodox Christian princes and local potentates lying in their path to submit to Ottoman overlordship (suzerainty) and contribute men, money and supplies to the Ottoman war machine, in return for lenient treatment (including retention of their landholdings, privileged social positions and Orthodox Christian religion). After the full subjugation of Serbia (including Kosova) by the 'infidel' Turks in 1455, Serbian epic poetry and religious art consciously nurtured a spirit of resistance and hopes of ultimate deliverance by depicting the Serbs as 'the chosen people of the New Testament – the "new Israel". Like the Hebrews in Babylonian captivity they would be led out of slavery to freedom' (Vickers 1998: 14).

During the 400 years of Turkish rule, there was some northward and westward displacement of Serbs out of Kosova into Croatia and Hungary. However, there was little large-scale persecution or conversion of Serb Christians, or large-scale Turkish settlement in Serbia, and the Ottoman 'millet' system of autonomy for religious communities allowed the Serbian Orthodox Church to remain largely intact. During the 1790s and early 1800s, the Belgrade *pasaluk* (as Serbia's new core province was known) was disrupted by Ottoman janissaries, whose unruly and predatory conduct precipitated a Serbian peasant/bandit uprising in 1804 led by a pig dealer and outlaw named Karadjordje (Black George) Petrovic. Karadjordje invoked the folk memories of the 1389 battle of Kosova and spoke of the need to free Serbia and Kosova of the Turkish 'yoke'. He summoned a Serbian Skupstina (assembly) in 1805 in order to adopt proposals for autonomy which were submitted to Constantinople for approval. However, the Sultan rejected them, and heavy-handed attempts to suppress the uprising using Muslim irregulars from Bosnia prompted the insurgents to solicit Russian backing and to mobilize wider participation in the revolt for several years. While Napoleon kept the Russians otherwise engaged in 1812–13, the Ottomans seized an opportunity to brutally crush the Serbian uprising in 1813. The severity of the repression and of the economic dislocation characteristic of this turbulent period precipitated another peasant uprising 'against unbearable local conditions' in 1815, led this time by Milos Obrenovic (reg. 1815–39). When Karadjordje secretly returned in 1817, Milos had him killed (Pavlowitch 2002: 30–2), thereby starting a long-lasting feud between the Karadjordjevic and the Obrenovic families. Milos then sought an accommodation with the Ottoman authorities and was granted local autonomy in return for payment of monetary tribute to the Ottoman. He thereby became an entrepreneurially successful big landowner who ruled his patch of the future enlarged Serbia in an authoritarian manner, but he used his power to prevent the emergence of (rival) large landowners and maintain the Serbian peasantry in possession of their smallholdings. Abundant land relative to population, rising pig exports to Austria and encouragement of immigration and colonization boosted his revenues, but his authoritarianism gave rise to a 'constitutionalist' movement that sought both to limit his powers and to share them with a seventeen-member council of notables. An inchoate Serbian national identity began to emerge during the 1820s and 1830s, as did an autocephalous (autonomous) Serbian Orthodox Church in 1832. However, the council so irked Milos that he abdicated and went into self-imposed exile in 1839. He was succeeded by his sons Milan, who died of tuberculosis within twenty-f ve days, and Mihailo, who was deposed by the Skupstina in 1842. The Skupstina then gave the vacant throne to Aleksandar Karadjordjevic (reg. 1842–59), the pliable son of Karadjordje. Aleksandar was courted by the Habsburg monarchy and, as a consequence, stayed out of the Crimean War of 1853–6, despite the Russophile leanings of the bulk of the population. This and other disputes led to his being deposed by the Skupstina in 1859. Milos Obrenovic, then aged seventy-nine, was recalled from exile, but died a year later. He was succeeded by his son Mihajlo, who was recalled to the throne and, during his second reign (1860–8), proved to be an able ruler. He established a regular army, bureaucracy and judiciary, expanded the state arsenal and secured the removal of the remaining Ottoman Turkish garrisons from Serbia in 1862 and 1867. However, he was assassinated by an unknown assailant in 1868.

Mihajlo was succeeded by his fourteen-year-old cousin, Milan Obrenovic (reg. 1868–89). He declared war on the Ottoman Empire in 1876, in support of a peasant rebellion in Bosnia, but had to be rescued by Russia from humiliating defeat. However, with Serb, Montenegrin and Bulgarian backing, Russia massively defeated the Ottomans in the Russo-Turkish War of 1877–8, through which Serbia obtained some significant territorial gains and international recognition as an independent state. The Berlin Congress of 1878 nevertheless seemed to foreclose any possibility of Serbia being able to incorporate the Bosnian Serbs into a 'Greater Serbia' (by allowing Austria-Hungary to occupy Bosnia-Herzegovina) and denied the Serbian state its cherished dreams of access to the Adriatic sea and a common border with Montenegro. Milan concluded very subservient pacts with Austria-Hungary in 1880 and 1881, turning Serbia into a vassal state, but declared it a kingdom in 1882. However, Serbian nationalists induced Milan to abdicate in 1889, because they strongly disapproved of his 'disreputable' love life, growing authoritarianism and increasingly unpopular subservience to Austria. For similar reasons, his successor, Aleksandar Obrenovic (reg. 1889–1903), was gruesomely murdered by members of the increasingly nationalistic Serbian army in 1903. Curiously, in spite of its grisly aspects, the coup of 1903 resulted in the establishment of a constitutional monarchy under King Petar Karadjordjevic (reg. 1903–14), effective government, strengthened finances and expanded education provisions. The new regime also ended the country's previous subservience to the Habsburg monarchy and instead realigned Serbia towards alliances with Russia and France (the two countries with which it has tended to maintain intermittent special relationships since that time).

From 1906 to 1911 Austria-Hungary imposed a prohibitive duty on the long-standing northward exportation of Serbian pigs across its territory to the major markets for pigmeat in Central Europe, in an attempt to make Serbia as subservient as it had been in the 1880s, but this 'pig war' stimulated Serbia to diversify its markets, trade routes and political ties. Austria-Hungary's formal annexation of Bosnia-Herzegovina in 1908 drove Serb politicians and newspapers to clamour for war against the Habsburg monarchy, but Russia's unwillingness to comply with Serbian wishes at that time postponed the impending showdown with Austria-Hungary until July–August 1914.

In the meantime, however, Serbia took part in the Balkan War of October 1912 to May 1913, which left Serbia in possession of Kosova, parts of what is now Albania and some predominantly Albanian-inhabited territory in Macedonia. These conquests carried Serbia for the f rst time well beyond the more *limited* (and some nationalists think *legitimate*) aim of fighting wars to liberate fellow Serbs living under 'alien rule'. Instead, these new conquests involved wholesale carnage, rape, pillage, arson and ethnic cleansing against hundreds of thousands of 'ethnic Albanians' (see Chapter 10). This is sometimes seen as *the start* of an unrelenting fight to the death between Serb and Albanians for control of Kosova and western Macedonia which has continued ever since, but actually it had already started in 1877–8, when Serbia occupied considerable predominantly Albanian-inhabited territory but was forced to relinquish it by the major European powers in 1878. In 1913 Serbia managed to hold its territorial gains for a couple of years, only to lose them again when it was defeated and occupied by the central powers during the First World War.

Archduke Franz Ferdinand (the heir to the Habsburg throne) made a visit to Sarajevo on 28 June 1914, provocatively timed to coincide with the anniversary of the 1389 battle of Kosova. The assassination of the archduke and his wife by the Bosnian Serb Gavrilo Princip precipitated the outbreak of the First World War, after Austria-Hungary gave Serbia an ultimatum containing demands that no self-respecting state could have accepted. Early in 1915, however, the Serbian 'David' astonished the world by heroically driving back the Austro-Hungarian 'Goliath' who had invaded Serbia and captured Belgrade during the latter half of 1914. But in October and November 1915 an unstoppable pincer attack by Germany, Austria-Hungary and Bulgaria obliged the Serbian army, government and royal family to retreat through Kosova and the freezing Albanian highlands towards the ports of Shkoder, Durres and Vlore, whence they were evacuated by the French navy to Corfu. During that epic retreat, nearly half the 300,000-strong Serbian army perished, and many more died of the disease on Corfu. The Serbs were lionized in the French and British press for their tenacity and bravery during the First World War (although we wonder how far the qualities involved really differed from those for which they were vilified in 1913 and during the 1990s). Overall during the Balkan Wars of 1912–13 and the First World War, around 750,000 Serbs perished (out of a total population of under 5 million in 1913) (Okey 1982: 154). Ultimately, however, the First World War brought about the disintegration of the Habsburg and Ottoman empires in 1918 and made possible the creation of a 'South Slav' state comprising elements drawn from both of those different empires.

The formation of the Yugoslav state

A multinational 'Triune Kingdom of Serbs, Croats and Slovenes' came into being in 1918, under the leadership of Serbia's Karadjordjevic dynasty and the nationalistic Serbian Radical Party government headed by Nikola Pasic. 'Yugoslavism' furnished the ideological inspiration behind the creation of the Triune Kingdom, which was renamed Yugoslavia in 1929. Serbia was the nucleus around which the kingdom coa lesced. Belgrade served as the capital, thanks to Serbia's leading roles in the Yugoslav struggles for independence from the Turks, in resisting further Austro-Hungarian imperial expansion into the South Slav lands, and in fighting the central powers in the Balkans during the First World War, although war-ravaged Serbia was far less developed than either Croatia or Slovenia and contributed less than half of inter-war Yugoslavia's territory and population. Non-Serbs (especially Croats) increasingly resented the Serbian chauvinism of these governing elites and the persistent use of the Serbian army, monarchy, bureaucracy and capital city to govern inter-war Yugoslavia largely as if it were simply a 'Greater Serbia'. The shooting of five Croatian oppositio leaders by a member of the governing Radical Party during a parliamentary session on 20 June 1928 exacerbated a major parliamentary crisis in 1928–9 (see Chapter 5).

King Aleksandar (reg. 1921–34) outlawed all ethnic and sectarian political parties and established a royal dictatorship in 1929. (The initially very successful Communist Party of Yugoslavia, established in 1919, had already been banned in 1920–1.) The Serbian General Petar Zivkovic, a key participant in the Serbian nationalist military coup in 1903, served as prime minister from 1929 to 1932 and was responsible only to the king. The country was officially renamed the Kingdom of Yugoslavia and wa reorganized into nine *banovini* (governorships) whose boundaries and names were deliberately designed *not* to correspond with those of historic territorial entities and identities, in a conscious attempt to obliterate all long-standing ethnic and territorial allegiances (Rothschild 1974: 237).

From September 1931 until the assassination of King Aleksandar in October 1934, there was a period of pseudo-parliamentary rule. The constitution of 1931 provided for a bicameral parliament, but banned overtly ethnic, religious and regional parties, required 'open' (not anonymous) balloting and stipulated that the party obtaining the largest number of votes was to receive two-thirds of the seats in the Skupstina, as well as its proportionate share of the remaining one-third of all seats. Half the members of the co-equal upper house (senate) were to be appointed by the king, while the other half were to be indirectly elected by electoral colleges for each *banovina*. In the firs elections to the new Skupstina on 8 November 1931, all 306 Skupstina seats were overwhelmingly 'won' by candidates on the Zivkovic government list, but this system lacked legitimacy even in the eyes of the Serbs, whose independent (but formally illegal) parties agitated for the restoration of a bona-fide system of representative democracy (Rothschild 1974: 242).

The two 'Alexandrine' regimes of 1929–31 and 1931–4 proved unable to cope with the consequences of the 1929–33 world depression, which roughly halved Yugoslavia's mainly agricultural export earnings, slashed state revenues and peasant incomes and greatly increased urban unemployment and rural underemployment. Ultra-nationalist terrorist bombing and assassination campaigns were carried out by the Bulgarian-based and virulently anti-Yugoslav IMRO and by Croatia's Catholic-fascist Ustasa (Insurrection) organization, which was established in 1929 and attracted financial and logistical support from Fascist Italy and the reactionary and 'revisionist' Horthy regime in Hungary. King Aleksandar was murdered by IMRO and Ustasa assassins in Marseilles during a state visit to France in October 1934.

During the regency of Prince Pavle Karadjordjevic (October 1934 to March 1941) and especially during the premiership of the Serbian nationalist Milan Stojadinovic (June 1935 to February 1939), depression-stricken Yugoslavia drifted into economic dependence on Nazi Germany, which became both a vital market for Yugoslav agricultural exports and the major supplier of much-needed industrial imports. This and other measures taken under Stojadinovic to stimulate mining, manufacturing, agricultural and infrastructural development helped to alleviate Yugoslavia's dire economic plight, but in February 1939 this dynamic prime minister was dismissed amid mounting alarm at his growing authoritarianism and fascist leanings, which also had become an obstacle to a much-needed accommodation with the Croatian Peasant Party.

From February 1939 to February 1941, Prince Pavle and Premier Tsvetkovic belatedly tried to defuse internal strife and pull back from the encircling Axis embrace. However, no compensatory Anglo-French military and economic assistance was forthcoming to back up the recurrent British and French exhortation of little Yugoslavia to 'stand up to' the growing might of Nazi Germany. Furthermore, while Tsvetkovic and Prince Pavle conceded extensive regional autonomy to Croatia in August 1939, this pact negotiated bilaterally with the Croatian Peasant Party impeded a true all-round decentralization and democratization of governance in Yugoslavia as a whole, to the anger of the Serbian, Bosnian and Slovene nationalist and liberal opposition parties.

Resistance and civil war in Yugoslavia, April 1941 to 1945

On 25 March 1941, bowing to mounting external economic and diplomatic pressure, Prince Pavle and Tsvetkovic acceded to the anti-Comintern pact promoted by the Axis powers. Two days later, however, they were overthrown by a Serbian nationalist military coup, which installed a young King Petar II on the Yugoslav throne and a nationalist General Simovic as prime minister. Hitler retaliated by ordering a punitive invasion and dismemberment of Yugoslavia, starting on 6 April 1941. Nazi Germany occupied northern Slovenia (which was directly incorporated into the Third Reich), most of Serbia and the Banat. Italy occupied southern Slovenia, Dalmatia and Montenegro, while Hungary annexed much of the Vojvodina and Bulgaria occupied Yugoslav (Vardar) Macedonia. The presence of nearly half a million resident ethnic Germans and almost half a million ethnic Hungarians in Yugoslavia during the 1930s considerably facilitated the German military occupation of large areas of Serbia and the Hungarian invasion of the Vojvodina, where most of the Magyars resided. The Yugoslav government and King Petar took refuge in London, where they established a Yugoslav government in exile, whilst in August 1941 Germany established a quisling government in Serbia under General Nedic. A puppet 'Independent State of Croatia' (the NDH), which included Slovenia and Bosnia-Herzegovina, was proclaimed on 10 April 1941 and was administered on Nazi Germany's behalf by the Croatian Catholic-fascist Ustasa in collaboration with reactionary sections of the Catholic clergy and some fascist Bosniak Muslims. Several hundred thousand non-Catholic Yugoslavs, mainly Serbs and Montenegrins living on NDH territory, were murdered by the Ustasa regime and its Catholic and Muslim collaborators between mid-1941 and late 1944 (see Chapter 5 for various estimates of the death tolls).

Wartime Yugoslavia also produced two major resistance movements: Serbian royalist-nationalist *cetniki* (bands) declared allegiance to Colonel Draza Mihailovic, but the more important Communist-led 'partisan' movement was headed by Josip Broz, alias Tito (1892–1980). This proved to be the only movement capable of draw-ing mass support from all sections of Yugoslav society. Both movements came close to being annihilated by the Axis powers and their collaborators in 1942–3. However, helped by Italy's switching of sides in September 1943, which resulted in the capture of many Italian weapons by the Communist-led partisans, Tito's forces grew to 300,000 by late 1943 and to 800,000 by May 1945. In November 1943, the Communist-dominated Anti-Fascist Council for the National Liberation of Yugoslavia (AVNOJ, established in November 1942) declared itself to be the supreme legislative and executive body of Yugoslavia. In May 1944 Winston Churchill announced that the Allies had decided to switch their support from Mihailovic (who 'has not been fght-ing the enemy') to 'Marshall Tito, because of his heroic and massive struggle against the German armies'. The partisans liberated all of southern and central Yugoslavia by late 1944 and the rest of Yugoslavia in early 1945, albeit with crucial Red Army assistance against German forces in the north-east. As each locality was liberated, it came under a Communist-controlled 'people's liberation committee'. By mid-1945, the embryonic new state had gained control of public transport, the banks and about 80 per cent of Yugoslavia's industrial sector. The land law enacted in August 1945 conf scated all holdings over 20 to 35 hectares (depending on the terrain). In August 1945 the Communists also launched a 'National Front', which allegedly obtained 90 per cent of the votes cast in single-list elections to a constituent assembly in November 1945. The constituent assembly abolished the monarchy and proclaimed a Federal People's Republic of Yugoslavia.

Serbia in the Communist-ruled Yugoslav Federation, 1945–90

Even though Serbs and Montenegrins had constituted the backbone of the Communist-led Yugoslav 'partisan' movement that liberated Yugoslavia from the murderous grip of the Axis powers and their Croat and Muslim collaborators, Josip Broz 'Tito', who wielded ultimate control over Yugoslavia from 1945 until his death in 1980, was determined not to allow Serbs to dominate the new Communist-ruled Yugoslavia to anything like the degree that they had dominated inter-war Yugoslavia. The Tito regime fostered a federal system within which power was progressively devolved to the six constituent republics (Croatia, Slovenia, Montenegro, Macedonia and Bosnia-Herzegovina, as well as Serbia) under the successive constitutions and constitutional revisions of 1945, 1953, 1963, 1965 and 1974. In addition, Tito further diminished the power of the Serbian Republic by steadily devolving power to the two substantial autonomous provinces of Kosova and Vojvodina located within it. The boundaries of the constituent republics were also drawn in such a way as to strongly favour the non-Serb ethnic groups at the expense of the Serbs. Substantial predominantly Serb-inhabited areas were incorporated into Croatia and Bosnia and were flatly denied the forms of provincial autonomy that were granted to the inhabitants of Kosova and Vojvodina. The Tito regime also deliberately fostered the Republic of Macedonia and a distinct Macedonian language, literature, identity and church in order to negate long-standing Serbian claims to the territory of 'Vardar Macedonia' and to its pre - dominantly Orthodox Slavic inhabitants and culture. A Republic of Montenegro, whose boundaries were deliberately drawn to include many Serb-inhabited areas which had never been part of Montenegro, was established for much the same purpose – to weaken the Serbs. Consequently, the widespread perceptions among Serbs that they were given a very raw deal by the Tito regime were not products of Serbian nation-alist paranoia, as is often implied by Western journalists and academics, but were well founded in fact. Serbs quite justifiably felt that, having 'won the war' and liberate Yugoslavia in 1944–5, they were subsequently cheated and robbed – and had 'lost the peace'. It was very convenient for the Tito regime that large sections of the Serbian 'establishment' and nationalist intelligentsia had been 'liquidated' by Croat and Bosnian Muslim fanatics between 1941 and 1944 and that the Serb nation was thus initially too debilitated to give strong expression to Serb grievances against the rum deal they had been given (Djilas 1991: 121).

Nevertheless, despite its active discrimination against the Serbs, the Tito regime intended Communist Yugoslavism and the federal system which it both embodied and promoted to provide a basis for 'national equality and harmonious relations among the nations of Yugoslavia' (Djilas 1991: 186). Many (perhaps most) Serbs seem initially to have acquiesced in this, to give it a try. Furthermore, so long as there was a united, monolithic, Yugoslav Communist party and regime with a complete monopoly of power, 'no disintegrative nationalist forces could come to prominence' (Djilas 1991: 186–7). It is also often suggested that so long as the hardbitten Serbian security supremo Aleksandar Rankovic was Tito's second-in-command (until 1966), Serbs felt reassured that Serbian interests would not be completely 'sold out'.

During the 1960s, however, power was devolved from the overarching Yugoslav Communist regime to the ruling parties and bureaucracies of the six constituent republics and the two autonomous provinces, fragmenting the former monolithic unity and facilitating the expression of hitherto suppressed national grievances (Djilas 1991: 187). The major landmarks in the reassertion of Serbian nationalism were: the forced resignation of Aleksandar Rankovic in 1966 (after it was discovered that he had been keeping even Tito himself under surveillance!); the major explosion of Kosovar Albanian discontent in 1968 and the greatly increased autonomy which Tito granted to Kosova in response; the expulsion of the Serbian nationalist writer Dobrica Cosic from the League of Communists in 1968 for breaking the taboos of Yugoslav Communism by giving expression to Serbian nationalist grievances concerning both Kosova and the blatant double standards involved in the Tito regime's treatment of Serbia and the Serbs as compared with the other constituent nations of the Yugoslav Federation; the major explosion of Kosovar Albanian discontent in 1981; the publication by a newspaper in 1986 of excerpts from an unfinished Memorandum writte by members of the Serbian Academy of Arts and Science (SANU), giving strident expression to Serbian nationalist grievances concerning Kosova and the position of Serbia and the Serbs in the Yugoslav Federation; and the inflammatory words of hitherto little-known Serbian Communist apparatchik, uttered during a visit to Kosova in 1987.

Kosova: the 'launchpad' for Slobodan Milosevic, 1987–90

On 24 April 1987 Slobodan Milosevic, the then seemingly colourless leader of Serbia's League of Communists, visited Kosova Polje (a largely Serbian suburb of Pristina, the largely Kosovar capital city of Kosova), ostensibly on a mission to defuse the mounting anger of the Kosova Serbs against their perceived harassment and mistreatment at the hands of the province's Kosovar majority. In the event, Milosevic delivered a rabble-rousing speech that further inflamed Serb feelings of victimization. 'This is your country, these are your houses, your fields and gardens, your memories,' he told his audience of anxious and disgruntled Serbs and Montenegrins.

> You are not going to abandon your lands because life is hard, because you are oppressed by injustice and humiliation. It has never been a characteristic of the Serbian and Montenegrin people to retreat in the face of obstacles... You should stay here, both for your ancestors and for your descendants ... Yugoslavia does not exist without Kosova . . . Yugoslavia and Serbia are not going to give up Kosova.
>
> (Judah 1997: 29)

The speech culminated with the emotive refrain: 'No one should dare to beat you!' The fact that this supposedly spontaneous speech in a dreary industrial suburb was broadcast on the main Serbian television news programme that evening (and repeatedly thereafter) suggests that it was part of a premeditated and carefully prepared plan to play the Serbian nationalist card for personal political advantage. Milosevic, who had never publicly spoken up for the Kosova Serbs before that fateful day, stole a march on his Communist and nationalist rivals and was suddenly catapulted to the forefront of a Serbian nationalist revival and a concerted endeavour to reassert Serbian dominance over Yugoslavia. 'Kosova was only the launch pad. The goal was Yugoslavia' (Silber and Little 1995: 47).

From autumn of 1987 through 1988 and 1989, Milosevic and his supporters and allies (in the state apparatus, in the JNA, in the media and in several sections of Yugoslavia's League of Communists) stage-managed a series of mass rallies and media events, through which Milosevic stirred up and exploited Serbian nationalism and irredentism in order to bolster his position and divert attention from the short-com-ings of Communist rule. Even though he ostensibly favoured a much more centralized, cohesive and Serb-dominated Yugoslavia, his pugnacious stance actually accelerated the disintegration of the federation. Milosevic's 'happenings of the people' and 'meetings of truth' exploited and publicized the increasingly embattled position of the Serb minority within Kosova and the allegedly beleaguered position of Serbia and the Serbs within Yugoslavia as a whole. This mobilization of Serbian nationalism and the accompanying 'anti-bureaucratic revolution' helped Milosevic to capture the presidency of Serbia in December 1987, to bring his own supporters to power in the autonomous province of Vojvodina in September 1988 and in the Republic of Montenegro in January 1989, respectively, and to oust the popular Kosovar Azem Vlassi from the leadership of the League of Communists in Kosova in November 1988. The forced resignation of Vlassi precipitated a week-long protest by Kosovar miners, factory workers and students demanding his reinstatement, but the Milosevic government refused to give way. Kosova's League of Communists was purged and gradually fell apart politically. On 3 February 1989 the Serbian Skupstina passed laws giving Serbia increased control over Kosova's police, judiciary and finances. In response, over 1,000 miners at the large Trepca mining and metallurgical complex at Mitrovica embarked on a hunger strike, demanding the resignation of Rahman Morina (the pliant successor of Azem Vlassi) and his chief collaborators. Kosova was brought to a standstill as more and more Kosovars went on strike. To break the deadlock Morina pretended to resign from the League of Communists along with Vlassi, but then had Vlassi imprisoned. There ensued a purge of Kosovar managers of large enterprises, while Kosova was placed under curfew. When Kosovars brought Kosova to a standstill once more, the Serb authorities declared a state of emergency and imposed martial law on the province (Vickers 1998: 229–35).

The major focus of Serb nationalist assertion and demands for greater centralization was the rescinding of the high degrees of 'provincial autonomy' which had been granted to the 'provinces' of Vojvodina and Kosova under the virtually confederal constitution of 1974. By the early 1980s, it appeared that the autonomous provinces of Vojvodina and especially Kosova had in many respects come close to attaining de-facto republican status and near parity with the six constituent republics of the Yugoslav Federation. Unfortunately for them, these two well-def ned and in many ways distinctive territories nevertheless remained formally part of the 'sovereign territory' of Serbia. During 1989 and 1990 this Achilles heel, combined with the failure of the other Yugoslav republics to put up an effective united front against them, helped Milosevic and his Serbian ultra-nationalist allies in the Serbian and Yugoslav security forces, state apparatus, academia and the media to substantially nullify the erstwhile far-reaching autonomy of these 'provinces'.

The epic struggle between the Serbs and the ethnic-Albanian-majority population for control of Kosova played a crucial role in the establishment, consolidation and eventual demise of the Milosevic regime. However, this province and the struggles within it need to be treated and understood in their own right, not least because it seems likely that Kosova will sooner or later gain international recognition as an independent Kosovar Albanian nation-state. Fuller consideration is therefore given to it in Chapter 10.

Vojvodina

According to the 1981 census, Vojvodina's 2 million inhabitants were 54.4 per cent Serb, 18.9 per cent Hungarian, 5.4 per cent Croat, 3.4 per cent Slovak, 2.3 per cent Romanian, 2.1 per cent Montenegrin, 0.9 per cent Ruthenes, while a sizeable 8.2 per cent declared themselves to be Yugoslav (Spiljevic 1985: 113). Prior to 1918 and again from 1941 to 1944, much of Vojvodina had been incorporated into Hungary, which had claimed to have 'historic' rights to the region. However, most of the region's hitherto dominant Hungarian landowners had their land expropriated during the early 1920s, while the remainder was expropriated by the Communist regime's land reforms in 1945–7, and many Hungarians either left voluntarily or felt that they were being driven out of Yugoslav-ruled Vojvodina during one or other of those periods. While it has not lacked inter-ethnic tensions, which were to surprisingly limited degrees aggravated by inflows of Serb refugees from conflict-stricken Croatia and Bosnia during the first half of the 1990s, Vojvodina remained relatively calm and pacific during the 1990s.

Serbia under Milosevic: the 1990s

On 16 July 1990 the ruling Serbian League of Communists (LCS) merged with its 'front organization', the Socialist Alliance of the Working People of Serbia. Together, they formed the Socialist Party of Serbia (SPS), led by Milosevic, which inherited the connections, patronage and fnancial and infrastructural assets of its predecessors and remained the dominant political organization in Serbia throughout the 1990s. By 1991 the SPS's total membership had shrunk to just half that of the LCS in 1989. Nevertheless, the 'rebranding' and 'relaunching' of the party in July 1990 did bring about a large influx of 'new blood': by late 1990 about one-third of the 430,000 members of the SPS were new recruits, and Milosevic went out of his way to promote 'new faces' to prominent positions, to create at least an outward appearance of renovation. Mihailo Markovic, the dissident Marxist (Praxis) philosopher and veteran critic of Tito, became vice-president of the SPS. The writer Antonije Isakovic, a co-author of the infamous ultra-nationalist SANU Memorandum in 1986, also became a prominent member (Miller 1997: 155).

Milosevic's only consistent goal was to remain in power. Although he gained infamy through his quest to incorporate Yugoslavia's fragmented Serb populations together in a 'Greater Serbia', this ambition always played second fiddle to his ruthles determination to retain power and office by whatever means came to hand. Durin the 1990s he variously deployed nationalism, warfare and his control of most of the Serbian media, not so much to mobilize support for his 'Greater Serbian' ambitions, but primarily in order to neutralize real or perceived rivals and opponents (Gordy 1999; Gagnon 2004).

The Serbian Skupstina legalized the formation of opposition parties in August 1990, in preparation for Serbia's first two-stage multiparty elections, which were held on 9 and 23 December 1990. These elections were announced at very short notice in late November 1990, giving other parties very little time to gear up for the contest. By then, dozens of new political parties had been launched. The most signifant were:

1. The Serbian Movement of Renewal (SPO, Srpski Pokret Obnove): a conservative nationalist party founded in spring 1990 and led by the wayward and fmboyant ultra-nationalist Vuk Draskovic. It had attracted between 15,000 and 25,000 members by late 1990 (Miller 1997: 155–8).
2. The Democratic Party (DS, Demokratska Stranka): founded in February 1990 and led by reform-minded but somewhat querulous and intransigent members of the Serb intelligentsia, many of whom adopted attitudes of contemptuous and elitist disdain towards the crude populism of Slobodan Milosevic and Vuk Draskovic, yet found it difficult to offer anything very appealing in its place. This party had between 10,000 and 15,000 members by late 1990, including the

academic Vojislav Kostunica, the writer Borislav Pekic and former dissident Marxist (Praxis) critics of Tito's Yugoslavia, such as Dragoljub Micunovic and Ljuba Tadic, but by the time of the election the party had already split into nationalist and anti-nationalist factions (Miller 1997: 155–8).

3. The Alliance of Reform Forces of Yugoslavia (ARFY, Savez Reformskih Snaga Jugoslavie): founded in June 1990 by Yugoslavia's liberal, cosmopolitan and reform-minded prime minister Ante Markovic, who (according to opinion polls) was at that point the most popular politician both in Yugoslavia as a whole and in Serbia, but whose popularity was about to be drowned by rising tidal waves of ethnic nationalism (Miller 1997: 155–8).

The crucial question during the summer of 1990 was whether a new Serbian constitution should be drawn up and ratified by the already-existing but still Milosevic controlled Skupstina in advance of the forthcoming multiparty elections, or whether this task should be delayed until after multiparty elections had taken place. This issue was submitted to a popular referendum on 1–2 July 1990, held at less than one week's notice. According to the widely questioned official results of the referendum, 97 pe cent of those who voted allegedly cast their votes in favour of entrusting the design of the new constitution to the Milosevic-controlled Skupstina, which in August and September 1990 speedily drew up and ratified a constitution conferring extensive and poorly limited powers on a directly elected president of the republic, who would be permitted to serve for two consecutive five-year terms of office. In addition, th Milosevic-controlled Skupstina shrewdly passed an electoral law in September 1990 establishing a British-style 'first-past-the-post' electoral system based on 250 single member constituencies, rather than proportional representation. This gave Milosevic and his allies successive majorities in the Skupstina, even though they never won a majority of votes in parliamentary elections. There were 160 seats 'in Serbia proper', 56 in Vojvodina and 34 in Kosova (Miller 1997: 158–9). In Kosova the ethnic Albanians (Kosovars) could be counted on to boycott the elections and thus hand an almost guaranteed victory to Milosevic's supporters amongst those members of the Serb minority in Kosova who turned out to vote, which was precisely what occurred time and again.

The first multi-candidate Serbian presidential election, 9 December 1990

Slobodan Milosevic convincingly won the 9 December 1990 presidential election in the f rst round. The pan-Serb but liberal-leaning nationalist Vuk Draskovic, leader of the SPO, came an unexpectedly poor second, while the vicious pan-Serb ultra-nationalist Vojislav Seselj came a distant f fth (see Table 6.2).

6.2 Serbian presidential election, 9 December 1990

Candidate	Share of vote (%)
Slobodan Milosevic (Socialist Party of Serbia, SPS)	63.3
Vuk Draskovic (Serbian Movement of Renewal, SPO)	16.4
Ivan Djuric (independent)	5.5
Sulejman Ugljanin (Party of Democratic Action, SDA)	2.2
Vojislav Seselj (independent ultra-nationalist)	1.9
Others	10.6

Note: Turn-out 71.5 per cent. Source: Miller (1997: 162).

Elections to the 250-seat Serbian parliament (Skupstina), 8 and 23 December 1990

Milosevic's SPS won a landslide victory in the first multiparty elections to the Serbia parliament on a platform advocating strong but pragmatic government, defence of Serb interests, a strong federation and economic security (the SPS was distinctly lukewarm towards economic reform). The first-past-the-post single-member constituency system, reinforced by a low and almost entirely Serb electoral turn-out in Kosova (18.6 per cent), hugely over-represented the SPS in the Skupstina, which served as a compliant and yet (by standard criteria) democratically elected parliament (see Table 6.3).

6.3 Serbian parliamentary election, 8 and 23 December 1990

	Share of vote in first round (%)	Seats
Socialist Party of Serbia (SPS, led by Milosevic)	46.1	194
Serb Movement of Renewal (SPO, led by Draskovic)	15.8	19
Democratic Party (DS)	7.4	7
Democratic Union of Vojvodina Hungarians (DZVM)	2.6	8
Party of Democratic Action (SDA, Muslim Slavs)	1.7	3
Alliance of Reform Forces of Yugoslavia (Markovic Party)	1.5	2

Note: Turn-out 71.5 per cent. Source: Gordy (1999: 36).

The emergence of the 'DEPOS' opposition alliance, early 1992

Several opposition parties took advantage of the de-facto cessation of the Serbo-Croatian war in January 1992 (pp. 202–4) to step up their attacks on the Milosevic regime. In February the Democratic Party launched a petition demanding the resignation of Milosevic and the election of a constituent assembly to draw up a more *liberal* democratic Serbian constitution. The signature-gathering campaign was backed by the SPO, New Democracy, the Serbian Liberal Party, the National Peasant Party and the Serbian wing of Ante Markovic's Alliance of Reform Forces of Yugoslavia, which was led by Vesna Pesic, and the petition was ultimately signed by 840,000 people (Thomas 1999: 111). These same parties also decided to support the SPO's plan for a mass protest rally at St Sava's Cathedral in Belgrade on 9 March 1992, the anniversary of the opposition rally that had seriously challenged the Milosevic regime in 1991. The 9 March 1992 protest rally was attended by 50,000 people and (contrary to Milosevic's wishes) was addressed by Patriarch Pavle, the head of the Serbian Orthodox Church, whose speech appealed for peace and national reconciliation and admonished the Milosevic regime: 'To you, all the shedding of blood and all the misfortune in the madness of this fratricidal war has not made plain the truth that out of such evil no good can come' (quoted in Thomas 1999: 112). The success of the rally encouraged the SPO, New Democracy, the Kostunica wing of the Democratic Party, the Serbian Peasant Party, the Serbian Liberal Party and prominent non-party intellectuals to launch an anti-Milosevic Democratic Movement of Serbia (known mainly by its acronym DEPOS), which held its inaugural meeting on 23 May 1992.

Formation of a (rump) Federal Republic of Yugoslavia, April–May 1992

In February 1992, in response to the break-up of the former Communist-ruled Yugoslav Federation, the leaders of the ruling SPS and of Montenegro's ruling Democratic Party of Socialists agreed to launch a new Federal Republic of Yugoslavia (FRY), comprising only the republics of Serbia (including the now only nominally autonomous provinces of Kosova and Vojvodina) and Montenegro. This proposal was reportedly approved by 96 per cent of those who voted in a referendum in Montenegro on 1 March 1992, on a 66 per cent turn-out (Cohen 2002: 209). The FRY was formally proclaimed on 27 April.

UN sanctions against the FRY

This new 'rump Yugoslavia' immediately became an international pariah, because of its aggression towards Slovenia and Croatia in 1991 and towards Bosnia from March/April 1992 onward. On 30 May 1992 the UN Security Council imposed a trade embargo on the FRY. The embargo excluded foodstuffs and medicines, but it included oil products and cigarettes. However, it was very weakly and unevenly enforced and thereby generated easy profits for sanctions-busting smugglers of oil products and cigarettes and fostered and enriched various Balkan mafias. The most notorious of these mafia networks were the ones controlled by the Bosnian Serb warlords-turned-gangsters Radovan Karadzic, Ratko Mladic and Arkan. Other sanctions against the FRY included the cutting of international air links to its main airports, the freezing of its public and private assets held abroad, reductions in the size of diplomatic missions to Belgrade and a ban on cultural, scientif and sporting contacts with Serbia and Montenegro. On 10 July 1992 NATO and the WEU invoked powers to stop and search Adriatic shipping, especially if cargoes were thought to be bound for Serbia via Montenegro. On 22 September 1992 the UN General Assembly refused to recognize the FRY as the legal successor to the old Communist-ruled Socialist Federation of Yugoslavia. On 16 November 1992 the UN Security Council voted for even tougher sanctions against the FRY, authorizing the use of force if needed. Stop-and-search powers were initiated along the Danube and in the Adriatic, while third-country transit traff c passing through Serbia or Montenegro henceforth needed permission from the UN sanctions committee; NATO and the WEU agreed to a full naval blockade of the Adriatic. On 16 June 1993 the FRY lost the seat it claimed to have inherited at the UN.

The economic hardships and international isolation resulting from the UN sanctions helped to intensify internal opposition to the Milosevic regime in some quarters, and some anti-war demonstrations began to take place (there had been earlier ones against government control of the media and harassment of the opposition).

Elections to the new bicameral federal parliament, 31 May 1992

The elections to the new federal institutions were formally boycotted by the main Serbian and Montenegrin opposition parties and by the Albanians of Kosova, with the result that the turn-out was only 55 per cent in Serbia and 57 per cent in Montenegro, and Milosevic and parties allied to him won a landslide victory. The distribution of seats in the 138-seat house of deputies is shown in Table 6.4.

6.4 Federal parliament election, 31 May 1992

Party	Seats
Milosevic's ruling SPS	73
The ultra-nationalist Serbian Radical Party (SRS)	33
Montenegro's Democratic Party of Socialists	23
Democratic Union of Hungarians of Vojvodina	2
League of Communists Movement	2
Independents	3

After the elections, in an attempt to broaden his support, Milosevic invited the elderly and eminent (albeit controversial) Serbian nationalist writer Dobrica Cosic to become president of the FRY, and brokered the election of Cosic to that office by th newly elected federal parliament.

The federal government headed by Milan Panic, July to December 1992

In an endeavour to curry favour with the West and get UN sanctions against the FRY lifted, Milosevic also brokered parliamentary acceptance of the wealthy and liberal-minded Yugoslav-American businessman Milan Panic as federal prime minister in mid-July 1992. Panic was a US citizen and a supporter of the US Democratic Party. Although born in Yugoslavia, Panic had emigrated to the USA in the 1950s and made a fortune in the pharmaceuticals industry. Initially, many observers expected Panic to act as a subservient stooge of the Milosevic regime, but he soon surprised most people (not least Milosevic himself) by the vigour and determination with which he pursued a much more liberal and conciliatory course in both foreign and domestic affairs. Panic championed recognition of all the other republics (including Croatia and Bosnia-Herzegovina) within their existing borders, implicit abandonment of the Bosnian and Croatian Serbs, the right of refugees to return home and an end to Serbian persecution and discrimination against ethnic Albanians in Kosova. In promoting Panic, Milosevic had seriously miscalculated, but the opposition parties were too slow and too deeply divided to take full advantage of this blunder. Once appointed, Panic could only be removed as federal prime minister with the support of majorities in both houses of the federal parliament, in one of which (the upper house) half the seats were allocated to representatives of Montenegro, most of whom supported Panic.

Federal President Dobrica Cosic also clashed with Milosevic by declaring his support for Prime Minister Panic during an unsuccessful vote of no confidence in the prim minister on 4 September 1992. Cosic further antagonized Milosevic on 16 October by demanding his resignation as president of Serbia, the disarming of paramilitary groups in Bosnia, and an end to FRY airforce sorties into Bosnia. Two days later Cosic also called for the lifting of the siege of Sarajevo and the city's demilitarization. On 20 October he even expressed willingness to hold war-crimes trials.

Serbian presidential elections, 20 December 1992

In late November, perceiving that Serbia's main opposition parties were still too disparate and divided to unite around a single candidate to challenge Milosevic, Panic decided to offer himself as a candidate in the forthcoming Serbian presidential election.

Serbia's electoral commission made repeated attempts to block Panic's candidacy, on the grounds that (as a Yugoslav-American) he had not lived long enough in the FRY, but in the end Serbia's supreme court allowed Panic to stand. Vuk Draskovic withdrew his own candidacy in order to avoid splitting the anti-Milosevic vote, but Panic's chances of success were impaired by his late and contested entry into the election. Milosevic garnered 53.2 per cent of the votes cast, comfortably beating Panic, who obtained 32.1 per cent (Thomas 1999: 132).

Elections to the Skupstina, 20 December 1992

The Albanian Kosovars boycotted the election, as did most of the Slav Muslims in the Sandzak (of Novi Pazar). CSCE observers declared the election 'seriously flawed'. The irregularities included media manipulation, the omission of at least 5 per cent of voters (mainly young people) from the electoral register, the granting of double votes to some voters (mainly married women registered under their married and maiden names), the use of unsealed ballot boxes and a lack of voting secrecy. The SPS lost ground but nevertheless remained the largest party, while Seselj's ultra-nationalist Serbian Radical Party (SRS) dramatically increased its representation (see Table 6.5).

6.5 Skupstina (Serbian parliamentary) election, 20 December 1992

	Share of vote (%)	*Seats*
Socialist Party of Serbia (SPS)	28.8	101
Serbian Radical Party (SRS)	22.6	73
Democratic Movement of Serbia (DEPOS)	16.9	50
Democratic Party (DS)	4.2	6
Democratic Union of Vojvodina Hungarians (DZVM)	3.0	9
Peasant Party of Serbia (SSS)	2.7	3
Democratic and Reform Democratic Party of Vojvodina	1.5	2
Citizens of Kosova-Metohija (Arkan and his associates)	0.3	5
Democratic Reform Party of Muslims	0.1	1
Others	14.0	0
Invalid ballots	5.8	0

Source: Gordy (1999: 47).

Elections to the lower house of the federal parliament, 20 December 1992

These broadly repeated the above pattern. The SPS obtained forty-seven seats, the SRS thirty-four, DEPOS twenty, the Democratic Party five, Montenegro's Democratic Party of Socialists f ve, Montenegro's People's Party four, and Vojvodina regional representatives three (Thomas 1999: 133).

Serbian local elections, 20 December 1992

The SPS established a more hegemonic ascendancy at local level, winning 59.4 per cent of local council seats. Even though the opposition parties proved more willing to cooperate and field joint candidates at local level (especially in Vojvodina) than at higher levels, DEPOS obtained only 10.9 per cent of local council seats and the

Democratic Party only 2 per cent, while the SRS obtained only 8 per cent (Thomas 1999: 133).

The aftermath of the December 1992 elections

On 29 December 1992 the Federal Prime Minister Milan Panic lost a vote of no confidence in the federal parliament. This was instigated by Seselj's SRS and supported by the SPS, which for a time acted in concert.

Dobrica Cosic was forced to resign as federal president on 31 May 1993, after losing a vote of confidence in the federal parliament instigated by the SRS and supported by the SPS. Cosic was accused of encouraging the Yugoslav Army (the Vojska Jugoslovenska or VJ) (in which he enjoyed support) to stage a coup and of being willing to cede most of Krajina to Croatia and of Kosova to the Kosovars.

The next day the police violently suppressed demonstrations in Belgrade, in which a policeman died. During the early hours of 2 June, the SPO leader Vuk Draskovic was arrested, badly beaten by the police and jailed for alleged obstruction of the police and incitement to riot. Western responses to these repressive measures were initially very muted, partly because the West was then seeking Milosevic's help in Bosnia. However, Milosevic granted Draskovic a pardon and ordered his release on 9 July 1993, in response to vociferous domestic protests and belated international pressure.

Mounting tensions between the SPS and the SRS ripened into mutual enmity during September 1993. The formation of a 'shadow cabinet' by the SRS on 3 September signalled that it was no longer willing to act as a subservient ally of Milosevic. On 20 September the SRS proposed a vote of no confidence in the Serbian government In retaliation, the SPS denounced the SRS as dangerous extremists who were trying to destabilize Serbia and undermine Serb government efforts to broker a peace in Bosnia by actively supporting paramilitary forces who were indiscriminately carrying out criminal acts of violence against Croats, Bosniaks and Serbs (Thomas 1999: 178–9).

Milosevic turned the tables on his opponents on 20 October 1993 by using his presidential powers to dissolve the Serbian parliament before the vote of no confence took place. This threw the divided opposition parties into disarray (Thomas 1999: 182). On 15 November New Democracy and the Civic Alliance of Serbia (GSS) joined the SPO in a reconstituted DEPOS, which was united in its opposition to continued warfare in Bosnia and in support of the international peace proposals. By contrast, the Democratic Party and Kostunica's Democratic Party of Serbia dissociated themselves from DEPOS and maintained their support for the secessionist stances taken by most Bosnian and Croatian Serbs.

The elections to the 250-seat Serbian parliament, 19 and 26 December 1993

The SPS obtained a reduced share of the vote but more seats, enabling it to continue to divide and rule (Table 6.6).

Taming the hyperinflation of 1992–3: Dragoslav Avramovic

The annual inflation rate soared to 9,237 per cent in 1992 and to a quite literally astronomical 116.5 to the power of 10 to the power of 12 per cent in 1993 (Table

6.6 Serbian parliamentary election, 19 and 26 December 1993

	Share of vote (%)	*Seats*
Socialist Party of Serbia (SPS)	36.7	123
Democratic Movement of Serbia (DEPOS)	16.7	45
Serbian Radical Party (SRS)	13.9	39
Democratic Party (DS)	11.6	29
Democratic Party of Serbia (DSS)	5.1	7
Democratic Union of Vojvodina Hungarians (DZVM)	2.6	5
Slav Muslim PDD and SDA	0.7	2
Serbian Unity Party (SSJ), led by Arkan	1.5	0
Others	7.3	0
Invalid ballots	4.0	0

Source: Gordy (1999: 49).

6.7). The hyperinf ation that occurred in the FRY in 1992 and 1993 was caused by the disintegration of the former Yugoslavia, the ensuing warfare and loss of monetary and fiscal control, and the economic sanctions imposed on the Yugoslav successo states, and a massive increase in money supply brought about by printing vast quantities of paper money to cover mounting budget deficits

The central bank governor Dragoslav Avramovic, a former World Bank officia and the chief architect of the stabilization programme, rapidly became 'a Serbian folk hero' for his success in combating hyperinflation (*The Times*, 30 April 1994, p. 13). On 24 January 1994 he launched a 'new dinar', which was to be backed by gold and hard currency reserves and convertible into Deutschmarks at par. The old Yugoslav currency was to remain in use for an interim period (initially exchange-able at a rate of 13 million old dinars to one new one). There was to be a new guaranteed minimum wage of 20 new dinars per month, and income in excess of that amount was to be taxed at a rate of 35 per cent. There were also steep rises in public-utility charges and penalties of three months to three years in prison for black-market hard-currency dealing.

The initial results exceeded all expectations and confounded the critics. Within three months, the uncontrolled printing of dinars had ceased, the monthly rate of inflation had fallen to zero, the 'new dinar' was holding its value, the authorities were energetically collecting taxes and, by March 1994, production had increased by 22 per cent compared with March 1993, even though the economy was still operating at about one-third of its 1989 level. As a result, empty shops were replenished and real incomes doubled (*FT*, 9 May 1994, p. 4). The annual inf ation rate in 1994 was a mere 3.3 per cent (Table 6.7).

However, excessive demands on the budget had not been eliminated, and by mid-1994 the money supply had begun to increase faster than foreign-exchange reserves (*FT*, 6 October 1994, p. 3). Monetary policy was relaxed after July 1994 in order to counter a renewed contraction in production (UN ECE 1995: 96). Furthermore, Avramovic's macro-economic stabilization programme had not been backed up by strong wage controls.

Faltering steps towards peace in Bosnia, mid-1994 to November 1995

After the Bosnian Serbs rejected the peace plan and canton system for Bosnia put forward by the six-power contact group in July 1994, the 'international community'

6.7 Serbia and Montenegro: selected economic indicators, 1990–2005

	1990	1991	1992	1993	1994	1995	1996	1997	1998	1999	2000	2001	2002	2003	2004	2005
								% rise/rates								
GDP	-7.9	-11.6	-27.9	-30.8	2.5	6.1	7.8	10.1	1.9	-18.0	5.0	5.5	3.8	2.7	7.2	5.0
Industrial output	-11.7	-17.6	-22.4	-38.2	1.3	3.8	7.6	9.5	3.6	-24.4	11.1	0.0	1.7	-2.7	7.5	0.0
Agricultural output	-7.0	9.7	-17.8	-3.2	6.0	4.1	1.5	7.3	-3.2	-2.0	-13.7	23.2	3.0	-6.0	19.4	–
Annual inflation	593.0	121.0	9237.0	*	3.3	78.6	94.3	21.3	29.5	37.1	60.4	91.1	21.2	11.3	9.5	17.2
Budget surplus (+) / deficit (−) (% of GDP)	–	–	–	–	–	–	–	–	–	–	-0.9	-1.3	-4.6	-3.4	-0.3	0.9
Unemployment	–	21.0	24.6	23.1	23.1	24.6	25.8	25.8	25.1	25.5	25.6	26.8	29.0	31.7	31.7	–
Foreign debt (% of GDP)	–	–	–	–	–	–	79.0	88.0	123.0	61.8	164.0	103.5	76.4	69.7	62.4	61.7
Share of private sector in GDP	–	–	–	–	–	–	–	–	–	–	40.0	40.0	45.0	45.0	50.0	55.0
FDI inflow ($ m)	–	–	–	–	–	–	–	740.0	113.0	112.0	25.0	165.0	562.0	1405.0	1028.0	2020.0
Foreign debt ($ bn)	–	–	–	–	10.6	11.0	11.5	11.8	12.2	10.7	11.4	11.9	11.8	14.3	14.9	16.0
Population (m)	–	–	–	–	10.5	10.5	10.6	10.6	10.6	8.4	8.3	8.3	8.3	8.3	8.3	8.3

Notes: Serbia and Montenegro not available separately. * 116.5 to the power of 10 × 12 (hyperinflation)!

Sources: Various issues of the annual EBRD *Transition Report*, supplemented by UN Economic Commission for Europe, *Economic Survey of Europe*; UN *World Economic and Social Survey*; and IMF *World Economic Outlook*. The figures for 2004 and 2005 are provisional estimates.

threatened to further intensify sanctions against the FRY. As a consequence, Milosevic began to retreat from his plans for the creation of a 'Greater Serbia'. He rather ineffectually imposed sanctions on the Bosnian Serbs on 4 August 1994, while the state-owned section of the Serbian media spewed forth abuse against Karadzic, who was henceforth regarded as a major thorn in Milosevic's side and an impediment to his overriding goal of holding on to power.

The Serbian economy, 1990–5

There was a massive contraction in the GDP of the FRY between 1990 and 1993 (see Table 6.7). Per-capita GNP fell from 3,060 dollars in 1989 to 350 dollars in 1993, by which time 60 to 70 per cent of the Serbian population lived below the officia poverty line and over half of Serbia's factories were temporarily closed (*FT*, 22 July 1993, p. 3). In real terms, the average monthly salary in Serbia in 1993 was only 10 per cent of the level fve years previously (*FT*, 18 December 1993). By 1994, industry was working at 20 to 30 per cent of its pre-war capacity, an estimated 40 per cent of all economic activity was occurring in the black market, and only agricultural output was holding up (*The Economist*, 12 February 1994, p. 36). Over 400,000 Serbs, mainly the talented and those in their prime, left Serbia between 1991 and 1996, depriving the Serbian economy of much-needed skills and expertise (*IHT*, 11 December 1996, p. 6) (see Table 6.7).

However, the relative resilience of Serbian agricultural output, Serbia's ongoing capacity to feed itself, the macro-economic stabilization programme of 1994 (discussed above), large remittances from Serbian émigrés living in Western Europe and North America, and the occurrence of positive economic growth in 1994 and 1995 helped Serbia's population and the Milosevic regime to surmount the massive economic crises of 1990–3. By the mid-1990s, roughly half the annual current account trade deficit of about 2 billion dollars was being covered by remittances from Serbs living abroad (*EEN*, 15 March 1996, vol. 10, no. 4, p. 4).

'Insider privatization', 1991–4, and its reversal in 1994–5

Privatization legislation was passed in August 1991. Privatization occurred mostly through management–employee buy-outs (EBRD 2000b: 9). In the summer of 1994 the opposition Democratic Party put forward a proposal for revaluation of enterprise assets in a bid to correct the 'injustices' of corrupt 'insider privatizations' carried out during the period of rampant inflation, when managers had been able to buy shares at absurdly low prices and thus obtained majority ownership of former socially owned capital 'for a trifle', whilst the vast majority of employees had been 'unable to par ticipate in the process because of their total pauperization'. As a result, the great majority of enterprises which had been transferred to private hands were 'resocialized'. By 1994 privatization had been completed in 1,785 enterprises, but under the property transformation revaluation act, privatization was 'annulled in 1,556 or 87 per cent of transformed enterprises, employing 80 per cent of the labour force in Serbia' (Lazic and Sekelj 1997: 1064). Most of the formerly self-managed firms became directly and incompetently controlled by Milosevic's cronies (*The Economist*, 14 December 1996, p. 44).

Milosevic's volte-face on Krajina and Bosnia, 1995

By 1994, it appears to have become fully apparent to Milosevic that his regime could not achieve the 'Greater Serbia' which he had set out to establish in 1991–2. Already by January 1992 Croatian military strength had recovered from the body blows inflicte on it by the war of August–December 1991 and was capable of taking back the territory it had lost, although President Tudjman's vain hopes that he and Milosevic could 'carve up' Bosnia between Croatia and Serbia restrained him from immediately pressing home the advantages of Croatia's new-found military strength at Serbia's expense (Mesic 2001: 11–12; Spegelj 2001: 35–6, 39; Tus 2001: 65–6). Tudjman realized in early 1995 that the Western powers had finally mustered the resolve not to allo the partition of Bosnia between Serbs and Croats. He finally unleashed Croatia's revanchist armed forces against the Republika Srpska Krajina (RSK) in the Blitzkrieg offensives of May and August 1995. Milosevic, realizing that his programme for a 'Greater Serbia' was unattainable, decided to cut his losses. He now 'not only failed to offer support to the beleaguered Serbs of the RSK', but also 'apparently ordered that the Krajina army should withdraw rather than offer sustained resistance to the Croats. As the army of the RSK pulled back from their positions they were followed by around 165,000 refugees, almost the entire Serb population of the Krajina' (Thomas 1999: 239).

However, the principal reason why Milosevic had to jettison his previous pan-Serb ambitions and allies in 1995 was that, contrary to the way they have usually been portrayed by the Western media, most Serbs had never given much (if any) support to the 'Greater Serbia' programme. As argued in an outstanding study of the Balkan wars of 1991 to 1995,

> Most of the population, while in favour of self-determination and ready to defend itself, had little predisposition to participate in aggression against their neigh-bours. The poor response to mobilization and limited commitment to the war effort of the average Serb, in particular, supports such an interpretation... Despite an overwhelming initial advantage in equipment and organization, the Serb war effort was beset by a low level of commitment, poor morale, personnel shortages, poor leadership and dysfunctional civil-military relations . . . Unable to reach a decisive victory, and faced with a collapse of morale and the ever more manifest possibility of defeat, Serb forces had no choice but to end the wars by coming to terms.
>
> (Magas and Zanic 2001: xxiv, xxix)

The Croatian former general Martin Spegelj, who was chief superintendent of the Croatian Army from 25 September 1991 to 1 January 1993 and one of the architects of Croatia's eventual victory over the Serbs, has also emphasized demographic reasons why Milosevic was unable to deliver on his initial promise to achieve a 'Greater Serbia':

> Serbs, because of their low birth rate, have very few young people to send to war. In peacetime the JNA ran at about 20 per cent of capacity, and in the event of war it needed to draft about 80 per cent non-Serb soldiers. In the north-western theatre in 1990, for example, some 30 per cent of the eighteen-year-old recruits were Albanians, 20 per cent Croats, 8 per cent Slovenes, 10 per cent Bosniaks,

a considerable number Hungarians, and only 15–20 per cent Serbs and Montenegrins, most of whom ... were not ready to risk their lives in a war against Slovenia and Croatia.

(Spegelj 2001: 24; cf. Tus 2001: 57)

While NATO carried out air strikes on Bosnian Serb forces, the foreign ministers of Bosnia, Croatia and Serbia reached agreement on the 'basic principles' of a political settlement in Bosnia on 8 September 1995. On 9 November, partly to reward Milosevic for his growing cooperation with Western peace initiatives, it was announced that the UN economic embargo on the FRY would be eased slightly.

The Dayton accords of 21 November 1995

Peace talks began on 1 November at the Wright-Patterson Airbase near Dayton, Ohio, USA. A peace agreement was finally initialled by presidents Izetbegovic, Tudjman and Milosevic on 21 November. (For full details, see Chapter 7.) The main points were as follows:

- Bosnia and Herzegovina (as it then became) was to be preserved as a single state within its present borders and with international recognition.
- It was to be divided into *two separate and largely autonomous territorial 'entities'*, with 51 per cent of the territory assigned to the Federation of Bosnia and Herzegovina (the FBiH), whose predominantly Bosniak and Croat population in 1996 was estimated at 2.5 million, while the other 49 per cent of the territory was allocated to the Republika Srpska (RS), whose predominantly Serb population in 1996 was estimated to be 1 million (*IHT*, 14 September 1996, p. 7).
- There was to be an 'effective' all-Bosnia central government, including a parliament, a three-member presidency, a constitutional court and single central bank.
- Refugees were to be allowed and encouraged to return to their old homes.
- Individuals charged with war crimes would be banned from participation in political and military life, and Bosnia, Croatia and the FRY would cooperate fully in the investigation and prosecution of war crimes.

Serbia after the November 1995 Dayton accords

Milosevic, having stirred up pan-Serbian nationalism from 1987 to 1990 and more intermittently in 1991–2, completely abandoned his former support for the Serbs outside Serbia in 1995 and sought in his own way to make the November 1995 Dayton settlement work. He seemed to believe that the defeat of the Bosnian Serb extremists would make his hold on power more secure. While promoting himself internation - ally as a guarantor of peace in the Balkans, at home Milosevic worked to stifle politica opposition and reassert state control over the economy. Harassment of the opposition was stepped up. Instead of reforming and restructuring the polity and the economy, Milosevic merely made cosmetic or tactical changes. He unceremoniously dumped many of the nationalists in his entourage and reactivated his earlier 'socialist' rhetoric. The FRY's economic position barely improved, partly because an 'outer wall' of UN sanctions would remain in place so long as Belgrade continued to repress the Kosovar Albanians and failed to cooperate fully with the ICTY (*IHT*, 6 March 1996, p. 7).

Elections to the federal parliament, 3 November 1996

Milosevic needed to win a majority in the federal parliament in order to make changes in the constitution of the FRY. By 1997 he would have completed two five-year term as president of Serbia, the maximum permitted by the Serbian constitution, and he wanted to gain a further lease of political life for himself by becoming president of the Serb-dominated FRY instead. He therefore wanted to change the federal constitution, both to maximize the representation of his SPS in the federal parliament (by switching from proportional representation to a first-past-the-post electoral system and to increase the powers of the office of president. His chances of success were greatly enhanced by the ongoing boycott of FRY and Serbian elections and institutions by the Kosovars, which virtually guaranteed that the SPS would win most of the seats in Kosova.

Prior to the election, several liberal or reform-minded opposition parties joined forces in the Zajedno (Together) coalition, comprising the SPO led by Vuk Draskovic, the DS led by Zoran Djindjic, the Democratic Party of Serbia (DSS) led by Vojislav Kostunica, and the Civic Alliance of Serbia led by Vesna Pesic.

On an electoral turn-out of 60 per cent, the distribution of seats in the 138-seat Chamber of Citizens (lower house) is shown in Table 6.8. If we exclude Montenegro from the calculations, the SPS-led coalition won 45 per cent of the votes cast in Serbia, the Zajedno coalition won 23.8 per cent, and the SRS won 19 per cent (Cohen 2002: 251).

6.8 Federal parliamentary election, 3 November 1996

Party	Seats
The SPS-led ruling coalition	64
The Democratic Party of Socialists of Montenegro, then allied to Milosevic	20
The ultra-nationalist Serbian Radical Party (SRS) led by Vojislav Seselj	16
The liberal reform-minded Zajedno coalition	22

The municipal elections held in Serbia on 3 and 17 November 1996 and Serbia's subsequent 'winter of discontent'

In the f rst round of local elections, which took place on 3 November 1996, no majority party emerged in 188 municipalities. This necessitated the holding of a second round of local balloting on 17 November 1996. The Zajedno alliance proved far more effective in these local elections than it had been in the federal elections. It claimed to have won in fifteen of the eighteen largest cities and towns in Serbia, includin Belgrade. 'The municipalities won by Zajedno accounted for 35.4 per cent of Serbia's population, 50 per cent of the employed workforce, and 63 per cent of the employees with higher degrees' (Cohen 2002: 251). However, electoral commissions and local courts began to declare the Zajedno victories to be invalid: they were annulled in all but one city (*IHT*, 6 December 1996, p. 9).

The attempt by the Milosevic regime to deny most of the opposition's victories in the local elections, combined with increased restrictions on university autonomy and liberties, unleashed a massive wave of street protests. Daily demonstrations began, f rst by students and later in the day by Zajedno supporters. These gradually attracted attention and (eventually) support from somewhat-surprised Western media and governments, which had hitherto tended to write off most Serbs as rabid adherents of authoritarian nationalism. The demonstrators were seemingly undeterred by the bitter cold of Serbian winter nights. The effectiveness of the opposition was enhanced by the fact that many of Serbia's municipal authorities (especially Belgrade city council) owned and operated television and radio stations, magazines and newspapers and managed to bypass state censorship of the news (*IHT*, 29 November 1996, p. 8). The largest demonstrations took place in Belgrade, sometimes involving a quarter of a million people, with some estimates going even higher. Although there were occasional clashes with the riot police, there was little loss of life. Demonstrations involving up to 40,000 people also took place in Nis, Serbia's second largest city – hitherto an SPS stronghold. This doggedly determined and courageous three-month-long confrontation with the Milosevic regime not only refuted the hitherto-standard Western media caricatures of the Serbs but also showed that large segments of the urban population were willing to *fight* for forms of freedom which most Westerners were lucky enough to be able to take for granted.

The regime staged fresh elections on 27 November. In twelve towns where Zajedno gains had been annulled, it won again. In Belgrade, Nis and Kraljevo, however, Zajedno boycotted the rerun elections (*The Guardian*, 9 December 1996, p. 2).

Organized groups of workers joined the opposition demonstrations for the fist time on 11 December. Workers downed tools in six factories in Belgrade, one in Nis and one in Mladenovac (*IHT*, 12 December 1996, p. 9). The Alliance of Independent Trade Unions of Yugoslavia and the smaller Nezavismost subsequently signalled their support for the opposition (*IHT*, 17 December 1996, p. 6).

Reversing its initial refusal, an OSCE delegation headed by the former Spanish prime minister Felipe González visited Serbia on 20–21 December. On 22 December a union of the free cities and municipalities of Serbia was established, with 'shadow' municipal governments being set up, and the Serbian privatization minister confirmed his resignation from the government (*EEN*, 31 December 1996, vol. 10, no. 25, p. 9).

The SPS organized a counter-rally in Belgrade on 24 December. Many of Milosevic's supporters were bused into Belgrade from the provinces, but only around 60,000 materialized, instead of the expected 500,000, and they were taken aback at how massively they were outnumbered by opposition protestors (*IHT*, 31 December 1996, p. 5).

Felipe González delivered the verdict of the OSCE investigation of the municipal elections on 27 December: 'the authorities and all political forces in Yugoslavia must accept and abide by the results of the local elections of 17 November'. Although the SPS and its allies had won a majority of the overall votes cast in the municipal elections, the OSCE investigators concluded that Zajedno had won in twenty-two disputed municipalities (nine in Belgrade and thirteen in other towns and cities). Thus OSCE supported all of Zajedno's claims, except in the case of Pozega.

Serbia's foreign minister Milan Milutinovic signed a letter to the OSCE on 3 January, conceding that the Zajedno coalition had won the election in three provincial towns and in 'nine municipalities in Belgrade' (out of sixteen), but reaffirming th SPS as the winner in six disputed towns (*IHT*, 4 January 1997, p. 7). These admissions were regarded as inadequate, both by the OSCE and by the domestic opposition.

On 7 January Serbia's supreme court recognized Zajedno's victory in the town of Lapovo; the next day the government acknowledged Zajedno's victory in Nis; and the following day the supreme court conceded that Zajedno had won in Vrsac, one of the six towns described on 3 January as having been won by the SPS *(The Guardian*, 11 January 1997, p. 14). On 11 January representatives of the government met student leaders and the government issued a statement that the will of the citizens 'must be fully respected' *(IHT*, 13 January 1997, p. 1), but on 13 January the local electoral commission in Nis again refused to recognize the opposition victory.

On 14 January the Belgrade electoral commission acknowledged that Zajedno had won 60 seats on the 110-seat Belgrade city council (with twenty-three going to the SPS-led coalition, ten awaiting a final decision and the remainder going to othe parties). The Nis electoral commission then reversed its previous stance and recognized the opposition victory there.

On 30 January, possibly in order to pave the way for a climbdown by Milosevic, the FRY president Zoran Lilic (a Milosevic loyalist) declared that 'The results of the elections should be recognized . . . everywhere the opposition won by the will of the people' *(Independent*, 1 February 1997, p. 15). Borisav Jovic, a close associate of Milosevic and a Serbian former member of the Communist Yugoslav presidency, also stated that the opposition victories in the local elections should be recognized (*The Guardian*, 31 January 1997, p. 14).

Riot police attacked demonstrators on 2 and 3 February. Patriarch Pavle appealed to the police 'to protect law and order and not those in power, who are sinking deeper and deeper, not knowing what they are doing' *(IHT*, 4 February 1997, p. 5).

Milosevic wrote to Prime Minister Mirko Marjanovic on 4 February:

> I propose that the Serbian government submit to parliament a draft emergency law which will proclaim as final, results of a part of local elections in Serbia i keeping with the findings of the OSCE mission. I wish to stress that the state interest of improving relations of our country with the OSCE and the international community far exceeds the importance of any number of council seats in a handful of towns.

During talks in France with the French prime minister, the three main leaders of Zajedno declared on 6 February that they would end the demonstrations and begin discussions on wider issues only when the Skupstina passed the emergency law. This finally took place on 11 February. The parliamentary session was boycotted by Zajedno, whose leaders stated that demonstrations would continue until the local councils were actually handed over to them. On 12 February student leaders vowed to continue their demonstrations until other conditions were met, notably the dismissal of the rector of Belgrade University. He resigned on 7 March, and the students ended their demonstrations. On 15 February Zajedno leaders called for a halt to demonstrations, but threatened to resume them if state controls on the media were not relaxed by 9 March 1997. On 21 February Zoran Djindjic was elected mayor of Belgrade.

The change in attitude of the Serbian Orthodox Church towards Milosevic was striking. From 1992 to 1996 the Orthodox bishops had adopted a generally passive or even approving stance towards the Milosevic government, had failed to condemn the three-and-a-half-year war in Bosnia-Herzegovina and had exhibited 'tacit support for the political aims of both the Krajina and the Bosnian Serbs' (*IHT*, 3 January 1997, p. 1). On 2 January 1997, however, an emergency meeting of the synod of the

Serbian Orthodox Church issued the following statement (signed by, among others, Patriarch Pavle):

> He [Milosevic] has already set us against the whole world and now wants to pit us against each other and trigger bloodshed just to preserve power. The Serbian Orthodox Church strongly condemns the falsifying of people's votes, the stiflin of political and religious freedoms, and especially the beating up and murder of people on the streets.

The statement called on the government to 'respect the results' of the local elections held on 17 November. The statement accused the regime of 'bringing the country and the nation to complete collapse and making people beggars', and of 'betraying' the Serbs of the Krajina and Bosnia.

Serbia after its winter of discontent, 1997

Unfortunately, the fractiousness of the opposition parties allowed this opportunity to cause permanent damage to Milosevic to slip through their fingers. In Serbia, Milosevic's writ still ran more or less unchallenged, especially after the Zajedno alliance collapsed in mid-1997, thanks in large measure to the ambition and wayward-ness of Vuk Draskovic and his wife Danica. The 100,000-strong police force had in effect become Milosevic's own praetorian guard. Serbia had been transformed from a regional power to a tawdry tin-pot dictatorship (*EEN*, 3 July 1997, vol. 11, no. 13, pp. 1–2).

Milosevic decided in June 1997 to change the constitution of the FRY, in order to increase the powers of the FRY presidency, which he wanted for himself. Montenegro's ruling Democratic Party of Socialists decided to oppose the proposed constitutional changes, because their main effect was substantially to reduce Montenegro's weight in the federation, but Milosevic was able to push through his constitutional changes against the wishes of the DPS because they were accepted by Montenegro's president, Momir Bulatovic, and by his supporters in the federal parliament. Milosevic was elected president of the FRY for the single four-year term permitted by the federal constitution on 15 July. He ran unopposed, the lower house voting eighty-eight for and ten against and the upper house voting twenty-nine for and two against, with many abstentions.

The Serbian economy after Dayton, 1996–9

Serbia's economy began to recover from 1995 to 1997. GDP rose by 6.1 per cent in 1995, 7.8 per cent in 1996 and 10.1 in 1997, before stagnating again in 1998 and contracting by 18 per cent in 1999. Industrial output followed suit (see Table 6.7).

In August 1996, *The Economist* commented that Milosevic appeared ready 'to dump his former socialist policies for "swift and brutal" privatization', in the belief that revenues from privatization would 'keep him and Serbia's ruling political and economic elite afloat for some time' *The Economist*, 31 August 1996, p. 37). On 9 June 1997, 29 per cent of Serbia Telecom was sold to Stet of Italy and 20 per cent to OTE of Greece, although the government retained a 'golden share' conferring a veto on important decisions (*FT*, 10 June 1997, p. 30). Milosevic used the proceeds mainly to clear backlogs of wages and pensions owed to workers and pensioners in time for the September 1997 elections to the Serbian parliament and presidency and to carry out emergency repairs to Serbia's crumbling infrastructure (*FT*, 20 October 1997, p. 2). In addition, the Skupstina approved a new privatization programme in June 1997, aiming to sell off 5,000 small and medium enterprises in order to attract foreign investment as well as to propitiate impoverished voters by handing out free shares in firms. About 90 per cent of industrial assets were still state-owned a that time.

The dinar was devalued by 69.7 per cent on 26 November 1996. On 26 January 1998 the dinar fell to 5.6 to the Deutschmark on the black market, due to a 50 per cent surge in money supply over the previous six months, as the Milosevic regime 'attempted to ease a liquidity crisis and pay workers and pensioners ahead of parliamentary and presidential elections' (*FT*, 27 January 1998, p. 3). On 1 April 1998 the off cial exchange rate was devalued by 45 per cent, from 3.3 dinars to the Deutschmark to 6. Black-market exchange rates were subsequently 6–6.3 to the Deutschmark *HT*, 2 April 1998, p. 13).

Unemployment was officially put at 26 per cent in 1997, but in reality it was ove 40 per cent and rising *FT*, Survey, 27 January 1998, p. 13). Many nominally employed workers were on forced leave, with little or no pay (*FT*, 29 May 1998, p. 3).

Elections to the 250-seat Skupstina, 21 September 1997

The turn-out was 57.5 per cent. The elections were boycotted by the Democratic Party (led Zoran Djindjic) and by the Civic Alliance of Serbia (led by Vesna Pesic). The OSCE concluded that the elections were 'fundamentally flawed', with widesprea vote-rigging and media bias in favour of the SPS-led coalition (*IHT*, 10 December 1997, p. 7). The final distribution of seats is shown in Table 6.9

6.9 Serbian parliamentary election, 21 September 1997

Party	Seats
SPS-led coalition (SPS, JUL and ND)	110
The ultra-nationalist SRS	82
The liberal-nationalist SPO	45
Five small parties[1]	13

Note:
1. Including one for Vojvodina Hungarians and one for Slavic Muslims in the Sandzak.

The four-round Serbian presidential election of 20–21 September, 5 October, 7 December and 21 December 1997

In the first round, Zoran Lilic (the former president of the FRY and a protégé of Milosevic) won 35.9 per cent of the vote, Vojislav Seselj (leader of the ultra-nationalist Serbian Radical Party) obtained 28.6 per cent, and the SPO leader Vuk Draskovic won 22 per cent.

The turn-out for the second round held on 5 October was only 48.97 per cent and thus below the minimum 50 per cent necessary for the vote to stand. Seselj won 49.1 per cent of the votes cast and Lilic 47.9 per cent.

A third round took place on 7 December. Although the turn-out was 51 per cent and the pro-Milosevic candidate Milan Milutinovic (who was then the foreign minister

in the federal government) won a larger share of the vote (41.5 per cent) than Seselj
(33 per cent), this was still below the 50 per cent share needed for the vote to stand.

A fourth round on 21 December finally produced a viable result. Milutinovic wo
59 per cent of the vote to Seselj's 37.5 per cent, on a turn-out of 50.53 per cent. The
OSCE described these elections as 'fundamentally flawed', especially in Kosova wher
despite the clearly visible Albanian boycott, a 'phantom army of Albanian voters'
had supposedly turned out to vote for Milutinovic! (*FT*, 22 December 1997, p. 2;
IHT, 23 December 1997, p. 10; Thomas 1998: 118).

The aftermath of the September 1997 elections

Perceiving that Milosevic and his allies had fallen far short of a parliamentary majority,
and presuming that the apparent enmity between the SPS and the SRS was insur -
mountable, Vuk Draskovic and the SPO turned their backs on the opposition parties
which had boycotted the parliamentary election (and were therefore not represented
in parliament) and sought to ingratiate themselves with Milosevic in the hope of
being invited into government. In the Belgrade city assembly on 30 September 1997
the SPO treacherously put forward a motion to oust the DS leader Zoran Djindjic as
mayor of Belgrade, claiming that he had abused his position to encourage an election
boycott. The motion was carried with support from the SPS and the SRS. In collusion
with the SPS and the SRS, the SPO also removed the Belgrade television station Studio
B from opposition control and sacked much of its existing staff. A number of protest
demonstrations ensued, but these were easily suppressed by riot police. The SPO, in
collusion with the SPS, subsequently 'sold city-owned flats dirt-cheap to its loyalists
(*The Economist*, Survey, 24 January 1998, p. 14).

During January and February 1998 the SPO led by Vuk Draskovic conducted
lengthy negotiations with prominent SPS offcials in an attempt to enter an SPS–SPO
coalition government. However, the increasingly violent confrontations between the
KLA and the Serbian security forces (backed by maverick paramilitary forces affiliate
to Vojislav Seselj's SRS and to Arkan) created an atmosphere of crisis that allowed
Milosevic to create a more congenial coalition with his former adversary Seselj instead
(Thomas 1998: 118). The SRS stole a march on the SPO on 24 March 1998 by joining
the SPS and the Yugoslav United Left in a coalition government. Vojislav Seselj
became one of five deputy prime ministers. The coalition had 187 of the 250 deputie
in the Serbian parliament. The SPO suddenly found itself left out in the cold, spurned
both by the Milosevic regime and by the other opposition parties. The formation of
this SPS–SRS coalition coincided with a ferocious counter-offensive against the KLA,
which had succeeded in establishing a virtual 'liberated zone' in the Drenica region
of Kosova in late 1997 and early 1998.

In May 1998 Milosevic instigated a new crackdown on the independent/dissident
sections of the media. 'The ban was disguised as a normal licensing decision . . . Of
thirty-eight independent radio and television stations that broadcast news . . . thirty-
five were shut down. Only three were granted new licences.' However, they were
now required to pay licensing fees of 12,000–15,000 dollars a month, which would
quickly put them out of business. All the other outlets granted frequencies either did
not broadcast news or were pro-Milosevic (*IHT*, 25 May 1998, p. 8).

A broad-based non-party student-based movement called Otpor (resistance) was
launched in October 1998 by a small group of about twenty activists (mainly students,
but also some young professional people) who had cut their teeth in the anti-Milosevic

protest movement of November 1996 to March 1997. Otpor sprang to life after the Milosevic regime tried to neutralize the universities as centres of revolt by drawing up a universities law which made rectors and deans appointees of the regime and which put pressure on university professors to sign contracts which many regarded as crude pledges of party loyalty. When the law came into force, the universities experienced a wave of sackings and resignations.

The 'purges' conducted by Milosevic, 28 October to 24 November 1998

Jovica Stanisic, the head of Serbia's public and state security department, was dismissed on 28 October 1998, after losing a political struggle against the architects of the campaign of repression both in 'Serbia proper' and in Kosova. Stanisic had been the leading pragmatist in Milosevic's entourage and had long resisted President Milosevic's authoritarian excesses. Over the previous two years he had been in conflict with the Serbian Radical Party leader Vojislav Seselj and Milosevic's wife Mirjana Markovic. He was replaced by Radomir Markovic, a member of Mirjana Markovic's Yugoslav United Left party (JUL). Along with Stanisic, a dozen top operational off cers of the security service were forced into retirement or removed. Also dismissed were Milorad Vucelic, vice-president of the ruling SPS, who had hitherto served as Milosevic's political disciplinarian, and (two days later) the air-force commander General Ljubisa Velickovic, who had protested against Milosevic's agreement to allow NATO surveillance f ights over Kosova (*FT*, 29 October 1998, p. 2; *IHT*, 26 November 1998, p. 5).

General Momcilo Perisic, the VJ's long-serving army chief of staff and joint architect of the war in Bosnia, was dismissed on 24 November 1998. Senior army off cers were reportedly unhappy with Milosevic's having agreed on 13 October to pull troops and armed police out of Kosova and to allow NATO surveillance flight over the FRY. General Perisic had publicly criticized Milosevic in October for allowing the FRY to become a pariah state and opposed the use of VJ troops against Kosovar civilians during the summer 1998 offensive in Kosova. General Perisic was replaced by General Dragoljub Ojdanic, a veteran of the 1991 siege of Vukovar and a member of the JUL (*IHT*, 26 November 1998, p. 5; *IHT*, 30 November 1998, pp. 1, 9).

Milosevic and four senior colleagues were indicted by the ICTY on 18 January 1999 for war crimes and crimes against humanity in Bosnia. They were charged with 'crimes against humanity – specif cally murder, deportation and persecutions – and with violations of the laws and customs of war'. The other indictees were: Milan Milutinovic, president of Serbia; Nikola Sainovic, deputy prime minister of the FRY; the VJ chief of staff General Dragoljub Ojdanic; and the FRY interior minister Vlajko Stojilkovic. This was the f rst time in history that this had happened to sitting heads of state (presidents Milosevic and Milan Milutinovic).

Vuk Draskovic foolishly accepted an offer from Milosevic to appoint him as a federal deputy prime minister with responsibility for international relations on 18 January 1999. Draskovic possibly deluded himself and his party that he could act as a restraining influence on the Milosevic regime, which was also in cohoots wit the violently ultra-nationalist SRS led by Seselj. In reality, Draskovic and the SPO merely brought themselves into further political and moral discredit by associating themselves with the large-scale ethnic cleansing and other atrocities carried out by the Milosevic regime against ethnic Albanians in Kosova in early 1999.

The Kosova war, March to June 1999

From March to June 1999 NATO unleashed a massive aerial bombardment against Serbia in response to the Milosevic regime's mounting atrocities in Kosova. For a full account of this war and its context, see Chapter 10 (pp. 544–56).

On 11 April 1999 unidentified gunmen killed the well-known opposition publishe Slavko Curuvija, the owner of the*Dnevni Telegraf* and the news biweekly*Evropljanin*, outside his apartment in Belgrade as he returned home from work. His papers had been heavily fined for breaching Serbia's restrictive information law, passed in Octobe 1998, and then had been banned. Curuvija had reregistered them in Montenegro and had them printed in Croatia, but their distribution in Serbia had been greatly curtailed (*IHT*, 12 April 1999, p. 8). Vuk Draskovic declared that 'Those who ordered and committed the murder have taken arms against Serbia more destructive than all the bombs of NATO. Let Slavko be the first and last victim of those who want to initiat a mad circle of fratricidal murder.' He was dismissed as federal deputy prime minister on 28 April (*The Times*, 29 April 1999, p. 19).

There were anti-Milosevic demonstrations by thousands of army reservists and their relatives in the industrial towns of Krusevac, Aleksandrovac and Raska in southern Serbia on 17–18 May and in the central city of Cacak and the northern industrial city of Pancevo on 19 May, all resisting further mobilization of reservists and demanding an end to the war and the recall of men sent from these towns to figh (*The Times*, 19 May 1999, p. 1). The protests had been triggered by the arrival of the bodies of reservists killed in Kosova just as more conscripts were being mobilized (*FT*, 19 May 1999, p. 1; 20 May 1999, p. 2). Thousands of Serbian troops deserted from their posts in Kosova and joined anti-war demonstrations in these towns (*IHT*, 21 May 1999, p. 1). The protests resumed in these same towns on 23–24 May, when thousands of reservists again disobeyed orders to return to Kosova, and spread for the first time to Kosova itself, especially the town of Lipljan which had been heavil bombed by NATO (*FT*, 25 May 1999, p. 2).

On 24 May 1999, the ICTY again indicted the FRY president Slobodan Milosevic, Serbia's president Milan Milutinovic, the FRY deputy premier Nikola Sainovic, the FRY minister of internal affairs Vlajko Stojilkovic, and the VJ chief of staff General Dragoljub Ojdanic on charges of 'crimes against humanity – specifically murder, deportation and persecutions, and with violations of the laws and customs of war', this time in relation to Kosova.

The political aftermath of the Kosova war, June 1999 to August 2000

In June 1999 Milosevic was obliged to accept and acknowledge defeat in the Kosova war (for details, see Chapter 10, pp. 554–6). While Milosevic and Serbia had taken a huge pounding from NATO bombers and artillery, both lived to fight another day and gained a degree of respect for that in some quarters.

The holy synod of the Serbian Orthodox Church issued the following double-edged appeal on 15 June 1999:

> Every sensible person has to realise that numerous internal problems and the isolation of our country on the international scene cannot be solved or overcome with this kind of government and under the present circumstances. Faced with the tragic situation in our nation and our country, we demand that the current

President of the country and his government resign . . . so that new officials acceptable at home and abroad can take responsibility for the people and their future . . . We also appeal to our brothers in Kosova to stay in their homes and not to leave their relics.

(The Guardian, 16 June 1999, p. 2)

Artemije, the Serbian Orthodox bishop of Kosova, spoke of the 'evil' committed by Serbs, claiming that 'We Serbs have lived in great pain and compassion at what was happening to our Albanian neighbours. We were sorry for every innocent victim.' However, he insisted that there was no collective guilt and reiterated the church's demand for Milosevic to resign (*FT*, 29 June 1999, p. 1).

An 'Alliance for Change' umbrella grouping of about thirty opposition parties staged the first of a series of anti-government demonstrations on 29 June, demanding the resignation of Milosevic and early elections. The Alliance for Change also attracted around 10,000 people to a rally in Kragujevac on 15 July (*The Guardian*, 17 July 1999, p. 17), while about 20,000 people attended a rally organized by Vuk Draskovic's SPO in Kragujevac on 17 July (*IHT*, 19 July 1999, p. 4). On 24 July Draskovic addressed a rally in Nis attended by around 25,000 people.

On 2 August 1999 an 'independent group of experts' led by economist Mladjan Dinkic outlined a plan for the formation of a transitional government to lead the FRY out of economic misery and prepare the way for new elections. The group called for a major rally to be held in the capital Belgrade on 19 August in support of this scenario. They declared that Patriarch Pavle and all opposition leaders and independent figures, including the former army chief General Momcilo Perisic, would be invited to attend. This so-called 'stability pact for Serbia' was drafted by a group of prominent Serb economists and academics, in response to the Balkan stability pact approved by Western leaders in Sarajevo. It argued that both the Milosevic regime and the opposition should agree to give up their aspirations to power for one year, during which free and fair elections would be be held. Mladjan Dinkic was the thirty-five-year-old leader of th Group of Seventeen organization of independent Yugoslav economists and an up-and-coming politician (*IHT*, 3 August 1999, p. 5).

Patriarch Pavle, other church dignitaries, the Group of Seventeen independent economists and Serbia's main opposition leaders, including Zoran Djindjic and Vuk Draskovic, met at the Patriarch's Belgrade seat on 9–19 August 1999. They agreed to take part in a mass anti-government rally in Belgrade on 19 August and to form a transitional government of experts that would prepare democratic and economic reforms and hold elections within a year. The rally was to be organized by Mladjan Dinkic and Predrag Markovic, authors of the so-called 'stability pact for Serbia'. They and Zoran Djindjic insisted that Milosevic would have to step down before any transition government could take over, whereas Vuk Draskovic argued for a transitional government involving a sort of power-sharing deal with Milosevic (*IHT*, 10 August 1999, p. 5; 11 August 1999, p. 4; 12 August 1999, p. 5). The holy synod of the Serbian Orthodox Church called on 11 August for the resignation of Milosevic as FRY president and of Milan Milutinovic as Serbia's president and for the formation of a transitional non-party 'government of experts' to prepare fresh elections and democratic and economic reforms (*IHT*, 12 August 1999, p. 5).

On 17 August Vuk Draskovic and the former army chief of staff Momcilo Perisic pulled out of preparations for the major anti-Milosevic rally scheduled for 19 August. Djindjic, the Alliance for Change and the Clinton administration wanted Milosevic to resign and to be delivered (perhaps within six months) for trial by the ICTY, while a transitional government of experts would serve for one year to prepare reforms and fresh elections. By contrast, Draskovic proposed either new internationally supervised elections for a government to replace Milosevic, or negotiations to form a transitional government that would render Milosevic a mere figurehead. Perisic wanted to see earl elections for a new government, placing him closer to Draskovic, who also favoured early elections (*IHT*, 18 August 1999, p. 2). Vuk Draskovic unexpectedly addressed the anti-government rally in Belgrade on 19 August and called for elections under international supervision. Draskovic declared that Serbia was 'in jail' because it was led by people who were totally ostracized by the world, but he chided the other opposition parties for making utopian plans for transitional governments which no one would recognize. When he left the speaker's podium, 'he was booed and jeered by many in the crowd' (*IHT*, 20 August 1999, pp. 1, 4).

On 3 October 1999 a truck swerved into Vuk Draskovic's car, killing his brother-in-law, and then struck the car behind him, killing three of his bodyguards, although Draskovic himself was only slightly injured. Draskovic claimed that this was an assassination attempt by the Milosevic regime. However, some people suggested that it was gang warfare, as Draskovic's brother-in-law was director of the board for municipal building sites in Belgrade, generally recognized as a corrupt source of rich pickings. The police found neither the truck's driver nor its current owner, lending credibility to Draskovic's claims (*IHT*, 15 October 1999, p. 6).

With Draskovic temporarily deactivated, the opposition parties reached agreement on 7 October on proposed terms for early elections, especially concerning the election laws and arrangements. These terms included a proportional voting system, a revision of electoral registers, the presence of domestic and foreign observers at all stages of the voting process, new electoral commission members, the replacement of a restrictive media law, new laws governing political parties and new 'international' rules on election campaigning (*IHT*, 8 October 1999, p. 2). Most opposition parties, with the major exception of the SPO, signed an agreement on electoral cooperation on 28 October. On 3 November the leaders of the oppositional Alliance for Change met with the US secretary of state Madeleine Albright, who pledged to suspend sanctions on oil deliveries and flights to Serbia in exchange for clean elections which woul evict Milosevic from power. However, the Milosevic regime derided this US proposal, pointing out that Milosevic expected to be re-elected and that the USA would in practice only recognize an election which Milosevic lost (*IHT*, 5 November 1999, p. 7; *IHT*, 6 November 1999, p. 4).

At a meeting organized by Vuk Draskovic's SPO on 10 January 2000, seventeen opposition parties agreed to join forces and to demand early elections at all levels of government by the end of April 2000.

Zeljko Raznatovic (alias Arkan) was shot dead at Belgrade's Intercontinental Hotel on 15 January 2000. A friend and a bodyguard were also killed. Intense speculation surrounded the assassination. It was widely believed that it was either a gangland killing or one ordered by Milosevic to ensure that Arkan would never be able to reveal what he knew about Milosevic's role in the Balkan wars. The (Montenegrin) FRY defence minister Pavle Bulatovic was shot dead in a Belgrade restaurant on 7 Febuary 2000. Again, there was intense speculation as to who was behind the killing, and why.

There was a further crackdown on the independent media in Serbia in March 2000, mainly utilizing a public-information law passed in 1998. Offcials shut down several

independent local television and radio stations for unspecified violations of the la
and in some cases confiscated their transmission equipment, while Belgrade's Studi
B faced a sudden state demand for a payment of 245,000 dollars. Thousands of people
took part in protests against these actions in Kraljevo, Pirot and Pozega. In addition,
several independent newspapers (including *Danas* and *Glas Javnosti*) suddenly faced
heavy fines and the popular evening paper, *Vecernji Novosti*, was brought under strict
government control (*IHT*, 17 March 2000, p. 5). The state-controlled media portrayed
the protestors as enemies of the state, and there was a new wave of military call-ups
(*FT*, 24 March 2000, p. 23).

A peaceful demonstration was staged by opposition parties in Belgrade on 14 April
2000. It called for early elections and attracted over 100,000 participants. Vuk
Draskovic and Zoran Djindjic not only attended but 'even' publicly shook hands.
The student organization Otpor also took part. On 15 May over 20,000 people, includ
ing both Zoran Dijndjic and Vuk Draskovic, attended an anti-Milosevic rally in
Belgrade (*IHT*, 16 May 2000, p. 9).

The Studio B television station and the B2-92 radio station, both owned by the
then SPO-controlled Belgrade city council, were seized on 17 May by the Serbian
government, which accused them of advocating an uprising against the authorities. The police also locked up the office of Radio Indeks, which was in the same
building, and those of the largest independent newspaper, *Blic* (*IHT*, 18 May 2000,
p. 5). In late May the Serbian education ministry banned all gatherings at universities
and decreed that the summer term was to end immediately (one week early) and
that students would be allowed to enter the universities only to sit their exams
(*Independent*, 27 May 2000, p. 16). About 10,000 people attended an opposition rally
in Belgrade on 27 May (*IHT*, 29 May 2000, p. 9).

Vuk Draskovic was shot and slightly injured at his holiday home in the sea-
side town of Budva (in Montenegro) on 15 June 2000. He blamed agents sent by
Milosevic, although there were also suggestions that the incident had been staged
by Draskovic in collusion with the Montenegrin government 'for their own purposes'.
Draskovic was quick to condemn other opposition parties 'for not reacting morerfnly
and sympathetically to the assassination attempt' (Cohen 2002: 402). Several people
were arrested by the Montenegrin police, who claimed that the suspects came from
Serbia.

On 6 July 2000 the federal parliament approved constitutional changes which
(i) provided for the direct election of the Yugoslav federal president and the upper
house of parliament; (ii) allowed two four-year terms for the president; and (iii) raised
the threshold for impeachment. The lower house passed the changes by ninety-fiv
votes to seven, while the upper house did likewise by twenty-seven votes to zero.
The changes were clearly designed to enhance Milosevic's chances of remaining in
power beyond July 2001, when his four-year stint as president of the FRY was due
to expire. Hitherto, the federal president had been elected by both houses of the federal
parliament and could only serve one four-year term, and the upper house of the federal parliament had been elected in equal proportions by the Serbian and Montenegrin
parliaments. The changes also transferred overall organization of federal elections
from the governments of Serbia and Montenegro (each within its own domain) to the
Milosevic-controlled federal government, thereby minimizing Milosevic's need for
Montenegrin support. Henceforth Montenegro would have 'no more weight than its
share of Yugoslavia's population – about 7 per cent' (*The Economist*, 15 July 2000,
p. 45). Even if Montenegro's President Djukanovic and his government were to call

for a Montenegrin boycott of the forthcoming federal elections, these elections could now take place anyway. This would allow Milosevic's Montenegrin allies, who were expected to attract at least 30 per cent support in Montenegro, to win all of Montenegro's seats in the federal parliament. Serbia's divided democratic opposition, most of which was then boycotting parliament and thus could not vote against the changes, appeared to be caught off guard by these moves (*IHT*, 7 July 2000, pp. 1, 8). After changing the electoral laws and arrangements to favour himself and the SPS, on 27 July Milosevic used his presidential powers to call for federal presidential and parliamentary as well as local elections to take place 24 September 2000 (*IHT*, 31 July 2000, p. 9).

An opinion poll conducted as late as May 2000 indicated that Milosevic was still Serbia's most popular individual politician (*FT*, 7 July 2000, p. 8) and that 'nearly 40 per cent of Serbs agreed that their leader, while imperfect, was better than any of his foes' (*The Economist*, 15 July 2000, p. 45). By August, however, other polls were indicating that over two-thirds of the electorate wanted Milosevic to be ousted (*IHT*, 31 August 2000, p. 9) and that the DSS leader Vojislav Kostunica would win a 42 per cent share of the vote as the joint candidate of a united opposition, as against 28 per cent for Milosevic (*The Economist*, 5 August 2000, p. 44). Vuk Draskovic told Radio B2-92 of Belgrade on 30 July that, having survived another assassination attempt in June 2000, he was not interested in taking part in the forthcoming elections.

Serbia's economy during and after the 1999 Kosova conflict

Serbia's real GDP fell by 18 per cent in 1999 (see Table 6.7). Even at the artificiall high off cial exchange rates, Serbia's GDP in 1999 was not much more than half its already depressed 1989 level. The recorded unemployment rate was over 30 per cent of the workforce in 1999, but the real rate was nearer 50 per cent (EBRD 2000b: 8). The NATO bombing in 1999 did relatively little damage to Serbian industry (less than 5 per cent of Serbia's industrial capacity was 'flattened'), but Serbia's physica infrastructure (especially bridges) and electricity supplies took a 'hard pounding'(*RCE*, December 2000: 40). A UN environmental-damage-assessment team stated in a report published on 14 October 1999 that there was no evidence that NATO bombing had caused an environmental *catastrophe* in Serbia, but it recommended immediate Western action to help clean up four major 'hot spots' of war-related environmental damage in heavily bombed industrial towns (notably Pancevo, Kragujevac and Bor) in order to protect the health of ordinary citizens, and it complained that NATO had not cooperated with its investigation into NATO's use of depleted uranium weapons (*FT*, 15 October 1999, p. 10).

The annual inflation rate for 1999 (37.1 per cent) was deceptively low, given tha the 1999 budget defcit had been fnanced by printing more paper money. Infationary pressures rose ominously in the second half-year. The government introduced strict price controls which curbed inflation statistically, but that simply induced producer to market their products under new names and with higher prices. In December 1999 China provided Serbia with 300 million dollars in grants and soft loans, but this only sufficed to support the dinar for a few months(*RCE*, April 2000, p. 48; *The Economist*, 5 February 2000, p. 45).

Serbia was unable to sell off state companies to earn foreign currency, partly due to continuing 'international' (i.e., Western) embargoes on trade and investment, while its efforts to collect debts amounting to roughly 3 billion dollars from Iraq and Libya proved fruitless. In the past, Milosevic had shored up political support by heavily subsidizing fuel and food prices. Having exhausted its financial reserves, his regim now blamed the new shortages and resurgent inflation on NATO's bombing campaig and on the panoply of international sanctions against Serbia, appealing to Serbia's long-standing sense of victimhood.

The agricultural sector, which accounted for nearly one-quarter of GDP, was stricken by drought in 2000. Serbia's external debt had risen to 12–14 billion US dollars by 2000, mainly through a build-up of debt-service arrears (EBRD 2000b: 8).

Between 300,000 and 350,000 educated professionals (mainly young adults) had left the FRY during the 1990s (*IHT*, 13 October 1999, p. 5; 25 October 1999, p. 6). The silver lining to this potentially debilitating loss was that it considerably reduced the number of people seeking work within Serbia, while greatly increasing the inflows of remittances from Serbians living in other countries. However, this Serb exodus was in large measure offset by substantial inflows of Serbian refugee from Croatia and Bosnia-Herzegovina, especially in 1995–6. There were up to 650,000 refugees from Bosnia and Croatia in Serbia by 1996 (*FT*, 6 August 1996, p. 7). Even though the FRY and Croatia resumed diplomatic relations in 1996, only 20,000 of the estimated 300,000 Serbs displaced from Croatia returned to their old homes during the late 1990s. Denied citizenship, the right to work, to vote or to own property in Serbia, they survived on handouts and on the charity of relatives and friends (*FT*, 30 December 1999, p. 4). The EBRD estimated in 2000 that there were about 900,000 refugees and internally displaced persons living in the FRY (*Transitions*, 2000, vol. 11, no. 6, p. 39), the vast majority in Serbia rather than in Montenegro.

Endgame: mounting opposition to Milosevic, August to October 2000, and the rise of Vojislav Kostunica

Sixteen opposition parties held a two-day meeting on 6–7 August 2000, aimed at organizing a united front against Milosevic. Fifteen opposition parties formally decided to back the democrat and moderate nationalist Vojislav Kostunica, the ffty-six-year-old leader of the centre-right DSS. Kostunica had begun his career as a university lecturer in constitutional law, but he had been dismissed from the law faculty of the University of Belgrade in 1974 for publicly supporting a senior professor who had been jailed for criticizing the Tito regime and for opposing the Yugoslav confederal constitution of 1974, on the grounds that it was unfair to the Serbs. After Tito's death, he coauthored the frst book that was allowed to be published in Yugoslavia advocating a multiparty system. In 1989, when Milosevic tried to coopt intellectuals and offered to renew employment for those who has been dismissed under Tito, Kostunica was one of the few who refused such blandishments. Instead, Kostunica took up the political f ght against Milosevic and joined with friends, including Zoran Djindjic, in forming the DS and was elected to the federal parliament. However, Kostunica found the DS insufficiently nationalistic and, in 1992, split off to set up his own DSS. He supported the Serb cause in the Croatian and Bosnian wars of the early 1990s and attacked Milosevic for betraying the Bosnian and Croatian Serbs by signing the 1995 Dayton accords (*FT*, 30 September 2000, p. 15;*IHT*, 12 October 2000, p. 8). Although a strong supporter of the rights of Serb minorities during Yugoslavia's dissolution, Kostunica never got involved in paramilitary activities.

For Serbs, Kostunica's virtues were many: 'a reputation for modesty, honesty and principle, a belief in democracy, a career untainted by any previous cooperation with the Milosevic regime, a clear patriotism and sense of nationhood, and a nuanced but sharply critical stance toward the United States and the Western countries that bombed Serbian targets' in 1999. His unassailable patriotism, his criticisms of the ICTY as a crude and corrupt instrument of 'victors' justice', his support for the Kosova Serbs, and his scepticism towards the West (especially the USA) 'made him a good choice for a democratic opposition accused over and over again by Mr Milosevic of being traitors in the pay of Washington and NATO' (*IHT*, 5 September 2000, pp. 1, 4).

Kostunica declared himself to be in favour of a form of state 'truth commission' of independent historians and experts to examine the crimes and victims of all the participants in the Yugoslav wars of the 1990s. He saw the ICTY as 'an instrument of American policy and not of international law'. He criticized the tribunal for refusing to examine the possibility that the rulers of the NATO countries had committed war crimes in authorizing the bombing of civilian targets in Serbia in 1999. He vowed not to hand over Milosevic to the ICTY for trial and refused to say whether he would hand over Radovan Karadzic and Ratko Mladic (*IHT*, 30 September 2000, pp. 1, 5). He promised to 'seek the withdrawal of NATO troops from Kosova' and 'not to cooperate' with the ICTY (*IHT*, 23 September 2000, p. 5).

At the meeting of opposition parties on 6 August 2000, Vuk Draskovic announced that his SPO was adopting the mayor of Belgrade, Vojislav Mihajlovic, as its presiden tial candidate, reversing a previously stated intention to boycott the presidential election. Mihajlovic was the grandson of General Draza Mihailovic, the commander of the Serbian nationalist-cum-royalist Cetnik resistance movement during the early 1940s, who had been executed by the Tito regime in 1946 for alleged cooperation with the Axis occupation forces. Draskovic had written a major biography of Draza Mihajlovic, who was a national hero and martyr in the eyes of many Serbian nationalists and monarchists. The leaders of the new Democratic Opposition of Serbia (DOS) coalition angrily accused Draskovic of conniving with Milosevic to undermine their efforts to unite the opposition parties behind a single presidential candidate and believed that he was angling to strike a deal with Milosevic. DOS supporters hoped that Vojislav Mihailovic, who was little known outside Belgrade, would prove incapable of diverting many votes away from the DOS candidate, Vojislav Kostunica (*IHT*, 7 August 2000, p. 6; *FT*, 7 August 2000, p. 7; *Independent*, 7 August 2000, p. 11).

The SPO announced on 24 August that it had decided to field its own candidate in the federal parliamentary elections (further reversing its previous commitment to a boycott) and not to team up with the DOS (*IHT*, 25 August 2000, p. 7).

The independent media announced on 25 August that Ivan Stambolic, Serbia's former president and Milosevic's erstwhile patron, had disappeared in mysterious circumstances. Stambolic had repeatedly declared that he would not run in the presidential election on 24 September, but he had recently attacked Milosevic in two blistering interviews broadcast in Serbia and Montenegro and was rumoured to be having second thoughts. His absence from politics since Milosevic organized an internal coup against him in late 1987 had given him an image of being above the intrigues and infighting of the opposition parties *The Guardian*, 5 September 2000, p. 13). On the same day, it was announced that, for the first time, Milosevic's wif Mirjana Markovic would stand as a candidate for the lower house of the federal parliament (*The Guardian*, 26 August 2000, p. 20).

In early September Vojislav Seselj announced that the SRS would not back Milosevic in a presidential run-off election, and on 8 September Zoran Lilic, the former

Yugoslav president and a long-time ally of Milosevic, confirmed that he had resigne from all his posts in the SPS (*The Times*, 15 September 2000, p. 17). Such developments generated the impression that key loyalists were dissociating themselves from President Milosevic in the wake of adverse opinion polls and the disappearance of ex-president Ivan Stambolic (*FT*, 22 September 2000, p. 22). The SRS announced on 13 September that it was cutting all ties to the regime. The SRS presidential candidate, Tomislav Nikolic, cited unacceptable levels of corruption in the coterie around Milosevic's wife and electoral malpractice by the SPS.

Meanwhile, the federal electoral commission had ordered the remnants of the independent media to stop distributing what it described as 'political propaganda for the opposition'. The opposition alliance was continually harassed, 'its campaign rallies banned, its grass-roots activists arrested and beaten', while the Milosevic propaganda machine portrayed them as 'traitors and fascists. Ludicrous tales of their alleged plots with NATO were revealed daily, to fuel the collective paranoia' and prepare the ground for more drastic measures against the opposition after the elections (*IHT*, 18 September 2000, p. 8). The most widespread fear was that the FRY constitution was so ambiguous that Milosevic could serve out his term as federal president until July 2001, even if he lost the federal elections (*The Guardian*, 21 September 2000, p. 2).

The Clinton administration announced on 16 September that the USA would be willing to lift its economic sanctions if the DOS coalition were to gain power (*IHT*, 19 September 2000, p. 6). Similarly, on 18 September EU foreign ministers issued a 'message to the Serbian people':

> We reaff rm that a choice leading to democratic change will entail radical change in the EU's policy with regard to Serbia. We will lift the sanctions against the Federal Republic of Yugoslavia; we will support the necessary economic and political reforms by providing Serbia with aid for its reconstruction and support reintegration . . . into the international community.
>
> (*The Guardian*, 19 September 2000, p. 17)

At the same time, a 'war-crimes trial' was initiated in Belgrade against the fourteen Western heads of government or state in countries involved in the NATO bombing of Serbia in 1999. The indictment named 503 civilians, 240 soldiers and 147 policemen killed by NATO bombing. The fourteen Western leaders were pronounced guilty on 21 September and sentenced to twenty years in prison.

Milosevic and Kostunica held campaign rallies in different parts of Belgrade on 20 September. About 150,000 people gathered in the city centre for Kostunica's rally, while Milosevic addressed a mere 15,000 people in a sports stadium (*IHT*, 21 September 2000, p. 6; *Independent*, 22 September 2000, p. 14).

In a televised interview on 21 September, the FRY prime minister Momir Bulatovic served notice that 'Under the constitutional law, the mandate of the president cannot be shortened. It will last until its expiry, which will be until mid-2001 *The Guardian*, 23 September 2000, p. 16). Thus Milosevic probably intended to continue to serve as FRY president even if he lost the federal elections, which looked increasingly likely (*FT*, 23 September 2000, p. 5).

The crucial elections of 24 September 2000

The Milosevic regime refused to allow Western observers into the country to monitor the elections, but it did invite teams from Russia, India and China. According to observers from the parliamentary assembly of the Union of Belarus and Russia, the FRY elections 'met all the requirements of international law' *CDPSP*, 2000, vol. 52, no. 39, p. 4).

The federal parliamentary election

The DOS alliance won over half the seats for Serbia in the chamber of citizens (the lower house) and exactly half the seats for Serbia in the chamber of republics (the upper house). However, the boycott of the federal elections by Montenegro's ruling Democratic Party of Socialists and its pro-independence allies gave the (pro-Serb and pro-Milosevic) Socialist People's Party a walk-over victory in Montenegro's seats in both houses of the federal parliament, thereby enabling Milosevic and his allies to retain overall control of both of these houses (see Table 6.10).

In this way, even though Milosevic lost the presidential election (see below), constitutionally it should have been possible for him to have ceded the federal presidency to Kostunica, while holding on to effective power by using his continued control of the federal parliament to get himself adopted as federal prime minister instead (Cohen 2002: 438). He could also have made use of his continuing control of the federal parliament to change the FRY constitution in order to curtail the powers of the president (Kostunica) while increasing his own powers as prime minister. Given these relatively feasible options, it is somewhat strange that Milosevic opted for the much riskier stratagem of using his influence over the federal electoral commissio to try to override the results of the presidential contest by declaring them invalid and holding a second (run-off) ballot, which he was likely to lose just as resoundingly as the first

6.10 Federal parliamentary election, 24 September 2000

Party/coalition	Chamber of citizens	Chamber of republics
In Serbia (including Kosova)		
The f fteen-party Democratic Opposition of Serbia	59	10
The SPS–Yugoslav United Left (JUL) alliance	44	7
Serbian Radical Party (SRS)	5	2
Alliance of Vojvodina Hungarians	1	0
Serbian Movement of Renewal (SPO)	0	1
In Montenegro		
Socialist People's Party (allied to the SPS)	28	19
Others	1	1

Source: Cohen (2002: 438–9) and *The Times*, 9 October 2000, p. 14.

The local elections held in Serbia

In the local elections, which were held in Serbia alone, the fifteen-party DOS allianc won a landslide victory, taking overall control of ninety towns and cities. In Belgrade the opposition won 96 of the 110 seats in the city council (Cohen 2002: 439).

The federal presidential election

On 25 September the SRS announced that Kostunica had won in the first round, wit 53.5 per cent of the vote, as against 37.9 per cent for Milosevic. However, the ruling SPS claimed that a second round would be needed, contending Kostunica had only won 45 per cent of vote, as against 40 per cent for Milosevic. The JUL, in which Milosevic's wife Mirjana Markovic played a leading role, went even further by claiming that Milosevic had won in the first round (by 56.3 per cent to 31.4 per cen for Kostunica). On 27 September the DOS claimed that the overall distribution of votes (in percentages of the total) had been as shown in Table 6.11(a). The DOS therefore claimed that Kostunica had won a first-round victory and that no run-of was called for. An opposition rally held in Belgrade on 27 September attracted more than 200,000 people, while opposition rallies elsewhere also attacted substantial crowds: Novi Sad, 35,000; Nis, 25,000; Kragujevac, 15,000; Kraljevo, 10,000 (*IHT*, 29 September 2000, p. 4).

However, on 28 September, after vacillating for three days, the official federal election commission (appointed by and responsible to the Milosevic-controlled Yugoslav parliament) claimed that the overall distribution of votes (in percentages of the total) had been as shown in Table 6.11(b).

Thus, according to the federal electoral commission, Kostunica had narrowly failed and a run-off ballot would have to be held on 8 October (*The Times*, 28 September 2000, p. 23). According to opposition members of the federal election commission, it had reduced the number of eligible voters by 600,000 'and made no effort to reconcile its results with those of the opposition' (*IHT*, 29 September 2000, p. 4). In Kosova, Milosevic's supporters claimed that Milosevic had obtained 140,000 votes, but the (NATO-led) KFOR (Kosova Peace Implementation Force) authorities in Kosova

6.11(a) Results of federal presidential election, 24 September 2000, according to the DOS

Candidate	Share of vote (%)
Vojislav Kostunica (Democratic Opposition of Serbia, DOS)	52.54
Slobodan Milosevic (SPS)	35.01
Tomislav Nikolic (Serbian Radical Party, SRS)	6.00
Vojislav Mihailovic (Serb Movement of Renewal, SPO)	2.99
Miroljub Vidojkovic (Affirmative Party	0.93
Invalid votes	2.35

Source: Cohen (2002: 438).

6.11(b) Results of federal presidential election, 24 September 2000, according to the federal electoral commission

Candidate	Share of votes (%)
Vojislav Kostunica (Democratic Opposition of Serbia, DOS)	48.96
Slobodan Milosevic (SPS)	38.62
Tomislav Nikolic (Serbian Radical Party, SRS)	5.79
Vojislav Mihailovic (Serb Movement of Renewal, SPO)	2.90
Miroljub Vidojkovic (Aff rmative Party)	0.92
Invalid votes	2.68

Source: Cohen (2002: 438).

insisted that fewer than 45,000 people had voted, that these had been almost entirely Serb, and that some of the polling stations from which votes were claimed to have come had never even opened (*The Guardian*, 30 September 2000, p. 2; *IHT*, 30 September 2000, p. 5).

The Serbian Orthodox Church (headed by Patriarch Pavle) issued a statement on 28 September addressed to 'Vojislav Kostunica, the elected President of Yugoslavia': 'Vojislav Kostunica and all the people elected together with him, when they take over the control of the state, its parliament and its municipalities, [should] do so in a peaceful and dignified way.' An opposition rally held on the afternoon of 29 Septembe attracted about 20,000 supporters. There were also rallies later on in Belgrade and elsewhere in Serbia. There were reports of some factories, schools and colleges closing, of some taxi drivers and truck drivers blocking roads, and of protests by some state media employees. The DOS alliance called for a campaign of civil disobedience, including a general strike, on 2–6 October.

Kostunica proposed an internationally monitored recount on 29 September, while miners at Serbia's huge open-cast coal mines at Kolubara (30 miles south of Belgrade) went on strike against the regime's attempts to invalidate Kostunica's first-round victory. They were joined on 1 October by coal miners at the Kostolac mine in eastern Serbia. The Kolubara mining complex employed about 17,500 people and provided the coal that generated more than half of Serbia's electricity. The miners claimed that their wages had been reduced from an average of about 150 Deutschmarks a month during the first half of 1999 to 70 Deutschmarks per month in mid-2000

Russia's President Vladimir Putin offered to mediate on 2 October: 'I am prepared to receive in the next few days in Moscow both candidates who have gone through to the second round . . . to discuss means of finding a way out of the curent situation.' However, Milosevic rejected this offer, while Kostunica criticized the Russian policy as 'indecisive and reluctant' and also US policy for 'indirectly bolstering Mr Milosevic by insisting that he remained an indicted war criminal' (*FT*, 3 October 2000, p. 9).

A campaign of civil disobedience began on 2 October, with strikes, rallies and road blocks. Support was patchy on the first day, but was strongest in some provincial towns and cities where the DOS had performed well in the elections. The DOS claimed that on 2 October a computer disk was thrown from a window in the Yugoslav statistics office and that the disk contained the election results from individual polling stations.

Kostunica visited the the Kolubara mining complex on 2 October and was greeted by the striking miners as 'president'. Later that day Milosevic sent the army chief of staff General Nebojsa Pavkovic to the mining complex to order the striking miners to return to work for the good of the nation. Despite variously yelling and cajoling, threatening punishments and promising a 10 per cent rise, General Pavkovic failed to end the strike. In the early hours of 3 October, the miners insisted that they would remain on strike until Milosevic accepted defeat. Later that morning Momcilo Perisic, the former army chief of staff who had been fired by Milosevic and had become a opposition leader, visited the striking miners to encourage them to continue their strike (*IHT*, 4 October 2000, pp. 1, 4). Later that day, the Belgrade prosecutor's office ordere the arrest of thirteen alleged organizers of the miners' strike, while the government warned that

> Any violent behaviour of individuals or groups that threatens citizens' lives, disrupts traffc and prevents industry, schools, institutions and health facilities

from carrying out their normal work, will be prosecuted by law .. . Special measures will be taken against the organizers of these criminal activities. These
measures will also apply to media that are financed from abroad and are breedin
lies, untruths and inciting bloodshed.

(IHT, 4 October 2000, p. 1)

The police made an unsuccessful attempt to take over the Kolubara mines on
4 October. They were foiled by the miners and their allies. The DOS alliance made
various demands, including the publishing of proper results by the constitutional court,
and gave Milosevic an ultimatum to resign by 3 p.m. on 5 October. Strikes spread.
The constitutional court responded by announcing that some of the voting in the
presidential election on 24 September had been annulled (*HT*, 6 October 2000, p. 1).

Serbia's 'October revolution', 5 October 2000

A popular revolution against the Milosevic regime took place on 5 October 2000.
Crucial was the participation of workers, who joined other groups such as students
and other intellectuals. Casualties were low. One demonstrator was killed accidentally
and one man died of a heart attack.

During the morning of 5 October the constitutional court declared that the first
round of the presidential election had been annulled and that a fresh election was
necessary. In Belgrade up to half a million demonstrators surrounded and stormed key
buildings, such as the federal parliament, the state-owned Radio Television Serbia
(RTS) and other electronic media services. Fires were started in the federal parliament
and RTS buildings. The off cial news agency Tanjug began to refer to Kostunica as
'President Kostunica'. The police offered little resistance and the army did not
intervene. Some police and soldiers even sided with the demonstrators.

The seemingly spontaneous storming of the federal parliament and the RTS on
5 October was actually the result of a carefully planned strategy, according to Velimir
Ilic, the mayor of Cacak, an opposition stronghold. At 7.30 a.m. on 5 October, a huge
column of protestors had set off from Cacak to Belgrade, led by Ilic. Most of the
participants were farmers and peasants, but they included off-duty army paratroopers
and police opposed to the Milosevic regime. As they marched, they were joined by
others. By the time the column reached Belgrade it was about 10,000-strong. These
were the people who led the storming of the federal parliament and RTS building.
The police defectors helped to break police cordons, opening the way for the protestors
to invade these symbolic buildings. Ilic nevertheless insisted that his associates who
broke into the federal parliament were not responsible for the f res started there. He
maintained that he did not inform the DOS alliance of his plans, but that he liaised
with the Otpor student movement and with fans of Belgrade's Red Star football club
(*Independent*, 9 October 2000, p. 12). Two off cers in an elite police unit in Belgrade
confirmed that over 100 active or former soldiers had spearheaded the storming of
the federal parliament and the RTS offices in the capital, in concert with sympatheti
police inside the buildings and with Velimir Ilic (*The Guardian*, 9 October 2000, p.
12). Ilic had assembled a core team of tough young men, including off-duty members
of the police and off-duty army paratroopers as well as workers, students and truck
drivers. He claimed that his personal pacts with two special police personnel in
Belgrade and two from Cacak had resulted in major segments of the police in the
capital siding with the demonstrators (*IHT*, 11 October 2000, p. 7).

A speech recorded by Milosevic was broadcast on 6 October:

> I congratulate Mr Kostunica on his electoral victory and I wish much success to all citizens of Yugoslavia. I intend to rest a bit and spend some time with my family and especially with my grandson Marko and after that to help my party gain force and contribute to future prosperity.

It was later revealed that the army chief of staff Nebojsa Pavkovic and senior colleagues had visited Milosevic on 6 October and ordered him to meet Kostunica, while the Russian foreign minister Igor Ivanov and President Putin congratulated Kostunica on his victory in the presidential elections. Igor Ivanov, who met Milosevic in person on 6 October, subsequently reported that during their meeting Milosevic had emphasized that he intended 'to seek a solution in a peaceful and legal manner', and that as the leader of Serbia's largest political party he intended 'to continue to play a political role in the country'. The constitutional court then reversed its previous stance by announcing that Kostunica had been the outright winner in the first round of the presidential election. Belarus offered political asylum to Milosevic. The army formally recognized President Kostunica as commander-in-chief and announced that it would not intervene in Serbian politics unless its bases or personnel were threatened (*EEN*, 2000, vol. 13, no. 1, p. 7).

Kostunica started putting together an interim ruling structure called the 'crisis committee for Yugoslavia', a quasi-government in which he invited representatives of Montenegro to participate. He also reaffirmed his election promises to hold full democratic elections within a year and to ask the newly elected federal parliament to write a new constitution (*FT*, 7 October 2000, pp. 1, 6, 12). Kostunica was formally sworn in as president on 7 October 2000.

Milosevic's brutish son Marko Milosevic, a millionaire underworld figure, fled fr a lynch mob in his hometown of Pozarevac, south-east of Belgrade, while his business properties were being looted (*The Guardian*, 9 October 2000, p. 12). He flew with hi wife and infant son on a JAT f ight to Moscow, where his uncle Borislav Milosevic was the FRY ambassador to Russia. He subsequently flew with his family to Beijing where he tried to enter China with a diplomatic passport but without a valid visa, as China and the FRY had an agreement allowing holders of diplomatic passports to enter each other's countries without visas. However, he was refused permission to enter, whereupon he and his family returned to Moscow (*FEER*, 19 October 2000, p. 14). Like Russia, China had already belatedly recognized Kostunica's victory.

Opposition activists took control of the national bank, the Serbian police and the customs off ce on 7–8 October, taking them out of the hands of Milosevic supporters. Zarko Korac, a leading member of DOS, admitted that the DOS was directly involved in these moves (*The Times*, 11 October 2000, p. 18).

The (Montenegrin) federal prime minister Momir Bulatovic and the Serbian interior minister Vlajko Stojilkovic resigned on 9 October 2000, while the Skupstina agreed to hold Serbian parliamentary elections on 17 December 2000. The powers of the federal authorities were much more modest than those of the Serbian authorities, who controlled most state revenues, the police and the constitutional court judges, who in turn played major roles in adjudicating the many disputes which arose (*FT*, 10 October 2000, p. 8).

As promised, the EU unconditionallly lifted most of the remaining sanctions against Serbia. Nevertheless, the EU maintained a freeze on state assets as well as a selective visa restriction in an attempt to prevent Milosevic and his cronies from escaping abroad with misappropriated Serbian assets (*IHT*, 10 October 2000, p. 1). The EU also offered aid estimated at about 2 billion US dollars for 2001 (*IHT*, 10 October 2000, p.1; *The Guardian*, 10 October 2000, p. 21).

From 9 October onward there were reports of growing numbers of employees turning against pro-Milosevic managers and demanding their resignation. There were forcible takeovers of the major banks and nearly all key companies and factories remaining in pro-Milosevic hands, as well as the state customs office. 'Eager to shor up his power base', Kostunica endeavoured 'to install his own supporters in charge of the country's most important institutions, including the police, judiciary, banks and state-run companies' (*IHT*, 11 October 2000, pp. 1, 7). Workers, rebels and opportunists rushed 'to seize businesses, assets and lucrative senior jobs in an uncontrolled raid on the power of the old regime'. Workers stormed the offices of factories, bank and the civil service, using threats and force to expel their old bosses (*The Times*, 11 October 2000, p. 18). At Belgrade University the teaching staff and students expelled the rector and other senior administrators (*FT*, 11 October 2000, p. 8). On 11 October Kostunica lamented that he was 'having almost as much trouble from my friends as from my enemies' and that some of the eighteen-party DOS coalition were making policy statements which had not been cleared with him and were using extra-legal procedures to take control of certain ministries and companies hitherto run by cronies of Milosevic. 'I cannot justify all that is going on … . On the surface there is a peaceful democratic transition, but below the surface there is a kind of volcano, not so controlled.' The wayward members of DOS were not so much eroding Kostunica's authority as compromising it. In particular, Kostunica and his aides complained that the Democratic Party led by Zoran Djindjic was trying to consolidate the popular revolt against Milosevic in ways that could sow confusion. The most blatant example was Djindjic's effort to put an ally and well-known businessman in charge of the customs office after ousting the old minister. The appointment of Djindjic's ally provoked an uproar among other political leaders in the DOS and was rescinded within a day. Djindjic also announced measures which Kostunica had not approved. For example, Djindjic had stated that the army chief of staff General Nebojsa Pavkovic would be dismissed, whereas Kostunica declared on 11 October that he had no inten tion of ousting General Pavkovic, who had became a popular hero for directing Serbian resistance to the NATO offensive against Serbia in April–June 1999. Kostunica stated he had no interest in stirring up a politically quiescent army. Djindjic had also announced that the economist Miroljub Labus would become provisional federal prime minister at the head of a government of technocrats, whereas Kostunica stated on 11 October that he would nominate a prime minister from Montenegro, as the constitution required (*IHT*, 12 October 2000, pp. 1, 4).

The SPS declared on 11 October that it intended to continue to govern Serbia until September 2001 since it had been elected on a four-year mandate and still headed Serbia's legally constituted government (there having been no parliamentary or presidential elections in Serbia at this time). The Serbian government would therefore 'ignore all the decisions of the so-called crisis committees'. State institutions, especially the prosecutor's office and the police, would 'take urgent action in accord ance with the law against the organisers and perpetrators of illegal actions'. The Serbian government authorized the Serbian prime minister Mirko Marjanovic to take over control of the interior ministry, which in turn controlled the police. It also demanded the reinstatement of four ministers and the restoration of its control over the state television and radio services.

The USA lifted its oil embargo and flight ban on Serbia on 12 October. James O'Brien, the special adviser to President Clinton for the Balkans, met President Kostunica, who affirmed that he would respect the November 1995 Dayton accord (which he had formerly condemned as a betrayal of Serb interests) as well as UN resolutions providing for ethnic Albanian self-government in Kosova. Kostunica also declared that 'If the will of the people of Montenegro is to not belong to the federation, this will be respected' (*IHT*, 13 October 2000, p. 11).

The increasingly divided SPS called for an exceptional congress on 25 November 2000, with some members openly calling for the removal of Milosevic as party leader.

On 14 October, after a week of talks between representatives of Kostunica, the DOS and the SPS-led Serbian government, an agreement was reached to share power in Serbia until new elections were held there on 24 December. Seven representatives of the SPS (including the president of Serbia, Milan Milutinovic) consented to this, but they also emphasized that they needed to consult with their party before they could sign a formal accord to this effect. Under this provisional agreement, the SPS-led government gave up its previous insistence on regaining control of the police and the interior and justice ministries (*IHT*, 16 October 2000, p. 2).

Kostunica attended an EU meeting hosted by the French government in Biarritz on 14 October. The EU promised emergency aid worth 200 million euros (170 million US dollars), to be used for purchase of food, medicine, fuel and similar items. Kostunica announced that he favoured changing the name of the FRY to Serbia-Montenegro and allowing the citizens of Serbia and Montenegro to express their wishes in a referendum on whether to remain within a federal union (*IHT*, 16 October 2000, p. 4). The next day, Crown Prince Aleksandar Karadjordjevic visited Belgrade for a meeting with President Kostunica (*The Times*, 16 October 2000, p. 17).

A transitional power-sharing arrangement for Serbia was formally agreed on 16 October. Fresh elections for the Serbian parliament were to be held on 23 December 2000. The SPS would retain the premiership but the premier would have to take decisions in consensus with deputy prime ministers from the DOS and the SPO. State television would be similarly run. The ministries of justice, fnance, information and the interior (the last of which was in charge of around 85,000 police) were to be jointly controlled by the DOS, SPS and SPO. The SRS refused to take part in this arrangement. No mention was made of the president of Serbia, Milan Milutinovic, whose mandate was not due to expire until 2002, nor of the minister of defence and the army high command.

President Kostunica visited Montenegro on 17 October, but he failed to persuade Montenegro's President Djukanovic to take part in a new federal government. Djukanovic applauded the movement towards liberal democracy in Serbia but insisted that he and his party would only take part in joint Serb-Montenegrin institutions after the two republics had redef ned their mutual relationship, which in turn would have to await the outcome of the Serbian parliamentary elections on 23 December. Nevertheless, Djukanovic stated that he and Kostunica had agreed to continue talks on the new relationship between their respective republics and he referred to Kostunica as president (in contrast to the previous month, when Djukanovic and the Montenegrin government had denounced the federal elections as illegal and had refused to recognize the election of Kostunica as president). At the same time, however, Djukanovic remained angry at plans by the DOS alliance to offer the federal premiership to his Montenegrin rivals in the Socialist People's Party, who had been long-standing supporters of Milosevic (*IHT*, 18 October 2000, p. 4). Miodrag Vukovic, a senior adviser to Djukanovic, warned: 'The present federation cannot be saved. What we want is a new partnership involving cooperation between two states. The new system could be something between a union and a confederation.' If that could not be attained, the only acceptable option would be complete independence (*IHT*, 19 October 2000, p. 7). On 27 October, Djukanovic wrote a letter to the UN secretary-general Kofi Annan proposing that Montenegro and Serbia should occupy separate seats in the UN. Montenegrin sovereignty, Djukanovic wrote, was the foundation 'of our initial proposal to President Kostunica, namely the proposal that acclaims the relationship of Montenegro and Serbia as an alliance of two internationally recognised states' (*IHT*, 22 November 2000, p. 5).

On 16 October the German federal intelligence service (BND) published a file o Milosevic alleging that he remained a 'boss of bosses' at the apex of a criminal organization that had salted away at least 100 million US dollars in purloined funds abroad. The file named a dozen senior Serbian politicians and over forty other peopl allied to Milosevic as members of a maf a that had bled the FRY dry for a decade or more. It alleged that Milosevic and his entourage constituted an organized criminal structure engaged in drug-dealing, money-laundering and other criminal acts. 'The near total control of key economic posts by Milosevic followers opened opportunities for illegal capital transfer for personal enrichment and f nancing for political plans – weapons purchases – and served as a camouflage for criminal activity – drug trade, the file claimed. Among the Milosevic cronies named in the report were the speake of the Skupstina, Dragan Tomic, the Serbian prime minister Mirko Marjanovic, and the former energy minister Dragan Kostic. The imposition of international sanctions on the FRY since 1992 had fostered 'massive smuggling operations . . controlled by Milosevic and his cronies, who made vast prof ts from it' (*Independent*, 17 October 2000, p. 13). The BND alleged that the sums involved 'could not have been obtained legally' and that Milosevic's private assets extended to Russia, China, Cyprus, Greece, Lebanon and South Africa. In Switzerland alone, 'it estimated his holdings at $100 million' (*The Guardian*, 17 October 2000, p. 15).

Kostunica visited Bosnia on 22 October 2000. This was the f rst such visit by a Serbian leader since 1992. He frst went to Trebinje in the Republika Srpska to attend, in a private capacity, the reburial of a Serb nationalist poet (a*Cetnik* supporter), who had died in the USA in 1943. Kostunica then visited Sarajevo, where he reaffirme his new-found support for the Dayton accords. He sought the rapid normalization of relations between Sarajevo and Belgrade (*HT*, 23 October 2000, p. 4), but he offered no apologies for Serb atrocities in Bosnia between 1992 and 1995.

The Skupstina approved an interim Serbian government headed by Milomir Minic, deputy chairman of the SPS, on 24 October. This lasted until after the December 2000 elections in Serbia.

On 25–26 October President Kostunica attended a summit of Balkan leaders in Skopje, at which the FRY was admitted into the Stability Pact for South-eastern Europe.

President Kostunica visited Russia on 27 October. President Putin congratulated him on having managed to lead Serbia out of a difficult situation without bloodshe and out of international isolation and promised a rapid resumption of the Russian energy deliveries to Serbia, which had been stopped earlier that year because Serbia owed Russia's natural gas monopoly Gazprom 300 million US dollars. Serb official estimated that to survive the winter Serbia urgently needed 600 million dollars in 'energy assistance'. Kostunica stated that 'Half the country's population is living without electricity and heating.' He proposed swapping commodities for the gas debt (*IHT*, 28 October 2000, p. 5). President Putin and Kostunica agreed to establish a group of experts to resolve the problems (*FT*, 28 October 2000, p. 10).

The FRY was readmitted to the UN on 1 November 2000. The USA, the UK, France and Germany restored normal diplomatic relations with Serbia on 17 November. President Kostunica went to the Monetenegrin capital Podgorica on 2 November to attend a meeting of the FRY supreme defence council, which President Djukanovic attended for the first time in years

The interim federal government headed by Zoran Zizic, 4 November 2000 to 29 June 2001

The federal parliament approved a new federal government headed by Zoran Zizic, the deputy leader of Montenegro's pro-Serb (and hitherto pro-Milosevic) Socialist People's Party, on 4 November 2000. Of the sixteen cabinet posts, the DOS was awarded nine (including the economics, foreign affairs and internal affairs portfolios). The other seven went to Montenegro's Socialist People's Party, including the posts of prime minister, defence minister and f nance minister. Djukanovic's Democratic Party of Socialists (DPS) was offered several posts, but declined them. Miroljub Labus, an American-trained economist who chaired the group of opposition economists and policy experts known as G17 Plus (which had drawn up the DOS economic programme), became the deputy prime minister responsibile for economic affairs. Goran Svilanovic, leader of the Civic Alliance and a long-time human-rights activist, became the foreign minister. Civic Alliance was the legal brain of the DOS and had been the most consistent anti-war party in Serbia since 1991. Zoran Zivkovic, the DOS mayor of Nis, became the interior minister.

Riots broke out in several Serbian prisons on 5 November and spread more widely on 7 November. The inmates demanded better conditions and that they should benefi from the amnesty promised by President Kostunica to Serbia's political prisoners, most of whom were ethnic Albanians from Kosova. Ethnic Albanians refused to participate in the riots, whereupon Kostunica announced an amnesty law for the hundreds of Kosovars imprisoned during the Kosova war of March–June 1999. The law was also to apply to political prisoners sentenced by the Milosevic regime for alleged 'terrorism' and to thousands of Serbian draft dodgers and deserters. The riots seemingly began after Serb prisoners heard that some 400 ethnic Albanians, roughly half of those still in Serbian jails, were being quietly released (*Independent*, 8 November 2000, p. 15).

A group of former senior members of the SPS launched a new Democratic Socialist Party on 20 November, but the same day Milosevic attended a televised meeting with SPS party colleagues, at which he made an appeal to SPS supporters to rally around him to 'save' the FRY from total disintegration. Serbia's president, Milan Milutinovic, who had been regarded as ready to break with Milosevic, was very noticeably present at the meeting (*The Times*, 22 November 2000, p. 21). At the special congress of the SPS in Belgrade on 25 November 2000, Milosevic was re-elected as the leader of the party. He was the sole candidate and obtained 85 per cent of the votes of the 2,300 delegates present (*Independent*, 27 November 2000, p. 15).

The FRY was formally invited to take part in an EU–Balkan summit meeting held in Zagreb on 24 November 2000, at which the Republic of Macedonia signed an SAA with the EU and Croatia formally opened negotiations towards an SAA. Kosova was represented at the summit by Bernard Kouchner, but there were no Kosovar representatives in attendance (*The Times*, 25 November 2000, p. 24). The EU had assumed prime responsibility for promoting reconstruction and stability in the Balkans and was offering the western Balkans – Macedonia, Croatia, Bosnia, Yugoslavia and Albania – assistance amounting to 4.65 billion euros from 2000 to 2006, in addition to the 200 million euros in emergency aid for energy, food and medicine which it had offered to Serbia to help it get through the winter of 2000–1. The EU assured Serbia's neighbours that the 200 million euros in emergency aid which Serbia had begun to receive was coming out of a special EU reserve*(The Economist*, 25 November 2000, p. 63).

The FRY was readmitted to the OSCE on 27 November 2000. In December 2000 the IMF readmitted the FRY (*FT*, 8 January 2001, p. 23) and the EBRD decided to allow the FRY to become a member with effect from 2001, when it would open a Belgrade office and become the first international financial institution ther *IHT*, 30 December 2000, p. 13).

On 8 December, Mladjan Dinkic, the governor of the FRY central bank, accused the Milosevic regime of having spirited 4 billion US dollars' worth of assets out of Serbia during the 1990s, mainly via banks in Cyprus (*The Guardian*, 9 December 2000, p. 25).

Elections to the Serbian Skupstina, 23 December 2000

On a disappointingly low electoral turn-out (58.8 per cent), the eighteen-party DOS coalition won nearly the two-thirds of seats needed to change the constitution. The results for parties which crossed the 5 per cent threshold are shown in Table 6.12.

6.12 Serbian parliamentary election, 23 December 2000

Party	Share of votes (%)	Seats
Democratic Opposition of Serbia (DOS)	64.4	176[1]
Socialist Party of Serbia (SPS)	13.5	37
Serbian Radical Party (SRS)	8.5	23
Serbian Unity Party (established by Arkan)	5.3	1

Note:
1. The two main components were the Democratic Party (DS) led by Zoran Djindjic (47 seats) and the Democratic Party of Serbia (DSS) led by Vojislav Kostunica (45 seats).

Source: Cohen (2002: 4).

The DOS-led Serbian government headed by Zoran Djindjic, 25 January 2001 to 12 March 2003

The formal inauguration of a DOS-led reformist government was frozen on 2 January 2001, when, following complaints from the opposition parties, the supreme court ruled that fresh elections had to be held on 10 January at nineteen of the country's 8,700 polling stations. However, the results merely confirmed the 23 December results (*IHT*, 12 January 2001, p. 4). The newly elected Skupstina convened for the first tim on 23 January. It approved a reform-minded DOS-led government headed by the DS leader Zoran Djindjic on 25 January. Djindjic promised transparency, the rule of law and economic liberalization (*FT*, 26 January 2001, p. 7).

During a visit to Belgrade on 25 January, the ICTY chief prosecutor Carla del Ponte rejected Serbian accusations that the use of cluster bombs and depleted-uranium munitions by NATO in its air strikes against Serbia during 1999 constituted a war crime. She maintained that there was no scientifi evidence to justify a war-crimes inquiry into NATO's use of such weapons in the Balkans: 'At this time their use is legal' (*Independent*, 26 January 2001, p. 13; *The Guardian*, 26 January 2001, p. 14). On the other hand, she was insistent that Milosevic should be investigated in relation to the deaths of the sixteen Serbian RTS employees killed by NATO bombs on 23 April 1999, because she was satisfied Milosevic had been adequately forewarned o this intended NATO air strike and had failed to get the building evacuated*The Times*, 27 January 2001, p. 16).

After her visit, Mrs del Ponte reported that 'Belgrade will not cooperate. They told me that we have no role there. If Slobodan Milosevic is ever to be tried it will never be in The Hague, only in Belgrade' (*IHT*, 1 February 2001, p. 8).

President Kostunica was in the process of setting up a Serbian war-crimes tribunal in Belgrade, which he clearly envisaged as an adequate and legitimate alternative to trying indicted Serbian war criminals at the ICTY in The Hague (*IHT*, 3 February 2001, p. 6). If the main purpose of holding such trials was to help heal social wounds and help Serbs to face up to the crimes committed by their compatriots and come to terms with these crimes, it would indeed have been far more effective and beneficia to have tried those accused of war crimes in Serbia, in accordance with Serbian standards of justice. Organizing trials far away, in accordance with alien procedures and standards of justice, largely defeats what should be the main purpose of the exercise. The presidential Truth and Reconciliation Commission was officially opened on 2 April, with a brief to examine the causes of the conicts in the Yugoslav lands during the 1990s (*IHT*, 4 April 2001, p. 5). However, this made it much more academic and bookish and much less effective in promoting the healing of social wounds and social reconciliation than the famous 'truth and reconciliation process' inaugurated by Archbishop Desmond Tutu in South Africa at the end of the apartheid regime. It started its work on 19 April.

Economic affairs after Serbia's revolution of 5 October 2000

In the immediate aftermath of the revolution of 5 October 2000, Serbia's inhabitants had to endure prolonged electricity shortages and blackouts and a sweeping price liberalization that raised the monthly inflation rate to 27 per cent (*IHT*, 14 November 2000, p. 7). Half of the workforce was unemployed and a third of the population lived below the officially determined subsistence level (*BCE*, May 2001, pp. 45–6). Positive economic growth had resumed (under Milosevic) in 2000, but in 2001 the GDP of the FRY was still only half the 1989 level (EBRD 2002b: 58). Serbia's largest enterprises were still 'largely unreformed and . . . characterised by substantial losses . . . widespread inter-enterprise arrears and barter arrangements'. Serbia still had 'no effective bankruptcy procedures' and, while there was a competition law, it had not yet been applied (EBRD 2000b: 9).

The new federal government, controlled by reformers from mid-October 2000, swiftly 'stabilized the currency, initiated foreign trade liberalization and abolished the system of preferential customs duties' (*FT*, 27 December 2000, p. 6). It declared the dinar to be fully convertible on 15 December 2000 and introduced a new series of bank notes (*EEN*, 2001, vol. 13, no. 2, p. 6). The multiple exchange-rate regime

was replaced by a managed float and current-account convertibility. The central
bank unified the exchange rates at roughly 30 dinars to the Deutschmark, close to th
black-market rate (EBRD 2001b: 142). In January 2001 the central bank announced
that the dinar exchange rate would be closely tied to that of the euro (EBRD 2003a:
80).

In January 2001 the Serbian finance minister Bozidar Djelic started to prepare
detailed economic programme in time for an international donors' conference which
was hosted by the EU and the World Bank in June 2001. The Djindjic government
initiated a review of earlier privatizations. The aim was to reverse or rectify numerous
'insider privatizations' and management buy-outs, which had given Milosevic's
cronies and the managers of publicly owned enterprises the possibility of acquiring
companies at knock-down prices. The government intended to decide what to do with
each company on a case-by-case basis (*FT*, 26 January 2001, p. 7).

The Serbian budget adopted in March 2001 set a public-sector deficit target of
per cent of GDP, compared with 13 per cent of GDP in 2000. To this end, public
expenditure was to be slashed, in a bid to reduce the annual inflation rate from 11
per cent in 2000 to 30 per cent in 2001. The government also froze ministers' salaries
and introduced salary caps for the public sector. The number of taxes was reduced
from 250 to 6, and new penalties were introduced for tax evasion (*BCE*, May 2001,
pp. 45–6).

Early in 2001 the World Bank estimated that the FRY would need to find 20.5
billion US dollars in external financing over the next five years in order to recov
from a decade of underinvestment, international isolation and war. The government
aimed for 5 per cent economic growth and 30 per cent inflation per annum in 2001

By mid-2001 almost all prices, other than those of bread, f our, electricity, water
and gas, had been liberalized. These measures were accompanied by strict macro-
economic stabilization policies, enforced by the central bank (EBRD 2001b: 20).
During 2001–2 the energy sector underwent major restructuring, including long-
delayed tariff increases. The average price of electricity was raised by 60 per cent in
April 2001, by 40 per cent in June 2001 and by 15 per cent in October 2001, in order
to bring charges closer to cost recovery levels.

The international donors' conference hosted by the World Bank and EU on 29 June
2001 pledged 1.28 billion US dollars in aid to the FRY, exceeding the original target
1.25 billion US dollars. The World Bank estimated that 1.3 million Serbs, or 12 per
cent of the population, lived in absolute poverty. Miroljub Labus, the deputy prime
minister in charge of economic reform and leader of the G17 Plus party, argued that
the FRY also needed substantial relief on its 12.2 billion dollar foreign debt and would
need a further 3 billion US dollars in economic assistance over the next four years
(*FT*, 30 June 2001, p. 1).

The ministers directly responsible for economic reform sought to distance them -
selves from the constant destructive feuding and bickering between President
Kostunica and Prime Minister Djindjic. They garnered widespread praise from
international financial organizations for the speed and effectiveness with which the
overhauled public finances, increased transparency and reformed the tax system
(*Transitions*, 2001, vol. 12, no. 2, pp. 35–6*FT*, 28 June 2001, p. 8). A firm clampdow
on cigarette- and petrol-smuggling boosted budget receipts and made lower tax rates
feasible, resulting in a 10 per cent increase in real wages in 2001. For the first time i
over ten years, pensions and wages were paid on time. Serbia, a haven for smuggling
into Europe, saw black-market sales drop from a 50 per cent market share in 2000 to

about 17 per cent in 2001 (*FT*, 4 October 2001, p. 10). A new labour law passed in December 2001 made it easier to hire and fire employees

The government and the central bank were able to introduce full current-account convertibility in May 2002 by abolishing all restrictions on payments and transfers for international transactions, other than some controls on short-term capital transactions (*FT*, 17 May 2002, p. 7).

Non-economic matters, 2001–2

The Djindjic government placed Slobodan Milosevic under twenty-four-hour police surveillance/protection from 1 February 2001. Moreover, a law adopted on 13 February 2001 curtailed the privileges of Serbian ex-presidents, thereby stripping Milosevic of the immunity from prosecution and many of the material benef ts which he had been hoping to enjoy. Henceforth it would be possible to strip ex-presidents of such privileges if they were sentenced to more than six months in prison by any court. The law provided only for a single security officer and one secretary to be placed at th disposal of a former president – no family members were to enjoy any privileges. The previous law on privileges had been introduced in 1998. It gave former Serbian presidents and all members of their families a lifelong entourage of dozens of state-paid bodyguards and secretaries and benefits covering all of their needs for a lifetim (*Independent*, 12 February 2001, p. 12). On 14 February the Serbian Skupstina repealed the restrictive and repressive public-information law enacted during Milosevic's media crackdown in 1998. It also voted to replace dozens of supreme court and municipal court judges, public prosecutors and other judicial officials. Some of these judicia officials asked to be relieved of their duties, but those who remained loyal to the Milosevic regime were fired *IHT*, 15 February 2001, p. 5).

The former head of RTS and close associate of Milosevic, Dragoljub Milanovic, was detained on 13 February, on suspicion having failed to act on an advance warning of the NATO air strikes on the RTS offices in Belgrade, in which sixteen of his staff were killed by NATO bombs on 29 April 1999 *[ndependent*, 14 February 2001, p. 16). He was released from detention on 23 April without charges being fled (*IHT*, 24 April 2001, p. 5), but on 2 August 2001 he was formally charged with causing the deaths of sixteen of his staff by deliberately failing to evacuate the RTS office when forewarned of the imminent NATO airstrike (*Daily Telegraph*, 3 August 2001, p. 18).

Radomir Markovic, the former head of Serbian state security, was arrested on 24 February in connection with investigations into the alleged attempt to kill Vuk Draskovic in a staged road accident on 3 October 1999. Branko Djuric, the former chief of police in Belgrade, and another policeman were also arrested.

The federal parliament passed legislation on 27 February to restore property which had been expropriated from the Karadjordjevic family (the former Yugoslav royal family) by Tito's Communist regime in March 1947 and to restore the family's Yugoslav citizenship (*EEN*, 2001, vol. 13, no. 3, p. 5). The family had fled to Londo in April 1941, when Nazi Germany invaded Yugoslavia. Three members were still alive: Crown Prince Aleksandar, his aunt Princess Jelisaveta, and his uncle Prince Aleksandar. Crown Prince Aleksandar was born in London in 1945 at Claridges Hotel, where the British government of the day had proclaimed Room 212 to be 'Yugoslav territory' so that he would be born a Yugoslav, but he had not visited Serbia until 1991. The exiled King Petar had died in 1970. Yugoslav citizenship was formally restored to Crown Prince Aleksandar on 12 March 2001, and in July 2001 Premier Djindjic informed him that the way was clear for his family to return and live in the Stari Dvor (Old Palace) and the Beli Dvor (White Palace) in Belgrade's fashionable Dedinje suburb (*The Times*, 13 March 2001, p. 20; 10 July 2001, p. 11).

On 28 February 2001 the Belgrade prosecutor's office initiated official investigations into allegations that Milosevic had smuggled gold worth 1.1 million US dollars from Serbia to Switzerland, notionally in the name of Greek and Cypriot firms, betwee 21 September and 2 November 2000. Inquiries were also under way into Milosevic's purchase of the Villa Mir, a very upmarket house which had been built for Tito in the chic Belgrade suburb of Dedinje in 1979 (*IHT*, 1 March 2001, p. 7; *The Economist*, 3 March 2001, p. 48).

A full bilateral political and economic cooperation agreement between the FRY and the Republika Srpska was signed on 5 March 2001 during a visit by President Kostunica to Banja Luka. This Serbian 'cosying up' to the Republika Srpska did not go down well in the West.

NATO decided on 8 March 2001 to allow Yugoslav (Serb) security forces to re-enter a small section of the buffer zone, the so-called the 'ground safety zone' (GSZ), in the borderlands between Kosova, 'Serbia proper' and the Republic of Macedonia (ROM). The NATO secretary-general George Robertson presented this as part of a gradual reduction in NATO commitments in the GSZ, which he claimed was being 'exploited by ethnic Albanian extremists as a base for attacking Serb policemen and for crossing between Kosova and Macedonia to attack Macedonian police' (*FT*, 9 March 2001, p. 20; 10 March 2001, p. 7). On 12 March NATO conf rmed that a limited number of Yugoslav army and ministry of interior troops would be allowed into the Presevo valley, a largely Albanian-inhabited area on Serbia's border with the ROM. A temporary cease-fire agreement was signed by the commanders of the liberation army of Presevo, Mevedja and Bujanovac (*The Times*, 13 March 2001, p. 21). This was another step towards the international rehabilitation of post-Milosevic Serbia.

Blagoje Simic, a former Bosnian Serb mayor, flew from Belgrade to surrender to the ICTY on 12 March 2001. Having adopted Yugoslav citizenship, he became the first Yugoslav citizen to give himself up in this way. Vladan Batic, Serbia's justice minister, announced on 20 March that Serbia would take steps to transfer non-Yugoslav citizens indicted for war crimes by the ICTY. Speaking after a meeting with Carla del Ponte, Batic also announced that he expected several more indictees to turn themselves in voluntarily. The USA had threatened Serbia with economic sanctions unless it began to cooperate with the ICTY by 31 March (*FT*, 21 March 2001, p. 10). Milomir Stakic, the Bosnian Serb former mayor of Prijedor in Bosnia, was arrested in Serbia on 23 March 2001 and handed over to the ICTY. He was wanted under a sealed indictment and was the f rst indictee to have been surrendered to the ICTY by the FRY authorities (*The Guardian*, 24 March 2001, p. 17). His arrest and extradition were apparently carried out without informing President Kostunica, who had repeatedly pointed out that extradition was illegal under the FRY constitution (*The Guardian*, 31 March 2001, p. 14).

In late March 2001 eight of Slobodan Milosevic's former associates were detained by police on charges of corruption, including Uros Suvakovic, a former head of Serbian state security, and Nikola Curcic, a former deputy head of the security police. The arrests brought to about fifteen the number of Milosevic's former associates held i custody (*The Guardian*, 28 March 2001, p. 11).

On 31 March the US government declared its readiness to certify that the FRY had started cooperating with the ICTY, thus meeting the requirements of US law and allowing US economic assistance to resume. The US Congress had earmarked 100 million US dollars for the FRY in 2000, half of it without conditions. Without certification, Yugoslavia would forfeit the other 50 million US dollars. The certification la demanded full compliance with the Dayton accords (*IHT*, 30 March 2001, p. 5).

Following a protracted exchange of gunfire between police and Milosevic's supporters in which no one was killed, Slobodan Milosevic was arrested at his Belgrade villa in the early hours of 1 April 2001 and taken to prison. Milosevic had declared that he would 'not go to jail alive' and had threatened to kill himself, his wife and his daughter, but negotiations proved effective. Milosevic's wife Mirjana and their daughter Marija remained at the villa. Later that day the Serbian justice minister Vladan Batic announced that Milosevic would be charged with abuse of power and fnancial corruption. The indictment stated that there was 'grounded suspicion' that Milosevic had 'committed crimes with the intention of securing benef ts for himself and a certain number of persons, to secure to his SPS party property and other benefits wit the aim of preserving that political party in power'. The indictment centred on 'the diversion of funds from customs accounts from 1994 onwards, supposedly to fund state companies, which resulted in illegal cash payments' to unnamed individuals (*FT*, 2 April 2001, p. 7). Milosevic also faced charges of organizing an armed group of people and inciting them to shoot at the police during the thirty-hour siege at the Villa Mir. The police also prepared criminal charges against Milosevic's daughter Marija, who had fired a pistol as the police drove her father away. Those arrested included officials of the SPS and the JUL, who were in possession of 'a small arsena of weapons and ammunition' (*IHT*, 3 April 2001, p. 5).

In court on 2 April 2001, Milosevic denied the charges of embezzlement from the state, but he admitted for the f rst time that he had covertly funded the Bosnian Serb and Croatian Serb armies during the 1990s:

> The investigation document states that I incited the highest ofĕials of the federal government to commit illegal acts and acquire gain for others from 1994 until 5 October 2000. But the people who profited were solely our state and people the defence of our country and economy . . [The money was] not stolen by anyone . . . As for the funds spent on weapons and ammunition and the other needs of the Bosnian Serb Republic Army and the Croatian Serb Republic Army, as these were state secrets they could not be shown in the budget, which is a public document. The same is true of the expenses for equipping the security forces and counter-terrorist forces.

However, the court turned down his appeal (*The Guardian*, 4 April 2001, p. 14; *The Times*, 3 April 2001, p. 15). The FRY asked Interpol to issue an international warrant for the arrest of Milosevic's son Marko in April (*IHT*, 5 April 2001, p. 5).

The US state department announced on 2 April that the USA would continue economic assistance to Serbia. The immediate effects were to secure the release of the above-mentioned 50 million US dollars of US aid and US support for Serbian membership of the World Bank and for a 260-million-dollar loan under negotiation with the IMF. But the USA also warned that, if the FRY did not cooperate with the ICTY, it would withhold support from the proposed international donors' conference to help rebuild the Serbian economy (*FT*, 3 April 2001, pp. 8, 18).

The registrar of the ICTY formally presented the Serbian authorities with a warrant for the arrest of Slobodan Milosevic on 5 April, in connection with the atrocities allegedly committed by Serbian security forces against ethnic Albanians in Kosova in 1998 and 1999. However, the Serbian justice minister Vladan Batic stated that he could not accept the warrant and redirected the ICTY registrar to the federal justice minister Momcilo Grubac, who on 6 April undertook to serve the warrant on Milosevic (*IHT*, 6 April 2001, p. 8; 7 April 2001, p. 2). Protestors led by Otpor also forced Mirjana Markovic and Marija Milosevic to leave the Milosevic family home in Pozarevac on 6 April (*The Guardian*, 10 April 2001, p. 14). On 12 April Milosevic was rushed from Belgrade's central prison to a military hospital complaining of chest pains, but army doctors found no evidence of heart disease (*IHT*, 13 April 200, p. 5), and he was returned to prison the next day. A Belgrade court delivered the ICTY indictment against Milosevic to his Belgrade prison cell on 3 May, but he refused to accept the document, which was left attached to the cell door (*IHT*, 4 May 2001, p. 12).

Tens of thousands of Serbs were granted rights of access to hitherto-secret police dossiers from 2 June 2001. Under a special decree, the Serbian government decided to make available to the public the files of so-called 'internal enemies, extremists and terrorists', as defned by the former Milosevic regime, including the former oppo sition leaders who were now in government, opposition sympathizers, prominent intellectuals, aid workers and journalists. Files had also been kept on people who contacted foreigners or frequently travelled abroad. In all, about 40,000–50,000 file were expected to be made available to the public, but analysts warned that Radomir Markovic (the former head of the state security police) had had time to destroy many key documents because he had been allowed to remain in office until January 2001, even though Milosevic had been deposed on 5 October 2000 (*Independent*, 2 June 2001, p. 15).

In an apparent reversal of his previous uncompromising nationalist stance, on 4–5 June President Kostunica appealed to his Montenegrin partners in the federal government to reconsider their opposition to a draft law permitting the extradition of persons indicted for war crimes by the ICTY, 'bearing in mind the highest national and state interests, primarily in regard to preserving the joint state' (the FRY). The Montenegrin diehard supporters of Milosevic, headed by Pedrag Bulatovic, opposed the extradition of any FRY citizen to the ICTY. The Montenegrins in the federal government had tentatively agreed that the FRY needed a law on cooperation with the tribunal, but had resisted a clause permitting Yugoslav citizens to be handed over to it against their will. They maintained that the ICTY was biased (*IHT*, 6 June 2001, p. 7). A deeply divided federal government fnally adopted a bill on cooperation with the ICTY on 14 June, while Montenegro's Socialist People's Party 'reluctantly dropped its objections' (*The Guardian*, 15 June 2001, p. 15). Opinion polls showed that public resistance to the extradition of Milosevic had 'melted away' (*FT*, 15 June 2001, p. 7).

Serbia's chief of police Dusan Mihajlovic announced on 5 June 2001 that investigators had started the exhumation of a mass grave site and that two other suspected sites were also being investigated. In May 1999 a truck containing eighty-six bodies had been dumped in the Danube. The remains had been removed from the river two weeks after the end of the NATO air strikes against Yugoslavia and buried at the site which was now being searched. Mihajlovic declared that ex-president Milosevic would be 'the key witness' in the impending court case (*IHT*, 6 June 2001, p. 7). Human-rights groups in Belgrade believed that the remains of up to 2,000 Kosovar Albanians may have been moved to Serbia by Serbian forces during the summer of 1999. Serbia's interior minister mentioned a possible figure of 1,000 buried at these three sites, but the ethnic Albanian community claimed that 4,000 members of their community were still unaccounted for from that time (*The Guardian*, 22 June 2001, p. 2).

In another volte-face, on 21 June the reformist leaders of the FRY announced the withdrawal of a bill on cooperation with the ICTY after Montenegro's Socialist People's Party decided to stick to its guns by opposing any law allowing the extradition of indictees to The Hague. However, the reformist federal interior minister Zoran Zivkovic declared that the ruling DOS alliance would find other ways to cooperat with the ICTY (*IHT*, 22 June 2001, p. 50). An opinion poll published in Belgrade on 21 June indicated that 46 per cent of those asked believed that Milosevic *should* be extradited to the ICTY. This was the first time that those in favour had outnumbere those opposed (*The Guardian*, 22 June 2001, p. 2). The next day, the federal govern- ment decided to issue a decree which, once adopted by the federal cabinet, would 'automatically become a legal measure that would enable all forms of cooperation' with the ICTY (*FT*, 23 June 2001, p. 7). As a cosmetic concession to Belgrade's constitutonal niceties, the word 'extradition' was not used in the decree. Instead, the process was described as a 'handing over'. Legal experts justified the decree on the basis that the FRY was a member of the UN and was thus obliged to implement the laws of UN-affiliated institutions *Independent*, 23 June 2001, p. 1). The decree was adopted by the FRY government on 23 June, taking advantage of the fact that the DOS alliance enjoyed a nine to seven majority within the cabinet. It transferred all authority and responsibility for extraditions from the federal authorities to those of the republics of Serbia and Montenegro and stipulated that suspects did not need f rst to be tried in local courts. A few dozen Milosevic supporters stood outside the cabinet office to protest against the passing of the decree. President Kostunica 'wa unhappy with the decree but was willing to accept it' (*IHT*, 25 June 2001, p. 7). Decisions on extradition were to be taken by three judges from a district or high court, and any appeal would have to be made within eight days. Five supreme court judges were to rule on any appeal within f fteen days (*The Guardian*, 25 June 2001, p. 2). The Serbian government invoked a little-known and rarely used article in Serbia's constitution which allowed Serbia to override federal law if it threatened Serbia's perceived interests.

On 25 June the federal justice minister filed court papers seeking the extraditio of Milosevic to the ICTY. Members of the SPS met with President Kostunica, who pronounced extradition of Milosevic to be 'a lesser evil' than the further impoverish ment of the FRY through the withholding of Western aid. An appeal by Milosevic's lawyers was to be heard by the constitutional court. The USA again warned that it wanted more details from Belgrade on its plans for Milosevic before deciding whether to take part in the projected aid donors' conference, while EU foreign ministers announced that the conference would only go ahead if Belgrade adopted the decree. EU officials also warned that, even if further aid was pledged at the conference, conditions would be set for the release of any funds and that these would include delivery of Milosevic to the ICTY. An opinion poll published on 25 June indicated that half of Serbia's citizens now favoured the extradition of Milosevic and only one-third opposed it, with the remainder undecided (*IHT*, 26 June 2001, p. 7; *FT*, 26 June 2001, p. 6). Thousands of Milosevic supporters gathered in Belgrade the next day to protest against the proposed extradition. President Kostunica reaffirmed that he woul prefer war criminals to be tried in Belgrade, but that pressure from Washington and from the majority of Serbia's democratic reformers had made this impossible (*Daily Telegraph*, 27 June 2001, p. 13).

The governments of Albania, Bosnia, Bulgaria, Croatia, Romania, Macedonia and the FRY signed an agreement on 27 June 2001, aimed at liberalizing trade in at least 90 per cent of goods traded between them, under the EU's Stability Pact for South-eastern Europe. Croatia, Bosnia and the FRY also reached agreement on measures to resettle the remaining 1.2 million refugees and displaced persons in their respective countries (*FT*, 28 June 2001, p. 8).

The Serbian government finally handed over Slobodan Milosevic to the ICTY o 28 June 2001. It had decided to ignore a constitutional-court ruling aimed at freezing the extradition process. The court had voted four to zero to freeze the government decree allowing extradition, and it had ordered all FRY and Serbian state institutions to take no action on extradition until it had decided whether the decree was con - stitutional. However, the court's four judges were all Milosevic appointees and Serbia's prime minister Zoran Djindjic claimed that its decision was invalid and endangered the country's survival. President Kostunica was only informed of the handover *after* the event (*The Times*, 29 June 2001, p. 1; *FT*, 29 June 2001, p. 1). This was the f rst time that a former head of state had ever been handed over for trial by an international court. About 2,000 to 3,000 Milosevic supporters, many of them elderly, protested in Belgrade's Republic Square (*Independent*, 29 June 2001, p. 1; *The Guardian*, 29 June 2001, p. 1). The extradition occurred only one day before the international donors' conference in Brussels. Nevertheless, the conference on 29 June duly rewarded Serbia for its 'compliant behaviour' by pledging 1.28 billion US dollars in additional aid to the FRY, slightly surpassing the official request for 1.25 billion US dollars (*FT*, 30 June 2001, p. 1).

Zoran Zizic resigned as federal prime minister on 29 June, declaring that the transfer of Milosevic to The Hague had humiliated the FRY. President Kostunica was also furious that the extradition had occurred without his knowledge and his DSS decided to withdraw from the eighteen-party DOS alliance, in both the federal and the Serbian parliaments (*FT*, 30 June 2001, p. 6). Zoran Djindjic replied that his move had been backed by all the ministers in his government except the one from Kostunica's party and that he had discussed the extradition with Kostunica and warned him that the Serbian government could not feel bound to obey an order from a constitutional court packed with Milosevic appointees. About 6,000 Milosevic supporters assembled in front of the federal parliament.

Carla del Ponte served an augmented list of charges on Milosevic on 29 June 2001, to take account of 'more facts and additional victims'. Milosevic and his four co-defendants were charged with responsibility for the deportation of 740,000 people from Kosova and for ordering the murder of 600 named victims. Mrs del Ponte also announced that the indictments could be amended again in future to include the results of exhumations of the mass graves discovered around Belgrade and additional charges stemming from the wars in Bosnia and Croatia. A charge of genocide was being considered (*IHT*, 30 June 2001, pp. 1, 4).

President Kostunica's office issued a carefully worded statement on 1 July 2001 denying he had had any prior knowledge of the Djindjic government's plans to extradite Milosevic. Djindjic denied this, stating that the president had been kept informed (*FT*, 2 July 2001, p. 6).

Milosevic appeared before the ICTY for the first time on 3 July 2001, for abou twelve minutes in all, having chosen to appear without defence lawyers. He declared that he considered the indictments against him to be 'false indictments' and the ICTY to be 'a false tribunal': 'It is illegal, being not appointed by the United Nations General Assembly. So I have no need to appoint counsel to [an] illegal organ... This trial's aim is to produce false justification for the war crimes NATO committed in Yugoslavia.' Given his refusal to plead, a plea of 'not guilty' was entered on his behalf (*FT*, 4 July 2001, p. 1). However, Milosevic had implicitly acknowledged the authority of the ICTY when, as president of Serbia, he had signed the Dayton accords in November 1995. These accords committed the signatories to cooperate in full with the ICTY, and in 1996 Milosevic had happily handed over an ICTY indictee named Drazen Erdemovic for trial by the selfsame court. On 13 July 2001 the Dutch government granted Mirjana Markovic a visa so that she could visit her husband in prison in The Hague.

Serbia's former police chief Radomir Markovic was charged on 20 August 2001 with involvement in the murder of four SPO members and the attempted assassination of Vuk Draskovic in the notorious car crash which occurred on 3 October 1999 (*IHT*, 21 August 2001, p. 5).

A major political crisis erupted in August 2001, when Kostunica accused Djindjic and his supporters of being involved in organized crime and threatened to pull his party out of the DOS-led government. In dozens of interviews Kostunica and members of his party accused the Djindjic government of colluding in and covering up evidence of corruption. Two DOS ministers tendered their resignations, but the DSS refrained from tabling a motion of no confidence, which (if carried) would have precipitate fresh elections. The dispute had blown up after a former state-security offial, Momir Gavrilovic, was killed in a gangland-style murder on 3 August, hours after he had allegedly been seen in Kostunica's off ce. Kostunica and his party claimed that he was shot because he possessed evidence linking Djindjic and his party to organized crime. The party followed these accusations with references to an article published in the Croatian newspaper *Nacional*, which claimed that Djindjic was connected to a businessman involved in lucrative tobacco-smuggling rackets. However, the central bank governor Mladjan Dinkic pointed out that Kostunica's party had failed to present any evidence for its claims against Djindjic. Several central-bank and finance-ministry officials threatened to resign if Kostunica's supporters gained th upper hand (*FT*, 23 August 2001, p. 6). On 21 August Dragan Karleusa, the deputy head of Serbia's organized crime unit, revealed what he claimed were details of Gavrilovic's dark past as a debt collector, an assassin and a paramilitary f ghter in Croatia and Bosnia. For a time these details appeared to assuage public anger against the Djindjic government. Karleusa stated that Gavrilovic, who had left the state-security police in 1999, was gunned down on a Belgrade street. A member of Kostunica's staff claimed that Gavrilovic had met with two of the president's advisers and had brought documents revealing government connections with organized crime. That information, which appeared to be uncorroborated, was seen as an attempt to damage Djindjic. Later reports suggested that Gavrilovic did indeed meet with Kostunica's aides, but only to discuss changes in the state-security police, with imputations that his murder shortly afterwards may have been directed against Kostunica (*IHT*, 25 August 2001, p. 2).

Kostunica's party refused to rejoin the Djindjic government. Its spokesperson Dusan Budisin claimed that the 'chain of criminality has remained unbroken, the narco-mafi untouched and the killings continue' (*Daily Telegraph*, 24 August 2001, p. 19). Kostunica himself stated: 'The fact is that crime has not been suppressed. It is rising and there are links . . . between the actions of certain segments of the state apparatus and the mafia, crime and certain clans' *IHT*, 25 August 2001, p. 2).

In a second appearance at the ICTY on 30 August, Milosevic exuded contempt and defiance, again refused to recognize the legitimacy of the court and criticized th conditions in which he was being held (*The Guardian*, 31 August 2001, p. 2).

At his third pre-trial appearance on 29 October Milosevic remained defiant. H refused to read the indictments against him, so they were read aloud in court to ensure that he had heard them. The 'Kosova' indictment against him had been revised to include charges of responsibility for widespread sexual assaults and claimed that Milosevic carried responsibility for the forced deportation of about 800,000 Kosovar Albanians (as against the 740,000 in the original indictment) to Serbia proper in 1999. It also added charges relating to new discoveries of bodies in mass graves near Belgrade. Milosevic still refused to appoint a defence counsel, in order to show his contempt for the court. The judges thereupon appointed three *amici curiae* (friends of the court) to act on his behalf *Independent*, 30 October 2001, p. 15). Milosevic also refused to enter pleas on the Croatia and Kosova charges. On his behalf, 'the court entered pleas of not guilty to a total of thirty-seven counts of crimes against humanity, breaches of the Geneva conventions and violations of the laws or customs of war' (*Independent*, 31 October 2001, p. 6). The clerk of the court also read out a new indictment on thirty-two counts of extermination, murder, torture, unlawful imprisonment, deportation and persecution in Croatia between August 1991 and June 1992 (*The Times*, 30 October 2001, p. 13).

On 6 November the constitutional court struck down a government decree provid ing for the handover of suspects to the ICTY, leaving the FRY with no legal basis on which to cooperate with the court. However, Carla del Ponte insisted that no special provision was needed to hand over suspects (*IHT*, 7 November 2001, p. 7). The ICTY praised the Serbian authorities on 9 November, when the Bosnian Serb twins Predrag and Nenad Banovic, who had been charged with beating and murdering detainees while they worked as guards at the Keraterm prison camp in north-western Bosnia in the 1990s, were extradicted from Belgrade to The Hague for trial by the ICTY.

From 10 to 12 November many members of Serbia's paramilitary special operations unit (the JSO), known colloquially as the 'Red Berets', went on strike at their training camp and blocked a main road into Belgrade with armoured cars, protesting that they had been tricked into arresting the Banovic twins. The JSO had been founded in 1991 by two high-ranking security police, Jovica Stanisic and Franco Simatovic. The JSO had about 300 members, many of whom were 'ordinary criminals'. It had been incorporated into the Serbian police force after the Dayton accords in November 1995 (*IHT*, 28 March 2003, p. 7).

Serbia's head and deputy head of intelligence, Goran Petrovic and Zoran Mijatovic, resigned on 14 November in the escalating row over cooperation with the ICTY, while the Serbian government placed the mutinous JSO/Red Berets under civilian control and launched an investigation into their demands for the resignation of the interior minister and a cessation of extraditions to The Hague until the federal parliament passed laws legalizing such extraditions. Prime Minister Djindjic accepted these resig- nations, but stood by the interior minister Dusan Mihajlovic, who also offered to resign in an attempt to defuse the protests (*FT*, 15 November 2001, p. 12). However, the Red Berets refused to submit to civilian control on 15 November and vowed to intensify their protests. Djindjic admitted that the state-security police had mishandled the situation by telling the Red Berets that the suspects to be arrested were common criminals rather than Serbs indicted by the ICTY, but also warned that the JSO would be disbanded if they persisted in refusing to submit to civilian control (*IHT*, 16 November 2001, p. 4).

In mid-November 2001 President Kostunica reluctantly accepted that the FRY and Serbia would have to cooperate with the ICTY and called for new laws to regularize the extradition of suspects (*The Times*, 19 November 2001, p. 17), whereupon on 16 November the Paris Club of creditor states agreed to reduce the FRY's 4.6 billion US dollars debt to them by 66 per cent (*IHT*, 17 November 2001, p. 13).

On 23 November the ICTY formally charged Slobodan Milosevic with committing genocide against the Bosnian people, in the third and most serious indictment brought against him. This charge would make him the first head of state ever to stand trial for genocide. The ICTY def ned genocide as 'acts committed with intent to destroy, in whole or in part, a national, ethnic, racial or religious group'. The indictment charged Milosevic on twenty-nine counts for multiple breaches of the Geneva conventions and crimes against humanity during the 1992–5 war in Bosnia, stating that 'Slobodan Milosevic participated in a joint criminal enterprise, the purpose of which was the forcible removal of the majority of non-Serbs, principally Bosnian Moslems and Bosnian Croats, from large areas of the Republic of Bosnia and Herzegovina' (*IHT*, 24 November 2001, p. 5).

Carla del Ponte declared on 28 November:

> Ratko Mladic is residing in the Federal Republic of Yugoslavia under the offial protection of the Yugoslav Army. As an officer of the Yugoslav Army, Genera Mladic is said to enjoy military immunity and he is being shielded from both national and international justice . . . Working with prime minister Djindjic and the Serbian authorities at the repubic level we have experienced good results .. . [But] cooperation at the federal level appears to be blocked for reasons of domestic politics.
>
> (*Independent*, 29 November 2001, p. 17)

At his fourth pre-trial appearance at the ICTY on 11 December, Slobodan Milosevic refused to enter a plea to the twenty-nine counts of genocide, complicity to commit genocide, crimes against humanity and other war crimes in Bosnia. The presiding judge therefore entered pleas of 'not guilty' on his behalf (*IHT*, 12 December 2001, p. 6). The prosecution had hoped to amalgamate charges for crimes in Kosova, Bosnia and Croatia into one trial, but the ICTY ruled that the Kosova trial should begin on 12 February, while the charges relating to Bosnia and Croatia would be heard later (*Independent*, 12 December 2001, p. 14).

During a trial held in December 2001, Pierre Bunel, a former French army com - mandant, denied having acted as a 'traitor' when he leaked NATO bombing plans to Belgrade during the Kosova war of March–June 1999. Bunel admitted to a Paris court that he had passed information from two NATO bomb-targeting documents to a Yugoslav officer, but he claimed that he had acted on orders from the French intelligence service, which asked him to persuade the Yugoslav officer that NATO' threat to bomb targets in Serbia was not a bluff and that the only way for the FRY to avoid massive bombings was to pull its security forces out of Kosova (*IHT*, 12 December 2001, p. 7). On 12 December 2001 he was convicted of treason and sentenced to f ve years in jail, three of which were then suspended.

President Kostunica announced on 27 December that he refused to accept the resignation of the army chief of staff, General Nebojsa Pavkovic, despite pressure from his coalition partners and from the international community. 'He offered to withdraw, but I asked him to stay because of reforms which he initiated and created' (*IHT*, 28 December 2001, p. 5). General Pavkovic had skilfully directed the Serbian war effort against NATO in 1999.

In January 2002, under renewed threat of forfeiting a billion of dollars of Western aid, Zoran Djindjic agreed to cooperate fully in the extradition of nearly a dozen Serbian indictees to the ICTY (*The Times*, 29 January 2002, p. 13).

The prosecution asked the ICTY on 30 January to reconsider a decision to hold two separate trials for Slobodan Milosevic. They wanted a single trial, arguing that all the charges added up to a single 'criminal enterprise' to create a Greater Serbia (*The Guardian*, 31 January 2002, p. 12). However, this was a somewhat questionable charge to press. Many states have been created by wars fought to bring most of the members of particular ethnic groups under a single jurisdiction (as a nation-state), but 'such wars of national unification' have rarely been regarded as 'criminal enter prises' (for example, Bismarck's wars to unify Germany, or Cavour's wars to unify Italy). Even though many people were killed in such wars, they are rarely described as 'criminal enterprises'. It would have been much sounder to have focused more narrowly on prosecuting Milosevic for the many gratuitous atrocities and acts of ethnic cleansing committed by forces acting on his orders as commander-in-chief.

Milosevic was finally allowed to defend his actions during the 1990s Balkan wars He accused the ICTY of mounting an 'evil and hostile attack' against him and demanded to be freed immediately, assuring the court that he would return to face trial: 'This is a battle I will not miss.' During his fe previous appearances, Milosevic had been silenced every time he tried to make a statement (*IHT*, 31 January 2002, p. 4). He signalled that he would conduct his own defence. He said of the indict - ments: 'I would call this an evil and hostile attack aimed at justifying the crimes committed against my country.' Carla del Ponte argued that Milosevic's plan to create a Greater Serbia underpinned all his crimes during the Balkan wars, which added up to 'one strategy, one scheme' to create a Greater Serbia by 'forced and violent expulsion of the non-Serb population' (*Independent*, 31 January 2002, p. 16). She also argued that it would be best for witnesses to have to testify only once: 'It is very important for the victims to have a single trial, because they can hear all the facts in the same procedure and see justice done at the same time' (*Independent*, 2 February 2002, p. 13). The ICTY agreed on 1 February to combine in a single trial the indictments against Milosevic relating to the three wars in the Balkans during the 1990s (Croatia, Bosnia and Kosova). His trial formally opened on 12 February 2002. He was the first head of state to be tried for *genocide*, but he was not the first head of state to be tried for *war crimes*: that was Admiral Karl Dönitz, who led Germany for a week after Hitler died, and was subsequently imprisoned for ten years.

On 25 February 2002, the authorities in Belgrade removed some impediments to the arrest of Ratko Mladic by stripping him of his army protection. He was told that the armed forces would 'no longer protect him'. He was rumoured to be continually moving from one safe haven to another in Serbia and in Serb-controlled eastern Bosnia. As a retired officer, he would henceforth come under the jurisdiction of Serbian civi authorities (*Independent*, 26 February 2002, p. 14). In March 2002, however, Carla del Ponte reaffirmed her belief that Ratko Mladic was living outside Belgrade unde the protection of the federal military (*IHT*, 22 March 2002, p. 3).

On 6 March 2002 judges turned down Milosevic's request for a temporary release from jail in order to assist him to mount his own defence. The presiding judge Richard May stated that the trial had commenced and the trial chamber was uncertain that Milosevic would continue to appear for trial, or that he would pose no 'danger to any victim, witness or others' (*IHT*, 7 March 2002, p. 5). On the same day, Carla del Ponte proposed that low- and middle-ranking war-crimes suspects should be tried by national courts, leaving international tribunals to deal only with high-profile case (*IHT*, 7 March 2002, p. 5).

As part of his defence, Milosevic claimed on 8 March that al-Qaeda militants had assisted Kosovar rebels to fight for independence from Serbia. He quoted fro an alleged FBI report, dated 18 December 2001, which he claimed proved that al-Qaeda had established a terrorist network in Kosova (*IHT*, 9 March 2002, p. 5).

Patrick Ball, an independent American statistician, testifed on 13 March that a systematic campaign by Serb security forces had resulted in the deaths of more than 10,000 Kosovar Albanians and that the pattern of refugee f ows from March to June 1999 clearly indicated that the blame lay with these Serbian forces, not NATO bombing or the KLA. His study, f nanced by the Ford Foundation, was based on the refugee f ows recorded by Albania's border guards and data collected by human-rights groups (*IHT*, 14 March 2002, p. 5). However, Milosevic questioned the authenticity of this documention, suggesting it had been planted as part of an ethnic Albanian propaganda campaign. Milosevic told Patrick Ball: 'I think you have been deceived' (*Independent*, 15 March 2002, p. 20). On 10 April Richard May, the presiding judge at the ICTY, gave the prosecution one year in which to conclude its case against Milosevic (*The Times*, 11 April 2002, p. 20).

In March 2002 Javier Solana brokered an agreement between Serbia and Montenegro to replace the FRY with a (looser) confederal State Union of Serbia. The details of this restructuring of the relationship between these two republics are pro - vided in the chapter on Montenegro, which was much more affected by this change than was Serbia. In the short term, the major political implication for Serbia was that the office of president of Yugoslavia held by Vojislav Kostunica was scheduled to disappear once the new state union entered into operation in 2003. This would in due course eliminate the standing and influence which Kostunica was enjoying in th post of federal president and would thereby increase the relative power of the Serbian prime minister Zoran Djindjic and his government.

On 14 March 2002 the VJ arrested an unidentifd US diplomat, a Serbian lieutenant colonel, a civilian and Momcilo Perisic, the former general and army chief of staff who had become Serbia's deputy prime minister, accusing them of involvement with espionage. Documents concerning Milosevic's roles in the 1990s Yugoslav conf icts were allegedly discovered in the unidentified US diplomat's briefcase and the arreste diplomat was allegedly in charge of the the US mission's relations with the ICTY. Western officials in Belgrade claimed that the diplomat had never seen the said documents before his arrest and that they therefore must been placed in his brief-case. The diplomat was released the next day, after being held incommunicado for fiftee hours and then made to appear before a military court. Perisic was kept in detention a day longer. Nebojsa Pavkovic, the general whom Milosevic had appointed to succeed Perisic and who had directed Serbia's war effort during the Kosova war, also announced on 14 March that he was planning to step down. President Kostunica was still refusing to dismiss Pavkovic, causing the US state department to become increasingly dis - illusioned with Kostunica and to cold shoulder him during his most recent visit to

Washington. On 15 March Premier Djindjic declared that the arrests were a 'first-rat scandal' and 'a blow to the country's credibility' (*IHT*, 16 March 2002, pp. 1–5).

The military authorities in Belgrade released Momcilo Perisic on 16 March. Nevertheless, a military court had forwarded criminal charges to military prosecutors and the military issued a statement that the arrested lieutenant colonel had passed confidential documents to Perisic, 'some of which he later passed on to a foreign citizen', and that the evidence pointed to a 'criminal act of espionage'. The US diplomat had also been charged before being released. The governments of the USA and Serbia accused the military of fabricating evidence and planting incriminating documents. Premier Djindjic also claimed that the military's intelligence arm had not consulted either its political superiors or the military leadership before carrying out the arrests. However, President Kostunica stated that 'According to everything I have learned so far, and I repeat so far, the legality of the procedure itself, from the standpoint of domestic procedure, is not disputable.' Federal military intelligence officers wer directly responsible to the off ce of the federal president (*IHT*, 18 March 2002, p. 6; *Independent*, 18 March 2002, p. 14). Claiming that he had been framed, Momcilo Perisic neverthless bowed to political pressure and resigned from the Serbian gov - ernment on 19 March. Both Kostunica and Djindjic asked Perisic to resign and to refrain from invoking his parliamentary immunity, to facilitate the offial investigation into what had gone on, and Perisic had agreed to this. The military still maintained that he had given the US diplomat documents 'relevant for the defence of the country', while other federal officials claimed that the documents could have been used agains Milosevic. Kostunica called on Djindjic to resign (*IHT*, 20 March 2002, p. 6). The USA subsequently obtained an apology from the federal government for the fact that its diplomat had been held incommunicado for fifteen hours. President Kostunica nevertheless insisted that there was 'concrete evidence' against Perisic, and Djindjic did not deny this (*The Economist*, 23 March 2002, p. 42).

Serbia's justice minister Vladan Batic announced on 27 March that the Serbian government would reinstate the decree allowing the automatic implementation of the ICTY statute, including rules allowing the extradition of indictees. He maintained that no specif c Serbian or FRY law to this effect was needed, because UN rules over-rode those of its member states. The move came a day after the federal constitutional court, still dominated by nationalists loyal to Milosevic and Kostunica, had ruled that ICTY statute could not be applied in the FRY. There were still fifteen ICTY indictee living in Serbia. The US congress had given the FRY until 31 March to cooperate fully with the ICTY or risk losing 120 million US dollars of aid. Batic also claimed that the Serbian government had fulfilled the other conditions set by the US congress, including the release of all ethnic Albanian political prisoners from Serbian jails and the severance of formal ties between Serbia and the Bosnian Serb military (*Independent*, 28 March 2002, p. 19; *IHT*, 30 March 2002, p. 2).

The Serbian authorities issued arrest warrants on 31 March for Serbia's incumbent president Milan Milutinovic and three other former close colleagues of Slobodan Milosevic: the former deputy prime minister Nikola Sainovic, the former interior minister and security chief Vlajko Stojilkovic, and the former army chief of staff, General Dragoljub Ojdanic. Justice Minister Babic maintained that it was up to the police to decide the rules governing the extradition of indictees and when and how to arrest them (*The Guardian*, 31 March 2002, p. 11).

Nevertheless, on 1 April 40 million US dollars in US aid to Serbia was frozen and US support for Serbia in organizations such as the IMF was suspended, because it was perceived that Serbia had still not complied *sufficiently* with the requirement to extradite its ICTY indictees. US congress laws and rules on aid donation specifie that indicted suspects must actually have been surrendered to the ICTY and that war-crimes investigators must actually have had full access to Serbian and FRY offial records. US secretary of state Colin Powell had the power to reverse the aid suspension if he saw that Serbia was fully complying (*FT*, 2 April 2002, p. 8; *IHT*, 3 April 2002, p. 5).

In a sudden volte-face, Montenegro's Socialist People's Party agreed on 9 April to a request from President Kostunica to support a new federal law legalizing the extradition of persons indicted by the ICTY, so long as it did not apply to persons indicted *after* the passing of this law, among others (*The Times*, 10 April 2002, p. 19). The forty-seat upper house of the federal parliament passed the new extradition law on 10 April. The next day the 138-seat lower house followed suit, by eighty votes to thirty-nine, with nineteen absences or abstentions. However, the new law only applied to suspects already indicted and no new names could be added. Radovan Karadzic and Ratko Mladic were unaffected by this law because they were not citizens of the FRY. The law *did* apply to about twenty suspects thought to be hiding in the FRY. Anyone indicted later could only be tried by courts within the FRY. In addition to allowing extradition, the law also granted UN prosecutors access to archives, witnesses and other sources relevant to their investigations of war crimes. Members of Kostunica's DSS and of Montenegro's Socialist People's Party (SNP) voted in favour of the bill, leaving only Milosevic's SPS, Seselj's SRS and other ultra-nationalists voting against it (*FT*, 11 April 2002, p. 11; *IHT*, 12 April 2002, p. 11). Very significantly, the new law also made provision for the FRY to pay for the defenc of indictees who surrendered voluntarily and to guarantee the appearance of these indictees before the ICTY if the court decided to set them free until their trials actually began (*Independent*, 12 April 2002, p. 13).

Vlajko Stojilkovic, who had been Serbia's interior minister and state-security chief from April 1997 to October 2000 and had been indicted for numerous crimes against humanity by the ICTY, shot himself in the head outside the federal parliament on 11 April, shortly after it had approved the new extradition law. He died on 13 April. While he was Serbia's interior minister from late 1997 to mid-1999, his special police forces had spearheaded the ethnic cleansing of Kosovar villages and he had frequently been seen in Kosova supervising his men. In February 2002 the federal parliament had stripped him of his parliamentary immunity, to allow his prosecution by Serbian courts (*FT*, 12 April 2002, p. 9; *The Guardian*, 12 April 2002, p. 15).

Miodrag Kovac, the federal health and labour minister and a member of Montenegro's Socialist People's Party, hanged himself in a Madrid hotel room on 12 April. FRY embassy officials in Madrid announced that he had left a 'very personal suicide note to his family and 'ruled out any link' with the Stojilkovic suicide. Nevertheless, Kovac's suicide note *did* state that he had 'trusted his party members too much'. He thus appeared to condemn his party for having voted in favour of the extradition law on 11–12 April, even though he himself had not been indicted by the ICTY. However, FRY police sources revealed that he *was* under investigation in relation to a pharmaceuticals-smuggling racket, and it is therefore possible that fear of prosecution *was* what drove him to suicide (*IHT*, 13 April 2002, p. 2; *The Times*, 13 April 2002, p. 20; *Independent*, 13 April 2002, p. 13).

It was announced on 15 April that General Dragoljub Ojdanic and Nikola Sainovic were prepared to surrender to the ICTY, because the federal parliament had passed the new extradition law. On 17 April the federal government gave twenty-three people indicted by the ICTY (including Radovan Karadzic and Ratko Mladic) until 22 April to give themselves up (*IHT*, 18 April 2002, p. 4). Six of the twenty-three decided to turn themselves in ahead of the deadline: General Dragoljub Ojdanic, Nikola Sainovic, Milan Martic – the former leader of the self-proclaimed Republic of Serb Krajina in Croatia, General Mile Mrksic, Captain Vladimir Kovacevic and the Bosnian Serb Momcilo Gruban. Serb officials stated that nearly all the others would be found an sent to the court within two weeks (*IHT*, 24 April 2002, p. 5).

The interior minister Zoran Zivkovic announced on 28 April that Serbia would provide the ICTY with a lot of information relating to the indictees, but also that there were matters that would remain 'state secrets, documents which will remain sealed for twenty to thirty years'. The interior ministry stated that it would decide how to respond to each ICTY demand for information on a case-by-case basis. ICTY officials would be allowed access to *some* state documents – not all (*IHT*, 29 April 2002, p. 5). On 21 May the USA certif ed that Serbian cooperation with the ICTY was sufficient for it to lift its embargo on 40 million US dollars in economic aid t Serbia.

A Belgrade court issued arrest warrants for seventeen Serbs charged with war crimes, including Radovan Karadzic and Ratko Mladic, on 9 May*IHT*, 10 May 2002, p. 5). Ranko Cesic, one of these 'wanted men', was arrested on 26 May. Serbia's first 'home grown' war crimes trial began on 11 June 2002. Ivan Nikolic was charged with 'war crimes against the civilian population', for having killed two Kosova Albanian civilians on 24 May 1999 when he was an army reservist. On 8 July he was sentenced to eight years in prison. Two other Serbian reservists for the army's anti-terrorist unit were charged with the murder of nineteen ethnic Albanians in Kosova in 1999 (*Independent*, 9 July 2002, p. 10). The maximum penalty for war crimes under Serbia's penal code was forty years in prison (*FT*, 9 July 2002, p. 7).

On 29 May President Kostunica withdrew over twenty members of his party from the boards of key state-run companies, claiming that the Serbian government had been involved in murky business deals, and threatened to call new elections – in yet another attempt to undermine and distance himself from the Djindjic government (*IHT*, 30 May 2002, p. 6).

Forty-five deputies belonging to the DSS walked out of the Skupstina and handed in their parliamentary identity cards on 12 June, in protest against a decision by the rest of Serbia's ruling coalition to deprive twenty-one of them of their parliamentary seats for poor attendance in parliament and to give these seats to rival parties. The DSS claimed that the Serbian parliament had become a sham, and their leader President Kostunica called for mass strikes and protests (*Independent*, 13 June 2002, p. 10).

On 21 June a Serbian court sentenced Dragoljub Milanovic, the former head of RTS, to a nine-and-a-half-year prison term for failing to protect the sixteen of his staff who were killed when NATO bombed its offices on 23 April 1999. The cour ruled that he had not ensured the safety of his staff, even though he had been forewarned that the building was about to be bombed (*IHT*, 22 June 2002, p. 3). The presiding judge pronounced him guilty of premeditated negligence towards the safety of his staff, but also declared that the sentence did 'nothing to absolve NATO'. Hundreds of important offices, ministries and installations had been regularly evacuated durin the air raids in 1999, but RTS had maintained 'full shifts throughout'. The court also established that plans to relocate the RTS had been shelved by Milanovic

(*Independent*, 22 June 2002, p. 12). Serbia's media had discovered in 2001 that employees who had good relations with the RTS management *were* forewarned of the NATO attack and stayed away from the buildings. Foreign media representatives who operated from the building were also forewarned. Milanovic's defence lawyer claimed that his client was 'only responsible in as much as he followed direct orders by the government and the head of state' (*The Times*, 22 June 2002, p. 17).

In a sudden volte-face, President Kostunica sacked the army chief of staff General Nebojsa Pavkovic (whom he had hitherto refused to dismiss) on 24 June and appointed the deputy army chief of staff Branko Krga in his place. NATO and Premier Djindjic had long been pressing for Pavkovic's removal, and Pavkovic accused Kostunica of bowing to 'undemocratic pressure from abroad' and taking 'personal vengeance' against him for having refused to take part in the presidential office's dirty tricks operations against Premier Djindjic during 2001, including a break-in at the Serbian government offices on the grounds that the Serbian authorities were bugging Presiden Kostunica and the army (*The Times*, 26 June 2002, p. 18). On 25 June about twenty generals and admirals isued a joint statement of support for General Krga. Kostunica had tried to spread responsibility for his removal of Pavkovic by seeking the backing of the federal security council, but Djindjic criticized the manner in which Kostunica got rid of Pavkovic because a stormy meeting of the federal security council on 24 June had actually *refused* to support Kostunica in this matter. Kostunica responded that he had acted within his presidential prerogatives (*IHT*, 26 June 2002, p. 12; 3 July 2002, p. 3).

During an interview in late June, Kostunica accused Djindjic of pushing priva - tization and economic liberalization in ways that showed that he and his followers 'do not care how people live. I favour a middle way.' He claimed Djindjic was a slave to IMF demands for budget cuts and hasty privatization of state companies which, even if they were ineff cient, provided employment in a depressed economy. He also insinuated that Djindjic was handing out contracts and property to cronies. Miroljub Labus, the federal deputy prime minister in charge of economic reform, replied that Kostunica was playing to the gallery while the Djindjic government made the diff cult decisions: Kostunica was 'a person who likes to show his links with the suffering, while others pay the price of getting the job done' (*HT*, 3 July 2002, p. 6).

Zoran Lilic, the former president of the FRY and Milosevic loyalist, was detained on 11 July and forcibly flown to The Hague after declining a subpoena to testify agains Milosevic at the ICTY (*The Times*, 12 July 2002, p. 18).

President Kostunica attended a meeting with the Bosnian president Beriz Belkic and the Croatian president Stipe Mesic on 15 July 2002. They pledged to rebuild peace, trust and trade between their respective countries and in the Balkans as a whole, to respect each other's borders, and to cooperate to increase trade, fight crime and help refugees to return to their former homes. However, whereas President Mesic had already apologized repeatedly and movingly for the atrocities committed by Croats against former compatriots during the 1990s, Kostunica pointedly refused either to apologize for the much greater atrocities committed by Serbs during the 1990s or to call on Radovan Karadzic to surrender to the ICTY (*IHT*, 16 July 2002, p. 5).

On 18 July a Serbian presidential election was called for 29 September 2002, in order to replace the incumbent Serbian president Milan Milutinovic, who was in The Hague facing charges of crimes against humanity. Milutinovic's term of office wa in any case due to expire in December. Miroljub Labus, the deputy prime minister in charge of economic reform, declared his candidacy in late July. In August the SPS chose sixty-nine-year-old Velimir 'Bata' Zivojinovic, one of Serbia's best-known actors and the star of several films about Yugoslav partisans fighting the Nazis, as i presidential candidate. On 23 August Vojislav Kostunica announced his own candidacy. This was not unexpected, since his post as president of the FRY was due to disappear in 2003 (*IHT*, 24 August 2002, p. 3).

A so-called 'anti-mafia' law was passed on 18 July, in order to establish a specia prosecutor's office, a new court department and a new detention unit to gather intelligence and wage war on organized crime, in an attempt to make a clean break with the security police of the Milosevic era (*FT*, 19 July 2002, p. 7).

In July 2002 Milosevic's daughter Marija renounced her Serbian citizenship in protest at what she saw as her country's betrayal of her father and announced that she would dedicate herself to campaigning for the independence of Montenegro. She had moved to the city of Cetinje, Montenegro's former capital, and had taken out Montenegrin citizenship. She could do this because her father was Montenegrin by birth (*The Times*, 20 July 2002, p. 11).

In August 2002, when Serbia received the final tranche of a 345-million-euro E aid package promoting key economic reforms (public expenditure control, tax policy and administrative reform, banking-sector restructuring and private-sector develop - ment), the EU Commission issued a favourable assessment of Belgrade's use of prior donations and announced it would give Serbia an additional 130 million euros (*FT*, 7 August 2002, p. 8).

The Council of Europe voted by 122 votes to 6 on 24 September to accept the FRY as a member, to take effect when Serbia and Montenegro ratifed a constitution for their new (much looser) state union (*Independent*, 25 September 2002, p. 16).

The Serbian presidential election, 29 September, 13 October and 8 December 2002

A turn-out of at least 50 per cent was needed for the vote to be validated, and a run-off ballot was to be held on 13 October if no one candidate obtained at least 50 per cent of the votes cast in the fst round. There were eleven candidates in the fst round, the turn-out was 55 per cent, and the front-runners were as shown in Table 6.13.

Seselj obtained twice as many votes as most opinion polls had predicted, not least because he received explicit support from Slobodan Milosevic and his SPS (*The Economist*, 5 October 2002, p. 44). Seselj, his SRS and the SPS urged their supporters to boycott the second round, in order to void the result (through a turn-out of less than 50 per cent) and thus give Seselj another chance (*IHT*, 4 October 2002, p. 5).

In the second round on 13 October 2002, Kostunica obtained 66.7 per cent of the votes cast, compared with 31.3 per cent for Labus, but the turn-out was only 45.5 per cent – less than the minimum 50 per cent required. The result was thereby declared void.

6.13 Serbian presidential election, 29 September 2002

Candidate	Share of vote (%)
Vojislav Kostunica (president of the FRY)	30.89
Miroljub Labus (Serbia's deputy prime minister)	27.36
Vojislav Seselj (leader of the SRS)	22.5

On 8 December 2002, three candidates took part in the third successive attempt to elect a president of Serbia. Vojislav Kostunica obtained 57.5 per cent of the vote. Vojislav Seselj obtained 36 per cent, and Borislav Pelevic (leader of the Serbian Unity Party founded by Zeljko Raznatovic, alias Arkan) came third. However, the 45 per cent turn-out was again too low to validate the result. Kostunica and his supporters claimed that the electoral registers contained hundreds of thousands of inaccuracies and included many people who were dead or had left the country during the Milosevic era, and that the actual voter turn-out as a proportion of those actually present and entitled to vote had been greatly understated as a consequence (*IHT*, 10 December 2002, p. ii). They did indeed have some genuine grounds for feeling that he had been cheated out of a rightful victory, but he also made wilder claims that the Djindjic government had 'added some 400,000 non-existent voters to the poll to ensure that the presidential poll would be invalid'. Kostunica appealed to the supreme court on 10 December (*The Economist*, 4 January 2003, p. 27). Zoran Djindjic and his DS had refrained from putting forward a presidential candidate of their own, allegedly on the calculation that the presidential impasse would be to their political advantage (*The Guardian*, 9 December 2002, p. 21). Djindjic also refused to endorse Kostunica's candidacy because his rival had continually attempted to use his presidential powers to bring down the government (*IHT*, 9 December 2002, p. 7). All these shenanigans severely distracted the Serbian government from some of the much-needed reform programmes which were being urged upon it by Western governments and the EU (*IHT*, 10 December 2002, Survey, p. ii).

When Milan Milutinovic's presidential mandate formally expired on 5 January 2003, Natasa Micic (the speaker of the Serbian Skupstina) took over as acting president until such time as a new president was elected. Natasa Micic thus became the first female president of Serbia. Since 1996 she had been an active member of Serbia's small Christian Democratic Party. She issued a decree postponing for six months any further attempt to elect a new president of Serbia. Ex-President Milutinovic surrendered voluntarily to the ICTY on 20 January 2003 (*IHT*, 21 January 2003, p. 4).

In late 2002 the USA started to unblock Yugoslav assets frozen during the 1990s under sanctions imposed against the regime of Slobodan Milosevic. Goran Svilanovic, the FRY foreign minister, announced that assets belonging to individuals and companies appeared to have been released. The funds still blocked were thought to include 'assets belonging to liquidated banks and the central bank of the defunct former Yugoslavia' (*FT*, 30 December 2002, p. 6).

Negotiations to replace the FRY with a looser state union broke down on 11–12 January 2003, when representatives of Serbia and Montenegro quarrelled over how to reframe the respective republics' relations with international financial institutions. IMF advisers wanted a new Serbian central bank (replacing the FRY central bank) to take charge of international dealings on behalf of both Serbia and Montenegro, but Montenegro vehemently opposed such a move (*FT*, 13 January 2003, p. 8). The EU foreign-policy supremo Javier Solana had announced on 28 November 2002 that, after months of stalled negotiations, Serbia and Montenegro had finally reached agreement in transforming the FRY into a confederal state union (*Independent*, 29 November 2002, p. 15).

Serbia was warned on 21 January 2003 that it would once again risk losing US financial and other support if it did not arrest and deliver to the ICTY the three 'most wanted' indictees: General Ratko Mladic, Major Veselin Sljivancanin and Colonel Miroslav Radic by the end of March (*IHT*, 22 January 2003, p. 3). The USA simultaneously promised to stop hounding Serbia and to relax the conditions it had attached to financial aid, if these three men were arrested by 31 March. The majo difficulty was that the Djindjic government had lost the backing of the FRY president Kostunica. Therefore, the DOS coalition could only muster a majority in the Skupstina by enlisting the support of some former Milosevic supporters, who were on the whole 'bitterly opposed to extradition' (*IHT*, 24 January 2003, p. 4).

Radomir Markovic was sentenced to seven years in jail on 30 January for his role in the attempt to assassinate Vuk Draskovic and in the murder of four of his aides in a staged car accident in October 1999. Draskovic denounced the outcome as a 'scandal', after the presiding judge concluded that the attempt on Draskovic's life had been an independent criminal act by two maverick members of the Red Berets, Nenad Bujosevic and Nenad Ilic, who were sentenced to fifteen years each for killin three members of Draskovic's entourage (including his brother-in-law). Markovic was only found guilty of covering up the crime by removing police records concerning the truck. The fourth defendant, Markovic's aide Milan Radonjic, was exonerated (*Independent*, 31 January 2003, p. 12).

The inauguration of the 'State Union of Serbia and Montenegro' ('Solania'), 4 February 2003

On 29 January 2003 the Montenegrin assembly had finally voted by fifty-four vot to seven to replace the FRY with a loose 'State Union of Serbia and Montenegro'. The change was also approved by the Serbian Skupstina (*Independent*, 30 January 2003, p. 12). It was ratified by the federal parliament in Belgrade on 4 February 2003. The constitutional charter of the 'State Union of Serbia and Montenegro' was passed in the upper house by twenty-six votes to seven, and in the lower house by eighty-four votes to thirty-one. A heated parliamentary debate took place. The creation of the state union owed much to tenacious lobbying by the EU foreign-policy supremo Javier Solana. It thus became known colloquially as 'Solania'. Vojislav Kostunica's term of off ce as president of the FRY was supposed to end when a new president of Serbia and Montenegro was elected by a new confederal parliament of Serbia and Montenegro. The state union was to have one army but two currencies, with Serbia using the dinar and Montenegro the euro. More than thirty federal institutions were to cease to exist, from the Yugoslav central bank to the federal ministries of financ and interior. Serbia and Montenegro, now called 'member states', were each allowed ten days to pass laws on the election of deputies to the projected 126-member parliament of Serbia and Montenegro. President Kostunica was allowed five days t select a date for elections to this parliament *FT*, 5 February 2003, p. 6;*IHT*, 5 February 2003, p. 3).

Vojislav Seselj was indicted by the ICTY on 14 February 2003. He was charged with fourteen counts of war crimes and crimes against humanity in Croatia, Bosnia and Serbia between 1991 and 1993. The ICTY was at a loss to explain how Seselj obtained prior knowledge of the indictment (he had already announced in advance that he would voluntarily fly to The Hague on 24 February). At his appearance before th ICTY on 26 February, Seselj refused to enter a plea, choosing instead to emulate Milosevic's show of defiance and contempt towards the court. Seselj reserved the righ to enter a plea within thirty days of his first appearance in court, after asking the prosecutors to clarify the indictment against him. He also denounced the charges against him as fabrications and followed Milosevic's example by opting to conduct his own defence, thereby attracting maximum publicity for his own cause and using the ICTY as a political platform (*IHT*, 27 February 2003, p. 5).

Zoran Djindjic narrowly survived what he said was an attempt to kill him on 21 February 2003, when a lorry cut across his motorcade. The lorry driver was arrested (*Independent*, 24 February 2003, p. 10). Djindjic suggested that the incident was linked to his government's efforts to stamp out organized crime, but there were also rumours that Djindjic himself had 'become too friendly with gangsters and may have become a target after falling out with them' (*The Economist*, 15 March 2003, p. 39).

Vojislav Kostunica stepped down as president of the FRY on 3 March, when parliamentary deputies from Serbia and Montenegro inaugurated the new confederal parliament of Serbia and Montenegro. The new president of the State Union of Serbia and Montenegro was Svetozar Marovic, who was elected unopposed and by prior agreement on 7 March. He was the deputy leader of Montenegro's Democratic Party of Socialists (*The Times*, 8 March 2003, p. 20).

The assassination of Premier Zoran Djindjic, 12 March 2003

Djindjic (aged fifty) was hit by two sniper bullets outside the main government building. The government immediately issued a statement that the assassination represented an attempt by the Zemun clan to halt the crackdown on organized crime (gangsterism) which Djindjic had initiated and that the assassination's purpose was 'to trigger fear and chaos in the country'. The government pinned the blame on Milorad Lukovic, a gangster warlord loyal to Milosevic, and several other prominent underworld figures *Independent*, 13 March 2003, p. 1; *The Times*, 13 March 2003, p. 12).

Lukovic was a former commander of the JSO. He was also the leader the Zemun clan/gang and had served in the French Foreign Legion, from which he had gained the nickname 'Legija'. When the Milosevic regime collapsed in October 2000, he had abandoned Milosevic and struck a sort of deal with Djindjic (reportedly to support the democracy movement in return for immunity from extradition to the ICTY). His forces had even assisted in the deportation of Milosevic to The Hague in June 2001. Under strong pressure from the West, however, Djindjic had begun a crackdown on Legija and his underworld associates. Serbia's government claimed that arrest warrants for Lukovic and other underworld bosses had been waiting to be signed by Djindjic on the day he was shot. The powerful Zemun clan/gang, which had about 200 known members, was also accused of abducting and murdering the former Serbian president Ivan Stambolic, attempting to assassinate Vuk Draskovic and carrying out over f fty murders (*FT*, 14 March 2003, p. 9; 19 March 2003, p. 11; *The Times*, 14 March 2003, p. 23). The Zemun clan/gang's main business was selling drugs. It reportedly controlled 80 per cent of the Serbian market. Serbia straddled an important transit route for drugs smuggled from the Middle East to Europe.

Legija himself, who had been accused of war crimes in Bosnia and Croatia, and Franko Simatovic, who led a paramilitary unit accused of many atrocities in Bosnia and Kosova, were rumoured to have been on the ICTY's wanted list. This may have motivated Legija to have Djindjic assassinated. Many Serbs thought that the West had contributed to Djindjic's death by pressing so hard for reform and extradition of persons indicted by the ICTY and by tying the delivery of desperately needed aid to compliance with these conditions. Serbia's press alleged that Djindjic had complex business interests, with reputed connections to the Surcin mafia *IHT*, 18 March 2003, p. 3).

Serbia's minority coalition government, which depended on tacit support from Milosevic's SPS for survival, declared a state of emergency (from 12 March to 22 April) and appointed deputy prime minister Nebojsa Covic as acting prime minister. Police and the military were given a free hand to arrest suspects without warrants and to detain anyone for up to thirty days without bringing charges. Like Djindjic, however, Covic incurred 'accusations from his opponents of getting too close to organized crime bosses' (*The Economist*, 15 March 2003, p. 39). By late March over 3,000 people had been arrested (*Independent*, 26 March 2003, p. 15).

On 14 March masked Serbian interior-ministry troops with machine guns surrounded a housing complex in Zemun belonging to Dusan Spasojevic, one of the Zemun gang's leaders and a former member of Milosevic's security services. Two bulldozers started demolishing the buildings and a nearby shopping mall. Two former senior members of Milosevic's security services, Jovica Stanisic and Franko Simatovic, were detained on 13 March. They were 'believed to have maintained significant infuence in police and mob circles even after Milosevic's ouster in October 2000'. A police statement claimed that three still unidentifed assassins and 'a criminal clan, as well as some other groups, mainly police-security structures from Milosevic's times', had been responsible for shooting Djindjic (*IHT*, 15 March 2003, p. 2; *FT*, 15 March 2003, p. 8).

Djundjic's funeral procession on 15 March drew half a million mourners on to the streets of Belgrade (*The Guardian*, 17 March 2003, p. 17). The next day, Zoran Zivkovic, the forty-two-year-old former federal interior minister and former mayor of Nis, was voted in by 128 votes to 100 to succeed Djindjic as prime minister of the DOS coalition.

The government headed by Zoran Zivkovic, March 2003–February 2004

On 18 March, Prime Minister Zivkovic described the assassination of Djindjic as a political act linked not only to the mafia and the former Milosevic regime, but als to existing 'political and financial structures' *FT*, 19 March 2003, p. 11;*The Guardian*, 19 March 2003, p. 115). On the same day acting president Natasa Micic dismissed the president of Serbia's supreme court and the republic's chief prosecutor*The Times*, 19 March 2003, p. 20). The next day, Milan Sarajlic, Serbia's deputy state prosecutor, was arrested for alleged links to the Zemun clan. Sarajlic admitted to 'having been on the payroll' of the Zemun clan and to having received 150,000 euros of the 1 million euros promised to him by the gangsters, according to a police statement. He had also damaged the investigation of the assassination of Djindjic by disclosing the where - abouts of a protected witness who had agreed to testify on the work of the Zemun clan. In addition, he had been responsible for the immediate release of Dejan 'Bugsy' Milenkovic, the driver of the lorry that had swerved into Djindjic's car on 21 February. The Serbian police claimed that Sarajlic had also admitted to obstructing investigations into a number of actual or attempted assassinations, including the killing of the anti-Milosevic journalist Slavko Curuvija and the attempt to kill Vuk Draskovic in 1999, the killing of Zika Petrovic (then general manager of Yugoslav Airlines) in 2000, and the murder of Serbia's deputy interior minister Radovan Stojicic in 1997

(*Independent*, 21 March 2003, p. 17). On 20 March the Skupstina also purged the judiciary of thirty-five Milosevic-era judges (including seven supreme-court judges) The justice minister Vladan Batic stated that: 'Inefficiency of courts allowed a numbe of killers and other criminals to dodge justice for years.' The judiciary was blamed for the poor handling of the investigation into the 21 February attempt to assassinate Djindjic, when his car had been pushed off the road and the driver of the lorry that swerved into Djindjic's vehicle had been immediately released. The Zivkovic government also ordered the suspension of two newspapers which it suspected of being funded by the Serbian mafia, including the mainstream newspaper *Nacional*, which had defied the state of emergency by publishing reports on the state's responses to the Djindjic murder (*Independent*, 20 March 2003, p. 14; *FT*, 20 March 2003, p. 10).

On 24 March the authorities arrested Zvezdan Jovanovic, a deputy commander of the Red Berets Special Operations Unit with links to the Zemun clan, claiming that he was the suspected assassin of Djindjic. They also arrested Sasa Pejakovic, whom they suspected of aiding Jovanovic, and found a German-made sniper rifle which (they suggested) might have been used to assassinate Djindjic. Jovanovic had f rst joined Serbia's paramilitary forces in 1991, when the JSO was commanded by Zeljko Raznatovic (Arkan). He joined the Red Berets in 1995. The Milosevic regime had not only encouraged criminals to fight in its notorious paramilitary units durin the Balkan conflicts of the 1990s, but had allowed them to participate in regular polic forces linked to underworld figures running lucrative drug-trafficking operations (*IHT*, 26 March 2003, p. 11).

The JSO was disbanded by the Zivkovic government on 26 March. The next day police claimed to have arrested at least f fteen of its members, including the Red Berets commander Dusan Marici. Other members were to be dismissed or transferred to other units. Two of the main people suspected of involvement in Djindjic's assassi nation died (rather conveniently) in a shoot-out with the police when officers tried t arrest them on 27 March. However, four of the alleged perpetrators of the Djindjic murder, all members of the JSO, were arrested. In all, about 1,000 people had by then been taken into custody, 400 of whom had been charged with offences (*ndependent*, 28 March 2003, p. 15; *Independent*, 29 March 2003, p. 18).

The fate of Ivan Stambolic

On 28 March the interior minister Dusan Mihajlovic announced that Serbian police had found the grave of the missing Serbian ex-president Ivan Stambolic, who was alleged to have been killed by the same Red Beret group suspected of having assas - sinated Zoran Djindjic. Stambolic had been viewed as a possible presidential candidate and as a threat to Milosevic's chances of re-election in September 2000. Stambolic had been abducted on 25 August 2000, while jogging in a Belgrade park. 'It is clear who ordered this crime,' Mihajlovic added, referring to Milosevic and his wife. Even though Stambolic had no plans to run in the 2000 elections, there was a widespread belief that Mirjana Markovic had considered him a strong potential opponent to her husband. Investigators suggested that Dusan Spasojevic and Mile (Milan) Lukovic were the Zemun clan leaders who had financed and organized the operation *IHT*, 29 March 2003, p. 7; *Independent*, 29 March 2003, p. 18). Mile Lukovic and Milorad Lukovic (Legija) were two unrelated people but both were high up in the Zemun gang. Stambolic had been director of the Yugoslav Bank for International Economic

Cooperation from 1988 to 1997 and by the time of his abduction was showing no signs of having any political ambitions. He supported Vojislav Kostunica for the FRY presidency (*Independent*, 29 March 2003, p. 24). On 29 March Serbian police stated that they had 'well-founded suspicions' that Mirjana Markovic was linked to the killing of Ivan Stambolic, and the next day Serbia's deputy prime minister Zarko Korac said that 'The killing of Ivan Stambolic was a paid, political killing. It is justified and logica to assume that the direct order for the killing came from the [Milosevic-Markovic] couple.' The order for the killing allegedly emanated from the security chief Radomir Markovic, but he was 'just the pawn in the couple's hands' (*Independent*, 31 March 2003, p. 13).

The former army chief of staff General Nebojsa Pavkovic was arrested on 1 April (*The Times*, 2 April 2003, p. 18), but Serbia's deputy prime minister Nebojsa Covic suggested that the arrest was linked to events in the past and not to the Djindjic assassination (*The Guardian*, 3 April 2003, p. 16).

Zvezdan Jovanovic, the JSO deputy commander who had allegedly f red the gun that killed Zoran Djindjic, claimed on 8 April that the Djindjic assassination was to have been the first of a series of planned killings aimed at toppling the Zivkovic government and restoring 'patriotic forces' (Milosevic's supporters) to power. He told investigators that these political killings were intended to sow chaos and panic among the population. A new transitional government would have ended Serbia's cooperation with the ICTY. Jovanovic claimed that he had acted on the orders of Milorad Lukovic. Investigations had begun into potential links between President Kostunica's office and Lukovic. Kostunica's security adviser Rade Bulatovic and the former chief of military intelligence General Aco Tomic were questioned about a meeting they had with Lukovic in December 2002 (*Independent*, 9 April 2003, p. 11). Bulatovic and Tomic, two of Kostunica's closest aides, were arrested on 8/9 April after police learned that they had met the gang bosses who planned the assassination of Djindjic. Lukovic was in hiding, but Spasojevic had been shot dead by police at the end of March. Kostunica denied any knowledge of such meetings. By then, more than 7,000 people had been arrested. The deputy prime minister Nebojsa Covic alleged that Vojislav Seselj had ordered the Djindjic assassination (*Daily Telegraph*, 10 April 2003, p. 18). On 13 April President Kostunica retaliated by reiterating his earlier accusations that Serbia's government appeared to be abusing the state of emergency, intended to facilitate the manhunt for those behind the assassination of Djindjic, to curb political freedoms. He also categorically denied that he or his party had any links with the gangsters and paramilitaries suspected of being responsible for the assassination. The two aides detained for alleged involvement in the assassination were not members of his party (*IHT*, 14 April 2003, p. 9).

A Belgrade court issued an arrest warrant for Mirjana Markovic on 18 April 2003, for failing to appear at her trial for abuse of power. However, she had left Serbia for Russia, ostensibly to visit her son and grandson, on 23 March. She had been charged with abuse of power for allegedly misusing her influence to ensure that her grandson' ex-nanny received a state apartment. She was also wanted for questioning vis-à-vis the murder of ex-President Stambolic (*IHT*, 19 April 2003, p. 7). By May she was the subject of an international warrant 'for her alleged involvement in the death of Ivan Stambolic' (*Independent*, 13 May 2003, p. 12).

The Zivkovic government lifted its forty-two-day state of emergency on 22 April. Reporting restrictions were lifted, allowing the Serbian media the right to criticize and analyse the full scope of government policy. Two mainstream newspapers had been suspended during the state of emergency and a magazine with alleged links to Milorad Lukovic was closed permanently, while other journalists had received 'warnings'. Police stated that they had pressed charges against over 1,000 individuals (*IHT*, 25 April 2003, p. 5). Another report claimed that during the state of emergency Serbia's police had questioned over 7,000 people and imprisoned over 2,000 suspected members of criminal gangs – the so-called 'mafia'. However, the government's critic feared that this crackdown on organized crime had been used to distracted the public from what some saw as 'Serbia's real problems: the continued impunity of those accused of war crimes'. No senior members of the Milosevic regime had yet been put on trial in Serbia for war crimes, and many observers had concluded that 'Djindjic was killed because he was ready to send more war crimes suspects to face trial .. . in The Hague.' Furthermore, not only critics of the government, but even some of its supporters, feared that the crackdown was becoming 'a political vendetta' focusing on Kostunica and his DSS (*IHT*, 22 April 2003, p. 5). Other reports claimed that over 10,000 people had been arrested during the state of emergency and that almost half of these had remained in custody (*The Guardian*, 30 April 2003, p. 15).

Charges were f led against Slobodan Milosevic, the former security chief Radomir Markovic and seven other people on 24 April, for alleged involvement in the Stambolic murder (*IHT*, 25 April 2003, p. 5). On 29 April, the Serbian authorities charged Milosevic, his former security chief and his former chief of staff with 'organizing a criminal group' which had tried to kill Vuk Draskovic in June 2000. Several members of the same underworld group were among forty-five suspects charged by police i connection with the Djindjic assassination (*IHT*, 30 April 2003, p. 6).

The interior minister Dusan Mihajlovic asserted that the Zemun clan was behind the Djindjic assassination, which had been carried out by a group of ffteen men. The Zemun clan wanted to create chaos and to install so-called 'patriotic forces' in power, he claimed, and their plot was called 'Stop the Hague'. Furthermore, the SRS leader Vojislav Seselj had instigated members of the Zemun clan to kill Djindjic, and Seselj's sudden decision to surrender to the ICTY in February 2003 had served as an alibi against suspicions that he was involved in the Djindjic assassination*Independent*, 30 April 2003, p. 12). In addition, Mihajlovic claimed that Aco Tomic and Rade Bulatovic were implicated in the Djindjic murder, because they had promised that the Serbian armed forces would not interfere in the *coup d'état* which was intended to follow on from it. They were charged with 'associating to commit hostile activities'. However, Mihajlovic also claimed that the investigation had uncovered no evidence of Milosevic having been involved in the assassination of Djindjic (*The Guardian*, 30 April 2003, p. 15).

In June 2003 Serbia granted visa-free entry to citizens of forty countries, including the USA, the EU states, the twelve EU accession states, Croatia and Slovenia. Croatia reciprocated with a promise to allow visa-free entry for Serbs, starting on 10 June*FT*, 6 June 2003, p. 12).

Dozens of Serbian nationalists and riot police were injured in battles on 13 June during the arrest of Major Veselin Sljivancanin, who had been indicted by the ICTY in 1995 for complicity in the massacre of 260 Croats near Vukovar in November 1991. He went into hiding after the fall of Milosevic in October 2000. The police clashed with hundreds of nationalist protestors, as well as members of the wanted man's family.

The USA had given Belgrade until 15 June to cooperate with the ICTY or risk losing political support and up to 110 million US dollars in economic aid in 2003*IHT*, 14 June 2003, p. 5). Two other members of the notorious 'Vukovar Three', Miroslav

Radic and Mile Mrksic (named on the same indictment), had already given themselves up to the ICTY (*Independent*, 14 June 2003, p. 10). The Serbian government had established a special prosecutor and special witness-protection schemes both to combat mafia-style gangsterism and to root out Serbs wanted for war crimes (*The Guardian*, 14 June 2003, p. 17).

In July 2003 opinion polls conducted in Serbia indicated that 60 per cent of Serbs now favoured full separation from Montenegro, where there was roughly 40–45 per cent support for full separation ('independence') from Serbia (*The Economist*, 19 July 2003, p. 31).

In July 2003 the Serbia authorities decided to give the ICTY about 6,000 pages of classified documents which could prove vital to the trial of Milosevic. If unexpurgated, these would provide prosecutors with full transcripts of the meetings of Serbia's supreme defence council (which Milosevic usually chaired) from 1991 to 2000 (*HT*, 12 July 2003, p. 2).

Serbia's central bank governor Mladjan Dinkic, two of the bank's three vice-governors and several department head resigned on 18 July 2003 in protest against controversial central bank reforms approved by the Skupstina. The resignations stripped Serbia's leadership of some of its most tough-minded economic decision-makers. Dinkic and his team were credited with pushing through the banking reforms which had tamed Serbia's previously uncontrolled inflation rate and with finding ways for Serbs to reclaim savings and other assets which had been frozen during the Milosevic era. However, they had run into conflict with the Zivkovic government i 2003, especially after Dinkic's private think-tank (G17 Plus) decided to convert itself into a political party which was sometimes critical of government policy and competed for support from much the same reform-minded constituencies as the governing DOS coalition. G17 Plus had been especially critical of laws approved by the Skupstina on 18 July, which Dinkic claimed would undermine the central bank's independence by giving the Skupstina powers to nominate and appoint the bank's senior officials However, the Zivkovic government replied that the bank's independence was not threatened and that the legislation merely involved prudent tidying-up or 'house - keeping', prompted by the transformation of the central bank into a solely Serbian institution after the dissolution of the FRY five months previously. Radovan Jelasic one of the resigning vice-governors, claimed the central bank's accomplishments had elicited suspicion and jealousy from the Zivkovic government, whose popularity was sagging. Dinkic had accused the government of corruption (*FT*, 19 July 2003, p. 7). However, it would have been naïve to suppose that there would be no comeback on his decision to abandon the political neutrality normally expected of a central bank governor by entering the political fray with a party of his own in competition with the government. The Skupstina appointed forty-one-year-old Kori Udovicki, a Yale-educated economist who had worked for the IMF, as the new governor of the central bank on 22 July. She pledged to continue Dinkic's anti-infation policies and initially commanded wide respect (*FT*, 23 July 2003, p. 9).

In July 2003, in a controversial parliamentary vote on media supervision, the Democratic Party turned to Milosevic's once-reviled SPS in order to outflank the smalle parties in the governing coalition, who refused to toe the government line. The Zivkovic government adopted new powers in the name of stability, following the assassination of Djindjic. Newspapers were now to be vetted before publication, which could now be blocked on grounds of 'national security' (*FT*, 29 July 2003, p. 8).

Serbia's miners, who had played a vital role in bringing down the Milosevic regime in October 2000 by going on strike in defiance of orders to the contrary, claimed tha the DOS government was betraying them 'by moving to restructure Serbia's coal and power industries without consulting them' (*FT*, 29 July 2003, p. 8).

During a visit to Washington in July 2003, Premier Zoran Zivkovic offered the US about 1,000 Serbian troops for service in Iraq or Afghanistan, but the USA did not immediately take up the offer (prudently so, given that Serb forces had recently engaged in 'ethnic cleansing' in Kosova). In 2002 the Serbian authorities had informed the USA of the location and plans of Yugoslav-built bunkers in Iraq (*The Economist*, 23 August 2003, p. 31; *IHT*, 20 December 2003, p. 3). In October 2003, Zivkovic again offered to supply NATO with 700 or more Serbian troops, this time for use in Afghanistan, presumably in a bid to curry favour with the USA (*FT*, 4 October 2003, p. 6).

On 4 September 2003 Serbia's justice minister Vladan Batic denied allegations by Amnesty International that suspects detained in connection with the assassination of Djindjic had been tortured by prison guards, but he did not rule out the possibility that some of the 4,500 suspects rounded up after 12 March may have been beaten in police stations. Amnesty International was pressing for an investigation (*IHT*, 5 September 2003, p. 5).

President Stipe Mesic of Croatia made a historic visit to Serbia and Montenegro on 10 September 2003, the first such visit since 1991. Svetozar Marovic, president of the State Union of Serbia and Montenegro, joined President Mesic in formally apologizing for 'all the evils' committed by citizens of their countries between 1991 and 1995, something that ex-president Kostunica had refused to do (*The Times*, 11 September 2003, p. 16). Among the thorniest issues was the return of refugees, including the 300,000 ethnic Serbs displaced from Croatia to Serbia. Croatia had registered 100,000 returns, but many of these had found their homes destroyed or possessed by new occupants and stayed only a short time before returning to Serbia (*FT*, 10 September 2003, p. 12). Regular flights between Zagreb and Belgrade wer re-established.

An indictment served by the Serb special prosecutor on 23 September charged Slobodan Milosevic, Radomir Markovic, General Nebojsa Pavkovic and Milorad 'Legija' Lukovic with masterminding the murder of ex-president Ivan Stambolic and an attempted assassination of Vuk Draskovic. Serbia's newly established special court tried Milosevic and his co-accused *in absentia*. Hitherto, the only accusation formally made against Milosevic had been for an illegal attempt to obtain a lot next to his house in Belgrade (*Independent*, 25 September 2003, p. 14).

Serbia's JAT airline reactivated flights between Belgrade and Sarajevo on 1 October, after a f ve-year interval, and offered to help Bosnia's grounded airline to resume operation. The new service was part of a plan to reconnect Belgrade with all the major cities in the region (*IHT*, 2 October 2003, p. 2).

On 20 October Carla del Ponte announced indictments against the former army chief of staff Nebojsa Pavkovic, the former corps commander Vladimir Lazarevic, the former police chief Vlastimir Djordjevic and the still active head of public security Sreten Lukic for crimes against humanity which they were alleged to have committed in Kosova in 1999. Prime Minister Zoran Zivkovic reacted very angrily to this, declaring that the indictments were a 'blow to reform in Serbia' and a 'drastic violation' of an informal agreement between the ICTY and Belgrade. He claimed that Carla del Ponte had assured the late Zoran Djindjic that there would be no new indict- ments based on the principle of command responsibility, but a spokesperson for Mrs del Ponte denied the existence of any such deal (*IHT*, 22 October 2003, p. 3). In Serbia these indictees were widely 'seen as heroes', so the government declared that it was in no hurry to arrest and extradite them (*ndependent*, 22 October 2003, p. 12). Serbia's interior minister Dusan Mihajlovic declared that he would not arrest or hand over Lukic, whom he praised for his crackdown on organized crime following the assassination of Djindjic. Serbia's police service planned an unprecedented public demonstration of support for its indicted supremo. Carla del Ponte had been warning the Serbs for six months beforehand that the indictments were on the way. The Serb authorities claimed on 23 October that they had conducted an unsuccessful manhunt for Ratko Mladic in Belgrade and four smaller Serbian towns and that they had been given to understand that, provided they hunted down the 'big fish' Ratko Mladic, they would be allowed to try the four 'smaller fish' in Serbia (*The Economist*, 25 October 2003, p. 45; *Independent*, 24 October 2003, p. 13).

About 10,000 workers led by a trade union with links to Slobodan Milosevic marched through Belgrade on 29 October, demanding the dismissal of the Zivkovic government, the holding of early parliamentary elections and a halt to privatization. The protest coincided with an attempt by nationalists and other Milosevic supporters to vote down the government in parliament (*HT*, 30 October 2003, p. 3). On the second day of demonstrations, several thousand workers marched to the parliament and three protestors were injured (*IHT*, 31 October 2003, p. 3).

On 13 November the Zivkovic government called for early elections to be held on 28 December, after the defection of two minor parties from the governing eighteen-party DOS coalition f nally wiped out its parliamentary majority. Zivkovic lamented that the reform programme had become 'bogged down' by obstruction – not so much from nationalists loyal to Milosevic as from the SRS and from within the DOS. 'We can no longer conduct reforms . . . And thus we will again demand the trust of the electorate.' The governing coalition had also been weakened by allegations of conflicts of interest and corruption (*FT*, 14 November 2003, p. 9; *IHT*, 14 November 2003, p. 3).

Another attempt to elect a Serbian president, 16 November 2003

There were six candidates in all, but the turn-out for the presidential election held on 16 November 2003 was only 39 per cent – again well below the 50 per cent needed to validate the outcome (*The Economist*, 22 November 2003, p. 49). Vojislav Kostunica's DSS contributed to this abysmally low turn-out by boycotting the elections. Furthermore, the distribution of votes cast was deeply disturbing. Dragoljub Micunovic, the seventy-three-year-old speaker of the joint parliament of Serbia and Montenegro and the candidate of the ruling DOS coalition, obtained only 1.8 million votes. This was 300,000 fewer than those for Tomislav Nikolic, the candidate and deputy leader of the ultra-nationalist SRS, which attacked the Zivkovic government's cooperation with the ICTY (*The Times*, 17 November 2003, p. 15; *The Times*, 18 November 2003, p. 20). Indeed, through their uncompromising insistence on Serbia's full cooperation with the ICTY, the Western powers had severely damaged the electoral standing of the reform-minded DOS coalition and came dangerously close to handing victory to the profoundly vicious and ultra-nationalist SRS. Almost as a death wish, the DOS coalition announced its formal dissolution on 19 November, six weeks prior to the parliamentary elections scheduled for 28 December (*IHT*, 20 November 2003, p. 4).

Seeking to capitalize on the alarming presidential-election outcome, on 1 December, Prince Aleksandar Karadjordjevic for the first time publicly proposed that the restoratio of a constitutional monarchy would 'make its citizens proud' and 'secure respect for Serbia, both at home and abroad' (*Independent*, 3 December 2003, p. 15).

On 12 December the ICTY banned Slobodan Milosevic from campaigning in Serbia's parliamentary election from his prison cell in the Netherlands, after he floute detention rules by recording a speech which was broadcast in Serbia. The ICTY imposed a similar ban on the SRS leader Vojislav Seselj, after he too broke the rules by speaking to supporters and journalists by telephone from Scheveningen jail. The ICTY announced that it would henceforth monitor all the telephone conversations of Milosevic and Seselj, other than those with diplomatic or legal officials or with thei families, in a bid to prevent them from campaigning in the media, and that it would ban them from seeing or speaking to off cials from their respective political parties during the next thirty days, because it was worried that this electioneering by ICTY indictees could undermine the court's standing in the former Yugoslavia. However, no legislation in Serbia banned people who had been indicted by a court or who were being tried from taking part in elections (*IHT*, 13 December 2003, p. 3). During a visit to Belgrade on 15 December, the EU foreign-policy supremo Javier Solana deplored the inclusion of Milosevic and three other people indicted by the ICTY on the official lists of candidates in the elections *IHT*, 16 December 2003).

The trial of thirty-six people collectively charged with organizing and carrying out the assassination of Zoran Djindjic began on 22 December 2003. The prosecution argued that gangland bosses with links to the JSO had tried to topple the Djindjic government and that Djindjic had been preparing a crackdown on organized crime at the time he was killed. Forty defence lawyers stormed out of the court on 24 December, when the presiding judge insisted on reading out to the court pre-trial statements which had supposedly been made to police by Zvezdan Jovanovic, a former JSO officer with links to the Zemun gang. Jovanovic was quoted as telling police that he personally had shot Djindjic, that he had done so to prevent further extraditions of indictees to the ICTY, and that Milorad 'Legija' Lukovic (the person accused of masterminding the assassination) had insisted that the assassination was necessary in order to halt the extradition process and the disbanding of the JSO (Lukovic himself was still on the loose). From the outset, defence lawyers for the thirteen suspects in the courtroom and the twenty-three others who were still at large sought to undermine the credibility of the prosecution case by arguing that the defendants had been tortured and beaten during the state of emergency from 12 March to 22 April. They protested against the use of confessions allegedly extracted from defendants by force and were able to exploit the fact that Amnesty International and other human-rights organizations had criticized the Serbian authorities for abuses which had allegedly occurred during the state of emergency, in which a total of 11,000 people were claimed to have been rounded up, including many members of opposition parties. The trial resumed on 25 December (*The Times*, 26 December 2003, p. 17).

Elections to the 250-seat Serbian Skupstina, 28 December 2003

Twelve parties and six coalitions contested the election. There was a moderately high turn-out (60 per cent). This was expected to benefit Zivkovic and his allies more tha the ultra-nationalists, because it meant that many opponents of the SRS and SPS who normally did not vote at all were in fact voting (*IHT*, 29 December 2003, p. 6; *FT*,

6.14 Serbian parliamentary election, 28 December 2003

	Share of vote (%)	Seats
Ultra-nationalists and the SPS:		
Serbian Radical Party (SRS, led by Seselj)	32.6	82
Socialist Party of Serbia (SPS)	9.0	22
The anti-Milosevic camp:		
Democratic Party of Serbia (DSS, led by Kostunica)	20.9	53
Democratic Party (DS, led by Boris Tadic)	14.9	37
G17 Plus (led by Miroljub Labus)	13.5	34
Serbian Movement of Renewal–New Serbia (led by Vuk Draskovic)	9.1	22

Source: Pavlovic (2004: 499).

29 December 2003, p. 5), but between them the ultra-nationalists and the SPS nevertheless obtained an alarming 41.6 per cent of the votes and 41 per cent of the seats (see Table 6.14).

The SRS and the SPS had 'benefited from a huge protest vote at the failure of th democratic reformers to stabilize the country, attack corruption or raise living standards. They also exploited the resentment of many Serbs towards the international war crimes tribunal' (*FT*, 30 December 2003, pp. 6, 14). Vojislav Seselj and Slobodan Milosevic headed the candidate lists of their respective parties. The SRS stated that Seselj would not be nominated initially for a parliamentary seat, but that an SRS deputy would vacate a seat for him if he was freed by the ICTY. The SPS did not formally decide before the election whether to allocate Milosevic a seat in parliament, but one day after the vote its leaders within Serbia announced plans to provide him with a seat (*FT*, 30 December 2003, p. 6).

Even though Serbia was facing enormous socio-economic problems, the dominant issue in the election was whether to cooperate with the ICTY. Antipathy towards the ICTY had increased considerably, especially since Carla del Ponte had issued new indictments against four members of the Serb security forces, including the police minister Sreten Lukic. Not only had the Zivkovic government refused to extradite these men, but parties across the political spectrum found it expedient to highlight their opposition to the ICTY and even to put up candidates who had been indicted by it. Sreten Lukic was a candidate for the Liberal Party and a member of the governing coalition, and had previously favoured cooperation with the ICTY. He was in second place on the campaign list of the Liberal Party led by the outgoing interior minister Dusan Mihajlovic, who had been among those responsible for Milosevic's arrest and subsequent deportation to The Hague, but had praised Lukic as 'a hero of the defence of our people in Kosova' (*The Guardian*, 27 December 2003, p. 18). The former army chief of staff Nebojsa Pavkovic was a candidate for the Socialist People's Party.

Although the four groups which had previously been united in opposition to Milosevic and the ultra-nationalists could still have combined to form a government enjoying majority support, the chronic tensions and bickering between them virtually precluded such an outcome. Kostunica's DSS refused to form a coalition with the DS, which it accused of crime and corruption. The third liberal-reformist grouping, G17 Plus, had profound disagreements with the Democratic Party but was willing to cooperate with Kostunica's DSS (*IHT*, 29 December 2003, p. 6). The SPO–New Serbia alliance campaigned for a monarchy, but it nevertheless positioned itself within the reform camp and broadly supported 'EU-orientated reform' *FT*, 9 January 2004, p. 6).

The four main reform-minded parties had all declared in advance that they would not cooperate with the ultra-nationalist SRS during or after the election. Despite his own strong pan-Serb and anti-ICTY leanings, even Vojislav Kostunica had enough good sense to announce during the election campaign that he could not support the SRS conception of a Greater Serbia (*IHT*, 30 December 2003, p. 3). However, these four shared little common ground and differed even on such key questions as whether to dissolve Serbia's 'state union' with Montenegro (*FT*, 29 December 2003, p. 5). Miroljub Labus, the G17 Plus leader and the DOS government's presidential candidate in 2002, had been at loggerheads with the Democratic Party since he had failed to receive the Democrats' wholehearted support. G17 Plus had left the government and became one of its most vociferous critics. The hard-nosed G17 Plus technocrats had long questioned the economic benefits for Serbia of a continuing link with Montenegro and had come out in favour of the two republics going their separate ways – a stance which was warmly welcomed by Montenegro's pro-independence lobby. However, the future of the 'state union' with Montenegro was not a key political issue in the election, and the 'Belgrade political establishment's self-absorption' together with its lack of enthusiasm for the largely EU-imposed 'state union' meant that (re)integration of the Serbian and Montenegrin economies and harmonization of Serbian and Montenegrin trade policies was not a high priority and was seriously behind schedule. Since the assassination of Djindjic, reform had 'stalled'. G17 Plus also cared little for Kosova. By contrast, Kostunica wanted to strengthen the 'state union' with Montenegro and cling on to Kosova. Kostunica ostensibly sought to concentrate on poverty relief, while his reformist rivals made contradictory proposals for jump-starting an economy whose industrial output had fallen by 3 per cent during 2003 (*The Economist*, 3 January 2004, pp. 21–2; *The World Today*, 2004, vol. 60, no. 1, p. 19; *FT*, 30 December 2003, pp. 6, 14).

The SRS openly called for the establishment of a 'Greater Serbia', pledged to sever diplomatic ties with Croatia, vowed to halt extradition of ICTY indictees to The Hague and benefited from the DOS government's failure to improve living standards (*IHT*, 29 December 2003, p. 6). It had toned down its rhetoric and adopted a populist, more socio-economic message, promising to turn away from 'brutal capitalism', to reintroduce price controls (especially on basic foodstuffs), to increase state pensions and welfare benefits, to create more public-service jobs and to restore Serbia's national pride. Its supporters were typically older and included many Serb refugees from Croatia, Bosnia and Kosova. Tomislav Nikolic, Seselj's deputy and acting head of the SRS, vowed that, even though his party remained committed to the creation of a Greater Serbia (including much of Croatia), 'it would seek to gain what it had failed to win in war by diplomatic means' *The Economist*, 3 January 2004, pp. 21–2).

The success of the SRS highlighted just how disappointed many Serbs were with the meagre results of three years of economic liberalization, the feuding between the diverse opponents of the former Milosevic regime and the constant allegations and revelations of governmental corruption. The DOS coalition had failed to become an effective force for change, giving many voters the impression that valuable time had been squandered. The outgoing deputy prime minister Nebojsa Covic publicly accepted that the DOS coalition had earned the punishment it received from Serbia's voters (*IHT*, 29 December 2003, p. 4).

With considerable justification, however, many members and supporters of the DOS government also blamed the Western powers for not having provided more development aid to help Serbia restructure its economy, polity and society and create jobs. The Western powers had made the tasks of the DOS coalition government almost impossibly difficult, not only through the actual meagreness of their economic suppor for Serbia's reconstruction-cum-reform programmes, but also through dogged and blinkered Western insistence that this beleaguered reforming government of a hugely damaged and debilitated country simultaneously had to comply fully and immedi- ately with the punitive fervour and obsessions of the Western-sponsored ICTY – a Procrustean bed that rapidly dissipated the reformers' initial popularity. This turned them into the most abject national traitors in the eyes of even the most moderate and reform-minded Serbian patriots/nationalists. Thus, at least partly out of sheer anger, frustration and disgust at the inability of the seemingly servile and impotent DOS government to retain or salvage Serbian dignity by securing Western consent to the imprisonment and prosecution of ICTY indictees in Serbia rather than in The Hague, large numbers of moderate and reform-minded Serbian patriots voted for either Kostunica's DSS or Seselj's ultra-nationalist SRS, both of which aimed to halt the extradition of Serbian indictees to the ICTY.

Post-election wrangling and stalemate, January–March 2004

Kostunica declared on 5 January 2004 that he favoured a national-unity government of all the parties represented in parliament, which would hold off ce on a caretaker basis for a limited time and draw up a new constitution, but several parties had already rejected that option (*IHT*, 6 January 2004, p. 8). On 27 January, when the new Skupstina convened for the first time, it failed to elect a speaker, after the DS refused to suppor either Kostunica's candidate or that of the SRS. Kostunica refused to form a coalition with the DS, on the grounds that it would 'discredit' the new administration among people who had voted for the nationalist DSS, the SPS or the ultra-nationalist SRS in protest against the Democrats' poor record on the economy and corruption. In a bid to break the deadlock, Kostunica hinted on 29 January that he might consider sharing power with the SPS, although he denied that talks had been initiated. He stated that he could join forces with the SPS 'in order not to stymie the creation of a new government and face the people with new elections'. He also acknowledged that the SPS possessed 'administrative skills that we opposition parties are all lacking' (*IHT*, 29 January 2004). After six weeks of stalemate, Serbia's divided anti-Milosevic parties in the end sought support from the SPS to elect Dragan Marsicanin, a prominent member of the DSS, as parliamentary speaker by 126 votes to 81 (*IHT*, 5 February 2004, p. 3).

On 20 February Vojislav Kostunica announced that he would try to form a minority government with support from G17 Plus, the SPO, the DS and, most controversially, from the SPS.

The Skupstina voted on 25 February to sack the central bank governor Kori Udovicki, less than a year after she had been given the job. However, Mrs Udovicki had maintained monetary discipline and her successor Radovan Jelasic (a former deputy governor) was expected to follow suit (*FT*, 26 February 2004, p. 10).

The minority government headed by Vojislav Kostunica, March 2004 onward

Prime-minister-designate Kostunica announced on 2 March that his proposed government would seek to put war-crime suspects on trial in Serbia, instead of sending them to the ICTY, and would try to negotiate an agreement with the ICTY to allow Serbs who had already been convicted by it to serve their sentences in Serbia rather than in Western Europe, although a report published by the OSCE in 2003 had claimed that Serbia's court system was 'not yet up to standard'. SPS officials made it clea that SPS support for a Kostunica-led government would be conditional on that government not handing over further indictees to the ICTY (*IHT*, 3 March 2004, p. 3). Kostunica also declared that the only way to secure the survival of the ethnic Serb minority in Kosova was through 'partition of Kosova into entities, or cantonization' (*Independent*, 3 March 2004, p. 22).

Kostunica's proposed minority-coalition government gained parliamentary approval on 3 March. It could count on the support of the fifty-three DSS deputies the thirty-four G17 Plus deputies, twenty-three SPO–New Serbia deputies and twenty-two SPS deputies, just suffcient to give it a working majority in the 250-seat Skupstina. It included members of Kostunica's DSS, G17 Plus and Vuk Draskovic's SPO–New Serbia. The former central bank governor Mladjan Dinkic became the new f nance minister. Dinkic criticized the previous economic policy, saying it favoured Serbia's tiny upper class and yielded only 1.5 per cent growth in GDP in 2003. The government put forward policies which it claimed would reduce unemployment from the off cial 32 per cent level. It promised a combination of steep tax cuts and proposals for expensive state-led investments, such as a 296 million US dollar scheme at the ageing Zastava vehicle plant (*FT*, 13 March 2004, p. 6; *The Economist*, 10 April 2004, p. 34). The DS leader Boris Tadic became the joint Serbia-Montenegro defence minister.

A high-profile war-crimes trial, the first of its kind to be held in Serbia, opened in Belgrade on 9 March 2004. Six men were charged with murdering 192 Croatian prisoners of war after the fall of Vukovar in November 1991. A spokesman for the ICTY stated that this trial could pave the way for a new division of labour, whereby the ICTY would prosecute the big fish and Serbian courts prosecuted the small fry. The ICTY had recently prosecuted the notorious 'Vukovar Three', Veselin Sljivancanin, Mile Mrksic and Miroslav Radic, who were charged with orchestrating the Vukovar massacre (*The Times*, 10 March 2004, p. 19).

Kujo Krijestorac, a key witness in the prosecution of thirteen people charged with direct responsibility for the assassination of Zoran Djindjic, was found murdered in his car in Belgrade on 9 March. He had earlier told investigators that he had seen and could identify the sniper who carried out the killing.

Sasa Cvyetan, a Serbian paramilitary who had taken part in the massacre of fourteen women and children in a Kosova backyard four days after the start of the NATO bombing in March 1999, was sentenced by a Belgrade court on 17 March to twenty years in prison (the maximum permitted by Serbian law). However, human-rights activists saw him as a fall guy for the commanders of the Serbian paramilitary police unit known as the Scorpions, who were still at large. Another of the accused, Dejan Demiovic, had escaped to Canada, where he was fighting against extradition proceedings (*The Guardian*, 18 March 2004, p. 10).

In Belgrade on 19 March, 10,000 people marched to St Sava Cathedral demanding that 'the international community' take measures to guarantee the safety of the residual

Serb minority in Kosova. Serbian sources claimed that seventeen Orthodox churches and monasteries had been burnt down by ethnic Albanians in Kosova since 17 March (*The Times*, 20 March 2004, p. 14).

The Skupstina decided on 30 March to provide generous financial assistance t Serbs indicted by the ICTY, including Slobodan Milosevic, partly to encourage more Serb indictees to surrender voluntarily to the ICTY. The legislation offered all Serbian indictees at the ICTY full public reimbursement of legal costs, loss of earnings, telephone bills, visa fees and mail costs, as well as assistance for spouses, parents and children to fly to and stay in hotels in The Hague *IHT*, 31 March 2004, p. 2).

Due to Serbia's continued refusal to cooperate fully with the ICTY, on 1 April the US congress froze 26 million US dollars of aid to Serbia (a token amount, since Serbia was expecting 1.3 billion US dollars from other sources). The EU delayed a long-awaited 'feasibility study' on future Serbian and Montenegrin membership of the EU, while NATO indicated that Serbia and Montenegro would remain excluded from its Partnership for Peace, which they had been hoping to join in June 2004 (*The Economist*, 10 April 2004, p. 34; *FT*, 9 April 2004, p. 6).

Milorad Lukovic, the suspected architect of the assassination of Zoran Djindjic on 12 March 2003, gave himself up to the Serbian police at his home in a Belgrade suburb on 2 May, after a year on the run. Five of the thirteen people charged with direct responsibility for the assassination were by then in police custody, including the alleged sniper. The Belgrade media speculated that he had struck a deal with the prosecutors or the government, by offering to provide further information about the killing in return for a reduced sentence. Lukovic was also accused along with other former and serving members of the JSO of involvement in the abduction and killing of ex-president Ivan Stambolic (*IHT*, 4 May 2004, p. 3).

The late Zoran Djindjic's sister was hospitalized on 16 May after two men had attacked her in her home and injected her with the sedative diazepam. She and her mother had been receiving death threats and warnings to stop the prosecution of Milorad Lukovic (*IHT*, 17 May 2004, p. 4).

On 10 June the ICTY chief prosecutor Carla del Ponte reported to the UN Security Council that Belgrade's cooperation with the court was 'almost non-existent' (*The Guardian*, 12 June 2004, p. 18).

The fifth and sixth successive attempts to elect a Serbian president, 13 and 27 June 2004

In order to ensure that whoever obtained a majority of votes cast would become president of Serbia, the rules were changed to do away with the requirement for a 50 per cent turn-out to validate the result. However, a run-off ballot between the two leading candidates proved necessary and was held on 27 June. In the frst round there were f fteen candidates and the voter turn-out was 45 per cent. The two front-runners were the SRS deputy leader Tomislav Nikolic, who obtained 30.4 per cent of the votes cast, and the DS leader Boris Tadic, who obtained 27.6 per cent. Boris Tadic, the leader of the Democratic Party and former joint defence minister of Serbia and Montenegro, was backed by Serbian liberals and the Western powers. Dragan Marsicanin, who was backed by Prime Minister Kostunica, obtained under 13 per cent of the votes cast, while Bogoljub Karic, a shady multimillionaire businessman and former crony of Milosevic, obtained over 16 per cent. Tomislav Nikolic promised that, if elected in the second round, he would halt further extraditions of Serbs to the ICTY and would seek to bring down the Kostunica government. The prominent economic reformer Miroljub Labus warned that he would pull G17 Plus out of the governing coalition if Nikolic won (*FT*, 14 June 2004, p. 6).

A new president of Serbia was finally elected on 27 June 2004. Boris Tadic obtaine 53.5 per cent of the vote, as against 45.1 per cent for Tomislav Nikolic, obtained on a 48.5 per cent turn-out. The elections had been marred by shooting incidents, and two leading contestants defied a UNMIK (UN Mission in Kosova) prohibition agains holding election rallies in Kosova.

The strong support for the ultra-nationalist Nikolic could be construed as evidence that over 30 per cent of voters still supported parts of the 'Greater Serbia' programme of the 1990s and were 'in denial about the nature of that project and the practical consequences for Serbs of carrying it out'. However, another interpretation was that this was in large part a protest vote against the ICTY, against the continuing dire state of the economy and against the failure to resolve the future of Kosova and Montenegro and the plight of 'stranded' Serb minorities in neighbouring states and in Kosova. The post-Milosevic governments had not yet succeeded in alleviating widespread poverty and unemployment, while at the same time small sections of the elite had become obscenely rich through highly corrupt and hastily prepared 'insider priva - tizations' and by working with foreign companies. There was considerable disgust with the selling of state assets to privileged buyers at knock-down prices as a way of generating quick privatization revenues, and with the fact that informal Milosevic- era networks were still intact in the political, military and paramilitary underworlds, despite some arrests of leading f gures (*The World Today*, July 2004, p. 20).

At his inauguration on 11 July 2004, President Tadic promised that his first priorit would be 'to bring Serbia closer to the EU' and that he would promote cooperation with the ICTY: 'It will show our real adherence to the values of the civilized world' (*Independent*, 12 July 2004, p. 22). He accepted that full and honest cooperation with the ICTY was the sine qua non for Serbia's political and economic integration with the West and that Ratko Mladic in particular had to be found and extradited (*FT*, 12 July 2004, p. 7).

In August 2004 a diplomatic row erupted between Serbia and Hungary, following attacks on the 300,000-strong ethnic Hungarian minority in the Vojvodina province of northern Serbia. The Hungarian government sent a strongly worded letter to Prime Minister Kostunica, calling on him to halt the violence and prosecute the perpetrators (*FT*, 11 August 2004, p. 5). The ethnic Hungarian minority had managed to coexist peacefully with the Serbs during the 1990s, but during 2004 they had suffered physical attacks, desecration of graveyards and numerous racist graffiti   *IHT*, 16 September 2004, p. 3).

The Montenegrin members of the Serb-Montenegrin 'National Council for Cooperation with the ICTY' resigned on 23 September 2004 in protest against Serbia's continued refusal to comply fully with ICTY demands. Montenegro was rightly concerned that its own progress towards membership of the EU could be jeopar- dized by continued Serbian defiance or foot-dragging (*IHT*, 24 September 2004, p. 3). That same month, however, having insisted in vain for over a year that Serbia and Montenegro had to dismantle their trade tariffs simultaneously and at the same pace, the EU Commission conceded a 'twin-track approach' which allowed the republics to negotiate with the EU in tandem, preserving their status as a single candidate state without requiring them to adopt identical legislation (*FT*, Survey, 14 December 2004, p. 31). This only temporarily assuaged Montenegrin concern.

A car carrying President Boris Tadic was rammed repeatedly by a black Audi on 1 December 2004, but his security officials were unable to stop the Audi from speedin off afterwards (*IHT*, 2 December 2004, p. 5).

Deputy prime minister Miroljub Labus threatened on 26 December 2004 that he would pull G17 Plus out of the governing coalition unless, by the end of January 2005, the government extradited to The Hague the ICTY indictees who were still at large in Serbia. The retired Serbian general Vladimir Lazarevic agreed on 29 January 2005 to give himself up voluntarily to the ICTY, where he was wanted for crimes committed by his troops against ethnic Albanian civilians in Kosova in 1999. He did so on 3 February. The government's official stance was that it would not arrest ICT indictees, but would leave it up to them to decide to turn themselves in voluntarily (*IHT*, 28 December, p. 3; *IHT*, 29 January 2005, p. 3; *IHT*, 4 February 2005, p. 5).

Milan Gvero, a retired sixty-seven-year-old Bosnian Serb general who had been an aide to Ratko Mladic and had been indicted for expelling and killing Bosniaks on the eve of the July 1995 Srebrenica massacre, gave himself up voluntarily to the ICTY on 24 February. His departure was 'sweetened by a significant cash payment' It had by then become an open secret that Kostunica's policy of persuading ICTY indictees to turn themselves in 'voluntarily' was backed up by payments of hundreds of thousands of euros to their relatives for their 'services to the homeland' (*Independent*, 25 February 2005, p. 22). Radivoje Miletic, another former Bosnian Serb army general and aide to Mladic, followed suit on 28 February. Momcilo Perisic, the sixty-year-old former army chief of staff (1993–8), did likewise on 7 March. His indictment detailed alleged crimes from August 1993 to November 1998, including attacks on civilians in Srebrenica, and stated that (as Mladic's superior) he knew of the plans to attack Srebrenica but did nothing to prevent it. However, General Perisic had been dismissed by Milosevic in 1998 for resisting the use of the VJ to crush the ethic Albanian insurgency in Kosova, and he had subsequent launched an opposition party which joined the DOS movement (*IHT*, 8 March 2005, p. 3). Mica Stanisic, a former police chief in the Bosnian Republika Srpska, surrendered to the ICTY on 11 March (*FT*, 12 March 2005, p. 9). Gojko Jankovic, a former Bosnian Serb para - military indicted for systematically raping Bosniak women, decided to give himself up to the ICTY on 13 March after five years on the run   *IHT*, 14 March 2005, p. 7). Until late 2004, according to his wife Milica, he had been living in Russia under a false identity and twenty-four-hour protection. He had been one of at least three ICTY indictees hiding in Russia (*IHT*, 15 March 2005). Drago Nikolic and Vinko Pandurevic, former Bosnian Serb off cers who had been indicted for genocide in the 1995 Srebrenica massacre, gave themselves up on 15 and 23 March. Kostunica was under intense international pressure to step up the extradition of suspects to the ICTY ahead of an EU report expected in early April 2005 on whether Serbia was fit to star negotiations on an SAA – the frst step towards EU membership (*IHT*, 21 March 2005, p. 3). Ljubomir Borovcanin, the deputy commander of the Bosnian Serb special police during the Srebrenica massacre, decided to give himself up after a meeting with Serbian officials on 29 March (*IHT*, 30 March 2005, p. 5). Sreten Lukic, the retired general who served as deputy interior minister in the Djindjic government between 2001 and 2003, 'surrendered' (somewhat involuntarily) on 4 April (*IHT*, 5 April 2005, p. 3). Vujadin Popovic, a Bosnian Serb officer implicated in the Srebrenica massacre, sur rendered the same week, bringing to thirteen the number of Serb and Bosnian Serb indictees who had surrendered since the start of 2005 (*FT*, 13 April 2005, p. 8). On 22 April General Nebojsa Pavkovic, the army chief of staff who had commanded

Serbia's armed forces very skilfully during the 1998–9 conflict in Kosova and wa widely regarded as a national hero in Serbia, agreed to surrender to the ICTY after spending several weeks in hiding (*IHT*, 23 April 2005, p. 5). He did so on 25 April. The Kostunica government achieved these numerous 'voluntary' surrenders by 'threatening some with arrest and negotiating deals with others, including promises of financial aid to their families' *IHT*, 16 May 2005, p. 3).

Ex-prime minister Zoran Zivkovic revealed on 18 March that unarmed CIA agents had participated in dozens of unsuccessful attempts by Serbian police to capture Ratko Mladic in 2003 and that a deal had been concluded on Serbian–US cooperation in the hunt for Mladic, with the aim of either catching Mladic or verifying that he was not hiding in Serbia (*IHT*, 19 March 2005, p. 5).

Montenegro's prime minister Milo Djukanovic proposed on 22 February 2005 that Serbia and Montenegro should retain loose links but be recognized as independent states. Vojislav Kostunica rejected this proposal out of hand the next day, calling it a 'gross violation of the Belgrade agreement' signed by the two countries (*IHT*, 24 February 2005, p. 4). On 28 February Montenegro's foreign minster Miodrag Vlahovic declared that Montenegro aimed to become a member of the EU and of NATO as an independent state, rather than as part of the State Union of Serbia and Montenegro (*IHT*, 1 March 2005, p. 7).

Vuk Draskovic, speaking as foreign minister of the State Union of Serbia and Montenegro, stated on 4 April that Ratko Mladic was hiding with the help of Serbian security services: 'It is only natural that the security services know where Ratko Mladic is. They know if he is in Serbia and they know if he is not . . . Without that kind of protection, without that kind of network, it would be impossible for Mladic to be invisible' (*FT*, 5 April 2005, p. 7).

The EU Commission announced on 12 April 2005 that it would recommend that formal negotiations be commenced with Serbia and Montenegro on an SAA, after a commission study concluded that the State Union of Serbia and Montenegro was fi to start such negotiations and had improved its cooperation with the ICTY sufficiently The recommendation was approved by the EU's foreign ministers (Council of Ministers) on 25 April, with a view to starting negotiations in November 2005.

Judges at the ICTY suspended the trial of Slobodan Milosevic for five days on 2 April, following medical reports that he was suffering from 'dangerously high' blood pressure (*IHT*, 21 April 2005, p. 10). During Milosevic's ongoing trial at the ICTY, on 1 June 2005 a video was shown of six Bosniaks being dragged from the back of a lorry by Serbian paramilitary police and then tortured and killed. The video was rebroadcast on Serbian television on 3 June. This was the first time that a visual recor of part of the infamous July 1995 Srebrenica massacre had been shown on television. The next day, the Serbian authorities arrested six members of the notorious Scorpions, a paramilitary police unit attached to the Serbian interior ministry. The film foot-age was highly significant because it showed that paramilitary police from Serbia proper (and not just Bosnian Serb forces) had taken part in the Srebrenica massacre. Carla del Ponte, the chief prosecutor at the ICTY, commented that the Scorpions were under the command of Serbia's interior ministry and had been transferred to Bosnia with the knowledge of the Serbian police (*The Times*, 3 June 2005, p. 47). A survey conducted shortly before the televising of this video had indicated that under half of Serbia's adult population believed that the Srebrenica massacre had even taken place (*Independent*, 3 June 2005, p. 28;*The Guardian*, 3 June 2005, p. 15). Prime Minister Kostunica swiftly condemned the killings, and on 7 October a Serbian court charged five of the arrested Scorpions with the murder of six Bosniaks in Srebrenic in Bosnia in July 1995 (*IHT*, 8 October 2005, p. 5).

On 29 June a Belgrade court found Radomir Markovic (Milosevic's former security chief), Milorad 'Legija' Lukovic (former head of the Serbian JSO and chief suspect in the Djindjic and Stambolic assassination trials) and three other former JSO members guilty of the attempted murder of Vuk Draskovic and the killing of four of his associates on 3 October 1999. Markovic was sentenced to ten years in prison, while the other three received fifteen-year terms. The sentences were the toughest yet serve by a Serbian court against Milosevic's henchmen. The prosecution had asked for forty-year prison terms for each of the suspects, the maximum sentence allowed by Serbian law. Milhalj Kertes, who had been one of Milosevic's chief hatchetmen during the 1990s, was sentenced to three years in prison for providing the armoured truck and the cash used in the crash (*IHT*, 30 June 2005, p. 3).

Radovan Karadzic's wife Ljiljana made an impassioned plea for him to surrender to the ICTY on 28 July, stating that 'her family could no longer live with the constant pressure applied by international and local security forces seeking his arrest' and that she had 'decided that the welfare of her family had to take priority'. His son Aleksandar had been detained for a week by NATO forces in Bosnia in July, due to his involvement in his father's support network (*HT*, 28 July 2005; *The Guardian*, 29 July 2005, p. 17).

Charges against Marko Milosevic for allegedly threatening an opponent with a chainsaw were dropped in August 2005, apparently as part of a deal to ensure that the SPS did not withdraw its support from Serbia's minority government, after the accuser claimed that 'he could no longer remember whether Marko Milosevic had threatened him'. However, the accuser's mother claimed that the accuser and his family 'had received death threats'. In June 2005 the authorities had also revoked an arrest warrant for Milosevic's wife Mirjana Markovic, who had been wanted on corruption charges and for questioning in relation to the Ivan Stambolic murder enquiry. Both were now free to visit Milosevic, whom they had not seen for over two years (*The Times*, 16 August 2005, p. 27; *Independent*, 20 August 2005, p. 22). However, after Mirjana Markovic failed to return from her self-imposed exile in Russia in order to appear for trial on corruption charges in Belgrade, a new international warrant for her arrest was issued on 15 September. The previous arrest warrant had been revoked in June, after her lawyer provided assurances that she would definitely attend this hearing. She ha left Serbia in 2003 amid charges that she had given government-owned luxury apartments to party off cials and that she had abused her influence to obtain a stat flat for a family nanny *IHT*, 16 September 2005, p. 5; *The Guardian*, 16 September 2005, p. 18).

The start of negotiations on an SAA between the EU and Serbia and Montenegro was given the 'green light' by a meeting of EU heads of government in Luxembourg on 4 October 2005. Technical negotiations began in November 2005, but no timetable or even timescale was set for the completion of these negotiations, which were very strongly linked to continued (Serbian) cooperation with the ICTY and to further political, economic, judicial and administrative reform in both countries. The main effects of the opening negotiations were to involve Serbia and Montenegro in a structured dialogue with and monitoring by the EU and to allow them increased access to EU funds. The intention was that, so long as Serbia and Montenegro remained constituent parts of the EU-brokered state union, the two countries would sign a single SAA, but with separate detailed annexes – one for each state. Furthermore, unless

Montenegro voted decisively in favour of full independent statehood (in the referendum on independence scheduled for 21 May 2006), Brussels was still expecting the two republics to accede to the EU as a single entity (*FT*, Survey, 12 July 2005, pp. 30–1).

On 4 November 2005, the Skupstina approved an agreement allowing NATO troops transit rights through Serbia and Montenegro to their bases in Kosova and Bosnia. Several other Balkan countries had made similar agreements with NATO, but this had been a particularly sensitive issue in Serbia (*IHT*, 5 November 2005, p. 4).

At the end of a two-year trial, on 12 December 2005, Serbia's special war-crimes tribunal found fourteen former members of a Serbian militia guilty of having executed about 200 Croatian prisoners of war at a pig farm in the village of Ovcara (near Vukovar) in November 1991. Eight of the defendants received twenty-year prison sentences, the maximum permitted under Serbian law. The others were given prison sentences

> ranging from five to fifteen years, including the only woman among the defendants, who was given a nine-year prison term. Two of the sixteen defendants originally indicted were acquitted. The trial in Belgrade was seen as a key test of the ability of Serbia's judiciary to deal with cases of war crimes committed by Serbs.
>
> (*IHT*, 13 December 2005, p. 3)

Thus far, the Serbian authorities had brought seven war-crimes cases to trial, five o them in the special war-crimes court which was partly fianced by the US government. According to some human-rights groups, however, these Serbian prosecutions had focused on middle-ranking army and police offcers, while many more senior offcers were not being challenged about their conduct in either the Bosnian, or the Croatian or the Kosovar conflict. Indeed, many who had been accused by human-rights groups of either ordering crimes or failing to prevent them were still 'at their posts' (*IHT*, 4 January 2006).

Carla del Ponte declared on 20 January 2006 that Ratko Mladic was 'hiding in Serbia under the protection of the army', and dismissed Serbian claims that he had fled to Russia. She announced that she wanted to start the trial of Mladic in July 2006, simultaneously with the other eight indicted for crimes committed during the 1992–5 war in Bosnia (*IHT*, 20 January 2006, p. 4). The EU's enlargement commissioner, Olli Rehn, reiterated that Serbia's integration with the EU could be frozen if it did not cooperate fully with the ICTY (*IHT*, 21 January 2006, p. 3). Serbia's justice minister Zoran Stojkovic responded by suggesting that ICTY investigators could participate in Serbian operations to track down Mladic, so that they could see for themselves 'that we are really trying to fufil our obligation' *IHT*, 21 January 2006, p. 3).

On 31 March 2006 the EU extended by one month – until 30 April – the deadline for Serbia to hand over Ratko Mladic to the ICTY after Carla del Ponte told EU offals that Belgrade was making progress in hunting him down. Olli Rehn reported that Mrs del Ponte had received a strong assurance from prime minister Vojislav Kostunica that Mladic would soon be arrested and transferred to the ICTY. The grace period allowed Rehn to proceed with the next round of SAA negotiations with Serbia and Montenegro, scheduled for 5 April, which the EU had threatened to freeze if Serbia failed to hand over Mladic. The State Union foreign minister Vuk Draskovic claimed on 30 March that Serbia's secret service knew where Mladic was hiding but had failed to arrest him (*IHT*, 1 April 2006, p. 3).

The EU suspended the SAA negotiations with Serbia on 3 May 2006 after Belgrade yet again failed (or, in effect, refused) to arrest Ratko Mladic and hand him over to the ICTY for trial. EU enlargement commissioner Olli Rehn announced the decision after consulting with Carla del Ponte. Ironically, the SAA negotiations had been proceeding well. Mrs del Ponte stated that the obvious conclusion was that she had been bamboozled when she was told at the end of March 2006 that the arrest of Mladic was 'a matter of days or weeks'. She added that she had received reports that the Serbian security services could have arrested Mladic at the end of January but refrained from doing so because the government wanted him to surrender voluntarily. However, there were suggestions in Belgrade that Kostunica had genuinely sought the arrest of Mladic but had discovered that 'his control over the security services was not suffient to deliver' (*IHT*, 4 May 2006, pp. 1, 8). It was indeed conceivable that the Kostunica government was not strong enough, either politically or morally, to override the obduracy of Serbia's security services.

In response to this major further setback to Serbian restructuring and reform, the G17 Plus leader Miroljub Labus announced his resignation as deputy prime minister and as head of Serbia's negotiating team. He blamed Prime Minister Kostunica for the government's failure to arrest and deliver Mladic. In his letter of resignation, Labus declared that the Kostunica government had 'betrayed the most important interest of the country and the citizens of Serbia' (*Independent*, 4 May 2006, p. 23). He also accused the Serbian security services of looking for Mladic 'everywhere except where he is hiding' (*The Times*, 4 May 2006, p. 19). It was unclear whether Labus's G17 Plus party would remain part of the governing coalition or whether it would withdraw the support of its thirty-one deputies in the Skupstina – a step that risked precipitating the government's collapse, because it only had a fve-seat parliamentary majority. The main justification for G17 Plus to continue to support the Kostunica government was that the collapse of that government could strengthen the political positions of the SPS and Vojislav Seselj's ultra-nationalist SRS. The hard line taken by Western governments, the EU and the ICTY on the handing over to the ICTY of persons indicted for war crimes and crimes against humanity had severely weakened the position of Serbia's more liberal alternatives to the intransigent Serbian nationalists in the SPS, the SRS and Kostunica's DSS. The political outlook was grim.

There were muted responses in Serbia to the referendum on Montenegrin inde - pendence on 21 May 2006, in which 55.5 per cent of Montenegro's eligible voters voted in favour of dissolving the increasingly dysfunctional State Union of Serbia and Montenegro. The nationalistic Serbian prime minister Vojislav Kostunica and his ruling Democratic Party of Serbia were long-standing opponents of Montenegrin independence, as were the SPS and the SRS. However, Serbia's President Boris Tadic, who would also have preferred Montenegro not to secede, probably spoke for most Serbs when he pragmatically accepted the referendum outcome on 23 May (*IHT*, 24 May 2006, p. 3).

A special session of the Montenegrin assembly formally declared Montenegrin secession from Serbia on 3 June 2006. Prime Minister Vojislav Kostunica flatly refuse to officially congratulate Montenegro on its attainment of independent statehood, and no Serbian officials attended Montenegro's independence ceremonies, but Serbia' defence minister nevertheless declared that the largely Serb armed forces of the defunct state union would accept Montenegrin independence and that all Serbian soldiers would withdraw from Montenegro within a week, while President Tadic graciously wished the people of Montenegro 'peace and stability and overall prosperity' on its route to EU membership and promised that Serbia would remain Montenegro's closest friend. Negotiations between Belgrade and Podgorica on how to divide up the joint assets and liabilities of the defunct state union were scheduled to take place during the summer of 2006. The negotiators would also have to decide the terms on which Montenegrins could continue to study or work in Serbia or use Serbian hospitals in future. On 5 June a special session of Serbia's Skupstina formally accepted the dissolution of the state union and unanimously declared Serbian independence, although Serbia's ultra-nationalist parties (headed by the SRS) and the SPS absented themselves from the vote, presumably in order to feel neither tainted nor bound by it (*IHT*, 6 June 2006, p. 3). Most Serbs nevertheless appeared to accept the secession of Montenegro from the state union with equanimity, not least because about 60 per cent of Serbs had also been in favour of dissolving the state union that had been foisted upon Serbia and Montenegro by Javier Solana and the EU in 2002–3 (see pp. 000). In accordance with the Serb-Montenegrin State Union's founding charter, Serbia became the official successor to the state union

Reforming and restructuring Serbia's economy, 2001–5

Liberalization of Serbia's foreign trade regime

During the first half of 2001 almost all non-tariff import restrictions were abolished but quantitative export restrictions were maintained for some agricultural goods. An action plan to harmonize trade, customs and excise regimes between Serbia and Montenegro by the end of 2005 was approved by the parliaments of both republics in the spring of 2003 and by the State Union parliament in August 2003. During 2004–5 virtually all import and export quotas were abolished (EBRD 2005b: 174).

On 27 June 2001 the governments of Romania, Albania, Bosnia-Herzegovina, Bulgaria, Croatia, Macedonia and Yugoslavia signed an agreement aimed at liberalizing trade in at least 90 per cent of goods traded between them, under the auspices of the EU's Stability Pact for South-eastern Europe (*FT*, 28 June 2001, p. 8). In March–April 2002 Serbia signed bilateral free trade agreements with Hungary, Romania, Bulgaria, the Republic of Macedonia and Bosnia-Herzegovina *FT*, 24 April 2002, p. 6).

Clearing the Danube

The Danube was off cially reopened to shipping on 29 November 2001, for the f rst time since May 1999 when bombs dropped by NATO aircraft destroyed the bridges over the river. Some parts of the Danube were still in need of further clearance work which was to be completed by mid-2002. In July 2000 the EU Commission had earmarked 23 million euros to pay 85 per cent of the projected 26 million euro cost of clearing the river of debris from bridges destroyed by NATO bombing (*IHT*, 27 July 2000, p. 6; *FT*, 30 November 2001, p. 13).

Foreign and internal debt

The FRY had an external debt of 12 billion US dollars in early 2001. This was equal to about 140 per cent of GDP, and debt-service payments far exceeded export earnings, pushing Serbia deeper into debt (*The Guardian*, 5 April 2001, p. 13). On 16 November 2001 Yugoslavia's official Paris Club creditors agreed to write down the 4.6 billio US dollar debt owed to them by 66 per cent (*IHT*, 17 November 2001, p. 13). In July 2004 the Serbian government reached an agreement on its outstanding debts with the London Club of commercial creditors, reducing the present value of these debts by 62 per cent (EBRD 2004b: 171–2). In addition, the state owed 4.5 billion US dollars in hard currency to its own citizens in 2001. Their hard-currency bank accounts had been frozen under Milosevic, plus as much again in dinar-denominated debts (*The Economist*, 17 February 2001, p. 50).

Reforms of the banking sector

About 80 per cent of the banking sector was still owned by enterprises under social ownership in 2000 (EBRD 2000b: 9) and was in crisis and failing to meet the needs of the real economy. The sector had over 4.81 billion US dollars in accumulated uncovered losses, 'equal to more than 40 per cent of the country's GDP', according to the central bank governor Mladjan Dinkic (*IHT*, 3 February 2001, p. 12). Insolvent banks were closed or placed under close supervision in 2001. Dinkic presided over twenty-three bank closures between October 2000 and September 2002, including the four biggest state banks in January 2002. The cost of the January 2002 bank closures was about 4 billion US dollars, equivalent to 1 per cent of GDP. Such closures denied ailing industries further access to addictive soft loans. Other banks were being prepared for privatization (EBRD 2002a: 56; *The Economist*, Survey, 14 September 2002, pp. 4, 7). The central bank became 'a largely independent institution' pursuing a monetary policy based on fully covering the money supply with foreign currency reserves. It ended the earlier practice of providing soft loans to insolvent state- or socially owned enterprises and to the government.

The introduction of euro notes and coins in the euro zone on 1 January 2002 boosted the commercial banking sector, as Serbs sought to convert Deutschmark savings into euros through the banks. In order to do so they were required to open bank accounts. Serbian banks estimated that as much as 800 million Deutschmarks were converted into euros during the frst two days after euro notes became available. Bank collapses, runaway inflation and government seizures of hard-currency savings had driven man Serbs away from bank accounts and the formal economy during the 1990s. The entry of selected foreign banks helped to restore confidence in the sector. From early 2002 however, foreign banks were not allowed to obtain new licences and could only enter the market by acquiring a Serbian bank (*IHT*, 18 January 2002, p. 5).

Under a law passed in January 2002, the ZOP payments bureaux operated by the national bank of Yugoslavia in order to maintain a state monopoly of financial transactions during the Communist era and under Milosevic were f nally closed in January 2003. Responsibility for processing payments was transferred to the com - mercial banks. This reform met EU requirements as well as an obligation to the IMF (*FT*, 6 January 2003, p. 6). The benef ts included the emergence of a more eff cient and less corrupt payments system and more commercially viable banking. Increased confidence in Serbian banks, combined with the growing presence of foreign banks and widespread use of the euro, 'lured hidden cash into the open' (*FT*, Survey, 28 January 2003, p. 13). Nevertheless, the state still had significant or majority share holdings in sixteen of the forty-seven major banks in 2004 (EBRD 2004b: 170–1).

Privatization

Privatization was almost at a standstill from 1999 to 2001. The country's large enterprises remained largely unreformed and accrued heavy losses. Soft budget constraints, widespread inter-enterprise arrears and barter arrangements were rife. State- and socially owned enterprises still controlled 80 per cent of industry's capital stock and employed almost 75 per cent of the industrial workforce in 2001.

In June 2001 the Serbian parliament adopted a new privatization law. At least 70 per cent of shares in state- and socially owned enterprises were to be sold to private investors. Employees would be allowed to acquire (free of charge) shares amounting to 15 per cent of an enterprise's capital, while a further 15 per cent was to be distributed free to adult citizens. Strategic investors were henceforth permitted to acquire majority holding (EBRD 2001b: 20, 142). In December 2001 three large Serbian cement plants were sold for 139 million US dollars to foreign strategic investors.

Auctions and sales of small and medium enterprises began in 2002, as did the restructuring of insolvent large enterprises employing 9.5 per cent of the labour force – by decentralizing them, exposing them to market forces and hardening budget constraints, in a bid to prepare them for future privatization (EBRD 2004b: 22–3). Serbia's privatization agency also made preparations in 2002 to sell the Zastava car plant to a foreign car maker in 2003, arguing that 'a successful sale of Zastava would make it easier to privatize the 48 other state companies that urgently need to be restructured' (*The Economist*, 17 August 2002, p. 57).

In 2002 Serbian prosecutors investigated corruption allegations concerning the sale of 29 per cent and 20 per cent stakes in Telekom Serbia to Telecom Italia and the Greek telecommunication corporation OTE, respectively, in 1997. Telecom Italia fended off 'allegations that the Milosevic-era deal involved millions of dollars in kick backs' by agreeing to sell its 29 per cent stake back to the Serbian government for 195 million US dollars in December 2002, while OTE negotiated to swap its 20 per cent stake in Telekom Serbia's fixed-line telephone service for a controlling stake in its mobile telephone arm (*Independent*, 30 December 2002, p. 7; *FT*, 15 July 2003, p. 8).

Receipts from privatization reached 1.3 billion euros in 2003, mostly through the sale of: controlling stakes in Serbia's two largest cigarette-rolling plants to Philip Morris International and British-American Tobacco; Beopetrol, the country's second largest retailer of oil products, to the Russian oil giant Lukoil; Serbia's Apatinska Pivara brewery to Belgium's Interbrew; Celarevo brewery to Denmark's Carlsberg; a majority stake in the smaller Pancevo plant to Turkey's Anadolu Efes; and the Smederevo steel works to US Steel, as well as smaller sales of oil-product enterprises. Hitherto, there had been little foreign investment in Serbia (*FT*, 27 October 2003, p. 10; *The Economist*, 23 August 2003, p. 31). During 2003, net FDI in Serbia amounted to nearly 1.4 billion US dollars, generated mostly by these large sell-offs in the tobacco, beer and oil sectors (EBRD 2004b: 170–1).

Privatization of small-scale enterprises through auctions proceeded steadily during 2003–4. By mid-2004, over 1,000 companies had been sold (out of a total of around 2,500) since the comprehensive programme had been adopted in 2001. In spite of political uncertainties, the pace of privatization accelerated even more after that. By mid-2005 about 1,250 Serbian enterprises had been privatized successfully. In 2004–5 about sixty large industrial conglomerates underwent major restructuring with the help of international donors, with the aim of preparing them for eventual sale. The privatization of socially owned companies was scheduled for completion by the end of 2006, and the privatization law was amended in June 2005 to allow the government to write off the debts of selected companies, in order to facilitate their sale (EBRD 2005B: 174).

Taxation and business environment

During the 1990s, the Milosevic regime had sequestered billions of Deutschmarks from citizens' hard-currency savings, and politically favoured companies were granted access to this scarce hard currency on very favourable terms. In June 2001, the Djindjic government introduced an excess-profit tax on the estimated 8.3 billion Deutschmar extra profits earned by individuals, such as Bogoljub Karic, who had enjoyed specia access to these loans (EBRD 2002b: 146–7; *FT*, 20 May 2002, p. 9).

For obvious reasons, there had been hardly any FDI in the Serbian economy under Milosevic, even during the years when his regime actively sought such investment (1994, 1997–8). A new federal foreign investment law in early 2002 promoted the equal status of foreign and domestic investors.

VAT was introduced into Serbia from 1 January 2005, and Serbia's corporate-tax rate was reduced from 14 per cent to 10 per cent, one of the lowest rates in Europe. Nevertheless, surveys indicated that the business environment remained unfavourable. There were continuing concerns about political instability, pervasive corruption, the poor functioning of the judicial system and limited access to capital for the private corporate sector.

Expansion of the private sector

The private-sector share of GDP rose from about 40 per cent in 2000–1 to about 55 per cent in 2005 (EBRD 2004b: 6, 172; EBRD 2005b: 4). No reliable estimates were available for the 1990s. However, such estimates understate the full importance of private (including unrecorded and illicit) activity. The black economy may have accounted for as much as 70 per cent of economic activity in 2000 (*The Economist*, 14 October 2000, pp. 31–2). In January 2003 Alexander Vlahovic, Serbia's minister of the economy and privatization, estimated that the shadow economy accounted for 40–50 per cent of GDP, down from 80 per cent in January 2000, and that 30–40 per cent of Serbia's workforce worked in the shadow economy (*FT*, Survey, 28 January 2003, p. 12). In 2004, the EBRD estimated that the informal economy accounted for 30–50 per cent of GDP (EBRD 2004a: 66).

Concluding reflections: the travails of political and economic reform and restructuring in post-Communist Serbia

Under Milosevic, the Serbs were deeply ensnared and implicated in the strongly vertical power structures, power relations and clientelism that have been the bane of all Balkan polities, economies and societies, with the significant exception of Sloveni (which has been excluded from this book partly for that reason). These structures were closely intertwined with the strongly clientelist 'ethnic collectivism' that has been the other major affliction of the Balkans. The Milosevic regime ran the Serbian econ omy like 'a giant government cartel, with ministers and political leaders wielding enormous influence in both the public and so-called private sector'. Clientelism reache out even to farmers, who were virtually obliged to engage in political activity in order to receive the seeds they needed (*Independent*, 7 August 1996, p. 9).

Milosevic promoted this tightly controlled state-run economy not so much out of ideological conviction as because he used centralized economic power as a means of retaining political control. Key segments of Serbia's economy, such as the energy sector, agriculture and international trade (including drug-, oil-product- and cigarette-smuggling), were controlled by Milosevic's unsavoury cronies. In 1996, for example, the general manager of Progres, which was both Serbia's biggest exporter and its leading importer of Russian gas, was the prime minister Mirko Marjanovic, while the parliamentary speaker Dragan Tomic headed Jugopetrol, Serbia's biggest liquid-fuel distributor. Because these companies represented major sources of personal enrichment, these politicians opposed any notion of a truly pluralistic and competitive market economy (*IHT*, 21 August 1996, p. 2). Radical economic reform of any kind would have struck at the heart of Milosevic's power base, which rested 'on a vast web of political and economic patronage' (*IHT*, 5 August 1996, p. 6).

Economically, post-Milosevic Serbia still has a huge mountain to climb. Even though the private sector was accounting for 55 per cent of Serbia's economy by 2005, and even though Serbia's valiant economic reformers have accomplished considerable economic liberalization and some economic restructuring (despite very meagre support from the West and endemic feuding between the reformist Democratic Party and Vojislav Kostunica's uncompromisingly nationalistic Democratic Party of Serbia), in 2004 Serbia's GDP was estimated still to be only 56 per cent of its already severely depressed 1989 level. Moreover, the official unemployment rate was stil nearly 30 per cent, although some of those recorded as 'unemployed' actually had jobs in the informal economy (EBRD 2005a: 64). Much of the economy is still under the control of criminals and gangsters; poverty and inequality have grown to alarming proportions; vital remittances from Serbs living abroad are seriously declining; and there appears to be only a faint and flickering light at the end of Serbia's very lon and grim tunnel.

To an even greater extent than in other post-Communist states in the Balkans, the strengthening and deepening of liberal democracy in post-Milosevic Serbia is being severely impeded by deeply entrenched 'vertical' power relations and power structures inherited from the former Communist regime, from its nationalist-cum-monarchist precursors, and (much more distantly) from Ottoman and pre-Ottoman times. These power relations and power structures were given a potent new lease of life by Milosevic's étatist authoritarian-nationalist regime and its shrewd exploitation of highly corrupt and clientelist ethnic collectivism. They were further reinforced by the violent paramilitary and gangster networks which Milosevic nurtured and used for his own ends. The victims of the Milosevic regime included not only the roughly 130,000 Bosniaks, Croats and Kosovar Albanians who perished at the hands of Milosevic's armed thugs and the many more who suffered injuries, bereavements, privations and expulsions (ethnic cleansing), but also (albeit to lesser degrees) the much-maligned Serb populations who found themselves deeply ensnared, exploited and implicated in numerous crimes by the Milosevic regime and its collaborators. Although there have been innumerable attempts to stigmatize the Serbs with collective guilt for the terrible atrocities carried out in their name by a vicious and callous minority of Serbs, these imputations of collective guilt are far from justified

Our account of post-Communist Serbia has deliberately highlighted the courage, tenacity and magnitude (as well as the tragic internal divisions, quarrels and mistakes) of the Serbian opposition to the Milosevic regime and its pernicious policies and practices, as well as the sickening regularity with which the Western powers aided and propitiated Milosevic far more than they assisted and supported the many Serbs who opposed him and his often brutal allies and henchmen. We have done this not in order to 'whitewash' the Serbs, many of whom have undeniably deserved the opprobrium which has been heaped upon them, but in order to redress important imbalances and try to set the record straight. Large numbers of Serbs resisted the Milosevic regime, by voting, canvassing, speaking and demonstrating against it, by draft-dodging, by deserting from the army, and by defying military orders – indeed, proportionately, much more so than Italians resisted Mussolini's Fascist regime, or than Germans resisted the Nazi regime, for example. The main Serbian opposition forces, divided though they were, displayed great spirit and dogged determination in their opposition to Milosevic. Unfortunately, the mass mobilizations of strong Serbian opposition to Milosevic in 1991, in 1992 and during the winter of 1996–7 were fatally weakened by the fact that they received hardly any effective or constructive support from the Western powers, who treated Milosevic as a pragmatist with whom they could 'do business'. Even the overthrow of Milosevic in autumn 2000 was accomplished by the sheer courage and determination of the Serb opposition, with precious little assistance from the West or anyone else. The frequent claims that Milosevic succeeded in mobilizing an allegedly illiberal and rabidly nationalistic Serb nation to actively demand, approve or applaud large-scale crimes against humanity and ethnic cleansing are thus extremely misleading. Rather than impugn the Serbs, many more of whom appear to have actively and courageously opposed Milosevic than actively supported him, it would be more just to point fingers at the pusillanimity of the Wester powers when faced with recurrent mass mobilizations of Serbian opposition against the Milosevic regime. In addition, both here and in our analyses of post-Communist Montenegro, Croatia, Bosnia-Herzegovina, Macedonia and Albania, it has been emphasized that the very 'leaky' or selectively enforced sanctions imposed on the Yugoslav lands by the Western powers contributed hugely to the emergence and enrichment of powerful smuggling, drug-dealing, arms-dealing and people-traffickin criminal networks, which now have established a deeply entrenched stranglehold on large parts of Serbia's economy, polity and society. The West's tendency to criticize and punish Serbia and the Serbs for the criminal consequences of Western actions is utterly hypocritical. The Western powers should instead be trying to make some amends by doing and paying a great deal more than they have done, in order to start undoing the huge and enduring damage which they (albeit unintentionally) inflicte on this benighted region during the 1990s.

A crucial test for Milosevic's successors has been whether they can 'establish the rule of law in a highly criminalized society', as this will indeed determine whether Serbia becomes 'a little Russia or a civilized European country' (*NYRB*, 2000, vol. 47, no. 18, p. 14). As recently as autumn 2004, Serbia's so-called 'mafia' network in business and the underworld were still financing major political parties and politicians, according to Dusan Mihajlovic, the leader of Serbia's Liberal Party. In his view, corruption had become so extensive that 'honesty becomes more of a burden and diligence is like putting your head on a block' (*IHT*, 14 September 2004, p. 3). Sadly, it is by no means clear that the Serbian political establishment and judiciary have either the strength, or the moral courage and resolve, or sufficient financial resources, to overcome the deeply entrenched criminalization and corruption of their economy, polity and society. It seems unlikely that they can do it without large-scale Western assistance, and yet the West seems much more preoccupied with punishing Serbia (by withholding resources) than with helping it. The Western powers even seem to delude themselves that punitive action is the best form of help. It is certainly a very cheap surrogate for real help!

In order to implement their reform and reconstruction programmes, it is actually not necessary for Serbia's reformers to win over or gain the acquiescence of the thuggish ultra-nationalist and the criminal gangster wings of the Serbian polity, economy and society. With sufficient Western support and assistance, it would be ver feasible for Serbia's reformers and moderate nationalists to marginalize and gradually neutralize the ultra-nationalist SRS, the much diminished SPS and their criminal or thuggish supporters. Regrettably, Western meanness and obduracy, combined with the undeniable limitations and bickering of the DOS coalition, rendered such a strategy virtually impossible from early 2001 to March 2003. This resulted in growing diversions from and resistance to the reform programme and culminated in the assassination of Premier Zoran Djindjic on 12 March 2003. This in turn led to a state of emergency from 12 March to 22 April 2003, an excessive (but understandable) crackdown on all perceived threats to the survival of the DOS coalition government, the consequent stalling of most reform and reconstruction programmes during the rest of 2003, and the massive defeat of the battered and decapitated DOS coalition in the 28 December 2003 parliamentary elections. The sanctimonious ICTY, as well as the Western governments and organizations which have unrelentingly backed it to the hilt, should not be allowed to escape their major share of responsibility for (i) having repeatedly placed the DOS coalition government in impossible positions; (ii) their roles in creating the situation which resulted in the assassination of Zoran Djindic and the resultant over-reaction, disintegration and discrediting of Serbia's reforming coalition; and (iii) the growing disgust and disillusionment of most moderate and reform-minded Serbs towards what came to be seen as a servile DOS coalition government.

In their seemingly blind and relentless pursuit of retribution against the perpetrators of admittedly terrible crimes against humanity during the 1990s, the Western powers and the ICTY helped to wreck the reform-minded DOS coalition. Given the nationalist intransigence of Kostunica and his DSS, the DOS coalition embodied the only realistic hope of rapidly and radically restructuring the 'vertical' power relations and power structures that had previously sustained and undergirded the Milosevic regime and its corrupt and vicious allies in the security forces, the SRS, irregular armed forces and numerous criminal networks. Western governments and the ICTY either failed or refused to see that, in order to make it feasible to implement fundamental and far-reaching political, judicial and economic restructuring and reconstruction in a profoundly damaged, debilitated and traumatized country, it was above all necessary to build, sustain and reward a broad reforming coalition which could successfully marginalize and neutralize the forces ferociously opposed to such changes. To have had any realistic hope of accomplishing this, the Western powers would have had to soft-pedal their preoccupation with indicting people for war crimes and crimes against humanity and bringing them to justice in a Western court, in order to make possible much-needed processes of coalition-building, societal reconciliation, burying of hatchets, political stabilization and economic recovery. Admittedly, some monstrous criminals might have escaped being imprisoned and tried by the ICTY as a result, or their capture might have been further delayed, yet Mladic and Karadzic have thus far evaded capture in any case, and Milosevic – shrewd to the last – managed to cheat his captors and largely escape punishment by dying before his trial was completed.

The crucial point is that*there was a great deal more at stake* than simply satisfying Western demands for retribution by bringing Serb indictees to increasingly discredited and counterproductive 'victors' justice' at the ICTY. The West's chosen priorities and instruments have greatly delayed and impeded the much-needed processes of social healing, reconciliation and facing up to and coming to terms with all that occurred under the Milosevic regime. It is in large part a consequence of these warped Western priorities and Western parsimony that Serbia missed its chance for a clean break with the past under the Djindjic government and now appears to be almost irretrievably mired in organized criminal networks, clientelism, protection rackets and corruption.

Consider what would have happened if the governments and parliaments that accomplished the celebrated post-Francoist 'transition' to democracy in Spain had been bedevilled by constant and imperious Western demands that they had to *begin* by rounding up everyone who had committed atrocities under Franco and sending them for trial, not in Spain in accordance with Spanish law and as part of Spain's coming to terms with the crimes committed under Franco and during the civil war, but at a smug and sanctimonious 'international' court located in northern Europe, and if Western support and acceptance of Spain into Western or Western-dominated organizations had been made conditional on Spain's full and immediate compliance with such demands. It would certainly have made Spain's 'transition' much harder and might even have wrecked it altogether, while the botched attempt by diehard Francoist security personnel to halt Spain's 'transition' in 1981 might have succeeded instead of ignominiously collapsing. Similarly, consider what would have happened if the West had insisted that the democratization of Chile after the termination of General Pinochet's dictatorship had had to*begin* by sending all the security personnel who had committed atrocities under the Pinochet regime for trial in a European or North American court, as a precondition for Western economic support and readmission of Chile into the Western-dominated 'international community' and international organizations. The process would almost certainly have stalled very quickly, with Pinochet's still-powerful security forces resuming control of government and the judiciary. Such examples help to make clearer the crass folly and ineptitude of the policies which the West has repeatedly adopted towards Serbia. They also suggest that the principal 'blame' for the limitations and failings of Serbia's political and economic liberalization and restructuring since the 'October revolution' in 2000 lies less with the Serbian people and Serbia's undeniably disunited and querulous reformers than with the utterly myopic stances adopted by the Western powers. It was *known from the outset* that Serbia's numerically preponderant reformers were very disunited and fractious on several major and highly emotive issues, including cooperation with the ICTY, the plight of the much-despised and highly vulnerable ethnic Serb minority in Kosova, the respective futures of Kosova and Montenegro and whether or not to restore the monarchy. This made it all the more imperative to exercise great caution and concentrate on building and rewarding societal reconciliation and broad reform-minded coalitions with generous Western support and assistance, rather than to concentrate on punishment and vilification. The fact that so much was at stake, an that the West could expect to incur much larger costs if the much-needed reform and restructuring of the Serbian polity and economy were to be successfully obstructed or reversed, made it all the more important to give the strongest possible backing to the reform-minded DOS coalition, instead of continually undermining it and ultimately contributing to the assassination of its only impressive and charismatic leader, Zoran Djindjic.

When Slobodan Milosevic died in detention on 11 March 2006, what stood out most clearly was the degree to which the media had 'personalized' the Milosevic regime, seeing it as the work of one man and the nation which was assumed to have adulated him. However, this man's fall from power in October 2000 and his death in March 2006 have proved that it would take much more than the removal of one man to fundamentally alter the corrupt, 'ethnic collectivist' and highly clientelistic 'vertical' power structures that have long ensnared the people of Serbia. Serbia's new governments since October 2000 have been a lot less authoritarian and repressive than was the Milosevic regime, but the window of opportunity to carry out a more radical and profound transformation of post-Milosevic Serbia appears to have been missed. Certainly, part of the 'blame' for this lies with the substantial Serb *minority* which continues to support or even actively engage in the activities, methods and conduct which maintain a corrupt and increasingly criminalized vertically structured polity, economy and society. Part of it also lies in the deep internal divisions and fractiousness of the reform-minded coalition which came to power between October 2000 and January 2001. However, the blind ineptitude of the West's policies towards Serbia also played a major part in undermining and ultimately helping to destroy the reforming coalition, through the excessive pressures and demands to which it was subjected by the ICTY, the international financial institutions and the USA and the EU. Most depressingly of all, even now that a major opportunity has manifestly been missed, none of the major players has been showing any inclination to analyse candidly what went wrong and to rethink their priorities and strategies. Instead, they are all merely helping to dig Serbia ever more deeply into a hole. The outlook is becoming increasingly bleak. Not only has the best internal window of opportunity to change Serbia fundamentally been missed, but the external context for such a change appears to be becoming less and less propitious. The most influential West European members o the EU appear to be succumbing to growing waves of 'enlargement fatigue' and xenophobia, both of which are making it less and less likely that the western Balkan states can realistically expect to be granted EU membership in the foreseeable future. If so, the EU will become much less capable of providing effective leverage and incentives for fundamental restructuring and reform, and the whole process of restructuring and reform in the western Balkans could not only lose all momentum, but even go into reverse. We hope to be proved wrong, but the portents are not good.

7   Bosnia and Herzegovina

The travails of coexistence

Introductory 'country profile'

Bosnia and Herzegovina is a small country with a total population of 3.8 million in 2004. It has a land area of 51,129 square kilometres, which is about a tenth of the size of France or just over a fifth of the size of the United Kingdom and former Yugoslavia About 70 per cent of the total land area is mountains or other high ground, most of which is forested, and only 13.6 per cent is arable. The high Dinaric Alps, which dominate the terrain, made internal communications difficult until the constructio of modern roads and railways in the later twentieth century. The country is on average 693 metres above sea level.

Bosnia and Herzegovina was home to 19 per cent of former Yugoslavia's popu - lation. It was one of the poorer Yugoslav republics. In 1988 its per-capita GDP was only 68 per cent of the Yugoslav average, only half the level for Croatia and one-third of the level for Slovenia (Lampe 1996: 332). In 2004, despite the devastating impact of the warfare of 1992–5, Bosnia's per-capita gross national income at pur-chasing power parity was 7,430 US dollars , still somewhat ahead of the Republic of Macedonia (6,480 US dollars) and Albania (5,070 US dollars), albeit far below countries such as Croatia (11,670 US dollars), Slovenia (14,810 US dollars) and France (29,320 US dollars) (World Bank 2005: 292). Offcially, 44 per cent of the workforce was unemployed in 2004, although it is sometimes argued that the existence of a very large 'grey economy' (amounting to nearly 40 per cent of GDP) may have reduced the 'real' unemployment rate to around 20 per cent of the workforce (CIA 2005). Nevertheless, 18 per cent of Bosnians still lived 'below the poverty line and another 30 per cent just above it' in 2005 (The Economist, 26 November 2005, p. 49), because much so-called 'employment' was very nominal or part-time and very poorly paid.

The capital city is Sarajevo, which had a population of 525,980 in 1991. Banja Luka, which had a population of 195,139 in that year, is the second city and capital of the predominantly Bosnian Serb Republika Srpska. Mostar, with a population of 126,067 in 1991 and about 105,000 today, is the capital of Croat-dominated Herzegovina, which comprises 18 per cent of the republic's territory. The other major towns are, in order of size, Tuzla, Zenica, Bihac, Doboj, Jajce, Travnik and Trebinje.

Who are the Bosnians?

Even though they speak a common and mutually comprehensible language (Serbo-Croat), the modern-day inhabitants of Bosnia and Herzegovina mainly belong to three distinct South Slavic ethno-cultural groups:

1. Since the mid-1960s, *Bosniaks* have been the largest ethno-cultural group in Bosnia, and by 2000 they comprised 48 per cent of the population by ethnic aff liation. They used to be referred to as 'Bosnian Muslims' or simply 'Muslims', because they have been predominantly (but by no means entirely) Muslim by religious affiliation and are primarily descended from South Slavs who converte from Christianity to Islam during the 415 years of Ottoman-Turkish Muslim rule in Bosnia (1463–1878).

2. Since the mid-1960s, *Bosnian Serbs* have been relegated to the status of second largest ethno-cultural group, and by 2000 they comprised only 37.1 per cent of the population by ethnic affiliation. They have been predominantly (albeit ofte very nominally) Eastern Orthodox Christians by religious affiliation. They wer the most numerous ethno-cultural group in Bosnia from the sixteenth or seventeenth century until the 1960s.

3. There has also been a substantial (albeit steadily shrinking) *Bosnian Croat* minority, which by 2000 made up only 14.3 per cent of the population. They are predominantly (albeit often very nominally) Roman Catholic and they consider themselves to be the 'original' South Slavic inhabitants of Bosnia, who lost their majority status as a result of the exodus of many Bosnian Catholics during the f fteenth and sixteenth centuries and the gradual conversion of many of those who remained either to Eastern Orthodox Christianity or to Islam during the Ottoman era (a process which Croat nationalists and 'national historians' have often portrayed as a form of 'apostasy' or religious and cultural 'desertion' and 'betrayal').

In 2000 40 per cent of the population was declared to be Muslim by religious aff li-ation, 31 per cent Eastern Orthodox Christian and 15 per cent Roman Catholic, while 14 per cent were declared to have other religious affiations or to be atheist or agnostic.

It strikes some people as odd that in Bosnia and Herzegovina the term*Muslim* came to be used as a 'marker' of*ethnic or ethno-cultural identity* as well as (and increasingly instead of) religious identity, and that the 'Bosnian Muslim' community has come to be off cially regarded primarily as an*ethnic* rather than as a religious group. However, this is not without parallels elsewhere. Being 'Jewish' originated as a religious identity, yet it has gradually become an ethno-cultural identity to which agnostics and even atheists can subscribe. Furthermore, amid the current wave of Islamophobia in the West, the term 'Muslim' is increasingly being used at least as much in a *cultural* (or even *racist*) sense as in a religious one. Many of the people who are being labelled 'Muslim' (and are increasingly incurring cultural and racial prejudice, harassment, discrimination or even special surveillance for 'being Muslim') are not in the least bit religious – indeed, some are atheists or agnostics. Considerations of this sort are highly relevant to the ethno-cultural group of South Slavs whom the former Yugoslav Communist regime began to categorize as 'Muslim' or 'Bosnian Muslim' by ethnicity/ nationality (*narodnost*) in the 1961 census and as a distinct nation (*narod*) in 1968 and in the 1971 census, and who became officially called Bosniak *Bosnjak*) during the 1990s (Malcolm 1994: 199; Bringa 1995: 27, 34–5). Many members of this 'Bosniak' group are not actively Muslim or are only very vaguely 'Muslim by culture' (rather than by active religious practice and belief. After forty-five years of avowedl atheistic Communist rule (1945–90), widespread membership of the ruling League of Communists, and the growth of consumerist materialism since the 1960s, many Bosniaks could more accurately be described as either agnostic or atheist, even if they nevertheless feel that they belong to a South Slav community distinguished and defined by the Islamicization of its ancestors under Ottoman rule

Even those Bosniaks who define themselves as 'Muslim' *by religion* as well as by ethnicity/nationality nevertheless see themselves as *South Slavs* and as *Europeans*. They indignantly reject any imputation that being Muslim somehow makes them non-Slavic or non-European. Just as there have long been Arab, Iranian, African and Chinese Christians, so it is perfectly possible to be simultaneously 'European' and 'Muslim' – this is *not* a contradiction in terms. However, partly in response to the growing (and increasingly *racist*) tendencies for European and American 'Islamophobes' to equate being 'European' or 'Western' with being Christian (at least by 'culture', 'descent' or 'heritage', if not by active religious belief or practice) and to equate being 'Muslim' increasingly with being 'non-European' or 'non-Western', members of Bosnia's 'Muslim' community have taken to calling themselves 'Bosniaks' rather than 'Bosnian Muslims'.

Before the First World War (and to diminishing degrees subsequently), 'Bosniaks' or 'Bosnian Muslims' were usually referred to as 'Turks' by virtue of their predominant (supposedly 'Turkish') religious affiliation, even though relatively few Turks ever settled in Bosnia and Herzegovina – and those who did usually felt themselves to be ethnically quite different from their South Slavic 'Bosnian' or 'Bosniak' co-religionists. Ironically, it was as confusing then to use an *ethnic* label (Turks) to designate to a *religious* group (Muslims) as it has recently been to use a *religious* label (Muslims) to designate an *ethnic* group (Bosniaks). The new ethnic nomenclature (Bosniaks) is less confusing for foreigners, although it does not do away with the paradox that their 'Muslim heritage' is all that differentiates 'Bosniaks' from Bosnian Serbs and Bosnians Croats.

It is only since the late nineteenth century that Bosnians have been differentiated from one another in this particular way. From late medieval times until the nineteenth century, the traditional *collective* regional/territorial appellation for *all* the inhabitants of Bosnia and Herzegovina was 'Bosnian' *(Bosanac)*, *irrespective* of their individual ethnic and religious affiliations (Bringa 1995: 34–5). Medieval and early modern 'Bosnians' were primarily identif ed by their *shared territorial* or *regional* identity and by their particular religious affiliation (either Catholic, or Orthodox or – later – Muslim), but they appear to have been regarded as a single ethnic group. Only since the nineteenth century, with the gradual emergence and intensification of nationalis and ethnic consciousness, has it become increasingly common to translate *religious* into *ethnic* aff liations: to assume that 'Catholic' must mean 'Croat', that 'Orthodox' must mean 'Serb', and that 'Muslim' must be an ethnic more than a religious identity or affiliation. Interestingly, the social anthropologist Tone Bringa reported that as recently as 1987–8 the inhabitants of the Bosnian villages which she was studying were still often identif ed as either *Orthodox* or *Muslim* or *Catholic*, but that these ostensibly *religious* labels were being used as *ethnic* labels (Bringa 1995: 21). This was not mental confusion, but simply a particular way of categorizing people and of thinking about such categories – hence the apt title of her book, *Being Muslim the Bosnian Way*.

Relatively little is known about the early history of Bosnia and Herzegovina. During the Bronze Age the area appears to have been settled by warrior tribes who came to be known to the ancient world as Illyrians and who are generally assumed to have spoken an Indo-European Illyrian language or languages, although no one can be sure of this since no texts or inscriptions in such a language have survived – we don't even know if they actually had a written language (see Chapter 2, p. 24). Roman incursions into the Illyrian domains began in 229 BC, ostensibly to protect Roman shipping in the Adriatic sea against Illyrian 'piracy', but also to consolidate Rome's dominion over the Adriatic region. Southern Illyria came under (mainly indirect) Roman control from 168 BC, mainly as a by-product of the crushing defeat that the Romans inflicted on the neighbouring kingdoms of Macedonia and Epirus in that year. Nevertheless, the region's inhabitants kept up sporadic resistance to Roman overlordship until AD 9, when Rome decided to crush them once and for all. Most of the territory of present-day Bosnia and Herzegovina was incorporated into the large Roman coastal province of Dalmatia, which was established at that time. The discovery of significant metal ores in Bosnia encouraged the Romans to build roads and develo important mining industries. The region thus became an integral part of the Roman Empire. This facilitated the spread of Christianity, which became the offial imperial religion in 313 AD.

When the Roman Empire was divided into eastern and western halves in 395, what is now Bosnia and Herzegovina came under the jurisdiction of the East Roman (Byzantine) Empire centred on Constantinople. From AD 455, however, Dalmatia experienced the depredations of successive waves of Germanic, Turkic and other 'barbarian' invaders, leading to gradual economic decline and deurbanization. This in turn opened the way for the first incursions of Slav migrants and predators fro the north during the sixth century and permanent settlement by pagan Slavic agricul- turalists during the seventh and eighth centuries. Bosnia was briefly annexed by a emerging Croatian kingdom in AD 925 and AD 960, but it changed hands repeatedly. The oldest surviving written mention of a territory called 'Bosona' (centred on the upper reaches of the river Bosna, as is Bosnia today) occurs in a handbook written by the Byzantine emperor Constantine Porphyrogenitus in AD 958. Difficult either to control or to unite because of its mountainous and relatively impenetrable terrain, fragmented into relatively autonomous tribal or clan units known as *zupe* or counties (each under the control of a warlord known as a *zupan* or count), and 'possessing neither well-def ned natural frontiers nor a strong nuclear area', Slavicized Bosnia appears not to have cohered into a distinct polity until the eleventh century (Darby 1968: 58). Nevertheless, Catholic missionaries from the Dalmatian coastal towns and Orthodox ones from the Byzantine domains began to Christianize Bosnia's Slavic inhabitants during the ninth century, and Bosnia may have come nominally under Roman Catholic ecclesiastical jurisdiction by the tenth century (Donia and Fine 1994: 17).

Bosnia's first strong ruler was Ban Kulin (reg. 1180–1204), who encouraged ric merchants from Ragusa (now Dubrovnik) to exploit Bosnia's signif cant metal ores (Malcolm 1994: 14). From 1168 to 1326, the area known as Hum or Zachumlje (roughly present-day Herzegovina) emerged as an independent statelet. The half- century following Ban Kulin's death in 1204 saw repeated attempts by Catholic Hungary to subjugate Bosnia with papal backing, amid Franciscan allegations that the nominally Catholic church in Bosnia was too lax and was allowing subversive Manichaean dualist heresies to flourish there. John Fine (1976) and Noel Malcol (1994) have argued cogently that these allegations were merely a smokescreen for Hungary's territorial ambitions, expressed in several Hungarian invasions of Bosnia between 1235 and 1241. The Mongol invasion of Hungary in 1241 saved Bosnia from likely destruction (Donia and Fine 1994: 18–19). In 1252, having made a swift recovery, Hungary's rulers persuaded the pope to place Bosnia's Catholics under the authority of the Hungarian archbishop of Kalocsa and a Hungarian-appointed bishop of Bosnia. However, the Bosnians refused to have anything to do with him and turned instead to an independent Bosnian church, which seems to have been founded around 1203 but now acquired much stronger support and infrastructure (Fine 1987: 146–7). Hungary's Catholic rulers and the Dominican Order alleged that this 'breakaway' Bosnian church was heretical (Manichaean/dualist) and a potential threat to Roman Catholic Christendom. Most historians of Bosnia and the Balkans have taken these allegations at face value, not least because these alleged heresies and the consequent Roman Catholic hostility to Bosnia and the Bosnian church offered convenient and superficially persuasive ways of explaining how and why so many Bosnians later converted to Islam under Ottoman rule. However, John Fine and Noel Malcolm have persuasively argued that this breakaway 'nativist' church was broadly Catholic (rather than radical or heretical) and that the only evidence to the contrary comes from highly suspect Hungarian, Dominican and Franciscan sources (Fine 1987: 17–18, 143–8, 280–2; Malcolm, 1994, Chapter 3). The Bosnian church accepted 'an omni - potent God, the Trinity, church buildings, the Cross, the cult of saints, religious art and at least part of the Old Testament', all of which were rejected by the Manichaean (dualist) Bulgarian Bogomils (Donia and Fine 1994: 23).

The biggest f aws in the frequent contentions that a heretical Bosnian church helped to pave the way for the subsequent conversion of many Bosnians to Islam under Ottoman rule are that (i) the Bosnian church had ceased to exist by 1459, whereas Ottoman rule only began in 1463 and the major conversions of Bosnians to Islam did not occur until 100 or 200 years later; and (ii) it is diff cult to see any substantive connection between the alleged Manichaean teachings of the breakaway Bosnian church and the subsequent willingness of many Bosnians to embrace Islam, since Manichaeism and Islam are as different as chalk and cheese!

Bosnia became considerably stronger under Ban Stjepan Kotromanic (reg*c*.1318–53), who allied himself with Hungary's King Robert of Anjou (reg. 1308–42) and his son Louis/Lajos I (reg. 1342–82). He annexed Hum (future Herzegovina) in 1326 and fortuitously presided over a boom in Bosnian silver-, lead-, copper-, zinc- and gold-mining. Srebrenica (the name means 'Silver') emerged to become the centre of the Bosnian silver-mining industry, which by the 1420s would account (with Serbia) for over one-fifth of Europe's silver output (Fine 1987: 283). In addition, annexation of Hum in 1326 gave Kotromanic control of the trade and customs duties of the valley of the river Neretva. Soaring revenues enabled him to build a strong army. Although he seems initially to have been Eastern Orthodox, he converted to Roman Catholicism during the 1340s. He befriended the leader of the Franciscan Order and allowed it to launch a proselytizing 'mission' in Bosnia (Fine 1987: 277, 281–2).

Kotromanic was succeeded by his fifteen-year-old nephew Tvrtko I (reg. 1353–91) who was obliged to take refuge in Hungary when Bosnian nobles brief y placed his younger brother on the Bosnian throne in 1366–7. However, Hungary helped Tvrtko to regain his throne in 1367. As under Kotromanic, burgeoning mining royalties and customs duties enabled Tvrtko to buy allies and rebuild a Bosnian army, helping him to reassert control over Hum and rebellious northern Bosnia. This, together with the defeat of a large Christian Slavic army by the Ottoman Turks at the battle of Maritsa and the final extinction of Serbia's Nemanjic dynasty in 1371, allowed Tvrtko to stake a claim to the vacant Serbian throne and to annexe the upper Drina and river Lim valleys (known today as the Sandzak region) in 1373–4. In 1377 he also seized the three coastal *zupe* between Ragusa and the bay of Kotor and had himself crowned

'King of the Serbs, Bosnia, Maritime and Western Areas'. In 1384 he annexed the bay of Kotor, a great natural harbour, and proceeded to conquer much of the Adriatic (Dalmatian) coast between Kotor and Zara (including the Adriatic islands of Brac, Hvar and Korcula) between 1384 and 1389 (Cirkovic 2004: 80–3). But these successes were short-lived.

The Ottoman conquest, 1388–1528

The Ottoman Turkish conquest of Bosnia was a protracted process lasting 140 years, involving a hugely debilitating series of raids, skirmishes and wars, from the defeat of a Turkish invasion force at Bileca in 1388 until the fall of the Hungarian-controlled fortress town of Jajce in northern Bosnia in 1528. On 15 June 1389 Bosnian forces participated in the legendary battle of Kosova, against the Ottoman Turks (see pp. 234 and 515). After Tvrtko I's death in 1391, his ineffectual successors were unable to hold the enlarged Bosnian polity together and fend off various encroachments on (or defections from) its territory. Venice seized control of almost all the Dalmatian coast by 1420, with the major exception of Ragusa. Hum seceded under its own duke (Herceg) in 1448 – hence its new name, Herzegovina, which was also used by the Turks. In 1451 the Ottomans captured the strategically located town of Vrhbosna, which blossomed into the beautiful city of Sarajevo under Ottoman rule. The Ottomans' capture of Constantinople in 1453 and their complete subjugation of Serbia in 1459 allowed them to step up their conquest of Bosnia. King Stefan Tomas (reg. 1443–61) appealed to the pope and Catholic Christendom for help in 1459. The pope insisted that the Bosnian church had to be completely suppressed as the precondition for any help, and its adherents were thus forced to choose between full subordination to the Catholic Church or exile. According to the papacy, most of the Bosnian Christians then submitted to the Catholic Church, while the rest were exiled. This capitulation to the Catholic Church was of no avail. King Stefan Tomas died in 1461 and was succeeded by his son Stefan Tomasevic (reg. 1361–3), who immediately appealed to the pope and indirectly to Hungary for help against the Turks. However, the irritated Ottomans invaded Bosnia and Herzegovina in 1463, while Catholic Christendom passively looked on. The Turks captured King Stefan Tomasevic, duped him into ordering Bosnia's fortresses to surrender (about seventy obeyed) and then beheaded him (Fine 1987: 583–5). King Matyas of Hungary seized his chance to occupy most of the major forts in northern Bosnia in late 1463 and thereby establish a Hungarian-controlled Banate of northern Bosnia, but most of this was lost to the Ottomans during the 1470s. The last stronghold (Jajce) was lost in 1527, after the decimation of Hungary's main armies at the battle of Mohacs in 1526. The Herceg of Herzegovina temporarily regained most of his possessions in Herzegovina in 1463, but finally los them to the Ottomans in 1483 (Fine 1987: 585–9).

Even before the fall of Bosnia in 1463, 'many Bosnians entered Ottoman service' (Fine 1987: 589). Given the ignominious dissolution of the Bosnian church in 1459 and a widespread sense that Bosnia had been repeatedly betrayed by Catholic Christendom, the disillusioned Bosnians were by then 'shaky Christians' (Fine 1987: 589). A Bosnian delegation that visited Venice in the wake of the Ottoman conquest to beg for Venetian assistance to liberate Bosnia stated that, if they had to choose between submission to Hungary and remaining under Ottoman control, they would prefer the latter (Donia and Fine 1994: 34). Contrary to the view that many Bosnian landlords converted to Islam in order to retain their lands and positions, Fine maintains that 'there is no evidence in the sources of any continuity in families between Bosnia's medieval and its post-conquest Muslim aristocracy' (Donia and Fine 1994: 41). Nevertheless, he warns against temptations to idealize the impact of Ottoman overlordship in Bosnia and the subsequent relationship between the native Bosnian elite and the Ottoman regime:

> the Ottoman conquest was bloody; many Bosnians were carried off as captives or killed, including many executed after the conquest . . . The members of the Bosnian nobility who were allowed to submit and keep their lands tended to be from second-level families. The great nobles who sought and were accepted into Ottoman service were usually removed from Bosnia and given land and posts in Anatolia.
>
> (Fine 1987: 590)

Bosnian society was much weakened as a result.

Bosnia and Herzegovina under Ottoman rule, 1463/83–1878

Under Ottoman rule, Bosnia and Herzegovina were divided in three *sandzaks* (districts) within the overarching *beglerbeglik* (province) of *Rumeli* (Rumelia, derived from the Balkan name for Byzantium as successor to Rome), whose central administration was seated in Sofia. The three Bosnian *sandzaks* went by the names of: (i) *Bosnia*, whose first administrative, garrison and commercial centre was the burgeoning Islamicized city of Sarajevo; (ii) *Zvornik*, which included parts of what is now eastern Serbia and was administered from the town of Zvornik; and (iii) *Herzegovina*, whose administration and garrison were based in Foca from 1470 to 1572 but then moved to Plevla until 1833. Around 1554 the whole of Bosnia was upgraded to *beglerbeglik*. Its main seat of administration was Sarajevo from 1554 to 1583, from 1640 to 1698 and from 1850 to 1878. From 1583 to 1640 the administrative centre moved to Banja Luka, in order to be 'closer to the action' as the Ottoman domains expanded northward, but Sarajevo remained the province's main commercial, craft-industrial and Islamic centre – hence the city's fine legacy of great buildings from that era. Sarajevo regaine its former administrative role from 1640 to 1698. However, after Habsburg forces succeeded in setting fire to Sarajevo in 1697, the administration moved to the tow of Travnik until 1850. Sarajevo nevertheless recovered and has remained Bosnia's spiritual and commercial capital to this day (Donia and Fine 1994: 48–58).

Islamicization and the ethnogenesis of the 'Bosniaks'

The Islamicization of Bosnia under Ottoman rule was gradual, non-coercive and incomplete. Ottoman tax registers indicate that Muslims made up less than 10 per cent of the population in central and eastern Bosnia in 1468–9. In 1485 the Ottoman *sandzak* of Bosnia still contained about 155,000 Christians and only 22,000 Muslims. By the 1520s, however, the Christian population had fallen to around 98,000, while the Muslim population had risen to about 84,000, and by the early seventeenth century Muslims were in a majority. Since 'there was no large-scale Muslim immigration into Bosnia', the Muslim population must have grown through 'conversions of Bosnian Christians to Islam', although there is no evidence of 'massive forcible conversion' of Bosnians to Islam (Malcolm 1994: pp. 52–4). Islamic doctrine explicitly demanded political and religious toleration towards Christians and Jews as fellow 'peoples of the Book' and fellow believers in 'the One God', *provided* they did not engage in violent resistance or treachery against Islam (if they did do this, however, they could legitimately be 'punished'). Furthermore, the military preoccupations of the Ottoman elite made them willing from the outset to leave much of their empire's important commercial, administrative, political, diplomatic and ecclesiastical business in largely unsupervised Christian hands. Indeed, since Islam prescribed that Muslims had to pay fewer and lower taxes than non-Muslims, the Ottomans knew that they had to rely disproportionately on their Christian subjects for revenue, and that Balkan Christians were therefore of far greater value to the Ottomans *as Christians* than they would have been as either forced or voluntary converts to Islam. Thus it was not necessary for Bosnians to become Muslims in order to prosper, nor was it necessary for Bosnian landowners to become Muslims in order to retain their landholdings (Malcolm 1994: 64–5). The spread of Islam was also related to the growth of new largely Muslim towns such as Sarajevo and Mostar. Slaves and serfs who converted to Islam could obtain their freedom and were especially likely to live in the expanding towns (Malcolm 1994: 65–7).

There was a large exodus of Roman Catholics seeking to escape growing fiancial deprivation and actual or imagined persecution (Malcolm 1994: 55–6). On the other hand, partly because of large inflows of Orthodox Christians from Turkish-occupie Serbia and partly because it was more favoured than the Catholic Church, the Eastern Orthodox Church actually gained large numbers of new adherents, spread to new areas and built many new monasteries and churches in Bosnia during the first centur of Ottoman rule (Donia and Fine 1994: 32, 37–40, 47). All the same, its ecclesiastical infrastructure remained weak and rudimentary. Divided between three rival churches (Catholic, Bosnian and Orthodox), none of which had established 'a proper system of parish churches and parish priests', Bosnian Christianity failed to put up a united front against the gradual Islamicization of a large share of the population. Mountainous terrain also put many villages beyond the reach of the skeletal infrastructure of the churches (Donia and Fine 1994: 36–7, 43–4; Malcolm 1994: 52–7, 70–1), and in Bosnia's remote and 'largely priestless' rural areas, Christianity probably became 'little more than a set of folk practices and ceremonies . . . The shift from folk Christianity to folk Islam was not very great; many of the same practices could continue, albeit with slightly different words or names .. . Many of the same festivals and holy days were celebrated by both religions.' Bosnian Muslims continued to venerate the Virgin Mary, Christian saints and icons, and often retained Christian names and patronymics (Malcolm 1994: 58–60; Donia and Fine 1994: 44). However, conversion to Islam did confer practical advantages. Christians could not file lawsuit against Muslims, nor could they give testimony against Muslims in Muslim courts, and by the eighteenth century the Ottoman regime mainly relied on Muslim offcials. Nevertheless, South Slav converts to Islam, rather than people of Turkish descent, made up the vast majority of Bosnia's Muslims – in contrast to Bulgaria, where most Muslims *were* of Turkish descent.

During the last century of Ottoman rule in Bosnia (1770s–1870s), there was growing political turbulence and social unrest – not so much among Bosnian Christians as among Bosnian Muslims, who reacted against the increasingly wayward and unruly *kapetans* and janissary corps (finally abolished and suppressed by the Ottoman in favour of a more modern conscript army in 1826) and against the emergence of powerful semi-autonomous Muslim lords (*pashas*). The resultant instability and conflict damaged the economy, encouraging landlords to try to compensate themselves by squeezing more income out of the increasingly impoverished peasantry, whether Christian or Muslim, but this nevertheless sowed growing Christian–Muslim antago- nism, intensified by growing Christian evangelical/missionary activities – includin church- and school-building (Malcolm 1994: 119–31).

Bosnia-Herzegovina under Habsburg occupation, 1878–1918

In 1878, as a by-product of the emergence and international recognition of fully independent Serbian, Romanian and Montenegrin states and an autonomous Bulgarian state (see pp. 76, 128–9 and 236), Bosnia-Herzegovina came under more efficient bu widely resented military occupation by the strongly Roman Catholic Austro-Hungarian Empire. The Austro-Hungarians encountered some armed resistance from Bosnian Muslims, initially supported by Orthodox Christians (against a common Catholic foe), but in the long run there was much more Muslim emigration than resistance. Tens of thousands of Muslims (perhaps over 100,000 by 1918) decamped to other parts of the still very extensive Ottoman Empire (Malcolm 1994: 138–40). Until 1908, Austria-Hungary pretended that Bosnia-Herzegovina was merely under a temporary 'military protectorate', intended to prevent it from falling into Serb, Bulgarian or Russian hands. From the outset, however, it pursued policies that implied long-term possession.

Bosnia-Herzegovina was confined to a quasi-colonial status *outside* the formal framework of the monarchy and was administered by offcials from the joint Austro-Hungarian ministry of finance. This arrangement resulted in neglect of peasant needs, mounting impoverishment and festering social problems. There was also high-profile support for the small Catholic (Croat) minority and the Catholic Church, in an 'unholy alliance' with the reactionary and oppressive Muslim landlord class and the conservative Muslim clergy – mainly to the detriment of the Orthodox Bosnians, who increasingly thought of themselves as Serbs. Up to 1918, over 80 per cent of the population of Bosnia-Herzegovina remained illiterate. In the Austrian population census of 1910, the religious affliations of the population of Bosnia-Herzegovina were declared to be 43.5 per cent Orthodox, 32.3 per cent Muslim, 22.8 per cent Catholic, 0.6 per cent Jewish and 0.8 per cent other affiliations (Donia and Fine 1994: 87)

The new Habsburg overlords were a lot more energetic in their efforts to develop the Bosnian economy than the Ottomans had been. By 1907 they had constructed 1,022 kilometres of railway, over 1,000 kilometres of highway, 121 bridges, chemical plants, iron- and steelworks, cigarette and carpet factories, model farms, a model vineyard, a *shariat* school to train judges for the Muslim law courts, nearly 200 elementary schools, three high schools, a technical school, a teacher-training college and an agri-cultural college, while also developing iron, copper and chrome mines and forestry. Free elementary education in state schools, in which members of each denomination were to receive separate religious instruction from their own clergy, was made compulsory in 1909, while 41,500 serfs bought their freedom between 1879 and 1913, although this still left over 93,000 families in bondage (Malcolm 1994: 141–4). However, these accomplishments did more to confirm than to refute the essentiall alien, disruptive and colonial character of Habsburg rule in Bosnia-Herzegovina and, whatever the material benefits, the previous equilibrium between Bosnia's Muslims Orthodox Christians and Catholics was fatefully disturbed by the sudden inf ux of large numbers of Catholic off cials, colonists, soldiers and clergy.

From 1882 to 1903 the Magyar official Benjamin Kallay ran the civil administratio of Bosnia-Herzegovina while also serving as the joint finance minister of Austria Hungary. Kallay endeavoured to foster a distinctive Bosnian national identity which could unite the area's Muslim, Orthodox Christian and Catholic inhabitants and keep them separate from their Serbian and Croatian neighbours (Malcolm 1994: 147–8). Had it been possible to keep Bosnia-Herzegovina completely sealed off from the outside world, such a policy might have succeeded. However, the policy did not elicit positive responses from the cosmopolitan and civic-minded Muslims of Sarajevo, who had long maintained relatively civil relations with their Orthodox Christian, Catholic and Jewish neighbours. Even though religious affiliations had not yet fully metamorphosed into separate national identities, it proved impossible to prevent Serbian and Croatian nationalist ideas and identifications from spreading among the Orthodo and Catholic populations of Bosnia-Herzegovina, not least through the 'networks of priests, schoolteachers and educated newspaper readers' which Austro-Hungarian policies fostered (Malcolm 1994: 148–9). Furthermore, government cooperation with the Muslim leadership in Sarajevo aroused suspicion and resentment among Christians who thought that they should now enjoy a monopoly of offial favour (Malcolm 1994: 145–7). At the same time, the monarchy's increasingly divisive and ham-fisted rul of Croatia (see pp. 186–8) and its attempts to lord it over the small kingdom of Serbia fanned the flames of both Serbian and Croatian nationalism, even within Bosnia-Herzegovina. Austria-Hungary's formal annexation of Bosnia-Herzegovina in 1908, abandoning the previous pretence of a temporary 'protectorate' over it, further inflame South Slav nationalism in Bosnia-Herzegovina itself as well as in Serbia, Croatia and Montenegro. This act seems to have supplied a principal motive for the fateful assassination of the Austrian crown prince (Archduke Franz Ferdinand) and his wife by a young Bosnian South Slav nationalist called Gavrilo Princip, during their state visit to Sarajevo on 28 June 1914. This provocatively fell on the anniversary of the battle of Kosova, which had become the most emotive date in the South Slav nationalist calendar. This assassination set in motion the diplomatic and military chain reactions that culminated in the outbreak of the First World War. 'It was in Sarajevo in the summer of 1914 that Europe entered the century of madness and self-destruction' (ICB 2005: 6).

Bosnia-Herzegovina in the first Yugoslavia, 1918–41

From 1918 to 1941 Bosnia was denied any *de jure* autonomy within the unitary Serb-dominated 'Kingdom of Serbs, Croats and Slovenes'. However, Mehmed Spaho, the leader of the ascendant Yugoslav Muslim Organization (JMO), skilfully exploited the divisions and rivalries between Serbs and Croats in order to gain a considerable measure of de-facto provincial autonomy for his region. When serfdom was abolished and much estate land was redistributed in 1919, Spaho fought to ensure that in Bosnia, predominantly Muslim landlords received compensation from the state. 'Roughly 4000 Muslim families were affected by this reform.' In addition, when the new Yugoslav state was carved up into thirty-three *oblasts* (territorial units), Spaho helped to ensure that the six Bosnian *oblasts* broadly corresponded to the previous Austro-Hungarian divisions (*kreise*) and their Ottoman predecessors (*sandzaks*). This helped to maintain Bosnia's regional identity through the 1920s. Nevertheless, the region remained a relatively neglected, impoverished and stagnant provincial backwater during the inter-war years, and its regional identity was damaged by the arbitrary *banovinas* established from 1929 to 1941 (Malcolm 1994: 163–9).

Bosnia-Herzegovina during the Axis occupation and partition of Yugoslavia, 1941–5

From April 1941 to early 1945 almost all of Bosnia-Herzegovina was formally incorporated into the Independent State of Croatia (NDH), which was formally governed by the Croatian fascist Ustasa. However, most of the strategically important coastal and lower-lying western areas (including Mostar and Foca) were, in practice, under Italian military occupation from April 1941 until September 1943, when Italy surrendered to the Western Allies. Similarly, many inland areas were under German military occupation until early 1945. In September 1943, moreover, German forces hurriedly and ferociously occupied the areas which had hitherto been controlled by the Italian military, in order to prevent these areas from falling (as a result of the Italian capitulation) either to the Western Allies, giving them a valuable foothold on the western Balkans, or to the Communist-led partisans, who in practice managed to seize much of the weaponry and ammunition abandoned or surrendered by the chaotically withdrawing Italian forces.

Many Bosnian Croats seem to have actively welcomed and collaborated with the Croatian Ustasa's programme of systematic ethnic cleansing and genocide, directed against Bosnian Serbs, Montenegrins, Jews and Roma (Gypsies). However, this programme of ethnic cleansing and genocide provoked the emergence of extremely fierce and tenacious South Slav resistance to the Ustasa, the Axis occupation forces and their mainly Croatian and Bosniak collaborators. This resistance came mainly from the Bosnian Serbs, who were driven to engage in a desperate, bare-knuckled fight to survive and retaliate against the massive crimes against humanity that were perpetrated against them by Croats and Bosniaks.

The appalling sufferings and loss of life which Bosniaks suffered at the hands of Bosnian Serbs between 1992 and 1995 have made it fashionable for the media and some academics to portray the Bosniaks in a somewhat idealized, rose-tinted light, as innocent victims of Serb aggression and (conversely) to regard Bosnian Serbs as monsters. However, black-and-white dichotomies of this sort rarely survive closer scrutiny, and the one that has been constructed between the Bosniaks and the Bosnian Serbs is no exception. Many Bosniaks were far from being innocent bystanders during the mass genocide and ethnic cleansing carried out against Bosnian Serbs between 1941 and 1944. In line with the thinking of Croatian 'integral nationalist' ideologues from Ante Starcevic (1823–96) and Josip Frank (1844–1911) to Franjo Tudjman (1922–99), the Croatian fascist Ustasa considered the Bosniaks merely to be 'Islamicized Croats' who had wrongfully been detached from the main body of the Croatian nation under Ottoman rule, and the Ustasa and their collaborators seized this opportunity to try to bring these so-called 'Islamicized Croats' back into the Croatian fold (see Chapter 5, p. 187). Many Bosniaks seem to have actively and voluntarily participated in the ethnic cleansing and genocide against the Bosnian Serbs and, to lesser degrees, Bosnian Jews and Roma, although their motives for doing so were far less clear than those of the Croats. Their forebears had occasionally been accomplices in Ottoman Turkish acts of repression and reprisal against Balkan Christians who challenged or defied Ottoman/Muslim rule, as was powerfully portrayed in Ivo Andric's Nobel prize-winning historical novel *The Bridge over the Drina* (1945), but that barely begins to explain the much greater scale and intensity of the Bosniak atrocities committed against Bosnian Serbs in 1941–4. In contrast to Kosova, where there undoubtedly had been many previous Serb atrocities against Muslim Kosovars, there was no comparable record of previous Serb atrocities against Muslims in Bosnia. Thus the barbarities perpetrated by Serbs against Bosniaks between 1992 and 1995 can *partly* be seen as a belated 'settling of accounts' for the atrocities which their parents and grandparents had suffered at the hands of the Bosniaks in the 1940s (LeBor 2003: 4). Taking account of the atrocities committed in Bosnia-Herzegovina and Croatia during the twentieth century as a whole, neither Croats, nor Serbs, nor Bosniaks come out well. If any ethnic group meted out much more ethnic cleansing and genocide than it incurred, it was probably the Croats, both in 1941–5 and (to lesser degrees) in 1992–5, even though the Croats seem to have escaped relatively lightly in recent apportionment of opprobrium by Western media, politicians and political and academic commentators. However, our concern is not to establish an invidious and ultimately specious 'hierarchy of blame', but rather to emphasize that none of these ethnic groups has had a clean record and that it is nearly always dangerous as well as unjust to suppose that particular ethnic groups can be cast exclusively in the roles of either villains or monsters, while other ethnic groups are treated essentially as innocent victims. Life is never that simple.

Nevertheless, it appears that around 8 per cent of Bosniaks perished between 1941 and 1945, whether in combat, or as a result of combat-related injuries, disease and malnutrition, or as a result of the increasingly savage Axis reprisals against the Communist and Bosnian Serb-led insurgency, as well as through savage Communist and Bosnian Serb reprisals against Bosniaks for their acquiescence or active complicity in the programme of ethnic cleansing and genocide carried out by the Croatian Ustasa regime and its collaborators (Goldstein 1999: 158; Lampe 1996: 380).

Bosnia-Herzegovina in the Communist-ruled Yugoslav Federation, 1945–90

After the Second World War, a Communist-ruled Republic of Bosnia-Herzegovina was established as a constituent part of the Socialist Federal Republic of Yugoslavia (SFRY) established by the victorious Communist-led partisans. Bosnia and Herzegovina underwent striking demographic changes during Communist rule. As a result of markedly higher birth rates and lower emigration rates among Bosniaks than among Bosnian Serbs and Bosnian Croats from the 1950s to the 1980s, Bosnian Serbs ceased to be the largest ethnic group in Bosnia by the late 1960s, while Bosnian Catholics were reduced to just 17.3 per cent of the population by 1991 and just 14.3 per cent by 2000. The resultant alteration in the relative strengths of these three groups was reinforced by the decisions of the Communist regime to reclassify Bosnia's 'Muslims' as a distinct *ethnic group or ethnicity* from 1961 onward and as a fully fledged *nation* from 1968 onward. Moreover, the Bosnian Serb ascendancy in the Bosnian League of Communists was increasingly challenged by the rising status and power of Bosniak Communists from the 1960s onward. Some Bosnian Croat and Bosnian Serb intel - lectuals, politicians and journalists clearly got feverishly worked up about these changing demographic power relations, with fearful and tragic consequences during the 1990s. However, this does not automatically mean that such anxieties and mentalities were shared by the population as a whole. They seem mainly to have been a syndrome of Bosnian Serb and Bosnian Croat nationalist intelligentisia.

The Yugoslav Communist regime was strongly committed to the industrializa-tion of Bosnia-Herzegovina. In particular, for strategic/geopolitical reasons, much of Yugoslavia's armaments industry was located in Bosnia-Herzegovina, which was perceived as a relatively secure 'Dinaric fortress' that could hold out against either a

Western or (more likely) a Soviet invasion. During the 1980s, '40 to 55 per cent of
the Bosnian economy was tied to military industries' and 60 to 80 per cent of the JNA's
physical assets were located in Bosnia, as were 68 per cent of its 140,000 troops
(Woodward 1995: 259). Partly as a result, Bosnia's per-capita levels of production,
income and consumption and its levels of educational provision, literacy, health care
provision and life expectancy rose dramatically between the 1950s and the 1980s.
However, it nevertheless remained one of the poorer Yugoslav republics and its
per-capita GMP fell from 83 per cent to 68 per cent of the Yugoslav average between
1953 and 1988 (Lampe 1996: 332–3), mainly because much of the increase in income
and output was almost literally 'eaten up' by the Bosniaks' high birth rates and rapid
population growth. This population explosion also far outstripped the capacity of
Bosnia's economy to create new jobs suitable for the large numbers of young people
who were entering the job market, with the result that the country experienced 22 to
23 per cent unemployment between 1985 and 1988 (Woodward 1995: 53). Bosnia's
unemployment rate would have been even higher if tens of thousands of Bosnian Serbs
and Croats had not emigrated from Bosnia between the 1960s and the 1980s.

Bosnia's political and socio-economic problems were greatly magnified by the
structuring – and hence segmentation – of Bosnian society along religious-cum-ethnic
lines. Until 1991 Bosnia's inter-communal power-sharing arrangements averted overt
inter-communal warfare, but the 'downside' was that they helped to perpetuate highly
clientelistic, corrupt, nepotistic, ethnic collectivist, and 'vertical' power relations and
power structures both in the political and in the economic spheres. Clientelism, corruption and nepotism became particularly rife in Bosnia due to the steadily intensifying
competition for goods, services and jobs, for each of which demand continually
outstripped supply. The magnitude of Bosnia's problems in these respects was revealed
to the outside world by the huge (billion-dollar) corruption, clientelism and nepotism
scandals which were exposed at the Agrokomerc agro-industrial and trading
conglomerate in 1987 (Malcolm 1994: 209–11; Woodward 1995: 87).

During the 1980s the ethnically divided leadership of Bosnia's League of Communists reacted nervously and heavy-handedly to growing expressions of nationalist
and religious activism among Bosnia's Muslims and Catholics (on the Catholic revival,
see above). After Bosnia's Muslim clergy engaged in increasingly outspoken criticism
of the Communist regime during the late 1970s and early 1980s and showed some
interest in Ayatollah Khomeini's Islamic revolution in Iran, the Communist leadership
issued warnings against 'pan-Islamism' and published reminders of the collaboration
of some Bosniak clergy with the ethnic cleansing and genocide carried out by the
Croatian fascist Ustasa in Bosnia during the Second World War. In addition, in 1983
thirteen Bosniaks were put on trial in Sarajevo, charged with 'hostile and counter-
revolutionary acts derived from Muslim nationalism'. The chief defendant was the
lawyer Dr Alija Izetbegovic, whose principal 'crime' was to have written an *Islamic
Declaration*, which was (falsely) alleged to have called for the establishment of 'an
ethnically pure Muslim Bosnian state'. The court was also reminded that Izetbegovic
had belonged to a 'Young Muslims' organization that had opposed the Communist-
led attacks on Islam in Yugoslavia during the later 1940s. For these alleged 'crimes',
Izetbegovic was sentenced to fourteen years in jail, reduced on appeal to eleven years.
Bosnia's most senior 'secular Muslim' Communist, Hadija Pozderac, played a prominent role in this Communist witch-hunt against Bosniak religious activists. Ironically,
in 1987 Pozderac's family was implicated in the above-mentioned Agrokomerc scandal
and he was forced to resign from his post as vice-president of the SFRY (Malcolm

1994: 208–9). Indeed, the numerous resignations precipitated by the Agrokomerc affair helped to discredit and create an ominous power vacuum in Bosnia's League of Communists just two years prior to the disintegration of the SFRY.

During the summer of 1990, following the disintegration of the League of Communists of Yugoslavia earlier in the year, Bosnia's League of Communists took no steps to prepare Bosnia to defend itself against potential Serb and Croatian aggression, even though regimes espousing the ideas of a 'Greater Serbia' and a 'Greater Croatia' had come to power in Serbia and Croatia, respectively. On the contrary, the Bosnian Communist regime allowed the JNA to 'confiscate the armaments' of Bosnia's locally controlled territorial defence forces 'without resistance' (Hoare 2001: 180).

The multiparty parliamentary elections of 18 and 25 November 1990

Amid a deepening economic crisis and mounting fears of potential incorporation of parts of the republic into an authoritarian-nationalist 'Greater Serbia' ruled by Slobodan Milosevic, Bosnia-Herzegovina held freely contested multiparty elections on 18 and 25 November 1990. The pattern of voting mainly divided along ethno-religious lines. The f nal distribution of seats in the 130-seat chamber of citizens (lower house) and in the 110-seat chamber of counties (upper house) of the parliament of Bosnia-Herzegovina is shown in Table 7.1.

7.1 Bosnia-Herzegovina parliamentary election, 18 and 25 November 1990

Party	Seats Chamber of citizens	Seats Chamber of counties
Party of Democratic Action (SDA, main Bosniak party)	43	43
Serbian Democratic Party (SDS, main Bosnian Serb party)	34	37
Croatian Democratic Union (HDZ, main Bosnian Croat party)	21	24
League of Communists–Social Democratic Party	15	4
Alliance of Reform Forces of Yugoslavia (SRSJ)	12	1
Muslim Bosniak Organization (MBO)	2	–
Democratic Socialist Alliance (DSA)	1	–
Ecological Movement (EP)	1	–
Socialist Youth Organization + Democratic Party (DS)	1	–
Serbian Movement of Renewal (SPO)	1	1

Source: Burg (1997: 133).

A non-Communist SDA–SDS–HDZ coalition government and a non-Communist 'collective presidency' were established in December 1990, with the Bosniak leader Alija Izetbegovic serving as 'president of the collective presidency'. This office was meant to rotate, but in December 1992 a clause in the constitution was invoked in order to allow Izetbegovic's tenure as 'president of the presidency' to continue for the duration of the 'Bosnian conflict' which erupted in April 1992. This coalition government was

> both unable and unwilling to organize the defence of Bosnia-Herzegovina in preparation for an attack by Serbia and the JNA. The Serb-nationalist SDS was violently opposed to any republican defence preparations and its central and local bodies cooperated with the JNA and Yugoslav security services in hindering such preparations as much as possible.

The SDA (Party of Democratic Action), led by President Izetbegovic, was therefore 'forced to organize its own clandestine resistance movement independently of the Bosnian state institutions' (Hoare 2001: 180), which was of course a major handicap. During 1991 Bosnia's industrial output fell by 16.2 per cent and the annual inflation rate was 117.4 per cent. Industrial output plummeted by a further 25 per cent in 1992 (UN ECE 1994: 52; UN ECE 1995: 70; *Business Europa*, April–May 1995, p. 60).

President Izetbegovic made a televised appeal to Bosnians on 10 October 1991 to refuse to serve in the JNA, i.e., to boycott the Serbian war against Croatia:

> It is your right and duty as citizens of Bosnia-Herzegovina not to respond to the call-up . . . I call upon you to find the courage to refuse to take part in these evi deeds. Remember, this is not our war. Let those who want it, wage it. We do not want this war.
>
> (quoted in Tus 2001: 58)

This principled solidarity with Croatia against Serb aggression contrasted with the remarkable lack of solidarity between Croatia and Slovenia against their shared Serbian foe (see Chapter 5, pp. 201–2).

When the Bosnian parliament adopted a 'memorandum on sovereignty' on 15 October 1991, most of the Bosnian Serb deputies walked out in protest. This memorandum implied that the parliamentary majority in Bosnia-Herzegovina would only accept either full sovereign independence or a loose Yugoslav confederation which would have to include Croatia and Slovenia to counterbalance Serbia.

With strong encouragement from the EC and the Badinter Committee, which had been established in 1991 to advise the EC on whether to recognize the independence of the individual Yugoslav republics, a referendum on whether Bosnia-Herzegovina should become an independent state took place on 29 February to 1 March 1992. The turn-out was only 63.4 per cent, because most Bosnian Serbs boycotted it, but 92.7 per cent of the votes cast were in favour of independence. The Bosnian Serbs and the Yugoslav military had foreseen that their opposition to an independent Bosnia was bound to be heavily outvoted, and they had long since started preparing to mount a military fight to separate the predominantly Serb-inhabited areas from the new Bosnia state and to maintain close links with Serbia. The opening shots in the incipient Bosnian conflict were fired when Serb paramilitary forces attacked Bosniak villages aroun Capljina on 7 March and around Bosanski Brod and Gorazde on 15 March. These minor attacks were followed by much more serious Serb artillery attacks on Neum on 19 March and on Bosanski Brod on 24 March (Magas and Zanic 2001: 360).

However, it appears that war was not unavoidable. The SDS and its leader Radovan Karadjic repeatedly approved and accepted the proposals emanating from the EC mediators Lord Peter Carrington and José Cutilheiro to keep Bosnia together as a single state, *provided* that it had very weak central institutions and functions and that the predominantly Serb-inhabited areas were allowed to retain high degrees of autonomy and close links with Serbia. Many 'Serbophobes' have regarded the Serb stance as an insincere or duplicitous smokescreen or decoy, intended to mask the ruthless and premeditated belligerent intentions of the Serb leaders in Bosnia, in the JNA and in Serbia itself (namely, most of the contributors to Magas and Zanic 2001, as well as Gow 1997). While it is quite conceivable that the Serb leaders in Bosnia, Serbia and the JNA were indeed duplicitous, it is equally conceivable that the vast majority of 'ordinary Serbs' in Bosnia were *not hell-bent on waging war* (this was very much the case in Serbia itself – see pp. 202, 243 and 253–4). Partly because of the much-publicized huge suffering of the Serbs during the Second World War, most Serbs were well aware of the immense destructiveness of modern warfare and of the imperative need to coexist peacefully with their Bosniak and Croatian 'cousins'. The broad Serb acquiescence in the drift towards war was probably at least partly attributable to a growing realization that the degrees of autonomy and leeway which the Bosniak SDA and its leader Alija Izetbegovic were prepared to concede at that time fell far short of Serb demands. In this sense, the 'Bosnian confct' of 1992–5 was what it took to make the Bosniaks and the Western powers see and accept the magnitude of the local autonomy and freedom of manoeuvre which would have to be conceded to the Serb community within Bosnia as the price of their acceptance of an independent Bosnian state. Even though the resultant highly devolved systems of governance have proved to be highly dysfunctional in post-Dayton Bosnia and Serbia, these may yet prove to be the only basis on which Bosnia can sustain inter-ethnic peace and avoid a return to mutually devastating warfare.

Under the 'Cutilheiro plan' brokered in Lisbon on 18 March 1992, the major parties agreed to 'cantonize' multi-ethnic Bosnia and Herzegovina along the lines of the Swiss federation. Bosnia-Herzegovina would comprise 'three constituent units based on national principles and taking into account economic, geographical and other criteria' (Gow 1997: 85). Under a revised plan jointly brokered by Lord Carrington and Cutilheiro, the Bosnian Serb and the Bosniak communities would each have acquired decentralized control of about 44 per cent of the country, with the far less numerous Bosnian Croats getting the remaining 12 per cent. In terms of 'economic value', however, the Bosniak share would have been much higher than 44 per cent, because the Bosniaks were preponderant in Bosnia's main towns and cities. The major obstacle to the implementation of this plan was that it was intrinsically non-viable. Because of centuries of migration, ethnic intermingling and intermarriage, discrete 'ethnic areas' were not readily distinguishable (Gow 1997: 80).

The 'Bosnian conflict', April 1992 to October 1995

More sustained fighting broke out in April 1992. The killing of a Bosniak civilia woman on 5 April 1992 by a sniper, while she was demonstrating in Sarajevo against the raising of barricades by Bosnian Serbs, is widely regarded as marking the start of warfare between the three major communities. The Bosnian Serbs had the massive initial advantages: JNA support and the fact that the local Bosniak-dominated territorial-defence forces had largely been disarmed by the JNA in summer 1990. When the EU and the USA recognized Bosnia on 7 April 1992, the Bosnian Serbs proclaimed an independent 'Serbian Republic of Bosnia' (the embryo of the subsequent

Republika Srpska), which strove to become part of a 'Greater Serbia'. Bosnian Serbs were widely criticized for this orientation. However, the Bosnian Serbs had just as much right to determine their own future as did the other constituent peoples of the SFRY. If it was internationally acceptable for the Croats, Slovenes, Bosniaks and other Yugoslav peoples to exercise their rights to national self-determination by seceding from the SFRY, then it was logically inconsistent to deny the Bosnian Serbs the same right to national self-determination by seceding from the Republic of Bosnia-Herzegovina, whether by setting up a republic of their own or by joining a 'Greater Serbia'. Having failed to prevent the Bosniaks and the Bosnian Croats from voting for secession from the SFRY, the Bosnian Serbs were (by the same logic) equally entitled to establish a republic of their own which could (if it chose) seek links with or inclusion in a Greater Serbia. Admittedly, the Bosniaks and the Western powers contended that rights of national self-determination only applied to the constituent republics of the SFRY, not to ethnic groups or peoples as such, and that the Bosnian (and the Croatian) Serbs therefore did not have the same rights to self-determination as most other Yugoslavs. However, in the Balkans and East Central Europe since the late nineteenth century, nations and national self-determination have been conceived in ethnic terms. We are second to none in arguing that this is an inherently destabilizing and conf ictual basis on which to endeavour to construct a political order (see Bideleux 1996: 285–90; Bideleux and Jeffries 1998: 407–18). Nevertheless, all parties have accepted that this is the basis on which it was decided to build the post-1918 political order in these regions and it is therefore encumbent on all parties to try to 'make the best of a bad job' by endeavouring to apply and uphold this principle as fairly and consistently as possible. To apply national self-determination to some ethnic groups while denying it to others involves dangerous double standards. Furthermore, all parties had long known full well that the Yugoslav Communist regime established the Republic of Bosnia-Herzegovina in 1945 and drew inter-republican boundaries in such a way as to include as much territory and as many Serbs as possible in the republics of Bosnia-Herzegovina and Croatia, in order to deprive Serbia of as much territory and population as possible, in conscious violation of the dominant principle of national self-determination. They also knew full well that by the late 1980s and early 1990s many Serbs were determined to rectify this widely perceived ethno-cultural injustice. In these circumstances, the Western-backed refusal of the Bosniaks and the Croats to allow the Bosnian and Croatian Serbs the same right of self-determination as they had invoked for themselves (and to revise the widely resented inter-republican boundaries established in 1945) was an open invitation to Serbia, the JNA and the Bosnian and Croatian Serbs to take matters into their own hands and to try to resolve these disputes by *force majeure*. We deeply mistrust the principle of national self-determination, but, for better or worse, we accept that it is the cardinal legitimizing principle on which the post-1918 political order in the Balkans has been built. Viewed in this light, the Western-backed refusal of the Bosniak and Croat political leaders to allow Bosnian and Croatian Serbs the same rights of self-determination as they invoked for their own people, as well as their Western-backed refusal to countenance any redrawing of political boundaries, bears part of the responsibility for the outbreak of warfare between Serbs, Bosniaks and Croats in 1991–2. Violations of the prevailing principle of national self-determination by Bosniaks, Croats and their Western backers also gave Serb nationalists strong inducements to seize control of whatever territories they inhabited and defensible corridors of territory connecting these to Serbia. We fully acknowledge that in doing this, Serb nationalists carried out appalling and unpardonable war crimes and crimes against humanity. Nevertheless, their stance was more consistent with the prevailing principle of national self-determination than were the stances taken by their opponents.

In June 1992, moreover, the Bosniak-dominated government of Bosnia-Herzegovina resolutely rejected 'cantonization' as a framework for accommodating and reconciling differences between the three main ethnic groups who inhabited the republic. So too did the Bosnian Croats, who unilaterally declared an autonomous 'Croatian Community of Herzeg-Bosna' on 5 July 1992. *There was thus not much difference in principle between the aspirations of the elected leaders of the three main ethnic communities in Bosnia-Herzegovina.* As Rogers Brubaker has put it, what occurred in Europe's post-Communist states in 1990–2 was a 'massive "nationalization" of political space' (Brubaker 1996: 3). The elected leaders of all three of the main communities subscribed to the inherently destabilizing and dangerous principle of national self-determination, and they all sought to apply that principle in whatever way would give their own ethnic group control of as much territory as possible. To varying degrees, the leaders of all three groups resorted to ethnic cleansing and acts of genocide in often vicious endeavours to attain their not greatly dissimilar goals. This was largely a consequence of the ruthless determination of these leaders to interpret and apply the principle of national self-determination to the (self shly perceived) maximum advantage of their own ethnic community at the expense of the other two, even though all the ethnic communities involved in these conflicts wer extensively intermingled rather than neatly concentrated in particular localities. Viewed in these terms, the conflict was an infernal zero-sum contest: one group's gain was another group's loss. Only if all the contending parties had been prepared to renounce the destructive principles of nationalism and national self-determination would it have been possible to have reconciled and accommodated the interdependent needs and aspirations of all of Bosnia's ethnic communities in a more cosmopolitan polity. Regrettably, the elected leaders of *all three* of the main communities in Bosnia were grimly determined to maximize national self-determination for their own community, in whatever way most favoured their own community at the expense of the other two. The biggest culprits were not particular individuals or ethnic com - munities, but the dangerous nationalist doctrines that drove the elected leaders of all three communities to become ever more ruthless in the pursuit of these pernicious principles.

Larger-scale warfare broke out between Croats and Bosniaks in central Bosnia in October 1992 and intensif ed in April 1993. At first the Bosnian Croats made mos headway, carrying out 'ethnic cleansing' of the areas they captured. The escalating conf ict rapidly attracted world attention and UN mediation. The UN Security Council declared an 'air-exclusion zone' (alias 'no-fly zone') on 9 October 1992 for militar f ights over Bosnia and Herzegovina. However, in the event of violations, there was only to be urgent consideration given to 'further measures necessary to enforce the ban'. There were 1,397 violations of the ban between 9 October 1992 and 1 January 1994 (*FT*, 1 March 1994, pp. 2, 22), but not one aircraft was shot down for violating the ban until 28 February 1994.

The so-called Vance–Owen plan of 28 October 1992, which was worked out in large measure by a working group headed by the Finnish diplomat and future president of Finland Martti Ahtisaari (Gow 1997: 235), proposed that Bosnia should be divided into ten largely autonomous provinces, with the three main ethnic groups (Muslim, Serb and Croat) having a majority in three provinces each, although all main groups were to be represented in provincial governments. If the USA and the EU had jointly imposed the Vance–Owen plan, the Serbs would have retained only 43 per cent of Bosnia, as against the 49 per cent granted by the Dayton plan, and Bosnia would have been maintained as a unitary state, rather than as an unwieldy and fragile confederation. On taking office in January 1993, the Clinton administration did much t undermine the Vance–Owen plan and fought shy of committing any forces to its implementation, ostensibly because it 'rewarded ethnic cleansing' by appearing to allow Serbs to retain control of 43 per cent of the republic's total land area. However, the settlement that Richard Holbrooke finally brokered at Dayton in November 1995 after the Bosnian conflict had been allowed to drag on for another twenty months awarded the Serbs 49 per cent of the republic's total land area – and even this was only achieved after the Croats had been allowed to get away with ethnically cleansing much of Herzegovina and Croatia.

The Bosnian Serb 'parliament' in Pale (located on high ground near Sarajevo) defie both Milosevic and the so-called 'international community' by refusing to accept the Vance–Owen plan in early 1993. A referendum held by the Bosnian Serbs on 15–16 May 1993 also overwhelmingly rejected the plan. Milosevic thereupon threatened sanctions against the Bosnian Serbs, but these were ineffectual.

The potential fall of Srebrenica to the Bosnian Serbs in spring 1993 evoked a strong international reaction. On 16 April 1993 the UN Security Council declared Srebrenica and its environs to be a 'safe area', i.e., an area which forces acting under UN auspices would make safe from 'armed attack or any other hostile act'. Several other Bosnian towns and their environs were also to be declared 'safe areas', including Sarajevo, Bihac, Gorazde, Tuzla and Zepa. On 11 May 1993, the Clinton administration in the USA made an unsuccessful attempt to persuade Europeans to support a 'lift and strike' strategy, i.e., to lift the arms embargo on the Bosnian government and to bomb the Serbs until Bosnian government forces were well enough armed to repel the Bosnian Serbs.

There was a Bosniak counter-offensive in the spring and summer of 1993, involving many Bosniaks who had themselves been victims of earlier cleansing. The Bosniaks felt that, since the international community had in effect accepted Serbian and Croatian 'facts on the ground' as a fait accompli in each case, survival meant having to resort to retaliatory large-scale 'ethnic cleansing' of their own. Nevertheless, Bosnian Serbs still controlled about 70 per cent of Bosnian territory in October 1993, whereas Bosniaks and Croats controlled only about 15 per cent each (although their shares included high proportions of the towns and other economically valuable territory).

A plan for Bosnia was put forward by Serbia and Croatia in June 1993. This envisaged a territorial division between three constituent republics and a highly consensual confederation of three constituent peoples, but there was intentionally nothing in these proposals to prevent the Serbs from creating a 'Greater Serbia' or the Croats from creating a 'Greater Croatia'.

On 4 June 1993 the UN Security Council approved the sending of troops to the six 'safe areas'. The troops were authorized to take necessary measures, including the use of force, if aid convoys were obstructed or if there were bombardments against the safe areas by any of the parties or armed incursions into them. However, the number of troops actually sent to protect the 'safe areas' was much lower than hoped for and there were substantial delays. Eight months after the UN Security Council authorized the dispatch of 7,600 peacekeeping troops in June 1993, only 5,000 had arrived in Bosnia.

NATO threats of air strikes were weakened by the conditions laid down. The UN Secretary-General Boutros Boutros Ghali had a veto. Normally he would have to approve any requests from the commander of UNPROFOR. The chances of actual air strikes taking place seemed remote, given the resistance to air strikes among UN commanders, which reflected their fears of retaliatory attacks on UNPROFOR troop already in Bosnia, the potential adverse effects of air strikes on the Geneva peace talks, and a disbelief in their effectiveness in deterring aggression. On 28 January 1994 Boutros Boutros Ghali delegated the authority to approve air strikes to his special representative in the former Yugoslavia, Yasushi Akashi.

In early 1994 President Clinton secretly gave his approval to covert arms shipments from Iran to the Bosniaks via Croatia, which of course took its share. However, this tacit US approval of military assistance to Bosnia (which breached the UN arms embargo against the Yugoslav successor states) was not publicly admitted until 5 April 1996 (*IHT*, 6 April 1996, p. 2). As early as the autumn of 1992, US officials had learne that Iran had opened an arms-smuggling route to the Bosniaks with Turkish assistance, and the Clinton administration turned a blind eye to this after taking office in Januar 1993 (*IHT*, 13 May 1996, pp. 1, 6). On 8 November 1996 the US senate intelligence committee formally conf rmed that President Clinton had approved a secret decision to do nothing to stop the smuggling of Iranian arms to the Bosniaks via Croatia. The committee admitted that senior Clinton administration officials misled the U congress, America's allies and the American people in this matter, but defended the administration's stance by affirming that it had broken no US laws, that the arms had helped the Bosniak goverment to survive, and that there was no tangible evi - dence that Iran's influence in the Balkans had increased as a result*IHT*, 9 November 1996, p. 2).

World attention was focused on Sarajevo on 5 February 1994, when a mortar bomb killed sixty-eight people in a marketplace and injured more than 200 others. In response, NATO gave a formal warning on 10 February 1994 that within ten days 'the heavy weapons of any of the parties found within the Sarajevo exclusion zone, unless controlled by UNPROFOR, will, along with their direct and essential military support facilities, be subject to NATO air strikes which will be conducted in close co-ordination with the UN secretary-general'. Unfortunately, disagreements emerged between NATO and the UN on 14 February 1994 over the 20 February deadline for surrender of heavy weapons and over what precisely was meant by 'control' of heavy weapons. The chain of authority for issuing air-strike orders was also insuff ciently clear. The Bosnian Serbs took advantage of this confusion to procrastinate and deepen the differences between NATO and the UN. NATO finally began to take military actio on 28 February 1994, when US f ghters operating under NATO auspices shot down four of the six Bosnian Serb jet aircraft that had been bombing targets in central Bosnia. This was not only the first enforcement of the 'air-exclusion zone' resolution, but also NATO's f rst ever combat mission.

In March 1994, Croatia's President Tudjman went along with the idea of a US-brokered Bosniak–Bosnian Croat federation linked economically to Croatia in a loose confederation. The federation would be split up into cantons. There would be a single army and a central government responsible for defence, foreign affairs and economic policy (including foreign trade), while the cantons would have authority over the police, education, housing and public services.

However, a large-scale Serbian assault on the Gorazde 'safe area', starting on 29 March 1994, turned into a f asco both for the UN and for NATO. NATO aircraft did not start bombing the Bosnian Serbs who were attacking Gorazde until 10 April 1994, and this failed to halt the Bosnian Serb advance. The Bosnian Serbs took full advantage of the divisions in 'the international community' and of the lack of UN troops on the ground by continuing to attack while pretending to negotiate. They fully gained full control of Gorazde on 17 April, while a cease fire was being announce by Karadzic and Yasushi Akashi. NATO gave the Bosnian Serbs a new ultimatum on 22 April, and a cease fire was announced on 23 April, after talks in Belgrade wit Bosnian Serb leaders. The Bosnian Serbs complied with the ultimatum suff ciently to head off further air strikes. Under new rules of engagement, it was agreed that the UN secretary-general would only need to approve a first air strike. A similar procedur was later agreed for the other 'safe areas' of Bihac, Srebrenica, Tuzla and Zepa.

On 25 April 1994 a so-called contact group of leading officials from the USA, Russia, the United Kingdom, France and Germany was established to coordinate responses to the conflicts in the Yugoslav lands. They were subsequently joined by Italy, whose close proximity gave it a major stake in achieving peace in former Yugoslavia. In July 1994 the contact group put forward a peace plan for Bosnia-Herzegovina, based on the concept of a federation split up into cantons but not solely along ethnic lines. However, the Bosnian Serbs rejected the plan and the territorial divisions put forward by the contact group, whereupon the 'international community' threatened to intensify their sanctions against the Bosnian Serbs and the FRY. This induced Milosevic to distance himself from the Bosnian Serbs and to shelve his plans for the creation of a 'Greater Serbia'. He rather ineffectually imposed sanctions on the Bosnian Serbs on 4 August 1994, while the state-owned section of the Serbian media spewed forth abuse against Karadzic, who was henceforth regarded as a major thorn in Milosevic's side.

Bihac effectively fell to Bosnian government forces on 21 August 1994, but on 8 September Bosnian Serbs launched a two-pronged attack on Bihac. On 26 October Bosnian government forces launched a successful counter-offensive in the Bihac area, and on 1 November Bosnian Croats began to help Bosnian government forces there and around Kupres in central Bosnia. Kupres fell to a combined Bosnian govern ment and Bosnian Croat attack on 3 November, but on 27 November the UN and NATO virtually sat on their hands while Bosnian Serbs captured the supposed 'safe area' of Bihac and held the UNPROFOR troops there as hostages.

The turning of the tide, 1995

The Croatian government, the Bosnian government and the Bosnian Croat militia agreed to form a military alliance on 6 March 1995. On 20 March Bosnian government forces launched a major offensive to capture Bosnian Serb positions on peaks around Tuzla and Travnik (the targets including communications towers). On 25 March the Bosnian Serbs shelled Mostar and Gorazde.

Eleven people were killed in Sarajevo on 7 May, when the area near the entrance to the tunnel which formed the city's lifeline to the outside world was shelled. The following day it was revealed that Yasushi Akashi and General Bernard Janvier had turned down a request from the UNPROFOR commander Lieutenant General Rupert Smith for air strikes on the Bosnian Serbs. On 24 May, nevertheless, Smith threatened air strikes against any transgressor if the following deadlines were not met: (i) all heavy weapons to cease firing in the Sarajevo exclusion zone by noon local time on 25 May and (ii) all such weapons to be located either outside the exclusion zone or in UN-controlled collection sites by noon on 26 May.

NATO jets attacked a Bosnian Serb ammunition dump near Pale on 25 May 1995, when four guns taken from a UN collection site were not returned. The Bosnian Serbs responded by shelling Sarajevo and four other 'safe areas', killing seventy-one civilians in Tuzla. The following day NATO jets launched another attack on the ammunition dump. The Bosnian Serbs retaliated by taking over 300 UN peacekeepers as hostages and using (unarmed) UN military observers as 'human shields' at likely targets of air strikes. An intervention by Milosevic on 2 June resulted in the release of 121 of the UN hostages (about a third of the total), but Bosnian Serb forces then took another sixteen UN personnel hostage and shot down a NATO (US) jet on routine patrol. The last twenty-six hostages were not released until 18 June, and Bosnian Serb forces shelled UN headquarters in Sarajevo on 2 July, seemingly deliberately.

The Srebrenica massacre, July 1995

Srebrenica became famous as the site of the worst acts of genocide carried out in Europe since the Second World War, mainly between 10 and 19 July 1995. On 6 July 1995 Bosnian Serb forces under General Ratko Mladic began an assault on Srebrenica. They blamed Bosnian government forces for launching raids out of the enclave. Two days later the Bosnian Serbs started overrunning UN observation posts in Srebrenica and briefly took Dutch troops prisoner. On 10 July the Bosnian Serbs issued an ultimatum to UN troops to leave Srebrenica. The next day they captured Srebrenica, despite two NATO air strikes on a Serb tank column. Srebrenica, the first 'safe area' to be declared was thus the f rst to fall. On 12 July the Bosnian Serbs began transporting civilians out of Srebrenica and separating out males over the age of sixteen to be 'screened for war crimes'. The UN Security Council unanimously passed a resolution demanding that Bosnian Serb forces should immediately withdraw from Srebrenica and that all parties should show full respect for Srebrenica's 'safe area' status.

A 155-page UN report on the mass murder perpetrated in Srebrenica was published in November 1999. The report stated that Bosnian Serbs had murdered around 7,600 Bosnian Muslim males over the age of sixteen in Srebrenica and that the UN's willing ness to negotiate with the Bosnian Serb leaders, Radovan Karadzic and General Ratko Mladic, had amounted to 'appeasement'. 'Through error, misjudgement and an inability to recognize the scope of evil confronting us', the report said, 'we failed to do our part to save the people of Srebrenica from the Serb campaign of mass murder.' The report reserved its harshest criticism for the UN leadership, particularly former secretary-general Boutros Boutros Ghali, his senior commander Lieutenant General Bernard Janvier from France, and his top envoy Yasushi Akashi from Japan. While the role of the future UN secretary-general Kof Annan in the tragedy was not clearly addressed in the report, he had already accepted that as head of the peacekeeping operation at the time he incurred much of the overall responsibility for the UN's failure in Bosnia. The report also questioned a great many UN decisions during the confict. The UN had by then acknowledged that its arms embargo had undermined the Bosnian army's ability to defend itself. The report strongly criticized UNPROFOR's persistent refusal of Bosniak requests for the return of the weapons which they had been forced to surrender and which would have afforded them some means of self-defence. 'The cardinal lesson of Srebrenica is that a deliberate and systematic attempt to terrorize, expel or murder an entire people must be met decisively with all necessary means, and with the political will to carry the policy through to its logical conclusion' (*IHT*, 16 November 1999, pp. 1, 10; *Independent*, 17 November 1999, p. 19).

The conclusion of peace, September–October 1995

Thirty-seven civilians were killed in a mortar attack on Sarajevo on 28 August. In retaliation, NATO launched Operation Deliberate Force on 30 August. NATO planes carried out a series of massive air strikes against Bosnian Serb targets, particularly around Sarajevo but also in Tuzla, Gorazde, Zepa and Mostar, while a newly established European 'rapid reaction force' shelled targets around Sarajevo, with the declared aim of clearing the exclusion zone of heavy weapons.

On 8 September 1995, while NATO carried out air strikes on Bosnian Serb forces, the foreign ministers of Bosnia, Croatia and Serbia reached agreement on the 'basic principles' of a political settlement in Bosnia. US special envoy Richard Holbrooke described the agreement as 'an important milestone in the search for peace'. On 18 September it was estimated that the Bosnian Serbs held around 50 per cent of Bosnia and Herzegovina. Control of the other 50 per cent was split more or less equally between the Bosnian government and the Bosnian Croats. The offensive in western Bosnia had virtually ceased by 21 September (*The Economist*, 4 November 1995, p. 55; *IHT*, 29 December 1995, p. 6).

US-led negotiations resulted in the signing of a cease-fire agreement on 5 Octobe 1995, but on 8 October it was reported that heavy fighting continued in northern Bosnia where troops from Croatia supported Bosnian government forces. The cease fire was further delayed on 9 October, because most of the preconditions had still not been met, but it fnally began on 11 October. It generally held, but fghting continued in a few places (e.g., around Sanski Most and Prijedor). On 18 October a UN aid convoy reached Gorazde from Sarajevo for the first time in two years. On 8 Novembe it was announced that a Russian combat brigade (about 1,500 troops) would participate in the peace implementation force.

The Dayton accords, 21 November 1995

Peace talks began on 1 November 1995 at the Wright-Patterson air base near Dayton, Ohio, USA. A peace agreement was finally initialled by presidents Izetbegovic, Tudjman and Milosevic on 21 November and the formal signing ceremony took place in Paris on 14 December. The main points were as follows:

1. Bosnia and Herzegovina was to be preserved as a single state within its present borders and with international recognition. The name of the country was to be changed from the 'Republic of Bosnia-Herzegovina' to 'Bosnia and Herzegovina'. The capital city of Sarajevo was to be reunited under federal authority, albeit divided into ten semi-autonomous districts.
2. Bosnia and Herzegovina was to be divided into two very separate and largely autonomous territorial 'entities': 51 per cent of the territory was assigned to the the FBiH, whose predominantly Bosniak and Croat population in 1996 was estimated at 2.5 million; and the other 49 per cent of the territory was allocated to the Republika Srpska, whose population in 1996 was estimated to be 1 million (*IHT*, 14 September 1996, p. 7). Within the FBiH, the Dayton accords gave 27 per cent of territory to the Bosniaks and 24 per cent to the Croats (*The Economist*, 20 January 1996, p. 24).
3. There was to be an 'effective' all-Bosnia central government, including a parliament, a three-member presidency, a constitutional court and single central

bank. The presidency and parliament would be chosen through free democratic elections, to be held under international supervision. The three-member presidency (one person to represent each of the main ethnic groups) would rotate, but with the FBiH providing the first 'president of the presidency'. The central authoritie would be responsible for foreign policy, foreign trade, common and international communications, inter-entity transport, air-traffic control, monetary policy, citizenship and immigration. To counter the threat of financial instability, it wa decided that for the first few years the new central bank would operate as a currency board, issuing domestic currency only against full foreign-exchange backing, and that there would be no domestic-bank financing of public expenditur (UN ECE 1996: 170).

4. Refugees were to be allowed and encouraged to return to their old homes.
5. Individuals charged with war crimes were to be banned from participation in political and military life; and Bosnia, Croatia and the FRY were required to cooperate fully with ICTY investigation and prosecution of war crimes.
6. A land corridor would link Sarajevo and Gorazde.
7. The future of Brcko and the Posavina corridor was to be submitted to international arbitration, but the Bosnian Serbs were awarded the area in western Bosnia around Sipovo and Mrkonjic Grad which they had lost in the summer of 1995.
8. A 'strong international force', which came to be known as the Implementation Force for Bosnia (IFOR) would supervise the separation of forces, which NATO christened Operation Joint Endeavour. The force was to number around 60,000, including roughly 20,000 US troops as well as Russian forces.
9. An international aid programme was to provide humanitarian relief, assist reconstruction and help refugees.
10. The agreement provided for a 'build-down' of weapons by those who had a great many arms, and a 'build-up' of the undersupplied Bosnian army *The Economist*, 30 March 1996, p. 20).

In the interim, until the holding of elections, Alija Izetbegovic remained president of the Bosnian presidency, while Haris Silajdzic remained prime minister of Bosnia and Herzegovina. The top posts within the Bosniak-Croat federation were held by president Kresimir Zubak, vice-president Ejup Ganic, prime minister Izudin Kapetanovic, and defence minister Vladimir Soljic. Radovan Karadzic remained the de-facto president of the Republika Srpska.

Many commentators angrily denounced the way in which the 'Bosnian Serbs' were allowed to retain 49 per cent of the territory of Bosnia-Herzegovina at Dayton, when they made up only about one-third of the total population. However, this righteous indignation overlooked two important considerations: (i) over half the territory of Bosnia and Herzegovina is made up of visually spectacular but economically barren and impoverished mountains; and (ii) most of the more economically valuable towns and cities and most of the small amounts of economically valuable farmland have remained in the hands of the (combined) Bosniak and Bosnian Croat majority through-out the post-Communist period, even at the height of the 'Bosnian conflict'. It is misleading to make judgements on this issue simply on the basis of the percentage distribution of 'land' or 'territory' between the main ethno-cultural groups, without taking into account the large variations in the economic potential and value of the 'land' or 'territory' which they held. Mainly as a legacy of the Ottoman and pre-Ottoman periods, the Bosniak and Bosnian Croat communities became and remained relatively prosperous and urbanized, whereas Bosnian Serbs mainly inhabited relatively impoverished and rural highland areas and therefore had a greater need for 'land' as the basis of their still mainly rural or small-town livelihoods. Indeed, the 'Bosnian conflict' of 1992–5 was in large part a civil war between town and country in which many educated middle-class Bosnian Serbs sided with the mainly town-based Bosniaks against rural Bosnian Serbs. It is by no means clear that the Bosnian Serbs got the better long-term territorial 'deal' at Dayton in 1995: much of what they obtained was relatively barren or impoverished terrain, whereas the Bosniaks and Croats retained control of the main towns and Bosnia's main coastal and lowland terrain (the areas with greater economic potential).

The human costs of the Bosnian conflict, 1992–5

Initially, estimates of the death toll from the Bosnian conflict exceeded 200,000. According to an article by Bosnia's prime minister Haris Silajdzic in the *International Herald Tribune* in February 1995: 'Seventy per cent of our country is occupied. More than 200,000 civilians have been killed, including 17,000 children. More than 400,000 people have been wounded. More than 2 million have been expelled from their homes. All this, and our pre-war population was only 4.3 million' (*IHT*, 23 February 1995, p. 8). In late 1995 the World Bank estimated that about 250,000 people had been killed, over 200,000 wounded, 13,000 permanently disabled, and 2.3 million displaced from their home regions (*Transitions*, November–December 1995, vol. 6, no. 11–12, p. 30). In early 1995 the UN high commissioner for refugees estimated that Serbs had expelled, killed or imprisoned 90 per cent of the 1.7 million non-Serbs who had been living in Serb-held areas of Bosnia (*IHT*, 5 January 1995, p. 6). More than 10,000 residents of Sarajevo had been killed and about 50,000 had been wounded (*IHT*, 6 April 1995, p. 7). The ICTY later put the number killed during the siege of Sarajevo (from early 1992 to 1995) at 10,500, of whom almost 1,800 were children (*IHT*, 30 December 1999, p. 2).

In February 2006, however, the Sarajevo-based Investigation and Documentation Centre (financed by Norway) announced, on the basis of its own very carefully documented estimates, that the number of people who perished in Bosnia and Herzegovina between 1992 and 1995 was around 100,000. About 70 per cent of the victims had been Bosniaks, about 25 per cent Serbs and 5 per cent Croats. This painstaking project of listing all the victims and displaying their names on the Internet was due for completion in April 2006 (*Independent*, 13 February 2006, p. 21).

These much lower estimates of the total death toll aroused considerable angst and controversy among Bosniaks, who had become accustomed to claiming and thinking that many more people had died and feared that the lower estimates would both diminish the world's perceptions of the enormity of the war crimes and the crimes against humanity committed by Serbs and reduce their chances of securing an international court judgment of (genocidal) collective guilt against the Serbs and enormous reparation payments from them. However, this is not a competition. The legal issues concerning whether genocide, war crimes and other crimes against humanity took place are not dependent on numbers. And it is both misleading and unjust to try to tar all Serbs with the same brush, by pronouncing them collectively guilty, as is emphasized in Chapter 6.

Even on the reduced estimates, the war in Bosnia killed vastly more people than did the ten-day war in Slovenia in July 1991, in which sixty-five people died, including thirty-seven JNA soldiers, twelve Slovene territorial-defence servicemen and police, and sixteen civilians (mainly Turkish truck drivers), while about 330 people were injured (Tus 2001: 46). The war in Croatia killed an estimated 20,000 people, about one-fifth of the number killed in Bosnia, and over 1 million people were displaced from their places of residence (*FT*, 3 March 1994, p. 22; *BCE*, March 1995, p. 15). On the other hand, terrible though it was, the Bosnian death toll was dwarfed by the 800,000 killed in Rwanda in 1994, by the millions who were killed in the Congo during the 1990s, and by the 300,000 or more who have been killed more recently in Darfur. These have been even greater tragedies, but the West has taken much less notice of them because the victims were not white Europeans and they lived in faraway countries.

'Displaced persons' and their return or non-return

In May 1996 it was estimated that around 2.5 million Bosnians had either left or been forcibly expelled from their homes since the beginning of the war in April 1992 (i.e., more than half of the 1991 population of 4,377,033 had been displaced). Of these, about 1.2 million were estimated to be living as so-called IDPs in other parts of Bosnia, mostly in areas controlled by armed forces of their own ethnicity, while about 600,000 were in other Yugoslav successor states. Of these, probably 450,000 were (mostly Serbian) refugees who had fled to Serbia and Montenegro. The other 700,00 refugees from Bosnia were in other European countries. Nearly half were in Germany, where the major 1960s–1980s emigration from Yugoslavia had established large émigré communities. As of May 1996, only 50,000 people, mostly IDPs, were thought to have returned to their old homes – many of which had either been damaged or demolished or had acquired new occupants (*The World Today*, June 1996, vol. 52, no. 6, pp. 144–5).

According to the UN High Commission for Refugees (UNHCR), only 550,000 of the 2.1 million people driven out of their homes by fighting and ethnic cleansing returned to their old homes during the fst three years of peace. Of the 1 million people who would be outnumbered by other ethnic groups if they were to return to their old homes, only 60,000 did so (*IHT*, 24 February 1999, p. 5). Most of the returnees were elderly people returning to Bosniak-controlled areas. In mid-1998 the Office of th High Representative (OHR) estimated that 75 per cent of refugees (about 600,000) were still abroad; and 85 per cent of IDPs (about 950,000) remained displaced from their pre-conf ict homes. Bosnia's total population was thought to be only 3.7 million in 1997, compared with almost 4.4 million in 1991 (*FT*, 4 July 2000, p. 8).

About 100,000 Serbs had abandoned their homes in Sarajevo during and imme - diately after the conflict. As of mid-2000, about 15,000 Sarajevo Serbs had returned The rate of return of refugees and IDPs to Bosnia was accelerated by the property laws introduced in 1998, which the OHR used to evict new occupants so that former owners could reclaim their property. Bosnian Serbs long blocked the return of refugees, but they became more compliant after the high representative Wolfgang Petritsch began dismissing local officials for obstructing the Dayton accords. By mid-2000 abou 220,000 had made claims for the return of their homes under the new property laws (*IHT*, 3 August 2000, p. 5). By late 2003, about 90 per cent of claims for return of property had been settled (*The Economist*, 20 December 2003, p. 56).

In September 2004, the UNHCR announced that over 1 million refugees and IDPs had returned to their former homes. Nearly 450,000 of these returnees were alleged to be so-called 'minority returnees', returning to areas in which they were in the minority, but the real figure may have been smaller

> Many people 'returned' only to regain possession of their property, which they then sold. Minority returnees may have stayed on in parts of the countryside, but the towns and cities are overwhelmingly dominated by one or other ethnic group ... Of Bosnia's pre-war Croat population of some 830,000, only half remain. Many, especially the young, have gone to Croatia, which, since independence, has offered them automatic citizenship.
>
> (*The Economist*, 26 November 2005, pp. 49–50)

Economic costs of the Bosnian conflict, 1992–5

There was massive destruction in the conflict zones, and massive dislocation in mos other parts of Bosnia-Herzegovina. In early 1996 the World Bank estimated Bosnia's unemployment rate to be between 50 and 60 per cent (*IHT*, 7 January 1997, p. 5). Per-capita income had fallen from 1,872 US dollars in 1991 to 524 US dollars in 1995 (*BCE*, September 1996, p. 80). Data collected by the World Bank in 1995 painted a very bleak picture. Around 45 per cent of all industrial plants, including perhaps 75 per cent of all oil ref neries, had been destroyed. A much higher percentage had been robbed of machinery and equipment. The surviving industry operated at 5 to 6 per cent of pre-war capacity, 78 per cent of electrical-generating capacity was out of commission, and coal production was less than 10 per cent of pre-war levels. Two-thirds of the housing stock, a third of all health-care facilities, half of all school buildings, a third of roads and about 40 per cent of bridges had been damaged or destroyed. Domestic food production satisfied only one-third of the country's requirements, and about 80 per cent of Bosnia relied on outside food aid. Water-borne diseases had become increasingly common (*Transitions*, November–December 1995, vol. 6, nos. 11–12, p. 30; *FT*, 21 December 1995, pp. 2, 13). The Bosnian government estimated that livestock herds had shrunk by 70 per cent (*IHT*, 29 January 1996, p. 9). Before the start of the conflict, 1.1 million of Bosnia's inhabitants ha been employed and 350,000 had been unemployed. In early 1996, by which time over one-third of the potential workforce had been killed, maimed or driven out of the country, the corresponding figures were 210,000 and 650,000 (*Transitions*, January–February 1996, vol. 7, no. 1, p. 5).

Anticipated reconstruction costs and foreign aid, 1996–9

In December 1995, the World Bank estimated reconstruction costs for Bosnia and Herzegovina at 4.9 billion US dollars, excluding rescheduling of its foreign debt (*FT*, 11 December 1995, p. 22). In early 1996 the World Bank, in association with the EBRD, the European Commission and UN agencies, proposed a 5.1 billion US dollar reconstruction programme over four years (1996–9 inclusive), with disbursements of roughly 1 billion US dollars in 1996, 1.6 billion US dollars in 1997, 1.4 billion US dollars in 1998 and 1.1 billion US dollars in 1999 (UN ECE 1996: 168).

Representatives of fifty countries attended a conference held on 12–13 April 199 on aid for the reconstruction of Bosnia hosted by the World Bank and the EU. They accepted the World Bank estimate that roughly 5.1 billion US dollars would be needed over four years, including 3.7 billion US dollars for the Bosniak-Croat federation and 1.4 billion US dollars for the (much smaller) Republika Srpska. At this conference an additional 1.23 billion US dollars were pledged, taking the total pledged for 1996 to 1.8 billion US dollars . The USA pledged an extra 219 million US dollars, bringing the total US contribution to around 550 million US dollars (*IHT*, 15 April 1996, p. 7). For 1996 alone, the EU as an organization pledged an extra 200 million US dollars, its member states 198 million US dollars, the World Bank 200 million US dollars, Japan 130 million US dollars, Canada 1.1 million US dollars, Muslim countries 144 million US dollars, other donor countries 79 million US dollars, the EBRD 70 million US dollars and the Islamic Development Bank 25 million US dollars (*Business Europa*, June–July 1996, p. 28). Each donor country would select its own preferred projects.

Post-Dayton Bosnia, 1996–2006

The governmental structures established for post-Dayton Bosnia and Herzegovina

1. The **three-member Bosnian presidency** was to comprise one directly elected representative from each of the three main ethnic communities (Bosniak, Bosnian Serb and Bosnian Croat). There was to be an annually rotating 'presidency of the presidency'. However, whether in the interests of stability or as a concession to the inflamed and inflated sensibilities of Alija Izetbegovic as the elected lead of the largest of the three main communities, it was decided that the term of office of the first 'president of the presidency' (Izetbegovic) would be for tw years. In principle, decisions were to be taken by the three-member presidency on the basis of unanimity. On a practical day-to-day basis, however, decisions could be taken with the support of just two members of this collective presidency, unless the third person declared that the 'national interests' of his or her ethnic group were threatened by that decision. In that event, the third person had to obtain the backing of two-thirds of the members of parliament from his/her half of FBiH in order to block the other decision arrived at by the other two presidents (*The Economist*, 21 September 1996, p. 50).
2. **The Republika Srpska** retained a presidency of its own, comprising a president and a vice-president, both of whom were to be directly elected on the basis of a single round of voting.
3. **The FBiH** also retained a two-member presidency of its own. Furthermore, this federation was divided into ten cantons, each of which also had an assembly of its own (444 seats in total). Under the Dayton accords, the Bosnian Croats were not allowed to rule both of the most ethnically 'mixed' cantons, namely Neretva (which includes Mostar) and Lasva-Vrbas. The other cantons within the FBiH are Una Sana, Posavina, Tuzla-Podrinje, Zenica-Doboj, Gorazde, West Herzegovina, Sarajevo and Tomislavgrad.
4. The forty-two-seat **house of representatives** of Bosnia and Herzegovina, the lower house of the central legislature, comprised twenty-eight seats for directly elected representatives from the FBiH and fourteen seats for directly elected representatives from the Republika Srpska (reflecting their 2:1 populatio ratio).

5. The fifteen-seat **house of the peoples** of Bosnia and Herzegovina, the upper house of the central legislature, comprised five Bosniak, five Croat and five Serb representatives, and was to be elected indirectly. Ten delegates were to be drawn from the house of representatives of the FBiH and five from the national assembl of the Republika Srpska.

6. In addition, the FBiH and the Republika Srpska were each to retain directly elected parliaments of their own. The FBiH had a bicameral parliament, comprising a 140-seat **house of representatives** (elected by proportional representation on a party list basis) and a sixty-seat **house of the peoples** (elected on a geographical basis, comprising thirty Bosniaks and thirty Croats and others). The Republika Srpska had a unicameral parliament: the eighty-three-seat national assembly.

7. There were also to be numerous **local councils** in both 'entities'. These were to be mainly responsible for providing local services (including police), deciding local housing policies, etc. These local councils comprised 109 *opstinas* (muni-cipalities) and about forty-one extra constituencies created where *opstinas* lay astride inter-entity boundaries. This gave rise to about 150 elective units of local government in due course.

8. All elections were to be by proportional representation, except for those to the three-member Bosnian presidency, to the house of peoples of the FBiH and to the presidency of the Republika Srpska, which were to be 'first past the post'

The immediate aftermath of the Dayton accords

The UN Security Council announced on 22 November 1995 that the arms embargo on the countries of the former Yugoslavia would be lifted over a six-month period and that economic sanctions on the FRY would be suspended for an initial six months. On 5 December NATO's foreign and defence ministers gave provisional approval to the sending of around 60,000 troops to Bosnia, including 20,000 from the USA, 13,000 from the United Kingdom, 10,000 from France and 2,000 from Russia. Other countries participating in the peacekeeping operation were Austria, Estonia, Latvia, Lithuania, Finland, Sweden, the Czech Republic, Slovakia, Hungary, Poland, Romania, Ukraine, Pakistan, Egypt and Malaysia. On 8 December the Bosnian government pledged to remove all foreign Muslim fighters from Bosnia within thirty days of signing the peac agreement in Paris, as the USA and the United Kingdom in particular feared 'Islamist' attacks on their troops.

The f rst major post-Dayton 'peace implementation conference' was held in London on 8–9 December 1995, in order to discuss how to proceed with the implementation of the civilian aspects of the Dayton settlement. The Swedish ex-premier Carl Bildt was appointed as the first 'high representative', whose functions were (i) to coordinate civilian aid and the reconstruction programme and (ii) to act as liaison between the civilian and military operations. Michael Steiner from Germany became the first 'deputy high representative'. A peace-implementation council (replacing th International Conference on the Former Yugoslavia) was to have a steering board comprising the G7 countries, Russia, the EU presidency, the European Commission and the Organization of the Islamic Conference. An OSCE mission was to prepare and conduct elections, while the UN high commissioner for refugees was to encourage and facilitate the return of refugees to their former homes.

The formal signing of the Dayton accords took place on 14 December 1995 in Paris. The UN Security Council approved the deployment of IFOR the following day. NATO formally took over responsibility for peacekeeping in Bosnia from the UN on 20 December 1995. The deadline for withdrawal from the frontlines, 19 January 1996, was considered generally to have been met. There was a similar deadline for the exchange of about 900 prisoners of war, but only about 220 of these prisoners had been released by then. The Bosniak government was the most reluctant to comply with this. On 15 January it postponed the first major exchange, demanding an explanation of what had happened to 24,742 people missing in Serb-held territory. About 4,000 were thought by the Bosniak government to be held in detention by Serbs, but the fate of the others was unknown, including some 5,000 men from Srebrenica (*IHT*, 16 January 1996, p. 6).

Bosnia's Bosniak prime minister Haris Silajdzic announced on 21 January 1996 that he would resign his position with effect from 30 January, because the Bosnian parliament had passed a law that reduced the number of ministries in the central government and thus weakened the central government's capacity to govern. On 13 April he announced the formation of a new 'Party for Bosnia and Herzegovina' (SBiH), committed to a genuinely multi-ethnic Bosnia. On 15 June, however, while he was campaigning for his SBiH, he was hit on the head with an iron bar by a supporter of the (Bosniak) Party of Democratic Action (SDA). Despite this severe head injury, he returned to high office as co-chairman of the cabinet after the September 1996 elections.

The presidents of Bosnia, Croatia and Serbia met contact-group members in Italy on 17–18 February 1996. All remaining prisoners of war were to be released forthwith, the Bosnian Serbs of Sarajevo were reassured that their freedom would be protected, and UN sanctions against the Bosnian Serbs were to be suspended once IFOR conf rmed that they were complying with the Dayton accords. Russia unilaterally lifted its UN-backed sanctions against the Bosnian Serbs on 23 February 1996. Four days later the UN suspended sanctions against the Bosnian Serbs, after IFOR had conf ned that they were complying with the zones of separation agreement.

President Izetbegovic was admitted to hospital on 22 February 1996 with heart trouble. His declining health, combined with his reluctance to relinquish his lead role to a younger f tter Bosniak leader and conciliator, complicated the quest for recon - struction and inter-communal reconciliation.

In late February 1996 an unarmed confederal police force (comprising Bosniak, Bosnian Croat and Bosnian Serb officers monitored by an international police forc and without powers of arrest) started to patrol Vogosca, the f rst of the f ve Serb-held suburbs of Sarajevo to change hands. However, most Bosnian Serbs had already left Vogosca. On 29 February the Sarajevo suburb of Ilijas was handed over to the control of the central state institutions. It was estimated that only around 2,000 of the previous 17,000 inhabitants of Ilijas were still living there. On 6 and 12 March, respectively, the Sarajevo suburbs of Hadzici and Ilidza also came under the control of the central state institutions. There had been reports of widespread intimidation, looting and arson by gangs of Bosnian Serb extremists, but there were also reports of intimidation of Bosnian Serbs and looting by Bosniak gangs. The Bosniak political leadership did too little to reassure the Bosnian Serbs in the five Serbian-held suburbs surround ing Sarajevo that they would be welcome to continue living there once the formal control of those suburbs had changed hands, while the Bosniak police exhibited some unwillingness to halt the intimidation of Serbs living in and around Sarajevo. The climax came when the Bosniak authorities largely excluded Bosnian Serbs and Croats from Sarajevo's new cantonal council (forty-f ve of the forty-seven seats were given to Bosniaks, while Serbs and Croats were allotted just one seat each). This prompted the city's widely respected Bosniak mayor Tarik Kupusovic to resign in protest(*IHT*, 18 March 1996, p. 6). On 19 March, nevertheless, Grbavica (the fifth hitherto Serb held suburb of Sarajevo) also came under control of the central authorities. Fewer than 2,000 (mostly elderly) inhabitants had remained there (*The Guardian*, 19 March 1996, p. 12; *The Times*, 20 March 1996, p. 15). There were varying estimates of how many Serbs in total remained in the five suburbs in question. The UN believed that onl 8,000–10,000 Serbs (between 10 and 12 per cent of the pre-war Serb population) were still there (*Independent*, 19 March 1996, p. 11). Various Western media reports suggested that roughly 60,000 Serbs had lived in these suburbs during the 1992–5 war, but that only 10,000–11,000 still remained in their old homes (*IHT*, 20 March 1996, p. 1; *The Times*, 20 March 1996, p. 15).

The Bosniak and Bosnian Croat leaders agreed on 30 March 1996 to strengthen the FBiH by establishing a customs union, a single state budget, a unitary banking system and a new flag. On 25 April they also agreed to establish a joint police forc and a network of human-rights monitors.

A subsequent meeting of the Peace Implementation Council on 13–14 June con - troversially decided to confirm that elections would be held as planned on 14 Septembe 1996 (the Clinton administration was particularly keen that they should go ahead). The final communiqué also declared that Karadzic 'should remove himself from the political scene'. On 25 June 1996 the chairman of the OSCE reluctantly gave his final approval for holding of elections in Bosnia on 14 September. Despite the 'extremely high risks', he declared, any delay 'could heighten political uncertainty and political division even more' (*IHT*, 26 June 1996, p. 6).

The USA 'certif ed' on 26 June 1996 that the Bosnian government had fulflled its obligations to expel the Iranian military units which had been established in Bosnia during the 1992-5 conflict, declaring that foreign Muslims had either left or been removed from the Bosniak army and security services (*IHT*, 8 July 1996, p. 5).

The US secretary of state Warren Christopher convened a meeting on 14 August, at which he persuaded presidents Izetbegovic, Tudjman and Milosevic to reaffirm their commitment to implementing the Dayton accords and (in the cases of presi-dents Izetbegovic and Tudjman) to strengthening the FBiH 'as the cornerstone of the peace process'. It was agreed that Herceg-Bosna would 'cease to exist' by 31 August 1996.

On 27 August, citing 'widespread abuse of rules and regulations', the OSCE postponed the local elections that had been scheduled for 14 September 1996. Criticism was especially levelled at the Bosnian Serbs and at the authorities in Serbia for the ways in which large numbers of Bosnian Serb refugees had been registered to vote in towns such as Brcko and Srebrenica, which had formerly had Muslim majori-ties. However, the election rules approved by the OSCE had given the three main nationalist parties (the Croatian Democratic Union, the Party of Democratic Action and the Serbian Democratic Party) a virtual monopoly on registering voters. The OSCE considered it necessary to postpone the local elections for the second time on 22 October 1996.

The problem of Radovan Karadzic in the Republika Srpska, May–September 1996

On 15 May 1996 Radovan Karadzic announced the 'dismissal' of the moderate Bosnian Serb prime minister of the Republika Srpska, Rajko Kasagic, who was willing to cooperate and negotiate with the leaders of the other ethnic groups in Bosnia and Herzegovina. In response, Kasagic declared that 'Karadzic is an illegitimate president because he was not elected by the people, as called for in the constitution, but only by a self-proclaimed parliament . . . The Dayton Agreement is the only future the Republika Srpska has' (*IHT*, 17 May 1996, p. 1). Nevertheless, the national assembly of the Republika Srpska voted overwhelmingly in favour of the dismissal of Kasagic, who was replaced by the hardline Bosnian Serb nationalist Gojko Klickovic. In a bid to circumvent international hostility to his continuing prominence in Bosnian politics, Karadzic announced that he would relinquish his role in foreign policy (as president of the republic) to the vice-president Biljana Plavsic, who was known as the Iron Lady because of her hardline Serbian nationalist views, while he would concentrate on rebuilding the economy, assisting the rehabilitation of Bosnian Serb refugees, and providing jobs for demobilized Bosnian Serb soldiers. However, there was considerable doubt as to whether such moves would diminish Karadzic's influenc (*IHT*, 21 May 1996, p. 5).

Karadzic was re-elected leader of the SDS on 29 June 1996, but the following day it was revealed that in a letter dated 26 June 1996 Karadzic had stated his intention to relinquish the presidency to Biljana Plavsic. She replied that Karadzic would remain president of the Republika Srpska until the elections scheduled for 13–14 September 1996, but on 3 July 1996 Karadzic declared that he would not be a presidential candidate and on 9 July he accepted the post of chairman of a newly established senate instead.

The ICTY issued international arrest warrants for Karadzic and Ratko Mladic on 11 July 1996, on charges of genocide and war crimes. The next day Richard Holbrooke went on a mission to persuade President Slobodan Milosevic to comply fully with the Dayton accords and to cooperate in removing Radovan Karadzic and Ratko Mladic from public life. Holbrooke warned Milosevic that failure to cooperate in this matter could result in 'the disenfranchisement of the SDS and the reimposition of sanctions' (*IHT*, 20 July 1996, p. 5). Robert Frowick, the American head of the OSCE's electoral mission in Bosnia, threatened that unless Karadzic stepped down fully as leader of the SDS, the party would be banned from taking part in the September 1996 Bosnian elections. Likewise, Admiral Leighton Smith, the commander of NATO forces in Bosnia, stated that he was prepared to seek out and arrest Karadzic if ordered to do so. He had the power and authority to reimpose international sanctions against the Republika Srpska. So did the high representative for Bosnia, Carl Bildt, but in Bildt's opinion the Dayton accords did not disqualify Karadzic from serving as leader of the SDS. This difference of interpretation became a major source of friction between Bildt and the USA and a major factor in Bildt's resignation as high representative in June 1997. On 19 July Milosevic capitulated to Western pressure and, in the presence of Milosevic and the FRY foreign minister Milan Milutinovic, Karadzic was made to sign the following statement, along with Momcilo Krajisnik, Biljana Plavsic and the Republika Srpska Serb foreign minister Aleksa Buha:

1. As of 19 July 1996 Dr Biljana Plavsic has assumed the office of Temporar
Acting President of Republika Srpska until completion of the elections of
14 September 1996.
2. Dr Radovan Karadzic states that he shall withdraw immediately and
permanently from all political activities.
3. As of 19 July 1996 Dr Radovan Karadzic relinquishes the office of Presiden
of the SDS and all the functions, powers and responsibilities of the President of
the SDS shall be frozen until the SDS chooses a new President. These powers
and responsibilities shall be taken over by Professor Buha.

The Western media, international organizations such as the World Bank and the EBRD,
and even some Western academic writers on Bosnia have often presented the continuing power and influence of Karadzic in the Republika Srpska as if it was base
on a deeply entrenched Bosnian Serb 'ethnic nationalism' and 'ethnic solidarity',
which allegedly encouraged Bosnian Serbs to overlook, condone or even applaud
Karadzic's overarching responsibility for Bosnian Serb war crimes and to resist all
endeavours to bring him to justice. Such interpretations are misleading. Karadzic's
continuing power and influence was based, not so much on the wildly exaggerate
'ethnic solidarity' of the Bosnian Serbs, as on his control of a large mafia-like gangste
network engaged in racketeering, illicit dealing and intimidation. In 1997 Chris Hedges
reported that Karadzic presided over a near-monopoly of the sale of gasoline, cigarettes
and other goods in the Republika Srpska. Karadzic controlled this near-monopoly
through two companies which he ran jointly with Momcilo Krajisnik, the Bosnian
Serb representative on the three-member Bosnian presidency. The two companies in
question were Centrex, which Karadzic had started in 1993 with the protection of the
police and the Serbian Democratic Party and which secured exclusive rights to import
and sell a variety of goods, and Selkt-Impex, which he launched in 1996 in league
with the interior ministry of the Republika Srpska, to handle imports and supplement
the salaries paid to the Bosnian Serb police by the Serbian-dominated FRY (*IHT*,
7 April 1997, pp. 1, 7). Many Bosnian Serbs were understandably afraid to oppose or
denounce Karadzic publicly, not because they revered him, but because they were still
controlled and intimidated by the informal, corrupt, thuggish and gangsterish state
within a state built up by Karadzic and his cronies. This, rather than Bosnian Serb
'ethnic solidarity', was the major obstacle to thoroughgoing democratization, economic
restructuring and liberalization in the Republika Srpska in particular and in Bosnia
and Herzegovina as a whole. Democratization, economic restructuring and liberalization were at odds with powerful, corrupt, brutal and deeply entrenched vested
interests, which resisted reforms that even hardline Bosnian Serb nationalists such as
Biljana Plavsic came to view as absolutely indispensable to the full economic recovery
of the Republika Srpska and to its eventual acceptance and integration into the EU.
Some of the newly elected Bosnian Serb leaders, including Biljana Plavsic, thus found
themselves increasingly at odds with Karadzic, whose blatantly flaunted power an
influence were a major embarrassment and a large obstacle to the 'normalization' of
political and economic life in the Republika Srpska and to its full acceptance by the
international community, including major aid donors and foreign investors. However,
on 12 September Plavsic called for the secession of the Republika Srpska from Bosnia
and its unification with the FRY. This call contravened the Dayton accords and th
following day she was forced by the OSCE to apologize and publicly retract.

The Bosnian presidential and parliamentary elections of 14 September 1996

The elections went ahead despite the many arguments put forward for postponing them, such as the likely retrenchment of ethnic divisions, the lack of progress made with regard to refugees wishing to return to their homes, the lack of independent media, widespread intimidation of opposition parties, and the accusation that the timetable was set to suit the November 1996 US presidential election. The election rules laid down by the OSCE somewhat imprudently gave the main nationalist parties (the SDA, the SDS and the HDZ) extensive control over local election commissions and the registration of voters. On election day OSCE supervision was minimal. International election monitors were each responsible for five polling stations. A senior official estimated that only 20 per cent of the voting would be watched (*IHT*, 14 September 1996, p. 7). The OSCE lacked sufficient resources and manpower to discharge th supervisory role which it had taken on. The electoral outcome was biased in favour of the three major nationalist parties. Registered voters who were not living in their former places of residence were given a three-way choice as to where to vote: where they used to live, where they now lived or where they would like to live. Because over 1 million Bosnian refugees and IDPs had not yet managed to return to their old homes but were not to be (as a consequence) unfairly deprived of their rights to vote, during these elections, refugees and IDPs respectively comprised 19 per cent and 18 per cent of those registered to vote (Chandler 1999: 117). Their votes were fiercel courted. There were many reports of pressure being exercised, especially by the Bosnian Serbs and Bosnian Croats, in order to induce people to vote either in the places where they currently lived or in areas that had been ethnically cleansed. However, reports of Bosniak intimidation also surfaced in, for example, Bihac. On election day the SDA threatened not to recognize the results in the Republika Srpska and the next day the Bosnian Serbs stopped counting for a while, alleging irregularities in the refugee and IDP balloting.

Thus, even though the election was generally peaceful, there was considerable unease about the vote itself. The electoral turn-out, estimated at 82 per cent by the OSCE, was suspiciously high in comparison with the estimated number of registered voters (2.92 million). On 23 September, therefore, the OSCE took the controversial decision to increase the figure for the total number of registered voters to 3.2 million although it resisted pressure for a recount. Its sub-committee had declared that there was 'a significant possibility of double voting, other forms of fraud, or counting irregularities' and therefore a recount was necessary.

The final election results were announced by the OSCE on 24 September 1996. As predicted, the vote divided mainly along ethnic lines. In the balloting for the three-member Bosnian presidency, Alija Izetbegovic was elected as the Bosniak repre - sentative, Momcilo Krajisnik was elected as the Bosnian Serb representative and Kresimir Zubak was elected as the Bosnian Croat representative. The voting figure were as follows: for the Bosniaks, Alija Izetbegovic 729,034 (runner-up: Haris Silajdzic, 123,784); for the Bosnian Croats, Kresimir Zubak 342,007 (runner-up Ivo Komsic, 38,261); and for the Bosnian Serbs Momcilo Krajisnik 690,373 (runner-up Mladen Ivanic, 305,803). Western commentators considered the size of the vote for Mladen Ivanic encouraging for the future, even though it was boosted by the votes of Bosniaks and Croats who chose to vote in the Republika Srpska. Ivanic was 'a socialist with links to Serbia's president, Slobodan Milosevic' and 'a staunch autonomist', but he nevertheless advocated cooperation and compromise with Bosnia's

Muslims and Croats (*The Economist*, 21 September 1996, p. 47; *IHT*, 19 September 1996, p. 10).

Between them, the three main overtly nationalist parties (the SDA, the SDS and the HDZ) won 86 per cent of the seats in the house of representatives, the lower house of the confederal parliament. Here the distribution of seats by party was as shown in Table 7.2.

7.2 All-Bosnian parliamentary election, 14 September 1996

Party	Share of vote (%)	Seats
Party of Democratic Action (SDA), led by Alija Izetbegovic	45.2	19
Serbian Democratic Party (SDS), led by Biljana Plavsic	21.4	9
Croat Democratic Union (HDZ), led by Kresimir Zubak	19.0	8
United List of Bosnia and Herzegovina[1]	4.8	2
Alliance for Peace and Progress	4.8	2
Party for Bosnia and Herzegovina (SBiH), led by Haris Silajdzic	4.8	2

Note:
1. This was a five-party coalition which included the Union of Bosnian Social Democrats. It was sometime characterized as 'centre-left', but in fact two of the parties were left-leaning, one was centrist and two were right-leaning. The distinguishing features of the United List were that its members drew support from all ethnic groups and that its platform was non-sectarian.

Vladimir Soljic and Ejup Ganic were elected president and vice-president, respectively, of the FBiH, but they had little power to influence policy decisions (Chandler 1999: 74). The final distribution of the 140 seats in the house of representatives of the FBiH was as shown in Table 7.3.

7.3 FBiH parliamentary election, 14 September 1996

Party	Share of vote (%)	Seats
SDA	55.7	78
HDZ	25.0	35
United List	7.9	11
Party for Bosnia and Croatia	7.9	11
Democratic People's Union	2.1	3
Croat Party of Rights	1.4	2

The f nal distribution of seats in the unicameral eighty-three-seat national assembly of the Republika Srpska was as shown in Table 7.4.

7.4 Republika Srpska national assembly election, 14 September 1996

Party	Share of vote (%)	Seats
SDS	54.2	45
SDA	16.9	14
Alliance for Peace and Progress	12.0	10
Serbian Radical Party (SRS)	7.2	6
Party for Bosnia and Herzegovina	2.4	2
United List	2.4	2
Democratic Patriotic Bloc of Republika Srpska	2.4	2
Serb Party of Krajina	2.4	2

Partial 'normalization' of Bosnia after the September 1996 parliamentary and presidential elections

The interior ministers of Germany's Länder decided on 19 September 1996 to start returning refugees to their old homes in Bosnia, with effect from 1 October.

Presidents Izetbegovic and Milosevic met in Paris on 3 October 1996 and pledged to establish full diplomatic relations between Bosnia and rump Yugoslavia. They also agreed to establish freedom of trade and transport and visa-free travel for their respective nationals and to refrain from 'political and legal acts which do not contribute to the improvement of friendly relations and cooperation'.

Momcilo Krajisnik and ten elected Bosnian Serb deputies boycotted the inauguration of Bosnia's three-member presidency and the house of representatives of Bosnia and Herzegovina on 5 October because it demanded an oath of loyalty to a unitary state of Bosnia and Herzegovina (*IHT*, 7 October 1996, p. 11), but on 22 October, Krajisnik met Izetbegovic and Zubak in Sarajevo for the first working session of th presidency and took the oath of loyalty. On the same day, the OSCE again postponed the holding of local elections, due to 'continuing political problems in municipalities across Bosnia' (*FT*, 22 October 1996, p. 2).

A meeting of Western foreign ministers with Bosnia's three-member presidency in Paris on 14 November 1996 adopted new 'guidelines' which committed the Bosnian presidency to establish 'as a high priority . . . all the joint institutions provided for in the constitution and to make them fully operational as soon as possible'. The guidelines also contained reminders that aid was dependent on 'the degree to which all the authorities of Bosnia and Herzegovina fully implement the peace agreement', including cooperation with the ICTY (*Independent*, 15 November 1996, p. 13). The next day, President Clinton announced that the USA would contribute about 8,500 troops to the follow-up force after the expiry of IFOR's mandate on 20 December 1996. 'We will propose to our NATO allies that by the June of 1998 the mission's work should be done and the forces should be able to withdraw.'

On 18 November 1996 NATO agreed to set up SFOR (the Stabilization Force for Bosnia), comprising 31,000 troops. On 13 December the UN approved a mandate for SFOR, while the German parliament approved the use of 2,000 German combat troops as part of SFOR, to operate in south-eastern Bosnia. This was the first tim since the Second World War that German combat forces had been allowed to take full part in a ground mission with Western allies, albeit jointly with French forces.

A peace-implementation conference held in London on 4–5 December 1996 further emphasized that international aid to Bosnia would be dependent on fulf lment of the Dayton accords. Increased assistance was to be given to the ICTY and to the investigation branch of the international police task force. The final communiqué also called for the establishment of an integrated telephone system and a single system of car number plates for the whole of Bosnia.

The first full session of the central Bosnian house of representatives took place o 3 January 1997. The Serb delegates who had boycotted the inaugural session in October 1996 had since then signed a 'solemn declaration' upholding the Bosnian constitution, but they continued to avoid taking an oath to it in a public ceremony (*IHT*, 4 January 1997, p. 2). The house of representatives approved, with just one abstention, the council of ministers proposed by the three-member Bosnian presidency: the two co-premiers were the Bosniak Haris Silajdzic and the Bosnian Serb Boro Bosic; the foreign minister was the Bosnian Croat Jadranko Prlic; the foreign-trade minister was the Bosniak Hasan Muratovic; and the minister of communications was the Bosnian Serb Spasoje

Albijanic. Each minister had two deputies and, overall, posts were distributed equally among the three ethnic communities.

The American lawyer Roberts Owen, chairperson of the arbitration tribunal on the town of Brcko, announced on 14 February 1997 that the tribunal would give its judgment no later than 15 March 1998 and that until then Brcko would be under international supervision. However, on 15 March 1998 it was announced that the judgment would be further delayed, until at least early 1999 (*IHT*, 16 March 1998, p. 1).

Agreement was reached on a power-sharing arrangement for Sarajevo on 28 March 1997, paving the way for the election of a city mayor. In a display of support for the peaceful coexistence of the city's differing ethno-cultural communities, Pope John Paul II visited Sarajevo on 12–13 April 1997 and met all three members of the Bosnian presidency.

The Bosnian Peace Implementation Council threatened to impose sanctions on 30 May, unless the Dayton accords were carried out in full. It also announced that from 20 June 1997 Carl Bildt's role as high representative for Bosnia would be taken over by Spain's former foreign minister Carlos Westendorp.

The power struggle in the Republika Srpska, November 1996 to September 1997

Biljana Plavsic, the recently elected Republika Srpska president, announced on 8 November that General Ratko Mladic and the rest of the Bosnian Serb general staff would at last be dismissed. Dr Plavsic was contemplating turning against Karadzic and Mladic and becoming much more subservient to the Western powers (in order to obtain lenient treatment for her own crimes against humanity, it later transpired). Mladic's successor as commander of the Bosnian Serb army, Major General Pero Colic, was sworn in on 10 November. On 11 November, however, about 100 high-ranking officers in the Bosnian Serb army declared their 'full support for the mai headquarters led by General Mladic, as they are the only ones to guarantee the survival of the Serb Republic' (*IHT*, 12 November 1996, p. 8). The Bosnian Serb military occupied a television transmitter until 18 November and Mladic did not finally resign his command until 27 November.

In early February 1997 President Plavsic placed an advertisement in Serbian newspapers, calling for an investigation into the export-import companies controlled by Karadzic and Momcilo Krajisnik. She stated on television that the Karadzic–Krajisnik companies, Centrex and Selk-Impex, were bringing in massive revenues from contraband and that Karadzic controlled a nationwide secret-police network. 'The consequence of this is an enormous accumulation of wealth by a relatively small number of our population . . . Do they think that the rest of the population will be their slaves?' (*The Times*, 5 July 1997, p. 17).

The Bosnian Serb leadership in Pale signed an agreement with the Serbian government on 28 February 1997 which included a promise of military cooperation. The agreement also spelled out cooperation on such matters as foreign trade, border traffic, citizenship and customs (*IHT*, 12 March 1997, p. 8). The Republika Srpska parliament ratified this agreement on 16 March, although President Plavsic urged its rejection on the grounds that it contravened the Dayton accords (*The Guardian*, 17 March 1997, p. 10).

President Plavsic dismissed the Republika Srpska interior minister Dragan Kijac, a Karadzic loyalist, on 27 June 1997, for refusing to deal with the corruption that had permeated the economy and enriched people such as Karadzic. However, his dismissal was rescinded the next day by the Republika Srpska prime minister. In retaliation, President Plavsic was briefly detained by Serbian police at Belgrade airport on 29 June, and the following day she was briefly detained by Republika Srpska police She accused Karadzic of still running the Republika Srpska and of plotting a coup. On 3 July she attempted to use her presidential powers to dissolve the Republika Srpska assembly and call fresh elections for 1 September 1997, declaring that the 'functioning of legal order' was 'in a serious crisis in almost all fields' and that th national assembly was 'carrying out orders from the informal centres of power', while the Republika Srpska police were 'organizing criminal activities' (*The Times*, 5 July 1997, p. 17). On 5 July the Republika Srpska assembly enacted measures designed to weaken the powers of the president, make impeachment easier and prepare the ground for a referendum on whether to dismiss her. The existing constitutional settlement stipulated that the assembly had to call a referendum if it wished to remove the president. President Plavsic was expelled from the ruling SDS on 19 July. The following day, in Doboj, she threatened to have Karadzic arrested for corruption and told supporters: 'Now is the moment to establish a democratic Serb state based on legality, because we belonged – and will again belong – to Europe' (*IHT*, 21 July, p. 5; *IHT*, 22 July 1997, p. 9).

It was announced on 8 August that the (paramilitary) 'special police' forces in the Republika Srpska were to be brought under the control of SFOR (where they were considered to be soldiers) or the UN international police task force (where they were considered to be police). These Bosnian Serb 'special police' units were then ordered to return to barracks or face seizure of their weapons, while SFOR carried out inspections. SFOR outlawed the provision of special police protection to indicted war criminals such as Karadzic and Mladic on 15 August (*IHT*, 16 August 1997, p. 2).

The Republika Srpska constitutional court on 15 August overruled President Plavsic's attempt to dissolve parliament and call early elections. One of the seven judges on this court later revealed that he had been beaten and ordered to vote against Plavsic. There were also rumours of others being intimidated. On 17 August two ministers in the Republika Srpska government, including the fiance minister, resigned. On 20 August SFOR troops, with Plavsic's consent, again took control of police stations in Banja Luka. Pero Colic, the Bosnian Serb army chief of staff, warned on 22 August that he would not remain a passive spectator if the Republika Srpska split. The next day the Republika Srpska government announced that it would henceforth regard all President Plavsic's decisions as 'irregular, illegitimate and non-binding'. However, IFOR issued what amounted to a decree that she had the right to dissolve the legislature and hold new elections (*IHT*, 20 August 1997, p. 5).

A large group of Bosnian Serb army commanders met with President Plavsic in Banja Luka on 26 August, but Colic and three other prominent commanders stayed away from the meeting (*Independent*, 27 August 1997, p. 8). The next day Plavsic also met Patriarch Pavle, the head of the Serbian Orthodox Church, while the Doboj television transmitter (north-east of Banja Luka) was captured by supporters of Plavsic and then retaken by supporters of Karadzic. Clashes occurred on 28 August between (US) SFOR troops and supporters of Karadzic in Brcko and Bijeljina, where pro-Plavsic police tried to take control of police stations. On the same day, Plavsic launched a new political party, the Serbian People's Union. The next day bombs were exploded in Banja Luka and Doboj, and one person was killed. On 1 September Karadzic supporters stoned SFOR troops who were guarding the television transmitter near Bijeljina.

The Republika Srpska army chief of staff Pero Colic met Dr Plavsic in Banja Luka on 3 September and subsequently referred to her as the 'supreme commander'. On 8 September SFOR troops and police loyal to Plavsic prevented numerous Karadzic supporters from attending a Serb nationalist rally in Banja Luka, but the following day SFOR troops rescued Karadzic supporters (including Momcilo Krajisnik, interior minister Dragan Kijac and prime minister Gojko Klickovic), who were being besieged by Plavsic supporters.

Plavsic and Krijisnik met Milosevic in Belgrade on 24 September and concluded an agreement to hold a parliamentary election in the Republika Srpska on 15 November 1997, as well as elections for its two presidential posts (those held by Plavsic and Krajisnik, respectively) on 7 December 1997. They also agreed that the Republika Srpska official radio and television broadcasts would henceforth emanate on alternat days from Banja Luka (the stronghold of Plavsic supporters) and Pale (the stronghold of Karadzic supporters), while the international authorities (the Office of the Hig Representative et al.) would be allowed a one-hour slot of their own each evening.

On 28 September Plavsic accused Karadzic of having transferred 49 million Deutschmark into foreign bank accounts (*The Times*, 29 September 1997, p. 14). Two days later the Pale faction of Bosnian Serbs led by Radovan Karadzic and Momcilo Krajisnik refused to endorse her decision to call parliamentary elections for 23 November rather than 15 November, as had been provisionally agreed with Milosevic in Belgrade (*EEN*, 1997, vol. 11, no. 19, p. 7). Plavsic and her supporters needed as much time as possible to get their forces organized for the election campaign, whereas it suited the coalition led by Karadzic and Krajisnik to have the election as soon as possible, in order to give their less-established opponents less time to get organized.

Starting in September 1997, the USA, SFOR, the OSCE and the Office of the Hig Representative intervened with increasing openness in support of President Plavsic, who had clearly struck some sort of deal with Bosnia's Western overlords, who for their part evidently expected Plavsic and her allies to do their bidding. The Pale-based Serbian Radio and Television network (SRT) 'was pressurised to sign up to a series of agreements' which were designed to reduce the inf uence of the SDS and raise the media profile of its rivals. The Udrivigo agreement of 2 September 1997 which was concluded between the deputy high representative and the commander of SFOR and Mocilo Krajisnik 'in his capacity as Chairman of the Board of Directors of SRT', stipulated that SRT would provide an hour of prime airtime each day for the less nationalistic political parties, provide the Offce of the High Representative (OHR) with a half-hour slot of prime viewing time, and would refrain from 'inflammator reporting' against SFOR and international organizations which supported the Dayton accords. A further agreement concluded between Biljana Plavsic, Momcilo Krajisnik and President Milosevic in Belgrade on 24 September further reduced 'the Pale faction's editorial control over SRT' (Chandler 1999: 126). In Belgrade on 13 October Krajisnik also yielded to Plavsic's insistence on holding the forthcoming parliamentary elections on 22–23 November rather than 15 November. During that autumn the USA also delivered 700,000 US dollars worth of equipment to the SRT studios in Banja Luka and provided 'media training and the services of a US government media expert to assist Plavsic in her campaign' (Chandler 1999: 127).

On 1 October, meanwhile, at the request of the high representative, SFOR troops seized control of four radio and television transmitters controlled by Karadzic supporters, namely those near Doboj and Bijeljina in the north, at Trebinje in the south-east, and Sarajevo in the centre, and handed them over to supporters of President Plavsic. On 16 October 'the Pale faction' managed to resume broadcasting from a new television transmitter, but this 'pirate' relay station was taken over by SFOR troops three days later. On 11 November SFOR troops also seized a police station in Doboj which was controlled by pro-Karadzic 'special police'.

David Chandler (1999) has portrayed all these interventions as unwarranted and somewhat scandalous Western interference in Bosnian Serb electoral politics. They were certainly invasive and they could be regarded as 'high-handed liberal paternalism', but such interventions were also quite plausibly defended on the grounds that they were designed to establish a more level playing field on which less nationalisti parties and viewpoints could obtain more equal media access and more balanced media coverage (ICG 1997), as Chandler partly concedes (1999: 112–13). Refraining from intervention would simply have left extreme nationalists in unchallenged control of most of the local media facilities.

The local elections held across Bosnia, 13–14 September 1997

On this occasion, would-be voters were allowed to register to vote either in the area where they had lived in 1991 (voting there either in person or by postal ballot) or in the place where they had been residing since June 1996. A resounding 89 per cent chose to register in their former abodes (*The Guardian*, 11 November 1997, p. 17). These local elections were overseen and organized by the OSCE. There were 2.5 million registered voters, including 400,000 outside Bosnia *IHT*, 15 September 1997, p. 10). In all, 83 parties, 9 coalitions and 159 independent candidates took part (*IHT*, 13 September 1997, p. 2). Voting took place in 136 municipalities and in 6 precincts in Mostar. During the two election days, the USA flew three aircraft over Bosnia whic were capable of broadcasting programmes explaining and advocating the Dayton accords and of jamming radio and television broadcasts hostile to the Dayton accords. The HDZ and the SDS did not carry out their threats to boycott the elections. However, the SNS, launched by President Plavsic, came into existence too late to be eligible to take part.

There were a dozen towns in which exiles won either a majority or a large share of the seats, e.g., Brcko, Dvar, Mostar and Srebrenica. In nine towns where the incumbent 'powers that be' had blocked duly-elected exiles or IDPs from taking office the OSCE itself chose the new mayors and it compelled multi-ethnic councils to meet (*The Economist*, 11 April 1998, p. 34). Through these local elections, the OSCE managed to oversee the installation of elected assemblies in all but two of Bosnia's 136 municipalities. One of the exceptions was Srebrenica, whose displaced Bosniak population (still living as refugees) elected a Bosniak-majority local assembly using the absentee voting system. In Srebrenica, Bosniak parties in theory won control of the town council by gaining twenty-f ve seats. In January 1998, however, the f rmly ensconced Bosnian Serb community blocked the arrival of the twenty-five Bosnia councillors and stoned the car of an OSCE official. On 6 April 1998 the OSCE suspended Srebrenica's elected town council and said it would appoint an administrator with wide powers (*The Economist*, 11 April 1998, p. 34).

These elections saw more than seventy parties win representation. However, only in Tuzla did non-ethnic parties manage to prevail. There were some positive developments, however. In the Republika Srpska the Bosnian Serb nationalist SDS did not capture as many votes as it was feared they would, although many disaffected former SDS supporters merely transferred their allegiance to the SRS, the Bosnian branch of Vojislav Seselj's SRS in 'Serbia proper'. Furthermore, some candidates standing for 'refugee return' were elected in parts of the FBiH, as was one in the Republika Srpska (Friedman 2000: 26).

The parliamentary elections held in the Republika Srpska, 22–23 November 1997

The turn-out for the November 1997 election was 77 per cent. These elections were fairly openly viewed by the USA, SFOR, the OHR and the OSCE 'as an opportunity to wrest legislative power from the Serb hardliners' (Chandler 1999: 125–6). With active US, SFOR and OSCE backing, more conciliatory and less nationalistic politicians did gain the initiative for a few years. The f ercely nationalistic SDS led by Momcilo Krajisnik and (unofficially) Radovan Karadzic won only twenty-four o the eighty-three seats in the national assembly, but this was partly compensated by increased support for the ultra-nationalist SRS. The still relatively new SNS founded by President Plavsic won fifteen seats (the same as the SRS). It decided to make common cause with the two small but more conciliatory independent parties and with the Bosniak-dominated Coalition for Bosnia and Herzegovina, which won sixteen seats, benefiting considerably from the postal votes of Bosniak refugees resident outside the Republika Srpska. The final distribution of seats in the eighty-three-sea national assembly of the Republika Srpska was as in Table 7.5.

The OHR, SFOR and the USA thereupon endeavoured to persuade the newly elected Republika Srpska assembly to back a non-party government of technocrats which would have been headed by the liberal-minded economics professor Mladen Ivanic (who was not even an elected deputy), but Ivanic was unacceptable to the SDS and the SRS and they managed to block his appointment. President Plavsic then proposed Milorad Dodik, the leader of the Independent Social Democrats (who held only two seats in the assembly), as the new premier of the Republika Srpska. However, Dodik was reviled by the nationalistic SDS and SRS deputies, who could not forgive his outspoken opposition to the war and his eagerness to cooperate fully with the OHR, SFOR and the Western powers. During the night of 17–18 January 1998, however, after the SDS 'speaker of the house' had adjourned parliament and the Bosnian Serb nationalist deputies had gone home to sleep, the other parties hurriedly reconvened and (with the active support of the OHR) voted in a government headed by Dodik. The SDS and the SRS denounced Dodik as a tool of the West and as a traitor to his

7.5 Republika Srpska national assembly election, 22–23 November 1997

Party	Share of vote (%)	Seats
Serbian Democratic Party (SDS)	28.8	24
Serbian Radical Party (SRS)	18.0	15
Serbian People's Union (SNS, led by Plavsic)	18.0	15
The SDA-led coalition (mainly Bosniak)	19.2	16
The Republika Srpska branch of Milosevic's Socialist Party	10.8	9
Bosnian Social Democratic Party	2.4	2
Independent Social Democrats (SNSD, led by Milorad Dodik)	2.4	2

Source: Chandler (1999: 77).

fellow Bosnian Serbs and refused to recognize the new government. However, the Dodik government managed to govern with the support of the Bosniak and Croat deputies, who travelled to sessions of the national assembly under UN protection.

Dodik blamed the economic problems of the Republika Srpska on the 'needless spite, nonsense and egoism' of its previous rulers. He pledged strict implementation of the Dayton accords, the establishment of a free press, an end to censorship, an end to state corruption, an acceleration of privatization and a separation of church and state. He also declared his intention to transfer the capital of the Republika Srpska from Pale, the old power-base of Radovan Karadzic and his supporters, to Banja Luka (*IHT*, 21 January 1998, p. 5; IHT, 22 January 1998, p. 8). On 31 January 1998 the Bosnian Serb parliament voted in favour of such a transfer.

The aftermath of the September and November 1997 elections

At a meeting of the Peace Implementation Conference held in Bonn on 9–10 December 1997, after two years of strong resistance to full implementation of the Dayton accords, the prerogatives of the high representative were augmented, empowering him to dismiss politicians and officials and to impose laws and interim solutions if necessary or when the major protagonists were unable to reach agreement. In addition, deadlines were set for various measures, such as the introduction of common car number plates throughout Bosnia and Herzegovina by the end of January 1998. On 18 December, moreover, President Clinton announced that US troops would stay in Bosnia beyond the June 1998 deadline:

> It is imperative that we not stop until the peace here has a life of its own, until it can endure without us . . . The progress in Bosnia is unmistakable, but it is not yet irreversible . . . If we pull out before the job is done, Bosnia will almost certainly fall back into violence, chaos and ultimately a war as bloody as the last one.
>
> (*The World Today*, 1999, vol. 55, no. 6, p. 8)

Momcilo Krajisnik signed a dual-citizenship agreement with the Yugoslav foreign minister Milan Milutinovic on 13 December 1997, and on 19 January 1998 the government of rump Yugoslavia granted recognition to the Milorad Dodik government in the Republika Srpska. Cocking a snook at his erstwhile Bosnian Serb allies in the SDS and the SRS, President Milosevic said that he believed that the Dodik government would 'cooperate completely' in the peace process and that he supported this (*IHT*, 22 January 1998, p. 8).

On 21 January 1998 the high representative imposed a solution for the design of a common currency that would be binding on both entities until they could reach agreement on a common design between themselves. The *konvertibilna marka* (convertible mark, exchangeable one for one into Deutschmarks) would in fact acquire two sets of designs. Banknotes would have both Cyrillic and Latin lettering, but one set would feature leading Bosniak and Croat historical and cultural figures, while the other would feature only famous Serbs. UN officials considered it unlikely that the *konvertibilna marka* would dethrone the Deutschmark as the medium for all major private business transactions. Nevertheless, it would eventually play central roles in all governmental transactions and it would have legal standing in both 'entities' (*IHT*, 22 January 1998, p. 5; *FT*, 22 January 1998, p. 2). The new *marka* came into circulation in June 1998.

In a similar vein, on 2 February 1998, Westendorp unveiled the imposed common vehicle number plates. The neutral design revealed neither ethnicity nor place of origin. On 22 April agreement was reached between all sides to re-establish a Bosnia-wide postal service. On 20 May Westendorp also imposed a new flag (as no consensus ha been reached on its design), and in July new passports became available, incorporating only minor variations to reflect linguistic differences between the two entities

In the Republika Srpska, meanwhile, despite his vilification by Bosnian Serb nationalists for his repeated condemnations of the war and his subservience to the Western powers, the relatively unknown thirty-nine-year-old premier Milorad Dodik quickly signed agreements to unify the Republika Srpska police with the Bosniak and Bosnian Croat forces, to issue common passports, to establish a common currency and car number plates and to draw up a proper budget. He dismissed numerous corrupt off cials, 'including customs officials, the head of the financial police, and the enti board of directors at the Bosnian power company and at Energopetrol, the fuel enterprise'. He also dismissed the directors of Bosnia's two oil refneries, of the iron mines in Ljubija and of the major brewery and cigarette factories in Banja Luka, and the nationalist editor of the state-owned daily newspaper *Glas Srpski*. In contrast to the ultra-nationalist Biljana Plavsic, whose cooperation was designed to save herself from being indicted for her war crimes, Dodik appeared to 'genuinely support the calls to rebuild a multi-ethnic Bosnia'. He endorsed an international plan to return large numbers of refugees to their old homes. He had formed a government in Banja Luka and announced that the seat of government would move there from the Karadzic stronghold in Pale. The EU gave Dodik's fledgling administration 6.7 million US dollars to pay back salaries and get down to work. Once a budget was drawn up, the Republika Srpska would become eligible for a large tranche of the 1.5 billion US dollars in aid pledged by the international community for Bosnia. It was announced that by 2 February 1998, with the assistance of EU customs inspectors, all border and customs stations would be in the hands of 'Dodik loyalists' who would 'divert tens of millions of dollars in revenue from Pale to newly established government bank accounts in Banja Luka'. Dodik insisted that all records and state documents be transferred there from Pale. Westendorp promised international intervention if this was not accomplished (*IHT*, 29 January 1998, pp. 1, 6).

A 'Sarajevo Returns Conference' was held on 3 February 1998 in Sarajevo, whose population was now 87 per cent Bosniak (whereas it had previously been split somewhat more evenly between Bosniaks, on the one hand, and Serbs and Croats, on the other). In the run up to the conference, foreign offcials in Bosnia had complained of the failure of all parties 'to implement repeated pledges to foster the rebirth of a multi-ethnic society'. In late 1995 both the FBiH and the Republika Srpska had 'enacted laws and regulations meant to freeze communal concentrations and obstruct the return of minority refugees to their pre-war homes'. The conference was called to highlight 'the failure of the government to allow – much less promote – minority resettlement' and to set a series of deadlines for the adoption of new laws and the resolution of dozens of housing disputes, in order to facilitate the return of thousands of minority refugees to Sarajevo. In order to ensure that their message was heard, American and European diplomats at the conference also planned to threaten to cut off tens of millions of dollars in aid if the new deadlines were not met. The principal obstacle to allowing minority refugees to return was a law enacted by the Bosniaks in late 1995 which had given former residents two weeks to reclaim their homes after the 22 December 1995 cease f re. If they did not meet this deadline, their property could be declared abandoned and given to someone else. Because the law was never publicized outside the country, hundreds of thousands of refugees had been left without means of legal redress. The FBiH parliament had also voted to deny refugees the right to return to thousands of apartments which had previously been owned by the JNA, by nullifying the contracts for the sale of those apartments to their pre-1992 occupants. The Bosniak army had 'declared many of the apartments abandoned and transferred them to favoured war veterans' (*IHT*, 3 February 1998, p. 4). The conference called for at least 20,000 Serbian and Croatian refugees to be allowed to resettle in Sarajevo by the summer of 1998, and the FBiH was given two weeks to revoke the 1995 legislation governing the return of property to Serbs and Croats. However, President Izetbegovic declared that he would not accept this demand unless the Republika Srpska was made to reciprocate (*IHT*, 4 February 1998, p. 6; 5 February 1998, p. 5; *The Guardian*, 5 February 1998, p. 11). A follow-up conference was held in Banja Luka on 28 April 1998, with all sides represented, in order to accelerate the return of refugees and IDPs.

The Bosnia-wide parliamentary and presidential elections of 12–13 September 1998

There was considerable delay before the results of the OSCE-organized elections for all offices above the municipal level were announced. Foreign observers criticize the conduct of these elections. 'Roughly 200,000 voters could not find their names o the register and had to be given special ballot forms . . . Computer glitches and late deliveries of ballot forms also caused large queues at many polling stations . . . They also attacked the poor security provided for parties campaigning in areas controlled by ethnic rivals.'

Nevertheless, the then head of the OSCE mission in Bosnia described the elections as 'the most successful' since 1995 (*The Guardian*, 15 September 1998, p. 16). The ethnic and confessional parties lost ground, although Izetbegovic retained the Bosniak seat in Bosnia's three-member presidency and Ante Jelavic of the HDZ obtained the Croat seat. The results of the parliamentary elections for the Bosnia and Herzegovina house of representatives are shown in Table 7.6.

Within the FBiH, the SDA-dominated coalition headed by Alija Izetbegovic lost its overall majority in the 140-seat house of peoples, dropping from eighty-eight to sixty-eight seats. The Croat nationalist HDZ also lost seats, while non-confessional parties such as the Social Democrats increased their representation (*FT*, Survey, 21 October 1998, p. iii). Nevertheless, the SDA and its coalition partners had still captured 48 per cent of the vote in the FBiH. The two biggest Croat parties between them won 23 per cent. The two Social Democratic parties, the biggest non-ethnic parties, took only 17.5 per cent between them (*FT*, Survey, 14 December 1999, p. 37) (see Table 7.7).

In the Republika Srpska, the ultra-nationalist Nikola Poplasen was elected president, beating Biljana Plavsic. Poplasen had been the commander of a Bosnian Serb militia unit during the 1992–5 conflict. His party was an offshoot of the Serbian deputy prim minister Vojislav Seselj's Radical Party of Serbia. During the election campaign Poplasen declared that he would use all constitutional means to unite the Republika Srpska with Serbia. Most voters chose Poplasen on the grounds that other candidates would permit the return of Muslims and Croats who were ethnically cleansed in the war *(The Guardian*, 26 September 1998, p. 19).

7.6 All-Bosnian house of representatives election, 12–13 September 1998

Party	Seats
SDA-Led 'Coalition for a Single and Democratic BiH' (KCD)	17
HDZ (Croat Democratic Community)	6
SDS (Serbian Democratic Party)	4
Serbian Radical Party (SRS)	2
Radical Party-Republika Srpska	1
SLOGA	4
Social Democratic Party (SDP)	4
Social Democrats of BiH	2
Democratic People's Union (DNZ)	1
New Croatian Initiative (NHI)	1

Source: Freedom House (2001: 114).

7.7 FBiH house of peoples election, 12–13 September 1998

Party	Seats
SDA-led 'Coalition for a Single and Democratic Bosnia and Herzegovina'	68
Social Democratic Party	19
Social Democrats of BiH	6
New Croatian Initiative (NHI)	4
Democratic People's Union (DNZ)	3
HDZ (Croatian Democratic Community)	28
Croat Party of Rights (HSP)	2
Socialist Party-Republika Srpska (pro-Milosevic)	2
Bosnia-Herzegovinan Patriotic Party	2
Democratic Party of Pensioners	2
Bosniak Party of Rights	1
Coalition of the Centre	1
Croat Peasants' Party	1
Bosnian Party (BOSS)	1

Source: Freedom House (2001: 114).

However, the more moderate Zivko Radisic (SP-RS) was elected to the post of Serb member of Bosnia's three-member presidency, beating the hardline SDS incumbent Momcilo Krajisnik. Moderates also largely held their ground in the national assembly election (see Table 7.8).

The aftermath of the September 1998 elections in the FBiH and in Bosnia as a whole

Bosnia and Croatia signed an accord on 23 November 1998, which gave Bosnia the right to use the Adriatic port of Ploce in return for granting Croatia free transit through Neum, a short section of the Adriatic coast (*FT*, 24 November 1998, p. 2).

A meeting of the Bosnian Peace Implementation Council held in Madrid on 15–16 December 1998 gave increased powers to the high representative, empowering him to block aid allocations or to bar parties and political leaders from running for election if they failed to cooperate. At the same time, a programme of economic, legal and political reforms was approved which aimed to reduce Bosnia's reliance on outside support (*FT*, 17 December 1998, p. 3).

7.8 Republika Srpska national assembly election, 12–13 September 1998

Party	Seats
SDS (Serbian Democratic Party)	19
SRS (Serbian Radical Party)	11
Socialist Party-Republika Srpska (SP-RS)	10
Radical Party-Republika Srpska (RS-RS)	3
SDA-Led 'Coalition for a Single and Democratic BiH' (KCD)	15
SNS (Serbian People's Union) (Biljana Plavsic's party)	12
Independent Social Democrats (SNSD)	6
Serbian Coalition for the RS	2
Social Democratic Party (SDP)	2
HDZ (Croatian Democratic Community)	1
New Croatian Initiative (NHI)	1
Coalition for King and Country	1

Source: Freedom House (2001: 115).

On 26 March 1999, in protest at the start of NATO bombing of Serbia on 24 March 1999, the Russian contingent in SFOR opted out of US command and established a command headquarters of its own (*EEN*, 1999, vol. 12, no. 16, p. 9). It was announced on 2 November 1999 that SFOR forces would be cut by one-third to 20,000 by April 2000 (*The Economist*, 19 August 2000, p. 35).

Wolfgang Petritsch, Westendorp's successor as high representative for Bosnia, dismissed twenty-two local politicians (nine Serbs, seven Bosniaks and six Croats) on 29 November 1999, mainly for obstructing the return of minority-group refugees (*FT*, Survey, 24 December 1999, p. 35).

Haris Silajdzic, the Bosniak co-premier of Bosnia and Herzegovina, called on 23 January 2000 for the Dayton agreement to be revised on the grounds that it was not being implemented. He stepped down from the co-premiership on 11 February (*EEN*, 2000, vol. 12, no. 22, p. 4).

It was announced on 8 March 2000 that Brcko would become a neutral multi-ethnic district with a multi-ethnic administration appointed by its 'international supervisor' (*IHT*, 9 March 2000, p. 5).

Aftermath of the November 1998 elections in the Republika Srpska

Despite winning the presidency, Poplasen's party won only eleven of the eighty-three seats in the assembly. Even in alliance with the SDS and other hardline Serb nationalists, it could muster only thirty-three seats, well short of a majority (see Table 7.8). Furthermore, the high representative Carlos Westendorp dismissed the vice-president from Karadzic's party for making bellicose statements about the possible repercussions in Bosnia of NATO's war against Serbia in Kosova.

Poplasen's room for manoeuvre was thus very limited. Since the nationalist coalition was well short of a majority in the assembly, the search for a new prime minister was a tense and protracted process which could well have led to fresh elections. In the meantime Milorad Dodik remained in office as caretaker prime minister with th tacit support of the Bosniak deputies who held the balance of power in the assembly.

On 14 November Poplasen invited Dragan Kalinic, a fellow hardliner who was close to Karadzic, to head a government, but only one member of parliament switched allegiance. The OHR and the Western powers wanted Milorad Dodik, whose party had increased its representation from two to six seats in the election, to remain prime minister of the Republika Srpska. They made clear that, if he did, the Republika Srpska would continue to receive Western economic assistance (it had already brought in some 240 million US dollars worth of aid since July 1997). Moreover, if the pressure worked and Dodik remained prime minister, the OHR and the Western powers would endeavour to ensure that he delivered on his promises – for example, he had said that he would let 70,000 Croat and Bosniak refugees back into the Republika Srpska during 1998, but so far only 2,000 had made it (*The Economist*, 21 November 1998, p. 46).

In an attempt to break the political deadlock after a hardline nationalist nominee for the premiership failed to win parliamentary approval, President Poplasen nominated Brane Miljus, a member of the Party of Independent Social Democrats led by Milorad Dodik (the incumbent prime minister), as Republika Srpska prime minister designate on 31 December 1998. However, Miljus was voted down by the Republika Srpska assembly on 25 January 1999.

Carlos Westendorp dismissed Nikola Poplasen as president of the Republika Srpska on 5 March 1999, justifying his action as follows:

> The destiny of the Bosnian Serbs is no longer controlled by Belgrade. Nor would the great majority of the Serbs who live in Republika Srpska wish it to be . . . President Poplasen had been warned . . . But from the moment of his election . . . he persistently abused his position to obstruct implementation of the Dayton peace agreement. Most serious was his refusal to nominate a viable candidate for prime minister . . . It has been evident for many months that only one member of the National Assembly can command a workable majority, and that is Milorad Dodik, the prime minister of the last administration, who has been acting as caretaker. His government has shown a willingness to comply with the demands of the peace process. Mr Poplasen, a hardliner of the old school, responded by refusing to sign legislation legally passed by a majority vote of the National Assembly. The f nal straw came when he sought to remove Mr Dodik . . . The decision [to remove him] has been further justified by his subsequent call for violent civil disobedience.
>
> (*IHT*, 15 March 1999, p. 10)

Dodik resumed his prime-ministerial duties once Serb anger cooled.

The Bosnia-wide local elections held on 8 April 2000

The turn-out was about 70 per cent. The results pointed to reduced support for the nationalist parties, especially in mainly Bosniak areas hitherto dominated by Izetbegovic's SDA, and confirmed a trend towards political moderation. The multi ethnic Social Democrats, who had hitherto controlled only the northern town of Tuzla, won control of most of the major Bosniak-dominated towns and cities, including Sarajevo. Nevertheless, nationalist parties continued to enjoy broad support in most of the mainly Serb-inhabited and Croat-inhabited areas (*HT*, 10 April 2000, p. 4;*IHT*, 11 April 2000, p. 4). Although the SDS remained the largest single party in the Republika Srpska, it was clear that its position had been eroded. Alija Izetbegovic announced on 6 June 2000 that he would step down from the three-member Bosnian presidency when his term of office expired in mid-October 2000. He was replaced b the Bosniak Zivko Radisic on 14 October 2000, but remained influential behind th scenes right up to his death in 2002.

Elections of 11 November 2000 to the all-Bosnia parliament, to the parliament and cantons of the FBiH, and to the assembly, presidency and vice-presidency of the Repubika Srpska

The elections were administered by the OSCE. As usual, voting generally divided along ethnic lines, although the non-nationalist and multi-ethnic Social Democratic Party led by Zlatko Lagumdzija gained strong support among Bosniaks and among educated, middle-class and cosmopolitan urban Croats and urban Serbs within the FBiH. However, nationalist parties still gained strong support among rural and small-town Bosnian Croats and Bosnian Serbs (see Tables 7.9 and 7.10).

High Representative Wolfgang Petritsch proclaimed that these elections had brought non-nationalists to power:

> The victory of Dayton and international engagement has been a lasting peace, a slow but perceptible lessening of fear in Bosnia and Herzegovina and an increasing focus among ordinary citizens on issues that really matter: jobs, a decent education for one's kids, a state that can do business with the outside world.
>
> (*IHT*, 26 March 2001, p. 10)

7.9 All-Bosnian house of representatives election, November 2000

Party	Share of vote (%)	Seats
Within the FBiH		
Social Democratic Party (SDP)	27.3	8
Party of Democratic Action (SDA)	27.0	7
Croatian Democratic Union (HDZ)	19.3	5
Party for Bosnia and Herzegovina (SBiH)	15.6	4
Democratic People's Union of Bosnia (DNZ BiH)	2.2	1
New Croat Initiative (NHI)	2.0	1
Others	6.6	1
Within the Republika Srpska		
Serbian Democratic Party (SDS)	39.7	6
PDPr (Party of Democratic Progress)	15.2	2
Party of Independent Social Democrats (SNSD)	10.6	1
Party of Democratic Action (SDA)	7.4	1
Socialist Party-RS (SP-RS)	5.7	1
Party for Bosnia and Herzegovina (SBiH)	5.4	1
Social Democratic Party (SDP)	5.2	1
Serbian People's Party –Biljana Plavsic (SNS-BP)	4.5	1
Others	6.3	0

Source: Freedom House (2002: 112).

7.10 FBiH house of representatives election, November 2000

Party	Share of vote (%)	Seats
Social Democratic Party (SDP)	26.1	37
Party for Bosnia and Herzegovina (SBiH)	14.9	21
Party of Democratic Action (SDA)	26.8	38
Croatian Democratic Union (HDZ)	17.5	25
Others	14.7	19

Source: Freedom House (2002: 112).

In the mainly Croat-inhabited areas of the FBiH (especially Herzegovina) the nationalist HDZ led by Ante Jelavic, the Croatian representative on the three-member Bosnian presidency, organized an unauthorized referendum, parallel to the off cial elections, asking Croats whether they backed its campaign for a Croatian 'third entity' or a mini-state of 'Herceg-Bosna' for the Bosnian Croats within FBiH. The HDZ claimed to have won 70 per cent support for this among the Bosnian Croats (*IHT*, 13 November 2000, p. 5). Despite declaring the referendum illegal, the authorities allowed it to go ahead.

In the Republika Srpska the nationalist SDS led by Dragan Kalinic became the biggest party, but it lacked an overall majority (see Table 7.11). The strong showing of the SDS was helped by widespread allegations of corruption against the current Western-backed prime minister Milorad Dodik. The Bosniaks 'split their vote almost equally' between the nationalist SDA and the multi-ethnic SDP (*The Guardian*, 16 November 2000, p. 19).

7.11 Republika Srpska national assembly election, November 2000

Party	Share of vote (%)	Seats
SDS (Serbian Democratic Party)	36.1	31
SNSD (Independent Social Democrats)	13.0	11
PDPr (Party of Democratic Progress)	12.3	11
SDA (Party of Democratic Action)	7.6	6
Party for Bosnia and Herzegovina (SBiH)	5.2	4
Social Democratic Party (SDP)	5.0	4
Socialist Party-Republika Srpska (SP-RS)	4.9	4
DSP	4.1	4
DNS	3.5	3
SNS, Biljana Plavsic	2.3	2
Others	6.0	3

Source: Freedom House (2002: 113).

Mirko Sarovic was elected president of the Republika Srpska with 50 per cent of the vote. Milorad Dodik came second with 30 per cent, having been 'perceived to have used Western protection as a cover for incompetence and misrule' (*The Economist*, 18 November 2000, p. 68). The Party of Democratic Progress was led by Mladen Ivanic.

The Bosnian Croat separatist movement, February–November 2001

On 28 February 2001 Ante Jelavic, the Croat member of Bosnia's three-member presidency, announced that Croats could no longer take part in the joint Bosniak–Croat FBiH, claiming that the ways in which the FBiH, the OHR and the Republika Srpska were implementing the Dayton accords had 'cut the Croats out of the picture': 'From today the Federation is a Bosniak national entity . . . without Croats' (*IHT*, 1 March 2001, p. 11). This decision to withdraw from the FBiH was endorsed on 3 March by a 'Croatian National Congress' in Mostar, which the HDZ had launched under its own control in 2000. The congress decided to set up a Croat 'inter-cantonal council', with legislative, judicial and executive powers. Jelavic said the new structure could be dismantled if, within fifteen days, the OHR revoked the electoral change made shortly before the November 2000 elections, which had favoured multi-ethnic parties and involved some reallocation of seats held by Bosnian Croats in local government from areas where the HDZ was strong to other districts (*FT*, 6 March 2001, p. 10). The 'Croatian National Congress' called on all Croats to quit their jobs in the FBiH army, police and other public services and establish an autonomous Croat statelet or 'third entity', most probably to prepare the way for eventual secession of the Croat-inhabited areas and their subsequent 'union' with Croatia. 'Short of money and losing support among a weary electorate', the HDZ made a desperate 'bid for survival (*IHT*, 17 April 2001, pp. 1, 9).

In response, on 7 March the high representative Wolfgang Petritsch dismissed Ante Jelavic and other senior Bosnian Croat officials and barred Jelavic from holding an elected off ce. Petritsch also dismissed Ivo Andric-Luzanski (a former president of the FBiH), Marko Tokic and Zdravko Batinic from their positions as vice-presidents of the HDZ and from various elected posts. Petritsch declared that Jelavic was less concerned with the interests of Croats than with 'the well-being and position of extreme nationalists, and perhaps even criminal elements in his party' (*FT*, 8 March 2001, p. 36). Nevertheless, the Bosnian Croat autonomists and separatists vowed to defy the OHR and to continue their pursuit of self-rule (*IHT*, 9 March 2001, p. 4). The Croat autonomists/separatists set up their own military headquarters on 28 March as a mutiny spread among Croat soldiers serving in the FBiH armed forces. Croat police and soldiers were warned that anyone who joined the illegal Croat structures could lose their jobs and pension rights (*The Guardian*, 29 March 2001, p. 17).

The Croatian separatist leadership succeeded in persuading several thousand Croat soldiers 'to desert the federal army, luring them with a promise of good pay' (*The Economist*, 14 April 2001, p. 40). On 7 April SFOR troops seized arms depots which had been held by the Croats since the end of the 1992–5 Bosnian conflict and reassure the outside world that the FBiH weapons stores remained 'safe and secure*The Times*, 7 April 2001, p. 18). The Croatian separatists pressed ahead, despite condemnation from the Croatian government in Zagreb, which was still footing the bills for the Croat components of Bosnia's armed forces. Intelligence sources in Zagreb estimated that 'half that money ended up in private hands' (*The Guardian*, 9 April 2001, p. 12).

SFOR troops and Bosnian police seized the Mostar headquarters and ten other branches of the Hercegovacka Banka on 6 April 2001, because it was being used by the Croat autonomists/separatists to bankroll their campaign to establish a separate Croatian 'entity'. The bank had been entrusted with the task of collecting taxes and customs duties on the government's behalf in the FBiH, but it had begun to withhold funds from the government (*The Economist*, 14 April 2001, p. 40). These police actions precipitated major riots in Mostar, where Croat mobs stoned SFOR troops, attacked employees of international organizations, stormed the banks and seized money and documents (*IHT*, 7 April 2001, p. 2), and in Grude, south-west of Mostar, where the rioters took eleven officials (auditors and their escorts) as hostages for more tha twelve hours and threatened to kill them. The hostages were not given up until the seized bank documents were returned (*The Guardian*, 9 April 2001, p. 12; *IHT*, 28 June 2001, p. 2).

Bosnia's HDZ and its Croatian congress had lost financial support after Croatia' HDZ lost the parliamentary elections in Croatia in January 2000. It also lost electoral support in the November 2000 parliamentary elections in Bosnia, whereupon the Bosnian HDZ prevented moderate Bosnian Croats from entering the FBiH government for three months after the elections, until the high representative Wolfgang Petritsch overruled their stalling tactics (*The Economist*, 14 April 2001, p. 40). Headquartered in Mostar, the Hercegovacka Banka had come to be controlled by a group of ethnic Croats known as the 'young generals'. These were men who had become rich during the 1992–5 Bosnian war by selling arms and food 'and were rewarded with appoint - ments to military rank, mostly without formal training'. Some were also senior offials of the Bosnian HDZ. Western investigators and the Bosniak police claimed that Bosnian HDZ officials, supporters and appointees were 'deeply involved in the region's lucrativ illegal trade in oil, contraband cigarettes and liquor, and stolen cars'. Large profits fro this illegal trade (as well as local tax revenues and the 'pensions' paid by the government of Croatia to Bosnian Croat war veterans) were being laundered by the Hercegovacka Banka. 'The 6 April confrontation underscored the new reality of peacekeeping in the Balkans: increasingly powerful alliances between ethnic nationalist politicians and organized criminals.' This resulted in violent confrontations between Croats and NATO soldiers and Western personnel in four Bosnian cities, in which twenty-nine Western and Bosnian participants were injured, 'several seriously' (*IHT*, 28 June 2001, p. 2).

Croatian war veterans blockaded the base of Divulje near Split (used by SFOR forces in Bosnia-Herzegovina) on 9 April 2001, in protest at 'international attempts to prevent self-rule by the Croatian community in Bosnia' and in support of Bosnian Croat demands for a separate state. They threatened to do the same at the port of Ploce and at other ports and bases used by SFOR to support its peacekeeping operation (*IHT*, 9 April 2001, p. 7).

On 15 April the FBiH defence minister Mijo Anic, a moderate Croat, claimed success in stemming Croat desertions from the federation's armed forces, 'reporting that around three-quarters of the soldiers in central and north-eastern Bosnia had gone back to barracks. In the hardline nationalist region of Herzegovina it was less than half.' SFOR announced that it had started prudentially removing heavy weapons from several Croat-controlled barracks and weapons depots (*The Guardian*, 16 April 2001, p. 13).

The authorities conducting investigations into the Bosnian Croat riots on 6–7 April brought charges against two Bosnian Croat police chiefs suspected of egging on the rioters, including the police chief of Mostar, Dragan Mandic (*IHT*, 17 April 2001, pp. 1, 9). A second SFOR-backed raid on the Hercegovacka Banka on 18 April resulted in new administrators being installed at the bank to prevent it from continuing to fund Croat self-rule institutions. Bosnian Croat deserters 'were then presented with an ultimatum to sign new contracts . . . Knowing that the Croat self-government could not pay them, most signed' (*FT*, Survey, 20 December 2001, p. 17).

During its ten-month boycott of the FBiH parliament, the HDZ 'tried every imaginable option to demand greater rights for its people'. In the end, faced with the indifference or even hostility of many ordinary Croats and with having nearly all its funding cut off by the determined actions of the international organizations and by Croatia's new government, the Bosnian HDZ reoccupied its seats in the FBiH parliament on 28 November 2001 (*FT*, Survey, 20 December 2001, p. 17). This crisis gave Bosnia's new Alliance for Change governments at the central and FBiH levels a very difficult and tense time through most of 2001. Built around Bosnia's Socia Democratic Party and Haris Silajdzic's Party for Bosnia and Herzegovina (SBiH), the Alliance for Change excluded Bosnia's major nationalist parties from government for the first time since the 1992–5 conflic

Republika Srpska after the November 2000 elections

The moderate Mladen Ivanic leader of the Party for Democratic Progress (PDPr), became prime minister in January 2001 in coalition with the SDS, which was the largest party in the national assembly (holding thirty-one of the eighty-three seats). The Ivanic government then embarked on 'a programme designed to reform the economy, attract investment and increase transparency' (*FT*, Survey, 20 December 2001, p. 17). Nevertheless, in deference to the nationalist sensibilities of his SDS coalition partners, Ivanic also tried to cultivate closer ties with Serbia and Montenegro. Thus the FRY president Kostunica was invited to Banja Luka, where he signed a full bilateral political and economic cooperation agreement on 5 March 2001. Serbia was still providing substantial funding for the Republika Srpska armed forces. Almost 4,000 off cers held dual rank in the FRY and Republika Srpska armies, and Serbia trained them and paid their salaries and pensions (*IHT*, 27 June 2001, p. 8).

There was major Bosnian Serb violence against Bosniaks in the town of Trebinje starting on 5 May 2001, during a ceremony to mark the start of the rebuilding of the Osman Pasa mosque, which had been destroyed by Bosnian Serbs during the 1992–5 conf ict. Angry Bosnian Serbs beat up dozens of Muslims and forced Western off cials to take refuge in the Islamic centre. Among the hundreds of people trapped there for hours were the American deputy high representative Jacques Klein as well as the British, Swedish and Pakistani ambassadors to Bosnia, who had come for the ceremony (*IHT*, 8 May 2001, p. 5). There was further violence by Serb extremists on 7 May, this time in Banja Luka, aimed at preventing the start of the rebuilding of the sixteenth-century Ferhadja mosque, the f nest of more than twenty mosques which had been destroyed there by Bosnian Serbs on 7 May 1993. On 18 June Bosnian Serb police clashed with hundreds of Bosnian Serb nationalist rioters attempting to disrupt another ceremony to mark the start of the rebuilding of a medieval mosque (*IHT*, 19 June 2001, p. 5).

There were international protests when, on 24 July 2001, the Republika Srpska police sent a bill of 176,000 pounds to the organizers of a ceremony commemorating the Bosniaks who had been massacred in Srebrenica in July 1995, arguing that the organizers should foot the bill for providing security (*The Guardian*, 25 July 2001, p. 15).

All-Bosnia affairs, March 2001–

On 12 March 2001, after four months of stalemate, the FBiH parliament voted in a new 'Alliance for Change' government headed by Alija Behman. However, Bozidar Matic resigned as premier of Bosnia's central government on 22 June, after the all-Bosnia parliament failed to adopt a new election law which the Council of Europe had demanded as one of the main conditions for admitting Bosnia and Herzegovina, in order to dispense with the need for OSCE and OHR monitoring of elections. The law in question was intended to lay down the principles governing elections at all levels. Nevertheless, such a law was later passed and on 22 January 2002 the Council of Europe's parliamentary assembly approved Bosnia's membership application.

The governments of Bosnia, Croatia and the FRY reached agreement on 27 June 2001 on measures to resettle the remaining 1.2 million refugees and displaced persons in their respective countries, for example, by providing returnees with house purchase and reconstruction loans on more favourable terms (*FT*, 28 June 2001, p. 8).

The al-Qaeda attacks on the World Trade Center and the Pentagon on 11 September 2001 (9/11) had significant political and military repercussions in Bosnia and Herzegovina. On 17 October 2001, the US and British embassies in Sarajevo, Mostar and Banja Luka and a British Council office in Sarajevo were shut down after receivin threats (*IHT*, 18 October 2001, p. 7). Among the dozens of Muslim 'suspects' detained and questioned by the Bosnian police and SFOR were six men of Algerian origin, who were subsequently accused of plotting to blow up the US embassy and planning other attacks on Americans in Bosnia. On 25 October SFOR announced that it had intercepted and cut off links from Bosnia to the al-Qaeda network (*IHT*, 25 October 2001, p. 4). However, the high representative, Wolfgang Petritsch, declared in the *International Herald Tribune*:

> Much has been made of the residual infuence of the Mujahidin fghters who stayed [in Bosnia] after the 1992–5 war. But no evidence has been produced that the country has served as a base for al-Qaeda. Allegations made by some Serbian extremists that the wars in the former Yugoslvia were fought to fend off Muslim fundamentalism are ridiculous. What is truly worthy of note is that the infuence of fundamentalist Islam in the Balkans has been so weak.
>
> (*IHT*, 28 November 2001, p. 7)

The US defence secretary Donald Rumsfeld proposed on 18 December 2001 that NATO's forces in Bosnia should be cut by one-third in 2002, arguing that this peacekeeping role was straining the USA and other NATO countries which had embarked on a 'war against terrorism'. NATO also announced a separate British proposal to create a unified command in the Balkans in order to facilitate further NATO-force reductions there. Rumsfeld nevertheless reaffirmed that there would b no unilateral US withdrawal from the Balkans (*IHT*, 19 December 2001, pp. 1, 8).

In December 2001, the UN decided to quash an investigation into whether offers from the UN international police task force had been involved in trafficking wome from Eastern Europe to Bosnian brothels, following disclosures that several police officers employed by the UN in Bosnia had been 'dismissed for sexual misconduct' (*IHT*, 28 December 2001, p. 5).

Bosnia officially announced on 4 January 2002 that it wanted to open negotiation for an SAA with the EU during 2002 (*FT*, 15 January 2002, p. 6), but it was still negotiating at the time of writing (2006).

In an operation coordinated with the Bosnian government, on 18 January 2002 US troops took custody of the six Algerian 'suspected terrorists' mentioned above (fiv of whom had acquired Bosnian citizenship) after a Bosnian court ordered their release from the Bosnian prison in which they were being held, on the grounds that there was insufficient evidence against them. The US military had claimed that the six Algerians were part of an Islamic group linked to the al-Qaeda network and had decided to fl them to the US military base at Guantanamo Bay (Cuba). However, to protect intelligence sources, the US was 'unwilling to disclose evidence that could be used against them in a trial'. As a result, the Bosnian court ruled that 'there was insufficient evidenc to continue holding the men'. The six released Algerians were then rearrested by the US military, who feared that a conventional extradition would have given the six men time to flee. Since 9/11, at least twenty people had been detained in Bosnia o terror-related suspicions. Several, including Egyptians and Jordanians, had been expelled to their home countries (*IHT*, 19 January 2002, p. 5). 'The five suspects wit Bosnian passports were stripped of their citizenship before they were turned over' (*IHT*, 24 January 2002, p. 6). Bosnia's political and judicial authorities, any of whom could at any time be dismissed (without right of appeal) by the high representative, were quite obviously too vulnerable to be able to stand up to American high-handedness. This was one of the many downsides of living under a NATO military protectorate. The USA may have had good grounds for its suspicions, but these were not disclosed. The OHR was struggling to promote the rule of law and respect for law in Bosnia, while at the same time the USA was making a mockery of due legal process.

EU foreign ministers agreed in principle on 28 January 2002 to take over the international police operations in Bosnia. A 500-member police force drawn from all EU member states would replace the UN-led international police task force, whose mandate expired at the end of 2002 (*FT*, 29 January 2002, p. 6).

Bosnia launched its first common identity card on 20 May 2002, and the next da it was agreed that Bosnia's armed forces would form a joint peacekeeping unit for UN missions overseas, including twenty personnel from each of the three 'entities'.

Paddy Ashdown, the widely respected former leader of the UK Liberal Democratic Party, succeeded the Austrian diplomat Wolfgang Petritsch on 27 May 2002 as high representative for Bosnia and Herzegovina. Lord Ashdown would also formally represent the EU in Bosnia, as well as be answerable to the Peace Implementation Council in which all the countries involved in the international protectorate over Bosnia were represented. Ashdown declared that his chief priority would be to promote the rule of law:

> It may well be that the grip of nationalism in Bosnia and Herzegovina is, slowly – too slowly – weakening. But the grip of criminality and corruption is strength ening . . . We must cut out the cancer at the heart of Bosnian society – organized crime . . . There must be nobody above the law and no place beyond the law in Bosnia and Herzegovina . . . Bosnian justice works too often for the powerful and the politically connected, not for ordinary people.
>
> (*IHT*, 28 May 2002, p. 12; *Independent*, 28 May 2002, p. 10)

The Western media assessments of Wolfgang Petritsch's performance as high representative were generally favourable. He had cajoled the Western-backed coalitions that won the elections in 2000 both in the FBiH and in the Republika Srpska into passing reforms and constitutional changes designed to guarantee equal rights – and equal public-sector job opportunities – for all three ethnic groups (*IHT*, 31 May 2002, p. 7).

The USA vetoed a UN Security Council resolution extending the UN peacekeeping mission in Bosnia on 30 June 2002, after the American demand that US peacekeepers had to be placed outside the jurisdiction of the International Criminal Court (ICC) was rejected. The ICC was due to come into operation on 1 July 2002. The USA gave the UN until midnight 3 July to find a political solution to the crisis. NATO insiste that the mandate for its peacekeeping mission in Bosnia came from the 1995 Dayton accords, rather than from the UN. However, it nevertheless recognized that loss of UN backing could affect the willingness of some countries to participate in the international protectorate over Bosnia. The German government warned that the 1,700 German soldiers would have to be withdrawn if the mandate expired (*IHT*, 2 July 2002, pp. 1, 10), and the Irish took a similar line. In reality, two distinct groups of foreign forces were involved in the protectorate over Bosnia: (i) the police force of 3,300 members, who were directly under UN control, which could potentially have ceased to exist without an extension of the UN mandate; (ii) the 19,000-member NATO-led force in Bosnia, which did not rest on UN authorization or funding. On 30 September 2002 a deeply divided EU agreed to allow its member states to strike their own bilateral deals with the USA granting US soldiers and officials immunity from the ICC, but in all cases with clauses providing explicit assurances that any American soldier or government official accused of a war crime or a crime against humanity would def nitely be brought to trial in the USA. This exemption was to be offered only to American soldiers or officials serving abroad (i.e., not to all US citizens living abroad) and there was to be no reciprocity, in order to deny EU nationals facing prosecution by the ICC the possibility of seeking sanctuary in the USA. By then twelve countries (including Israel, Romania, East Timor and Tadjikistan) had already signed bilateral deals to this effect with the USA (*The Economist*, 2 October 2002, p. 46). The Bush administration then set about 'trying to line up countries one by one to pledge not to extradite Americans' to the ICC (*IHT*, 8 August 2002, p. 1). It made muscular use of a provision in its new anti-terrorism law, warning other countries that they could forfeit all US military assistance if they signed up to the ICC without pledging to protect Americans serving in their countries from its reach. On 12 July a compromise UN resolution

> drew on an existing article in the 1998 Rome Statute under which the International Criminal Court was created, declaring that, for one year, the court would not open proceedings against any UN peacekeeping personnel from countries that did not accept the court. The country would have to renew the request after that for it to be continued.

This compromise cleared the way for the UN Security Council to renew the mandate of the UN peacekeeping mission in Bosnia (*IHT*, 15 July 2002, p. 6).

The presidents of Bosnia, Croatia and the FRY held a summit meeting in Sarajevo on 15 July 2002. They pledged to rebuild peace, trust and trade and promised to respect each other's borders, to cooperate in their fight against crime and to help refugee return to their old homes. However, President Vojislav Kostunica of Yugoslavia refused either to apologize for Serb atrocities during the 1991–5 Yugoslav conflict or to call on Radovan Karadzic to surrender to the ICTY in The Hague (*IHT*, 16 July

2002, p. 5). In August, Carla del Ponte, the chief prosecuting judge at the ICTY, accused SFOR of 'not having made a "real effort" to arrest Radovan Karadzic' (*HT*, 24 August 2002, p. 3).

On 6 August 2002 a British tribunal ruled that Kathryn Bolkovac, an American former member of the UN police in Bosnia, had been dismissed unfairly after she had reported to her superiors that UN officials, international aid workers and colleague were directly involved in the use of women and children as sex slaves in Bosnia, in collusion with Balkan sex traffickers *IHT*, 8 August 2002, p. 3). She had disclosed that 'UN peacekeepers went to nightclubs where girls as young as fifteen were forced to dance naked and to have sex with customers and that UN personnel and international aid workers were linked to prostitution rings in the Balkans'*The Times*, 7 August 2002, p. 13).

An off cial report on the 1995 Srebrenica massacre, commissioned by the Republika Srpska and published on 3 September 2002, provoked Bosniak outrage and an international furore by flatly denying that such a 'massacre' had ever taken place, by suggesting that Bosniaks had imagined or fabricated the massacre, and by claiming that 'only' 1,500 people had been killed – mostly in combat (*The Guardian*, 4 September 2002, p. 14).

Bosniaks were further enraged on 2 October 2002, when Biljana Plavsic, who had been indicted for crimes that included wilful ethnic cleansing and genocide, pleaded guilty to just one of the eight charges laid against her and – in return for pleading guilty (she was the first indictee to do so) – secured the official dropping of the other sev charges (*FT*, 3 October 2002, p. 9). Dr Plavsic had initially pleaded innocent, but, following a highly controversial round of plea bargaining, changed her mind and pleaded that she was guilty, but (only) of 'persecutions on political or religious grounds'. This was still categorized as a 'crime against humanity', but it was one of the lesser charges against her. She also expressed her 'full and unconditional remorse' (*The Guardian*, 3 October 2002, p. 14). Dr Plavsic was transferred to Sweden in June 2003 to serve a relatively comfortable 11-year prison sentence.

The Bosnia-wide parliamentary and presidential elections of 5 October 2002

These elections were the first to be held for full four-year parliamentary terms (instea of just two years, as hitherto), and were the f rst since 1996 not to be held under the auspices of the OSCE. Nevertheless, more than 400 international observers watched the elections, and they subsequently declared that they 'met international standards' (*IHT*, 7 October 2002, p. 3). The electoral turn-out was only 55 per cent, the lowest level since the Dayton accords. This was attributed partly to the fact that these elections were the sixth in seven years. However, Bosnians were suffering not only from 'election fatigue', but from a growing realization that participation in elections actually had little impact on political outcomes – including the policies pursued in the wake of those elections, partly because of the inbuilt 'immobilism' of consociational power-sharing systems of government, and partly because of the overarching and increasingly interventionist tutelage exercised by the high representative, who had the power to act as the Western 'pro-consul' in Bosnia.

There were dramatic reductions in support for the reformist and non-sectarian Social Democratic Party (under Zlatko Lagumdzija) which had led the Alliance for Change coalition, and significant increases in support for some of the nationalist parties (the SDA and the SRS), although in the parliamentary elections Bosnian Croat voters punished the HZD for its abortive separatist shenanigans. Overall, 'Nationalist parties ... capitalized on the loyalty of their hardline supporters, while many moderate voters stayed at home' (*FT*, 7 October 2002, p. 8). Support for nationalist parties increased sufficiently at the all-Bosnia level and in the FBiH parliament to put nationalists back in overall charge, while in the Republika Srpska reductions in support for the Serbian nationalist SDS and Socialist Party-Republika Srpska (SP-RS) were offset by increased support for the ultra-nationalist Serbian Radical Party. Greatly increased support for Milorad Dodik's moderate Party of Independent Social Democrats was partly offset by reduced support for the Republika Srpska prime minister Mladen Ivanic's moderate PDPr. Most of the smaller parties in the Alliance for Change coalition failed to win re-election at all, partly due to the 3 per cent thresholds employed in Bosnia's proportional representation systems (see Table 7.12).

The voting patterns in the elections to the parliaments of the FBiH and the Republika Srpska broadly reflected those indicated above for the central house of representatives. In both 'entities' the party composition of parliaments remained quite fragmented, with numerous smallish parties gaining representation despite the 3 per cent threshold. This was not merely a reflection of Bosnia and Herzegovina's high degree of ethnic fragmentation. What was equally striking was the existence of several rival nationalist or quasi-nationalist parties competing for the support of each of the competing ethnic groups. While this situation strengthened the relative bargaining positions of minorities and impeded the (re-)emergence of one-party authoritarianism, by the same token it made for relatively weak or unstable government, instead of consolidating support around two to four dominant parties which could provide stronger, more stable and more decisive government. This constellation of forces reduced the dangers

7.12 All-Bosnian house of representatives election, 5 October 2002

	Share of votes (%)	
	October 2002	November 2000
Within the FBiH		
SDA (Bosniak nationalists)	32.4	(27.0)
HDZ (Croat nationalists)	15.9	(19.3)
SBiH (Party for Bosnia and Herzegovina)	16.2	(15.6)
Social Democratic Party	15.7	(27.3)
BOSS (Bosnian Party)	2.6	(–)
SPU (Pensioners' Party)	2.5	(–)
DNZ BiH (Democratic People's Union, BiH)	2.3	(2.2)
NHI (New Croatian Initiative, moderate Bosnian Croats)	1.9	(2.0)
HDU	2.2	(–)
Within the Republika Srpska		
SDS (Serb nationalists)	33.7	(39.7)
SNSD (Dodik's Independent Social Democrats)	22.4	(10.6)
PDPr (Ivanic's Party for Democratic Progress)	10.4	(15.2)
SDA (Bosniak nationalists)	7.3	(7.4)
SRS (Serbian Radical Party) (nationalists)	4.8	(–)
SP-RS (Socialist Party RS) (Serbian nationalists)	4.3	(5.7)
Party for Bosnia and Herzegovina	3.9	(5.4)

Source: Freedom House (2003: 153).

of a 'tyranny of the majority', but it was also very unpropitious for vigorous enact-ment and implementation of much-needed radical reforms and restructuring, unless there emerged unwonted levels of cross-party cooperation to achieve such changes. The outcome thus put a high premium on cross-party cooperation to overcome the potential dysfunctional effects of political/ethnic fragmentation.

Nationalist candidates won the first-past-the-post elections to Bosnia's three-member presidency: Sulejman Tihic (of the SDA) won 37.3 per cent of the Bosniak votes, just narrowly beating Haris Silajdzic (34.8 per cent), who championed a cosmopolitan multi-ethnic Bosnia; Mirko Sarovic (of the SDS) obtained 35.5 per cent of Bosnian Serb votes; and Dragan Covic (of the HDZ) won 61.5 per cent of the Bosnian Croat votes. The presidency of the Republika Srspska was won by the SDS candidate, Dragan Cavic (not to be confused with Dragan Covic), with only 35.9 per cent of the votes cast. But constitutional changes imposed by the OHR obliged the Republika Srpska president henceforth to 'cohabit' with two non-Serb vice-presidents: one Croat, in this instance Ivan Tomljenovic (Social Democrat), and one Bosniak, in this instance Adil Osmanovic of the SDA (Freedom House 2003: 152, 154).

At the presidency level, therefore, Bosnia's governance again became dependent on the degree of willingness of the elected leaders of the three main ethnic communities to cooperate constructively with one another. Fortunately, the three newly elected mem-bers of this presidency professed to be amenable to economic reform, economic integration and eventual Bosnian membership in the EU, and they quickly demonstrated an 'increased willingness by Bosnia's nationalists to identify points of common interests and to accept positive policy changes' (*FT*, Survey, 12 November 2002, p. 31).

The aftermath of the October 2002 elections

The central government of Bosnia and Herzegovina imposed an indefinite ban on all exports of arms and military equipment on 29 October 2002, after it came to light that the Republika Srpska had been violating the UN arms embargo against Iraq. The move followed the resignation of the Republika Srpska's Bosnian Serb defence minister and its army chief of staff (*IHT*, 30 October 2002, p. 5).

The EU announced on 16 December 2002 that it would be ready to take over the SFOR mission in Bosnia by mid-2004 (*FT*, 17 December 2002, p. 6). On 1 January 2003 the European Union Police Mission (EUPM) took over the role of the UN International Police Task Force (UNIPTF) set up in 1995 to oversee law enforcement in post-Dayton Bosnia, as well as the training of Bosnia and Herzegovina's 20,000-member police forces. The 900 (unarmed) EUPM personnel would wear berets and armbands with the EU's insignia (twelve gold stars on a blue background), as well as their own national uniforms.

On 13 January 2003 the Bosnian central parliament approved a new coalition government dominated by Bosniak, Bosnian Serb and Bosnian Croat nationalist parties working in tandem. The new prime minister, Adnan Terzic of the Bosniak SDA, announced that his government would accelerate economic change, uphold the rule of law and seek closer ties with the EU (*IHT*, 14 January 2003, p. 3). The unexpectedly high degree of cooperation between the nationalist SDA, SDS and HDZ largely confounded critics who had previously supposed that these parties could never work together effectively. They unified the command structure of the country's once riva Bosniak–Croat and Bosnian Serb armies and intelligence services and took steps to curb corruption and black-marketeering by introducing a Bosnia-wide VAT.

In March 2003 the human-rights chamber of Bosnia and Herzegovina, a panel of Bosnian and international judges, ordered the Republika Srpska to pay more than 2 million US dollars in compensation for the massacre of over 7,000 Bosniaks at Srebrenica in 1995. It was anticipated that a Srebrenica memorial would absorb most of the compensation money, half of which was to be paid immediately, 'with the rest spread over the next four years'. The DNA identification programme set up by the International Commission of Missing Persons, which was badly in need of money, was unlikely to get any. The project had identified more than 1,500 of th 30,000 people still unaccounted for. The judges also ordered the Republika Srpska government to provide more information about the location of mass graves (*IHT*, 8 March 2003, p. 2).

SFOR handed over Naser Oric, a Bosniak, to the ICTY in April 2003. He had led the Bosniak defence of Srebrenica before it fell in 1995. The ICTY had indicted him for the 'murder and cruel treatment' of Serb prisoners, as well as burning and plundering about f fty Bosnian Serb villages between 1992 and 1995 (*FT*, 12 April 2003, p. 12). This indictment implied that not even the infamous Srebrenica mass-acre was a completely cut-and-dried 'evil versus good' crime. It had been preceded by smaller crimes against humanity perpetrated by Bosniaks against Bosnian Serbs in the Srebrenica area. On 15 April Oric was charged with 'six counts of violations of the law and customs of war, including murder, cruel treatment, wanton destruction and plunder in eastern Bosnia'. Bosnian Serbs accused him of 'killing about 2,000 Serbs from villages around Srebrenica', including responsibility for 'the so-called "Bloody Christmas" massacre in January 1993, when dozens of women and children died in the village of Kravice' (*IHT*, 16 April 2003, p. 6).

Russia announced in April 2003 that it would withdraw its 320 peacekeeping troops from Bosnia and 650 from Kosova, due to financial concerns and a lack of a war threat in the Balkans (*IHT*, 16 April 2003, p. 6).

The US deputy defence secretary Paul Wolfowitz declared on 22 May 2003 that 'September 11 has clearly changed the stakes for the United States in dealing with security issues in those areas that could be sanctuaries for terrorists' and that Bosnia was not 'just any failed state around the world, but one with a Moslem population in the heart of Europe' (*HT*, 23 May 2003, p. 3), thus confirming the belief in US defenc circles that Bosnia was a potential haven for Islamist terrorists.

In early June 2003 Bosnia signed a bilateral deal exempting US soldiers and official in Bosnia from the jurisdiction of the ICC (*The Guardian*, 12 June 2003, p. 13). In March 2004 it was announced that in September an ethnically mixed team of thirty-six Bosnian mine clearers would join the US-led military occupation forces in Iraq for one year. These were partly symbolic gestures of subservience to the USA, intended to gain favour.

The OHR froze the bank accounts of Radovan Karadzic's wife, their two children, his brother and ten other people on 7 July, because they had allegedly been helping him to evade arrest (*IHT*, 8 July 2003, p. 7).

Thousands of Bosniaks gathered at the newly built memorial centre at the site of the July 1995 Srebrenica massacre on 11 July 2003, 'to commemorate the eighth anniversary of Europe's worst atrocity since World War II and lay to rest 282 of its victims'. This was also the first time that a Bosnian Serb delegation, led by Prim Minister Dragan Mikerevic of the Republika Srpska, attended such a ceremony. Premier Mikerevic also announced that his government had commissioned a new and more candid report on the massacre (*HT*, 12 July 2003, p. 2). In mid-2003 Bosnian

Serbs comprised 95 per cent of the population of Srebrenica. The 1991 census had recorded 27,572 Bosniaks as living there, but thus far only 1,720 had returned to the town (*Daily Telegraph*, 20 September 2003, p. 22). In September 2003, at an even bigger memorial service for the victims of the 1995 Srebrenica massacre attended by 20,000 people (including ex-president Bill Clinton), the leaders of the Bosnian Serb SDS announced that the Bosnian Serbs had finally abandoned dreams of a Greate Serbia. Likewise, the leaders of the Bosnian Croat HDZ declared that the Bosnian Croats had also abandoned their dreams of uniting Bosnia's Croat-inhabited areas with Croatia. For his part, Bosnia's Bosniak prime minister appealed for peace and reconciliation between Bosnia's three main communities. In its report on this apparent sea change in attitudes, *The Economist* emphasized that all Bosnians now held similar passports and could move freely around their country, that Serbia and Croatia no longer posed military threats to Bosnia, and that Bosnia's armies had been reduced to very small numbers, but that this progress was still very incomplete and fragile. Although opinion polls showed that fear of inter-ethnic tension and conflict had largely been superseded by more immediate and mundane worries about unemployment (not least because roughly 40 per cent of Bosnians were unemployed), new fears were emerging that the economic outlook was so dire that it could easily rekindle the seemingly doused f ames of inter-ethnic tension and conf ict in the future – the more so as the earlier torrent of foreign reconstruction aid was now drying up (*The Economist*, 27 September 2003, p. 44).

In September 2003, partly in order to improve Bosnia's chances of being accepted into NATO's 'Partnership for Peace' programme (PfP), the leaders of Bosnia's Bosniak, Serb and Croat communities surprised the world by thrashing out an agreement to integrate their respective armed forces and command structures more fully. The agreement had yet to be ratified by the parliaments of the FBiH and th Republika Srpska, but that negotiations had even got this far was a major break-through. A central Bosnian defence ministry was to be established. Each of the two 'entities' would continue to have its own army, but all soldiers would wear the same uniform, swear the same oath, serve under the same flag and operate under a single command and control structure. Bosnia's armed forces were to be cut from nearly 20,000 soldiers to just 12,000. There was also to be a 75 per cent reduction in the number of reserves, and conscription was gradually to be curtailed. The hope was that these proposed reforms would be rewarded by Bosnia's acceptance into the PfP (*The Times*, 6 October 2003, p. 14). These reforms obtained the necessary parliamentary approval in December 2003.

The death of seventy-eight-year-old Alija Izetbegovic on 19 October 2003 marked the departure of the last of the nationalist leaders who had presided over 'the Bosnian conflict' of 1992–5. It was announced at his funeral on 22 October that the ICTY would stop investigating his alleged war crimes.

On 13 November 2003 Svetozar Marovic, the Montenegrin president of the State Union of Serbia and Montenegro, formally expressed his deepest regret for 'every evil act of misfortune that anyone in Bosnia-Herzegovina was exposed to because of Serbia-Montenegro' and declared that it was the duty of South Slav politicians to foster 'an atmosphere of forgiveness' (*The Times*, 14 November 2003, p. 24).

NATO's defence ministers agreed on 1 December 2003 to reduce the SFOR forces in Bosnia and Herzegovina from 12,000 to 7,000 by March 2004, while Bosnia's leaders agreed on 3 February 2004 to reduce its armed forces from 19,800 to 12,000 soldiers (*IHT*, 4 February 2004, p. 4). Later that month the Bush administration announced that the USA had decided to withdraw its remaining 1,200 soldiers from Bosnia by the end of 2004 (*FT*, 19 February 2004, p. 15).

SFOR and OHR officials froze the assets of ten prominent Bosnian Serbs on 9 February 2004, accusing them of having run a support network for Bosnia and Herzegovina's most wanted criminals for years. These ten individuals included the former president of the Republika Srpska, Mirko Sarovic, and several senior police officials. They were also barred from travelling to the USA. Describing Radovan Karadzic's supporters as a criminal gang, SFOR and the OHR declared that his successful efforts to elude capture had been financed by 'corruption, money launderin and extortion' (*IHT*, 10 February 2004, p. 8).

Dragan Mikerevic, the prime minister of the Republika Srpska, publicly warned Bosnian Serbs on 8 April 2004 to be 'ready to accept the truth whatever it is', apropos the July 1995 Srebrenica massacre. He was referring to the imminent publication of the findings of the commission which the Republika Srpska had established in January (*IHT*, 9 April 2004, p. 4). On 16 April Paddy Ashdown dismissed General Cvjetko Savic, the Republika Srpska army chief of staff, for his failure to provide information needed by the Republika Srpska commission investigating the Srebrenica massacre. He also dismissed Dejan Miletic, the Head of Republika Srpska Secretariat for Relations with the ICTY and Research on War Crimes, for his lack of cooperation with the ICTY. On 11 June the Republika Srpska finally published the long-awaite report of a largely Bosnian Serb commission of investigation into the 1995 Srebrenica massacre. The report stated that the commission had established that 'several thousand' Bosniaks had been 'liquidated in a way which represents grave violations of international humanitarian law' in Srebrenica between 10 and 19 July 1995 and that the Bosnian Serb perpetrators had tried to cover up the worst atrocity committed in Europe since the Second World War (*HT*, 12 June 2004, p. 8). The report also provided information on thirty-two mass graves (eleven of them previously unknown and containing up to 2,000 corpses) and for the first time implicated Serbia proper in th massacre, 'noting that Serbian police units were ordered to take part' (*The Guardian*, 14 June 2004, p. 15). Paddy Ashdown had warned that he would sack the Bosnian Serb leaders 'if they failed to acknowledge the truth' that everyone else already knew (*The Economist*, 19 June 2004, p. 47).

NATO leaders formally agreed on 28 June 2004 to hand over the peacekeeping operation in Bosnia to the EU. This was to be 'the EU's most ambitious military operation to date'. However, since over 80 per cent of SFOR troops were already from EU member states, this 'changing of the guard' would involve more form than substance. SFOR would become EUFOR, employing much the same military forces as before. The 7,000-member EUFOR operation in Bosnia was to be commanded by the UK, a leading member of NATO. The EU was already running a 300-member peacekeeping operation in Macedonia (where the EU took over from NATO on 31 March 2003) and a substantial police-training mission in Bosnia (the EUPM). Both directly and through its major NATO members, EUFOR would also be able to call and rely upon back-up from NATO planning, facilities, logistical support, sur-veillance operations, intelligence and command and control systems, under the aegis of the deputy head of NATO's military planning division (*FT*, 27 April 2004, p. 8). Furthermore, despite the formal handover to the EU, NATO was to retain a small military presence of its own in Bosnia, 'to help with military reforms, fight terroris and keep up with the hunt for war crimes suspects' (*IHT*, 29 June 2004, p. 3; 5 July 2004, p. 6). Indeed, a superpower as Islamophobic as the USA was unlikely to remove itself completely from a country which (on the evidence of its own pronouncements) it regarded as a potential haven and breeding ground for Islamist terrorists.

Paddy Ashdown suspended sixty Bosnian Serb politicians and officials from thei posts and froze the bank accounts of the SDS and several leading Bosnian Serb companies on 30 June 2004, claiming that the SDS and senior members of the Republika Srpska government were colluding to ensure that Radovan Karadzic was not arrested and handed over to the ICTY. Those suspended included Dragan Kalinic (who was the leader of the SDS and also the speaker of the Republika Srpska parliament) and Zoran Djeric, the Republika Srpska's interior minister. 'Several mayors, senior police commanders and members of parliament were also suspended.' The OHR claimed that 'Bosnian Serb government officials had been shifting public funds into their ow criminal networks as well as to support Karadzic' (*IHT*, 1 July 2004, p. 3). Ashdown ordered the transfer of SDS party funds to the Bosnian state, switched half a million euros of public funding from the SDS to organizations committed to protecting human rights and tracking down war criminals and announced the setting up of a commission to review the structure of police forces in Bosnia. Thirteen names were also added to the EU visa blacklist against people alleged to be helping indicted war criminals. A special audit was also ordered into the Bosnian company Srpske Sume to find out whether it had been used 'to finance criminal or war criminal networks'. That same week a NATO summit stated that it would not allow Bosnia to join its PfP pro-gramme, due to the power and influence of 'obstructionist elements in the Republika Srpska' (*The Times*, 1 July 2004, p. 18; *The Guardian*, 1 July 2004, p. 2). Ashdown declared: 'The Republika Srpska has been in the grip of a small band of corrupt politicians and criminals for far too long . . . We have to get rid of the cancer of obstruction and corruption.' During the 1992–5 conf ict, he maintained, the SDS had become 'a network of criminality, infiltrating and corrupting almost every institutio . . . Nearly a decade after the war it is still linked to the organized crime that robs this country' (*The Times*, 1 July 2004, p. 18; *The Guardian*, 1 July 2004, p. 2).

The Republika Srpska's official panel investigating the Srebrenica massacre acknowledged on 14 October 2004 that Bosnian Serb forces had killed more than 7,000 Bosniaks in Srebrenica in 1995. It was the f rst time that the panel or any previous Republika Srpska body had given a death toll (*IHT*, 15 October 2004, p. 4;*Independent*, 15 October 2004, p. 26). On 10 November the Republika Srpska government issued a statement expressing sympathy for 'the pain of relatives of the Srebrenica victims and . . . sincere regrets and apologies over the tragedy which has happened to them', and that the Republika Srpska government was determined to 'face the truth about the tragic conflict in Bosnia-Herzegovina' and to take 'decisive steps to force all persons who committed war crimes to face justice' (*Independent*, 11 November 2004, p. 27; *The Times*, 11 November 2004, p. 49).

The leader of the 'Mothers of Srebrenica', the association formed by families of the victims of the July 1995 Srebrenica massacre, announced on 12 November 2004 that they would file a lawsuit seeking over 2.6 billion US dollars in compensation fro the Republika Srpska, Serbia and Montenegro (*IHT*, 13 November 2004, p. 5).

The EU assumed control of the peacekeeping operation in Bosnia on 2 December 2004, taking over from NATO. EUFOR, comprising about 7,000 troops drawn from twenty-two of the twenty-five EU member states and from ten non-EU countrie (such as Chile and Canada), was expected to remain for around three years. NATO was to retain about 300 soldiers in Bosnia as a backup to the EU (*IHT*, 2 December 2004, p. 2).

Paddy Ashdown dismissed six Bosnian Serb police officers and three other Bosnia Serb officials in the Republika Srpska on 16 December 2004 and froze their bank accounts, for having failed to pursue and having obstructed the arrest of people indicted for war crimes (*IHT*, 17 December 2004, p. 5). He claimed to have evidence that Ratko Mladic had not only been sheltered by old army colleagues, but had been on the Republika Srpska army payroll until recently (*The Guardian*, 17 December 2004, p. 17). In his view, the Republika Srpska's 'failure to arrest a single war crimes fugitive in nine years was a "cold, hard fact" that put the government in fundamental breach of Dayton' (*IHT*, 18 December 2004, p. 3).

Dragan Mikerevic, the notably moderate Bosnian Serb prime minister of the Republika Srpska, resigned on 17 December 2004. He had gone to great lengths to apologize for Bosnian Serb atrocities and to make his compatriots face up to the truth about the Srebrenica massacre and to the need for reconciliation. However, he resented the sanctions and dismissals imposed on the Republika Srpska and on the SDS for their failure to arrest and extradite the indictees sought by the ICTY and for his refusal to enact the police and army reforms demanded by Paddy Ashdown(*IHT*, 18 December 2004, p. 3; *FT*, 18 December 2004, p. 6). Whether it was wise of Ashdown to have driven this relatively moderate and conciliatory Bosnian Serb leader, who had been the f rst to show the degree of moral courage needed to acknowledge unreservedly the Bosnian Serbs' full responsibility for the Srebrenica massacre, to resign the premiership of the Republika Srpska at this difficult juncture, only time will tell. Th next day Mladen Ivanic, the Republika Srpska foreign minister, and Borislav Paravac, the Bosnian Serb member of Bosnia's three-member presidency, also resigned. Although all three included Ashdown's demands, dismissals and sanctions among their reasons for resigning, some observers thought that the dispute was 'more deeply rooted in the desire among Bosnian Serbs to resist the consolidation of government institutions in Bosnia' (*FT*, 20 December 2004, p. 6).

On 8 January 2005 the Republika Srpska president Dragan Cavic asked Pero Bukejlovic of the ruling SDS to form a government. Bukejlovic's programme aimed at 'resolving social issues, speeding up the privatization process and improving cooperation with the tribunal at The Hague' (*IHT*, 10 January 2005, p. 3). The Republika Srpska delivered a Bosnian Serb indicted for war crimes and crimes against humanity to The Hague for the first time on 16 January 2005, after the USA had cancelled 10 million US dollars in aid due to the lack of arrests. Savo Todovic, charged on eighteen counts of war crimes and crimes against humanity, had voluntarily surrendered to Bosnian Serb police and was then transferred to The Hague. He had been in charge of a prison camp in which up to 300 inmates had been killed during the 1992–5 war (*FT*, 17 January 2005, p. 6; *The Guardian*, 17 January 2005, p. 13).

A special court was inaugurated in Sarajevo on 9 March 2005 to take over cases from the ICTY in The Hague. Bosnia was the f rst country in the former Yugoslav lands to be entrusted with such cases. Local courts in the South Slav states had some times been allowed to try minor cases, but the indictments first had to have the approval of the ICTY. The new war-crimes court in Sarajevo was established with international help, was monitored by the ICTY, and was initially staffed by inter - national judges and prosecutors, with Bosnian judges and prosecutors only gradually taking over. The aim was to allow the ICTY to concentrate on high-profile cases(*IHT*, 10 March 2005, p. 3).

Paddy Ashdown dismissed the Bosnian Croat Dragan Covic from Bosnia's three-member presidency on 29 March 2005, 'for refusing to step down in the face of serious corruption charges'. His offences were said to have been committed between 2000 and 2003, while Covic was deputy prime minister of the FBiH (*IHT*, 30 March 2005, p. 5). Covic denied the charges against him. About 150 senior Bosnian politicians and officials had been dismissed from their jobs between 1998 and March 2005. Ashdown had been especially willing to use his powers of dismissal, sacking sixty people in June 2004 and another nine in December 2004(*Independent*, 30 March 2005, p. 22).

The Republika Srpska authorities stated on 31 March 2005 that they were investigating nearly 900 of their own government state officials in order to determin whether they had played any role in the July 1995 Srebrenica massacre. The officia Republika Srpska commission of inquiry had given Bosnia's state prosecutors the names of 892 people accused of taking part in the killings. The list had been drawn up on the insistence of Paddy Ashdown, following the increasingly candid off cial acknowledgement by the Republika Srpska between June and December 2004 that Bosnian Serbs were responsible for the killings. The Republika Srpska courts had not yet charged anyone with the killings, but human-rights groups pointed out that the large number of off cials, soldiers and politicians accused of involvement suggested that many of them might still be in power (*IHT*, 1 and 2 April 2005).

On 1 June 2005, at the continuing trial of Slobodan Milosevic by the ICTY, a videotape was shown of six Bosniaks being dragged from the back of a lorry by Serbian paramilitary policemen, tortured and then shot dead. The video was broadcast on Serbian television on 3 June. This was the first time that a visual record of part of th Srebrenica massacre had been seen by millions of South Slavs, and it provided proof that paramilitary police from Serbia proper (and not just Bosnian Serbian troops, as previously claimed) had taken part in the massacre. A survey conducted shortly before the video was broadcast indicated that under half the population of Serbia believed that the Srebrenica massacre had even taken place (*Independent*, 3 June 2005, p. 28; *The Guardian*, 3 June 2005, p. 15).

The war-crimes tribunal established in Bosnia and Herzegovina began to prosecute war-crimes cases in September 2005. In October 2005 it stated that it expected the number of its prosecutions in connection with the 1995 Srebrenica massacre to increase dramatically, after the Republika Srpska authorities gave it a list of over 19,000 Bosnian Serb soldiers, police officers and officials who had allegedly been involv in the massacre. The accompanying report stated that 17,342 soldiers participated in the capture of Srebrenica and in the subsequent killings. It also listed 55 defence ministry administrators, 209 civil protection workers and 34 drivers as having been involved (*IHT*, 6 October 2005, p. 4).

For the f rst time, on 18 November 2005, a court in the Republika Srpska capital Banja Luka found three ethnic Serb former policemen guilty of having killed six Muslims, including two women, in March 1994. The two defendants present were each sentenced to twenty-year jail terms, while the third was sentenced *in absentia* to fifteen years in prison *IHT*, 19 November 2005, p. 4).

On the tenth anniversary of the Dayton accords (21 November 2005), Western officials initiated negotiations to rewrite the agreement and accelerate the country's eventual integration into the EU and NATO. The next day, under intense US and European pressure, Bosnia's three-member presidency, as well as religious leaders and the leaders of the eight main parties representing the Bosniak, Croat and Serb communities, signed an outline agreement to press for constitutional changes to create a stronger central government by March 2006. This came hard on the heels of an announcement that the EU would open SAA negotiations with Bosnia on 25 November. In a joint statement, the Bosnian leaders also called on persons indicted by the ICTY to surrender to it, on pain of arrest. The Bosnian parties stated that the envisaged constitutional changes were 'only the first steps' and that further consti tutional amendments would be necessary if Bosnia was to be capable of meeting the EU's accession criteria (*FT*, 22 November 2005, p. 14; *IHT*, 23 November 2005, pp. 1, 8). Bosnian leaders agreed to 'streamline' the tripartite presidency and strengthen the central parliament. 'The essence of the US plan is to strengthen a central government and national parliament at the expense of the Entities', in readiness for the next round of elections in October 2006. The EU also emphasized that Bosnia needed to undertake constitutional reforms to become 'a fully functioning and viable state' if it was ultimately to achieve accession to the EU'(*he Guardian*, 23 November 2005, p. 16). In the event, however, the consensus broke down and the proposed reforms were only partly implemented.

On 14 December 2005 the seventy-fve-year-old German former minister for postal services Christian Schwarz-Schilling was designated as the next high representative in Bosnia and Herzegovina in succession to Paddy Ashdown, with effect from 1 February 2006. He became an expert on the region through working as a mediator following Bosnia's 1992–5 war and supervising the return of refugees to their former homes (*IHT*, 15 December 2005, p. 2). He vowed to use his powers to impose laws and remove obstructive officials only as a last resort. He declared

> Progress will only be irreversible when Bosnians take responsibility for the peace process. It is my task as Bosnia's last High Representative to oversee the transition from today's quasi-protectorate to local ownership .. . There are . . . limits to what can be achieved by imposition and these limits have almost certainly been reached . . . I have seen impressive changes as a result of the efforts of local people and institutions . . . But today tried-and-tested mechanisms, in particular in the form of the EU's pre-accession negotiations but also NATO's Membership Action Plan, exist to focus the minds of Bosnian leaders on required reforms . . . While clearly Bosnia has a long way to go, the goal of eventual membership in these institutions should be sufficiently powerful to help Bosnians overcome division and shape their own destiny.
>
> (*IHT*, 2 February 2006, p. 9)

Bosnian economic affairs since 1995 (post-Dayton)

Starting from very low levels in 1995, initial recovery was rapid in the FBiH, but it proceeded much more slowly in the Republika Srpska. During 1996 the GDP of the FBiH rose by 35 per cent, inf ation was low, and unemployment fell to between 50 and 60 per cent of the workforce (from a peak of 90 per cent in 1995), but the Republika Srpska had virtually zero growth, received only 2–3 per cent of Western aid for Bosnia, still suffered from high inflation and around 90 per cent unemployment, and its average wages were only about one-third of the levels in the FBiH. Bosnia's GDP (the combined GDP of the two 'entities') was about one-third of its pre-war level in 1996 and industrial output was about 10 per cent of its 1991 level (*Focus: Eastern Europe*, 3 March 1997, p. 71; *IHT*, 1 September 1997, p. 8; *Transitions*, February 1997, vol. 8, no. 1, p. 11).

GDP continued to recover in 1997, with the FBiH reporting 37 per cent economic growth. Growth continued to be driven by the electricity-generating, food-processing and construction sectors (EBRD 1998a: 33). However, industrial production was still only 15 per cent of its pre-war level and many people still relied on help from soup kitchens. Indirect (not direct) taxes were the government's main revenue sources. Much of the Republika Srpska's farmland lay idle (*IHT*, 11 December 1997, pp. 13, 17). Apart from the railways, which were nominally unified throughout the country other utilities (electricity, post and telecommunications) were still run as three separate organizations, one for Bosniaks, one for Croats and one for Bosnian Serbs, and unemployment was still around 40 per cent (*FT*, Survey, 21 October 1998, pp. iii–iv). Inflation was tamed with astonishing rapidity. In 1994 the annual rates of consumer price inflation were 780 per cent in the FBiH and 1,061 per cent the Republika Srpska but strong anti-inflation action from 1995 to 1998 eliminated inflation in the form and reduced it to only 14 per cent in the latter by 1999.

However, poverty remained rife. According to a World Bank survey published in late 2001, 19 per cent of the total population were living below 'the general poverty line' and another 30 per cent were living only just above that level (EBRD 2003b: 125). Bosnia's real GDP in 2004 was still only about 60 per cent of its 1989 level (EBRD 2005a: 13). In 2003 the off cial unemployment rate was around 42 per cent but, according to Dirk Reinermann (the World Bank's representative in Sarajevo), 'only 16 per cent of Bosnians had no work at all' (*The Economist*, 20 December 2003, p. 56). In 2004 the official unemployment rate was still around 42 per cent and, althoug many of the formally unemployed actually had jobs in the informal sector, the 'real' rate of unemployment was still high, 'probably close to 20 per cent' (EBRD 2004a: 34). In late 2005 unemployment officially stood at 43 per cent, but the World Ban still argued that, if the grey economy was factored in, the real rate of unemployment was 16 –20 per cent. Nevertheless, 18 per cent of Bosnians still lived 'below the poverty line and another 30 per cent just above it' (*The Economist*, 26 November 2005, p. 49). Bosnia's central bank estimated that the informal sector was equivalent to about 38 per cent of recorded GDP in 2003 (EBRD 2004b: 107).

Remittances from abroad played a crucial role in sustaining Bosnia's partial economic recovery. By 2003, remittances from Bosnians working abroad amounted to 2 billion convertible marks a year, exceeding Bosnia's annual receipts of foreign aid (*FT*, Survey, 23 November 2004, p. 34).

Economic policy, 1995–2005

The Bosnian government pronounced the Deutschmark an official currency (exchange able at 100 dinars each) on 9 November 1995. IMF membership was approved on 21 December 1995. The IMF backed a plan whereby the new central bank was to operate for at least six years as a currency board. This meant that currency in circulation plus commercial bank deposits with the central bank were required to be limited to what could be fully covered by holdings of foreign currency. Guided by the IMF and the EU Commission, the OHR initiated a so-called 'quick-start' package in 1996. Under pressure from the OHR and the IMF, the Bosnian parliament approved it on 20 June 1997. It involved the establishment of a central bank, a common currency, a customs union and common external tariffs (*The Economist*, 28 June 1997, p. 43). It was designed to tame inflation and rapidly restore Bosnia's internal trade and financial institutions. Bosnia's Bosniak, Serb and Croat leaders agreed to establish a single central bank and a new currency, albeit with different designs for each area

(*Transitions*, June 1997, vol. 8, no. 3, p. 30). The Central Bank of Bosnia and Herzegovina started operations in August 1997, with Peter Nicholl, a New Zealander, as governor. On 21 January 1998 the high representative Carlos Westendorp imposed a solution for the design of the *konvertibilna marka*. The value of the new *konvertibilna marka* (KM, convertible mark) was to be pegged one for one to the Deutschmark. The 'entities' were not legally obliged to take on the KM, but all budgetary operations involving the central government had to be conducted in the new currency (EBRD 1997b: 157). The central bank launched the KM on 22 June 1998, to gradually replace three existing currencies: the Croatian kuna, the Bosnian dinar and the Yugoslav dinar. From mid-1998 the KM began to be used for official payments in both entities. Acceptance of the KM was quickest in the Bosniak-majority areas and slowest in the Bosnian-Croat areas. In the Republika Srpska over 50 per cent of commercial bank deposits were in KM by 1999 (EBRD 1999a: 34). Furthermore, the government and public-sector entities were to refrain from financing expenditures through domesti bank loans.

In 1999 the FBiH enacted a law requiring each firm that had been in existence i 1991 to pay 'waiting list' money to each worker who had been on (or even 'eligible' to be on) a waiting list to become an employee of that frm in 1991. The total liability would have been 600 and 800 million KM, if it could have been enforced (this was unlikely, since it would have driven almost every large company in the FBiH into bankruptcy). The law was revised following international protests. During the Communist era, many unemployed workers had been given fictional jobs which involved 'doing nothing for around 30 per cent of the normal wage'. Of the 15,400 employees in the FBiH coal mines, for example, 2,260 were on such 'waiting lists', i.e., the lists of temporarily laid-off workers who were paid about 30 per cent of their salaries to sit at home (*FT*, Survey, 14 December 1999, pp. 35–6). This 'waiting list' phenomenon was symptomatic of how weighed down by social protectionism the Bosnian economy still was. In June 2000 the governments of both entities announced their commitment to revising labour laws to reduce 'waiting lists' and the severance costs for those already on them, to establish more f exible provisions on f xed-term contracts and less restrictive provisions on cancelling employment contracts. These changes were approved by the FBiH parliament in August 2000 (EBRD 2000b: 142). In Republika Srpska in late 2000 the OHR amended the existing labour law to reduce compensation payments to employees on 'waiting lists', in order to increase the attractiveness to investors of enterprises undergoing privatization. Yet there remained contractual obligations on investors to maintain specifed levels of employment (EBRD 2001b: 122–3).

An agreement reached with the IMF in 1999 envisaged phasing out the old payments bureaux inherited from the Communist regime by the end of 2000. The old system prevented banks from offering payments services and provided countless opportunities for bureaucratic interference, control, transaction charges and bribe-taking (EBRD 1999b: 198–9). In 2000 the High Representative Wolfgang Petritsch lamented that the governance of the economy of Bosnia and Herzegovina was still 'to a large extent the same as it was in the days of Communism. Many of the old . . . structures are still in place . . . The banking system, in many cases on the verge of bankruptcy, is also in dire need of overhaul', and 'state companies, like the payment bureaux, are a cash-cow for the major political parties' (*The World Today*, 2000, vol. 56, no. 4. p. 24). In January 2001 Bosnia's payment system finally shifted from the old payments bureau to making payments via commercial banks.

The advent of euro notes and coins on 1 January 2002 boosted the weak banking sector as Bosnians sought to convert Deutschmark savings into euros. This led to the withdrawal of the Deutschmarks which had been circulating alongside the KM and accelerated the growth of bank deposits, which also resulted from (more trusted) foreign banks taking over Bosnian banks (*FT*, 10 January 2002, p. 7).

After the October 2002 elections Paddy Ashdown and his advisers *imposed* twelve economic reforms which Bosnia's parliaments had voted down during their previous term. These reforms aimed to strengthen Bosnia's economic institutions by 'increasing transparency, improving the poor quality of statistics, clarifying land ownership and better regulating the banking system'. They included moves to introduce VAT in place of sales taxes and reductions in direct taxes, to encourage a major switch from illicit to open, legal and taxable economic activity. The OHR aimed to simplify (new) business registration by opening 'one-stop shops' and internet-based registration and thus to revive the lagging privatization process, curb official corruption and increas competition in sectors where it had been restricted. This was a form of 'economic shock therapy'. Support was forthcoming from the three main nationalist parties which had previously obstructed reforms; a more hard-nosed neo-liberal economic policy consensus was emerging (*FT*, Survey, 12 November 2002, p. 31). Kemal Kozaric, a Bosnian economist, succeeded Peter Nicholl as governor of the central bank in January 2005. Monetary policy continued to be guided by the currency board of the central bank.

Internal and external trade liberalization and realignment

Progress towards creating 'a single economic space' within Bosnia and Herzegovina was slow. Steps taken towards this goal included an agreement between the two entities in June 1999 to harmonize excise taxes (implemented from March 2000) and decisions by both entity parliaments in May 2001 to equalize their sales-tax rates. Direct tax rates were lower in the Republika Srpska, and valuation of goods for customs purposes differed between the entities, which also had different foreign-investment laws. A harmonized income-tax law was introduced in January 2000 (EBRD 2001b: 122–3). In February 2003 an indirect tax policy commission was established to focus on how best to set up a single customs administration and administer VAT on an all-Bosnia basis rather than at entity level. The underlying aims were to promote tax reform and create a unif ed 'single economic space' (EBRD 2003b: 124). In April 2004 the two entities signed an agreement to work towards the elimination of all barriers to inter-entity trade and the introduction of a Bosnia-wide VAT (to replace existing entity sales taxes) from January 2006 (EBRD 2004b: 106). The central Bosnian authorities, rather than the two entities, began collecting customs duties in 2004. A Bosnia-wide VAT registration process was launched in July 2005, in order to inaugurate the Bosnia-wide VAT system from January 2006 (EBRD 2005b: 110).

In September 2000, EU foreign ministers approved an EU package granting duty-free access to 95 per cent of imports from Bosnia, along with Albania, Croatia, Macedonia and Montenegro. The package included abolition of tariffs on most industrial and farm products exported to the EU, but some restrictions remained on western Balkan exports of fish products and wine to the EU (*FT*, 19 September 2000, p. 10). On 19 December 2000 Bosnia and Croatia signed an agreement that eliminated customs duties on Bosnian goods entering Croatia and reduced duties on Croatian goods entering the Bosnian market (*IHT*, 20 December 2000, p. 19). The governments of Bosnia, Bulgaria, Croatia, Romania, Macedonia, Albania and the FRY signed an agreement on 27 June 2001 aimed at liberalizing at least 90 per cent of visible trade between them by 2006, under the auspices of the EU Stability Pact for South-eastern Europe (EBRD 2001b: 122–3).

Privatization of industry and services

Before 1992, the economy of Bosnia and Herzegovina was dominated by ten large conglomerates which were jointly responsible for over half of GDP. Shares in self-managed 'socially owned' enterprises were nationalized during the 1992–5 conflict passing into the hands of the FBiH and the Republika Srpska in their respective domains, but enterprise directors retained effective control of 'their' enterprises. Public enterprises owned the largest banks in both entities and were their largest depositors and borrowers (EBRD 1998b: 156).

A privatization law was adopted by the FBiH in October 1997. It envisaged that privatization of small enterprises would be followed by the sale of strategic enterprises (electricity, water supply, transportation, mining, forestry, telecommunications and public service and media), and that the state would settle its obligations to citizens by issuing vouchers that could be used to buy assets offered for sale through auctions and public tenders. The Republika Srpska embarked on mass privatization in 1996, under a scheme that was criticized by international observers and was subsequently cancelled by a new government in early 1998. In June 1998 a new privatization law was passed, resembling the one in the FBiH.

Prior to 1999, however, still no state-owned enterprise had yet been privatized and no bank had been restructured (EBRD 1999a: 34). Privatization was relaunched in 2000. In the FBiH small-scale privatization was about two-thirds complete by mid-2002, with 214 companies sold out of 322, but fewer than 200 of the 1,034 large-scale companies earmarked for sale had been sold by mid-2002. A Sarajevo stock exchange opened on 12 April 2002. In the Republika Srpska, 119 out of 276 of the small enterprises for sale and 154 of the 648 large enterprises earmarked for sale had been fully privatized by the end of June 2002. Sales were mostly to the public through vouchers and to management–employee buy-out teams. A stock exchange opened in Banja Luka on 14 March 2002 (EBRD 2002b: 126–7). By May 2003 about 78 per cent of small enterprises in the FBiH and 55 per cent those in the Republika Srpska had been privatized, but only fifteen out of fifty-six large enterprises in the FBiH and only four out of ffty-two large enterprises in the Republika Srpska, 'highlighting the problems of vested interests and corruption in blocking sales' (EBRD 2003b: 124–5). The privatization of banks was virtually completed in the Republika Srpska and close to completion in the FBiH by 2003 (EBRD 2003b: 124–5). Foreign banks now controlled 90 per cent of bank capital (*FT*, Survey, 23 November 2004, p. 35). This reduced the number of banks to thirty-three by 2004 (EBRD 2005b: 110). Overall, the private-sector share of GDP rose from 35 per cent in 1999 to 40 per cent in 2001, 45 per cent in 2002, 50 per cent in 2003 and 55 per cent in 2005 (see Table 7.13).

Foreign direct investment

FDI was deterred by delays to harmonization and liberalization of business laws in the two entities, which in turn contributed to delays in starting negotiations on an SAA with the EU. Moreover, Bosnia still had not passed any laws on restitution of

7.13 Bosnia and Herzegovina: selected economic indicators, 1993–2005

	1993	1994	1995	1996	1997	1998	1999	2000	2001	2002	2003	2004	2005
							% rate/rise						
GDP	-40.0	-40.0	20.8	40.0	37.0	10.0	9.6	5.5	4.3	5.3	4.0	5.7	5.0
Industrial output	–	–	33.0	38.1	51.4	18.5	12.1	9.4	-2.0	11.5	3.8	12.0	10.5
Agricultural output	–	–	-9.7	28.4	22.8	8.6	–	–	–	–	–	–	–
FBiH inflation rate	–	780.0	-4.4	-24.5	14.0	5.1	-0.9	1.9	1.9	-0.2	0.2	-0.3	2.1
Republika Srpska inflation rate	–	1,061.0	12.9	16.9	-7.3	2.0	14.1	14.0	7.0	1.7	1.8	2.2	2.7
Budget surplus (+)/deficit (–) (as % of GDP)	–	–	-0.3	-4.4	-0.5	-6.9	-4.8	-3.1	-2.5	-4.1	-1.7	-1.9	0.1
Unemployment rate (end-year)	–	–	–	–	37.0	38.0	39.3	39.6	40.3	40.9	42.0	–	–
Foreign debt as % of GDP	–	–	180.0	132.0	119.0	72.0	66.2	59.2	47.4	37.7	33.3	31.1	30.2
Share of private sector in GDP (%)	–	–	–	–	–	–	35.0	35.0	40.0	45.0	50.0	50.0	55.0
Population (m)*	4.1	4.2	4.2	4.1	4.2	4.2	3.8	3.8	3.8	3.8	3.8	3.8	3.8
FDI inflow (net, $ m)	–	–	–	–	–	–	177.0	150.0	130.0	266.0	382.0	490.0	400.0
Foreign debt ($ bn)	–	–	3.4	3.6	4.1	3.0	3.1	2.8	2.4	2.1	2.4	2.6	2.7

Notes: Population 1993–8 includes refugees temporarily resident in other countries; 1999–2005 excludes refugees resident in other countries. Estimates only (no census since 1991).

Sources: Various issues of the annual EBRD *Transition Report*, supplemented by UN Economic Commission for Europe, *Economic Survey of Europe*; UN *World Economic and Social Survey*; and IMF *World Economic Outlook*. Figures for 2004 and 2005 are provisional estimates.

(or, failing that, compensation for) property confiscated by the Communist regime after 1945. As a consequence, the legal standing of claims made by those whose property had been confiscated after the Second World War remained unclear, and this element of uncertainty was a disincentive to new investment.

FDI was negligible until 2002/3, when it became more substantial (see Table 7.13). A string of acquisitions made Slovenia the only significant foreign investor in Bosni before then (*FT*, 10 July 2001, p. 6). Germany's Heidelberger Zement bought 51 per cent of Kakanj (Bosnia's biggest cement maker), the Zenica steelworks was bought by the Kuwait Investment Agency, and Volkswagen invested 50 million Deutschmarks in producing Skoda cars in Sarajevo. Birac, a giant alumina producer in the Republika Srpska, restarted production in 2003, having been bought by the local investment arm of Lithuania's Ukio Bankas (*FT*, Survey, 11 November 2003, p. 35).

Concluding reflections: assessing the problems and accomplishments of post-Dayton Bosnia

Peace has been achieved, much of Bosnia's infrastructure has been rebuilt, human rights are more-or-less being respected, and (within narrow limits) the rule of law and elective government have been established. In November 2002 the UN high representative Paddy Ashdown emphasized that

> Since 1995, in this country of 3.7 million people, more than 800,000 refugees have returned; and 300,000 have gone back to parts of the country where they now represent an ethnic minority. In many places ethnic cleansing has been reversed. A new human right has been created in Bosnia and Herzegovina – the right of refugees to return to their homes. This is unique in European history. Ethnic cleansing has taken its toll, but Serbs, Croats and Moslems still intermingle ... The answer to the divisions raised by borders is not to redraw them, but to make them increasingly irrelevant, as we have done in the EU.
>
> (*IHT*, 16 October 2002, p. 7)

'When the Dayton peace accords were signed there were 430,000 people under arms; today there are 22,000' (*IHT*, 5 November 2002, p. 9). In July 2004 the World Bank published an assessment which described Bosnia and Herzegovina, for the firs time, as a 'transition country' in the mould of the new Central and East European democracies which a decade previously were just turning towards the EU. The country had transcended 'post-conflict' status and it could now start following the lead of th new EU member states (*FT*, Survey, 23 November 2004, p. 33).

However, in late 2005 slightly over half of the 2.2 million people displaced by the Bosnia conf ict of 1992–5 still had not returned to their former homes*The Economist*, 23 November 2005). Moreover, it is by no means certain that Bosnia's political leaders have the degree of will – or even the desire or strong incentives – to overcome the now generally acknowledged dysfunctionality of the political and governance struc- tures established and entrenched by the Dayton accords of November 1995, sufficientl to enable them to undertake the far-reaching restructuring and reforms needed to make Bosnia eligible for an SAA with the EU and official candidate status – let alone E membership in due course.

Unfortunately, even though impressive advances had been made on some fronts, the accomplishments remain very dependent on foreign (mainly Western) tutelage and aid, and there is only so much that a pervasively 'controlling' Western tutelage can achieve. It is inherently difficult to prepare a country to become genuinely *independent* by subjecting all the major decisions, policies, policy frameworks and the governing political and economic philosophies to Western tutelage. All the infrastructure that has been (re)built and the elements of 'good governance' that have been 'imported' and imposed by external agents have not generated much investment in sustainable (new or revived) economic activities that can reduce Bosnia's dependence on external aid, generate much 'real' and sustainable new employment, and reduce Bosnia's poverty and dependence on illegal economic activities and criminal networks. This in turn reinforces the continuing dominance of vertical power relations, vertical power structures and highly clientelistic and often criminalized 'ethnic collectivism' (still better understood more as a form of power relations and power structure than as a set of attitudes or mentalities), which in turn lie at the root of all Bosnia and Herzegovina's difficulties. There are no indications that these fundamental, fateful problems are being tackled at all, or are even adequately recognized and understood. All the Western tutelage and the billions of dollars/euros in foreign aid that have gone into post-Dayton Bosnia have only been treating the external *symptoms* of its deep-seated problems, rather than their underlying *causes*.

Bosnia is acutely afflicted by 'rent-seeking behaviour'. This is often attributed to a particular mentality or mindset, falling back on cheap and easy cultural caricatures and stereotypes of particular peoples. However, the root problems reside in the ways in which the polity, the economy and the society are structured, which in turn give rise to the patterns of behaviour which foster the cultural stereotypes and caricatures which some observers mistakenly regard as the root problems. The main problem is that the power structures, the ways in which society is structured, and therefore the structure of opportunities and incentives in Bosnia do not encourage Bosnian entrepreneurs to seek to enrich themselves by producing more and by developing and using more efficient methods, because property, contracts, rewards and risks are still too uncertain and insecure. This in turn is due partly to the continuing power and magnitude of organized criminal economic networks, partly to the weakness of the rule of law, and partly to the high degree to which the population remains ensnared by highly clientelistic, ethnic collectivist and vertically structured power relations and power structures. In this predicament, the lines of least resistance for Bosnian entrepreneurs are to obtaining 'rents' (income obtained from control of resources that are – often artificially – in short supply). This is done, for example, by exploiting shortages, cornering markets, fostering local monopolies, dealing in various banned or contraband commodities, and engaging in or submitting to various forms of racketeering, including classic Mafa-style protection rackets, with the aim of maximizing short-term rather than highly uncertain and insecure long-term gains to themselves and society.

As early as August 1996, the prominent US columnist Jane Perlez lamented that

> The leaders of Bosnia, Serbia and Croatia have refused to loosen their grip on the economies that gave each of them a power base during the war . . . By perpetuating their fiefdoms built on spoils and patronage, the politicians are obstructing the economic changes – and development of entrepreneurs and regional markets – that could help dilute the virulent nationalism that propelled the conflict . . . All over the region loans to start businesses remain almost unattainable from government-controlled banks. Still persisting are the import-export licences and tariff barriers from which politicians-cum-war-profeers made

fortunes. Air, rail and telephone links that would help citizens move about and foster businesses are slow in coming because there is fear of competition damaging to government monopolies.

(*IHT*, 21 August 1996, p. 2)

In November 1998 Mike O'Connor similarly complained that,

With the ravages of war still very obvious and an economy still run by Communist-era rules, doing business in Bosnia remains so unattractive that there is very little foreign investment. The economy survives in large part on international aid and the money spent to support foreign organizations and tens of thousands of foreigners working here . . . Bosnian politicians refuse to provide the kind of business environment that most large foreign investors demand. Foreign economists say there is often favouritism in the way taxes are collected and laws are applied. They say the lack of a commercial banking system or privatization also keeps investors away . . . Bosnian leaders allow, and often profit from, corruption, tax evasion and tax regulations so burdensome that companies often must bribe officials or break the law

(*IHT*, 23 November 1998, p. 4)

In October 1999 Robert Barry, the head of the OSCE mission to Bosnia and Herzegovina, pointed out that

While slow and steady progress has been made on the political front – as the monopoly of the ruling nationalist parties slowly gives way to political pluralism – much less progress has been made towards creating a functioning market economy in Bosnia . . . With the benefit of hindsight, it is clear that the inter national community made a fundamental mistake at the beginning of the Dayton implementation process in 1996. Too much emphasis was placed on physical reconstruction and not enough on fundamental economic reform. The conse - quences are all too visible. Bosnia's rule of law, investment climate and economic strength is among the worst in Central and Eastern Europe... Bosnia has become dangerously donor-dependent. A large part of the problem is that the Bosnian leadership has so far been unwilling to commit itself to the task of building a market economy. Instead, it seeks to consolidate its control over the economy, which provides it with funds and sources of patronage.

(*FT*, 22 October 1999, p. 23)

In 1999 the economists Daalder and Froman opined that

Bosnia's leaders show little commitment to the type of reforms necessary to create a prosperous, or at least sustainable, economy . . . They have maintained control and tolerate, if not participate in, a system rife with corruption – all in the service of what they define to be their nationalist political interests. . Multiple approvals by a wide array of petty officials are required for almost any type of economi activity, opening the door to widespread graft. Taxes are unevenly collected . . . And according to one senior member of the judiciary, 90 per cent of the judges are viewed as compromised and needing to be replaced. The result is an economy that has grown almost completely dependent on foreign aid.

(Daalder and Froman 1999: 109)

Also in 1999 Jeffrey Smith focused on the scale and the damaging effects of the black economy and gangsterism.

> Criminal gangs – using skills gained circumventing blockades and embargoes during the 1992–5 Bosnian war – are smuggling in thousands of cartons of untaxed cigarettes and unknown quantities of illegal drugs .. . They have also established well-protected corridors for trafficking in stolen cars from Western Europe an prostitutes from Eastern Europe. Unofficial markets 'have mushroomed through out the country' . . . 40 per cent to 60 per cent of the Bosnian economy appears to be based on black-market commerce. This has fuelled the rise of a wealthy criminal class that wields enormous political influence and annually diverts hundreds of millions of dollars in potential tax revenue to itself. Although there is little evidence of direct diversion of foreign aid to private hands, the siphoning off of public revenue has helped ensure the country's continued dependence on outside assistance for many years to come.
>
> (*IHT*, 27 December 1999, p. 5)

In its more impersonal 'offcialese', the EBRD has identifed analogous problems:

> The economy is burdened with the pervasive influence of bureaucracy and b the lack of capital and unclear governance in the state sector . . . Delays in the privatization process have limited access to investment finance and given rise to asset stripping (often through the creation of 'joint ventures' between state and private firms). Private businesses generally face a difficult or even hosti tax and administrative environment that has shed little of its socialist legacy. Inconsistent tax treatment tends to distort competition . . . The Council of Ministers has wide discretionary powers to grant tax exemptions, a system which is prone to abuse and has contributed to unfair competition. Business legislation in both entities remains a patchwork of sometimes inconsistent laws and regulations, dating back mostly to the Socialist Federal Republic of Yugoslavia and to wartime administrations.
>
> (EBRD 1999b: 198–9)

Other observers have focused on the scale of fraud and misappropriation of public funds, including foreign aid. By 1998, up to a billion dollars had disappeared from public funds or had been stolen from international aid projects through fraud carried out by the Bosniak, Croat and Serb nationalist leaders who keep Bosnia rigidly partitioned into three enclaves, according to an investigation by a US-led anti-fraud unit set up by the OHR. Not all of this missing money was stolen from Bosnian public funds. Much was lost through the failure of offcials in Bosnia to collect taxes, 'either through corruption or mismanagement' (*IHT*, 18 August 1999, pp. 1, 4;*IHT*, 21 August 1999, p. 2).

In April 2005 the influential International Commission on the Balkans conclude that the effects of the Western 'quasi-protectorates' in Bosnia and Kosova were 'debilitating' because,

> With no real stake in these territories, international representatives insist on quick results to complex problems; they dabble in social engineering but are not held accountable when their policies go wrong. If Europe's neo-colonial rule becomes

further entrenched, it will encourage economic discontent; it will become a
political embarrassment for the European project.

(ICB 2005: 11)

The governmental structures which were established in post-Dayton Bosnia and
Herzegovina can fruitfully be regarded as an experiment in non-majoritarian 'consociational democracy' which sought to accommodate, reconcile, reassure and safeguard
the interests of the separate and potentially conflicting ethno-cultural communitie
that were fated to live intermingled in a single yet deeply fractured polity. The
overriding necessity was to try to achieve some form of non-violent 'coexistence'
or mutual modus vivendi, in other words a framework that gave equal protection,
respect, recognition and scope for expression and fulfilment to the interests, concerns
rights, values and identities of each of the constituent ethno-cultural communities
as well as the two confederal 'entities' that make up this polity. The system which
was worked out was and remains exceedingly complex, arcane and cumbersome.
Many commentators have come to regard it as a hugely debilitating impediment to
desperately needed radical reforms, economic restructuring and economic develop -
ment (see, for example, Gligorov 2001). In large measure, these 'consociational'
structures have 'locked' and further institutionalized Bosnia's citizens into their
respective ethno-cultural communities, in effect into a new form of ethnic*apartheid*,
instead of knitting them together and transcending their differences. This is the major
intrinsic drawback or 'downside' of the concept of 'consociational democracy' coined
and popularized by the well-known Dutch political scientist Arendt Lijphart since
the 1960s. Nevertheless, in deeply fractured and divided polities, such structures
can sometimes be the only feasible way of circumventing the potential violent and
destructive inter-communal conflict, even if they are exceedingly complex, cumber
some, inimical to radical reform, economic restructuring and inter-communal inte -
gration, and conducive to 'lowest common denominator' politics. They can*only* take
measures which *each* of the constituent communities is willing to accept and to live
with. It is diffcult for them to reach (let alone execute) the bold majoritarian decisions
which are sometimes the only way to overcome systemic gridlock.

Most of the many critics of the terms of the Dayton settlement have berated and
bemoaned the resultant immobilism or structural gridlock and the entrenched attitudes,
mentalities and power structures which this helped to maintain or even deepen.
However, it has to be remembered that the overriding need and concern in 1995 was
to devise a system which would get *all* the main parties 'on board', and which each
of them could live with, in order to bring the terrible fratricidal fighting to an end, t
reduce the likelihood that f ghting might erupt all over again in the near future, and
to buy time for the economic reconstruction and recovery which it was (rather
optimistically) hoped would help to heal old wounds and reconcile diverse peoples
to living and working together again. The hope was that, like the peoples of the EU,
the peoples of Bosnia and Herzegovina would be gradually welded together (and
their mutual animosities sublimated) by shared prosperity. A large part of the problem
is that shared prosperity isn't happening and doesn't look likely.

In principle, the post-Dayton structures were not unlike the systems of governance
and decision-making which have evolved for not dissimilar reasons within the Swiss
Federation and (since the 1950s) within the EC and the EU. These too were designed
to safeguard and accommodate potentially conflicting interests, concerns and value
within a deeply fractured and multilingual Swiss confederation and within a European

states system which had long displayed strong in-built propensities to violent and self-destructive warfare.

Sadly, there are very strong indications that full economic reconstruction and recovery, as well as far-reaching (re)integration in the sense of reconciling and transcending entrenched inter-ethnic differences and mutual mistrust, are precluded by the existence of these complex, cumbersome and increasingly dysfunctional post-Dayton structures. These have tended to 'lock' people into narrowly ethnic compartments, structures and mindsets. As a result, people are disinclined to 'move on'. This has impeded the vital political and economic reforms and the far-reaching economic restructuring that are needed in order to nurture a more vigorous private enterprise economy and to overcome the polity's still dangerously high levels of unemployment and poverty. If this continues to be the case (as, regrettably, seems most likely), then the inter-ethnic tensions and the social problems which are festering as a result of this debilitating 'structural gridlock' could well erupt into another bout of inter-ethnic warfare – the very thing that the Dayton negotiations sought above all to prevent. The post-Dayton settlement seems to have reproduced within Bosnia and Herzegovina, on a smaller (but not much less dangerous) scale, the systemic and inter-ethnic gridlock that blocked much of the economic reform and restructuring that was so desperately needed in the SFRY during the 1970s and 1980s and which ultimately helped to blow it apart with such explosive force during the 1990s. If this is allowed to happen, all the efforts and commitments which most (if not all) parties seem to have made in good faith at Dayton and subsequently to rebuild a more prosperous and harmonious multicultural Bosnia and Herzegovina will have been in vain.

A violent denouement is not unavoidable. For the moment, however, it appears that the strength and the concentration of both local and international 'political will' needed to carry out radical economic, political and social restructuring and avert yet another major human tragedy of this sort are conspicuously lacking. The vote for independence in Montenegro on 21 May 2006, combined with international acceptance of that outcome, encouraged even the supposedly moderate and pro-western Bosnian Serbs led by the RS prime minister Milorad Dodik to step up demands to be allowed unfettered national self-determination, including the right to secede from Bosnia and Herzegovina or even to join a 'Greater Serbia' – and gave a boost to Bosnian Croat dreams of union with Croatia. The Bosnian confederation thus remained perilously close to gridlock and/or dissolution.

8   Macedonia

Towards a bi-national state?

Introductory 'country profile'

The (Former Yugoslav) Republic of Macedonia (ROM) is a small state with a land area of 25,733 square kilometres (about one-tenth of the size of the UK and of the former FRY, and about one-twentieth of the size of France), with a population of only 2 million in 2005. It is a mountainous and extensively forested country, with twenty-four mountains exceeding 2,000 metres above sea level. Much of the economically active population engages in agriculture, especially dairy farming, but agriculture only accounted for 11 per cent of GDP in 2004. Agriculture is concentrated in the valley of the river Vardar, which runs from north-west to south-east and on into Greece and the Aegean sea, and in the valleys of its tributaries, with consider - able irrigation. There is some production of rice and tobacco, the latter supplying cigarette factories in Prilep, Skopje and Kumanovo. The river valleys enjoy warm Mediterranean summers, but the highlands get bitterly cold in winter. The country has significant deposits of zinc, lead, copper, chrome and nickel ores and considerabl hydroelectric power potential, which served as the basis for the promotion of signifant metallurgical and electro-metallurgical industries by the former Communist regime, as well as deposits of non-metallic minerals (asbestos, mica, coal, quartz and gypsum). There are also significant food-processing, textile, clothing, footwear, chemicals, timber-processing and bus-building industries. However, industry only contributed 26 per cent of GDP in 2004, whereas services accounted for 63 per cent and agriculture 11 per cent. Officially, 38 per cent of the workforce was unemployed in 2004 (thir quarter), but many of those registered as unemployed were actually engaged in the large 'black economy'. Recorded per-capita GDP amounted to only 7,100 US dollars in 2004, at purchasing power parity, but this omits income generated by the 'black economy' (CIA 2005). The republic's major cities are the capital Skopje (population *c.*600,000 or *c.*30 per cent of the total population), Bitola, Tetovo, Gostivar, Kumanovo, Titov Veles, Kicevo, Prilep, Strumica, Stip and Ohrid.

Who are the Macedonians?

According to much-disputed population census returns, the ethnic composition of the ROM's population has been as shown in Table 8.1. The 1991 census was boycotted by many Albanians, Turks and Roma, who claimed that it would not be conducted fairly and accurately by the dominant Slavic Macedonians. Leaders of the ethnic Albanian community regularly asserted thereafter that ethnic Albanians actually comprised 35 to 40 per cent of the population and that the ROM ought to be

8.1 Ethnic affiliations of population of Macedonia, 1981–200

(% of total)	1981	1991	1994	2002
(Slavic) Macedonians	67.0	64.6	66.5	64.2
Albanians	19.8	21.0	22.9	25.1
Turks	4.5	4.8	4.0	3.5
Roma	2.3	2.7	2.3	1.9
Serbs	2.3	2.1	2.0	1.2
Others	4.1	4.8	2.3	1.8

Sources: Spiljevic (1985: 90), Europa (1992: 335), Perry (1997: 226) and CIA (2005).

reconstituted either as a bi-national 'dual-identity' state (Slav Macedonian and ethnic Albanian Macedonian) or simply as the state of the citizens of the ROM (the formulation embodied in an inter-communal framework agreement in August 2001), rather than as the state of the Slavic Macedonians – the formulation embodied in the firs post-Communist constitution adopted in November 1991. A repeat census, held under international supervision in summer 1994, was also boycotted by most ethnic Albanians and to lesser degrees by the ethnic Turk and ethnic Serb minorities. This yielded the following results: total population was given as 1,936,877, within which Slavic Macedonians accounted for 1,288,330 (66.5 per cent) and ethnic Albanians for 442,914 (22.9 per cent). Ethnic Albanian leaders still insisted that the number of ethnic Albanians was closer to 800,000 (around 40 per cent of the population), but some foreign observers regarded such claims with scepticism (*EEN*, 1995, vol. 9, no. 10, p. 2). The internationally monitored census conducted in November 2002 indicated that ethnic Albanians comprised only 25.1 per cent of the population.

There has been considerable dispute over the use of the terms 'Slav(ic) Macedonians' or 'Macedonian Slavs'. The more nationalistic Slavic Macedonians vehemently demand to be called simply 'Macedonians', both because they regard themselves as constituting the 'Macedonian nation' and because they regard the terms 'Slav' and 'Slavic' as *racial* rather than as *ethnic* designations. However, this would entail acceptance of a narrowly 'ethnic' conception of the nation in question and also of the Slavic Macedonians' claims to 'ownership' of the ROM (as is undoubtedly the intention behind the demand). Against this, we uphold a more inclusive 'civic' conception of the nation and the nation-state, because in principle the ethnically and linguistically Albanian, Turkish and Gypsy inhabitants of the ROM have as much right to be considered 'Macedonians' and 'citizens of the ROM' as do its ethnically Slavic inhabitants (for most of whom the Slavic Macedonian language is the 'mother tongue'). By the same token, the ROM 'belongs' just as much to its long-standing ethnically and linguistically Albanian, Turkish and Gypsy inhabitants as it does to its ethnically and linguistically Slavic ones. In our view the terms 'Slav' and 'Slavic' should pri - marily be used as *linguistic* rather than as *ethnic* or *racial* designations, if only because the peoples of the Balkan Peninsula are in reality *mongrels*, as are most of Europe's inhabitants. They are the products of so many centuries of 'racial' and 'ethnic' mixing, assimilation and interbreeding that it is virtually meaningless to try to assign them to (spurious) distinct 'racial' categories. What they have had in common far outweighs what separates them.

In view of these complications, we shall distinguish the Macedonian-speaking Slavic citizens and inhabitants of the ROM from the ethnically and linguistically Albanian, Turkish, Gypsy and Serb ones by referring to them not as *Macedonians* (because we do not accept that they have any exclusive, prior, titular or proprietorial claim to that republic), but as *Slavic* or *Slav Macedonians*. This is not to their liking, but (like the EU, the OSCE and NATO) we do not accept their claims to a privileged position within the ROM. The privileges which they long claimed were the prime reason for the violent inter-ethnic conflict that afflicted the ROM from February September 2001. Until the implementation of the so-called Ohrid framework agreement of August 2001, Slavic Macedonians occupied more than 90 per cent of public-sector jobs and made up more than 90 per cent of the police force and 90 per cent of the university-student population, even though the ROM was home to substantial ethnic and linguistic minorities amounting to about one-third of the population (*HT*, 8 June 2001, p. 8).

The ethnic and linguistic mix is more or less matched by the diversity of religious affiliations, with the Slavic Macedonians traditionally inclining towards Eastern Orthodox Christianity (although there are also some Muslim and a few Protestant Macedonian Slavs), whereas the ethnic Albanians, Turks and Roma have traditionally inclined towards Islam (although a few of each adhere to Christian denominations). However, religious observance has plummeted in recent decades. In the 2002 census, only 32.4 per cent of the population were returned as Macedonian Orthodox Christians and only 16.9 per cent were returned as Muslims, while just 0.2 per cent were returned as non-Orthodox Christians and 50.5 per cent were returned as having either no religious affiliation or other religious affiliations (CIA 2005

The ROM is *only one part* of a considerably larger group of territories which for around 2,500 years have intermittently borne the 'umbrella name' of Macedonia. The ROM is centred on the Vardar river basin and is often referred to as *Vardar Macedonia*. That name is often useful, to distinguish this area from the 'other Macedonias'. Part of western Bulgaria has come to be known as *Pirin Macedonia* (after the Pirin mountains which are its main topographical feature); and a large part of north-eastern Greece is also known as Macedonia – and will henceforth be referred to as *southern Macedonia* or *Greek Macedonia*.

'Vardar Macedonia' prior to the 1990s

As a result of the use of the name 'Macedonia' for several quite distinct regions and peoples, the history of 'Macedonia' as a land or group of lands with a distinct name and identity is the most contested and controversial of any of those considered in this book. There have also been very heated disputes over the history and provenance both of the ancient and strongly Hellenized pre-Slavic inhabitants of all three sections of 'Macedonia' and of the more recently settled and much less Hellenized 'Slavic Macedonians', as well as over who can legitimately lay claim to what. There has been a particularly long and fierce debate about whether the Slavic Macedonians are a sub-species of the Bulgarian nation, a sub-species of the Serbian nation, or a nation in their own right, just as there are ongoing and highly charged debates over whether the ancient pre-Slavic inhabitants of 'Macedonia' were 'Greeks' or were a people (or even a cluster of peoples) who were originally – and may even have remained – quite distinct from 'the Greeks'. Greeks have long based their claims to (southern) Macedonia on ancient Macedonia's significant links and affinities with ancient Greece, on medieval Macedonia's close links and affinities with the Greek dominated Byzantine Empire, and on the growing numerical preponderance of people who have considered themselves to be ethnic Greeks in southern Macedonia in recent times. Against this, some classical scholars and many Slavic Macedonians contend that, despite their close links with ancient Greece, the ancient Macedonians were a people distinct from the ancient Greeks, and that the modern Greeks have little or no right to claim or appropriate the illustrious past and ancestral homelands of 'the ancient Macedonians' for themselves. Some Slavic Macedonian nationalists go further still and incense Greek nationalists and some Western classicists by insisting that the illustrious historical, cultural and territorial heritage of ancient Macedonia (Alexander the Great and all that), and even that of the 'Macedonian' territories which later came under Byzantine rule, somehow pertains or 'belongs' to the modern Slavic Macedonians, who have thereby acquired a 'glorious past' which many or most of their early modern ancestors never 'knew' they had.

It is neither necessary nor possible to resolve these major bones of contention here. All that needs to be known for present purposes is that the Slav ancestors of the Slavic Macedonians who currently reside in the (Former Yugoslav) ROM appear to have settled in this area between the sixth and eighth centuries AD, that this area had previously been substantially Hellenic or Hellenized and part of the Byzantine Empire's domains, that parts of this territory have also been (among) the long-standing homelands of the modern ethnic Albanians and their ancestors, that Vardar Macedonia also played central roles in the formation and Christianization of medieval Serbia, that during the late nineteenth century it became the object of rival territorial claims by Serbia, Bulgaria and Greece, and that during the twentieth century many or most of the ethnic Albanians living in Vardar Macedonia and in Kosova also decided to stake 'proprietorial claims' to the western sections of Vardar Macedonia for themselves.

During the late nineteenth century, all three of the territorial sections of Macedonia (Vardar, Pirin and Greek) were mostly very poor and had very mixed populations comprising largely Orthodox Christian Slavs, largely Orthodox Christian Greeks, some Orthodox Christian Romanians (Vlachs), some Jews, some partly Christian and partly Muslim Roma, some Muslim Slavs, and many Muslim ethnic Albanians and Turks. Albanian, Turkish, Roma and Slav Muslims may well have comprised as much as half of the population. However, the interests of the Muslim inhabitants in Vardar Macedonia were increasingly overridden or ignored after the decisive defeat of the Ottoman Empire in the Russo-Turkish War of 1877–8, which signalled the start of the terminal phase of the protracted decline of Ottoman imperial ascendancy in the region.

As one of the last parts of Europe to be 'liberated' from Ottoman rule, Vardar Macedonia also became a major battleground in the Balkan Wars of 1912 and 1913. The victory of the Balkan states over the Ottoman Turks in 1912–13 ended over 400 years of Ottoman dominion over the Balkans. As a result of these victories, Greece took possession of southern Macedonia, while Serbia grabbed and brutally subjugated the semi-Albanian province of Kosova. However, Serbia and Greece helped to thwart Bulgaria's expectation that it would gain possession of Vardar Macedonia, thereby reneging on the deal which they had struck with Bulgaria just prior to their joint declaration of war against the Ottoman Empire, with the result that Bulgaria quite rightly felt that it had been double-crossed by its erstwhile allies. Although Greece subsequently lost possession of southern Macedonia during the two world wars, it regained it from 1918 to 1941 and again in 1945. Southern Macedonia now appears to be enduringly part of Greece, not least because the Greeks have either driven out or assimilated most of its formerly quite numerous Slavic inhabitants (whom the Greek state has consistently refused to recognize as a separate ethnic group or nationality), in addition to driving out most of its formerly very numerous Turkic and Muslim inhabitants and replacing them with large numbers of ethnic Greeks (mostly ethnic Greek refugees who had been expelled from Anatolia during the 1920s).

During the inter-war years, Vardar Macedonia languished economically as a landlocked and impoverished backwater of the Serb-dominated Yugoslav kingdom. At the same time, Bulgarian nationalists who bitterly resented having been 'cheated' out of acquiring Vardar Macedonia in 1912–13 and in 1918–19, together with the terrorist and ultra-nationalist IMRO established in 1893, repeatedly engaged in aggressive endeavours to (re)acquire Vardar Macedonia for Bulgaria, on the basis of their claims that the Macedonian Slavs were a sub-branch of the Bulgarian nation. IMRO *komitas* (brigands) carried out political assassinations, terrorized villages and exacted tribute, while claiming that they were fighting either for the creation of an independent Macedonian state or for Vardar Macedonia to be reunited with Bulgaria (including Pirin Macedonia).

The language of the Slavic Macedonians is indeed close to Bulgarian in its vocabulary, although it is in some respects closer to Serbian in its grammar. However, the experience of somewhat rapacious and heavy-handed Bulgarian military occupation during the two world wars seemed to convince the Slavic inhabitants of Vardar Macedonia that perhaps they were not Bulgarians after all and that their interests could be better served and protected within the more commodious framework of a Yugoslav federation.

From 11 October 1941 to August 1944 the inhabitants of Vardar Macedonia made significant contributions to the Communist-led resistance to the German-backed Bulgarian occupation of their land (as well as to fascist rule in other parts of Yugoslavia). On 2 August 1944, at the monastery of Prohor Pciinski, the first meeting of the Communist-controlled Anti-Fascist Council of National Liberation of Macedonia, comprising 116 delegates from all over Macedonia, formally decided that Vardar Macedonia would become one of the six semi-autonomous constituent 'republics' which would make up the Yugoslav federation established by the Communist-led partisan movement and the Communist Party of Yugoslavia in 1945. Despite considerable opposition from Serbs, the Yugoslav Communist leadership succeeded in persuading most Yugoslavs to accept that the Macedonian-speaking Slavic inhabitants of Vardar Macedonia were in reality neither Bulgarians nor Serbs, but were instead a nation in their own right. The SFRY vigorously fostered a distinctive, newly devised Macedonian Slavic written language, as well as a mass-education system and a Macedonian Slavic culture and identity based upon that language. Even Greece appeared to tacitly recognize the existence of a Slavic Macedonian nation in 1949, in return for a tacit cessation of Yugoslav support for the Communist-led guerrilla forces (parts of which were Macedonian Slavic) in the Greek civil war of 1945–9.

In 1958, with the backing of the Yugoslav Communist regime, an archdiocese of Ohrid was re-established. In 1967, moreover, the Orthodox Christian community in the ROM broke away from the Serbian Orthodox Church (of which it had hitherto been part) and established an autocephalous (self-governing) Macedonian Orthodox Church. This further strengthened the claims of the Slavic Macedonians to be a nation in their own right rather than a junior branch of the Serbian nation. However, partly because this ecclesiastical secession further curtailed Serbian pretensions to dominance of Yugoslavia, it was vehemently opposed by the Serbian Orthodox Church, by the Orthodox patriarchate in Istanbul, and by the other major Orthodox churches, and this has remained the case ever since. Nevertheless, this merely persuaded the embattled majority of Macedonian Orthodox Christians to dig in their heels, and since then any attempt by some Macedonian Orthodox Christians to reunite parts of their church with the Serbian Orthodox Church have been treated as tantamount to treason. In July 2005, despite protests from human-rights organizations, the Slav Macedonian archbishop Jovan Vraniskovski was sentenced to thirty months in prison for attempting to establish an 'Orthodox archdiocese of Ohrid' affiliated to the Serbia Orthodox Church, which a Macedonian court interpreted as grounds for convicting him of 'inciting ethnic and religious hatred' (Stavrova and Alagjozovski 2005i).

Even though during the Communist era the ROM received considerable transfer payments (subsidies) and public investment in infrastructural modernization and in the promotion of new metallurgical, textile, footwear, tobacco and food-processing industries, it remained the poorest republic and the second poorest region of the Communist-ruled SFRY (only the autonomous province of Kosova was poorer). In 1990 its per-capita GDP was only half the Croatian level and one-third of the Slovene level, and on official statistics, 23 per cent of the workforce was unemployed. Skopj was devastated by a major earthquake in 1968.

The ROM was also afflicted by growing tension between the dominant Slavic Macedonians and the under-privileged and increasingly restive and assertive ethnic Albanians, whose increasingly nationalistic aspirations to Albanian-language educational and cultural institutions of their own were strongly stimulated by the mobilization of autonomist nationalism among ethnic Albanians in Kosova in 1968 and 1981, as well as by subsequent Yugoslav persecution and repression of Kosovar Albanian nationalism during the 1980s and 1990s. The ethnic Albanians in the ROM and in Kosova displayed growing mutual support/solidarity in their parallel struggles against Slav hegemony and in making joint demands for some sort of union, possibly as an ethnic Albanian 'seventh republic' within the SFRY. The establishment of such a republic would have facilitated the development of joint or shared higher education and cultural institutions using Albanian in place of South Slavic languages, as well as the conduct of politics and administration and the provision of broadcasting and legal services in Albanian. That could well have assisted some sort of Yugoslav federation to have survived the secession of Slovenia and Croatia in 1991, but any such option appears to have been unacceptable to Serbian as well as Slav Macedonian nationalists.

During these same decades, the Slavic Macedonian leadership became unnerved by the (re)emergence of aggressively expansionist Serbian nationalism, as Serbian nationalists reverted to calling Vardar Macedonia 'South Serbia' and threatened to (re)incorporate it into a 'Greater Serbia'. Some Slavic Macedonians responded by becoming more fiercely nationalistic themselves. From October 1989, football crowd supporting Vardar (Skopje's main football team) started chanting 'We ght for a united Macedonia!' and 'Solun is ours!' ('Thessaloniki is ours!'), and in February 1990 the poet Ante Popovski launched the Movement for All-Macedonian Action and instigated large demonstrations in Skopje to protest against the perceived persecution of Slav Macedonians in Greece and Bulgaria. With a programme harking back to the old ultra-nationalist IMRO (which had been suppressed or driven underground by the Communist regime after 1945), a new pan-Macedonian nationalist party called Internal Macedonian Revolutionary Organization–Democratic Party of Macedonian National Unity (IMRO-DPMNU) held its founding congress in Skopje in June 1990 and elected the twenty-six-year-old unemployed graduate Ljubco

Georgievski as its leader. Helped by financial backing from the Slav Macedonian diaspora in North America and Germany, this swiftly established itself as the major nationalist party in the ROM.

Politics after the end of Communist rule

The upsurge of Slav pan-Macedonian nationalism, the backwash from the anti-Communist revolutions of 1989–90 in East Central Europe and Bulgaria and Romania, anxieties concerning the aggressive pan-Serbian nationalism which had emerged in Serbia, and doubts as to whether this poor, small and deeply divided republic could survive the incipient disintegration of the SFRY – all these factors helped to persuade the republic's increasingly nervous and defensive League of Communists (then led by Petar Gosev) to permit vigorously contested multiparty elections to be held in November and December 1990.

The elections to the unicameral 120-seat parliament (Sobranje) on 11 and 25 November and 9 December 1990

The turn-out was 85 per cent in the first round and 80 per cent in the second, and the distribution of seats and votes is shown in Table 8.2.

8.2 Macedonian parliamentary election, 11 and 25 November and 9 December 1990

Party	Share of vote (%)	Seats
IMRO-DPMNU (Pan-Macedonian nationalists led by Ljubco Georgievski)	31.7	38
League of Communists of Macedonia–Party of Democratic Change[1]	25.8	31
Party for Democratic Prosperity[2]/National Democratic Party[3]	18.4	22
Alliance of Reform Forces and Young Democratic Progressive Party[4]	15.0	18
Socialist Party of Macedonia	3.3	4
Party for Complete Emancipation of the Roma	0.8	1
Others	5.0	7

Notes
1. These reform-minded Communists were renamed the Social Democratic Union of Macedonia in 1992.
2. A Titoist ethnic Albanian party.
3. An ethnic Albanian nationalist party.
4. Supporters of the Yugoslavist reform programme of Yugoslav premier Ante Markovic.

Source: Perry (1997: 233–4).

The 'government of experts' headed by Nikola Kljusev, January 1991 to July 1992

Since no party came remotely close to winning a majority and the largest party (IMRO-DPMNU) was very short of personnel competent to hold ministerial office, a technocratic 'government of experts' was formed with cross-party support. The firs priority of the Kljusev government was to try to curb hyperinflation (1,664 per cen in 1992) by launching a new currency (the denar) and a stringent austerity programme, as a by-product of which the ROM became monetarily independent from the rest of the SFRY (Perry 1997: 235).

On 25 January 1991 the parliament declared the ROM to be a 'sovereign territory' (but not yet an independent state), and on 27 January it elected the prominent Slav Macedonian Communist Kiro Gligorov to serve as the first president of the republic Ljubco Georgievski, the twenty-seven-year-old leader of IMRO-DPMNU, was elected to serve as vice-president, but he resigned from that post in October 1991, complaining that he and his party had been politically marginalized, despite being the largest political faction.

Under President Gligorov's paternalistic but initially quite liberal and enlightened tutelage (he firmly supported power-sharing with the ethnic Albanians and a marke economy), the Slav Macedonian majority sought to cooperate closely with the Bosniak leaders in Bosnia and Herzegovina and to share power with the elected representatives of the ethnic Albanian minority during the first half of 1991, in a vain endeavour t preserve the SFRY.

However, when it finally became clear in July 1991 that the SFRY was being tor apart by inter-republican confrontation, suspicion and rivalry, President Gligorov and the republic's other leaders decided to hold a referendum on national independence on 8 September 1991. Even though many members of the disgruntled Albanian and Serb minorities boycotted the referendum, there was a turn-out of 75.7 per cent and a 95.3 per cent 'yes' vote. The following month the Yugoslav People's Army accepted this verdict with equanimity and unilaterally withdrew the bulk of its forces, weaponry and other equipment from the republic, initially for use in Croatia, leaving the ROM with very little military force at its disposal – as was fully exposed when ethnic Albanian insurgency erupted in 2001.

In preparation for independence, parliament adopted a new constitution on 17 November 1991. Because this constitution subsequently became a major bone of contention not only between the Slavic Macedonian majority and the republic's sub-stantial ethnic Albanian community, but also between the ROM and Greece, it needs to be considered in some detail. The preamble of the constitution described the ROM as the 'national state of the Macedonian people, in which full equality as citizens and permanent coexistence with the Macedonian people is provided for Albanians, Turks, Vlachs, Roma and other nationalities living in the Republic of Macedonia', with the intention of promoting 'peace and a common home for the Macedonian people with the nationalities living in the Republic of Macedonia'. This constitution, which was promoted by a president and a government prudently committed to maintaining Titoist traditions of peaceful inter-ethnic coexistence and inter-ethnic cooperation and harmony, studiously refrained from referring to ethnic Albanians, Turks, Vlachs and Roma as 'ethnic minorities' or 'national minorities' and used the word 'nationalities' instead, in an attempt to avoid either portraying them as, or making them feel that they were, disadvantaged or second-class citizens. Furthermore, although Article 7 stated that 'The Macedonian language, written using its Cyrillic alphabet, is the officia language in the Republic of Macedonia', it added that

> In the units of local self-government where the majority of the inhabitants belong to a nationality, in addition to the Macedonian language and Cyrillic alphabet, their language and alphabet are also in official use, in a manner determined by law. In the units of local self-government where there is also a considerable number of inhabitants belonging to a nationality, their language and alphabet are

also in official use, in addition to the Macedonian language and Cyrillic alphabet under conditions and in a manner determined by law.

Nevertheless, the ethnic Albanian community did feel slighted and seriously disadvantaged by the new constitution and the conception of the republic which it embodied. Even though the constitution went some way towards establishing equal rights and status for all citizens of the ROM, there were important omissions and shortfalls, and at the same time the constitution quite clearly endeavoured (albeit inconsistently) to privilege the Slavic Macedonians, the Macedonian language and alphabet, and the Macedonian Orthodox Church. The Slav Macedonian majority was attempting to have its cake and eat it, to proclaim 'ethnic equality' (in the preamble) and the idea that the republic was a state of all its citizens (in Articles 2 and 4), yet at the same time to stake out a privileged, titular and proprietorial claim to that state, its identity and its main institutions.

Although the constitution made provision for the recognition and use of the languages of the non-Slavic 'nationalities' in some primary and secondary schools (Article 48) and as second offcial languages (alongside Macedonian) in areas where such 'nationalities' constituted over 50 per cent of the population (Article 7), prominent ethnic Albanians considered this threshold to be excessively high (under internal armed and Western diplomatic pressure it was reduced to 20 per cent in August 2001). In addition, the constitution made no provisions for the recognition and use of these languages in parliament, in law courts, in centrally provided public services, or in public broadcasting. Although Article 48 also stated that 'Members of nationalities have a right freely to express, foster and develop their identity and national attributes' and guaranteed 'the protection of the ethnic, cultural, linguistic and religious identity of the nationalities' and their 'right to establish institutions for culture and art, as well as scholarly and other associations for the expression, fostering and development of their identity', there was no recognition of their right either to have universities of their own or to have instruction in their own languages in higher education. Since primary and secondary schools were expected to remain segregated along ethno-linguistic lines (each ethnic group having had its own schools in Communist-ruled Yugoslavia), this omission seemed designed to deny the non-Slav 'nationalities' equal access to higher education, in a country where access to most elite, managerial and professional occupations and most positions of power had by then become closed to those without degrees from higher-education institutions.

Prior to the 1990s, fortuitously, the existence of the SFRY and freedom of movement across it had enabled the ROM's able and upwardly mobile ethnic Albanians to circumvent this potential blockage of their opportunities for 'advancement' by pursuing degree courses taught and examined in Albanian at the University of Pristina in Kosova, after which (in principle at least) they could either return to the ROM or move elsewhere in the federation to pursue graduate careers. Largely as a consequence, in 1989–90 ethnic Albanians (who comprised over 22 per cent of the population) made up only 1.7 per cent of all university students and only 3.9 per cent of all higher-education students in the ROM (Szajkowski 2000: 252). From 1991 onwards, however, the breakup of the federation, the escalation of ethnic Albanian unrest and Serb repression in Kosova, and new restrictions on movement across newly erected borders virtually ended this possibility and greatly increased the demand for higher education taught and assessed in Albanian within the ROM. Yet the conspicuous absence of provision for this in the November 1991 constitution was subsequently interpreted by the Slav Macedonian majority as a constitutional *prohibition* on higher education taught and examined in Albanian, to the considerable detriment of able and ambitious ethnic Albanians. Furthermore, although Articles 19 and 20 promised freedom of religious confession, worship and conscience and outlawed parties and associations encouraging or inciting 'military aggression or ethnic, racial or religious hatred or intolerance', they singled out the Macedonian Orthodox Church (and no other religious denomination) for special mention and thus implicitly gave it a privileged status.

As a consequence of all this, the majority of ethnic Albanian deputies in parliament opposed the new constitution in the vote on 17 November 1991. Thereafter, the ethnic Albanian political parties mounted steadily growing campaigns throughout the 1990s and early 2000s for the establishment of an ethnically neutral state granting genuinely equal rights and status to all its inhabitants – or, failing that, either a 'bi-national state' of Slavic Macedonians and ethnic Albanians or a decentralized federal state. Some ethnic Albanians went further and aspired to bring about the secession of the largely Albanian-inhabited northern and western areas of the ROM and their 'union' with largely Albanian-inhabited Kosova, either to form a second Albanian state or to unite both of these areas with the Republic of Albania. However, these latter groups appear to have remained a small minority within their own community, and the dominant aspiration of ethnic Albanians in the ROM has been towards power-sharing and equality of opportunity, rather than secession and political union with ethnic Albanians elsewhere.

Parliament formally declared the ROM's independence on 21 November 1991. First Bulgaria, then Turkey, Russia and China formally recognized the ROM by its chosen name. However, EU recognition of the republic as an independent state was blocked by Greece's vehement objections to the use of the name 'Republic of Macedonia', to the design of the republic's flag, and to certain passages in the ne constitution. Successive Greek governments maintained that the use of the name 'Macedonia' (i) made implicit claims to an ancient Macedonian cultural heritage that allegedly 'belongs' to modern Greece and (ii) made implicit territorial claims to Greek-inhabited 'southern Macedonia'. In addition, Greece took exception to Article 49 of the constitution, which stated that 'The Republic cares for the status and rights of those persons belonging to the Macedonian people in neighbouring countries, as well as ex-patriates, assists their cultural development and promotes links with them', alleging that this carried a latent threat of unwarranted intervention in Greek internal affairs (its outrageous treatment of its Slavic Macedonian minority). Finally, Greece objected to the fact that the design of the national flg incorporated the Star of Vergina, a sunburst symbol which had been found in 1977 on a gold casket in the tomb of Philip II of Macedon and which was also associated with his son Alexander the Great, complaining that the ROM was thereby staking a further claim to a historical heritage which allegedly 'belonged' to Greece. Recurrent Slav Macedonian denials that the republic had any designs on current Greek territory were of little avail. Ever since, however, Greece has adamantly refused to give up its objection to the republic's un-qualified use of the name 'Macedonia', and it has repeatedly warned that it will veto any attempt by the EU to recognize it by that name or to allow the republic to enter the EU under that name. To its credit, however, in the spring of 1992 Greece firml rejected a proposal from Slobodan Milosevic to carve up the ROM between Greece and the rump FRY (*FT*, 13 November 1992, p. 3; Perry 1997: 232).

The Kljusev government was brought down by a vote of no confidence in July 1992 mainly due to IMRO-DPMNU's desire for a 'political' government headed by itself.

However, IMRO-DPMNU proved unable to form a government with sufficient parliamentary support to govern. It therefore fell to the former Communists, now renamed the Social Democratic Union of Macedonia (SDUM), to put together a new coalition government (Perry 1997: 235).

The centre-left government headed by Branko Crvenkovski, October 1992 to November 1994

After much wrangling, a new government was finally put together by the thirty-year old former Communist Branko Crvenkovski, whose ascent was 'fast-forwarded' by President Gligorov. With just one four-year interruption from late 1998 to late 2002, Crvenkovski has been the dominant figure in the republic's politics ever since. With Gligorov's backing, Crvenkovski helped to maintain inter-ethnic peace by giving four cabinet posts to leading members of the ethnic Albanian parties (Perry 1997: 235). This established a pattern that has persisted ever since. With the partial exception of Montenegro, the ROM was the only former Yugoslav republic that managed to keep out of the inter-republican and inter-ethnic warfare that ravaged the former federation during the f rst half of the 1990s. This was in large measure due to the dogged deter-mination of large components of the Slav Macedonian and the ethnic Albanian elites to maintain the Titoist tradition of inter-ethnic power-sharing and to actively restrain their respective communities from resorting to violence. This helped to keep the fric-tions between the Slav Macedonian majority and ethnic Albanians within manageable bounds. For example, when four ethnic Albanians died in a clash with the police on 8 November 1992, the repercussions of the incident were not allowed to escalate out of control. The same was true when, on 10 November 1993, two ethnic Albanian deputy ministers were accused (along with a number of other people) of plotting armed rebellion and encouraging predominantly Albanian-inhabited western Macedonia to secede from the ROM. On 2 July 1994 all twenty-three ethnic Albanian deputies walked out of parliament over the jailing of ten ethnic Albanians for allegedly forming paramilitary units in order to overthrow the government, but again the two sides managed to resolve their differences peacefully.

However, this good fortune was also attributable to the far-sightedness shown by the NATO states *here* (in contrast to the rest of former Yugoslavia) by committing military 'monitors' to the republic expressly to reduce the risks that it could either replicate or get sucked into the inter-republican and inter-ethnic conf icts that were aff icting the rest of former Yugoslavia. The main reason why the NATO states were so much more prepared to take timely and far-sighted preventive action in ROM than in other parts of former Yugoslavia seems to have been the realization that, if inter-republican or inter-ethnic conflict had been allowed to spill over into the ROM it would be exceedingly diff cult to conf ne it to former Yugoslavia. It could easily have sucked in Albania and Bulgaria, which in turn could easily have drawn in Greece and Turkey, thereby sparking off a much larger and more dangerous regional conflagration in the so-called 'powder keg of the Balkans'. The so-called 'international community' (largely a euphemism for the Western powers) therefore swiftly obtained UN authorization to install a small international force in the ROM in order to help secure its borders and bolster its stability. On 25 November 1992 the UN Security Council decided to send a dozen observers to assess the prospects for a peacekeeping force, and this was followed by a decision to send 700 military observers to monitor the ROM's borders with Kosova and Albania.

On 8 April 1993, after interminable wrangling, the ROM was finally admitted a the 181st member of the UN using the provisional name of the 'Former Yugoslav Republic of Macedonia' (FYROM). The permanent name was supposed to be the subject of international arbitration, but Greece withdrew from the formal negotiations as early as October 1993. Germany, France, the Netherlands, Denmark, Italy, Finland and Japan finally established formal diplomatic links with the FYROM (under tha name) in December 1993.

Greece's prime minister Andreas Papandreou announced on 16 February 1994 that his government had decided to suspend the activities of its consulate in Skopje and the movement of goods to and from the ROM via the port of Thessaloniki, 'except those that are absolutely necessary for humanitarian reasons, such as food and medicines'. Greece's finance ministry later stipulated that the embargo would appl to all customs points in Greece (*IHT*, 28 March 1994, p. 6). Since Thessaloniki normally handled 70 to 80 per cent of Macedonia's imports and exports, the trade embargo had crippling effects on this very poor and landlocked statelet. The much richer and stronger Greek state was shown in an utterly mean-spirited and bullying light. The imposition of this trade embargo was somewhat surprising because, as late as January 1994, there had been hints of a more conciliatory approach by the Greek government. However, on 31 March 1994 over a million Greeks demonstrated in Thessalonki in support of non-recognition of the ROM. Greece's actions aroused considerable frustration and anger among its EU partners. On 6 April 1994 the EU gave Greece a week to lift its blockade or face a referral to the EU court of justice for violation of EU trade laws, but the Greek government did not respond. Unfortunately, the EU's own rules and procedures prevented it from obliging the Greek state to desist from its childish yet extremely damaging behaviour towards the ROM. On 29 June 1994 the court of justice refused the EU's request for an emergency interim injunction, which it deemed could only be granted on the grounds of 'grave and irreparable harm' to the EU itself.

The Party of Democratic Prosperity, hitherto the main party of the ethnic Albanians living in Macedonia, underwent a split at the party congress held on 13 February 1994, when the radical faction led by Arben Xhaferi broke away and founded a rival ethnic Albanian party which before long became known as the Party of Democratic Action.

The parliamentary elections of 16 and 30 October 1994

The turn-out in the f rst round was 78 per cent. There were long delays before the results were published, allegedly due to 'technical factors', including inadequate electoral rolls. The off cial electoral commission admitted that 10 per cent of voters were not on constituency registers, but they were nevertheless permitted to vote. International observers were far from happy with the situation, but thought the election results should nevertheless stand.

In the first round of voting, the two main opposition parties obtained much lowe shares of the votes than had been anticipated. IMRO-DPMNU, which remained an ultra-nationalist party but at the same time favoured more rapid privatization and economic liberalization, won only 14.4 per cent of the votes cast. The Democratic Party, which had been founded in 1993 by the former Communist leader Petar Gosev and campaigned on a platform of clean government, tax cuts, accelerated privatization using a voucher scheme, refusal to accept the principle of collective rights for the Albanian minority, and opposition to federalism and the granting of local cultural and territorial autonomy to ethnic Albanians, won only 11.2 per cent of the votes cast. Alleging serious irregularities, the Democratic Party of Macedonia and IMRO-DPMNU decided to boycott the second round held on 30 October, when the turn-out was only 57.5 per cent. As a result of this opposition boycott of the second round, the Alliance for Macedonia, comprising the Social Democratic Union of Macedonia (SDUM), the Liberal Party and the Socialist Party, gained 95 of the 120 seats in parliament. The final distribution of seats is shown in Table 8.3

8.3 Macedonian parliamentary election, 16 and 30 October 1994

Party	Seats
Social Democratic Union of Macedonia (SDUM)	58
Liberal Party	29
Party for Democratic Prosperity (PDP, ethnic Albanian party)	10
Socialist Party of Macedonia	8
National Democratic Party (ethnic Albanian party)	4
Democratic Party of Macedonia (led by Petar Gosev)	1
Social Democratic Party of Macedonia	1
Party for the Complete Emancipation of the Roma	1
Democratic Party of Turks	1
Independents	7

Source: Perry 1997: 236.

The presidential election held on 16 October 1994

As expected, the presidential election was won on the f rst ballot by the incumbent Kiro Gligorov, with 52.4 per cent of the votes cast. The main challenger, the IMRO-DPMNU leader Ljubco Georgievski, received only 14.5 per cent. However, there was a high percentage of spoiled ballots.

The centre-left government headed by Branko Crvenkovski, November 1994 to November 1998

For the sake of inter-ethnic harmony, the (ethnic Albanian) Party for Democratic Prosperity, which had won ten seats, was given four cabinet posts – the same number as the Liberal Party, which had won twenty-nine seats. In addition, ethnic Albanians were appointed to important diplomatic posts in Germany, Belgium and Switzerland, to the constitutional court and to high positions in the armed forces. All of this caused much consternation in the (largely Slavic) Liberal Party, which 'gradually moved to a semi-oppositional posture within the ruling coalition' (Perry 1997: 237), while the under-represented opposition parties engaged in various extra-parliamentary resistance campaigns.

Ethnic Albanians opened a private Albanian university in Tetovo on 16 February 1995, in defiance of a state prohibition on any such action. An Albanian protester was shot dead, the founder of the university was arrested and imprisoned, and the republic's ethnic Albanian deputies began a boycott of parliament(*HT*, 7 March 1995, p. 8). Nevertheless, both of the major ethnic communities were careful not to let the situation get completely out of hand, and four months later the founder of the university was released on bail (*FT*, Survey, 7 July 1995, p. 36). Faced with these frictions, President Gligorov worked commendably hard to maintain ethnic harmony and the integrity of the country, and the Slavic Macedonian camp showed a degree of self-restraint. Although the premises of the unofficial Albanian university in Tetovo remained closed, its lecturers were allowed to teach people in their homes, increased numbers of ethnic Albanians were accepted at Skopje University, and degrees from the University of Tirana (in Albania) were accorded official recognition in the RO (*The Economist*, 6 April 1996, p. 45).

Faced with mounting international condemnation of its behaviour towards the ROM, Greece unilaterally relaxed its trade embargo on the ROM in December 1994, for example by allowing through fuel for humanitarian purposes. On 4 September 1995 it was simultaneously announced in Washington, Athens and Skopje that the Greek and Macedonian foreign ministers were to meet to take steps towards 'the creation of a basis for friendly relations between the two countries'. The issue of the ROM's name had yet to be resolved, but other disputes were settled. The Star of Vergina was to be removed from the Macedonian flag, while sections of the Macedonian constitution considered by Greece to be threatening were to be amended. In return Greece would lift its economic embargo, and both Greece and the USA would establish diplomatic relations with the ROM. An agreement to this effect was signed on 13 September and ratif ed by the ROM parliament on 9 October. Greece lifted its economic embargo on the ROM on 15 October 1995.

President Gligorov narrowly survived an assassination attempt on 3 October 1995, when a car bomb exploded in Skopje. He was severely hurt and lost his right eye. At first Slav Macedonian ultra-nationalists were blamed, and later 'the mafia' (*The Economist*, 6 April 1996, p. 45). Gligorov himself became convinced that 'the impulse came from outside his country and that it was not a personal attack but an effort to destabilize Macedonia and keep it out of Western institutions' (*IHT*, 19 April 1996, p. 8). Later, however, Gligorov's endeavours to bring the black economy under control were 'reliably thought to have inspired the attempt on his life' (Szajkowski 2000: 261).

The parliamentary speaker Stojan Andov, leader of the Liberal Party, took over temporarily as acting president of the republic and increasingly clashed with Premier Crvenkovski. Gligorov's temporary incapacity and fears that he might not be willing or able to resume the presidency threatened seriously to destabilize Macedonian politics. However, partly because of these fears, Gligorov resumed his presidential role in January 1996.

During 1997 and the first half of 1998 Prime Minister Branko Crvenkovski face mounting criticism and his governing centre-left coalition came under mounting strain over alarmingly high unemployment rates (42 per cent in 1997, 41 per cent in 1998), rampant corruption, insider privatization, dysfunctionally high levels of taxation, failure to attract foreign investment, and the slow pace of reforms aimed at giving ethnic Albanians, Turks and Roma equal status with Macedonian Slavs. During 1997 the Tat savings house collapsed amid widespread accusations of corruption and involvement by government off cials, the deputy governor of the central bank was arrested on charges of abusing his authority, and several ministers were dismissed following further scandals, including the collapse of several pyramid investment schemes (*The Economist*, 31 May 1997, p. 4;*FT*, Survey, 17 December 1997, pp. i–ii). The continuing ethnic divide between the dominant Macedonian Slavs and the underprivileged ethnic minorities left both camps feeling that their interests had been poorly served (Fraenkel 2001: 262).

In mid-February 1997, thousands of Slav Macedonian students began protests against a law designed to promote increased use of the Albanian language in the pedagogical (teacher-training) faculty in Skopje. These protests 'turned into organized daily rallies of up to 10,000 people' (*EEN*, 30 March 1997, p. 6). The law had been passed under strong pressure from the USA, the EU and EU member states. It merely permitted the use of Albanian as one of the languages of tuition in just one branch of the republic's main university, in very incomplete and long-overdue recognition of the linguistic rights and aspirations of the republic's large ethnic Albanian minority (*The Economist*, 29 March 1997, p. 54).

Parliament passed a law on 8 July 1997 restricting the use of non-Macedonian flag and permitting the flags of ethnic minorities to fly outside municipal buildings on on public holidays. The next day three people were killed and over 200 were injured when violence erupted in the predominantly ethnic Albanian towns of Tetovo and Gostivar, as police tried to prevent the flying of the Albanian national flag. The defi ethnic Albanian mayor of Gostivar insisted on flying this flag alongside the ROM flag outside the town hall. However, the SDUM-led government still managed to retain the support of the moderate PDP, partly by setting up a parliamentary commission to investigate the riots (*FT*, Survey, 17 December 1997, p. ii). On 17 September 1997 the mayor of Gostivar was sentenced to thirteen years in jail for not carrying out orders to lower the Albanian flag from public buildings in Gostivar, but the sentence was later reduced to seven years. The mayor of Tetovo received a two-and-a-half-year prison term for a similar offence (*The Economist*, 7 March 1998, p. 54). The Democratic Party of Albanians (DPA) withdrew from parliament on 13 April 1998 in protest against the ongoing imprisonment of the ethnic Albanian mayors of Gostivar and Tetovo (*EEN*, 1998, vol. 12, no. 5, p. 6).

In December 1997 the UN Security Council extended the mandates of UNPREDEP (the UN preventive force stationed in the ROM) by nine months, until the end of August 1998, but the troops were supposed to be withdrawn 'immediately thereafter'. President Gligorov was in favour of extending the mandate for a longer period (*FT*, Survey, 17 December 1997, p. iii).

The two-stage election to the 120-seat parliament, 18 October and 1 November 1998

Under a new electoral law, eighty-five seats were to be contested on a first-past-th post basis, but thirty-five were to be filled by proportional representation (with a 5 per cent threshold). There were numerous reruns due to electoral irregularities (*The Economist*, 7 November 1998, p. 56).

The main contenders were:

1. The incumbent Social Democratic Union of Macedonia (SDUM), which had governed in partnership with the moderate (ethnic Albanian) PDP during the preceding six years.
2. The IMRO-DPMNU, led by thirty-four-year-old Ljubco Georgievski, who talked of attracting 1 billion US dollars of foreign investment and of compensating citizens of the ROM for losses they had incurred in financial scams. By this tim IMRO-DPMNU had renounced its former ultra-nationalist stance, had entered a previously unthinkable electoral alliance with the main ethnic Albanian parties in an attempt to supplant the SDUM, and was presenting itself as a party of peace. This apparent metamorphosis of the IMRO-DPMNU into a moderate centre-right party owed much to Vasil Tupurkovski, a US-educated international lawyer,

former leader in Yugoslavia's Communist Youth movement, and former member of the rotating federal presidency of the former Communist-ruled SFRY, who had founded the Democratic Alternative in 1998 and worked especially hard to persuade IMRO-DPMNU to abandon its traditional hostility towards the ROM's large Albanian minority and to break with its past by fighting the election campaign primarily on economic issues. Georgievski cast off IMRO-DPMNU's former wild image and stressed the need to crack down on corruption, make the ROM less risky for investors, foster opportunities to build small businesses and create jobs. He even promised to introduce a law banning discrimination against ethnic minorities (*The Economist*, 7 November 1998, p. 56).

3. The Democratic Alternative, a new pro-business party founded and led by Vasil Tupurkovski. During the mid-1990s he had served as ROM's special envoy to the USA. In 1998 he pledged to bring in 1 billion US dollars in foreign invest - ment to reduce unemployment and speed the ROM's transition to a market economy, with the assistance of ethnic Macedonians in the USA and Australia. He declared: 'Macedonia should become a high-quality agricultural producer and food-processor supplying markets abroad. The way to beat unemployment is to encourage development of family-sized agri-business units' *FT*, 2 November 1998, p. 4; *FT*, 3 November 1998, p. 2). Tupurkovski brokered the above-mentioned 'unholy alliance' between the previously ultra-nationalist IMRO and the ethnic Albanian parties.

4. The Liberal Democratic Party, formed on 19 April 1997 by merging the Democratic Party and the Liberal Party and led by Petar Gosev, the former leader of the League of Communists of Macedonia.

5. The main ethnic Albanian parties: the moderate PDP; and the more radical DPA led by Arben Xhaferi.

See Table 8.4 for the distribution of seats following the election.

8.4 Macedonian parliamentary election, 18 October and 1 November 1998

Party	Seats
IMRO-DPMNU, led by Ljubco Georgievski	49
Party for Democratic Prosperity (PDP)	14
Democratic Alternative (DA), led by Vasil Tupurkovski	13
Democratic Party of Albanians (DPA), led by Arben Xhaferi	11
SDUM	27
Liberal Democratic Party	4
Socialist Party	1
Party for the Complete Emancipation of the Roma	1

Source: Fraenkel (2001: 263).

The centre-right governments headed by Ljubco Georgievski, December 1998 to 13 May 2001

After the election, Georgievski invited the DA, the PDP and the DPA to join with IMRO-DPMNU in a coalition government. One of his first concessions to the PD and the DPA was to offer to release the former mayors of Tetovo and Gostivar, who were still serving prison sentences for having raised Albanian flags outside their respective city halls. According to Arben Xhaferi, there was also an agreement to give increased powers to elected local authorities and to establish a state-funded university in which instruction would be primarily in Albanian. Having previously argued that the ROM's ethnic Albanians might have to secede in order to secure equal political rights, Xhaferi now argued that they had to learn to work together with Macedonian Slav politicians. It seemed that even the most nationalistic Slav Macedonians and ethnic Albanians had begun to accept that this landlocked country, sandwiched between Serbia, Albania, Greece and Bulgaria, would remain poor and isolated unless its leaders learned to work *together* instead of *against* one another (*IHT*, 1 December 1998, p. 5). The imprisoned mayors of Tetovo and Gostivar were freed in March 1999 (*FT*, 29 March 1999, p. 2).

Georgievski's 'business-friendly' premiership initially displayed considerable boldness and openness, which aroused high expectations and gave a brief boost to foreign direct investment and economic growth. In return for ROM diplomatic recognition of Taiwan, the Taiwanese government contributed 20 million US dollars towards the construction of the ROM's first free-trade zone in 1999 (BCE 1999: 36) On 25 September 1999 Greece's state-run Olympic Airways began regular flights between Athens and Skopje and on 10 November 1999 Greece and the ROM launched a 90 million US dollar project to build a 220-kilometre oil pipeline from the northern Greek port of Thessaloniki to Skopje. This would link refineries controlled by Helleni Petroleum, the partly privatized Greek energy group, in Thessaloniki and Skopje. It was to be completed in 2001 (*FT*, 11 November 1999, p. 14).

A landmark 'declaration of cooperation' was signed by Georgievski and Prime Minister Ivan Kostov of Bulgaria on 22 February 1999. It was signed in two copies, in the official languages of both countries. This allowed Georgievski to claim that 'the Bulgarian side for the first time had agreed to an explicit endorsement of the Macedonian language', while Kostov was able to tell the Bulgarian public that Macedonian was 'merely a technical variation of Bulgarian'. On Bulgarian insistence, the declaration contained an undertaking by the ROM side never to invoke Article 49 of the ROM constitution (which obliged the ROM to care for the status and rights of Macedonians in neighbouring states) as a pretext for interference in the internal affairs of Bulgaria. This was an exact copy of the formula used (with the same aim) in the interim agreement between the ROM and Greece in 1995. The parallel declarations also included stipulations that each would suppress the activities of institutions and private citizens fostering violence or hatred directed at the other. Under the agreement, Bulgaria was to donate military equipment to the ROM. Other agree - ments included the promotion and protection of investments, trade cooperation, international road traff c and air services. A defence cooperation agreement was signed with Bulgaria on 12 March, and a free-trade agreement on 13 October 1999.

The influx of 360,000 Kosovar Albanian refugees the during Kosova war of March–June 1999 'noticeably widened social and political f ssures within and among Macedonia's ethnolinguistic communities' (Fraenkel 2003: 402). The war aroused fears among the Macedonian Slav majority that the balance of population and power in the ROM would be changed dramatically in the ethnic Albanians' favour. However, the ethnic Albanian community within the ROM accommodated and looked after the 360,000 Kosovan refugees and then calmed 'the Slav majority's fears of being swamped' by helping Kosovar families to return home again in June–July 1999 (*FT*, Survey, 19 February 2001, p. 14).

The presidential elections held on 31 October, 14 November and 5 December 1999

In order to win, a candidate had to obtain over 50 per cent of the votes cast. Both of the front-runners favoured integration with the EU and improved relations with Greece. Tito Petrovski, the candidate of the SDUM, led in the first round with 33 per cent o the vote. Boris Trajkovski, the candidate of IMRO-DPMNU, came a poor second with 22 per cent of the vote (*IHT*, 2 November 1999, p. 7). However, Trajkovski won the run-off election on 14 November, with 53 per cent of the vote. Unusually for a Slav Macedonian, Trajkovski had studied theology in the USA, where he rejected Communism and was ordained as a Methodist (Protestant) minister. This was expected to go down well with many Americans. Second-round support from the ethnic Albanian minority contributed decisively to his victory. However, the SDUM claimed that there had been widespread electoral fraud in western Macedonia, where most ethnic Albanians lived. OSCE election monitors conceded that there had been 'irregularities in some western districts' (*FT*, 16 November 1999, p. 12), and on 27 November the supreme court annulled the election results in 230 polling stations (out of 2,793 in total), involving more than 160,000 voters (about 10 per cent of the 1.6 million electorate). Trajkovski nevertheless won the rerun elections on 5 December and was sworn in on 15 December.

Parliament passed a law on 25 July 2000 allowing for higher education in the Albanian language. The government, under Western pressure, then allowed the construction of a 50 million-dollar private university in Tetovo to provide higher education in Albanian for up to 2,500 students. The new university, sponsored by 'the international community', was due to open in Tetovo in October 2001. Some courses were to be taught in Albanian, while others were to be taught either in English or in Macedonian (*FT*, 6 March 2001, p. 10).

The local elections of 10 September 2000

These were easily won by the opposition parties. IMRO-DPMNU performed least well in the larger towns and cities, where the effects of an unemployment rate of between 25 and 35 per cent and austerity measures cutting thousands of public-service jobs and privatizing or closing down forty major loss-making state enterprises were most keenly felt. International monitors described the ballot as having been 'marred by security incidents, irregularities and intimidation' (*FT*, Survey, 19 February 2001, p. 11; *IHT*, 12 September 2000, p. 6).

Feuding between coalition partners and five acrimonious cabinet reshuffles in 2000 culminated in the departure of Vasil Tupurkovski's DA from the governing coalition on 23 November. Georgievski announced a new cabinet on 30 November, following a coalition agreement between the IMRO-DPMNU, the DPA and the LDP. The DPA became the government's main coalition partner and acquired five cabine portfolios, including the economics ministry. Bedredin Ibrahimi, general-secretary of the DPA, became deputy prime minister. The DA's role as a business-friendly liberal coalition partner was taken over by the LDP, whose Srgjan Kerim became foreign minister.

The ethnic Albanian insurgency, late January to September 2001: the rise of the national liberation army (UCK)

Ethnic Albanian insurgents fired a rocket-propelled grenade at a train in the ROM o 27 January 2001, carried out a spate of armed attacks on ROM police stations during February 2001 (*FT*, Survey, 19 February 2001, p. 11), and clashed with ROM forces on 18 and 26–28 February 2001.

Three Slav Macedonians and an undisclosed number of ethnic Albanians died in mortar attacks and small-arms fire between a self-proclaimed national liberation arm (UCK – Ushtria Climatare Kombetare) and the ROM army in the village of Tanusevci on the ROM side of the Kosova–Macedonian border on 7 March 2001. During the late 1990s Tanusevci had been an important base for the KLA and was used both as a transit point for the smuggling of arms and for training rebels. In 2000 Tanusevci became a clearing house for the supply of arms to the Liberation Army of Presevo, Medvedya and Bujanovac (UCPMB) operating in the largely Albanian-inhabited Presevo valley area of southern Serbia, about 30 kilometres away. As tensions increased, a training base was again set up by the UCPMB. In September 2000 ROM military vehicles were fired upon near the village. Most prominent Kosovar Albania politicians such as Adem Demaci (a former spokesman for the KLA) and Ahmed Ceku (head of the Kosova Protection Corps) dissociated themselves from the UCPMB and the UCK, which undoubtedly recruited elements of the formally disbanded KLA. Many guerrillas in Tanusevci openly admitted to being former KLA fighters. Two distinc groups of ethnic Albanians were involved in initiating the insurgency of 2001: those in southern Serbia and western Macedonia who considered themselves to have been disenfranchised and impoverished by the governments in Belgrade and Skopje, and those responsible for f nancing, arming and organizing the insurgency. A very small hard core of veterans was fghting to create a 'Greater Kosova' which could eventually be united with Albania to form a 'Greater Albania'. Although considerable attention was given to pan-Albanianism in the West, it attracted very little support amongst ethnic Albanians (Kola 2003). However, some of the proponents of pan-Albanianism were 'motivated not by national ideology but by profit. Many entrepreneurs make money from instability, which allows them to control markets and continue their trade in illicit drugs, consumer items and women' (*The World Today*, 2001, vol. 57, no. 4, pp. 10–12).

The emergence of the UCK was evidently affected by developments not only in Kosova, but also in the Presevo valley area of southern Serbia. On 26 January 2000 two ethnic Albanians were killed by Serbian police in Dobrosin, located just inside the Serbian border in the Presevo valley, in what was called the ground safety zone (GSZ). Soon afterwards ethnic Albanian guerrillas calling themselves the UCPMB appeared in the village, naming themselves after three districts in southern Serbia populated by around 100,000 ethnic Albanians. 'Politically they were linked to the Popular Movement for Kosova, the LPK, a tiny party of deeply committed ethnic Albanian nationalists which had, however, been instrumental in creating the Kosova Liberation Army (KLA) in 1993.' It is conceivable that, until the fall of Milosevic on 5 October 2000, the US troops who oversaw this area

> may have been less than diligent in choking off supplies to the UCPMB because anything that helped destabilize Milosevic was deemed to be a good thing ... Several key members of the LPK were Macedonian Albanians. They included

> Fazli Veliu, the LPK chairman through much of the 1990s, and Bardhyl Mahmuti,
> a key organizer and fund-raiser who lived in exile in . . . Switzerland. In 1993 a
> meeting of ethnic Albanian activists took place in Kicevo in western Macedonia
> . . . and there a decision was made to move towards active armed resistance. The
> result, in August of that year, was the formation of the LPK and in turn the KLA.

After the Kosova war of March–June 1999, moderate LPK members such as Bardhyl
Mahmuti argued that the LPK had achieved its purpose and should be disbanded, but
'a hard core of LPK members decided to keep the old party alive'. Such people played
major roles in setting up both the UCPMB and the UCK. In the ROM the political
leader of the UCK was Ali Ahmeti, who had previously been a major organizer of
supplies for the KLA in 1997–9.

> Ever since the end of the Kosova war many of the Macedonian Albanian LPK
> men had been agitating to start a conflict in the ROM. Many of their old comrades
> now in powerful Kosova parties or even in the civil administration, tried to
> dissuade them, arguing that a new war would not be in the interests of Kosova.

However, the founders of the UCK rejected these appeals and orchestrated an armed
insurgency in western Macedonia. In all their official declarations, however, the UC
leaders emphasized that they only wanted 'rights for Macedonia's Albanians and not
the breakup of the state' (*NYRB*, vol. 48, no. 8, pp. 36–7).

In Skopje in February 2001, some supporters of the ethnic Albanian insurgents in
western Macedonia launched a National Democratic Party (NDP), whose programme
called for a federal ROM. The leader of the new party was Kastriot Haxhirexha (*Daily
Telegraph*, 12 March 2001, p. 11; *Daily Telegraph*, 13 March 2001, p. 16). The UCK
insurgents and the National Democratic Party both wanted the ROM to become a
bi-national federation, with ethnic Albanians taking full control of western Macedonia,
where most of them lived. Fadil Bajrami, a former member of the DPA and a founder
member of the NDP, stated: 'We have waited ten years for the Albanians to get their
rights and it has not happened . . . We see a federation, along the lines of Belgium, as
the future in Macedonia' (*FT*, 31 March 2001, p. 8).

The veteran reporter Jonathan Steele emphasized that the brewing conflict was 'not
just a dispute between Albanians and Macedonians', but 'also a dispute among
Albanians'. Prominent ethnic Albanian politicians, in Kosova and Albania as well as
in the ROM,

> all condemned the gunmen . . . Apart from four Albanian and two Macedonian
> MPs, the entire [Macedonian] parliament condemned the 'armed groups of
> extremists' . . . and called for foreign military help. The motion was supported
> not only by the Albanian party in government but also by the Albanian oppo-
> sition Party of Democratic Prosperity. So the gunmen operating in the hills
> above Tetovo represent a minority. That said, it does not follow that a large number
> of Macedonia's Albanians do not support their goals, as opposed to their violent
> methods. Before and since independence in 1991 Albanians have regularly criti-
> cised the lack of language rights for their community and discrimination in public
> service jobs . . . Arben Xhafari, now the leading Albanian moderate in Macedonia,
> is a jail veteran from flag protests going as far back as 1968. Calls for federalisatio

within Macedonia . . . have long been canvassed by some Albanians, though always rejected by Macedonian [Slavic] politicians on the grounds they would be the first step to secession

(The Guardian, 19 March 2001, p. 18)

In mid-March 2001 UCK insurgents called for international mediation to secure their aims, including a division of the ROM into two federated entities dominated by ethnic Albanians on the one hand and Slav Macedonians on the other. The UCK proclaimed that they were battling to put an end to 'systematic discrimination', and they demanded 'the right to create their own police force, army, schools and parliament in a Macedonian federation of two states' (*IHT*, 21 March 2001, pp. 1, 6). The UCK insisted that it was 'not seeking to break up the Macedonian state but merely to secure equal rights for the Albanians'. Nevertheless, the Tetovo branch of the UCK warned that it would 'fight if necessary', in order to achieve 'the transformation of Macedoni into a federation' (*The Times*, 21 March 2001, p. 19). This was mainly a response to the fact that, for better or worse, Macedonian politics was structured along ethnic collectivist lines. There was 'no multi-ethnic political party' (*IHT*, 28 March 2001, p. 4).

The UCK enjoyed widespread support among rank-and-fle ethnic Albanians, who considered that they had been treated as second-class citizens by the Slav Macedonian majority and sympathized with UCK demands for enhanced political and economic rights (*IHT*, 19 March 2001, p. 7). UCK insurgents declared their intention to take over western Macedonia in order to bring about a federation, although sceptics retorted that the real objective was to join an enlarged independent Kosova (*The Guardian*, 19 March 2001, p. 2). What was being 'played' out in the ROM was 'the last unresolved issue of the Balkans conflict: the Albanian question', i.e., how to accommodate th national aspirations of the 2.5 million ethnic Albanians who had been left stranded in states adjacent to Albania (*FT*, 24 March 2001, p. 11).

Tim Judah contended that, even though no major party within Albania was explicitly calling for the creation of a 'Greater Albania', there was nevertheless an active 'Albanian question' in Kosova, in the ROM, in southern Serbia and, to a smaller degree, in Montenegro. He nevertheless contended that

> the teeth of a relatively few hardliners can be drawn if Albanians feel their rights are represented in the countries in which they live, if they believe that Kosova will, one day, be independent, and, most important of all, if they can prosper in a south-eastern Europe where borders may soon come to mean as much as they do today between Germany, France and Luxembourg . . . That phrase 'to make borders unimportant' is much heard now in the Balkans from people who want both ethnic unity and an end to f ghting.

(NYRB, vol. 48, no. 8, pp. 36–7)

In May 2001 Fazli Veliu, one of the founders of the UCK, 'threatened to broaden their conflict with ROM security forces' unless the UCK were brought into negotiation on the republic's future. Veliu, fellow members of Switzerland's significant Albania diaspora, members of the KLA and ethnic Albanian political exiles in the USA, Germany and Switzerland had planned the creation of the UCK. As the president-in-exile of the People's Movement of Kosova, Veliu had also been one of the founders of the KLA (*The Guardian*, 21 May 2001, p. 10).

At a Balkan summit in Skopje on 23 February 2001 President Boris Trajkovski and the Yugoslav president Vojislav Kostunica initialled a long-awaited treaty definin the border between the ROM and Serbia (*The Economist*, 3 March 2001, p. 48). This agreement led to stricter border patrols, 'sparking clashes between Macedonian police and ethnic Albanian smugglers' (*FT*, 19 March 2001, p. 10). On 1 March the ROM parliament ratified this treaty by eighty-nine votes to nine, in spite of tensions ove the occupation of the mountain village of Tanusevci by ethnic Albanian nationalists from Kosova. The PDP voted against ratification, on the grounds that the politica parties in Kosova had not been consulted (*FT*, 2 March 2001, p. 8).

The EU, working in tandem with NATO, lined up a solid front of international support behind the ROM government and President Trajkovski. The EU foreign-policy supremo Javier Solana and NATO secretary-general George Robertson cooperated closely. The crisis in the ROM became the first test of a new formula in transatlantic cooperation, whereby a newly capacitated EU foreign-policy team would take the lead in handling a European security problem and NATO would play smaller sup - porting roles – in this instance, both inside the ROM and as a major presence across the border in Kosova (*IHT*, 23 March 2001, p. 4). On 2 March NATO reassured Macedonia that it was closely monitoring the actions of a force of about 100 ethnic Albanian insurgents who had occupied the village of Tanusevci. NATO also reaffimed its commitment to maintaining the territorial integrity of the FRY, which still had nominal jurisdiction over Kosova and Montenegro (*IHT*, 3 March 2001, p. 2).

The killing of three Macedonian soldiers on 4 March 2001 led the ROM to close its border with Kosova. On 5 March it was announced that the UCK's operations were not confined to Tanusevci but included the forests around it. NATO 'started beefng up security along Kosova's border with Macedonia amid growing concern that the region could face fresh instability' (*IHT*, 6 March 2001, p. 6). The Bulgarian president Petar Stoyanov offered to send troops to assist the ROM army, and he sent a military equipment convoy to the ROM on 8 March (*Independent*, 9 March 2001, p. 13).

On 8 March, as part of an operation coordinated with Macedonian military forces through the night and morning to fush out ethnic Albanian rebels from their mountain base, some 300 (mostly American) international peacekeepers occupied Tanusevci, which they found empty and abandoned (*IHT*, 9 March 2001, pp. 1, 4). On the same day NATO decided to allow Yugoslav (Serb) security forces to re-enter a small section of the so-called GSZ at the junction of the borders between Kosova, Serbia and Macedonia. Thus began a signif cant step in the international rehabilitation of post-Milosevic Serbia. NATO's secretary-general George Robertson announced that it was 'the first step in a phased and conditioned reduction' of NATO commitments in the GSZ (*FT*, 9 March 2001, p. 20). The GSZ was being 'exploited by ethnic Albanian extremists as a base for attacking Serb policemen and for crossing between Kosova and Macedonia to attack Macedonian police' (*FT*, 10 March 2001, p. 7).

On 14 March, several hundred FRY troops and special police units, monitored by NATO officials, were allowed to start patrolling a 25-square-kilometre area of th GSZ buffer zone in the Presevo valley. This area separated off the insurgents in the Presevo valley from those in northern Macedonia (*IHT*, 15 March 2001, p. 5). Concurrently, the UCK expanded its insurgency from the sparsely populated countryside to the outskirts of Tetovo (*IHT*, 15 March 2001, p. 5). Around 200 ethnic Albanian rebels were also reported to be involved in fighting which took place in an around the village of Lavce in the hills above Tetovo. Support for the rebels was reported to be 'almost universal' among ethnic Albanians in these villages and in Tetovo (*IHT*, 16 March 2001, p. 4). Mortar shells hit the main square in Tetovo on 16 March. Tetovo, which was 80 per cent ethnic Albanian, had a police force which was 90 per cent Slavic Macedonian. Rauf Ramadini, the ethnic Albanian police commander in Tetovo, was replaced by a Slavic Macedonian on 17 March(*The Times*, 19 March 2001, p. 13).

In a stage-managed display of inter-ethnic unity, the ROM parliament held a three-day debate from 16 to 18 March, which ended with a condemnation of the UCK attacks on Tetovo and an appeal for international military assistance against the insurgency, albeit with a stipulation that this should not include troops from neighbouring countries. The motion called for 'wider dialogue' among the 'relevant forces' in Macedonia and condemned the 'armed groups of extremists' (*The Guardian*, 19 March 2001, p. 13). Except for four Albanian and two Macedonian Slavic deputies, the entire parliament (including the DPA and the PDP) supported the motion (*The Guardian*, 19 March 2001, p. 18).

At that time NATO's 3,000-strong presence in the ROM was limited to logistical support troops. On 19 March George Robertson declared that:

> What is required is the isolation of those who are undermining the democratic process, and we can do that with KFOR on the Kosova side of the border, cutting off lines of supply . . . We will not contemplate the changing of borders through violence and we will not contemplate the breakup of the Former Yugoslav Republic of Macedonia.
>
> (*Independent*, 20 March 2001, p. 13)

Officially the Macedonian army had around 15,000 men, including some 1,400 reservists, but Western diplomats put the number of 'combat-capable' soldiers at no more than 1,200 (not vastly greater than the UCK forces). Although around 30 per cent of the army's conscripts were ethnic Albanians and about 10 per cent were Roma, Turks and other minorities, about 90 per cent of the officers were Slavs. The government could also call on 350 special police and 450 gendarmes trained in riot control and paramilitary operations (*The Guardian*, 26 March 2001, p. 13; *The Guardian*, 22 March 2001, p. 2).

On 20 March the government postponed a planned military offensive aimed at ending the insurgency around Tetovo in order to allow civilians twenty-four hours to vacate a series of villages occupied by the rebels. The pause was based in part on intelligence information provided by the USA and Germany, which were flying pilotless military reconnaissance drones over the area from bases in Kosova. The security forces preparing for the offensive were predominantly Slav Macedonian, and they were receiving weapons from Greece and Bulgaria (*IHT*, 21 March 2001, pp. 1, 6). France also sent a battery of pilotless drones to monitor the border between Kosova and Macedonia, and intelligence gathered by the drones was passed to KFOR commanders and 'shared with the Macedonian authorities' (*IHT*, 22 March 2001, p. 4). The 'terrorists' were given twenty-four hours to cease hostilities or leave the ROM (*Independent*, 21 March 2001, p. 13).

The DPA and the PDP issued a joint declaration on 20 March: 'We call on the groups that have taken up arms on the territory of our state to lay down their arms and return to their homes peacefully. We condemn the use of force in pursuit of political objectives.' They also urged the government to speed up the implementation of measures it had already agreed on to improve inter-ethnic relations, especially the creation of an Albanian university in Tetovo and the establishment of an Albanian-language television channel (*Daily Telegraph*, 21 March 2001, p. 15; *Independent*, 21 March 2001, p. 13).

During a visit to Macedonia on 20 March, Javier Solana encouraged the ROM government to take a hard line: 'Nothing and I mean nothing will be obtained by violent means . . . It is a mistake to negotiate with the terrorists and we do not recommend it'; 'The terrorists have to be isolated. All of us have to condemn and isolate them' (*Independent*, 21 March 2001, p. 13; *The Guardian*, 21 March 2001, p. 14).

Ali Ahmeti, the political spokesperson of the UCK, made the following pro-nouncement on Kosova's RTK television on 21 March 2001: 'We, the general staff of the National Liberation Army, announce a unilateral ceasefe and we open the road for dialogue . . . We shall respond to force if fired upon' *The Times*, 22 March 2001, p. 14). Ahmeti had been a founder of the KLA, had served as a local commander under Haradinaj in western Kosova, and had been a key figure in organizing the KLA's gun-runnning and logistics (*Independent*, 24 March 2001, p. 14). There was no government reaction to the offer, and the ROM security forces reclaimed some ethnic Albanian rebel positions in the mountains around Tetovo on 22 March. However, 'the government came under pressure from EU officials and opposition parties to abandon an all-out offensive' (*The Guardian*, 23 March 2001, p. 15). Although ROM forces continued to fire on ethnic Albanian insurgent positions outside Tetovo as the EU intensifed diplomatic efforts to end the confict, they showed no sign of launching an all-out offensive against the UCK (*FT*, 23 March 2001, p. 10). The EU had a signifcant carrot to offer for the exercise of restraint, as the ROM was due to sign an SAA with the EU in April. The SAA required the signatory state to work for 'peaceful resolution of its internal conf icts' (*The Guardian*, 24 March 2001, p. 17).

President Trajkovski took part in a European Council meeting of the EU heads of state and government in Stockholm on 23 March. They promised to 'stand by Macedonia in this critical moment in its history' and urged it to respond to the insurgency 'in a restrained and proper manner' (*The Times*, 24 March 2001, p. 17). Russia's president Vladimir Putin, who also attended this EU summit, declared: 'Today we are witnessing exactly the same situation in Macedonia [as in Chechnya]' (*IHT*, 24 March 2001, p. 2). He urged the West 'to deal with Albanian insurgents in Macedonia in the way Moscow acted in Chechnya, arguing that the use of force [was] the only way to prevent a destabilization of the region' *Independent*, 24 March 2001, p. 14). NATO secretary-general George Robertson declared that it was essential to 'marginalize' the ethnic Albanian insurgents 'whose objective – as it had been in Kosova and southern Serbia – was to provoke a reaction that would drag in outside forces' (*The Guardian*, 24 March 2001, p. 17).

On the same day, the three most prominent political leaders of the Kosovar Albanians, Ibrahim Rugova, Hashim Thaqi and Ramush Haradinaj (the former senior field commander in the KLA and currently leader of the Alliance for the Future of Kosova), signed a statement drafted by EU officials

> We, the leaders of the political parties in Kosova, call on the extremist groups which have taken up arms on the territory of Macedonia to lay them down imme-diately, and to return to their homes peacefully. We urge the Macedonian

government to show restraint and to address and resolve the grievances through peaceful and democratic means.

Under pressure from the EU, ROM security forces conducted only sporadic shelling of rebel positions, and the UCK did not respond to such attacks for several days (*The Guardian*, 24 March 2001, p. 2; *IHT*, 24 March 2001, p. 2).

Two Ukrainian MI-24 helicopter gunships arrived in the ROM on 23 March and were pressed into action the next day, firing rockets at insurgents in the hills. Tw transport helicopters also flew in from Ukraine and two more arrived later (*The Guardian*, 26 March 2001, p. 13;*The Times*, Supplement, 28 March 2001, p. 3). ROM forces launched a concerted tank, artillery and infantry offensive on 25 March. Several strategic villages were taken without apparent loss of life. If the operation continued to go well, off cials stated privately, President Trajkovski would call for all-party nego-tiations on legal and constitutional changes to satisfy long-standing ethnic Albanian grievances (*IHT*, 26 March 2001, pp. 1, 8). However, the PDP suspended its partici-pation in parliament and urged the DPA to pull out of the governing coalition, although the leaders of both parties emphasized their willingness to negotiate over Albanian demands for equal rights (*The Times*, 27 March 2001, p. 16).

On 26 March ROM government forces continued to move carefully through the hills above Tetovo, consolidating their control of villages which had been held by UCK rebels for nearly two weeks. However, after the combined artillery and infantry assault on 25 March most of the UCK fighters had abandoned their positions unde the cover of night and, although sporadic gunf re and explosions could still be heard in the hills, the operation had caused few government or civilian casualties. ROM off cials promised that there would be aid to villagers to repair or rebuild any damaged houses. George Robertson and Javier Solana came to Skopje on the night of 26 March, offered further NATO and EU support, praised the ROM for its 'proportionate military response to the rebels', and encouraged it to act swiftly to show the ethnic Albanians that progress was possible 'without the gun'. NATO announced that it would form a new group of about 400 British and Scandinavian soldiers to help patrol the border with Kosova, while the British government announced that it would provide unmanned reconnaissance planes (*IHT*, 27 March 2001, p. 7). However, a gathering of over 10,000 Kosovar Albanians in Pristina on 26 March to mark the twentieth anniversary of the March 1981 Kosovar revolt against Serb rule in Kosova turned into a demonstration of support for ethnic Albanian rebels in the ROM (*FT*, 27 March 2001, p. 9).

Javier Solana underlined EU support for inter-ethnic dialogue on 27 March by making a high-profile visit to Tetovo. After talks with local Albanian political leaders he declared that 'the fghting is over ... it is time for dialogue .. . An important message to the rebels is that the best thing they can do is lay down their weapons and start a political life.' During his visit to Tetovo, Solana held talks with the DPA leader Arben Xhaferi, before walking through the town square arm in arm with the mayor Ismail Murtezan (*FT*, 28 March 2001, p. 8).

Nevertheless, violence was what had given the ethnic Albanian insurgents global attention, international standing and even a modicum of legitimacy. It would be hypocritical to try to pretend that this was not the case. If they had not resorted to violence, few people would have taken much notice of them, and the agenda of ROM politics would have continued as before.

Contrary to the widespread caricatures of this region as one riven by ethnic hatreds, a striking feature of this confict in the ROM was the self-restraint shown by most Slav

Macedonian and ethnic Albanian newspapers. On the whole, newspapers on both sides refrained from crude hatemongering and libel against the other side. An editorial in the Albanian daily *Fakti* appealed to the insurgents to lay down their arms, warning that 'Their desire to consolidate the rights of Albanians could very easily boomerang with destructive effects for the future of Albanians.' The Slavic Macedonian press also endeavoured not to offend the ethnic Albanian minority. Indeed, the crisis increased the momentum for all-party negotiations to deal with underlying grievances of the ethnic Albanians (*FT*, 28 March 2001, p. 8).

Javier Solana and Chris Patten, the EU commissioner for external relations, visited Skopje on 2 April to promote or even impose the idea of a round-table 'Europe Committee', designed to resolve the country's bitter inter-ethnic tensions and pave the way for the signing of the EU–ROM SAA in Luxembourg the following week (*The Guardian*, 2 April 2001, p. 13). This initiative followed intense negotiations among the ROM's political leaders. Solana insisted the EU would not lead the negotiations but would act as a 'facilitator' (*FT*, 2 April 2001, p. 7). President Trajkovski invited leaders of all of the ROM's political parties to take part in the talks which began on 2 April. However, the PDP refused to send a representative, because 'We want the meetings to be well prepared with a defnite agenda and we want international mediation', even though the EU had declined to play the role of mediator (*FT*, 3 April 2001, p. 8).

By early April, however, the UCK was recruiting ethnic Albanians in western Macedonia so as to open up a second front. In Albania camps previously used by the KLA were being reopened (*The Guardian*, 5 April 2001, p. 13). The UK foreign secretary Robin Cook few to Skopje on 5 April to step up the pressure on all parties to give and take in the proposed negotiations. However, when he proclaimed that 'We want to help Macedonia defeat the terrorists', Xhaferi roundly rejected Cook's use of the word 'terrorist', pointing out that the insurgents 'cannot be terrorists because they have uniforms and a front line – and they have not attacked civilians. We have an uprising' (*Independent*, 6 April 2001, p. 14).

On 9 April 2001, at a meeting of EU foreign ministers in Luxembourg, the long-heralded SAA was duly signed with the ROM. The SAA held out an offer ('per - spective') of eventual EU membership, provided Macedonia introduced a wide range of reforms to enhance its capacity to meet and fully comply in due course with the associated challenges and requirements. However, EU foreign ministers firmly but politely declined Macedonia's request for immediate recognition as an officia candidate for membership. At this meeting in Luxembourg, the elected leaders of the Macedonian Slav community were also formally given until the next meeting of EU heads of government (the European Council) in Gothenburg in June 2001 to reach agreement with the elected leaders of the ethnic Albanian minority on the institutional reform and political restructuring of the ROM in order to accommodate more fully the rights, aspirations and interests of its ethnic minorities, especially the Albanians. Prime Minister Ljubco Georgievski agreed to produce a progress report for the Gothenburg European Council and promised to meet the June deadline for improved inter-ethnic relations. The EU specified several immediate political priorities, includin the opening of the long-awaited new university with an Albanian-language element by August, the setting up of an Albanian-language television channel, and the devolution of power to directly elected local authorities (*Independent*, 10 April 2001, p. 12; *The Guardian*, 10 April 2001, p. 14).

On the same day, OSCE monitors in the ROM complained to the government about 'the arrest and beating of scores of ethnic Albanian civilians, and the vandalizing of dozens of houses, by security forces "cleaning up" after the offensive against Albanian guerrillas' (*The Guardian*, 10 April 2001, p. 14). The next day the ROM established 'a commission to guarantee equal treatment' of its ethnic minorities and 'to investigate ways to fight organized crime' *The Guardian*, 12 April 2001, p. 14).

After ethnic Albanian demands that the ROM constitution be rewritten to guarantee minorities equal status with majority Slavs were rejected by the Slav-dominated ROM government, which argued that such changes would lead to a de-facto division of the ROM, eight members of the republic's security forces were killed near the Kosova border on 28 April (*IHT*, 30 April 2001, p. 6).

About 700 Macedonian Slavs carried out a pogrom against ethnic Albanian and Slav Muslims in the town of Bitola (170 kilometres south-west of Skopje) early on 1 May 2001, attacking their shops, bakeries and restaurants, after the funerals of four of the Macedonian Slav police off cials killed by ethnic Albanians on 28 April (*FT*, 2 May 2001, p. 8; *The Times*, 2 May 2001, p. 12; *The Guardian*, 2 May 2001, p. 13). In addition, in Skopje a man eating in an ethnic Albanian pizzeria was shot dead and a machine gun was fired at the Albanian embassy *The Times*, 4 May 2001, p. 16). The pogroms resumed the following night and destroyed at least ten shops. The Albanian government, which had condemned the killing of Macedonian offcials by UCK insurgents, condemned the attack on its embassy in Skopje(*HT*, 3 May 2001, p. 7; *FT*, 3 May 2001, p. 8).

President Trajkovski visited Washington on 1–3 May 2001 to obtain US approval and support for a coalition government uniting Macedonia's main political parties until new elections could be held in 2002. On 2 May Trajkovski 'won backing from President George Bush for the government's strategy of trying to resolve grievances through dialogue' (*FT*, 4 May 2001, p. 6).

ROM government forces unleashed a fresh assault on ethnic Albanian insurgents in the north on 4 May. Military offcials accused the insurgents of using 3,500 people, mostly women and children, as 'human shields' in the villages of Vaksince and Slupcane (*IHT*, 5 May 2001, p. 2). It was unclear how many civilians stayed there of their own free will and how many were coerced into remaining in these villages. Helicopter gunships, tanks and mortars pounded the villages of Slupcane and Vaksince on 5 and 6 May, after the expiry of a deadline for civilians to leave (*The Guardian*, 7 May 2001, p. 10). Government forces called on civilians to leave the villages in the firing line, promising to hold fire for several hours each morning. However, most o the civilians at risk refused offers of safe escort out of the area by the International Red Cross on 6 May (*Independent*, 8 May 2001, p. 11).

The government announced on 5 May that it was starting consultations on whether to declare a state of war. This would have given the president the power to rule by decree and appoint a new government, the government the power to seal the borders, ban public gatherings and impose curfews, and wide-ranging powers to the security forces. However, a declaration of war could occur only with the approval of a two-thirds majority in the 120-member parliament (*IHT*, 7 May 2001, p. 5), and President Trajkovski was known to be opposed to declaring a state of war. EU and NATO offi cials rushed to Skopje on 6 May to try to convince the government not to declare a state of war. Even though there were genuine fears of civil war, and even though many young ethnic Albanians had stated that they backed the insurgents, very few had joined up and there had been no civilian resistance when the ROM armed forces forced the insurgents into retreat (*Independent*, 7 May 2001, p. 12). On 7 May the DPA leader Arben Xhaferi warned that the DPA would leave the coalition if a state of war was proclaimed, while the UCK 'offered a ceasefire in exchange for direct talks with th government' (*Independent*, 8 May 2001, p. 11).

On 7 May government forces pounded the ethnic Albanian insurgents with helicopter gunships, but the government backed off from declaring a state of war. Instead, ROM party leaders redoubled their efforts to form a national unity government, as an alternative way to undermine the insurgents. A senior member of the PDP said his was the only party that had not consented to join the unity government, but he insisted that the PDP would not relent until the indiscriminate shelling of insurgent-held villages ceased. A session of parliament which would have debated whether to introduce a state of war on 8 May was postponed, under pressure from the EU and NATO (*IHT*, 8 May 2001, p. 5).

The SDUM agreed to join the government on 8 May, thus expanding the ruling coalition to 96 of the parliament's 120 members (*The Guardian*, 12 May 2001, p. 17).

On 10 May Ljubco Georgievski and Serbia's prime minister Zoran Djindjic met in Skopje and pledged 'to work together to fight ethnic Albanian "terrorists" activ on both sides of the border with Kosova' (*IHT*, 11 May 2001, p. 5). Arguing that a 'prolonged ceasefire would allow the terrorists to regroup', Georgievski gave the PDP until 11 May to make up its mind about joining the new coalition which would be announced in parliament on 12 May. The EU urged the PDP to comply (*Independent*, 11 May 2001, p. 15). The PDP finally gave way and agreed to join with the two main Slavic political parties and the DPA to form a rainbow coalition on 11 May, but the insurgents swore to f ght on until they were invited to participate in talks on settling the grievances of the ethnic Albanians. Government forces extended a cease f re on a daily basis, but Georgievski rejected the PDP's calls for a truce/(*HT*, 12 May 2001, p. 2).

The 'unity government' headed by Ljubco Georgievski, 13 May to September 2001

The new government claimed to represent almost 90 per cent of the electorate, on the basis of votes cast at the 1998 general election. One of its first acts was to postpon a population census from May to October 2001. The Albanian minority had claimed that the results of the 1994 population census had been rigged by the Slav majority and wanted the next census to be conducted under closer international scrutiny and control. For their part, Slav Macedonian off cials complained that ethnic Albanians had been pouring into the ROM from Albania and Kosova, lured by the ROM's relative prosperity. Many Slav Macedonians argued that these ethnic Albanian immigrants had no automatic right to ROM citizenship, that they could diminish the previous numerical predominance of the Slavs and hence their control of the republic, and that they should therefore neither be counted in the census nor registered as potential voters (*The Guardian*, 14 May 2001, p. 17).

On 14 May, during a short break in the fighting, humanitarian workers organize by the International Committee of the Red Cross evacuated about 100 ethnic Albanian civilians from besieged villages in northern Macedonia, but many of the evacuees denied that they had been misused or forced to stay by the insurgents (*IHT*, 15 May 2001, p. 5).

The new 'unity government' ordered its forces briefly to cease attacking ethni Albanian insurgents on 15 May, but warned that they would face a full-scale assault in two days' time unless they cleared out of their strongholds in northern villages by 17 May. Until then government forces would only attack when attacked (*IHT*, 16 May 2001, p. 5). When 17 May arrived, however, government forces held their fire Sporadic clashes occurred up to noon on 17 May, but the front line remained generally quiet thereafter (*IHT*, 18 May 2001, p. 5). President Trajkovski claimed that the cease fire was working, as ethnic Albanian civilians were leaving the villages/*Independent*, 18 May 2001, p. 14). On 18 May army artillery briefly broke the unofficial cease f by targeting insurgent positions near the border with Kosova, but their guns fell silent after six volleys, suggesting that the government was honouring a pledge to act with restraint (*IHT*, 19 May 2001, p. 2). There was further (sometimes heavy) fighting i northern Macedonia on 21 May and in the Tetovo area on 23 May. The defence ministry claimed that at least 1,000 civilians remained in besieged northern villages, even though hundreds had been evacuated by the Red Cross (*Independent*, 22 May 2001, p. 13). There were fears that insurgents retreating from the Presevo valley in Serbia might join forces with those in the ROM. KFOR therefore promised an amnesty to insurgents who handed themselves in, promising that they would thereupon be released (*Independent*, 23 May 2001, p. 15). On 23 May the Bulgarian government called for an international force to be sent to Macedonia to help defeat the insurgents (*Independent*, 24 May 2001, p. 20). Western intelligence sources estimated that the UCK had 2,000 members, but UCK commanders claimed to have 6,000 (*The Guardian*, 25 May 2001, p. 14).

In Prizren (in Kosova) on 23 May 2001 the US diplomat Robert Frowick, who was serving as the personal envoy of Mercea Geoana, the Romanian foreign minister and then chairman of OSCE, secretly brokered a deal between Ali Ahmeti, the political spokesperson of the UCK, and Arben Xhaferi and Imer Imeri, the leaders of the two ethnic Albanian parties, with the help of Veton Surroi, the editor of a lead- ing Kosova newspaper. The deal called for the insurgents to halt all fighting in exchange for amnesty guarantees and a right of veto over imminent political deci - sions on the rights and status of ethnic Albanians in the ROM (*IHT*, 26 May 2001, p. 2). The next day the USA, the EU, NATO and the ROM government denounced the agreement, even though a senior US diplomat had helped to negotiate it, declaring that the insurgents had no right to take part in such negotiations (*FT*, 25 May 2001, p. 10; *The Times*, 25 May 2001, p. 14). However, some Balkan specialists suspected Frowick was acting on behalf of the USA, which apparently considered that EU efforts to promote dialogue in Skopje were failing to make headway (*FT*, 26 May 2001, p. 8). Frowick's efforts culminated in a statement, signed by Ali Ahmeti, Arben Xhaferi and Imer Imeri, calling for the UCK to be integrated into civilian life and to be implicitly though not directly involved in the round-table negotiations. However, the EU urged the DPA and the PDP to distance themselves from the insurgents and repudiate the secret peace document, and it defended the ROM government's right to use force in suppressing the UCK, while urging restraint (*FT*, 28 May 2001, p. 6; *The Guardian*, 29 May 2001, p. 19). Despite the official condemnations and dis- avowals, this deal did pave the way for the actual settlement that was reached in August, so the pretended disgust and repudiations should be taken with a considerable pinch of salt!

Government forces captured the insurgent stronghold of Vaksince on 26 May and launched a heavy barrage against the village of Matejce the next day. There were reports of refugees being beaten by Macedonian forces (*Daily Telegraph*, 28 May 2001, p. 13). There were also reports that as many as sixty civilians had died in the recent fighting, but the police 'insisted that they were all rebels, some of them in civilia clothing' (*IHT*, 28 May 2001, p. 5).

A NATO and EU foreign ministers meeting in Budapest on 30 May urged the ROM government to use 'proportionate' force in response to violence and to introduce an amnesty for UCK insurgents. At the same time, the government was assured of support and was promised that no one expected it to negotiate with gunmen (*The Economist*, 2 June 2001, p. 45; *FT*, 31 May 2001, p. 10; *Independent*, 31 May 2001, p. 14).

On 31 May, in what appeared to be a major policy shift, Prime Minister Ljubco Georgievski announced that the ROM could rewrite its constitution to declare the ethnic Albanians to be a constituent nation and their language a second official lan guage, while President Trajkovski offered an amnesty to the UCK insurgents, provided they laid down their weapons. All except those who had organized the insurgency or killed Macedonian police or soldiers would qualify, and NATO would provide a safe corridor for their retreat into Kosova. In addition, the Macedonian Orthodox Church would lose its privileged place in the constitution. These concessions were offered under pressure from NATO and Javier Solana. After a meeting with President Trajkovski, Arben Xhaferi also announced that the plan involved demilitarizing the rebels and reintegrating them into society (*The Guardian*, 1 June 2001, p. 13; *IHT*, 1 June 2001, p. 5; *IHT*, 2 June 2001, p. 9).

On 3 June, however, ROM army helicopters pounded insurgent positions in the north and ground troops fought them on the ground, while Georgievski declared that the broad-based coalition government was 'barely functioning' and suggested the next day that early elections might be needed to end the political impasse and the continu ing insurgency (*IHT*, 4 June 2001, p. 7; *IHT*, 5 June 2001, p. 5). A gunman opened fire on the office of President Trajkovski on 6 June, and Macedonian Slavs and Albanians ceased to venture into each other's areas in Skopje (*Independent*, 7 June 2001, p. 12). Prime Minister Georgievski threatened to declare a state of war and assume emergency powers, and backtracked on his previous offer to change the constitution and give Albanians more rights, claiming that he had been speaking 'cynically' just to show the pressure the ROM was under from the international community and the 'blackmail' it faced from the ethnic Albanian parties (*IHT*, 7 June 2001, pp. 1, 4). 'The EU quickly intervened to urge Macedonia not to declare war' (*FT*, 7 June 2001, p. 9). The two main Macedonian Slav parties were vying for elec toral advantage ahead of early elections mooted for September 2001. Henceforth Georgievski reverted to the ultra-nationalism for which IMRO-DPMNU had been renowned before 1998 and began to criticize the SDUM for urging restraint (*The Guardian*, 7 June 2001, p. 12).

Macedonian Slavs staged another pogrom in Bitola on the night of 6–7 June, smashing and burning dozens of houses and shops belonging to ethnic Albanians. The police said about 100 houses were damaged and a mosque was set on fire. Bitola had a mixed population of Macedonian Slavic Christians, Slavic Muslims and ethnic Albanians. The Albanians, at about 3 per cent, were Bitola's smallest group (*IHT*, 8 June 2001, p. 4). The next day the Human Rights Watch organization accused the Macedonian police of having taken part in the pogrom, which it said was clearly intended to force Albanians to flee from Bitola, as they had done after the pogro there in April (*Independent*, 8 June 2001, p. 17).

The Macedonian government redoubled its offensive against ethnic Albanian insurgents on 8 June, ignoring their offer of a cease fire. UCK fighters appeared uniform in an outlying suburb of Skopje. Prime Minister Georgievski withdrew his call for a declaration of war, but continued his belligerent ranting. Meanwhile, President Trajkovski announced that he was preparing a peace plan to present to parlia-ment that would offer a partial amnesty to rebel fighters to persuade them to withdra and end the conflict *IHT*, 9 June 2001, p. 2).

The UCK took control of Aracinovo, only 10 kilometres east of Skopje, on 8–9 June. A UCK commander threatened to use 120-millimetre artillery pieces to blast Skopje and its airport and the ROM's largest petroleum refinery, unless the militar stopped their indiscriminate shelling of ethnic Albanian villages in which the insurgents were based (*IHT*, 11 June 2001, p. 2). By 10 June, 29,000 people had crossed the border from the ROM into Kosova since February 2001 (*FT*, 11 June 2001, p. 9).

The ROM government and the UCK both declared brief cease fires on 11 June t alleviate two 'humanitarian disasters': water shortages in the city of Kumanovo and food shortages in the villages affected by f ghting (*IHT*, 12 June 2001, p. 5).

On 12 June leaders of the ROM's four main political parties agreed to start nego-tiating at a lakeside retreat in Ohrid to try to agree on political changes (*FT*, 13 June 2001, p. 9). The next day a plan emerged for a joint statement by the political leaders on the substance and timetable for changes meant to elevate the status of the ethnic Albanian minority. Under consideration was a proposed amendment to the ROM constitution that would grant equal status to the ethnic Albanians and the majority Slavs. 'Officials also said the plan could include a series of new government commit ments to rebuild towns destroyed by fighting, construct new schools and permit expanded international monitoring of the Macedonian police and army.' The plan was similar to the one signed in Prizren (the main city of Kosova) in May by Ali Ahmeti, drafted by Robert Frowick and the editor of a leading Kosova newspaper, Veton Surroi, in consultation with the leaders of the ROM's ethnic Albanian political parties. It called for

> a ceasefire followed by a month-long period of rebel disarmament, plus a government-approved amnesty for former fighters. The arms were to be hande over to local politicians and international off cials, who would in turn pass them to the government. Police and army forces would re-establish control of rebel-held territory under international supervision.
>
> (*IHT*, 14 June 2001, p. 4)

The ROM government on 14 June offcially asked NATO to help disarm the UCK, while pledging to discuss Albanian demands to change the country's constitution, but dismissed as 'absolutely unacceptable' UCK demands for a general amnesty, a place in reform talks and the chance to join the army and police. President Trajkovski asked for NATO troops to oversee the disarmament of the UCK (*IHT*, 15 June 2001, p. 5).

On 15 June the UCK extended a twelve-day truce with ROM government forces until 27 June 'to create conditions for dialogue'. Georgievski expressed support for the peace plan. However, as his political support weakened, he had adopted an increasingly strident tone and was suspected of having backed the formation of Slav Macedonian paramilitary groups and the arming of Slav Macedonian reservists (*FT*, 16 June 2001, p. 9; *IHT*, 16 June 2001, p. 2). The next day the EU agreed to appoint a special envoy to the ROM to oversee implementation of political reforms (*FT*, 18 June 2001, p. 6).

NATO states announced on 20 June that they were prepared to send up to 3,000 troops to the ROM for a limited time to help disarm the UCK once a peace agreement was reached to ensure a cessation of hostilities. The disarmament force would be a 'coalition of the willing', in response to calls for assistance by the Macedonian government. It would not require a UN Security Council mandate. President Trajkovski announced that peace talks between Slav and ethnic Albanian representatives had reached an impasse because the ethnic Albanians were 'practically asking for a two-nation state . . . They have no sincere intention of conducting a dialogue and finding effective and acceptable political solutions.' He accused them of holding out 'in the expectation that the international community will intervene and support their unrealistic political demands' (*IHT*, 21 June 2001, pp. 1, 6).

A government official asserted on 21 June that the main stumbling block was Arben Xhaferi's insistence on a federal structure for the ROM (*IHT*, 22 June 2001, p. 5), while Bulgaria confirmed that 'its army special operations units were conductin an exercise near the Macedonian border' (*The Guardian*, 22 June 2001, p. 14). NATO sources stated that the ethnic Albanians 'appeared to be hoping that an intervention force would be sent to police a division of the country' and were demanding 'the right to veto all laws' (*The Times*, 22 June 2001, p. 17; *Independent*, 23 June 2001, p. 15).

ROM government forces launched a heavy offensive against UCK positions just north of Skopje on 22 June. The renewed f ghting caused another surge of refugees into Kosova, bringing the total there to more than 50,000 (*IHT*, 23 June 2001, pp. 1, 4).

Javier Solana announced on 24 June that the two sides had agreed to a limited cease f re. The next day UCK insurgents pulled out of Aracinovo under a NATO-brokered deal. The alliance then sent at least four trucks to the village to take out weapons belonging to the rebels. Aracinovo became a demilitarized zone. The EU appointed the French former defence minister François Leotard as its envoy to Macedonia and warned the government not to count on new fiancial aid unless it settled its differences with its ethnic Albanian opponents (*IHT*, 26 June 2001, p. 7).

At least 3,000 Slav Macedonian protestors, some throwing stones, gathered in front of President Trajkovski's residence in Skopje to demand his resignation on 25 June. 'The crowd included armed police reservists and soldiers' (*The Times*, 27 June 2001, p. 14; *The Times*, 30 June 2001, p. 16). Over 5,000 Slav Macedonians then marched through Skopje, protesting against Western involvement in the conflict, firing guns in the air, occupying the parliament building for several hours, an burning EU and OSCE f ags and pictures of Javier Solana (*IHT*, 27 June 2001, p. 5; *IHT*, 28 June 2001, p. 8). 'The police . . . did not intervene to stop the storming of Parliament' (*Independent*, 28 June 2001, p. 3). Later that week Slav Macedonian paramilitary groups known as the Lions began to daub menacing graffiti on walls in Skopje and ethnic Albanian businessmen received death threats. 'Civilians with criminal links started to appear with guns from the government's arsenal' (*The Economist*, 30 June 2001, p. 44).

Over 100,000 people had been displaced by the conflict by 26 June *FT*, 27 June 2001, p. 10). In addition, numerous arrests and police beatings of ethnic Albanians had been reported since ethnic Albanians began their insurgency. Sporadic fightin continued in several regions on 2–3 July and by then an estimated 105,000 people had been displaced, including more than 65,000 who had fled to Kosova *IHT*, 4 July 2001, p. 4).

President George W. Bush signed an executive order on 27 June barring Americans from any transactions involving the property of any known ethnic Albanian insurgents

and restricted their entry into the USA (*HT*, 28 June 2001, p. 4). The next day President
Trajkovski and other ROM officials appealed to EU leaders to follow President
Bush's lead.

On 5 July the ROM government announced an open-ended cease fire with ethni
Albanian insurgents, to pave the way for a peace deal and the deployment of a 3,000-
strong NATO peacekeeping force. Cease-fire agreements were signed forthwith by Pande Petrevski, the ROM's chief of general staff, and Ali Ahmeti for
the UCK (*Independent*, 6 July 2001, p. 11). The deal consisted of two linked agreements, one between the UCK and NATO, the other between the ROM authorities
and NATO. The UCK signalled that it would be prepared to disarm, but only after a
political-constitutional settlement (*The Guardian*, 6 July 2001, p. 11). The agreement
signed between the UCK and NATO indicated that NATO had decided 'to negotiate
directly' with the UCK, 'previously branded "terrorists" by both NATO and the EU'
(*FT*, 6 July 2001, p. 6).

Chris Patten, the external relations commissioner, pledged on 10 July that the
ROM would obtain additional aid worth more than 50 million euros from the EU
if it implemented a settlement between its Slav and ethnic Albanian citizens, on top
of the 42 million euros that had already been earmarked for the ROM in 2001 (*The
Guardian*, 11 July 2001, p. 14; *Independent*, 11 July 2001, p. 11).

From 11 July, the UCK established roadblocks in and around Tetovo, in effect
taking control of many suburbs and surrounding villages, while accusing the government of sending armed civilians and Serbian, Ukrainian and Bulgarian mercenaries
to hunt them down. NATO warned the insurgents that any attack either on Skopje or
on its airport could be taken as an attack on itself. The Slav Macedonian camp was
deeply split. The hawks led by prime minister Ljubco Georgievski and interior minister
Ljube Boskovski controlled the militarized police force. The doves led by President
Trajkovski believed that these hardliners had instigated the violent protests in Skopje
on 25 June. The hawks were also believed to be backing paramilitary organizations
who were preparing to attack ethnic Albanian civilians (*he Economist*, 14 July 2001,
p. 44). Georgievski declared on 18 July that the draft proposals put forward by the
USA and the EU were a 'blatant violation of Macedonia's internal affairs' and would
mean 'carving up the country'. He accused the West of siding with the Albanian
insurgents and giving them logistical support. 'What we have on the table is a document
tailored to break up Macedonia' (*IHT*, 19 July 2001, p. 5).

With the help of François Leotard and an American mediator, James Pardew,
tentative agreement was reached on 19 July for talks to begin at expert level the next
day (*IHT*, 20 July 2001, p. 5). The negotiations envisaged that, at the local level,
a minority language could be used officially if 20 per cent or more of the population
spoke it (*FT*, 20 July 2001, p. 8). However, having made major progress on constitutional changes, increased representation for Albanians in the public services
and more power for local authorities, negotiations 'stalled on a single issue: recognition of Albanian as a second official language'. Many Slav Macedonians believed
that language was 'a stalking horse for their country's disintegration'. They claimed
it would 'create a new constitutional order in which the state would eventually
be federalized under the guise of Western-imposed multiethnicity'. They pointed to
a history of ethnic Albanian ambivalence towards the ROM, including demands for
'territorial autonomy' and, more recently, 'internal self-determination'. Bilingualism
would 'breed, not bury, separatism', they argued. For ethnic Albanians, however,
that fear missed the point. They argued that Slav Macedonians had to make signifant

concessions on the hegemonic position of the Macedonian language in order to make possible a new civil equality. There were several minorities with vested interests in such an outcome. This was not just a country of Slav Macedonians and ethnic Albanians. Roma, Turks, Vlachs, Serbs and others together made up 10 per cent of the population. The Slavic Macedonian language would remain the lingua franca of this ethno-culturally diverse state, but ethnic Albanian negotiators wanted Albanian to be usable in parliament and government institutions when requested and to become a second official language in areas where ethnic Albanians constituted over 20 pe cent of the population, as well as increased Albanian representation in the republic's police force (*IHT*, 21 July 2001, p. 4; *FT*, 27 July 2001, p. 7).

On 24 July the ROM government accused the NATO countries of directing the UCK with the goal of turning the ROM into an international protectorate, while in Skopje crowds of people who claimed that insurgents had forced them out of their homes and villages on 23 July staged angry protests outside the parliament (*IHT*, 25 July 2001, p. 4). These refugees were joined by Slav Macedonian residents of Skopje 'in an anti-Western rampage, stoning the US, British and German embassies, trashing a McDonald's and a British Airways office, and setting cars ablaze' *IHT*, 26 July 2001, p. 8). The UCK strengthened its grip on Tetovo and its environs on 25 July, while Macedonian Slav demonstrators again attacked the British, German and American embassies and set fire to vehicles belonging to UN and EU agencie (*Daily Telegraph*, 26 July 2001, p. 18). Georgievski sent a letter to President Boris Trajkovski urging him to order an all-out military strike to drive the insurgents back (*IHT*, 26 July 2001, p. 1). The same day, the USA obtained a commitment from Ukraine to stop supplying arms to the ROM (*Independent*, 26 July 2001, p. 12).

NATO persuaded ROM government and UCK forces to reinstate a cease f re on 25 July. In return, the UCK agreed to withdraw from territory it had occupied since the truce on 6 July and to allow displaced villagers to return to their homes. For its part, the government said its forces would exercise restraint around Tetovo (*FT*, 26 July 2001, p. 6). Nevertheless, thousands of people fled from Tetovo after the government warned the UCK to withdraw from the city or face a full-scale offensive, and at least eleven ethnic Albanian civilians were killed (*Independent*, 26 July 2001, p. 12). Ethnic Albanian forces began to withdraw from their positions as George Robertson and Javier Solana arrived on yet another crisis mission to the ROM *Daily Telegraph*, 27 July 2001, p. 19). The interior ministry announced that it was charging eleven ethnic Albanians with war crimes, including the UCK's political leader Ali Ahmeti, who had signed the new cease fire *IHT*, 27 July 2001, p. 1).

The Ohrid negotiations, 28 July to 13 August 2001

Western diplomats shuttled between the main political leaders on 27 July, laying the groundwork for direct negotiations to start in relative tranquillity beside Lake Ohrid the next day. The talks were to have been resumed in Tetovo, but the atmosphere there was too fraught (*IHT*, 28 July 2001, p. 2). The status of the Albanian language and ethnic Albanian demands that locally elected authorities be allowed to appoint and control local police forces remained major sticking points. The negotiators were still proposing that Albanian should become an official language wherever ethnic Albanians made up more than 20 per cent of the population (*FT*, 30 July 2001, p. 5). On 30 July the ROM prosecutor's office ordered the detention of eleven ethnic Albanians, including Ali Ahmeti (*IHT*, 31 July 2001, p. 4).

The UCK took advantage of the NATO-brokered cease fire to move into village around Tetovo under the very noses of Western observers and government forces, having already seized most of Tetovo itself. The UNHCR estimated that 30,000 refugees had by then been displaced inside the ROM, while more than 76,000 ethnic Albanians had fled to Kosova. An OSCE report documented 'kidnappings, dis-appearances and beatings of ethnic Slavs and of Albanians employed by official bodies'. Many Slavic Macedonians bitterly criticized NATO for not having adequately disarmed members of the KLA after the war with Serbia, thereby allowing former KLA members to foment rebellion in the ROM (*FT*, 31 July 2001, p. 8). Although US 'failure' to police south-eastern Kosova and its border with the ROM more assiduously after the Kosova crisis of 1998–9 was widely seen as having allowed ethnic Albanian militants to mount their insurgency in the ROM, giving rise to a widely held impression that the USA secretly favoured the ethnic Albanians against the Slav Macedonians, in reality the US army had been 'merely afraid to expose its soldiers to danger' (*IHT*, 25 August 2001, p. 4).

At this time, Ljube Boskovski, the hardline Slav Macedonian interior minister, was distributing thousands of arms to Slav Macedonian 'self-defence units'. Some members of the ROM government may even have had a political interest in prolonging the crisis. Vladimir Milcin, head of the liberal George Soros-funded Open Society Institute in Skopje, accused Prime Minister Georgievski of 'using Slav nationalism to def ect public opinion from a series of financial scandals' which were damaging his party*FT*, 31 July 2001, p. 8).

Michael Gordon reported that on paper the ROM army numbered 16,000, with several thousand paramilitary police, but military experts reckoned that the two forces had fewer than 2,500 well-trained fighters between them – insufficient to fight effectively on the two fronts simultaneously. These forces were weak because, after the ROM declared independence in 1991, the federal authorities based in Belgrade had removed all their troops and weapons from the republic, which now had to build up a new military force from scratch. It had undertaken 'a small buying spree in Ukraine, acquiring a small f eet of MI-24 helicopter gunships, MI-8 helicopters equipped with rocket launchers, Sukhoi 25 attack planes and BM-21 truck-mounted rocket launchers' (*IHT*, 7 July 2001, p. 5).

The ROM government closed the border with Kosova on 1 August, temporarily halting NATO supply convoys to KFOR, but the restriction was lifted within hours. KFOR depended on supplies transported overland from the Greek port of Thessaloniki. Since mid-1999 there had been about 4,000 NATO troops (KFOR Rear) based in the ROM, in addition to the intelligence and training personnel stationed there since 1994, when NATO signed a PfP with the ROM. KFOR Rear provided essential military, transport, food supplies and logistics backup for the 40,000 KFOR troops in Kosova (*FT*, 7 August 2001, p. 6).

Western mediators declared a breakthrough on 1 August: 'Albanian would now be accepted as an official language in areas where 20 per cent of the population is ethnic Albanian' and it would 'also be acceptable in parliament' (*IHT*, 2 August 2001, p. 5). On the next day (Macedonia's 'national day'), speaking at the monastery in southern Serbia at which Vardar Macedonia had agreed on 2 August 1944 to become a constituent republic in a Communist-ruled SFRY, Prime Minister Georgievski voiced the hope that these negotiations would end with a plan to avert a new Balkan war, but warned that signing that document while our territories are occupied by terrorists would be a shameful agreement . . . We must take back our occupied territories because we cannot close our eyes to the fact that we are talking under the threats of guns . . . All the Albanian extremists in Kosova, southern Serbia, Macedonia and Montenegro have only one goal, the creation of a Greater Albania... Unfortunately today we have a strong and decisive people but indecisive leadership.

(*IHT*, 3 August 2001, p. 4)

Another breakthrough was reached on 5 August, with an agreement on changes in the police force. The numbers of ethnic Albanians in the police force were in the future to reflect the country's ethnic mix (ethnic Albanians then made up only 5 pe cent of the 6,000 police). In return, the Skopje government would retain overall control of the police services. The plan also envisaged the deployment of dozens of international police experts to help carry out the reform. The Slav Macedonian leaders also agreed to the prescription of a minimum of minority votes needed to pass laws in parliament and to the earmarking of public funds for Albanian-language higher education (*IHT*, 7 August 2001, p. 4). This compromise, brokered by Javier Solana, meant that 500 new ethnic Albanian police off cers would be appointed in the ROM and trained by Western police, with another 500 to be appointed in the future (*Independent*, 7 August 2001, p. 9).

On 6 August talks stalled on the difficult issues of disarming the UCK (especiall the timing) and providing an amnesty for these insurgents (*IHT*, 7 August 2001, p. 4). The deadlock was broken the next day, when the Macedonian Slav leaders dropped demands for a quick disarming of the insurgents (*IHT*, 8 August 2001, p. 5). The emerging deal gave ethnic Albanians greater rights in return for the complete dis - armament of the UCK and required the republic's parliament to ratify the terms of the deal within forty-five days of its signing. However, a breakaway group, the Albanian National Army (Armata Kombetare Shquiptare or the AKSh), condemned the agreement and vowed 'to fight on' *IHT*, 13 August 2001, p. 1).

The ROM's leading politicians initialled the Ohrid framework agreement on 8 August. The political and military components of the agreement were skilfully synchronized: parliament had to pass the laws needed to enshrine the offers of greater rights to the Albanians to the same timetable that the insurgents handed over their weapons (*The Guardian*, 11 August 2001, p. 18). The formal signing was scheduled for 13 August. On the evening of 8 August 'a small group of protesters marched on the US embassy in Skopje to express unhappiness at US pressure to reach a settlement. Several hundred people gathered outside the parliament and demonstrators also blocked the main roads.' The government imposed a curfew on Prilep to head off possible unrest there, but conflict reignited in Tetovo *IHT*, 9 August 2001, pp. 1, 5; *FT*, 9 August 2001, p. 5). Albanian insurgents fought government forces for control of Tetovo on 9 August. By the next day, the scale of the f ghting throughout north-western Macedonia and north of Skopje was threatening the planned signing of the framework agreement (*FT*, 11 August 2001, p. 8). At least seven Macedonian Slav soldiers were killed by landmines on 10 August. The AKSh claimed that it had carried out the attack to avenge the deaths of five ethnic Albanians in Skopje on 8 Augus (*The Times*, 11 August 2001, p. 11). However, after the heaviest fighting seen thu far (spreading to within 5 kilometres of the outskirts of Skopje), on 12 August the ROM government called a unilateral cease fire *FT*, 13 August 2001, p. 6).

The signing of the Ohrid framework agreement, 13 August 2001

The Ohrid framework agreement, signed by the republic's political leaders in Skopje at a low-key ceremony attended by George Robertson and Javier Solana, included the following elements:

1. Amendments to the preamble of the constitution to delete reference to (Slavic) Macedonians as the only 'constitutional' people and to make the ROM a 'civic society', comprising and belonging to all its citizens.
2. Introduction of a 'double majority' system in parliament, requiring that half of the lawmakers voting on a measure must come from at least one minority group for it to be enacted.
3. Making Albanian the second official language in communities where ethnic Albanians made up more than 20 per cent of the population.
4. Provision of state-funded higher education in the Albanian language wherever ethnic Albanians comprised more than more than 20 per cent of the population. (Previously the state had funded only lower education in Albanian in such communities.)
5. Proportional representation of ethnic Albanians in the constitutional court and of Albanians and other minorities in government administration and the police.
6. Ethnic Albanians to select police commanders in communities where ethnic Albanians constituted a local majority.
7. Stronger and wider powers to be given to locally elected authorities (munici - palities).
8. Provision for a census in late 2001 to ascertain the ethnic composition of the population.
9. Equal status to be given to the Orthodox, Muslim and Catholic faiths.
10. An amnesty to be granted to militants who had not committed indictable crimes during clashes with government forces.

The ROM parliament was allowed forty-five days to approve the reforms after th president presented them to parliament on 16 August. 'Operation Essential Harvest', to collect weapons voluntarily surrendered by the ethnic Albanian rebels, was scheduled to last a maximum of thirty days and was to involve around 3,500 British-led NATO personnel. The EU and NATO had proposed that all insurgents were to be free from the prospect of prosecution unless they were indicted by the ICTY, but the ROM government considered this too lenient and wanted a start on disarmament before any amnesty (*Independent*, 14 August 2001, p. 9). The EU Commission promised to approve a 30 million-euro package to support the agreed reforms and to convene a donors' meeting in conjunction with the World Bank to drum up further aid for the ROM, provided the agreement was ratified and implemented. The 30 millio euro would be drawn from a 5.5 billion-euro fund for the Balkans for 2000–6 and would be on top of the 42 million euros already earmarked for the country in 2001 (*FT*, 15 August 2001, p. 5).

Despite the signing of the Ohrid framework agreement, heavy fighting continue in the north (*IHT*, 14 August 2001, p. 1), and at least nineteen government soldiers and as many insurgents had died in fighting since the accords were initialled on 8 August. Most of Tetovo remained under UCK control (*Daily Telegraph*, 14 August 2001, p. 13).

On 14 August the UCK leader Ali Ahmeti signed an agreement to turn over weapons to NATO soldiers, after receiving assurances of an amnesty and of political reforms. 'President Trajkovski was offering an assurance that rebels would not be prosecuted . . . Only those liable for prosecution at the UN war crimes tribunal would be excluded from the amnesty', but to become binding, any amnesty would have to be approved by the ROM parliament (*IHT*, 16 August 2001, p. 1). NATO officials announced tha the ROM government had promised, in a status-of-forces agreement defining NATO' mission in Macedonia, to 'strictly abide by international human rights standards' and, after the NATO arms-collectors left, to accept OSCE and EU monitoring (*The Guardian*, 18 August 2001, p. 2).

By 20 August, the US government was financing 'an intense political advertisin and lobbying campaign . . . to secure parliamentary passage of a peace deal . . . regarded with deep skepticism by Macedonian political parties and the Macedonian public', but whose ratification would require a two-thirds majority in parliament t amend the constitution (*IHT*, 17 August 2001, pp. 1, 6). In protest, from 19 August angry members of the Macedonian Slav majority blocked the main KFOR supply route into Kosova (*IHT*, 20 August 2001, p. 1).

Since mid-August there had been f erce debate over how many weapons should be collected from the UCK insurgents under the disarmament drive. The ROM armed forces proposed the collection of 8,000 guns, but the UCK volunteered to give up 2,500 (*The Guardian*, 22 August 2001, p. 10). NATO envisaged collecting roughly as many weapons as there were UCK insurgents, but there was widespread scepticism regarding the proportion of weapons that would actually be handed over (*The Times*, 22 August 2001, p. 11). On 18 August *The Economist* estimated that at least 200 people had been killed and 100,000 displaced by fighting in the ROM since February 2001 (*The Economist*, 18 August 2001, p. 11).

On 21 August NATO foreign and defence ministers decided to send a full 3,500-soldier taskforce into Macedonia. Major-General Joseph Ralston, the commander of NATO forces in Europe, told the NATO Council that the cease fire was 'generall holding, with incidents declining both in intensity and numbers' and emphasized that the danger of waiting, and perhaps seeing the cease fre unravel, 'was greater than the danger to NATO troops of going in immediately' (*IHT*, 22 August 2001, p. 4).

On the same day, an explosion badly damaged a church within the fourteenth-century Orthodox monastery of St Atanasie and the Holy Virgin in the village of Lesok in the north-west, one of the most revered Orthodox Christian buildings in the ROM. However, this was 'one of the few attacks on religious buildings' during the six months of fighting. In early August a mosque in Prilep had been set on re by Macedonian protestors, and several mosques in rebel-held villages north of Kumanovo had been badly damaged by months of shelling by government forces, but neither the Macedonian Slavs, who were predominantly Orthodox Christians, nor the ethnic Albanians, who were predominantly Muslim, had 'made religion an overt part of the conflict' *IHT*, 22 August 2001, p. 4; *The Guardian*, 22 August 2001, p. 10).

On 22 August the ROM government claimed that the insurgents possessed 85,000 weapons, vastly more than the UCK had agreed to hand over to the NATO disarmament taskforce (*IHT*, 23 August 2001, p. 1). Major-General Gunnar Lange, the Danish commander of the NATO taskforce, admitted that he had received 'intelligence reports that new shipments of weapons were already on their way to the rebels from Kosova' (*Independent*, 23 August 2001, p. 12). Nevertheless, 'NATO off cials conceded that they did not expect the guerrillas to hand over all their weapons' (*The Guardian*, 23 August 2001, p. 11).

NATO announced on 24 August that a deal had been reached with the insurgents to surrender 3,300 weapons, and that it hoped to start collecting weapons on 27 August. NATO officials played down the significance of the precise figure, 'arguing that point of the mission is to build trust – to persuade the ethnic Albanian and Macedonian sides to use the arms handover as their first mutual confidence-building measure' (*IHT*, 25 August 2001, p. 2). Indeed, the important point was 'not the numbers' but the fact that the UCK was 'giving up a significant capability' *The Times*, 25 August 2001, p. 16). On 26 August Prime Minister Georgievski called the agreed figure 'humiliating' and alleged that the true figure for weapons in UCK possession was closer to 60,000, but Major-General Gunnar Lange emphasized that the figure of 3,300 weapons which the insurgents had agreed to surrender was 'very close' to NATO's own estimates of the number held and that, in addition, the rebels planned to hand over 110,000 rounds of ammunition *IHT*, 27 August 2001, pp. 1, 6;*The Times*, 27 August 2001, p. 9).

The f rst stage of the three-stage disarmament process, the collection of one-third of the 3,300 weapons to be surrendered by UCK insurgents, was conducted suc - cessfully between 27 and 30 August (*IHT*, 31 August 2001, p. 6). In three days 1,470 weapons were collected (*Daily Telegraph*, 1 September 2001, p. 20). Among Macedonian Slavs, however, NATO was 'consistently demonized as an ally of the rebels' (*IHT*, 28 August 2001, p. 4), and the population became 'deeply suspicious of the United States, the EU and NATO' (*IHT*, 31 August 2001, p. 5). Many Slavic Macedonians saw the framework agreement as a sell-out and resented the deploy- ment of 3,500 NATO soldiers to implement it. 'Among the most resentful' were the 67,000 Slavic Macedonians who, according to the government estimates, had fle their homes (*FT*, 28 August 2001, pp. 1–2). An*FT* editorial reported: 'Sections of the Slav population and the Macedonian government feel betrayed. They abandoned their traditional allegiance to the Serbs during the 1999 Kosova conflict and backe NATO. They expected a reward. Instead, they were pressed to sign a peace deal that they regard as tilted toward the ethnic Albanians' (*FT*, 29 August 2001, p. 14).

On 31 August, while appealing to the ROM parliament to support the Ohrid framework agreement and to adopt reforms promoting and protecting minority rights, President Trajkovski requested the return of the UN peacekeeping force stationed in the country during the 1990s and called for international recognition of 'Republic of Macedonia' as the country's name (*IHT*, 1 September 2001, p. 2). By 2 September violence had 'virtually stopped' (*FT*, 3 September 2001, p. 10). By then there were f fty OSCE peace monitors in the ROM (*The Times*, 3 September 2001, p. 13). The OSCE was preparing to send 150 and the EU had promised thirty (*IHT*, 6 September 2001, p. 4).

The ROM parliament voted, by a margin of ninety-one to nineteen (well above the requisite two-thirds majority), to start drafting amendments to the constitution grant- ing greater rights to the ethnic Albanian minority on 6 September 2001. This vote, following nearly a week of heated and acrimonious debate, merely began the legislative process. Detailed clause-by-clause discussion would ensue until the final vote, whic would again require a two-thirds majority. In parliament many deputies made lengthy speeches highly critical of the government and of the Western-mediated plan, while 'Macedonia's security council rejected a proposal to allow any international military force to take over after NATO's thirty-day operation'. Nevertheless, this vote suffed to trigger a second round of disarmament of the insurgents, involving the collection of a further one-third of the agreed weapons total (*IHT*, 7 September 2001, p. 7; *IHT*, 8 September 2001, p. 5; *FT*, 7 September 2001, p. 9). This proceeded successfully from 7 to 13 September.

An informal meeting of EU foreign ministers on 9 September decided to back the deployment of another NATO-led force to protect up to 200 peace monitors in the ROM after operation 'Essential Harvest' ended. There was disagreement over whether such a force should be backed by a UN mandate and uncertainty over whether the ROM government would accept another NATO mission without UN consent. Within the EU, only Britain dismissed the need for a UN mandate – a view it shared with the USA. Most EU members believed that a UN mandate would confer international legitimacy on the operation and allow non-NATO countries to participate in a mission whose scope and duration had yet to be decided. This willingness to support the installation of another NATO-led force in the ROM reflected the vie within the EU that the ROM was still unstable and that any 'security vacuum' (the term used by EU foreign ministers) could be exploited by either side, rendering the peace monitors more vulnerable to attack. Support for a NATO-led force also put paid to a proposal by the French EU special envoy François Leotard that the EU could lead a force to protect the monitors who would assist the return of refugees to villages where control was contested. It was confirmed on 9 September that Leotard had hande in his resignation with effect from 8 October, but EU officials insisted that this resignation 'had nothing to do with the proposal' (*FT*, 10 September 2001, p. 1). 'EU diplomats said they feared that the Slav-dominated government would crack down on rebels . . . once the disarmament mission has finished' (*The Guardian*, 10 September 2001, p. 10). On 10 September a ROM government spokesman stated: 'We have nothing against NATO forces being part of an international force with a UN mandate with a mission to protect the ROM's borders with Kosova and Albania' (*IHT*, 11 September 2001, p. 7).

By 10 September over 36,000 ethnic Albanian refugees had returned from Kosova to the ROM, while another 45,000 remained in Kosova, but 'virtually none of the 30,000 or so' (Slavic) Macedonian refugees had returned to their homes (*FT*, 11 September 2001, p. 8).

NATO announced on 13 September that it had collected 2,135 (over two-thirds) of the 3,300 weapons to be surrendered by ethnic Albanian insurgents, despite the threat posed to disarmament by Slavic Macedonian paramilitaries. At the same time Slavic Macedonian opponents of the Ohrid framework agreement sought a refer endum on the proposed reforms, but the ROM parliament indefinitely put off debat on whether to hold such a referendum (*IHT*, 14 September 2001, p. 10; *The Times*, 14 September 2001, p. 11).

The Economist reported that the weapons collected by NATO included 'few serious items: ground-to-air missiles, rocket- and grenade-launchers, snipers' rifes. The rebels have buried many others, NATO suspects.' However, it also pointed out that Slavic Macedonian police reservists had not had to hand back 'the 10,000 or so Kalashnikovs' which interior minister Ljube Boskovski and his friends had distributed in spring 2001 and that the interior ministry's 'legitimate anti-terrorist police', known as the Tigers, were 'recruiting hard'. However, only 10 per cent of those attracted by its colourful advertising were being accepted, with the result that the rest were joining 'the Lions and other dubious groups', who in provincial towns were 'extorting money from businesses, buying off local police and other offcials, and chasing out of town those who might support President Boris Trajkovski and others trying to build peace' (*The Economist*, 15 September 2001, p. 42).

President Trajkovski stated on 14 September that any further installation of foreign troops in the republic would need a UN mandate and would be needed only to seal the border with Kosova. The Slav Macedonians who had been forming paramilitary units clearly wanted all foreign troops to leave, in order to 'have a free hand' to deal with the ethnic Albanian insurgents once they had been disarmed (*The Guardian*, 15 September 2001, p. 17).

Although the cease fire was holding, by 14 September about 22,000 Slavic Macedonians had fled from ethnically mixed towns and villages since the Ohrid framework agreement was signed, whereas almost 35,000 displaced ethnic Albanians had returned home, according to the UNHCR. This and the increasingly nationalistic tone of the local media was strengthening the widespread Slav Macedonian view that the accords were 'biased in favour of the Albanian minority' and were 'a step towards partition', as well as the pressure on MPs to submit the accords to a referendum. Leaders of the two main Slav Macedonian parties supported the accords but were allowing their MPs a free vote. NATO admitted that about a third of the Kalashnikov rif es it had collected were unserviceable (*The Guardian*, 15 September 2001, p. 17).

The ROM government stated on 17 September that it would accept a small NATO security force after the weapons collection was completed and would ask the OSCE to increase its monitoring presence. Branko Crvenkovski, the leader of the pro-Western SDUM, warned that his party could pull out of the fragile coalition government if parliament voted for a referendum on the Ohrid framework agreement (*IHT*, 18 September 2001, p. 9). The next day NATO sources warned that 'A delay of some months to organize and carry out a referendum seems to us to be a very serious danger for the political stability we are trying to reach.' The UCK leader Ali Ahmeti gained considerable Western respect by giving assurances that the UCK insurgents would 'continue to surrender their weapons even if the ROM government stalled on implementing political concessions' (*Daily Telegraph*, 19 September 2001, p. 12).

On 19 September the ROM parliament put off the start of crucial constitutional amendments to secure peace with the ethnic Albanians in order to debate whether to submit the deal to a referendum. 'Deputies insisted that a vote on whether to hold a referendum should come first.' However, Javier Solana warned that 'two months woul be needed to organize a referendum and this would put us in a difficult situation' because the insurgents had already surrendered 'two-thirds of their declared arsenal to NATO troops' (*IHT*, 20 September 2001, p. 9). The parliament then decided to postpone its decision on a referendum until 26 September, whereupon NATO proceeded with the third and final phase of the weapons-collection process from 20 to 26 September.

On 24 September the ROM parliament approved in principle the fifteen con - stitutional amendments required by the Ohrid framework agreement, albeit sometimes by considerably less than the two-thirds margin that they would require for final ratification. Ethnic Albanian leaders warned that altering the reforms or submitting them to a referendum would renew the conflict, while NATO reported that by the the insurgents had turned in 92 per cent of their declared weapons stockpile, three days before the end of the mandated thirty-day disarmament period. The most controversial amendment replaced the reference to the 'national state of Macedonian people' in the preamble to the constitution with the words 'a state of its citizens'. Final ratif cation would clear the way for legislation to decentralize power and to recruit ethnic Albanians into the police force 'in proportion to their one-third presence in the population' (*IHT*, 25 September 2001, p. 9).

NATO announced the end of its weapons-collection mission on 26 September and agreed to provide a much smaller follow-on force, ostensibly to protect international peace monitors who would observe the implementation of the peace settlement. However, the 'real reason' was that the international community believed that 'a symbolic NATO presence alone will do much to prevent further fighting' (*Independent*, 27 September 2001, p. 16; *IHT*, 27 September 2001, p. 5). The NATO mission had gathered a total of 3,875 weapons and 397,625 items of ammunition, including mines and explosives (*Daily Telegraph*, 27 September 2001, p. 23).

Germany got ready on 27 September to take command of a NATO mission for the first time in its history, after the alliance ordered the deployment of 1,000 soldiers to protect 280 civilian peace monitors following the expiry of its thirty-day mandate to collect UCK weapons. Germany was to provide 600 of the 1,000-strong force, 450 of whom had already arrived (*IHT*, 28 September 2001, p. 4). The same day, Ali Ahmeti declared:

> The signal has been given to all former fighters that they should reintegrate as civilians of this country ... Last night at midnight the National Liberation Army was formally disbanded and all the former fighters have become ordinary citizen of this country once again ... We want all the displaced people to return to their homes, whatever their background ... For us it is of key importance to have an amnesty for our fighters, for them to reintegrate into society
>
> (*IHT*, 28 September 2001, p. 4)

By then over 55,000 of Macedonia's war refugees had returned home, but repatriating the rest would 'depend in part on setting up ethnically mixed police patrols', according to the UN high commissioner for refugees, Ruud Lubbers. About 97,000 people remained displaced (*IHT*, 29 September 2001, p. 7).

Western officials reacted angrily on 3 October when interior minister Ljube Boskovski announced moves to retake control of rebel-held areas on 4 October, 'ignoring calls to wait until a Western-brokered peace deal was implemented and a promised amnesty for the rebels agreed'. In addition, the Slav-dominated parliament halted the ratification and implementation of the needed constitutional amendments following the success of the NATO weapons-collecting mission and the withdrawal of most of its troops and refused to resume the process until the UCK accounted for several missing Macedonian Slavs (*Independent*, 4 October 2001, p. 16).

Slav Macedonian police entered three Albanian villages on 4 October, but they backed off elsewhere 'after meeting resistance'. Western officials 'warned the government against moves that could reignite violence' and the EU commissioner for external affairs, Chris Patten, announced that a donors' conference scheduled for 15 October to consider increased financial aid to the ROM was 'absolutely inconceivable' until the conduct of the Macedonian Slavs improved (*IHT*, 5 October 2001, p. 4; *IHT*, 6 October 2001, p. 2). Patten accused the parliament of having broken its promise to complete the ratification process by the previous week *The Guardian*, 5 October 2001, p. 18). On 5 October Javier Solana and Chris Patten met ROM leaders in Skopje and insisted that they honour the Ohrid framework agreement. The police then announced that 'they would stop entering ethnic Albanian-populated villages and that any future restoration of government authority in the contested areas would be carried out in cooperation with NATO, the EU and OSCE' (*IHT*, 6 October 2001, p. 5). The same day the ICTY announced that it was sending the ROM government 'a list of alleged war crimes committed by the ROM army and police, accompanied by a request that it investigate the hardline interior minister, Ljube Boskovski'. The European Council of Humanity, Action and Cooperation (ECHAC) had gathered eyewitness accounts of alleged killings, kidnappings, torture and the systematic destruction of mosques by the police, the army and paramilitary groups, who had used the conflict with the UCK 'as an excuse to launch a systematic campaign to force ethnic Albanians out of the country'. In addition, ECHAC alleged that during May and June there had been deliberate shelling of civilian targets. ECHAC stated it would also produce a collection of eyewitness accounts of abuses and crimes committed by the UCK (*The Guardian*, 6 October 2001, p. 19).

President Trajkovski's office announced on 9 October that there would be no arrest of former UCK gunmen who had given up their weapons, unless they were charged with war crimes by the ICTY. Ethnic Albanian politicians declared that this assurance was insuff cient to ensure the former insurgents' safety. The government had listed a series of incidents for which former insurgents would still be prosecuted, including several ambushes of security forces and the bombing of a hotel. The PDP demanded that an amnesty be enshrined in a law passed by the parliament, and NATO official stressed that only the ICTY should have the right to prosecute former insurgents for war crimes (*The Guardian*, 10 October 2001, p. 10). On 11 October former UCK leaders reiterated demands for the proposed amnesty to be passed into law and for the release of all ethnic Albanians detainees (*IHT*, 13 October 2001, p. 5).

Ethnic Albanian deputies boycotted a key meeting of parliament on 9 October, in protest against Slav Macedonian attempts to revise some provisions of the Ohrid accords by retaining specif c references to the Macedonian Orthodox Church and the Slav Macedonian people in the revised constitution (*IHT*, 10 October 2001, p. 6).

On 16 October President Trajkovski condemned 'certain groups of deputies' for continuing to block the requisite constitutional amendments. It was unclear whether he was blaming the delays on hardline Macedonian Slav nationalist deputies who were bent on blocking or diluting the amendments, or on the ethnic Albanian deputies who were boycotting parliament. However, Trajkovski was partly responsible for the delay. The president was constitutionally required to review all legislation proposed prior to its submission to the legislature. Instead of presenting parliament with all f fteen amendments for enactment as a package, Trajkovski had forwarded only nine. This led ethnic Albanian deputies to boycott key parliamentary meetings (*IHT*, 17 October 2001, p. 6).

The UNHCR announced on 17 October that at least 60,000 people had yet to return to areas they had left when UCK insurgents took over. The government estimated that 44,000 people, almost two-thirds of them Slavs, were still displaced within the country, while the UNHCR estimated that almost 20,000 ethnic Albanians were still in Kosova and Serbia (*The Guardian*, 18 October 2001, p. 20). On 21 October President Trajkovski approved a plan for the deployment of ethnically mixed police units to areas which had been under UCK control, following talks with NATO and EU representatives (*IHT*, 22 October 2001, p. 5). The next day ROM police units cautiously started re-entering a few former UCK-controlled areas under international supervision. Twelve lightly armed policemen drove patrol cars into five villages, f anked by monitors and liaison experts from NATO, OSCE and the EU. The police units, comprising six Slav Macedonians and six ethnic Albanians, made token patrols, but only through primarily Slav-inhabited northern districts (*FT*, 23 October 2001, p. 12).

NATO, EU and OSCE envoys had to rescue Macedonia's fragile peace process yet again on 12 November, after three policemen were killed by ethnic Albanians in an ambush outside the village of Trebos in the north-west (the AKSh claimed responsibility for the deaths). The Western envoys blamed the hardline interior minister Ljube Boskovski for provoking the violence ahead of the crucial vote in parliament to ratify the framework agreement: (i) by disregarding previously agreed procedures before moving police into the site of an alleged mass grave, which the government claimed held the bodies of thirteen Slav Macedonians kidnapped by the UCK during the summer, and (ii) by authorizing the arrest of seven former insurgents, alleging they were in possession of weapons which were supposed to have been handed in. Police units were withdrawn from Trebos later that day, while the envoys also secured the release of thirty-nine Slav Macedonians held by ethnic Albanians (*FT*, 13 November 2001, p. 14).

Parliament f rst voted separately on each of the fifteen constitutional amendment required by the Ohrid framework agreement on 16 November, and then voted over - whelmingly in favour of amending the constitution as a whole to incorporate the changes. In the final version of the preamble, the four major parties agreed to defi the republic as comprising 'all citizens' of 'the Macedonian people, as well as citizens living within its borders who are part of the Albanian people', among others. President Trajkovski declared an amnesty for the former insurgents, soon after parliament ratifd the amendments. All former insurgents, including about 120 detainees and convicts, were to be covered by the amnesty, except those indicted by the ICTY (*IHT*, 17 November 2001, p. 3). The same day, the AKSh announced the start of a 'war for the liberation of all Albanian territories in former Yugoslavia'. However, it admitted to having only a few dozen members (*The Guardian*, 17 November 2001, p. 18).

The three SDUM ministers (for defence and foreign affairs and a deputy premier) withdrew from the unity government on 21 November. The party's leader Branko Crvenkovski stated that SDUM did not want to share the blame for 'a catastrophic economic policy, crime, corruption, political party feudalism. These things even escalated during the conflict . . . It is true that the international community has urged us to remain in the government. But we cannot act as babysitter for Georgievski and Boskovski and clean up their dirty work.' Crvenkovski had long warned that the SDUM would return to opposition once the Ohrid framework agreement was approved by parliament. The Liberal Democratic Party also withdrew its minister (for health) from the government (*The Guardian*, 22 November 2001, p. 18; *Independent*, 22 November 2001, p. 18).

The parliamentary leaders of the Macedonian Slavs and the ethnic Albanians agreed on 26 November to postpone the forthcoming parliamentary elections from 27 January 2002, the date specified in the Ohrid framework agreement, to April (*IHT*, 27 November 2001, p. 6). On 28 November President Trajkovski announced that he would give 'strong consideration' to a three-month extension of the NATO military mission, which was scheduled to end on 26 December (*IHT*, 29 November 2001, p. 8).

Parliament decided by eighty-five votes to four on 24 January 2002 to give electe local authorities a greater say on budgetary matters, pubic services, culture, education and health, in order to pave the way for the holding of an international donors' conference on 12 March (*IHT*, 25 January 2002, p. 5).

Despite the headway achieved, in early February the ROM remained 'divided by roadblocks, gunfire and deep mistrust. Many ethnic Albanian villages and neighbour hoods that violently broke away from government control .. . remain off-limits to the police. International negotiators painstakingly negotiate, hamlet by hamlet . . Progress is slow and the police have reentered only 30 per cent of 120 insurgent villages'*IHT*, 6 February 2002, p. 5). Parliament finally passed an amnesty law on 7 March 2002 President Trajkovski's amnesty had not been legally binding in the law courts (*IHT*, 9 March 2002, p. 5).

The one-day aid donors' conference held by the European Commission and the World Bank on 12 March 2002 to reward the ROM for having started to implement and follow the Ohrid framework agreement generated aid commitments totalling 515 million US dollars, over twice the amount anticipated (*FT*, 13 March 2002, p. 10).

Having tried unsuccessfully in early 2002 to persuade all parties to take part in a so-called 'coordination council' to monitor implementation of the Ohrid frame- work agreement, the former UCK leader Ali Ahmeti launched a new party called the Democratic Union for Integration (DUI) on 5 June 2002. He said it would be 'open to all ethnic groups' and dedicated to f ghting the organized crime which was 'corrupting politics on both sides of Macedonia's ethnic divide' (*Independent*, 6 June 2002 p. 13; *IHT*, 15 June 2002, p. 5). Several parliamentary members of the PDP and the DPA defected to the DUI, which also succeeded in galvanizing into activity many ethnic Albanians who had previously felt politically alienated or apathetic. The ethnic Albanian DPA, which had been tainted by its close association in government with the corrupt and wayward IMRO-DPMNU, rapidly lost members and support to the DUI. DUI supporters pointed out that, through six months of inter- communal violence, followed by cultivation of the EU and NATO, Ahmeti had accomplished more to promote ethnic Albanian rights and status than either the DPA or PDP had done during the previous ten years of subservient cooperation with Slav-dominated governments (Fraenkel 2003: 407, 409).

Parliament overwhelmingly approved nine new laws which made Albanian the republic's second off cial language on 19 June. The laws authorized the use of Albanian in all governmental business and the use of Albanian as well as Macedonian in the census to be held in November 2002 (*Independent*, 20 June 2002, p. 11; *FT*, 24 June 2002, p. 7).

The Georgievski government issued a warrant for the arrest of Ali Ahmeti for war crimes on 29 August. Ahmeti's DUI was expected to do well at the forthcoming parliamentary election, and the hardline nationalist interior minister Ljube Boskovski had repeatedly promised to have Ahmeti arrested (*The Guardian*, 14 September 2002, p. 15).

The election to the 120-seat parliament, 15 September 2002

The turn-out was 73.1 per cent (Fraenkel 2003: 410), the highest of the four elections since 1991. The OSCE fielded 900 election observers *The Guardian*, 16 September 2002, p. 14). The election appeared to be largely free of violence. 'Only a few iso- lated shooting incidents were reported during twelve hours of voting' (*IHT*, 16 September 2002, p. 5). Although the OSCE condemned a rash of pre-election kidnap- pings and killings, it called the election 'a major step towards stability, reconciliation and democracy' (*Independent*, 16 September 2003, p. 9). See Table 8.5 for the results of the election.

8.5 Macedonian parliamentary election, 15 September 2002

Party	Seats
The 'Together for Macedonia' Alliance	60
(SDUM, led by Branko Crvenkovski)	(43)
(Liberal Democratic Party, LDP)	(12)
(Others)	(5)
IMRO-DPMNU, led by Ljubco Georgievski	33
Democratic Union for Integration (DUI), led by Ali Ahmeti	16
Democratic Party of Albanians (DPA), led by Arben Xhaferi	7
Party for Democratic Prosperity (PDP, ethnic Albanian)	2
National Democratic Party (NDP, ethnic Albanian)	1
Socialist Party of Macedonia	1

Note: turn-out was 73 per cent.

Source: Fraenkel (2003: 410).

The SDUM and its allies (who together obtained 41 per cent of the votes) accused Ljubco Georgievski's IMRO-DPMNU (which obtained 23 per cent of the votes) of mismanaging the economy, indulging in widespread corruption and exacerbating the previous year's crisis (*FT*, 17 September 2002, p. 7). However, even though the IMRO-DPMNU lost the election, 'the influence of their supporters in Macedonia's still pervasive criminal underworld' remained 'powerful' (*The Economist*, 21 September 2002, p. 40). Ali Ahmeti's UDI, which championed inter-ethnic reconciliation, obtained 12 per cent of the vote (*IHT*, 17 September 2002, p. 3).

Despite winning half the seats in parliament, Branko Crvenkovski's 'Together for Macedonia' coalition was determined to share power with at least one of the ethnic Albanian parties. The nationalist and anti-Communist DPA preferred to have nothing to do with the ex-Communist SDUM and PDP, which in turn looked askance at the DPA's four-year association with the tawdry, nationalistic and inept IMRO-DPMNU (1998–2002). For its part, the PDP was a spent force. Therefore, even though most Slavic Macedonians had regarded Ali Ahmeti and his closest associates as 'terrorists' from February to September 2001, Crvenkovski invited the DUI to become his main partners in government. Crvenkovski justified this choice by saying: 'The alternativ is much worse: inter-ethnic confrontation' (Fraenkel 2003: 411).

The centre-left 'government of guns and roses' under Branko Crvenkovski, October 2002 to April 2004

The new government became known as the government of 'guns' (DUI) and 'roses' (emblem of the SDUM). The DUI was given four of the fourteen ministries: justice, transport, education and health. On 1 November 2002, seventy-two deputies voted in favour of the government and twenty-eight against (*IHT*, 2 November 2002, p. 5).

In early 2003 Ljubco Georgievski was pushed into relinquishing the leadership of IMRO-DPMNU, in response not only to the severe electoral trouncing that it experienced in September 2002, but also to the increasingly disreputable corruption generated by Georgievski's wayward, personalistic and clientelistic leadership. Nevertheless, even after he stood down, Georgievski continued to command considerable support in certain sections of the party which he had led for thirteen years. He had played a major role both in the grooming and in the f nal selection of his successor, IMRO-

DPMNU's former finance minister Nikola Gruevski. Georgievski apparently though he could control him from behind the scenes. However, Gruevski was a much more stable and measured politician who dispelled the whiff of corruption and transformed IMRO-DPMNU into a moderate centre-right conservative party, which employed the more technocratic, managerial and prosaic language of its Western counterparts.

In a landmark decision to initiate the EU's first-ever military operation, on 14 December 2002 a meeting of EU and NATO ministers and officials decided tha the EU would soon take over from NATO the military mission of protecting the peace monitors and helping to maintain peace in the ROM. At the same time, NATO launched a new mission in Macedonia, to assist the republic with military reforms (*FT*, 16 December 2002, p. 6). On 20 January 2003 President Trajkovski officiall asked the EU to take over the hitherto NATO-led peacekeeping operation in the ROM in March 2003 (*IHT*, 21 January 2003, p. 3). The EU-led force was to remain open to troops from other countries, such as Turkey (*IHT*, 28 January 2003, p. 3). On 17 March NATO formally agreed to hand over its peacekeeping role in the ROM to the EU. The EU had hoped to take over the ROM mission in late 2002, but the move was delayed by a dispute between Greece and Turkey over how to assure EU access to NATO intelligence, logistics, planning, and command and control systems (*IHT*, 18 March 2003, p. 1).

The 345-member European force formally took over from NATO on 31 March 2003. The force, which was under French command, included 200 soldiers who were to be deployed mostly near the Kosova border. The operation, christened 'Concordia', was scheduled to last six months in the first instance and was to be carried out in close cooperation with NATO, which retained a token presence in the ROM and promised 'to take over again if things get nasty' (*FT*, 2 April 2003, p. 10; *The Economist*, 5 April 2003, p. 48).

In June 2003 the ROM sent troops to take part in the US-led occupation of Iraq. No major political party in the ROM challenged this support for the USA during 2003 and 2004 (Stavrova and Alagjozovski 2004c). At the end of June 2003 the ROM government also agreed to refrain from extraditing any Americans wanted for trial by the newly established ICC. The USA had threatened to halt 10 million US dollars in military aid unless the ROM agreed that American citizens should be exempt from the ICC's jurisdiction (*Independent*, 1 July 2003, p. 9). Subsequently, several hundred citizens of the ROM took jobs in Iraq, working for the occupation authorities.

The ROM weathered a major security crisis on 7 September 2003, when members of the AKSh clashed with Macedonian security forces on the border with Kosova, leaving two ethnic Albanian gunmen and one civilian dead. These clashes followed two weeks of increased tension in the north-west, where hundreds of policemen had surrounded two villages near Kumanovo in order to arrest a former UCK commander accused of kidnapping offences. The operation was allegedly overseen by represen-tatives of the EU stabilization force and the OSCE (*The Guardian*, 8 September 2003, p. 15; *IHT*, 8 September 2003, p. 5).

The AKSh aspired to unite the ethnic Albanians living in Macedonia, Kosova, Serbia, Montenegro, Greece and Albania proper. In the long run it envisaged the creation of a Greater Albania encompassing all ethnic Albanians. In April 2003 Michael Steiner, the German diplomat in charge of the UN protectorate in Kosova, officially declared the group a terrorist organization, after it blew up a bridge in northern Kosova. It had occasionally attacked the Serbian army in southern Serbia, and it had claimed responsibility for blowing up a courthouse in the Macedonian town of Struga in February 2003, but it had stepped up its activity in August and early September 2003, killing several people along the ROM's border with Kosova. However, the AKSh appeared to have little popular support. Its core consisted of fifty to seventy cigarett smugglers drawn from both sides of the border with Kosova, and their increased violence appeared to be prompted largely by a desire to prevent the police from shutting down their smuggling routes and capturing them. Nevertheless, the ethnic Albanian deputy Hisni Shaqiri warned that the DUI would withdraw from the coalition government if the police or soldiers killed any ethnic Albanian civilians, while the DUI leader Ali Ahmeti complained that the SDUM had not consulted its ethnic Albanian coalition partners sufficiently over how to respond to the AKSh's attacks (*The Economist*, 13 September 2003, p. 43).

The EU military mission to the ROM withdrew at the end of its term on 15 December 2003, leaving behind a small police mission (*IHT*, 4 March 2004, p. 8).

President Trajkovski and several members of the government died in a plane crash in bad weather in mountainous southern Bosnia on 26 February 2004, en route to an international investment conference in Mostar. Trajkovski had won wide respect for his relatively neutral stance during the crisis of 2001 and for his efforts to integrate ethnic Albanians into the republic's body politic. At the time of the crash Prime Minister Branko Crvenkovski was in Dublin to formally submit the ROM's application for membership in the EU, but he and his delegation immediately rushed back to Skopje for emergency cabinet meetings and for President Trajkovski's funeral, which took place on 5 March. Numerous high-level foreign delegations attended, hundreds of thousands of mourners lined the funeral route, and the president of the EU, Romano Prodi, publicly urged the ROM to persevere with its application for EU membership, which (according to opinion polls) enjoyed 87 per cent support among adults (Stavrova 2004a). The speaker of the ROM parliament, Ljubko Jordanovski, took over as acting president.

The ROM finally submitted its application for membership of the EU on 22 Marc 2004. Reinforcing the impact of the SAA signed in April 2001, this important step gave added impetus to (and the prospect of even greater rewards for) the republic's programmes of political and economic reform and restructuring. EU membership was supported by about 87 per cent of the ROM's adult citizens (Stavrova 2004a).

The two-round presidential election of 14 and 28 April 2004

Foreign election monitors declared this to have been the most peaceful election campaign for several years. Prime Minister Branko Crvenkovski (SDUM) and Sasko Kedev (IMRO-DPMNU) were the main candidates. There were also two Albanian candidates. Ljube Boskovski, the hardline nationalist former interior minister, wanted to run, but failed the ROM's residency requirements. Crvenkovski's election cam - paign focused on pledges to lead his country into the EU and NATO. IMRO-DPMNU, which had been accusing the Crvenkovski government of betraying Slav Macedonians by giving too many concessions to ethnic Albanians, changed tack and focused on criticizing the government's economic policies, which it tried to blame for the ROM's 37 per cent unemployment rate (*IHT*, 15 April 2004, p. 3). In the first round, on a turn-out of only 55.2 per cent, Crvenkovski gained 42 per cent of the votes, Sasko Kedev obtained 34 per cent, and the two ethnic Albanian candidates obtained 14 per cent (Gezim Ostreni, DUI) and 8.6 per cent (Zudi Xhelili, DPA) (Stavrova 2004b).

After the second round, the state electoral commission declared Branko Crvenkovski to have won with 62.7 per cent of the vote, as against 37.3 per cent for Sasko Kedev, on a turn-out of only 53.8 per cent – just above the 50 per cent needed to validate the result. Opposition leaders refused to accept the state electoral commission's offi cial turn-out figure (claiming that it was nearer 46 per cent) and asked for the vote to be annulled. International observers also complained of irregularities. OSCE observers reported stuffing of ballot boxes at 4 per cent of the polling stations unde observation and cases of armed groups intimidating voters (*FT*, 30 April 2004, p. 9). They nevertheless concluded that the election had been 'generally' democratic (*IHT*, 30 April 2004, p. 4).

The centre-left government headed by Hari Kostov, May to November 2004

The elevation of Crvenkovski to the presidency made it necessary to choose a new prime minister. The choice fell on the conscientious and hard-working interior minister Hari Kostov (a Vlach), who was committed to completing the reforms required by the 2001 Ohrid framework agreement and by the ROM's quest for EU membership. He was close to Crvenkovski, but was somewhat disadvantaged by not having been a member of the SDUM.

On 2 May 2004 the nationalistic former minister of the interior Ljube Boskovski was charged with having instigated the killing of seven Pakistani 'economic migrants' near Skopje in March 2002 in an attempt to 'show the United States that the government was actively supporting the campaign against terror'. At that time Boskovski had claimed that the killings were a 'major success in war against international terrorism', that the seven alleged 'mujahideen' from Pakistan and India had planned to attack Western embassies before going on to 'inf ltrate the West', that they had been killed when they opened fire on a police patrol, and that the UCK sympathized with militan Islamic groups, including al-Qaeda. However, police investigations concluded that the seven people killed were illegal economic migrants who had had the misfortune to pass through the ROM, where they were assassinated by the police on Boskovski's orders for political purposes. Boskovski denied the charges against him. He was still a parliamentary deputy, but the public prosecutor demanded his arrest and a parliamentary committee removed his parliamentary immunity (*IHT*, 3 May 2004, p. 3; *Independent*, 3 May 2004, p. 3). On 4 May he fed to Croatia, where he also had citizenship. Ljubco Georgievski, who had been prime minister at the time and Boskovski's close ally, denied any knowledge of the killings (*IHT*, 17 May 2004, p. 3). Croatian police arrested and imprisoned Boskovski on 31 August 2004. Boskovski was also indicted by the ICTY on 14 March 2005 for his alleged role in a clash between ROM security forces and ethnic Albanian insurgents in August 2001, in which seven ethnic Albanian civilians had been killed and ninety had been arrested and then brutally beaten up by Macedonian police for forty-eight hours (Stavrova and Alagjozovski 2005e). This was the first time the ICTY had indicted a citizen of the ROM. Boskovski was still being held in custody in Croatia for his alleged role in the murder of the seven Asian economic migrants in 2002 (*IHT*, 15 March 2005, p. 3). However, on 22 April 2005, a court in the ROM acquitted the three former senior police officers and a business associate accused of carrying out the murder of thes seven Asians, allegedly on Boskovski's orders (*IHT*, 23 April 2005, p. 5). Their release, due to there being insuff cient evidence, was hailed as a major victory by the Slav

Macedonian nationalist opposition parties and newspapers, who claimed that the charges against them and against Boskovski had been cooked up as an act of revenge by the then prime minister Hari Kostov, whom Boskovski had accused of financia wrongdoings. During 2005 Slav Macedonian nationalists (including members of the Macedonian Slav diaspora) collected money and organized fund-raising celebrity concerts to help finance the legal defence of Boskovski, whom they regarded as a national hero who had carried out his patriotic duty in taking punitive actions against ethnic Albanians (whether combatants or civilians) during the insurgency of 2001 (Stavrova and Alagjozovski 2005h). Slav Macedonian nationalists claimed that Boskovski's co-defendant in the ICTY trial, the former police officer Johan Tarculovski had been extradited to The Hague illegally, since the republic's constitution prohibited the extradition of Macedonian citizens, and that the ICTY was guilty of double standards in pursuing charges against Boskovski and Tarculovski, while not actively pursuing charges against former members of the UCK for their alleged crimes. These alleged double standards reportedly further soured relations between Slav Macedonian nationalists and the ethnic Albanian community in early 2005. On the other hand, the ROM government's willingness to prosecute Slav Macedonian nationalists and to cooperate with the ICTY (regardless of whether this was just or unjust) ingratiated it with the USA and the EU and contributed to the EU's positive response to the republic's application for EU membership (Stavrova and Alagjozovski 2005e). Thus political calculations may have overridden considerations of what was just in these cases.

During the summer of 2004, with new local elections due to be held on 17 October, it became necessary to complete the legislative implementation of the 2001 Ohrid framework agreement by transferring considerable powers from the central govern-ment to locally elected authorities and by making Albanian a second official languag in municipal districts where ethnic Albanians constituted 20 per cent or more of the population. The alternative would have been to hold local elections while keeping the existing distribution of powers and without enacting legislation to make Albanian an off cial language wherever ethnic Albanians made up 20 per cent or more of the population. However, this would have broken the Ohrid framework agreement, angering the EU and the USA and possibly jeopardizing the republic's chances of further integration into the EU and NATO. Therefore, the EU special envoy Søren Jessen Petersen and the US ambassador Lawrence Butler worked closely with the three main parties in the coalition government to broker mutually acceptable terms for the implementation of the rest of the agreement – no mean feat. It was decided to combine extensive decentralization of powers and the strengthening of minority-language rights with a major redrawing of municipal boundaries and a reduction in the number of municipalities from 123 to 80, both to create more viable and equitably sized units of about 20,000 citizens per municipality and to add a number of ethnic Albanian-populated suburbs and villages to urban areas in which Slav Macedonians were often only narrowly in the majority or, in other cases, only slightly above 80 per cent of the population (and therefore monolingual). As a result of the proposed redrawing of boundaries, ethnic Albanians would become the majority in 16 out of the 80 new municipalities (instead of in 28 of the 124 existing local authorities). Furthermore, the inclusion of several ethnic Albanian suburbs within metropolitan Skopje would raise the ethnic Albanian share of the capital's population above 20 per cent, thereby requiring Skopje to become an officially bilingual and bicommunal city. In addition redistricting would result in Turkish becoming a second official language in three municipalities and Roma and Serbian becoming second official languages in two mor cases. The new municipal authorities would locally administer public services (including schooling, health care and local policing), local cultural affairs, local planning and local economic development (Stavrova 2004e and 2004f).

The SDUM-led coalition finally reached long-delayed agreement on a package of new laws on 13 July 2004. However, these reforms still needed parliamentary approval and were strongly opposed by many Slav Macedonian nationalist newspapers and politicians, especially IMRO-DPMNU and the Slav Macedonian diaspora, who portrayed it both as a form of corrupt gerrymandering and as a mortal threat to the Slav Macedonian nation (*FT*, 16 July 2004, p. 6; *The Economist*, 7 August 2004, p. 36).

In Struga, a somewhat rundown resort town of 36,000 inhabitants on the shores of Lake Ohrid in south-western Macedonia, the police used tear gas and rubber bullets to quell Slav Macedonian riots against the decentralization and minority-rights reforms on 23 July. The defence minister Vlado Buckovski and the SDUM leader Nikola Kurciev were trapped inside the party's local headquarters, surrounded by a hostile crowd lobbing Molotov cocktails. Slav Macedonians had hitherto controlled Struga's town council, but the new laws would result in control passing to the town's ethnic Albanian majority (*IHT*, 24 July 2004, p. 3). The town of Kicevo would be similarly affected in 2008.

The World Macedonian Congress, a Slav Macedonian diaspora organization headed by Todor Petrov and dedicated to protecting 'Macedonian identity', had launched a nationwide petition for a referendum on the redistricting component of the reforms, with the aim of blocking their enactment. Under the Macedonian constitution, they only needed to collect 150,000 signatures to force a referendum to be held*The Times*, 6 November 2004, p. 62). In Skopje on 26 July around 20,000 Slav Macedonians demonstrated against the proposed changes, which were portrayed as a partition of Macedonia along ethnic lines and the virtual break-up of the country. Many Slav Macedonians feared that increased autonomy for the ethnic Albanians in the north and west of the country would allow them 'to secede and join a greater Albania' (*Daily Telegraph*, 28 July 2004, p. 13). On 3 August, faced with more than 160 oppo sition amendments to the proposed legislation, local elections were postponed from 17 October to 21 November (*IHT*, 4 August 2004, p. 5).

The controversial legislation was passed by sixty-one votes to seven, with fifty two abstentions, on 11 August (*IHT*, 13 August 2004, p. 4). In response, the Slav Macedonian community in Struga threatened 'to declare independence' if the new laws were introduced there (*IHT*, 30 August 2004, p. 3). On 1 September 2004 the government acceded to the petition to hold a referendum on the proposed redistricting reforms and scheduled the referendum for 7 November.

It was revealed on Al-Jazeera television on 18 October 2004 that two Macedonian construction workers in Iraq had been beheaded. A videotape had been made of the beheading, but it was not shown in full because of its graphic nature. Nevertheless, even in the aftermath of this grisly event, no major party seriously questioned Macedonian participation in the US-led occupation regime in Iraq. During the same month Macedonians were told that their country's collaboration in the US-led occupation of Iraq was not in itself sufficient to enhance its chances of gaining admission to NATO. Simon Lunn, the secretary-general of the parliamentary assembly of NATO, stated that

Whether you will get an invitation [to join NATO] in 2006 depends on reforms in the Justice Department, visible fight against organized crime and corruption and the rights of ethnic minorities. Above all, the state of the economy . . . must improve. You have to have some economic growth, and you have to reduce the high rate of unemployment.

(Stavrova and Alagjozovski 2004c)

On 3 November, shortly before the referendum on the Macedonian 'Law on Territorial Organization', the USA announced that it would henceforth recognize the republic by its preferred name, the Republic of Macedonia, dropping the prefix 'Forme Yugoslav'. However, the move sparked outrage in Greece and was seen as a blatant attempt to influence the outcome of the referendum by offering a sop to Slav Macedonian nationalists (*IHT*, 5 November 2004, p. 3). The EU refused to follow suit. The government urged the supporters of the reforms to boycott the referendum, in order to keep the turn-out below the minimum 50 per cent required to validate the result and make it binding. Prime Minister Kostov announced that he would not vote and would resign if the referendum succeeded. Michael Sahlin, the EU's new special envoy to the ROM, warned that if the referendum succeeded it 'would cause constitutional turmoil' and delay the country's entry into the EU and NATO and 'create a climate for those who believe in violence to exploit'. Nevertheless, IMRO-DPMNU gave its support to the referendum organizers and urged its supporters to vote against the redistricting reforms (*The Times*, 6 November 2004, p. 62; *IHT*, 6 November 2004, p. 3).

Although 96 per cent of voters voted against the redistricting reforms on 7 November 2004, the turn-out was only 26.2 per cent, due to the combined support of the government, the EU, the USA and the ethnic Albanian community for a mass boycott. 'Even in areas without any ethnic Albanians, turn-out was below the required 50 per cent' (Stavrova and Alagjozovski 2004d). The result was therefore neither valid nor binding. The question on the ballot asked voters whether they wanted to keep current boundaries or to accept the government's proposed revisions. It was the redrawing of boundaries, rather than decentralization per se, which had excited the fiercest opposition

In spite of defeating the opposition to the proposed reforms and winning US recognition of the ROM by its preferred name, Prime Minister Hari Kostov resigned unexpectedly on 15 November, after less than six months in off ce. He complained that other much-needed reforms had been delayed and alleged diffculties in working with the ethnic Albanian DUI. He complained that 'One of the coalition partners . . . is promoting partisan interests, nepotism and corruption' and that the DUI's preoccupation with decentralization and single-minded promotion of the interests of its own constituency, to the exclusion of all else, was getting in the way of economic modernization. He also complained of a lack of consensus and teamwork in the governing coalition, including internal disputes over efforts to join the EU and NATO (*The Times*, 16 November 2004, p. 40;*IHT*, 16 November 2004, p. 6;*FT*, 17 November 2004, p. 11).

The centre-left government headed by Vlado Buckovski, December 2004 to July 2006

Vlado Buckovski, the SDUM defence minister and party vice-president, was elected leader of the governing SDUM on 26 November and became prime minister-designate on 28 November 2004, although he was not confirmed in office until mid-Decembe His declared priorities were to hasten the republic's integration into the EU and NATO by completing the reform programme begun by his predecessors. He was chosen in preference to three other candidates for these posts. This was the first contested electio for the SDUM, as Crvenkovski had been elected unopposed four times between 1991 and 2003 (Stavrova and Alagjozovski 2004e).

Buckovski immediately faced a major challenge to his authority. For two months an armed band of former UCK insurgents took control of Kondovo, an ethnic Albanian district on the outskirts of Skopje, demanding a new amnesty for those former UCK members who had not been covered by previous amnesties and economic assistance for the many former UCK members now living in poverty. The DUI leader Ali Ahmeti and the DPA leader Menduh Thraci met up with these former UCK gunmen on 6 December and endorsed their demands. However, Buckovski and his justice minister stood firm, arguing that the previous amnesties had been implemented in full, and faced down the challenge in order to maintain their own authority and the rule of law. The Buckovski government endeavoured to be even-handed by also refusing to pander to Ljubco Georgievski's demands for amnesties to be granted to the indicted former interior minister Ljube Boskovski and to those Slav Macedonians who had been members of notorious paramilitary and special police units during 2001 (Stavrova and Alagjozovski 2004f).

The municipal elections held on 13 and 17 March and 10 April 2005

In the first round there were widespread irregularities, including the stuffing of ball boxes, group voting, abuse of proxy voting and failure to sign election lists, according to OSCE and Council of Europe election monitors. Scuffles between election worker shut down at least three polling stations in the first round. Prime Minister Buckovsk held a meeting of political parties and called for improvements in electoral conduct in the second round, but the IMRO-DPMNU leader Nikola Gruevski described this as a 'whitewash' (*IHT*, 14 March 2005, p. 7; *FT*, 14 March 2005, p. 8).

The OSCE reported that voting in the second round occurred in a 'generally orderly manner', but that there were nevertheless thirty instances of ballot-box-stuffing an fifty of irregular proxy voting. Procedures had been 'bad' or 'very bad' in 14 per cent of the polling stations observed, including intimidation outside polling stations. Many of the problems had occurred in the western and northern regions, where rival ethnic Albanian parties accused each other of trying to disrupt the election. After the second round, Michael Sahlin (the EU special envoy to the ROM) warned that the republic could not hope to be allowed to enter the EU unless its conduct of elections improved dramatically. A third round of voting was held on 10 April at one in ten polling stations, thereby allowing about one-third of voters to cast their ballots again, but still there were widespread reports of electoral irregularities. In all three rounds, moreover, turn-outs were on the low side (for example, 28 per cent in Skopje on 10 April). Overall, the big loser was democracy itself (Stavrova and Alagjozovski 2005f).

The economy, 1990–9

The ROM had been the poorest republic in the SFRY during the 1980s, and its economy had therefore relied considerably on subsidies from the richer republics – primarily from Slovenia and Croatia. Net financial transfers to the ROM via the federal budge of the former SFRY in the late 1980s amounted to about 6 per cent of the ROM's GDP (UN, *World Economic and Social Survey*, 1996, p. 33). Furthermore, even before the violent disintegration of the Yugoslav Federation plunged the ROM into even greater economic hardships (mainly because it was thereby cut off from its main established suppliers of goods and services, from the main established markets for its products and from the federal subsidies on which it had come to rely to fund large parts of its public infrastructural and income-support programmes), the country was already suffering from a roughly 25 per cent adult unemployment rate. It was therefore hit very hard by the massive economic crisis that accompanied the breakup of the federation (see Table 8.6).

Monetary and exchange rate policies during the 1990s

The Yugoslav dinar was withdrawn in April 1992 and replaced by coupons. A new currency, the denar, was introduced in May 1993. Officially the new denar was allowe to float from the beginning of 1994, but in practice it remained closely aligned to the Deutschmark. The exchange rate of the new denar was more or less stable in 1994–6, but it was devalued by 14 per cent in July 1997 (EBRD 1997b: 169). There after, the exchange rate was in effect pegged to the value of the Deutschmark (EBRD 1999b: 218).

There was almost full current-account convertibility by 1994. Controls remained on the capital account, but the liberalization of foreign trade was well advanced (EBRD 1994: 25, 109). By 1996, import licensing and quantitative import restrictions had been removed for 96 per cent of import categories (the remaining restrictions were mainly on chemicals, steel and some foodstuffs), and auctions were held for imports still subject to quotas. All residual quantitative restrictions on imports were removed in November 1996 (EBRD 1996b: 151; EBRD 1997a: 29).

Price liberalization and macro-economic stabilization during the 1990s

As elsewhere in former Yugoslavia, the explosive combination of monetary laxity and price liberalization resulted in hyperinfation (1,664 per cent) in 1992. However, the subsequent combination of monetary stringency, income controls and opening the economy to international competition succeeded in dramatically reducing the annual inflation rate to low levels from 1995 onward (see Table 8.6). The ROM's f rst two macro-economic stabilization packages were introduced in the spring and autumn of 1992. A third one (sponsored by the IMF) was introduced in December 1993. There was also a heavy reliance on wage controls. In April 1993, wages were frozen for six months, a stringent incomes policy was in force from late 1993 to late 1996 (EBRD 1994: 25; EBRD 1996b: 151), and another six-month wage freeze was applied to publicly owned enterprises from July to December 1997.

Liberalization of prices proceeded steadily during the early 1990s, although a 'notif cation requirement' remained for milk, municipal rents, water and central heating (EBRD 1994: 25). By 1995, 80 per cent and by 1996, 90 per cent of prices in the

8.6 Republic of Macedonia: selected economic indicators, 1990–2005

	1990	1991	1992	1993	1994	1995	1996	1997	1998	1999	2000	2001	2002	2003	2004	2005
								% rise/rate								
GDP	-9.9	-7.0	-8.0	-9.1	-1.8	-1.2	1.2	1.4	3.4	4.3	4.5	-4.5	0.9	2.8	4.1	3.5
Industrial output	-10.6	-17.2	-16.0	-14.3	-9.7	-8.9	5.0	2.9	4.4	1.7	9.4	-4.6	-0.8	5.1	-2.1	6.7
Agricultural output	-10.2	17.6	0.4	-20.4	7.8	2.3	-2.9	0.0	3.9	0.9	1.0	-10.8	-2.0	4.8	4.9	3.0
Annual inflation	608.0	115.0	1,664.0	338.0	126.0	16.0	2.5	0.8	2.3	-0.7	5.8	5.3	2.4	1.1	-0.3	0.1
Unemployment	23.0	25.0	26.0	28.0	30.0	36.0	39.0	42.0	41.0	32.4	32.1	30.5	31.9	36.7	37.2	36.5
Budget surplus (+) / def cit (−) (as % of GDP)	–	-3.6	-9.8	-13.4	-2.7	-1.0	-1.4	-0.4	-1.7	0.0	2.5	-6.3	-5.6	-0.1	0.7	0.3
Foreign debt as % of GDP	–	16.0	33.0	33.0	25.0	24.0	25.0	31.0	40.0	40.6	43.2	43.5	43.4	39.5	38.3	39.7
Private-sector share of GDP (%)	15.0	15.0	15.0	35.0	35.0	40.0	50.0	50.0	55.0	55.0	55.0	60.0	60.0	60.0	55.0	65.0
Private-sector share in employment (%)	–	–	–	–	–	–	–	–	–	45.0	45.0	50.0	50.0	50.0	55.0	–
FDI (net inf ows) ($ m)	–	–	0.0	0.0	24.0	12.0	12.0	18.0	175.0	32.0	176.0	439.0	77.0	97.0	156.0	97.0
Foreign debt ($ bn)	–	0.7	0.8	0.8	0.8	1.1	1.1	1.2	1.4	1.5	1.5	1.5	1.6	1.8	2.0	2.3
Population (m)	–	–	2.2	2.2	1.9	2.0	2.0	2.0	2.0	2.0	2.0	2.0	2.0	2.0	2.0	2.0

Sources: Various issues of the annual EBRD *Transition Report*, supplemented by UN Economic Commission for Europe, *Economic Survey of Europe*; UN *World Economic and Social Survey*; and IMF *World Economic Outlook*. Figures for 2004 and 2005 are provisional estimates.

retail price index were free of controls, including retail prices of all basic goods other than bread, but guaranteed base prices remained for wheat, sugar, sugar beet, sunflowe and tobacco (EBRD 1995b: 42; EBRD 1996b: 151). A reform programme worked out and initiated with IMF and World Bank support in January 1994 not only reduced inflation and the budget deficit (Table 8.6), but initiated large-scale privatization an bank restructuring.

Privatization during the 1990s

Under the reform programme championed by the Yugoslav federal government headed by Ante Markovic in 1990–1, privatization proceeded further in the ROM than in any of the other Yugoslav republics. The principal participants were enterprise employees who received 'internal' shares (Koevski and Canning 1995: 5, 33).

A law on the transformation of enterprises with social capital was enacted in June 1993. The 1,517 enterprises involved in the first stage of privatization accounted for over 50 per cent of total corporate assets. A total of 414 enterprises, including public utilities, were excluded from the first stage (Koevski and Canning 1995: 9–11). Although the main emphasis was on privatization by sale, discounts were made available to present and former employees, citizens were allowed to use the hard-currency deposits frozen in 1990, and former owners (or their heirs) whose property had been conf scated by the Communist regime were to be compensated. The initiative for commencing privatization was to rest with the enterprise (workers councils and/or the boards of directors), but enterprises failing to meet prescribed deadlines would be privatized by the privatization agency. The deadlines for presenting privatization plans were December 1994 for small and medium enterprises and December 1995 for larger ones (Koevski and Canning 1995: 33).

Over 90 per cent of small enterprises were already privately owned by 1994 (EBRD 1994: 24). In 1994 eighty-four large enterprises were privatized (EBRD 1995a: 56). In addition, a special restructuring programme was introduced in 1994 to restructure the twenty-five largest loss-making enterprises. These included utilities, *agro-kombinats*, mines and textile, chemical and electrical machinery enterprises (EBRD 1996b: 150–1). By mid-1995 more than half of the republic's enterprises (representing at least half of the former state assets in the enterprise sector) had been privatized through management and employee buy-outs (EBRD 1995b: 23). By the end of 1997 almost all enterprises designated in 1993 for privatization had completed the process, representing more than three-quarters of all enterprises. Management and employee buy-out remained the most common method (EBRD 1998a: 35).

According to the EBRD, 'Improvements in corporate governance have been slow. This is due in part to the prevalence of management and employee buy-outs in the privatization process, which can act as a hindrance to enterprise restructuring.' Up to March 1998, enterprises sold to outsiders 'accounted for less than 15 per cent of employees in privatized enterprises', while foreign investors were deterred by high political risks in the region – their participation in the privatization process 'amounted to less than 2 per cent of equity privatized'. In addition, financial discipline had bee weakened by banks continuing to lend 'to loss-making enterprises with a poor debt service record and by an ineffectual bankruptcy law inherited from the former Yugoslavia' (EBRD 1998b: 166–7). A new and ostensibly more stringent bankruptcy law came into effect from May 1998, but application of the new law was slow, especially with regard to large enterprises.

From 1998 there emerged a greater emphasis on sales of enterprises to outsiders, including foreign investors. The intention was to privatize infrastructure on a case-by-case basis (EBRD 1998b: 166–7). Privatization of banks and large industrial and service enterprises was still slow.

Foreign direct investment during the 1990s

The ROM attracted little FDI during the 1990s (Table 8.6). It was inhibited by regional instability, doubts regarding the stability of the fledgling Macedonian state and a legal prohibition on ownership of land by foreigners (Koevski and Canning 1995: 14). Greek companies accounted for about half the total up to 1997 (*FT*, Survey, 17 December 1997, pp. iii–iv). In 1999, Hellenic Petroleum SA agreed to invest 190 million US dollars in Okta, Macedonia's main energy company, to double Okta's annual refining capacity and build a 90 million US dollar 220-kilometre pipeline t carry crude oil from Thessaloniki to Skopje (*FT*, 11 November 1999, p. 14). By 2001, Greek companies had invested about 250 million US dollars in the ROM (*The Economist*, 3 March 2001, p. 51), despite the initial bad blood between the neighbours. Total foreign investment increased sharply in 1998, but fallout from the crises of late 1998 to mid-1999 in Kosova caused several planned deals to be postponed in 1999 (EBRD 1999b: 219).

Despite the slow pace of privatization of industry during the 1990s, the relatively rapid growth of private enterprise (especially in service activities) ensured that the private sector accounted for half of GDP by 1996 – or earlier still, if the black economy is taken into account (see Table 8.6).

The biggest problem: unemployment during the 1990s

The official unemployment rate mounted steadily from 26 per cent in 1992 to 42 pe cent in 1997 (Table 8.6), although the real rates may have been lower because many people who were recorded as unemployed actually worked in the unrecorded 'grey' (informal) and 'black' (illicit) sectors. In January 1998 the government implemented a programme to stimulate employment by granting concessions on social-security contributions (EBRD 1998b: 166).

Agriculture and agri-business during the 1990s

Most of Macedonia's farmland was already in private hands under the Communist regime, and in 1996 private farmers were producing about 75 per cent of agricultural output on smallholdings with an average size of only 2.8 hectares (*FT*, Survey, 15 November 1996, p. ii). However, the privatization of publicly owned agriculture-related enterprises lagged behind the rest of the economy, although the pace quickened between 1996 and 1999.

Most processing of agricultural products was still carried out by some 200 *agro-kombinats*, publicly owned conglomerates that controlled some 15 per cent of agricultural land in 1996. Some had diversified into hotels, transport and tourism. law enabling the privatization of *agrokombinats* was passed in April 1996 (EBRD 1996b: 150–1), and their assets were split up and sold in 1997. Processing facilities, livestock and agricultural assets were offered for sale, with preference given to bids from managers and employees. State landholdings were not put up for sale. Instead, the *agromombinats'* holdings were to be made available on five-year leases. By Ma 1998, 70 per cent of all agriculture-related enterprises (representing about 40 per cent of employment in the sector) had been privatized, mostly to existing managers and farmers, and the rest were scheduled for privatization by the end of 1998 (EBRD 1998b: 166; EBRD 1999b: 218–19).

A law was passed in April 1998 to allow restitution of land and assets expropriated by the Communist regime after 1945. A land law passed in 1999 abolished restrictions on the permitted size of landholdings and gave impetus to the enlargement of exist-ing farms (EBRD 2000a: 54), but it was bound to take a lot of time and money to consolidate the ROM's smallholdings into larger and more remunerative undertakings. ROM agriculture was likely to continue to be based on under-capitalized, small-scale and low-income peasant farming for the next decade or two, at the very least, *faute de mieux.*

Economic affairs after the crises of 1999–2001

According to the EBRD, from 1998 to 2000 the ROM had been 'one of the fastest reforming countries' in the region, 'with signif cant progress being made on priva -tization, banking reform and institutional reform', but 'the increased uncertainty' caused by the Kosova crisis of 1998–9 and its violent repercussions in the ROM in 2000–1 'led to a slowdown in reform' (EBRD 2001b: 28). The insurgency of 2001 and also the economic costs of repressing that insurgency jeopardized macro-economic stability and prospects for growth. 'In order to fiance increased military expenditure, in June 2001 the government introduced a tax on financial transactions', which wa applied throughout the second half of 2001 (EBRD 2001b: 146).

Since 1999, monetary and exchange-rate policy was based on a de-facto peg of the denar to the euro (in place of the former peg to the Deutschmark, after it was superseded by the euro). In its *Transition Report* for 2005, the EBRD affirmed tha 'The exchange rate remains stable in line with the long established Central Bank policy of a de-facto near-peg of the denar to the euro' (EBRD 2005b: 131).

A new law enacted in April 2001 (with effect from October 2002) liberalized foreign-exchange operations, in particular for (hitherto negligible) non-resident portfolio investment. In April 2003 the ROM joined the WTO. Along with the free-trade agreements initialled with all Balkan countries in 2001–2, WTO membership reinforced the country's relative openness to trade. The average import tariff rate fell to 14.6 per cent and all quantitative restrictions on imports were removed, 'with the exception of some tariff-free quotas consistent with WTO rules' (EBRD 2003b: 144).

ROM economic policy has been characterized by relatively stringent neo-liberal monetary and fiscal orthodoxy and subservience to the IMF and the World Bank. This has attached overriding priority to achieving and maintaining low inf ation and interest rates, both for the sake of stability, predictability and low-risk premia and to curry favour with the USA and the EU. However, the ROM's rates of economic growth have remained substantially lower than those in states such as Albania, Romania, Bulgaria and Croatia (see Table 1.2). Vladimir Gligorov, a leading critic of the ROM's adherence to such cautious neo-liberal economic orthodoxy, has argued that some-what looser monetary and fiscal policies and acceptance of slightly higher inflati and managed depreciation of the denar would have fostered greater international competitiveness and faster economic growth (Gligorov 1998, 1999, 2006).

Contrary to such views, Laza Kekic has argued that the ROM's main problems

> are not policy related. Rather they have to do with regional instability – to which,
> because of its size, location and multi-ethnic makeup, [it] is extremely sensitive
> . . . On the other hand, because of regional instability, loss of savings and financia
> scandals, the authorities had to aim for a higher degree of stability to rebuild
> confidence than would otherwise have been the case. The evidence that exchange
> rate policy hurt competitiveness and was responsible for low export growth is
> also weak.
>
> (Kekic 2001: 197–9)

In other words, circumstances which lay beyond its control would still have caused
the ROM to experience relatively slow economic growth even if it had adopted looser
or more expansionary monetary, exchange rate and fiscal policies

For whichever reason (policy or circumstances), the ROM has reaped meagre
rewards for its semi-voluntary and semi-obligatory pursuit of neo-liberal monetary
orthodoxy, low inflation and a fixed exchange rate. Nevertheless, in 2005 the
Buckovski government launched a drive to increase economic growth and job creation
and to reduce the gaping external-trade def cit by establishing a 'one-stop shop' for
registering new companies, cutting down on red tape, granting customs exemption
for re-exports and, above all, promoting increased labour-market flexibility. This
last objective was pursued through a new labour law (July 2005) which increased
the freedom of employers to hire and fre workers, encouraged and facilitated the use
of fixed-term and part-time contracts, strengthened employers vis-à-vis organized
labour, reduced paid sick leave, regulated annual leave entitlements and made health
insurance for unemployed workers conditional on their registering with the national
employment agency (EBRD 2005b: 130). Thus, the underlying economic philosophy
remained strictly neo-liberal, putting its trust in freer market forces to overcome market
failings and imperfections, in continuing subservience to the business-friendly neo-
liberal orthodoxies of the World Bank and the IMF. Whether orthodox economic
neo-liberalism would suff ce to overcome the poor economic growth and job-creation
record of the ROM economy only time would tell.

Privatization and foreign direct investment, 1999–2005

The privatization of large-scale enterprises accelerated in 1999–2000. By May 2000
1,572 enterprises had been privatized and a further 138 privatizations were underway (EBRD 2000b: 162–3). The government sold 51 per cent of the f xed-line state
telecommunications company Macedonian Telecommunications to the Hungarian
f rm Matav in early 2001 (EBRD 2001a: 64). By 2002 the share of private capital in
the ROM banking system had risen to 84.3 per cent (EBRD 2002b: 150–1).

In early 2001 the ROM government decided to discuss and to vet all foreign-
investment projects, as well as the spending of windfall earnings from the sale of
publicly owned enterprises to foreign investors/firms, with the international financi
institutions (including the EBRD and the IFC) and with foreign embassies, especially
those of the USA and the EU, in further subservience to Western interests*FT*, Survey,
19 February 2001, pp. 11–12).

Also in early 2001 the government drew up an action plan, with assistance from
the World Bank, to privatize forty large loss-making enterprises by June 2002. Each

enterprise was treated on a case-by-case basis and was to be either financially restructured and fully privatized, or else closed down. The state remained a major stakeholder in a number of large industrial loss-makers and was having great difficult in either selling or closing them, although eight were sold by international tender in 2001–2 (EBRD 2002b: 150–1). The privatization of large loss-making enterprises was relaunched in 2002 (EBRD 2003b: 144–5). The privatization agency, which the government had intended to close by April 2004, remained open into 2005 and continued to sell shares in state-owned enterprises through the stock exchange. When the privatization agency closed down in late 2005, the remaining state holdings in enterprises were transferred to other public institutions.

In 2004 and 2005, inflows of FDI in the ROM remained low, because 'investor continue to be deterred by the small market size and perceived risk'. They remained 'mainly concentrated in utilities, mining and metal processing' (EBRD 2004b: 127; EBRD 2005b: 130–1).

The relative resilience of the ethnic Albanian community

Under Communist rule, the ROM became industrialized and the state bureaucracy greatly expanded. However, jobs in both of these sectors went overwhelmingly to Slavic Macedonians. As a result, ethnic Albanians suffered less than Slav Macedonians did from the virtual collapse of public-sector enterprises during the early 1990s. By the same token, however, the ethnic Albanian population, which had been largely excluded from the public sector in the Communist era, also found itself excluded from the privatization process – especially from the management buy-outs and 'insider privatizations' which yielded rich pickings for the chosen few. The ethnic Albanian community therefore continued to send its young men to work abroad, to develop private farming and private businesses (including an informal family-based fnancial banking system) and to rely relatively heavily both on remittances from émigré communities and on livelihoods obtained from the black economy (*FT*, Survey, 19 February 2001, p. 14). Another consequence was that ethnic Albanians were less affected than Slav Macedonians by the economic disruptions resulting from the Kosova war in 1999 and the insurgency in 2001.

In view of the ROM's gaping external-trade deficits, it is worth mentioning tha the republic has been kept afloat financially not only by modest inflows of West economic aid and FDI, but even more substantially by the remittances of émigré workers, most of whom appear to be ethnic Albanians rather than Slav Macedonians. High unemployment, low wages, scarcity of jobs and the still deeply entrenched discrimination in favour of Slavs to the detriment of ethnic Albanians has driven large numbers of ethnic Albanians to seek work in other countries (mainly in the EU, but also in Iraq), in most cases without severing their family ties to the ROM.

Concluding reflections

Towards EU membership?

Prior to the 1990s, over half the ROM's exports regularly went to the other Yugoslav republics, and much of the rest went to other Communist states. The ROM sought to compensate for the loss or contraction of these relatively soft and sheltered mar - kets by embarking on a gradual economic reorientation towards and integration with the EU.

On 18 September 2000 EU foreign ministers approved a package of measures granting duty-free access to EU markets for 95 per cent of exports from Macedonia, Albania, Bosnia, Croatia, Serbia and Montenegro. The package included abolition of tariffs on imports of most industrial and farm products into the EU, although a few quantitative restrictions would remain on exports of fish products and wine to th EU (*FT*, 19 September 2000, p. 10).

At an EU–Balkan summit held in Zagreb on 24 November 2000, a so-called SAA was concluded between the EU and the ROM, which was the first western Balkan stat to enter such an agreement. The SAA was signed in Luxembourg on 9 April 2001 (during the insurgency!) and entered into force on 1 April 2004. It was a new form of association agreement designed to deal with the particular challenges posed by the proposed gradual integration of western Balkan states with the EU by striving to promote political dialogue, intra-regional (i.e., Balkan) cooperation, 'the four free-doms', approximation of the republic's legislation with the European Community *acquis communautaire*, and wide-ranging cooperation in all areas of EC policy. Other than for wine, veal and f sheries products (on which import-quota restrictions would continue), ROM exports were to be granted immediate free access to EU markets, while in return the republic agreed gradually to eliminate its own tariffs on EU exports over the next ten years, with the target of establishing free trade between the EU and the ROM in all industrial and most agricultural products by 2011. For textiles and steel, the country's biggest exports, the liberalization timetable was less than ten years. Import quotas on agricultural and fishery products were to be abolished on both sides when the agreement was signed, but there was no timetable for further tariff liberalization in those sectors (EBRD 2001b: 146).

On 27 June 2001 the governments of the ROM, Albania, Bosnia-Herzegovina, Bulgaria, Croatia, Romania and the FRY signed an agreement to liberalize trade in at least 90 per cent of goods trade between them, under the auspices of the EU's Stability Pact for South-eastern Europe, with the aim of enhancing intra-regional stability, integration and economic growth (*FT*, 28 June 2001, p. 8). However, mainly because of the predominant 'hub-and-spoke' nature of the economic and political relationships between the EU and the Balkan states (not least because of the EU's insistence on dealing with each state individually/separately with regard to its gradual economic and political integration into the EU economy and civil association), it is inherently unlikely that very much intra-regional integration will be accomplished between the Balkan states until *after* (rather than *before*) their admission to full membership of the EU. No matter how much the EU tries to *exhort* intra-regional Balkan integration, this is vastly outweighed by the powerful effects of dealing with each state individually/separately prior to granting full membership.

In December 2001, two reports written by independent French and Italian con - sultants on behalf of EuropeAid, which was set up by the EU commissioner for external affairs, Chris Patten, earlier that year to speed disbursement of EU aid and to develop a long-term strategy in the Balkans, concluded that the European Commission's aid programmes to the ROM and Albania lacked clear strategies, were bogged down in bureaucratic delays and infighting, competed with other international financial institutions and, thus far, had brought little benefit. In the case of the ROM, whic had received nearly 500 million euros over the previous decade, the commission had ignored the need to establish institutions that would bring different ethnic groups together. It had also failed to tackle the corruption rampant in the administration, or to address the poor pay and the politicization of the public administration, or to build up civil-society institutions (*FT*, 10 December 2001, p. 6).

The ROM submitted an application for membership of the EU on 22 March 2004. In response, the EU Commission president Romano Prodi personally delivered to prime minister Hari Kostov a 300-page questionnaire on 1 October 2004. This contained no less than 3,000 questions to be answered about the ROM's state of preparedness to become an official candidate for EU membership, with entitlements to EU pre-accessio assistance. About 1,000 people worked on producing 14,000 pages of answers to these questions, and these were proudly delivered to Brussels on 14 February 2005.

On 9 November 2005, after conducting a searching preliminary assessment of the ROM's answers to the questions and of its suitability, the EU Commission recom - mended that the republic's official candidacy should be accepted by the European Council on 15 December 2005. The EU enlargement commissioner Olli Rehn travelled to Skopje to deliver the commission's 'opinion' in person to the ROM government. The commission carefully refrained from specifying a start date for formal member- ship negotiations, but commission officials non-bindingly indicated that they wer unlikely to begin before 2007. They emphasized that the ROM would have to make 'considerable progress' before such negotiations could start, especially with regard to well-conducted and fair elections, a more effective fight against corruption and organized crime, the attainment of higher and more sustained economic growth and fuller employment, and the strengthening of administrative capacity and judicial independence and efficiency. It appeared that the major reason for waiting until 200 to decide when to begin formal membership negotiations was that the next parlia- mentary election was due in September 2006, and the commission especially wanted to see how well these elections would be conducted before committing itself to a start date for formal negotiations. Commission officials warned that the EU would sho 'zero tolerance' for widespread electoral irregularities in the next parliamentary election, which would be treated as 'the ultimate test of Macedonia's maturity as a democracy' (*FT*, 9 November 2005, p. 8; Stavrova 2005; Stavrova and Alagjozovski 2005m). Unfortunately, the June 2006 election campaign was marred by substantial violence and intimidation.

In view of the fact that the ROM had been the poorest of the former Yugoslav republics and still had an offcial unemployment rate of 37.7 per cent in the third quarter of 2004, to have reached this stage so soon after the demise of Communist rule in 1990 and the massive insurgency of February–September 2001 was a remarkable achievement. This also reflected the special interest in and strenuous support for th ROM which had consistently been displayed by the EU, in large measure because of the importance of the republic to the peace, stability and westward orientation of South-eastern Europe as a whole. This EU decision on the ROM also sent an encour- aging signal to other western Balkan states that serious candidacy for EU membership was a credible aspiration, while at the same time giving the ROM access to significan EU pre-accession funds and, in addition, encouraging foreign investors to start investing in the republic with greater confidence that it really could become a full member of the EU by 2012 or 2013.

However, since the Treaty of Nice adopted in 2000–1 does not permit the EU to expand beyond twenty-seven members unless a new EU treaty is adopted and ratifie in order to help the EU cope with the pressures and strains of further enlargement, the ROM's strenuous efforts to become eligible for EU membership could yet turn out to have been in vain. For this reason, the high hopes of eventual EU membership, which the EU has actively been encouraging in the ROM and other western Balkan states since October 1999 (and even more strongly since June 2003), could yet prove to be false ones, if the existing EU members prove incapable of agreeing on and ratifying a new EU treaty – or, alternatively, if EU members opposed to further EU enlargement continue to use non-ratification of a new E   treaty as a means of blocking further enlargement. If such a state of deadlock were to persist, the negative repercussions on political and economic morale and prospects in the ROM and other western Balkan states could inflict incalculable damage on the whole region

The ROM's wars on corruption, fraud and organized crime

In the early 1990s, the ROM prided itself on being much less corrupt than most Balkan states. However, the rigid and bureaucratic payments system inherited from the Communist regime (known as the ZOP), together with the countless fees payable and authorizations required for travel and residency documents, telephone lines, medical treatment, business licences and the like, fostered abundant opportunities for payment and extortion of bribes, which seriously encumbered and slowed down all kinds of activity (not just economic ones). Furthermore, the SDUM, during its long tenure of off ce from 1991 to 1998, fostered clientelistic patronage networks, cronyism and insider privatization. Similarly, UN sanctions against the FRY (primarily Serbia) during the 1990s fostered a luxuriant growth of sanctions-busting smuggling, rack - eteering and gangsterism in the ROM, as elsewhere in the post-Communist Balkans.

IMRO-DPMNU won the 1998 election in large measure on a promise to increase prosperity and inflows of FDI by 'decapitating the octopus' of SDUM corruption. T make a f nal break with the old ZOP payments system, a new payments system centred on an inter-bank clearing system owned and run by the banks was put in place in July 2001. For six months, the two payments systems operated in parallel, but the ZOP was finally liquidated at the end of 2001 (EBRD 2002b: 150–1). However, most o the promised anti-corruption legislation and measures to control money-laundering were not enacted until 2002, the year in which IMRO-DPMNU lost office. By the corruption, fraud and racketeering were even more rampant under Ljubco Georgievski, Ljube Boskovski and their cronies than they had ever been under the SDUM. In 2002 opinion surveys indicated that most of the republic's citizens saw corruption as being even more destructive than the inter-ethnic conflict of 2001 had been (Fraenkel 2003 430–2). In the run-up to the parliamentary election of September 2002, the International Crisis Group published two major reports, entitled*Finance Peace in Macedonia, Not Corruption* and *Macedonia's Public Secret: How Corruption Drags the Country Down*, both of which documented how deeply mired in corruption the country had become under IMRO-DPMNU. They probably dealt æoup de grâce to Georgievski's chances of re-election.

Branko Crvenkovski was returned to office in September 2002 in large part to d the jobs that Georgievski had promised to do but didn't. Premier Crvenkovski publicly acknowledged the high levels of corruption and organized crime and, in a campaign to convince voters that his new government would not simply slip back into the bad habits of the 1990s, he established an initially powerful and independent anti-corruption commission in October 2002 and required all ministers and senior public officials t disclose all their assets and business interests. To encourage others, he also instigated high-profile arrests and prosecutions of the most conspicuously corrupt members of the preceding IMRO-DPMNU regime: Dusko Avramovski from the privatization agency, Vojo Mihajlovski from the national health fund, the former defence minister Ljuben Paunovski and the former economy minister Besnik Fetaj. In addition,

Crvenkovski's successor Hari Kostov secured the passage of a strong law on prevention of money-laundering in July 2004. After that, however, the anti-corruption drive lost momentum. The anti-corruption commission lost its independence under a legal amendment passed in July 2004, whereupon the head of that commission accused the government of having given up the fight against corruption and the investigation an prosecution of corruption and fraud cases was drastically curtailed (Tsekov 2005: 11–13). If the ROM's governing elites are genuinely intent on gaining admission to the EU, they will have to relaunch the offensive against corruption, fraud and organized crime in earnest. Otherwise, the country is in effect being held hostage by corrupt, clientelistic and often criminal and ruthless networks which currently control large swathes of the economy, the police, the courts and the bureaucracy. This is a major problem which needs to be brought under control (if not eliminated) before the ROM can safely be admitted to the EU, i.e., without running the risk that the EU would thereby incorporate such a problem into its own structures and operations.

The economy

The ROM underwent a very severe economic crisis during the frst half of the 1990s. Even though sanctions were poorly enforced, ROM participation in UN sanctions against the FRY also imposed costs and delayed economic recovery. Per-capita income fell from 2,200 US dollars in 1990 to 1,600 US dollars in 1994 (BCE 1995: 42), and by 1996 most enterprises were working at less than half their capacity (UN ECE 1996: 168). After the ROM's admission to the IMF in December 1992 and to the World Bank in December 1993, substantial foreign aid was mobilized. When an agreement on economic reconstruction was signed in February 1994, a standby loan of 80 million US dollars was arranged, inflation was reduced and the denar was stabilized, but at considerable cost in terms of lost output and employment. In 1994 the ROM's GDP was only about 65 per cent of its 1992 level (Pettifer 1995: 56). Officially, unemployment rose to over 30 per cent of the total workforce in the mid-1990s (see Table 8.6), but in practice more than 40 per cent of the workforce was either formally unemployed or on forced leave from factories that had shut down (*FT*, 14 October 1994, p. 2).

Macedonia's economy began a belated recovery from 1996 to 2000 (see Table 8.6). Although the ROM was among the countries hardest hit by the 1998–9 Kosova crisis (mainly through its negative impact on trade and the influx of over 360,000 Kosova refugees), the negative effects were mercifully short-lived and economic recovery resumed strongly during the second half of 1999 (EBRD 2000a: 5). The inter-ethnic conf icts that erupted within the ROM itself in 2001 reduced GDP and the output of both industry and agriculture by about 10 per cent, but the negative impact of conflic was again mercifully short-lived. By 2004, the ROM's GDP had recovered to about 80 per cent of its 1989 level (EBRD 2005b: 48).

The ROM has continued to have alarmingly high official unemployment rates since the mid-1990s, but it is increasingly argued that these official rates fail to mak suff cient allowance for unrecorded employment in the informal grey economy and in the illicit black economy. Taken together, these amounted to 20 to 40 per cent of GDP in 1997 (*FT*, Survey, 17 December 1997, p. ii). In 2003, according to the EBRD estimates, the largely unrecorded 'informal sector' amounted to 'around 40 per cent of GDP' (EBRD 2003b: 145). In 1996 Macedonia's ministry of finance claimed tha the real unemployment rate was 'only' between 22 and 24 per cent (*FT*, Survey, 15 November 1996, p. iii), in contrast to the officially recorded rate of 39 per cent at tha time. Nevertheless, even an unemployment rate of 22–24 per cent was very grim and demoralizing for the unemployed. High unemployment was also the main reason for the World Bank 'finding' that 22 per cent of the ROM's population were living i poverty in 2005, while 133,000 of its inhabitants were even without reliable access to basic foodstuffs (Stavrova 2005).

Democratization and liberalization

In the final analysis, the most striking aspect of the ROM experience since the earl 1990s is not the fact that the country has undergone so many crises, problems and hardships, but that, in spite of all its buffetings and sufferings, it has nevertheless held together, has persevered with strikingly liberal economic policies and has remained broadly consensual, liberal and democratic. Indeed, despite appearing relatively weak, impoverished and vulnerable at the outset, the ROM has been rather more consistently liberal (both politically and economically) than any of the other Yugoslav successor states, other than Slovenia, and it skilfully and prudently avoided getting sucked into the destructive warfare that resulted from the disintegration of Communist Yugoslavia. In spite of coming under huge pressure from the champions of violent and intemperate ethnic collectivism, the principal elected leaders of its two largest 'nationalities' have repeatedly bent over backwards to defuse or pull back from the explosive potential for violent inter-ethnic conflict which has been built into the structure and compositio of this precarious multi-ethnic state from the outset.

The most important feature of the civil war between ethnic Albanian insurgents and ROM security forces between February and August 2001 is not that this threatened the integrity and survival of this state, but rather that the conflict was actively containe and overcome by a conscious determination on both sides to exercise self-restraint. There was a tragic loss of over 100 lives on both sides, but a conf ict which could easily have escalated into a massive catastrophe costing tens of thousands of lives was averted by the willingness of both sides to negotiate and compromise. Since that time, a culture of dialogue has taken root and seems to be steadily growing stronger and deeper (TOL, 8 November 2004).

Interestingly, in 2004 the EU foreign-policy supremo Javier Solana, who played a leading role in brokering the Ohrid framework of 2001 (and, less fruitfully, the State Union of Serbia and Montenegro in 2002–3), told the Serbian prime minister Vojislav Kostunica that the 'Macedonian model of decentralization is better than cantonization' and that 'Macedonia could serve as a model for Kosova' (Stavrova 2004a). In effect, the Macedonian model of decentralization is a microcosm of the Spanish 'state of autonomies' (*estado de las autonomías*), which succeeded in decentralizing power and granting extensive local autonomy without either creating a federal state or showing special favour to particular ethnic groups above the rest. (In a sense, this is a variation on Joseph Chamberlain's 1890s' conception of 'Home rule all round'.) This model might also prove suitable for Bosnia and Herzegovina, as an alternative to the cumbersome and centrifugal 'confederal' model which was established there by the November 1995 Dayton accords.

At the same time, it is important not to idealize or to be complacent about the vaunted 'Macedonian model'. It has its limitations.

> Contrary to the view of Macedonia's 'peace architects', the country's conflic cannot be remedied exclusively by addressing procedural issues and structural inequities. Rather, any effective solution must address the deep sense of violated

identity felt equally strongly by both [Slav] Macedonians and [Macedonian] Albanians and the accompanying resentments these groups harbour about the distribution of the state's economic, political and social resources.

(Fraenkel 2003: 404)

The ROM's heterogeneous ethnic groups, interests and aspirations are gradually being accommodated and provided with secure channels of expression, but a long time will elapse before we can be sure that they are truly knitting together into a robust civil association. For the time being, it appears that the very widely supported aspiration to meet the requirements of membership as laid down by the EU is chiefly what i holding this fragile and increasingly decentralized multi-ethnic polity together.

The ROM has been plagued by the power of gangsters and black-marketeers, by the relatively weak rule of law, by pervasive and multifarious forms of corruption and crime, and by the high incidence of electoral irregularities. Nevertheless, since 2001 the country has also displayed an increasingly pervasive belief that all major political differences and disputes should be vigorously debated and negotiated in public and that they should ultimately be resolved by negotiation and the ballot box, rather than simply by recourse to violence. The major challenges ahead are to establish the rule of law and to curb corruption, fraud, electoral malpractice and the power of gangster networks sufficiently to satisfy the requirements of EU membership, whic for its part should provide suffcient incentives and pre-accession assistance to facilitate the meeting of those challenges.

Serious public engagement with political issues and debate has remained strikingly high, as have levels of popular participation in democratic political institutions, organizations and processes. This is in marked contrast to some formally 'consolidated' democracies such as Poland and the Czech Republic, where the initial post-1989 enthusiasm for and engagement with democratic political debate and participation has given way to profound and widespread disillusionment and apathy, reflected in lo levels of political participation and even lower levels of engagement in public debate on major issues of public policy. Thus, paradoxically, while some of the formally 'consolidated' democracies in East Central Europe are in some senses undergoing a profound 'crisis of democracy', the formally very 'unconsolidated' democracy which has emerged in the ROM appears to be in a rude and vigorous state of health, despite its formal deficiencies. This is a salutary warning against attaching undue importance to relatively static formal criteria of democratic consolidation along the lines propounded by Juan Linz and Alfred Stepan (1996: 5–13). While it is true that in states such as Macedonia, Albania and Bulgaria, the almost routine occurrence of electoral irregularities has resulted in fairly frequent reruns and recounts of democratic ballots, these rough-and-ready expressions of democratic politics are nevertheless being pursued with great zest and it is becoming the case that for these countries (to borrow a recurring refrain in Linz and Stepan 1996) 'democracy is the only game in town'. They may play it rough, but they nevertheless play the game with remarkable vigour and engagement. The parliamentary election held on 5 July 2006 was won by IMRO-DPMNU, which had been reformed into a moderate liberal-conservative centre-right party by Nikola Gruevski (see p. 451). The OSCE concluded that, even though the election campaign had been marred by violence and intimidation, the poll itself had been peacefully and well conducted. However, Prime Minister Nikola Gruevski's exclusion of parties representing the ethnic Albanian minority from his government threatened to rekindle damaging inter-ethnic tensions.

9   Montenegro

To be or not to be?

Introductory 'country profile'

Montenegro (Black Mountain) is a very small country with a land area of 13,812 square kilometres – only 5.7 per cent of the size of the UK or 2.5 per cent of the size of France. At the time of the 2003 census, it had only 616,000 inhabitants. Montenegro is as mountainous as its name implies. According to an old Montenegrin ballad, 'When God finished making the world, He found that he had a great many rocks left in Hi bag; so He tumbled the whole lot on to a wild and desolate bit of country – and that is how Montenegro was formed' (Darby 1968: 73). Limestone (*karst*) scenery makes up large parts of the terrain, which bears an uncanny resemblance to 'apple crumble' and gives rise to widespread aridity, as most surface water disappears (sooner or later) down 'swallow-holes' into subterranean caverns, lakes and rivers. Although much of Montenegro is breathtakingly beautiful and has immense potential for tourism, it was one of the poorer and less industrialized parts of the SFRY. It accounted for 5.4 per cent of the land area and 3 per cent of the population but only 2 per cent of the GMP of the SFRY in 1989, when Montenegro's per capita GMP was roughly 73 per cent of the Yugoslav average (EEN, 1995, vol. 9, no. 10, p. 4).

During the Communist era the capital of Montenegro was known as Titograd, but in the early 1990s it reverted to its pre-Communist name, Podgorica. It had a population of 152,288 in 1991. The other major towns were Niksic (74,821 in 1991), Bijelo Pole (55,145), Berane (45,662, formerly known as Ivangrad) and the port of Bar (37,331) (Europa 1992: 341). Small and picturesque Cetinje was the charming but remote mountain capital of Montenegro before 1918 and it is still the 'spiritual capital' of Montenegro, as the seat of the prince-bishopric and the later principality and kingdom which gave birth to the 'modern' Montenegrin statelet which repeatedly expanded its territory with Russian moral, material and military support between 1715 (more strongly 1799) and 1913.

Who are the Montenegrins?

Montenegrins and their forebears have long spoken Serb as their 'mother tongue'. During the eighteenth and nineteenth centuries, Montenegrins were widely perceived to be 'mountain Serbs', i.e., Serbs who had merely evolved somewhat differently from the main body of Serb-speaking peoples due to their location in a very mountainous territory whose relative inaccessibility had allowed them largely to avoid coming under the varying degrees of direct Ottoman Turkish rule which befell most of the Balkan Slavs from the late fifteenth to the early nineteenth century (or later, in most cases)

Until a breakaway autocephalous (autonomous) 'Montenegrin Orthodox Church' was re-established in 1993 (there having previously been one from 1855 to 1920), most of its population declared an (increasingly nominal) affiliation to the autocephalou Serbian Orthodox Church. It has therefore long been a matter of debate among Montenegrins, Serbs and outside observers whether the Montenegrins are a nation in their own right or a 'branch' of the widely scattered and highly variegated Serbian 'nation'. This 'existential question' was seemingly given a definitive answer in th referendum helf on 21 May 2006, when just over 55 per cent of the votes were cast in favour of Montenegro becoming a fully independent state. Nevertheless, it was also clear that for a while at least the inhabitants of Montenegro would remain quite deeply divided on this crucial issue.

The proportion of Montenegro's population which has chosen to identify itself as 'Montenegrin' (rather than as 'Serb') has fictuated dramatically over time, as have the proportions that have chosen to identify themselves as 'Yugoslavs', as 'Orthodox Christian' (Slavs) or as 'Muslim Slavs' (see Table 9.1). The ways in which the inhabi tants have thought about themselves and have chosen to identify themselves (not necessarily the same thing!) must therefore have depended as much or more on calcu lations of personal advantage or disadvantage or considerations of political expediency, than on more 'substantive' changes in ethnicity or ethnic affiation. Indeed, the unusu ally large variations in ethnic affiliation (over time) in Table 9.1 must have mainl reflected changes in self-identification, because since the terrible upheavals and carnag of 1941–5 Montenegro (unlike some other parts of former Yugoslavia) has not been the scene of *major* assaults on particular groups or *major* net inward or outward migrations by particular groups.

Although over 70 per cent of the population were declared to be Orthodox Christians in the November 2003 census, these were divided between the Serbian and the break-away Montenegrin Orthodox churches (*FT*, 15 July 2000, p. xviii). As late as 1991, moreover, nearly 20 per of the population were declared to be Muslim by religious affiliation. Of these, about two-thirds were Muslim Slavs (mainly living in or near the Montenegrin section of the Sandzak of Novi Pazar), while about one-third was ethnic Albanians (mainly living in southern areas which could have become part of a 'Greater Albania' but which were annexed by Montenegro in the nineteenth and twentieth centuries). Muddying the waters still further, while 59.7 per cent were declared to have the 'Serbian' language as their mother tongue in the November 2003 census, 22 per cent were declared to have 'Montenegrin' as their mother tongue. We say 'were declared', because here, as elsewhere, 'heads of household' rather than all individual members of the population filled in the census forms on which the censu

9.1 Ethnic affiliations of population of Montenegro, 1953–200

(% of total)	1953	1961	1971	1981	1991	2003
Montenegrins	86.6	81.4	67.1	68.5	61.9	40.6
Serbs	3.3	3.0	7.5	3.3	9.3	30.1
Albanians	5.6	5.5	6.7	6.5	6.6	7.1
Muslim Slavs	–	6.5	13.3	13.4	14.6	4.3
Croats	2.3	2.2	1.7	1.2	1.0	1.1
Yugoslavs	1.5	0.3	2.1	5.7	4.2	–
Others	0.7	1.1	1.6	1.4	2.4	16.8

Sources: Ravkovic (2004), Spiljevic (1985: 96) and Europa (1992: 341).

figures on ethnic, linguistic and religious affiliation were supposedly based. It shoul also be mentioned that the population and ethnic-affiliation data which were occa sionally put out by the Montenegrin state in the late nineteenth and early twentieth centuries were almost wholly misleading and useless, because Montenegro's rulers at that time did not want the outside world to know quite how *few* 'Montenegrins' there were! The actual census returns were closely guarded state secrets. Moreover, it is quite conceivable that even the supposedly 'reliable' Montenegrin census data published since 1953 have been products of unusually large degrees of distortion and manipulation by the authorities or heads of households in this still highly 'patriarchal' society.

Supposed precursors of the modern Montenegrin polity

Modern nationally self-conscious 'Montenegrins' have long been taught to think of themselves as descendants of Slavs who frst arrived in the territory that is now known as Montenegro during the sixth century and settled there in more substantial numbers during the seventh and eighth centuries. The pre-existing population of these territories probably comprised various peoples, many of whom may have spoken a so-called 'Illyrian' language, but they were not necessarily an Illyrian people or ethnic group, as no one knows for certain whether such groups or even such a language ever existed (as explained in Chapter 2, pp. 23–6). We can be more certain that the pre-existing population included substantial admixtures of Latin-speaking or Greek-speaking former 'Roman' inhabitants from various parts of the former west Roman Empire and the ongoing east Roman (Byzantine) Empire – especially in the still-surviving towns, which were mostly ports and f shing villages along the Adriatic coast. There were also residues of transient Celtic settlers and various Turkic, Iranian and Germanic peoples who had at various times preyed upon relatively rich but vulnerably exposed west Roman or Byzantine domains or settlements. The new Slav settlers almost certainly intermingled and ultimately interbred with the pre-existing inhabitants, were converted to Christianity by them and produced new cultural syntheses and hybrid peoples and identities. During the ninth and tenth centuries, a statelet known as Duklja emerged on parts of what is now the territory of the Republic of Montenegro. During the eleventh century, another Slavic or partly-Slavic state which came to be known as Zeta emerged in an area straddling what is now Herzegovina as well as parts of present-day Montenegro. The name 'Montenegro' began to be used occa sionally from the end of the thirteenth century, but for a long time it only referred to the highland area around Mount Lovcen, which looms over the town of Cetinje. During the f fteenth century, Cetinje served as the last mountain refuge or redoubt of Zeta's ruling Crnojevic family, whose power was being terminated by Ottoman Turkish raids and encroachments from the south and east and Venetian ones along the coast. In 1499, however, most of inland Zeta fell under Ottoman Turkish suzerainty, while the coastal region centred on the large and beautiful natural harbour of the bay of Kotor came under Venetian control until 1797, when it passed into Austro-Hungarian hands.

During the four to five centuries of Ottoman dominion over the South Slav lands the relatively mountainous, widely forested and remote terrain around Cetinje and Mount Lovcen remained a refuge for fugitives, outlaws and bandits and became more widely known as Montenegro. Its relatively inaccessible terrain and very limited intrinsic value (other than great scenic beauty!) allowed it considerable de-facto independence, despite repeated Ottoman raids, during which most of the 100,000 or so inhabitants would melt into the mountains and forests, reappearing when it again became safe to do so. Montenegrins made disproportionately large contributions to keeping alive a rich South Slavic tradition of epic verse, legend and song.

The small and rudimentary Montenegrin polity centred on the Eastern Orthodox monastery at Cetinje came under the control of the energetic bishop Danilo Petrovic, a member of the Njegos clan, from 1696 until his death in 1737. He visited Peter the Great of Russia in 1715, forged close ties with the Russian Orthodox Church hierarchy and secured long-lasting Russian diplomatic recognition and ecclesiastical, material and financial patronage for his diocese and polity. This enabled him and his successor to transform his emerging statelet into a hereditary possession which remained in the hands of the Petrovic family and the Njegos clan from 1715 to 1918. Until 1852, this small realm was organized as a prince-bishopric. Because Orthodox bishops and the monks from whom they were recruited were required to be unmarried and celibate, the hereditary succession ran from uncle to nephew rather than by the more usual patrilineal descent. Abundant evidence of Montenegro's heavy dependence on Russian military, material, fnancial and ecclesiastical patronage is on display in the fascinating Orthodox monastery-museum in Cetinje. A high proportion of its most striking or ostentatious exhibits originated as donations from Russia. Bishop Petar Petrovic Njegos II (reg. 1830–51) was a celebrated reformer/innovator and a prolific writer o romantic nationalist verse. His poem 'The Mountain Wreath', a somewhat bloodthirsty celebration of the epic Serbian-cum-Montenegrin struggle against the Ottoman Turks, has remained the most revered literary work in the Serb language, especially among the more nationalistic, Turkophobic and Islamophobic Serbs and Montenegrins. His successor Danilo Petrovic Njegos II (reg. 1851–60) renounced ecclesiastical authority and instead obtained recognition at home and abroad (still primarily from Russia) as a secular hereditary prince, thereby becoming free to marry and have children. His successor, his nephew Prince Nikola (reg. 1860–1918) upgraded his expanding but very poor principality to the status of a kingdom in 1910.

As a Russian 'client statelet' in the western Balkans, Montenegro was repeatedly augmented in size between 1799 and 1913. Montenegro's major territorial expansions came about: (i) through joint operations with Russia against the Ottoman Empire in 1799; (ii) in conjunction with Russia's victory over the Ottoman Empire in the Russo-Turkish War of 1877–8, which also resulted in general European (and not just Russian) recognition of Serbia, Montenegro and Romania as fully independent states and Bulgaria as a virtually independent state; and (iii) through the resounding combined victory of Montenegro, Serbia, Bulgaria and Greece over the Ottoman Empire in the Balkan Wars of 1912–13.

However, the principality's military successes were not undergirded by successful economic development. On the contrary, def cient economic opportunities focused its best talents on military, political and literary endeavours, mostly in Serbia but also in Bosnia, establishing a strong Montenegrin presence in the middle and upper reaches of Serbian and Bosnian society. The chronic cash-strapped condition of Montenegro was affectionately satirized as the fictitious but thinly disguised principality of 'Pontevedro' in Franz Lehar's operetta*The Merry Widow* (1905). However, the underlying realities were more grim. The dire poverty of Montenegro's agricultural resource base also gave rise to very high rates of emigration (both to Serbia and to the USA) and endemic rural depopulation, which in turn contributed to the breakdown of the highland clan systems and their codes of honour, which had been the social basis of

Montenegrin society hitherto. This process was vividly described by the most famous Montenegrin, the gifted writer and former Yugoslav Communist politician Milovan Djilas (see Djilas 1958).

Like Serbia, Montenegro was allied to the *entente* against the central powers during the First World War. Despite putting up a very brave fight against a much larger foe it fell under Austro-Hungarian occupation and suffered proportionally massive loss of life and devastation, while King Nikola and his family went into exile. In 1918 Montenegro was militarily annexed and fully absorbed by the Serb-dominated Triune Kingdom of Serbs, Croats and Slovenes, which was renamed Yugoslavia in 1929. The ascendant Serbs prevented the return of King Nikola from exile, and for twenty-five years Montenegro ceased to exist as a political entity in its own right. During the inter-war years it languished as an economically depressed political backwater and continued to suffer from net emigration and widespread rural depopulation.

Montenegro's relatively inaccessible forests, mountains and gorges and its traditions of feisty independence helped to make it one of the main centres of Communist-led 'partisan' resistance to the Axis occupation of Yugoslavia during the Second World War. The partisans in Montenegro suffered terrible privations and Axis reprisals and came close to being wiped out completely more than once, but they fought on with extraordinary courage, stoicism and feats of endurance. As a result, the Montenegrins acquired further renown as doughty South Slavic 'freedom fighters', with a stature ou of all proportion to their small numbers. Since 1993, however, Montenegro's inhabitants have somewhat lived down their previous reputation as fierce fighters for Serbi causes, mainly by endeavouring to dissociate themselves from Serb belligerence in Bosnia, Croatia and, above all, Kosova and by seeking to evade military service outside Montenegro.

In 1945, a war-ravaged but territorially expanded Montenegro was 'resurrected' and 'reinvented' as one of the constituent republics of the Communist-ruled SFRY. This was part of President Tito's drive to 'cut Serbia down to size' by depriving it of as much territory and population as possible, but it was also in recognition of the disproportionately large Montenegrin role in the Communist-led partisans' victory over German Nazism and Croatian fascism. One consequence of this is that most of the territory of the Republic of Montenegro which has existed since 1945 had either *never* or only *briefly* been part of the Montenegrin dynastic statelet which existed from 1715 to 1918. It is for these reasons that much of present-day Montenegro is populated by peoples whose forebears never thought of themselves as 'Montenegrins', but on the contrary thought of themselves (or were identified by others) as Serb, Albanian, Muslim Slavic or Croat, or simply as Orthodox, Muslim or Catholic. Modern Montenegro has literally been cobbled together as the combined result of military-cum-political opportunism and Russian patronage between 1799 and 1913 and political expediency-cum-opportunism since 1945. This is not so unusual – many of the world's so-called nation-states have been cobbled together in similarly opportunistic ways and have 'discovered', 'invented' and inculcated spuriously ancient 'national' identities and pedigrees for themselves after the event. Nevertheless, the still quite recent creation of a much-enlarged and far-from-prosperous Republic of Montenegro helps to explain why opinion polls have regularly indicated that nearly half of Montenegro's inhabitants do not identify with Montenegro in terms of ethnic-cultural or ethno-national allegiance, and do not regard 'Montenegrins' as a nation separate from the 'Serb' nation. Instead, these people have tended to identify either with Serbia, mainly in the eastern and northern areas which were annexed to the Cetinje-based statelet during the nineteenth century, or with Albania, in the case of the roughly 7 per cent ethnic Albanian minority which mainly inhabits the southern areas that were annexed by the Centinje-based statelet in the late nineteenth and early twentieth centuries.

Although the Yugoslav Communist regime vigorously promoted industrialization, especially heavy and extractive industries, Montenegro did not acquire a highly industrialized economy, and its banking sector remained underdeveloped. From 1972 onward, Montenegro's industrial sector was dominated by Kombinat Aluminijuma Titograd (KAT), the giant bauxite-processing and aluminium-smelting enterprise located just outside Titograd (Podgorica). In addition, the port of Bar, major electric power plants and a spectacular high-altitude railway (running through the mountains from Bar to Podgorica and Belgrade) were built primarily to serve the needs of KAT, which during the 1980s accounted for nearly half of Montenegro's export earnings, consumed about 60 per cent of Montenegro's electricity output and accounted for most of the freight traffic on the republic's railways and passing through the port o Bar. Together with the port, the railway and its electricity suppliers, KAT accounted for about half of Montenegro's GDP. Other than Russia, Montenegro was believed to have Europe's largest reserves of bauxite (aluminium ore).

A semi-private tourism sector fourished during the 1980s, as Montenegro belatedly began to cash in on the spectacular beauties of its coastal and mountain scenery and the quaint charm of some of its smaller towns. It also had a significant merchant-shipping fleet, which generated *c*.25 per cent of its foreign-exchange earnings during the 1980s.

By 1990, while Montenegro was still under Communist rule, Montenegrin agri - culture, housing and small-scale service activities were already to considerable degrees in private hands. In addition, Montenegro had a f ourishing illegal 'black economy' and an equally flourishing semi-legal but unofficial 'grey economy' or 'informal sector each of which added at least 10 to 20 per cent to offcially recorded economic activity (possibly much more, as by definition 'black' and 'grey' economies are under-recorded)

The 'Montenegrin uprising' of 10 January 1989

The Titoist leadership of the League of Communists of Montenegro (LCM) and of the republic's presidency were ousted on 10 January 1989 by supporters of Slobodan Milosevic's so-called 'anti-bureaucratic revolution', led in Montenegro by Momir Bulatovic. As a result, Bulatovic became the new leader of the LCM, replacing the Titoist incumbent. Following the example of the Milosevic regime in Serbia, Bulatovic used the LCM's domination of Montenegro's main institutions to amend the existing constitution to provide for (i) a unicameral parliament (the Montenegrin assembly) elected on a first-past-the-post basis and (ii) a relatively strong directly elected pos of president of Montenegro, both of which he could conf dently expect to control.

The first multiparty presidential elections, 9 and 23 December 1990

In the run-off contest between the two leading candidates on 23 December, the LCM leader Momir Bulatovic resoundingly defeated the candidate of the Alliance of Reform Forces of Montenegro, affiliated to the party launched by the liberal-cosmopolitan an reform-minded SFRY prime minister Ante Markovic. The results of the concurrent parliamentary elections are shown in Table 9.2.

9.2 Montenegrin parliamentary election, 9 and 16 December 1990

Party	Seats
League of Communists of Montenegro (LCM)[1]	83
Alliance of Reform Forces of Montenegro	17
Democratic Coalition of Muslims and Albanians[2]	13
People's Party (Narodna Stranka)	12

Notes:
1. Renamed the Democratic Party of Socialists (DPS) in June 1991.
2. Comprising the Equality Party, the (Bosniak) Democratic Action Party and the (ethnic Albanian) Democratic Alliance.

Source: Europa (1992: 341–3).

In 1991 President Bulatovic appointed Milo Djukanovic (aged twenty-nine) as prime minister of Montenegro. Despite the reputation that Djukanovic acquired after 1996 as a prominent critic of Milosevic, Bulatovic and Montenegro's continu- ing political association with Serbia, Djukanovic had played a prominent role in Milosevic's 'anti-bureaucratic revolution' and appeared to be a fervent supporter of Bulatovic and Milosevic (Cohen 2002: 380).

Growing Montenegrin support for Serbia, 1990–2

Unlike the governments of the republics of Macedonia and Bosnia and Herzegovina, the Bulatovic regime initially aligned itself quite closely with Serbia when the hitherto Communist-ruled SFRY began to disintegrate from January 1990 onward. The Montenegrin member of the federation's collective presidency resigned in protest in March 1991 when Serbia's request for a state of emergency was refused. Branko Kostic, his pro-Serb Montenegrin replacement, chaired the illegitimate 'rump' presidency (representing only Serbia, Montenegro, Kosova and Vojvodina) from October 1991. During the same month, however, President Bulatovic accepted the Italian-brokered EC proposals for peace with Croatia and for the (re-)establishment of a very loose Yugoslav confederation (which Serbia's Milosevic regime contemp- tuously rejected). In addition, the Montenegrin government objected to the use of Montenegrin citizens in Serbia's war with Croatia, and the Montenegrin assembly approved a declaration of Montenegrin sovereignty. Some Montenegrin forces never theless participated in Serbia's war against Croatia, especially in the utterly callous and unnecessary JNA siege/shelling of Dubrovnik, which served no other military purpose than to inflict grief and physical damage on this 'jewel of the Adriatic'. Western observers and commentators were particularly incensed by this cynical and gratuitous vandalism.

In a Montenegrin referendum held on 1 March 1992, 96 per cent of the votes cast were in favour of remaining part of a rump FRY, comprising only Montenegro and Serbia (including Kosova and Vojvodina). The turn-out was 66 per cent, but the referendum was boycotted by Montenegro's substantial Muslim Slav and ethnic Albanian minorities. On 27 April 1992 Serbia and Montenegro inaugurated the new FRY, which comprised 44 per cent of the area and 39 per cent of the population of the former Communist-ruled federation. Montenegro accounted for only about 6 per cent of the population of the FRY (*The Economist*, 23 July 1994, p. 42).

The elections to the FRY parliament, 31 May 1992

The turn-out in Montenegro was 57 per cent, compared with 55 per cent in Serbia. Montenegro, because of its small size, had only 23 seats in the 138-seat house of deputies (lower house) of the FRY parliament, and these were all won by the ruling Democratic Party of Socialists. Milan Panic, the Yugoslav-American millionaire who served as FRY prime minister from mid-July to 29 December 1992, soon turned into a Western-backed rival and challenger to President Milosevic and came to depend on the backing of the Montenegrin representatives in the FRY parliament to retain office Panic could not have survived the votes of confidence held on 4 September and 2 November without the support of Montenegro's representatives in the upper house of the FRY parliament (the chamber of citizens), in which they held half the seats.

The election to the eighty-five-seat Montenegrin assembly, 20 December 1992

9.3 Montenegrin parliamentary election, 20 December 1992

Party	Seats
Democratic Party of Socialists (DPS)	46
People's Party	14
Liberal Alliance of Montenegro	13
Serbian Radical Party	8
Social Democratic Party of Reformists	4

The two-round presidential election of 20 December 1992 and 10 January 1993

Momir Bulatovic gained 43 per cent of the votes in the first round, whereas Brank Kostic (who favoured even closer ties with Serbia) obtained 24 per cent. In the second round Bulatovic was re-elected with 63.3 per cent of the votes, while Branko Kostic obtained 36.7 per cent.

Montenegro's gradual estrangement from the Milosevic regime and Serbia, 1993–2000

By late 1992 most of the initial Montenegrin support for pan-Serb belligerence during the breakup of the former SFRY had given way to growing misgivings and 'shame at the role Montenegrins had played' in that process (Miller 1997: 179). For a while, therefore, even President Momir Bulatovic distanced himself from his 'godfather' President Milosevic. An attempt to declare Montenegrin independence no longer seemed out of the question, even though it seemed certain that Serbia and the VJ would have forcibly suppressed any such a move.

From 1993 to 1995, moreover, Serbia maintained an embargo on food supplies to Montenegro, which the Milosevic regime accused of having re-exported food from Serbia to neighbouring states (including Albania) which it considered hostile to the Serbs. Because of the UN-sponsored international economic sanctions against the FRY, this Serbian food embargo severely exacerbated food shortages, retail price inflation and recourse to black-market activities in Montenegro. This further stimulated Montenegrin criticisms of Serbian 'domination'. There was also growing resentment among Montenegrins at being tarred with the same brush as Serbia by the 'international community', as well as towards the profoundly damaging economic fallout from the Bosnian conflict and from the UN economic sanctions against the FRY. These sanctions slowly but surely helped to deliver much of the Montenegrin economy into the hands of increasingly powerful criminal gangs, smugglers and black-marketeers, who increasingly dealt in illegal arms and drugs shipments, stolen cars, and sanctions-busting trade in fuels and cigarettes. As in Bosnia, Macedonia, Croatia, Kosova and Serbia, these mafia-like criminal networks quite rapidly gained control of 30–5 per cent of the economy (the estimates vary considerably), engaged in widespread intimidation and protection rackets, acquired extensive control over many public institutions and increasingly undermined the ability of most inhabitants to 'make honest livings'. The effects were deeply corrupting and corrosive.

A large part of the trouble was that the UN, the USA and the EU and its member states applied sanctions in very uneven, selective, dishonest and incomplete ways, thereby fostering, enriching and empowering criminal networks on a massive scale in the FRY and in adjacent states. Subsequently, the UN, the USA and the EU and its member states (utterly hypocritically) 'blamed' this dire state of affairs on the govern ments, 'cultures' and 'mentalities' of the post-Communist Balkan states, accusing them of being 'soft on crime' and too ready to accept and indulge in corruption, black-marketeering and criminal activity, instead of honourably acknowledging that Western-instigated sanctions and the very erratic and 'leaky' ways in which they were applied bore prime responsibility for these profoundly damaging developments. Adding insult to injury, ever since then the post-Communist Balkan states have repeatedly been chastised and 'punished' in various ways for these scourges, whose growth to such pervasive and damaging proportions has largely stemmed from the sanctions which were so unevenly and counterproductively imposed on the Yugoslav successor states by the West. It is therefore scarcely surprising that, from 1993 onward, growing numbers of Montenegrins sought to dissociate Montenegro as much as possible from Serbian, Bosnian and Croatian belligerence and the deeply damaging, corrupting and criminalizing effects of 'leaky' Western sanctions, although by then the worst consequences were so strongly entrenched that it has proved extremely difficult to escape or overcome them. The point of these comments is not to 'white-wash' the conduct of the peoples and governments of Montenegro and its neighbours, who were by no means beyond reproach. Rather, it is to draw attention to the shirked responsibility and moral hypocrisy of the Western powers, which have repeatedly chastised and penalized the post-Communist Balkan states for problems of criminality, corruption and other misconduct which were in large measure fostered by Western policies (especially sanctions). Instead of chastisement and punishment, these states need and deserve much greater Western economic assistance to overcome the huge and still ongoing damage that has been infl cted on them by the West during the 1990s. The chief culprits are seeking to deflect attention from their own culpability by continually finding fault with the Balkan states which were among the victims an have in large measure become hostage to the rich and powerful criminal smuggling and trafficking networks that were fostered by the 'international' (i.e., Western) sanctions regimes during the 1990s.

Prime Minister Milo Djukanovic appeared initially to have been a staunch supporter of the broadly pro-Milosevic stance taken by President Bulatovic and gradually to have become disillusioned, frustrated and resentful towards the hegemonic behaviour of Serbia and the Milosevic regime towards Montenegro and with the profound economic damage and international isolation that were being inflicted on Montenegr by UN sanctions against the FRY and by Montenegro's continuing close association with Serbian aggression, economic sclerosis and hyperinflation. No doubt partly t further his own political ambitions, Djukanovic began to adopt a much more detached or even critical stance towards the Milosevic regime, Bulatovic and Montenegro's ongoing ties with Serbia. Nevertheless, until Serbia was convulsed by major political confrontations between Serbian opposition forces and the Milosevic regime from late November 1996 to March 1997, Djukanovic trod carefully and avoided any open breach with Milosevic. Even after he publicly voiced support for Serbia's opposition forces against the Milosevic regime in December 1996, he still refrained from advocating outright Montenegrin secession from the FRY, not least because Montenegro's inhabitants had become (and have remained) deeply polarized into pro- and anti-independence camps and because Milosevic still had the power to topple or undermine the much weaker Montenegrin government and to order a Serbian invasion or military takeover of Montenegro. Nevertheless, in October 1993 the Djukanovic government did allow UN monitors to start patrolling Montenegro's borders with Bosnia (ostensibly in order to police and enforce more scrupulously the very 'leaky' sanctions which the 'international community' had decided to impose on the Bosnian Serbs from 8 May 1993 onward) and announced that it would welcome a mission from the OSCE (*Independent*, 26 October 1993, p. 12). Montenegro's representatives in the FRY parliament also supported the FRY prime minister Milan Panic and the FRY president Dobrica Cosic against the Milosevic regime from September to December 1992 and tried (unsuccessfully) to keep President Cosic in off ce when he was ousted by the Serbian Radical Party (SRS) and Milosevic loyalists on 31 May 1993.

Another expression of the growing desire of many Montenegrins to distance themselves from Milosevic's Serbia was the re-establishment of an autocephalous Montenegrin Orthodox Church 31 October 1993. This met with strong resistance from the Serbian Orthodox Church (into which the former Montenegrin Orthodox Church had been forcibly merged in 1920) and from Europe's other major Orthodox churches, which since then have staunchly refused to recognize this 'breakaway Montenegrin church' (as they see it). Father Antonije Abramovic, who had lived in Canada for over forty years, was appointed as the patriarch of the new church.

Montenegrin grievances towards Serbia increased still further during 1994 and 1995, because neither the Montenegrin nor the FRY governments were able to halt (let alone reverse) the devastating economic contraction and surge in poverty and unemployment which had begun in 1991–3. In addition, Montenegrins increasingly refused to serve in the VJ when they were called up for military service. In some cases, whole units withdrew. During a visit to Cetinje in October 1995, President Momir Bulatovic's car was stoned by protestors demanding Montenegrin secession from the FRY. Nevertheless, despite mounting unrest, the Democratic Party of Socialists was able to hold on to power in the parliamentary elections of November 1996 (see Table 9.4).

9.4 Montenegrin parliamentary election, 3 November 1996

Party	Seats
Democratic Party of Socialists (led by Milica Pejanovic-Djurisic)	45
National Accord (People's Party + Liberal Alliance of Montenegro)	19
Party of Democratic Action (Muslim Slav party)	3
Democratic Alliance of Montenegro (mainly ethnic Albanian party)	2
Democratic Union of Albanians (ethnic Albanian party)	2

Source: Freedom House (1998: 656).

Increasingly open Montenegrin support for the anti-Milosevic opposition movements in Serbia, November 1996 to March 1997

Montenegro's (oppositional) national accord alliance held a rally in Podgorica on 26 November 1996 in support of Serbian mass demonstrations against the Milosevic regime. On 5 December even President Momir Bulatovic publicly criticized the Milosevic regime's attempts to invalidate the opposition victories in Serbia's local elections (*EEN*, 1996, vol. 10, no. 24, p. 8). The following day the Montenegrin authorities stated that 'The annulment of democratic elections belongs to the practice of totalitarian regimes' (*IHT*, 7 December 1996, p. 5). On 29 December Montenegro's premier Milo Djukanovic sent a letter of support to the Serbian students leading mass protest against the Milosevic regime (*EEN*, 1996, vol. 10, no. 25, p. 9).

Premier Djukanovic brought out into the open a growing rift between himself and President Bulatovic over Milosevic on 21 February 1997. He declared that 'Milosevic's policy is not the policy for the future of the people of Serbia and Yugoslavia' and that Milosevic should be removed from 'any offce in Yugoslavia's political life'. On 24 March, after a barrage of criticism for these statements, Djukanovic was forced to resign as deputy chairman of the governing Democratic Party of Socialists (DPS). The following month, however, President Bulatovic and seventeen pro-Milosevic deputies in the Montenegrin assembly left the DPS and formed a separate parliamentary faction. The People's Party also split. Its leader Novak Kilibarda, who opposed Milosevic and favoured secession from the FRY, retained the allegiance of five deputies

On 23 June 1997, when Milosevic suddenly decided to change the constitution of the FRY to provide for the direct election of the FRY president (in order to strengthen his own chances of getting elected to that post) and also to increase the powers of the FRY president (his future self), Montenegro's governing DPS decided to accept Milosevic's candidacy for the FRY presidency but to oppose his proposed constitutional changes, because their main effect was to substantially reduce Montenegro's weight in the federation. The existing system under which the FRY president was chosen by the two houses of the FRY parliament gave Montenegro a de-facto veto over the choice of president, thanks to the equal representation of Serbia and Montenegro in the upper house of the FRY parliament. By making the FRY president directly elected, however, Montenegro's tiny electorate was bound to be hugely out-voted by the much larger Serbian electorate. Milosevic was nevertheless able to push through his constitutional changes against the wishes of the ruling DPS, because the changes were accepted by President Momir Bulatovic and his supporters in the FRY parliament. However, this precipitated moves within the DPS to curb the power of Momir Bulatovic and oust him from the presidency.

In July 1997 Milica Pejanovic-Djurisic became chairman of the DPS, while the DPS adopted Milo Djukanovic as its candidate in Montenegro's forthcoming presidential election. Djukanovic declared that the FRY

> should be a country of deep reforms, a developed democracy . . . integrated into the world economy . . . President Bulatovic feels that we do not have the right to show much initiative, and that we should have great respect for Slobodan Milosevic. However, a passive stance such as this will only lead to an unconditional acceptance of Yugoslavia the way Mr Milosevic and Serbia see it.
>
> (*Moscow News*, 19 June–2 July 1997, p. 4)

The Montenegrin presidential elections of 5 and 19 October 1997

In the f rst round, Milo Djukanovic, contrary to poll predictions that he would trounce President Bulatovic, trailed by 145,337 votes to 147,609. The other six candidates won fewer than 13,000 votes between them. Turn-out was a respectable 67 per cent. During the campaign Djukanovic refrained from advocating Montenegrin indepen - dence. Instead, he declared that Montenegro should have equal status with Serbia within the FRY (*EEN*, 1997, vol. 11, no. 19, pp. 1–2). On 19 October 1997, however, Djukanovic won the second round with 173,099 votes to Bulatovic's 166,771, on a turn-out of 75 per cent. The OSCE concluded that, even though there had been 'imperfections and infractions', on the whole 'the elections at the polling station level were well-conducted' and the result broadly reflected the will of the electorate. Bulatovic, whose presidential term was not due to expire until 15 January 1998, accused Djukanovic of interfering in voter registration and of involvement in cigarette-smuggling. Djukanovic retaliated by accusing Bulatovic of embezzlement.

In Podgorica on 14 January 1998, riot police broke up a demonstration by pro-Bulatovic supporters accusing Djukanovic of electoral fraud. Djukanovic was sworn in as president of Montenegro the next day. The long political ascendancy of Momir Bulatovic thus gave way to that of Milo Djukanovic.

The Montenegrin economy, 1991–8

Following the imposition of UN sanctions against Yugoslavia in 1991–2, Montenegrin industries mostly either closed down or reduced their production to about 20 per cent or less of capacity. The KAP, the huge bauxite-processing and aluminium-smelting enterprise outside Podgorica, worked at about 20 per cent of capacity from 1992 to 1995. Montenegro's merchant-shipping fleet lay stranded or impounded around th world. The war with Croatia plus UN-inspired sanctions against the Yugoslav belligerents caused a complete collapse of Montenegro's tourist industry, which had just begun to 'take off' during the 1980s (the country's coastal scenery, mountains and river gorges are spectacularly beautiful). Unemployment far exceeded 15 per cent, but was hard to quantify (*EEN*, 1995, vol. 9, no. 6, p. 3).

KAP, 'with its under-capitalized bauxite mines, worn out railways and 1972-vintage aluminium smelter', was kept under public ownership and management until 1998, by which time it had run up large accumulated losses of 157 million US dollars. Years of heavy losses and non-transparent transactions had 'drained the economy' by imposing heavy losses on the railways, the electricity company, banks and other creditors. In 1998 the Swiss-based firm Glencore was awarded a controversial fiv year 'management contract', which was concluded in secret (without an open tender or public bidding process) and involved 'a local trading company with close ties to Montenegro's ruling circles'. The contract to run the bankrupt enterprise guaranteed an annual payment to Glencore. Glencore was also permitted to set a timetable for the privatization of the enterprise, in which it would have the right of first refusal an the right to sell any asset without having to obtain prior government approval, while KAP's debts were rescheduled (*FT*, 8 December 1998, p. 2; *FT*, Survey, 10 July 2001, pp. 14–15).

Elsewhere in the industrial sector, Montenegro initiated a privatization process during the early 1990s by transferring state-owned assets to a number of state funds which by 1996 had become majority shareholders in about 350 enterprises (EBRD 2000b: 9). The prevalent approach to privatization in Montenegro was to transfer majority ownership to three state-managed funds, with employees retaining a minority holding. Ten per cent of each enterprise's shares were allocated to its employees, who were given the right to buy an additional 30 per cent at heavily discounted prices. The remaining 60 per cent was split between three state-managed funds: the devel - opment fund received 36 per cent, the pension fund 18 per cent and the unemployment fund 6 per cent. These funds were required by law to sell their stakes within fe years of the restructuring of an enterprise, with a minimum 20 per cent to be sold each year. By mid-1996, this first phase, begun in 1991, was almost complete with 96 per cen of enterprises transferred from social ownership to ownership by these funds and by employees (*Business Europa*, September–October 1996, p. 17).

By early 1996 Montenegro had privatized 90 per cent of its industry (other than KAP), whereas in Serbia 90 per cent of industry remained state-owned (*EEN*, 1996, vol. 10, no. 4, p. 4). For the first time, moreover, Montenegrin wages were higher than Serbian wages (*The Economist*, 14 December 1996, p. 44). Prior to 1998, however, the only significant sale of a Montenegrin enterprise to a foreign strategic investor wa the purchase of Niksic brewery by Interbrew of Belgium in 1997.

The war of attrition between Djukanovic and Milosevic, 1998

In retaliation for the Montenegrin voters' rejection of Bulatovic in the presidential election, Milosevic economically blockaded Montenegro. New border controls were erected between Montenegro and Serbia, and Serbia rerouted its maritime imports and exports from Bar in Montenegro to Thessaloniki in Greece. Meanwhile, Momir Bulatovic launched a new party, the SNP of Montenegro, drawn mainly from the pro-Serbian wing of the DPS, on 21 April 1998.

Radoje Kontic, the (ethnically Montenegrin) prime minister of the FRY, was dismissed by votes of no confidence in both houses of the FRY parliament on 18 May 1998. Although Kontic was formally accused of incompetence, Djukanovic claimed that in reality Kontic was being punished for having refused to declare a state of emergency in Montenegro when Bulatovic lost the Montenegrin presidential election in October 1997 (*IHT*, 19 May 1998, p. 6). The next day the Montenegrin assembly declared the removal of Kontic illegal and voted not to recognize the new FRY government, in which Milosevic had appointed Momir Bulatovic to the post of prime minister. However, Bulatovic was approved by both houses of the FRY parliament, in which the only representatives from Montenegro were members of Bulatovic's new party (*EEN*, 1998, vol. 12, no. 6, p. 8).

In retaliation, the Montenegrin assembly replaced the six deputies from Montenegro in the upper house of the FRY parliament with six new nominees and passed a resolution requiring them to follow the instructions of the Montenegrin assembly(*EEN*, 1998, vol. 12, no. 6, p. 2). It also announced that it would no longer respect laws promulgated by the FRY parliament, that it would not recognize the new FRY prime minister, and that it would ignore the dictates of Milosevic. It accused Milosevic of trying to undermine the Montenegrin government by suspending pension payments and FRY funds to Montenegro (*IHT*, 29 May 1998, p. 2).

Elections to the Montenegrin assembly, 31 May 1998

The turn-out was 76.5 per cent and OSCE observers considered that the election had been 'generally well conducted' (*FT*, 2 June 1998, p. 2), but there was concern over the pro-Djukanovic bias in the Montenegrin media and the anti-Djukanovic bias in much of the Serbian media (*The Guardian*, 2 June 1998, p. 12). See Table 9.5 for the distribution of seats and votes cast.

9.5 Montenegrin parliamentary election, 31 May 1998

	Share of votes (%)	Seats
The 'To Live Better' coalition (DPS, SDP and People's Party)	48.9	42
including: Democratic Party of Socialists	–	(30)
People's Party	–	(7)
Social Democratic Party	–	(5)
SNP (led by Momir Bulatovic)	35.6	29
Liberal Alliance of Montenegro (openly secessionist)	6.2	5
Democratic Alliance of Montenegro (mainly ethnic Albanian party)	1.6	1
Democratic Alliance of Albanians (ethnic Albanian party)	1.1	1
Others	6.6	0

Source: www.montenet.org/politics/parties, accessed 5 November 2005.

President Djukanovic's 'To Live Better' coalition won a more convincing victory than most observers had expected. It formed a coalition government headed by Filip Vujanovic in June–July 1998, with the support of the Liberal Alliance of Montenegro and one ethnic Albanian deputy.

On 12 June, President Djukanovic called for Kosova to be granted substantial autonomy and for the involvement of OCSE mediators in the talks on its future, warning 'Montenegro will not be dragged into internal confcts on Yugoslav territory. If a conflict flares up we will recall our army recruits from Kosova'(*BCE*, June 1998, p. 20).

The Montenegrin assembly passed a new law on Montenegrin representation in the chamber of republics (the upper house of the FRY parliament) on 16 June. Henceforth all Montenegrin deputies in that chamber were to be elected on a first-past-the-pos rather than on a proportional-representation basis, thus depriving Momir Bulatovic's SNP of representation in the FRY parliament (*FT*, 18 June 1998, p. 3). Next day, the Montenegrin assembly also resolved that Montenegrin national servicemen should be withdrawn from Kosova and that the contact group's 12 June recommendations for Kosova should be implemented (*EEN*, 1998, vol. 12, no. 7, p. 8).

The Montenegrin government resolved on 23 July 1998 unilaterally to issue export and import licences independently of the FRY government (*EEN*, 1998, vol. 12, no. 9, p. 5), and on 3 August the Montenegrin government decided to suspend all contacts with the FRY government until Momir Bulatovic stood down as FRY prime minister, warning that a referendum on Montenegro's secession from the FRY was possible (*IHT*, 4 August 1998, p. 7).

During the autumn of 1998, Montenegro's political leaders continued to find way to needle the Milosevic regime, for example by printing newspapers and magazines banned by the Serbian authorities and then smuggling them into Belgrade by bus, train and plane and by halting Montenegrin transfers of tax revenue to the FRY government, which the Montenegrin government and parliament claimed had not been legally constituted since May. The Montenegrin government also took over the tasks of licensing mass media, levying customs duties and approving imports and exports from its territory. It diverted roughly 1 million US dollars in FRY taxes to fund its pension fund (because Belgrade had not provided funding for the previous four months). It also announced plans to open its own 'liaison' off ces in five foreign capitals an began to negotiate separate trade deals with Western states (having won permission to tap international f nancial institutions under a partial exemption from international sanctions against Serbia). It licensed a radio station to begin transmissions into Serbia and was considering adopting a separate Montenegrin currency. In November 1998, in a bid to reassert its jurisdiction over the media, Serbia levied a 300,000 US dollar fine against the publisher of *Monitor*, a Montenegrin magazine that had illustrated an article about Serbia with a picture of a student group calling for national resistance. Montenegrin officials announced that the fine would not be enforced. However, because of the strong allegiance that a large minority of Montenegro's inhabitants still maintained towards the FRY and its armed forces, Djukanovic and his governing coalition cast themselves as supporters of a reformed FRY, rather than as champions of its further disintegration. Polls taken in autumn 1998 found Montenegrins to be deeply divided on the issue of greater independence, with about 30 to 35 per cent in each camp. President Djukanovic therefore stipulated that, before Montenegrin independence could be attained, it would need to be supported by two-thirds of the population, partly in order to diminish the serious risk that a vote for independence could precipitate major social unrest (*IHT*, 28 November 1998, p. 7). (Djukanovic appeared to have forgotten about this prudent concern during the run up to the May 2006 referendum on Montenegrin independence, when he initially held out for the issue to be resolved by a simple majority on a minimum 41 per cent turn-out.)

Towards Montenegrin 'independence by installments', 1999

By January 1999 Montenegro had ceased payment of any taxes or dues to the FRY institutions and all formal participation in FRY decision-making, and customs duties were accruing directly to the Montenegrin exchequer. In mid-January two border-crossings were opened between Montenegro and Croatia, despite strong opposition from Belgrade. In practice the (largely Serbian) VJ, in the form of the Second Army based in Podgorica, was the only FRY Yugoslav institution which the Montenegrin government still recognized. On 4 March Montenegro announced that it was unilaterally abolishing entry-visa requirements.

On 24 March, the first day of the Kosova war (24 March to 10 June 1999), the government of Montenegro announced that it would not recognize the Milosevic regime's declaration of an 'imminent state of war', fearing that this was but a prelude to a state of emergency that would enable the FRY government to invoke sweeping powers over Montenegro (*FT*, 25 March 1999, p. 2).

The US state department continued to express fears that Milosevic might provoke violence in Montenegro in order to give the estimated 12,000 VJ troops there an excuse to oust the elected government, which had declared its neutrality in the Kosova conflic (*IHT*, 6 April 1999, p. 1). Javier Solana warned Milosevic on 2 April that NATO had 'plans to stop' any attempt to overthrow or unseat President Djukanovic (*FT*, 3 April 1999, p. 1).

The FRY military prosecutor hit back at Montenegro on 18 April by opening criminal-court proceedings against deputy prime minister Novak Kilibarda of Montenegro on the charge of 'undermining' Yugoslavia (*EEN*, 1999, vol. 12, no. 16, p. 10). The next day the (largely Serbian) VJ headquarters stepped up the pressure by delivering a letter to the Montenegrin government, ordering it to place Montenegro's police directly under FRY military command. The order elicited an instant rejection from President Djukanovic. Tension increased further when forces of the second corps of the VJ moved to close the Debeli Brijeg border-crossing between Montenegro and Croatia (near Herceg Novi). Croatia's ambassador to the UN complained of an incursion by up to 300 mainly Serbian troops into the UN-monitored demilitarized zone in the Prevlavka peninsula, whose possession was disputed between Croatia and Montenegro, and demanded the withdrawal of these troops from the area (*FT*, 22 April 1999, p. 2). The border-crossing was soon reopened, after these troops had closed it for two days, but the VJ kept a post just inside the border in order to deny access to foreigners not in possession of valid FRY entry visas (*FT*, 23 April 1999, p. 2).

On 15 May 1999, amid the escalating conflict between Serbia and NATO and ethni Albanians in Kosova, the VJ closed Montenegro's border with Albania, in order to prevent Kosovar Albanian refugees from crossing into Albania (*IHT*, 17 May 1999, p. 6). The VJ also placed checkpoints on the border between Montenegro and Bosnia and Herzegovina, in an attempt to prevent Montenegrin and Serbian recruits and reservists from draft-dodging, as by then only about 20 per cent of would-be recruits and reservists from Montenegro were complying with military call-up notices (*The Times*, 17 May 1999, p. 9). On 21 May hundreds of residents of Cetinje gathered to protest against the arrival of some 1,300 VJ reservists. This provocative move came a day after the VJ had closed all of Montenegro's main frontier-crossings, confiscatin Italian aid and turning back trucks carrying supplies because the drivers had no FRY visas. The VJ trained artillery on the town and set up checkpoints on surrounding roads. President Djukanov had warned: 'The regime in Belgrade wants to install the Yugoslav army as a dictatorship power in Montenegro.' At that time, the Montenegrin government controlled *c.*10,000 police in Montenegro, whereas Milosevic controlled *c.*20,000 VJ troops in the republic (*FT*, 22 May 1999, p. 2).

On 26 May Montenegro demanded the withdrawal of VJ troops, control over its own economy, and the right to conduct its own foreign policy, but the VJ continued to flex its muscles and set up periodic roadblocks (*IHT*, 12 July 1999, p. 4). In an attempt to gain increased Western backing by complying with Western stipulations, on 30 June Djukanovic also told a rally in Niksic that Montenegro would hand over to the ICTY 'anyone indicted for war crimes who happens to be in the territory of Montenegro' (*IHT*, 3 July 1999).

On 2 July 1999 the NATO secretary-general Javier Solana warned that, while NATO was not in favour of Montenegro becoming independent from Serbia, NATO would take action if Milosevic tried to provoke a conflict in Montenegro. According

to the NATO commander General Wesley Clark, Milosevic was sending reinforcements into Montenegro and putting ethnic Serbs and political allies of Momir Bulatovic
into positions of authority there (*IHT*, 3 July 1999, p. 5). Meanwhile, President
Djukanovic said that the Montenegrin government was waiting patiently for Serbia's
reply to its proposal to redefine their partnership and warned that Montenegro woul
go it alone if Serbia adhered to its 'retrograde' stance (*IHT*, 3 July 1999). On 9 July
the Tanjug news agency announced that representatives of Milosevic's Socialist
Party of Serbia and Djukanovic's DPS would meet the following week to discuss
Montenegro's demands, which included Montenegrin control of any VJ units based
on its own territory, the right to choose the FRY prime minister (since Serbia had
chosen Milosevic to be the FRY president), and the right to adopt a currency board
of its own, with fnancial backing from the West (*IHT*, 12 July 1999, p. 4; *FT*, 14 July
1999, p. 2). These talks between Montenegro and Serbia on redefiing their relationship
began on 14 July. President Djukanovic went into the negotiations declaring:

> I want first of all to see Montenegro as a democratic country, economically
> developed and integrated into Europe. If Montenegro can achieve this in its present
> status as a member of the Yugoslav Federation, then that is good. If that should
> prove impossible, however, then the issue of independence will be imposed as
> an inevitable alternative.
>
> (*IHT*, 15 July 1999, p. 6)

On 5 August 1999 the Montenegrin government approved a set of draft proposals
redefining its relations with Serbia and warned that, if these were rejected, a referendum
on independence would be held in Montenegro. The main proposals were:

1. To change the name FRY to Association of the States of Montenegro and Serbia,
    or Commonwealth of Montenegro and Serbia.
2. To replace the FRY government with a six-member 'council of ministers'.
3. To replace the current two-chamber FRY parliament with a single house, with
    equal numbers of seats for Montenegro and Serbia. This unicameral assembly
    would choose the FRY president, but with both republics retaining a veto.
4. To give Montenegro its own defence ministry and army command. Recruits from
    Montenegro were to serve only in Montenegro, and troops on Montenegrin soil
    would no longer be commanded from Belgrade. The defence council was to be
    jointly chaired by the presidents of Montenegro and Serbia, a unanimous decision
    was to be necessary to declare either war or a state of emergency, and command
    over the FRY armed forces (VJ) was to alternate between Montenegro and Serbia
    every two years.
5. To allow Montenegro to have its own foreign ministry, foreign policy and
    currency.

> (*IHT*, 6 August 1999, p. 4; *FT*, 6 August 1999, p. 2;
> *The Economist*, 14 August 1999, p. 32)

Prime Minister Filip Vujanovic stated that these draft proposals would allow
Montenegro to 'secure democratic and economic development' and join European and
world institutions without 'harming' Serbia, but the Serbian deputy prime minister
and ultra-nationalist Vojislav Seselj warned that the VJ would intervene if Montenegro
tried to secede from the FRY. President Djukanovic gave Serbia six weeks to accept
or reject Montenegro's proposals (*IHT*, 6 August 1999, p. 4).

However, Montenegro's coalition government was deeply divided on the issue of independence. The DPS's main coalition partner, the Social Democratic Party, favoured outright independence, whereas the smaller coalition partner, the People's Party (with the notable exception of its leader Novak Kilibarda), wanted to maintain a union of some sort with Serbia. These divisions, which were mirrored to some degree with the DPS, allowed President Djukanovic to procrastinate or sit on the fence (Roberts 1999: 13). At that time, opinion surveys showed that 35 to 40 per cent of Montenegro's 680,000 inhabitants favoured retaining an association with Serbia, while a similar proportion wanted complete independence. However, Serbia never formally replied to the Montenegrin proposals of 5 August 1999 to restructure the constitutional relationship between the two republics. Even though Djukanovic had promised to hold a referendum on independence if Serbia did not reply to those proposals within six weeks, nine months later he announced that he was not in a hurry (*IHT*, 25 May 2000, pp. 1, 5; *IHT*, 19 September 2000, p. 6).

The FRY government was reshuffled on 12 August 1999. Momir Bulatovic remained prime minister, but seven ministers were dismissed and twelve new ones (including five from the ultra-nationalist Serbian Radical Party) were brought in, expanding the cabinet to twenty-seven members. All the new ministers were on a list of 308 prominent South Slav politicians, officials and businessmen who were barred from travelling to the West, and none of them were members of Montenegro's ruling DPS.

There were further negotiations between the DPS and the Socialist Party of Serbia and its allies (including the Yugoslav United Left and the Radical Party) on 25–26 October 1999. The Serb delegation was led by Vojislav Seselj, Serbia's deputy prime minister and leader of the Serbian Radical Party, who again warned that separation would lead to a 'bloody war' and would provoke another NATO intervention in the Balkans (*FT*, 26 October 1999, p. 12). However, the talks again yielded no results (*FT*, 30 October 1999, p. 5).

Meanwhile, Montenegro took further unilateral steps towards de-facto independence. On 29 October, its assembly adopted a new citizenship law which gave applicants the right to hold Montenegrin as well as Yugoslav citizenship, provided they had lived in Montenegro for ten years consecutively prior to the application (*FT*, 30 October 1999, p. 5). On 24 November the Montenegrin government declared the airports in Podgorica and Tivat to be Montenegrin state property and took them out of the hands of the Yugoslav airline JAT. On 25 April 2000, furthermore, a memorandum of understanding and cooperation was signed with Albania during a visit by the Albanian foreign minister (*EEN*, 2000, vol. 12, no. 23, p. 7).

In response to such actions, the FRY air-traffic directorate and the VJ seized control of Podgorica's airport and suspended traffic into and out of Montenegro for twelv hours on 8 December 1999. They also raised objections to the building of a hangar in the military part of the airport for use by the helicopters and aircraft of the Montenegrin government and police. However, air traffic returned to normal the following day. I early March 2000 a television station connected to the United Yugoslav Left, the party of Milosevic's wife Mirjana Markovic, began broadcasting pro-Serbian propaganda using military television transmitters, and a new pro-Serbian paramilitary unit was set up within the VJ in Montenegro. This 'Seventh Military Police battalion' was made up of pro-Milosevic Montenegrins, and it included 900 trained saboteurs and special forces (*Daily Telegraph*, 7 March 2000, p. 23). On 25–26 March, under pressure from Belgrade, Djukanovic announced that his government had agreed to allow VJ troops to join Montenegrin police at checkpoints along Montenegro's borders with Albania and Kosova, partly because Montenegro had received no security or economic guarantees from the West. Nevertheless, Djukanovic reaffirmed his opposition to th creation of a special military battalion numbering about 1,000 men within the Yugoslav Second Army based in Podgorica, warning: 'They are in fact a paramilitary unit and their party association is unanimous ... They are devoted to Mr Milosevic. Over 50 per cent of them have criminal records. They are not being retained to protect the country but to overthrow the government' (*IHT*, 29 March 2000, p. 6).

In May 2000 Milosevic still had as many as 20,000 soldiers stationed in Montenegro, including paramilitary forces believed to be far better trained and equipped than Montenegro's growing police force of some 15,000 (*IHT*, 25 May 2000, p. 5), but the Montenegrin police and the VJ nevertheless 'staged joint military exercises to show tensions had eased' after the stand-off over control of Podgorica airport (*FT*, 2 June 2000, p. 8). However, tensions flared up again on 31 May 2000, when President Djukanovic's security adviser Goran Zugic was assassinated.

The local elections held in Podgorica and Herzeg Novi on 11 June 2000

OECD observers were satisfied. The turn-out was 75 per cent. President Djukanovi hoped that his ruling three-party 'To Live Better' coalition would defeat both the anti-independence SNP and the pro-independence Liberal Alliance, thus keeping his options open on the highly contentious independence issue. The VJ kept tensions high by holding military exercises in Montenegro. On 9 June Podgorica was awash with speculation after a Russian newspaper reported that Milosevic planned to create a new Yugoslavia made up of eight cantons, in which Montenegro would have equal status with regions within Serbia. At the same time, members of the pro-Yugoslav SNP were increasingly unhappy with Belgrade's dominance of their party (*FT*, 10 June 2000, p. 6). About one-third of Montenegro's population lived in Podgorica, so these two local elections involved about a third of the electorate (*Independent*, 13 June 2000, p. 16).

The results reflected the political divisions in Montenegro over the union with Serbia. In Podgorica the 'To Live Better' coalition won twenty-eight of the fifty-fou seats (a gain of one); the pro-Milosevic 'Yugoslavia Coalition' obtained twenty-two seats (a loss of one); and the Liberal Alliance obtained four seats. In Herceg Novi the 'Yugoslavia Coalition' won nineteen of the thirty-f ve seats (a gain of six); the 'To Live Better' coalition obtained fourteen seats; and the Liberal Alliance obtained two seats. Montenegro's pro-Serb constituencies were mainly concentrated in cities close to the Serbian border. However, the population of Herceg Novi included large numbers of retired VJ officers and Serbian migrants and refugees from Bosnia, Herzegovina, Croatia and Kosova (*The Guardian*, 13 June 2000, p. 15). Some voters expressed dissatisfaction with corruption scandals involving the ruling parties (*FT*, 13 June 2000, p. 10). Furthermore, Djukanovic and the Montenegrin government had improved relations with neighbouring Croatia by reopening a border crossing near Herceg Novi and broadening cooperation with Dubrovnik, but Herceg Novi's new mayor based his campaign on promises to oppose such cooperation*Independent*, 13 June 2000, p. 16). The results were a blow for the Liberal Alliance, which had pre-cipitated these elections 'by pulling out of government-led local coalitions, hoping to improve its showing and press for anti-corruption measures and an early independence referendum' (*IHT*, 13 June 2000, p. 5). However, the result was generally greeted with relief within Montenegro and in the West. It was felt that a more one-sided outcome would have been destabilizing. The West had 'offered Montenegro just enough support to give Milosevic pause about invading the republic', but had refrained from offering 'a blanket security guarantee that might embolden Montenegro to separate so definitel from Belgrade as to provoke a war' (*IHT*, 10 July 2000, p. 8).

Deepening constitutional crisis, 2000

On 6 July 2000 the Montenegrin government, parliament and president rejected constitutional changes enacted by the Milosevic-dominated FRY parliament in June 2000, which provided for both the FRY president and the upper house of the FRY parliament to be directly elected, allowed the same individual to serve two consecutive four-year terms as FRY president, raised the threshold for impeachment, minimized Montenegro's weight in determining political outcomes and made it much easier for Milosevic to seek election to another term as FRY president. Hitherto, the FRY president had been elected by both houses of the FRY parliament and could only serve one four-year term, while the upper house of the FRY parliament had been elected by the parliaments of Serbia and Montenegro and had comprised equal numbers of representatives of Serbia and Montenegro. The move to elect its members directly in effect annulled the balance stipulated in the FRY constitution of 1992. Henceforth Montenegro's weight in the FRY elections and political decision-making would in effect be limited to its 7 per cent share of the FRY population, nullifying its previous claims to 'sovereign equality' with Serbia. The constitutional amendments also transferred control of the conduct of FRY presidential and parliamentary elections from the officials of the Serbian and Montenegrin governments to those of the FR government, effectively ending Montenegro's share in the organization and conduct of FRY elections. The changes were obviously designed to give Milosevic a strong chance of remaining in power beyond July 2001, when his current term as indirectly elected FRY president was due to expire (*The Economist*, 15 July 2000, p. 45; *IHT*, 7 July 2000, pp. 1, 8; *Independent*, 7 July 2000, p. 13).

In response, President Djukanovic announced that Montenegro would not take part in the FRY elections scheduled for 24 September 2000, and on 8 July the chairman of the FRY supreme court declared that in effect the FRY no longer existed (*EEN*, 2000, vol. 12, no. 24, p. 5). On 8 July the Montenegrin assembly also passed the following 'resolution on the protection of the rights and interests of the Republic of Montenegro', which had been submitted to it by the Montenegrin government in draft form on 7 July:

1. The parliament shall not recognize and accept any legal or political act whatsoever passed by the legislative, executive and judicial authorities of the federal state without the participation of the lawful and legal representatives of Montenegro.
2. The parliament shall not recognize and accept amendments of the constitution of the FRY, as the amendments were adopted by the illegal and illegitimate federal parliament, against the majority will of the citizens of Montenegro and flagrantl violating the constitutional right of the Republic of Montenegro as an equal constituent of the federal state.
3. The parliament calls upon all the state authorities to act, within the framework of their constitutional and legal powers, in accordance with this resolution and

not to implement any decisions whatsoever adopted by the illegitimate and illegal federal authorities and to undertake all the normative and other measures necessary for the protection of interests of the citizens and the Republic of Montenegro and unhindered functioning of its legal system.

4. The parliament calls upon all the state authorities of the republic, especially the ministry of internal affairs, political parties, bodies and institutions to contribute through their activities to preserve peace, as well as members of the Yugoslav army not to allow themselves to be abused against the citizens, institutions and state authorities of the Republic of Montenegro.

5. The parliament calls upon the citizens of Montenegro, citizens and democratic forces of Serbia as well as the international community to help in finding peacefu solutions to the problems existing between Montenegro and the state authorities of Serbia and the federation, respecting the will of citizens.

> (http://www.montenet.org/aktuelno/resolution,
> accessed 5 November 2005)

On 10 July President Djukanovic declared that 'Yugoslavia no longer exists' and that Montenegro would not take part in FRY elections scheduled for September 2000 (*The Guardian*, 11 July 2000, p. 15). Montenegro was in the process of establishing a large and well-armed force of special police and there were at least 10,000 police in active service, but the armed forces of the FRY stepped up border patrols and, except for one crossing, closed the border with Bosnia. The SNP and the government started talks to reduce tensions (*FT*, 19 September 2000, p. 10).

The FRY presidential and parliamentary elections held on 24 September 2000

In early September President Milo Djukanovic decided to encourage a boycott of the forthcoming FRY elections. This suited both Milosevic and Djukanovic by protecting President Djukanovic's political base while at the same time making it easier for Milosevic to retain control over the new FRY parliament, which in turn was likely to further reinforce secessionist sentiment in Montenegro (this was similar to the logic underlying the Kosovar Albanian boycott). Conversely, if Milosevic were to be beaten by the Serbian democratic opposition, it would become more difficult to get Western support for a breakup of the FRY. Nevertheless, while the Djukanovic regime off cially discouraged the state media from reporting on the election campaign, it still allowed those Montenegrins who wanted to do so to take part in the election, in order to avoid open conf ict with the 35 to 40 per cent of Montenegro's popula- tion in favour of continued union with Serbia (*IHT*, 13 September 2000, p. 11). There were fears in Podgorica that Milosevic would manipulate the pro-Serbian minority in Montenegro to engineer a pretext for some sort of Serbian military intervention in Montenegro (*IHT*, 19 September 2000, p. 6). Negotiations were therefore initiated between the Djukanovic regime and the pro-Serbian Socialist People's Party (SNP) to allow those citizens who wished to do so to vote in regular polling booths. However, the pro-Serb camp suddenly rejected the supervision of the polling stations by Montenegro's security forces. As a result of the ensuing deadlock, the pro-Serbian camp in Montenegro organized its own balloting 'with no restrictions on multiple voting or other forms of fraud' (*The Economist*, 16 September 2000, p. 63).

With under 7 per cent of the FRY's population, Montenegro was bound to have very little weight in determining the outcome of the FRY elections. Partly for this reason, only 24 per cent of the Montenegrin electorate took part and, among Montenegro's political parties, only the (pro-federation and pro-Serb) SNP led by Momir Bulatovic gained representation in the FRY parliament (Freedom House 2002: 431–2).

The repercussions of the September 2000 FRY elections and the demise of the Milosevic regime in Serbia

Montenegro's governing coalition parties decided in late October 2000 that legal preparations for a referendum on independence should be in place by the end of the year and that the proposed referendum should be held by 30 June 2001 (*EEN*, 2000, vol. 13, no. 1, p. 4), but in practice these preparations were not followed through.

President Djukanovic stated that 'The serious dilemma we are faced with is: do we follow the illusion of a common state, which in the meantime has been left with only a few compromised and abused functions, or the reality of two functioning states.' He described Montenegro's existing relationship with Serbias as 'unsustainable' and promised a referendum on the issue during the first half of 2001 (*Independent*, 25 November 2000, p. 15).

On 28 December 2000 President Djukanovic again rejected Montenegro's continued participation in the FRY as it was then constituted. This prompted the seven People's Party deputies to withdraw their support from the coalition government, depriving it of its parliamentary majority (*The Guardian*, 30 December 2000, p. 18).

On 20 February 2001 Djukanovic called an early parliamentary election for 22 April 2001. On 24 February, in preparation for the imminent election, the SNP elected Predrag Bulatovic as its new leader (replacing Momir Bulatovic), and on 24 March the SNP and the People's Party forged a pro-Serbian 'Together for Yugoslavia' electoral alliance (*EEN*, 2001, vol. 13, no. 4, p. 7).

On 12 April 2001, in a blatant attempt to sway the election outcome, the 'Contact Group' (comprising the USA, Britain, Germany, France, Italy and Russia) issued a joint statement supporting 'a democratic Montenegro within a democratic Yugoslavia' and warning that the Contact Group would 'deprive Montenegro of political and financial support' if it seceded from the FRY and pursued the goal of independence (*IHT*, 13 April 2001, p. 4; *FT*, 21 April 2001, p. 5). Considering that the FRY had until recently been controlled by politicians whom f ve of these six powers regarded as guilty of ethnic cleansing and other crimes against humanity, this act of international blackmail was in some respects quite outrageous. Why should any group of people have been made to feel obliged to remain within a federation with such a monstrous record, and why should their attempts to secede have resulted in threats of punishment by the major Western states? At the same time, however, it is possible to understand the Contact Group's fears that any Montenegrin attempt to attain increased inde - pendence at that time might well have resulted in military intervention by the rump VJ and yet another Balkan war, which the Contact Group could only have halted through a military intervention of their own. In effect, the Montenegrins were being threatened with severe punishment if they failed to do the bidding of the major powers by biding their time.

Elections to seventy-eight seats in the Montenegrin assembly, 22 April 2001

There was a high (82 per cent) turn-out and the preliminary assessment of the OSCE was that the election had been 'pluralistic, accountable and transparent', but despite the presence of around 3,000 monitors, there had been some reports of irregularities and the state-run media were unduly under Djukanovic's control (*IHT*, 24 April 2001, p. 5; *The Guardian*, 23 April 2001, p. 13). During the campaign, Montenegrin official complained that the FRY authorities had re-established the custom barriers between the two republics which had been abolished after Milosevic was ousted in October 2000, and Carla del Ponte, the chief prosecutor at the ICTY, handed over sealed indictments giving the names of senior Montenegrin politicians and officials who wer alleged to have been parties to the bombardment of Dubrovnik during the autumn of 1991 (*Independent*, 21 April 2001, p. 13).

Djukanovic pledged that if the parties favouring greater independence won a two-thirds majority in the assembly, he would hold a referendum on independence on 13 June 2001. He put forward the vision of a loose union of Serbia, Montenegro and neighbouring states pursuing free trade, jointly participating in peacekeeping, and jointly using the euro (*IHT*, 23 April 2001, p.10; *FT*, 23 April 2001, p. 6). Both the VJ and the federation's civilian leadership affmed that they would not inter vene militarily to prevent Montenegro from leaving the federation (*IHT*, 24 April 2001, p. 5).

However, Djukanovic's 'Victory for Montenegro' coalition was damaged by ongoing foreign and opposition claims that he had allowed Montenegro to become a paradise for cigarette- and arms-smugglers and sex-traff ckers. Italian investigators and newspapers linked Djukanovic's administration to an organized tobacco-smuggling ring. They claimed that dozens of criminals enjoyed Montenegrin state protection and that smuggling amounted to 50 per cent of Montenegro's GDP (*Independent*, 21 April 2001, p. 13; *FT*, 10 August 2001, p. 7). The opposition naturally benef ted from these allegations, although President Djukanovic subsequently wrote to the *Financial Times* to deny them (*FT*, 15 August 2001, p. 5).

Djukanovic's Victory for Montenegro coalition, which favoured greater inde - pendence for Montenegro, won 42 per cent of the votes cast and thirty-six seats in the seventy-eight-seat assembly, well short of the forty-six seats needed to change the constitution or ratify a pro-independence referendum result (see Table 9.6).

9.6 Montenegrin parliamentary election, 22 April 2001

Party	Seats
Democratic Party of Socialists (DPS)	30
Social Democratic Party (SDP)	6
Liberal Alliance of Montenegro	6
Club of Albanian Parties	2
SNP (led by Predrag Bulatovic)	19
People's Party	11
Serbian People's Party	2

Source: Freedom House (2002: 431).

The Liberal Alliance of Montenegro, which favoured immediate and outright independence/secession, won 7.7 per cent of the votes and six seats. The Democratic Union of Albanians, which won 2.6 per cent of the votes and two seats, also backed independence. If the governing coalition had been broadened to include the Liberals and the Albanian minority, these parties would have had a substantial parliamentary majority. However, the Liberals uncompromisingly insisted on holding an immediate referendum on independence as the price of their support, even in the absence of the two-thirds majority needed to make this a viable option. Djukanovic wanted a more independent Montenegro, but only in order to negotiate a looser union in which Serbia and Montenegro would be equal partners (despite their disparate sizes). Polls suggested that up to 60 per cent of Montenegrins supported independence, but this fell short of the two-thirds majority needed to hold and win a referendum on independence and get the result ratif ed by a two-thirds majority in parliament – and in any case fiv major Western states had threatened to punish Montenegro if it tried to become an independent state (*BCE*, June 2001, p. 42). The result was a deadlock. The Together for Yugoslavia coalition, which favoured retaining the existing federal union with Serbia, won 40.7 per cent of the vote and thirty-two seats, just enough to block the parliamentary ratif cation of a referendum verdict in favour of independence.

The minority centre-left government headed by Filip Vujanovic, June 2001 to April 2002

On 20 May 2001 the DPS formally turned down the unworkable coalition terms offered by the Liberal Alliance of Montenegro (*EEN*, 2001, vol. 13, no. 5, p. 7). On 22 May, however, Montenegro's constitutional court ruled that a referendum on independence could be validated by a simple majority rather than a two-thirds majority (*EEN*, 2001, vol. 13, no. 5, p. 7). On 30 May Filip Vujanovic was asked to form a minority government. The secessionist Liberal Alliance agreed to support it provided it agreed to hold a referendum on independence within six months (*The Times*, 31 May 2001, p. 10). During June and July 2001 the new Vujanovic government talked of holding a referendum on independence by January 2002, but President Djukanovic continued to urge flexibility on the issue. He was getting on well with the new Serbian prim minister Zoran Djindjic, who expressed his willingness to discuss a looser Yugoslav federation within which Serbia and Montenegro would be 'independent in all but name' (*The Economist*, 7 July 2001, p. 49). Djukanovic proposed

> new democratic relations between our two independent states which should be applicable to relations between all the former Yugoslav states. It would be based on free trade, the euro as a common currency and visa-free travel. We also propose the demilitarization of Serbia and Montenegro with joint command of the reduced army.
>
> (*FT*, Survey, 10 July 2001, p. 13)

However, on 19 September 2001 the Vujanovic government and President Djukanovic refused to attend talks in Belgrade on the future of Yugoslavia, because they objected to the proposed participation of the FRY prime minister Dragisa Pesic, a leading member of the Montenegrin opposition SNP (*The Guardian*, 20 September 2001, p. 17).

The creation of the State Union of Serbia and Montenegro ('Solania'), March 2002

On 14 March the EU foreign policy supremo Javier Solana succeeded in brokering an agreement between the Serbian and Montenegrin governments to remain united in a FRY state and to drop the name 'Yugoslavia' in favour of the 'State Union of Serbia and Montenegro'. The agreement put off until 2006 the holding of any referenda on whether the two republics should separate from each other completely. Serbia and Montenegro would retain separate currencies, economic systems and customs services, but they would share some weakish joint institutions, including a common presidency, parliament, supreme court, defence establishment and five ministries (ones for foreig affairs, human rights, defence). Elections were scheduled for autumn 2002 to choose a parliament, which would in turn elect a president of the federation (*IHT*, 15 March 2002, p. 1; *The Economist*, 23 March 2002, p. 42). The agreement was contingent upon ratification by the parliaments of the two republics and by the FRY assembly President Djukanovic claimed that the rotation of senior official positions would 'ensure the protection of Montenegro's interests in international institutions', including the alternation of representatives from Montenegro and Serbia in their shared seat at the UN. He also stated he did not rule out the holding of a referendum in Montenegro to ratify the agreement (*The Times*, 15 March 2002, p. 20). A new FRY constitution would enter into force by the end of 2002 at the latest. The council would be responsible for foreign affairs, defence, international economic relations, and protection of human and minority rights. The economic systems of both republics would gradually be harmonized with EU rules (*FT*, 15 March 2002, p. 6).

Solana (perhaps rashly!) claimed that the deal marked 'an important step forward for the stability of the region and Europe' and that this was 'not an end of anything, but the beginning of a new chapter that we will write together and bring you member-ship of the EU' (*Independent*, 15 March 2002, p. 20). Presidents Kostunica and Djukanovic afterwards jointly attended the two-day EU European Council in Barcelona on 15–16 March.

The parliaments of Serbia and Montengero on 9 April approved the proposed termination of the FRY and the establishment of a looser union. The Montenegrin parliament approved the agreement by fifty-eight votes to eleven. Members of Montenegro's Social Democratic Party, which supported outright independence, had threatened to withdraw from the Montenegrin government if the agreement was adopted and was planning to resign the next day. A constitution was to be drafted to create a new 'Union-level' parliament, presidency, council of ministers and army, subject to another round of parliamentary approval by both republics (*IHT*, 10 April 2002, p. 9).

Vujanovic resigned as prime minister on 19 April 2002, after both the Social Democratic Party and the Liberal Alliance of Montenegro withdrew their support from his minority government in protest against the new modus vivendi worked out with the Serbian government. However, the Liberals simultaneously indicated their willingness to take part in talks on the formation of a fresh government*The Guardian*, 20 April 2002, p. 16).

On 31 May 2002 the agreement was ratified by the FRY parliament by seventy four votes to twenty-three in the lower house and by twenty-three votes to six in the upper house. A constitutional commission had yet to flesh out the details of the ne state union. It was originally envisaged that a constitution would be ready for approval by the three parliaments in June 2002, but this target date was not met (*IHT*, 1 June 2002, p. 2; *The Times*, 1 June 2002, p. 20).

The local elections held on 15 May 2002

Contrary to expectations and despite being hit by the withdrawal of support from two other pro-independence parties, the ruling DPS increased its support at local level, while the pro-Yugoslav opposition led by the SNP lost support (*FT*, 17 May 2002, p. 7). These elections, which took place everywhere except Podgorica and Herceg Novi, involved an 'unholy alliance' between the pro-independence Liberals and the pro-Serb SNP, which 'agreed to pool resources to secure the selection of anti-Djukanovic mayors and local councils' (*FT*, Survey, 11 July 2002, p. 17). This imprudently turned the election into a referendum on Djukanovic, who evidently remained Montenegro's most popular politician. However, on 30 May, a magistrate in the Italian city of Bari accused Djukanovic of having 'promoted, directed and organized' a Mafia-style gang which had been smuggling at least 1,000 tonnes of contraband cigarettes a month from Montenegro to Italy up to the year 2000 (*The Times*, 31 May 2002, p. 21). This Camorra gang was the Neapolitan counterpart to the Sicilian Maf a.

Elections to the Montenegrin assembly, 20 October 2002

Seven coalitions and three parties competed for the seventy-f ve seats allocated by proportional representation, but with a 3 per cent threshold. The OSCE deemed these elections to have been 'free and fair', with only a few minor incidents of violence being reported, and the turn-out was high, at 75 per cent (Pavlovic 2004: 490).

The 'Coalition for a European Montenegro', comprising the DPS led by President Djukanovic and the SDP, favoured greater (but not outright) independence for Montenegro and obtained 47.9 per cent of the votes cast and thirty-nine seats. The 'Together for Change' coalition, which favoured maintaining the FRY union with Yugoslavia and comprised the SNP, the People's Party and the Serbian People's Party, obtained 38.4 per cent of the votes cast and thirty seats, while the pro-independence Liberal Alliance of Montenegro declined to 5.7 per cent of the votes cast and four seats. The 'Albanian Coalition', comprising the Democratic Union of Albanians, the Democratic Movement of Montenegro and Democratic Prosperity, obtained 2.4 per cent of the votes and two seats (Pavlovic 2004: 501). In the wake of his sub-stantial victory in the parliamentary elections, Djukanovic stood down as president of Montenegro and took up the more powerful post of prime minister at the head of a DPS–SDP coalition government. However, this necessitated the holding of a presidential election on 22 December, in order to select a new president of Montenegro.

The presidential elections held on 22 December 2002, 9 February 2003 and 11 May 2003

The front-runner for the post was Filip Vujanovic, who favoured full sovereign statehood for Montenegro, had served as prime minister in 2001–2 and subsequently served as speaker of the Montenegrin parliament. He was challenged by ten other candidates, mostly independents, all of whom won fewer than 7 per cent of the votes cast (*IHT*, 23 December 2002, p. 4). However, despite winning 83.9 per cent of the votes cast, Vujanovic failed to get elected because the turn-out of 45.9 per cent was below the 50 per cent required by the constitution. This necessitated a rerun of the presidential election on 9 February.

Much of the electorate had refrained from voting on 22 December, both in protest at the state of the economy and because of the claims of an unnamed Moldovan woman that she had been enslaved for years and forced to have sex with powerful Montenegrin business and political leaders. This prostitution scandal rocked Montenegro's political establishment and strained relations within the coalition government. The deputy public prosecutor Zoran Piperovic, who was directly implicated in these allegations, was forced to resign despite his protestations of innocence. Furthermore, the SNP, after its heavy defeat in the October parliamentary election, did not field a candidat but called for an election boycott, further depressing the turn-out (*Independent*, 23 December 2002, p. 7).

In the rerun of the presidential election on 9 February 2003, the turn-out of 47 per cent was still below the minimum required 50 per cent. The opposition SNP and a few other groups again fielded no candidate(s) and again called for a boycott *IHT*, 10 February 2003, p. 7), while the OSCE criticized the DPS for ordering civil servants and state employees to vote for its candidate *The Guardian*, 11 February 2003, p. 13).

However, on 27 February the Montenegrin parliament revised Montenegro's electoral law to abolish the requirement of a minimum turn-out of 50 per cent. No new threshold was set in the amendment, which was approved by fifty-three votes to one, with twenty-one absences or abstentions (*IHT*, 28 February 2003, p. 3). On 11 May 2003, at the third attempt, Filip Vujanovic won 64.2 per cent of the votes cast, compared with 31.4 per cent for Miodrag Zivkovic and 4.4 per cent for Dragan Hajdukovic, and thus f nally became president.

The Montenegrin economy, 1998–2002

A new privatization plan in Montenegro was approved in 1998, leading to the estab-lishment of a privatization council. The plan targeted about 300 enterprises, most of which were to be privatized either by a mass voucher scheme or by international tender (EBRD 2000b: 9).

During the 1990s, however, Western sanctions, bank collapses, government seizures of hard-currency savings and high taxes on legal employment had distorted competition and pushed more than 40 per cent of the Montenegrin economy into the shadows, encouraging illegal activities such as the smuggling of cars and cigarettes in breach of trade sanctions on the FRY. In addition, over 40,000 people worked in 350 loss-making state enterprises, while 42,000 worked in a bloated civil service. A World Bank study estimated that another 15,000–25,000 workers were on job waiting lists or unpaid leave (*FT Survey*, 10 July 2001, pp. 14–15).

The political changes of 2000–1 gave new impetus to Montenegrin privatization (EBRD 2001a: 28). Privatization was more advanced in Montenegro than in Serbia, but progress had slowed down in the late 1990s. The government planned to accelerate the process by (i) public-tender privatization of fifteen to twenty large enterprises (ii) a mass-voucher privatization programme for 240 medium companies; (iii) batch-sale privatization of thirty-three companies; and (iv) liquidation of about thirty insolvent companies (EBRD 2001b: 143). The mass-voucher privatization scheme, covering about 27 per cent of state property, was officially completed in Februar 2002. Most mass-privatization shares came to be held by six privatization funds. At the same time, international tenders were prepared for majority stakes in nineteen large companies (EBRD 2002b: 147).

On 2 November 1999 Montenegro decided to make the Deutschmark its officia currency in a bid to shield its economy from soaring inflation in Serbia and the resultan fall in the value of the Yugoslav dinar. Basic goods such as bread, milk, petrol and power were to be priced in Deutschmarks, and citizens would receive their salaries and pensions in Deutschmarks, from 4 November. This was to be an interim arrangement prior to the introduction of a separate currency, the marka (*IHT*, 2 November 1999, p. 7).

Montenegro launched the marka in January 2002. It traded alongside the Deutschmark at par. Both currencies would be legal tender and all government transactions could be carried out in either of them. Businesses would be free to use the currency of their choice. A currency board, governed by one Montenegrin and four personnel from G7 countries, was established to strictly regulate the system. The quantity of markas in circulation would not be allowed to exceed the value of Montenegro's foreign-currency reserves, which were to be held either in Deutschmarks or euros (*FT*, 30 October 1999, p. 5). The Yugoslav dinar was to be phased out completely by the end of that month.

The introduction of the Deutschmark paved the way for the biggest economic reforms to date, by facilitating the establishment of a separate Montenegrin central bank, reform of the banking system and the replacement of ZOP, the centralized clearing system inherited from the former Communist-ruled FRY. The demise of ZOP terminated a state monopoly and replaced it with competition between the largely privatized banks (*FT*, Survey, 10 July 2001, p. 14). The Yugoslav National Bank in Belgrade retaliated by blocking all payments between Serbia and Montenegro. Some 18,000 pensioners living in Montenegro who relied on pensions from Belgrade had their payments blocked; 8,000 military employees and 2,000 civil servants were in the same boat. In addition, Serb police stopped dozens of trucks carrying fresh food from crossing into Montenegro, while Montenegrin businessmen who were owed money by f rms in Serbia had no way of retrieving it (*The Economist*, 4 December 1999, pp. 48, 51).

The prices of staple consumer goods such as bread and milk were partially liberalized in 2001. Bread and milk prices increased by nearly 60 per cent in January 2001 and by a further 100 per cent in August 2001. Post and telecommunications charges were raised by nearly 100 per cent in June 2001. Transportation, telecommunications and municipal services charges were also de-controlled (EBRD 2001b: 142).

Serbia imposed a full economic blockade in March 2000, further tightening the economic noose on Montenegro, which traditionally relied heavily on Serbia for supplies. Since 1999 the Montenegrin government had been forced to import grain supplies from Slovenia and Croatia, which were considerably more expensive than those from Serbia (*Daily Telegraph*, 7 March 2000, p. 23).

The re-monetization of the Montenegrin economy, 2002–3

The introduction of euro notes and coins on 1 January 2002 and the concurrent demise of the Deutschmark forced hundreds of thousands of Montenegrins to give up their holdings of Deutschmarks and convert them into euros. Partly to boost a previously weak banking sector, the conversion rules were designed to push Montenegrins into opening bank accounts. It became a legal requirement for sums in excess of 10,000

Deutschmark (5,112 euros) to be converted through the banks (*FT*, 10 January 2002, p. 7). The Montenegrin authorities limited the amount of Deutschmarks people could exchange for euro notes to 10,000 Deutschmarks per transaction. Any larger amount had to be deposited in a bank account. However, streetwise Montenegrins believed that their 'local fat cats' had already offloaded their Deutschmarks the previous year, and they expected 'some of this money to return as foreign investment' (*The Economist*, 12 January 2002, p. 38).

Thus the euro quickly became the 'de-facto currency' in Montenegro, as in other parts of former Yugoslavia. A billboard near the Central Bank of Montenegro proclaimed: 'The Euro. Our currency'. By the end of March 2002 stores were accepting payment only in euros. The 'euro rush' was much bigger than anticipated, perhaps because the banks made it easy for people who wanted to do so to 'hide their wealth'. All that customers had to do was show 'a national identity card – no questions asked, no money tracing, no fees'. As in Serbia, people could simply send money in packs of 10,000 Deutschmarks by courier. 'Money laundering is also big business. Montenegro registered more than 500 offshore "banks", a remarkable number for a country with only 700,000 inhabitants' and these were 'allowed to transfer money into and out of the country without disclosing the money's origins'. This, in a country where a very high proportion of the economy was 'unofficial', 'based on activities like cigarette smuggling and corruption as well as legitimate income that people hide from tax collectors' (*IHT*, 18 January 2002, p. 5).

From January 2002 Montenegro became a 'de-facto thirteenth member of the euro zone . . . Instead of the DM 250–300 million believed to be in circulation or taken out from under mattresses, no less than DM 900 million was presented for exchange into the new currency . . . The conversion process was seen as a unique opportunity to attract savings into new accounts with banks', which were henceforth (in theory) expected to operate 'according to European standards of transparency', while teams of US- and EU-funded technical experts drew up 'impressive-looking laws and regulations designed to guarantee the fair treatment of foreign investors and minority shareholders and clean up and modernize the banking system' (*FT*, Survey, 11 January 2002, p. 18). In 2003 the euro had become 'the sole legal currency' (EBRD 2003a: 80).

These changes paved the way for, and greatly facilitated, a further major change in Montenegro's domestic payments system at the end of 2003: the transfer of responsibilities for handling payments from the bureaucratic and corrupt ZOP to the commercial banks. This substantially reduced the scope for political-cum-bureaucratic control of the economy and, hence, the scope for racketeering and bribe-taking by corrupt state bureaucrats, politicians and their Mafia-style intermediaries. The governor of Montenegro's central bank estimated that 'one-third of the Montenegrin economy remained "hidden" in 2002. However, economic reforms were luring private enterprise back into the light.' In August 2002 the government simplified company registration, and simplification and reductions in taxation were expected to draw business into th open (*FT*, Survey, 1 July 2003, p. 32).

Montenegro under the centre-left government headed by Milo Djukanovic, November 2002 onward

On 29 January 2003 the Montenegrin assembly voted to abolish the FRY by fifty-fi votes to seven and to replace it with a looser 'State Union of Serbia and Montenegro'.

The change was also approved by the Serbian Skupstina, but it had not yet been ratifie by the FRY parliament in Belgrade (*Independent*, 30 January 2003, p. 12).

The inauguration of the 'State Union of Serbia and Montenegro' ('Solania'), 4 February 2003

On 4 February 2003 the FRY parliament approved the constitutional charter of the loose 'State Union of Serbia and Montenegro'. A heated parliamentary debate took place, even though the constitutional charter was adopted by large majorities in both houses (*IHT*, 5 February 2003, p. 3). The creation of the state union owed so much to tenacious brokerage and lobbying by Javier Solana that it became known colloquially as 'Solania'. The constitutional charter was passed in the upper house by twenty-six votes to seven, and in the lower house by eighty-four votes to thirty-one. Vojislav Kostunica's term of office as president of the FRY was scheduled to end when a ne president of Serbia and Montenegro was elected by a new 'parliament of Serbia and Montenegro', but this had yet to be elected. The 'state union' was to have one army but two currencies, with Serbia using the dinar and Montenegro the euro. More than thirty FRY institutions were to cease to exist, from the Yugoslav central bank to the FRY ministries of finance and interior. Serbia and Montenegro, now called 'member states', were each allowed ten days to pass laws on the election of deputies to the projected 126-member 'parliament of Serbia and Montenegro', and President Kostunica was allowed five days to settle on a date for elections to that parliamen (*FT*, 5 February 2003, p. 6).

The fall of the Milosevic regime in October 2000 had also paved the way for the rapid removal of the Milosevic-era trade barriers against Montenegro by the post-Milosevic governments of Serbia and the FRY (*BCE*, June 2001, p. 42).

From mid-June 2003 until October 2004, the SNP, the Serbian People's Party, the People's Party and the Liberal Alliance of Montenegro boycotted the Montenegrin assembly, ostensibly in protest against a decision by the Djukanovic government to suspend live television coverage of debates in the Montenegrin assembly, misusing regulatory broadcasting laws passed by both government and opposition parties in September 2002. Even though the government partially gave way and allowed cameras to be brought back in for a few sessions, the opposition parties launched a united campaign of meetings and other protests in Podgorica and broadened their demands to include the calling of an early parliamentary election (Ramusovic 2004a: 1). The opposition attempted to weaken Djukanovic and his government in much the same way that the DPS simultaneously endeavoured to weaken the State Union of Serbia and Montenegro by refusing to sanction direct elections to the FRY presidency and the FRY parliament, in large part from fear that the reluctance of secessionist-minded Montenegrins to take part would simply hand the pro-Serb and pro-union parties a landslide victory in such elections, which were the only ones which the pro-Serb and pro-union opposition parties could hope to win. The government argued that it would not be worthwhile to directly elect the state union's president and parliament until it had been amply demonstrated that the state union enjoyed suffient popular support and political viability to survive. At the same time, the Montenegrin government deliberately made little attempt to harmonize its laws, customs duties and other taxes with those of Serbia, in an ultimately successful attempt to pressurize the EU into agreeing to treat and assess Montenegro separately from Serbia – on their respective merits, rather than as a single 'harmonized' unit. Not surprisingly, by July

2003 opinion polls in Serbia were indicating that 60 per cent of Serbs now favoured full separation from Montenegro, although only about 40–45 per cent of the inhabitants of Montenegro supported full separation from Serbia (*The Economist*, 19 July 2003, p. 31).

Prime Minister Djukanovic came under greatly increased pressure on 9 July 2003 to 'come clean about his alleged involvement in tobacco smuggling after Italian prosecutors linked him with an organized crime racket'. The public prosecutors' offic in Naples had named him 'as a linchpin in the illicit trade which used Montenegro as a transit point for smuggling cigarettes across the Adriatic Sea into Italy and into the hands of the mafia for distribution across the EU'. Djukanovic denied the allegation at a press conference held on 9 July. However, when the Montenegrin prosecutor's office forwarded the report to an investigating magistrate, he ruled that no charges could be brought against Djukanovic because of his immunity from prosecution as a member of the Montenegrin assembly. Nevertheless, in a lawsuit conducted in New York, the EU Commission named Djukanovic in connection with a money-laundering conspiracy allegedly masterminded by the US tobacco giant R. J. Reynolds. The EU was suing R. J. Reynolds for allegedly selling its product to the maf a, which then smuggled it untaxed into the EU, but R. J. Reynolds denied the accusations (*The Guardian*, 11 July 2003, p. 16). Djukanovic was also accused of using a Swiss bank to salt away large amounts of money. All these accusations merely gave further encouragement to Djukanovic to seek international acceptance that Montenegro was a sovereign state, out of fear that the state-union authorities could conceivably have overridden the legal immunity conferred on Djukanovic by the Montenegrin assembly. At the same time, public discontent and industrial strife were growing, in large part because about one-third of Montenegrin adults of working age were unemployed and the government was poised to prune the country's bloated civil service*The Economist*, 19 July 2003, p. 31).

In September 2003 the UN human-rights commissioner for Serbia-Montenegro criticized the Montenegrin authorities for failing to charge the former deputy public prosecutor Zoran Piperovic and three other men in the Moldovan sex-trafficking case and for closing the case 'for lack of evidence' *(Independent*, 5 September 2003, p. 13).

The pro-Serb SNP and Serbian People's Party urged Montenegro's inhabitants not to cooperate with the population census held in November 2003, because they feared that the Montenegrin authorities would try to under-record the proportion of the population which considered itself to be Serbian rather than part of a separate (albeit predominantly Serb-speaking) Montenegrin nation.

The Montenegrin assembly voted on 24 March 2004 to lift the immunity from prosecution of Miodrag Zivkovic, the leader of the opposition Liberal Alliance, whom Djukanovic was suing for making accusations that he had received the services of the Moldovan woman involved in the sex-traffcking case *(Independent*, 25 March 2004, p. 23).

From 1993 to 2003, politics in Montenegro had largely focused on the pros and cons of political independence. By April 2004, however, following two years of scandal and economic hardship, support for the parties that favoured greater indep endence had declined significantly. Opinion polls now showed only 41 per cent in favour o independence, 39 per cent against and 20 per cent undecided. Dragisa Burzan, Montenegro's foreign minister, claimed that Montenegro had incurred political costs caused by Serbia's failure to cooperate fully with the ICTY and major economic costs that resulted from being obliged by the EU and by the 'state union' which the EU had brokered to harmonize its economy with that of Serbia.

As a result of this political gridlock, a new political force was emerging. Nebojsa Medojevic, head of a think tank called the Group for Changes (GZP), argued that Montenegrin aspirations towards greater independence should be put on hold and that a cross-party 'government of technocrats' should be formed in order to halt the severe decline in living standards that was afflicting Montenegro. Medojevic said h favoured independence, but contended that Montenegro was not yet ready for it. In his view, Montenegrins were being 'cheated by crony privatizations' and Montenegrin economic statistics were either fraudulent or at best half truths. There was also growing public hostility to the Russian companies which were trying to buy up the Montenegrin companies being privatized. The GZP was not yet a political party, but it modelled itself on G17 Plus in Serbia, which began as a think tank but had become a party in government. Opinion polls indicated that for a short while the GZP became a strong third-party contender (*The Economist*, 10 April 2004, p. 34).

Gunmen killed Dusko Jovanovic, the editor of the Montenegrin newspaper *Dan* (*The Day*), which was embroiled in more than a dozen lawsuits, on 28 May 2004. Jovanovic had been indicted by the ICTY in 2003 for revealing the identity of a protected witness involved in the trial of Slobodan Milosevic, but these charges were subsequently dropped after Jovanovic published an apology. *Dan* was frequently critical of the ruling coalition headed by Milo Djukanovic (*IHT*, 29 May 2004, p. 8). In 2001 it was the first local paper to reprint a series of articles from the Croatian press detailing the allegations that cigarette-smuggling was thriving in Montenegro under Djukanovic. In November 2002, it had also been the first newspaper to publis the claims of a traffcked Moldovan woman that a number of prominent Montenegrin politicians and officials had been exploiting her as a sex slave. Djukanovic had fil a lawsuit against Jovanovic and his newspaper in connection with these stories, and a court hearing had been due to begin in June 2004.*Dan* also served as a mouthpiece for the opposition SNP and supported a continued union with Serbia. However, *Dan* stoked up political diff culties for the Djukanovic regime, not so much through its views on the future of the republic's relationship with Serbia, but mainly through its dogged campaign to expose alleged corruption and scandals involving Djukanovic and his cronies. It consistently maintained that the prime minister and his allies were linked to sex-traffi king, cigarette-smuggling and other maf a-style activities. For their part, Djukanovic's supporters retorted that *Dan* was more committed to slanderous mud-slinging than to the truth and that dozens of libel cases had been launched against it in recent years. Jovanovic had received numerous death threats and was the firs newspaperman to be executed mafa-style in Montenegro (*Independent*, 29 May 2004, p. 27; *The Economist*, 5 June 2004, p. 37).

From 29 to 31 May 2004 thousands of protesters marched through Podgorica chanting 'Milo, murderer', accusing Djukanovic of involvement in the murder of Jovanovic, and demanding that the government find the killers*Independent*, 1 June 2004, p. 21). Nevertheless, the Djukanovic government faced little competition from the main opposition parties, which continued to boycott the Montenegrin assembly (*FT*, Survey, 29 June 2004, p. 32).

In October 2004 the SNP and the Serbian People's Party were induced partially to abandon their boycott of the Montenegrin assembly by the restoration of live television coverage of assembly sessions, international insistence that the boycott merely polarized opinion and did not serve or foster democracy, and fear that a continued boycott would exclude them from the assembly's deliberations on whether the state-union parliament should be elected directly or indirectly, given that the constitutional charter of February 2003 had specified the state-union parliament should be directly electe two years after the charter's adoption (i.e., from March 2005 onwards). However, the government parties insisted that any such elections would be a distraction from the more important tasks of seeking more rapid integration into the EU and of resolving whether to perpetuate the increasingly dysfunctional State Union of Serbia and Montenegro, whose existence allegedly complicated more than it assisted processes of reform and rapprochement with the EU.

However, the pro-independence Liberal Alliance of Montenegro and the People's Party continued to boycott the assembly altogether, partly in protest against the Montenegrin government's promotion of plans to construct a major dam in the upper reaches of the spectacularly beautiful 80-kilometre Tara canyon in order to increase cheapish electricity supplies to the giant aluminium-smelting plant near Podgorica (which contributed 40 per cent of Montenegro's GDP) and to the neighbouring Republika Srpska. The Tara canyon had been declared a UNESCO World Heritage site in 1977, and the opposition to the plan to dam the top end of it was partly con- servationist and partly concerned to cash in on the canyon's potentially lucrative tourist potential (Ramusovic 2004d).

Concluding reflections

Privatization and 'selling out' to foreigners

Between 2002 and 2005, the privatization of Montenegro's economy was largely completed, and a number of its major enterprises were bought by foreigners. During the first three-quarters of 2005, Montenegro received FDI amounting to approximatel 376 euros per inhabitant (ICG 2005c: 7), but whether this is cause for celebration or grounds for concern is open to debate.

The largest privatization to date was the sale of 54 per cent of the oil company Jugopetrol Kotor, Montenegro's main importer and distributor of oil products, to Hellenic Petroleum of Greece in late 2002–3 (*FT*, Survey, 29 June 2004, pp. 32–3). Privatization in the hotel and tourism sector was far advanced by 2003 (EBRD 2004b: 170). A UK-based investor acquired a majority stake in Zeljezara Niksic, the major steelworks, in spring 2004. During 2005 a majority stake in Telekom Crne Gore, the fixed-line telecommunications company with a stake in mobile-phone operator ProMonte, was sold to Hungary's Magyar Telecom for 114 million euros, and a 65.4 per cent stake in KAP (the giant aluminium complex outside Podgorica) was sold to a subsidiary of the Russian aluminium firm Rusal for 235 million dollars. The privatization of Montenegro's banks was 'virtually' completed by the sale of Podgoricka Banka and Montenegro Bank, which accounted for 20 per cent of the Montenegrin banking sector and increased the proportion of banking-sector capital in private ownership to 85 per cent. By mid-2005, with almost all of its industries now in private ownership, Montenegro claimed to have the lowest corporate tax rate in Europe (EBRD 2005b: 174; *FT*, Survey, 29 June 2004, pp. 32–3; *FT*, Survey, 12 July 2005, p. 30).

Selling off all major industrial, public-utility and banking enterprises to 'respect- able' foreign owners is sometimes perceived to be a rapid and effective way of importing 'international' (Western) management cultures, introducing Western stand- ards of business conduct and transparency and preventing the 'commanding heights' of the economy from falling under the control of local clientelistic and criminal networks. It often receives extravagant praise from the EBRD, the World Bank, the IMF, the EU, the *Financial Times* and other Western international organizations. It certainly opens up and 'internationalizes' the economy in certain respects. However, it has also placed the Montenegrin economy largely under foreign (mainly Western) control, vastly reducing the scope for meaningful democratic control by Montenegrins over an economy which is no longer 'their own' (because it has largely been sold off to foreigners). It also limits the scope for democratic debate, accountability and even scrutiny in the economic sphere, because power and decision-making in relation to the economy is no longer primarily located in Montenegro. Furthermore, whether selling everything in sight to foreigners will actually generate meaningful economic growth and jobs and reduce poverty for Montenegrin citizens (as distinct from simply importing growing numbers of footloose and extremely well-paid expatriate Western executives) remains to be seen.

The Republic of Macedonia, which has had the strongest and most consistent record of selling everything imaginable to foreigners (mainly Westerners) and of slavishly following the neo-liberal orthodoxies and advice propounded by Western-dominated international organizations, has achieved not only the lowest inf ation rate but also one of the lowest rates of economic growth and job creation in the region. Western international organizations such as the EBRD nevertheless proclaim the Macedonian economy a 'great success' because Westerners have acquired control of just about everything that matters – and never mind that 37 per cent of Macedonians are unemployed and see little prospect of economic growth in forms that create real employment for locals. It is obvious from EBRD reports that their main criteria of success are low inf ation, how easy it is to hire and especially fe locals, and how completely anything of value has been transferred to Western ownership. In examining the post-Communist Balkan economies, we could be forgiven for being reminded of the northern 'carpet-baggers' who descended on the American South after the Civil War, cheaply buying up anything of value that had survived the conflict, while most of the 'poor white southerners as well as the 'liberated' slaves languished in chronic unemployment and poverty, but nevertheless thought they were 'doing a great job'. The main question is: 'a great job for whom?'. In relation to the Balkans, Western international official seem to assume that Westerners know how to run things properly, but again the question is: 'properly for whom?'.

Towards EU membership?

Opinion polls conducted during the summer of 2005 indicated that at least 80 per cent of Montenegrins wished to join the EU (*FT*, Survey, 12 July 2005, pp. 30–1). Most Montenegrins clearly perceive that EU membership, along with the 21 May referendum on independence, offers Montenegro the best chances of escaping from the baleful clutches of Serbia and overcoming the highly clientelistic and often criminalized vertical power structures which are the major impediments to a truly liberal polity and economy in their country. Even Montenegro's prime minister Djukanovic, who has repeatedly been accused of being deeply implicated in clientelistic networks that are making money out of illegal cigarette-smuggling and prostitute-trafficking seems to have made determined efforts since 1997 to lead his country towards the EU and national independence in a concerted endeavour to free it from control by Serbian-style 'maf as'. It is unclear how much (if any) substance there is to the recurrent allegations against him. However, if the allegations are true, the main thrusts of his policies in government appear to be directed towards 'kicking the habit'.

During a visit to Montenegro on 10 March 2000, the EU commissioner for external relations, Chris Patten, promised to boost planned EU assistance (60 million euros) by a further 5 million euros to fund infrastructure projects. As part of the ostracized, Serb-dominated FRY, Montenegro was not allowed to receive much aid from most 'international institutions, but Patten's 5 million euro package avoided being chan- nelled through either the Serbian or the FRY government by being directly targeted to specific projects in Montenegro, including a new bridge at Mora and a new road linking Podgorica to its airport' (*Independent*, 11 March 2000, p. 14). By mid-2000 the EU (together with the USA) had delivered 450 million Deutschmarks in aid to Montenegro, and a further 280 million Deutschmarks were promised for 2001 (*FT*, Survey, 10 July 2001, p. 13).

As part of its endeavour to promote more vigorous development and intra-regional trade in the western Balkans taken as a whole, on 18 September 2000 EU foreign ministers approved a package granting duty-free access to 95 per cent of its imports from Montenegro (along with imports from Albania, Bosnia, Croatia and Macedonia). In particular, Montenegro was to be allowed to export its aluminium to EU countries duty free (*FT*, 19 September 2000, p. 10; *The Times*, 19 September 2000, p. 14).

The State Union of Serbia and Montenegro brokered by the EU in 2003–4 was designed, among other things, to harmonize the external trade policies and regulations of these two entities, especially vis-à-vis the EU itself and adjacent Balkan states. In June 2004 it was reported that it had 'already reached compromises on hundreds of tariffs' but that harmonization was 'proving difficult on fifty-six others', main 'staple food products protected in Serbia but imported tariff-free by Montenegro'*FT*, Survey, 29 June 2004, p. 32).

In September 2004 the EU conceded to Montenegro the right to negotiate the details of its progress towards membership of the EU separately from Serbia, even though they were still to be regarded as one country. Having insisted for over a year that Serbia and Montenegro had to reduce and harmonize their respective trade tariffs and barriers, which was bedevilled by foot-dragging and intransigence, the EU now endorsed a 'twin-track approach' which would allow the two republics to negotiate with the EU *in tandem*, 'seeking status as a single candidate state without adopting the same legislation'. Each republic was henceforth to be asked individually to harmonize its legislation with EU regulations (*FT*, Survey, 14 December 2004, p. 31).

At least partly in response to this major sea change in Montenegrin relations with the EU, on 23 September 2004 Montenegro's deputy interior minister Pedrag Boskovic announced that the Montenegrin members of the council for cooperation with the ICTY were resigning in protest against what they described as Serbia's failure to cooperate in handing over indicted persons to the tribunal. He claimed that Montenegro did not want to impair its own progress towards membership of the EU (*IHT*, 24 September 2004, p. 3). The resignations appeared to be an effort by Montenegrins to offload o to Serbia all the blame for non-compliance with the ICTY.

The start of negotiations on an SAA between the EU and Serbia and Montenegro was given the 'green light' by a meeting of EU heads of government in Luxembourg on 4 October 2005. Technical negotiations began in November 2005, but no timetable or even timescale was set for the completion of these negotiations, which were very strongly linked to continued (Serbian) cooperation with the ICTY and to further poli- tical, economic, judicial and administrative reform in both countries. The main effects of the opening negotiations were to involve Serbia and Montenegro in a structured dialogue with and monitoring by the EU and to allow them increased access to EU funds. The intention was that, so long as Serbia and Montenegro remained constituent parts of the EU-brokered state union, the two countries would sign a single SAA, but with separate detailed annexes – one for each state. The major EU institutions and member states were evidently hoping that the State Union of Serbia and Montenegro would somehow survive in a form that would allow these two countries to join the EU as a single entity, rather than as two separate states (*FT*, Survey, 12 July 2005, pp. 30–1). There were fully understandable concerns in the EU Commission that the ongoing fragmentation and multiplication of small Balkan states was bound to further complicate the major challenges posed by EUintimations and even solemn assurances that all the Balkan states would be welcomed into the fold in due course. However, Montenegro's 55.5 per cent vote in favour of full independent statehood in the referendum held on 21 May 2006 drove the final nail into the State Union's coffi thereby exposing the EU's striking lack of subtlety and realism in this matter. Montenegro's attainment of independence has also further encouraged many Kosovars, Bosnian Serbs and Bosnian Croats to think in similar terms, increasing the potential for further 'Balkanization' of the Balkans during the twenty-f rst century.

Living under the sway of criminal networks

In 2004 Montenegro's central bank governor estimated that the illegal 'black economy' still accounted for roughly 30 per cent of economic activity, and that the unoff cial 'grey economy' also accounted for about 30 per cent of GDP (*FT*, Survey, 29 June 2004, pp. 32–3). These f gures imply that large parts of the Montenegrin economy are under the control of criminal networks that engage in various forms of racketeering, do not pay taxes and are neither fiancially nor legally accountable to the civil service, the judiciary and democratically elected politicians, which in turn substantially limits the scope for democracy, for a fully functioning welfare state (for lack of public funding), and for proper protection and regulation of terms of employment and working conditions. Although Western governments f nd it convenient to blame Montenegro or its governing institutions for this state of affairs, much of the blame should really be assigned to the West and the Western-dominated UN.

The fundamental dysfunctionality of the State Union of Serbia and Montenegro and the case for secession

There was an ever-growing range of arguments in favour of Montenegro becoming an independent state. From the outset, the Republic of Montenegro has had its own political system and institutions, which have operated quite independently from those of Serbia. Montenegro 'harbours no unfulflled territorial ambitions', and the Badinter Commission, which was established in 1991–2 to draw up and assess criteria that could guide EU decisions on whether to grant recognition to each of the individual Yugoslav republics as independent states, concluded that Montenegro merited such recognition, if it sought it (ICG 2005c: 6, 15). Furthermore, its substantial ethnic Albanian minority was adequately represented in parliament and in government, was not visibly subject to systematic discrimination or persecution and received appropriate protection of and respect for minority rights. In addition, during the 1990s most Montenegrins became more and more alienated from the actions and policies of the Milosevic regime, from which they tried increasingly to dissociate their country. Montenegrins increasingly refused to serve in the VJ when called up for military service, and from 1993 onward the Montenegrin government began to insist that recruits from Montenegro could not be required to serve outside their country or expected to be party to Milosevic's dirty business. From 1994 onward Montenegro developed its own direct trade and other dealings with Western countries, in an attempt to mitigate the damage it was incurring from UN/Western sanctions against the FRY (of which it was still formally a part). Since the mid-1990s Montenegro has pressed ahead with privatization, economic reform and restructuring, leaving Serbia far behind, although 'There is a strong feeling in Podgorica that its opportunity to advance faster toward EU membership is held hostage to Serbia's often retrograde policies' (ICG 2005c: i). In a largely successful endeavour to insulate itself from the inflationary consequences of Serbia's belligerenc and economic policies, Montenegro made the Deutschmark its off cial currency in 1999 and adopted the euro as its de-facto currency in 2002. As a result, Montenegro has become a low-inf ation economy (2 per cent per annum in 2005), whereas Serbia has remained a high-inflation economy (14.5 per cent per annum, 2002–5). By th late 1990s, the Montenegrin government and parliament had ceased to regard FRY laws (let alone Serbian ones) as having any legal force in Montenegro. Unlike Serbia, moreover, 'The Montenegrin government and its institutions have harboured no one indicted for war crimes on their territory and have repeatedly made it clear that they will arrest any such persons and cooperated fully with the ICTY' (ICG 2005c: 6). Since the late 1990s, Montenegro has developed a separate taxation system, its own customs-collection service and trade policies and its own census authority. For several years now, it has had its own foreign minister, foreign policy, diplomatic service, national flag, national anthem and public holidays. Premier Milo Djukanovic has argued that the Serbian and Montenegrin economies are uncomfortable bedfellows. Not only do they already have separate currencies, tax regimes and trade rules, but they are also pulling in different directions. Serbia's economy still has a major agricultural sector, whereas the Montenegrin economy is increasingly reliant on tourism. Serbia therefore attempts to protect its farmers from cheap food imports, whereas Montenegro endeavours to buy food from the cheapest sources, 'no matter where we import from' (*IHT*, 3 March 2006, p. 3). To almost all intents and purposes, therefore, Montenegro is already functioning – and must therefore be viable – independently. The only standard trappings of statehood which it has lacked an army and a defence ministry of its own.

Most important of all, the state union which Javier Solana had foisted on Serbia and Montenegro largely against their wishes had become increasingly dysfunctional. The state union appeared to be 'equally unpopular in each of its constituent parts' (ICG 2005c: i). Political and especially governmental activity in Montenegro had become increasingly geared towards blocking the activities, curbing the power, and under - mining the eff cacy and legitimacy of the state union, whose maintenance only a 30–40 per cent minority of Montenegro's population desired.

This in turn caused Montenegrin politics to become unhealthily polarized into pro- and anti-state union camps. Montenegrin governments increasingly 'resisted all attempts at forming an effective and functional central state union government, fearing it would lead to Serbian domination', and for the same reason no new elections took place to the state union parliament, even though the term of office of the existing on had expired in 2002 (ICG 2005c: 8). Most worryingly, Serbia's armed forces, police and other state security forces were still laws unto themselves and were not yet fully subject to civilian (let alone democratic) control (ICG 2005b: 6–7). Montenegrins therefore had strong grounds for resenting being tied involuntarily to such a state by the state union framework, largely under pressure from Javier Solana and the EU. For these reasons among others, Montenegro's citizens amply deserved to be allowed and even encouraged to break free and be judged on their own merits, instead of being lumped in with Serbia. This was not a matter of pandering to Montenegrin nationalism (which is not intrinsically better than any other form of nationalism!), but rather of allowing Montenegro's inhabitants to be as free and as democratic as they could be in their difficult and constrained circumstances

There were a few redeeming features to this situation. 'Much of Serbia's political elite continue to look at the world through the distorted lens of Milosevic-era nationalism, with its xenophobia, sense of victimhood and denied entitlement', whereas 'Montenegro's governing elite has broken with the past [in these respects] and taken a broader European perspective' (ICG 2005c: 6). Nevertheless, the dominant orientations of Montenegrin government and politics were to varying degrees distractions or diversions from more constructive forms of political-cum-governmental activity, especially the fundamental political and economic reforms and restructuring which post-Communist Balkan states need most urgently. Within Montenegro, this was most manifest in the continuing power of organized criminal networks, the continuing control of the Djukanovic regime and its allies over the media, the strongly entrenched dominance of a single political party over Montenegrin politics, and the highly clientelistic 'verticality' of Montenegrin power relations and power structures, notwithstanding the extensive privatization and marketization of the Montenegrin economy. Indeed, economic change had taken place in ways that reinforced rather than challenged Montenegro's still strongly vertical power relations and structures and the dead hand of clientelistic, corrupt and essentially conservative elites.

Nevertheless, there were also good grounds for concern about the potential repercussions of the Montenegrin vote for independence on 21 May 2006. The independence issue was highly divisive. The Kostunica government in Serbia and Serbian nationalists in both Montenegro and Serbia were strongly opposed to Montenegrin secession, even though the loose union linking Serbia and Montenegro was widely viewed as dysfunctional (even among Serbian nationalists!). Some Serbian nationalists warned of civil war within Montenegro or war between Serbia and Montenegro if secession were to be approved in the referendum. During 2005 Serbia's premier Vojislav Kostunica repeatedly scoffed at the idea of Montenegrin independence: 'How can Montenegro be independent? Its entire population is smaller than Belgrade's.' He also started demanding that the 260,000 or more Montenegrin nationals resident in Serbia (most of whom had lived there for decades) should have the right to vote in the independence referendum. Premier Djukanovic dismissed this out of hand, as it was obviously intended to render the referendum unwinnable (*FT*, Survey, 12 July 2005, pp. 30–1).

The Venice Commission, a Council of Europe body whose recommendations on democratic governance are regarded as authoritative, concluded in December 2005 that Montenegro's referendum law – requiring a straight majority result on a turn-out of at least half the electorate – was entirely acceptable and in line with good European practice. However, these rules were unacceptable to Montenegro's pro-Serb opposition parties, and Javier Solana appointed Miroslav Lajcak, a Slovak diplomat, to mediate between the government and the opposition (*The Guardian*, 27 February 2006). As a compromise, Lajcak proposed that any referendum had to be endorsed by 55 per cent of those voting; and that to be valid, at least 50 per cent of the electorate would have to take part. Javier Solana and EU foreign ministers (the EU Council of Ministers) quickly backed Lajcak's proposal.

Pro-independence politicians in Montenegro were infuriated by the EU stance, pointing out that few referendums had ever had to achieve a 50 per cent turn-out and a 55 per cent 'yes' vote for the result to be deemed valid. Clearly it was going to be exceedingly difficult for the pro-independence camp to win by the required margin Foreign critics also pointed out that the terms the EU insisted on were more exacting than the referendum rules followed by most EU member states. For example, Sweden and Malta would not have become EU members if the same conditions had been applied to their membership referendums. Opinion polls in Montenegro indicated a 55–45 split in favour of independence. Djukanovic clearly felt that he could narrowly lose a vote conducted on Brussels' terms. Instead, he proposed adopting the Danish rule that 41 per cent of the electorate must vote 'yes' for a referendum to be valid. He evidently thought he could persuade 41 per cent of the electorate to vote in favour (*The Guardian*, 27 February 2006).

The EU supported Lajcak's proposal and called on the Montenegrin government to end its opposition to the proposed terms. It threatened that, unless Montenegro accepted the Lajcak plan, it would not allow international monitoring of the referendum by the OSCE. Montenegro's opposition parties decided on 25 February to back the rules proposed by the EU, at least partly on the calculation that these rules seemed to give them a very good chance of defeating the independence drive.

However, Prime Minister Djukanovic continued to hold out for his preferred rules and, firmly committed to independence, lobbied furiously for the Brussels terms t be changed. On 23 February he warned that 'The EU formula contains a virus dangerous for stability of society when it comes to the implementation of the results ... The formula harms basic democratic principle. The decision should belong to the majority, not the minority' (*The Guardian*, 27 February 2006; *IHT*, 27 February 2006, p. 3). He was right. If the referendum had produced a majority in favour of independence, but of less than 55 per cent or on a turn-out below 50 per cent, there would have been a grave risk that Montenegrin politics would become deadlocked and crisis-stricken. Under the EU's rules, Montenegro would be obliged to remain within a state union that did not work and few people liked. The EU would then have to deal with a crisis of its own making.

At the end of the day, however, a country as small and as weak as Montenegro had little option but to submit to the EU's ruling and latent blackmail. On 2 March 2006, Montenegro's parliament unanimously approved the holding of a referendum on 21 May 2006 on whether Montenegro should become independent from Serbia, on the rules proposed by the EU. At least 50 per cent of Montenegro's 466,000 eligible voters would have to take part in the referendum and at least 55 per cent would have to vote for independence for the result to be deemed valid and binding. Djukanovic announced that, if the pro-independence camp failed to win the referendum, 'he would resign immediately' (*IHT*, 3 March 2006, p. 3).

The State Union of Serbia and Montenegro was utterly dysfunctional and the vote for secession in reality merely gave formal recognition to an already viable and 'really existing' Montenegrin state, which needed to break free from the baleful power and inf uence that Serbia still had over it. The real dilemma was that successful attainment of Montenegrin independence would add to the ongoing 'Balkanization' of the former Yugoslav territory, the repeated amoeba-like proliferation of small states. The problems concern *not* the intrinsic political and economic *viability* of small states (which is already being demonstrated in practice by states such as Slovenia, Malta and Montenegro), but the proliferation of small states and the difficulties this poses fo their eventual integration into the EU. This *proliferation* of small states means that the EU is likely to face in due course the major institutional absorption problems of admitting at least nine separate Balkan states: Bulgaria, Romania, Croatia, Macedonia, Montenegro, Albania, Serbia, Bosnia and Herzegovina (assuming it holds together as one state, formally), and Kosova. This will pose major problems for voting procedures, representation, institutional viability and the balance between large and small states within the EU. It will also add to the vexations of nations such as the Catalans, the Basques, the Scots and the Welsh, who are considerably more numerous than the Montenegrins, the Slav Macedonians and the Albanians, for example, and yet won't be anywhere near as well represented and able to champion their interests in the EU because they have been denied states of their own. However, the EU will just have to cross those bridges when it comes to them.

The Landmark Referendum on Montenegrin Independence, 21 May 2006

On a turnout of 86.3 per cent (Montenegro's highest since the early 1990s), 230,711 people (55.5 per cent of voters) voted in favour of independence, while 184,954 (44.5 per cent) voted against. There were just 2,090 votes above the 55 per cent threshold required to validate secession in accordance with the EU-brokered ground-rules. The Montenegrin government and the official Montenegrin Orthodox Church backed independence, as did most members of Montenegro's ethnic Albanian, Muslim Slav and ethnic Croat minorities. The opponents mainly identified themselves as ethni Serbs and saw no real distinction between Serbs and Montenegrins. Members of the Montenegrin diaspora and Montenegrin citizens temporarily working or studying in Serbia were allowed to take part in the voting, but Montenegrins permanently resident in Serbia were not. 'Unionists' alleged that the Montenegrin government found ways to f nance the homecoming of thousands of Montenegrins who *favoured* independence. Many proudly paid their own way, but many were given free tickets, paid for by unnamed benefactors. However, the Serbian-controlled state railways also offered free railway tickets to Montenegrin migrant workers and students to encourage them to return to Montenegro to vote *against* independence. The EU suspension of SAA negotiations with Serbia in early May 2006 (see p. 319) boosted the pro-independence campaign by corroborating Premier Djukanovic's claims that an independent Montenegro stood a better chance of achieving EU membership than one linked to Serbia (*FT*, 19 May 2006, p. 6, and 22 May 2006, p. 8). Serbia's president Boris Tadic acknowledged the referendum outcome on 23 May and appealed for a swift resolution of disputes in order to 'remove all doubt' and 'make the results fial' (*IHT*, 24 May 2006, p. 3). The Montenegrin economist Nebojsa Medojevic subsequently announced the launching of a new political party to mobilize those Montenegrins who favoured independence but were against Milo Djukanovic, whom he accused of creating 'a Colombia on the Adriatic, a paradise for tycoons', at least some of whom had made fortunes out of cigarette smuggling, drug-dealing and people traffickin (*The Economist*, 27 May 2006, p. 44).

Montenegro's Declaration of Independence, 3 June 2006

On 3 June a special session of the Montenegrin Assembly, boycotted by pro-Serb parties, unanimously endorsed the referendum outcome and declared Montenegrin independence. Montenegro, the first newly independent state of the twenty-first century, was to be a 'multi-ethnic, multi-cultural and multi-religious society . . based on the rule of law and a market economy'. Its paramount goals would be integration into the EU and NATO, and it would immediately initiate procedures for gaining admission to the UN and other international organizatons in its own right. Serbia's nationalistic prime minister Vojislav Kostunica pointedly refused to congratulate Montenegrins on the referendum outcome. Nevertheless, Serbia's defence minister quickly announced that the armed forces of the defunct state union would accept Montenegrin independence and that all Serbian soldiers would withdraw from Montenegro within a week, while Serbia's President Boris Tadic wished the people of Montenegro 'peace and stability and overall prosperity' on their way to European integration and promised that Serbia would remain Montenegro's closest friend. Negotiations between Belgrade and Podgorica on how to disentangle the two states, how to deal with property rights, military facilities and work permits, how to divide up joint debts and federally owned property, how to finance future Montenegrin us of Serbian hospitals, and how to fund Montenegrin students who had hitherto studied free of charge at Serbian universities, got off to a quick start. On 5 June a special session of Serbia's *Skupstina* accepted the dissolution of the state union and unanimously declared Serbian independence, although its ultranationalist parties and the SPS absented themselves from the vote so as to feel neither tainted nor bound by it (*IHT*, 6 June 2006, p. 3). Most Serbs nevertheless accepted Montenegro's secession from the state union with good grace, not least because Montenegro had a somewhat longer history of independent statehood than Serbia, and opinion polls had long shown that around 60 per cent of Serbs favoured dissolution of the defunct state union foisted upon them by the EU (see p. 305), further confirming that most Serbs have much th same common-sense pragmatism and bread-and-butter priorities as do most other Europeans, including Montenegrins.

10 Kosova

The forging of a nation and a state

Introductory 'country profile'

Kosova has long been a fiercely contested borderland between Serbia and Albania. I has a land area of 10,908 square kilometres, amounting to only 4.3 per cent of the territory of former Communist Yugoslavia, 4.5 per cent of the size of the UK and 2 per cent of the size of France. Kosova was the poorest area within former Yugoslavia. By 1988, Kosova's GDP per capita was only 27 per cent of the Yugoslav average, 13 per cent of the level for Slovenia and 31 per cent of the level for Croatia, while its unemployment rate was an appalling 53 per cent – or three times the 17 per cent rate for Yugoslavia as a whole (Lampe 1996: 332–3; Woodward 1995: 52–3).

Kosova may have had a population of around 2 million in 2004, but no one really knows, because no reliable population census has occurred there since 1981. In 2004 Kosova's ministry of trade and industry's working hypothesis was a population of 2.4 million, its ministry of environment and spatial planning was basing its plans on a population of 2.2 million, whereas the ministry of finance and economy was basin its assumptions, calculations and decisions on a resident population of about 1.8 million (Bradley and Knaus 2004: 5). In 1981, 77.4 per cent of the population were declared to be Kosovars (ethnic Albanians), 13.2 per cent were Serbs, 1.7 per cent Montenegrins, 3.7 per cent (Slavic) Muslims, 0.8 per cent Turks, 0.2 per cent Yugoslavs, and 3 per cent had other ethnic affiliations (Spiljevic 1985: 108). In 1991 it was estimated tha about 90 per cent of the inhabitants were Kosovars, while about 10 per cent were regarded as 'Serbs', a category that presumably subsumed other Slavs (primarily Montenegrins and Bosniaks) (Yugoslavia 1992).

From 1918 until the Kosova war of 1999, however, the international community repeatedly upheld Serbia's 'historic' territorial claims to Kosova. As a result of Serbia's victories during the Balkan Wars of 1912–13, Kosova fell under a Serbian military occupation which was resumed after both world wars and reappeared during the death throes of Tito's Yugoslavia (Lampe 1996: 94). This in effect denied the region's inhabitants the right to self-determination, during a century in which national self-determination came to be regarded as a fundamental human right and (for better or worse) as the main basis on which new states could be legitimated. Since 1912 (albeit rarely before then), the predominantly Muslim and ethnic Albanian inhabitants of Kosova have repeatedly locked horns with their Serbian overlords, who are predominantly Eastern Orthodox Christians.

Who are the Kosovars? Who are the Kosova Serbs?

Ethnic Albanians not only comprise the vast majority of the population in Kosova. They have also been brought up to believe that their nation is the oldest in the Balkans, directly descended from the ancient Dardanians *(Dardanae)*, a branch of the so-called 'Illyrian peoples' who had allegedly inhabited most of the western Balkans (including Kosova) for many centuries before the arrival of Slavic 'interlopers' on the scene during the seventh centuryAD. This in turn has encouraged ethnic Albanians to believe that their ethnic group rightfully has a 'prior claim' to several partly Slav-inhabited areas of the western Balkans, especially Kosova and north-western Macedonia, and to regard the Slav inhabitants as relatively recent military usurpers of these 'ethnic Albanian homelands'. In addition, Kosova has been important to many ethnic Albanians because of the pivotal role it played in the Albanian 'national awakening' which took place between the 1850s and 1912 (see pp. 23–8).

On the other hand, Serbian Orthodox Christians and nationalists regularly refer to Kosova as 'the cradle of the Serb nation'. A long tradition of melodramatic Serbian epic poetry, folksong and religious art has celebrated Kosova as a Serbian 'spiritual homeland' within which medieval Serbian kings and princes built great Orthodox Christian churches and monasteries, fought famous battles for their faith and for their kith and kin, and were buried. Kosova is regularly referred to as 'the crucible of Serbdom', and the Serbian Orthodox Church as well as Serbian epic songs and poetry kept this notion of 'Serbdom' alive through more than four centuries of Ottoman rule (1455–1912) and subsequently.

Many Serbian nationalists and 'national' historians dispute the modern ethnic Albanians' claims to lineal descent from the ancient Dardanians and Illyrians. They make very plausible counter-claims that the modern Albanian ethnic group is *not* ancient but only emerged between the fourteenth and nineteenth centuries and that it comprised fresh *admixtures* of *diverse* 'ethnic strains', including Illyrians, Thracians, Dacians and Vlachs. There is no conclusive evidence that a people unambiguously identifiable as 'Albanian' constituted a majority of the population in Kosova prior to the Ottoman conquest. Even the relatively pro-Albanian histories of Kosova written by Miranda Vickers and Noel Malcolm concede that the region probably had a predominantly Orthodox Christian and Slavic population from the eighth to the mid-nineteenth centuries (Vickers 1998: 1–4, 16, 18; Malcolm 1998: 55–7). While it is just about conceivable that the people who lived in the Kosova lowlands   *before* the successive inflows of Slavs into the area between the eighth and the thirteenth centurie may have *some* recognizable connections to modern ethnic Albanians (although the evidence for such a claim is weak), there can be little doubt that any 'proto-Albanians' who were displaced from Kosova by these large inflows of Slav settlers would hav mingled and interbred extensively with the other inhabitants of the areas to which they were dispersed (including Slavs, Vlachs, Dacians and Thracians). Therefore, whoever they were, it is highly unlikely that the people who supposedly 'returned' to Kosova between the sixteenth and the nineteenth centuries were *the 'same'* as the people who were displaced from Kosova by the Slav settlers between the eighth and thirteenth centuries.

However, it is equally plausible that substantial proportions of the Slavs who settled in Kosova gradually intermingled, interbred and assimilated with its previous inhabitants, regardless of whether these inhabitants were (or were descended from) 'Illyrians', Dardanians, Dacians, Thracians or even 'proto-Albanians'. The occurrence of so many centuries of mixing, cross-cultural 'borrowing', interbreeding and blurring of ethnic differences makes it rather silly to try to draw clear-cut pseudo-biological distinctions between the diverse ethnic groups in Kosova and adjacent areas. Like most human beings, they must largely have been 'mongrels'.

There also appears to be little substance to Serb claims that Kosova was 'the cradle of the Serbian nation'. The earliest *expressly Serbian* stronghold and Orthodox ecclesiastical centre was not in Kosova, but rather in nearby *Raska* (Darby 1968: 90; Malcolm 1998: 43–5). Like Kosova, Raska was later to become another predominantly Muslim enclave in the Balkan Peninsula, known to many students of modern European history as the *Sandzak of Novi Pazar* (this being the name it acquired under Ottoman rule – it is now known simply as Sandzak for short). Furthermore, the earliest expressly Serbian polity was centred *not* on Kosova, but on the medieval principality of Zeta, which occupied much of what is now known as Montenegro and Herzegovina (see p. 234). Nevertheless, Kosova did acquire a 'sacred' and 'mystical' significance i Serbian self-understanding and history, because it was only *after* the medieval Serbian Orthodox Church established a new bishopric at Pec in Kosova in 1297 that the medieval kingdom of Serbia reached its fullest fruition and maximum extent. This expansion of Serbian power and inf uence was indeed accompanied by considerable displacement of the non-Orthodox and non-Slavic inhabitants of Kosova, Zeta and north-western Macedonia, while many of the prior inhabitants who continued to live in these areas were (quite heavy-handedly or somewhat involuntarily) 'converted' to Serbian Orthodox Christianity and thus gradually 'Serbianized'. Furthermore, every single ruler of medieval Serbia built and endowed at least one major monastery (usually including at least one in Kosova), whether in an attempt to sanctify his rule or, in the case of the Stefan Dusan 'the Great' (1331–55), to atone for having gained the throne by murdering his father. All of these medieval Serbian rulers were subsequently canonized, with the notable exception of the patricidal/ regicidal Stefan Dusan, while the legal code promulgated by the latter in 1349 required all of the kingdom's subjects (even non-Serbs) to be baptized into the Serbian Orthodox Church. This cast medieval Serbia's rulers in the role of defenders of the faith and extirpators of heresy. A major consequence was that much of southern Kosova became the property of Orthodox Christian monasteries. Serbs therefore frequently refer to the region as 'Kosova and Metohija', which was its official name during much of the twentieth century. The suff 'Metohija' (land of monasteries) staked an implicit Serbian Orthodox claim to the territory.

In recent times, Serbian nationalists, especially those who profess to be Orthodox Christians, have tended to claim (and may even believe) that these illustrious monastic complexes and the relics of those who founded them or died defending them have established 'eternally sanctified' Serbian claims to these lands, even though they ar now overwhelmingly inhabited by Muslim Kosovars – in much the same way that some Zionist zealots believe that their 'Holy Places' and all that the Jews have suffered on account of their special identity and faith have established eternal Jewish rights to 'the Holy Lands' which for over 1,300 years have been mainly inhabited by Arabs. Indeed, partly for this reason (as well as because many Jews and Serbs identified with one another as fellow victims of fascist acts of genocide in the 1940s), during the Yugoslav conflicts of 1991–5 there was fairly overt Jewish identification with t Serbian cause. On 4 March 1989 Matija Beckovic, who was then president of the Serbian Writers' Association, declared that Kosova's soil had absorbed so much Serbian blood and had been home to so many sacred Serbian relics and graves that it would 'remain Serbian land, even if not a single Serb remains there' (quoted in Ramet 1997: 142).

1389 and all that

The rapid disintegration of the medieval kingdom of Serbia following the death of Stefan Dusan in 1355 contributed to a Balkan power vacuum that was soon to be filled by the advance of the Muslim Ottoman Turks up the Balkan Peninsula. Their major victories over Christian forces occurred at Adrianople (Edirne) in 1364, in the Maritsa valley in 1371, at Nis in 1386 and at Nicopolis in 1396. However, it was the battle of Kosova plain on 28 June 1389 that passed into legend as a titanic clash between the Ottoman Turks and a grand coalition of Serbian, Bulgarian, Albanian, Bosnian and Wallachian Orthodox Christian forces, as a result of which the last vestiges of Serbian power and chivalry perished. In reality, both sides suffered heavy casualties and had to withdraw at the end of the day. The Serbian leader Prince Lazar died in the battle, but the Ottoman Sultan Murad was also slain (allegedly by a Serb assassin) during its immediate aftermath. Serbian national mythology maintains that one of the Serb leaders, Vuk Brankovic, deserted with his troops to the Turkish side, but this claim is not corroborated by Ottoman accounts. Formally, the battle was a draw, and the Ottoman advance into the Balkans was but briefly delayed. Nevertheless, thi battle and the myths woven around it gradually became focal points of South Slavic (especially Serbian and Montenegrin) traditions of epic verse, folksong and painting which idealized the killing of non-Serb and non-Montenegrin neighbours, romanti - cized the burning of non-Serb and non-Montenegrin villages, and attributed major misfortunes to the treacherous acts of 'Judas f gures', thereby fostering a 'betrayal syndrome' and recurrent calls for vigilance against 'traitors'. All of this was quite ruth-lessly exploited by twentieth-century Serbian nationalists for nefarious Machiavellian purposes.

Soon after 1389, the Serbian Orthodox patriarch Danilo ascribed the following 'immortal' and much-quoted words to Prince Lazar on the eve of battle:

> It is better to die in battle than to live in shame. Better it is for us to accept death from the sword than to offer our shoulders to the enemy. We have lived a long time for the world; in the end we seek to accept the martyr's struggle and to live forever in heaven. We call ourselves Christian soldiers, martyrs for godliness.

Thus, in the words of the Serbian epic song 'The Downfall of the Serbian Empire' collected by the major Serbian philologist and nationalist Vuk Karadzic (1787–1864), Prince Lazar exchanged his earthly empire for the 'empire of heaven' (Judah 1997: 38–9). Lazar's (alleged) remains were initially buried in Pristina, Kosova's main city, but in 1401 or 1402 his widow had them transferred to the monastery which Lazar had founded at Ravanica. This became the centre of a devotional cult which attracted pilgrims from all over Serbia during the early modern era. In 1690 Serbian monks retreating from the Turks evacuated Lazar's remains first to Hungary and then in 1697 to a monastery at Srem (Sremska Ravanica).

In modern times there has been a deliberate resuscitation of the long dormant cult of the 1389 battle of Kosova, which has served to make 28 June the most impor-tant day in the Serbian 'national calendar'. The cult was revived by the Serbian government at the time of the battle's 500th anniversary on 28 June 1889, which was commemorated with considerable pomp and ceremony. The Serbian foreign minister of the time, Cedomil Mijatovic, declared: 'An inexhaustible source of national pride was discovered on Kosova. More important than language and stronger than the Church, this pride unites all Serbs in a single nation . . . We bless Kosova because the memory of the Kosova heroes upheld us, encouraged us, taught us, and guided us' (Emmert 1989: 15). Commemorative church services were held, a Prince Lazar medal was struck, and about 30,000 pilgrims visited the remains of St Lazar at the monastery of Sremska Ravanica in Srem. This in turn gave rise to a spate of turgid poems, plays and paintings on the subjects of Kosova, St Lazar and medieval Serbia, right up to the First World War (Judah 1997: 68–9).

Europe paid a colossal price for the morbid and obsessive Serbian cult of Kosova on 28 June 1914, when a group of Serb nationalists decided to 'avenge Kosova' by assassinating the Austrian Habsburg crown prince Franz Ferdinand during his state visit to Sarajevo, thereby setting in motion the chain of events that precipitated the First World War. In 1942 the German occupiers of Serbia helped to spirit Lazar's (supposed) remains away from Sremska Ravanica and the attentions of marauding Croatian fascists to the relative safety of Belgrade. They were kept there until 1987, when they were ceremonially paraded around numerous shrines, churches and monasteries in various parts of Serbia and Kosova, before being returned to Ravanica in time to commemorate the 600th anniversary of the battle of Kosova plain on 28 June 1989 (Judah 1997: 38–9). This commemoration was stage-managed by Serbia's president Slobodan Milosevic, as part of the mobilization of Serbian nationalism and religious bigotry through which he consolidated his power in Serbia in 1987–9. Unfortunately, the modern Serbian nationalist and Serbian Orthodox obsession with Kosova has continued to focus attention on the past rather than the future and has repeatedly diverted the country from carrying out urgently needed internal reforms and political modernization.

A mere thirteen years after the 1389 battle of Kosova, Ottoman power was temporarily broken by the Central Asian armies of Timur the Lame (Tamerlane) in 1402–3. However, the Balkan Christians failed to take full advantage of this, and Ottoman power recovered by the 1420s. The Ottomans inf icted swingeing defeats on Balkan and Hungarian Christian forces at Varna in 1444 and at a second (and much more decisive) battle of Kosova plain in 1448, prior to capturing Constantinople in 1453. After the full subjugation of most of Serbia (including Kosova) by the 'infidel Turks in 1455, Serbian epic poetry and religious art consciously nurtured a spirit of resistance and fostered hopes of ultimate deliverance by depicting the Serbs as 'the chosen people of the New Testament – the "new Israel". Like the Hebrews in Babylonian captivity they would be led out of slavery to freedom' (Vickers 1998: 14)

The fundamental long-term change that occurred in Kosova during Ottoman rule (1455–1912) was the substantial expansion of its increasingly Islamicized ethnic Albanian Muslim population, which in turn reduced the relative importance (though not the absolute size) of the area's Serbian Christian population. 'The Ottomans found it convenient to entrust the administration of Albanian territories to native pashas or beys (*begs*), but no single ruler held sway over all Albanian lands: one would be played off against another' (Hall 1994: 4). Serbian historians and nationalists have tended to claim that the hitherto-preponderant Serbs were displaced northwards by active Albanian Muslim and Turkish colonization, as well as by flight from Ottoman-inspire religious discrimination, oppression and Islamicization. However, perspectives of this sort are highly misleading. While there was indeed some intermittent Ottoman persecution of Serbs and other Christians, this usually took the form of punitive measures against Serb/Christian uprisings or Christian support for military incursions by powers such as the Habsburg or tsarist empires. On the whole, the Ottomans valued the Orthodox Church as a partner and as a useful instrument of social control, and they conspicuously refrained from large-scale forcible colonization and Islamicization in the Balkans. Although there was some hostility towards Catholics and the Catholic Church in the Ottoman Balkans, this emanated as much from the Orthodox Church as from the Ottoman and Islamic hierarchies (Bideleux and Jeffries 1998: 64–81). There was a significant exodus of Serbs from Kosova in 1690–1 and a smaller one i 1739, after the Habsburgs had instigated but failed to assist abortive revolts against the Ottomans. However, the religious and 'national' significance of the so-called 'grea migration' of 1690 has been dramatized and blown up out of all proportion by Serbian religious and nationalist paintings portraying large numbers of Serbs being led out of Kosova by the Serbian Orthodox patriarch Arsenije III, in the manner of Moses leading the Israelites out of Egypt. Noel Malcolm has persuasively argued that the refugees must have included many Catholics and Albanians as well as Serbs and Montenegrins, that no more than half of them hailed from Kosova, and that the exodus could not have been headed by Patriarch Arsenije because he 'was not even in Kosova at the time' (Malcolm 1998: 139–62). Some of the Serbs and Montenegrins who remained in Kosova converted to Islam and then (as Muslims) became assimilated into the growing Albanian and Turkish communities. Much of the depletion of the Serbian population of Kosova was caused by plague and other epidemic diseases, rather than by repression, persecution or involuntary displacement. When land-hungry ethnic Albanians and other non-Slavic peoples moved into Kosova, they did so mainly to fill a demographic vacuum. Furthermore, the inexorable rise in the proportion of Muslims in the population was not entirely attributable to a displacement of Christian Slavs by Muslim Albanians and Turks. The Islamicization of the ethnic Albanians took place not overnight, but gradually and non-coercively, over several generations. On some calculations, Muslim Albanians and Turks may already have outnumbered Christian Slavs in Kosova by about 60:40 by the late nineteenth century. Nevertheless, an Albanian/Muslim preponderance was probably not established before the nineteenth century, and it may not have become marked until the major Balkan uprisings and wars of 1875–82, which precipitated substantial outflows of Serbian and Montenegri refugees (Malcolm 1998: 194, 230).

Kosova and the nineteenth-century 'Albanian national awakening'

During the late nineteenth century, Kosova was one of the main centres of nascent Albanian nationalism. The Catholic Church and Albanian diaspora communities in Italy, Romania, Istanbul and the USA began to sponsor Albanian-language schools and publications in Italy and in the Albanian-inhabited territories of the Ottoman Empire. For the Albanian nationalists who were 'formed' and educated by these schools, the Italian *Risorgimento* and the emergence of independent Serb, Montenegrin, Greek and Bulgarian nation-states provided inspiring role models as well as potential threats to Albanian cultural autonomy and identity. Many ethnic Albanians became particularly alarmed when, profiting from Russia's military victories over the Ottoman Empire in the Russo-Turkish war of 1877–8, Serbia and Montenegro grabbed large swathes of Albanian-inhabited territory, including parts of Kosova.

In June 1878 various local Albanian potentates held an emergency meeting at Prizren in Kosova, where they launched a proto-nationalist League of Prizren to mobilize resistance against further encroachments on Albanian 'homelands' and to press for the unification of the four Albanian*vilayets* (Shkoder, Monastir, Janina and Kosova) into a single autonomous administrative unit under continuing Ottoman suzerainty and protection. Most Western accounts of this movement maintain that the majority of politically aware Albanians did not wish to see the Ottoman Empire dismembered, because it served as a shield against larger predatory neighbours. Nevertheless, Albanian nationalists and 'national' historians have tended to assume that an Albanian proto-national identity had come into existence long before this and that it was just waiting to be 'awakened' into fully fledged national consciousness

Under pressure from the Berlin Congress of June 1878, Serbia was forced withdrew its forces from Kosova, although Montenegro was allowed to keep the Gusinje region. However, the manifest inability of the Ottomans to preserve the integrity of their Balkan domains, combined with growing Albanian alarm at the repressive and central izing disposition of the absolutist Sultan Abdul Hamid II (1878–1908), resulted in a massive rebellion against the beleaguered Ottoman authorities in the Albanian *vilayets* in August 1878, followed by further anti-Ottoman demonstrations in 1879. A major Kosovar uprising organized by the League of Prizren succeeded in expelling the Ottoman administration from Kosova, western Macedonia and the Sandzak of Novi Pazar in early 1881. However, the league was bloodily suppressed by Ottoman occupation forces later that year, and Kosova in effect remained under repressive martial law thereafter, not least because of the occurrence of further ethnic Albanian insurrections in Kosova in 1884, 1889, 1901 and 1903. The breakdown of law and order, Ottoman attempts at repression, and considerable outfows of Serbs contributed to Kosova's economic stagnation during this period. Serbian nationalist accounts have tended to claim that as many as 150,000 Serbs left Kosova between 1878 and 1912, but Noel Malcolm cogently argues that a total of about 60,000 is more plausible, considering that there may only have been 150,000 Serbs living in Kosova in 1878 (Malcolm 1998: 230)!

Some Kosovar political leaders actively participated in the Young Turk revolution of 1908, which ended the absolutist regime of Sultan Abdul Hamid II, in the vain expectation that the Young Turks would grant the Albanians large degrees of provincial autonomy, the right to use and to be educated in their own language (hitherto denied) and the restoration of their traditional privileges with regard to taxation and the bear ing of arms. However, Kosovar potentates mistrusted the Young Turks' plans for a constitution, census registration (seen as a step towards obligatory military service and regular taxation) and increased centralization of power. It appears that the great majority of the Kosovar leaders of the League of Prizren were motivated more by *clan particularism* than by modern *nationalist* doctrines (Vickers 1998: 62–6). In October 1908 Austria-Hungary formally annexed Bosnia-Herzegovina, which it had held under military occupation since 1878, partly to forestall any (re)assertion of Young Turk or Serbian claims to it. This further exacerbated tensions in the Balkans and focused Serbian and Montenegrin attention on opportunities for southward expansion into Kosova and Macedonia.

By the summer of 1909 several Kosovar clans were again up in arms against the Young Turk authorities, who took five months to pacify Kosova. Large numbers o Kosovar insurgents and their relatives took refuge in neighbouring Montenegro and Serbia, whose governments readily gave weapons and succour to the refugees in the hope of enticing these predominantly Muslim Albanians to join an imminent South Slav and Greek crusade to oust the Ottomans from the Balkans. In 1910 and 1911 there were further Kosovar insurrections against the punitive taxes, village-burning, public floggings and other repression inflicted by over 20,000 Young Turk troops. This strif resulted in an exodus of tens of thousands of Serbs, Montenegrins and Kosovars from Kosova, as well as further escalations of Kosovar guerrilla warfare against the Young Turk forces and increased deliveries of arms and money from the Serbian and Montenegrin governments to the Albanian insurgents. This Serbian and Montenegrin support for the insurgent Kosovar clans, which briefly fostered fairly *amicable* relations between the South Slav and ethnic Albanian inhabitants of Kosova, finally persuade the Young Turks to promise greater political and cultural autonomy for the Kosovars in the near future. However, these promises rang hollow and few Kosovars retained much trust in the increasingly beleaguered Young Turk regime.

Between January and September 1912, while the Ottoman Empire was still reeling from defeat by Italy in Tripolitania (Libya) in 1911–12 and growing numbers of ethnic Albanians were deserting from the Ottoman armed forces, ethnic Albanian insurgents captured Prizren, Pec and Pristina in Kosova, as well as Skopje (now capital of the ROM) and various towns in central and southern Albania. However, Kosovar clan leaders rejected a Serbian offer of local cultural autonomy for Kosova within an envisaged Greater Serbia, fearing that this would precipitate a wholesale partition of the Albanian homelands between the South Slav nations and Greece if they were to triumph militarily over the Ottomans. The Kosovar clan chiefs preferred to play for time in order to build up their own self-defence forces by talking to the Serbian and Montenegrin governments and accepting their offers of military and financial assistance, while at the same time accepting the promises of full autonomy and free elections emanating from a new Ottoman government under Moukhtar Pasha, which claimed to be opposed to the centralization and Turkifation policies of the temporarily deposed Young Turks (Vickers 1998: 70–4).

Any remaining Albanian hopes of attaining Albanian autonomy under Ottoman protection were snuffed out by the lightning victories of 350,000 Montenegrin, Serb, Bulgarian and Greek troops over much smaller Ottoman forces in the Balkan War of October–November 1912. During this war Serbia occupied north-western Macedonia and most of Kosova, while Pec and Djakovica were captured by Montenegro. Realizing that the 'Albanian homelands' were in grave danger of being partitioned between Serbia, Montenegro and Greece, eighty-three self-appointed representatives of the Albanian nation assembled at Vlore on 28 November 1912 and issued an Albanian declaration of independence. Lacking modern weapons and coordination, clan-based Albanian guerrilla forces proved unable to evict the Serbian and Montenegrin occupying forces. However, Austria-Hungary, which was determined to prevent Serbia from gaining a foothold on the Adriatic coast, threatened to intervene on the Albanians' behalf. To pre-empt a widely feared Austro-Hungarian occupation of Kosova or the creation of a 'Greater Albania' (including Kosova) under Habsburg patronage, a conference of ambassadors was hastily convened in London in December 1912 to determine the size and shape of the embryonic Albanian state and to place it under multilateral 'great power protection'. In the ensuing negotiations, Austria-Hungary supported the ethnic Albanian delegation's demands for the inclusion of Kosova, Shkoder, Janina and north-western Macedonia in an emerging Albanian state. However, it was widely feared that such a state might result in a further expansion of Austro-Hungarian power and infuence in the Balkans and thus goad Serbia, Bulgaria,

Greece and Montenegro into further pre-emptive wars, possibly with Russian backing. Austria-Hungary was persuaded to acquiesce in Serbia's acquisition of much of north-western Macedonia during the Balkan War of July 1913 (in addition to most of Kosova, which it already held), while Greece acquired southern Epirus (including Janina). In return, Russia persuaded Serbia to withdraw its troops from the Adriatic coast, Montenegro was forced to yield Shkoder to the embryonic Albanian state, and Greece was required to drop its claims to Korca, Gjirokaster and Saranda. In Albanian eyes, however, 'a far from complete Albanian state' had come into existence. Kosovars, in particular, 'felt slighted', because they had spearheaded the armed struggle against the Ottomans from 1909 to 1912. The boundaries of the emerging Albanian state reflected a compromise between the claims put forward by Greece and Serbia, on the one hand, and those urged on the Albanians' behalf by Austria and Italy, on the other (Hall 1994: 11). Over half of the ethnic Albanian inhabitants of the western Balkans were left outside the new Albanian state. As in 1878, concern to preserve peace in Europe (not unjustifiably) took precedence over nationalist claims and ethnic considerations (Vickers 1998: 84). Nevertheless, the decision to leave over half of the ethnic Albanians outside Albania did not buy peace for long. Most of the states involved in this decision were about to be drawn into yet another Balkan war, which rapidly escalated into the First World War.

The Serbian and Montenegrin occupation of major portions of Kosova during the Balkan War of October–November 1912 was accompanied by wanton atrocities against the area's predominantly Muslim and Albanian inhabitants. The invading Serb forces provocatively referred to Kosova as 'Old Serbia' and treated its predomi-nantly ethnic Albanian inhabitants as if they had no right to be there. A Serbian soldier later recorded what he had thought and felt as his unit fought to 'liberate' Kosova from the Turks during the Balkan War of 1912:

> The single sound of that word – Kosova – caused an indescribable excitement. This one word pointed to the black past – five centuries. In it exists the whole of our past – the tragedy of Prince Lazar and the entire Serbian people. Each of us has created for himself a picture of Kosova while we were still in the cradle. Our mothers lulled us to sleep with songs of Kosova, and . . . our teachers never ceased in their stories of Lazar.
>
> (Emmert 1989: 20)

The advancing Serb forces attacked not only the Ottoman army but also the region's Albanian and Turkish civilian inhabitants. The Russian revolutionary Leon Trotsky, who was working as a war correspondent in the Balkans, received the following account from a Serb army officer

> The horrors actually began as soon as we crossed the old frontier . . . Entire Albanian villages had been turned into pillars of fre . . . In all its fiery monoton the picture was repeated the whole way up to Skopje . . . Among the mass of soldiers you see Serb peasants who have come from every part of Serbia. On the pretext of looking for their sons and brothers, they cross the plain of Kosova – and start plundering.
>
> (Trotsky 1980: 267–8)

In 1914 the Carnegie Endowment for International Peace published its *Report of the International Commission to Inquire into the Causes and Conduct of the Balkan Wars* which, among other things, described the 'ethnic cleansing' perpetrated by Serbs and Montenegrins against the Albanians of Kosova and north-western Macedonia in terms which gruesomely prefigured the accounts of atrocities committed by Orthodox Serb and Montenegrins against Bosnian and Albanian Muslims during the 1990s:

> Houses and whole villages were reduced to ashes, unarmed and innocent populations massacred *en masse*, incredible acts of violence, pillage and brutality of every kind – such were the means employed by the Serbo-Montenegrin soldiery, with a view to the entire transformation of the ethnic character of regions inhabited exclusively by Albanians . . . Since the populations of the countries about to be occupied knew, by tradition, instinct and experience, what they had to expect from the armies of the enemy and from the neighbouring countries to which these armies belonged, they did not await their arrival but fled. Thus, generally speaking, the army of the enemy found on its way nothing but villages which were either half deserted or entirely abandoned. To execute the orders for extermination, it was only necessary to set fire to them. The population, warned by the glow o these f res, fled in haste. There followed a veritable migration of peoples . . All along the railways interminable trains of carts drawn by oxen followed one another; behind them came emigrant families and, in the neighbourhood of the big towns, bodies of refugees were encamped.
>
> (Carnegie Endowment for International Peace 1914: 51)

Such accounts need not imply that inter-ethnic confict and ethnic cleansing should be regarded as endemic to the region. On the contrary, for long periods Serbs and Montenegrins had coexisted quite peacefully or even amicably with Albanians, Turks, Vlachs, Roma (Gypsies) and Jews. Nevertheless, there were well-rehearsed patterns of violence and counter-violence which f ared up intermittently and were becoming all too familiar to many of the region's inhabitants. These patterns need not be attributed to alleged innate aggressiveness, ancient ethnic or religious hatreds or lack of civility among Balkan peoples, nor even to the multi-ethnic and multi-denominational charac ter of the Balkan Peninsula. Rather, they were mainly attributable to the peninsula's long-standing role as a marchland and battleground between major Christian powers and the Ottoman Empire. Its inhabitants were repeatedly encouraged and incited to rebel and to commit barbaric acts against 'the other side' by European 'great powers' with imperialist aspirations in the Balkans. It is also striking that during the protracted 'war of attrition' between the Ottomans and Europe's so-called 'Christian powers', Christians and Muslims often fought on both sides, somewhat negating representations of this as 'religious warfare'. It had much more to do with the interactions of 'great power' ambition and rivalry and 'small power' vassalage, than with religion per se.

'Sideshow': Kosova and the First World War

Early in 1915 the Serbian 'David' astonished the world by heroically driving back the Austro-Hungarian 'Goliath', which had invaded Serbia and captured Belgrade during the latter half of 1914. In October and November 1915, however, an over-whelmingly powerful multi-pronged invasion by Germany, Austria-Hungary and Bulgaria finally obliged the Serbian army, the government and the royal family t retreat through Kosova and the freezing cold Albanian highlands towards the ports of Shkoder, Durrës and Vlorë. From there they were evacuated by the French navy to Corfu, where many died of disease and malnutrition. During this epic retreat, in which nearly half the 300,000-strong Serbian army perished, some Kosova Albanians took revenge for the sufferings and atrocities which the Serbs had perpetrated against them in 1912–13 (Judah 1997: 100). However, it appears that most of the Serb deaths were caused by hunger, disease, frost-bite and Albanian reluctance to assist their erstwhile oppressors, rather than by Albanian atrocities (Malcolm 1998: 260; Vickers 1998: 91–2).

From late 1915 to September 1918, most of Kosova and north-western Macedonia came under an exceptionally rapacious Bulgarian military occupation, during which notorious atrocities were committed against ethnic Albanians by Bulgarians and Macedonian Slavs (Crampton 1997: 143–5; Vickers 1998: 92). By contrast, the parts of Kosova which fell under Austro-Hungarian occupation were encouraged to regard the Habsburg Empire as a protector against actual and potential Serb, Montenegrin, Bulgarian, Greek and Italian encroachments and depredations and were allowed to establish hundreds of Albanian-language schools and fly the Albanian flag (Hall 1994: 4)

During October and November 1918, as the First World War ended in defeat for the central powers and their protégés, Kosova was recaptured by Anglo-French-backed Serbs and Montenegrins, who proceeded to burn and bombard thousands of Kosovar homes and to terrorize, drive out or kill many thousands of Kosovar inhabitants (Vickers 1998: 93–5). Some Albanian accounts contend that, overall, the Serbs drove 150,000 Kosovars out of Kosova between 1912 and 1920 (Lampe 1996: 371). However, since Serbia had lost about 800,000 lives (one-quarter of its population) during its Herculean struggle against the central powers (Petrovich 1976: II, 662–3; Lampe 1996: 107), it is conceivable that Serbs were somewhat desensitized to the Kosovars' suffering. In the eyes of the victorious Allies, moreover, the 'heroic Serbs' could do no wrong. The creation of a Greater Serbia was regarded as a hard-won reward for a superhuman war effort against the common foe – the central powers. Serb representatives at the Paris Peace Conference of 1919–20 got away with insistently referring to Kosova as 'Old Serbia' or 'southern Serbia', in a successful endeavour to deny the legitimacy of Albanian claims to this predominantly Albanian-inhabited territory (Lampe 1996: 114–15).

In response, influential Kosovars organized a committee for the national defenc of Kosova in November 1918, and from then until 1924 there existed a major Italian-backed Kosovar resistance movement known as the Kachaks (derived from the Turkish word for outlaw, *kachmak*). Starting in 1922, however, the Kachak movement began to be repressed by the ascendant Albanian clan chief, Ahmed Zogu. The dictator-ship he established in Albania in December 1924 received some initial Yugoslav support, in return for his cooperation in the rapid and bloody suppression of the Kosova committee and the Kachaks (Vickers 1998: 1000–1). In July 1921 Kosovar leaders petitioned the League of Nations to unite Kosova with Albania, claiming in their seventy-two-page submission that 12,371 Kosovars had been killed and 22,000 imprisoned since 1918. The League's Commission of Enquiry replied that violations and misinterpretations had been committed on both sides; and, since both parties expressed willingness to avoid further violations in the future, it left it at that (Vickers 1998: 98).

Inter-war Yugoslavia accomplished little to assimilate, expel, accommodate or reconcile its substantial ethnic Albanian minority, whose problems were for the most part ignored or left to fester. During the early 1920s there was a drive to assimilate the Kosovars through state schooling conducted exclusively in Serbo-Croat. 'Albanians were denied the right to use their Albanian language for all official matters or in any form of cultural activity.' From the mid-1920s, however, state policy changed to discouragement of any form of state education for the Kosovars, in the hope that dependence upon their under-funded private Muslim *mektebs* (primary schools) and *medreses* (secondary schools) would 'keep the Albanians backward and ignorant' (Vickers 1998: 103). Partly as a consequence, over 80 per cent of inter-war Kosovars remained illiterate, rural and agricultural. Inter-war Yugoslavia also attempted to pressurize its Albanian (and Turkish) Muslim minorities to emigrate en masse. Noel Malcolm has estimated that between 90,000 and 150,000 'Albanians and other Muslims' emigrated from Kosova between 1918 and 1941 (Malcolm 1998: 286). Miranda Vickers contends that the number of ethnic Albanians who emigrated from inter-war Yugoslavia was between 200,000 and 300,000, but she also points out that this was less than the numbers of Serbs, Croats and Slovenes who emigrated to the USA in the same period (Vickers 1998: 119). In 1938 Turkey and Yugoslavia initialled an agreement to transfer 200,000 so-called 'Turkish Muslims' from southern Yugoslavia to Turkey, but the agreement was neither ratif ed nor implemented, due to the deteriorating international situation (Judah 1997: 88).

Despite this Kosovar emigration and the settlement of some 60,000–70,000 Serb and Montenegrin colonists in the region during the 1920s and 1930s, ethnic Albanians outnumbered Serbs and Montenegrins in Kosova by about 2:1 (Lampe 1998: 371; Malcolm 1998: 282). According to the 1921 census, 64 per cent of Kosova's 436,929 inhabitants spoke Albanian as their mother tongue; according to the 1931 census, the proportion was 62.8 per cent (Vickers 1998: 95, 116). Serbs and Montenegrin colonists were mostly settled on land taken from the Kosovar community, through the forced redistribution of (i) estates belonging to big landowners and Muslim religious institutions, (ii) supposedly 'abandoned' communal land and (iii) land for which Kosovars could not prove ownership. However, many of the new Serb and Montenegrin settlers felt unwelcome and found it difficult to make a living in thi impoverished region, with the result that much of the land they were awarded was eventually sold back to ethnic Albanians. Kosovars were more hostile towards these *newcomers*, who were unfamiliar with the Albanian language and customs, than they were towards Serbs and Montenegrins born and bred in Kosova. 'Native' Kosova Serbs and Montenegrins, 'who often spoke Albanian, were used to collaborating with Albanians, and had adopted some of their customs', also somewhat resented the favours bestowed upon the new settlers (Malcolm 1998: 281; Vickers 1998: 106–8). King Aleksandar's reorganization of Yugoslavia into nine administrative units known as *banovinas* in 1929 involved an attempt to dissipate Kosova's historic regional identity by dividing the region between three separate*banovinas,* centred on the non-Kosovar towns of Cetinje, Skopje and Nis, respectively.

There was very little industrial development in inter-war Kosova. A few lead and zinc mines, a smelter and a refinery were developed by foreign firms during the 1930 primarily at Trepca near Mitrovica. As elsewhere, however, mining was associated with grinding poverty and harsh exploitation, rather than with prosperity. Otherwise, the only significant industrial activities which emerged in inter-war Kosova were thre small power plants, five sawmills, ten flourmills and two brick kilns (Vickers 199 109). Kosova's valuable nickel, cadmium, bauxite, chrome, lignite and manganese deposits were not opened up until the Communist era. Nevertheless, the commence-ment of mining during the 1930s fostered the emergence of a small industrial proletariat in Kosova, and the Communist-run miners' union successfully organized a twenty-day strike at Trepca in May 1936. The following year, the Communist Party of Yugoslavia (CPY) established a regional committee for Kosova, as an offshoot of the Communist Party regional organization for Montenegro. By 1938 Communist Party cells had been established in Pec, Pristina, Prizren and Djakovica, but only 23 of the 239 CPY members in Kosova were ethnic Albanians (Vickers 1998: 114–15). By April 1941 CPY membership in Kosova had risen slightly to 270, but only 20 of these were Albanians (Malcolm 1998: 300).

The Kosovars strike back, 1941–4

Following the dismemberment of Yugoslavia by Germany, Italy, Hungary, Bulgaria and the so-called Independent State of Croatia in April 1941, Kosova's important mining districts (especially Trepca) passed under German administration, while some of its eastern districts were assigned to Bulgaria. The Trepca mines supplied 40 per cent of the lead consumed by Nazi Germany during the Second World War (Malcolm 1998: 301). However, most of Kosova was incorporated into an Italian-controlled Greater Albania, and Albanian became the off cial language of administration and instruction. Fascist Italy presented itself as the liberator and protector of the Albanians and as the creator of a unified Albanian state. At the same time, tens of thousands o Serbs and Montenegrins (especially the recently settled colonists) were driven out of their homes and off their land, often ending up dead or as forced labourers in Kosovar-run mines or labour camps, while scores of Serbian Orthodox churches were wantonly destroyed (Malcolm 1998: 293–9, 305; Vickers 1998: 122)

Those Serbs and Montenegrins who fought the Italians and their Albanian collaborators in Kosova initially gravitated towards the Serbian nationalist Cetniks, whose primary allegiances were to the beleaguered Orthodox Church and to the royalist government in exile. The partisan resistance movement established and led by the CPY failed to attract many Kosovar supporters. The local Communist cells continued to be dominated by Serbs and Montenegrins, and most Kosovars regarded the CPY as a tool of Slav supremacism. In August 1942 the CPY had merely 463 members in Kosova, only 12 per cent of whom were Kosovars, and as late as January 1944 only about 400, only 45 of whom were Kosovars. No specifically Albanian partisa detachment was established in Kosova until September 1942. Kosova's Communist cells also had great difficulty in establishing and maintaining contact with the embryonic Communist Party of Albania (CPA), which was formally founded in November 1941 (Vickers 1998: 125–8, 140).

There was collaboration between Kosovars and the Axis forces at various levels. However, the dominant motivation was

> neither ideological sympathy with Fascism or Nazism, nor any interest in the wider war aims of the Axis Powers, but simply the desire of many Albanians to seize the opportunity offered by the collapse of Yugoslavia to gain more power over their own territory and reverse the colonizing and Slavicizing policies of the previous two decades.
>
> (Malcolm 1998: 296)

Few ethnic Albanians were willing to fight outside their own homelands and man harboured misgivings about the long-term intentions of Fascist Italy and mistrusted its cooperation with the Serbian quisling regime headed by General Milan Nedic. These misgivings, coupled with mounting food shortages, inflation and economic collapse, eventually encouraged growing numbers of ethnic Albanians in Kosova and elsewhere to look more favourably upon the activities of the Yugoslav and Albanian Communist partisans during late 1942 and 1943. In September 1942, anxious not to be upstaged by the CPA and the CPY, Albanian conservative nationalists launched the Balli Kombetar (BK, National Front), which was opposed to fascist control of Albania and Kosova but committed to the continued union of Albania with Kosova. At Mukje in August 1943, however, the BK and the CPA agreed on co-operation to liberate an 'ethnic Albania' which would include Kosova. In response, the CPY bluntly informed the CPA of its intention to keep Kosova within a new Yugoslavia which would be 'a country of free people' with 'no place in it for national subjugation of the Albanian minority', and warned the CPA to dissociate itself from the profoundly fickle BK (Vickers 1998: 131)

The CPY's interventions in Albanian politics, combined with the CPA's subservience to the older and much stronger CPY, contributed to a rapid deterioration of relations between the BK and the CPA. The incipient BK–CPA rift was exacerbated by the concurrent capitulation of Italy to the Allies on 8 September 1943, which unleashed a battle for control of the territories that had been under Italian occupation. Unfortunately, instead of surrendering to the Allies (who were not well placed to step into the Italians' shoes), most of the Italians in the western Balkans simply surrendered to the German forces, which moved rapidly to fill the power vacuum created there b Italy's collapse. Germany also gained the goodwill of the BK and many Kosovars by pledging to keep Kosova united with Albania. Dzafer Deva, the most powerful f gure in the BK, swiftly declared his allegiance to Germany, launched a second League of Prizren in Kosova on 16 September 1943, and placed the BK's newly established paramilitary units at the service of the Germans. The most notorious of these were the Kosova regiment and the SS Skanderbeg division, both of which engaged in sav-age attacks on Kosova Serbs and Montenegrins. The upshot was that tens of thousands of Kosova Serbs and Montenegrins were killed, terrorized or driven out of Kosova by BK forces between September 1943 and November 1944, when overall control of Kosova finally passed from the retreating Germans to the victorious Yugoslav Partisan (Lampe 1998: 223; Vickers 1998: 140–1).

Meanwhile, at a conference held at Bujan in western Kosova between 31 December 1943 and 2 January 1944 to launch a National Liberation Committee for Kosova, the CPY and the CPA exhorted the Kosovars to join the struggle against fascism in the expectation that victory would pave the way for union between Kosova and Albania within the framework of a broader Balkan or Yugoslav-Albanian federation. However, both Tito and his chief plenipotentiary in Kosova, Vukmanovic Tempo, subsequently wrote letters criticizing the Bujan conference for raising issues and expectations which (in their view) were damaging diversions from the war effort and should prop erly have been put to one side until the war was over. Even Enver Hoxha agreed that 'the question of the future of Kosova and other Albanian-inhabited regions in Yugoslavia should not be raised during the war' (Hoxha 1981: 137). Tito seems to have calculated that he could not afford to alienate Yugoslavia's dominant Serbs by allowing any form of union between Kosova and Albania or secession of Kosova from Serbia. Milovan Djilas, the eminent Montenegrin writer who was part of Tito's inner circle of CPY leaders during the 1940s, subsequently argued that the long-term solution to the long-standing tensions between the Serbs and the Albanians lay in the creation of a relatively large Albanian republic within an overarching Yugoslav-Albanian federation:

> unification – with the truly voluntary agreement of the Albanian leaders – would not only be of direct value to both Yugoslavia and Albania, but would also finall put an end to the traditional intolerance and conflict between Serbs and Albanians Its particular importance . . . lay in the fact that it would make possible the amalgamation of our considerable and compact Albanian minority with Albania as a separate republic within the Yugoslav-Albanian Federation. Any other solution to the problem of the Albanian minority seemed impracticable to me, since the simple transfer of Yugoslav territories inhabited by Albanians would arouse violent conflict in the Communist Party itself
>
> (Djilas 1963: 112)

However, Djilas's relatively accommodating attitudes towards ethnic Albanians were not widely shared among the dominant Slavs in the CPY, who quite blatantly favoured Yugoslav ascendancy over ethnic Albanians. The CPY and the partisan movement were overwhelmingly South Slav movements which recruited very few Kosovar adherents between 1942 and 1945 (Vickers 1998: 125–8, 140). Both tended to give much lower priority to Kosovar than to South Slav interests and did little to prevent Kosovars from being callously and brutally treated by Serbs and Montenegrins.

When Kosova was f nally 'liberated' by Yugoslav partisans in late 1944, many Serbs and Montenegrins took revenge against the Kosovars – not least against those who had served in the Kosova regiment and the SS Skanderbeg division. Wealthy ethnic Albanians and actual or alleged 'collaborators' with the Axis powers had their property expropriated, along with the property of Muslim and Christian religious institutions. These measures, combined with Serbian settling of old scores against Albanians, precipitated a large-scale Kosovar rebellion from December 1944 to February 1945, at the end of which Kosova was placed under martial law. It has been claimed that between 36,000 and 47,000 ethnic Albanians were killed in Yugoslavia between 1944 and 1946 (Vickers 1998: 148), but Noel Malcolm has shown that such claims were greatly exaggerated (Malcolm 1998: 312).

Kosova under Yugoslav Communist rule

In July 1945 the CPY organized a Communist-dominated 'Assembly of National Representatives of Kosova and Metohija' in Prizren. This dutifully voted for the 'voluntary' union of Kosova with the new Socialist Federal Republic of Yugoslavia (SFRY), even though ethnic Albanians made up only 0.16 per cent of CPY members at that time (Vickers 1998: xix, 144). While the Serbs, the Croats, the Slovenes, the Montenegrins and even the Macedonian Slavs were recognized as fully fledged 'nations', each entitled to their own republic, Yugoslavia's ethnic Albanians were treated merely as a 'nationality' rather than a fully f edged 'nation' with the right to form a republic of their own (Malcolm 1998: 327–8). There were subtle gradations. Recognition as a 'nationality' was a lower status than recognition as a 'nation' or even a 'national minority'. Until they were recognized as a full-blown 'nation' in their own right, rather than as a mere 'nationality', they could not even obtain recognition as a 'national minority'. In addition, Yugoslavia's ethnic Albanians were to be lastingly divided between the three predominantly Slavic republics of Serbia, Macedonia and Montenegro, which further diluted their numerical weight and their capacity to influence decision-making within the SFRY. So-called 'Kosova and Metohija', containing the largest concentration of Albanians within the SFRY, was to become a mere appendage to the Republic of Serbia, with very limited regional autonomy.

However, having 'pacified' Kosova and subordinated it to the Serbian republic, th regime sought to reconcile the Kosovars to Communist rule. The 1948 census had revealed that 74 per cent of Kosova Albanians above the age of ten were illiterate and, in order to remedy this, the Communist regime established hundreds of new Albanian-language schools during the late 1940s and into the 1950s, despite severe shortages of appropriate textbooks and of teachers capable of providing instruction in Albanian. In 1945 there had been barely 300 Kosovar teachers in Kosova's 392 schools (Malcolm 1998: 318; Vickers 1998: 152–3). Higher education continued to be available only in other parts of Yugoslavia, where Serbo-Croat was the medium of instruction. At this stage, however, it would have been impossible to recruit enough suitably qualified ethnic Albanians in Kosova to staff an Albanian-language universit in the SFRY. The regime also promoted Albanian cultural societies, libraries, museums, theatres, drama groups, music and dance, following the examples of the union republics in the Soviet Union.

At the same time, however, Albanian Muslims and Orthodox Christians alike were subjected to extensive and intrusive surveillance and occasional harassment by the Uprava Drzavne Bezbednosti (UDB), the state-security police headed by Aleksandar Rankovic, who was the Serbian vice-president of Yugoslavia and the major 'power behind the throne'. In 1956 about 56 per cent of UDB officers in Kosova were Serbs 28 per cent were Montenegrins and only 13 per cent were Kosovars. Kosovars also remained under-represented in key occupations. Serbs and Montenegins, who comprised 27 per cent of Kosova's inhabitants in 1953, held 68 per cent of 'administrative and leading positions' and constituted about 50 per cent of factory workers and LCY members at that time. In 1971, when Serbs and Montenegrins comprised only 21 per cent of Kosova's population, they retained 52 per cent of all managerial positions; and, as late as 1981, when they constituted only 15 per cent of the population, Serbs and Montenegrins still held 30 per cent of all public-sector jobs (Malcolm 1998: 321, 323, 326, 337). Most Serbs continued to refer to all Muslims – whether ethnic Albanian, ethnic Turk or Bosnian – as 'Turks', a habit dating back to Ottoman times. Under some off cial pressure,

> between 1945 and 1966 roughly 246,000 people emigrated to Turkey from the whole of Yugoslavia. More than half that total was probably from Macedonia . . . Detailed figures for Kosova are not recorded, but a total in the region of 100,000 for the whole of that period may not be an unreasonable guess.
>
> (Malcolm 1998: 323)

Nevertheless, by the mid-1950s a more educated and politically assertive generation of Albanian intelligentsia had come to prominence, headed by the writer Adem Demaci (b. 1936). His novel *Serpents of Blood* (1958) was a condemnation of the Albanian tradition of blood feuds which had divided whole communities for generations. For his vocal championship of Kosovar rights, and for protesting against the pressures on ethnic Albanians to emigrate to Turkey under the pretence that they were 'Turks', he was given prison sentences in 1958, 1964 (f teen years) and 1976 (f teen years). During the early 1960s, Demaci headed a secessionist Revolutionary

Movement for the Unification of the Albanians, boasting around 300 members. B
the time of his final release from prison in April 1990 (by which time he had bee
incarcerated for over twenty-seven years), he had come to be regarded as Kosova's
'Nelson Mandela'.

Many Kosovars were harassed by the security police during the late 1950s and early
1960s for illegally unfurling Albanian flags, for demanding greater political and
cultural autonomy for Kosova, for protesting against the (not-altogether-voluntary)
emigration of so-called 'Turks', or for resisting the mandatory surrender of firearm
to the Serb police in 1956. There were some modest concessions in the new Yugoslav
constitution of 1963, which for the first time referred to the Kosovars as one of
Yugoslavia's 'nationalities' rather than merely as a 'national minority', to Kosova as
an 'autonomous province', and to its erstwhile 'regional council' as a 'provincial
assembly'. On the other hand, the Kosovars were still not seen as constituting (part
of) a 'nation' with the right to a republic of their own, and the precise constitutional
status of Kosova's provincial assembly was still regarded as a matter to be determined
by the parliament of the Republic of Serbia (Vickers 1998: 157, 160).

The political atmosphere in Kosova became markedly freer and more relaxed after
Aleksandar Rankovic was ousted in July 1966 (Lampe 1998: 284–5). The fall of
Rankovic was perceived as a serious setback for the Serbs, and this boosted Kosovar
confidence as well as Serb paranoia. By 1968 inexpensive paperbacks in the Albanian
language were flooding off the presses of the main Kosovar publishing house
Rilindja, while a thaw in Yugoslav relations with Albania (partly resulting from
the 1960s Soviet–Albanian rift and the Warsaw Pact invasion of Czechoslovakia
in 1968) gave rise to a large inflow of books from Tirana into Kosova, some of whic
spoke of Kosova as part of a Greater Albania. In 1968 there were also symposia
in Pristina and Tirana to commemorate the 500th anniversary of the death of the
Albanian 'national hero' Skanderbeg. However, in May 1968 two prominent members
of the LCS central committee, the writer Dobrica Cosic and the historian Jovan
Marjanovic, complained that Kosovars were openly irredentist, that Kosova Serbs and
Montenegrins were suffering systematic discrimination in public employment,
and that this discrimination was causing growing numbers of Slavs to leave the province. This was an ominous portent of things to come, but for the time being the
Communist leadership in Serbia held out against such expressions of Serb paranoia,
and both men were 'condemned by their colleagues for being "nationalistic" and
opposed to "self-management" ' (Vickers 1998: 165–6).

Simmering Kosovar grievances boiled over in late 1968. In August of that
momentous year, the major Kosovar Communist newspaper*Relindja* floated the idea
that Kosova should be raised to the status of a republic – on a par with Montenegro,
Macedonia and Bosnia-Herzegovina (Lampe 1998: 297). On 27 November 1968,
student demonstrations which culminated in the smashing of cars and windows and
the chanting of separatist slogans took place in Pristina, Gjilan, Pudujevo and Urosevac.
Soldiers and tanks were quickly moved on to the streets. The unrest quickly spread
to north-western Macedonia, especially the city of Tetova, where Albanian nationalists
drew international attention to the serious political under-representation of ethnic
Albanians (a quarter of the population) in the ROM and demanded that the Albanian-
inhabited areas of Kosova, southern Montenegro and north-western Macedonia
be united in a single Albanian Republic within the SFRY (Vickers 1998: 167).

Although the ringleaders of the 1968 unrest were tried and imprisoned, the Yugoslav
Communist regime nevertheless made significant concessions in an endeavour

to assuage Kosovar resentments. The Serbian suffix 'Metohija' (with its implicit Serbian Orthodox claim to the territory) was dropped from the name of the region, which was redesignated the Socialist Autonomous Province of Kosova. In January 1969, moreover, the Serbian parliament granted Kosova a legislature and a supreme court of its own, while the Albanian, Turkish and Serbo-Croat languages were accorded equal status within the province. A university teaching in Albanian as well as in Serbo-Croat was inaugurated in Pristina in late 1969, on the basis of several 'faculties' which had already been established there as subsidiaries of the University of Belgrade. By 1979 the University of Pristina had 30,000 students and over 1,000 lecturing staff (Malcolm 1998: 326). The League of Communists of Kosova (LCK) was given greater autonomy and clearance to restaff most of the province's official posts with Kosovars More radically, the new federal constitution of 1974 devolved political power to Yugoslavia's constituent republics and to the two socialist autonomous provinces of Kosova and Vojvodina. These last finally became constituent components of the SFRY with direct representation and voting rights on the major federal bodies, and were no longer subject to the legal jurisdiction of the Republic of Serbia within which they were still nominally located. Their provincial assemblies were given a veto in 'all matters that affected them' (Vickers 1998: 178).

However, neither side was entirely happy with these compromises. Serbs com - plained that the Kosovars (who comprised only 8 per cent of the population of the Republic of Serbia) had been granted extensive autonomy, whereas the Croatian Serbs (who comprised 15 per cent of the population of the Republic of Croatia) were denied any comparable autonomous region(s) within Croatia. Moreover, as a result of the granting of provincial autonomy to Kosova, about 21 per cent of the Serbs within the Republic of Serbia no longer lived directly under the jurisdiction of the Serbian government in Belgrade. Kosova Serbs and Montenegrins began to feel that they were being disadvantaged by this and by a growing preference for employees who could speak and write both Serbo-Croat and Albanian. Indeed, by 1981 over two-thirds of LCK members and three-quarters of Kosova's police were Kosovars. At the same time, Kosovars complained that the 1974 constitution fell well short of granting them their own sovereign republic and that it continued to describe them as a 'nationality' rather than as a fully fledged 'nation'. In official Yugoslav parlance, 'A nation . . . was potentially a state-forming unit . . . A nationality . . . on the other hand, was a displaced bit of a nation, the main part of which lived elsewhere: it could not be a constituent nation in a federation' (Malcolm 1998: 327–8). In 1975 and 1976 scores of Kosovars (including Demaci) received long prison sentences for organizing or associating with underground separatist movements with names such as the Kosova National Liberation Movement, the Revolutionary Movement of United Albanians, and the Marxist-Leninist Communist Party of Albanians in Yugoslavia (Malcolm 1998: 326–7; Vickers 1998: 179–81).

In 1978, however, a Kosovar (Fadil Hoxha) was for the first time elected vice-president of the nine-member state presidency of the SFRY and (along with the president of the Kosova provincial committee, Mahmut Bakalli) to the ruling presidium of the LCY (Vickers 1998: 183). This fostered a partly naïve belief that Kosovars were at last able to influence and participate more fully in the Yugoslav *political* system, on a less unequal footing than in the past. Precisely for this reason, perhaps, Kosovars began to shift their attention from narrowly political and constitutional griev-ances to their increasingly glaring *economic* disadvantages and to misgivings about the nature and implications of the Yugoslav *economic* system.

As a percentage of the Yugoslav average, Kosova's per-capita gross social product (GSP) fell from 43 per cent in 1953 to 32 per cent in 1971 and 27 per cent in 1988, whereas the corresponding figures for Slovenia (the richest of the Yugoslav republics rose from 175 per cent in 1953 to 187 per cent in 1971 and 203 per cent in 1988 (Lampe 1996: 328). Thus, the basic economic disparity between the richest and the poorest areas of Yugoslavia was perceived as having widened from 4:1 in 1953 to 6:1 by 1971 and nearly 8:1 by 1988. Such statistics, published in the official Yugoslav statistical yearbooks, fuelled a belief that the Kosovars were seriously disadvantaged economically by the Yugoslav economic system and were doomed to fall ever further behind Yugoslavia's richer republics and regions.

In reality, such figures greatly overstated the degree to which Kosova was fallin behind Yugoslavia's richer areas. Thus in 1977 Kosova's per-capita GSP was calculated to be only 30 per cent of the Yugoslav average, yet Kosova's average per-capita 'personal income' was reported to be 86 per of the Yugoslav average at about that time (1976) (Bideleux 1987: 180). The calculation of GSP involved a great deal of double, treble and even quadruple counting of output, especially in the more industrialized areas such as Slovenia and Croatia, and it seriously underestimated the importance of income in kind and the size of the black economy in the 'clannish' rural areas of Kosova, Macedonia, Bosnia and Montenegro. GSP was an exceptionally flawed national-income concept, yet the Communist regime nevertheless liked it because it gave rise to very inflated growth statistics for an industrializing economy

Various 'social indicators' also suggest that in important respects Kosova was actually catching up with the richer republics, rather than falling behind. By 1978, 57 per cent of Kosova's population was classed as urban. By then a modern road network had been built, electricity and running water had been made available to all but the remotest villages, nearly 95 per cent of Kosova's children were receiving elementary schooling, and there was one doctor per 2,009 inhabitants (compared with one per 8,527 in 1952). Kosova's average life expectancy rose from forty-five years in the immediat post-1945 period to sixty-eight years by 1980 (Pippa and Repishti 1984: 131–3).

Unfortunately, these same improvements in health care, sanitation, education and life expectancy also contributed to a population explosion and to Kosova's relatively high levels of unemployment, which rose from 18.6 per cent in 1971 to 27.5 per cent in 1981 and 57 per cent in 1989 (Vickers 1998: 189, 223). The scale of the unemployment problem was exacerbated by the overriding priority that the Communist regime accorded to the development of relatively capital-intensive extractive industries and electric-power generation, which were quite unable to create new employment opportunities fast enough to keep pace with a rapidly expanding population of working age and the drift of labour off the land into the towns. At the same time, the persistence of a substantial minority of illiterate adults reduced the employability of this section of the population. The adult illiteracy rate in Kosova fell from 62.5 per cent in 1953 to 41 per cent in 1961 and 32 per cent in 1971, but it was still 17.6 per cent in 1988 (Bideleux 1987: 180; Lampe 1998: 333). Lampe attributes the persistence of lamentably high adult illiteracy rates to a continuing shortage of Kosovar schools and school-teachers, combined with 'the patrimonial practice of keeping females away from schools' (Lampe 1998: 296).

There were major student protests in Pristina in March 1981 against the poor standard of university catering and the overcrowding of university dormitories. These demonstrations also sparked off more generalized urban riots and political demands for Kosova to have full 'republican' status and rights of secession. Some Serbs and

Montenegrins were assaulted, shops were looted, cars and houses were set on fire and a convent attached to the Serbian Orthodox patriarchate at Pec was burned down. Schools and factories were closed, while thousands of troops took to the streets to enforce a curfew. In May 1981 a student occupation of the University of Pristina's dormitories was dispersed by police using tear gas and resulted in a temporary closure of the university. The Yugoslav media portrayed Kosova as a hotbed of irredentism and hostility to Serbs and the Communist regime, while the leadership of the LCK was criticized for its lack of 'vigilance' and 'firmness'. Ten or eleven people wer killed, according to official reports, many more were injured and thousands of Kosovar were imprisoned or expelled from the LCK (Malcolm 1998: 334–6; Vickers 1998: 197–200). Ironically, the rapid expansion of higher education for Kosovars since 1969 had produced severe overcrowding of university facilities and soaring graduate unemployment. The new university in Pristina was churning out graduates faster than the province's capital-intensive industries and already over-staffed enterprises could absorb them; and this, combined with the overarching Yugoslav economic crisis of the early 1980s, intensified competition between educated Kosovars and Serbs fo scarce white-collar jobs (Lampe 1998: 211–12).

More ominously, the Kosova riots of 1981 helped to set in motion the Serbian nationalist backlash that gathered pace throughout the 1980s and helped to tear the SFRY apart. At the congress of the LCS later in 1981 two leading Serb politicians, Ivan Stambolic and Draza Markovic, declared that Serbs should be able to defend their rights without fear of being branded as nationalists and Great Serb chauvinists. From 1982 onwards, Serbian nationalist writers such as Vuk Draskovic, Dobrica Cosic, Antonije Isakovic and Veselin Djuretic became increasingly bold in their historical revisionism and in their attacks on Titoist cosmopolitanism (Tanner 1997: 211–12). Tens of thousands of Serbs attended the funeral of Aleksandar Rankovic on 20 August 1983, 'in what became the f rst mass protest about the status of Serbs in Kosova and in Yugoslavia generally' (Vickers 1998: 218).

Serbs and Montenegrins also voiced increasingly strident concern at the decline of the combined Serb and Montenegrin share of Kosova's population from 27.4 per cent in 1961 to 20.9 per cent in 1971, 15.0 per cent in 1981 and an estimated 10 per cent in 1991, while that of the Kosovars rose from 67 per cent in 1961 to 73.7 in 1971, 77.5 per cent in 1981 and an estimated 90 per cent in 1991 (Lampe 1996: 330). These changes had little to do with migration or the displacement of people, whose scale was greatly exaggerated by alarmist Serbian nationalists. The principal reason for the changing composition of Kosova's population was that from the 1960s and 1980s Kosovar birth rates were more than double those of the Serbs and nearly double those of the Montenegrins, while at the same time the Kosovars were experiencing a dramatic rise in life expectancy and a corresponding decline in death rates. As a result, the Kosovar rate of natural increase was nearly three times the Yugoslav average by the late 1970s. In response, Serbian nationalists stridently denounced the so-called 'demographic genocide' of the Kosova Serbs by the more prolific Kosovars There were also defamatory allegations that Kosovars were subjecting the province's embattled Serb and Montenegrin minorities to various forms of harassment, dis-crimination, sexual assault and intimidation.

On 24 April 1987 Slobodan Milosevic visited Kosova as the relatively new and little known leader of the LCS, ostensibly to calm the Kosova Serbs' anger at their perceived mistreatment at the hands of the locally ascendant Kosovars. In the event, however, he delivered an infammatory speech, which culminated in his most famous and emotive catchphrase: 'No one should dare to beat you!' Repeatedly broadcast on Serbian television, this speech catapulted Milosovic to the forefront of the Serbian nationalist revival and Yugoslav politics. Largely on the strength of this, he became president of Serbia in December 1987 and his allies took control of Vojvodina in September 1988 and Montenegro in January 1989. Milosevic also managed to get the popular Kosovar Communist boss Azem Vlassi replaced by the pliant but unpopular Kosovar police chief Rahman Morina in November 1988.

The forced resignation of Vlassi precipitated a week-long protest by Kosovar miners, factory workers and students demanding his reinstatement, but the Milosevic government refused to give way. The LCK was purged and gradually fell apart, curtailing the Kosovars' capacity to resist Belgrade politically. On 3 February 1989 the Serbian parliament passed laws giving Serbia increased control over Kosova's police, judiciary and finances. In response, over 1,000 miners at the large Trepca mining and metallurgical complex at Mitrovica embarked on a hunger strike, demanding the resignation of Rahman Morina and his most prominent collaborators. Kosova was brought to a standstill as more and more Kosovars went on strike. To break the deadlock Morina pretended to resign along with Vlassi, but then immediately had Vlassi imprisoned and carried out a purge of Kosovar managers of large enterprises, while the province was placed under curfew. When Kosovars brought Kosova to a standstill once more, Serb-controlled security forces declared a state of emergency (Vickers 1998: 229–35).

In March 1989, with Kosova under emergency rule, both the Serbian parliament and Kosova's intimidated provincial assembly passed constitutional amendments which restored Kosova to Serbian legal, political and economic control. At least twenty-eight Kosovars died and many more were wounded in the subsequent riots. The Communist leaders in Montenegro, Macedonia and Vojvodina supported Serbia's actions in Kosova, while the Bosnian leadership passively acquiesced. The only vocal opposition emanated from Slovenia. Azem Vlassi was subjected to a show trial in October and November 1989, which precipitated renewed student and industrial unrest thoughout Kosova. In January 1990 initially peaceful demonstrations by thousands of Kosovar students and workers gradually turned into violent attacks on cars, buses and trains and violent confrontations with the security forces, in which at least thirty-one people died and hundreds were injured. During 1990, as the SFRY broke up into several separate states, Serbian troops and police were left in sole control of Kosova (Vickers 1998: 235–6, 241–2).

On 5 July 1990 Kosova's provincial assembly was physically ejected from its building. Some of the deputies briefly reassembled on the steps outside to proclaim a Republic of Kosova within the SFRY, but outside Serbian control, whereupon the Serb authorities formally dissolved Kosova's government, occupied its radio and television stations and took direct control of the province, with the approval of the SFRY federal presidency. *Rilindja*, the main Kosovar daily newspaper, was shut down in August 1990 along with all the province's Albanian-language radio and television stations. Kosovar theatres, libraries, museums, art galleries, dance groups and fi m units were also purged or closed down, while school curricula were 'Serbianized' and Kosovar teachers were sacked before the start of the new school year. On 28 September 1990 Serbia promulgated a new republican constitution which annulled the autonomous status of Kosova, whereupon defiant deputies from Kosova's dissolve provincial assembly adopted a constitution for an underground 'Republic of Kosova' at a secret gathering in the town of Kacanik (Vickers 1998: 245–7).

During 1990 the Serbian authorities either purged or closed down various public enterprises employing large numbers of Kosovars and allowed some to be taken over by Serbian enterprises. They also passed laws requiring enterprises to recruit at least one Serb for every Kosovar employed and requiring Kosovar employees to sign 'loyalty letters' proclaiming their allegiance to the Republic of Serbia, on pain of dismissal. In response Kosovar trade unionists launched an autonomous Alliance of Independent Trade Unions of Kosova to fight for the reinstatement of dismisse Kosovar workers and to provide them with moral and financial assistance out of a 'solidarity fund'. This was funded by voluntary contributions from Kosovar firms employees and, above all, *Gastarbeiter* (guestworkers) living in the EC (Vickers 1998: 246, 249).

From April 1990 onwards most Kosovars embraced non-violent passive resistance, with encouragement from the Democratic League of Kosova (LDK) launched in December 1989. Dr Ibrahim Rugova, then president of the Kosova Association of Writers, became the leader of the LDK. The LDK, which rapidly became the para - mount Kosovar political movement, initially aspired to republic status for Kosova within a confederal Yugoslavia. In an attempt to close ranks against their Serb oppressors, thousands of Kosovars took part in open-air ceremonies to terminate long-standing blood feuds. By the spring of 1991, the LDK had offces in Stuttgart, Zurich and Brussels and claimed to have 700,000 members. In partnership with other Kosovar parties, the LDK held an unofficial referendum on the independence and sovereignt of Kosova in late September 1991. It claimed that, on an 87 per cent turn-out, 99 per cent had voted in favour of independence for Kosova. The 'Republic of Kosova' was recognized by Albania in late October 1991. The LDK's parallel 'Republic of Kosova' applied (unsuccessfully) for recognition as a state by the EC on 23 December 1991 (Malcolm 1998: 347–50; Vickers 1998: 248–54).

In Albania, meanwhile, Dr Sali Berisha's Democratic Party (DP) initially encour aged Kosovar secessionism in the belief that, with Western economic and technical assistance, a non-Communist DPA-ruled Albania would soon be able to unite with Kosova. The DPA's founding programme (1990) called for 'democratic union' with Kosova, and in March 1992 Berisha told his supporters that the DPA 'will not stop fighting until her dream of uniting the Albanian nation comes true'. As an Albanian northerner (Gheg) with extensive family connections in Kosova, Berisha gave union with Kosova a higher priority than did Albanian southerners (Tosks). His emphasis on Albanian unif cation also usefully attracted substantial donations to DPA election funds from Kosovar *Gastarbeiter* in Western Europe and from the over 400,000-strong Albanian-American community in the USA. However, after he became president of Albania in 1992, Berisha backtracked, because much-needed Western economic assistance became increasingly conditional on (i) Albanian non-interference in the affairs of former Yugoslavia and (ii) formal support for the inviolability of existing frontiers. Furthermore, as the death agonies of the SFRY escalated into warfare in 1991–2, many Kosovar males evaded military service in the JNA either by going into hiding within Kosova or by slipping across the mountains into Albania, where 'they quickly began to control several areas of economic activity, most notably car imports, drug dealing and gun-running. Kosovar immigrants bore some responsibility for the spiralling crime rate and the growth of mafia-type activities that became so prevalen during Albania's early transition period' (Vickers 1998: 255–9, 269). It thus became prudent for Albania to try to keep Kosova at arm's length.

The University of Pristina was rapidly 'Serbianized' from September 1991 onward.

Kosovar students were debarred from entering, and to enforce this all university buildings were put under police guard. Some 7,000 Serbian and Montenegrin students (along with a few Greeks) were allowed to continue their higher education, which was henceforth conducted solely in Serb. From November 1991, however, Kosovars began to organize their own Albanian-language 'parallel university', for which they gradually obtained modest financial support from the Albanian diaspora in the EC There also sprang up a 'parallel school system' staffed by Kosovar teachers dismissed from the state schools. By 1994 this was providing a rudimentary education in private houses, churches, restaurants and garages for two-thirds of Kosova's 450,000 children of school age. However, the system was acutely underfunded and its teachers were very poorly and irregularly paid. Pupils and parents gradually became disaffected with the system, not least because the certificates and diplomas provided carried little weigh or recognition among prospective employers. 'For Kosova Albanians the "parallel" education system became a metaphor of prison and freedom at one and the same time' (Kostovicova 1999: 12).

Since most Kosovars were systematically excluded from public employment and hence from official social and medical insurance, there also emerged a similarly makeshift 'parallel health service' staffed by Kosovar doctors and nurses dismissed from Kosova's public hospitals and polyclinics. Notwithstanding the receipt of some financial assistance and medical supplies from the Albanian diaspora and foreign charities, the 'parallel clinics' had to be run on a shoestring (often without proper equipment, sanitation, reliable power supplies or even clean running water). Consequently, infant mortality and the incidence of diseases such as polio and tetanus increased (Vickers 1998: 152, 262, 275). At the same time, Kosovars were subjected to frequent power cuts and water restrictions, while growing numbers of sacked or unemployed Kosovars were evicted from housing owned by local communes or former employers.

In some respects, ironically, the economic position of Kosova's Serbs and Montenegrins deteriorated even more than that of the Kosovars. Growing exclusion from public-sector employment forced most Kosovars to engage in various sorts of private activity, much of it in the informal 'grey economy' or even in the illicit 'black economy'. Closely knit kinship structures and strong determination and solidarity in the face of adversity helped many Kosovars to make a success of private enterprise, whether as traders, shopkeepers, restauranteurs, contractors, gunrunners or drug dealers. Serbs and Montenegrins, by contrast, were increasingly dependent on the public institutions and state enterprises, which all but collapsed under the impact of war, sanctions, shortages, corruption and rampant inflation, with the result that their real wages and salaries were but a fraction of what they had been in 1990 and were often heavily in arrears. Along with the costly wars with Bosnia and Croatia, the forcible subjugation of Kosova was a colossal drain on Serbian resources, reportedly absorbing more than one-ffth of Serbia's public expenditure. Furthermore, Kosova's poverty, insecurity and economic contraction severely reduced any conceivable returns on these expenditures, whether to Serbia as a whole or to Serbian enterprises operating in Kosova. Thus, grimly clinging on to Kosova contributed to the impoverishment of Serbs as well as Kosovars. Moreover, contrary to Western media and some academic portrayals of the Serbs, Kosova was never a hugely popular 'cause' among Serbs (Malcolm 1998: 351–3; Vickers 1998: 253, 277–8, 299). Indeed, despite recurrent attempts by the Serbian government to persuade or direct Serb refugees to settle in Kosova (especially after the displacement of about 200,000

Croatian Serbs from Croatia to Serbia in August 1995), it seems that no more than about 25,000 of these remained in Kosova for any length of time. Kosova had become too poor, too dangerous and too alien and unwelcoming for most Serbs – and Serbian state support for Serb colonists had long been too erratic and unreliable. Similarly, instead of straining at the leash to kill or dominate their neighbours, growing numbers of Serbs sought to resist or evade military service against neighbouring peoples, whether in Croatia, Bosnia or Kosova (see pp. 202, 243 and 253–4). Control and domination of Kosova was the project of a voluble Serbian nationalist minority with strong power bases in the security forces, the media and the state apparatus, but nonetheless a minority.

During 1991 and 1992 the Serbian authorities began to arm Kosova's embattled Serb and Montenegrin minorities and encouraged the formation of paramilitary forces such as Vojislav Seselj's 'White Eagles' and Arkan's 'Tigers'. Seselj, the leader of the ultra-nationalist Serbian Radical Party, was awarded a professorship at Pristina University, and in 1994 Arkan (alias Zeljko Raznatovic) was elected to a seat in the Serbian parliament from a constituency in Kosova. While *arming* Kosova's Serbs and Montenegrins, the Serb authorities sought to *disarm* the Kosovars. This reinforced Rugova's appeals for non-violence, as he explained in April 1992:

All our weapons have been taken away by the Serbian police. We are not certain how strong the Serbian military presence in the province actually is, but we do know that it is overwhelming and that we have nothing to set against the tanks and other modern weaponry in Serbian hands. We would have no chance of successfully resisting the army. In fact the Serbs only wait for a pretext to attack the Albanian population and wipe it out.

(quoted in Vickers 1998: 264)

In May 1992 Rugova presided over unofficial 'parallel elections' in which his LD obtained 574,755 votes (76.4 per cent of the total), the Parliamentary Party of Kosova (led by Adem Demaci) won 36,549 votes (4.9 per cent), the Peasant Party of Kosova won 23,682 votes (3.2 per cent), the Albanian Christian Democratic Party won 23,303 votes (3.1 per cent), and independents won 24,702 votes (3.3 per cent). Rugova, as the sole presidential candidate, was elected president of the Republic of Kosova with 99.5 per cent of the votes cast. (These elections were naturally boycotted by Kosova's Serbs and Montenegrins.) Despite the presence of eight monitoring groups from the EC and the USA, there was considerable Kosovar discontent at the way in which Rugova and the LDK marginalized rival politicians and parties. The fact that Kosova's f rst 'parallel parliament' did not actually meet further strengthened Rugova's hegemony over Kosovar political life. Lamentably, the Kosovar boycott of Serb and FRY elections handed most of Kosova's seats in the Serbian and FRY parliaments to the SPS and hardline Serbian nationalists. If the Kosovars and the LDK had vigorously contested these elections, President Milosevic would have faced a much more hostile parliament (Vickers 1998: 260–1, 280).

It is often overlooked that in large measure Rugova and the LDK were able to organize a 'parallel state' with its own schools, health care, elections and other institutions because the Milosevic regime allowed them to do so. The Milosevic regime had various authoritarian features, but it never established a one-party 'totalitarian' state. It harassed rival political parties and movements, but it allowed them to exist, function and put out some literature. In the case of Rugova and the LDK, Milosevic may well have calculated that it was greatly to his advantage to allow Kosovar apostles of non-violence a relatively free hand, in order to limit or delay the growth of more violent and dangerous insurgency and free up most of the Serbian and FRY police and armed forces for use against Croatia, Bosnia and the very considerable Serb opposition to the Milosevic regime. It is also conceivable that Milosevic was influence by the public warning delivered by the US President George Bush on 25 December (Christmas Day) 1992: 'In the event of conflict in Kosova caused by Serbian action the United States will be prepared to employ military force against the Serbs in Kosova and in Serbia proper' (*New York Times*, 28 December 1992).

By early as 1993, however, there was growing Kosovar frustration and resentment towards Rugova's rejection of violent resistance, combined with his intransigent non-cooperation with and non-participation in Serbian institutions. His stance had resulted in Kosova becoming almost completely sidelined in international negotiations on former Yugoslavia. The LDK evidently had no real strategy beyond boycotting off cial institutions and electoral processes, and non-violent passive resistance was clearly leading nowhere. Many Kosovars became even more disillusioned with what came to be seen as Rugova's almost fatalistic *passivity* (as distinct from more militant and principled Gandhian *pacifism*) after the Dayton accords of November 1995, because the West did not make the lifting of international sanctions against Serbia and Montenegro conditional upon steps being taken to resolve the Kosova problem. On the contrary, external pressure for a solution to the Kosova crisis was curtailed in order to secure Serb support for the peace agreement in Bosnia and Herzegovina. 'The Kosova Albanians received nothing from the settlement. This was a huge disappointment... Kosovan Albanians were resentful that they were now to be locked into a Serb-dominated [rump] Yugoslavia' (Crampton 2002: 271). Internationally, the 'Kosova question' was being reduced to questions of respect for autonomy and human rights, with almost no international recognition of Kosovar aspirations to self-determination and independence (Vickers 1998: 269–71, 283–7). After Dayton, only some minor sanctions were retained against Serbia until such time as it (merely) improved its human-rights record in Kosova. Thus, not just in Serbia but in Kosova, 'the Dayton settlement had the general effect of strengthening Milosevic's rule' (Malcolm 1998: 353).

Battles over education

Agreement was reached on 2 September 1996 to end the Kosovar boycott of state schools, which had begun in 1990. Kosovar students were to move from the parallel (underground) system operating from private houses to public educational estab - lishments in Kosova (*EEN*, 1997, vol. 11, no. 7, p. 5). However, the reintegration of education made little headway in practice, and tensions continued to run high in the educational f eld. For their part, Kosova's Serb minority had understandable misgivings about schools that issued diplomas stamped 'Republic of Kosova' (*The Economist*, Survey, 24 January 1998, pp. 14–15).

When Rugova 'banned' Kosovars from staging street demonstrations, his critics first challenged him in the education sector, which was deemed to be the flagship o his strategy of non-violent resistance to Serb domination but actually giving Kosovars a very third-rate education (Kostovicova 1999: 12). A car bomb seriously injured the (ethnic Serb) dean of the University of Pristina on 16 January 1997. The SPS mayor of Pristina blamed 'Albanian terrorists', and the media in Albania confrmed that the

KLA had claimed responsibility for the bombing *IHT*, 21 January 1997, p. 4). Around 3,000 students from the underground Albanian university, formed in 1989, took part in peaceful protests in Pristina on 1 October 1997, demanding that Pristina University be returned to Kosovar control. The demonstration was broken up by FRY riot police (*IHT*, 20 October 1997, p. 5). Similar protests were similarly broken up by riot police on 30 December 1997 and on 4 January 1998, in Pristina and elsewhere.

There were Serb demonstrations in Pristina on 23 March 1998 against an agreement to reintegrate Serb and Kosovar education in Kosova. There was to be a phased return of ethnic Albanian pupils and university students to state educational facilities by 30 June 1998. Serbs and Albanians, respectively, were to be taught in morning and afternoon shifts in their own languages with their own curricula, but using the same buildings and back-up services. Ethnic Albanians were to have access to dormitories and dining rooms by the end of September 1998 *FT*, 24 March 1998, p. 2; *The Times*, 24 March 1998, p. 14). However, the agreement was nullified by the mounting conflic

The rise of the Kosova Liberation Army and the drift towards war

In 1982 numerous Kosovar students and young workers were driven into emigration/ exile among the 500,000 or so Kosovar *Gastarbeiter* by Yugoslav repression of the Kosovar nationalist unrest which had erupted in 1981. A small group of these young Kosovars, who had come to the conclusion that Kosova could only attain freedom through an armed struggle, founded the Levizja Popullore e Kosoves (Popular Movement for Kosova, mainly known by its Albanian initials, LPK). Following small secret conferences which they held in the Republic of Macedonia in late 1992 and in Pristina in early 1993, they launched the Ushtria Climitare e Kosoves (Kosova Liberation Army, KLA), which carried out its frst attack in 1993. It received income or donations from small businesses, smuggling, drug-dealing and the Albanian diaspora. The first significant breaches in Kosovar non-violence occurred in 1995 and 1996, but as yet only in the form of isolated incidents or attacks (Vickers 1998: 278, 290–2, 296).

The armed insurgency in Albania during the spring of 1997 put into circulation *c*.700,000 weapons of various sorts, seized from Albanian arms depots, and many of these found their way across the relatively porous mountain frontier between Albania and Kosova. In November 1997 the KLA repelled an armed offensive by Serb police and, in so doing, effectively established a 'liberated zone' in the Drenica region (Thomas 1998: 118). During the winter of 1997–8 the KLA overran numerous police stations, seized scores of automatic weapons, attacked many police patrols and checkpoints and claimed responsibility for assassinations of over fifty Serbian policemen and officials, as well as of ethnic Albanians suspected of collaborating with the Serbian authorities. Rugova, while still calling for an independent Republic of Kosova, condemned the KLA's use of force (*IHT*, 3 March 1998, p. 5).

One of the leading Kosovar insurgents in 1997 and early 1998 was Adem Jashari, a 'local tough' based in the village of Prekaz in central Drenica, who 'liked to get drunk and go out and shoot Serbs'. In retaliation, Serbian military police killed seventeen Kosovars during raids on the Drenica region on 28 February 1998, and on 4 March they killed about eighty Kosovars (mainly members of the Jashari clan) during a siege of the Jashari clan stronghold. In response to these assaults,

the KLA began to despatch arms and uniforms over the border from Albania,
...village militias began to form, and clan elders . . . decreed that now was the
time to fight the Serbs. Whether they were KLA or not, they soon began to cal
themselves the KLA . . .The KLA . . . punched through a supply corridor to the
Albanian border and soon found itself in control of most of Drenica and part of
the Decani region along the border.

(Judah 1999: 23–4)

In retaliation, nearly 100 killings were carried out by hundreds of heavily armed
Serbian police and military units during March 1998, and 'more than half of the victims
were women and children ... The Serbs, rather than hunt down armed groups, blasted
villages into rubble' (*IHT*, 18 March 1998 p. 4; *IHT*, 23 March 1998, p. 5; *IHT*,
24 March 1998, pp. 1; *IHT*, 7 April 1998, p. 6).

Representatives of the 'Contact Group' (the USA, Russia, France, Germany, the
UK and Italy) met in London on 9 March 1998 and decided to stop supplying Serbia
with any equipment that could be used for internal suppression and terrorism and to
ask the UN Security Council to impose a comprehensive arms embargo on the FRY.
The five Western members of the group agreed to deny visas to those responsible
for repression in Kosova and to halt government-financed export credits for trade and
investment (including funding for privatization, the proceeds of which were considered
likely to be used to finance the Milosevic regime). Russia's representatives stated
that the Russian government would reconsider its stance if the repression continued.
FRY assets abroad were to be frozen by the five Western powers from 25 March
(the date of the Contact Group's next meeting, due to take place in Washington), if
the repression continued. All six member states condemned the 'unacceptable use
of force' by the Serb police, but they also condemned the 'terrorist actions' of the
KLA and agreed that Kosova should be granted autonomy but not independence. They
issued a statement that within ten days Milosevic should take 'rapid and effective
steps to stop the violence and engage in a commitment to find a political solution t
the issue of Kosova through dialogue', that special police units should be withdrawn
from Kosova, that the OSCE, the International Committee of the Red Cross, Contact
Group diplomats and the UNHCR should be allowed access to Kosova, and that
the ICTY should consider extending its enquiries to Kosova (*IHT*, 10 March 1998,
pp. 1, 6; *FT*, 10 March 1998, p. 1).

In response, on 10 March the Serbian government offered an 'open dialogue'
with 'responsible' Albanian representatives from Kosova. Ibrahim Rugova replied
on 11 March that 'the best, the optimal and most viable solution and the best for the
region and the neighbouring countries – Albania, Serbia, Macedonia and the rest
– would be an independent Kosova with all guarantees for the local Serb population and Serb interests in Kosova' (*The Guardian*, 12 March 1998, p. 14). A
Serbian delegation arrived in Pristina on 12 March offering the Kosovars 'the highest
level of autonomy', but Rugova sensed a trap and replied that they had been given
no prior warning or invitation and that they wanted an outside mediator: 'This offer
is not all serious. It was made just to ease outside pressure on Serbia' (*FT*, 27 April
1998, p. 21).

As the sole candidate, Rugova was re-elected as de-facto president of the informal
Kosova republic on 22 March 1998. There were also elections to its 130 parliamentary
seats. Serbia deemed the elections illegal but neither interfered in them nor prevented
them, as it could have done. Rugova's prominence suited Milosevic.

The Contact Group agreed on 25 March to extend the deadline for compliance with its demands, including the full withdrawal of Serb-dominated special police units from Kosova and the start of unconditional dialogue with representatives of the ethnic Albanian community. It warned that, if its demands were not met within four weeks, it would 'take steps to apply further measures' (*IHT*, 26 March 1998, pp. 1, 4).

The UN Security Council imposed an arms embargo on the FRY on 31 March 1998, condemned Serbia's use of 'excessive force' and urged Belgrade and the Kosovar leadership to enter into 'meaningful dialogue on political status issues', aiming at 'an enhanced status for Kosova which would include a substantially greater degree of autonomy and meaningful self-administration'. Serbia's president Milan Milutinovic flew to Pristina on 7 April to offer the Kosovars a 'dialogue', but Kosovar leaders spurned the offer and demanded foreign mediation and the removal of Serbian paramilitary police from Kosova.

Milosevic shrewdly held a referendum in Serbia on 23 April 1998, asking the question: 'Do you accept foreign representatives taking part in resolving the problems of Kosova and Metohija?'. The turn-out was 73.1 per cent, and foreign involvement was rejected by 94.7 per cent of the votes cast (*IHT*, 25 April 1998, p. 1).

The Contact Group decided on 29 April 1998 to freeze FRY assets held abroad, but Russia dissented from a threat to block new foreign investments in Serbia if it did not agree to a framework for 'status negotiations' on Kosova by 9 May. The ban on foreign investment was implemented on 9 May, only to be suspended again on 18 May. The US diplomatic emissary Richard Holbrooke succeeded in persuading Milosevic and Rugova to meet in Belgrade on 15 May, when they agreed to hold further negotiations in Pristina on 22 May.

Between March and June 1998 the KLA unleashed a major guerrilla offensive which gained control of about one-third of Kosova (*IHT*, 4 July 1998, p. 10). Western governments initially appeared to welcome the emergence of these 'terrorists' as a new (and for the West seemingly costless) way of increasing the pressure on Milosevic to restore Kosovar autonomy. Western officials met KLA representatives and demanded that these 'terrorists' be represented in negotiations between the Kosovars and the Serbian government. By June 1998 the KLA had *c*.2,000 fighters (*IHT*, 7 June 1999, p. 7). In early summer 1998 NATO threatened to increase its presence and hold military exercises in Albania and the ROM, but then backtracked in the face of practical military difficulties, Russian opposition and the unexpected strength o the KLA.

NATO foreign ministers issued a joint statement on 28 May 1998: 'The status quo is unacceptable. We support a political solution which provides an enhanced status for Kosova, preserves the territorial integrity of Yugoslavia and safeguards human and civil rights of all inhabitants of Kosova, whatever their ethnic origin' (Jeffries 2002b: 442). They also approved military exercises in and training for Albania and the ROM, an increase in the size of the UN force in the ROM from 800 to 1,050, continued Western military presence there after the expiry of the UN mandate on 31 August 1998, and contingency planning for preventive deployments on the Kosova border.

In early June 1998 Serbia launched an all-out military and police offensive against Kosovar insurgency. In response, on 4 June Rugova called off a dialogue with the Serb authorities which was due to start the following day, and on 8 June the EU strongly condemned Serbia for 'a campaign of violence going far beyond what could legitimately be described as a targeted anti-terrorist operation'. It banned new investment in Serbia (Montenegro was exempted), jeopardizing a 1 billion US dollar Italian–Greek investment in Serbian telecommunications. The USA followed suit (*FT*, 9 June 1998, p. 2). The Contact Group (including Russia) condemned the 'massive and disproportionate use of force' by the Milosevic regime and demanded an immediate cessation of the repressive action by Serb military forces against Kosovars, the withdrawal of Serb security forces from the region, unimpeded access for international monitors and observers, measures to help refugees return home, and 'rapid progress' in talks with Kosovar leaders. If Serbia did not comply, NATO promised 'further measures to halt the violence and protect the civilian population, including those that could require the authorization of a United Nations Security Council resolution', but this time it also warned Kosovar extremists to desist from violence. The USA, the UK, Germany, France, Italy, Canada and Japan also banned JAT flights, but the ban remained a dead letter. Concrete action was largely deferred until after Milosevic had met with Boris Yeltsin in Moscow on 16 June. In Moscow Milosevic agreed to allow EU observers into Kosova, to guarantee the safe return of refugees and access for aid agencies, and to accept a monitoring unit (composed of US, Russian, Austrian and Polish diplomats) in Kosova. Meanwhile, NATO held air exercises in Albania and the ROM along the border with Kosova on 15 June, while the EU again banned JAT fights to EU countries and did so yet again on 29 June. However, this ban did not become effective until 16 September (*FT*, 31 October 1998, p. 4).

The KLA named Adem Demaci, the leader of the Parliamentary Party of Kosova who had spent over twenty-seven years as a political prisoner and had close ties with Kosovar militants in Switzerland, as their political representative on 13 August 1998. He then resigned as chairman of the Parliamentary Party of Kosova (*FT*, 17 August 1998, p. 3).

In July and August Serbia's continuing military and police offensive destroyed many thousands of Kosovar homes. The Serbs were accused of resorting to 'genocide' and 'ethnic cleansing', but prior to August 1998 there were no verified reports of atrocities of Bosnian dimensions. About half of the refugees remained within Kosova, but the rest took refuge in Albania, the ROM and Montenegro, whose government explicitly dissociated itself from the Milosevic regime. The UN-CR estimated that 30,000 Kosovars had fled to Montenegro and another 13,000 to northern Albania b mid-August 1998, and that over 10 per cent of Kosova's population had been displaced from their homes. Kosovar sources admitted that the Serb counter-offensive had brought 159 villages and hamlets which had been controlled by insurgents back under government authority, and that most of the residents had f ed. Once civilians left an area, the Serb police then looted and burned abandoned Kosovar homes, farms and businesses (*IHT*, 17 August 1998, pp. 5, 8). 'The KLA appeared to have been crushed. Realising that it could not take on the far more heavily armed Serbs, the KLA simply melted into the woods' (Judah 1999: 25).

On 2 July 1998 the USA announced the formation of the monitoring unit agreed in the 16 June talks between presidents Milosevic and Yeltsin in Moscow. It comprised US, Russian, Austrian and Polish diplomats. Richard Holbrooke began a fresh round of diplomacy in the region on 3 July, and the monitoring unit began its patrols in Kosova on 6 July 1998. Contact Group proposals for a constitutional settlement were presented on 8 August 1998. Kosova was to have broad autonomy, either as a 'special part' of Serbia or as a 'constituent unit' of the FRY. 'Kosova would be obligated not to secede unilaterally and Belgrade would be obligated not to alter Kosova's status unilaterally.' Kosova would have 'constitutionally protected signif cant legislative, executive and judicial powers, including control of local police' and its own taxation, flag, emblems and international relations. The Contact Group also expressed 'its willingness to provide political, economic, technical and other support for the implementation of such an agreement' (*FT*, 13 August 1998, p. 2).

On 23 September the UN Security Council approved (with China abstaining) a Franco-British resolution demanding an immediate cease fire, cessation of 'all actio by security forces affecting civilians', immediate withdrawal of 'security units used for civilian repression' and 'rapid progress on a clear timetable for peace talks', with further measures to be taken in the event of non-compliance. The resolution referred to the 'enforcement provisions' of Chapter 7 of the UN Charter (a Chapter 7 resolution is militarily enforceable) (*IHT*, 24 September 1998, p. 7).

The Holbrooke–Milosevic agreement, 13 October 1998

By early October an estimated 800 lives had been lost and 300,000 people (15 per cent of the population) had been driven from their homes (*IHT*, 3 October 1998, p. 1). Foreign television coverage of the 250,000 or more Kosovars camped helplessly and vulnerably on hillsides aroused an international outcry. Like the Bosnia conf ict of 1992–5, the inter-ethnic conflicts in Kosova in 1997–8 sharpened US–EU tensions on security matters and exposed 'a European incapacity to mount a concerted response to a crisis in Europe without American leadership' (*IHT*, 11 November 1998, p. 7).

Holbrooke met with Milosevic on 5 October 1998 and threatened US/NATO air strikes against Serb security forces in Kosova unless their offensive was curtailed. An agreement between Holbrooke and Milosevic was announced on 13 October 1998, and NATO reserved the right to use air strikes to ensure compliance. The agreement included: the introduction of an international team of 2,000 unarmed monitors ('compliance' or 'verif cation' monitors) from the OSCE, made up of US, EU and Russian military experts and backed up by NATO reconnaissance flights over Kosova maintenance of a cease fire; withdrawal of Serb heavy weapons; the withdrawal of Serb security forces (both soldiers and special police) to the positions they held before March 1998 (it was left unclear which forces were to be withdrawn from Kosova and which merely returned to barracks); the police force in Kosova was to be run by local authorities and to reflect the ethnic composition of the local population relief agencies were to work unhindered; refugees were to return to their homes; elections (to be monitored by the OSCE) were to take place within nine months; the ICTY was to send a mission but was not to have jurisdiction on Yugoslav territory (i.e., permission would be needed to extradite suspects); and the 'main elements' of an agreement on political autonomy were to be reached by 2 November 1998. 'Neither Belgrade nor NATO wanted allied forces on the ground' (*IHT*, 15 October 1998, pp. 6, 8, 10). The US diplomat William Walker, who had served from 1997 to 1998 as the UN transitional administrator in eastern Slavonia, was chosen to head the OSCE verification mission in Kosova

General Wesley Clark, NATO supreme commander in Europe, signed a deal with Yugoslav military on 15 October, authorizing the penetration of FRY airspace by NATO planes. The next day NATO extended the deadline for the withdrawal of Serb security forces from 17 October to 27 October, in order to allow the OSCE time to make the necessary arrangements. The same day the Bundestag resolved by 503 votes to 63 (with 18 abstentions) to commit German fighter planes to any NATO air strike on Serbia. This was the f rst time that the German federal republic had approved the potential use of force outside NATO territory without a UN mandate(*IHT*, 17 October 1998, p. 2). U2 planes began reconnaissance missions over Kosova and Serbia proper on 18 October.

NATO announced on 26 October that it had obtained written commitments from Milosevic to cut back the Serbian military presence in Kosova and to lift roadblocks by 27 October, just ahead of the NATO deadline. Key provisions included the departure of all extra units of the special military police, leaving fewer than 5,000 men. Regular Serbian forces were to be kept to a ceiling of 10,000 personnel, all in barracks which they would leave only after giving prior notice to the OSCE monitors. Heavy weapons, down to mortars, were to be stored. The sole exceptions to these curbs were to be 1,500 border guards, needed to patrol against arms-smuggling and to conduct normal border functions (*IHT*, 27 October 1998, p. 6). On 27 October NATO deemed Serbian compliance to be suffcient not to commence air strikes. 'As the Serbs pulled back, the KLA advanced to fill the vacuum' (Judah 1999: 25)

Kosova's tenuous two-month cease f re collapsed entirely on 24 December after Serbia sent tanks into Podujevo in search of KLA fighters, after eleven days of comba in which both sides showed that they no intentions of resolving their differences peacefully (*Independent*, 26 December 1998, p. 5). By January 1999 the KLA had evolved from 'a ragtag peasant resistance movement' into a 'high-tech, mobile guerrilla force' (*IHT*, 2 January 1999, p. 2). There were about 600 monitors in Kosova by then and the intention was to have 2,000 in place by the end of January 1999 (*IHT*, 26 December 1998, pp. 1, 5). Overstepping their formal mandate, instead of merely 'observing' or 'verifying', the monitors mediated local clashes, brokered cease f res and started to investigate the disappearance of hundreds of missing civilians. The OSCE, the UN and even Russia rallied behind them (*FT*, 23 January 1999, p. 11).

The Racak massacre, 15 January 1999, and its aftermath

It was discovered on 16 January that forty-five Kosovars (including three women an a child) had been killed the day before, allegedly by Serbian forces, in the village of Racak. Most had been shot at close range in the head and stomach. On 17 January a team of Finnish forensic scientists sent to investigate these events declared Racak to have been the site of a 'crime against humanity'. The next day the Milosevic regime ordered William Walker to leave the country within forty-eight hours, after he bluntly accused Serb security forces of having carried out a massacre of ethnic Albanians at Racak. When General Clark and General Klaus Naumann (chairman of NATO's military committee) met Milosevic on 19 January 1999, they warned him that Serbia faced air strikes unless it fully complied with its undertakings on Kosova. Walker then received a twenty-four-hour extension of the expulsion order. Even Moscow joined in the condemnation of Walker's expulsion (*FT*, 20 January 1999, pp. 2, 18).

On 21 January William Walker def ed the expulsion order, and Finnish forensic experts were allowed to start examining the corpses at Racak (*FT*, 22 January 1999, p. 2). The next day the expulsion order was suspended ('frozen') and a report by the international monitors concluded that the massacre had been an act of revenge by Serbian security forces for the killing of four of their own men (*IHT*, 23 January 1999, p. 4). Western recordings of Serbian telephone conversations indicated that the Racak massacre had been carried out on orders from Belgrade and implicated the deputy prime minister Nikola Sainovic and General Sreten Lukic, Kosova's senior police commander, in it (*IHT*, 29 January 1999, p. 10; *The Times*, 29 January 1999, p. 17).

In response, the UN secretary-general Kofi Annan warned: 'The international community should have no illusions about the need to use force when all other means have failed. We may be reaching that point once again in the former Yugoslavia.' On 22 January the Contact Group condemned the 'mass murder' in Racak and 'set the goal of early negotiations on a political settlement with direct international involvement'. The principles included 'effective self-government for the Kosovar Albanians', including their own political, legal, judicial and police powers, 'with the final statu of Kosova to be decided at least three years later through some form of referendum' (*IHT*, 25 January 1999, p. 6).

The Rambouillet conference and accords, 6 February to 18 March 1999

On 29 January 1999, the Contact Group summoned representatives of the Yugoslav/ Serbian governments and of the Kosovars to a conference which was to start no later than 6 February in the Chateau de Rambouillet near Paris. Three weeks were to be allowed for the achievement of a negotiated settlement. The representatives were expected to make adequate progress on a deal involving 'substantial autonomy' (but not independence) for Kosova within a week, and to conclude the deal within another week. The conference was to be co-chaired by the British and French foreign secretaries, Robin Cook and Hubert Vedrine, with the assistance of the US envoy Christopher Hill, the EU envoy Wolfgang Petritsch and the Russian envoy Boris Mayorsky. The Contact Group's draft peace proposals gave sweeping powers to the head of the OSCE's Kosova verification mission, including the powers to remov and appoint officials in the administration and judiciary, to shut down existing institutions, to supervise elections to be held within nine months, and to set up its own broadcasting network. Kosova's status was not defned in the proposals, but for an interim period of three years the territory was to be granted 'a high degree of self-government', with the option of also holding posts in the governments of Serbia and the FRY, respectively (*FT*, 2 February 1999, p. 1). It was envisaged that the head of the OSCE team in the province would have powers similar to those of the high representative in Bosnia. However, the proposals envisaged that Serbia or the FRY would retain formal control over foreign, defence, trade, monetary and fiscal policy and that sovereignty over the province would not be affected. The OCSE verificatio team then had 1,070 members operating in Kosova, increasing to the originally proposed 2,000 once a peace settlement was approved (*IHT*, 3 February 1999, p. 5). A revised draft stated that all paramilitary groups, including the KLA, were to be disbanded within three months of a peace settlement being signed, instructed Serbia to reduce its police-force strength in Kosova from around 10,000 to 2,500 immediately, and envisaged that the head of the Kosova verifcation mission would set a timetable for the remaining police to leave as soon as a new force ref ecting Kosova's ethnic composition was formed. The federal army was then to be scaled down to just 1,500 and confined to three garrisons and to patrols along the border with Albania and th Republic of Macedonia (*FT*, 6 February 1999, p. 2).

The sixteen-member ethnic Albanian negotiating team at Rambouillet included the LDK leader Ibrahim Rugova, Rexhep Qosja (leader of the United Democratic Movement, which aspired to a 'Greater Albania' and had close links to the KLA), Veton Surroi (publisher of *Koha Ditore*, the largest circulation newspaper in Kosova), Hashim Thaqi (head of the KLA's political directorate), Azem Syla (the top military commander of the KLA), Jakup Krasniqi (a member of the KLA directorate, which held together the network of local KLA warlords), Xhavid Haliti (the key Tirana-based organizer of the KLA, overseeing the flow of arms from the mountains of norther Albania into Kosova) and Bujar Bukoshi (the Germany-based major KLA fund-raiser among ethnic Albanians living abroad). The thirteen-member Serbian/Yugoslav delegation included: Ratko Markovic, deputy prime minister of Serbia; Nikola Sainovic, federal Yugoslav deputy prime minister; another deputy prime minister and representatives of Kosova's various minority groups, including Muslim Slavs, a Turk, a Gypsy and an Egyptian.

While fighting continued in Kosova, the Rambouillet negotiations started as planne on 6 February. Serbia's president Milan Milutinovic joined the talks on 11 February. The Contact Group decided on 14 February to extend the peace negotiations for another week, setting a frm deadline for 20 February, at which time they were extended until 23 February (2 p.m. GMT).

The sticking points in the negotiations were (i) Serbian objections to provisions for a NATO-led peacekeeping force, and (ii) ethnic Albanian demands for a referendum on Kosova's future status after three years. The Contact Group insisted throughout that the peace plan should not predetermine Kosova's fial status. Instead it envisaged that, after a three-year period of autonomy, Kosova would get international support in negotiating its future status with Belgrade. Midway through the negotiations, the Kosovar delegation seemed ready to accept this deliberately open-ended formulation. However, the Kosovar delegation later backtracked, asserting that the plan had to include provisions for a referendum on Kosova's future status, which (given the ethnic composition of Kosova's population) was bound to result in an overwhelming vote for independence. On 20 February, confronted by ethnic Albanian refusal formally to endorse the proposed settlement, the US secretary of state Madeleine Albright warned the Kosovar delegation: 'We had never said that there would be bombing of the Serbs if there was a "no" answer also from the Albanians.' She simultaneously berated Milosevic for refusing to discuss the plan for NATO forces to police the settlement. The British foreign secretary Robin Cook similarly warned that air strikes against Serbia were 'not going to help' to provide stability in Kosova if Kosovars refused to accept the autonomy offer. The proposed political blueprint for Kosova was formally accepted by Serbia's president Milan Milutinovic (*IHT*, 22 February 1999, pp. 1, 4).

On 23 February the peace talks were suspended until 15 March, when a 'peace implementation conference' was to be convened in Paris. The international mediators reported that there was a 'consensus' on autonomy for Kosova, but that both sides had refrained from signing any agreement. The ethnic Albanian delegation said that it needed to hold 'technical consultations' with its 'political and military' base in Kosova, because the formal proposals did not refer to a referendum after three years, but merely included a reference to 'taking into account the political will of the local population' and the 1975 Helsinki Final Act. The chief Kosovar opponent of the proposed settlement was Adem Demaci, the official KLA political spokesperson, wh had refused to attend the talks. Demaci's objections swayed Hashim Thaqi, who put pressure on other delegates to oppose the deal. This set back by at least three weeks the Western plan to gain Kosovar approval and use it as a lever to pressure Belgrade to accept the deal or face NATO air strikes (*IHT*, 25 February 1999, pp. 1, 6). The Kosovar delegation announced on 24 February the formation of a 'provisional government', to be made up equally of the two main Kosovar parties and the KLA

and led by a prime minister to be chosen by the KLA, which was to hold office unti
elections took place nine months after a peace accord was signed (*FT*, 25 February
1999, p. 2). Hashim Thaqi was named as head of a provisional Kosovar government
on 1 March, until a peace accord was signed and elections were held for a Kosova
parliament (*IHT*, 4 March 1999, p. 6). The following day, Adem Demaci resigned as
political representative of the KLA, having lost the support of KLA regional
commanders in Drenica (*FT*, 3 March 1999, p. 2). Rugova and Demaci were thus being
marginalized within the Kosovar camp.

US intelligence reported on 25 February that Serbian military strength in Kosova
had risen to 'more than double' the levels permitted by the Holbrooke agreement
with Milosevic on 13 October 1998. The Serbs had more than 25,000 troops and police
deployed in Kosova, plus a growing force of 7,500 troops backed by 200 tanks
just north of the province. The US secretary of state Madeleine Albright and
General Wesley Clark warned that NATO was ready to strike if these Serbian forces
crossed into Kosova. The same day, China vetoed an extension of the mandate of
the 1,100-member UN preventative deployment force (UNPREDEP) in the Republic
of Macedonia until 31 August 1999, not least because on 27 January 1999 the ROM
had opened diplomatic relations with Taiwan. The ROM was providing logistical
support for the civilian monitors in Kosova as well as a base for NATO operations
in the region (*IHT*, 26 February 1999, pp. 1–5).

Richard Holbrooke met Milosevic on 10 March 1999 but failed to persuade him
to accept NATO troops in Kosova. When peace negotiations formally resumed in Paris
on 15 March 1999, while heavy f ghting continued in Kosova, the Kosovar delegation announced that it was now willing to sign up to the internationally brokered
proposals. These provided for (i) a 100-seat assembly that would control taxes and
public expenditure, represent all of Kosova's ethnic communities and elect a president,
who in turn would nominate a prime minister; (ii) thirty local councils, which would
be responsible for such issues as law enforcement, schools, medical care and land
use; (iii) a seperate judiciary for Kosova; and (iv) a review of the whole arrangement
after three years by an international meeting which would determine a mechanism
for a final resolution of Kosova's status, taking account of the will of the people
and 'the opinions of relevant authorities' (*FT*, 16 March 1999, p. 3; *IHT*, 16 March
1999, p. 8).

The plan was to be enforced by a NATO-led force, the Kosova peace implementation force (KFOR), comprising around 28,000 troops. The VJ would have to
leave the province, except for 1,500 border guards who would be confined to a
5-kilometre zone bordering Albania and Macedonia and operate under rules enforced
by NATO troops. The FRY police presence would be limited to 2,575 people for
one year, operating under the direct control of the Kosova verification mission. B
the end of that year, a 3,000-member new local police force would have been trained
and would include members of the KLA, who were required to surrender their heavy
weapons to NATO-controlled storage depots and were banned from carrying light
weapons or wearing insignia (*IHT*, 11 February 1999, p. 8; *IHT*, 12 February 1999,
p. 10). An annexe to the Rambouillet accords stated that 'NATO personnel shall enjoy,
together with their vehicles, vessels, aircraft and equipment, free and unrestricted
passage and unimpeded access throughout the Federal Republic of Yugoslavia,
including associated airspace and territorial waters' (*IHT*, 11 June 1999, p. 7). Such
a stipulation would have been unacceptable to most states – not just Serbia.

During February and again in March 1999 the US secretary of state Madeleine

Albright had made two unpublicized telephone calls to Milosevic to suggest a face-to-face meeting in Geneva, at which the US administration would be willing to discuss changes in the Rambouillet accords, in order to offer 'every reasonable opportunity to resolve the Kosova crisis diplomatically' (*FT*, 30 September 2000, p. i.; *FT*, 7 October 2000, pp. i, ix). According to the Pentagon, by 18 March, 30,000–40,000 Serbian troops were deployed in and around Kosova (*IHT*, 19 March 1999, p. 1).

The countdown to war, 18–24 March 1999

On 18 March representatives of the ethnic Albanian delegation signed the Rambouillet accords, but Russia's mediator Boris Mayorsky refused to sign as a witness and the negotiations were terminated the following day, since the Milosevic regime had also refused to sign. This signalled the start of a major new offensive by nearly 40,000 Serbian soldiers and security forces based in and around Kosova (*IHT*, 22 March 1999, p. 6). On 22 March Richard Holbrooke made a final attempt to clinch a deal with Milosevic to avert a war, but by the following day it was clear that his mission had failed. On 23 March the FRY declared an 'immediate threat of war' and sacked the second most powerful figure in the VJ, General Alexander Dimitrijevic, head of military security (*FT*, 24 March 1999, p. 1). The same day the Russian prime minister Yevgeny Primakov, who was flying to the USA in an attempt to broker a deal to aver a war, turned around in mid-flight following a telephone conversation with US vice president Al Gore, because the latter could not assure him that NATO would not start bombing Serbia during his planned visit to Washington.

NATO's air war against Serbia, 24 March to 9 June 1999

NATO began its missile and air attacks on Serbia on 24 March 1999. The NATO decision to launch air strikes had to be made unanimously. Once made, however, no individual NATO member could reverse that decision, although objectors could of course withhold their own military forces (*FT*, 30 March 1999, p. 2). The USA provided roughly 80 per cent of the planes involved in the bombing campaign, reflecting the huge gap, in terms of both offensive capability and political resolve, between the USA and the EU states. This was the first time in its fifty-year histo that NATO had waged war on a sovereign nation. It also represented a momentous (perhaps ominous) transformation or reinvention of what had originally been conceived as a purely defensive alliance to protect Western Europe from a 'Soviet threat' which had ceased to exist. The American columnist Flora Lewis claimed that this was 'the f rst war that was not for conquest, or defence or the imposition of political power, but to assert standards of behaviour . . . The war with Serbia to stop tyranny and ethnic cleansing in Kosova was a milestone' (*IHT*, 18 March 2000, p. 8). This war was also the f rst time since 1945 that German aircraft took part in military combat operations. However, Russia and China (among others) perceived the war to be both unwarranted and illegal (ironically, in breach of norms of international law which had been promoted largely by the same Western states that were now breaking them, and had previously been derided by the states now upholding them!). Russia temporarily suspended its cooperation with NATO and its participation in the PfP programme.

On the first day of the war, NATO alleviated anxieties in nearby Albania, Bulgaria Macedonia, Slovenia and Romania by providing written assurances that it would consider any military strikes against them by Serb forces to be 'unacceptable'. Interestingly, NATO officials confirmed that Javier Solana's letters to this effect we out *before* the Serbian government warned Romania, Albania, Hungary, Bulgaria and Macedonia to refrain from supporting the impending NATO offensive or the Kosovar insurgents (*IHT*, 25 March 1999, p. 5). On 11 April the Albanian government decided to give NATO 'rights to control all our air spaces, ports and any other kind of military infrastructure in Albania' (*HT*, 12 April 1999, p. 1). (Montenegro's stance and vulnerabilities during the Kosova war are discussed in Chapter 9.)

During Phase 1 of the war (24–27 March), NATO's chief targets were Serbian air defences and command and control systems. Its bombing strategy was (and has continued to be) criticized for initially targeting a few high-profile targets, in the hop that this would swiftly incapacitate the Serbian security forces and that Milosevic would use this as an excuse to capitulate early on. If this was what the leaders of the NATO states were hoping for, they seriously misjudged both Milosevic and the resilience and resourcefulness of the Serb security forces, who not only continued to operate but even escalated their rates of killing and ethnic cleansing. The then German foreign minister Joschka Fischer later famously recounted that, when he visited Belgrade just before NATO started its bombing campaign, Milosevic told him: 'I am ready to walk on corpses, and the West is not. That is why I shall win*HT*, 4 June 1999, p. 8). In other words, Milosevic was calculating that the NATO states (not Serbia!) would be the first to give up the fight. There were indeed serious and openly paraded tensions and strains between NATO members which could quite conceivably have brought the bombing offensive to an early halt. Not only was there the usual tension between French Gaullist *amour-propre* and American determination to 'do it their way'. Even more seriously, the British and (to lesser degrees) the French government and military were arguing, on the basis of hard lessons learned from their (by then considerable) *shared* experiences of difficult peacekeeping operations in the western Balkans, that it could be extremely hazardous for NATO to rely exclusively on its massive superiority in airborne weaponry and that it would be much more prudent either to combine or to swiftly follow up the aerial bombardment of Serb forces and installations with a*ground offensive* designed to wrest control of Kosova from the Serb security forces and the KLA as soon as possible, with the multiple aims of (i) pre-empting the real dangers of intensified ethnic cleansing an mass murder by bestial men of violence on both sides, (ii) minimizing or at least reducing the civilian casualties and 'collateral damage' resulting from exclusive reliance on aerial bombardment, which (if not backed up by a ground offensive) would mainly have to be conducted either by night or from great heights, with consequent loss of accuracy, and (iii) restoring order in Kosova as soon as possible, to protect civilians from a potentially hazardous power vacuum. A swift or almost concurrent NATO ground offensive was probably the only strategy that could have prevented the Serb security forces from carrying out their 'Operation Horseshoe', the programme for systematically murdering or driving out Kosovars, which the Milosevic regime had adopted in October 1998 and which brought about the initial dramatic escalation in mass murder and ethnic cleansing after 24 March 1999 (causing a major crisis within NATO ranks), instead of the reductions anticipated by NATO planners and Western public opinion. Nevertheless, the US, Greek, Italian and German governments remained 'politically allergic' to any offensive deployment of NATO ground forces in Kosova, mainly because of fears of the domestic political impact of incurring military casualties and the dangers of getting bogged down in a protracted ground war.

This, together with the persistently declared unwillingness of several NATO members (especially the USA) either to combine or to quickly follow up the initial bombing campaign with a large-scale invasion of Kosova by ground forces and the initial escalation of mass murder and ethnic cleansing in Kosova, resulted in major soul-searching and mutual recriminations within and between NATO states and forces in late March and much of April 1999 and came close to handing Milosevic a victory.

On 27 March 1999 NATO announced that Phase 2 of the bombing campaign was to begin, including attacks on Serbian ground forces in Kosova. However, these attacks were not nearly as decisive and led to far fewer losses in Serbian troops and weaponry than NATO strategists had anticipated, partly because the Serb military made very effective use of camouflage, decoys and dummy targets (such as bogus tanks and armoured cars). Ironically, these ploys had originally been devised to outwit a potential Soviet invasion of Communist Yugoslavia.

It was only during Phase 3, when NATO stated bombing infrastructure and other economic and communications targets within Serbia proper, that Milosevic began to buckle – and even this took much longer than anticipated. Phase 3 began on 3 April 1999, when the interior ministry building in Belgrade was attacked. Other targets included power stations, oil refineries, bridges, government buildings, television stations and allegedly dual civilian/military factories (e.g., cars and armaments). They were considered legitimate targets not only because they helped the war effort, but also because their destruction was (perhaps mistakenly) thought likely to strike at the roots of the economic power of Milosevic and his cronies. NATO bombs and missiles knocked out the electricity supply in most of Serbia for several hours on 3 May (*IHT*, 4 May 1999, p. 1).

On 1 April 1999 Yugoslav state television showed film of a meeting between Milosevic and Ibrahim Rugova, during which Rugova signed an agreement and appealed for an end to NATO air strikes. On 5 May, however, Rugova and his family flew to Rome as guests of the Italian government. He subsequently explained that he had effectively been a prisoner in Belgrade, that the agreement had no meaning, and that he had signed it and made his appeal for an end to NATO attacks under duress and to protect his family (*HT*, 18 May 1999, p. 7;*The Guardian*, 18 May 1999, p. 5). This episode did not lastingly damage either his political standing or his reputation for personal integrity.

The major arguments for and against waging war on the Milosevic regime

NATO's decision to wage war on the Milosevic regime in March 1999 was and has remained highly controversial. For one thing, NATO never sought a UN Security Council resolution to authorize its bombing campaign, because it was obvious that Russia and China would simply have vetoed it. The campaign was therefore at least partly in breach of international law. There were also serious and legitimate misgivings and criticisms concerning the way in which the NATO bombing campaign was conducted – especially the great height at which NATO planes flew, making it harde to bomb legitimate Serbian military targets with precision and to minimize civilian casualties and 'collateral damage'. It was also extremely problematic that some NATO states (especially the USA itself) felt the need from the outset to declare openly that an invasion of Kosova by NATO ground forces was out of the question because of the politically unacceptable casualties which such forces could have incurred,

although it is not difficult to appreciate the domestic political constraints operatin
on NATO governments and the serious differences of opinion between NATO
members on this matter. In addition, it is undeniable that the start of NATO's bombing campaign triggered a terrible escalation of the killing and 'ethnic cleansing' of
Kosovars by Serbian troops and police, which the bombing had ostensibly been
initiated to halt.

With regard to claims that the NATO offensive was an unwarranted violation of
Serbia's sovereignty over Kosova, it can be argued that Serbia's claims to sovereignty
over Kosova were (and remain) seriously open to question. From 1945 to 1992 the
SFRY (rather than Serbia) had exercised effective jurisdiction over Kosova. This
was what had enabled the SFRY to grant Kosova virtual autonomy and the same
voting rights as the fully fledged republics in the SFRY during the 1970s and 1980s
Unfortunately, after the former SFRY ceased to exist, both *de facto* and *de jure*, 'the
international community' muddied the waters by repeatedly (and imprudently)
acknowledging Serbian claims to sovereignty over Kosova – contrary to the repeatedly
expressed wishes of the overwhelming majority of Kosova's inhabitants, whose elected
leaders repeatedly demanded either membership of a loose confederation of equal
and sovereign peoples and states or (failing that) full independence. Serbia's claims
to have inherited the SFRY's sovereign jurisdiction over Kosova carry no more weight
than would a Russian claim to have inherited the sovereign jurisdiction of the former
Soviet Union over its non-Russian 'union republics'.

In any case, supporters of NATO's military offensive against the Milosevic regime
asserted that humanitarian considerations should override the usual respect for state
sovereignty, both legally and morally, given that almost 1,000 Kosovar civilians had
already been killed and over 300,000 Kosovars had *already* been driven from their
subsequently looted or destroyed homes by Serbian security forces between February
1997 and February 1999,*before* the start of NATO bombing. Indeed, NATO was open
to criticism for not having acted*much sooner* to try to halt this campaign of systematic
mass murder and ethnic cleansing. NATO emphasized that its actions were in keeping
with the spirit of previous UN Security Council resolutions (those passed on 31 March
1998 and 23 September 1998), and that on 26 March 1999 the Security Council had
rejected by twelve votes to three a Russian resolution calling for an immediate cessation
of bombing and a return to negotiations (China supported Russia's stance). The UN
rules were deficient in that they did not allow a clear-cut decision either way

Most tellingly of all, however, the opponents of NATO's decision to wage war on
the Milosevic regime have seemingly refused to consider what would have happened
if NATO had *not* gone to war. Milosevic would have had *carte blanche* to carry out
unconstrained attacks and ethnic cleansing against hundreds of thousands of Kosovars.
There is little doubt that large-scale human-rights violations and loss of life would
have continued unchecked. The 'Operation Horseshoe' programme for systematically 'cleansing' Kosova of its Kosovar population is known to have been prepared
and decided on by the Milosevic regime in October 1998 (*IHT*, 21 July 1999, p. 4).
'Horseshoe was designed to produce a permanent solution, and was launched even
before the Rambouillet discussions' (*IHT*, 15 April 1999, p. 6). Therefore, the opponents of NATO's bombing campaign have remained open to the *counter-charge* of
having been unwilling to take or even to propose any credible or effective action
to try to halt the systematic killing and cleansing of large numbers of Kosovar civilians
by the security forces of the Milosevic regime. The steadily increasing moral,
diplomatic and economic pressures applied to the Milosevic regime from March 1997

to February 1999 had already conspicuously *failed* to halt its murderous campaign. Milosevic repeatedly agreed to desist, but repeatedly resumed this campaign as soon as he thought that he could get away with it. The NATO states found themselves forced to choose between taking decisive military action or passively watching the Milosevic regime carry out systematic mass murder and ethnic cleansing without hindrance. The choice fell to the NATO states, not out of any spurious claims to moral superiority, but because they were the only ones capable of taking effective action, given that the UN Security Council was being paralysed by Russian and Chinese vetoes and the EU was militarily impotent. As Ibrahim Rugova cogently stated in retrospect:

> Some people in NATO countries criticised their governments for intervening. Fortunately for us they were ignored . . . We knew that if the bombing stopped Milosevic would win and we would all pay a dreadful price . . Another criticism of the NATO air campaign in Kosova at the time was that it created rather than averted a humanitarian crisis there. People are today saying the same thing about the military campaign in Afghanistan. But in Kosova, as in Afghanistan, what many people failed to realise was that the humanitarian crisis had begun much earlier . . . [In both cases] military action was the only way to create the conditions for resolving the humanitarian crisis . . . Without NATO's intervention and determination [in Kosova,] hundreds of thousands would still be living in tents all over Europe . . . The uncomfortable reality is that military force is sometimes necessary to protect human rights and enforce the rule of law . . . Military force brought an end to four years of suffering in Bosnia. It reversed the ethnic cleansing that had begun in Kosova on a massive scale in 1998.
>
> (*Daily Telegraph*, 20 November 2001, p. 24)

The journalist and historian Noel Malcolm, who has long been one of the most eloquent and erudite champions of the Kosovar cause, took a similar stance. He reckoned that during the twelve months preceding 24 March 1999 'Serb forces had driven more than 300,000 Albanians out of their homes – homes which, in many cases, they then looted and burnt. Roughly 2,000 people had been killed' (*Daily Telegraph*, 24 March 2000, p. 28). The writer Salman Rushdie also trenchantly answered NATO's critics:

> I supported the NATO campaign in Kosova, finding the human rights evidenc in favour of intervention to be powerful and convincing. Many writers, intel - lectuals, artists and left-leaning *bien-pensants* thought otherwise. One of their arguments was, if Kosova, then why not [also intervene] in Kurdistan? Why not Rwanda or East Timor? Oddly, this kind of rhetoric actually makes the opposite point to the one it thinks it's making. For if it would have been right to inter- vene in these cases, and the West was wrong not to, then surely it was also right to defend the Kosovans, and the West's previous failures only serve to emphasize that this time, at least, they – 'we' – got it right. The anti-intervention camp's major allegation was and is that NATO's action in fact precipitated the violence it was intended to prevent; that, so to speak, the massacres were Madeleine Albright's fault. This [stance] seems to me both morally reprehensible – because it exculpates the actual killers – and demonstrably wrong. Set emotion aside and look at the cold logistics of Milosevic's massacre. It quickly becomes apparent that the atrocity was carefully planned. One does not make detailed plans to wipe out thousands of people just in case a speedy response to a Western attack

should be needed. One plans a massacre because one intends to carry out a massacre. True, the speed and enormity of the Serbian attack took the NATO forces by surprise . . . That doesn't make it right to blame NATO. Murderers are guilty of the murders they commit, rapists of their rapes.

(Rushdie 2002: 312–13)

Even though the motives for the NATO intervention against Serbia over Kosova were by no means entirely altruistic (they surely included concerns to give NATO a new role in European affairs and a new *raison d'être*), this need not automatically imply that either the intervention itself or its outcomes were detrimental or unjustified Our own support for NATO's decision to wage war on the Milosevic regime has more recently been reinforced by private conversations with some liberal-minded members of the Serbian intelligentsia who lived through the NATO bombing of Belgrade. Whilst Serb nationalists have continued to condemn the NATO bombings, more liberal-minded Serbs have tended to accept that (i) this fearful bombing campaign was actually the only means by which the pernicious plans of the Milosevic regime could have been halted; (ii) it rapidly became blindingly obvious to the regime and to the population at large what the prime targets were most likely to be; and (iii) the Milosevic regime was actively tipped off in advance by some NATO personnel, in attempts to ensure that these buildings and installations were evacuated before the bombs and missiles struck. Although some members of the French security services were later publicly vilified by their anglophone allies for having passed supposedl vital information to the Serb intelligence services during the bombing campaign, in this Machiavellian world one cannot rule out the possibility that these members of the French security services were in fact acting on NATO's behalf, because it was not in NATO's interests to be seen to be inflicting 'too many' human casualties (civilia or otherwise) on the Serbs in this David and Goliath contest, for fear of arousing Western public sympathy for the Serbs. Furthermore, the subsequent arrest and prosecution in 2001 of Dragoljub Milanovic, the former head of Serbian state television, on the charge of having failed to act to save the lives of sixteen of his staff when he was clearly warned in advance that the building in which they worked was shortly to be attacked by NATO (*Independent*, 14 February 2001, p. 16) provided very concrete evidence that NATO was itself engaged in passing information about targets to the Milosevic regime in attempts to reduce civilian loss of life.

At the same time, even though there were strong arguments in favour of NATO intervention in Kosova in 1999, this Western intervention (like that in Bosnia in 1994–5) stands out in retrospect as a quantum leap in the trend towards a new 'human rights imperialism'. It refected a growing willingness of Western military powers to throw their weight around, to dictate to others, and to intervene militarily in the internal affairs of much weaker sovereign states – all in the name of the protection and promotion of human rights and the rights of threatened and oppressed ethnic and religious groups. This has increasingly provided Western powers with countless pretexts to intervene militarily almost anywhere they choose in the 'non-Western world'. In this perspective, even though the NATO intervention in Kosova in 1999 can be justified in terms of the particular moral choices to be made in the specific circumstances prevailing at that time and place, it can at the same time be seen as representing an ominous step down a slippery slope towards new and more obviously questionable forms of Western imperialism, such as the US-led occupation of Iraq. Alternatively, it could be seen as a dangerous throwback to older traditions of Western military imperialism and interventionism in the name of protecting the rights of particular religious and ethnic groups, with which the Balkans had been all too familiar between the 1870s and 1913 and again in 1918–20. Either way, the Kosova war has become enmeshed in many-layered moral ambiguities.

The tortuous termination of the Kosova war

Among the factors contributing to Milosevic's eventual capitulation were the build-up of NATO forces in countries such as adjacent Albania and the Republic of Macedonia, coupled with increasingly credible NATO warnings that no options were being ruled out. Of the three new members of NATO (Poland, Hungary and the Czech Republic), the Polish government proved very supportive of the NATO bombing campaign and the Hungarian government was not far behind, but the Czech political establishment had major misgivings. The *governments* (though *not the populations*) of the countries that were at that time actively *seeking* NATO membership (Albania, Bulgaria, Croatia, Romania, Slovenia and Slovakia) also strongly supported the NATO campaign and in return garnered valuable new US and EU support for their eventual inclusion in both NATO and the EU. The hitherto lack - lustre and unpromising Romanian and Bulgarian candidatures for NATO and EU membership were suddenly transformed during 1999, partly as a direct consequence of their support for this NATO campaign.

Although NATO leaders and officials continued to rule out a ground invasion o Kosova, or using any ground forces that would have to 'f ght their way in', Javier Solana announced on 3 April that plans were being studied for NATO to send an 'escort force' numbering 60,000 or more into Kosova in order to protect returning refugees. Although this would occur only *after* Yugoslav forces had been compelled to withdraw from Kosova by the sheer weight of NATO's bombing and missile attacks, it could occur before any peace deal was signed. To halt the bombing, Solana stated, the Milosevic regime had to 'stop all repressive and combat activity and withdraw its forces from Kosova, and accept arrangements in which all refugees can return safely to Kosova under protection of an international security force'. However, NATO officials later had to 'clarify' that the statement reflected Solana's personal views and had not been officially authorized by NATO. It reflected the tenor of inform discussions between the five NATO members of the Contact Group, who were 'co ordinating the international community's response' to the Kosova crisis (*FT*, 5 April 1999, p. 2). NATO offcials announced on 4 April that it would commit ground troops to help Albania and Macedonia cope with the growing Kosovar exodus from Kosova – roughly 350,000 refugees (*IHT*, 5 April 1999, p. 1).

The nineteen NATO foreign ministers issued a joint statement on 12 April 1999, warning that air strikes would continue until Milosevic agreed to: (i) ensure a veriable halt to all military action and the immediate cessation of violence and repression; (ii) accept the stationing of an international military presence in Kosova; (iii) ensure the withdrawal of Serb military, police and paramilitary forces from Kosova; (iv) guarantee the unconditional and safe return of all refugees and displaced persons, and unhindered access to them by humanitarian aid organizations; and (v) provide credible assurances of his willingness to work on the basis of the Rambouillet accords and in conformity with international law and the charter of the UN. The statement went beyond the Rambouillet accords in demanding the withdrawal of *all* Serbian military forces from Kosova (*IHT*, 13 April 1999, p. 6).

The Bulgarian government agreed on 21 April to a NATO request for Bulgaria's oil pipeline to Serbia to be cut off (*HT*, 23 April 1999, p. 4). The next day Romania's parliament resolved, by 225 votes to 21 (with 99 abstentions) to accept NATO's request for unrestricted use of its airspace, while Slovenia announced that it would allow NATO forces to cross its territory if ground troops invaded Kosova(*T*, 23 April 1999, p. 2). On 25 April the Bulgarian parliament approved the opening of Bulgarian airspace to NATO planes, while the Slovak government announced the opening of its airspace to the aircraft and offered NATO ground access along a rail and highway corridor as well (*IHT*, 26 April 1999, p. 5). The Hungarian government and parliament followed suit, and on 3 May the Hungarian parliament explicitly affirmed that NATO plane would be allowed to make strikes operating directly from Hungarian bases, despite attempts by some socialist deputies to impose limitations (*T*, 4 May 1999, p. 2). The next day the Bulgarian parliament did likewise (*FT*, 5 May 1999, p. 20).

When NATO celebrated its fiftieth anniversary on 23–25 April 1999 (although i was actually founded on 4 April 1949), only one of the forty-three governments invited to attend the celebrations declined the invitation (Russia, in protest at NATO's bombing of Serbia). The f nal communiqué of the NATO summit stated that 'Milosevic must withdraw from Kosova his military, police and paramilitary forces' (the word 'all' was now missing) and that NATO had given security assurances to seven 'frontline states' (*IHT*, 3 May 1999, p. 8; *FT*, 26 April 1999, p. 1).

On 6 May 1999 the foreign ministers of the G8 countries (including Russia) adopted the following *general principles* for a political solution to the Kosova crisis:

1. Immediate, verifiable end of violence and repression in Kosova
2. Withdrawal of Serbian military, police and paramilitary forces from Kosova.
3. Deployment of effective international civil and security presences in Kosova, endorsed and adopted by the UN and capable of attaining the common objectives.
4. Establishment of an interim administration for Kosova under UN Security Council auspices, to ensure conditions for a peaceful and normal life for all Kosova's inhabitants.
5. The safe and free return of all displaced persons and unimpeded access to Kosova for humanitarian aid organizations.
6. A political process towards (i) the establishment of an interim political framework agreement providing substantial self-government for Kosova, taking full account of the Rambouillet accords and the principles of sovereignty and territorial integrity of the SFRY and neighbouring states and (ii) the demilitarization of the KLA.
7. A comprehensive approach to the economic development and stabilization of the Balkans.

In order to implement these principles the G8 foreign ministers instructed their political directors to prepare a draft UN Security Council resolution, and the G8 presidency was authorized to inform the Chinese government of the results of this meeting.

On 7 May the Chinese embassy in Belgrade was bombed, killing three Chinese journalists and wounding twenty-seven other Chinese. This precipitated three days of angry demonstrations and mob attacks on US and UK embassies in China. NATO described the bombing as a 'terrible accident' resulting from 'faulty' targeting information which mistook the building for the quasi-military Yugoslav federal directorate of supply and procurement, an explanation which the Chinese government and media did not accept. China suspended cooperation with the US on stopping proliferation of weapons of mass destruction, discussions about human rights and high-level military contacts. On 30 July the USA agreed to pay 4.5 million US dollars in compensation to the families of those killed or wounded by the bombing. On 16 December 1999 it also agreed to pay 28 million US dollars in compensation for the embassy building (characteristically, putting a higher value on a mere building than on human lives), while China agreed to pay 2.9 million US dollars in compensation for damage to US diplomatic buildings by Chinese demonstrators (*IHT*, 17 December 1999, p. 4). In April 2000 the CIA fired an intelligence officer and reprimanded six managers f errors that led to the bombing. NATO claimed that an outdated street map had been used for targeting its bombs (*IHT*, 10 April 2000, pp. 1, 5), but the Chinese foreign ministry rejected this explanation (*FT*, 11 April 2000, p. 12).

On 24 May the ICTY indicted the FRY president Slobodan Milosevic, Serbia's president Milan Milutinovic, the FRY deputy premier Nikola Sainovic, the FRY minister of internal affairs Vlajko Stojilkovic, and the VJ chief of staff General Dragoljub Ojdanic, on charges of 'crimes against humanity – specifically murder, deportation and persecutions, and with violations of the laws and customs of war' in Kosova. This was the f rst time in world history that sitting heads of state had been indicted by an international court.

NATO approved plans on 25 May to increase the projected size of its proposed peacekeeping force in Kosova (KFOR) to about 48,000 troops, in place of the previously envisaged figure of 28,000, thereby fuelling debate about the potential launching of a ground invasion. While still insisting that NATO soldiers would enter Kosova only to enforce a peacekeeping mandate, NATO secretary-general Javier Solana affirmed that 'All options remain open'. NATO leaders sought to foster ambiguity concerning the scope of the envisaged NATO mission. At that point, there were still only about 14,000 NATO troops in the ROM and about 8,000 more in Albania, where they were helping to look after Kosovar refugees. Britain was the leading advocate of expanding NATO's ground forces sufficiently to be able t 'enter Kosova even without the consent of the Belgrade government', once the Serb forces had been suffciently battered by bombing. By contrast, the US, German, Greek and Italian governments remained strongly allergic to any suggestion of committing NATO ground forces to Kosova without Serb and UN Security Council consent(*HT*, 26 May 1999, p. 10; *FT*, 26 May 1999, p. 2).

Victor Chernomyrdin, the former Russian premier who had been appointed as President Yeltsin's special envoy to Serbia on 14 April, made a breakthrough during an eight-hour negotiating session with Milosevic in Belgrade on 28 May 1999. He persuaded Milosevic to accept that troops from NATO states which had not taken part in the bombing of Serbia could take part in an international peacekeeping force in Kosova after the war ended (Crampton 2002: 275). Hitherto, Moscow had sup - ported Milosevic's acceptance of a lightly armed peacekeeping force, including Russian forces and troops from neutral nations, but excluding units from NATO countries, for post-war Kosova (*IHT*, 29 May 1999, p. 1). After attending an EU–US summit in Bonn on 31 May to 1 June, Chernomyrdin returned to Belgrade on 2 June to present revised peace proposals to Milosevic, together with the Finnish president and EU envoy Martti Ahtisaari. President Ahtisaari read the entire non-negotiable document out aloud to Serbia's rulers, answered their questions about it, told Milosevic to discuss the terms with his colleagues and demanded an answer the next day (*IHT*, 5 June 1999, p. 4). The French health minister Bernard Kouchner, a physician who gained international fame as director of Medecins sans Frontières, was named as the UN secretary-general's special representative for Kosova and as the first head of th proposed UN mission in Kosova (UNMIK) on 2 June. He took up his post there on 15 July.

The peace terms accepted on 3 June 1999

1. Immediate and verifiable end of violence and repression in Kosova
2. Verifiable withdrawal from Kosova of all military, police and paramilitary forces according to a rapid time schedule.
3. Deployment in Kosova, under the aegis of the UN, of effective international civilian and security presences.
4. The international security presence with substantial NATO participation must be deployed under unifed command and control and authorized to establish a safe environment for all people in Kosova and to facilitate the safe return to their homes of all displaced persons and refugees.
5. Establishment of an interim administration for Kosova as part of the international civilian presence under which the people of Kosova can enjoy substantial autonomy within the FRY to be decided by the security council of the UN. The interim administration is to provide transitional administration while establishing and overseeing the development of provisional democratic self-governing institutions to ensure conditions for a peaceful and normal life of all inhabitants in Kosova.
6. After withdrawal an agreed number of Yugoslav and Serbian personnel will be permitted to return to perform the following functions: liaison with international civil mission and international presence, marking/clearing minefelds, maintaining a presence at Serb patrimonial sites, maintaining a presence at key border-crossings.
7. Safe and free return of all refugees and displaced persons under the supervision of the UNHCR and unimpeded access to Kosova by humanitarian aid organizations.
8. A political process towards the establishment of an interim political framework agreement providing for a substantial self-government for Kosova, taking full account of the Rambouillet accords and the principles of sovereignty and territorial integrity of the FRY and the other countries of the region, and the demilitarization of the KLA. Negotiations between the parties for a settlement should not delay or disrupt the establishment of democratic self-governing institutions.
9. Comprehensive approach to the economic development and stabilization of the crisis region. This will include the implementation of a stability pact for South-eastern Europe with broad international participation in order to further promotion of democracy, economic prosperity, stability and regional cooperation.
10. Suspension of military activity will require acceptance of the principles set forth above in addition to agreement to other, previously identified, required elements which are specified in the footnote. A military-technical agreement will then b rapidly concluded.

Withdrawal: Procedures for withdrawals, including the phased, detailed schedule and delineation of a buffer area in Serbia beyond which forces will be withdrawn.

Footnotes to Item 10: Footnote (1) concerned equipment associated with returning personnel, terms of reference for their functional responsibilities, the timetable for their return, delineation of their geographical areas of operation, rules governing their relationship to international security presence and international civil mission and 'other required elements': a rapid and precise timetable for withdrawals, meaning, e.g., seven days to complete withdrawal, air defence weapons to be withdrawn outside a 25-kilometre mutual safety zone within forty-eight hours. Return of personnel for the four functions specified above was to be under the supervision of the internationa security presence and limited to a small agreed number (hundreds not thousands). Suspension of military activity was to occur after the beginning of verifiable with drawals. The discussion and achieving of a military-technical agreement was not to extend the previously determined time for completion of withdrawals. Footnote (2) referred to the composition of the international peacekeeping force (KFOR) to be stationed in Kosova. NATO considered an international security force with 'sub-stantial NATO participation' to mean one with NATO at its core, under the unifed command and control, and under the political direction of the North Atlantic Council, albeit in consultation with non-NATO participants. All NATO members, NATO partners and other countries were to be eligible to contribute to the international security force. The NATO units were to be under NATO command. However, Russia considered the Russian contingent would not be under NATO command and that its relationship to 'the international presence' would be governed by relevant additional agreements.

The FRY government and the Serbian parliament accepted the proposals (other than the footnotes to item 10) on 3 June (*IHT*, 8 June 1999, p. 8). The SRS leader and Serb deputy premier Vojislav Seselj opposed the proposals in parliament and vowed to quit the government as soon as NATO troops entered Kosova (*IHT*, 4 June 1999, p. 2).

On 8 June the foreign ministers of the G8 countries agreed on a draft resolution to be presented to the UN Security Council. The following sequence of events was envisaged: (i) signature of the military-technical agreement; (ii) swift verifiable star of the Serb military withdrawal; (iii) a pause in NATO bombing; (iv) adoption of the resolution by the UN Security Council; (v) deployment of peacekeeping forces; (6) formal termination of the NATO air campaign upon completion of the Serb military withdrawal. Events 2, 3 and 4 were meant to be almost simultaneous, to make it possible to comply with the Russo-Chinese insistence on a cessation of NATO bombing *before* the passing of the UN resolution.

NATO stopped bombing Serbia on 9 June, when the military-technical agreement was signed on NATO's behalf by Lieutenant General Sir Michael Jackson, the British commander of NATO's Rapid Reaction Force and KFOR, while two federal Yugoslav generals signed on behalf of the FRY. Dragoljub Ojdanic, the VJ chief of staff, could not participate because he had been indicted for war crimes by the ICTY. Concessions to the FRY military included an extension of the time allowed for the withdrawal of their forces from seven to eleven days. There was to be a 5-kilometre-wide buffer zone (the so-called 'ground security zone' or GSZ) along Serbia's borders with Kosova and Macedonia, and a 25-kilometre-wide 'no-fly zone'

The formal suspension of NATO bombing was announced on 10 June, after the start of the FRY military withdrawal from Kosova had been verified. UN Resolutio 1244, which embodied the peace terms agreed on 3 June (with minor amendments), was approved by the UN Security Council on 10 June 1999 by fourteen votes to none and one abstention (China).

However, NATO military commanders were taken by surprise when Russia rushed the first foreign peacekeeping troops (a convoy of fifty vehicles and nearly 200 soldier into Kosova from northern Bosnia early on 11 June. The US deputy secretary of state Strobe Talbott turned back to Moscow in mid-flight after hearing about the Russia troop deployment. Russia's foreign minister Igor Ivanov assured him that the Russian soldiers were merely preparing to assume positions along the northern rim of Kosova and did not plan to enter Kosova without coordinating their moves with NATO commanders. In fact Russia sought to gain a sector of its own, preferably in the north where Serbian religious shrines and many of Kosova's Serb inhabitants were most heavily concentrated, but NATO commanders feared that the creation of a specifically Russian sector would quickly result in the de-facto partition of Kosova. NATO had divided the Kosova map into five sectors which were be controlled by NATO forces from the USA, Britain, France, Italy and Germany, respectively (*IHT*, 12 June 1999, pp. 1, 4).

When Russia tried to f y six aircraft containing 600 paratroopers to Kosova from Russia on the evening of 11 June, the governments of Hungary, Bulgaria and Romania refused Moscow's requests for permission to cross their air space (*FT*, 15 June 1999, p. 4; *IHT*, 16 June 1999, p. 1). Russian forces from Bosnia nevertheless succeeded in reaching Pristina airport during the early hours of 12 June, whereas NATO forces did not start moving into Kosova until later that day. The Russian forces were welcomed by Kosova Serbs and blocked off Pristina airport. This resulted in a stand-off with NATO forces. Russia's move was widely seen as an attempt to outmanoeuvre NATO's refusal to allocate it a sector of its own, as well as an attempt to divide Kosova into Serb and Kosovar sectors. It remained unclear who had ordered the rapid influ of Russian troops, as the Russian foreign minister Igor Ivanov announced that his ministry 'had not been informed about the move' (*FT*, 14 June 1999, p. 2).

It later transpired that Lieutenant General Sir Michael Jackson had refused to carry out an order from NATO's supreme commander Wesley Clark to get NATO forces into Pristina airport ahead of the Russians, reportedly replying: 'No, I'm not going to do that. It's not worth starting World War Three' (*IHT*, 11 September 1999, p. 1). Jackson's non-compliance with Clark's order occurred under a rarely invoked NATO procedure allowing a NATO officer to get his own country's authorization to disobe an order from a superior NATO officer from another member state. It appears that the Blair government opposed the use of British troops to seize Pristina airport ahead of the Russians (*IHT*, 14 September 1999, p. 4). By mid-June Britain had committed 13,000 troops to Kosova, France 9,000, Germany 8,000 and the USA 7,500 (*IHT*, 19 June 1999, p. 1).

The US defence secretary William Cohen reached an agreement with his Russian counterpart Marshal Igor Sergeyev on 18 June to add 3,600 Russian troops to KFOR, which would ultimately comprise over 50,000 personnel. To save Russian face, Russian troops were allowed to control the grounds of Pristina airport, although air traffic and airspace remained under UK control. The agreement also provided for Russian troops to operate within the USA, German and French sectors of Kosova, but made no provision for a separate Russian sector (*IHT*, 21 June 1999, pp. 5, 8). Russian troops were exempted from having to apprehend people accused of having committed war crimes or crimes against humanity (*IHT*, 1 July 1999, p. 5). On 5 July NATO and Russian negotiators agreed more detailed terms for deploying peacekeepers in Kosova, although the details were not disclosed. Russian officials claimed that th accord stated that Russian troops would not serve directly under NATO command, but instead would accept – and by and large execute – NATO orders issued through a Russian liaison officer located at NATO headquarters in Brussels. After the agreement was signed, however, Russia's forces began to argue that they should be allowed to follow Russian orders, not NATO ones, according to Western officials (*IHT*, 6 July 1999, pp. 1, 4).

The Cologne summit, 18–20 June 1999, and the Stability Pact for South-eastern Europe

The G8 countries met in Cologne from 18 to 20 June, although President Yeltsin arrived only for the final day. President Clinton and other Western leaders made it clear tha Serbia would be ineligible for *reconstruction* funds so long as President Milosevic remained in power, but the Cologne declaration nevertheless opened the way for immediate *humanitarian* aid to the entire Balkan region, including Serbia. The eight leaders also endorsed an EU-sponsored stability pact for South-eastern Europe (*IHT*, 21 June 1999, pp. 1, 6). 'There were no specifics on how much money would be involved, although it was accepted that Europe should pay the lion's share' (*FT*, 21 June 1999, p. 3). Javier Solana announced on 20 June that all Serbian troops and police had completed their withdrawal from Kosova eleven hours before the deadline and that he was therefore definitively terminating NATO's bombing campaign *IHT*, 21 June 1999, p. 5).

Human casualty figures during the Kosova war

The NATO bombing campaign ended without a single NATO combat casualty. Two NATO planes were shot down (including a vastly expensive US stealth bomber), but in both cases the pilots were rescued. Two US pilots were killed in a training accident involving Apache helicopters.

In early June 1999 NATO estimated that 5,000 Serbian servicemen had been killed and 10,000 wounded during the bombing and missile campaign (*FT*, 4 June 1999, pp. 1–2). However, on 10 June President Milosevic stated on Serbian state television that the Serbian security forces had lost only 462 soldiers and 114 policemen during the eleven-week war, while on 21 July the VJ chief of staff General Dragoljub Ojdanic claimed that only 524 security personnel had been killed and a further 37 were listed as missing (*IHT*, 22 July 1999, p. 5). It will shortly become clear that Milosevic's claims regarding casualties and war damage on the Serb side were more accurate than NATO's (see p. 559).

The UK foreign office claimed on 17 June 1999 that at least 10,000 Kosovars had perished at Serb hands in Kosova between 25 March and 10 June 1999 (*Independent*, 18 June 1999, p. 3), and the UNMIK chief administrator Bernard Kouchner claimed on 2 August that mass graves containing an estimated 11,000 bodies were scattered across Kosova (*IHT*, 3 August 1999, p. 5). By mid-August 2000, however, UN forensic investigators searching for the bodies of ethnic Albanians killed by Serbs in Kosova during the war expected the final toll of confirmed killin to be between 4,000 and 5,000 – or less than half the totals previously alleged by NATO and the UN (*The Times*, 19 August 2000, p. 13).

Conflicting estimates of war damage

The US defence secretary William Cohen and General Henry Shelton, the chairman of the joint chiefs of staff, claimed on 11 June 1999 that NATO warplanes had flow just under 10,000 bombing runs, dropping 23,000 bombs and missiles, and that NATO bombing and missile attacks had destroyed 450 artillery pieces, 220 armoured personnel carriers, 120 tanks, more than half of the FRY's military industry, and 35 per cent of the country's electricity-generating capacity (*IHT*, 12 June 1999, p. 5), whereas the VJ claimed only to have lost thirteen tanks (*FT*, 19 July 1999, p. 2).

On 22 June 1999, however, NATO began to acknowledge that its air power had knocked out much less Serbian military equipment in Kosova than it had previously claimed (partly because it had been duped by the Serbs' adroit use of dummies and decoys) and that the nearly 47,000-strong Serb armed forces were a lot less demoralized at the end of the war than earlier NATO accounts had suggested (*IHT*, 23 June 1999, p. 1). General Wesley Clark admitted on 16 September that only 26 'actual tank wreckages' had been found by NATO, although NATO commanders still insisted that they had confirmed evidence of 93 Serb tanks, 153 armoured personnel carriers an 339 military vehicles having been destroyed (*IHT*, 17 September 1999, p. 5). A suppressed internal US air force report later admitted that there had been only 58 accurate strikes during the war, rather than the 744 'confirmed' by NATO at war' end. This special investigation team also discovered that, while the US top brass had boasted that NATO forces had disabled around 120 tanks, about 220 armoured personnel carriers (APCs) and up to 450 artillery and mortar pieces, the true f gures were probably that NATO had only hit 14 tanks, 18 APCs and 20 artillery and mortar pieces – figures very close the losses admitted by the VJ *Independent*, 8 May 2000, p. 12). These low figures for damage to Serbia's armed forces suggested that, overall NATO's colossal aerial bombardment of Serbia must have inflicted vastly more damage on civilian than on military targets and that it must have been the damage to civilian targets rather than those to Serbia's largely unscathed security forces which ultimately forced Milosevic to capitulate. Thus massive NATO aerial frepower won the war, but not in ways of which it should be especially proud.

A report issued by the New York-based Human Rights Watch on 6 February 2000 estimated that 503 Serbian civilians had been killed by NATO bombs and missiles during the war. The report concluded that NATO may have breached the Geneva Convention in five areas: (i) use of cluster bombs (which spray small bombs over wide area) near populated areas; (ii) attacks made on targets of questionable military legitimacy, including the Serb Radio and Television head offe in Belgrade, the New Belgrade heating plant and seven bridges which were not on major transportation routes and had no military functions but were bombed during daylight hours when civilians were most likely to be crossing them; (iii) failure to take adequate measures to warn civilians of strikes; (iv) failure to take suff cient precautions when attacking mobile targets, including seven attacks on convoys or transportation links; and (v) failure to take suffcient measures to verify that targets did not have concentrations of civilians. The report estimated that one-third of the deaths and half the casualties investigated could have been avoided if NATO had abided by the Geneva Convention rules (*Independent*, 7 February 2000, pp. 1, 3; *IHT*, 8 February 2000, p. 7). In June 2000 Amnesty International published a similarly scathing critique of NATO's conduct of the war, accusing it of major violations of the rules of war preached by the West itself, of deliberate attacks on civilian targets, of taking insufficient precautionary measures to avoid unnecessary loss of civilian lives, and of continually giving over-riding priority to the safety of fighter planes and their pilots' lives at the cost of civilia lives (*IHT*, 8 June 2000, p. 1; *Independent*, 7 June 2000, p. 17).

The ICTY chief prosecutor Carla del Ponte nevertheless declared on 2 June 2000 that 'Although some mistakes were made by NATO, I am very satisfied tha there was no deliberate targeting of civilians or unlawful military targets by NATO during the bombing campaign' (*IHT*, 3 June 2000, p. 1; *The Guardian*, 3 June 2000, p. 21).

The KLA demilitarization agreement, 21 June 1999, and its aftermath

A detailed demilitarization agreement drawn up by NATO officers and KLA commanders was signed by Lieutenant General Sir Michael Jackson for NATO and by Hashim Thaqi for the KLA. It stipulated the *immediate cessation of all hostile acts by the KLA*, including the firing of weapons, the use of explosive devices, th placing of mines, the use of barriers or checkpoints, the conducting of military, security or training activities, the attacking, detaining or intimidation of civilians, the con - f scation or violation of property, reprisals, counter-attacks and all movement of 'armed bodies' into neighbouring countries (Albania and the ROM).

Within four days of signing, the KLA was to close all fighting positions, entrenchments and checkpoints on roads and mark minefields and booby traps, whil a joint implementation commission was established with representatives from the KLA and the NATO-led forces.

Within seven days, the KLA was to (i) establish secure weapons-storage sites to be verified by NATO forces, for all weapons except for pistols and licensed huntin shotguns; (ii) clear minefields and booby traps; (iii) vacate fighting positions; and (iv) assemble its members in locations approved by NATO commanders. KFOR permission would be needed for KLA members to leave these areas, and they agreed to carry weapons only in the designated assembly areas, with only commanders and their bodyguards permitted to be go about armed outside them. If KLA members ventured out, they were not to carry weapons or wear uniforms or insignia. Commanders, however, were still allowed to wear their uniforms and carry pistols when on official business and to be accompanied by three bodyguards each (*IHT*, 30 June 1999, p. 4; *IHT*, 1 July 1999, p. 10).

Within thirty days, all KLA members not of 'local origin' were to withdraw, the KLA were to store all prohibited weapons in registered sites, and KLA members would no longer be permitted to carry prohibited weapons, including all automatic rif es, any weapon 12.7 millimetres or larger, and all missiles, mines, grenades or other explosives. Once these weapons were stored they were to be under the joint control of the KLA and NATO for sixty days, after which NATO would assume complete control. No weapons were to be carried within 2.4 kilometres of main roads, principal towns, cities and borders.

Within ninety days, the KLA was to have completed the process of demilitarization and to have stopped wearing military uniforms and insignia, and KFOR permission would be needed for any training or parading. The agreement envisaged the 'formation of an army in Kosova along the lines of the US National Guard in due course, as part of a political process designed to determine Kosova's future status'. It would have a core of 4,000 professionals plus reservists. Clause 8 of the agreement threatened 'military action as deemed appropriate' by the commander of KFOR for any KLA member in breach of the agreement.

The KLA was then reckoned to comprise in the region of 9,000 hardened fighters plus 30,000 irregulars who joined after being driven from their homes in the spring of 1999. General Jackson emphasized that the demilitarization pact was 'a unilateral undertaking' on the part of the KLA and not a formal pact or two-way contract with NATO, unlike the one which Serbia's military had signed with NATO (*HT*, 22 June 1999, pp. 1, 7). Aided by the demilitarization pact, the squabbling and ineffectiveness of the Kosovar moderates and the disarray of a UN administration short on personnel and awaiting the promised police, whom UN member states were slow to send, the KLA was able to seize control of most of Kosova in June and July 1999. In the absence of a strong international presence, the KLA established a network of self-appointed ministries and local councils, seized businesses and apartments and collected taxes and customs payments. UNMIK had initially received only 156 of the planned deployment of 3,100 police (*IHT*, 30 July 1999, p. 1). Organized criminal networks and supporters of the KLA took advantage of the 'law and order vacuum' created by the long delay in deploying UN civil administrators and the expected 3,000-strong international police force to impose their own coercive and intimidatory forms of organization 'at street-level in towns and villages across Kosova' (*T*, 2 August 1999, p. 3). Gangs in Pristina, some of which had suspected links to the KLA, simply appropriated apartments, real estate, businesses, fuel supplies and cars from Kosovars and Serbs, who had almost no means of obtaining legal redress (*Independent*, 2 August 1999, p. 9).

This outcome bore out the official British and (to a lesser extent) French view tha the liberation of Kosova from the murderous Milosevic regime should have been carried out by aerial bombardment *in conjunction with major ground forces*, which could have quickly f lled the vacuum left by the forced withdrawal of the Serbs and by the further collapse of public order, instead of simply relying on the American strategy of smashing Kosova's economic and societal infrastructure to smithereens through colossal aerial bombardment and then naïvely hoping that the liberated province would be administered by law-abiding liberals rather than by thugs. There were no quick and easy 'technological fixes' for political and societal breakdown, a the USA belatedly began to learn the hard way in Iraq and Afghanistan. Simple-minded US reliance on bombing and pounding an already run-down society into submission naturally created a power vacuum which, in the absence of adequate ground forces and police, was most readily f lled by corrupt and clientelistic gangster networks and warlords.

Ibrahim Rugova received a warm welcome from cheering crowds in Pristina on 15 July 1999, when he returned to Kosova (*IHT*, 16 July 1999, p. 4). Within hours, however, he left again for Italy, thus jeopardizing the fst session of the UN-appointed advisory Kosova transitional council on 16 July. The UN had delayed the opening session by several days to allow Rugova to attend, but he instructed the LDK to boycott it (*The Guardian*, 17 July 1999, p. 17). However, Rugova returned to Kosova again with his family on 30 July, declaring that this time he intended to stay. He attended a meeting of the multi-ethnic advisory transitional council on 21 August, but Hashim Thaqi did not.

In September 1999 a civilian force called the Kosova Corps began to emerge out of the disbanding KLA. It was officially intended to cope with infrastructure rebuilding, ceremonial duties, humanitarian assistance and disaster relief (for forest fires, earthquakes, mountain rescue). KLA officers nevertheless saw this as the potential core of a future national army. There was a 19 September deadline for the complete demilitarization of the 9,000 uniformed and gun-carrying KLA 'regulars'. However, the Kosova Corps was intended to have only 3,000 regular members and 2,000 part-timers, with a military structure drawn from the principal commanders and brigades of the disbanding KLA (*IHT*, 4 September 1999, p. 2; *FT*, 9 September 1999, p. 2). After a personal appeal by General Wesley Clark and a concession from NATO allowing the organization to be called the 'Kosova Protection Corps', on 20 September the KLA leaders accepted a plan to transform the erstwhile KLA members into a civil defence organization. After the deadline for decommissioning KLA weapons expired on 19 September 1999, General Sir Michael Jackson obtained a promise from the disbanding KLA leadership that the KLA would officially ceas to exist at midnight on 21 September. Agim Ceku, the former KLA chief of staff, was to be the head of the Kosova Protection Corps (*IHT*, 22 September 1999, p. 5). By October 1999, however, the political leadership which emerged from the KLA began to suffer a collapse of popular support (according to voter surveys and senior ex-KLA figures), due to popular backlash against the widespread abuse of power by former insurgents (*IHT*, 18 October 1999, p. 10).

UNMIK announced on 3 September 1999 that it was dropping the Serbian dinar and that from 4 September all official dealings would be in Deutschmarks. All taxe would henceforth be collected in Deutschmarks and withheld from the Serbian Republic. The decree merely legalized the de-facto situation. In Kosova, as in much of the Balkans, the Deutschmark was already the main currency in daily use (*The Times*, 4 September 1999, p. 19).

EU foreign ministers agreed on 5–6 September 1999 to ease the international sanc tions imposed on Kosova and Montenegro, by exempting them from the oil embargo and the EU ban on commercial fights, while failing to obtain agreement on an 'energy for democracy' initiative, which would have provided Serb municipalities controlled by opponents of Slobodan Milosevic with fuel (*FT*, 6 September 1999, p. 2).

Serb leaders in Kosova pulled out of the UNMIK civilian advisory body on 22 September 1999, in protest against the creation of the Kosova Protection Corps and its dominance by ethnic Albanians. The Kosova Serb leaders nevertheless decided to remain in contact with UNMIK administration, despite leaving the transitional council (*FT*, 23 September 1999, p. 2).

The interim administrative council established by UNMIK and the Kosovar leaders, 15 December 1999

The UN chief administrator Bernard Kouchner signed a power-sharing agreement with Kosovar leaders on 15 December 1999, creating an interim administrative council until elections were held. It was expected to absorb all existing administrative structures and to be in operation by 31 January 2000. Under the agreement, Ibrahim Rugova, Hashim Thaqi and Rexhep Qosja were to work in concert with the UN, the EU, the OSCE and the UNHCR. The new body had fourteen functional departments which were intended to function like government ministries and would rebuild the war-shattered province. This pact with the Kosova leaders was a tacit recognition by UNMIK that it was unable to administer the province effectively without their participation. No representatives of the dwindling Serbian community took part in the launch of these arrangements (*IHT*, 16 December 1999, p. 6; *The Guardian*, 16

December 1999, p. 17). Soon afterwards, the KFOR commander General Klaus Reinhardt ordered his soldiers into the streets in force because, faced with a major crime wave and the growth of gansterism, the 1,800-member UN police force was unable to cope (*IHT*, 22 December 1999, p. 4). Bernard Kouchner believed that a force of 6,000 officers was necessary (*The Guardian*, 6 December 1999, p. 12). The Eurocorps, which had been set up in 1995 by France and Germany and was later joined by Spain, Belgium and Luxembourg, provided about 350 officers out of a total headquarters staff of around 1,000 and was put in command of KFOR on 18 April 2000.

Members of Kosova's Serb national council decided on 2 April 2000 to end their six-month boycott of the province's main post-war institutions and to send representatives to two multi-ethnic bodies set up by UNMIK, although these representatives were only to be observers and their participation would be reviewed after three months (*IHT*, 3 April 2000, p. 6). A split occurred in Kosova's Serbian population, with the Mitrovica representatives opposing a decision by other leaders to cooperate with the interim administrative council (*IHT*, 6 April 2000, p. 4). On 4 June 2000 the Serb national council decided to suspend the participation of Serb observers in the interim administrative council and other joint bodies, in protest against a spate of killings of Serbs. They demanded that the Security Council implement more stringent security measures and the establishment of 'functional self-rule' in areas occupied by Serbs (*The Guardian*, 5 June 2000, p. 15). Moderate Serbs later decided to return to the interim administrative council, provided it implemented UN commitments to send anti-terrorist police to Serb areas targeted by Kosovar extremists and to admit more Serbs into the Kosovar-dominated police force (*The Guardian*, 26 June 2000, p. 14).

The OSCE announced on 24 July 2000 that fewer than 1,000 Serbs, out of the estimated 105,000 who remained in Kosova, had registered to vote in the municipal elections scheduled for 28 October. By contrast, over 1 million Kosovars had registered to vote. Potential Serb voters in Kosova were threatened in various ways by representatives of the Belgrade regime, 'including long-term persecution should they return to Serbia, arrest on espionage charges, random violence and suspension of pensions' (*Independent*, 25 July 2000, p. 12).

UNMIK reluctantly agreed on 4 September that, because Kosova remained formally a province of Serbia, residents of Kosova could vote in the crucial FRY presidential and parliamentary elections held on 24 September 2000, which finally put an end to the Milosevic regime. Kosova's Serb population saw considerable benefs to keeping the Milosevic regime in power, because the salaries or pensions of Kosova Serb teachers, administrators, police, health workers and pensioners were still being paid by Belgrade (*The Times*, 13 September 2000, p. 17).

Municipal elections, 28 October 2000

These elections to Kosova's thirty municipalities were largely peaceful. The turn-out of registered voters (including only 1,000 Serbs) was 79 per cent (*IHT*, 8 November 2000, p. 13). There were candidates from the Bosniak, Gorani, Turkish and Ashkalia-Roma minorities, but no Serb and Serbophone Roma candidates. To circumvent the Serb boycott, Bernard Kouchner made clear his intention to appoint Serbs to some municipalities (*The Guardian*, 28 October 2000, p. 19).

Ibrahim Rugova's LDK won 58 per cent of the votes cast and control of twenty-one municipalities. Hashim Thaqi's PDK won 27.3 per cent of the votes cast and control of six municipalities. Ramush Haradinaj's Alliance for the Future of Kosova (AAK) won 8 per cent of the vote. All three of these Kosovar parties demanded full independent statehood for Kosova. However, while Rugova's LDK advocated non-violence, tolerance and cooperation with other parties, Thaqi's PDK took a hardline nationalist stance. Most of his supporters were young, but his popularity had declined because many voters now associated his party with a violent underworld of crime and corruption. Former KLA members were accused of taking over ordinary people's homes and businesses at gunpoint, using violence against political opponents, foment-ing a climate of lawlessness, which resulted in almost daily killings, and generally abusing their power (*IHT*, 30 October 2000, p. 9; *The Economist*, 4 November 2000, p. 68). Ramush Haradinaj's AAK sought to steer a middle course (*T*, 28 October 2000, p. 10).

Releases of Kosovar political prisoners held in Serbian prisons

During the Kosova war of March–June 1999 the Milosevic regime had moved an estimated 2,000 Kosovar political and other prisoners from prisons in Kosova to prisons in Serbia (*IHT*, 28 February 2001, p. 7). In December 1999 a court in Nis had convicted a Kosovar, Dr Flora Brovina, of terrorism for alleged links to the KLA and sentenced her to seven years in prison, but Serbia's supreme court quashed her conviction on 7 June 2000 (*IHT*, 8 June 2000, p. 5). In October 2000, President Kostunica arranged a pardon for her, but she refused to leave jail unless the other Kosovar political prisoners were released too (*IHT*, 26 October 2000, p. 4). Dr Brovina was finally released along with fifteen other prisoners in November 2000

On 26 February 2001 the FRY parliament passed a long-awaited amnesty law. UNMIK officials and human-rights organizations had long called for the release o the 650 Kosovars still held in Serbian prisons. Human-rights organizations considered *c*.570 of these to be political prisoners. The new law amnestied those convicted of conspiring against the state, but not those convicted of acts of terrorism. The other main benef ciaries of the law were an estimated 28,000 young Serbs and Montenegrins who had f ed abroad to avoid military service during the wars in Croatia, Bosnia and Kosova. Approximately 200 of the imprisoned Kosovars had been charged with terrorism and their cases were to be reviewed separately. After reviewing their cases, however, the Serbian justice minister Momcilo Grubac asked President Kostunica to pardon some who had been convicted on insuff cient evidence. In particular, a group of 143 men from the town of Djakovica had been convicted as a group, apparently without evidence, after several policemen were killed (*IHT*, 28 February 2001, p. 7). A Belgrade court ruled on 23 April 2001 that their original mass trial had followed 'faulty procedures' and that their sentences should be reviewed. However, new trials were considered highly unlikely, and these 143 Kosovars were released from Serb prisons and allowed to return to Kosova on 25 April. The Red Cross alleged that 281 Kosova Albanians were known still to be in Serbian prisons, and that a further 3,526 people were still unaccounted for, including 2,746 Kosova Albanians, 516 Serbs, 137 Roma, and 127 others (*IHT*, 26 April 2001, p. 7; *Independent*, 26 April 2001, p. 17). On 16 March 2002 the Serbian authorities handed over most of their remaining Kosovar prisoners to NATO troops at the Kosova border (*IHT*, 27 March 2002, p. 5).

Kosova under Hans Haekkerup as UNMIK chief administrator, 2001

Bernard Kouchner's term of office as the UNMIK chief administrator in Kosova expired on 13 January 2001, and his successor, the former Danish foreign minister Hans Haekkerup, took up his post two days later.

In April 2001 Serbs blocked traffic in Kosova to protest against a new policy o collecting excise taxes on goods entering Kosova. Protesters put up roadblocks in Mitrovica and nearby border-area towns denouncing 'customs points' intended to cut them off from Yugoslavia. However, UNMIK responded that the new revenue posts were not customs points but merely an attempt to collect duty on previously untaxed cigarettes, fuel, liquor and luxury items, in a Kosova which was awash with black-market merchandise (*IHT*, 18 April 2001, p. 6).

The provisional 'constitutional framework', inaugurated 14 May 2001

Hans Haekkerup unveiled a constitutional framework for provisional self-government in Kosova on 14 May 2001 and announced that elections to a legislative assembly would be held on 17 November. The assembly was to have 120 seats, including ten reserved for Serbs and ten for Kosova's other minorities. The assembly would elect a president, who would nominate a prime minister, who would form a government. The assembly would have powers in health, education and environment, but ultimate executive authority remained with the UN's chief administrator, who would be able to dissolve parliament. UNMIK would also retain power over taxes, public spending and the judiciary and remain responsible for the Kosova Protection Corps. This framework would allow Kosova's Albanians and Serbs – if the latter would participate – to run the territory until both were ready for final-status negotiations. However, th Kosova Serb leadership rejected the constitutional framework out of hand, declaring that it would boycott the elections and that it wanted a veto in the parliament*FT*, 15 May 2001, p. 11; *IHT*, 24 May 2001, p. 7).

Elections for the new 120-seat Kosova national assembly, 17 November 2001

There was a 5 per cent threshold for ethnic Albanian parties. The mandate was for three years. The OSCE declared the elections to have been peaceful and well conducted. The turn-out was 65 per cent among ethnic Albanians, 46 per cent among ethnic Serbs, and 63 per cent overall (*FT*, 19 November 2001, p. 12). See Table 10.1 for the results.

10.1 Kosovan parliamentary election, 17 November 2001

Party	Share of votes (%)	Seats
Democratic League of Kosova (LDK, led by Ibrahim Rugova),	46.2	47
Democratic Party of Kosova (PDK, led by Hashim Thaqi)	25.5	26
Alliance for the Future of Kosova (AAK, led by Ramush Haradinaj)	7.8	–
Povarak ('Return', a group of Kosova Serb parties)	11.0	22

After the election, the Serb exodus from Kosova continued. The economy of the Serb enclaves relied mainly on subsistence agriculture, petty trade and humanitarian aid. KFOR convoys made life in the enclaves possible, even ensuring food supplies, but all attempts to establish an UNMIK administration in northern Mitrovica were vehemently blocked by local protests. Paramilitary groups called 'bridge watchers' prevented many residents in the north from participating in the November election to the Kosova assembly. Turn-out was a mere 7 per cent in Mitrovica, despite over two-thirds of eligible voters having registered to vote. Many Kosova Serb teachers, doctors and municipal workers drew salaries from both Belgrade and UNMIK. Civil courts for the Serb enclaves were relocated across the border (Mateeva and Paes 2002: 19–21). Rada Trajkovic, the leader of the Serbian group in the newly elected assembly, declared their willingness to enter a coalition 'with all people of goodwill, who are ready to prevent discrimination against the Serb community' (*IHT*, 5 December 2001, p. 7).

The assembly held its inaugural session on 11 December. Hashim Thaqi's PDK walked out, delaying the election of a president, but under Haekkerup's temporary chairmanship the assembly chose the LDK member Nexhat Daci to serve as its de-facto speaker (*Independent*, 11 December 2001, p. 14). On 13 December the assembly again failed to elect a president, after both the PDK and the AAK refused to vote and Ibrahim Rugova secured only forty-nine votes, far less than the required two-thirds majority. The PDK was prepared in principle to vote for Rugova, but only if and when a power-sharing arrangement was agreed between them (*Independent*, 14 December 2001, p. 17). There was another failed attempt to elect a president on 10 January 2002. Rugova received fifty-one votes, still ten short of the simple majorit needed on that occasion. The other Kosovar parties continued to boycott the voting until a power-sharing agreement was reached (*IHT*, 11 January 2002, p. 4).

On 28 December 2001 Hans Haekkerup announced his resignation for personal reasons as the UNMIK chief administrator, with effect from the end of 2001. 'His young family apparently left the tense atmosphere of Pristina with much relief' (*The Economist*, 26 January 2002, p. 43). His deputy Charles Brayshaw took over until it was announced on 21 January 2002 that Michael Steiner (from Germany) would be the new UNMIK chief administrator.

Kosova under Michael Steiner as UNMIK chief administrator, January 2002 to July 2003

Kosova's assembly finally voted in a president (Ibrahim Rugova), a prime minister and a ten-minister cabinet on 4 March 2002. The prime minister, forty-seven-year-old Bajram Rexhepi, was a moderate member of Hashim Thaqi's party and had been a f eld doctor for the KLA and a respected former mayor of Mitrovica. A coalition deal gave Rugova's LDK the fnance, education, culture and transport and communi-cations portfolios, while Thaqi's PDK took the trade and public services portfolio. The coalition of Serb parties was given the agriculture ministry. On 8 March Nebojsa Covic, Belgrade's special envoy for Kosova, accused prime minister Bajram Rexhepi of having taken part in the torture and decapitation of a Serb soldier by the KLA in May 1999, but Dr Rexhepi denied the charges (*The Times*, 9 March 2002, p. 20).

The NATO states agreed on 10 May 2002 to reduce their peacekeeping forces in Kosova from 38,000 to 33,200 by mid-2003 (while those in Bosnia and Herzegovina were to be cut to 12,000), because the security situation had improved considerably.

The military perceived the remaining security threats to be from criminal networks and lightly armed extremists, rather than from military or paramilitary forces. This was followed by a crackdown on former KLA members suspected of having committed major crimes, as UNMIK had been widely accused of failing to tackle crimes committed by former KLA members. In June UN police detained six senior ex-KLA personnel on charges of having killed fellow Kosovars in June 1999 (*The Economist*, 22 June 2002, p. 44). In August UN police arrested Rustrem Mustafa (known by his *nom de guerre* Remi) and charged him with having abducted and imprisoned at least five people during the 1997–9 conflict in Kosova. On 12 August the AAK lead and former KLA commander Ramush Haradinaj was charged in connection with a shooting incident which took place in 2000 with a Kosovar family which supported a party rivalling his own. Six other Kosovars, including his brother Daut, were also indicted on the same charge (*The Guardian*, 15 August 2002, p. 14;*IHT*, 15 August 2002, p. 3). British troops detained three former KLA members on 17 February 2003 and handed them over for trial by the ICTY, for atrocities allegedly committed in Kosova in 1998–9. This was the first time the ICTY had detained former member of the KLA.

Local elections held in Kosova on 26 October 2002

The Kosovar turn-out was 57 per cent and the Serb turn-out was 20 per cent – a large increase on previous local elections, but still very low, despite promises from Michael Steiner that they could benefit from a plan to devolve power to local authorities (including Serb-dominated ones) and from increased investment if they became politically engaged. As a result of these disappointing turn-outs, UNMIK plans to decentralize power and encourage investment were deferred (*The Economist*, 2 November 2002, p. 46). Rugova's LDK won outright control of eleven of the thirty local councils (including Pristina), but its support had slipped. Support for Thaqi's PDK rose, giving it outright control of four municipalities and scope to control at least four others together with smaller parties (*IHT*, 4 November 2002, p. 4).

A group of largely ethnic Serb-populated municipalities located mainly in the north of Kosova announced on 20 January 2003 that they were establishing a 'union' with its own president, assembly and flag, but UNMIK declared this move illegal and prevented it from going ahead. In June 2003 it was reported that about 230,000 Serbian and other refugees from Kosova were living in Serbia and Montenegro and that only 7,000 such refugees had returned since 2000 (*The Economist*, 28 June 2003, p. 82). Only about 100,000 Serbs had remained in Kosova, mostly in small enclaves surrounded by Albanian villages and in larger groupings along the border with 'Serbia proper' (*IHT*, 15 August 2003, p. 5). In October 2004, however, the Berlin-based think tank European Stability Initiative argued that there were only 65,000 Serb refugees from Kosova in Serbia (rather than the 220,000–230,000 widely claimed) and that many of Kosova's Serbs had sold their properties with no intention of returning. It also suggested that Serbs still living in Kosova numbered 128,000, rather the 100,000 or so which was widely assumed, and that two-thirds of Kosova's Serbs actually lived in the south and in relatively scattered and isolated rural communities, rather than in the northern towns or in neat enclaves (*The Economist*, 16 October 2004, p. 44).

In April 2003 Russia notified KFOR that it would start withdrawing its peacekeeping forces from the Balkans within two months, both for fnancial reasons and due to a perceived absence of a war threat in the Balkans. Russia had 650 peace-keepers in Kosova and 320 in Bosnia. The last Russian forces left Kosova on 24 July 2003 (*IHT*, 16 April 2003, p. 6; *IHT*, 25 July 2003, p. 5).

Michael Steiner added the Kosovar 'Albanian National Army' (ANA) to the UN's official list of terrorist organizations on 17 April after it claimed responsibility for blowing up a railway bridge in a Serb-inhabited part of northern Kosova. Two suspected bombers were killed by the blast. The move meant that members of the group could be jailed for up to forty years (*IHT*, 18 April 2003, p. 4).

Kosova under Harri Holkeri as UNMIK chief administrator, July 2003 to May 2004

Harri Holkeri, a former prime minister of Finland, succeeded Michael Steiner as chief administrator of UNMIK in July 2003.

Two Kosova Serb youths, aged eighteen and nineteen, were killed and four others injured on 13 August when a gunman opened fire on them while they were swimmin in the Bistrica river near the Albanian village of Zahac, close to the Serbian enclave of Gorazdevac (near Pec). Italian KFOR soldiers were guarding them at the time (*FT*, 14 August 2003, p. 6). Harri Holkeri appointed a special international prose - cutor to head the investigation of the incident, which leaders of the Serbian community in Kosova feared could thwart their efforts to lure back to Kosova the 200,000 or so Serbs who had taken refuge in 'Serbia proper' (*IHT*, 15 August 2003, p. 5). No one was sure who was responsible for this incident and others like it, but the prime suspect was the so-called ANA (*The Economist*, 23 August 2003, p. 31). Violent inter-ethnic clashes began to occur daily after this incident.

Serb and Kosovar leaders met face to face for the first time since 1999 for UN sponsored talks on 14 October 2003, but both sides remained intransigent. The meeting took place in Vienna and was mediated by UN officials, in the presence of the E commissioner Chris Patten and the EU foreign-policy supremo Javier Solana. These UN-sponsored talks were 'supposed to avoid the contentious issue of Kosova's future status' and were 'intended merely to pave the way for future negotiations on everyday issues burdening Kosova, such as energy supplies, transportation, missing persons and the return of refugees ... International mediators stressed that the final status of Kosov would be determined by the UN Security Council' (*IHT*, 15 October 2003, p. 3). President Rugova and Nexhat Daci, the speaker of the Kosova assembly, insisted on outright independence for Kosova, but the Serb team (which included Serbia's deputy prime minister Nebojsa Covic) rejected this out of hand. Nevertheless, the two sides did agree to establish 'working groups focusing on issues including energy supplies, telecommunications, refugee returns and missing persons' (*FT*, 15 October 2003, p. 8). Further talks were scheduled for November. Over the next year or so, the major refrain of the UNMIK protectorate was 'standards before status'. It was argued that Kosova's rulers and inhabitants would have to raise their standards of practice and observance with regard to democratic and human rights before the UN would endeavour to settle the territory's eventual status, because only when a viable multi-ethnic Kosova had been built could the question of its future status be addressed. It was agreed in December 2003 that an assessment of Kosova's headway in raising its 'standards' could be initiated in the summer of 2005 *FT*, 22 March 2004, pp. 16–17).

In early March 2004 Vojislav Kostunica, the newly elected prime minister of Serbia, called for the 'cantonization' of Kosova (regarded as coded language for partition along ethnic lines), but he later changed his language to emphasize more ethnically neutral 'decentralization'. On 16 March he protested that human-rights abuses against Serbs in Kosova were a daily occurrence and that the only way to stabilize the situation was through 'decentralization and institutional guarantees' for Serbs and other non-Albanian minorities in Kosova (*The Guardian*, 18 March 2004, p. 10).

The Serbian former paramilitary Sasa Cvyetan, who had taken part in a massacre of fourteen ethnic Albanian women and children in Kosova on 20 March 1999, was sentenced to twenty years in jail (the maximum sentence available) in a landmark trial in Belgrade on 17 March. However, human-rights observers saw him as a fall guy for a notorious Serbian special police unit called the Scorpions. Dejan Demiovic, another of the accused, had escaped to Canada, where he was fighting extradition proceedings (*The Guardian*, 18 March 2004, p. 10).

The resurgence of inter-ethnic violence, 17–18 March 2004

On 15 March 2004 a nineteen-year-old Serb was wounded by gunshot in the village of Caglavica near Pristina. The next day, possibly in retaliation, two ethnic Albanian boys were drowned in the icy river Ibar, which runs through the ethnically divided city of Mitrovica, and a nine-year-old boy went missing after the three of them were chased by a gang of Serbs with fierce dogs, according to the testimony of the missin boy's thirteen-year-old brother. The subsequent police investigation furnished no corroborating evidence for this account of what happened (*Independent*, 22 March 2004, pp. 20–1). Nevertheless, whether this account was accurate or not, on 17 March reports of this tragedy sparked off a major explosion of violent discontent, which had been brewing for some time among ethnic Albanians, especially the numerous unemployed, impoverished and politically frustrated former KLA members. Their anger was directed not only against the remaining pockets of ethnic Serbs living in Kosova, but also against KFOR, the UNMIK protectorate and the officials and polic who served it.

As a result, on 17 March Serbs and Kosovars exchanged grenades and heavy gunf across the river Ibar, killing at least six people, while about 800 ethnic Albanians broke police/NATO roadblocks and attacked the mainly Serb village of Caglavica, setting houses on fire, and eleven French peacekeepers were wounded – one fatally – by stone and shrapnel from a hand grenade. In the western village of Belpolje, Kosovars drove out Serb residents and set fre to houses, while in Pec Kosovars attacked the regional UN headquarters and damaged UN vehicles. Clashes between Serbs and ethnic Albanians also occurred in several other towns in the region, including Kosova Polje and Lipljan. The unrest even spread to Belgrade, where Serbian demonstrators set on fire the city's seventeenth-century mosque *IHT*, 17 and 18 March 2004, pp. 1, 8).

NATO ordered the deployment of 1,100 extra troops to Kosova from Britain, Italy and the USA on 18 March, in an attempt to stem a wave of inter-ethnic violence, while in Obilic, Mitrovica and Prizren Serb houses and Orthodox churches were set alight by mobs. The burnt-out wrecks of UN vehicles served notice that the violence was as much focused on UN and NATO forces as on Kosova's Serb minority. Most of the victims of violence appeared to be Serbs *IHT*, 19 March 2004, pp. 1, 8). Vojislav Kostunica accused Kosovars of mounting an 'attempted pogrom and ethnic cleansing' against the Serbian minority (*The Times*, 19 March 2004, p. 1). The Belgrade media reported that all ethnic Serbs had been forced out of Prizren and Obilic, and more mosques were set alight in Serbia (*FT*, 19 March 2004, p. 8).

Gregory Johnson, the US admiral and commander of NATO forces in southern Europe who on 18 March took control of the security operation, described the violence as clearly orchestrated 'ethnic cleansing' and claimed that the goal of its organizers was to rid Kosova of its few remaining Serb enclaves. A surprise outcome of the attacks was that many Kosova Serbs came to regard US troops are their best protection against Albanian attacks. 'American troops were called in . . .. to help disperse marauding Albanians after eight hours of clashes with UN police and peacekeepers. Within fifty minutes of the US troops' arrival the crowds had fled*IHT*, 20 March 2004, p. 3).

On 19 March, the third day of mob violence, the Serbian defence minister Boris Tadic warned that Serbia could abandon its hands-off approach to Kosova if NATO failed to protect the ethnic Serb minority from ethnic Albanian mobs, although Tadic's subsequent demand that Serbian troops be allowed into Kosova was rejected. Few Serbs accepted the Kosovar leaders' claims that the violence had exploded spontaneously, even though Kosova's ethnic Albanian prime minister Bajram Rexhepi appealed to the rioters to desist (*FT*, 20 March 2004, p. 6). The view among international policy-makers was that Kosovar hardliners had orchestrated this upsurge of violence in order to advance their agenda of an independent and Serb-free Kosova. The violence subsided on 20 March, as KFOR acted more robustly to stem the trouble and Kosovar political leaders intensified their appeals for an end to the figh ing. The father of the drowned boys publicly asked that their funeral be a quiet and dignified affair and not an excuse for further rioting. His moving appeal was echoe by Kosova's interim government and by UNMIK. Caglavica was placed under the protection of Swedish troops, and the government set up a fund to repair the 110 homes and 16 Serb churches destroyed (*The Times*, 22 March 2004, p. 12; *Independent*, 22 March 2004, pp. 20–1).

The UN estimated that 28 Serbs had been killed, 3,600 had been rendered homeless and over 1,000 had been driven from their homes or evacuated from trouble spots. Some sought refuge in Serbia proper. In addition, seventy-two UN vehicles and forty-one churches or monasteries had been destroyed during March 2004 (*The Guardian*, 20 March 2004, p. 16; *FT*, 22 March 2004, p. 7; *IHT*, 31 March 2004, p. 8). In July 2004 the New York-based human-rights organization Human Rights Watch published a scathing report entitled 'Failure to Protect: Anti-Minority Violence in Kosova, March 2004'. It strongly criticized KFOR and the UN police for having 'failed catastrophically to protect minorities during the widespread rioting' during March 2004. Among other charges, it accused the NATO-led forces of locking their gates and standing by during riots that had left 19 dead, 900 wounded, 4,100 people displaced, 27 churches and at least 550 homes destroyed. The report also accused the international community of being in 'absolute denial about its own failures in Kosova'. This had been the biggest test for NATO and the UN in Kosova since 1999, and they had failed it. However, a NATO off cial in Kosova claimed that KFOR had 'quickly stabilized the situation within hours during the riots', had prevented a civil war, and had chosen to save lives rather than buildings. More than 1,200 of those who fled the pogroms had found temporary refuge inside KFOR's military bases (*HT*, 27 July 2004, p. 3;*Independent*, 27 July 2004, p. 23). Serbian leaders claimed that the mob attacks in March 2004 had given Belgrade 'the moral authority to insist that Albanians be denied independence and be obliged to accept autonomy instead, under Serbian sovereignty'*IHT*, 23 March 2004, p. 5).

In an interview published in the*Financial Times* on 19 April 2004, Kosova's interim prime minister Bajram Rexhepi warned that his provisional government would seek separation from Serbia in September 2005 if the UN had not made substantive headway on the province's status by then. 'If we wait until September 2005 and we see they are buying time, probably we will unilaterally move for a referendum on independence or a declaration of independence,' he stated, while maintaining that he would prefer to see a gradual transition to self-rule agreed with the UN. He suggested that 'Kosova's political transition could start with two years of "monitored independence". This would allow a provisional government to assume full control while continuing to face strict international scrutiny' (*FT*, 19 April 2004, p. 9).

On 29 April the Serbian parliament adopted a plan put forward by Premier Kostunica to give the Serbs in Kosova five Serbian autonomous regions which woul be all but independent from the province, whose final status was to be 'left open' (*Independent*, 30 April 2004, p. 29; *The Economist*, 22 May 2004, p. 39).

In May 2004, Amnesty International published a report entitled 'Does That Mean I Have Rights?', covering the period 1999–2003. It claimed that UN police and NATO peacekeepers were generating 'as much as 80 per cent' of the income of the illegal sex trade in Kosova and that 'members of the international community' made up '20 per cent of the people using traffcked women and girls'. As a result of the infux of thousands of NATO troops, Kosova had become 'a major destination country for women trafficked into forced prostitution. A small-scale local market for prostitu-tion was transformed into a large-scale industry based on trafficking, predominantl run by criminal networks.' The burgeoning sex trade and sex slavery in Kosova resembled similar phenomena in Bosnia. In March 2004 the UN department of peacekeeping in New York had acknowledged that KFOR had come to be 'seen as part of the problem in traffcking rather than the solution', although UNMIK described the Amnesty report as 'highly unbalanced' (*FT*, 7 May 2004, p. 8; *The Guardian*, 7 May 2004, p. 14).

The UN administrator Harri Holkeri resigned for health reasons on 25 May 2004, two months before the end of his one-year mandate. He had recently been admitted to hospital in Strasbourg suffering from fatigue (*FT*, 26 May 2004, p. 8). Holkeri, who was sixty-seven, had been widely criticized for his lacklustre performance and carried the can for the resurgence of inter-ethnic violence during March 2004. During his brief tenure, the UN headquarters in New York had increasingly intervened in Kosova's affairs, irritating Kosovar politicians who felt that decisions were being taken away from Kosova, and the economy had continued to go downhill, partly due to a botched privatization plan. Public services and utilities remained chaotic, with frequent water and power cuts, organized crime was growing fast and the unemployment rate was approaching 70 per cent (*FT*, 27 July 2004, p. 9).

Holkeri had been Kosova's fourth UN administrator in five years. The US diploma Charles Brayshaw again temporarily stood in as the acting chief administrator of UNMIK. After a f ying start in its f rst year, UNMIK had

> lost its way under a succession of uninspiring – or arrogant – leaders. Whereas Bernard Kouchner was seen as too lenient towards acts of Albanian revenge against Kosova's small Serb minority, his successor, Hans Haekkerup of Denmark, was seen as anti-Albanian .. . Michael Steiner of Germany was disliked by almost everybody for his autocratic style.
>
> (*The Guardian*, 26 May 2004, p. 15; *Independent*, 26 May 2004, p. 23).

In the fourth annual report on human rights in Kosova, published on 12 July 2004 by Kosova's Polish ombudsman Marek Antoni Nowicki, both UNMIK and the Kosovar leadership were extensively criticized for having failed to achieve even a minimum level of guaranteed rights and freedoms, especially for the Serbian minority. Much of the report focused on the inability of Serbs and other minorities to live, travel and work freely in the province. They were still largely confined to their homes relying on militarily escorted transport for occasional visits to other places, and the representation of non-Albanians in Kosova's civil service was too low (*IHT*, 14 July 2004, p. 3).

Following the pogroms of March 2004 (to the time of writing) Kosova Serbs boycotted Kosova's provisional parliament and government, and the official talks between the governments of Kosova and Serbia on 'doable' issues were not resumed. Nevertheless, leading f gures from both sides met eight times unofficially during th first half of 2004, albeit outside Kosova, and in June 2004 advisers to Kosova's prime minister Bajram Rexhepi and president Ibrahim Rugova met their Serb counterparts in Greece (*The Economist*, 26 June 2004, p. 45).

Kosova under Søren Jessen-Petersen as UNMIK chief administrator, August 2004 to June 2006

Restoring self- and public confidence in UNMIK was the major challenge for Søre Jessen-Petersen, the Danish diplomat and former head of the EU mission in the ROM who become the new chief administrator for UNMIK in August 2004. On 23 August Søren Jessen-Petersen and General Walter Schwimmer, the secretary of the Council of Europe, signed documents calling for the protection of minorities and prevention of torture, applying the Council of Europe's human-rights treaties and providing for monitoring the implementation of those human-rights principles in Kosova (*IHT*, 24 August 2004, p. 5).

The elections to Kosova's 120-seat parliament, 23 October 2004

Serbia's prime minister Vojislav Kostunica and the head of the Serbian Orthodox Church urged Serbs to boycott the forthcoming elections in Kosova. Kostunica also accused UNMIK of pandering to Kosovar extremists. Kosova remained very tense, with the Serbs who lived in isolated enclaves facing daily harassment by Kosovars (*IHT*, 30 July 2004, p. 3). Serbia's Western-orientated president Boris Tadic was the only prominent Serb who volubly supported international calls for Serbs to resume participation in Kosova's political institutions (*IHT*, 23 October 2004, p. 3). The turn-out for Kosova's registered voters was 53 per cent, but under 1,000 Serbs (only 0.3 per cent) voted. See Table 10.2 for the distribution of votes and seats.

The government headed by Ramush Haradinaj, 3 December 2004 to 8 March 2005

With forty-seven seats in the 120-member assembly, the LDK was well short of an overall majority. On 2 December, therefore, the LDK struck a power-sharing deal with the AAK. President Rugova appointed the AAK leader and former rebel commander Ramush Haradinaj to the post of prime minister, even though he had recently been questioned by the ICTY war-crimes investigators. The next day Kosova's parliament

10.2 Kosovan parliamentary election, 23 October 2004

Party	Share of votes (%)	Seats
Democratic League of Kosova (LDK), led by Ibrahim Rugova	45.4	47
Democratic Party of Kosova (PDK), led by Hashim Thaqi	28.9	29
Alliance for the Future of Kosova (AAK), led by Ramush Haradinaj	8.4	9
The Citizens Movement ORA (Hour), led by publisher Veton Surroi	6.2	7

Note: in addition, ten seats were reserved for representatives of the Serbs and ten for representatives of smaller minorities, including Roma, Bosniaks, Montenegrins and Turks.

Source: Terdevci (2005).

approved the choice of Ramush Haradinaj as prime minister by seventy-two votes to three, while the PDK abstained. In return, parliament re-elected Rugova to the presidency (*IHT*, 4 December 2004, p. 3). Haradinaj promised to give himself up to the ICTY if he was indicted, but also warned that he could not guarantee Kosova's stability in that eventuality (*FT*, 4 December 2004, p. 6). On 9 December Serbia's justice minister Zoran Stojkovic warned that Haradinaj would be arrested on war-crimes charges if he ever set foot in Serbia (*IHT*, 10 December 2004, p. 7).

On 13–14 February 2005, Serbia's president Boris Tadic made a visit to Kosova, the first by a Serb head of state since 1999. This was billed as a fact-finding tour, b Tadic addressed Serb crowds in village after village, including some of the most isolated and impoverished Serb communities, but there were no meetings with Kosovar leaders (*IHT*, 15 February 2005, p. 3).

Haradinaj suddenly resigned as prime minister on 8 March 2005, and the following day he 'surrendered' to the ICTY, which had (as feared) indicted him for war crimes allegedly committed while he was a KLA commander in 1998–9. Haradinaj seemed conf dent that he could prove himself 'innocent of any crime'. However, the Serbian authorities had charged him with several hundred killings and kidnappings. NATO hurriedly increased its peacekeeping forces in Kosova by 1,000 troops, fearing that the announcement could set off general unrest or clashes between Kosovars and the Serb minority (*IHT*, 9 March 2005, pp. 1, 8). Haradinaj was the second former KLA commander to be indicted by the ICTY. On 14 March he was formally charged with 'superior responsibility for the rape, murder and torture of Serb and Gypsy civilians by Albanian separatists under his control' and also of 'personally participating in beatings and torture, including the abuse of Albanian civilians who were believed to have collaborated with Serbs' (*IHT*, 15 March 2005, p. 3).

Despite Haradinaj's 'terrorist' past, he had quickly gained respect as an effective, flexible and dynamic prime minister. The premature termination of his premiership by the ICTY was widely regretted, because Kosova had seemed poised to break out of the vicious circles that had impeded progress towards constructive dialogue and reconciliation between the Kosovar and Serb camps (*The Economist*, 2 April 2005, p. 38). This was yet another illustration of the disruptive and sometimes highly counter-productive impact of the Western determination to give a higher priority to retribution than to the promotion of reconciliation and constructive dialogue within deeply fissure societies. Nevertheless, on 11 March officials from Serbia and Kosova agreed to resume low-level dialogue the following week, thus ending the four-month Serb boycott on bilateral meetings with Kosovar officials *FT*, 12 March 2005, p. 9).

President Rugova survived an apparent assassination attempt on 15 March, when a bomb exploded while his convoy was passing through Pristina. A shadowy Kosovar dissident group claimed responsibility for the attack, although Serb responsibility could not be discounted (*The Economist*, 2 April 2005, p. 38).

The coalition government headed by Bajram Kosumi, 23 March 2005 to 1 March 2006

Bajram Kosumi was sworn in as the new prime minister of Kosova's interim government on 23 March (*The Times*, 24 March 2005, p. 41). He was a former student leader who had previously served as environment minister and had not been an insurgent. He had spent almost ten years in prison for his role in the peaceful protests in Kosova in 1981–2. 'For the f rst time since Kosova elected a government of its own in 2001, there are no known former KLA men in power' *The Economist*, 2 April 2005, p. 38). In an attempt to kick-start further efforts at inter-ethnic reconciliation, Slavisha Petkovic, a Kosova Serb who had been an IDP before returning to Kosova, was made head of a ministry for returnees and ethnic communities, which was given a budget of 14 million euros – the third biggest budget of any ministry. In addition, Patriarch Pavle, the head of the Serbian Orthodox Church, agreed to accept the 4.2 million euros which had been offered by the Kosovar government in the summer of 2004 for the repair of damage inficted by rioters on Orthodox churches in March 2004 (*IHT*, 15 April 2005, p. 6).

There were three synchronized bomb blasts in central Pristina on 2 July 2005 (at the UNMIK headquarters, at the Kosova headquarters of the OSCE and at Kosova's parliament building), but no one was injured. In addition, a government building shared with the Serbian Democratic Party in the northern town of Zubin Potok was damaged by a bomb explosion on 4 July. The bombs were aimed at impeding Kosova's path towards independence from Serbia, according to President Rugova and Prime Minister Kosumi. Such violence was calculated to damage the chances of a positive evaluation of Kosova's readiness for self-government by the Norwegian diplomat, lawyer and 'special envoy' Kai Eide, to whom the UN secretary-general KofAnnan had entrusted the task of assessing whether Kosova had made sufficient advances on democratic an human rights 'standards' to start negotiations on its future 'status'. Eide's review was scheduled for completion by September 2005 (*IHT*, 4 and 5 July 2005, pp. 3–4). The report was expected to assess whether sufficient steps had been taken to establish functioning democratic institutions, to protect minority rights, to promote economic development, to ensure the rule of law, to provide freedom of movement and to guarantee property rights (*IHT*, 8 October 2005, p. 3).

Kai Eide submitted his report on 4 October 2005 and recommended an early start to 'final-status' negotiations. On 7 October Ko Annan announced that he would notify the UN Security Council that he wanted to start discussions on the status of Kosova: 'The question concerns independence or autonomy . . . Naturally, I cannot say now what the result will be . . . The question of independence is on the table, the question of autonomy is on the table' (*IHT*, 7 and 8 October 2005, p. 3). On 24 October the UN Security Council decided to initiate formal 'final status' nego tiations on Kosova, which were considered most likely to lead to so-called 'conditional independence' or 'independence without full sovereignty' for Kosova. The UN secretary-general Kof Annan announced that Finland's former president and veteran 'Balkan specialist' Martti Ahtisaari was to be his special envoy in charge of these negotiations (*The Guardian*, 25 October 2005, p. 18).

At the end of November 2005 the ICTY for the first time convicted a former KLA insurgent of murder, torture and cruel treatment during the KLA insurgency of 1997–9, although it acquitted two other such people. Haradin Bala was imprisoned for thirteen years, but Fatmir Limaj and Isak Musliu were acquitted of abducting and murdering suspected collaborators and Serbian civilians. The arrest of these three former insurgents in early 2003 had precipitated protests among Kosovars, many of whom regarded them as freedom fighters *IHT*, 1 December 2005, p. 7).

President Ibrahim Rugova died of lung cancer at the age of sixty-one on 21 January 2006. The UN-mediated talks on Kosova's future status had been scheduled to start in Vienna on 25 January, but their start was postponed by the UN until 20 February in order to allow the Kosovars time to choose a new president-cum-chief-negotiator. UN and Western leaders appealed for calm and unity in Kosova, while the Serbian government voiced concern that Rugova's successor might not share his commitment to non-violence. No other Kosovar politician had been held in such high regard. He had won international respect through his unswerving and principled adherence to peaceful opposition to Serb dominance, whereas many other Kosovars in leadership positions had risen to prominence though the KLA insurgency of 1997–9. Rugova's death therefore left a major vacuum in Kosova's faction-ridden political scene (*IHT*, 22 January 2006, pp. 1, 4–6). Since Rugova had not groomed a successor within the LDK, Nexhat Daci (the speaker of the Kosovar parliament) served as acting president until a successor was elected.

Very nearly half the population of Kosova turned out for Rugova's funeral. Almost 1 million people braved freezing temperatures. Unusually for the Balkans, Rugova's funeral was held without any religious rites. The ceremony was held at the 'martyr's graveyard' memorial complex, where other heroes of the Kosovar nationalist movement had also been buried. It was widely believed that Rugova's rumoured conversion to Catholicism was the main reason for the absence of religious rites. Although born into a Muslim familiy, he had not been seen in a mosque for years and, contrary to Muslim tradition, his body had lain in state in an open casket at the Kosova parliament building, but it was feared that non-Muslim funeral rites might have disturbed the predominantly Muslim Kosovars (*Independent*, 27 January 2006, p. 23). Only two representatives of Kosova's Serb minority attended the funeral. Serbia's president Boris Tadic asked to be allowed to attend, but his request was rejected because it referred to Kosova as 'part of Serbia's territorial patrimony' (*IHT*, 27 January 2006, p. 3).

Fatmir Sejdiu, a ffty-four-year-old law professor and secretary-general of the LDK, was unanimously elected as leader of the LDK on 30 January 2006. He was the only candidate. Western diplomats had pressed for rapid selection of Rugova's successor, fearing that a protracted contest could disrupt the talks on Kosova's 'fal status' (*IHT*, 31 January 2006, p. 8). The parliament elected Sejdiu as the province's new president on 10 February, paving the way for the temporarily postponed UN-mediated 'fina status' negotiations to start on 20 February. Sejdiu declared that independence from Serbia was non-negotiable, but he pledged to make Kosova a state guaranteeing minority rights and one that is 'at peace with itself and with its neighbours' (*IHT*, 11 February 2006, p. 6).

Prime Minister Bajram Kosumi, his deputy Adem Salihaj and the speaker of the Kosova assembly Nexhat Daci resigned on 1 March 2006. The Kosumi government had incurred international criticism for inefficiency and a perceived failure to take effective steps to build a democratic and multi-ethnic society capable of fully accommodating the Serb and other minorities in Kosova (Terdevice 2006).

The new prime minister was Agim Ceku, the former KLA military chief of staff, who since September 1999 had been in charge of the Kosova Protection Corps (KPC), mainly comprising former KLA members (see pp. 560–62). Ceku's skilful management of the conversion of the core of the KLA into the formally civilian KPC impressed Western diplomats and earned him a reputation for being competent, focused, hard-headed and easy to work with. Based on considerable experience of talking and dealing with him, both the EU foreign-policy supremo Javier Solana and the UNMIK chief administrator Søren Jessen-Petersen expected Ceku to be a leader with the strength and stature to reinvigorate Kosova's government, to give a high priority to 'decentralization'/minority rights and to persuade fellow Kosovars that formal independence would only be feasible if they were prepared genuinely to safeguard and respect the rights of minorities – especially Serbs. The Kosova assembly approved Ceku's appointment by sixty-five votes to thirty-three (the ten Serb representative were still boycotting the assembly), a larger margin than for his predecessors. His previous role as head of the KPC had precluded a party aff liation, but on becoming prime minister he joined the AAK and aimed to maintain the ruling LDK–AAK coalition. Unprecedentedly, he delivered his acceptance speech to the assembly not only in Albanian but also in Serbian and English. This was seen as a good portent. At the same time, the senior LDK member Kole Berisha became the new speaker of the Kosova assembly, and Lutf Haziri became the new deputy prime minister as well as local government minister. However, the two main Kosovar opposition parties (the PDK and ORA) argued that these changes were merely 'cosmetic', since all other ministers retained their posts (Terdevci 2006). In a subsequent interview, Ceku declared: 'I want to be seen as the prime minister of all Kosova's citizens' (*IHT*, 17 April 2006, p. 3). It remained to be seen whether this clean sweep of Kosova's top four leadership positions (including the presidency) would reinvigorate the governance of Kosova during 2006, the most critical year since 1999, or whether the sceptics would be vindicated.

In April 2006 Serbia's government, which was still paying the salaries of Serbian public employees in the Serbian enclaves in Kosova (enabling many to collect two salaries – one local and the other from Serbia), ordered all such persons to resign from any responsibilities with UNMIK on pain of forfeiting their Serbian paychecks (*IHT*, 17 April 2006, p. 3). Søren Jessen-Petersen resigned as UNMIK chief adminis trator in late June 2006, amid criticisms that he was too indulgent and close to Kosovar leaders and that Kosova was heading down a blind alley.

Concluding reflections on Kosova: towards an illusory 'independence'?

Notwithstanding Serbian nationalist and Serbian Orthodox insistence that Kosova remained an inalienable part of Serbia's 'territorial patrimony', by early 2006 it was fully conceivable that Kosova would gain some sort of 'conditional independence' in late 2006 or during 2007, despite substantive fears in some quarters that such a move could destabilize large parts of the Balkans yet again. The fears of renewed or increased destabilization in the Balkans arose because (i) such a move could revive or encourage the endeavours of the large ethnic Albanian minority in north-western

Macedonia to obtain increased autonomy, to obtain redefinition of the ROM as a dual-identity Slav/Albanian state, or even to secede from the ROM and unite either with an ethnically Albanian 'Greater Kosova' or with a 'Greater Albania', any one of which could undermine the fragile modus vivendi (the Ohrid framework agreement) negotiated between the ethnic Albanian and Macedonian Slav communities within the ROM in 2001; (ii) it could evoke pre-emptive or retaliatory military action by Serbia, since many (perhaps most) Serbs clearly regard Kosova as part of Serbia's 'sovereign', 'ancestral' and 'sacred' 'patrimony'; (iii) any of these possibilities would set precedents and examples which could further encourage the restive Bosnian Serbs and Bosnian Croats to try to secede from the highly fragile federated Republic of Bosnia and Herzegovina; (iv) such changes would further intensify the rivalries, mutual suspicions, tensions and uncertainties which already bedevil relations between peoples and states in the Balkans; and (v) by further increasing the fragmentation ('Balkan - ization') of the region into an even greater number of very small, relatively poor, mutually mistrustful and barely viable states, such changes and tensions would make it even more difficult to integrate the south-western Balkans (and perhaps even Bulgaria, Romania and Croatia) into the EU in due course. The least likely of these alarming scenarios, at least in the short term, are moves to establish a 'Greater Kosova' incorporating the north-western areas of the ROM inhabited mainly by ethnic Albanians, still less a 'Greater Albania', uniting Albania, Kosova and north-western Macedonia within a single state. The Albanian-born-and-educated writer and broadcaster Paulin Kola has published an important book which quite cogently argues that there has never been much practical interest in or support for the creation of a 'Greater Albania' within the present-day Republic of Albania (Kola 2003). However, public-opinion surveys conducted in late 2004 somewhat contradicted Kola's claims, finding 'a relatively high acceptance of the idea of a "Greater Albania" among the Albanian populations of both Kosova and Albania', although 'a great majority of Albanians in Macedonia reject the idea of dividing the country' and '77.5 % of ethnic Albanians (and 85 % of ethnic Macedonians) support the territorial integrity of the Macedonian state' (International Commission on the Balkans 2005: 17–18, 43–5). The least predictable factor was whether Serbia would peacefully acquiesce in international recognition of Kosova's formal sovereignty and independence, or whether it would react aggressively, especially after Montenegrin secession from the State Union.

On the other hand, it was equally conceivable that international recognition of an independent Kosovar state would create a fait accompli or 'facts on the ground', to which, after several rounds of ritual pro forma protests, its deeply disaffected neighbours would simply accommodate themselves, thereby defusing intra-regional tensions and rivalries and strengthening the very fragile stabilization that had occurred in the wake of the major insurgencies in Albania in 1997, in Kosova in 1997–9 and in the ROM in 2001. Furthermore, the UNMIK chief administrator Søren Jessen-Petersen cogently argued that, both politically and legally, 'the international community' and the UN Security Council's Resolution 1244 kept Kosova in a damaging state of limbo from June 1999 to 2005; that uncertainty about its future status acted as a major deterrent to investment and job creation in Kosova, for both foreign and domestic investors; and that 'early resolution of the status question will finally allow Kosov and the wider region to bury the past and focus on urgent social and economic priorities. It will also allow Kosova and its neighbours to speed up their journey toward Europe' (*IHT*, 24 October 2005, p. 8).

The great dilemma was that the outcomes could conceivably lean in either direction, with no means of knowing in advance what the repercussions would be. Unless backed up by a continuing pre-emptive commitment of quite substantial international peacekeeping forces to the region, there was some risk that international recognition of Kosova as an independent state could be as hazardous and destabilizing as was the over-hasty international recognition of Croatian and Slovene independence in January 1992 and Bosnian independence in April 1992. The strong hope in the EU (and to a lesser extent in the USA) was that the solemn promise given at the Thessaloniki European Council in June 2003, that Serbia, Macedonia and Bosnia would eventually be included in the EU, would prove sufficiently enticing and conducive to 'good conduct' to enable the recognition of Kosova's 'conditional independence' to take place without causing major ructions among its neighbours. Unfortunately, this leverage was jeopardized by the growing xenophobia and enlargement fatigue in most of the EU states, combined with major uncertainties over whether the EU states would agree on and ratify a new EU treaty to facilitate furter EUenlargement. According to the EU Treaty of Nice, agreed in 2000 and ratified in 2001, such a treaty was the sin qua non for any further enlargement of the EU beyond twenty-seven member states – i.e., beyond Bulgaria and Romania. As a result, the promise of eventual EU membership was in danger of ceasing to be an incentive which the EU could offer to the western Balkan states with much conviction, credibility or certainty. Indeed, it might already have become undeliverable, and there were growing risks that this could seriously diminish the chances of a harmonious settlement of the four major unresolved 'f nal status' issues in the Balkans: the future status of Kosova and Montenegro and the future cohesion (or otherwise) of Bosnia and the ROM.

Even more to the point, even if Kosova were to attain some sort of conditional independence in late 2006 or during 2007, that would mark only *the beginning* (not the end) of grim and protracted struggles to resolve its truly appalling problems and to surmount its de-facto economic, political and military dependency upon the West for its very existence. Since the 1980s, Kosova's economy has been in dire straits. It is not even remotely viable as the economy of a genuinely independent (i.e., self-supporting) state. According to Kosova's own statistical off ce, 57 per cent of the population of working age was unemployed in December 2002, and the number of recorded unemployed continued to rise steadily from then until late 2005 (*Kosova-report*, 13 December 2005). During 2005, estimates of Kosova's unemployment rate ranged from 30 per cent to 70 per cent, the government was near-bankrupt, and the economy was expected to contract by a further 2 per cent, having contracted steadily since 2003 (*IHT*, 8 October 2005, p. 3).

In 2004 a hard-headed UN-sponsored assessment of the state of Kosova's economy arrived at some appallingly bleak conclusions: 'apart from building materials, some furniture production and a small food-processing sector, there is hardly any local manufacturing'; any economic recovery that had taken place since 1999 had taken the form of foreign-aid-funded public construction, public administration and retailing; any 'GDP growth in Kosova's economy was driven by external transfers, rather than ... any lasting increase in the productivity of Kosova's enterprises', and was 'therefore unsustainable'; in 2003 'Kosova's imports totalled €968.5 million, while exports (mostly mushrooms, timber and scrap metal) amounted to only€36.3 million'; besides foreign aid, nearly half of Kosova's total income in 2002 came in the form of remittances sent home by the Kosovar diaspora; 'Kosovo households received more cash income from relatives abroad than they did from working in Kosovo'; but, 'with the route to new emigration to the EU now blocked, there is a substantial risk that remittance income will decline in the coming years'; and finally, even including thos engaged in subsistence agriculture and in the

> large grey sectors in construction, trade and services, the total employment for Kosovo is only 325,000, whereas the working age population is around one million. This means that the employment rate (i.e. the numbers employed expressed as a percentage of the working age population) is less than a third . . . Every person employed is obliged to support five or six household members. In this environment, making household savings to finance business investment becomes extremely difficult . . . At the same time, Kosovo has the youngest population in Europe, with 36,000 [additional] young people pressing onto the labour market every year. There is simply no possibility that domestic employment creation will absorb this increase in the labour supply in the near future

As a result, 'the next generation of young Kosovars has very little to look forward to' (Bradley and Knaus 2004: 7–11). No wonder the 'international community' and UNMIK were in such a hurry by 2005 to shut up shop and pull out. The only burgeoning Kosovar businesses were organized crime and the sex trade, no doubt partly because they involved very low capital overheads, while the previous external escape hatches for Kosova's rapidly multiplying surplus people were being ever more tightly closed by mounting (increasingly xenophobic) Western immigration restrictions.

There have been well-founded fears that this dire economic situation could severely exacerbate or even reignite the Balkans' still simmering inter-ethnic tensions. In April 2005 the International Commission on the Balkans rightly emphasized that the resurgence of inter-ethnic unrest in Kosova in March 2004 was a f ashing warning-light:

> the status quo is not only unsustainable, it might also drive the region towards a new period of highly dangerous instability . . . Time is running out in Kosova. The international community has clearly failed in its attempts to bring security and development to the province . . . The events of March 2004 amounted to the strongest signal yet that the situation could explode. Since then UNMIK has demonstrated neither the capacity nor the courage to reverse this trend. Serbs in Kosova are living imprisoned in their enclaves with no freedom of movement, no jobs, and with neither hope nor opportunity for meaningful integration into Kosova society . . . The lack of leadership in Belgrade has contributed to the plight of the Kosova Serbs . . . The Albanian leadership in Kosova must also share its part of the blame for failing to show any real willingness to engage in a process of reconciliation and the development of multi-ethnic institutions.
>
> (International Commission on the Balkans, 2005: 19–20)

All of the major players, as well as the results of their activities, come out of these assessments very badly. The UN Security Council decision on 24 October 2005 to initiate formal 'final status' negotiations on Kosova was thus made *amid and despite* grave doubts over its economic and political viability as a state. At that time Kosova was in no sense 'ripe' or 'ready' for independence, nor had it made much meaningful headway towards meeting the desired standards of democracy, rule of law, respect and protection for human and minority rights, or even the most minimal personal security (see ICG 2005a: 4, 8–10). Rather, the decision to initiate negotiations to settle Kosova's final status was merely based on correct (but frighteningly negative) percep tions that the existing arrangements had failed, were not working or had become untenable. The UN decision to move towards some form of independent statehood for Kosova was thus an attempt by the 'international community' to extricate itself from this costly and highly embarrassing impasse by offloading ultimate responsibilit for managing the nightmarish mess which it had inherited and perpetuated on to Kosovar elites, which had thus far exhibited much greater eagerness to exercise perquisites and patronage than responsibility and respect for minority rights. The nascent Kosovar state was therefore most likely to remain entrapped not only in and by the evils of unreconstructed, corrupt, clientelistic and clannish ethnic collectivism and 'verticality of power', but also in and by chronic economic, political and military dependence on the West. As far ahead as could be foreseen, Kosova's economy and the state which it was*unable* to support through its own meagre resources were bound to remain dependent upon a far from dependable Western life-support machine.

It does not necessarily follow that any decision to grant Kosova conditional inde-pendence would be wrong or stupid, but it needs to be borne in mind that the degrees of formal independence and sovereignty which could be granted to Kosova will be even more illusory, deceptive and insubstantial than usual. At most, Kosova will be what Robert Jackson (1993) aptly termed a 'quasi-state'. Moreover, Kosova is most likely to remain a pressure-cooker in grave danger of exploding; and, if it does explode, its contents are likely to get splattered across a Europe which is so self-absorbed and so engorged in consumerism that it barely notices the dire problems which are brewing and festering in its own backyard.

11 The post-Communist Balkans, the West and the EU

Major challenges and contradictions between rhetoric and reality

The central political and economic challenges (some would say requirements) in the post-Communist Balkan states, as in most of the former Soviet republics, are to move away from the ascendancy of often gangsterish 'power clans' based upon massive and clientelistic power relations and corruption, the primacy of 'ethnic collectivism' and what Russians call 'the verticality of authority', towards 'horizontally structured' civil societies and civil economies based upon limited government, the rule of law and 'level playing fields'. As this book has repeatedly argued, such changes are require to lay the indispensable foundations for more liberal, accountable and law-governed forms of democracy and capitalism. Since 1999, the prospect of eventual EU membership has been giving the formerly Communist-ruled Balkan countries the most powerful opportunities, incentives, support and political leverage to make these very diff cult changes. This is the main reason why such changes have latterly been making so much more headway in the Balkans than in most of the former Soviet republics, which have been given much less reason to hope that they can realistically aspire to EU membership in the foreseeable future (although that hasn't stopped some of the latter from indulging in a lot of wishful thinking).

Up to a point, it is necessary to insist that the post-Communist Balkan states must 'put their own houses in order' first, as a precondition for entry into the EU, becaus it is of paramount importance for the EU to maintain its own institutional viability – otherwise, it will cease to function effectively and all parties (even the new members) will lose out. Nevertheless, this must not be allowed to obscure the important (albeit paradoxical) fact that the post-Communist Balkan states can best be assisted to put their houses more fully in order by admitting them to the EU and its stringent rules and disciplines, which is a strong argument for admitting them sooner rather than later. The resultant change of context and transformation of power structures is what will most fully enable them to escape the vicious circles of the dysfunctional power struc tures, power relations, behaviour and practices which they have inherited from past regimes, whether Byzantine, Ottoman, nationalist or Communist. Balkan political, social and economic development has been most seriously impaired by these power structures, together with the dysfunctional incentive and opportunity structures which they fostered, rather than by the allegedly dysfunctional attributes and consequences of Balkan culture, mentalities, attitudes or behaviour, which are most likely to be profoundly altered by entry into the EU. Change those power structures and power relations, and societal incentive structures, opportunity structures, mentalities, mindsets and attitudes will gradually adjust to the new order. The growing commodifcation of culture(s) and identities reinforces this (See Bideleux 2001b: 20–2).

Since mid-1999, the EU Commission and nearly all the governments of EU member states have demonstrated a growing determination to assess all applicants strictly in accordance with defensible and transparent criteria: the 1993 'Copenhagen criteria', which stipulated 'stability of institutions guaranteeing democracy, the rule of law, human rights and respect for and protection of minorities, the existence of a functioning market economy as well as the capacity to cope with competitive pressure and market forces within the Union', along with 'the candidate's capacity to take on the obligations of membership', supplemented by the 1995 'Madrid criteria', which stipulated that new members must possess the administrative-cum-judicial capacity to implement and comply with the obligations of membership (primarily the 80,000 pages of EU legislation, the *acquis communautaire*). This is a relatively fair and square way of dealing with the candidate countries. They have been clearly notified where the goal posts are and what they need to do to become eligible for membership. However, it also needs to be much more fully recognized that this mode of enlargement is massively regressive in the sense that it places most of the enormous 'burdens of adjustment' on Europe's poorest and most troubled countries rather than on its richest and most stable and comfortable ones. Greatly increased 'pre-accession aid' for candidate states would help to mitigate this huge intrinsic imbalance.

In each of the new member states, as well as in the current and prospective candidate states, the 'Copenhagen criteria' and 'Madrid criteria' have helped to foster growing cross-party consensuses on macro-economic policies, privatization, restructuring of institutions and industries, judicial and legal reform, and promotion and protection of human and minority rights, which in turn has helped to promote the rule of law, equal citizenship (equal civil rights and equality before the law), political stability, democracy and the development of more 'level playing fields' and more fully marketized and liberalized economies. This in turn has helped slowly to restructure and reorientate these candidate countries away from the prevalence of 'vertical' power relations and power structures, from the primacy of 'primordial' ethno-cultural ties and from clientelistic and 'ethnic collectivist' conceptions of the polity, towards stronger horizontally structured impersonal ties and civil societies and civil economies based upon the rule of law.

The Copenhagen European Council in December 2002, which decided to allow the eight East Central European states to enter the EU in May 2004, also decided that Bulgaria and Romania would be admitted either in 2007 or, if it were to be decided in October 2006 that they were not yet ready, in 2008. At the Thessaloniki European Council held in June 2003, the governments of the EU-15 committed themselves in principle to gradually integrating the western Balkan states (Croatia, Albania, Serbia–Montenegro–Kosova, Macedonia, and Bosnia and Herzegovina) into the EU in unspecified ways in due course, albeit without making any binding commitment to precise timescales. In October 2005 it was decided to allow Croatia (along with Turkey) to start official membership negotiations in early 2006, with a view to potentia Croatian entry in 2009, and to recognize Macedonia as an off cial candidate for EU membership, although no timetable was as yet agreed for the start of formal member ship negotiations. In October 2005, moreover, the EU also initiated formal negotiations for SAAs with Serbia and Montenegro. Bosnia was considered not yet ready to begin such negotiations but Albania in February 2006 signed an SAA, ratified by the EU i June 2006.

The EU decision to grant official candidate status in October 2005 to the ROM which had been the poorest of the former Yugoslav republics, experienced a massive insurgency in 2001 and still had a 37 per cent unemployment rate in 2004, sent a strong signal to other western Balkan states that EU membership was a credible aspiration.

Economically, by imparting greater certainty of its future access to rich markets and inclusion in very robust and stable EU-wide frameworks of rules and policies, it was likely to encourage both foreign and domestic investors to invest in the republic with greater confidence. It also gave the ROM access to significant EU pre-accession fund

The significance of Europe's emerging supranational cosmopolitan legal order

The emerging supranational cosmopolitan legal order of the EU is consummating the shift from an 'old Europe' of often primordial 'vertical' power relations and power structures, to a 'new Europe' based on the 'horizontally structured' ties of civil association and rule of law, which are the sine qua non of any truly *liberal* democracy and *liberal* capitalism. It is in this regard that both the requirements and the consequences of EU membership can do most to transform the Balkan polities, by fostering 'horizontally structured' civil societies and civil economies based on the rule of law, equal civil rights for all permanent residents, and the equality of all individuals before the law, for the frst time after more than 2,000 years of unbroken 'verticality of power'.

EU membership would make it easier for the Balkan peoples and states to transcend the limitations of the nation-state and 'ethnic collectivism' by incorporating them into the large, stable, predictable and much more commodious framework of a resilient supranational cosmopolitan legal order within which every person enjoys full civil and legal equality as a member of an ethnic and religious minority – there being no ethnic or religious group remotely large enough to dominate the EU (even Germany, the largest member, now makes up less than a quarter of the population of the enlarged EU). Within the EU, all citizens increasingly enjoy the same fundamental rights and liberties and are increasingly subject to the same laws and obligations, because EU legislation now accounts for well over half of all the laws applicable within its member states. The nation-state, no matter how it is internally structured and no matter how fully it is committed to the recognition and protection of minority-group rights, always contains dominant and subordinate (under-privileged) ethnic and religious groups. No matter how 'liberal' or 'democratic' a liberal democracy might become, its laws are still likely to embody the interests, preferences and aspirations of the dominant ethnic, religious or racial group and to give less weight or consideration to those of minority groups. Legislation to protect and respect minority rights does not eliminate the underlying problem, but merely discourages it from baring its claws too blatantly. By contrast, even though it has not succeeded in muzzling European racism and Islamophobia, the EU framework has the capacity to transcend and do away with the distinction between dominant and subordinate ethnic and religious groups. In the words of Romano Prodi, the former president of its commission, the EU offers a 'model of a consensual pooling of sovereignty in which every one of us accepts to belong to a minority' (Prodi 2000: 7). This is how EU membership can most effectively help to liberate the prospective Balkan members of the EU from the baleful legacies of ethnic and religious collectivism (including the nationalist doctrines which were largely imported from the West), in much the same way that it is doing for most of the peoples and states in Western and East Central Europe.

The relatively autonomous forms of liberal democracy which are widely (but perhaps mistakenly) thought to have prevailed in Western Europe from the late 1940s to the 1970s are increasingly being challenged by the mutually reinforcing impact of globalization, economic liberalization, privatization, regional integration, the growth of regulatory and judicialized governance, and the dilution and growing fragmentation of the specifically 'national' or 'nationwide' identities, cultures and political constituencies which previously helped 'national' democracies to cohere. The self-styled liberal democracies in Western Europe have never been much more than various forms of 'elective oligarchy' (Burnheim 1985), but latterly the future survival of even this relatively meagre and formal version of liberal democracy is increasingly in jeopardy. Regional integration may have contributed in some small measure to the erosion or restriction of the scope for representative liberal democracy in Europe and hence to the mounting concern about 'democratic deficits'. However, regional integratio is only one of many factors involved. By way of compensation, the existence of the EU and its capacity for entrenching fundamental rights and freedoms within a strong overarching legal framework offers the most promising means of *mitigating* the seemingly inexorable reductions in the scope for democratic control, scrutiny, accountability and deliberation, which are resulting from forces and trends which either have escaped or are simply beyond the control of Europe's peoples, states and democratic mechanisms.

The EU is essentially a supranational legal order which has been consensually nego tiated between its member states. The classic hallmarks of statehood are monopolies or near-monopolies of the means of coercion (organized violence), taxation, public education (identity formation), and adjudication of disputes between citizens. The EU remains a long way from possessing any of these crucial monopolies or near-monopolies, even though it has acquired *some* of the emblems of statehood (legislative and regulatory powers, a flag, an anthem and a currency). The EU is not and has never been conceived as a supranational form of European *democratic* polity, for the perfectly sound reason that such a polity is almost certainly even less realizable at the supranational level than it has been within Europe's so-called nation-states. No useful purpose can be served by calling for the EU to become more democratic or by pretending that it already is more democratic than it is really capable of being. Dishonest or deluded calls and pretences of this sort can only further increase popular cynicism and misgivings towards it, without substantially reducing or mitigating the underlying problems. What EU citizens could usefully be made much more aware of is the major degree to which its supranational legal order now offers the most robust and free-standing 'horizontal' framework for the legal protection of fundamental rights and freedoms in existence anywhere in the world. It isn't merely based on the rule of law. *It is the rule of law – nothing more, nothing less.* To a unique degree, that is its def ning feature and its greatest advantage over any other system of governance yet devised. This has powerfully reinforced and contributed to the growing dispersal and decentring of power, as well as the promotion of European peace and prosperity, thereby assisting the survival of whatever degrees of liberal democratic control, scrutiny, participation and accountability are still possible at the national and subnational levels in a world increasingly dominated by hugely powerful transnational, unelected and unaccountable global economic forces and highly networked but also largely unaccountable 'information societies'. The 'rule certainty' fostered by the EU is the basis of an unprecedentedly impersonal, impartial and pervasive *rule of law*, which in turn is the foundation stone of limited government, the decentring and dispersal of power, equality before the law, and security of person, property and contract – in a word, liberalism. It is also fostering a new 'culture of rights' (civil and legal), which is revolutionizing the roles of the judiciary and law in the new EU member states in East Central Europe (Drucker and Drukerova 2005). It can do the same in the Balkans.

The legitimating purpose of the EU is not the construction of some sort of supra-national democratic polity – that is an unrealizable utopian dream, rendered impossible by (among other things) the EU's sheer size, its unavoidable governmental and legal complexity, and the absence of a united EU-wide *demos* to serve as the basis of an EU-wide democratic polity. Nor is its legitimating purpose to try to impose the will, the values or the aspirations of a majoritarian coalition of groups and interests on Europe's variously conceived minorities – this would simply represent a highly dysfunctional supranational 'tyranny of the majority'. Instead, the legitimating pur-poses of the EU are (i) to maintain a strong liberal-cosmopolitan supranational legal framework within which a rich, productive and dynamic diversity of groups and interests can coexist peacefully and can each pursue or promote their own chosen projects and aspirations with the minimum of mutual impairment, friction and conflict and (ii) thereby to facilitate the survival of whatever degree of liberal democratic control, scrutiny, participation and accountability is still possible at the national and subnational levels. The EU exists to safeguard, accommodate and profit from the rich cultural, political, ideological, social and scientific *diversity* which has been the hallmark and saving grace of modern Europe, rather than to foster or impose common or uniform 'European' goals and values and a common European cultural identity. Its oft-repeated goal is to promote an emphatically pluralist 'ever-closer union of European peoples', not to foster a unitary European people (*demos*). Thus the core purpose of the EU is not to promote a common European identity, or a common European identity, or a common European culture, or even common European values, as so many Europhiles (and Europhobes!) misguidedly believe, but rather to make possible the thriving and peaceful coexistence of a rich and vibrant diversity of identities, cultures and values.

The development of the EU as a supranational legal order, combined with the effects of globalization, economic liberalization and privatization, is in effect leading its member states towards liberal conceptions of limited government and the rule of law, resting upon a legal order whose primary functions are to foster high levels of rule-certainty, stable expectations, low-risk premia, security of persons and property, 'level playing fields', toleration, non-discrimination and increased legal protection of individual rights and liberties. There are no foolproof protections but these are probably the strongest ones.

The nature of the supranational legal order which has gradually emerged in Europe since the sixteenth- and seventeenth-century 'wars of religion', and which was put on a much stronger footing by the founding of the European communities during the 1950s, has been shaped by the necessity 'to work out principles of coexistence among individuals and groups committed to different conceptions of truth and the good', and by 'the gradual discovery that, in the absence of agreement on ends, agreement on procedures is required if destructive conflict is to be avoided' (Nardin 1983: 318). In practice the twenty-fve member states of the EU are united *not* by common projects and shared interests or values, but rather by their acceptance that they are all equal members of a civil association defined by adherence to a common set of rules, law and procedures designed to allow each to pursue their own interests and goals with the minimum of mutual impairment, friction and conflict

The value of changing the framework within which inter-communal problems and conflicts are to be resolved

The problems of 'ethnic collectivism' and inter-communal conflict which have afflict the Balkans cannot be fully resolved or overcome within the unduly constrictive or 'boxed in' framework of the sovereign nation-state. They can only be fully resolved by radically changing the framework within which the peoples involved coexist, by placing them on completely equal legal and civil footings within the cosmopolitan supranational legal order and 'level playing field' which constitute the essence of th EU, which is little more or less than the rule of law. The ongoing construction of a supranational cosmopolitan legal order, rather than the pursuit of illusory utopian conceptions of 'cosmopolitan democracy' or the potentially dangerous legal protection of group rights, is the way forward for the EU and the basis on which it can help to defuse many (albeit not all) of Europe's potentially explosive inter-communal problems. Enlarging the framework of coexistence to the point where no single group can dominate and every group is a minority offers the maximum scope for devising, adopting and elaborating institutions, policies and laws that can come closest to achieving impartiality between such groups. That is the great unsung virtue of the EU and its major contribution to *the very possibility* of a truly civilized coexistence or *convivencia* in Europe. A spurious 'consensus on values' is *not* what Europe needs. The growing ethnic, racial and religious diversity of most European societies makes that largely unattainable, even if it were desirable. But such a consensus, a Europe based on 'common values', is not even desirable, because that would reduce the cultural and political pluralism which has been the foundation stone of European liberalism and European economic, scientif and technological creativity and dynamism (Jones 1983; Nardin 1983). Rather, what Europe needs are common institutions and a common legal/procedural framework within which differences and conf icts of interests and values can be negotiated. 'We do not need common values in order to live together in peace. We need common institutions in which many forms of life can coexist' (Gray 2000: 6).

The problems of ethnic and religious collectivism and inter-communal conflict i the Balkans can be mitigated or alleviated, but they cannot ever be fully resolved or surmounted within the confining framework of the nation-state, regardless of whethe it is 'civic', 'ethnic', 'consociational' or even federal. Such problems can only be radically surmounted or defused by moving beyond the highly problematic and constricting framework of the nation-state to the much larger, more commodious and more cosmopolitan supranational legal framework of the EU, wherein (i) for inescapable demographic reasons, there can be no dominant ethnic group and therefore everyone is on the same footing in being part of a minority group; and (ii) everyone, irrespective of ethnicity, colour or creed, is increasingly subject to the same body of secular and cosmopolitan EU rules, norms and laws.

This approach can be seen as a further application of Jean Monnet's approach to resolving Europe's problems. In his *Mémoires,* Monnet wrote that

> I understood that it was often vain to try to resolve problems which did not exist on their own but were the product of circumstances. It is only by changing the circumstances that we can change the situation of which they are the causes. Rather than using up my energy on the things which offered the most resistance, I got into the habit of looking for what it was in the environment that created this resistance in the first place and then changing it

(Monnet 1976: 420–1).

The implication is that, if problems cannot be resolved within the parameters of the nation-state, then one must break out of the impasse by changing the framework. This is the biggest benefit which inclusion in the EU could offer to the Balkans

The EU implicitly rests upon the belief that societies should primarily be based upon and held together by impersonal law, interests and contractual relations of the 'civil' and 'horizontal' Lockean variety, rather than by 'vertical' power relations, power structures and clientelistic or 'primordial' ties of religion, race, ethnicity and kinship. Religious, ethnic and racial collectivism are fundamentally at odds with the civil liberal-cosmopolitan legal order, ethos and requirements of the EU. In the long term, the European integration project could be seriously damaged or even jeopardized if it were to admit too many societies which continue to be based upon and held together by such 'vertical' power relations, power structures, clientelism and primordial ties. Changing the basis of Balkan societies is proving very diffcult, but it is essential and this may be more palatable and somewhat easier to achieve *after* their admission to the EU than while they are still waiting to be admitted.

The EU has often been likened to the Austro-Hungarian Empire, which was similarly held together by a supranational rule of law and in which no single ethnic group held an absolute majority – i.e., every group was a minority group. However, the cosmo politan universalism of the EU is a major advance on the ethnic particularism, the parochial narrow-mindedness, widespread religious bigotry and segregation, and the often-stultifying Catholic absolutism and Catholic collectivism which were hallmarks of the Habsburg monarchy, which *did* have dominant (albeit non-majoritarian) ethnic groups and a dominant collectivist religion. EU law, which has direct effect and supremacy in the member states, is the only currently existing legal framework in the world within which 'cosmopolitan law-enforcement' can be rendered fully operational.

Thomas Mann famously called for the 'Europeanization of Germany' as a safeguard against the 'Germanization of Europe', and this was central to German policy from Adenauer to Kohl. Germany became enmeshed and embedded in 'European' political and economic structures in order to avert any future resurgence of the old demons of German nationalism and racism. By the same token, the most valuable form of Europeanization of the Balkan Peninsula will be to enmesh and embed it in larger European political and economic structures which will help to keep its own 'inner demons' of religious and ethnic collectivism at bay. The resultant shift of emphasis from unfettered sovereignty and representative democracy to a supranational liberal legal order that sets considerable prudential limits on national sovereignty and democ racy, far from signifying some huge sacrifce or retrograde step (as many Europhobes and radical democrats would have us believe), is actually the greatest gift that the Western European states can confer on their 'eastern cousins'. The alternatives foregone are only illusions (or delusions) of national sovereignty, mere fig leaves that barely conceal the reality of inescapable 'democratic deficits' at all levels of governance (not just at the EU level), since all of Europe is becoming increasingly unable either to control or to hold to account global capitalism, a transnational security community (NATO), transnational firms and transnational flows of capital, information, ideas and technology.

Europe's potential 'tiger economies'

There are also major economic dimensions to the prospective integration of the post-Communist Balkan states into the EU. In 2004 the French car manufacturing firm

Renault, which bought Romania's state-owned Dacia car plant in 1999, launched the successful Dacia Logan model. It was planned to produce 250,000 of these cars and a further 150,000 assembly kits during 2005, targeting markets in East Central Europe, the Balkans, the CIS, Turkey and the Middle East. The cars were priced at only 5,700–8,000 euros (depending on choice of engine and fittings). The workforce at the Daci car plant were paid one-tenth of the wages of their West European counterparts (Ameriei 2004). This development, like the Czech Skoda car plant bought and relaunched by Volkswagen, vividly illustrates the potential for Balkan and East Central European countries to become Europe's 'tiger economies' on the basis of relocation of manufacturing from high-cost locations in Western Europe to low-cost ones further east. Balkan and East Central European workers may be as educated and skilled as their West European counterparts, yet they work for far lower wages and their strong drive to prosper makes many of them highly motivated and adaptable. The major impediments to relocation of sophisticated West European manufacturing operations to countries such as Romania (much more than to the more highly developed East Central European countries) lie in the serious inadequacies of their infrastructure and a shortage of fully dependable suppliers of the many bought-in inputs required by such operations. However, such constraints can to some degree be circumvented by building up fully integrated manufacturing complexes in and around the new production bases in the Balkans and East Central Europe. West European workers and trade unions understandably view such relocation of manufacturing eastwards with considerable apprehension, because it has already resulted in significant loss of manufacturing jobs in Western Europe, especially in high-cost Germany. The main response to such misgivings must be that service industries and knowledge-intensive industries already account for over 70 per cent of GDP in Western Europe, and that the economic future of high-income West European countries lies primarily in even greater specialization in service and knowledge-intensive activities – rather than in manufacturing, most of which can be done at much lower cost elsewhere. Relocating manufacturing eastwards to countries such as Romania represents a major net efficiency gain for Europe as whole, and thereby helps Europe to compete more effectively with much lower-waged producers in Asia and in the Americas. The Balkans and East Central Europe can provide an educated but still low-waged manufacturing workforce, while Western Europe can provide the requisite finance, technology, organizational know-how, design, marketing, distribution and other service- or knowledge-intensive products, while also reaping welfare gains from the increased availability of cheaper manu - factured goods from the east, whether for its own consumption or for export overseas. And the more that the Balkans and East Central Europe prosper on this basis, t he more valuable they can become as markets for West European products (mainly, but not exclusively, services). Luddite resistance to relocation of West European manufacturing to the Balkans and East Central Europe may not preserve West European manufacturing jobs for long, but is more likely to result simply in such jobs being lost altogether in the face of ever-intensifying competition from lower-waged producers outside Europe. It is partly for these reasons that a further enlarged and fully integrated EU is much more likely to survive and prosper than one which continues to exclude the Balkans. The same logic favours the eventual/gradual inclusion of countries such as Turkey, Ukraine, Moldova, Georgia, Armenia and Azerbaijan as well.

Economically, the most important aspect of the EU's relations with the Balkan former Communist states is not the amount of EU aid and structural funding that is granted to them, but rather the degree to which these states are willing and able to sign up to and participate in the rules and practices of the EU. Successful transitions from largely state-run and state-owned industrial systems to decentralized market systems that foster autonomous entrepreneurial behaviour and decision-making not only depend upon the promotion of appropriate and effective macro-economic policies and economic infrastructure, but also require well-defined rules for integrating th decisions of decentralized agents. Most important of all is *rule certainty* for all economic agents, in order to stabilize expectations and thereby to reduce risk, risk premia, interest rates, the costs of borrowing and transaction costs, and to increase business confidence and both domestic and foreign investment. Private FDI can be especially valuable, in so far as it transfers technologies, products and management and marketing techniques, although at the same time we must beware of the ways in the major international financial organizations disgracefully and simplistically equate 'success with selling off everything possible to foreign (mainly Western) f rms, as discussed in Chapters 8 and 9 (pp. 462–3 and 503–4).

It is in these respects that EU membership and preparations for entry can do most to promote the development of market economies and a liberal order in the Balkans, even though in the process the scope for national democratic sovereignty and account ability is being and will continue to be curtailed in important respects. Both are reinforced by increased adherence to and confdence in the prevalence of rule-governed and law-governed behaviour. EU membership brings increased certainty, clarity, transparency, uniformity and impartiality with regard to the rules that will govern economic and political activity within and between its member states. These rules, which f gure prominently in the conditions of membership, offer reassurance and encourage ment to private entrepreneurs and investors. These have been the major factors in the huge inf ows of foreign capital into Spain, Portugal and Ireland since they became members of the European Community (even outweighing the economic benefits conferred by the more highly publicized infows of EU 'structural funds'). The scope for reaping such gains remains intrinsically greater for poorer countries and regions than for richer ones, provided they can muster and sustain the levels of fiscal and monetary discipline and entrepreneurial responsiveness that will allow them to participate fully in the EU's stringent but bracing supranational framework of law and rules. This, rather than the very limited EU 'financial transfers' (structural funding available, is the main reason to hope that the large disparities between rich and poor states can be reduced by EU membership. This is also a reason to admit the Balkan former Communist states to the EU as soon as feasible, without waiting for them fully to 'put their own houses in order' before entry. The widespread assumption that only advanced economies can master the disciplines and reap the benefits of the adven of the euro is nonsense. Montenegro has been using the euro as its main currency since 2002, Bulgaria is preparing to do so from 2010, and both Bulgaria and Macedonia have been operating 'currency boards' tied to the euro since 2002. These countries, rather than those that already have strong and stable currencies, are the ones that stand to gain the most from European monetary union increased stability and certainty, and reduced risk premia.

Caveats: contradictions between rhetoric and reality

So far, this concluding chapter has focused on the virtues of integrating the post-Communist Balkan states with the EU and the ways in which the EU can assist these states. However, it is also crucial to bear in mind the attendant rigours, downsides and contradictions between rhetoric and reality, if only to show greater awareness, sympathy and understanding for the predicament in which the post-Communist Balkan states are placed and the various barriers which have yet to be overcome.

EU assessments of the capacity and willingness of the post-Communist Balkan states to meet the so-called 'Copenhagen criteria' and the 'Madrid criteria' are likely to be very *stringent and exacting*, as has already been seen in the cases of Romania and Bulgaria, and there is *no guarantee* that any of these states will be admitted. Unfortunately, the longer that most of the Balkan states are obliged to wait before being admitted to the EU, the higher the entry requirements are likely to become and the larger and the more onerous the *acquis communautaire* will become. Furthermore, the larger the number of countries that *succeed* in gaining entry into the EU, the greater would be the relative marginalization of those left waiting outside it. This will make it all the more important to admit even the 'laggards' as soon as feasible, in order to minimize the duration of this interim period of growing exclusion and marginalization of non-members.

In addition, the EU's attempts to foster intra-regional stability, integration and economic growth among the post-Communist Balkan states (including Moldova) may well rest on unwarranted expectations. On 27 June 2001 the governments of Albania, Bosnia-Herzegovina, Bulgaria, Croatia, the ROM, Romania, the FRY and Moldova signed an agreement to liberalize trade in at least 90 per cent of goods trade between them, under the auspices of the EU's Stability Pact for South-eastern Europe, with the aim of enhancing intra-regional stability, integration and economic growth. However, mainly because of the predominant hub-and-spoke nature of the economic and political relationships between the EU and the Balkan states (not least because of the EU's insistence on dealing with each state individually/separately with regard to its gradual economic and political integration into the EU economy and civil association), it is inherently unlikely that very much intra-regional integration will be accomplished between the Balkan states until *after* (rather than *before*) their admission to full membership of the EU. This is consistent with the experience of the Iberian peninsula and (so far) East Central Europe. No matter how much the EU tries to *exhort* intra-regional Balkan integration, this is vastly outweighed by the powerful effects of dealing with each state individually/separately prior to granting full membership.

It is still widely assumed that the post-Communist Balkan states should only be allowed into the EU *after they have 'sorted out their problems'* – not before. This is a complacent and misconceived way of looking at their problems and predicaments. It is highly unlikely that their economic problems, the anxieties of their ethnic and religious minorities, their political fragilities, their social problems, their security anxieties, their law-and-order defcits and their civil-rights defcits can be substantially alleviated or overcome within narrowly 'national' frameworks.*'National' frameworks are part of the problem to be solved, not part of the solution.* Durable resolutions of their problems can probably only be attained within the broader, stronger, more commodious, more secure, more law-governed, more civil and more stable framework that membership of the EU and its supranational legal order can provide. Excluding these countries from the EU until they have 'sorted out their problems' will only cause their problems to fester and periodically erupt, to the detriment not only of their own populations (who have already suffered far more than was 'really necessary') but of Europe as a whole.

Admittedly, there could be considerable costs or risks in allowing these countries to join the EU in advance of their resolving their major economic, legal, ethnic and political problems, but there are even greater costs and risks attached to leaving them to 'stew in their own juices' outside the EU. As in the 1990s, the rest of Europe will continue to be unable to insulate itself from the fallout from these problems, and *only the EU has the capacity to break the vicious circles and to transcend the limited parameters and horizons within which these countries are currently trapped. They must therefore be allowed to enter the EU before long, in order to alter fundamentally the frameworks within which their problems are tackled and thus to deal with the root causes of those problems rather than merely with their outward symptoms or consequences.* Having argued along these lines since 2001 (Bideleux 2002a, 2002b and 2005a), it is encouraging to see that this line of reasoning has been adopted in the influential April 2005 report by the International Commission on *The Balkans in Europe's Future*.

Unfortunately, the so-called 'enlargement fatigue' expressed in the referenda in which the French and the Dutch rejected the proposed EU constitution in May and June 2005 respectively has made it less likely that Balkan states (other than Bulgaria, Romania and possibly Croatia) would be allowed to enter the EU in the near future, although for the time being the EU has courageously and wisely chosen to ignore this 'enlargement fatigue' and to persevere with preparations for further eastward enlargement (including Turkey). However, Croatia is now unlikely to be admitted until 2010, and the next entrants may have to wait until 2014. It will be tempting, and in some ways quite appropriate, to aim for a 'western Balkan enlargement' of the EU on 28 June 2014, the centenary of the assassination of Archduke Franz Ferdinand and his wife, because this event was the catalyst which precipitated the outbreak of a world war that profoundly changed the course of European and especially Balkan history. Many of the problems and conficts of the post-Communist Balkans have more to do with the 'unfinished business' of the First World War and its aftermath tha with the legacies of Communist rule. Indeed, even the advent of Communism as a major force in Balkan history owed a great deal to the consequences of the First World War, especially the Russian revolutions of 1917.

Western hypocrisy vis-à-vis Balkan criminal networks

It appears that the UN, the USA and the EU either do not understand or do not wish to understand the nature, depth and durability of the harm that they have inflicted o large numbers of mostly innocent people through the imposition of economic sanctions on belligerent or rogue states during the 1990s. The harm has been especially severe in the case of the Yugoslav successor states, where sanctions were not (and usually could not be) rigorously policed and enforced. Consequently huge and highly profiable opportunities were created for smugglers and criminal gangs to become rich and powerful through arms- and drug-traff cking, sanctions-busting, racketeering and dealing in contraband, to the vast long-term detriment of the great majority of the population in the countries subjected to sanctions. Once entrenched, these increasingly mafia like criminal networks are fearfully difficult to curb or uproot. They deeply corrup and gain growing control of many public institutions, run protection rackets and increasingly cow or intimidate much of the population. The UN, the USA and the EU have rubbed even more salt into these externally inflicted wounds when, instead o blaming themselves and the sanctions they have imposed for the growing subjection of these countries to pervasive control by criminal networks, they have usually had the brazen hypocrisy to defect all the 'blame' and to impose further 'punishment' on to the governments and populations of the targeted countries for allegedly being too 'soft' on the criminal activities, gangs, networks and corruption which these (mainly Western) economic sanctions have luxuriantly fostered, and from the long-term effects of which the targeted countries have a devil of a job escaping.

Admittedly, sound justifications *can sometimes* be put forward for the imposition of economic sanctions against countries or regimes that are perpetrating violent evils against their own or other countries' inhabitants, especially if such sanctions can achieve certain desired goals without recourse to outright military intervention and potentially greater human suffering and loss of life. However, in these cases it is then morally incumbent on the countries or organizations which arrogate to themselves the right to apply such sanctions also to accept in full their own responsibility (i) to police and enforce those sanctions very scrupulously and carefully; (ii) to minimize the likelihood that those sanctions will simply enrich and empower criminal gangs and networks that undermine and prey upon innocent people who are trying to make 'honest livings'; and (iii) after the perceived need for such sanctions has passed, to be prepared to provide and foot the bills for all the massive help which the successor governments and the populations of the targeted countries will almost always need and deserve in order to overcome the profoundly undermining, corrupting and criminalizing effects of those sanctions, instead of simply 'blaming' and 'punishing' those governments and populations for the resultant growth of criminal activity, mafia networks and large-scale corruption. The UN, USA and EU have exhibited deplorable propensities for repeatedly 'blaming' and 'punishing' the populations and successor governments of countries which they have subjected to crippling, corrupting and criminalizing sanctions for the pervasive and deeply undermining criminalization, brutalization and corruption which often directly results from such sanctions.

Not so Nice

The biggest potential obstacle to further 'eastward enlargement' of the EU is that the Treaty of Nice (agreed in December 2000) does not permit the EU to expand beyond twenty-seven members unless a new EU treaty is adopted and ratified in order to hel the EU cope with the pressures and strains of further enlargement. This means that all the strenuous efforts which the western Balkan states and Turkey are making in order to become eligible for EU membership and all the high hopes of eventual EU membership which the EU has actively aroused in the western Balkan states and Turkey since October 1999 (and even more strongly since June 2003 and October 2005) could yet prove to be false ones, if the existing EU members prove incapable of agreeing on and ratifying a new EU treaty – or, alternatively, if EU members opposed to further EU enlargement were to use non-ratif cation of such a treaty as a means of blocking further enlargement. If, for lack of a ratified treaty to facilitate further enlargement, the EU were to become unable to admit any more members after Bulgaria and Romania, that would mean that it had been negotiating with Turkey and the western Balkan states on a false prospectus, urging them towards an unattainable goal. This in turn would cause major crises within the western Balkan states and Turkey and in their relations with the EU states, from which they could take a decade or more to recover. If such a state of deadlock were to persist, the negative repercussions on political and economic morale and prospects in the western Balkan states and Turkey could inf ict incalculable damage on the whole region.

However, as the International Commission on the Balkans fully acknowledged in *The Balkans in Europe's Future* (2005), the still festering ethnic, legal, social and economic problems of these countries were very unlikely to subside or 'go away', and prosperous Western Europe is not able to insulate itself from the backwash from those problems, as it discovered during the 1990s. Therefore, the case for admitting these states by about 2014, in order to help resolve or defuse those problems, and for removing the legal and institutional obstacles to wider European integration and EU enlargement will have to be made as cogently as possible – both for the sake of the Balkans and Turkey and for the sake of Europe as a whole.

Under powerful pressure from West European xenophobic demands for increasingly stringent migration restrictions and asylum controls, the new south-eastern and eastern frontiers of the enlarged EU have been fortified and policed in a manne mildly reminiscent of the old 'iron curtain' or, even more aptly, the old *cordon sanitaire* established between Europe and the Ottoman Empire during the eighteenth and nineteenth centuries. This has been accomplished at considerable cost to the (relatively poor) new and prospective member states, as one of the many obligations they were required to accept as a condition of acceptance into the EU. While liberal-minded West Europeans like to blame this on the xenophobia of politicians and the media, the latter were mainly responding to public opinion. Xenophobic parties have been gaining strong electoral support in countries such as France, Italy, Belgium, the Netherlands, Denmark and Austria. Fear of West European xenophobia has induced the vast majority of West European governments to introduce increasingly tough restrictions on immigration (even from new member states, in blatant violation of the proclaimed liberal ethos of European integration) and to insist that new members follow suit. In some west European states where xenophobic parties are not yet strong (e.g., the UK and Spain), governments are nonetheless increasing immigration restrictions pre-emptively.

As a result of the new east–west barriers to movement which are being erected across Europe on the insistence of supposedly liberal West European states, those Balkan and East European states which were left stranded to the south and east of the EU's new frontiers are becoming even more marginalized and economically disadvan taged (relatively speaking) than they had been before the first 'eastward enlargement of the EU in May 2004 – not least because the eight East Central European countries to which they had enjoyed relatively unimpeded 'visa-free' access during the Communist era and the 1990s became full members the EU in May 2004, and as part of the conditions of admission to the EU, these new members were obliged to establish stringently policed new barriers (including expensive high-tech electronic surveillance systems) against potential 'illegal' immigration and asylum-seeking from the Balkans, Turkey and the CIS states, which were regarded as both sources and conduits for such 'illegal' migration. As a result, the official EU rhetoric and hype about *gradual integration* of the post-Communist Balkan states and Turkey with the EU is being contradicted by the grim reality of the EU states' actual growing restrictions on movement for the inhabitants of those states wishing to travel to the EU (whether for tourism, on business, as 'economic migrants' fleeing poverty and unemployment, o to some extent even for study). The high visa charges, other documentation costs, requirements of proof of pre-booked accommodation and return flights, requirement of proof of cash reserves and credit-worthiness, all add to the barriers to movement, which are keeping many would-be travellers and migrants increasingly 'bottled up' in places such as Kosova and Bosnia, unable to move in pursuit of greater opportunity.

This growing discrepancy between rhetoric and reality will foster increasing disillusionment and resentment towards the EU if it is not rectified

However, the biggest and the most uncomfortable of the various contradictions that have become ever more apparent during the writing of this book is the glaring discrepancy between the rhetoric of Western liberalism, democracy, equal rights and equal respect, on the one hand, and the harsh realities of arrogant, self-serving and paternalistic Western tutelage, on the other. The often damaging and humiliating degrees to which the post-Communist Balkan states have been 'told what to do', boxed in, patronized and used by innumerable highly paid Western officials and executive (often in the name of liberalism, democracy and human rights) is very disturbing. The degrees of tutelage have increased over time. During the early 1990s, the Balkan states were for the most part left to fend for themselves, and Westerners mainly conf ned themselves to offering gratuitous advice on matters on which they were often quite remarkably ill-equipped to do so. Since the Western intervention in the Bosnia conf ict in 1994–5, however, Western tutelage has gradually become more insistent and comprehensive. Since the Kosova war of March–June 1999, the West has gone to excess in the degrees to which it has tried to 'micro-manage' and dictate the processes of change in the Balkans described in this book. Bosnia and Kosova have latterly been 'lorded over' by Western quasi-colonial regimes. The EU states, the EU itself, the ICTY, the USA and the international financial institutions have become eve more insistently prescriptive and inclined to monitor very closely the degrees to which the post-Communist Balkan states are complying with their demands, so that they can be rewarded or punished as the West sees fit. The scale and intensity of these operations has latterly been quite breathtaking, and we can only imagine how deeply such comprehensive and high-handed Western tutelage is resented. Unfortunately, given the enormous disparities in wealth and power between Western and post-Communist Balkan states, it is difficult to see how these very unequal and condescending power relations can be avoided or overcome, but we can at least increase awareness of what is occurring.

This in no way downplays the importance of the changes in internal power relations and power structures which have been highlighted as the central theme of this book, nor the importance of the prospect of EU membership in helping to bring these changes about. The existence of the EU and pursuit of EU membership have become the major sources of change, both by altering the incentive and opportunity structures for Balkan elites and by giving them greatly increased political and economic leverage to bring about highly signif cant reform and restructuring of post-Communist Balkan polities, economies and societies. However, it is possible to differentiate between the important new structural contexts, incentives, opportunities and leverage, which are the main drivers of change, and the more mixed blessings of the Western officials, executives interests, attitudes and behaviour involved in creating the new structures, incentives, opportunities and leverage. Western missionary, crusading and imperialist traditions die hard, it seems, especially in relation to the Balkans.

Bibliography

Periodicals and reports

Newspapers, journals and reports regularly cited in the text have been abbreviated as follows:

BCE   *Business Central Europe*
CDPSP   Current Digest of Post-Soviet Press
DIW   Deutsches Institut für Wirtschaftsforschung (Berlin)
EEN   *Eastern Europe Newsletter* (latterly renamed *Eastern Europe*)
EBRD   European Bank for Reconstruction and Development
EIU   Economist Intelligence Unit
FEER   *Far Eastern Economic Review*
ICG   International Crisis Group reports
IMF (*WEO*) International Monetary Fund *World Economic Outlook*
FT   *Financial Times*
IHT   *International Herald Tribune*
NYRB   *New York Review of Books*
TOL   Transitions Online (www.tol.cz)
UN ECE   United Nations Economic Commission for Europe

Books and journals

Aagh, A. (1998) *The Politics of Central Europe*, London: Sage Publications.
Ali, R. and Lifschultz, L. (1994) 'Why Bosnia?', *Third World Quarterly*, vol. 15, no. 3.
Allcock, J. (2000a) 'Constructing the Balkans', in Allcock and Young (eds) (2000), pp. 217–40.
—— (2000b) *Explaining Yugoslavia*, New York: Columbia University Press.
Allcock, J. and Young, A. (2000) *Black Lambs and Grey Falcons: Women Travelling in the Balkans*, Oxford: Berghahn Books.
Almond, M. (1994) *Europe's Backyard War: The War in the Balkans*, London: Mandarin.
Ameriei, R. (2004) 'Romania: The Not-Quite 5000-Euro Car', TOL, 22 September.
—— (2005a) 'Romania: Ghosts from the Past', TOL, 20 June.
—— (2005b) 'Romania: Limited Exit', TOL, 14 October.
—— (2005c) 'Romania: Optimism and Caution', TOL, 3 November.
—— (2006) 'Romania: The Persistence of Scandal', TOL, 23 January.
Andric, I. (1945, 1949) *The Bridge over the Drina*, Belgrade: Prosveta and London: George Allen & Unwin.
Åslund, A. and Sjöberg, Ö. (1991)*Privatization and Transition to Market Economy in Albania*, Stockholm: Stockholm Institute of Soviet and East European Economics, Working Paper no. 27.
Bakic-Hayden, M. (1995) 'Nesting Orientalisms: The Case of Former Yugoslavia', *Slavic Review*, vol. 54, no. 4, pp. 917–31.

Banac, I. (1984) *The National Question in Yugoslavia*, Ithaca, NY: Cornell University Press.

Bartlett, W. (1996) 'From Reform to Crisis: Economic Impacts of Secession, War and Sanctions in the former Yugoslavia', in Jeffries (1996b), pp. 151–72.

Bell, J. D. (1977) *Peasants in Power: Alexander Stamboliski and the Bulgarian Agrarian National Union, 1899–1923*, Princeton, N.J.: Princeton University Press.

—— (1997) 'Democratization and Political Participation in "Postcommunist" Bulgaria', in Dawisha and Parrott (1997), pp. 353–402.

Berend, I. (1986) 'The Historical Evolution of Eastern Europe as a Region', *International Organization*, vol. 40.

Berend, I. and Ranki, G. (1974) *Economic Development in East-Central Europe in the Nineteenth and Twentieth Centuries*, New York: Columbia University Press, vol. 40, no. 2, pp. 329–46.

Berkeley, B. (2001) *The Graves Are Not Yet Full*, New York: Basic Books.

Bethell, N. (1974) *The Last Secret*, London: André Deutsch.

Bieber, F. (2003)*Montenegro in Transition: Problems of Identity and Statehood*, Berlin: Nomos.

—— (2004) 'Bosnia-Herzegovina', in Freedom House (2004), pp. 124–53.

—— (2005) *Post-War Bosnia: Ethnicity, Inequality and Public Sector Governance*, Basingstoke: Palgrave-Macmillan.

Biberaj, E. (1991) 'Albania at the Crossroads' *Problems of Communism* (September–October).

Bideleux, R. (1987) *Communism and Development*, London: Methuen. First published 1985.

—— (1990) 'Agricultural Advance under the Russian Village Commune System', in R. Bartlett (ed.) (1990) *Land Commune and Peasant Community in Russia*, London: Macmillan, pp. 196–218.

—— (1994) 'Alexander II and the Emancipation of the Serfs', in P. Catterall and R. Vine (eds) *Europe 1870–1914*, London: Heinemann.

—— (1996) 'Introduction', 'The Southern Enlargement of the EC: Spain, Portugal and Greece', 'The Comecon Experiment', 'Bringing the East Back In' and 'In Lieu of a Conclusion: East Meets West', in Bideleux and Taylor (1996), pp. 1–21, 127–53, 174–204, 225–51, 281–95, respectively.

—— (1998) 'La Grèce: Ni intérêts nationaux, ni idéaux fédéralistes', in A. Landuyt (ed.), *Europe: fédération ou nations*, Paris: SEDES, pp. 205–27.

—— (2000) 'Dopo la democrazia: l'Unione Europea come ordine giuridico liberale sovranazionale', in A. Landuyt (ed.)*L'Unione Europea tra rifflessione storica e prospettive politiche e sociali*, Sienna: Protagon Editori, pp. 15–48.

—— (2001a) 'Civil Association: The European Union as a Supranational Liberal Legal Order', in M. Evans (ed.) *The Edinburgh Companion to Contemporary Liberalism*, Edinburgh: Edinburgh University Press, pp. 225–40.

—— (2001b) 'What Does It Mean to Be European? The Problems of Constructing a Pan-European Identity', in G. Timmins and M. Smith (eds) *Uncertain Europe*, London: Routledge, pp. 20–40.

—— (2001c) 'Europeanization and the Limits to Democratization in East-Central Europe', in G. Pridham and A. Agh (eds) *Prospects for Democratic Consolidation in East-Central Europe*, Manchester: Manchester University Press, pp. 25–53.

—— (2002a) 'The New Politics of Inclusion and Exclusion: The Limits and Divisions of Europe', in A. Plesu and L. Boia (eds) *Nation and National Ideology: Past, Present and Prospects*, Bucharest: New Europe College, pp. 28–49.

—— (2002b) 'Extending the European Union's Cosmopolitan Supranational Legal Order Eastwards: The Main Significance of the Forthcoming "Eastward Enlargement of the European Union" ', in M. M. Tavares Ribeiro (ed.)*Identidade Europeia e Multiculturalismo*, Coimbra: Quarteto, pp. 129–64.

—— (2003) 'Imigração, Multiculturalismo e Xenofobia na União Européia: Para um Estado Policial Europeu?', in M. M. Tavares Ribeiro (ed.)*Europa em Mutação*, Coimbra: Quarteto, pp. 243–61.

—— (2004) 'Tra oriente e occidente: la Grecia e l'integrazione europea', in A. Landuyt (ed.) *Idee d'Europa e integrazione europea*, Bologna: Il Mulino, pp. 299–342.

—— (2005a) 'The Balkans and the European Union: A Difficult Road', in A. Landuyt and D Pasquinucci (eds) *Gli allargamenti della CEE/UE, 1961–2004*, Bologna: Il Mulino, pp. 659–83.

—— (2005b), 'Denmark's Ambiguous Roles in the Eastward Enlargement of the European Union: From Copenhagen to Copenhagen', in A. Landuyt and D. Pasquinucci (eds) *Gli allargamenti della CEE/UE, 1961–2004*, Bologna: Il Mulino, pp. 263–87.

Bideleux, R. and Jeffries, I. (1998) *A History of Eastern Europe: Crisis and Change*, London: Routledge.

Bideleux, R. and Taylor, R. (eds) (1996) *European Integration and Disintegration: East and West*, London: Routledge.

Bjelic, D. and Savic, O. (2002)   *Balkan as a Metaphor: Between Globalization and Fragmentation*, Cambridge, Mass.: MIT Press.

Boia, L. (2001) *Romania*, London: Reaktion Books.

Booth, K. (ed.) (2001) *The Kosovo Tragedy: The Human Rights Dimension*, London: Frank Cass.

Borenzstein, E., Demekas, D. and Ostry, J. (1993) 'An Empirical Analysis of the Output Decline in Three Eastern European Countries', *IMF Staff Papers*, vol. 40, no. 1.

Bose, S. (2002) *Bosnia after Dayton*, London: Hurst.

Bowers, S. (1989) 'Stalinism in Albania: Domestic Affairs under Enver Hoxha' *East European Quarterly*, vol. 22, no. 4.

Bradley, J. and Knaus, G. (2004) 'Towards a Kosovo Development Plan: The State of the Kosovo Economy and Possible Ways Forward', Pristina: UNMIK/Economic Strategy and Project Identification Group (ESPIG)

Brankovic, A. and Nenadovic, A. (2002) 'Undertaking a Difficult Ttransition in Yugoslavia' *Transitions*, vol. 13, no. 3.

Bringa, T. (1995) *Being Muslim the Bosnian Way*, Princeton, N.J.: Princeton University Press.

Brooks, K. and Meurs, M. (1994) 'Romanian Land Reform, 1991–93' *Comparative Economic Studies*, vol. 36, no. 2.

Brown, J. (1970) *Bulgaria under Communist Rule*, New York: Praeger.

—— (1991) *Surge to Freedom: The End of Communist rule in Eastern Europe*, London: Adamantine Press.

Brubaker, R. (1996), *Nationalism Reframed*, Cambridge: Cambridge University Press.

Burg, S. (1997) 'Bosnia Herzegovina: A Case of Failed Democratization', in Dawisha and Parrott (1997), pp. 122–45.

Burnheim, J. (1985), *Is Democracy Possible?* Cambridge: Polity Press.

Brzezinski, Z. (1967) *The Soviet Bloc*, Cambridge, Mass.: Harvard University Press.

Business Central Europe (BCE) (1995) *The Annual: 1995–96*, London: The Economist Group.

—— (1997) *The Annual: 1997–98*, London: The Economist Group.

—— (1998) *The Annual: 1998–99*, London: The Economist Group.

—— (1999) *The Annual: 2000*, London: The Economist Group.

—— (2000) *The Annual: 2001*, London: The Economist Group.

Carlson, S. and Betts, W. (2001) 'Albania', in Freedom House (2001).

—— (2002) 'Albania', in Freedom House (2002).

Carnegie Endowment for International Peace (1914), *Report of the International Commission to Enquire into the Causes and Conduct of the Balkan Wars*, Washington, D.C. (reissued in 1993).

Catchlove, D. (1972) *Romania's Ceausescu*, Tunbridge Wells: Abacus Press.

Chandler, D. (1999) *Bosnia: Faking Democracy after Dayton*, London: Pluto Press.

Chary, F. B. (1972), *The Bulgarian Jews and the Final Solution, 1940–44*, Pittsburgh, Pa.: University of Pittsburgh Press.

CIA (2005) *World Factbook*, http://www.cia.gov/cia/publications/factbook/, accessed 16 October 2005.

Cirkovic, S. (2004) *The Serbs*, Oxford: Blackwell.

Clague, C. and Rausser, G. (eds) (1992)*The Emergence of Market Economies in Eastern Europe*, Oxford: Blackwell.

Clissold, S. (ed.) (1968) *A Short History of Yugoslavia*, Cambridge: Cambridge University Press.

Cochrane, N. (1988) 'The Private Sector in East European Agriculture',   *Problems of Communism*, March–April.

—— (1993) 'Central European Agrarian Reforms in a Historical Perspective',   *American Journal of Agricultural Economics*, vol. 75, no. 3, pp. 851–6.

Cohen, L. (1993, 1995), *Broken Bonds: Yugoslavia's Disintegration and Balkan Politics in Transition*, Boulder, Colo.: Westview Press.

—— (1997) 'Embattled Democracy: Postcommunist Croatia in Transition', in Dawisha and Parrott (1997), pp. 69–121.

Cohn, L. (2002) *Serpent in the Bosom: The Rise and Fall of Slobodan Milosevic*, Boulder, Colo.: Westview Press.

Cole, A. (2005) *French Politics and Society*, 2nd edn, Harlow: Pearson-Longman.

Coles, P. (1968) *The Ottoman Impact on Europe*, London: Thames & Hudson.

Covic, B. (ed.) (1991) *Croatia between War and Independence*, Zagreb.

Crainic, N. (1938), 'Programmul statului etnocratic', in his*Ortodoxie si etnocratie*, Bucharest: Cugetarea (reissued in 1987), pp. 245–71.

Craiutu, A. (2000) 'Light at the End of the Tunnel: Romania', in Pridham and Gallagher (2000), pp. 169–94.

Crampton, R. (1994) *Eastern Europe in the Twentieth Century*, London: Routledge.

—— (1997) *A Concise History of Bulgaria*, Cambridge: Cambridge University Press.

—— (2002) *The Balkans Since the Second World War*, London: Longman.

Crowther, W. (1988) *The Political Economy of Romanian Socialism*, New York: Praeger.

Cungu, A. and Swinnen, J. (1999) 'Albania's Radical Agrarian Reform'*Economic Development and Cultural Change*, vol. 47, no. 3.

Daalder, I. and Froman, B. (1999) 'Dayton's Incomplete Peace'*Foreign Affairs*, vol. 78, no. 6, pp. 106–14.

Danforth, L. (1995) *The Macedonian Conflict*, Princeton, N.J.: Princeton University Press.

Darby, H. C. (1968), Chapters 1–8 of Clissold (1968), pp. 8–153.

Dawisha, K. and Parrott, B. (eds) (1997) *Politics, Power, and the Struggle for Democracy in South-East Europe*, Cambridge: Cambridge University Press.

Deak, I. (2000) 'The Debate over Fascism and Resistance in Hungary', in Deak et al. (2000), pp. 39–73

Deak, I., Gross, J. and Judt, T. (eds) (2000) *The Politics of Retribution in Europe: World War II and its Aftermath*, Princeton, N.J.: Princeton University Press.

Dedijer, V. (1967) *The Road to Sarajevo*, London: Macgibbon & Kee.

Deletant, D. (1998) *Romania under Communist Rule*, Bucharest: Civic Academy Foundation.

Djilas, A. (1991), *The Contested Country: Yugoslav Unity and Communist Revolution, 1919–1953*, Cambridge, Mass.: Harvard University Press.

Djilas, M. (1957) *The New Class*, London: Thames & Hudson.

—— (1958) *Land without Justice*, New York: Harcourt Brace Jovanovich.

—— (1963) *Conversations with Stalin*, Harmondsworth: Penguin.

Djukic, S. (2001) *Milosevic and Markovic: A Lust for Power*, Montreal: McGill-Queens University Press.

Donia, R. and Fine, J. (1994)   *Bosnia and Herzegovina: A Tradition Betrayed*, London: Hurst.

Dragovic-Soso, J. (2002) *Saviours of the Nation: Serbia's Intellectual Opposition and the Revival of Nationalism*, Ithaca, N.Y.: McGill-Queens University Press

Drakulic, S. (1993), *The Balkan Express: Fragments from the Other Side of War*, New York: Norton.

Drezov, K., Gokay, B. and Kostovicova, D. (eds) (1999) *Kosovo: Myths, Conflict and War*, Keele: Keele European Research Centre.

Drucker, J. and Druckerova, A. (2005) 'Czech Republic', in Freedom House (2005).

Dyker, D. and Vejvoda, I. (eds) (1996) *Yugoslavia and After*, London: Longman.

EBRD (1994) *Transition Report*, London: European Bank for Reconstruction and Development.

—— (1995a) *Transition Report Update* (April), London: European Bank for Reconstruction and Development.

—— (1995b) *Transition Report*, London: European Bank for Reconstruction and Development.

—— (1996a) *Transition Report Update* (April), London: European Bank for Reconstruction and Development.

—— (1996b) *Transition Report*, London: European Bank for Reconstruction and Development.

—— (1997a) *Transition Report Update* (April), London: European Bank for Reconstruction and Development.

—— (1997b) *Transition Report*, London: European Bank for Reconstruction and Development.

—— (1998a) *Transition Report Update* (April), London: European Bank for Reconstruction and Development.

—— (1998b) *Transition Report*, London: European Bank for Reconstruction and Development.

—— (1999a) *Transition Report Update* (April), London: European Bank for Reconstruction and Development.

—— (1999b) *Transition Report*, London: European Bank for Reconstruction and Development.

—— (2000a) *Transition Report Update* (May), London: European Bank for Reconstruction and Development.

—— (2000b) *Transition Report*, London: European Bank for Reconstruction and Development.

—— (2001a) *Transition Report Update* (April), London: European Bank for Reconstruction and Development.

—— (2001b) *Transition Report*, London: European Bank for Reconstruction and Development.

—— (2002a) *Transition Report Update* (April), London: European Bank for Reconstruction and Development.

—— (2002b) *Transition Report*, London: European Bank for Reconstruction and Development.

—— (2003a) *Transition Report Update* (April), London: European Bank for Reconstruction and Development.

—— (2003b) *Transition Report*, London: European Bank for Reconstruction and Development.

—— (2004a) *Transition Report Update* (April), London: European Bank for Reconstruction and Development.

—— (2004b) *Transition Report*, London: European Bank for Reconstruction and Development.

—— (2005a) *Transition Report Update* (April), London: European Bank for Reconstruction and Development.

—— (2005b) *Transition Report*, London: European Bank for Reconstruction and Development.

Ekmecic, M. (1980) 'Serbia's War Aims', in D. Djordjevic (ed.) *The Creation of Yugoslavia, 1914–1918*, Santa Barbara, Calif.: Clio Books.

Emmert, T. (1989) 'The Kosovo Legacy', in *Serbian Studies*, vol. 5, no. 2, pp. 1–20.

Estrin, S. (1983) *Self-management: Economic Theory and Yugoslav Practice*, Cambridge: Cambridge University Press.

—— (1991) 'Yugoslavia: The Case of Self-Managing Market Socialism' *Journal of Economic Perspectives*, vol. 5, no. 4, pp. 187–94.

Europa (1992) *Eastern Europe and the Commonwealth of Independent States 1992*, London: Europa Publications.

Financial Times (various surveys):

Albania: 21 July 1994; 2 October 1995; 19 February 1997; 23 February 2000; 18 December 2002; 18 May 2004.

Bosnia-Herzegovina: 21 October 1998; 14 December 1999; 20 December 2001; 12 November 2002; 11 November 2003; 23 November 2004; 15 November 2005.

Bulgaria: 7 December 1984; 27 October 1988; 17 May 1991; 5 May 1993; 13 October 1994; 21 October 1997; 8 March 1999; 2 October 2002; 16 November 2004.

Croatia: 30 May 1996; 28 May 1997; 7 July 1998; 10 July 1999; 19 June 2001; 24 June 2002; 17 June 2003; 13 July 2004; 7 June 2005.

Macedonia: 7 July 1995; 15 November 1996; 17 December 1997; 19 February 2001.

Montenegro: 10 July 2001; 11 July 2002; 1 July 2003; 29 June 2004; 12 July 2005.

Romania: 3 May 1994; 25 May 1995; 9 July 1996; 25 June 1997; 28 September 1998; 3 October 2001; 14 October 2003; 23 February 2005.

Serbia: 28 January 2003; 14 December 2004.

Yugoslavia: 18 June 1984; 21 December 1984; 21 June 1985; 17 December 1985; 17 June 1986; 16 December 1986; 22 December 1987; 22 June 1988; 6 December 1988; 29 June 1989; 5 December 1989; 6 July 1990; 17 December 1990; 27 June 1991; 27 January 1998 (Federal Republic of Yugoslavia).

Fine, J. V. Jnr. (1976) *The Bosnian Church: A New Interpretation*, Boulder, Colo.: Westview Press.

—— (1983) *The Early Medieval Balkans*, Ann Arbor, Mich.: University of Michigan Press.

—— (1987, 1994) *The Late Medieval Balkans*, Ann Arbor, Mich.: University of Michigan Press.

Fischer-Galati, S. (1975) 'The Communist Take-Over of Romania', in Hammond (1975), pp. 310–20.

Forto, E. (2003) 'Croatia', in Freedom House (2003), pp. 196–214.

—— (2004) 'Croatia', in Freedom House (2004), pp. 174–95.

Fraenkel, E. (2001) 'Macedonia', in Freedom House (2001).

—— (2003) 'Macedonia', in Freedom House (2003).

Freedom House (1998) *Nations in Transit 1998*, New York: Freedom House.

—— (2001) *Nations in Transit 2001*, New York: Freedom House.

—— (2002) *Nations in Transit 2002*, New York: Freedom House.

—— (2003) *Nations in Transit, 2003*, New York Freedom House.

—— (2004) *Nations in Transit 2004*, Lanham, Md.: Rowman & Littlefield

—— (2005) *Nations in Transit, 2005*, New York: Freedom House.

Friedman, F. (2000) 'Dayton, Democratization and Governance: Electoral Dilemmas in Bosnia's Peace and Security', *International Relations*, vol. 15, no. 1, pp. 22–9.

Frydman, R., Rapaczynski, A., Earle, J. et al. (1993) *The Privatization Process in Central Europe*, London: Central European University Press.

Gallagher, T. (2001) *Outcast Europe: The Balkans, 1789–1989*, London: Routledge.

—— (2005) *Theft of a Nation: Romania since Communism*, London: Hurst.

Gagnon, V. (2004) *The Myth of Ethnic War: Serbia and Croatia in the 1990s*, Ithaca: Cornell University Press.

Georgiev, V. (1966) 'The Genesis of the Balkan Peoples',   *Slavonic Review*, vol. 44, pp. 285–97.

Gerolymatos, A. (2004) *The Balkan Wars*, Staplehurst: Spellmount.

Giatzidas, E. (2002) *An Introduction to Post-Communist Bulgaria: Political, Economic and Social Transformation*, Manchester: Manchester University Press.

Giddens, A. (1985) *Nation State and Violence*, Cambridge: Polity Press.

Glenny, M. (1999) *The Balkans 1804–1999*, London: Granta Books.

Gligorov, V. (1998) 'Patterns of Divergence in the Western Balkans', Vienna Institute for International Economic Studies, Monthly Report no. 5.

—— (1999) 'Macedonia: Stability under threat', in P. Havlik et al., *The Transition Countries in 1999*, Vienna: Vienna Institute for International Economic Studies.

—— (2001) 'Bosnia and Herzegovina', in Verememis and Daianu (2001), pp. 132–9.

—— (2006) Interview with Biljana Stavrova, 'A Decisive Year for Integration', TOL, 2 March.

Goldstein, I. (1999) *Croatia: A History*, London: Hurst.

Goldsworthy, V. (1998) *Inventing Ruritania*, New Haven, Conn.: Yale University Press.

Good, D. (1984) *The Economic Rise of the Habsburg Empire, 1850–1914*, Berkeley, Calif.: University of California Press.

—— (1994) *Economic Transformation in Central and Eastern Europe*, London: Routledge.

Gordy, E. (1999) *The Culture of Power in Serbia*, Pennsylvania, Pa.: Pennsylvania State University Press.

Gow, J. (1997) *Triumph of Lack of Will: International Diplomacy and the Yugoslav War*, London: Hurst.

Gow, J. and Carmichael, C. (2000) *Slovenia and the Slovenes*, London: Hurst.

Gray, J. (2000) *The Two Faces of Liberalism*, Cambridge: Polity Press.

Graybow, C. (2002) 'Croatia', in Freedom House (2002), pp. 140–53.

Gross, J. T. (2000) 'Themes for a Social History of War Experience and Collaboration' and 'A Tangled Web: Confronting Stereotypes Concerning Relations between Poles, Germans, Jews, and Communists', in Deak et al. (2000), pp. 14–35 and 74–129.

Gulde, A. M. (1999) 'The Role of the Currency Board in Bulgaria's Stabilization', *Finance and Development*, September.

Guldescu, S. (1970) *The Croatian-Slavonian Kingdom, 1526–1792*, The Hague: Mouton.

Haddock, B. and Caraiani, O. (1999) 'Nationalism and Civil Society in Romania', *Political Studies*, vol. 47, pp. 272–94.

Hall, D. (1994) *Albania and the Albanians*, London: Pinter.

Hammond, T. (ed) (1975) *The Anatomy of Communist Takeovers*, New Haven, Conn.: Yale University Press.

Havel, V. (1994) *Towards a Civil Society: Selected Speeches and Writings, 1990–1994*, Prague: Lidove Noviny Publishing House.

—— (1996) 'The Hope for Europe', *New York Review of Books*, 20 June, pp. 38–41.

Held, J. (ed.) (1992) *The Columbia History of Eastern Europe in the Twentieth Century*, New York: Columbia University Press.

Higley, J. and Gunther, R. (1992) *Elites and Democratic Consolidation in Latin America and Southern Europe*, Cambridge: Cambridge University Press.

Hitchins, K. (1994) *Rumania, 1866–1947*, Oxford: Clarendon Press.

Hoare, M. A. (2001) 'Civilian–Military Relations in Bosnia-Herzegovina 1992–1995', in Magas and Zanic (2001), pp. 178–99.

Hoen, H. (ed.) (2001) *Good Governance in Central and Eastern Europe: The Puzzle of Capitalism by Design*, Cheltenham: Edward Elgar.

Holbrooke, R. (1999) *To End a War*, New York: Modern Library.

Hoxha, E. (1981) *With Stalin*, Tirana.

Hristov, H. (1985) *A History of Bulgaria*, Sofia: Sofia Pres

Huntington, S. (1993) 'The Clash of Civilizations?', *Foreign Affairs*, summer 1993.

—— (1998), *The Clash of Civilizations and the Remaking of World Order*, London: Touchstone, pp. 22–49.

Hupchick, D. (2002) *The Balkans: From Constantinople to Communism*, New York: Palgrave Macmillan.

ICB (International Commission on the Balkans) (2005)*The Balkans in Europe's Future*, Sofia Centre for Liberal Strategies, April.

ICG (1997) *Media in Bosnia and Herzegovina: How International Support Can Be More Effective*, ICG Report, 7 March, Sarajevo: International Crisis Group.

—— (2004) *Pan-Albanianism: How Big a Threat to Balkan Stability?*, Tirana/Brussels: Europe Report no. 153.

—— (2005a) *Kosovo: Toward Final Status*, Brussels: Europe Report no. 161, 24 January.

—— (2005b) *Macedonia: Not Out of the Woods Yet*, Brussels: Europe Briefing no. 37, 25 February.

—— (2005c) *Montenegro's Independence Drive*, Brussels: Europe Report no. 169, 7 December.

—— (2006) *Macedonia: Wobbling toward Europe*, Brussels: Europe Briefing no. 41, 12 January.

Ioanid, R. (2000) *The Holocaust in Romania: The Destruction of the Jews and Gypsies under the Antonescu Regime, 1940–1944*, Chicago, Ill.: Ivan Dee.

Ionescu, G. (1964) *Communism in Romania, 1944–1962*, Oxford: Oxford University Press.

Jackson, R. (1993) *Quasi-States: Sovereignty, International Relations and the Third World*, Cambridge: Cambridge University Press.

Jarvis, C. (2000) 'The Rise and Fall of Albania's Pyramid Schemes'*Finance and Development*, vol. 37, no. 1.

Jensen, E. (1937) *Danish Agriculture: Its Economic Development*, Copenhagen: J. Schultz Forlag.

Jeffries, I. (ed.) (1981) *The Industrial Enterprise in Eastern Europe*, New York: Praeger.

—— (1990) *A Guide to the Socialist Economies*, London: Routledge.

—— (1993) *Socialist Economies and the Transition to the Market: A Guide*, London: Routledge.

—— (1996a) *A Guide to the Economies in Transition*, London: Routledge.

—— (ed.) (1996b) *Problems of Economic and Political Transformation in the Balkans*, London: Pinter.

—— (2002a) *Eastern Europe at the Turn of the Twenty-First Century: A Guide to the Economies in Transition*, London: Routledge.

—— (2002b) *The Former Yugoslavia at the Turn of the Twenty-First Century: A Guide to the Economies in Transition*, London: Routledge.

Jelavich, B. (1983a) *A History of the Balkans (Volume I)*, London: Cambridge University Press.

—— (1983b) *A History of the Balkans (Volume II)*, London: Cambridge University Press.

Jelavich, C. and Jelavich, B. (eds) (1963) *The Balkans in Transition*, Berkeley, Calif.: University of California Press.

—— (1977) *The Establishment of the Balkan National States, 1804–1920*, Seattle, Wash.: University of Washington Press.

Jones, E. (1981) *The European Miracle*, London: Cambridge University Press.

Jouan, V. (2003) 'Albania', in Freedom House (2003).

Judah, T. (1997) *The Serbs: History, Myth and the Destruction of Yugoslavia*, New Haven, Conn.: Yale University Press.

—— (1999) 'The growing pains of the Kosovo Liberation Army', in Drezov et al. (1999), pp. 21–5.

Kajsiu, B. (2004) 'Albania', in Freedom House (2004), pp. 28–49.

Kann, R. (1950a) *The Multinational Empire*, Vol. I, New York: Columbia University Press.

—— (1950b) *The Multinational Empire*, Vol. II, New York: Columbia University Press.

—— (1974) *A History of the Habsburg Empire, 1526–1918*, Berkeley, Calif.: University of California Press.

Kaplan, R. (1993) *Balkan Ghosts: A Journey Through History*, New York: St Martin's Press.

Karpat, K. (ed.) (1990) *The Turks of Bulgaria: The History, Culture and Political Fate of a Minority*. Istanbul: ISIS Press.

Kaser, M. (1981) 'The Industrial Enterprise in Bulgaria' in Jeffries (1981).

—— (2001) *Albania*, London: Economist Intelligence Unit.

Kekic, P. (2001) 'Former Yugoslav Republic of Macedonia (FYROM)', in Veremis and Daianu (2001), pp. 186–202.

King, R. (1980) *History of the Romanian Communist Party*, Stanford, Calif.: Hoover Institution Press.

Koevski, G. and Canning, A. (1995)   *Privatization in the Former Yugoslav Republic of Macedonia*, Heriot-Watt University: Discussion Paper no. 95/10.

Kola, P. (2003) *The Search for Greater Albania*, London: Hurst.

Kormos, C. (1944) *Rumania*, Cambridge: Cambridge University Press.

Kostovicova, D. (1999) 'Albanian Schooling in Kosovo', in Drezov et al. (1999), pp. 12–20.

Krastev, I. (2004) *Shifting Obsessions: Three Essays on the Politics of Anticorruption*, Budapest: Central European University Press.

Krastev, I., Dorosiev, R. and Ganev, G. (2004a) 'Bulgaria', in Freedom House (2004), pp. 154–73.
—— (2005) 'Bulgaria', in Freedom House (2005).
Kupchan, C. (2005) 'Independence for Kosovo', *Foreign Affairs*, vol. 84, no. 6, pp. 14–20.
Lampe, J. (1996) *Yugoslavia as History*, Cambridge: Cambridge University Press.
—— (2006) *Balkans into Southeastern Europe*, New York: Palgrave Macmillan.
Lampe, J. and Jackson, M. (1982) *Balkan Economic History 1550–1950*, Bloomington, Ind.: Indiana University Press.
Lazic, M. and Sekelj, L. (1997) 'Privatization in Yugoslavia (Serbia and Montenegro)*Europe-Asia Studies*, vol. 49, no. 6.
LeBor, A. (2003) *Milosevic: A Biography*, London: Bloomsbury.
Linz, J. and Stepan, A. (eds) (1978) *The Breakdown of Democratic Regimes*, Baltimore, Md.: Johns Hopkins University Press.
—— (1996) *Problems of Democratic Transition and Consolidation: Southern Europe, South America and Post-Communist Europe*, Baltimore, Md.: Johns Hopkins University Press.
Logoreci, A. (1977) *The Albanians*, London: Gollancz.
Lovrenovic, I. (2001) *Bosnia: A Cultural History*, London: Saqi Books.
Lydall, H. (1987) *Yugoslav Socialism: Theory and Practice*, Oxford: Oxford University Press.
—— (1989) *Yugoslavia in Crisis*, Oxford: Clarendon Press.
McFarlane, B. (1988) *Yugoslavia: Politics, Economics and Society*, London: Pinter.
McGowan, B. (1997) 'The Age of the Ayans', in H. Inalcik and D. Quataert (eds)*In Economic and Social History of the Ottoman Empire, Vol II, 1600–1914*, Cambridge: Cambridge University Press, pp. 637–758.
McIntyre, R. (1988) *Bulgaria: Politics, Economics and Society*, London: Pinter.
Magas, B. (1993) *The Destruction of Yugoslavia: Tracking the Break-up 1980–92*, London: Verso.
Magas, B. and Zanic, I. (eds) (2001)*The War in Croatia and Bosnia-Herzegovina 1991–1995*, London: Frank Cass.
Malcolm, N. (1994) *Bosnia: A Short History*, London: Macmillan.
—— (1998) *Kosovo: A Short History*, London: Macmillan.
Mann, M. (1988) *States, War and Capitalism*, Oxford: Blackwell.
—— (2004) *Fascists*, Cambridge: Cambridge University Press.
—— (2005) *The Dark Side of Democracy: Explaining Ethnic Cleansing*, Cambridge: Cambridge University Press.
Marmullaku, R. (1975) *Albania and the Albanians*, London: Hurst.
Mateeva, A. and Paes, W.-C. (2002) 'Kosovo: Trapped in its own Maze', *The World Today*, vol. 58, no. 7, pp. 19–21.
Mazower, M. (2001) *The Balkans*, London: Pheonix Press.
Meier, V. (1999) *Yugoslavia: A History of its Demise*, London: Routledge.
Mesic, S. (2001) 'The Road to War', in Magas and Zanic (2001), pp. 3–13.
Miller, J. (2001) 'The Bulgarian Currency Board', *Comparative Economic Studies*, vol. 43, no. 1.
Miller, N. (1997) 'The Republic of Macedonia: Finding its Way', in Dawisha and Parrott (1997), pp. 226–84.
Miller, W., White, S. and Heywood, P. (1998)*Values and Political Change in Postcommunist Europe*, Basingstoke: Macmillan.
Mitic, A. (2005), 'Standing by Enlargement', TOL, 13 October.
Mitrany, D. (1930) *Land and the Peasant in Romania*, London: Oxford University Press.
—— (1951) *Marx against the Peasant: A Study in Social Dogmatism*, Chapel Hill, N.C.: University of North Carolina Press.
Monnet, J. (1976) *Mémoires*, Paris: Fayard.
Montias, J. (1967) *Economic Development in Communist Romania*, Cambridge, Mass.: MIT Press.

Moore, P. (1984) 'Bulgaria', in T. Rakowska-Harmstone (ed.)*Communism in Eastern Europe*, 2nd edn, Bloomington, Ind.: Indiana University Press, pp. 186–212.

Mungiu-Pippidi, A. (2004) 'Romania', in Freedom House (2004), pp. 440–61.

—— (2005) 'Romania', in Freedom House (2005).

Nardin, T. (1983) *Law, Morality and the Relations of States*, Princeton, N.J.: Princeton University Press.

Nye, J. (2004) *Soft Power*, New York: Public Affairs.

O'Donnell, G. (1996) 'Delegative Democracy', in L. Diamond and M. Plattner (eds)*The Global Resurgence of Democracy*, 2nd edn, Baltimore, Md.: Johns Hopkins University Press.

OECD (1992) *Bulgaria: An Economic Assessment*, Geneva: OECD.

Okey, R. (1982)*Eastern Europe, 1740–1980: Feudalism to Communism*, London: Hutchinson.

Oren, N. (1973)*Revolution Administered: Agrarianism and Communism in Bulgaria*, Baltimore, Md.: Johns Hopkins University Press.

Osmova, M. and Faminsky, I. (1980)*Ekonomika zarubezhnikh stran: Sotsialisticheskie strani*, Moscow: Visshaya shkola.

Owen, D. (1996) *Balkan Odyssey*, London: Victor Gollancz.

Palairet, M. (1997), *The Balkan Economies c. 1800–1914*, Cambridge: Cambridge University Press.

—— (2001) 'The Economic Consequences of Slobodan Milosevic', *Europe-Asia Studies*, vol. 53, no. 6.

Pano, N. (1992) 'Albania', in Held (1992), pp. 17–64.

—— (1997) 'The Process of Democratization in Albania', in Dawisha and Parrott (1997), pp. 285–352.

Parekh, B. (1993) 'The Cultural Particularity of Liberal Democracy', in D. Held (ed.)*Prospects for Democracy*, Cambridge: Polity Press, pp. 156–75.

Pashko, G. (1991) 'The Albanian Economy at the Beginning of the 1990s', in Sjöberg and Wyzan (1991).

—— (1993) 'Obstacles to Economic Reform in Albania', *Europe-Asia Studies*, vol. 45, no. 5, pp. 907–21.

—— (1996) 'Problems of the Transition in Albania, 1990–94' in Jeffries (1996b), pp. 63–82.

Pavlovic, D. (2004) 'Serbia-Montenegro', in Freedom House (2004), pp. 490–520.

Pavlowitch, S. (2002) *Serbia: The History behind the Name*, London: Hurst.

Peranic, B. (2005) 'Croatia', in Freedom House (2005).

Perry, D. (1997) 'The Republic of Macedonia: Finding its Way', in Dawisha and Parrott (1997), pp. 226–84.

Petrovic, P., Bogetic, Z. and Vujosevic, Z. (1999) 'The Yugoslav Hyperinflation of 1992–94 Causes, Dynamics and Money Supply Process', *Journal of Comparative Economics*, vol. 27, no. 2.

Petrovich, M. (1976) *A History of Modern Serbia, 1804–1918*, New York: Harcourt Brace Jovanovich, 2 vols.

Pettifer, J. (ed.) 1999 *The New Macedonian Question*, London: Palgrave.

—— (1995) 'Macedonia: Still the Apple of Discord', *The World Today*, vol. 51, no. 3.

Pinson, M. (ed.) (1996) *The Muslims of Bosnia-Herzegovina*, Cambridge, Mass.: Harvard University Press.

Pippa, A. and Repishti, S. (1984) *Studies on Kosovo*, New York: Columbia University Press.

Pollo, S. and Puto, A. (1981) *A History of Albania*, London: Routledge & Kegan Paul.

Poulton, H. (1995) *Who are the Macedonians?*, London: Hurst.

Pralong, S. and Apostol, M. (2002) 'Romania', in Freedom House (2002).

—— (2003) 'Romania', in Freedom House (2003).

Prescott, L. (1986) 'Farming Policy in Albania', *Albanian Life*, no. 2 (no. 35 in the series).

Pridham, G. and Gallagher, T. (eds) (2000) *Experimenting with Democracy: Regime Change in the Balkans*, London: Routledge.

Prifti, P. (1978) *Socialist Albania since 1944*, Cambridge, Mass.: MIT Press.

Prodi, R. (2000) '2000–06: Shaping the New Europe: Presentation to the European Parliament', *Bulletin of the European Union*, Brussels, Supplement 1/2000, pp. 5–13

Prout, C. (1985) *Market Socialism in Yugoslavia*, London: Oxford University Press.

Pundeff, M. (1992) 'Bulgaria', in Held (1992), pp. 65–118.

Putnam, R. (1993) *Making Democracy Work: Civic Traditions in Modern Italy*, Princeton, N.J.: Princeton University Press.

Puto, A. (2006a) 'Albania: How's Your Health?', TOL, 13 February.

—— (2006b) 'Albania: Time to Deliver', TOL, 27 February.

Qirezi, A. (2004) 'Albania', in Freedom House (2004).

Raikin, S. (1998) 'Bulgaria', in Ramet (1998), pp. 224–50.

Ramet, S. (1997) *Whose Democracy? Nationalism, Religion and the Doctrine of Collective Rights in Post-1989 Eastern Europe*, Lanham, Md.: Rowman & Littlefield

—— (ed.) (1998) *Eastern Europe: Politics, Culture and Society since 1939*, Bloomington, Ind.: Indiana University Press.

Ramusovic, A. (2004a) 'Montenegro: Back to Parliament', TOL, 27 October.

—— (2004b) 'Montenegro: My Beautiful Launderette?', TOL, 1 November.

—— (2004c) 'Montenegro: Barbarians at the Gate', TOL, 2 December.

—— (2004d) 'Montenegro: Stemming the Tide', TOL, 20 December.

Roberts, E. (1999) 'Trouble Ahead', *World Today*, vol. 55, no. 12.

—— (2005) *Realm of the Black Mountain: A History of Montenegro*, London: Hurst.

Roberts, H. (1951) *Romania: Political Problems of an Agrarian State*, New Haven, Conn.: Yale University Press.

Rocker, R. (1937) *Nationalism and Culture*, Los Angeles, Calif.: Rocker Publications.

Romania (1974), *Romania*, Bucharest: Editura Enciclopedica Romana.

Romania Factbook (2000) *Romania Factbook 2000*, <http://www.factbook.ro>, accessed 7 June 2005.

—— (2005) *Romania Factbook 2005*, <http://www.factbook.ro>, accessed 7 June 2005.

Ronnas, P. (1989) 'Turning the Romanian Peasant into a New Socialist Man: An Assessment of Rural Development Policy in Romania', *Soviet Studies*, vol. 41, no. 4.

—— (1991a) 'The Economic Legacy of Ceausescu', in Sjöberg and Wyzan (1991).

—— (1996) 'Romania: Transition to Underdevelopment', in Jeffries (1996b), pp. 13–32.

Roper, S. (2000) *Romania: The Unfinished Revolution*, Amsterdam: Harwood.

Rose, R. (1992) 'Toward a Civil Economy', *Journal of Democracy*, vol. 3.

Rothschild, J. (1974) *East-Central Europe between the Two World Wars*, Seattle, Wash.: University of Washington Press.

—— (1989) *Return to Diversity: A Political History of East-Central Europe since World War II*, London: Oxford University Press.

Rushdie, S. (2002) *Step across this Line*, London: Vintage.

Sakwa, R. (2002) *Russian Politics and Society*, 3rd edn, London: Routledge.

Schnytzer, A. (1982) *Stalinist Economic Strategy in Practice: The Case of Albania*, London: Oxford University Press.

Shafir, M. (1985) *Romania: Politics, Economics and Society*, London: Pinter.

Shevtsova, L. (2005) *Putin's Russia*, Washington, D.C.: Carnegie Endowment.

Siani-Davies, Peter (2005) *The Romanian Revolution of December 1989*, Ithaca, N.Y.: Cornell University Press.

Silber, L. and Little, D. (1995) *The Death of Yugoslavia*, Harmondsworth: Penguin.

Sirc, L. (1979) *The Yugoslav Economy under Self-Management*, London: Macmillan.

Sjöberg, Ö. (1996) 'The Regional Effects of Economic Transformation in Albania', in Jeffries (1996b), pp. 83–109.

Sjöberg, Ö. (1991) *Rural Change and Development in Albania*, Boulder, Colo.: Westview Press.

Sjöberg, Ö. and Wyzan, M. (eds) (1991) *Economic Change in the Balkan States: Albania, Bulgaria, Romania and Yugoslavia*, London: Pinter.

Skendi, S. (1967) *The Albanian National Awakening, 1878–1912*, Princeton, N.J.: Princeton University Press.

Skrubbeltrang, F. (1953) *Agricultural Development and Rural Reform in Denmark*, Rome: UN Food and Agriculture Organization (FAO).

Spegelj, M. (2001) 'The First Phase, 1990–92: The JNA Prepares for Aggression and Croatia for Defence', in Magas and Zanic (2001), pp. 14–40.

Spiljevic, M. (ed.) (1985) *Facts about Yugoslavia*, Belgrade: Beogradski izdavacko-grafick zavod.

Stavrianos, L. (1958) *The Balkans since 1453*, New York: Holt, Rinehart & Winston.

—— (1963) 'The Influence of the West on the Balkans', in Jelavich and Jelavich (1963)

Stavrova, B. (2004a) 'One Step Closer to the EU', TOL, 29 March.

—— (2004b) 'Influential Voting Bloc', TOL, 19 April

—— (2004c) 'Crvenkovski Victory Confirmed', TOL, 3 May

—— (2004d) 'The Opposition: In Opposition to Itself', TOL, 14 July.

—— (2004e) 'A Rush to Compromise', TOL, 19 July.

—— (2004f) 'Drawing the Line', TOL, 16 August.

—— (2004g) 'Poets Clash over Renowned Festival', TOL, 26 August.

—— (2005) 'Catching the Train', TOL, 14 November.

—— (2006a) 'From the Brink of War to the EU's Door', TOL, 9 January.

—— (2006b) 'A Date with Democracy', TOL, 25 January.

Stavrova, B. and Alagjozovski, R. (2004a) 'Fixing the Economy', TOL, 7 October.

—— (2004b) 'Filling in the Blanks', TOL, 11 October.

—— (2004c) 'In the Face of Iraq Deaths', TOL, 22 October.

—— (2004d) 'A Sigh of Relief', TOL, 8 November.

—— (2004e) 'Coalition of the Temporarily Willing', TOL, 29 November.

—— (2004f) 'Paramilitary Greeting', TOL, 13 December.

—— (2005a) 'Everyone Running', TOL, 7 February.

—— (2005b) 'One Mile to Go', TOL, 14 February.

—— (2005c) 'Remembering a Peacemaker', 3 March.

—— (2005d) 'Fair Elections for Faster Integration', TOL, 14 March.

—— (2005e) 'From Skopje to The Hague', TOL, 21 March.

—— (2005f) 'Business as Usual?', TOL, 18 April.

—— (2005g) 'A Capital Name', TOL, 5 May.

—— (2005h) 'Crimes and Misdemeanors', TOL, 20 May.

—— (2005i) 'Court Takes Bishop', TOL, 11 August.

—— (2005k) 'An Uneasy Anniversary', TOL, 25 August.

—— (2005l) 'Have Arrest Warrant, Won't Arrest', TOL, 29 August.

—— (2005m), 'Time to Open the Waiting Room's Door?', TOL, 7 November.

Stoianovich, T. (1960) 'The Conquering Balkan Orthodox Merchant', *Journal of Economic History*, vol. 20, no. 2.

—— (1967) *A History of Balkan Civilization*, New York: Knopf.

Sugar, P. (1971) 'External and Domestic Roots of Eastern European Nationalism', in Sugar and Lederer (1971), pp. 3–54.

—— (1977) *Southeastern Europe under Ottoman Rule, 1354–1804*, Seattle, Wash.: University of Washington Press.

—— (ed.) (1995) *East European Nationalism in the Twentieth Century*, Washington, D.C.: American University Press.

Sugar, P. and Lederer, I. (eds) (1971)*Nationalism in Eastern Europe*, Seattle, Wash.: University of Washington Press.

Swinnen, J. (1999) 'The Political Economy of Land Reform Choices in Central and Eastern Europe', *Economics of Transition*, vol. 7, no. 3.

Sword, K. (ed.) (1990) *The Times Guide to Eastern Europe*, London: Times Books.

—— (ed.) (1991) *The Times Guide to Eastern Europe*, 2nd edn, London: Times Books.

Szajkowski, B. (2000) 'Macedonia: An Unlikely Road to Democracy', in G. Pridham and T. Gallagher (2000).

Tamas, G. M. (1996), 'Ethnarchy and Anarchism',*Social Research*, vol. 63, no. 1, pp. 172–83.

Tanner, M. (1997)*Croatia: A Nation Forged in War*, New Haven, Conn.: Yale University Press.

Taylor, A. J. P. (1976) *The Habsburg Monarchy, 1809–1918*, Chicago, Ill.: University of Chicago Press.

Terdevci, F. (2004) 'Kosovo: Premier Games', *TOL*, 22 November.

—— (2006) 'Kosovo: No Clean Sweep', *TOL*, 13 March.

Thomas, R. (1998) 'Choosing the Warpath', *World Today*, vol. 54, no. 5.

—— (1999) *Serbia under Milosevic: Politics in the 1990s*, London: Hurst.

Thompson, S. (1993) 'Agrarian Reform in Eastern Europe following World War I: Motives and Outcomes', *American Journal of Agricultural Economics*, vol. 75, no. 3.

Tiltman, H. (1934) *Peasant Europe*, London: Jarrolds.

Tismaneanu, V. (1997) 'Romanian Exceptionalism? Democracy, Ethnocracy and Uncertain Pluralism in Post-Ceausescu Romania', in Dawisha and Parrott (1997), pp. 403–49.

Todorov, T. (2001) *The Fragility of Goodness: Why Bulgaria's Jews Survived the Holocaust*, London: Weidenfeld & Nicolson.

Todorova, M. (1997) *Imagining the Balkans*, Oxford: Oxford University Press.

Tolstoy, N. (1978) *Victims of Yalta*, London: Hodder & Stoughton.

Toynbee, A. (1935–54) *A Study of History*, 10 vols, London: Oxford University Press.

Trosky, L (1980) *The Balkan Wars, 1912–1913*, New York: Monad Press.

Trotsky, L. (1937) *The Revolution Betrayed*, New York; reprinted, Pathfinder Press, 1972

Tsantis, A. and Pepper, R. (1979) *Romania: The Industrialization of an Agrarian Economy under Socialist Planning*, Washington, D.C.: World Bank.

Tsekov, G. (2004) 'Macedonia', in Freedom House (2004), pp. 378–97.

—— (2005) 'Macedonia', in Freedom House (2005).

Turnock, D. (1986) *The Romanian Economy in the Twentieth Century*, London: Croom Helm.

Tus, A. (2001) 'The War in Slovenia and Croatia up to the Sarajevo Ceasefire', in Magas an Zanic (2001), pp. 41–66.

UN Economic Commission for Europe (1992) *Economic Survey of Europe in 1991–92*, New York: United Nations.

—— (1993) *Economic Survey of Europe in 1992–93*, New York: United Nations.

—— (1994) *Economic Survey of Europe in 1993–94*, New York: United Nations.

—— (1995) *Economic Survey of Europe in 1994–95*, New York: United Nations.

—— (1996) *Economic Survey of Europe in 1995–96*, New York: United Nations.

—— (1997) *Economic Survey of Europe in 1996–97*, New York: United Nations.

—— (1998a) *Economic Survey of Europe 1998*, no. 1, New York: United Nations.

—— (1998b) *Economic Survey of Europe 1998*, no. 2, New York: United Nations.

—— (1998c) *Economic Survey of Europe 1998*, no. 3, New York: United Nations.

Vachudova, M. (2005) *Europe Undivided: Democracy, Leverage and Integration after Communism*, Oxford: Oxford University Press.

Verdery, K. (1996) *What was Socialism and What comes Next?*, Princeton, N.J.: Princeton University Press.

Veremis, T. and Daianu, D. (eds) (2001) *Balkan Reconstruction*, London: Frank Cass.

Vickers, M. (1998) *Between Serb and Albanian: A History of Kosovo*, London: Hurst.

—— (1999) *The Albanians*, London: Taurus.

Vickers, M. and Pettifer, J. (1997)*Albania: From Anarchy to a Balkan Identity*, London: Hurst.

Vucinich, W. (1962) 'The Nature of Balkan Society under Ottoman rule', *Slavic Review*, vol. 21, no. 4, pp. 597–616.

—— (1963) 'Some Aspects of the Ottoman Legacy' in Jelavich and Jelavich (1963), pp. 81–114.

—— (1965) *The Ottoman Empire: Its Record and Legacy*, Princeton, N.J.: Van Nostrand.

Wachtel, A. (1998)*Making a Nation: Literature and Cultural Politics in Yugoslavia*, Stanford, Calif.: Stanford University Press.

Weber, E. (1964) *Varieties of Fascism*, New York: Van Nostrand.

Wilkes, J. (1992) *The Illyrians*, Oxford: Blackwell.

Woodward, S. (1995) *Balkan Tragedy*, Washington, D.C.: Brookings Institution.

World Bank (1996) *World Development Report 1997: From Plan to Market*, New York: Oxford University Press.

—— (2005) *World Development Report 2006*, Oxford: Oxford University Press.

Wyzan, M. (1989) 'The Small Enterprise and Agricultural Initiative in Bulgaria: A Comment on Robert J. McIntyre', *Soviet Studies*, vol. 41, no. 4.

—— (1991) 'The Bulgarian Economy in the Immediate Post-Zhivkov Era', in Sjöberg and Wyzan (1991).

—— (1996) 'Economic Change in Bulgaria since the Fall of Communism', in Jeffries (1996), pp. 45–62.

—— (1998) 'The Political Economy of Bulgaria's Peculiar Post-Communist Business Cycle', *Comparative Economic Studies*, vol. 40, no. 1.

Yugoslavia (1992) 'The National Composition of Yugoslavia's Population, 1991', *Yugoslav Survey*, no. 1, pp. 3–24.

Zacharia, F. (1998) 'The Rise of Illiberal Democracy', *Foreign Affairs*, vol. 76, no. 6, pp. 22–43.

Zimmerman, W. (1995) 'The Last Ambassador: A Memoir of the Collapse of Yugoslavia', *Foreign Affairs*, vol. 74, no. 2.

Index

acquis (communautaire) 117–18, 170–1, 226, 465, **582, 590**.

'administrative and judicial capacity' 70, 117 121, 165, 170–3, 177, 466, 582

Adriatic Sea/islands 25, 66, 71, 184–5, 208, 236, 246, 332, 334, 374, 473, 501, 519–20

Afghanistan links 65, 119–20, 168, 226, 306, 550, 561

agriculture 22, 24–5, 30–4, 38–9, 42–4, 46, 52–3, 68–9, 71, 73, 77, 80, 88–90, 95, 97–8, 100–3, 123, 127–8, 131–2, 138–40, 146, 148–9, 152, 183–5, 209, 214, 233, 238, 251–2, 267, 324, 332, 398, 405, 459, 461–2, 468, 474, 476, 507, 566, 579; agricultural producer cooperatives (APCs, collectivized agriculture) 34, 37, 43, 52–3, 89–90, 97–8, 138, 146

Agrokomerc scandal (1987) 341–2

Ahmeti, Ali 424, 428, 433, 435, 437–8, 442, 445–6, 449–50, 457

Ahmeti, Vilson 42–3

Ahtisaari, Marti 346, 554, 575

Akashi, Yashuki 348–50

Albania xviii, 3, 5–6, 18, **22–89**, 123, 163, 181–2, 218, 236–7, 512–13, 517–22, 524–6, 528, 533–4, 537–40, 544, 546–7, 552, 560, 577–8, 582, 590; 'Greater Albania' aspirations 23–4, 32–3, 423, 425, 440, 451, 455, 472, 519, 524, 528, 543, 577; 'Albanoi' 25–6

Albanians (including ethnic Albanians in Kosova and ROM) xviii, 4, 6, 10, 16, **22–89,** 192, 200–1, 233, 236–7, 240–2, 244, 246–8, 253–4, 260–3, 276, 278, 283, 285–6, 289, 292–3, 295, 313, 315, 324, **405–57,** 464, 469–70, 472, 475–81, 484, 486, 491, 493–6, 506, 509, **512–80**

Algerian detainees in Bosnia 381–2

Aleksandar Karadjeordjevic, Prince 235

Aleksandar Karadjeordjevic, King 237–8

Aleksandar Obrenovic, Prince 236

Alia, Ramiz 34–46, 59

Alliance for the Future of Kosova (AAK) 564–7, 572–3, 576

Alliance of Reform Forces of Yugoslavia

(*Savez reformskih snaga Jugoslavije,* SRSJ or ARFY) 196–7, 244–5, 342, 411, 476–7

Al-Qaeda 292, 381–2, 453

Andric, Ivo 339

Annan, Kof 277, 350, 542, 773–4

Antonescu, Ion 84, 133–7, 140, 168–70

Arkan (Zeljko Raznatovic) 246, 248, 250, 260, 264, 279, 298, 302, 535

Armata Kombetare Shquiptare (AKSh,) 440, 448, 451–2

Ashdown, Paddy 382, 389–93, 396, 399

Ataka 120–2

Austria xvi, xviii, 2, 13, 14, 21, 27, 29, 56–7, 68, 77, 81, 128–30, 172, 174, 184–5, 188–9, 192, 198, 200, 228–30, 235–7, 337–8, 357, 382, 516, 519–21, 540, 593

Avramovic, Dragoslav 249–50

Axis Pact/Powers 33, 81–2, 84–5, 133–5, 175, 190, 238–9, 268, 339–40, 475, 524–6

Badinter Committee 343, 506

Babic, Milan 196

Balkan wars 2, 129, 188, 237, 253, 264, 291, 408, 474, 512, 520; Balkanization and Balkanism 1–3, 509, 577; Maria Todorova 3

basic treaty (1996) 152–3

Balli Kombetar (BK, in Albania and Kosova) 32, 48, 525

Basescu, Traian 126, 157, 160, 171, 175–9

Belgrade 189, 194–5, 208, 233, 237, 245–6, 249, 254–7, 260, **262–320**, 349, 366–75, 423, 439, 476, 485–90, 494, 498, 500, 508, 516, 521, 529, 532, 539–48, 551–4, 559, 563–6, 569–70, 579.

Berend, Ivan 3, 80, 85, 132, 136

Berisha, Sali 37, 42, 45–65, 69–71, 533

Berlin Congress (1878) 11, 76, 128, 236, 518, 566

Beron, Petur 99

Berov, Lyuben 101–2

Bessarabia *see* Moldova

Bihac 206, 329, 347, 349, 362

Bildt, Carl 357, 360, 365

Bitola 405, 431, 434

Black/grey economy 18, 100, 175–6, 180, 215, 230, 323, 329, 394, 402, 405, 418, 461, 464, 468, 476, 506, 530, 534, 554,579

Black Sea 73, 119, 125, 139, 168, 176

Bobetko, Gen. Janko 222

Bodnaras, Emil 135

Bolsheviks and Bolshevism 29, 81, 130, 133

Boris (Khan) 74

Boris III (Tsar) 78–82

Bosanski Brod 343

Boskovski, Ljube 437, 439, 444, 446–9, 452–4, 457, 467

Bosnia (and) Herzegovina xvi, 3–7, 13–15, 182, 187–9, 200–4, 206, 210–13, 216–19, 221–2, 227, 229, 234–40, 243, 246–55, 257–8, 261, 267, 277, 279, 283–4, 287–91, 293, 296, 299, 300, 306, 310, 315–18, 324, **329–404**, 412, 469, 474–5, 479–81, 486, 489, 491, 515, 518, 527, 530, 532, 535–6, 541, 550–51, 557, 566, 568, 571, 577–8, 582, 590, 593–4; Bosnian Church 333–4; Bosniaks (Bosnian Muslims) 13–16, 182, 187–92, 200–4, 206, 218, 221–2, 233, 249, 253, 290, 315–17, 324, **329–404**, 412, 469, 521, 532, 563, 573, 593; Bosnian Serbs 50, 192, 206, 236, 246, 250, 252, 254, 257, 283–4, 289, 293, 315–16, **329–404**, 480, 577; Bosnian Croats 206, 211–2, 217, 219, 221, 290, **329–404**, 577

Boutros Ghali, Boutros 348, 350

Brasov 125, 140, 183

Bratianu, Constantin 133; Bratianu, Ionel 130–1

Brcko 352, 359, 365–6, 368, 374–5

Bucharest 125, 128–9, 136, 139, 142–3, 145–6, 149–50, 153, 155–7, 159, 161–2, 164, 168, 171, 175–7

Bukovina (Bucovina) 130–8

Budisa, Drazen 195, 204, 207, 216–17, 221–2

Bufi, Ylli 41–3, 5

Bukovski, Vlado 457, 466

Bulatovic, Momir 258, 269, 274, 476–85, 492

Bulatovic, Pavle 264

Bulatovic, Predrag 285, 492–3

Bulatovic, Rade 303–4

Bulgaria, Bulgarians 2–3, 5–7, 9, 13, 16, 18, 20–1, 28–9, 35, 63, 65, 72, **73–124**, 129–30, 132–3, 135–6, 138–9, 163, 168, 170, 172–3, 177–9, 181–2, 188, 192, 221, 233–4, 236–9, 287, 320, 333, 336–7, 396, 407–11, 414–15, 421, 426–7, 433, 436–7, 462, 465, 470, 474, 509, 515, 517, 519, 521–2, 524, 546–7, 552–3, 557–8, 582, 589–92; Bulgars 74–5

Bulgarian Agrarian National Union (BANU) 78, 96

Bulgarian Communist Party (BCP) 79, 81, 83, 85–6, 94; Bulgarian Socialist Party (BSP) 94, 96, 99–117, 120–3

Bush, George (Senior) 536; Bush, George W. 169, 383, 388, 431, 436–7

Byzantine empire xvii, 9, 25–6, 74–5, 141, 184, 234, 332, 335, 407–8, 473, 581; *see also* Eastern Orthodox Church/Christianity

Cacak 262, 273

Cantons/cantonization 250, 312, 344, 346, 348–9, 356, 359, 376, 378, 469, 489, 568

Carol I, Prince/King 129–31

Carol II, Prince/King 132

Carrington, Peter (Lord) 344

casualties (human costs of wars) 32, 43, 84–5, 143, 190–1, 206, 208, 350, 353–5, 390, 429, 547–8, 551, 558–60

Ceausescu, Nicolae 138–42, 147, 159; 'systematization' programme 140–1

Ceku, Ahmed 423, 562, 576

centrally planned economy *see* command economy

Cermak, Gen. Ivan 207, 226

Cetinje 297, 471, 473–5, 480, 486, 503

cetniki (cetniks) 198, 239, 268, 524

Chernomyrdin, Viktor 554

China 34, 138–9, 141, 266, 270, 274, 277, 414, 541, 545–6, 548–9, 553–4, 556

Chervenkov, Vulko 87

Chirac, Jacques 158, 175

Churchill, Winston 84, 239

Ciorbea, Victor 153, 157–80

civil economies 5, 7, 143, 181–2, 230, 581–3, 624; civil society/societies xv, 5, 8–10, 64, 72, 111, 141, 143, 179, 181–2, 230, 465, 581–3

Clark, Gen. Wesley 487, 541–2, 545, 557, 559, 562

clientelism 1, 8, 18, 132, 141, 156, 180–2, 323–4, 327, 341, 587

Clinton, Bill 119, 159, 264, 269, 276, 347–8, 359, 364, 370, 388, 558

Codreanu, Corneliu 130

collaborators/collaboration 2, 31–3, 46–9, 75, 82, 84–7, 133, 136, 169, 187–92, 239, 242, 339–41, 455, 523–6, 532, 537, 573, 575, 601

command economy (centrally directed economy) 18–20, 88–9, 94, 147

Comecon (CMEA) 88–9, 94, 138

Communist Party of Albania (CPA, 1942–6) 31–2, 524–5, 529

Communist Party of Romania (CPR) 134–7, 141–3, 145, 173

Communist Party of Yugoslavia (CPY) and its regime 32–3, 190, 198, 240, 243, 282, 292–4, 330, 340, 345, 409–10, 462

Constantinescu, Emil 150–64

Constantinople (Byzantium, Istanbul) 25, 73, 75–7, 127–8, 185, 235, 332, 334–5, 409, 517

Contact Group 250, 349, 484, 492, 538–40, 543–4, 552

Cook, Robin 430, 543–4

Copenhagen and 'Copenhagen criteria' 7–8, 36, 170–1, 582, 590, 597, 602

Corfu 50, 237, 522

corruption 1, 5, 8, 10, 16, 18, 45–6, 51, 58, 61, 63–6, 69–71, 103, 105–6, 110, 112–24, 130–2, 141, 151, 156–8, 164–6, 170–82, 207, 213, 219, 224, 226, 230, 269, 283–4, 288, 305, 307, 309–11, 317, 322–7, 341, 365–6, 370, 382, 386, 389–91, 396–7, 401–2, 418, 420, 448, 450–1, 456, 465–8, 470, 479, 489, 499, 502, 534, 564, 581, 592

Cosic, Dobrica 240, 247, 249, 480, 528, 531

Covic, Nebojsa 301, 303, 310, 566, 568

Cozma, Miron 146, 149, 157, 161–2, 176–7

Crainic, Nichifor 11, 598

Craiutu, Aurelian 143–4, 180–1, 598

Crampton, Richard 86–7, 536

crime, criminality, gangs and criminalization xvi, 4, 5, 8, 14, 36, 45, 47, 50, 54–9, 64–6, 68–70, 72, 85–7, 103–4, 106, 113, 118–19, 121–3, 126, 142, 169, 172–3, 177–9, 191–2, 203, 208, 210, 218–23, 227–32, 246–7, 249, 253–4, 261–2, 264, 268–9, 277, 280, 283–5, 288–97, 299–309, 312, 315, 318–19, 324–8, 339, 341, 346, 350, 352–3, 358, 360–1, 365–6, 371, 378–9, 382–4, 387–92, 400, 402, 431, 436, 438, 441, 447–50, 454, 456, 466–8, 470, 479, 486, 489, 492–3, 496, 501, 504, 506–7, 533, 542, 554, 556–7, 561, 563–4, 567, 569, 571–3, 579, 581, 591–2

Crimean War 128, 235

Croatia 3–6, 9–10, 12–13, 15, 66–7, 182, **183–232**, 237–40, 243, 245–7, 249, 253–4, 262, 267, 278–9, 284, 287–91, 295–6, 299–300, 304, 306, 310, 312, 318, 320, 325, 329, 332, 338–49, 351–2, 354–5, 358–9, 373–4, 377–81, 383, 388, 396, 400, 410, 312, 453, 458, 462, 475, 477, 479, 482, 485–6, 489, 498, 502, 509, 512, 516, 529–30, 534–6, 552, 577–8, 582, 590–91; fascist Independent State of Croatia (NDH, 1941–44) 187, 190–3, 195, 198–9, 226, 239, 339, 524

Croatian Democratic Union (HDZ): in Croatia 195, 197–8, 201, 203–28; in Bosnia 342, 362–3, 372–3, 376–80, 385–6, 388

Croatian People's Party (HNS) 204–5, 216

Croatian Sabor *see* Sabor

Croatian Social-Liberal Party (HSLS) 195, 204, 207, 216–17, 221–2, 225

'Croatian Spring' 193–5

Croatian Party of Rights (HSP): in Croatia 187, 204, 207, 216, 225; in Bosnia 363, 373

Croatian Peasant Party (HSS) and precursors 187–90, 204, 207, 216, 225, 230, 238

Crvenkovski, Branko 415–19, 445–57, 467–8

CSCE 36, 248; *see also* OSCE

currency boards 106, 108, 113, 117, 121, 394, 396, 487, 498, 589

Cutilheiro, José 344

Cuza, Prince Alexandru Ioan 128

Cyprus 3, 228, 277, 279

Cyril (St.) and Cyrillic script/alphabet 28, 73–5, 126, 186–7, 193, 211, 370, 412–13

Czech Lands/Republic and Czechoslovakia 2, 12, 72, 74, 77, 81, 139, 159, 179, 193, 357, 470, 528, 552, 588

Dacia and Dacians 24, 127, 137, 513

Dacia Logan cars 588

Dalmatia 184–9, 194, 198, 203, 239, 332, 334

Danube and Danubian Plain 73, 125, 127–8, 246, 285, 320

Dayton accords 351–65 and 218, 221, 254, 276–7, 284, 288–9, 368, 370, 378, 392, 399, 469, 536

debt: public 6, 106, 218, 321; foreign debt 6, 34, 44, 51–2, 66, 90, 93–5, 99–101, 106, 117, 139–40, 147–9, 154, 209, 218, 251, 266–8, 281, 290, 321, 323, 355, 398, 459–60

Demaci, Adem 423, 527, 529, 535, 540, 544–5

democracy and democratization xv, xvi, 1, 5, 7–17, 20, 36–7, 39–40, 42, 47, 70, 72, 85, 87, 93, 96, 110, 114, 122, 131–2, 136–7, 141, 143–4, 179–80, 212, 226, 230–2, 238, 274–6, 300, 324–8, 352, 361, 399–404, 449, 457, 466, 469–70, 492, 503–4, 506–10, 555, 568, 574–80, 581–94; delegative democracy 180; illiberal democracy 180; consociational democracy 403–4

Democratic Convention of Romania (CDR) 150–1, 153, 155–6

Democratic League of Kosova (LDK) 533, 535–6, 538, 543–67, 572–6

Democratic Movement of Serbia (DEPOS) 245, 248–50

Democratic National Salvation Front (FDSN) 150–5; *see also* National Salvation Front

Democratic Opposition of Serbia (DOS) 268–76, 278–31, 315, 326–8

Democratic Party (DS, in Serbia) 243, 245, 248, 250, 255–60, 266–311, 326–8

Democratic Party (DP, in Albania) 37, 39–42, 45–71

Democratic Party (PD, in Romania) 153, 166–7, 171–2, 174–9

Democratic Party of Albanians (DPA, in Macedonia) 419–24, 427, 429, 431–3, 449–50, 457

Democratic Party of Serbia (DSS) 250, 255, 266–81, 287–91, 293–300, 303–21, 326–8

Democratic Party of Socialists (DPS, in Montenegro) 258, 278, 477–510

Democratic Union for Integration (DUI, in Macedonia) 449–52, 456–7

Democratic Union of Hungarians of Romania (UDMR) 144, 146, 150–1, 155–7, 166–7, 172, 174, 176

Democratic Union of Vojvodina Hungarians (DZVM) 245, 248, 250

Denmark and Danes 14, 57, 98, 131, 174, 192, 322, 416, 519, 565, 571–2, 593

Deutschmark (DM) 108–9, 196, 213, 250, 259, 272, 281, 321, 323, 367, 370, 394–6, 458, 462, 498–9, 507, 562

diaspora(s) 22–3, 71, 195, 204, 207, 216, 224, 227, 411, 425, 454–5, 517, 534, 537, 578

Dimitrov, Filip 99–102

Dimitrov, Georgi 85, 87

Dinkic, Mladen (Mladjan) 263, 279, 288, 305, 312, 321

Djilas, Milovan 17, 186, 475, 525–6

Djindjic, Zoran 223, 255, 259–60, 263–75, 279–317, 320–26

Djukanovic, Milo 265–6, 276–8, 316, 477–509

Dobrev, Nikolai 106–7

Dobrudja (southern) 80, 85, 129–30, 132, 136

Dodik, Milorad 369–71, 374–5, 377, 385

Dogan, Ahmed 109, 114

Dracula, Count (Vlad the Impaler) 168

Drakulic, Slavenka 12–13

Draskovic, Vuk 243–9, 255, 258–68, 282, 288, 299–301, 304, 306, 309, 312, 316–18, 531; his wife Danica 258

Dubrovnik (Ragusa) 183, 185, 202, 206, 228, 332, 334, 477, 489, 493

East Central Europe 5, 7–8, 10–16, 20–1, 74, 77, 85, 98, 117, 122, 135, 153–4, 163, 175, 180, 195, 345, 411, 470, 582–4, 588, 590, 593

Eastern Orthodox Church/Christianity xviii, 9–10, 25–7, 29, 49, 74–6, 78, 91, 115, 126, 142, 144, 161–2, 183, 186–8, 190–2, 225, 234–5, 240, 245, 257–8, 262–3, 272, 313, 330–3, 336–8, 366, 407–10, 413–14, 434, 441–2, 447, 462–3, 472, 474–5, 480, 504, 512–7, 521, 524, 527–8, 530, 569, 572, 574, 576; Church Slavonic 74–5

Ecoglasnost 82, 110

economic growth 5,6, 34, 44, 47, 88, 95, 103, 111, 117, 139, 148, 157, 194, 209, 218, 220–1, 225, 229, 251–2, 267,

280–1, 321, 394, 421, 456, 459, 461–6, 504, 530, 578, 583, 590

Eide, Kai 574

Elbasan 25, 36, 56

ethnic cleansing xv, 2–3, 14, 16, 31, 183, 190–2, 198, 203, 207, 218, 223, 236, 261, 291, 294, 306, 324–5, 339–41, 346–7, 354, 384, 399, 492, 521, 540, 546–50, 569–70

ethnic collectivism 5, 7–9, 10–16, 140–1, 180–2, 197, 230–1, 323–4, 400, 469, 580–81, 583, 586–7

ethnic affiliations of populations 22, 74, 125 183, 191, 233, 314, 330, 406, 472–3, 512

ethnic strife xvi–xviii, 3, 11–16, 27, 144–5, 180–2, 197–201, 231, 238, 341, 403, 407, 415, 467, 469, 513–46, 569–70, 586–7

ethnocracy and the ethnocratic state 11–13, 16

EU Commission 61, 108–10, 116–18, 121, 123–4, 159, 163–5, 168–70, 172–3, 177–8, 181–2, 224, 226, 228–9, 297, 314, 316, 318–20, 355, 357, 394, 430, 441, 446, 449, 465–7, 501, 508, 568, 581, 583, 591–2

EU Constitutional Treaty 123, 466–7, 568, 591–2

euro (currency) 121, 219, 281, 299, 321–2, 462, 493–4, 499–500, 507, 589

'Europe Agreements' 101, 151

EBRD 5–6, 21, 34, 43–4, 50–3, 61, 66–71, 97–8, 100–5, 109, 121, 125, 147–50, 154–5, 158, 162, 172, 179–80, 209, 213–16, 218, 229–30, 251–2, 266–7, 279–81, 320–4, 355–6, 361, 393–8, 402, 458–69, 483, 497–9, 503–4

EC (1958–93) and EU (1993–) 4, 7–8, 21, 42, 48–9, 51, 55–7, 61–5, 67, 70, 94, 101, 103, 108–12, 114–25, 144, 151–4, 158–82, 203, 205–6, 212–13, 217, 219, 221–32, 269, 274–328, 343–4, 347, 355–5, 361, 366, 371, 381–470, 479, 487, 495–6, 498–510, 539–94; European Union Force (EUFOR) 389–90; European Union Police Mission (EUPM) 386, 389

exclusion zones 346, 348–9, 351

fascism and neo-fascism 12, 30–3, 37, 78–9, 83–6, 92, 130–40, 165–6, 168, 187, 190–3, 195, 199, 213, 226, 231, 238–9, 269, 325, 339, 341, 409, 475, 514, 516, 524–5

Fatherland Front (Bulgaria) 83–9

Federation of Bosnia and Herzegovina (FBiH) 254, 351–2, 356–9, 362, 404

Federal Republic of Yugoslavia (FRY, 1992–2003) 206, 219, 221–2, 246–300, 320–8, 349, 352, 357, 360–1, 380–1, 383, 396, 414, 426, 465, 467–8, 477–500, 535–61, 564, 590

Ferdinand of Saxe-Coburg-Gotha, Prince (later King) 77–8, 129–31
Filov, Bogdan 81–2
Fino, Bashkim 56–7, 59, 61–2
First World War 9, 29, 77–8, 129–30, 188–9, 236–7, 338, 408–9, 475, 516, 520–22, 591
Foca 335, 339
foreign direct investment (FDI) 39, 44, 53, 66, 68, 71, 90, 95, 148, 154, 178, 209, 212, 215, 251, 322–3, 397–9, 459, 461, 464, 467, 503, 589
Former Yugoslav Republic of Macedonia (FYROM) *see* Republic of Macedonia
Framework Agreement (Macedonia, 2001) *see* Ohrid Framework Agreement
France xviii, 2, 10–11, 14–16, 57, 64, 128, 126, 131, 153, 158, 166, 169, 175, 186, 237–8, 257, 276, 290, 364, 436, 444, 451, 522, 543, 547, 551, 554, 557, 561, 569
Franz Ferdinand (Archduke) 188, 236, 338, 591
Frowick, Robert 360, 433, 435
Funar, Gheorghe 150–6

Gaj, Ludevit 186
Gallagher, Tom 134, 139, 143–5, 150, 154
genocide, Holocaust xv, xvi, 2–3, 14, 16, 46–8, 57, 59, 125, 134, 149, 169, 171, 178–9, 190–3, 198, 231, 287, 290–1, 315, 339–41, 346, 350, 353, 360, 384, 514, 531, 540
Georgiev, Colonel Kimon 79, 83–4
Georgievski, Ljubco 411–12, 417, 419–22, 430, 432, 434–5, 437–9, 443, 448–51, 453, 457, 467
Germany 2, 13, 18, 23, 31–2, 55, 57, 77, 80–5, 108–9, 124–5, 129, 132–5, 163, 169, 172, 179, 183–4, 195–6, 198, 200, 203, 213, 222, 228–30, 237–9, 250, 259, 272, 278, 281–2, 291, 321, 323, 349, 354, 357, 364, 367, 370, 394–6, 399, 411, 416–17, 425, 427, 446, 458, 462, 492, 498–9, 507, 521, 524–5, 538, 540, 544, 557, 562–3, 566, 571, 583, 587–8
Ghegs (Albania) 26, 29, 33
Gheorgiu-Dej, Gheorghe 136–8
Glagolitic script/alphabet 74–5
Gligorov, Kiro 412, 415–19
Gligorov, Vladimir 462
González, Felipe 256
Gorazde 343, 347–9, 351–2, 356
Gorbachev, Mikhail 8, 35, 39, 88, 96, 149
Gosev, Petar 411, 416–17, 420
Gostivar 405, 419–21
Gotovina, General Ante 207, 221, 224, 227–9
Greater Romania Party (PRM) xii, 144, 151–2, 155–6, 166–7, 171, 174
Greece and Greeks 1, 10, 20–1, 22–31, 33, 35, 37, 48–50, 55, 57, 60, 67–8, 71, 80,

83, 85, 126–9, 184, 188, 234, 258, 277, 283, 322, 405–18, 421–2, 427, 439, 451, 456, 461, 473–4, 483, 503, 517, 519, 522, 533, 539, 547
Ground Security Zone (GSZ) 283, 423, 426, 556
Group for Changes (GZP) 502
Groza, Petru 136–8
Gruevski, Nikola 451, 470
Gypsies *see* Roma.
G7 (Group of 7) 357, 498
G8 (Group of 8) 553, 556, 558
G17 Plus (Serbian think-tank/party) 278, 281, 305, 309–15, 319, 502

Habsburg Empire xvi, 11, 27, 128, 185–9, 198, 235–7, 335, 337, 516–19, 521, 587, 600, 602, 607; *see also* Austria.
Haekkerup, Hans 565–6, 571
Haradinaj, Ramush 428–9, 564–7, 572–3
Havel, Vaclav 11
HDZ: see Croatian Democratic Union
Helsinki Final Act 36, 48, 109, 163, 544
Hercegovacka Banka (HB, in Bosnia) 378–9
Herceg-Bosna 359, 377
Herceg-Novi 489
Holbrooke, Richard 347, 351, 360, 539–40, 545–6
Holkeri, Harri 568, 571
Holocaust *see* genocide.
hostages 349–50, 379
horizontally structured power relations/structures xv, 1, 5, 8, 10, 72, 141, 180–2, 230, 581–4, 587
Hoxha, Enver 32–5, 42, 525; his wife Nexhmije Hoxha 35, 45
Hum (Herzegovina) 235, 333–4; *see also* Bosnia and Herzegovina
Hungary 2, 84–5, 90, 125, 130, 132–4, 139, 142–4, 147, 152–3, 159, 169, 179, 182, 190, 213, 228, 235, 238–9, 242, 314, 320, 332–4, 357, 503, 515, 524m 547, 552, 557, 598

Iasi 125, 128, 140, 163
Ilic, Velimir 273, 296
Iliescu, Ion 134, 142, 145–6, 149–50, 164–70, 176–82
Illyrians, Illyria and Illyricum 23–8, 184, 186, 331–2, 473, 513; Illyrian Provinces and Illyrianism 186
IFOR 352, 357–8, 364, 366
industry and industrial development 7, 17–19, 25, 30–2, 34, 36–7, 39, 42–4, 51, 67–8, 73, 77, 80, 86–90, 94–5, 97, 100–5, 139, 148, 187, 194, 208–9, 214–18, 230, 238–9, 241, 247, 251–2, 258–9, 262, 266–7, 272, 306, 310, 321–3, 332–3, 335, 340–1, 343, 355, 393, 396–8, 405, 410, 461, 464, 468, 471, 476, 482–3, 501, 503–4, 512, 523
Indzhova, Reneta 102

inflation 17, 34, 42, 44, 50, 71, 90, 94–7
103–4, 106, 108, 139, 148–9, 154–5,
158, 167, 170, 196, 208–9, 213, 218,
249–52, 266–7, 280–1, 305, 321, 343,
393–4, 398, 411, 458–60, 462–3, 468,
479–80, 498, 504, 507, 525, 534
inter-ethnic strife: *see* ethnic strife
International Commission on the Balkans
(ICB) 4, 24, 402–3, 577, 579, 591–2
IMF 50, 59, 67–8, 99–101, 105, 107, 109,
115, 117, 139, 154, 158, 167, 196, 212,
279, 284, 294, 296, 298, 305, 321,
394–5, 458, 460, 462–3, 468, 504
International Crisis Group (ICG) 368, 503,
507, 580
Internal Macedonian Revolutionary
Organization (IMRO, VMRO) 79, 190,
238, 409
Internal Macedonian Revolutionary
Organization-Democratic Party for
Macedonian National Unity (IMRO-
DPMNU, VMRO-DPMNE) 410–12,
414–52, 455–7, 467, 470
International Criminal Court (ICC) 383,
387, 451
ICTY 207–8, 212, 217–32, 254, 261–2, 264,
268, 280, 283–300, 303–19, 326–8,
352–3, 360, 364, 383–4, 387–93, 441,
447–8, 453–4, 486, 493, 502, 505–7,
541, 554, 556, 560, 567, 572–3, 575, 594
Internally displaced persons (IDPs) 221–2,
354–5, 363, 368, 372, 574
Iraq links 3, 120, 169, 175, 226–7, 266, 306,
386–7, 451, 464, 551, 561
Iron Guard 130–1, 133–4
Isarescu, Mugur 154, 164–5
Istrian Democratic Assembly (IDS) 216, 225
Italy and Italians xviii, 2, 9, 23, 26–32, 35,
38, 42, 45–6, 51–9, 61, 64, 66–8, 71, 83,
80–1, 126, 128, 138, 163, 174, 183–5,
187–90, 207, 216, 220–1, 223, 229–30,
238–9, 258, 291, 325, 339, 349, 416,
465, 477, 486, 492, 496, 501, 517,
519–20, 524–5, 538, 540, 557, 561, 569,
593
Ivanic, Mladen 362, 369, 377, 380–1
Izetbegovic, Alija 200, 203, 206, 254,
341–4, 351, 356, 358–9, 362–4, 372,
375, 388

Jackson, Lt.-General Sir Michael 556–7,
560, 562
Janvier, General Bernard 348–50
Jajce 329, 334
Jasenovac death camp 190, 224, 246
Jelacic, Josip (Ban of Croatia) 186, 193, 195
Jelavic, Ante 373, 377–8
Jessen-Petersen, Søren 454, 572, 576–7
Jews and anti-Semitism 12, 74, 81–2, 84,
125, 129–30, 133–4, 149, 169, 171, 187,
190–2, 226, 336, 339, 408, 514, 521; *see
also* genocide.

Jiu Valley coal mines (Romania) 140, 146,
149, 155, 157, 161–2, 177
JNA (the Yugoslav People's Army,
1945–91) 195, 198–9, 201–3, 241, 253,
341–5, 354, 372, 477, 533
John Paul II, Pope 74, 116, 162, 191, 365
Jovanovic, Dusko 502
JSO (Special Operations Unit, 'Red Berets')
289–90, 299–303, 308, 317
judiciary and judicial capacity 7, 46, 58, 65,
70, 76, 110, 116–21, 123, 136–7, 153,
170, 172–3, 177–8, 197, 211, 215–16,
219, 232, 235, 242, 275, 282, 302,
317–8, 323, 325–8, 378, 382, 401, 466,
490, 506, 532, 540, 543, 545, 565, 582,
584
JUL: *see* Yugo-Left party.

Kadare, Ismail 35
Kallay, Benjamin 338
KAP (*Kombinat Aluminijuma Podgorica*),
formerly KAT, *Kombinat Aluminijuma
Titograd*) 476, 482–3, 503
Karadjeorje (Black George) Petrovic 235;
Karadjordjevic dynasty 235–8, 308
Karadzic, Radovan 246, 252, 268, 294–5,
317, 326, 349–50, 352, 359–61, 365–71,
374, 383, 387, 389–90
Karadzic, Vuk 515
KFOR 271, 427, 433, 439, 442, 545, 554,
556–7, 560–61, 563, 566–71
Khuen-Herdervary, Count 187
KLA 72, 260, 292, 423–5, 428, 439,
536–45, 547, 553, 555, 560–69, 573–6
Kljusev, Nikola 411–14
Knin 196–7, 205–6, 226
Kolubara coal mine (Serbia) 272–3
Kosor, Jadranka 227
Kosova and Kosovars 2, 4–5, 7, 15, 22–4,
27–31, 33, 50, 55, 59, 61, 72, 163, 181,
192, 203, 208, 221, 229, 233–7, 240–2,
244–9, 163, 181, 192, 203, 208, 221,
229, 233–7, 240–2, 244–9, 255, 260–3,
266, 268, 270–1, 276–9, 283–95, 300,
306, 309–18, 324, 327, 334, 338–9, 374,
387, 402, 408, 410, 413–15, 421,
423–47, 451–2, 461–9, 475, 479, 484–6,
489, 491, 509, **512–80**, 582, 593–4;
Battle of Kosova (1389) 235–6, 334,
338; 2nd Battle of Kosova (1448) 516;
Kosova Polje (Field) 241, 569; Kosova
Protection Corps 423, 562, 565, 576
Kostov, Hari 453–6, 466–8
Kostov, Ivan 103, 107–13, 119–22, 421
Kostov, Traiko 87
Kostunica, Vojislav 243, 245, 249, 255,
266–81, 287–321, 326–8
Kosumi, Bajram 574–5
Kotor (Bay of) 333–4, 473
Kouchner, Bernard 279, 554, 558, 562–5,
571
Kozloduy power station 110,116

Kragujevac 233, 263, 271
Krajisnik, Momcilo 360–70, 373
Kraljevo 256, 265, 271
Krajina (part of former Military Frontier
    region) 186, 196–8, 200, 205–6, 227,
    249, 253, 257–8, 295
Khrushchev, Nikita 34, 88
Kucan, Milan 196, 202, 206
Kulin (Ban) 332–3
Kumanovo 405, 435, 442, 451
Kun, Bela 130
Kupres 349
Kutle, Miroslav 218–19

Labus, Miroslav 275, 278, 281, 296–7,
    309–10, 314–15, 329
landlordism 75–8, 189, 335–8; in Bulgaria
    75; in Romania 127–9; in Croatia 185–6
Lazar, Prince 515
LDK *see* Democratic League of Kosova
League of Communists of Kosovo (LCK)
    529, 531–2
League of Communists of Serbia (LCS) 243,
    528, 531
League of Communists of Yugoslavia
    (LCY) 195–6, 527, 529
Leotard, François 436–7, 444
Liberal Party (LS, in Croatia) 216, 225
Lilic, Zoran 257, 259, 268, 296
London Club 101, 321
LPK 423–4, 537
Lukanov, Andrei 94–6, 100, 104–5
Lukovic, Milorad ('Legija') 300, 302–3,
    306, 308, 313, 317
Luxembourg (European Councils) 108, 159,
    317, 425, 430, 465, 505, 563

Macedon (kingdom of) 184
Macedonia (Vardar, Republic of ~, ROM)
    and Macedonian Slavs xviii, 3–6, 10, 16,
    23–4, 27–8, 31, 33, 49–50, 63–7, 73,
    75–6, 79, 81–2, 85, 100, 182, 190, 219,
    223, 234, 236, 239–40, 283, **405–70**,
    477, 479, 504, 509, 514, 518–22,
    526–32, 537–8, 543, 545–7, 552, 556,
    576–8, 582, 589
Macek, Vladko 189–90
Madgearu, Virgil 131
Madrid criteria 7, 582, 590
Mafias/gansterism 14, 51, 104–5, 122–3,
    164, 166, 246, 277, 289, 301–2, 361,
    400, 418, 479, 496, 499, 501–2, 533,
    591–2; *see also* crime
Magyars 75, 126–7, 182, 185–7, 239; *see
    also* Hungary; Magyarization 186–7
Majko, Pandeli 60–2, 64
Malcolm, Noel 332–3, 336, 513, 526, 550
Maniu, Iuliu 131–3, 137
Mann, Michael 16, 141
Marjanovic, Jovan 528
Marjanovic, Mirko 257, 275, 277, 324
market mechanisms and marketization xv,

xvi, 5, 8–10, 17–20, 37, 39, 41–2, 52–4,
    68–70, 93–4, 96–7, 101–5, 110, 117,
    122, 143, 146–7, 150–1, 154, 160, 162,
    165, 170, 179, 214–15, 224, 226, 230–2,
    322, 396–402, 458–64, 581–4, 587–94
Markac, General Mladen 226
Markov, Georgi 116
Markovic, Ante 196–7, 203, 244–5, 411,
    460, 476
Markovic, Mihailo 243
Markovic, Mirjana (Mira, wife of Slobodan
    Milosevic) 261, 268, 271, 285, 288,
    302–3, 317, 469
Markovic, Predrag 263
Markovic, Radomir (Rade) 261, 282, 285,
    299, 303–4, 306, 317
Marovic, Svetozar 388
Martic, Milan 205, 295
Matyas Hunyadi (King) 334
Matvejevic, Predrag 195
Mazowiecki, Tadeuz 205
Media xv, 9, 10, 15, 38–9, 46, 55, 65, 106,
    140, 142, 153, 169, 172–4, 197–212,
    216, 241–3, 246, 248, 253, 255–60,
    264–5, 272–3, 303, 305, 308, 328,
    339–40, 361–2, 367–8, 484–5, 493, 531,
    593
Medjugorje 194
Medojevic, Nebojsa 510
Mehdani, Rexhep 58
Meksi, Alexander 45, 55, 59
Mesic, Stipe (Stjepan) 201, 203–4, 217–19,
    221–24, 226–29, 296, 306
Meta, Ilir 62–6, 69
Methodius (St.) 74; *see also* Cyril (St)
Migration and migrants 4, 24, 36, 38, 49,
    65–6, 71, 332, 344, 453, 489, 521, 531,
    593
Mihai (King) 132–3, 135–7, 176
Mihajlo Obrenovic 235–6
Mihajlovic, Dragoljub ('Draza') 239
Mihajlovic, Dusan 285
Mihajlovic, Vojislav 268, 271
Mikerevic, Dragan 389–91
Milan Obrenovic 236
Milanovic, Dragoljub 282, 295–6, 551
Milos Obrenovic 235
Milosevic, Marija 284–5, 297
Milosevic, Marko 185, 274, 317
Milosevic, Slobodan 6, 15, 182, 197, 200,
    203, 205, 208, 217–18, 223, **241–317**,
    321–8, 342, 347, 349–51, 359–60, 362,
    364, 367, 369–70, 373, 392, 414, 423,
    426, 476–93, 500, 502, 506–7, 516,
    531–2, 535–6, 538–54, 558–9, 561–4
Milutinovic, Milan 256, 259–63, 276, 278,
    293, 296, 298, 360, 370, 539, 544, 554
Mineriadas 146, 149, 157, 161–2, 176–7
Mitrovica 242, 523, 532, 563, 565–6, 569
Mladenov, Petur 82–6
Mladic, Ratko 198, 246, 268, 290–5, 298,
    307, 314–19, 326, 350, 360, 365–6, 391

Mohacs (1526 battle of) 334
Moisiu, Alfred 65
Moldavia 126–8, 138
Moldova (Bessarabia) 3, 6, 111, 125–6, 132, 168, 176, 497, 501–2, 588, 590
Monnet, Jean 586
Montenegro (Zeta) xvi, 3, 5, 22–3, 26, 28–9, 33, 54, 67, 72–3, 76, 129, 182, 188, 213, 223–4, 228, 230, 233–4, 236, 239–40, 242, 246–8, 255, 258, 262, 265–8, 270, 274–8, 285–6, 292, 294, 297–300, 305–7, 310, 312–14, 316–20, 325, 327, 338, 354, 380, 388, 390, 396, 415–16, 440, 451, 465, 469, **471–510**, 514, 517–20, 524, 526, 528, 530, 532, 536, 539–40, 547, 562, 567, 578, 582, 589
Morina, Rahman 242, 532
Mostar 329, 336, 339, 349, 351, 356, 368, 378–9, 381, 452
Movement for Rights and Freedoms (MRF) 96, 99–100, 112, 120
Mushanov, Nikolai 79
Muslims, Islam and Islamophobia 9–10, 26–7, 30, 74–6, 81, 90–2, 187, 190–1, 233, 239, 248, 259, 330–3, 335–41, 357, 359, 363, 372, 380–2, 387, 392, 407–8, 431, 434, 453, 474, 477, 512, 516–17, 521, 523, 527, 583; Islamicization 335–7
Mussolini, Benito 30–1, 325

Nano, Fatos 38, 41–2, 45–6, 56–69
Nastase, Adrian 157, 166–7, 174–6, 178
nationalism 7, 11–17, 22, 27–9, 76–9, 90–2, 130, 133–4, 138–45, 186–7, 193–201, 203–4, 217, 220, 238, 240–4, 254, 256, 331, 338, 341, 346, 361, 382, 400, 409–11, 423–35, 439, 507–8, 515–21, 576–80, 586–7.
National Liberal Party (PNL, in Romania) 130–3, 137, 145–6, 150, 160, 166–7, 171–2, 174–6
National Salvation Front (FSN, Romania) 142–53, 180
NATO 56, 61–2, 65–6, 103, 107–8, 110, 112, 114–20, 152–3, 158, 163, 168–9, 181, 202, 206, 208, 211–12, 217, 219, 221–2, 225–7, 246, 254, 261–2, 264, 266–9, 271, 275, 280, 282–3, 285, 288, 290–2, 295–6, 298, 302, 306, 312–13, 316–18, 320, 335, 348–52, 357–8, 360, 364, 374, 379, 381–3, 388–90, 392–3, 403, 407, 409, 415, 426–9, 431–9, 441–51, 454–7, 486–8, 535, 539–42, 544–62, 564, 566, 569–71, 573, 587
Nazis/Nazi Germany 3, 31–2, 74, 80–2, 84–6, 126, 132–4, 169, 187, 192, 226, 238–9, 282, 297, 325, 475, 524; Nazi-Soviet Pact (1939) 81, 132
Nedic, General Milan 239
Nemanja dynasty 234
New Croatian Initiative (NHI, party in Bosnia) 373, 376, 395

New Democracy (ND, party in Serbia) 245, 249
Njegos clan/dynasty 474
Nikola (Prince/King) 474–5
Nikolic, Tomislav 269, 271, 295, 307, 310, 313–15
Niksic 471
Nis 233, 256–7, 263, 271, 278, 302, 515, 523, 564
Noli, Bishop Fan 29–30, 37
Norac, General Mirko 207, 220
Novi Sad 227, 233, 271

Obrenovic dynasty 235–6
Odjanovic, Gen. Dragoljub 261–2, 295, 551, 554, 556, 558
Office of the High Representative (OHR, i Bosnia) 354, 367, 369, 375, 378, 381–2, 386–7, 289–90, 394–6, 402
Ohrid: negotiations and 'framework agreement' (2001) 407, 435, 438, 440–1, 443–9, 453–5, 469, 577; town and lake 405, 409–10, 438, 455
Omonia (Democratic Union of the Greek minority, in Albania) 37, 40, 42, 48–9
operation essential harvest 441
orphans (Romania) 140, 171
OSCE 36, 47–8, 56–8, 60–3, 112, 166, 174, 180, 211–12, 216, 256–60, 279, 312, 357, 359–62, 364, 367–9, 372, 376, 381, 384, 401, 407, 422, 430, 433, 436, 439, 442–3, 445, 447–9, 451, 453, 457, 480, 482, 484, 493, 496–7, 508, 538, 541–3, 562–3, 565, 574.
Otpor (Resistance) 260–1, 265, 273, 285
Ottoman Turks/Empire xv – xvii, 2, 26–8, 75–7, 91, 127–9, 141, 180, 185–6, 188–9, 198, 234–7, 324, 330–9, 352, 408, 471, 473–4, 513–21, 527, 581, 593
Owen, David 202, 346–7

Pale (Bosnia) 347, 350, 365, 367–8, 370–1
Panic, Milan 247–9, 478, 480
Pannonia, Pannonian Plain: see Danubian Plain
Papandreou, Andreas 416
Pardew, James 437
Paris Club creditors 100–1, 290, 321
Partisans (1941–45): in Albania 33, 525; in Yugoslavia 191–2, 195, 239, 297, 339–40, 475, 525–6
Party for Bosnia and Herzegovina (SBiH) 358, 363, 376–7, 380, 385
Party of Democratic Action (SDA) 225, 244–5, 342–4, 358, 362–3, 369, 372–3, 375–7, 385–7
Party of Democratic Progress (PDPr) 376–7, 380, 385
Party for Democratic Prosperity (PDP) 417, 419–20, 426–7, 429–30, 432–3, 447, 449–50

Party of Independent Social Democrats (SNSD) 369, 373, 376, 385
Party of Labour of Albania (PLA, Albania's Communist Party, 1946–91) 32–43, 45–6, 48
Party of Romanian Social Democracy (PDSR) 152–6, 164–66
Party of Social Democracy (PSD) 167–77
Parvanov, Georgi 106, 108, 115, 121
Pasalic, Ivic 212, 219, 222
Pasic, Nikola 237
Pasko, Gramoz 37, 42–3, 51
Passy, Solomon 114
Patrascanu, Lucretiu 135–6
Patten, Chris 64, 430, 437, 446, 465, 505, 568
Pavelic, Ante 187, 190–2
Pavkovic, Gen. Nebojsa 272, 274–5, 291–2, 296, 303, 306, 309, 315
Pavle (Orthodox Patriarch, Serbia) 245, 257, 263, 272, 366, 574
Pavle Karadjeorgjevic (Regent, Prince Paul) 190, 238
PDK (Democratic Party of Kosova) 563–7, 573, 576
perestroika (Gorbachev's USSR) 35, 39, 88, 96, 140
Perisic, Gen. Momcilo 261, 263–4, 272, 292–3, 315
Pesic, Vesna 245, 255, 259
Petar Karadjeorgevic (King) 236
Petar II Karadjeorgevic (King) 238
Petkov, Nikola 83, 87, 99
Petritsch, Wolfgang 354, 374, 376, 378–9, 381–2, 395, 543
Petrom 162
Petrovic dynasty (Montenegro) 474
Partnership for Peace (PfP, NATO-led, 1994–) 152, 212, 219, 313, 388, 390, 439, 546
Phanariot regime 127–8
Pirinski, Georgi 103, 106
Plavsic, Biljana 360–1, 363, 365–9, 371–3, 376, 384
Podgorica (formerly Titograd) 278, 320, 471, 476, 481, 482, 485, 488–9, 491, 496, 500, 5002–3, 505, 507
Podkrepa (Support, trade union) 92, 96
Poland 2, 72, 81, 90, 133, 140, 143, 147, 149, 159, 169, 179, 357, 470, 552
Pomaks (Islamicized Slavs) 74, 76, 09–1, 93
Ponte, Carla del 221, 224, 227–8, 280, 283, 287, 289–92, 306–7, 309, 313, 316, 318–19, 483, 560
Popescu Tariceanu, Calin 157, 175–9
Poplasen, Nikola 372–5
Popov, Dimitar 96–100
population data 5, 22, 27, 73–4, 44, 81, 91, 93, 95, 125–6, 148, 183, 209, 233, 251, 329–30, 398, 405–7, 459, 471–3, 512, 517, 523, 527, 529–31, 533
power relations and power structures xvii,

xviii, 1, 5–21, 72, 96, 102, 105–6, 118, 122–3, 128, 135–7, 141–3, 180–2, 200, 210, 214–5, 217, 230–1, 240, 252, 323–8, 340–1, 361, 382, 467–8, 470, 479, 497, 504–6, 571, 580–84, 587, 591–2, 594.
Pozderac, Hadija 341–2
Presevo Valley 423
Preslav 75
Prevlaka peninsula 223
Princip, Gavrilo (assassin) 236
Pristina 241, 413, 429, 515, 519, 524, 528–30, 533, 535–82, 557, 561, 566–7, 569, 574
privatization 5, 7, 39, 41–5, 51, 59, 67–9, 71, 100–3, 105, 107–10, 113, 115, 118, 212, 147, 151, 154, 156–60, 162, 164, 166, 172, 175, 177, 179–81, 210, 213–15, 217–18, 229–30, 252, 256, 258–9, 261, 281, 296, 307, 314, 321–3, 370, 391, 395, 401–2, 416, 418, 460–4, 467, 483, 497, 502–3, 507, 571, 582, 585
Progress Towards Accession reports (EU), 110, 116–18, 164–5, 170, 173, 396, 505, 571, 573, 582, 585
Prussia   129
Purges 87, 140, 193, 261
Putin, Vladimir 8, 272, 274, 278, 428
Pyramid schemes 53–5, 58–9, 68, 71, 418

Qosja, Rexhep 543, 562

Racak massacre 542–3
Racan, Ivica 195–6, 207, 216–25, 230
Radic, Stjepan and Ante 187, 189
Rama, Edi 62, 66
Rambouillet Conference (1999) 543–5
Rankovic, Aleksandar 193, 240, 527–8, 531
Raska 234, 262, 514
Raskovic, Jovan 196–7
Raznatovic, Zeljko *see* Arkan.
Red Army (Soviet) 86, 133–5, 239
'Red Berets': *see* JSO
religious affiliations 27, 73–4, 126, 183, 330–1, 337, 407, 472
religious strife xviii, 3, 27, 189, 403
remittances 4, 51–4, 66, 71, 194, 252, 267, 324, 394, 464, 578
Republika Srpska (RS) 219, 253–4, 277, 283, 315, 329, 345, 351–2, 356–99, 503
restitution 52, 97–8, 100–1, 149, 155, 160, 167, 173, 214, 229, 397, 462
retribution 86, 100, 223, 326–7, 573
revolutions 3, 10–11, 16, 28, 35, 77, 79, 92, 130, 135, 138, 142–5, 186, 242, 273, 280, 327, 341, 411, 476–7, 518, 591
Rehn, Olli 70, 123, 318–19, 466
Robertson, George (Lord) 283, 426–9, 438, 441
Roma (Gypsies) 74, 76, 90–1, 110, 117, 119, 121, 125, 130, 173, 177–8, 233,

339, 405–8, 411–12, 417–18, 420, 427, 438, 455, 521, 563–4, 573
Roman Catholic Church, Catholicism and Catholics 9–10, 26–7, 33, 36, 74, 126, 129, 142, 162, 183–8, 190–4, 198, 238–9, 333–41, 441, 475, 517, 575, 587
Romans and the Roman empire 23–5, 75, 127, 184, 332, 335, 473
Roman, Petre 142, 146, 149–51, 153–7, 162, 177
Romania and Romanians 2–3, 5, 6, 9, 11–13, 16, 18, 20–1, 27, 29, 35, 63, 72, 76, 83–6, 89, 102, 108–11, 116, 118–19, 121, 123, **125–82**, 233, 242, 320, 357, 383, 408, 411, 433, 462, 465, 509, 517, 546–7, 552, 557, 577–8, 582, 587–8, 590–92
Rose, General Sir Michael 141
RTS 273, 280, 282, 295–6
Rugova, Ibrahim 428, 533–75
rule of law xvi, 1, 5, 7–8, 21, 70, 122, 124, 131, 180–2, 212, 226, 230, 325, 182, 399–401, 457, 470, 550, 574, 579, 581–7
Russia xvi, xvii, 7–8, 28, 73, 75–8, 80, 86, 102–5, 108–9, 115, 125–6, 128–31, 176, 205, 207, 235–6, 270, 272, 274, 277, 303, 315, 317–18, 322, 324–5, 337, 349, 351–2, 492, 502–3, 517, 520, 538–43, 546, 548–50, 553–4, 556–8, 567–8, 581, 591
Russo-Turkish war (of 1877–8) 28, 76, 128–9, 236, 408, 474, 517

'safe areas' 347–50
Sainovic, Nikola 261–2, 293, 294–5, 542, 544, 554
Salonika *see* Thessaloniki
Sanader, Ivo 222, 225–8
Sanatescu, General Constantin 135
sanctions 50, 52, 54, 91, 104, 246–54, 264, 267, 269, 274, 277, 283, 298, 325, 347, 349, 357–8, 360, 365, 391, 467–8, 478–82, 485, 497, 507, 534, 536, 490–1, 495
Sandzak (of Novi Pazar) 234, 248, 472, 509, 514, 518
Sarajevo (Vrhbosna) 188, 217, 236, 247, 263, 277, 306, 329, 334–8, 341, 344, 347–59, 364–5, 368, 371–2, 375, 381, 383, 391, 394, 397, 399, 516
Sarovic, Mirko 377, 386, 389
Saxecoburggotski, Simeon *see* Simeon II
SBiH: see Party for Bosnia and Herzegovina
Schwarz-Schilling, Christian 393
Second World War xv, 2, 32–3, 50, 69, 74, 80, 85, 87, 119, 132–6, 138, 171, 190–1, 193, 195, 340–1, 344, 350, 364, 389, 399, 475, 524–6
'self-management' 17, 193, 214, 252
Serbia xvi, 2–6, 10, 13, 15, 23, 26, 28–9, 54, 72–6, 125, 129, 182, 184, 187–218, 223–9, **233–328**, 333–8, **342–69**, 372–7,

380–1, 385, 388–92, 400, 407–11, 423–8, 432–3, 437, 439–40, 447, 451,455, 465, 467, 469, **472–578**, 582
Serbian Academy (SANU) 241, 243
Serbian Democratic Party (SDS) 196–7, 225, 342–3, 360–91
Serbian Movement of Renewal (SPO) 243–5, 255, 259–71, 263–5, 268–71, 276, 288, 311–12, 342
Serbian Peoples Union (SNS) 216, 368–9, 373, 376–7
Serbian Radical Party (SRS) 247–50, 255, 259–61, 268–71, 276, 279, 294, 297, 304, 307–13, 319–20, 326, 342, 363, 369–70, 373
serfdom 127–8, 338
Seselj, Vojislav 244, 248–9, 255, 259–61, 268, 294, 297–9, 303–4, 308–11, 319, 369, 372, 487–8, 535, 556.
Shehu, Mehmet 34–5
Shkoder 35–6, 40, 48, 59, 237, 518–20, 521
Sibenik 183
Silajdzic, Haris 352–3
Simeon (Tsar, 893–927) 75, 234
Simeon II (Tsar/King, Simeon Saxecoburggotski) 83, 87, 99, 109, 111–14, 120
Simovic, General Dusan 238
Sisak 183, 206
Skenderbeg (Gjergj Kastrioti) 26
Skopje 234, 277, 405, 410, 418–19, 421, 423–4, 426, 429–41, 446, 452–5, 457, 461, 466, 519–20, 523
Slavonia 184, 186–90, 198, 203, 206–8, 210–11, 541
Slovenia 1, 20–1, 71, 118, 159, 179, 189–92, 197–8, 202–3, 213, 228, 230–1, 237–40, 246, 254, 304, 323, 329, 343, 353, 399, 410, 458, 469, 498, 509, 512, 529–32, 546, 552–3
Smith, Lt-General Rupert 349
Social Democratic Union of Macedonia (SDUM) 415, 417, 419–20, 422, 432, 434, 445, 448, 450–2, 455, 457, 457, 467
Social Democratic Party (SDP): in Albania 45–6, 54, 58–9, 63; in Bulgaria 79; in Romania 174; in Croatia 197, 204, 207, 210–11, 216–18, 225; in Bosnia 373, 376–7; in Montenegro 484, 493, 496
Social Democratic Union (USD) in Romania 153, 155–6, 160
Socialist Federal Republic of Yugoslavia (SFRY) 404–5, 409–13, 420, 439, 458, 471, 475–8, 526–35
Socialist Party of Albania (SPA) 41–2, 45, 47, 54, 57–70
Socialist Labour Party (PSM) 151–3
Socialist People's Party (SNP) 294, 483–4, 489, 491–4, 496–7, 500–3
Socialist Party of Serbia (SPS) 243–50, 255–61, 266, 269–71, 275–9, 284, 286,

294, 297, 301, 305, 308–9, 311–12, 317, 319–20, 326, 386, 535–6
Sofia 82, 93, 106–7, 111, 115, 119, 121, 30
Sofianski, Stefan 10
Solana, Javier 292, 298–9, 308, 320, 426, 428–30, 434, 436, 438, 440–1, 445–6, 469, 486, 495, 500, 507–8, 546, 552, 554, 558, 568, 576
Soviet Republics (former) 8–9, 10–11, 581
Spaho, Mehmed 338
Spegelj, Martin 199–202, 204, 253–4
Srebrenica 315–17, 333, 347, 349–50, 358, 380, 384, 387–92
Stability Pact for South-Eastern Europe 63, 111, 167–8, 221, 263, 277, 287, 320, 397, 555, 558, 590
SAAs 61, 65, 70, 219, 228, 230, 278, 315–9, 346, 381, 393, 397, 399, 428, 430, 452, 465, 505–6, 554, 575, 582
SFOR 364, 366–89
Stalin and Stalinism 17, 34, 60, 84–5, 87–9, 133, 135–8, 140
Stambolic, Ivan 268–9, 3004, 306, 313, 317, 531
Stamboliski, Aleksandur 77–9, 102
Stanisic, Jovica 261, 289, 301
Starcevic, Ante 187, 339
State Union of Serbia and Montenegro (2003–6) 298–328, 495–510
Stefan Dusan (Serbian ruler) 234, 514–15
Stefan Tomas (King of Bosnia) 334
Stefan Tomasevic (King of Bosnia) 334
Stefan Uros III (Serbian ruler) 75, 234
Steiner, Michael 357, 451, 566–8, 571
Stjepan Kotromanovic (Ban of Bosnia) 333
Stepinac, Archbishop/Cardinal Alojzije 191–2, 194
Stojadinovic, Milan 238
Stoloyan, Theodor 150–1, 171, 175
Stoyanov, Petar 105–15, 426
Strossmasyer, Bishop Josip 186
Sugar, Peter 12, 14, 127, 460
Surroi, Veton 433, 435, 543, 573

Tadic, Boris 312–15, 319–20, 570, 572–3, 575
Tetovo 405, 417–22, 424–9, 433, 437–41
Thaci, Hashim 428, 543–4, 560–67, 573
Thessaloniki (Salonika) 25, 410, 416, 421, 439, 461, 483, 578, 582
Thrace/Thracians 24, 75–6, 80–2, 85, 127, 457, 412
Timisoara 125, 142–4, 152
Tirana 29, 32, 36, 38, 40–2, 54–7, 59–66, 70–1, 418, 528, 543, 601
Tirgu Mures 144–6
Tito (Josip Broz) and Titoism 34, 87, 192–3, 195, 199, 239–41, 243–4, 267–8, 282–3, 405, 411–12, 415, 422, 471, 475–6, 512, 525, 531
Tokes, Laszlo 142
Tosks (in Albania) 26, 29, 33, 42, 533

trade unions 36, 38, 41, 50, 92, 96–7, 106, 115, 149, 155, 159, 167, 213, 220, 256, 287, 307, 533, 588
trafficking and smuggling 14, 54–5, 63–5 68, 104, 117–19, 121, 123, 168, 172–3, 178, 277, 281, 288, 294, 302, 324–5, 348, 381, 402, 423, 452, 467, 479, 482, 485, 493, 496–9, 501–2, 505, 537, 542, 571, 591
Trajkovski, Boris 422, 426, 428–9, 431, 433–8, 442–3, 445, 447–9, 451–2
Transylvania 127–32, 134, 136, 140–2, 144–5, 153, 162, 182
Travnik 329, 335, 349
Treaty of Nice 466, 578, 582
Trnovo 75; ~ Constitution (1879), 76
Trepca 242, 523–4, 532
Trotsky, Leon 17, 530
Tsankov, Professor Alexander 79, 83
Tsvetkovic, Dragisa 238
Tudjman, Franjo 15, 182, 187, 190–91, 195–54, 339, 348, 351, 359
Tudor, Corneliu Vadim 140, 151, 155–6, 161–2, 165–7, 171–2, 174–5
Tupurkovski, Vasil 420–22
Turkey and Turks, 3, 9, 23, 26–8, 35, 57, 65, 68, 70, 73–7, 82, 91–3, 108, 114, 121, 125, 127–9, 185, 213, 234–7, 322, 330–1, 333–4, 405–8, 412, 414–15, 417–18, 427, 438, 451, 474, 512–21, 523, 527–8, 582, 588, 591–3
Tus, Anton 202–4, 253–4, 343, 354
Tuzla 329, 347, 349–51, 356, 368, 375
Tvrtko I (King of Bosnia) 333–4

UCK 443–57
UK 5, 33–4, 42, 50, 57, 84, 131, 137, 163, 183, 192–3, 228, 233, 237–8, 283, 381, 384, 429, 438, 441, 444, 492, 538, 540–41, 543–4, 547, 553–4, 556–7, 561
Ukraine 3, 8, 73, 83, 115, 125, 138, 158, 357, 429, 438–9, 588
Unemployment 6, 34, 44, 95, 139, 148, 209, 218, 251, 267, 321, 398, 459
Uniate Church 162
Union of Democratic Forces (UDF, Bulgaria) 92–122
UNHCR xiv, 354–5, 439, 445, 447, 538, 555, 562
UNPTF) 186
UNMIK 314, 555, 558, 561–80
UNPREDEP 419, 546
UNPROFOR 205, 348–50
USA 23, 27, 33–4, 50, 65, 113, 119, 125, 139, 154, 168–9, 171, 176–7, 195, 205, 208, 217, 224, 254, 264, 268–9, 276–8, 283–6, 293, 295, 298, 304, 306, 328, 344, 347, 349, 351, 356–7, 359–60, 364, 367–9, 382–3, 387–9, 391–3, 418–20, 422, 425, 427, 433, 437–9, 444, 451, 454, 456, 462–3, 474, 479, 492, 505,

517, 523, 533, 535, 538–40, 546–8, 554, 557, 561, 569, 578, 591–2, 594
Ustasa 187, 190–9, 213, 226, 231, 238–41

Vacaroiu, Nicolae 151–5
Vance-Owen Plan (Bosnia) 346–7
Vasile, Radu 160–4
Vatra Romaneasca 144
Velchev, Colonel Damian 79
Velchev, Milen 113–4, 117
Vergina (Star of ~) 414, 418
Verlaci, Shefqet 29
Verticality of power/authority xvii, 1, 5, 7–10, 14–16, 72, 89, 122–3, 141, 180–2, 180–2, 230–1, 323–4, 326, 328, 341, 400, 504, 580–83, 587
Videnov, Zhan 102–6
VJ (Yugoslav Army, FRY) 249, 261–2, 292, 315, 389, 478, 480, 485–9, 492–3, 506, 545–6, 554, 558–9
Vlachs 22, 75, 91, 233, 408, 412, 438, 453, 513, 521
Vlassi, Azem 242, 532
Vlore 28, 30, 54–9, 237, 519, 521
Vojna Krajina (Military Frontier) 186
Vojvodina 5, 125, 184, 233, 239–40, 242–50, 259, 270, 314, 477, 529, 532
Vujanovic, Filip 228, 484, 487, 494–7
Vukovar 183, 202–3, 261,304, 312, 318

Walker, William 541–2
Wallachia 75, 127–8, 515
Westendorp, Carlos 365, 371, 374–5, 395
Western Europe(ans) xviii, 3–4, 11, 12, 15–16, 55–6, 66, 70, 124–5, 166, 252, 312, 328, 402, 533, 546, 583–8, 593–4

Wilson, Woodrow 11, 29
World Bank 64, 67, 102, 139, 150–1, 250, 353, 355–6, 361, 441, 449, 460, 462–3, 468–9, 497, 504

xenophobia 3–4, 16, 90–1, 124, 131, 143, 328, 507, 578, 593
Xhaferi, Arben 416, 420–1, 430–6, 450
Xoxe, Koçi 33

Yalta Conference (1945) 136–7
Yeltsin, Boris 540, 554, 558
Young Turks 28, 77, 518–19
Yugoslav Army (FRY): *see* VJ.
Yugoslavism 186–7, 193, 196–7, 237, 240, 411
Yugoslav People's Army: *see* JNA.
Yugo-Left (JUL) 260–1, 270–1, 488

Zadar 183, 205
Zahumlje (Hum): 234, 333–4
Zajedno (Together) coalition 255–8
Zagreb 183, 186–9, 191–5, 203–12, 219–21, 278, 306, 378, 465
Zemun gang 300
Zenica 329, 356, 399
Zepa 313, 347, 349, 351
Zeta: *see* Montenegro.
Zhivkov, Todor 35, 88–94, 99, 116
Zivkovic, Zoran 278, 286, 295, 301–9, 316
Zizic, Zoran 278, 287
Zhelev, Zheliu 92–3, 96, 99–100, 102, 105
Zogu, Ahmed (King Zog) 29–33, 46, 58, 65, 621; son Leka ('Leka I') 58, 65

Lightning Source UK Ltd.
Milton Keynes UK
UKHW020002040919
349086UK00006B/38/P